C.P.A. LAW REVIEW

Under the 1978 Uniform Commercial Code

Text, Previous C.P.A. Law Examination Questions, and the Author's Model Answers

JOSEPH L. FRASCONA, J.D.

Member of the New York, Colorado, and Federal Bars and Professor of Business Law, University of Colorado

Sixth Edition

1981

RICHARD D. IRWIN, INC. Homewood, Illinois 60430

Irwin-Dorsey Limited Georgetown, Ontario L7G 4B3

ISBN 0-256-02465-0
Library of Congress Catalog Card No. 80–82096

Printed in the United States of America

1 2 3 4 5 6 7 8 9 0 MP 8 7 6 5 4 3 2 1

To My Students

PREFACE

The author is glad to know that the previous editions of this book have been so helpful to so many users that the demand is for another edition. Many features make this sixth edition of outstanding importance and value. (1) The material is current with authoritative up-to-date references. The tentatively approved draft of Restatement (Second) of Contracts, 1980, has been the basis for much rewriting of Part Two on Contracts. Also, much new material has been added reflecting pertinent changes in business law, a large amount of which has been the subject of recent questions on the business law part of the Uniform C.P.A. Examinations. (2) Part Five on Bankruptcy has been completely rewritten with an analysis of the new Bankruptcy Reform Act of 1978, now called the Bankruptcy Code to distinguish it from the previous Act. (3) Part Thirteen on Public Law has been expanded to include an analysis of the Foreign Corrupt Practices Act of 1977 with its emphasis on Accounting Standards, Foreign Corrupt Practices by Issuers and Domestic Concerns, and Disclosure as an amendment to the Securities Exchange Act of 1934. This joins the material, new in the fifth edition, on Federal Securities Regulation, Antitrust, and Regulation of the Employer and Employee Relationship, so frequently the subject of questions on the examinations. (4) In Part Three on Sales, the area of Product Liability is carefully discussed. (5) This edition retains the widely appreciated and very helpful innovation in the last edition of the basic concept of "the transferee gets only what the transferor has" rule and its exceptions before detailed discussion under Sales, Negotiable Documents of Title, Commercial Paper, and Investment Securities. (6) Most of the chapters and many sections open with careful summaries of the text material as an excellent basis for review. (7) The Frequency Chart is up-to-date as of the

May 1980 Uniform C.P.A. Examination. (8) The text has many illustrative diagrams. (9) The author has brought to the text many of the teaching techniques successfully used in his classes. (10) A large number of recent Uniform C.P.A. Examination questions have replaced former questions, with the author's model answers. Most of the Problems at the ends of the chapters have been retained because of their particular excellence for classroom and study purposes.

While there are various books on the market which are mainly *outlines* of business law for use by examination candidates in business law, in the author's opinion they apparently presuppose that the candidates have both an excellent and extensive background in business law. The author has found that, while in some instances such a background has been acquired, nevertheless in most cases there is an inadequate background on which to base a review. It is for this reason this book is written, to provide only that pertinent text material necessary to establish the necessary business law background, and to provide many chapters and section summaries to serve as a review of the text.

The author wishes to express his deep appreciation to the many people throughout the country who have been so helpful with their excellent, constructive comments. Some people who should be gratefully recognized in particular are: Gaylord A. Jentz, professor of business law at the University of Texas at Austin; Telford F. Hollman, professor of business law at the University of Northern Iowa; and Oscar J. Miller, professor of law and librarian, School of Law, University of Colorado. This edition of the book could not exist without the constant wisdom, understanding, knowledge, encouragement, and yeoman work of the author's wife, Jean Ezard Frascona, LL.B.

The author acknowledges with appreciation the following: 1. The American Institute of Certified Public Accountants, for its permission to reprint C.P.A. Examination questions, and to quote from its booklets on *Information for CPA Candidates* and the *Code of Professional Ethics;* 2. The American Law Institute, for its permission to reprint portions of the following materials copyrighted by it on the dates indicated: *Restatement of the Law, Second, Agency,* Volume 1, 1958; *Restatement of the Law, Second, Torts,* Volume 2, 1977; *Restatement of the Law, Second, Trusts,* Volumes 1 and 2, 1959; *Restatement of the Law, Second, Contracts,* Tentative Drafts 1–7, Revised and Edited 1973, and Tentative Draft No. 9, pages 19–21, April 8, 1974; 3. the National Conference of Commissioners on Uniform State Laws, for permission to reprint portions of the Uniform Partnership Act, and the Uniform Limited Partnership Act; 4. The Lawyers Co-operative Publishing Co., for its permission to quote from *American Jurisprudence.*

JOSEPH L. FRASCONA

Cumulative Frequency Chart

		Personal Property				Security			
Examination Date	Contracts	Nature and Acquisition	Bailments	Sales	Commercial Paper	Property Security Transactions	Suretyship	Bankruptcy	Agency
May 1980	1(20),3		4b(4)	1(27)(29) (32)–(34)(37) (38)(46),4a	1(15)(19) (21)–(25) (30)	4	1(36)(39)(41) (42)(44)	1(3)(10)(31) (35)(42)	5a,b
Nov. 1979	1(2)–(5)(7)	1(35) (43)		1(1)(7)–(9) (11)(13)	3	1(22)–(26) (39)(40)	4	1(15),4b	1(12)(31) (33)(50)
May 1979	1(6)(8)–(13)(17) (35)			1(33)–(39) (44)	1(25)–(32)	1(6)(14)(15) (18)(20)–(22)	1(1)(5)(7)	1(6)(16)(19) (22)–(24)(50)	1(40)(45), 2b(1)
Nov. 1978	1(27)–(30)(49), 5a,c,d			1(31)(35) (36),5a,b	1(42)(44)– (47)(50)	1(43),2a	1(20)(21) (24)(25)	2b	3a,b
May 1978	1(13)(15)(16)(19) (21)(22)(26)(42) (44),2a(4),3a			1(14)(36)– (41)(43)	2	1(23)(28) (49)(50)	1(45)(46)	1(23)–(25) (32)(46)	1(1)–(5) (10)
Nov. 1977	1(3)(5),4	2(20) (25)	2(25)	7	3(33)–(40) (43)	2(21)(22) (24)(26)(28)	1(4),2(17)– (19)(27)	2(23)(29)– (32)	1(4),5
May 1977	3(33)–(36)			3(42)(43) (45)–(48)	2(17)–(21) (25)(26)	2(29), 7a1C,b	2(30)–(32)	7a	2(22)–(24) (27)(28)
Nov. 1976	3(33)–(38) (40)(45)			1(5)–(7)(9) (12),3(35)	5a(1) (2),b	3(44), 6a	2(24)(26) (27)(30)–(32)	2(18)(19) (28)	2(20)–(22)(25) (29),5a(3)(4)

Cumulative Frequency Chart (*continued*)

Examination Date	Business Organizations		Insurance	Real Property	Wills and Decedents' Estates	Trusts	Accountant's Legal Responsibility	Public Law			
	Partnerships	Corporations						Federal Securities Regulation	Antitrust	Regulation of the Employer and Employee Relationship	Taxation
May 1980	5c,d(1)(2)	1(6)–(9) (12)–(14) (16)(49)	1(43)(45)–(48)	1(11)(26)	1(40)	1(28) (50)		2b,5d(3)	1(1)(2)(4) (5)	1(17)(18)	1(7),2a, 5d(4)
Nov. 1979	1(14)(16)–(19)(30),5a	1(30),2	1(12)(38) (45)	1(10)(41)	1(20)	1(44) (46)(47)	5	1(27)–(29) (32)	1(6)(21)(34)–(37)(42)	1(48)(49)	
May 1979	4	3	1(2)–(4)	5			2	1(43)(48) (49)	1(41)(42) (46)	1(47)	
Nov. 1978	1(16)–(18) (23)(26)	1(9)(10) (14)(15) (18)(19) (22)	1(7)(8) (13)	1(34)(41) (48)	1(34) (39)	1(37) (38)(40)	1(2)–(4) (32),4b (2)	1(11)(33) 4	1(1)(5) (6)(12)	3c	
May 1978	5	4	1(14)(17) (18)(20)	1(27)(29) (31)	1(34)	1(30) (33)(35)	3a,b(1)	1(6)(11), 3b(2)	1(7)–(9) (12)	1(1) (47)(48)	
Nov. 1977	1(4)(7)(8) (11)(12)(16)	2(20),6, 7c	1(2)(10), 3(47)			3(44)	1(5),3(42)	1(1)(6)(9), 6b(1)	3(41)(45) (46)(48)	1(13)–(15	
May 1977	4b,5	1(10)–(12)(15)	1(5)–(9)	3(36)–(40) (44)	3(41)		4	1(1)–(4),6		1(13)(14) (16)	
Nov. 1976	1(8)(10) (11)(13)–(15)	4	6b,c	3(41)–(43)			1(1)–(3), 3(39)(46)	1(4)(16), 4a,7	2(17) (23)	3(47)(48)	

CONTENTS

Part Three
PERSONAL PROPERTY

A. Nature of Personal Property

B. Acquisition of Personal Property

C. Bailments

D. Sales

E. Commercial Paper

Part Seven
BUSINESS ORGANIZATIONS

A. Partnerships

B. Corporations

Part Eight
INSURANCE

Part Nine
REAL PROPERTY

Part Ten
WILLS AND DECEDENTS' ESTATES

Part Eleven
TRUSTS

Part Twelve
ACCOUNTANT'S LEGAL RESPONSIBILITY

Part Thirteen
PUBLIC LAW

A. Federal Securities Regulation

B. Federal Antitrust Laws

C. Regulation of the Employer and Employee Relationship

INTRODUCTION

The objective of the Business Law part of the Uniform Certified Public Accountant Examination "is to test the candidate's knowledge of legal problems inherent in business transactions and the accounting and auditing implications of such problems. . . . Candidates are expected to recognize the existence of legal problems and the applicable basic legal principles,"[1] and to apply these principles to factual situations as contained in the examination questions. If the candidate using this book will make a careful examination of the summary headnotes preceding various chapters and sections, followed by a careful reading of the explanatory text, he should have the necessary knowledge of business law to cope with the examination. But he must apply it *carefully and completely.*

The examination "generally consists of multiple-choice questions and problem-type questions" which "are often set in an accounting or auditing environment and answers may involve integration with financial or managerial accounting and auditing knowledge."[2] Some recent examination questions and the author's model answers occur at the end of many portions of the book to illustrate their varying formats and provide helpful answers for review in content and method of answering. In the case of essay questions, the author recommends an umbrella approach as the method to be used generally in answering a question. At the top of the umbrella is the protruding staff point; that point is the precise answer to the question. The metal frame holding the spread fabric is the principle of law, the metal stem is the fact or facts with the

[1] *Information for CPA Candidates,* AICPA (1979), pp. 10, 11.

[2] Ibid., pp. 3, 5.

metal rods connecting the metal frame to the stem tying the principle of law to the facts, and the handle of the umbrella is the summary sentence with the answer's conclusion. Several principles of law may be involved. As an illustration see, under Contracts, November 1975 examination question 4a and its answer.[3] The umbrella approach, with its graduated application of the principle of law to a legal question, is but the scientific approach of applying rules to facts. Some essay questions ask that the issues be stated and then that they be discussed and applied to the facts in the questions. This is but the umbrella approach in a slightly different format. A *logical approach* to an essay question is vitally important for accuracy and completeness, and for best utilization of time. The reader should examine all the previous examination questions and the author's model answers in this book for help in developing this logical umbrella approach.

[3] Below, pp. 133–34.

Part One: Introduction to the Uniform Commercial Code

Chapter 1

BACKGROUND, DEFINITIONS, AND PRINCIPLES OF INTERPRETATION

Background

The Uniform Commercial Code, referred to as the "UCC," is the most recent product of society to further clarify and make uniform the law in *commercial transactions concerning personal property* throughout the United States. Prior to the Code, the desire of the various states for uniformity of various aspects of law prompted the formation of the National Conference of Commissioners on Uniform State Laws. Each state has representation on this body, which, after extensive study, formulated and recommended to each state for its adoption a proposed uniform law covering a particular area where uniformity was desired. To the extent of adoption by the various states, uniformity was achieved. In this way there was adopted the Uniform Negotiable Instruments Act, Uniform Warehouse Receipts Act, Uniform Sales Act, Uniform Bills of Lading Act, Uniform Stock Transfer Act, Uniform Conditional Sales Act, Uniform Trust Receipts Act, and many other uniform laws.

While these uniform laws served very well, nevertheless with the passage of time it was realized that those uniform laws dealing with various aspects of *commercial transactions concerning personal property* needed updating in order to reflect the evolutionary progress of commercial transactions in society, and that a greater uniformity of law in this area was needed among the various states. The National Conference of Commissioners on Uniform State Laws combined with The American Law Institute, a body of outstanding judges and lawyers, to produce a Uniform Commercial Code "(a) to simplify, clarify and modernize the law governing commercial transactions; (b) to permit the continued expansion of commercial practices through custom, usage and agreement of the parties; (c) to make uniform the law among the various jurisdictions."[1] After various amendments, the 1978 Official Text is the standard reference work adopted by 49 states and in part by Louisiana.[2] The Code replaces the uniform laws mentioned in the above paragraph together with various miscellaneous state statutes on commercial transactions. Practicing accountants should carefully note changes in the Code which presently exist in each state.

It should be observed very carefully that the Code is concerned only with *commercial transactions concerning personal property*. Thus it does not disturb other branches of the law, except that *to the extent they deal with any aspect of such commercial transactions they supplement, and are modified by, the Code which governs*. For example, the law of contracts deals with many kinds of contract, such as contracts to render services, contracts to sell an interest in land or goods, and contracts to sell commercial accounts receivable; the Code changes the law of contracts *to sell goods and commercial accounts receivable*. Also, it should be noted that Section 1–103 of the Code provides that, unless displaced by Code provision, the principles of law and equity, including the law merchant, shall apply and *supplement* the Code provisions. It should be noted carefully that the UCC in turn *supplements* the Uniform Consumer Credit Code (referred to in this book as U3C), which is dominant over the UCC.[3]

The Code consists of 11 Articles, each of which is subdivided into Parts, each Part having various Sections. References are by Section, each reference having three numbers—first the Article, then the Part, and lastly the Section. For example, the reference "Section 2–201" means that the material is in Article 2, Part 2 of that Article, Section 1 of that Part. Each Article deals with one facet of an overall commercial transaction. The Articles are:

1. General Provisions.
2. Sales.
3. Commercial Paper.
4. Bank Deposits and Collections.
5. Letters of Credit.
6. Bulk Transfers.
7. Warehouse Receipts, Bills of Lading and Other Documents of Title.
8. Investment Securities.
9. Secured Transactions; Sales of Accounts, and Chattel Paper.
10. Effective Date and Repealer.
11. Effective Date and Transition Provisions.

Parties to a transaction may, by their agreement, vary the legal effect of the Code except as the Code prohibits such variance.[4] For example, 1–102(3) of the Code provides that "the obligations of good faith, diligence, reasonable-

[1] UCC 1–102(2).

[2] Effective 1975, Louisiana adopted Code Articles 1, 3, 4, 5.

[3] See U3C, sec. 1.103.

[4] But cf. U3C, sec. 1.107, which generally prohibits a consumer from waiving or foregoing rights or benefits under that Act.

ness and care prescribed by the Act may not be disclaimed by agreement but the parties may by agreement determine the standards by which the performance of such obligations is to be measured if such standards are not manifestly unreasonable." Also, the parties may agree that the law of any state or nation shall apply and govern their contract rights and duties as long as *the transaction bears a reasonable relation to such state or nation;* i.e., the state or nation ordinarily must be where a significant enough portion of the making or performance of the contract is to occur or occurs. However, 1–105(2) of the Code limits this right of the parties and specifies the applicable law in certain instances in connection with: rights of creditors against sold goods; bank deposits and collections; bulk transfers; investment securities; and secured transactions. Also, a party to a transaction may waive or renounce, in whole or in part, his claim or right against the other party arising out of an *alleged breach;* but to be effective as a release the waiver or renunciation if *oral* must be supported by *consideration,* or if *in writing* it must be *signed and delivered* by the aggrieved party *without any requirement of consideration.*

Definitions

Various words and terms are clearly defined in the Code. Those which are applicable generally throughout the Code are defined in 1–201, and those which are particularly applicable to a specific Article are defined in the introductory sections to such Article. In the event of conflict between the definitions of a term occurring in two or more Articles, which does occur because the same word has different meanings in different contexts, *it is very important to remember that the definition in a specific Article governs for that Article.* For example, the definitions of "goods" are different under the Sales portion of the Code (2–105(1)), the Documents of Title portion (7–102(1)(f)), and the Secured Transactions portion (9–105(1)(h)). It is for this reason that the word "goods" is not included among the terms generally applicable throughout the Code (1–201). Again, it should be emphasized that *these definitions are applicable to the Code and not to other branches of the law not concerned with commercial transactions except as the Code refers to such other branches of the law.* For example, 1–201(11) of the Code defines "Contract" as meaning "the total legal obligation which results from the parties' agreement as affected by this Act and any other applicable rules of law." Some of these definitions are new, some modify, and some are basically the same as those previously used. *All definitions, whether of general or particular application to a specific Article, should be examined with great care because they control the meaning of the words used by parties in their dealings with each other.*

Principles of Interpretation

In addition to various definitions to assist in clarifying the meaning of terms, the Code lays down certain fundamental rules of interpretation for general use. Thus, prima facie authenticity, genuineness, and truth of the facts stated is accorded to documents issued by third parties as authorized or required by the contract, e.g., a bill of lading issued by a carrier or a policy of insurance issued by an insurer as parties by their contract have agreed is to be issued by such third party carrier or insurer.[5] Also the Code provides for an obligation of good faith by the parties to a commercial transaction;[6] concepts of "reasonable time" and when action is taken "seasonably";[7] course of dealing and usage of trade;[8] performance or acceptance under reservation of rights;[9] and a very important option by a party to accelerate the other party's payment or performance at will when, in good faith, he believes that the other party will not perform.[10]

[5] UCC 1–202.
[6] UCC 1–203.
[7] UCC 1–204.
[8] UCC 1–205.
[9] UCC 1–207.
[10] UCC 1–208.

Part Two:
Contracts

Chapter 2

CONCEPT AND CLASSIFICATION

SECTION I. CONCEPT OF CONTRACT

A contract is a promise or set of promises creating a legal duty of performance. A promise is a manifestation of intention that something shall or shall not happen. An agreement is not a contract, but is one of the four requisites of a contract. Quasi contract signifies that there is no contract but that a duty to perform is imposed by law as though there were a contract.

The law of contracts is concerned with promises and their legal effect. It would seem that any discussion of contracts should include: what a contract is; how contracts are formed; special kinds of contract in which third persons not parties thereto have a beneficial interest; proper proof of the existence of a contract; when a contract becomes performable by each of the parties; when nonperformance is wrongful and the legal remedies available to the injured party; and lastly, when a contract is terminated. Accordingly, this will be the order in which the subject will be discussed.

The subject of contracts is governed by the Common Law,[1] in the absence of statutory provision. The Uniform Commercial Code is a statute, operating in the area of its coverage. As stated previously,[2] the Code is concerned only with *commercial transactions concerning personal property* and does not disturb other branches of the law except that, to the extent that they deal with any

---

[1] The Common Law consists of those principles, rules, and usages which are sanctioned by the courts and found in their judicial decisions, and which are not dependent upon constitutional or legislative expression for their authority.

[2] See above, p. 2.

aspect of such commercial transactions, they are modified by the Code. *They supplement the Code.* Thus, to make a sale of goods under the Sales portion of the Code it is necessary to make a contract. Accordingly, the Code is supplemented by the law of contracts.

Definition of Contract

A *"contract" is a promise or set of promises creating a legal duty of performance.* It is a person's *promise* which induces action and reliance, and it is the *promise* to which the law attaches legal significance. Accordingly, by "contract" is meant a promise with a legal duty to perform its terms. Some promises create such a legal duty of performance, while others do not (e.g., a promise to commit a crime). If more than one promise is made and they all relate to the same transaction, they all constitute the contract. Promises not relating to the same transaction are separate contracts. There must be at least two parties to a contract; but there may be only one promise, as where A promises B compensation for performance of a service which B then performs. Both A and B are parties to the contract—A because he made the promise and B because he relied on it—although there is only one promise. B is under no duty to perform because he did not make a promise, he rendered a service; but once he does perform, then A's promise becomes performable according to its terms. It is the promise which is the contract and which is sought to be enforced.

The Promise

A *"promise" is an undertaking that something shall or shall not happen.* A promise is made by the promisor to the promisee. A *representation* is a statement of a *past or present fact* made to induce formation of a contract, while a promise is of *future conduct.* A's statement to B that X ship has arrived, which then induces the formation of a contract between A and B, is a representation. A *warranty* is essentially a promise or affirmation of a state of things, such as a statement that goods are or shall be of a certain quality.[3]

The concept of "conditions" has undergone a change in the Restatement (Second) of Contracts, sections 250–55. By the change, a condition is an event uncertain to occur but which must occur before performance becomes due under a contract. (A's promise in a contract with B to reimburse B for any loss he sustains by fire imposes no duty on A to perform until damage occurs by fire.) The terms "condition precedent," "condition concurrent," and "condition subsequent" are not used as such in the Restatement, however, since they still are used by the courts and, generally, the same legal effects occur, a few brief words about them at this point are in order. Basically, a condition is an event or a fact on the happening or nonhappening of which a promissory duty of immediate performance either arises or is extinguished. A's promise in a contract with B to reimburse B for any loss he sustains by fire imposes no duty

[3] See below, p. 231.

on A to perform until damage occurs by fire. A's promise has a *condition precedent* to duty of performance—namely, fire loss to B. A's promise may have a *condition subsequent* the occurrence of which extinguishes the duty to perform the promise. Using the illustration immediately above, A's promise may also provide that, if A rejects B's claim for fire loss and B does not sue A within a specified period of time thereafter, A will have no duty to perform his promise. The necessity of B's suit within the specified period of time is a condition subsequent, and its nonoccurrence extinguishes A's duty to perform his promise. There is also a *condition concurrent*, e.g., a buyer's performance of his promise to pay the purchase price of goods and the seller's delivery of the goods are to occur simultaneously. The subject of conditions is considered in detail later.[4]

An expression may take the form of a promise but not be a promise because it does not manifest an intention that something shall or shall not happen. Such expressions are called "*illusory promises*" and have no legal effect as a promise. An employer's statement that he will pay the employee whatever salary the employer sees fit is not a promise to pay a salary.

A contract can be only executory because it is to be performed in the future. The phrase "*executory contract*" means that the promise or promises have not all been performed, while "*executed contract*" means that the promise or promises subsequently have been performed and no promissory duty remains.

The promise must be manifested by physical conduct. The conduct may be an *express promise*, as by an oral or written word, a gesture, a sign, or other manner. An *implied promise* is a promise implied from conduct, just as a promise to pay is implied from the act of a customer gesturing to the vendor and carrying away merchandise from the vendor's counter. *Silence* is not an expression; but under certain exceptional circumstances, discussed later,[5] silence may have legal effect as an expression of acceptance. *Express contracts* are promises expressly given, while *implied contracts* are promises implied from conduct. There is no difference in legal effect between such contracts. Implied contracts are sometimes called "contracts implied in fact," distinguishable from "contracts implied in law."

Quasi contract (as though there were a contract) differs markedly from implied contracts and signifies that the name of a legal duty or obligation is imposed by law for reasons of justice and not because of any promise to perform. It is not a contract, because it lacks a promise and an agreement. Furthermore, damages are measured differently for breach of contract and for quasi contract, the damages for quasi contract being the reasonable value of what has been rendered. Illustrations of quasi contract are: obligations of parental or marital support; the obligation to surrender benefits received through unjust enrichment; and the obligation of an infant to pay the reasonable value of necessaries he has received.

A promise must create a legal duty to perform what has been promised. It

---

[4] See below, pp. 93–102.

[5] See below, pp. 29–30.

must create a *legal obligation,* not just a moral obligation, in order to be a contract. Not all promises create legal obligations. Promises which are not contrary to law and which are supported by consideration are sanctioned by the law and become legal obligations. Promises are contrary to law when they are contrary to the law as provided by statute, or contrary to public policy as declared by the courts for reasons of social welfare and justice. Such promises are illegal and do not create legal obligations. They cannot be called contracts and are called merely *illegal promises.*

Agreement

A promise by itself has no legal effect. It is the *reliance on, and compliance with,* the promise by someone else which causes the law to impose a duty of performance on the promisor. The promisor bargains his promise for something in return, and, when the promisee signifies his assent to the promise, there is an agreement. Accordingly, with but few exceptions, discussed later,[6] a contract must have an agreement manifested by the parties thereto. An *agreement* is a *manifestation of mutual assent* by two or more persons each to the other. This is often called a "meeting of the minds."

The courts are concerned only with the *expressed* intents of the parties, for that is the basis on which persons deal with each other and reach agreement. Their unexpressed mental intents are of no importance. There may be a manifestation of mutual assent when the parties are not mentally in accord. (A offers to sell B the house at 111 Walnut Street. There is only one 111 Walnut Street. B accepts, thinking of another house as 111 Walnut Street. The parties have manifested mutual assent to 111 Walnut Street and, accordingly, there is an agreement.)

While a contract requires an agreement, not every agreement is a contract. An agreement contemplating performance of illegal conduct or for an illegal purpose is void; and, as it does not create any legal obligation, it cannot be a contract. *The term "agreement" should not be confused with the term "contract."*

SECTION II. CLASSIFICATION OF CONTRACTS

A formal contract has a certain written form. An informal contract, "simple contract," may be oral or written. A promise can request in return only three things: (1) an act; (2) a forbearance; or (3) a return promise. A *unilateral* contract consists of a promise and, in exchange, an act or a forbearance. A *bilateral* contract has only mutual promises. A *voidable* contract is one in which one or more of the parties has the power to avoid the contract. An *unenforceable* contract has no legal remedy for its enforcement. In a *divisible* contract, performance of less than all the obligations on one side will become

[6] See below, pp. 61–67.

due by performance of less than all the obligations on the other side. An *indivisible* contract provides that performance of all the obligations on one side will become due only by performance of all the obligations on the other side.

Formal and Informal Contracts

All contracts may be classified broadly as either *formal* or *informal* contracts. Formal contracts are called such because of their exceptional form, such form alone determining their validity as contracts. There are four kinds of formal contract: *negotiable instruments, contracts under seal, recognizances,* and *letters of credit.*[7] *Negotiable instruments* are drafts, checks, negotiable promissory notes, and certificates of deposit under the Code. Warehouse receipts and bills of lading running to bearer or to the order of a specified person under the Code are *negotiable documents of title* and are considered formal contracts in the same category as negotiable instruments. These negotiable instruments and negotiable documents of title are promises expressed in a certain form. While corporate certificates of stock are of a negotiable character under the Code, they do not usually contain promises and, therefore, are not contracts. *Contracts under seal* originated long before informal contracts and consist of the promisor's delivery of a contract in writing with a seal attached. They were called "deeds," "specialities," or "covenants." No consideration was necessary for a sealed instrument. Today the seal has greatly diminished in importance, and in most states the distinction between sealed and unsealed contracts is absolished. A *recognizance* is an undertaking made in court that payment will be made unless a certain condition occurs. One of the purposes of a recognizance is to assure attendance in court at a future day.

Informal contracts are all contracts which are not formal contracts. They are sometimes called "simple contracts" and may be oral or written.

Unilateral and Bilateral Contracts

Contracts are classified more particularly as *unilateral, bilateral, voidable,* and *unenforceable.* All these contracts may be either under seal or be informal contracts. A *unilateral contract* is one in which only an act or a forbearance is rendered in return for a promise. A *bilateral contract* is one in which there are only mutual promises between the parties to the contract. By definition, a contract consists of a promise or set of promises creating a legal duty of performance. The promise or promises constitute the contract—not the manifestation of mutual assent or the consideration, which are necessary elements in the formation of the contract. A unilateral contract may have more than one promise on *one* side, and a bilateral contract may have more than one promise on *each* side. In unilateral contracts, only the promisor is bound by the con-

[7] See below, pp. 224, 304.

tract; while in bilateral contracts, all promisors are bound to each other. If the promisor requests and receives a return promise from someone other than the promisee, or the promisor requests the promisee to make a return promise to someone other than the promisor which the promisee does, there cannot be a bilateral contract, inasmuch as each party must be a promisor and a promisee to the other. There can be a unilateral contract, however.

Voidable Contracts

At the time of its inception the contract may be *voidable,* but not "void." A contract means that a promise creates a legal duty. A void promise creates no legal duty and, therefore, cannot be a contract. The phrase "void contract" is a misnomer, a contradiction in terms, and should be avoided. A voidable contract has a promise which creates a duty to perform. *It is a contract in which one or more parties has the power to avoid the contract by manifesting his election to do so.* It is subject to the same obligations as a contract not voidable, and it differs only in the existence of a power to avoid the contract. Only the party who has this power of avoidance may exercise or waive it. By his exercise of this power, the contract is rescinded and made void. By his waiver of this power, the power thereby ceases to exist and the contract no longer is subject to it. By waiving this power, the party is said to "ratify" the transaction. Illustrative of grounds for avoidance are: infancy, duress generally, undue influence, fraud in inducing the formation of a contract, and a party's nondisclosure of facts when there is a legal duty to do so as in transactions between fiduciaries and beneficiaries.

Unenforceable Contracts

An unenforceable contract is a contract with no legal remedy for its enforcement. The contract exists, nevertheless, because the law recognizes its performance as a legal duty. Illustrations are: contracts in which the remedy of enforcement is gone, as where a statute of limitations bars the right of recovery; and contracts which do not comply with the statutory requisites of proof of the contract, as where a contract which is within the statute of frauds fails to comply with its requirements.

Divisible Contracts

A divisible contract is a contract which provides that performance of less than all the obligations on one side will become due by performance of less than all the obligations on the other side. An indivisible contract provides that performance of all the obligations on one side will become due only by performance of all the obligations on the other side. For example, a contract for the construction of a building for a fixed price to be paid to the builder in installments as he completes each story of the building is a *divisible* contract. If the contract provided that the total cost of constructing the building would be paid on the completion of the whole building, it would be an *indivisible* contract.

SECTION III. REQUISITES OF CONTRACT

A contract has four essential elements: (1) two or more parties with contractual capacity, (2) manifestation of mutual assent, (3) consideration, and (4) legally valid transaction. These four elements will be considered in turn, in the order indicated, in the chapter immediately following.

Before beginning a detailed discussion of the law of Contracts, it should be carefully noted that in the new Restatement (Second) of Contracts, 1980, many of the new concepts of contract and agreement expounded in the Uniform Commercial Code (particularly in Article 2 on Sales) are now incorporated in the Restatement.

Chapter 3

FORMATION OF CONTRACTS

SECTION I. PARTIES WITH CONTRACTUAL CAPACITY

Parties to a contract may be natural or juristic persons. An infant's contract is voidable by him during his infancy or within a reasonable time (usually fixed by statute) after he becomes an adult, except that if the contract involves land he can disaffirm only within a reasonable time after he becomes an adult, provided, in some states, he returns or tenders the return of what he has received if he still has it, irrespective of its form. Under the Code on Sales of goods, the adult's transfer of goods, which he purchased from an infant, to a good faith purchaser for value before the infant disaffirms, cuts off the infant's power to disaffirm as to such purchaser and the infant cannot regain the property from him. The infant may ratify (waive his power to disaffirm) only after he becomes an adult. His retention and *use* after majority implies ratification, as does the expiration of a reasonable time after majority. An infant's contract for necessaries may be disaffirmed, but he must keep the necessary and is liable in quasi contract for its reasonable value. He is liable for his torts and crimes, and a contract fraudulently induced by him is voidable by the adult party. A mentally incompetent person's contracts are voidable by him, but a person adjudicated to be mentally incompetent has no capacity to contract. Whether a drunkard's contract is voidable by him depends upon the degree of his intoxication.

Parties with joint rights or joint obligations are one legal unit, and they sue or are sued collectively as a unit. Unless the parties expressly or impliedly indicate to the contrary, two or more parties who *together* promise the *same* performance to the *same* promisee or promisees are jointly bound. There are two exceptions: (1) if a written promise made together by more than one person uses solely the first person singular, the parties are jointly and severally

liable; (2) when two or more persons sign a negotiable instrument as maker, acceptor, drawer or indorser and as part of the same transaction, they are jointly and severally liable.

Persons

One of the four essential elements in the formation of a contract is parties with contractual capacity. Parties to a contract may be either natural or juristic persons. Natural persons are human beings. Juristic persons are legal entities designated or personified as such by law. Corporations, political subdivisions such as state and county, partnerships, and other associations with a legal entity are persons, in the sense that they can be parties to a contract.

Persons with Partial Capacity to Make a Voidable Contract

Juristic persons are limited to the powers granted to them and, accordingly, have capacity to contract as limited by such powers. Aliens may contract, but the contracts and contractual powers of enemy aliens are regulated by federal statute. Convicts serving long terms of imprisonment have their contractual powers limited by statute in many states. A married woman (feme covert) had no power to contract at common law, but today she is fully capable to contract. Infants, the insane, and drunkards in certain cases, have partial capacity to make voidable contracts. Each of these last three will be considered.

Infants. An infant, or minor, is a natural person male or female, who has not yet attained his majority. Today, in almost all states an infant is a person under 18 years of age, although in a few states the age of majority is still 21 years. Exceptions are made by statutes which provide different ages at which people enter into a contract of marriage, enlist in military service, or execute wills.

Disaffirmance. An infant is legally capable of making a contract; but, because of his immaturity and inferiority in bargaining astuteness, as compared with adults, an infant's contracts are *voidable* at his election. Except for the power of avoidance, an infant's contract is like any other contract and is subject to the same rules of law. The infant's privilege of avoidance, or of "*disaffirmance*" as it is often called in the case of infants' contracts, is absolute and personal only to the infant. Disaffirmance is an expression of intention to rescind or to avoid the contract and may be made expressly, or impliedly by conduct indicating avoidance. Once disaffirmance occurs, the contract is avoided and cannot be ratified subsequently. On disaffirmance, the adult party to the contract is entitled to whatever the infant received under the contract if the infant still has it, regardless of its changed form. If the infant no longer has what he received under the contract, in most states he can disaffirm anyway. If the infant still has what he received under the contract or what he has received in exchange therefor, in some states he must tender its return to the adult as a condition to disaffirmance, although most courts do not impose this as a condition.

An *executed* contract may be avoided during minority or within a reasonable period of time after majority, except a conveyance of real property which cannot be avoided during minority. State statutes usually specify what is a reasonable time; otherwise it is a question of fact for the jury. If the contract is *executory* on the infant's side, no expression of disaffirmance is necessary and the contract is unenforceable against him unless he ratifies the contract.

Generally, the effect of disaffirmance is to restore the parties to their position immediately prior to making the contract. However, if the property to which the infant is entitled is unavailable and has depreciated in value at the time of disaffirmance, there is a conflict among the courts as to whether the infant is entitled only to the value at the time of disaffirmance or he is to be made whole. A problem arises if, prior to disaffirmance, the adult party to the contract had transferred to a third person the property acquired from the infant. At Common Law the infant could disaffirm and regain the property, even if the transferee were a good faith purchaser for value. This is still true today, except in the case of a good faith purchaser for value of *goods* from whom the infant cannot regain the property. The exception applies only to a good faith purchaser for value and only to goods, as provided in 2–403(1) of the Code: "A person with voidable title has power to transfer a good title to a good faith purchaser for value." (I, an infant, sold and delivered goods to A, an adult. A's sale and delivery of the goods to G, a good faith purchaser for value, cuts off I's power of avoidance *as to G*, who obtains good title to the goods.)

Ratification. The infant's waiver of his power of avoidance is called "*ratification*" or "affirmance," and is a manifestation of assent to the contract. Ratification may occur only after majority and may be express, or implied from the infant's affirmative or negative conduct. *Retention and use after majority* of what the infant has received under the contract implies ratification. Failure to exercise the power of avoidance within a statutory, or in the absence of statute a reasonable, period of time after majority impliedly waives the power. The infant cannot ratify part of the contract and also disaffirm part of it. Ratification cannot occur if, at the time, the infant is ignorant of some material fact.[1] The effect of ratification is merely to remove the power of avoidance; the contract is not disturbed by it.

Necessaries. Although an infant may avoid his contracts, he is liable in quasi contract for the reasonable value of *necessaries* he has *received.* On disaffirmance, an infant must retain the necessaries he has received and may recover from the adult what he has paid in excess of the market value. A "necessary" is that which is actually and reasonably needed for the personal general welfare of the infant, considering his status in life, at the time the contract was made by him. Food, clothing, lodging, medical care, and, to a

[1] For the effect of ignorance of a material fact on ratification in agency, see below, p. 575. See also below, p. 67.

certain extent, education are included among necessaries. An ordinary education is usually essential to an infant's welfare; but whether higher education is a necessary depends upon the circumstances in each particular case. A purchase of clothes might be a necessary in one case and not in another, depending on the status in life of the particular infant, the clothes he had previously, the price of the new clothes, and other factors.

Torts and Crimes. An infant, except one of tender years, is liable for his torts or wrongs just as is anyone else. Commission of a tort by an infant in connection with a contract does not preclude the infant from exercising his power to disaffirm the contract, although some courts hold to the contrary. The usual type of tort committed by an infant is deceit by misrepresentation of age. If the infant's tort is independent of the contract, such as deceit inducing the formation of a contract, the infant is liable for the damage caused by the tort. If the infant's tort is a part of the contract, as a warranty in a sales contract, the infant is not liable for the tort. A contract induced by fraud is voidable at the election of the party defrauded; and, if the infant has perpetrated such fraud, *the adult* may avoid the contract.

When Not Voidable. Public policy, as provided by statute or declared by the courts, has recognized the desirability that certain contracts of infants should not be voidable because of such infancy. Examples are: a contract of marriage; a contract of enlistment in military service; and a contract to do that which the infant was under a legal duty to do and which he could be legally compelled to do. Many states by statute recognize that self-supporting infants often engage in business and, accordingly, provide that such contracts are binding with no power of avoidance if the contract was reasonable and provident from the infant's point of view. Also by statute in many states, infants above a specified age are permitted to procure life insurance with certain specified persons as beneficiaries (e.g., mother, father, brother, sister), but they are deprived of any power to avoid such insurance contracts. While an infant partner may disaffirm a contract of partnership and a contract made by the partnership, nevertheless, he cannot thereby disturb the availability of his capital contribution to firm creditors and to his partners.

Emancipation of an infant means that the parents have given up their right to the custody and income of the infant and that the infant is self-supporting. Emancipation may be done expressly, or impliedly—as by marriage or enlistment in military service with parental consent. Emancipation does not affect the infant's limited capacity to make contracts nor, in the absence of statute to the contrary, his right to disaffirm contracts.

The Mentally Incompetent. Mental incompetency may occur from a variety of causes—e.g., defective birth, accident, disease, old age. A person is mentally incompetent when, because of his mental illness or defect, he cannot comprehend the nature and consequence of the transaction. If a guardian for him is appointed by a court, this is an adjudication that he has no capacity to contract because he has such an extreme degree of mental incompetence that he cannot manifest assent to the transaction; only the guardian can contract.

Unless a guardian is appointed, the mentally incompetent person has partial capacity to contract and his contracts are voidable at his election with a reasonable time after he regains competency and learns of the contract. An exception of when there is no power of avoidance is if the contract is fair, the other contracting party does not know of the mental incompetency, and either the contract is partially or totally executed or the circumstances have so changed that it would be inequitable to permit a power of avoidance. The law applicable to infants applies generally to mentally incompetent persons. On regaining competency, the former incompetent may ratify the contract thereby waiving his power of avoidance.

Drunkards. Intoxication does not of itself make voidable a contract made by a drunkard. The degree of intoxication is important. If the intoxication is so extreme that the drunkard cannot manifest assent to the transaction, there is no capacity to contract and no contract. If the intoxication is not that extreme but it is such that the drunkard does not appreciate the nature and consequences of the transaction of which the other party is aware, the contract is voidable by the drunkard. If the drunkard has some understanding of the transaction and the other party being aware of the intoxication took advantage of it, then again the contract is voidable by the drunkard. Promptly after becoming sober, the drunkard can ratify the voidable contract and thereby waive his power of avoidance.

Multiple Promisors and Promisees—Joint, Several, and Joint and Several Parties

A contract requires two or more parties. If two or more parties to a contract are promisors or promisees of the *same* performance, such parties may be joint, several, or joint and several promisors or promisees. The *intentions* of the parties determine whether their obligations or rights are joint, several, or joint and several. Joint means collective, a unit. Parties with joint rights are one legal unit and sue collectively as a unit. If they have joint obligations, they are sued collectively as a unit.

Joint Liability. Unless the parties expressly or impliedly indicate to the contrary, two or more parties who *together* promise the *same* performance to the *same* promisee or promisees are *jointly* bound. For example, partners in a partnership make their contracts with third persons and are bound jointly to them. The partners are an entity for the purpose of that contract. If the parties express no intention in dealing with third parties as to how they wish to be bound, then their contract will be interpreted in light of the terms thereof and the circumstances surrounding its formation in order to determine their intention. *If no intention is expressed or implied to third parties, they are joint parties.* The manner and extent to which the parties agree *among themselves* that the obligation is to be borne does not preclude a joint obligation to third persons with whom they have contracted. In order to promote uniformity in the various branches of the law, *two exceptions are made to this principle of* *law if the parties do not indicate their intentions. First,* if a written promise made together by more than one person uses solely *the first person singular* the parties are *joint and several.* (A writing with the words "30 days after date *I* promise to pay to X $50" is signed by A, B, C, and D.)[2] *Second,* when two or more persons sign a negotiable instrument as maker, acceptor, drawer or indorser and as a part of the same transaction they are jointly and severally liable on the instrument.[3] They sue and are sued as a group. The discharge of joint debtors is discussed later.[4]

Several Liability. Unless the parties expressly or impliedly indicate to the contrary, two or more parties to a contract who promise the same performance by making *separate* promises, or who promise to make such performance *separately,* to the same promisee or promisees, are *severally* bound. "We each promise," "each of us promises," "we severally promise," are commonplace expressions indicating the intention to be bound severally.

Joint and Several Liability. Unless the parties indicate to the contrary, two or more parties who promise, in the same contract, the same performance to the same promisee or promisees, and who *also* make such promises separately or promise separate performance, are *jointly and severally bound.* "We and each of us promise" illustrates a joint and several liability. By statute in many states, obligations which are joint are interpreted to be joint and several,[5] unless the parties have expressed a contrary intention.

Joint, Several, and Joint and Several Rights. Just as two or more parties may be jointly, severally, or jointly and severally liable as co-obligors, so two or more parties may have joint, several, or joint and several rights as co-obligees. Unless the promisor indicates to the contrary, his promise of performance to two or more parties creates several rights if the interests of the promisees are separate and distinct, or joint rights if the promisees have only a single interest in the performance. (A contracted with B, C, and D, a partnership, to erect a building on their land. A's promise created joint rights in B, C, and D.)

SECTION II. MANIFESTATION OF MUTUAL ASSENT

One of the four requisites for a contract is an *agreement*, which is a manifestation of mutual assent by the parties, occurring by offer and acceptance. The test of the meaning of any manifestation is what a person in the position of the addressee reasonably could understand it to mean. An *offer* is a promise proposed in exchange for an act, forbearance, or a return promise. An *auction* is with reserve unless indicated to be without reserve. At an auction with reserve, a bid is an offer; if without reserve, a bid is an acceptance, subject to no

---

[2] See below, p. 322.

[3] Ibid.

[4] See below, pp. 121–22.

[5] With respect to liabilities of partners, see below, p. 656.

higher bid being made. A bid may be withdrawn at any time before the fall of the hammer. An offer terminates in four ways: (1) Its *acceptance.* (2) Its *expiration* by the offer's express or implied terms; or, prior to acceptance, by supervening death of the offeree or offeror, destruction of the thing required by the contract, or illegality. (3) Its *revocation* by the offeror prior to its acceptance, effective on the offeree's *receipt* of notice of the revocation. An *option* is an irrevocable offer as prescribed in the option contract. Under the Code on Sales of goods, a "*firm offer*" is a written, signed offer by a merchant to buy or sell goods and to keep his offer open for no more than three months; consideration is *not* required. An offer for a unilateral contract implies a subsidiary offer to keep the main offer open if the offeree begins performance. (4) Its *rejection* by the offeree, which is his manifestation of an intent not to accept the offer, effective on the offeror's receipt of the rejection. A counteroffer requires a change in the offer's terms and is a rejection. However, under the Code on Sales of goods, additional terms by the offeree do not prevent the agreed-upon-terms from creating a contract, the additional terms being new offers for addition to the contract, with special effect if the contract is between merchants.

An acceptance is the offeree's manifestation of assent to the offer in reliance on and in compliance with the offer. Silence is not a manifestation of assent, with certain exceptions. A confirmation of receipt of an offer is not an acceptance, except that under the Code on Sales of goods a written confirmation is an acceptance. An acceptance of an offer for a bilateral contract must be communicated to the offeror. Unless the offer indicates otherwise, it implies acceptance in any manner and by any medium reasonable under the circumstances. Unless the offer for a unilateral contract requires notice of acceptance, an accepting offeree need not notify the offeror of acceptance, unless the offeree can believe that the offeror cannot reasonably ascertain that performance has occurred, in which event he must notify the offeror or the offeror's duty to perform is discharged. *Estoppel* consists of one person's holding out of a material fact, and the other person's material change of position in reasonable reliance on the holding out. If the offeree misrepresents any existing fact which is essential to the formation of a contract, and the offeror reasonably relies on it and changes his position, the offeree is estopped from asserting the reverse of what he misrepresented.

"Fraud" is the intentional misrepresentation of fact, or the intentional nondisclosure of fact in violation of a legal duty to disclose, with intent to induce a contractual mistake. "Material misrepresentation" means an innocent misrepresentation, or innocent nondisclosure in violation of a legal duty, of material facts. Fraud or material misrepresentation in the "procurement" (misrepresentation of the nature of the act engaged in) precludes the formation of a contract. Fraud in the "inducement" or material misrepresentation causes the contract to be voidable at the election of the party to whom misrepresentation has been made. The innocent party can, expressly or impliedly, either waive or exercise his power of avoidance. Failure to avoid promptly causes waiver. Except

when there is a legal duty to speak, a party has no obligation to disclose that of which the other party is ignorant. A fiduciary has a legal duty to disclose to the person for whom he is a fiduciary. Generally, duress, coercion, and undue influence make a contract voidable. Generally, a unilateral mistake does not preclude the formation of a contract. Mutual mistake prevents the formation of a contract on only two occasions.

The time and place where a contract is made is the time and place where the last act necessary to make a contract has occurred by offer and acceptance, and it is the law of that place which will determine its status as a contract. Generally, the parties may agree that the law of any state shall apply and govern their contractual rights and duties if that state has a substantial relationship to the parties or to the transaction. Under the *parol evidence rule*, when a contract is in writing, any oral or written agreement made prior to such written contract, and any oral agreement made contemporaneously with the written contract, which contradicts (varies or adds to) such written contract, are inadmissible in evidence.

In order to have a contract there must be a bargain consisting of a manifestation of mutual assent and consideration, although there are exceptions. At this time we are concerned with the manifestation of mutual assent.

Parties must agree to a transaction, and such agreement must be manifested. In forming an informal contract, parties manifest to each other their mutual assent by offer and acceptance. An offer contains a promise which is bargained for something specific in return—conduct consisting of *performance* of an act or a forbearance (failure to act), or conduct in the form of a return *promise.* An acceptance is the rendition of what was requested in the offer, manifesting assent through compliance with the offer and in reliance thereon. If the conduct requested by the offer and rendered is a *return promise,* the contract is *bilateral;* if the conduct is *performance* (either an act or a forbearance), the contract is *unilateral.* In case of doubt whether the offer invites the formation of a bilateral or of a unilateral contract, the offer is interpreted by the courts as inviting a bilateral contract.

Offer

Expression of Intent to Contract. An offer manifests a willingness to enter into a bargain. An "offer" may be defined as a promise *proposed in exchange* for conduct consisting of an act or a forbearance, or a return promise. An offer is a complete[6] proposal. An offer is made by an offeror to an offeree. The offer may be expressed wholly or partly by words, writings, acts, or other conduct and must be communicated to the offeree. The offeror's expressed intent to

[6] But see a different rule for Sales under the Code, below, p. 202.

contract, as reasonably understood by the offeree, is important—not the offeror's unexpressed mental intent. The offeror's expression is tested objectively. Could a person in the position of the offeree reasonably understand the expression to invite certain conduct (act, forbearance, or return promise) in exchange for the promise? If he can, the expression is an offer. If the addressee knows, or reasonably should know, from the expression or from the circumstances at the time of the expression that the utterer does not thereby intend to make an offer, there is no offer.

Inadequate Expressions. An expression made in anger, jest, or excitement, if so understood by the addressee, does not constitute an offer because the circumstances surrounding its utterance would not lead the addressee to understand the utterer to intend an offer—an intent to contract. Similarly, negotiations (preliminary explorations) do not constitute offers. They are inducements inviting offers. Advertisements, published price lists, and merchants' circulars, indicating that goods are for sale, are not offers; they invite offers. Quotations,[7] estimates, trade inquiries and answers thereto, *usually* are not offers. *Invitations* to bid on work or on property to be sold are not offers. The *bids* usually are offers. Expressions or negotiations which are incomplete, vague, or indefinite, in that normally included terms are omitted, do not constitute offers. The phrase "$40 per week and a fair share of the profits of the business" is indefinite and not an offer. An offer must be a *complete proposal* contemplating definite and certain conduct, nothing remaining to be done but to accept the offer and thereby create a definite obligation. However, the law invokes the standard of reasonableness whenever it can in order to make a promise sufficiently definite to be legally enforceable. Thus, omission of a provision for the time within which performance is to occur, or for the amount of the purchase price, does not necessarily render the promise indefinite and ineffective as an offer. The law interprets the intent to be for a reasonable time or a reasonable amount—namely, the fair value. If the terms of the promise exclude such an interpretation, the promise is indefinite and is not an offer. It should be noted that a promise is sufficiently definite if it refers to extrinsic facts for completeness.[8]

A problem sometimes arises when an indefinite or vague promise is made and, in reliance thereon, complete or partial performance is made by the addressee. There are two possible solutions. First, if the promisor benefits from the performance, he then has a quasi-contractual obligation to pay a fair value for the benefits he received. Second, it is possible that the performance made definite the otherwise indefinite promise. (X tells Y that he will pay Y $80.00 per day for work when X wants him. Later, at X's request, Y works for X. There is a unilateral contract at $80.00 per day for each day Y worked. Although X's

---

[7] But see "firm offers," p. 25, ftn. 12, and pp. 202–3.

[8] However, under UCC 2–204(3): "Even though one or more terms are left open a contract for sale does not fail for indefiniteness if the parties have intended to make a contract and there is a reasonably certain basis for giving an appropriate remedy."

expression was too vague to be an offer because indefinite in time, yet Y's performance made X's offer definite as to when Y was to work.)

Auctions. Advertisements of an auction are not offers but invitations to appear and bid. An auction is with reserve unless indicated to be without reserve. At an auction "*with reserve*" a bid is an *offer*, and the auctioneer reserves the right to accept or reject any bid. If the auctioneer waives this right, it is an auction without reserve, and the auctioneer by announcing that it is an auction without reserve and by putting up the property for sale thereby makes an offer to sell to the highest bidder. At an auction *without reserve* a bid is an *acceptance* of the auctioneer's offer, subject to the condition subsequent that no higher bids are made. In an auction without reserve, the auctioneer need not put the goods up for sale and, if no bid is made within a reasonable time, he can withdraw any item that he has already put up. Also, before a bid is made he may announce that the auction is no longer without reserve. The auctioneer may do this just as any other offeror may withdraw or change his offer before acceptance. In an auction, whether with or without reserve, the bid may be withdrawn by the bidder before the auctioneer manifests his acceptance by the fall of the hammer or in other customary manner.[9] A bidder's retraction does not revive any previous bid.

Writings—Memorial or Contract. If the expression or manifestation under the circumstances reasonably leads the addressee to understand that the utterer does not intend it as a proposal binding upon him until the utterer manifests a further assent, it is not an offer. Difficulty is encountered, however, when the parties contemplate a subsequent writing. Do the parties intend the writing to be the contract, requiring their signed assent thereto; or do they intend it to be a memorial of the oral contract, or of the several writings constituting a written contract already made? If the writing is to be *the contract*, then the utterer's expression is not an offer. If the writing is to be a *memorial*, then the utterer's expression was an offer which has been accepted resulting in a contract. It is essentially a problem of interpretation of the intention of the parties as expressed by them. If the parties agree to a writing which shall contain solely the provisions already agreed upon, the contract has been made and the writing is merely a memorial thereof. If the agreement is incomplete, contemplating subsequent inclusion of necessary details at the time of the writing, the preliminary agreement constitutes merely negotiations and the writing is to be the contract.

Duration. An offer is legally operative—that is, capable of being accepted—until terminated. Termination may occur in four ways: *expiration*

---

[9] UCC 2–328: "(2) A sale by auction is complete when the auctioneer so announces by the fall of the hammer or in other customary manner. Where a bid is made while the hammer is falling in acceptance of a prior bid the auctioneer may in his discretion reopen the bidding or declare the goods sold under the bid on which the hammer was falling.

"(4) If the auctioneer knowingly receives a bid on the seller's behalf or the seller makes or procures such a bid, and notice has not been given that liberty for such bidding is reserved, the buyer may at his option avoid the sale or take the goods at the price of the last good faith bid prior to the completion of the sale. This subsection shall not apply to any bid at a forced sale."

of the offer, *revocation* of the offer by the offeror, and either *rejection* or *acceptance* of the offer by the offeree. If the offer has expired or has been revoked, there no longer is any offer for the offeree to consider. *Until expiration or revocation, there is an offer outstanding which the offeree may either reject or accept.*

Expiration of Offers. An offer may expire: pursuant to the terms of the offer; by delay in the communication of the offer; by supervening legal incapacity of the offeror or offeree to make a contract; by supervening destruction of a specific person or thing required for performance of the proposed contract; or by supervening illegality.

An offer may specify its duration. On the expiration of that time the offer is terminated. There is a difference of opinion as to the duration of an offer which ambiguously expresses the time within which acceptance must occur. (A mailed written offer specifies that the offeree has eight days in which to accept or to reject the offer. Do the eight days begin to run from the date the offer was written or from the date of its delivery to the offeree?) However, whether or not the utterer's expression constitutes an offer and what constitutes the terms thereof are determined by *what the addressee reasonably can understand the expression to mean.* The offeree should realize that the offeror *may* have intended the offer to begin from the date the offer was written or orally expressed. Accordingly, while some courts have held to the contrary, the better view is that such an offer begins to run from the date of its writing or oral expression and not from the date of its communication to the offeree.

If no time is expressed in the offer, then it is implied that the offeror intended its duration to be for a reasonable time. A reasonable time is determined by taking into consideration the nature of the offer and the circumstances under which it was made, of which the offeree either knows or reasonably should know. If the offer is for a unilateral contract, a reasonable time for acceptance is the time in which the act or forbearance can reasonably occur. If the offer is for a bilateral contract, what may be considered to be a reasonable time for acceptance varies. When the parties are not at a distance from each other, or are conversing over the telephone, a reasonable time for acceptance does not extend beyond the time of the occasion; acceptance must occur immediately or the offer thereupon expires. When the parties are at a distance from each other, a reasonable time for acceptance is determined by the haste by which the offer was sent, whether the subject matter is subject to rapid fluctuations in price, and the requirements of usage. Generally, in commercial transactions time is of the essence, and a reasonable period of time for acceptance of an offer sent by mail is return mail, the same day in which the offer was received.

Where communication of the offer has been delayed by fault of the offeror or of the communication channel utilized by the offeror, the offer expires if the time in which to accept has been expressed in the offer and has been exceeded or if a reasonable period of time to accept has elapsed and this is known or should be known by the offeree. If the offeree does not know, or has no means of knowing, of the delay, the period of time of acceptance is extended as though the delay had never occurred. If the offeree knows of the delay but the time expressed in the offer has not elapsed or if no time is expressed in the offer and a reasonable time has not gone by, the offeree may accept within the period of time remaining. The postmark on the letter, the date on the letter, and other circumstances surrounding the transmission of the offer are considered in determining whether the offeree had reason to know of the delay.

It is implied in an offer that, at the time of acceptance: the *offeror* is alive and legally capable of entering into a contract; where the proposed contract required the existence of a *specific* person or thing, that such person or thing was in existence; and the proposed contract would be a legally *valid* transaction. If between the time an offer is made and the time when a manifestation of assent is made by the offeree the offeror should die, the offer expires at that moment. An offeree takes the risk that the offeror is alive at the time of his acceptance. Inasmuch as an insane person is legally capable of making a voidable contract in most states, supervening insanity of the offeror, if not known to the offeree, does not affect the duration of the offer. If it is known to the offeree prior to his acceptance, the offer generally is considered void. As an offeree is required for an offer, the offeree's supervening death precludes acceptance and the offer thereby expires. Supervening insanity of the offeree, if known to the offeror, terminates the offer; if it is not known to the offeror, the offer continues in existence. If a specific thing required by the proposed contract for its performance is destroyed *prior to acceptance* of the offer, the offer expires. (A offers to supply B with all the goods produced by X factory. Prior to B's acceptance, X factory is destroyed. The offer has expired because the continued existence of X factory was required by the offer and by the proposed contract.) Generally, an agreement to perform an illegal transaction is legally void and therefore cannot create a contract. If the contemplated transaction *becomes* illegal subsequent to the making of the offer, the offer expires inasmuch as it cannot result in a contract.

Revocation of Offers. An offer for an informal contract, except for certain irrevocable offers, *may be revoked by the offeror at any time prior to acceptance.* Once acceptance has occurred an offer cannot be revoked, because the offer and acceptance have merged into an agreement creating a contract. Even though an offer expressly states a specific time in which to accept or states that the offer will not be withdrawn, it is still revocable at any time prior to acceptance.

No specific form of revocation by the offeror is required. It may be express, as by parol or writing, or may be implied from conduct. Any expression by the offeror which states or implies an intention not to be bound by the offer constitutes a revocation; the word "revoke" is not necessary.

A revocation is ineffective and does not terminate an offer until the revocation is received by the offeree.[10] Communication of the revocation may be

[10] See UCC 1-201(26)(27). See below, pp. 206–7.

made by the offeror or by the offeree's acquisition of reliable information of the offeror's expression of revocation. Information is reliable when a reasonable man would believe it to be true or when it should reasonably cause him to make inquiry. (A offers to sell certain land to B. Subsequently, before any acceptance by B, A sells such land to C. B learned of the sale. B no longer can accept. The offer has been revoked by A's expression of intent to revoke—the sale from which such intent is implied—and by the communication of such intent through B's acquisition of knowledge of the sale.) The offeree receives the revocation when it comes into his possession either personally, through his agent authorized to receive communications for him, or by deposit in a place authorized by him for deposit of this or similar communications. Deposit in the offeree's door mailbox or on his office desk, or delivery to his office secretary is communication. There can be no *effective* revocation without communication of notice to the offeree either by the offeror or by the offeree's acquisition of such knowledge, with one exception. When an offer is made to people unidentified to the offeror, the better view is that the offer may be revoked even though the offerees do not receive actual notice of the revocation, as long as the offeror takes all reasonable means under the circumstances to give the offerees such notice. Use of the same channel for revocation as for making the offer, with a similar degree of publicity, usually is sufficient. A newspaper publication of an offer for reward may be revoked by the same degree of newspaper publicity of revocation. Use of a different channel, such as radio, for revocation of a newspaper published offer might not reach the offerees, who might not be expected to hear a radio revocation. If the offeror later learned the identity of the offerees, publication in any form would, in itself, be insufficient; direct, individual communication would have to be made by the offeror.

Sometimes there is difficulty in determining whether an offer is divisible, in that it invites a series of acceptances each acceptance to create a new contract, or contemplates a single acceptance covering a series of acts to be performed under the one contract. If the offer is divisible, it may be revoked except as to contracts formed by acceptances which have already occurred. This is often the case in suretyship.[11]

An offer is irrevocable by the offeror or by his death or insanity if it is an option, or if it has resulted in part performance or tender of part performance in reliance thereon. An irrevocable offer is exposed to the power of acceptance

PROMISE

1. Offer to sell land for $10,000.

2. Promise to keep the offer to sell open for 30 days.

[11] See below, pp. 485–86.

just as any revocable offer, the difference being that, in the case of an irrevocable offer, a legal duty not to revoke is present which will be enforced. This duty exists because an express or implied contract has been made in which the offeror promises to keep the offer open.

Option. An offer is a promise proposed in exchange for an act, forbearance, or a return promise. If a promise does not request anything in exchange, it is not an offer; it is just a promise. A promise may consist of two parts, the first part being an *offer* to make an overall contract, and the second part being a *promise* to keep the offer in the first part open for a period of time. (A offers to sell certain land to B for $10,000 and states he will keep his offer open for 30 days.) If B accepts the offer within 30 days, A's offer to sell and B's acceptance of *that offer* create a contract for the sale of the land. However, before B's acceptance, A may terminate his promise to keep the offer to sell open and revoke his offer to sell without being liable for so doing. But if A's *promise* to keep the offer open asks for *consideration*,[12] i.e., an act, forbearance, or a return promise, then A's promise to keep the offer open becomes an *offer subsidiary* to A's *main offer* to sell. (A offers to sell certain land to B for $10,000 and states he will keep the offer open for 30 days if B will pay A $200 for this privilege. If B pays A $200, B thereby *accepts* A's *subsidiary offer*, creating a *contract* to keep the main offer open. A's *main offer* is now *irrevocable* by A for the 30 days, and is called an option.)

Accordingly, *an option is an irrevocable offer as prescribed in the option contract.* The essence of an option is that it is an irrevocable offer for the period of time expressed in the option contract; and if no period of time is expressed, then for a reasonable period of time.

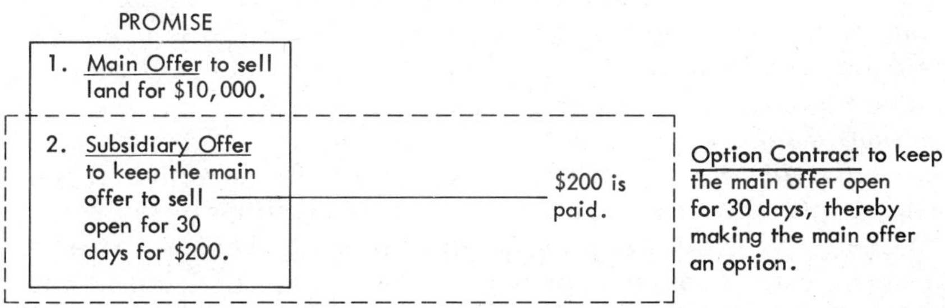

In this connection, if an offer for a *unilateral contract* is made and, in reliance thereon, *part performance* occurs or is *tendered*, can the offer be revoked by the offeror or terminated by his death or insanity? (A offers to pay B

[12] UCC 2–205: "Firm Offers. An offer *by a merchant* to buy or sell goods in a *signed writing* which by its terms gives assurance that it will be held open is not revocable, for lack of consideration, during the time stated or if no time is stated for a reasonable time, but in no event may such period of irrevocability exceed *three months;* but any such term of assurance on a form supplied by the *offeree* must be *separately signed by the offeror.*" (Author's italics.)

$100 to dig a ditch. B has dug part of the ditch when A dies, becomes insane, or wishes to revoke his offer.) An offeror may revoke his offer before acceptance occurs. Acceptance of an offer for a *unilateral* contract is *full* performance of the act or forbearance requested. Part performance is not acceptance of the offer. The offeror's promise is in exchange for performance of an act or a forbearance and, until performance occurs, there is no acceptance and no contract, and the promisor cannot be compelled to perform his promise. *When there is doubt concerning the meaning of the offer as to whether it requests a unilateral or a bilateral contract, the courts will interpret the transaction as a bilateral contract,*[13] thereby protecting both parties. (A offers to pay B $100 for rendering certain services, to which B replies "I'll do it," or "All right," or words of similar import. The expressions of A and B create a *bilateral* contract.) However, when the offer clearly contemplates a unilateral contract and part performance occurs, can the offeror revoke the offer? Inasmuch as the offeror may limit his offer as he wishes, if the terms of the offer indicate that the offeror may revoke, clearly the offer is revocable at any time before full performance. *If the offer contains no such indication, once part performance occurs or is tendered in reliance on the offer* there is an option contract, and the main offer now is *irrevocable by the offeror, by his death, or by his insanity.* The reasoning is that an offer for a unilateral contract implies a *subsidiary offer* to keep the main offer open if performance is begun. *Beginning of performance* is the act called for by the subsidiary offer and is consideration therefor, resulting in an option contract to keep the main offer open for the indicated time, or for a reasonable time if no time is indicated. Similarly, an offer for a unilateral contract implies a subsidiary offer to accept a *tender* of part performance, and once the tender of part performance is made there is an acceptance of the subsidiary offer, and an option contract is formed to keep the main offer open. It should be noted carefully that preparation to tender and preparation to perform do not constitute tender or part performance.

Rejection of Offers. *Rejection of an offer by the offeree terminates the offer immediately upon the offeror's receipt of the rejection.* If the offeror reasonably could infer from an offeree's expression, either by word or conduct, that the offeree does not intend to accept the offer, there is a rejection. The offeree's manifestation of rejection may expressly state a rejection, or it may be such conduct as to indicate to the offeror an intention to reject. A refusal to consider the offer any further is conduct implying no intent to accept. Similarly, a *counteroffer* implies a rejection. A "counteroffer" is an expression by the offeree of a new offer regarding the same subject matter as the original

---

[13] UCC 2–206: "(1) Unless otherwise unambiguously indicated by the language or circumstances

(a) an offer to make a contract shall be construed as inviting acceptance in any manner and by any medium reasonable in the circumstances;

(b) an order or other offer to buy goods for prompt or current shipment shall be construed *as inviting acceptance either by a prompt promise to ship or by the prompt or current shipment of conforming or non-conforming goods. . . .*" (Author's italics.)

offer, but containing different terms.[14] To constitute an offer, the counteroffer must contain all the elements of an offer. A *conditional acceptance* is a counteroffer if it contains the elements of an offer. However, an *inquiry* by the offeree whether the offeror would consider other terms, or an offeree's request for further details, are not counteroffers, since they do not imply an intent to reject.

The rejection must be received by the offeree in order to be legally effective. Does receipt mean actual receipt of the rejection by the offeror, similar to revocation which the offeree must receive to be legally effective; or merely deposit in the channel of communication authorized by the offeror, similar to the manner of effecting an acceptance? If an offer is sent by mail, the offeree mails a rejection, and then the offeree telegraphs an acceptance which the offeror receives before the rejection, does the mailing of the rejection terminate the offer? The rejection is not effective when mailed by the offeree, subject to the offeree's power to accept provided the offeror receives the acceptance before he receives the rejection. An acceptance sent subsequent to a previous rejection is solely a counteroffer, unless it arrives first, in which event it is an acceptance. If an acceptance is followed by a rejection, the rejection arriving first, later discussion[15] indicates that, although an acceptance is legally effective when mailed, nevertheless, if the offeror innocently *relies* on the earlier received rejection and changes his position before receipt of the acceptance, the offeree is estopped to allege the acceptance.

Acceptance

An "acceptance" is the offeree's manifestation of assent to an offer in reliance on, and in compliance with, the offer. The manifestation of mutual assent by the parties through offer and acceptance is essential to the formation of a contract. Once an acceptance occurs, there no longer is an offer; the acceptance merges with the offer, resulting in an agreement and in a contract if the other necessary elements are present. An acceptance is the consideration or price for the promise stated in the offer. Only the offeree to whom the offer is made may accept it.

Expression of Intent to Accept. The *form* of acceptance is that required by the offer and is either a promise or conduct other than a promise—namely, an act or forbearance. Unless the offer indicates and *insists* to the contrary, it invites acceptance in any form reasonable under the circumstances.

Performance and Part Performance in Unilateral Contracts. The offer for a unilateral contract is a promise which requests an act or forbearance from the offeree. A unilateral contract is formed only by performance on the part of the offeree. Performance means complete performance, and nothing else consti-

[14] See below, p. 30, ftn. 17.

[15] See below, p. 32.

tutes an acceptance of a unilateral offer. However, as previously pointed out,[16] an offer for a unilateral contract is interpreted legally to imply a subsidiary offer promising to keep the main offer open for the time stated in the main offer, or for a reasonable time if no specific time is stated, and promising to accept a tender of part or full performance by the offeree. The *beginning* of performance, or a tender of *part* performance, by the offeree is an acceptance and performance of *the subsidiary offer* resulting in an option contract to keep the main offer open and irrevocable for that time. On performance or tender of performance the main offer thereby is accepted, a contract is formed, and the promisor is obliged to perform his promise.

Performance and Tender of Performance in Bilateral Contracts. The offer for a bilateral contract is a promise which requests a return promise from the offeree. The offeree must give the return promise requested by the offer in order to form a contract; nothing else suffices except performance or tender of performance within the time in which the return promise of acceptance was to be made. Performance is a sufficient acceptance complying with the offer because, inasmuch as the primary purpose of the offer was to obtain performance, the promise of performance being a temporary expedient to assure such performance, the offeror cannot complain if he obtains the performance primarily desired. Part performance is not an acceptance of an offer for a bilateral contract. However, a tender of performance is an offer to perform and thereby is a promise to perform, which is what the offer requests. The tender is an acceptance.

Objective Test of Acceptance. The acceptance, as a manifestation of intent to accept, must be expressed clearly so that the offeror reasonably can understand it to constitute an acceptance of his offer. It is only when the parties—offeror and offeree—can understand the manifestation of each other to be in accord that there is an offer and an acceptance. If the offeree reasonably can understand the offeror's expression to be an offer, and the offeree's manifestation of assent thereto is reasonably clear to the offeror, there is a contract. It is immaterial that the offeree's mental and manifested assents are at variance; *the manifested assent controls.* The offeree may be ignorant of the nature, terms, and proper interpretation of the writing to which he assented; but if he reasonably could have ascertained the same, his negligence in not doing so and his resulting ignorance do not prevent the formation of a contract.

An offeree is held responsible for his examination of the terms of an offer made to him. His assent to such terms is an acceptance and such terms are a part of the contract, irrespective of whether or not he has examined and knows them. If he knows or reasonably should know that the contents of writings are a part of the offer, he should be aware that such writings contain contract terms; and his acceptance of such writings without objection is an implied acceptance of the contract terms contained therein. Some writings do, and some do not, purport to contain contract terms. Bills of lading, warehouse receipts, and telegraph message blanks are examples of writings which, throughout most of

[16] See above, pp. 25–26.

the United States, are held to purport to contain contract terms, and persons accepting them without objection are held to have impliedly assented to their terms. Whether or not a ticket of passage (e.g., railroad ticket) purports to contain contract terms depends upon the purpose and appearance of the ticket. If it is meant merely to show the beginning and ending points of passage, it does not purport to contain contract terms; while if it is covered with print and writing suggesting conditions concerning passage, it does purport to contain contract terms. With respect to baggage checks, the decisions are in conflict, but by the majority view the baggage check does not purport to contain contract terms. There is disagreement also on whether or not printed material on tags attached to goods, on catalogues, on letterheads, on invoices, and the like purport to contain contract terms. *The test on all this is whether or not the recipient of the writings reasonably can believe that the writings contain contract terms.* Of course, writings containing contract terms which are received by the offeree *after* the contract has been made are not binding upon him, unless he either expressly or impliedly agrees to reformation of the contract by his acceptance of such writings.

Silence. What an expression manifests is tested by what the addressee reasonably can understand it to mean. The same is true of silence. If an offeror reasonably can understand an offeree's silence to mean assent, then such silence is a manifestation of assent and an acceptance. *Silence, generally, is not a manifestation of assent.* An offeree is under no obligation to reply to offers or to do anything with services or property proffered or left with him, and his silence does not constitute assent.

There are exceptions, however, when an offeree's silence coupled with either activity or inactivity does constitute a manifestation of assent and, therefore, an acceptance.

1. Silence Coupled with Activity. Silent use implies acceptance. If the offeree receives property knowing, or having reasonable cause to know, that compensation is expected in return and, instead of rejecting such property, he exercises *dominion* over it, his silence is coupled with activity which manifests assent and is an acceptance. By "dominion" is meant the exercise of ownership by use, sale, destruction as opposed to discarding, or by other ways.

2. Silence Coupled with Inactivity. An offeree's silence and inactivity make more difficult a determination of the meaning of such silence. When the offeror indicates to the offeree that the latter's silence and inactivity will constitute acceptance and the offeree, understanding this, is silent thereby *intending* to accept, there is an acceptance and a contract. The parties may *agree* that silence shall be a manifestation of assent. An offeree, by *previous dealings* with the offeror or otherwise, may have led the offeror reasonably to believe that the offeree's silence and inactivity constitute a manifestation of assent; and if the offeror reasonably understands the offeree's present silence and inactivity to constitute assent, there is an acceptance. Thus, where an offeree *solicits* an offer, often in the form of an order, under circumstances which, because of the relations of the parties or otherwise, cause the offeror reasonably to believe that the offeree's silence is intended as a manifestation of assent, the offeree must indicate his rejection of the offer to the offeror within a reasonable time or his silence will constitute an acceptance. By court decision, and by statute in some states, insurance companies must notify applicants of rejection of their applications within a reasonable period of time; otherwise such delay constitutes acceptance. If an offeree receives property knowing, or having reasonable cause to know, that compensation is expected in return and, instead of rejecting it, he does nothing but takes the *benefit* of it, in the absence of statute to the contrary his silence and inactivity are held to manifest assent.

Adequacy of an Expression of Acceptance. A purported acceptance is legally inadequate and is not an acceptance if it does not comply exactly with the offer,[17] with the exceptions discussed previously in connection with part performance of an offer for a unilateral contract and the rendition of performance instead of a promise requested by an offer for a bilateral contract;[18] and with the additional exception, discussed later,[19] of an acceptance being effected by the offeror's receipt of the acceptance even though an improper channel of communication was used by the acceptor. An offer requesting an act is not accepted by a return promise. An expression of acceptance which is not clear or is equivocal, so that the offeror reasonably cannot understand it to constitute an acceptance, is not an acceptance. A *confirmation* that the offer has been received is not an acceptance.[20] If the offer requests the offeree to indicate a choice of amount or time of delivery, the acceptance must so indicate; "I accept" is not an acceptance in this instance. If an offer of reward is made for information leading to the apprehension of a criminal and for his conviction, both information and conviction are necessary for the acceptance of the unilateral offer. An expression of acceptance which also qualifies the acceptance or makes it *conditional* on something else happening is not an acceptance but is a rejection and a counteroffer instead. However, a qualified or conditional expression of acceptance should be distinguished from an expression of accep-

---

[17] UCC 2–207: "Additional Terms in Acceptance or Confirmation. (1) A definite and seasonable expression of acceptance or a written confirmation which is sent within a reasonable time operates as an acceptance even though it states terms additional to or different from those offered or agreed upon, unless acceptance is expressly made conditional on assent to the additional or different terms.

(2) The additional terms are to be construed as proposals for addition to the contract. *Between merchants* such terms become part of the contract unless:
   (a) the offer expressly limits acceptance to the terms of the offer;
   (b) they materially alter it; or
   (c) notification of objection to them has already been given or is given within a reasonable time after notice of them is received.

(3) Conduct by both parties which recognizes the existence of a contract is sufficient to establish a contract for sale although the writings of the parties do not otherwise establish a contract. In such case the terms of the particular contract consist of those terms on which the writings of the parties agree, together with any supplementary terms incorporated under any other provisions of this Act." (Author's italics.) See below, pp. 203–04.

[18] See above, p. 28.

[19] See below, pp. 32–33.

[20] But see ftn. 17, above.

tance which *requests* a change in the terms of the offer; the latter is an acceptance, the former is not. The two can be distinguished by asking the question: Does the expression of acceptance *require* a change in the offer's terms for the acceptance to take effect? If the answer is in the negative, it is an acceptance; if in the affirmative, it is not an acceptance. (A offers to sell goods to B for $1,000. B replies: "I accept, if the price is $900." There is no acceptance, but rather a counteroffer because the terms of the offer are qualified and the purported acceptance is qualified. Instead, B replies: "I accept, but you must give me good title." There is an acceptance, as a vendor impliedly warrants he has title[21] and the offer makes such an implied warranty; the reply has not changed the offer. Instead, B replies: "I accept, but I *hope* you will send the goods in 10 days rather than in 20 days." There is an acceptance, since the reply does not *require* the goods to be delivered in 10 days.)

Knowledge of Offer for Acceptance. An acceptance is made by the offeree with knowledge of the offer and with an intent to accept that offer. Without such knowledge of a prior offer, an offeree cannot intend to accept that of which he does not know. If performance is begun before an offeree learns of the offer, rendering the remainder is not acceptance because the complete performance as an acceptance was not made in reliance on the offer.

Communication of Acceptance. An acceptance, as a manifestation of assent, is in compliance with the offer. If the offer is for a *bilateral* contract, the offer requests a return promise which must be communicated to the offeror. If the offer is for a *unilateral contract*, the offer requests an act or a forbearance which need not be communicated to the offeror if not required by the offer. First, communication of acceptance in bilateral contracts, and then in unilateral contracts will be discussed.

In Bilateral Contracts. The parties contemplating a bilateral contract may or may not be at a distance from each other. Earlier discussion[22] indicated that when the parties are not at a distance from each other, or are conversing over the telephone, the occasion requires an immediate communication of a manifestation of assent, if the offer does not provide otherwise. In the case of a telephonic acceptance, the transaction is the same as though it were taking place between the parties in each other's presence, and the acceptance must be heard by the offeror to form a contract.

When the parties are at a distance from each other, the offer will indicate either expressly or impliedly the channel by which the acceptance is to be communicated to the offeror. If an offer *authorizes* the use of a specified channel by which to transmit an acceptance, the offer makes that channel the agent of the offeror for such purpose. By placing the acceptance in such channel, knowledge of such acceptance is given to the offeror through its agent. Unless the offer states to the contrary, the law interprets an offer to imply authority to *use* a *proper* mode of communication; and the moment such chan-

[21] See below, p. 233.

[22] See above, p. 22.

nel is used, the offeror has knowledge of the acceptance and the offer has been complied with. Deposit of the acceptance in the proper channel forms the contract, unless the offer provides to the contrary. A contract is formed at that place where the last act necessary to form the contract occurs, and at that very time. If the offer expressly *prescribes* the *exclusive* method of transmitting an acceptance thereby making it a *condition* of acceptance, then no other method can be implied. If the offer expressly requires the offeror's *receipt* of the acceptance, then it cannot be inferred from the offer that mere use of the proper channel is sufficient; the acceptance must be *received* to be effective as such. When the offer does not expressly indicate the channel of communication to be used for acceptance by the offeree, then the offer is interpreted to imply use of the same channel as for the offer, or whatever channel is customarily used for transactions of that nature at the place where the offer is received.[23]

It is incumbent on the offeree to observe every reasonable precaution for the safe transmission of his acceptance. A letter of acceptance must be addressed properly and must be stamped. When the proper channel for acceptance is other than by mail—e.g., telegraph, railway express—and that channel does not require prepayment for transmittal, such fact does not affect the propriety of the dispatch even though a delay in delivery may be occasioned thereby. If the offeree knows or has reason to know of interruption in the authorized channel of communication, his use of that channel resulting in nondelivery of his acceptance is not compliance with the offeror's requirement that the offeree take reasonable precaution in his transmittal of the acceptance, and no contract is formed.

An acceptance dispatched for transmittal by a channel not expressly or impliedly authorized by the offer is ineffective, unless received by the offeror in the same time as by use of the authorized channel. When so received by the offeror, the acceptance is then treated as a timely acceptance effective as of the date it was sent. Similarly, a misdirected acceptance is ineffective unless it is received by the addressee without undue delay in the same time as if properly directed. However, the offer expressly may so limit or *prescribe* the method of communicating an acceptance as to make it the *exclusive* method and a *condition* of acceptance that, even if the offeror receives an expression of acceptance in an unauthorized manner, the expression does not constitute an acceptance. (A offers to sell goods to B if B personally will appear at A's office and accept before a stipulated time. There cannot be an acceptance unless B appears, personally, before that time, and accepts.) It is sometimes difficult to determine whether the offer *prescribes* or *suggests* a manner of acceptance. If it *prescribes,* the manner of acceptance must comply exactly with the offer; nothing else, not even the offeror's receipt of the acceptance, will suffice. If it *suggests,* then *use* of the suggested channel is sufficient of itself; use of a

[23] See Restatement (Second) of Contracts, 1980, sec. 66. Also see UCC 1–201(38) for "Send"; and above, p. 26, ftn. 13. See also above p. 22 f.

channel *other* than the one suggested is ineffective, *unless* the offeror received the acceptance within the same time as if the suggested channel had been used.

In Unilateral Contracts. An offer for a unilateral contract is accepted by performance. The offeree has no obligation to notify the offeror of performance, unless the offer requires notice. If the offeror does not require notice, then he has the burden of ascertaining whether performance has occurred. *However, when the offeror does not know of the performance within a reasonable time* and he *cannot ascertain with reasonable promptness and certainty whether performance has occurred, and the offeree knows or has reason to know this, the offeree must exercise reasonable diligence in notifying the offeror,*[24] *or the offeror's duty to perform is discharged.* For example, under the law of suretyship, if S offers to C that if C will advance credit to D to purchase lumber from C and D does not pay C then S will pay C, C has the duty to notify S of each purchase by D from C on credit within a reasonable time after each such purchase, and C's failure to do so will discharge S from liability as a surety on each such contract.[25] There *is a contract* by the offeree's performance, but giving such notice is a condition precedent to the offeror's duty *to perform* his promise and is a condition subsequent discharging his duty to perform his promise. Notification of performance is accomplished by utilizing any reasonable means of communication, regardless of whether the addressee ever receives the notice. If the offer is for a bilateral contract and the offeree performs or tenders performance instead of making a return promise, such performance or tender thereof must be made within the same time in which the offer could be accepted by a return promise in order to constitute an acceptance.

Estoppel. A person may misrepresent a material fact. When one person represents or "holds out" to another person a material fact and the other person changes his position materially to his prejudice in reasonable reliance on the holding out, the first person is prohibited in law or "estopped" to deny what he had asserted previously. This principle of law is called "estoppel."[26] Its purpose is to prevent the obvious injustice which would otherwise result. (T stole O's horse and offered it for sale to B, who was ignorant of the theft and did not know that the horse belonged to O. O told B that it was not O's horse. In reliance on O's statement, B paid T and bought the horse from him. O is estopped to assert his title to the horse against B.) It should be noted carefully that estoppel has two ingredients: *a holding out by one person to another of a material fact; and the other person's material change of position in reasonable reliance on the holding out*.

In the law of contracts, an offer ceases if acceptance does not occur within the expressed or implied time of its duration, and it cannot be accepted there-

[24] Sending such notice by any reasonable means of communication, irrespective of whether or not it is received by the offeror, is sufficient notice.

[25] See below, pp. 485–86.

[26] See below, pp. 147, 567–68. *Cf.* promissory estoppel, below pp. 66–67.

after. Any subsequent manifestation of acceptance is a new offer. If the offeree dates his purported acceptance as of a time in which acceptance could occur, when in fact he is too late, there is no acceptance, because the offer has expired. Should the offeror reasonably rely on the purported acceptance, the offeree will be *estopped* from asserting a defense of delay as negativing acceptance. In other words, the offeree previously having falsely asserted the date of his acceptance to be correct, and the offeror having relied on the offeree's assertion and believing that a contract has been formed, the offeree is prevented from varying from his original assertion. Any other approach would be manifestly unfair to the innocent offeror. To state it more broadly, if the offeree misrepresents any existing fact which is essential to the formation of a contract, and the offeror reasonably *relies* on it and changes his position, the offeree is estopped from asserting the reverse of what he misrepresented. (A mails an offer to B. B mails an acceptance and then telegraphs a rejection, the telegram arriving first. A, relying on the telegram, changes his position. A then receives B's acceptance. Although a contract was formed when the acceptance was mailed, A's ignorance of this and his reliance and change of position induced by the telegram estop B from alleging his acceptance.)

Fraud and Material Misrepresentation

Misrepresentation is a manifestation of what is not in accordance with fact. A contractual mistake may occur as a result of intentional or unintentional misrepresentation, usually made by one of the parties to the transaction; or it may occur without any such misrepresentation. Here we are concerned with such misrepresentation; later we will consider contractual mistake without such misrepresentation.[27] Sometimes this subject is treated under various headings, e.g., "reality of consent" and "genuineness of consent." While the parties have manifested mutual assent, nevertheless an element of reality or genuineness appears to be lacking.

The subject of misrepresentation at times is discussed by text writers separately from offer and acceptance. However, it seems more feasible to consider misrepresentation along with duress, undue influence, and mistake under the heading of "mutual assent" because these subjects essentially are concerned with offer and acceptance. Some of these subjects preclude the formation of a contract, while others do not affect the formation of a contract but create a power to avoid a contract. These subjects will be discussed at this time, in the order indicated above.

When the term "fraud" is used, it may refer to a misrepresentation in connection with the law of torts or the law of contracts. In the law of torts, fraud is called "deceit," which is a tort,[28] and has a meaning slightly different from

[27] See below, pp. 40–41.

[28] Deceit, sometimes described as "actionable fraud," may be defined as a misrepresentation of a material fact made by a person with knowledge of its falsity and with intent to mislead another

fraud as used in the law of contracts. The same transaction may involve the tort and contractual fraud.

In the law of contracts *fraud* signifies *intentional* misrepresentation of fact to induce a contractual mistake. It may be defined as a misrepresentation of fact made by one person with the *intent* to induce another person to make a mistake in making, or in refraining from making, a contract. An intentional nondisclosure of facts when there is a duty to disclose, coupled with the intent to induce the mistake, is also fraud. Fraud may be stated more inclusively as the *intentional* misrepresentation of fact, or the *intentional* nondisclosure of fact in violation of a duty to disclose, with *intent* to induce a contractual mistake. If the misrepresentation, or the nondisclosure in violation of duty, is not intentional but innocent, then there is no fraud. However, there is a legal effect to such innocent misrepresentation or nondisclosure if the facts concerned are *material* facts. The term "*material misrepresentation*" means an *innocent* misrepresentation, or *innocent* nondisclosure in violation of a legal duty, of *material* facts. It should be noted that in fraud the fact need not be material; any fact is sufficient. Misrepresentation is a manifestation of what is not in accordance with fact. A material fact is a fact of such importance that, if known at the time of its representation, it would likely have influenced the conduct of a reasonable person.

Types of Fraud and Material Misrepresentation. Fraud and material misrepresentation are inoperative unless they produce a contractual mistake. They may either preclude the formation of a contract or render a contract voidable, depending on the type of fraud or material misrepresentation which occurs. There are two types: fraud or material misrepresentation *in the procurement*—which precludes the formation of a contract; and fraud or material misrepresentation *in the inducement*—which causes the contract to be voidable at the election of the party to whom the misrepresentation has been made.

Effect of Fraud or Material Misrepresentation in the Procurement—No Contract. Fraud or material misrepresentation *in the procurement* (also called "fraud in the factum," "fraud in the execution," or "fraud in the inception") means that the fraud or material misrepresentation consisted of a misrepresentation of the *nature of the act* in which the injured party engaged. An example of fraud in the procurement is a misrepresentation that the paper to be signed has certain provisions or is of a certain character when, by subtle substitution, the paper signed contains different provisions or is of a different character. If the substitution of the paper were made innocently, it would be a material misrepresentation but not fraud; however, the result in both cases would be the same. The injured party is misled in his belief that his act was not a manifestation of assent to any transaction, or that his manifestation of

---

person by inducing the latter to act in a particular business transaction in reliance thereon, which causes the other person so to act in justifiable reliance thereon and thereby to suffer pecuniary damage.

assent was made to a particular transaction when, in fact, it was made to another transaction not intended by him. If the injured party is *not negligent* and reasonably relies on the fraud or material misrepresentation, there is *no contract.* If he is *negligent,* there is no fraud or material misrepresentation in the procurement; but there is a *contract* which, because of the fraud or misrepresentation in the inducement, is *voidable* at his election. (A cannot read the writing before him. B misrepresents the terms or the character of the writing to A. A has no opportunity to have someone other than B read it to him, or the person reading it is in collusion with B and misrepresents also. A signs. There is no contract.) In the foregoing illustration, if A had the opportunity to have the writing read to him by some impartial person and does not avail himself of this opportunity, he is negligent and there would be a voidable contract.

Effect of Fraud or Material Misrepresentation in the Inducement—Voidable Contract. Fraud or material misrepresentation *in the inducement* (also called "fraud in the treaty") means that the fraud or material misrepresentation consisted of something inducing the *formation of the contract.* (A's intentional misrepresentation of his available manufacturing equipment in a contract to manufacture, or of his financial position in obtaining an extension of credit, or of the book value of shares of stock in a contract for their sale, or his contractual promise made with no intention to perform it, which induces B to make a contract, is fraud in the inducement creating a contract *voidable* at B's election. If the misrepresentations were made innocently, there would be material misrepresentation with the same result.) There is a manifestation of mutual assent to do certain things, and a contract is created. The contract's *formation, not its subject matter,* was induced by the fraud or material misrepresentation. If the injured party as a reasonable man has relied on this inducement, the contract is voidable at his election. *When the word "fraud" is used without qualification it signifies fraud in the inducement.* When a *third person not a party to the contract,* by fraud or innocent material misrepresentation induces an innocent party to contract with another innocent party, the injured party may avoid the contract unless the other innocent party has already materially changed his position in reliance on the contract.

Exercise of the Power of Avoidance. The injured party may exercise his power of avoidance, or may affirm the contract and thereby extinguish such power. If he chooses to avoid, he must avoid the entire transaction. He cannot avoid part and affirm part unless it is a severable contract, one divisible part of which has been completely performed, when he can affirm the performed part and avoid the rest of the contract.

The injured party may avoid or affirm expressly or impliedly. The power of avoidance must be exercised *promptly* after the injured party learns of the fraud or material misrepresentation. It is a condition of disaffirmance, with certain exceptions not discussed here, that the injured party promptly offer to return the consideration he has received under the contract. Avoidance is implied from the wronged party's retention of property he was to deliver, or his reacquisition of property he already has delivered, under the contract after he has learned of the fraud or material misrepresentation. Affirmance may be made expressly or may be implied from his failure to notify the other party promptly, or from his exercise of dominion over the consideration he has received, after he has learned of the fraud or material misrepresentation. It should be noted that, if there is solely a material misrepresentation—i.e., the material misrepresentation was innocently made—and the misrepresented fact becomes a fact prior to the exercise of the power of avoidance, the power thereby ceases to exist.

Remedies. On avoidance the injured party has a right in *quasi contract* for the value of the performance he has rendered and, when a judgment for such value would be inadequate, a right to restitution or specific restoration of the land or things which he has delivered under the contract, at his election. Specific restoration will not be decreed against a subsequent bona fide purchaser for value of goods.[29] Until the power of avoidance is exercised, the other party to the contract has title to the property, although the title is subject to the power of avoidance. A sale of the title to a bona fide purchaser for value without notice of the power of avoidance cuts off this power. When there is fraud or material misrepresentation in the procurement and the injured party has been negligent, resulting in a voidable written contract, the injured party may rescind the contract by exercising his power of avoidance or he may obtain a decree reforming the writing to what it was represented to be.

Misrepresentation by Nondisclosure and by Opinion. Before leaving the subject of fraud and material misrepresentation a brief comment should be made about nondisclosure and about misrepresentation of opinion.

In the absence of a legal duty to speak, a party has no obligation to disclose that of which the other party is ignorant. Probably the most common instances in which a duty arises in connection with contracts are: when there is a fiduciary relationship between the parties wherein one party is acting on behalf of the other, such as between principal and agent, partners, trustee and beneficiary, executor and beneficiary, attorney and client, suretyship, director and the corporation; and when an innocent material misrepresentation is made, but before the contract is concluded the party misrepresenting learns of the misrepresentation, there is a duty to disclose the misrepresentation to the other party. Failure to disclose in violation of a duty is a material misrepresentation that there is nothing to disclose, thereby causing the contract to be voidable at the election of the party to whom disclosure should have been made. This type of misrepresentation is an illustration of what is called "constructive fraud," which is fraud as a matter of law and which occurs by failure of one party to exercise good faith in dealing with another. In contrast is what is called "actual fraud," which is intentional and direct fraud by one party upon another as a fact.

An "opinion" is a fact. The assertion that one has an opinion is an assertion of a fact—namely, that he has an opinion. An expression of opinion is subject to

---

[29] See UCC 2-403(1), and below pp. 147–48.

interpretation either as a statement of absolute truth—a fact—or as an expression of a belief in a fact. If the latter, then reliance upon such a statement is not justified because the representation of opinion is not a *material* fact and the addressee reasonably cannot rely upon it. (A, a layman, says that a certain provision is the law. As a layman, his expression of the law is understood only as his opinion, his belief that such is the law. The opinion cannot reasonably be relied on and is not the subject of fraud or material misrepresentation.) In the foregoing illustration, if A had been a lawyer, his expression is an assertion of a fact of which he should have knowledge. When an opinion is expressed by one who professes to be an expert on the subject matter, his opinion can reasonably be relied on, and such opinion may be the basis of fraud or material misrepresentation. (A, an expert on certain subject matter, misrepresents such subject matter with the intent to induce a contractual mistake. His misrepresentation is fraud.)

Compulsion to Disclose under U3C. In 1968, the federal Consumer Credit Protection Act (CCPA) became law. Title I is called the Truth-in-Lending Act, with the purpose of assuring "a meaningful disclosure of credit terms so that the consumer will be able to compare more readily the various credit terms available to him and avoid the uninformed use of credit" (section 102). Its purpose is consumer protection, and persons granting consumer credit must disclose certain required data concerning credit charges. The Board of Governors of the Federal Reserve System prescribes regulations to carry out the purposes of the Title. Chapter 2 is concerned with "Credit Transactions," and section 123 provides that the Board shall except from federal disclosure requirements under Chapter 2 "any class of credit transactions within any State if it determines that under the law of that State that class of transactions is subject to requirements substantially similar to those imposed under this chapter, and that there is adequate provision for enforcement." Accordingly, to create state law, in 1974, the National Conference of Commissioners on Uniform State Laws approved of a revised final draft of the Uniform Consumer Credit Code, hereinafter referred to throughout this book as "U3C" so as not to confuse it with the UCC (Uniform Commercial Code), which covers only *commercial transactions concerning personal property*. The U3C is a comprehensive consumer protection law for state adoption covering only *consumer and other credit transactions*. The U3C is much broader in its coverage than the CCPA. Pertinent references to the U3C appear in the footnotes throughout this book. It should be noted carefully that the UCC *supplements* the U3C, which is dominant over the UCC.

Duress

Duress is concerned with *wrongful pressure*, either through the use of *physical force* or an *improper threat*, to induce formation of a contract. The threat may be of a wrongful act to the addressee, his family, or business associate. Fear from the improper threat is not measured by what would cause fear to a reasonable man but, rather, by what would cause fear to the particular addressee; it is a subjective test. A threat of a civil suit made in good faith with an honest belief in the claim is not an improper threat. There is a difference of view on whether or not a threat of criminal proceedings is an improper threat. By the preferred view, such a threat is improper. A threat of physical force is improper. A threat to induce an exchange of performance which would result in unfairness would be improper.

The varying effect of duress is determined by state law. Improper pressure by *physical force* compelling a person against his will to appear to manifest assent is duress and *precludes the formation of a contract* because there is no manifestation of assent. (A grasps B's hand and forces B to sign his name to a document.) However, if the wrongful pressure consists of an *improper threat* which induces a person to manifest assent *when he has no reasonable alternative* but to do so, there is duress and the resulting contract is *voidable* by the wronged party. If there is a reasonable alternative, there is no duress and the resulting contract is not voidable by the threatened person. (A improperly threatens to sue B unless B discharges A from a claim which B has against A. B assents to discharge A and contracts with A. A's threat is wrongful pressure, but since B can defend the civil suit he has a reasonable alternative, there is no duress, and the resulting contract is not voidable by B. B could have refused so to contract with A and defend against A's suit.) Duress may be practiced by one person inducing a second person to contract with a third person. The contract is voidable by the second person, unless the third person acted in good faith without reason to know of the duress, relying on the transaction or giving value, in which case the contract is not voidable. (A's duress on B induces B to sell his land to C, who acted in good faith promising to pay B the purchase price. A is not C's agent. The contract is not voidable by B.)

Undue Influence

"Undue influence" is another form of wrongful persuasion, rendering the transaction *voidable* at the election of the injured party. Undue influence is unfair persuasion by the exertion of influence obtained through the relationship between the parties and does not involve any fear. Undue influence may be defined as *unfair persuasion by the exertion of influence obtained either through domination over another, or by the reliance of one party on his relation with the wrongful party whereby the latter will not act contrary to the former's best interests and welfare.* It is the improper utilization of this influence which is unfair persuasion or undue influence. (A induces B, his son, to sign a contract with him, knowing that it is to B's great disadvantage to do so. A has utilized his parental relationship to his son's unreasonable disadvantage, which is undue influence. The contract is voidable by B.) Reliance on another's previous advice, the relationship of principal and agent or trustee and beneficiary, creates a duty in the person trusted not to exercise his influence unduly by unfair persuasion to the other party's disadvantage. If there is a fiduciary relationship between the parties—e.g., one party is either a trustee, executor, administrator, or guardian and the other is the beneficiary of this relationship—the transaction must be fair and reasonable and assented to by all the parties who must be legally capable of participating in the transaction; otherwise the transaction is voidable. Exercise of this power of avoidance and remedies thereunder are the same for duress and undue influence as in fraud and material misrepresentation.

Mistake

A contractual mistake is an erroneous belief in the existence of a fact *at the time the parties bargained with each other.* Mistake here is not the same as poor judgment or what occurs in the future. The mistake may occur as a result of fraud, material misrepresentation,[30] or without fraud or material misrepresentation. We here are concerned with contractual mistake without fraud or material misrepresentation.

The effect of a *unilateral mistake* was discussed previously under "Objective Test of Acceptance."[31] A unilateral mistake does not affect the enforceability of a contract or the formation of a contract, unless assent is given in ignorance of the nature, terms, or proper interpretation of a writing and such assent is given without negligence, in which event there is no contract. However, if a contracting party has reason to know of a mistake by the other party made at the time the contract is made, or if in the court's discretion the consequences of the mistake would be so serious as to cause enforcement of the contract to be unreasonable against the mistaken party, the courts will give relief to the mistaken party.

Mutual mistake by the expiration of offers which prevents formation of a contract was discussed previously.[32] However, a contractual mistake other than by fraud or material misrepresentation may make a contract voidable. A distinction should be made where the contract is made *voidable* by the mutual mistake of the parties or by only one party. When both parties make the same mistake regarding a fact on the basis of which their contract was made and the mistake will materially affect the exchange of the performances which the parties agreed upon, the party adversely affected may avoid the contract unless he undertook the risk of the mistake. (A contracts to sell certain land to B, both parties erroneously assuming that there is timber on the land. The contract is voidable by B, but not by A.) However, if the mistake is in an erroneous expression in a written contract of what the parties had previously agreed upon, then the remedy of reformation[33] is available and the contract is not voidable by either party. Risk is undertaken by a party if he agrees to take it, or

[30] See above, pp. 34–36.

[31] See above, p. 28 ff.

[32] See above, p. 23.

[33] See below, p. 43.

he acts on knowingly limited knowledge, with respect to a fact on which he is mistaken.

If either party's manifestation of intent is *ambiguous* or *uncertain* and this fact is *unknown* or *known* to the parties, and the parties attach different meanings to the manifestation, there is no contract even though each party mistakenly believes from the manifestations that there is agreement. Both parties acted reasonably in making their differing interpretations of the innocently appearing, but in fact ambiguous or uncertain, manifestation. If both parties know, or reasonably should know, of the ambiguous or uncertain nature of the manifestation, they are on notice of a possibility of differing interpretations being mistakenly made by each other which would not result in a contract. If solely one party knows of the uncertainty or ambiguity, he is bound by the reasonable interpretation put upon it by the other party; but this is not a situation of mutual mistake because *both* parties have not made a mistake.

Interpretation of Agreements

Once parties have manifested their intents, there is the problem of determining the meaning of their manifestations. After the meaning has been determined, legal effects flow from such determination. There are legal rules, called "standards of interpretation," which are applied in order to determine the meaning of what the parties have said or written, to determine their intents. Some of these rules follow:

1. In oral agreements, the meaning of the words or other manifestations used is that meaning which the utterer reasonably should know the addressee would understand from the employment of such manifestations. In written agreements, often called "integrations" to signify that the parties have reduced their agreement to a writing, the meaning which a reasonable person acquainted with the circumstances surrounding its formation would ascribe to the terms used is the meaning which would be applied to the writing.
2. If a word or other manifestation is ambiguous:
   a. If the ambiguity is unknown or known to both parties,
      (1) If each party gives a different meaning to the manifestation, there is no agreement for want of a manifestation of mutual assent.
      (2) If each party gives the same meaning to the manifestation, there is an agreement because of a manifestation of mutual assent and an accord in mental intent on the ambiguity.
   b. If the ambiguity is known, or should be known, to only one party, the meaning innocently attached to it by the other party is the meaning applied to the agreement and the first party is bound thereby.
3. The common, ordinary meaning of the language used everywhere applies.
4. Technical terms are given their technical meaning.
5. The manifested purpose of the parties is a very important factor in determining the parties' intentions.
6. A lawful, rather than an unlawful, interpretation will be given to the manifestations.

7. If the language used is susceptible of more than one meaning, and the above rules do not solve the difficulty, the language is interpreted most strongly against the party employing it. This is because the addressee of ambiguous words will interpret them as best suits himself.
8. Where there is inconsistency between printed or typewritten and handwritten provisions, the meaning of the latter prevails. If the inconsistency is between printed and typewritten provisions, the meaning of the latter prevails. If the inconsistency is between figures and written words, the meaning of the latter prevails.
9. If general terms are followed by specific terms, the specific provisions control and qualify the meaning of the general terms.
10. The circumstances surrounding the transaction are considered in interpreting the manifestations which occurred. Usage is a part of the circumstances.[34]

Law Applicable to Contracts. ***Under the Law of Contracts.*** The time and place where a contract is made is the time and place where the last act necessary to make a contract has occurred *by offer and acceptance.* It is the law of that place which will determine its status as a contract. Generally, the parties may *agree* that the law of any state shall apply and govern their contract rights and duties if that state has a substantial relationship to the parties or to the transaction.[35]

Under the Code. Under the Code, with certain exceptions, the parties may *agree* that the law of any state or nation shall apply and govern their rights and duties as long as the transaction bears a *reasonable relation* to such state or nation, i.e., the state or nation ordinarily must be where a "significant enough portion of the making or performance of the contract is to occur or occurs."[36] Also, under UCC 1–205(5), "An applicable usage of trade in the place where any part of performance is to occur shall be used in interpreting the agreement as to that part of the performance."

Parol Evidence Rule

The parol evidence rule is not a rule of interpretation nor of evidence. It is a rule with one simple purpose—to establish or determine what manifestations were made in written form. Once parties reduce their agreement to a writing intending that the writing is to constitute their contract, any oral (parol) or written agreement made prior to such written contract, and any oral agreement made contemporaneously with the written contract, which *contradicts* (varies or adds to) such written contract, are inadmissible in evidence and cannot be proved. In other words, a written contract is the final manifested intention of the parties, and it will not be contradicted by prior agreements or by contem-

[34] See UCC 1–201 (3) for "Agreement," and UCC 1–205 for course of dealing and usage of trade.

[35] See Restatement (Second) of Contracts, 1980, sec. 64, Comment d, and sec. 65, Comment c; Conflict of Laws and Restatement (Second) 1969, sec. 187.

[36] UCC 1–105. But see U3C, sec. 1.201.

poraneous oral agreements. Two important factors should be noted carefully: first, that the parties intend the writing to be a contract; and, second, that the terms of the written contract cannot be contradicted by any prior agreements or by contemporaneous oral agreements.

The writing must be a contract. If the writing is not a contract, then the parol evidence rule is inapplicable. Evidence is admissible to show that the parties do not intend the writing to be a contract, that the writing is not to be effective as a contract until a later time or on the occurrence of a contingency; or that the writing is void or voidable; or illegality, duress, mistake, lack of consideration. Such evidence does not contradict any written contract; it proves that the writing is not a contract or that it is voidable.

A written or oral contract may be modified or extinguished by a *subsequent* oral or written contract, and such subsequent contract is admissible in evidence to show the modification or nonexistence of the previous contract. It should be noted that writings which are executed as part of a single transaction are to be read and interpreted together as one agreement.[37]

Reformation. "If a written contract or conveyance does not reflect the intentions of the contracting parties because of a mistake of fact as to its contents or a mistake of law as to its legal effect, the writing may be reformed and extrinsic evidence not otherwise admissible to vary the writing is admissible solely for the purpose of reforming the contract so as to correct the mistake and reflect the intentions of the parties. But both parties must have been so mistaken, or one must know that the other was mistaken. However, a change of position by a person in reliance on the writing may preclude reformation, except reliance by persons who take the writing subject to equitable interests, such as asignees and transferees of instruments not of a negotiable character. The process by which a written contract is changed by court decree to reflect the previous intentions of all the contracting parties not properly expressed in the writing is called Reformation."[38]

SECTION III. CONSIDERATION

A promise is not a contract unless it is supported by *consideration.* Consideration is that which is rendered in compliance with the requesting promise. Consideration must be a legal detriment to the person rendering it or a legal benefit to the promisor. It is a legal detriment if the person rendering the consideration was under no previous legal obligation to do so. A promise is tested by what it promises. When there is a disputed (honestly believed) or an unliquidated (not ascertained in an amount) claim or defense, there is consideration for a promise in settlement. The following are exceptions, when consideration and agreement are not required: (1) The debtor's promise (express or implied) to pay a *particular* contractual debt barred by the Statute of Lim-

[37] See UCC 3–119 concerning negotiable instruments.

[38] Joseph L. Frascona, *Agency* (Englewood Cliffs, N.J.: Prentice-Hall, Inc., 1964), p. 19.

itations. (2) A bankrupt debtor's promise to pay a contractual debt from which he is dischargeable in bankruptcy, called "reaffirmation." The promise may be made only after a hearing before the bankruptcy judge and only before a bankruptcy discharge is granted. (3) A promise to pay a contractual obligation voidable by the promisor. (4) Some promises to perform obligations not existing previously. (5) Some promises to perform an obligation even though there is a failure of condition. (6) Promissory estoppel.

Common Law

The doctrine of consideration is a creature of English Common Law. Prior to 1285 an informal contract was not recognized by the English courts and the doctrine of consideration was unknown. Contracts under seal were recognized and enforced because of their formal nature and not because of the presence of consideration. After 1285 an informal contract was recognized and legally enforced, but consideration had to be present. Today, *a promise is unenforceable as a contract unless it is supported by consideration,* with certain exceptions.

Conduct Exchanged for a Promise

The new Restatement (Second) of Contracts has rearranged and rephrased much of the subject matter of the law of contracts, and also has brought the law up to date reflecting changes as the law developed.

The concept of consideration is that which is bargained and exchanged for a promise, namely conduct consisting of either performance by an act or a forbearance, or a return promise. (A promises B $100 if B will *perform work* for A. A's promise is bargained and exchanged for an act, namely B's doing the work. Doing the work is consideration for A's promise to pay making A's promise enforceable as a legal obligation.) In short, it is what the promise asks for and gets. There must be an exchange, a bargain. We will later find that there are exceptions when a promise is enforceable as an obligation without the requirement of consideration, and even without an agreement, in order to achieve justice. Often consideration is considered to mean the price for a promise. In the above illustration, A's promise to pay is being sold or exchanged for a price, namely B's work. Or A may promise to pay B if B will *refrain* or *forbear* from doing something. B's forbearance is the consideration or price for A's promise. Or A may promise to pay B for A's act or forbearance, but A's promise requests that B *promise* so to act or forbear. B's *return* promise is the consideration for A's promise, just as A's promise is the consideration for B's promise making B's promise enforceable as an obligation. There is an exchange.

However, not every act, forbearance, or return promise is consideration. Only when the person rendering the act, forbearance, or return promise *was under no previous legal obligation to the promisor to do so* does the act, forbearance, or return promise constitute consideration and make the requesting promise a legal obligation and enforceable as a contract. In the above illustrations, B was not under any previous legal obligation to A so to act, forbear, or give his return promise and, therefore, they constitute consideration. They are the price or "value" for the promise. (P promises $50 to S, a sheriff, if S will do a particular thing which the law already compels him to do by virtue of his office. S's performance is the act requested but is not consideration because S's act is only what S had to do. P in effect has obtained nothing in exchange for his promise. P's promise is not supported by consideration and is unenforceable.) Accordingly, the legal principle emerged that for a promise to be enforceable as a contract it must be supported by *consideration.* Courts often use the term "valuable consideration," which means consideration.

Value—Detriment or Benefit. The courts have indicated clearly what is meant by "value"; it is a *legal* value, as distinguished from an actual value. By legal value is meant something *which did not have to be given up or done previously* but which was rendered (usually by the promisee) as consideration for a promise, or something *to which the promisor was not entitled previously* but which he received as consideration for his promise. In the above illustrations, B's act, forbearance, or return promise was a *legal detriment to him* and is consideration for A's promise. Consideration may have legal value and, therefore, be legally sufficient even though it has no actual value. (A, for sentimental reasons, offers to buy a certain map of his town from B for $10. The map may have no actual value at all; yet B's delivery of the map to A is an act which B was not obligated to do previously and, therefore, is a legal detriment to him and consideration for A's promise to buy.) Courts do not inquire into the adequacy or actual value of the act, forbearance, or promises as fixed by the parties; that is for the parties to determine. Courts are concerned solely with legal value—namely, the legal detriment that has been experienced in compliance with the promise or the legal benefit received by the promisor. In a leading case the promisor requested the promisee to refrain from using tobacco and drinking liquor until the promisee became 21 years of age, in return for which the promisor would pay the promisee $5,000. The promisee abstained in compliance with the promise. The promisor contended that the promisee experienced no detriment, but rather a benefit in so abstaining, and that the promisor received no benefit from the promisee's forbearance. The court, holding that the promise was supported by consideration and enforceable, said:

> . . . . the promisee used tobacco, occasionally drank liquor, and he had a legal right to do so. That right he abandoned for a period of years upon the strength of the promise of the testator that for such forbearance he would give him $5,000. We need not speculate on the effort which may have been required to give up the use of those stimulants. It is sufficient that he restricted his lawful freedom of action within certain prescribed limits upon the faith of his uncle's agreement, and now having fully performed the conditions imposed, it is of no moment

> whether such performance actually proved a benefit to the promisor, and the court will not inquire into it; but were it a proper subject of inquiry, we see nothing in this record that would permit a determination that the uncle was not benefited in a legal sense. [*Hamer* v. *Sidway*, 124 N.Y. 538, 546, 27 N.E. 256, 257 (1891).]

It is the detriment experienced by the promisee or the benefit received by the promisor, performed as requested by the promise, which causes the courts to enforce the promise as a contract. It is that *kind* of an act, forbearance, or return promise which is the consideration or the price for which the courts look.

Mutuality of Obligation. Only promises require consideration. In unilateral contracts the promise requests an act or forbearance. In bilateral contracts, one promise requests another promise. Each of the parties relies on the other's promise as assuring performance of what is stated in the promise. Each promise is examined to determine whether it is consideration for the other promise. *A promise is consideration for another promise if it is a legally binding obligation. It is legally binding if it promises an act or forbearance which would be consideration by itself for a unilateral contract and if it is legally valid.* A promise to pay a due debt is not consideration because the duty to pay was already owing and, therefore, the promise is not binding. A promise to perform a criminal act for another promise to pay for such performance is invalid and, therefore, is not binding. Similarly, a promise by one who has no legal capacity to contract is void—e.g., the promise of a person adjudicated to be mentally incompetent is void, and in some states a married woman's promise to act as surety for her husband is void. When the promises are binding obligations, there is a contract. The courts speak of these binding promises as "mutual obligations" and of "mutuality of obligation" being present. What is meant is that each of the promises is consideration for the other because each is a legal obligation to perform consideration. If one of the promises is not a legal obligation, there is no mutuality of obligation, no consideration for the other promise, and, therefore, no contract. An illusory promise precludes the existence of mutuality of obligation because it is not a promise and, therefore, is not consideration.

Consideration

In determining whether a promise is supported by consideration, it is important to determine whether *the promise requests* an act, forbearance, or a return promise which was rendered in reliance on the promise. If this has occurred there is consideration. The rest of this section on consideration is concerned, first, with a detailed discussion of consideration; second, a detailed discussion of when conduct is not consideration; and third, the exceptional situations when consideration and agreement are not required to make a promise enforceable as a legal obligation.

Defined. "Consideration" may be defined as *that act, forbearance, or return promise requested and rendered in exchange for a promise.* Whatever is requested by the promise must comply with the promise and be rendered in reliance on the promise, as in the case of acceptance of an offer, in order to constitute consideration. An acceptance is consideration for the promise in the offer. Rendering the thing requested without knowledge of the promise is a gift by the promisee. (A promises to pay B $100 for B's horse. B, ignorant of the promise, gives the horse to A. B's act is a gift, since B did not act in reliance on the promise and had no expectation of anything in return.) The thing rendered must be exchanged as the price for the promise and be induced by the promise.

Illusory Promises. The return promise must be a promise in fact and not merely a promise in form. A promise is a manifestation of intention that something shall or shall not happen. An expression in the form of a promise which does not so manifest is not a promise. It is called an "illusory promise" or "apparent promise." An illusory promise is not consideration. (A "promises" to buy and B promises to sell all the oil which A may "desire" to order from B during one year at a fixed price. A's "promise" is illusory because it does not undertake to do anything. It does not promise to order; and, even if A does order, he does not promise to order from B. Accordingly, A has not given a return promise as requested, and B's promise is unenforceable for lack of consideration.) Illusory promises are nugatory because it lies within the power of the promisor, at his election, to do nothing. If the expression manifests an intention that an act or forbearance will occur, it is a promise and, therefore, is consideration, regardless of any choice which the utterer may reserve to himself. (A promises to sell to B all the goods he manufactures, and B promises to buy from A whatever goods A produces. A's promise at first appears to be illusory in that A may or may not manufacture goods; A does not undertake to manufacture. But A's promise is not illusory because, even though he has such choice, nevertheless, he has undertaken that, in the event he manufactures goods, he will sell them only to B. A has promised to sell *exclusively* to B.) Promises to "buy from you all I may require" or "sell to you all I may produce" are not illusory, since they undertake to buy or sell *exclusively,* even though the other features of each promise are illusory in that nothing may be required if the buyer's business does not function, or nothing may be produced if the seller's business does not operate.

Gratuitous Promises. A promise which is gratuitous is unenforceable for lack of consideration; it requests nothing in return. It is sometimes difficult to determine whether a promise is gratuitous or whether the promise requests consideration in return. A promise may state a condition which may be either a price for the promise or merely an act to effectuate a gift. If the promisee reasonably can believe that the condition expressed in the promise requests something as consideration, the courts so interpret the promise. Promises to contribute to charity, usually in the form of subscription or pledge, are essentially gratuitous in that they ask for nothing in exchange and people understand the intention of such promises as gratuitous. Because such promises are not supported by consideration, they should be unenforceable. However, because the courts strongly favor enforcement of charitable subscriptions, an exception to the requirement of consideration is made, called *promissory estoppel.* Although the charitable promise requests no consideration, yet if such a promise reasonably can be expected to induce reliance thereon and such reliance in the form of an act or forbearance occurs, the promisor is estopped or barred from setting up the absence of consideration and the promise is enforceable. Contracts under seal constitute another exception to the requirement of consideration in those few states where the seal still has its Common Law effectiveness. However, the seal still can be used to authenticate a signature, such as a corporate seal; and the seal may even be a signature when the party intends it as such. Under the Code, the Common Law effect of the seal is abolished. Also, a party to a transaction may waive or renounce, in whole or in part, his claim or right against the other party arising out of an *alleged* breach of contract; but to be effective as a release the waiver or renunciation *if oral* must be supported by consideration, or if *in writing* it must be signed and delivered by the aggrieved party *without any requirement of consideration.*[39]

"Past" Consideration. There is no such thing as "past" consideration, although some of the courts use this phrase.[40] Consideration is the price requested by, and exchanged for, the promise. An act or forbearance rendered *prior* to the making of the promise is not consideration for the promise, although such act or forbearance sometimes is referred to as "past" consideration to indicate that it occurred in the past or prior to the making of the promise. (X renders certain services for Y. Subsequently, Z promises X to pay for those services. X's services are not consideration for Z's promise, which is, therefore, unenforceable.) However, a subsequent promise may be evidence of the value of the previous act or forbearance. (A requests B to do a certain act, which B does in reliance on A's request. Subsequently, A promises B $100 for B's act. A's request implies a promise to pay the reasonable value of B's act, and B's performance is consideration for A's implied promise to pay such reasonable value. B's act is not consideration for A's *subsequent* promise, and A's subsequent promise is unenforceable for lack of consideration. A's subsequent promise is evidence of what A estimates to be the reasonable value of B's act.) An antecedent debt does not constitute consideration for a debtor's new promise to pay the debt. However, an antecedent or pre-existing debt constitutes value for a promise which is in the form of a *negotiable instrument*—e.g., check or negotiable promissory note—because under the Law Merchant,[41] which origi-

---

[39] See UCC 1–107.

[40] By state *statute*, "past" consideration may be recognized and, if it is the basis of a written promise, it causes the promise to be enforceable.

[41] The Law Merchant is that body of customs and usages of merchants sanctioned by the courts. Initially, this body of law was developed in English mercantile courts, and subsequently it became a part of the Common Law as recognized and declared by the Common Law Courts. Thus, the Law Merchant, along with the Common Law and Equity, became a part of the heritage of the

nally developed separately from the Common Law, the concept of consideration was unknown and it was commercially desirable to enforce a negotiable instrument.

"Moral" or "Good" Consideration. What is often called "moral" consideration or "good" consideration is not consideration at all, and a promise based upon either of these is unenforceable for lack of consideration. (A, "in consideration of B's love and affection," promises to pay B $1,000. The promise is unenforceable for lack of consideration.) No price is being exchanged for the promise. The "moral" consideration is nothing more than an indication of the motive prompting the promise.

Motive. Motive for making the promise should not be confused with consideration. If the promisor is motivated by his friendship with the promisee in promising to sell an article at a price lower than its actual value, and the promisor receives the requested act, forbearance, or promise in return, his promise is enforceable. Motive cannot be substituted for consideration, although it may explain why the consideration is so small.

Failure, Compared with Want, of Consideration. Failure of consideration should be distinguished from lack or want of consideration. If a bilateral contract has been formed by the exchange of promises and one of the promises is not performed, such nonperformance is a failure of consideration and the other promise thereby becomes unenforceable. Failure of consideration indicates that a contract has been formed, but one of the promises was not performed. Lack or want of consideration indicates that no contract has been formed because a promise was not supported by consideration, e.g., I'll give you $100.

By Whom and to Whom Consideration Is Rendered. Consideration may be given by the promisee or anyone else, and may be given to the promisor or to anyone he designates. If a promise requests consideration and the consideration is provided as requested, it is immaterial whether the consideration was to be provided by the promisee or by someone else. (A promises B $100 if C will do a certain act. In reliance on A's promise, C performs the act. C's act is consideration for A's promise. A just as well could have requested B to perform the act instead of C.) Similarly, the promise may request the consideration to be rendered to the promisor or to someone else. (A promises B that, if B will extend credit to C, A will pay B if C does not pay B. B extends the credit. B's act is consideration for A's promise, even though the consideration was rendered to C.) (A promises B that, if B will forbear instituting legal proceedings against C, A will pay B $100. B forbears. B's forbearance is consideration for A's promise.)

Third Party Intended Beneficiary Contracts. A third party intended beneficiary contract is a contract made between two persons for the purpose of

---

American colonies and of each of the later independent American states. Since a merchant's promise to pay an antecedent debt was enforceable under the Law Merchant, today the Code provides that "value" for a promise causing it to be enforceable may be consideration or an antecedent or pre-existing debt. For example, see UCC 1–201(44) (b) and 3–303(b).

benefiting a third person who is not a party to the contract and who provides no consideration. The third person is called a "beneficiary." (A promises B that, if B will lend A $100, A will pay $100 to C in 10 days. B lends A $100. A's promise is supported by consideration—namely, B's delivery of $100 to A. C is a beneficiary of the contract in that A is to pay $100 to him.) Third party intended beneficiary contracts create no difficulty regarding consideration. They raise the sole problem of whether the beneficiary should be permitted to enforce the promise made in his favor. This problem is discussed later,[42] under the separate subject of third party intended beneficiary contracts.

Recital of Consideration. ***Informal Contracts.*** If a written contract does not recite the consideration, it can be proved that the consideration was given. If a written agreement recites that the consideration has been given, the recital is *prima facie* evidence of that fact. However, a false recital that consideration has been given cannot evade the legal requirement of consideration, and the recital can be proved to be false. If the recital of consideration be false but a *promise* to pay the consideration can be implied, then the promise to pay the consideration is deemed consideration to support the other promise. (A, an insurance company, issues a policy to B insuring B's premises against fire, such policy stating it is effective only when B has paid the premium and falsely reciting that the premium has been paid. B accepts the policy. The falsity of the recital of payment can be shown; but inasmuch as B's promise to pay the premium can be *inferred* from B's acceptance of the policy, B's *implied* promise is the consideration supporting A's promise to insure.)

Conduct Usually Is Consideration, with Exceptions

Usually the requested conduct of an act, forbearance, or return promise is consideration, and usually it is both a detriment to the promisee and a benefit to the promisor. The exceptions are easily understood, because they involve the only situations when the consideration is neither a detriment nor a benefit.

The following acts or forbearances are not consideration for a promise: performance of an undisputed legal duty previously owing to the promisor directly, or indirectly as a member of the public; forbearance to assert, or the surrender of, an invalid claim or defense when the person forbearing or surrendering has no reasonable belief in its possible validity; and transfer of fungible goods or money in exchange for a promise to transfer a larger or smaller amount of the same thing at the same time and place.

The following promises, whether initial or return, are not consideration: a promise to do an act or to forbear which the promisor has reason to know would not be consideration for a unilateral contract; a promise containing alternatives of performance at the election of the promisor, at least one of such alternatives not being consideration for a unilateral contract; and a promise not binding or

---

[42] See below, pp. 74–77.

not capable of becoming binding, except when unenforceable or voidable solely by operation of law.

All these exceptions when there is not consideration for a promise can be summed up as follows:

1. Performance of an undisputed legal duty previously owing to the promisor.
2. Forbearance to assert, or surrender of, an invalid claim or defense not honestly and reasonably believed to be valid.
3. Mutual transfer of things of the same nature in different amounts at the same time and place.
4. A promise is not consideration for another promise if:
   (a) It is to perform the above acts or forbearances.
   (b) It promises an *alternative* of performing either the above acts or forbearances or something which is consideration, *at the election of the promisor.*
   (c) It is not binding, except for certain legal privileges accorded by operation of law.

Each of these acts, forbearances, and promises will be examined in turn.

Exception 1—Undisputed Legal Duty Previously Owing to Promisor. *An act or forbearance which is undisputedly and legally owing to the promisor is not consideration for a promise.*[43] (A owes B money. B promises A a horse if A will pay his debt to B. A pays his debt. A's payment is the act requested by the promise. A's payment is not consideration, however, because it did not constitute a detriment to A, inasmuch as he was already obligated to pay B; nor is it a benefit to B, because B already was legally entitled to it. B's promise is not supported by consideration and, therefore, is unenforceable.) The act requested and rendered is not consideration because neither a detriment nor a benefit is present. A creditor's promise to discharge his debtor if the debtor pays part of the indebtedness is not supported by consideration if such part payment is made. The creditor is entitled to payment of the entire amount of the indebtedness. His promise, in effect, is to excuse the debtor from paying a portion if the debtor will pay the rest. The promise requested an act of part payment, but inasmuch as the act was a legal duty owing to the promisor, it is not consideration for the promise to excuse a part of the debt. Therefore, *a promise to accept a lesser sum in satisfaction of a greater sum undisputedly owing to the promisor is not supported by consideration.* To state the principle more broadly and in another way, any promise to accept part of what is legally owing in satisfaction of it all, or to give something more than the contract requires in order to obtain performance of the other party's promise, is not supported by consideration and is unenforceable. (Under a contract between A

[43] But see below, p. 117, ftn. 4, concerning the binding effect in some states of an unsealed signed writing, without consideration, purporting to modify or discharge an existing legal obligation. For under the Code, see above, p. 48.

and B, A is to design and superintend the construction of certain buildings for B for a commission of 5 percent on the cost of the buildings. Subsequently, B desired the construction of an additional building and entered into a contract with C whereby C was to design and supervise the construction of the additional building for a commission of 5 percent of its cost. A refused to perform his contract with B unless B promised to give A 5 percent of the cost of the additional building in addition to C's 5 percent. B so promised. A then performed his contract and demanded the additional 5 percent. B's promise to pay A the additional 5 percent is unenforceable because it is not supported by consideration. B's promise requested an act, namely, A's performance of his contract with B. However, A's act was a legal duty previously owing to B; and as its performance did not constitute a detriment to A or a benefit to B, it is not consideration for B's promise.)

Part Consideration. A promise may request something, part of which is consideration and part of which is not consideration. That part which is consideration will cause the promise to be enforceable; the fact that the other part is not consideration is immaterial. (A owes B money. B promises to discharge A if A will pay a certain portion of the indebtedness and deliver A's horse to B. A complies with the promise. B's promise requested two acts: part payment and delivery of a horse. These acts were rendered. Although the act of part payment is not consideration because it is a legal duty already owing to B, nevertheless, A's delivery of the horse was not previously owing and is consideration to make B's promise enforceable.) Illustrations of this principle are numerous. Although a creditor's promise to discharge a debtor for part payment by the debtor is unenforceable for lack of consideration if such part payment is made, yet, if the creditor requests and receives something *in addition* to that legally owing, then his promise is enforceable because the addition is consideration. A debtor's part payment in a manner different from that required by the indebtedness obligation, as requested by the creditor, is consideration for the creditor's promise of discharge because the manner of paying is different from that required by the previous legal duty. A promise to pay a greater amount than that required by a contract, in exchange for a return promise by the other contracting party to perform his contract and to do additional work, is supported by consideration; the promise of additional work is consideration. A contract between creditor and debtor whereby an *interest-bearing* obligation is extended in time is supported by consideration. The consideration for the creditor's promise to postpone the date of payment consists of the debtor's promise to pay interest for a longer period of time and to pay the principal at a later date. That portion of the debtor's promise which assured payment of the principal promised performance of an act already due and, therefore, is not consideration. That portion of the debtor's promise assuring the payment of interest for a longer period of time than was required previously is consideration, making the creditor's promise enforceable.

Negotiable Instruments. Although it would seem that a creditor's promise to discharge a debt if the debtor will give to the creditor his negotiable instrument for the *full* amount would not be enforceable because it is not supported by consideration when such instrument is given—for the reason that the instrument is merely a new promise to pay what is already owing—such is *not* the case with respect to negotiable instruments. The law of negotiable instruments developed under the Law Merchant, separate from the Common Law. The Code reflects the Law Merchant by providing that a negotiable instrument is supported by *value* if the consideration supports a simple contract or there is an antecedent obligation. Accordingly, inasmuch as a debtor's negotiable instrument for the *full* amount is enforceable, the delivery of the instrument to the creditor in exchange for the latter's promise to accept it in full satisfaction of the debt is value for such promise. The debt is thereby discharged and the debtor has a new obligation—to pay the instrument. In the absence of any specific agreement a negotiable instrument for the full amount is not absolute payment but, rather, conditional payment—it is accepted on condition that it is paid. If the instrument is not paid, the original debt still exists; if it is paid, the original debt is discharged.

Although a debtor's instrument for a *smaller* amount is not consideration for the creditor's promise of discharge of the total amount due, yet, if a third person's signature (either as co-maker, co-drawer, or indorser) appears thereon, the debtor is discharged from the debt. The creditor's promise to discharge is supported by two promises—namely, the debtor's promise to make part payment, which is not consideration because it is already legally owing; and the third person's promise to pay the face amount of the instrument, which is consideration for the creditor's promise because it was not previously owing. This type of instrument is called a "secured instrument" because the third person's obligation to pay is additional security to the creditor that the debt will be paid. It is clear that a creditor's promise to discharge a debtor if a third person pays the whole or a part of the debt, or if a third person delivers his negotiable instrument for such amount to the creditor, is supported by consideration if such act is performed.

Compositions. A "composition" outside of bankruptcy[44] is an agreement whereby an insolvent or financially embarrassed debtor agrees with some or all of his creditors that, on his immediate payment to each of them of a part of his indebtedness to each, each will discharge the debtor. The consideration for the promises of the assenting creditors is usually either the promise of each creditor to forego a portion of his claim, or the debtor's forbearance or promise of forbearance to pay them more than an equal proportion of their claims. Composition agreements are socially useful and desirable and are enforced. Under the Bankruptcy Code, a composition is permitted between a debtor and his creditors with the approval of the court and only under chapters 7 and 13 is the individual debtor discharged from liability for such debts. The statute here represents public policy.

---

[44] For compositions (plans) under Chapters 11 and 13 of the Bankruptcy Code, see below, pp. 536, 533.

Prior Duty Owing to Public. A promise which requests as consideration that which is already owing to the public is not supported by consideration and is unenforceable. The person owing a legal duty is called the *obligor,* and the person to whom the obligation is owing is called the *obligee.* An obligor incurs no detriment to himself by rendering the promise to perform or by performing, inasmuch as he already was legally obliged to do so. Similarly, as the promisor is a member of the public, such legal duty was owed to him by the obligor and does not constitute a benefit to the promisor. People are under a legal duty not to commit torts, crimes, or other illegal acts; and forbearance from commission of such illegal acts, or performance of such illegal acts, or a promise to forbear from or to perform such acts, does not constitute consideration for a promise. A common carrier's promise to carry goods is not consideration for a shipper's promise to limit the carrier's liability for negligence, because common carriers are under a legal duty to carry goods for the public. There is an exception in the case of finders. Although a finder becomes an involuntary bailee under a legal duty to hold the property for the owner, nevertheless, the courts have held that an offer of reward for the return of the property is enforceable regardless of the doctrine of consideration. It should be noted carefully that, if the promise requests and receives from the obligor something, however small, in excess of his legal duty, such thing is consideration and, accordingly, the promise is enforceable.

Prior Duty Owing to Third Persons. The great majority of American courts hold that performance of, or a promise to perform, an obligation already owing to third persons (obligees) is not consideration for a promise of another person requesting such performance. A minority of American courts and the English courts hold it is consideration. The conflict reduces itself to the simple question of whether a legal benefit to the promisor constitutes consideration. Usually benefit and detriment occur together; but in the case of a prior legal duty owing to third persons, there is no detriment. (A is under a contractual duty to B to build a building. A refuses to perform. C promises A $1,000 if A will perform his contract with B. A performs in reliance on the promise. Under the minority view, A's performance is consideration for C's promise; the majority of American courts hold it is not consideration. A's performance was no detriment to A because he was under a legal duty to B to perform. However, under the minority view, A's performance is a benefit to C, for C obtained a performance to which he was not entitled previously.) The American courts consistently have stated that what constitutes a detriment to the promisee or a benefit to the promisor is sufficient to render a promise enforceable. In view of such statements by the American courts and their application by the English courts, and because a person who has sold his promise and received what he requested in exchange should pay for the benefit received, it is submitted that the minority American view is preferable. There is no question that, if a person *pays* consideration to the obligor for the latter's promise to perform his duty to the third party obligee, such payment is consideration for the obligor's promise, which is then enforceable by the person who has paid the obligor.

Exception 2—Invalid Claim or Defense Not Honestly and Reasonably Believed to Be Valid. *A forbearance to assert, or the surrender of, an invalid claim or defense made by a person who has no honest belief in the possible validity of such claim or defense is not consideration for the promise requesting it.* People have the legal right to institute legal proceedings for recovery on claims which they assert, be the claims valid or invalid. It is for the courts to determine the validity or invalidity of such claims. A promise to pay for forbearance to assert, or for forbearance from continuing to assert, such claim must be supported by consideration to be enforceable. If the claim is invalid, such forbearance or surrender gives nothing and is not consideration for the promise. Does it make any difference that the person so forbearing or surrendering honestly believes that the claim is valid when in fact it is invalid? The law says it does make a difference. If a person honestly believes that he has a valid claim, his giving up the right to institute legal proceedings thereon is a detriment to him and is consideration for a promise requesting such forbearance. Similarly, it constitutes a detriment to forbear continuing a legal proceeding already begun on the claim, or to surrender such a claim. If a person asserting an invalid claim has no honest belief in its validity, he gives up nothing detrimental to himself. The same principle applies to legal defenses. If the defense is invalid, it is not consideration; but if the person claiming the defense honestly believes that the defense is valid, his waiver of, or promise to waive, such defense is consideration for the initial promise requesting it. Accordingly, *any forbearance to assert, or any surrender of, an invalid claim or defense is not consideration, unless the person forbearing or surrendering honestly believes the claim or defense to be valid, in which case the forbearance or surrender is consideration.*

Disputed Claims. Claims may be disputed or undisputed. *A claim is disputed if it is honestly believed not to be valid by the party against whom the claim is asserted.* When a claim is undisputed, a promise to discharge the claim for payment of a lesser amount than what is due is not supported by consideration, on the ground that a promise to accept a lesser sum in satisfaction of a greater sum is not supported by consideration. There was a previous legal obligation to pay the entire amount; and, accordingly, there is no consideration for the promise to forgive a part of what is owing. However, when the claim is disputed, a promise to discharge the claim on payment of a compromised amount is supported by consideration if the payment is made. The reason is that the promisee thereby gives up an amount which he does not feel he is obligated to do. (A and B disagree on how much A owes B. A *honestly* claims it is $10, while B claims it is $20. Actually, B's claim is correct. They compromise on $15, and A pays $15 in return for B's promise to discharge the debt. B's claim is disputed, and A paid more than he felt was due. A's payment is a detriment and is consideration for B's promise.) It is immaterial that the actual amount owing was smaller or larger than the compromise amount. It is what a party honestly believed he was giving up or getting which is important and which constitutes the detriment or benefit. Courts do not inquire into the compromise amount except to see that it is a bona fide compromise. Accordingly, *a compromise of a disputed claim is enforceable.*

Liquidated and Unliquidated Claims. A claim may be liquidated or unliquidated. *A claim is liquidated when the amount is either: fixed by the parties, certain, or ascertained by mathematical computation or by operation of law.* (A sold and delivered goods to B for $200. A claims B owes him $200. B honestly asserts that he has, and A honestly asserts that B has not, paid the $200. A's claim is *liquidated* inasmuch as its amount is fixed, but the claim is *disputed* by each party as to its payment.) If the claim is liquidated and undisputed, the full amount of the claim is owing and a promise to accept a lesser amount in satisfaction of the total amount due is unenforceable. If the claim is liquidated but disputed, a compromise agreement for a stipulated amount will be enforced. (A owed B $20 but he honestly asserted he had paid it. B disagreed. They compromised that, if A would pay B $5, B would discharge A. A paid B the $5. B's promise is enforceable. The amount owed was certain, $20. The dispute was concerned with its payment.) If the claim is unliquidated, whether disputed or not, a promise of discharge on payment of an amount agreed by the parties is enforceable on payment of such amount. (A's car injured B, and B claims $1,000 damages. B promised to discharge A on payment of $1,000. A paid B $1,000. B's promise is enforceable. The claim was unliquidated.) Therefore, *payment of an unliquidated claim or payment of a disputed claim in the amount stipulated by the promise of discharge is consideration for such promise.*

Exception 3—Transfer of Like Goods or Money in Different Amounts. *The transfer of fungible goods or money in exchange for a promise to transfer a larger or smaller amount of the same thing at the same time and place is not consideration.* It is obvious that parties who agree to a mutual transfer of things of the same nature, in the same condition, but in different amounts at the same time and place, cannot intend to enter into a bona fide bargain. The transaction is probably a disguise for a gift by one party for the difference in amount. However, if there is the smallest difference in the time or place of each party's delivery, or in the quality or nature of the goods, or in any other way, then the contract is enforceable if the parties intended a bona fide agreement of exchange. The Code defines "fungible goods" as "goods of which any unit is, by nature or usage of trade, the equivalent of any other like unit." In the absence of any difference other than amount in the things sought to be exchanged, the delivery of such things is not consideration for a promise requesting it.

Adequacy of Consideration. The law does not inquire into the adequacy of the consideration agreed upon by the parties; it is concerned only with the consideration and whether fraud, duress, or undue influence is present. The difference between adequacy and consideration is that adequacy is concerned with the *actual* value of the thing requested and rendered, while consideration is concerned with its *legal* value in terms of *legal detriment* and *legal benefit.* The parties may agree to buy and to sell goods at a price which is above or below the market value. They may fix as consideration any price they wish just so long as there is a bona fide intent to bargain and to exchange what amounts to a detriment or a benefit so that consideration is present to make the promises enforceable.

The subject of adequacy of the consideration often arises in assignments or in the transfer of documents. A person may desire certain rights which he believes belong to another, and he promises a consideration to the other for assignment to him of *whatever rights* the promisee may have. After the assignment has taken place, the promisor may find that the promisee did not have the particular right desired. The promisor cannot raise the question of inadequate consideration when the promisee seeks to enforce the promise. The promisor must perform his promise even though he received an assignment of no value to him. The assignment is consideration, for it constituted a detriment to the promisee in that he gave up something he did not have to give up, and a benefit to the promisor in that he received something to which he was not previously entitled, regardless of the actual value to either party. If the promisor requested the assignment to him of *that particular right*, his promise is unenforceable for lack of consideration until that right is assigned. Similarly, a promise may request transfer of *a paper* or *document*, believing it to have a certain actual value. On transfer of the paper requested, the promisor finds it does not have the value he anticipated. His promise is enforceable because the transfer of the paper was consideration. If the promisor had requested the transfer of a paper containing *a certain right*, his promise is unenforceable for lack of consideration until that paper containing that right is transferred. Both parties may agree to effect a transfer of *a certain paper* containing *a certain right*. On transfer, it is found that the paper does not contain such right. There is no contract because of a mutual mistake of fact that the paper contained a particular right. Similarly, a promise of discharge may request the promisee's negotiable instrument—e.g., check, negotiable promissory note. If the promisor clearly indicates that the instrument alone is the consideration requested (which is unusual), then, regardless of whether the instrument is ever paid, the promise is enforceable. If the promisor does *not* clearly so indicate (which is the usual case), then the law interprets the intent of the parties to be that the consideration requested is *the money* indicated in the instrument and the promise is unenforceable for lack of consideration until the instrument is paid. In the latter situation the instrument is called "conditional payment."

Exception 4—Promise to Render What Is Not Consideration for a Unilateral Contract. *A promise to do an act or to forbear, which the promisor has reason to know would not be consideration for a unilateral contract, is not consideration for another promise. Every promise is tested by what it promises;* it must promise consideration in order to be enforceable as a contract. A promise *itself* can undertake to perform an act or forbearance. It may *request in exchange* an act, forbearance, or return promise. Whether a promise contemplates a unilateral contract by requesting an act or forbearance, or contemplates a bilateral contract by requesting a return promise to perform an act or to forbear, the *initial promise* must promise consideration in order to be enforceable. A return promise is not in itself consideration; *it* must promise an act or forbearance which is consideration. If an act or forbearance is not consideration, a promise promising it or requesting a return promise to perform it, and the return promise to perform it, are unenforceable because such promises are not supported by consideration. If the performance is consideration for a contract, the promise of performance is likewise consideration. As an illustration, performance of an act previously owing to the promisor, or a return promise to perform such act, does not constitute consideration in support of the initial promise; while performance of an act not previously owing to the promisor, or a return promise to perform such act, does constitute consideration in support of the initial promise. Inasmuch as a return promise must be supported by consideration, the initial promise also must undertake to perform an act or forbearance which is consideration for a unilateral contract.

Reasonable and Honest Belief of Consideration. Difficulty arises when the promisor of what is not consideration for a unilateral contract honestly believes that it is consideration for a unilateral contract. (A asserts an invalid claim against B. B promises A $100 if A will forbear asserting his claim. A forbears. A's forbearance is not consideration for B's promise, since it is no detriment to A and no benefit to B because the claim is invalid. If A honestly believed that the claim was valid at the time he forbore, his forbearance constitutes consideration because *he gave up a right to assert or litigate what he honestly believed to be a claim, which is a detriment to him.*) The law is concerned with what a party honestly believes when he enters into an agreement. Performing an act which he honestly believed he did not have to do (A honestly believing he had paid B the $50 debt, when he really had not, but paying $25 in reliance on B's promise of discharge), or forbearing to do something he honestly believed he did not have to do (forbearing to assert an invalid claim which he honestly believed to be valid, in reliance on a promise to pay), or promising to do such act or forbearance honestly believing he was under no obligation so to promise—all constitute consideration. Accordingly, to state the rule in a positive form, *a promise to render what is not consideration for a unilateral contract is not consideration for a bilateral contract unless the promisor honestly believes that it is consideration in which case his promise is consideration for a bilateral contract.*

Exception 5—Promise with an Alternative of No Consideration. *A promise containing alternatives of performance at the election of the promisor, at least one of such alternatives not being consideration for a unilateral contract, is not consideration for another promise.* A promise must undertake to perform an act or forbearance which would be consideration for a unilateral contract in order for the promise to constitute consideration for another promise. A promise which *reserves to the promisor* a choice of several performances, each of which is consideration, constitutes consideration because there *shall* be performance and the performance *shall* be consideration. If one of the alternative performances *reserved by the promisor* is not consideration, there is no certainty that the promisor will perform consideration, and that fact renders the promise itself not to be consideration. *A promise must undertake to perform consideration as a certainty, not as a possibility, for it to be consideration.*

However, a promise which undertakes alternative performances, one of which is consideration, *at the election of the promisee* is consideration. The promise assures the promisee a certainty of performance of consideration if the promisee so desires.

Promises containing alternatives, one of which is not consideration, at the election of the promisor are not by reason of that fact illusory. The word "promise" has been used in its proper legal sense, as a manifestation of intention that something shall or shall not happen. (A promises B to deliver a horse to B or to pay his debt to B, if B will promise to discharge the debt. B promises. A's promise contains two alternatives at A's election: to deliver a horse or to pay the debt. The first alternative is consideration, since delivery of the horse was not a previous legal obligation. The second alternative is not consideration, since it was a legal obligation previously owing. As the election of the alternatives lies with A, A's promise is not consideration for B's promise, and there is no contract. A's promise does undertake to perform one of two acts; and even though one is not consideration, nevertheless, it does *promise* an act.) An illusory promise does not undertake to perform anything. (A promises to buy and B promises to sell all the coal which A may wish to order from B at $25 per ton during one year. B's promise is to supply coal to A at that price in amounts as A may order during that year, which act is consideration and makes the promise consideration. A's expression is not a promise; it is illusory, because it does not undertake to perform anything. A's expression is not consideration for B's promise and no contract results.)

In the last illustration, one promise was not and the other was consideration. If the promise which is not consideration were performed, there would be a unilateral contract because the act of ordering coal is consideration as an acceptance of the promise to sell, which is outstanding until revoked or rejected. Similarly, if one of the two parties to a promissory agreement has no legal capacity to contract but performs his promise, there is a unilateral contract, since such *performance* was consideration for the other party's promise. Only a promise requires consideration in order to be enforceable.

Exception 6—Promises Not Binding. *A promise which is not binding or capable of becoming binding, except when unenforceable or voidable solely by operation of law, is not consideration for another promise.* Each promise in a bilateral *contract* is consideration for the other because it is a legal obligation; it is a binding promise. A bilateral promise is binding if it promises an act or forbearance which is a detriment or benefit and if it is legally valid. When a party reserves to himself the option of performing or not performing, the promise is illusory and obviously not binding because there is no promise to enforce. The law accords to infants, and to parties who have been defrauded, the power of avoidance at their election. *The granting of such a privilege does not affect the existence of the contract,* which continues until the privilege is exercised. Such contracts are called "voidable contracts." Inasmuch as a party has the option of performing or not performing his promise, the promise is illusory and not binding. Nevertheless, promises otherwise binding, but *which are made voidable solely by operation of law,* are treated as consideration because the purpose of the legal privilege is to give the power of avoidance to certain people in all fairness *to them.* If they wish to exercise the power, justice can be obtained. If they do not wish to exercise the power, then that is their right. Were the law to hold arbitrarily that promises made voidable solely by operation of law did not constitute consideration, the law would be superimposing its will upon the party sought to be protected and would be depriving him of the right to avoid exercising the protection. Accordingly, a promise which is *voidable* solely by operation of law is not, for that reason, not consideration for another promise. For the same reason, promises otherwise binding but which are made *unenforceable* solely by operation of law are treated as consideration. Illustrations of such unenforceable promises are: promises which are within, but do not comply with, the statute of frauds requiring the promise to be proved in certain enumerated ways for it to be recognized and enforced by the courts; and promises which have not been enforced within the period allowed under a statute of limitations.

Summary of Consideration

What Is Consideration. A promise may request as consideration an act, forbearance, or a return promise. A promise is unenforceable unless the consideration requested is rendered. There is consideration if the act, forbearance, or return promise has a legal value, as distinguished from an actual value. Consideration has a legal value if it constitutes a legal detriment to the person rendering it, usually the promisee, or a legal benefit to the person to whom it is rendered, usually the promisor. A legal detriment is the performance of something which the promisee was under no previous legal obligation to do. A legal benefit is the performance of something to which the promisor was not legally entitled previously. While the courts speak of detriment and benefit as consideration, there is serious conflict when benefit alone is sought to be applied as consideration. Usually, what is a detriment to one is also a benefit to the other, and the conflict is avoided. *All promises which are supported by a detriment or benefit are enforceable* as a contract.

What Is Not Consideration. *Every act, forbearance, or return promise requested and rendered is consideration except for a few situations when it is not consideration.* Accordingly, once it has been established that an act, forbearance, or return promise is present, examination should be made in order to determine if it is a detriment and benefit. An act or forbearance which is a previous legal obligation owing to the promisor is not consideration unless it is disputed by the promisee, in which event its performance is consideration. If an undisputed duty is owing by the promisee to a person other than the promisor, the majority, but not to be preferred, view is that its performance is not consideration for the promise. A forbearance to assert an invalid claim or defense is not consideration unless it is honestly believed to be valid by the promisee, in which event it is consideration. A bargain must be bona fide, and a transfer of fungible goods or money in exchange for a promise to transfer a larger or smaller amount of the same thing at the same time and place is not pursuant to a bona fide bargain and, therefore, is not consideration for the promise. Every promise given in exchange for another promise must constitute a legal obligation to be consideration for the other promise. The promises must be mutually obligatory to result in a contract. A promise is a legal obligation if it promises what would be consideration for a unilateral contract—namely, an act or forbearance which constitutes a detriment or benefit—and if it is legally binding on the promisor. A promise undertaking to perform an act or forbearance which is not consideration for a unilateral contract is not consideration for another promise. That which is not consideration for a unilateral contract has just been discussed. A promise reserving election in the promisor of alternative performances is a promise in that it undertakes to perform one of the alternatives. If one of the alternatives is not consideration for a unilateral contract, the promise is unenforceable; it does not undertake for a certainty that consideration will be performed, it does not promise value and, therefore, it is not consideration. If at least one of the alternatives is consideration and the election is in the promisee, the promise is consideration because of the obligation to perform consideration if the promisee so chooses. A promise which is not binding because it is illegal or is made by one who has no legal capacity to bind himself by it is not consideration. However, promises which are made voidable or unenforceable solely by operation of law are treated as consideration, even though they are illusory in that the privileged protection may be asserted in lieu of performance at the election of the promisor. A promise voidable or unenforceable solely by operation of law is an exception to the rule requiring a promise to be binding in order to be consideration. The act or forbearance must constitute a legal detriment or a legal benefit for it, or a binding promise, to constitute consideration.

When Consideration and Mutual Assent Are Unnecessary

There are certain promises which are enforceable although consideration[45] and mutual assent are not present. They are definite exceptions to the doctrine of consideration and to the requirement of mutual assent. The reason for such exceptions lies in the necessity for avoidance of obvious injustice and in the development of the law. A certain brief background is necessary to understand the reasons for these exceptions.

---

[45] UCC 2–205 provides that *merchants'* signed, written, firm offers to buy or sell goods for a period not exceeding three months are enforceable without consideration. See above, p. 25 ftn. 12.

Background. The courts developed the concept that if *a rule of law* subsequently causes a previous promise to become unenforceable, a subsequent *express* promise to perform the previous contractual obligation now barred by a rule of law would be *enforceable without any consideration.* Thus, if the statute of limitations barred enforcement of a promise, or if a promise to pay a debt was no longer enforceable because it had been discharged in bankruptcy, a subsequent express promise to perform the obligation would be enforceable. The new express promise itself is enforceable *according to its terms.* Inasmuch as the new promise can impose any limitations it wishes and also usually expressly promises to pay the debt and not to waive the statute, the *new promise* is the source of obligation and not the prior obligation barred by the statute.

Once the courts had decided to enforce a new express promise to perform an obligation barred by a rule of law, it was an easy step to imply such a promise from conduct. Today the new promise may be express or implied in fact. There is greater opportunity to imply such a promise when the statutory bar is the statute of limitations than there is when it is the Bankruptcy Code. It should be noted carefully that the new promise must refer to a prior obligation which had the elements of *contract,* not of tort. If an action on a *tort* is barred by the statute of limitations or discharged under the Bankruptcy Code, a new promise with respect to such tort must be supported by new consideration.

It was recognized that there were other situations or types of case in which promises should be held binding without consideration. The compelling motive was to avoid injustice. One of these situations involved *new promises of ratification* to perform existing *voidable* contractual obligations *not barred by any rule of law.* Illustrations of such contracts are contracts made by persons with partial capacity to contract, such as infants, to whom the law accords a power of avoidance because of their relatively inferior bargaining position; and contracts made under the influence of fraud, duress in some cases, or undue influence, a power of avoidance being accorded to those who have been wronged. A *new promise* by the person who previously had partial capacity to contract, or by the wronged person, *to perform the existing contract ratified the contract and eliminated the power of avoidance.* Another situation involved *new promises ratifying previously unauthorized acts* which did not necessarily create obligations binding on the promisor. An illustration is a contract purportedly made by one acting as an agent for a principal when in fact there was no agency relationship, yet the promisor subsequently ratified the purported contract by his promise to perform it. Still another situation involved *new promises* to perform obligations previously discharged because of a *failure of a condition* on which performance of the old promise was dependent, such condition mainly bearing on the time or manner of performance. Illustrations are: a surety's contract with a creditor in which the creditor is required to notify the surety of default by the principal debtor, the notice of default is not given and the surety is discharged, but the surety subsequently promises the creditor to perform the discharged contract; and a fire insurance policy requiring notice of fire loss within a specified period of time after such occurrence, the notice is not given and the insurer is discharged, but the insurer subsequently promises to perform the discharged obligation. A further situation involved gratuitous promises to perform something not previously obligatory and requesting nothing in return, the promisor reasonably expecting reliance on his promise, which subsequently occurs. This is known as the "*doctrine of promissory estoppel.*" An illustration is a gratuitous promise made to a charity contemplating the erection of a structure and, subsequently, work on the structure is begun.

All of these new promises, whether relating to contractual obligations barred by rules of law, ratifying voidable or unauthorized contracts, relating to previously discharged contractual obligations, or creating new obligations as in the case of promissory estoppel, will be considered in turn.

Promises Regarding Previous Contractual Obligations for the Payment of Money Barred by the Statute of Limitations. *A voluntary promise to perform a contractual or quasi-contractual obligation for the payment of money, which obligation is either presently enforceable, or presently unenforceable solely because of the statute of limitations, is enforceable without consideration and without mutual assent.* The promise must express an intent to make payment of all or part of such debt, whether it be liquidated or unliquidated, already barred by statute or not. *The effect of such a promise is to extend the statutory period beginning from the date the new promise is performable according to its terms.* The promise must be made by the debtor (obligor) or his authorized agent to the creditor (obligee), his surety or co-principal. A promise made by a joint debtor does not bind his co-debtors, but a promise made by a partner prior to dissolution binds the partnership. The promisor's *ignorance of material facts* at the time the promise is made renders the promise not binding, although *ignorance of the legal effect* of such facts does not affect the enforceability of the promise. The promise must *specify the indebtedness* to which it relates in order *for the statutory bar to be waived as to that particular indebtedness.* If the promise specifies several debts to which it is to be applied, the statutory bar is waived as to all of such specified debts. If the promise specifies an account stated, the statute is waived as to that account stated, all the items therein being set forth in one balance or account. If the debtor does not specify to which of several debts the payment is to be made, the creditor may apply it to any or all of such debts,[46] but *the statute is not waived as to any debt* because the payment *did not specify* to which debt it was to apply.

A promise may impose any conditions, and such conditions limit the performance of the promise. The waiver of the statute of limitations, or a promise so to waive, is a *detriment* and constitutes consideration for a promise in exchange. A debtor's promise to pay a lesser amount than that due and barred by the statute of limitations in exchange for the creditor's promise to accept

---

[46] See below, p. 114 ff.

such lesser amount is consideration for the creditor's promise because the debtor has experienced a *detriment* in waiving the statute of limitations. A promise to waive the statute and to pay a lesser amount than due *if the creditor will accept it* is not binding until the promisee complies with the promise's request by manifesting acceptance. A promise to pay a barred debt less an invalid claim asserted against the promisee is binding only to the extent of the difference between the barred debt and the invalid claim. If the promise requests the creditor's acceptance of such a proposition, then the promise is ineffective until the condition of acceptance has been made. A promise to pay a barred debt by installments is binding only on the occurrence of the due date of each installment.

The new promise to pay may be *express* or *implied* in fact; and it must be in writing in most states except in those few instances when it may be implied from the debtor's part payment, or from his issuance of a negotiable instrument or his giving of collateral security for any part or all of the indebtedness or for interest due thereon. The written promise must be signed by the promisor or his authorized agent. If the new promise is supported by consideration, the promise is enforceable whether oral or written, just as in any unilateral or bilateral contract. Most states *imply a promise to pay* from either of the following, unless the circumstances preclude such implication:

1. An acknowledgment of the existence of a debt.
2. Payment of part of the debt, the issuance of a negotiable instrument—e.g., check, negotiable promissory note, draft—or the delivery of collateral security for part or all of the debt or for interest due thereon.

Any such acknowledgment or transfer as indicated above cannot imply a promise to pay if the debtor's manifested intent is to the contrary. An acknowledgment of the debt expressing an inability to pay it does not imply a promise to pay. However, an acknowledgment of the debt expressing a *present* inability to pay implies a promise to pay it in the future and is binding when the promisor becomes able or on the expiration of a reasonable time under the circumstances. An acknowledgment of the debt expressing inability to pay before the expiration of a year implies a promise to pay on the expiration of a year, and the statute is waived or extended to begin to run all over again on the expiration of the year. *The statute begins to run on a new promise from the time performance is due on the new promise.*

An express promise not to plead the statute of limitations as a defense to any action begun in the future for the recovery of a claim is valid and implies a promise to pay if the express promise is made *after* maturity of the claim. If such a promise is made *before* a claim's maturity, it is interpreted to mean a perpetual forbearance from pleading the statute, which is void. It is illegal to agree to limit, for an unreasonable period of time, a right to enforce a possible future claim. If the promise is made *after* maturity of the claim, then such a promise not to plead the statute is valid, for it is interpreted to mean a new promise to pay, which extends the statute. A promise to extend the statute beyond the next statutory period is valid.

It should be noted that the promise must be voluntarily made. It is not interpreted to be a voluntary promise if made under oath or in a pleading defending an action; nor is a judgment which is not by default or confession[47] considered a voluntary promise.

Promises Regarding Previous Contractual Obligations for the Payment of Money Barred by a Discharge under the Bankruptcy Code. *A promise to pay part or all of a contractual debt dischargeable under the Bankruptcy Code, made after a hearing before the bankruptcy judge and before a discharge in bankruptcy, is enforceable without consideration and without mutual assent.* The promise is called a "reaffirmation." The promise does *not* waive a discharge if made *prior* to the beginning of bankruptcy proceedings, which is the filing of a voluntary or involuntary petition in bankruptcy. The effect of the promise is to waive discharge of the *specified* debt if such discharge should occur. In general, the promise is governed by the same principles applicable to a promise waiving the statute of limitations. A promise to waive a discharge of a particular debt implies a promise to pay that debt; and, in the event of discharge in bankruptcy from such debt, the new promise is binding, effectively waiving the discharge.

Promises to Perform Voidable Obligations. *A promise to perform a contractual obligation voidable by the promisor is enforceable without consideration and without mutual assent.* Such a promise is binding and extinguishes the power of avoidance. In most states the promise need not be in writing. The waiver of such power of avoidance is called "ratification" or "affirmance" of the contract. The promise to perform the voidable obligation has a binding effect only if the power of avoidance has not been exercised previously by the promisor. The time within which an infant or a mentally incompetent person may exercise this power is indicated in a discussion of infants and mentally incompetent persons as parties with limited capacity to contract.[48] The time for exercise of the power in the case of fraud, duress in some cases, and undue influence is indicated in a discussion of voidable contracts under manifestation of mutual assent.[49]

Modification of Executory Contract. Often the parties to a contract may wish to modify and make adjustments in their contract which is still executory in that it is not yet fully performed on either side. A problem of consideration arises. (A contracts to pay B a price for digging a cellar for A. When B discovers that large rock is in the way, A agrees with B to pay B a fixed additional amount to do the job, which B than does. Can B enforce the contract for the changed, increased amount? The Restatement (Second) of Contracts, section 89D, provides that A's modified promise to pay the increased amount is enforceable

[47] For confession of judgment, see below, p. 321, ftn. 34.

[48] See above, pp. 13–16.

[49] See above, p. 36 ff.

because the modification is "fair and reasonable in view of the circumstances not anticipated when the contract was made.")

Promises to Perform Obligations not Existing Previously. Ratification by a promise to assume an obligation not previously borne by the promisor also is enforceable without consideration or assent in many instances. A few examples are: a principal's ratification of an act performed on his behalf by one who was not his agent; a principal's ratification of an unauthorized act of his agent; and a promise to pay the original debt together with interest not exceeding the maximum legal rate, in substitution for an illegal usurious agreement.

Promises of Performance of Discharged or Dischargeable Duties. *A promise is binding without consideration and without mutual assent which undertakes to perform an obligation conditioned on something which has not happened if the condition was not an essential element in **performance** of the obligation and merely fixes the **time** or **manner** of performance.* Again, justice is served best if promises of this character, whether made before or after failure of the condition's occurrence, are enforced without consideration and without mutual assent. Illustrations of such promises are: a surety's expressed promise, or acknowledgment of a duty, to perform his suretyship obligation which has been discharged by conduct of the principal debtor or creditor; a promise to be liable by a party whose secondary liability on a negotiable instrument was discharged because he had not received due notice of dishonor or because improper presentment was made; and an insurer's promise that notification of loss in a manner other than as prescribed by an insurance contract will be proper.

Promissory Estoppel. The Restatement (Second) of Contracts, section 90, provides: "*A promise which the promisor should reasonably expect to induce action or forbearance on the part of the promisee or a third person and which does induce such action or forbearance is binding if injustice can be avoided only by enforcement of the promise.*" The doctrine of *promissory estoppel* is an exception to the rules requiring a manifestation of mutual assent and consideration in order to form a contract, and is designed as a device to achieve justice when the situation requires relief and no other legal remedy is available.

A gratuitous promise is not an offer, since it proposes nothing in exchange for the promise and, consequently, cannot be accepted. Without an acceptance there is no consideration, and the promise is unenforceable. Yet, often such promises are made which the promisor has reason to know may induce a substantial change of position by the promisee and which does induce such change of position in justifiable reliance thereon. In equity, such promises are enforced to achieve justice in certain cases involving land. A gratuitous promise to convey land which has induced the promisee to enter and make improvements upon the land and a gratuitous promise not to foreclose on a mortgage have been held binding in equity. At law the principle is well established that a gratuitous promise not to assert a defense, or a gratuitous promise to waive a contractual condition in favor of the promisee, which induces a change of position in reasonable reliance thereon, is binding. Accordingly, the presently enunciated principle of promissory estoppel includes these and all cases in which gratuitous promises of the nature described induce the change of position indicated in such principle.

The principle of promissory estoppel is a substitute for the requirement of consideration in the situations covered by it. It has pertinent application to charitable subscriptions. At any time prior to reliance thereon, the gratuitous promise may be revoked or withdrawn. Once reliance occurs or partial reliance has begun, the promise is binding. (A subscribes $100 to a fund to build a church. Before the erection of the church is begun, the promise is revocable. Once the erection is begun, the promise is irrevocably binding.) The principle has been extended to other than charitable subscriptions. (A promises $1,000 to B, knowing that B needs the money for a certain purpose. B relies on the promise and changes his position materially in reliance on the promise to accomplish that purpose. A's promise is binding.)

It should be noted carefully that *promissory* estoppel is a term used to estop a party from setting up lack of manifestation of mutual assent and lack of consideration as a defense to suit on his *promise*. It is not a true estoppel. "Estoppel" has been discussed previously[50] and means that a misrepresentation of a material fact has been made, reasonable reliance thereon has occurred, and the utterer of the misrepresentation is now estopped from denying the truth of what he previously had misrepresented. (A, in response to an inquiry by B, states that a certain horse is not A's, when in fact it is A's horse which has been stolen by C. In reliance on A's statement, B purchased the horse from C. A is estopped to assert that the horse is his.)

Here, as in all the other promises binding without manifestation of mutual assent and consideration, previously discussed, *ignorance of material facts renders the promise either unenforceable or merely voidable, there being a difference of view on this point.*

Contracts under Seal

In many states where the seal still has its Common Law significance and the sealed promise is binding without consideration,[51] a contract under seal is enforceable without a manifestation of mutual assent. A seal is any substance, writing, sign, or impression affixed to a writing and intended as a seal by the promisor. The promisor may affix the seal or adopt one already there.

---

[50] See above, pp. 33–34.

[51] But see below, p. 117, ftn. 4, concerning the binding effect in some states of an unsealed signed writing, without consideration, purporting to modify or discharge an existing legal obligation.

SECTION IV. LEGALLY VALID TRANSACTION

The transaction must be legal. It is illegal if its formation or performance is contrary to law by being opposed to statute, or to public policy as declared by the courts. Usury is the taking of interest on a loan in excess of that maximum interest permitted by law. Statutes in many states prohibit the formation or performance of agreements on Sunday. Agreements in unreasonable restraint of trade are illegal. Restraint is unreasonable in the following instances if: it is in excess of what is reasonably necessary in time, area, or subject matter to protect the person to be benefited by the restraint, or imposes undue hardship on the restricted person; it tends to create a monopoly or to control prices; it unreasonably restricts the alienation (transfer) of property; or if it restrains competition not in connection with the sale of a business and its goodwill or similar transaction. A wager is illegal, as is an agreement to interfere with governmental processes.

A transaction is legally valid when the agreement is not legally void. An illegal agreement is void, generally, because usually it creates no legal duty or obligation to perform. *An agreement is illegal when its formation or performance is contrary to law by being opposed to statute, or to public policy as declared by the courts.*

Effect of Illegal Agreements

Illegal agreements *usually are void* either because the statute so provides or because the courts will not enforce the agreement as against public policy. The reason why the courts usually refuse to enforce an illegal agreement is because the plaintiff usually is a wrongdoer and courts deny relief to a wrongdoer. If the plaintiff is not a wrongdoer, then, in certain cases, the courts will grant relief, even by enforcing the agreement if justice so requires. The following are some of the principles in effect among courts regarding relief under illegal agreements:

1. If a statute bars recovery under an illegal agreement, then the courts can give no relief. If no statute bars recovery, then it is within the discretion of the courts to determine whether relief is justified and the kind of such relief.
2. Ordinarily, no recovery will be granted to either party under an illegal agreement. If the agreement is executed, it will not be opened; if it is executory, it will not be enforced.
3. Relief and recovery will be permitted to a party under an illegal agreement for whose protection and benefit the law exists. Recovery may be by rescission of the agreement and restitution of what has been parted with by the protected party, or by enforcement of the agreement and an award of damages for its breach. (A issues to B a policy of insurance containing terms which are contrary to law enacted for the benefit of people like B. On the occurrence of

the event insured against, relief should be given to B as the law was enacted for his benefit. Here the most appropriate relief would be enforcement of the policy.)

4. When one party justifiably is ignorant of the facts which make the agreement illegal and the other party is not ignorant, the ignorant party may refuse to perform after he has learned of the facts and may recover damages for breach of the executory portion of the agreement (the loss he sustained or the profit not made thereunder), or regain what he previously has performed or its value at the rate under the agreement. If both parties are ignorant, then relief is given only to the extent of performance already rendered, at the agreed rate.

5. When part of an agreement is valid and part illegal, if the main purpose of the agreement will not be affected, the valid portion of the agreement will be enforced by the courts. An agreement consisting of several valid distinct parts, all of which are supported by an illegal act, forbearance, or return promise, is illegal and unenforceable as a whole. If one of such parts is supported by a valid consideration, that part is valid and enforceable.

6. If an agreement is legally valid but by a change of law it becomes illegal, all contract rights of performance and damages for breach which arose prior to the change of legal status continue in existence. Recovery is limited to the extent of the agreement prior to the change of legal status.

7. Once an agreement is illegal, it continues to be illegal unless a change in law specifically validates such agreement, or the fact causing the transaction to be illegal and of which both parties were ignorant at the time of the transaction is changed, no longer barring the agreement as illegal.

8. When something has been rendered under an illegal agreement but the illegal provisions are still executory, the party who has rendered the thing may recover what was rendered. (Under an illegal gambling agreement, A delivered his money bet to B, a stakeholder. A may recover the money from B at any time prior to B's delivery of it to the other party to the agreement.)

Kinds of Illegal Agreement

There are various kinds of illegal agreement. A faw of the more important ones will be considered here.

Commission of Crimes and Torts. Inasmuch as the law provides public punishment for the commission of a crime and civil relief for the commission of a civil non-contractual wrong, called a "tort," agreements which contemplate performance of a crime or tort are illegal. Examples of such torts are: battery, assault, defamation (slander or libel), deceit, infringement of trademark or trade name.[52] Generally, a person may contract that another shall not owe a

[52] It should be noted that while persons may deal or refuse to deal with other persons as they choose, in the absence of statute to the contrary (e.g., the federal Civil Rights Act of 1964), they may not, unless privileged, induce *other persons* to refuse to deal, to refuse to continue a business relationship, or to breach their contracts with third persons. Society recognizes the interest of persons to enter into business relations with each other, and it protects this interest by denouncing

duty of care to the plaintiff's interest and that the other will not be liable for harm to the plaintiff's interest caused by conduct of the defendant which, but for the contract, would constitute negligence. The parties are free to contract as they wish, provided it is not illegal. An agreement is illegal if it provides against liability: for intentional infliction of harm; or for negligence with respect to performance of a public duty for compensation (e.g., railroad transporting goods or passengers for hire, public warehouseman for hire), or with respect to the employer's liability for harm negligently caused to an employee while acting within the scope of his employment.

Violation of Statute. Agreements which are prohibited by statute are illegal. Statutes may make such agreements illegal by prohibiting either the formation or the performance of such agreements. The prohibition of such formation or performance may be made expressly, or impliedly by providing penalties therefor, making it a crime, or requiring a license therefor. When a statute requires a license, an examination must be made of the legislative intent to determine whether the purpose of the statute was to protect the public or to obtain revenue. If the former, then an agreement violating the statute is illegal; if the latter, then usually the agreement is considered valid.

Usury. Usury is the taking of interest on a loan in excess of that maximum interest permitted by law. Three elements are necessary for usury: a loan of money, to be repaid, with interest in excess of that permitted by law. At Common Law there was no legal maximum of interest on a loan of money. Today, by statute,[53] most states provide for a maximum rate of interest on a loan and the taking of interest in excess of such rate is usury. Usurious agreements are illegal in most states. Such statutes usually specify two rates of interest: the legal rate and the maximum rate. When a contract provides for interest but does not specify the rate, the legal rate is applied.[54] The maximum rate is the highest rate permitted in that state. The rates of interest vary among the states.[55]

The effect of usury also varies among the states, as follows:

1. Forfeiture of principal and all interest.
2. Forfeiture of all interest.
3. Forfeiture of that portion of the interest in excess of what is permitted by law.
4. Forfeiture of interest, and a civil penalty is imposed on the lender to repay to the borrower double the interest charged.

---

such interfering inducements as wrongful and tortious. Inducing either breach of contract or refusal to deal are, therefore, torts and may be defined as intentionally and without privilege causing another person by inducement or otherwise to breach his contract, to refuse to continue a business relationship, or to refuse to deal, with a third person, which is a legal cause of special damage to the third person.

[53] See U3C, sec. 1.108, governing extension of consumer credit.

[54] UCC 3–118(d) prescribes, in the case of negotiable instruments, "the judgment rate at the place of payment. . . ."

[55] See U3C, sec. 2.401, Article 3, Part 2, for maximum charges on loans.

5. Usurious interest once paid cannot be recovered.
6. Usury is a crime.

Because of public policy the various states except certain transactions from the usury rule. The following are usual exceptions:

1. Small personal loans for short duration may exact interest rates higher than those permitted by law for ordinary loans.
2. An innocent mistake in calculating interest resulting in interest in excess of the permitted rate. Only such excess is forfeited.
3. Addition of proper service charges to the interest due.
4. Deduction of interest at the permitted rate in advance of the loan.
5. Loans to corporations in excess of the permitted rate.
6. Imposition of collection charges in addition to permitted interest in the event of the borrower's default.
7. A higher price for bona fide credit sales than for cash sales.
8. Purchase of an annuity.
9. Discount of commercial paper by sale.
10. Calculation of interest on the basis of 360 days in the year.

Often a form different from a loan is utilized to color the nature of a transaction and thereby attempt to avoid the usury law. The courts examine a transaction and the circumstances surrounding its formation to determine the intent of the parties and to see if the transaction is meant to be usurious. When the transaction is in the form of a sale, the courts require an intent to loan on the part of the one advancing the credit before they will consider the transaction usurious. Some of the subterfuges attempted to evade the usury laws are as follows:

1. Requiring the borrower to antedate his note to effect a usurious transaction.
2. The charging of fictitious fees in connection with the loan.
3. The sale on credit by the lender to the borrower of property far in excess of its fair value, the borrower to realize the cash by its sale.
4. Improper statement of the amount of the loan or of the rate of interest in the loan transaction.
5. Compelling the borrower to repay to the lender part of the loan immediately on making the loan.
6. The sale of property by the borrower to the lender at a low price on the condition that the borrower is to buy it back later at a higher price.

Sunday Statutes. In the absence of statutory provision to the contrary, contracts can be made and performed on Sunday. Many states have statutes which prohibit the formation or performance of agreements on Sunday. The extent of such statutes varies greatly. Such statutes usually except agreements to marry and agreements made of necessity or for charity. Matters of health, saving of property, religious ministry, and household work come within the exception. If a contract is made on other than a Sunday but performance is to occur on a Sunday, then, if performance on Sunday is not material to the contract, the contract is interpreted as requiring performance on the next day when performance is legally permissible. Such an agreement is legal. An offer made on Sunday and accepted on Monday creates a contract on Monday. An agreement made on Sunday but subsequently agreed to on Monday creates a contract on Monday, if all the elements of a contract are present, because the parties agreed anew and thereby created their contract.

Unreasonable Restraint of Trade. Agreements in *unreasonable* restraint of trade are illegal.[56] The law permits contracts in restraint of trade, which is the restraint of competition in business or restraint in the exercise of one's occupation; yet such restraint must not be unreasonable. Restraint is unreasonable: if it is in excess of what is reasonably necessary in time, area, or subject matter to protect the person to be benefited by the restraint, or imposes undue hardship on the restricted person; if it tends to create a monopoly or to control prices; if it unreasonably restricts the alienation of property; or if it restrains competition not in connection with the sale of a business and its goodwill or similar transaction. While the courts are more ready to countenance restraints where they are part of a contract involving the sale of a business and goodwill than where they are part of an employment contract, nevertheless the restraint must not be more than is reasonably necessary to protect the person to be benefited by the restraint.

Wagers. A wager is an agreement in which: the parties have no legal interest in the subject matter; one party is to win at the expense of the other; and performance of the agreement is subject to the condition of a fortuitous event. Gambling agreements and lotteries are wagers. Wagers are illegal in most states by statute. An insurance contract is not a wager because the insured has a legal interest to protect, either his property or his life and health, and by the insurance contract he is shifting to the insurer for consideration the insured's risk of harm to, or destruction of, such interest. If the insured has no legal interest, the agreement is illegal as a wager.[57] Speculative business agreements are valid, whether they be for the purchase of securities on margin or for "futures," provided the agreement does not preclude delivery of the subject matter and does not contemplate settlement dependent on the rise and fall of the market price. If the agreement precludes such delivery and contemplates such settlement, the agreement is a wager and illegal. However, the courts are in conflict concerning the validity of a hedging agreement for commodities, which is a common business transaction today precluding such delivery and contemplating such settlement. The purpose of the hedging agreement is to protect the value of commodities already acquired from being affected by a change in market prices. It would seem that such a transaction is of social value and should be protected; the federal courts, as well as some state courts, have held the hedging contract as valid and not contrary to public policy.

---

[56] See below, pp. 841–47.

[57] See below, p. 743.

Inasmuch as the federal courts are concerned with this type of agreement in enforcing federal interstate commodity regulatory legislation, the federal view appears to be preferable.

Interference with Governmental Process. Interference with governmental processes is improper, and agreements so to interfere are illegal. An agreement providing for unfair influence of a public official in carrying out a public duty is illegal. Fairly influencing such official is proper, and agreements so to influence are valid. (A employs B to urge favorable support by C, a congressman, of a legislative bill. Such an agreement is valid. However, if the agreement provided for the rendition of favors or of bribery, the agreement is illegal.) An agreement to pay a potential witness in a legal proceeding more than he is entitled to by law, unless he is an expert witness, is illegal. An agreement to conceal a crime, to testify falsely, to suppress evidence, or to induce assertion of a claim known to be false is illegal. An agreement to do business with an alien enemy residing in the enemy country or to aid an alien enemy country is illegal.

Chapter 4

CONTRACTS AND THIRD PARTY INTENDED BENEFICIARIES

Only the parties to a contract may enforce it, except for third party intended creditor or donee beneficiary contracts and for assignments.

SECTION I. THIRD PARTY INTENDED BENEFICIARY CONTRACTS

When a contract is made (1) with the manifested intention that it is to be performed to and for the benefit of a third person (2) who is either a creditor or donee of the promisee, there is a third party intended creditor or donee beneficiary contract which is enforceable by the beneficiary against the promisor. An incidental beneficiary cannot enforce the contract. The promisor's obligation cannot be varied as against a donee beneficiary unless the contract permitted variations; but it can be varied as against a creditor beneficiary unless the beneficiary has changed his position materially in reliance on the benefit conferred before he learns of the variation.

Contracts are binding upon the parties thereto and create rights and duties among those parties. Such parties are in "privity of contract" and may enforce the terms of their contract among themselves. A contract may provide that benefits are to be rendered to persons not parties thereto, called a "third party intended beneficiary contract."[1] Such a contract is enforceable by the third person only under certain circumstances.

[1] See UCC 2–318: "Third Party Beneficiaries of Warranties Express or Implied," in the sale of goods.

Requirements

There are two requirements. First, *the contract must be made with the manifested intention that it is to be performed to and for the benefit of a third person not a party to the contract,* called the third party intended *"creditor beneficiary"* or the third party intended *"donee beneficiary."* It is not necessary that the creditor or donee beneficiary be identified at the time the contract is made in order to create rights in the beneficiary under the contract. Illustrations are: a building contract for the benefit of the laborers and materialmen to be hired by the building contractor; a contract for the benefit of employees; and a contract for the benefit of the promisee's children surviving him. Second, *the beneficiary must be either a creditor of the promisee who is to obtain the benefit under the contract or a donee of such promisee.* In a *creditor beneficiary contract,* the performance of the promise is to satisfy the promisee's *duty* to the beneficiary. In a *donee beneficiary contract,* the performance of the promise is to make a *gift* to the beneficiary of the performance owed by the promisor to the promisee.

Types of Third Party Intended Beneficiary

Contracts may create three types of third party beneficiary: donee, creditor, and incidental. Only the first two beneficiaries can enforce the contract. The type of beneficiary in each contract is determined by the *intention* of the parties as expressly or impliedly indicated in the contract and the circumstances surrounding its formation.

Donee Beneficiary. A third party beneficiary under a contract which has the *purpose* of making a *gift* to the beneficiary of a right against the promisor, not due or believed to be due by the promisee to the beneficiary, is a *"donee beneficiary."* A donee beneficiary receives as a gift from the promisee a right against the promisor under the contract. (A and B contract whereby A the supplier contracts to supply B the purchaser with goods for $1,000, which B promises he will pay to C. B is under an obligation to C, the donee beneficiary of the contract who may enforce it against B. The contract was made and intended for the benefit of C, who is a donee of A the promisee.)

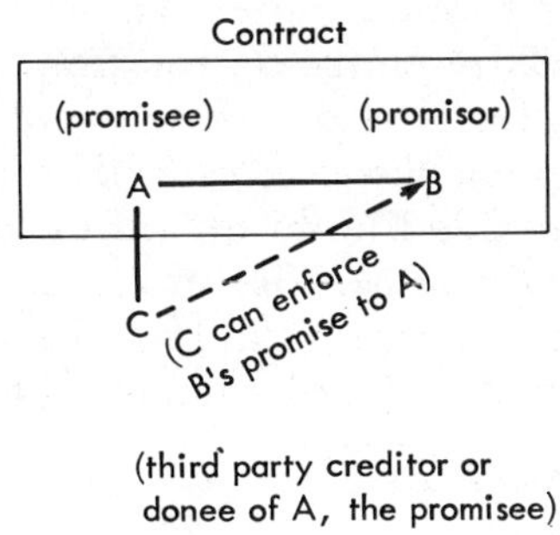

Creditor Beneficiary. A third party beneficiary under a contract in which the *purpose* is to confer on the beneficiary a right against the promisor, not as a gift but in order that the promisor's performance will satisfy a *duty* actually, or believed to be, *owing by the promisee to the beneficiary,* is called a "*creditor beneficiary.*" A creditor beneficiary is a creditor of the promisee and receives a right against the promisor in order to satisfy the promisee's obligation due to the beneficiary. (A owes C $100. A lends $100 to B on B's promise to A that B would pay $100 to C in satisfaction of A's debt to C. B is the promisor, A is the promisee, and the contract was made specifically for the benefit of C, who is a creditor of A the promisee. C is a creditor beneficiary.) The right was not conferred on the creditor as a gift but in satisfaction of the claim; so the creditor is a creditor beneficiary. However, a right against the promisor may be conferred on the promisee's creditor as a gift, making him a donee beneficiary. The express or implied intention of the contracting parties is the test. (A owes C $1,000 and D $5,000. A and B contract whereby B promises: to pay C $50 as an expression of appreciation for waiting so long; to pay D $5,000 in satisfaction of A's indebtedness to D; and to pay $1,000 to E, who is A's brother. C, although a creditor of the promisee, is a donee beneficiary, for the intention is to pay the $50 as a gift rather than as payment on the indebtedness. D is a creditor beneficiary. E is a donee beneficiary.)

Incidental Beneficiary. A person who will benefit incidentally by the promisor's performance under a contract in which such person is *not intended* to be a beneficiary and, therefore, is neither a donee nor a creditor beneficiary is called an "*incidental beneficiary.*" (A, a wholesaler, and B, a retailer, contract whereby A promises to sell and B promises to buy certain of X Company goods. X is an incidental beneficiary.) Since the contract was *not made with the intention* that it be for his benefit and he is neither a creditor nor a donee of the promisee, he cannot enforce the contract to which he was not a party.

Rights of Donee and Creditor Beneficiaries

In the great majority of states, donee and creditor beneficiaries have a direct right against the promisor for the enforcement of his promise. Incidental beneficiaries have no rights under the contract. The donee and creditor beneficiaries have a right against the promisor subject to whatever defenses the promisor has against the promisee under the contract. The contract may be voidable at the election of the promisor, the promisor's duty of performance may have been discharged because of failure of consideration,[2] or the contract may be unenforceable against the promisor. The promisor's defenses under the contract should be available to him regardless of whether or not there are any donee or creditor beneficiaries. The promisee may have defenses to the creditor beneficiary's claim against him. The promisee's ignorance of the invalidity or unenforceability of such a claim does not affect the creation of rights

[2] See below, p. 116.

in the beneficiary as either a creditor or donee beneficiary. If the intent was that the promisor's performance was to satisfy a claim, then the beneficiary is a creditor beneficiary regardless of whether or not he had a claim. The promisee has determined that the debt exists, and the promisor cannot refute such a determination. The promisor cannot set up against the creditor beneficiary defenses available to the promisee as against the beneficiary, except in one type of case. If the contract between the parties provided that the promisor was to be liable for payment of the promisee's debts, then the promisor is to determine which debts may be properly asserted by the creditor beneficiary and the promisor may set up the promisee's defenses. (A assigns his business to B under a contract whereby B assumes all of A's debts. B can set up A's defenses to any debts asserted.)

Variation of Promisor's Obligation

The donee or creditor beneficiary may disclaim or assent to the benefit conferred. Assent is presumed unless the beneficiary disclaims within a reasonable period of time after learning of the benefit conferred. Once disclaimer occurs, the beneficiary's right is extinguished as of the time the contract was made. The promisor's duty is then performable to the promisee, unless such performance is rendered impossible by the disclaimer. Disclaimer can be set aside if it is a fraud on creditors of the beneficiary.

The promisor and promisee have the power to discharge or modify the promisor's duty unless: their contract prohibits this; or the beneficiary has changed his position materially in justifiable reliance on the promise before he knows of the discharge or modification. (A takes out a policy of insurance on his life, naming C as a donee beneficiary, *reserving* the power to change the beneficiary. C's rights as a donee beneficiary are defeasible by A, who subsequently may arrange with the insurance company for a change of beneficiary.)[3]

When the creditor beneficiary learns of the contract made for his benefit, since the promisor now is a surety for the debtor promisee, the creditor becomes subject to the rules of suretyship.[4] (D owes C $1,000. X contracts with D to pay D's debt to C. If C modifies his contract with D without X's assent, X may be discharged from his promise.)

SECTION II. ASSIGNMENT OF CONTRACT RIGHTS AND DELEGATION OF CONTRACT DUTIES

Contract *rights are assignable* and contract *duties are delegable*, unless the contract is *personal* in character. This occurs when either (1) the assignment or delegation is prohibited by law, or (2) the contract expressly or impliedly prohibits assignment or delegation. Under the Code, a contractual provision prohibiting the assignment of an *account* is void.

[3] For assignment of interests under life insurance contracts, see below, p. 758.

[4] See below, pp. 495–96.

A contract is impliedly personal in character and contract *rights* are impliedly *nonassignable* without the *obligor's* assent if: (1) the personal skill, discretion, judgment, or personal taste or fancy of the obligor is involved; or (2) assignment would impose material additional risks or burdens on the obligor or change his duty. An assignee acquires the rights of his assignor and is subject to the obligor's defenses against the assignor. If the obligor receives notice of an assignment, his duty is to perform to the assignee. However, under the law of contracts and the Code, *when assignment of an account is made for the purpose of security*, unless the obligor receives notice of the assignment and the assignee *demands* payment, the obligor may properly pay the assignor and thereby be discharged of his debt. As assignment may include express, and does include implied, warranties.

A contract is impliedly personal in character and contract *duties* impliedly *nondelegable* without the *obligee's* assent if: (1) the personal skill, discretion, judgment, or personal taste or fancy of the obligor is involved; or (2) delegation would vary materially the performance due to the obligee under the contract. If the delegated person contractually *assumes* the obligor's duty, a third party creditor beneficiary contract is created for the benefit of the obligee. Under the Code, unless indicated to the contrary, an assignment of an entire contract and its acceptance by the assignee is interpreted as an assumption of the duties by the assignee. If the obligee agrees to accept a third person in place of the obligor, there is a *novation* which is (1) a new contract (2) in which one of the parties was not a party to the old contract and (3) which immediately discharges the old contract.

A contract creates rights and duties. The party having rights is called the "*obligee*" and the party owing duties is called the "*obligor.*" Contract rights may be transferred, just as other property, and such a transfer is called an "*assignment.*" The right assigned is called a "*chose in action*" (thing in action), because it is a right of action on the contract, a claim, e.g., an account receivable. *Contract duties may be delegated but not assigned,* because a party with contract duties cannot avoid his obligations merely by transferring them. An assignment is made by a person called an "assignor" to a person called an "assignee." In the assignment of contract rights, no particular form of assignment is necessary; it may be oral or in writing, as long as there is a manifestation of intent to transfer such rights. The assignment may be of the entire right or of only a portion, called a "*partial assignment.*" (X owes Y $100. Y assigns $50 of the debt to Z.) An assignment is distinguished from a contract *to* assign in that the latter promises a future assignment of a right and creates a present right to such assignment in the future. An assignment is effective when the assignee acquires the assignor's right to the obligor's performance. It is not necessary for the assignee to inform the obligor of such assignment in order to make it effective, nor need the person to whom duties are delegated notify the obligee of such delegation. *Contract rights may be assigned and duties delegated unless the contract is personal in character,* which occurs when either:

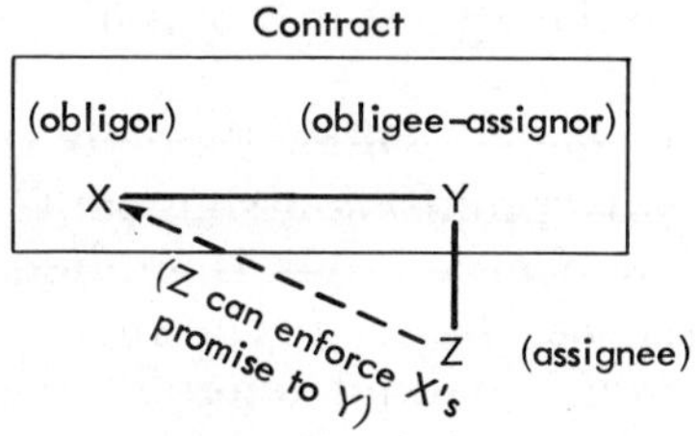

1. *Assignment or delegation is prohibited by law* because it is contrary to statute, or to public policy as declared by the courts. It is for this reason that a public employee cannot assign future compensation or delegate performance of his public duties and that a person with a government pension cannot assign it.

2. The contract expressly or impliedly prohibits assignment or delegation.[5]

Assignment of Rights

Rights under a contract *not personal* in character are assignable. However, assignment is not possible unless there is a contract right capable of assignment. Future rights expected to arise under an *existing* contract, such as compensation for employment,[6] are assignable; but expected future rights under a contract not in existence cannot be assigned, in the absence of statute to the contrary.

Personal Contracts Are Nonassignable without the Obligor's Assent. A contract may or may not be personal in character. It is personal in character when its assignment is prohibited either by law or by the contract, expressly or impliedly. If prohibited by law, the contract cannot be assigned in any case. If prohibited by the contract, it cannot be assigned without the *obligor's* assent. *A contract which is personal in character other than by law is nonassignable by the obligee without the obligor's assent.*

Under the Code. It should be noted very carefully that the sale or assignment of *accounts* is governed by the Code. The Code favors assignment freely of accounts, and while a clause in a contract precluding assignment *of the contract* is valid, nevertheless "A term in any contract between an account

[5] UCC 2–210(3): "Unless the circumstances indicate the contrary a prohibition of assignment of 'the contract' is to be construed as barring only the delegation to the assignee of the assignor's performance."

[6] But under U3C, sec. 3.305: "A creditor may not take an assignment of earnings of the consumer for payment or as security for payment of a debt arising out of a consumer credit transaction. An assignment of earnings in violation of this section is unenforceable by the assignee of the earnings and revocable by the consumer. This section does not prohibit a consumer from authorizing deductions from his earnings in favor of his creditor if the authorization is revocable, the consumer is given a complete copy of the writing evidencing the authorization at the time he signs it, and the writing contains on its face a conspicuous notice of the consumer's right to revoke the authorization."

debtor and an assignor is ineffective if it prohibits assignment *of an account*. . . ."[7] (Author's italics.)

Impliedly Personal Contracts. Often there is difficulty in determining whether a contract impliedly prohibits assignment.[8] A contract is impliedly personal in character and the contract right is impliedly nonassignable without the obligor's assent if: *only the obligor promisor is to perform or control the acts required by the contract*, meaning generally the obligor's personal skill, discretion, judgment, or personal taste or fancy; *or assignment would impose material additional risks or burdens on the obligor or change his duty.* (E employs S as his secretary, or A employs B as an artist to paint A's portrait, or X employs Y as his business representative. These contracts are of a personal character, and rights thereunder cannot be assigned by E, A, or X without the consent of S, B, or Y, respectively.) The right to fire protection in a contract of fire insurance is of a personal character because the insured's reliability as an insurance risk is an element considered by the insurer in issuing the policy, and the right to fire insurance is impliedly nonassignable. By the majority view, the purchaser under a contract *to purchase* on the *personal unsecured* credit of the purchaser cannot assign his contract right to make such purchase because credit was extended only to such purchasing party, and substitution of another party would subject the seller to a risk of loss through credit which he had not previously undertaken. In a contract for the sale of a business, the seller's promise not to compete with the buyer is interpreted to apply to the one owning the business, and the buyer may assign this right to such restraint to a subsequent purchaser of the business without thereby imposing any additional burdens on the seller. The usual type of assignment is of the right to be paid money, the right to have a contractor erect a building, and the right of restraint from competition, to mention only a few examples. These rights do not involve any personal skill, discretion, judgment, or personal taste or fancy and, therefore, are not personal in character; nor do they involve the imposition on the obligor of any materially increased burdens or risks.

Revocation of Assignment. An assignment may be made for value—i.e., for consideration—or it may be made gratuitously. By the former, the assignment is irrevocable and the right passes from the assignor to the assignee. The right acquired by a gratuitous assignment is revocable by the assignor or by his death unless: the assignee has already realized on the assignment by payment. An assignor of a revocable or voidable assignment may revoke or avoid such assignment by a subsequent assignment of the same right. An assignment cannot be foisted on an unwilling assignee who may refuse or disclaim the assignment within a reasonable period of time after he learns of it. An assignment is ineffective without the assignee's manifestation of assent, except when the assignment is for value or made with a token necessary to the obligor's performance.

---

[7] UCC 9–318(4).

[8] For assignment of a contract for the sale of goods under the Code, see UCC 2–210.

Rights Acquired by Assignment. An assignee acquires the rights of his assignor; he stands in the shoes of his assignor; and the assignee may sue in his own name. If the assignor has a claim which has a priority in payment from the obligor's insolvent estate, assignment of the claim includes the priority feature. An assignee takes the assigned right subject to all defenses, setoffs, and counterclaims available to the obligor as against the assignor obligee which accrued before the obligor has notice of the assignment.[9] (A contract between A and B is voidable by B. A assigns the contract right to C. B may avoid the contract.)[10] However, even if the obligor receives notice of the assignment, he still can be discharged by impracticability, illegality, failure of a condition, or present or prospective failure of performance by the obligee.

Notice of Assignment to the Obligor. While an assignee is not required to give to the obligor notice of assignment in order to effect an assignment, his failure to do so may affect his recovery on the right because third parties would be adversely affected. Ignorance of such assignment may cause the obligor to pay the obligee or the obligee's judgment creditor instead of the assignee, which discharges the obligor. If the obligor receives notice of the assignment, he must perform to the assignee. Further, the obligee may assign the same right successively to different assignees. If the obligor innocently pays the first assignee who appears before him, not knowing of any previous assignment, the obligor is discharged. As between the two assignees, who has the assigned right? The first assignment in time transferred the right to that assignee. If the first assignment is revocable, then the subsequent assignment revoked the prior assignment. If the first assignment is irrevocable, a second assignee, who is either a gratuitous assignee or an assignee for value but with notice of the previous assignment, obviously should not be able to prevail over the assignee prior in time. However, if the second assignee is one for value and without notice of any prior assignment—i.e., a bona fide purchaser for value in good faith without notice of the prior assignment—whether or not he may prevail over the first assignee depends upon the jurisdiction. In some states the assignee who first gives notice of assignment to the obligor prevails. By the better view the assignee first in time prevails, unless a subsequent innocent assignee for value *obtains* payment or other performance from the obligor before the obligor has notice of the prior assignment. In short, as between an assignee and the obligor, the assignee acquires the right defeasible by the innocent obligor rendering performance to the obligee, to the obligee's judgment creditor, or to an assignee subsequent in time. As between an assignee and either a judgment creditor of his assignor or an assignee subsequent in time, the assignee prior in time has the right defeasible only by the obligor's innocent *performance* to such judgment creditor or subsequent assignee.

An assignee may prefer that the obligor pay to the assignor, and the assignee trusts the assignor will then pay to him. However, an assignee may prefer that

---

[9] But see U3C, sec. 3.404, and below, pp. 433, 447–48.

[10] For a discussion of the assignment of accounts under the Secured Transactions Article of the Code, see below, pp. 447–48.

the obligor pay directly to the assignee. Because of this, under the law of contracts and also under the Code, *when the assignment of an account is made for the purpose of security,* unless the obligor *receives* notice of the assignment and the assignee *demands* payment, the obligor may properly pay to the assignor and thereby be discharged of his debt. The assignee would then have to recover the money from the assignor. *An assignee should give actual notice to the obligor and demand payment or performance from the obligor in order to protect his right, although such notice is not required in order to make an assignment effective as between the assignor and the assignee.*[11]

Warranties. An assignment may include express warranties and, by operation of law, the following implied warranties as enumerated in section 165 of the Restatement (Second) of Contracts:

> (1) Unless a contrary intention is manifested, one who assigns or purports to assign a right by assignment under seal or for value warrants to the assignee
> (a) that he will do nothing to defeat or impair the value of the assignment and has no knowledge of any fact which would do so;
> (b) that the right, as assigned, actually exists and is subject to no limitations or defenses good against the assignor other than those stated or apparent at the time of the assignment;
> (c) that any writing evidencing the right which is delivered to the assignee or exhibited to him to induce him to accept the assignment is genuine and what it purports to be.
>
> (2) An assignment does not of itself operate as a warranty that the obligor is solvent or that he will perform his obligation.
>
> (3) An assignor is bound by affirmations and promises to the assignee with reference to the right assigned in the same way and to the same extent that one who transfers goods is bound in like circumstances.
>
> (4) An assignment of a right to a sub-assignee does not operate as an assignment of the assignee's rights under his assignor's warranties unless an intention is manifested to assign the rights under the warranties.

Delegation of Duties

Duties under a contract not personal in character are delegable.

Personal Contracts Are Nondelegable without the Obligee's Assent. A contract is personal in character when delegation of duties thereunder is prohibited either by law or by the contract, expressly or impliedly. If prohibited

---

[11] See UCC 9–318(3). For a discussion of the effect of an assignment of an account on other creditors of the assignor, see Secured Transactions, below, pp. 447–48. UCC 9–205 should be noted at this point: "Use or Disposition of Collateral Without Accounting Permissible. A security interest is not invalid or fraudulent against creditors by reason of liberty in the debtor to use, commingle or dispose of all or part of the collateral (including returned or repossessed goods) or to collect or compromise accounts or chattel paper, or to accept the return of goods or make repossessions, or to use, commingle or dispose of proceeds, or by reason of the failure of the secured party to require the debtor to account for proceeds or replace collateral. This section does not relax the requirements of possession where perfection of a security interest depends upon possession of the collateral by the secured party or by a bailee."

by law, contract duties cannot be delegated in any case. If prohibited by the contract, the duties cannot be delegated without the *obligee's* assent. *Duties under a contract which is personal in character other than by law are nondelegable by the obligor without the obligee's assent.*

Impliedly Personal Contracts. Often there is difficulty in determining whether a contract impliedly prohibits delegation of its duties. A contract is impliedly personal in character and contract duties impliedly nondelegable without the obligee's assent if: the obligee promisee has a *substantial interest* in having *only the obligor promisor perform or control the acts required by the contract,* meaning that, generally the obligor's personal skill, discretion, judgment, or personal taste or fancy; *or delegation would vary materially the performance due to the obligee under the contract.* Under the heading "*Impliedly Personal Contracts*" on page 80 above, the first illustration refers to employment between E and S, A and B, X and Y. Neither S, B, nor Y could delegate his respective duties without the assent of E, A, or X, respectively. A building contractor can delegate his contract duty to erect a building for the other party because no special skill is involved, but a building contractor with certain special or unusual skills could not delegate his duty. A member of a professional athletic team could not delegate his duties, nor could an officer in a corporation. Because the duty cannot be delegated does not preclude the assignment of a right by the obligor. (In the illustration of E and S, A and B, X and Y, although neither S, B, nor Y could delegate his duties nor E, A, or X assign his rights to performance by the other parties, nevertheless, the employees could assign their rights to compensation.)

Effect of Delegation. The obligor's delegation of a contract duty authorizes the delegated person to perform the duty. Such delegation does not extinguish the duty of the obligor to the obligee under their contract. The delegated person may have the *option* of performing the duty, or he may *assume* performance of the duty. He may also refuse to consent to such delegation. It is difficult sometimes to determine whether there is an assumption of the duties. By the better view and under the Code,[12] unless indicated to the contrary, *the assignment of an entire contract and its acceptance by the assignee is interpreted as an assumption of duties by the assignee and as creating a third party creditor beneficiary contract.*[13] Some courts hold to the contrary, that an assumption of duties must be expressly manifested.

Novation

The obligor, the obligee, and the delegated person may contract together to extinguish the obligor's duty in exchange for the assumption of such duty by the delegated person. Repudiation by the obligor of his duty, coupled with the assumption of such duty by the delegated person and the obligee's silent

[12] UCC 2-210(4). Also see below, pp. 207–8.

[13] See above, p. 76 f.

acceptance of performance by such delegated person with knowledge of such repudiation, operate to extinguish the obligor's duty. The obligee could accept the substituted performance and inform the obligor or the delegated person that he did not thereby waive his right to continue to hold the obligor liable for performance of his duty; the obligor's duty would not be extinguished. The extinguishment of the obligor's duty and the substitution of another person in his place is accomplished by a *novation*. *A novation is a new contract in which one of the parties was not a party to the old contract and which immediately discharges the old contract.* Until novation occurs, the obligee can hold both the obligor and the delegated person who *assumed* the duty liable for the performance of such duty.[14]

---

[14] The obligee is a third party creditor beneficiary of the contract between the obligor and the delegated person who assumed the duty and, thus, he may enforce the contract. See above, p. 76 f.

Chapter 5

STATUTE OF FRAUDS

The statute of frauds is a "proof" statute requiring a proper writing to prove a contract. An executory contract under the statute is *unenforceable* unless the contract is evidenced by a proper writing and is signed by the party to be charged with performance or by his lawfully authorized agent. Under the law of contracts, the following contracts are within the statute: (1) a contract of an executor or administrator to answer personally for a duty of his decedent; (2) a contract to answer for the duty (debt, default, or miscarriages) of another person; (3) a contract made in consideration of marriage, not between the parties to be married; (4) a contract to transfer, buy, or pay for an interest in land; (5) a contract not performed by any party to it and which *cannot* be performed within one year from the date of its formation. *For contract* (2): *a.* The contract must be to answer for the debtor obligor's duties; the surety promisor must not *assume* the obligor's duty. *b.* The surety's promise must be made to the creditor obligee. *c.* The contract must be made primarily for the benefit of the obligor, not the surety. *For contract* (5), generally the year begins to run from the end of the day when the contract was made and expires at midnight on the anniversary date of the contract's formation. Contracts performable on a contingency which may or may not happen within a year are not within the statute. The writing may be one writing or a series of related writings. The writing may be the written contract itself, or any note or memorandum thereof. It must state: (1) the names of the parties (or describe them); (2) the subject matter; (3) indicate that a contract was made between the parties; and (4) the essential terms and conditions of each promise and to whom made.

Under the Code, various provisions require a writing to prove a contract thereunder. For example, an oral contract for the sale of goods for the price of $500 or more is proved by a memorandum which must: (1) evidence a contract for the sale of goods; (2) be signed by the party to be charged or by his lawfully authorized agent; and (3) specify a quantity of goods.

Background

Each state has a statute of frauds as a part of its law. The statute of frauds is concerned not with frauds but rather with *certain methods of proof necessary to establish the existence of certain kinds of contract* in order to prevent the occurrence of fraud through perjured testimony to prove the existence of such alleged contracts. The statute provides that a contract of the kind indicated therein is *unenforceable* unless proved in a certain specified way. There are slight variations in the statutes of the various states, but for the most part they are alike. It is a "proof" statute. If the contract has been executed, there is no longer any reason for the statute and it then is inapplicable.

Contents of the Statute

The statute of frauds applies only to informal, executory contracts. A contract within the provisions of the statute is *unenforceable* unless proved as prescribed. Failure to comply with the requirements of proof affects enforceability, not validity, of the contract. The following five types of contract are *unenforceable unless the contract is evidenced by a proper writing, signed by the party to be charged with performance or by his lawfully authorized agent:*

1. A contract of an executor or administrator to answer personally for a duty of his decedent.
2. A contract to answer for the duty (debt, default, miscarriages) of another person.
3. A contract made in consideration of marriage, not between the parties to be married (e.g., father's promise to pay groom to marry daughter).
4. A contract to transfer, buy, or pay for an interest in land.
5. A contract not performed by any party to it and which *cannot* be performed within one year from the date of its formation.

Under the Code. There are other types of transaction the enforceability of which is governed by the Code: a contract for the sale of goods for the price of $500 or more (UCC 2–201); a contract for the sale of securities (UCC 8–319); a security agreement for a non-possessory security interest (UCC 9–203); a contract for general intangibles, e.g., goodwill, royalty rights, rights to performance (UCC 9–106), and contracts for various types of security transaction (UCC 9–104),[1] for more than $5,000 are governed by UCC 1–206. Reference

[1] See below, pp. 422–23.

should be made to those specific areas in the text to determine the proof necessary to make such contracts enforceable.

Contract to Answer for the Duty (Debt, Default, or Miscarriages) of Another Person. There is no difficulty in understanding the first and third types of contract. The second type of contract is concerned with the relationship among three people: a creditor or obligee, a principal debtor or obligor, and a surety:

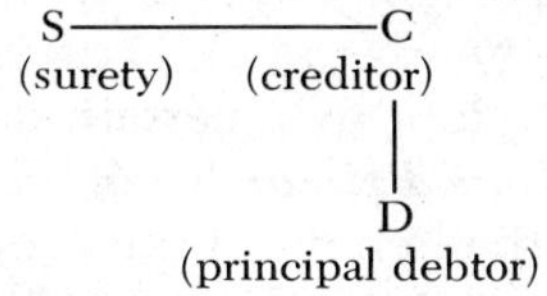

A "surety" is a person who makes his credit available to another, a debtor; and if he is compelled to pay because of the debtor's default, he has a right to be reimbursed by the debtor. (S contracts with C that, if C will sell goods to D on credit and D does not pay, then S will pay C. C sells the goods to D who does not pay C. When S has paid C, S has a right to be reimbursed by D.) *When the surety contracts with the creditor whereby the surety will pay the creditor if the debtor fails to pay, the contract is within the statute.*

The Contract Must Be for the Promisor (Surety) to Answer for the Debtor's Duty. If the contract does not appear to be for this purpose and the creditor has no reason for knowing otherwise, then the contract is not within the statute. (S and D agree that they will sign a contract with C for the purchase of certain goods to be deliverable to S. S and D have agreed that the goods will then be turned over to D, inasmuch as the only reason for S's participation in the contract is to induce C to sell the goods because of S's financial reliability. D will then reimburse S for the contract price. C is ignorant of this surety relationship between S and D. An oral contract is made by S and D with C. The contract is not within the statute. S did not promise to answer for D's duty; he *assumed* it. S and D are *both debtors* to C under the contract.) If the promisor contracts to *assume* the debtor's duty, he thereby makes the duty his own and is not answering for the debtor's duty. He may do the latter by so contracting with the creditor, by a novation, or by doing so originally whereby he and the debtor become jointly liable to the creditor for an obligation. An oral contract between the promisor and the creditor whereby the promisor *undertakes to pay* the debtor's debt is not a contract to answer for the debtor's debt; the promisor has assumed and made the debt his own, and the contract is enforceable although oral. An unconditional promise to pay is different from a promise to pay *if* the debtor fails to pay. The first promise creates an absolute liability on the promisor for the debt; the second promise creates a contingent liability to answer for the debtor *if he* defaults. The first promise is not within the purview of the statute; the second is.

The Surety's Promise Must Be Made to the Creditor and Be Collateral to the Debtor's Duty. The surety's promise must be made to the creditor because the contract is to answer to the creditor for the debtor's duty. It is immaterial that the debtor's duty is voidable at his election, for, until avoidance, the duty is still owing. (D, an infant, makes a contract with C. S contracts with C to answer for D's default. S is bound.) A promise by one who holds the debtor's property to deliver it to the creditor is not a promise to answer for the debtor's duty as contemplated by the statute. The debtor's duty need not be in existence at the time the surety's promise is made to the creditor. (S orally *contracts* with C that, if C will sell goods to D on credit and D does not pay, then S will pay C. C sells the goods to D.) (D owes C money. S *contracts* with C that, if D does not pay his debt by a certain date, S will pay it.)

The Contract Must Be Made Primarily for the Benefit of the Debtor. A contract made primarily for the benefit of the promisor and not for the benefit of the debtor is not within the statute. (D owes C money. C is about to proceed against D's property on the debt. X contracts with C that, if C will forbear from proceeding against D's property for a certain period and if D does not pay by that time, then X will pay. C forbears. Whether or not the contract is within the statute depends on X's relationship to D. If X is also a creditor of D and made the contract so that D's business would not be ruined and, if given time, D could pay X and C, then the contract is not within the statute. It was made for X's benefit and not for D's benefit. If X is only a friend of D and made the contract to help D get on his feet, then the contract is within the statute.) However, if the promisor is a *paid surety*, e.g., an insurance company acting as a surety;[2] the contract is held to be within the statute, inasmuch as the purpose of the statute is to include this type of promise irrespective of premium benefit.

Contract to Transfer, Buy, or Pay for an Interest in Land. A contract to transfer, buy, or pay for an interest in land is within the statute because of the great importance of land and the temptation to commit perjury to prove a contract for its sale. The statute covers interests in land. Easements, leases, mining rights, and the building of a railroad, in connection with land, are illustrations of interests in land. Licenses for the use of land are not interests in land. A theater ticket is merely a license to enter upon the land. A contract for board and lodging and a contract to erect a building or to make improvements on land are not contracts for an interest in land. They are merely contracts relating to the land. A "lease" is a contract for the sale of an interest in land, but most state statutes provide that a lease for a period less than a year is not within the statute and is enforceable if oral. Oil, gas, minerals, or a structure (e.g., building) affixed to land are land; but a contract for their sale, contemplating their severance from the land *by the seller* after the formation of the contract, causes them to be treated as goods *for the purpose of the contract.*[3]

---

[2] The insurance company may be acting as a *surety* or as an *indemnitor*. If a surety, it is within the statute; if an indemnitor, it is not within the statute. For the distinction between surety and indemnitor, see below, pp. 480, 488; 749, 745 ff.

[3] See UCC 2–107(1), and below, pp. 199–200. *If the buyer is to sever*, these are considered contracts affecting land and thus the statute of frauds and the recording of land rights are applicable to them.

Such a contract is not considered as dealing with interests in land and, therefore, is not within the statute. Similarly, a contract for the sale of *a house,* but not of the land underneath it, contemplates severance from the realty and is not within the statute. A contract to give a mortgage is within the statute because a mortgage is an interest in land. A mortgage is different from the indebtedness it secures; it is a right to sell the land on the debtor's default and to apply the proceeds in satisfaction of the indebtedness. A contract to sell the debt is not within the statute even though the mortgage follows the indebtedness.

A contract to sell an equitable interest in land is within the statute (e.g., a contract to sell land creates an equitable interest in land in favor of the buyer because, in a court with equity powers, he can compel the seller to convey the land to him). While some courts consider an option to buy land as not creating such an interest in land until the buyer accepts under the option, other courts hold that the option of itself creates such an interest.

Part Performance. Part performance of a contract for the sale of land or of an interest therein may take the contract *out of the statute* and permit its enforcement, depending upon the nature of the part performance, as in the following instances:

1. *Seller's conveyance to the buyer.* When that portion of an oral contract requiring performance by transfer of an interest in land has been executed, the courts do not consider the contract as any longer within the statute, and they will enforce the remaining unexecuted portion of the contract. (A contracts orally with B for the purchase of B's land, A to pay the price 30 days after B has conveyed the land to A. B conveys the land to A, but A defaults in making payment. The contract is no longer within the statute of frauds and is enforceable by B.)

2. *Seller's delivery of possession to buyer and either buyer's payment or buyer's substantial improvements on the land with seller's consent.* By the better view, when under an oral contract a purchaser of land or of an interest in land acquires or retains *possession* of the land with the consent of the vendor *and pays* a portion or all of the purchase price, *or* a purchaser with the consent of the vendor makes *valuable improvements* thereon, the contract is specifically enforced[4] by the courts. Many courts consider permitted possession of the land sufficient to justify specific enforcement of the oral contract. The courts do this, regardless of the statute, in order to prevent the perpetration of injustice and fraud on the buyer. A buyer who pays a part or all of the purchase price but makes no valuable improvements and does not obtain possession may not enforce the oral contract and is entitled solely to the return of what he has rendered or its reasonable value as a quasi-contractual right. The purchase price need not be money; it may be services, chattels, or land.

Contract Not Performable within One Year. There have been conflicting interpretations of that portion of the statute which provides for contracts not

[4] See below, p. 110 f.

performable *within* one year from the making thereof. The first difficulty is in the calculation of the one-year period. The law disregards fractions of a day. In calculating the one-year period some courts have disregarded the legal fiction of disregarding a fraction of a day and have computed exactly the period of one year. The better view[5] is to disregard the fraction of a day so as to be most favorable to enforcement of the contract. Accordingly, the year begins to run from the end of the day when the contract was made and expires at midnight on the anniversary of the date of the contract's formation. All courts hold that a bilateral contract for a year, in which performance is to begin the day the contract is made, is not within the statute. By the better view, if performance is to begin the day after the contract was made, the contract is not within the statute. All courts agree that, if performance is to begin at any time later than the day following the contract's formation, the contract is within the statute. It should be noted that the date of the contract's formation is the date when the last act necessary to create the contract occurs. *The above discussion relates solely to executory bilateral contracts. A unilateral promise is not within the statute*, regardless of the period of time for the performance called for, because there is no contract until such performance occurs.

The second difficulty is in the determination of what contracts are not to be performed within the year's time. All courts agree that, if the contract literally *cannot* be completely performed within the year by the mode of performance agreed upon, then the contract is within the statute, regardless of the expectations and views of the parties concerning the probability of performance within the year. An illustration is an oral contract to sell a number of crops from the same land when it is physically impossible to grow that many crops from that land in one year. If performance within one year were conceivably possible by a method of performance different from the one contemplated by the parties in their contract, some courts hold the contract not to be within the statute, but most courts hold to the contrary. Contracts performable on a contingency which may or may not happen within a year are not within the statute, regardless of the duration of such contracts. Illustrations of such contracts are: insurance contracts on life or property, regardless of the term of years, because the contingency may occur within the year and the promise to pay become performable; and a contract to support another for life, because death may occur within a year and the contract thereby be performed. However, a contract to support another, or to forbear, for a term of years is within the statute. While it is true that a promise to support another for five years is discharged by the promisee's death, yet the *promise* has not been performed; its further *performance* is excused. In contrast, a contract to support for life is *performed* on the promisee's death. For the same reason, a contract not to compete for a period in excess of one year is, by the better view, within the statute.

Courts are in disagreement concerning the status of a contract performable on one side but not on the other within one year. (A and B orally contract

[5] See Restatement (Second) of Contracts, 1980, sec. 198, Comment c.

whereby A is to render his performance now, e.g., pay money, and B is to render his performance over a period of 18 months.) Because the entire contract cannot be performed within one year, it is clearly within the statute. However, most courts hold that, if one side of the contract is performable within one year and such performance occurs within one year, the contract no longer is within the statute. Many courts hold that performance on one side within the year is not enough; if the remaining promise on the other side still is not performable within the year, the contract is still within the statute. The Restatement (Second) of Contracts, section 198, provides that performance on one side, made *at any time,* takes the contract out of the purview of the statute. In any case, if all or part performance is rendered on one side of an oral contract which is unenforceable, the party who has performed has a right of restitution of what he has rendered or the reasonable value thereof on the ground of quasi contract in order to prevent unjust enrichment.

The Writing

All five types of contract may be proved by a writing evidencing the contract, signed by the party to be charged with performance or by his lawfully authorized agent. Generally, in the absence of statute to the contrary, the writing may be the written contract itself, or any note or memorandum thereof. The memorandum is sufficient if made at any time before a legal action is begun on the contract. (A and B make a signed written contract. On its expiration A and B orally contract to renew the contract previously made and now expired. The previous contract is a memorandum evidencing the subsequent oral contract.) It may be a formal or informal writing and may be one writing or a series of related writings. If there is more than one writing, either all the writings must be attached to the signed writing or the signed writing must refer to all the other writings. (A writes to B complaining about B's failure to perform an oral contract within the statute of frauds and sets forth all the data regarding such contract. B's answering signed letter refers to A's letter and admits the formation of such a contract but refuses to perform it. B's signed letter refers to A's letter, and the two writings constitute the memorandum sufficient to satisfy the statute and to prove the oral contract. The contract is enforceable by A against B. If B were seeking to enforce the oral contract against A, A's signed letter would be the memorandum.) The memorandum need not have been intended by the party as a memorandum of the contract.

The memorandum must be *signed* by the party to be charged with performance or by his lawfully authorized agent.[6] Signature means any mark, sign, printing, or writing intended by the party making or adopting it to be his signature[7] authenticating the writing as his. It may occur anywhere on the writ-

[6] See below, p. 588, for the legal effect when an agent does not identify his principal in the memorandum signed by the agent.

[7] Under UCC 1–201(39): " 'Signed' includes any symbol executed or adopted by a party with present intention to authenticate a writing."

ing; and it is different from the word "subscribe," which means that the signature must occur at the bottom of the document. The memorandum may be asserted to prove the contract only against the party who has signed it. In the second illustration given in the paragraph above, if B had never answered A's letter, A could not assert the oral contract against B; but B could assert the contract against A and prove the contract by A's signed letter, which is a memorandum signed by the party to be charged—namely, A. One contracting party cannot authorize the other party to sign the memorandum for him because of the temptation to assert authority fraudulently. However, a third person may be authorized to sign for both parties. In sales by auction, the auctioneer impliedly is authorized by both seller and buyer to prepare and sign on their behalf a memorandum of sale *immediately* after the sale.

Generally, in the absence of statute to the contrary, the signed writing must: indicate the parties, or provide a description sufficient for their identification; reasonably identify the subject matter of the contract; be sufficient to indicate that a contract was made between the parties; and state with reasonable certainty the essential terms and conditions of each promise and to whom made.[8] The memorandum is sufficient even though it omits terms which are implied or supplied by law. (A is the agent of C, and B is the agent of D. C and D have made an oral contract within the statute of frauds. A and B are authorized to execute a memorandum of the contract, which they do, signing as "C" and "D." The memorandum is sufficient to prove the contract against C or D.) Omission of any essential data causes the writing to be insufficient as a memorandum. A writing naming the parties but not indicating their relationship (e.g., who is the buyer and who the seller) is defective. A memorandum which has been destroyed or lost may be proved by other evidence.

[8] Under UCC 2–201(1), the memorandum must evidence a contract for the sale of goods; it must be signed by the party to be charged; and it must specify a quantity.

Chapter 6

CONDITIONS

A condition is an event uncertain to occur but which must occur before performance becomes due under a contract. An absolute promise has no conditions as to its *immediate* performance; time is not a condition. A conditional (dependent) promise is *immediately* performable only when something other than a lapse of time must occur. There are three conditions: (1) *condition precedent*—the condition must occur before there is a duty of immediate performance of the conditional promise; (2) *condition concurrent*—a condition which is to occur simultaneously with another condition, each a condition to performance of a promise; (3) *condition subsequent*—a condition which, if occurring subsequent to the rise of a duty of immediate performance of a conditional promise, extinguishes such duty.

Nonperformance of a promise is a failure of *condition.* Unless expressly agreed to the contrary, the effect of nonperformance depends upon what has been done by the nonperforming party. If nothing has been done, there is a failure of *consideration* and the injured party is *discharged.* If something has been done, the effect of the nonperformance depends upon the materiality of the nonperformance. If a *material nonperformance*, then there is a failure of condition, failure of *consideration*, and the injured party is *discharged.* If a *nonmaterial nonperformance*, then there is a failure of condition, substantial performance, and the injured party must perform his promise less any damage he sustained by such failure. If the main purpose of the contract has been performed or not defeated, there is substantial performance and a failure to perform is nonmaterial; otherwise the failure to perform is material.

Prospective failure of consideration occurs when, after the contract is made, a strong likelihood of material nonperformance by a promisee arises. Examples

are: the promisee's repudiation or insolvency and the promisor's material change of position in reliance thereon; destruction or impairment of the requisite subject matter of the contract, or of the requisite means of performing the contract, making impracticable rendition of substantial performance by the promisee. If the promisee's failure of consideration is excused by the promisor, then the promisor's duty of performance still exits and he is not dependent upon the promisee's performance as a condition.

Nature and Importance

A recent change in the terminology and concept of "condition" is that a condition is an event uncertain to occur but which must occur before performance becomes due under a contract. Basically, a condition is an event or fact on the happening or nonhappening of which a promissory duty of *immediate performance* either arises or is extinguished. (A promises to pay B $100 for the construction of a shed. A has no duty of *immediate performance* of his promise until the condition for such performance has occurred—namely, B's construction of the shed.) (A insures B's house against fire, the policy providing that failure of the insured to bring an action against the insurer for fire loss within a prescribed period of time after the insurer has rejected the claim shall terminate the insurer's duty to pay. Fire occurs and B presents his claim, which A rejects. B does not bring an action against A within the prescribed time. A's promissory duty of immediate performance—i.e., to pay B for the fire loss—has been extinguished by B's failure to sue within the prescribed time, which is a condition extinguishing A's duty.) The subject of conditions is the key to the comprehension of performance and nonperformance, breach of contract, and discharge from the duty of performing one's promise. In brief, the occurrence or nonoccurrence of a condition determines whether or not a party has a legal duty of *immediately performing* his promise.

Absolute and Conditional Promises

All promises are either absolute or conditional. They differ as to when a duty of *immediate performance* arises in each case. A promise performable only after the lapse of a certain period of time is an absolute promise. There are no conditions to its immediate performance; *the law does not consider a lapse of time as a condition.* A promise is conditional when something other than a lapse of time must occur. A promise which is not absolute is conditional. (A promises to pay B $1,000 on the expiration of 30 days, and B promises to deliver goods two months after such payment. A's promise is absolute, payable at the end of 30 days, and subject to no conditions. B's promise is conditional, no duty of immediate performance arising until two months after payment.) A conditional promise may have as a condition either the performance of another party's promise or the occurrence of an event or act. Conditional promises are often called "dependent promises" because there is no duty of their immediate performance until the occurrence of the condition on which such performance is dependent.

Classification of Conditions

Conditions Precedent. Conditions may be *precedent, subsequent,* or *concurrent;* and they may be either expressly stated or implied in fact from the contract, or implied in law. *A condition precedent is a condition which must occur before there is a duty of immediate performance of the conditional promise.* (A promises to pay B $10,000 on the arrival of a certain ship. Arrival of the ship is a condition precedent.) When the condition of a promise is the promisor's satisfaction of the performance of the condition, it is a problem of interpretation as to whether the satisfaction means *personal satisfaction,* or the *reasonable satisfaction of a person in the promisor's position.* Satisfaction is concerned solely with the performance of the condition, and nothing else. (A contracts with B for the purchase of a suit to be made by B to A's satisfaction for $95. B manufactures a suit for A. A, without examining the suit, expresses his dissatisfaction. A's satisfaction is a condition precedent to A's immediate promissory duty to pay. A has not indicated any satisfaction or dissatisfaction *of the performance,* and his repudiation of the contract subjects him to damages for its breach.) Regardless of whether the satisfaction is interpreted as personal or as reasonable, the promisor must act in good faith and cannot be arbitrary or capricious. In the event of doubt as to which satisfaction is meant, reasonable satisfaction is implied by law as the intent of the parties. If the purpose of the contract is the personal taste, fancy, preference, or convenience of the promisor, then the satisfaction is personal and, until he is personally satisfied, there is no duty of immediate performance of his promise. Whether or not another person would reasonably be satisfied is irrelevant. If the purpose of the contract is to accomplish a routine, ministerial, or mechanical result, then the satisfaction is that of a reasonable man in the promisor's position. An architect's certificate is issuable on the architect's reasonable satisfaction. (A contracts with B for B's construction of a building. On completion B is to obtain a certificate of satisfaction from C, an architect, and deliver it to A, who will then pay B $10,000. C's satisfaction of performance is reasonable satisfaction. If C's dissatisfaction is unreasonable, B need not produce the certificate in order to obtain the $10,000.) A promise to do something on the demand of the promisee is conditional on the making of such demand, except that, when the promise is to pay the promisor's money debt, the promise is not interpreted as conditional and the promisee need make no demand in order to hold the promisor liable. This is an odd exception which has come into the law. While the demand for payment of the debt need not be made, yet a demand for interest thereon is a condition precedent which must be made. It should be noted that a contract which does not expressly state when it is to be performed is impliedly performable within a reasonable time.

Conditions Subsequent. *A condition subsequent is a condition which, if occurring subsequent to the rise of a duty of immediate performance of a* *conditional promise, extinguishes such duty.* (A insures B's house against fire, the policy providing that B is to notify A of any loss by fire within a prescribed period of time thereafter or A's duty to pay will cease, and further providing that, if B's claim is rejected, B must sue A within a prescribed period of time thereafter or A's liability will cease. B's notice to A of fire loss is a condition precedent to the creation of any duty of immediate performance of A's conditional promise. On giving such notice A's duty arises; but it may be extinguished by B's failure to sue A within the prescribed period of time after his claim has been rejected, which is a condition subsequent.) A condition subsequent to the duty of immediate performance should be distinguished carefully from a *condition subsequent to the creation of a contract* but *before the duty of immediate performance arises.* (A insures B's house against fire, the policy providing that, if gasoline is kept on the premises, the policy is void. If gasoline is kept on the premises, the contract is ended. The gasoline provision is a condition subsequent to the creation of a contract.)

Conditions Concurrent. *Conditions concurrent are conditions which are to occur simultaneously, each a condition to performance of a promise.* (A contracts with B for the purchase of B's house for $10,000, the transfer of the deed and payment to occur at the same time. Transfer of the deed is the condition of the immediate promissory duty of performance by A, and payment is the condition of the immediate promissory duty of performance by B. Performance of each promise is a concurrent condition.)

Implied Conditions. Implied conditions may be implied in fact or implied in law. A condition implied in fact is implied from the contract of the parties. (A and B contract whereby A is to supply coal to B for one year; and B agrees to buy such coal exclusively from A as B requires it, for a certain price payable by B. It is implied in fact that a condition for the performance of A's promise is notice from B of his requirements.) A condition implied in law is a condition implied by the courts, when necessary, to assist in interpreting the contract. Conditions implied in law are concerned mostly with the order in which promises are to be performed.

Conditions Implied in Law—Order in Which Promises Are Performable.

1. The law implies that, in the absence of anything in the contract to the contrary, mutual promises are concurrently conditional *if they can be performed simultaneously* with the knowledge of both parties. (A and B contract whereby A is to deliver certain goods to B on a certain date. B is to pay A $100, but the contract does not state when such payment is to be made. The law implies that payment is to be made at the time of delivery. Performance of each promise is concurrently conditional.) If parts of such promises can be so performed, performance of each part is concurrently conditional. This applies to installment contracts.

2. However, *when a material part of the contract is to be performed on one side by installments and the last installment can be performed simultaneously with full performance by the other side,* such last installment and full performance are concurrent conditions. (A contracts with B for the sale of land

whereby A is to pay for the purchase price by installments. The payment of the last installment by A and the transfer of the deed by B are concurrent conditions.)

3. *If performance of one promise will extend over a period of time, while the other promise, by its terms, is not to extend over any period of time,* performance of the promise taking time is implied as a condition precedent to performance of the other promise which will not take any time to perform. An illustration is an employment contract in which the employee is to receive a salary, the employee's services taking time to perform but not the employer's payment of salary. The employee's performance is a condition precedent to payment by the employer.

Failure of Condition

There is no immediate duty to perform a conditional promise until the condition occurs. The effect of failure of the condition to occur depends on whether or not the condition was *promised.* Damages are available to an injured party against a party who has wrongfully failed to perform his promise. *If the condition was not promised,* the failure is not a breach of any contractual duty and there can be no damages for breach of promise—i.e., of contract; the promise dependent on the condition's occurrence is extinguished. In the illustration of the fire insurance policy with the condition that, if gasoline were kept on the premises, the contract would be void, no promise was made that gasoline would not be kept on the premises; occurrence of the condition discharges the insurer from any duty to perform his promise, but he has no action for damages against the insured because the insured has neither made nor breached any promise regarding the presence of the gasoline. However, when a condition is *promised* and fails to occur, the injured promisor has no duty to perform his conditional promise (the promisee has not performed the condition, nor is he ready, willing, and able to perform); except that the courts make a distinction between performance and substantial performance of the condition which directly affects the duty of performing the conditional promise.

Degrees of Nonperformance. "Performance" means complete performance. "Nonperformance" means a failure of performance, whether in small or great degree. When performance has not occurred, whether or not the injured party is discharged from his promissory duty to perform depends upon the express terms of the contract and the law regarding discharge of the duty of performance. *If the parties have provided expressly* in their contract that failure of performance in any detail whatsoever discharges the duty of the injured party, then any defect in performance discharges such duty. The parties have expressed themselves; it is their contract, and the law will not act contrary to their intentions. *If there is no such express provision,* the courts examine what has been done by the nonperforming party under the contract. In the event that *nothing has been done* in performing under the contract, then there is a *failure of consideration discharging* the injured promisor from any duty of performance. *When something has been done* under the contract but it is not performance, the courts are more inclined to see whether the conditional promisor got substantially what he was to receive under the contract. *If substantial performance has occurred, the promisor's duty of performance is not discharged; if no substantial performance has occurred, there is a failure of consideration and his duty to perform is discharged.* Restating this in another way, anything less than substantial performance creates a *material* failure of performance; substantial performance creates a *nonmaterial* failure of performance. *A material failure of performance* does not entitle the nonperforming promisee to any right of performance by the conditional promisor because there has been a *failure of consideration*. A *nonmaterial failure of performance* entitles the nonperforming promisee to performance of the conditional promise but subjects the promisee to damages for breach of contract if the nonperformance was wrongful.

Test of Materiality of Nonperformance. Often it is very difficult to determine whether or not the nonperformance is material. Determination of materiality is a question of fact for the jury. The thought is often expressed that, *if the main purpose of the contract has been performed, or not defeated*, then there is *substantial* performance and the failure to perform is *nonmaterial;* otherwise the failure to perform is *material*. *Wilful* failure to perform is a weighty factor inclining the courts to treat the failure to perform as material and discharging any immediate duty of performance of the injured promisor's conditional promise. Building a house with pine floors instead of oak floors, and installation in a building of a different brand of pipe equal in quality to that specified by the contract, have been held to be substantial performance. Delay in performance is material nonperformance only when time is of the essence. The parties may expressly provide in their contract that time is of the essence. In business contracts, time is of the essence. The circumstances surrounding the formation of the contract may indicate that time is of the essence. Installment contracts for the sale of goods are governed by the Code, and the effect of nonperformance in an installment is discussed later under Sales.[1]

Failure of Consideration. The promisee's less than substantial performance is a material failure of performance which constitutes a *failure of consideration* discharging the conditional promisor's duty of performance. The conditional promisor's right of action against the nonperforming promisee for damages for wrongful nonperformance is predicated on the assumption that the promisor can perform his promise. If, after the promisee's nonperformance, it appears that the promisor could not perform his promise, then the promisor's right of action is extinguished. (E and A made an employment contract on February 1, A's employment to begin March 1. On February 15, E repudiated the contract. On February 25, A died. While E had breached the contract thereby creating in A a right to damages from E, nevertheless, A's death prior to the date when A's performance was to begin extinguishes A's right, acquired

[1] See below, p. 260.

by his estate, to bring such action.) Failure of consideration discharges the duty of the conditional promisor regardless of his ignorance of the existence of such failure of consideration. (A refuses to perform his contract with B, not knowing of B's material nonperformance. A has not acted improperly. B's material nonperformance was a failure of consideration discharging A's duty to perform.)

Prospective Failure of Consideration. When a strong likelihood of *material nonperformance* by the promisee arises subsequent to the formation of the contract, in some instances the promisor's duty of performance should be discharged and in other instances the promisor should have the opportunity to change his position materially in reliance thereon and thereby to be discharged of his duty of performance. This is called "prospective failure of consideration." However, if prospective failure of consideration is wrongfully caused by the conditional promisor, his duty to perform is not discharged. Prospective failure of consideration may occur in the following ways:

1. The obligor promisee's manifestation of an intention not to render substantial performance (called "repudiation") *and* the obligee promisor's material change of position in reliance thereon. The promisee can retract his manifestation before the promisor's material change of position in reliance thereon and thereby cause the situation to be the same as it was prior to the manifestation. Failure of the obligor promisee to give to the obligee promisor, at his request, adequate assurance of performance when reasonable grounds have arisen causing the promisor to believe that the promisee will substantially breach his contract, can be treated by the promisor as a repudiation by the promisee.[2]

2. The obligor promisee is insolvent under the law of contracts and under the Uniform Commercial Code when he "either has ceased to pay his debts in the ordinary course of business or cannot pay his debts as they become due or is insolvent within the meaning of the federal bankruptcy law;"[3] or he has been adjudicated bankrupt, or bankruptcy proceedings are pending against him; or his property is in receivership, or receivership proceedings are pending against him; *and* the obligee promisor has materially changed his position in reliance thereon before performance by the promisee occurs, is tendered, or is secured.[4] However, if the contractual obligation of the insolvent or bankrupt promisee is to render *personal* services and his insolvency or bankruptcy will *not* interfere with his rendition of such services, the promisor may not consider such insolvency or bankruptcy as a prospective failure of consideration and his duty to perform is not discharged.

---

[2] See below, pp. 265–67 for discussion of the Right to Adequate Assurance of Performance under UCC 2–609(1), applicable here.

[3] Restatement (Second) of Contracts, 1980, sec. 276; UCC 1–201(23).

[4] It should be noted that a promisee's insolvency or bankruptcy discharges the promisor of his obligation to continue to extend credit to the promisee, unless security is given to assure performance by the promisee. It should be noted also that, if the promisee is a debtor in bankruptcy, if the trustee in bankruptcy does not assume or reject an executory contract or unexpired lease of the debtor within 60 days after the order for relief, or within such additional time as the court, for cause, within such 60-day period, fixes, then such contract or lease is deemed rejected. (See below, p. 525.)

3. In a contract to sell certain land or goods to the promisor purchaser, the promisee vendor contracts to sell the same to a third person, or so encumbers the same as to cause the promisor reasonably to believe that the promisee will not be able to remove the encumbrance by the time performance to the promisor becomes due. The promisor is not required to change his position materially to be discharged of his duty to perform; but by doing so the promisor precludes the promisee from canceling such discharge by his subsequent reacquisition of the land or goods, or removal of the encumbrance, before the time performance to the promisor becomes due.

4. The promisor purchaser neither knows nor has reason to know at the time a contract is made to sell him certain land or goods that the promisee vendor does not own the same *and*, on learning of this fact while it still continues, the promisor materially changes his position in reliance thereon.

5. Destruction or impairment of the *requisite* subject matter of the contract, or of the *requisite* means of performing the contract, making impracticable rendition of substantial performance by the promisee. (A contracts with B to paint *B's building*, which subsequently is destroyed accidentally; A's duty to paint the building is discharged. Or X contracts with Y for the purchase of a product to be made by a *certain* factory or *certain* person, and subsequently the factory is destroyed or the person dies; X's duty to purchase is discharged.)

6. Death or physical incapacity of the obligor promisee of a *personal service contract* rendering his performance impossible, or the promisor's material change of position in reliance on the physical condition of the promisee as making the latter's personal performance reasonably improbable. Whether or not a contract is for personal services is determined by whether or not the duty of performance is delegable.[5]

7. Supervening illegality of contractual performance by the promisee.

Excused Failure of Consideration. Previous discussion[6] has indicated that *failure of consideration by material nonperformance* of the promisee *discharges* the conditional promisor's duty of performance. However, if the promisee's failure to perform has been *excused*, then the promisor's duty of performance still exists and he is not dependent upon the promisee's performance as a condition. When the promisor has excused the promisee's material nonperformance, he is deemed to have waived it. If the promisee substitutes a performance *materially* different from what the contract called for, the promisor's acceptance of the promisee's material nonperformance with knowledge of such, or his implied acceptance by his retention of such material nonperformance for an unreasonable period of time, *excuses the failure of consideration* and imposes upon the conditional promisor the duty of performing his promise. (A contracts with B for the purchase of a certain machine for $100. The machine which is delivered to A is *materially* defective. A knows of the defect but retains the machine for an unreasonable period without objecting to B. A has excused the failure of consideration and is under a duty to pay the $100.)[7] However, acceptance of material nonperformance is *not*, in itself, a manifesta-

[5] See above, p. 82.

[6] See above, p. 98 f.

[7] For excused failure of consideration under the Code on sales of goods, see below, p. 263.

tion of assent to further material nonperformance, *unless the frequency of such acceptance reasonably induces the promisee to believe that such material nonperformance is satisfactory to the promisor and the promisee changes his position materially in reliance thereon.* (A issued a noncancelable policy of insurance to B which provided that annual premiums must be paid in advance at the home office of A. For ten years B had paid the premium each year by mailing a check to the home office, which accepted it. B mailed a check for the eleventh premium to A, which A never received. On the expiration of the due date, A informed B that the policy was canceled. B immediately tendered the eleventh premium and requested reinstatement of the policy. A must accept the check and reinstate the policy. A's promise to insure required payment at the home office. By accepting mailed checks for ten years, which A did not have to do, A induced B to believe that such manner of performance was satisfactory to A. B's material change of position in reliance thereon by sending mailed checks to the home office is excusable nonperformance.) It should be noted that, if the promisor of a contract to be performed within a specified or a reasonable time waives the requirement or condition of such time or indicates he is willing to extend such time without specifying the length of the extension, he subsequently must inform the promisee of a reasonable time within which his performance is to occur if it is to have the same effect as though it were originally a term of the contract. In this way nonperformance which has been excused previously can be stopped from continuing indefinitely.

Other instances of excused material nonperformance are:

1. The promisor's manifestation of an intention not to render substantial performance (called "repudiation") or his manifestation of doubt concerning his ability to render substantial performance, which has induced nonperformance by the promisee or failure of the condition to occur. The promisor's retraction of his manifestation before the promisee's material change of position in reliance thereon extinguishes the effect of the manifestation as excusing material nonperformance by the promisee.
2. The promisor's hindrance or prevention of the promisee's performance or of occurrence of the condition which otherwise would have occurred, provided such hindrance or prevention was not caused or justified by the promisee's financial condition or by his conduct.
3. *Continued acceptance* by the promisor of defective performance (e.g., delivery of defective installments) is such as causes the promisee reasonably to believe that such performance is satisfactory to the promisor and the promisee materially changes his position in reliance thereon.
4. Excusable impracticability of performance by the promisee which would discharge the promisee's duty of performance,[8] the promisor's duty to perform having arisen and the condition of its performance serving only to determine the time when such performance is to occur.[9]

---

[8] See below, p. 123 f.

[9] As an illustration of this kind of excusable material nonperformance, C, creditor, is to return to D, debtor, certain security of the debtor at which time D is to pay his debt to C. The security is destroyed through no fault of C. D's promise to pay C is performable without the condition of C's surrender of the security.

5. The promisee's inability to produce a required architect's, or other expert's, certificate because of the architect's unreasonable refusal to deliver such a certificate to the promisee or because the architect is physically unable to do so.

Ordinarily, the promisor may reject material nonperformance without stating any reason therefor, and the giving of an insufficient reason is immaterial. However, if such rejection reasonably induces the promisee not to perform, which he could have done in proper time, then the promisor impliedly waives or excuses nonperformance. An illustration of this is the tender of payment by check[10] or in other form which is not legal tender when payment is to be made in legal tender. Rejection of nonlegal tender for this reason without explanation misleads the promisee, since he could have obtained such legal tender in proper time if he had been informed of the reason for the rejection. The promisor has excused the promisee's performance, and the promisor is under a duty to perform his promise.

Importance of Nonperformance to Conditions and Breach of Contract. Nonperformance is of importance to the subjects of conditions and breach of contract in different ways. In conditions, actual or prospective *material failure of performance affects the promisor's duty of performance;* it does not create a right of action for damages for such failure. In breach of contract, *any wrongful failure of a promised performance creates a right of action for damages.* Accordingly, conditions are important in connection with the promisor's duty of performance and, if *promised* and *wrongfully* not performed, are important as constituting a breach of contract.

[10] For payment by check in contracts for sale of goods under the Code, see below, p. 254.

Chapter 7

BREACH OF CONTRACT

Wrongful nonperformance of a promissory duty is a breach of contract, which may be a material breach or a nonmaterial breach. Repudiation may occur at the time performance is due, or prior to that time called "anticipatory repudiation." Both are a material breach, the latter being a breach, even though performance is not yet due, which can be withdrawn before the innocent party has changed his position materially in reliance thereon. Nonperformance is wrongful if there is no legal justification or excuse therefor. The injured party can waive a nonmaterial or material breach, or treat a material breach as a nonmaterial breach; but if it is a material breach by repudiation, the injured party cannot waive the breach and also continue to perform under the contract. Breach may create three remedies—damages, specific performance, and restitution. (1) *Damages* is the money judically awarded as compensation for injury or harm sustained. There are *nominal* damages, *punitive* damages (not awarded for breach), and *compensatory* damages for loss sustained or gains lost caused by the breach. Damages are fixed as of the time the breach occurred, except in the case of an anticipatory breach when damages are fixed as of the time when performance was to have occurred. The injured party has a duty to mitigate damages. (2) *A decree of specific performance* of a contract (an injunction) is available *if damages at law are inadequate.* It will be awarded in contracts for: the transfer of interests in land; unique chattels or intangibles, or interests therein; or services in certain cases. (3) *Restitution* is to restore an injured person to his original position prior to the particular transaction. The injured party has an election of these three remedies, subject to certain limitations.

Wrongful Nonperformance

Wrongful nonperformance of a promissory duty under a contract is a breach of promise and, therefore, a breach of contract. The law is concerned only with the *wrongful* nonperformance of a contractual duty and does not impose liability for excused nonperformance. A breach occurs on the failure to perform an *immediate* duty under the contract.

On breach of contract an *immediate* right of action for such breach becomes available to the injured party against the wrongfully nonperforming party. The extent of this right of action depends upon the materiality[1] of the breach. A material breach is a breach of the entire contract, often called a "total breach," which creates a right to remedies (damages, specific performance, or restitution) which may be substituted for the rights under the contract; while a nonmaterial breach is a breach of only a part of the contract, often called a "partial breach," which thereby creates a right of action only for damages for the partial breach. A nonmaterial breach means that there has been substantial performance or nonmaterial failure of performance with no excuse for incomplete promised performance; it creates only the right of action for damages, the contract remaining in existence and the injured party still having the duty of performing his promise. A breach of contract is material if either: substantial performance is not rendered when due; substantial performance which otherwise would have occurred is prevented or hindered by the other party; or the breach is accompanied or followed by a repudiation of the contract.

Repudiation. A party may repudiate his duty to perform under the contract. Repudiation is a manifestation of an intention not to render *substantial* performance of a contractual duty; it may be made expressly or impliedly by conduct. An *express* repudiation must be made to the other party or to any other beneficiary of the performance due under the contract, and it must clearly indicate such unwillingness to perform substantially. Repudiation is *implied* from voluntary conduct which causes substantial performance to be either actually or apparently impossible. *When unjustified repudiation accompanies or follows a breach of contract, it characterizes the breach as a material breach.* The injured party not only is discharged from the duty of performing his promise, but he also acquires a right of action for such breach. Until the injured party materially changes his position in reliance on the repudiation, the repudiating party may withdraw his repudiation. Withdrawal of the repudiation still leaves the nonperformance and a right of action therefor, the extent of which is determined by whether the nonperformance is a material, or a nonmaterial, breach. Reliance by material change of position may be made expressly or impliedly by conduct indicating an intent to do so. An illustration of implied reliance is: the injured party's bringing an action for the breach; or his purchase elsewhere of an article or services similar to that promised and not rendered; or his sale of the subject matter of the contract.

---

[1] See above, p. 98.

Anticipatory Breach. Unjustified repudiation may occur not only at the time when the duty is to be performed but also prior to such time; the latter is called an "anticipatory breach." Anticipatory breach is not really a breach because a *breach occurs only on a failure to perform an immediate duty under the contract.* However, a party's unjustified repudiation of his duty *to perform* under the contract exposes the injured party to a risk of nonperformance which he had not contemplated previously. He should not continue under a duty of performing his promise when the other party has indicated clearly wrongful refusal to perform his promise, if the injured party so wishes. The wrongful character of this repudiation stamps it as a breach by anticipatory repudiation. Accordingly, an anticipatory breach gives to the other party *the right to change his position materially in reliance thereon and thereby be discharged* of his duty to perform his promise *and preclude the repudiator's withdrawal of his repudiation.* Until such reliance, the repudiation can be withdrawn. Timely withdrawal of the repudiation restores the parties to their status immediately prior to the anticipatory breach.[2] There remains no right of action to the other party because no duty of immediate performance has been breached. (On January 10, A contracted with B to buy a certain horse, the price to be paid and the horse to be delivered on January 30. On January 15, B sold the horse to C. On January 20, A, relying on B's sale to C, bought a horse from D. On January 25, B repurchased the horse he sold to C. On January 30, B tendered the horse to A. A refused to take it and refused to pay for it. B's sale to C was an implied repudiation constituting an anticipatory breach. A's purchase on January 20 was an implied material change of position in reliance on such breach thereby precluding B's withdrawal of his repudiation. B's tender of performance on January 30 was ineffectual. If A had not changed his position by January 25 and he knew of B's repurchase of the horse, B's repurchase would have been a withdrawal of the repudiation and A's duty to perform would have continued to exist with no right of action against B.) Tender of performance after material change of position in reliance on an anticipatory breach is ineffectual to restore the injured party's duty to perform his promise; the latter's duty is discharged. Withdrawal of the repudiation must be brought to the attention of the injured party before his reliance on the anticipatory breach in order to be effective. If the repudiation was made expressly, then the repudiator must inform the injured party; if made impliedly, then notice obtained by the injured party from any source is sufficient.

A party's insolvency and his manifestation of doubt concerning his ability to render substantial performance are not nonperformance; their occurrence gives to the other party an *opportunity* to discharge his contractual duty to perform by changing his position materially in reliance thereon, as discussed previously under "Conditions,"[3] but they do not constitute an anticipatory breach, for two reasons. First, anticipatory breach is concerned with a party's

---

[2] See UCC 2–611.

[3] See above, p. 93 ff.

manifested *voluntary unwillingness* to perform, and is a breach of contract creating a right of action because of the *wrongful refusal* to perform. Second, breach of contract is concerned with a right of action for wrongful *nonperformance*, and not with the *possibility of nonperformance*.

Anticipatory breach creates an immediate right of action for the breach of contract. The assertion of this right by bringing an action is a material change of position in reliance on the breach. Failure to exercise this right gives to the repudiator an opportunity to withdraw his repudiation; and, for this reason, the statute of limitations does not begin to run on the right of action until the time when there is a failure to perform an immediate duty under the contract.

When Nonperformance is Wrongful. Nonperformance is wrongful when there is a contractual duty to render immediate performance, performance has not been rendered, and there is no legal justification or excuse for such nonperformance. Accordingly, except for anticipatory breach, there cannot be a breach of contract if a contractual duty of immediate performance has not yet arisen, or the duty has been discharged. Discharge of a contractual duty may occur not only by failure of condition, discussed previously,[4] but in other ways, discussed later.[5]

Waiver

Waiver is the relinquishment of a known right. In the discussion of conditions,[6] it was indicated that the conditional promisor could excuse the condition on the occurrence of which performance of his promise was dependent. The excuse of such condition was, in effect, a waiver.[7] Similarly, after the occurrence of a breach of contract, the injured party may waive defective performance or nonperformance by manifesting, either expressly or impliedly, his intention not to insist on performance. The injured party can waive a nonmaterial breach or a material breach, or treat a material breach as a nonmaterial breach—e.g., accepting materially defective performance—except that, in the case of a material breach by repudiation, the injured party cannot waive the breach and also continue to perform under the contract.[8] Delay in asserting a right of action for a breach, and delay in changing one's position materially in reliance on a material breach, do not imply a waiver. Neither is the injured party's urging of performance after a breach a waiver of such breach.

Remedies

Breach of contract is wrongful nonperformance, creating an immediate *right of action for damages* for such breach. There are two other remedies

[4] See above, p. 97 ff.

[5] See below, p. 114 ff.

[6] See above, p. 100 ff.

[7] See UCC 2–208, 2–209.

[8] See below, p. 108.

which are available for proper cases: *specific performance* and *restitution*. These remedies are forms of relief to help the injured party, damages being a form of relief at law, and specific performance and restitution forms of relief in equity. These three forms of relief have different objectives. *"Damages" is the money judicially awarded as* compensation for *injury* or harm sustained. By "injury" is meant the invasion of another person's interest. Here the interest is in performance of the contract and the injury is the interference with the interest by nonperformance. Injury is distinguished from the words "damage" and "harm," which mean *loss* or tangible and material detriment. A decree of "specific performance" seeks to compel performance of the contract according to its terms as much as possible. "Restitution" means the return of what has been rendered, or its value, in order to place the parties in the positions they occupied prior to the contract's formation. These three remedies will be considered in turn.

Damages. Damages may be *nominal* or *trivial, exemplary* or *punitive,* or *compensatory.*

Nominal Damages. Immediately on breach of contract a right to an action for damages arises. The right exists although no damage has been sustained, and statutory nominal damages will be awarded if an action is begun. Such damages are trivial and indicate that *injury without damage has occurred.* (A and B contract for the sale of a horse for $50. B refuses to take the horse, which is worth $75. A has suffered no damage.)

Punitive Damages. A judicial award for malicious, wanton, or intentionally wrongful conduct, which is in excess of compensation for injury or damage, is called "exemplary" or "punitive" damages. Punitive damages are not available for breach of contract.

Compensatory Damages. Compensatory damages are to compensate the injured party for loss sustained or gains lost caused by the breach. The wrongful party should be liable only for the damage which he reasonably should or could foresee would naturally flow from the breach. If he knows or should know at the time the contract is made that breach may cause damage to the other party greater than the damage which would ordinarily occur, breach causing such damage makes him liable therefor. Such damage is called "special damage," which must be pleaded specially as well as proved. (A and B contract for the sale of certain gaskets. A, the seller, knows B has a contract to supply these gaskets to C. A breaches the contract. A is liable for the loss of profit which B would have made under his contract with C, as well as the loss which B may have experienced under his contract with A. If B were involved in litigation with C because of his failure to supply the gaskets, A would be liable for this damage also.)[9] In contracts for the sale of real or personal prop-

[9] See UCC 2–715(2). It should be noted carefully that while general damage and special damage describe the loss or harm experienced, they are reflected in the judicial award of general damage*s* or special damage*s*. General damage*s* are concerned with loss which usually accompanies the injury complained of; pleading the injury gives the defending party sufficient notice of the damage which need not be pleaded. Special damage*s* are concerned with loss which does not usually accompany the injury complained of and which must be pleaded specially as well as proved.

erty, damages are measured by the difference between the contract price and the market price at the time when performance was due. In contracts for services, the measure of damages depends upon who is the injured party. If an employee has been improperly discharged under a contract, his damages are his salary due up to the time of his discharge plus his salary under the remainder of the contract, less what he has earned by other employment since the breach and what prospective earnings he can make in other employment for the remainder of the contract period. When a contract for services is for the life of the employee, the duration of the contract is measured by the employee's health and expected span of life, as determined by mortality tables at the time of the breach. If the employer is the injured party, his damages are the difference between the contract rate and what he must pay a substitute for the same services. Whatever expense is saved to one party by the other party's breach is deducted from the damages. (A contracts to manufacture an article for B for $1,000. After A has begun to manufacture, B repudiates the contract. A's damages are measured by $1,000 less the expense which A still would have to incur to finish the article. To state it in another way, A could recover the expense he has already incurred plus his loss of profit.)

Damages are fixed as of the time the breach occurred, except in the case of an anticipatory breach when damages are fixed as of the time when performance was to have occurred. On the occurrence of a *nonmaterial* breach the injured party immediately acquires a right of action for damages, but he must continue performance under the contract. If the breach is *material,* the injured party has a right of action for damages for such breach. He may treat a material breach other than by repudiation as a nonmaterial breach and continue performance, his right of action for damages being reduced to the damages for a nonmaterial breach. (A and B contract for the delivery of goods by installments. B's first deliveries are materially defective. The breach is material. A retains the goods delivered without objecting to B, or objects to B but retains the goods and awaits further deliveries. A has a right of action for damages for the defective deliveries he has already accepted.) When a material breach occurs by repudiation, the injured party cannot waive the breach and continue to perform under the contract. He must not perform any further.[10] He may change his position materially in reliance on the material breach by repudiation and thereby preclude the repudiator's withdrawal of his repudiation. Suit is such a change of position. His damages are for the *entire* contract. Alternatively, he may rescind the contract and demand restoration to his original position prior to the formation of the contract. The right of rescission is a quasi-contractual right of restitution. *Immediately on breach of contract there arises the duty to mitigate damages.* (A employs B for one year. After six months A discharges B without cause. B must seek employment elsewhere for the remaining six months; and his earnings therefrom, or what he could have

[10] See UCC 2–704(2), and below, p. 275, when the aggrieved seller may complete the manufacture of unfinished goods on the buyer's default in order to avoid loss.

earned in that period, are deducted from the amount of salary he would have received for the remainder of the contract's duration. B's damages are for such loss in earnings for that period.) Breach of contract for the payment of money causes interest to accrue for the amount due from the time of such breach, unless the parties have provided to the contrary in their contract. Such interest is a part of the damages and is computed at the legal rate. If the parties provide in their contract for liquidated damages, interest accrues thereon.

Liquidated damages are the judicial award of that certain amount of money *fixed by the parties* as reasonable compensation for damage caused by wrongful conduct where it is difficult to determine the extent of such damage. They are fixed by agreement *before* a breach occurs. The amount must not be a penalty to deter such conduct but, rather, it must be compensatory. A provision for a forfeiture is void. (A and B contracted for the sale of oil to be delivered to B in 50-gallon drums. The contract provided that the drums were to be returned to A; and, if not returned, $5 was to be paid for every drum not so returned. The $5 provision was meant to be an indication of liquidated damages. If the drums reasonably were worth much less, the provision might be considered a forfeiture and therefore invalid.) Contracts for the sale of real estate usually provide that the amount of the buyer's deposit will be the liquidated damages in the event the buyer defaults and does not pay the balance of the purchase price.

In building construction contracts, if substantial performance has been rendered by the builder in good faith, damages will be either replacement cost or the difference between the value of what was to be performed and what was performed, whichever involves the lesser economic waste. (Under a contract between A and B, A installed pipe in a building which differed from the pipe specified under the contract only in the brand name. A may recover from B the contract price for his substantial performance less the damage sustained by B. B has not experienced any damage and the benefit to B by replacing the pipe would be far outweighed by the hardship occasioned thereby to A. The usual test of replacement cost would not be used here.)

Specific Performance. The object of a decree specifically enforcing performance of a contract is to achieve, as nearly as possible, the effect contemplated by the contract. A decree of specific performance is a form of equitable relief. It is an *injunction* granted against a party who has breached, or is threatening to breach, a contract *when damages at law would be inadequate* as relief to the injured party. The issuance of a decree lies solely within the discretion of the court handling each particular case. From the applied discretion of the courts certain guiding principles have emerged. Courts will not issue a decree of specific performance of a contract in favor of a party who has materially breached the contract. Both a decree for specific performance of a contract and an award of damages for the remainder of the contract may be made in the same case if such relief is deemed necessary. An agreement will not be specifically enforced if it is illegal or if enforcement would be contrary to public policy or welfare. An agreement to create an illegal monopoly will not be specifically enforced. A contract in which one party has the power of avoidance will not be ordered specifically enforceable against such party, inasmuch as that party has the legal power to nullify the effect of the decree. Courts will consider the difficulty of enforcing a decree before issuing one.

Land. Contracts are usually for the transfer of property or interests therein, or for the rendition of services. In contracts for the transfer of interests in land a decree of specific enforcement is available only when the land has not yet been transferred. The vendor may compel the vendee to accept the transfer and to make payment therefor, and the vendee may compel the vendor to transfer the land. Inasmuch as the vendor can be compelled to transfer, the vendee should be compelled to accept transfer. If the land has been transferred but the vendee refuses to make payment, a decree of specific enforcement will not be issued, although a judgment for the money is obtainable by the vendor.

Chattels and Intangibles. Courts consider the following factors in determining the adequacy or inadequacy of damages for breach of contract for the transfer of chattels and intangibles or of interests therein: the sentiment associated with, and the unusual character of, the chattel or intangible; the availability of a substitute chattel or intangible;[11] the difficulty in estimating damages; and the probability of realizing on any award of damages. *No decree of specific performance will be issued unless the chattel or intangible is unique* (e.g., family heirlooms or works of art), or other proper circumstances exist where damages for nondelivery would be inadequate. Patents and copyrights are unique. Stock in a corporation is not unique; but if the same stock is not otherwise available for purchase and failure to acquire those particular shares will have a harmful effect that cannot be compensated by an award of damages, then such shares are unique and a decree will be issued. (A owns 48 percent, B owns 49 percent, and C owns 3 percent, of the shares in a corporation. A contracts with C for the purchase of his 3 percent of the shares. C refuses to transfer his shares to A. A can obtain a decree of specific performance because no other shares are available and C's shares are necessary to give A control of the corporation, which control is not contrary to public policy.)

Personal Services. *Contracts for personal services are contracts of such a character that performance is nondelegable.*[12] Contracts made with artists, sculptors, musicians, doctors, lawyers, accountants, ball players, teachers, cooks, and valets are illustrations of contracts of a personal character. A decree of specific enforcement will never be issued for such contracts because of the difficulty of enforcement, the probability of creating an unworkable and undesirable relationship between the parties, and the U.S. Constitution's prohibition of involuntary servitude.

Injunctions are of two kinds: *mandatory* and *prohibitory.* A mandatory

---

[11] For specific performance under the Sales provisions of UCC 2–716, see below, p. 283.

[12] For delegation of duties, see above, p. 82 f.

injunction compels the performance of an affirmative act and is called a "decree of specific performance" when used in the law of contracts. It will not be issued in contracts of personal service. A prohibitory injunction compels or enjoins the nonperformance of an act and, in the law of contracts, is a decree enforcing a negative promise. (A contracts to work for B and not for C. An injunction restraining A from working for C is a prohibitory injunction.) A promise not to render personal services for anyone else may be express or implied in a contract. If not implied, then a prohibitory injunction would not be issued. If implied, it is unusual for a prohibitory injunction to be issued in a personal service contract case unless irreparable harm will result. Courts generally will not issue such an injunction with the primary intention of enforcing the affirmative promise. Nor will a court usually issue a prohibitory injunction when its effect will be to deprive a person of the means of making a living. A court will consider the type of employment contract, the probability of a renewal of good employer-employee relations, the harm which will be caused in the event of issuance or nonissuance of an injunction, and the inadequacy of other legal remedies. Irreparable harm seems to be the overall test of whether or not a prohibitory injunction will issue in personal service contract cases. (A, an auditor well known for his ability to detect defalcation in business firms, was employed by B, a firm of accountants, to work for them for a certain period. A refused to perform under the contract. B cannot obtain a mandatory injunction. B probably could not obtain a prohibitory injunction enjoining A from working elsewhere because no irreparable harm will result by A's employment elsewhere. A is not unique, and another accountant with his qualifications can be found. A's employment by some other firm of accountants will not affect B's business seriously.) (A, a well-known opera star, contracts with B to sing in B's theater for a specified period and not to sing in any competing theater. A refuses to perform and contracts to sing in a competing theater. B cannot obtain a mandatory injunction but can obtain a prohibitory injunction preventing A from singing in the competing theater because of the irreparable harm which otherwise would be caused to B. If A were to sing in a noncompeting theater, the prohibitory injunction would not be issued.) Violation of either a mandatory or a prohibitory injunction is a contempt of court; and the violator could be penalized by fine, imprisonment, or both, by the court which issued the injunction.

Restitution. Restitution is a noncontractual remedy made available in the law of contracts and is designed to restore an injured person to his original position prior to the particular transaction. It applies to other fields of law as well as to contracts. In the law of contracts, its purpose is to restore an injured party to his original position prior to the formation of the contract which is *materially breached* by the other party.

Restitution applies *when* (1) *the complaining party has rendered some performance which the other party has received under the contract,* (2) *the other party has materially breached the contract,* (3) *the performance due from the other party is other than for the payment of a liquidated debt, and* (4) *the complaining party promptly tenders the return of whatever he has received and still has.* The complaining party can obtain the reasonable value of what he has rendered less the benefit that he has received from what was rendered to him by the defending party under the contract. The complaining party's expenses in preparing to perform the contract do not constitute anything that the defending party has received. A mistaken overpayment of money can be reacquired by restitution.

A party in materially breaching his contract may leave unperformed either the payment of a liquidated debt—i.e., money—or something else. An action for damages for breach of contract will give adequate relief to the complaining party if the remaining performance due is the payment of a liquidated debt, but often it will not give adequate relief if the remaining performance is of a different nature. Restitution in money, either paid by the complaining party or as the reasonable value of what he has rendered and what is received by the defending party, is available as an alternative remedy to an action for damages only if the *remaining* performance or some part thereof due from the defending party is other than for the payment of a liquidated debt. (A employs B at $50 per week for ten weeks. B works one week, and then A repudiates the contract. B can bring an action for damages for breach of contract but cannot ask for restitution for the reasonable value of his week's work.) (A and B contract for the sale of land to A, who pays the purchase price of $10,000 at the time of the contract, a deed to be delivered by B to A in 30 days. B repudiates the contract. A can get restitution of the $10,000 he paid.) If only a part of the remaining performance due from the defending party is not for payment of a liquidated debt, restitution is available. (A and B contract whereby A is to render certain services to B for which B will pay $1,000 and convey certain land to A. A renders the services, and B then repudiates the contract. A may get restitution for the reasonable value of his services.) Specific restitution of land, or unique chattels or unique choses in action, may be allowed only if all other remedies are inadequate and justice so requires, if the property still exists, and if the property has not been sold by the defending party to a bona fide purchaser for value.

The complaining party must act promptly after breach by the defending party and tender the return of whatever he has received and still has, unless he has previously disposed of the property without knowledge of the breach by the defending party, or unless the property is worthless. Unreasonable delay extinguishes the remedy of restitution. Acceptance of defective performance with knowledge of such defectiveness makes restitution unavailable. The performance must be accepted or rejected; acceptance precludes subsequent rejection. Disclaimer by a beneficiary in a third party beneficiary contract of the performance due him under the contract gives the promisee a right of restitution for what he has rendered to the promisor.

Election of Remedies. Restitution is available only when a material breach has occurred by the defending party. Where restitution is available, the complaining party has a choice of remedies between an action for damages for breach of contract or restitution. When specific performance also is available, the election of remedies must be made between restitution and damages and between restitution and specific performance.

In connection with election of remedies it should be noted that the occurrence of misrepresentation making a contract voidable also requires an election of remedies. The contract may be either avoided (rescinded) or affirmed. Exercise of the power of avoidance discharges the contract; and the remedy of restitution is available to recover what the complaining party has rendered, or its value, under the contract. Affirmance of the contract causes the complaining party to retain what he has received and accepted; and, if the misrepresentation amounts to fraud, the complaining party has an action for damages for the tort of deceit.[13] There is a difference of opinion as to the measure of such damages. In most states the "loss of bargain" rule applies whereby the measure of damages is the difference between the market value of what the defrauded party has received at the time of such receipt and the value that the property was represented to have. If the defrauded party still owes part of the purchase price, such amount owing will be deducted from the damages to be awarded. In the minority of states the "out-of-pocket" loss rule is applied under which the measure of damages is the difference between the purchase price and the market value of what was purchased as of the date of receipt of such property. Damages "for breach of warranty is the difference at the time and place of acceptance between the value of the goods accepted and the value they would have had if they had been as warranted, unless special circumstances show proximate damages of a different amount."[14]

---

[13] See above, p. 34, ftn. 28.

[14] See UCC 2–714(2), and below, pp. 282–83.

Chapter 8

DISCHARGE OF CONTRACTS

Termination of a contractual duty is called a "discharge." This may occur in the following ways:

a. *By act of the parties:* (1) Performance. (2) Failure of a condition precedent, occurrence of a condition subsequent, unexcused failure or prospective failure of consideration, material breach of contract, improper refusal of a valid tender of performance. (3) Release and contract not to sue, supported by consideration. Under the Code, a party's renunciation or waiver of a claim or right against the other contracting party arising out of an alleged breach is effective as a release: if oral, must be supported by consideration; if a signed writing, no consideration is required. (4) Mutual rescission. (5) Accord, and accord and satisfaction. (6) Novation. (7) Account stated. (8) Assignment. The assignment of a right and either the assignee's notice of assignment to the obligor, or such notice *and* demand for payment if the assignment is of an account for the purpose of security, discharges the debtor's duty to the assignor and makes it performable to the assignee. (9) Exercise of a power of avoidance. (10) Fraudulent material alteration of a written contract, fraudulently made without the assent of the other contracting party. (11) Discharge of joint debtors. A promisee's discharge of a joint promisor discharges all the joint promisors, unless the discharge *reserves* rights against the other joint promisors, in which case the reservation operates as a promise not to sue that joint promisor, and the others are still liable.

b. *By operation of law:* (1) Judgment. (2) Arbitration award, enforceable in the courts. (3) Bankruptcy discharge. (4) Statute of Limitations. Failure to institute legal action on a matured claim within the prescribed statutory period of time bars legal enforcement of the claim and, in effect, discharges the

debtor's duty to perform. (5) Excusable impracticability. Promised performance may be a *physical* impossibility or *impracticable* because of the extreme and unreasonable expense, difficulty, loss, or injury to one of the parties which may be involved. The promisor's *subjective* inability does not excuse his nonperformance, and his duty is not discharged. *Existing* impracticability when the promise was made prevents the promise from creating a duty and, therefore, from becoming a contract. But *supervening* impracticability of performance by the promisor discharges his contractual duty to perform as well as that of the other contracting party.

The termination of a contractual duty is called a "discharge." A "contract" is a promise or set of promises creating a legal duty of performance. Discharge of a contractual duty discharges the promise and, therefore, discharges the contract. Discharge may occur by act of the parties or by operation of law.

By Act of the Parties

Discharge of a contractual duty by act of the parties may occur in the following ways: *performance, failure of condition, material breach of contract, mutual agreement, assignment, exercise of a power of avoidance, and fraudulent material alteration of the contract.*

Performance. Performance, meaning complete performance, of a contractual duty discharges that duty. When there is more than one matured debt and the debtor makes a payment, the creditor must apply the payment as directed by the debtor at or before the time of such payment. If no such indication is given by the debtor, then the creditor may apply the payment to any or all of the matured debts or distribute such payment among them,[1] provided he does so within a reasonable period of time and gives notice to the debtor of such application within a reasonable period of time. The creditor's subsequent suit on the debts, or his sending of a statement of the status of such debts, is notice to the debtor of his application of such payment. The creditor cannot apply such payment to an immature debt or to a disputed or illegal claim. He can apply the payment to a debt barred by the statute of limitations, but, if the payment is insufficient to satisfy the debt, the statute is not waived as to the remainder still due. If neither the debtor not the creditor indicates to which of such matured debts the payment is to be applied, the law in most states is that the payment is to be applied as is most just. Usually, the payment is applied first to overdue interest, then to the earliest unsecured matured debt, and finally to the earliest secured debt, to which the creditor might have applied

[1] But see below, p. 492, for the effect in Suretyship if the surety advances the money to the principal debtor for payment to the creditor and the creditor knows this.

such payment. An appropriation once made cannot be changed except by the assent of both parties. Such assent may validate a previously improper application of payment. A debtor's silence for an unreasonable period of time after his receipt of notice of the application of a payment is interpreted as assent to such application, whether made properly or improperly.

Failure of Condition and Material Breach of Contract. As discussed previously under "Conditions,"[2] the duty of performance of a promise may depend upon the occurrence of a condition precedent, the nonoccurrence of a condition subsequent, or performance of a return promise. Unexcused failure of a condition precedent to occur prior to the time when performance of the promise is due discharges the promise. Occurrence of a condition subsequent discharges the promise. When the condition is the performance of a return promise, a promise is discharged by either: a material breach of contract; an unexcused failure of consideration—i.e., material nonperformance—or an unexcused prospective failure of consideration. It should be reiterated here, although previously discussed in "Conditions," that, once a material breach or an unexcused failure of consideration has occurred, the promissory duty is discharged without any change of position, while for *prospective* unexcused failure of consideration a material change of position in reliance thereon generally is necessary in order to discharge the promissory duty. Repudiation is a material breach of contract, and a material change of position is unnecessary except to preclude the repudiator from withdrawing his repudiation.

A promisor's improper refusal of a valid tender of performance by a promisee under a bilateral contract is a waiver of such performance, and the promisor has a duty to perform his promise without the occurrence of performance by the promisee. The tender has the effect of performance. The promisee's duty of performance is discharged, except when such performance is the payment of money. The effect of an improper refusal of a valid tender of performance by the payment of money is to halt the running of interest on the amount unpaid and to cause the creditor to pay for the court costs of any later suit he may bring to collect such payment from the debtor.[3] A tender is an unconditional proffer by one party to perform, with present ability to do so, what he is required to do under a bilateral contract or what is requested in an offer for a unilateral or a bilateral contract. When a tender is made in response to an offer for a unilateral or a bilateral contract, the tender is an acceptance and a contract is formed.

Mutual Agreement. By agreement between the parties an existing contractual duty may be discharged. Such an agreement may apply to different types of situation, and, accordingly, it has a different name to identify each situation. The situations to be discussed here are: *release and contract not to sue*, *mutual rescission*, *accord and satisfaction*, *novation*, and *account stated.*

---

[2] See above, p. 93 ff.

[3] For the effect of an improper refusal of a valid tender of performance by the payment of money in the law of: Commercial Paper, see below, p. 502; Security, see below, pp. 470, 494.

Release and Contract Not to Sue. A release is a voluntary relinquishment of a right by its owner to the person against whom it is exercisable. Relinquishment of a right discharges its correlative duty. A release is not a contract because it is not a promise of future performance; it operates immediately in accordance with its terms. If the terms specify a condition precedent before the release is to be operative, the release is ineffective as a relinquishment of a right until the occurrence of the condition. Although a release is not a contract, *in the absense of statute to the contrary it must be supported by consideration*, or be under seal in those few states preserving the Common Law effect of a seal.[4] In the absence of statute to the contrary, a release need not be in writing and may be oral, although in practice it usually is in writing so as to assure future proof of the release. If the release is in writing, it must be executed and *delivered* in order to be effective. A *general release* relinquishes all existing rights of the owner to the person against whom they are exercisable, and may include future and contingent claims. A *mutual release* is a discharge by each of two or more parties to the other or others, the consideration for each discharge being the discharge or discharges given by the others. The validity of a release may be attacked for fraud, duress, undue influence, mutual mistake, lack of capacity so to release, and lack of consideration. A receipt differs from a release in that a receipt is a written acknowledgment or admission that some thing has been received.

It should be noted carefully that, under the Code, the Common Law effect of the seal is abolished. Also, a party to a transaction may waive or renounce, in whole or in part, his claim or right against the other party arising out of an *alleged* breach; but to be effective as a release the waiver or renunciation *if oral* must be supported by consideration, or if *in writing* it must be signed and delivered by the aggrieved party *without any requirement of consideration.*[5]

The release may contain terms providing for the discharge of a future right. This portion of the release is a contract not to sue or not to enforce a right when it arises; it is a contract to forbear permanently. The terminology may be in the form of a release, a covenant not to sue, a promise, or a waiver. A contract not to sue permanently has the same net effect as a release. A contract not to sue may appear separate from inclusion in a release.

Mutual Rescission. A contract may be rescinded and all rights and duties thereunder discharged. When the parties to the contract agree to rescission, it is called "mutual rescission." The agreement to rescind is operative to discharge the duties immediately, and no promise is made of future action. Although the agreement of rescission is not a contract, there must be a *manifestation of mutual assent and consideration.* The parties may manifest mutual

[4] However, because the Common Law effect of the seal as a method of causing a release or promise without consideration to be enforceable has largely disappeared and with it the opportunity of making a binding gratuitous discharge of an existing legal obligation, by statute or judicial decision in some states a signed written unsealed release or promise concerning an existing legal obligation, indicating an intention to be bound thereby, is enforceable without consideration.

[5] UCC 1–107.

assent by a writing, by words, or by other conduct. Failure to object to another party's expressed intent to rescind may indicate assent. However, if repudiation is made by one party, the other party's silence or failure to object is not an expression of assent to rescission. A contract containing a term or terms inconsistent with a term or terms in a previous contract is interpreted as an agreement of mutual rescission of such prior term or terms.

The consideration for mutual rescission is found in the mutual giving-up of rights to performance under the contract by each party, each relinquishment being consideration for the other. Each party must be entitled to some performance by the other, whether it be complete or part performance. If one party has completely performed, there cannot be mutual rescission without additional consideration because, while the party who has performed gives up his right to return performance, yet the other party has no right to give up in exchange.

Mutual rescission does not involve restitution unless the parties so agree. In the absence of any provision for restitution in their agreement of mutual rescission, the parties are left where they find themselves at the moment of rescission.

Accord and Satisfaction. An *accord* is a *new contract* whereby the parties to it agree to a specified *performance in the future as satisfaction* of an existing duty owing between them *under a previous contract.* (A owes B $100 under a previous contract. A and B contract whereby A agrees to deliver and B agrees to take a horse in 30 days in satisfaction of the debt.) The previous contract is not discharged, but performance under it is suspended pending performance under the new contract. *Performance of the new contract* discharges the new and old contracts and is, therefore, a "satisfaction" of such contracts. Failure to perform the new contract has an effect dependent upon who breaks the new contract. If the debtor breaks the new contract, the creditor has the alternative remedies of suing on the new, or on the old, contract. If the creditor breaks the new contract, the debtor still has the duty of performing under the old contract; but the debtor may sue for damages for breach of the new contract or, in a proper case, obtain specific performance of the new contract. When the creditor has breached the new contract, specific performance of the accord usually is given as the best way to avoid circuity of action and to avoid the difficulty of ascertaining the debtor's damages at law.

Satisfaction is that performance which discharges a contractual obligation. Either *the accord itself* or *performance of the accord* may constitute the satisfaction of the previous contract, depending on the *intention of the parties to the accord.* An "accord and satisfaction" means that the accord itself is a satisfaction of the previous contract discharging it.

When the parties to an accord clearly manifest an intent that the accord is to be also a satisfaction, no problem is present, the accord constituting also a satisfaction of the previous contract which is now discharged by the accord and satisfaction. However, it is difficult sometimes to determine from the accord whether or not the parties intended it to be also a satisfaction. Unless the circumstances are to the contrary, it is but reasonable to infer that a creditor does not intend merely to exchange his present undisputed liquidated[6] claim or undisputed overdue unliquidated claim for a new claim against his debtor. However, the circumstances may be such as to lead to the inference that the creditor does wish an accord and satisfaction. Accordingly, the law provides that, in case of doubt of the creditor's intention, if the previous contractual duty is *undisputedly* either to pay a *liquidated* debt or to perform an *unliquidated matured* obligation, the accord is solely an accord; otherwise the accord is also a satisfaction. (D owes C $1,000. D delivers his check for $1,000 to C. Because a check is deemed conditional payment in the absence of agreement to the contrary, the original contract debt is not discharged until the check is paid. The check is an accord but not a satisfaction until the check is paid.)

Debtors often offer to settle the claims of their creditors by sending their checks therefor. There cannot be any accord or accord and satisfaction without the creditor's acceptance of his debtor's offer. An offer to settle a disputed or unliquidated claim by sending a check therefor[7] is accepted by the creditor when he cashes it or otherwise manifests his assent to it; and an offer of something other than money to settle the disputed or unliquidated claim is accepted by the creditor when he expressly accepts it, or impliedly accepts it by exercising dominion over it. Such acceptance creates a contract of accord which is also a satisfaction. It must be manifested clearly to the creditor, however, that what has been sent is in satisfaction, otherwise there is no accord or agreement on the performance as satisfaction of the prior contractual obligation.

There is a conflict of authority regarding the effect of a creditor's *retention* of a debtor's check voluntarily sent by the debtor and indicated to be in full satisfaction of a *disputed* claim. Most courts hold that the mere silent retention is an implied acceptance creating an accord on that amount as due and payable. Other courts hold that there is no acceptance. All courts would agree that cashing the check was an accord, and payment a satisfaction of the claim. Unless the parties agree to the contrary, a contract to *take* a check or a negotiable promissory note for the *undisputed* full amount due, or a check or note for *less* than the amount claimed if the claim is *disputed* or *unliquidated*, is solely an accord, and satisfaction is to occur on payment of the check. A creditor cannot cash a check sent in settlement of a disputed or unliquidated claim and declare he is not accepting it as satisfaction. He must either accept or reject, and cashing the check or exercising dominion over whatever else he has received in settlement creates an accord and satisfaction.

Novation. A novation is a *new contract* in which one of the parties was not a party to the old contract and which immediately discharges the old contract.[8]

---

[6] A claim is liquidated when the amount is either fixed by the parties, certain, or ascertained by mathematical computation or by operation of law. A claim is disputed if it is honestly believed not to be valid by the party against whom the claim is asserted. (See above, p. 55 ff.)

[7] For consideration, see above, pp. 55–56.

[8] The new party's *assumption* of the previous contractual obligation is not a promise to answer for the debt, default, or miscarriages of another under the statute of frauds. See above, p. 87 ff.

It is an accord and satisfaction in which a new party participates. (A owes B money under a previous contract. C contracts with A and B that he will pay the debt in consideration of B's release of A. There is a new contract, the old A/B contract is discharged, and the new debtor, C, is being substituted for the old debtor, A.)

Account Stated. *An account stated is an account which has been settled and the matured items and balance agreed to by the parties* either expressly, or impliedly by failure to object thereto within a reasonable period of time after receipt of a statement of such account. The account stated discharges all matured debts up to the date of the account stated. *An account stated is open to correction for innocent mistake, unless in the meanwhile the other party has changed his position in reliance on the account stated.* (A receives his monthly bank statement with canceled checks and does not notice the forgery of his signature to one check payable to C. C has cashed the check and is solvent until A discovers the forgery, at which time C is insolvent. A requests B, the bank, to correct his bank balance and to add the amount of the forged check. A cannot regain such amount. There is an account stated between A and B; and though an innocent mistake has been made, B has relied on A's silence by refraining from doing anything and would be prejudiced in recovering from C, who is now insolvent.)[9]

An account stated must be distinguished from other types of account which have nothing to do with discharge of contracts. An *account* is a detailed statement of debits and credits between parties, usually arising out of contract or some fiduciary relationship. A *current running account* is an open or unsettled account; it has not been finally closed or stated. In the absence of agreement between the parties, statute, or trade custom or usage, interest cannot be charged on such an account because the amount due is uncertain; and it is not until the amount is certain that interest may be charged. In the case of an account stated, however, in the absence of any contrary agreement between the parties, interest may be charged, inasmuch as the amount due is certain. A *mutual account* is one which, pursuant to agreement between the parties, involves mutual credits. Each party's side of a mutual account may be set off against the other, and only the balance is recoverable. An *account rendered* is an account presented by the creditor to the debtor for his examination and acceptance.

Assignment. The subject of assignment has been discussed previously.[10] It was pointed out that, if the obligor receives notice of an assignment, his duty to perform to the assignor is discharged and his duty now is to perform to the assignee. If the obligor does not receive such notice and innocently performs to the assignor who tortiously and silently accepts it, he is discharged of his contractual duty. However, when assignment of an account is made for the purpose of security, if the obligor receives notice of the assignment and the

---

[9] See below, pp. 405–6.

[10] See above, pp. 79 ff., especially p. 82 f.

assignee's *demand* for payment, then the obligor's duty to perform to the assignor is discharged; his duty now is to perform to the assignee. If no demand is made, the obligor is still obligated to the assignor and his payment to the assignor discharges him of his contractual duty. A delegation of duty is not an assignment.

Exercise of a Power of Avoidance. Voidable contracts are subject to rescission by exercise of the power of avoidance on the part of the party who has such power. Previous discussion has indicated when voidable contracts are created.[11] Exercise of the power of avoidance discharges the contract and may give rise to a right of restitution.

Fraudulent Material Alteration of Contract. A fraudulent material alteration of a written contract, made by a party to the contract with *intent* to alter materially his rights or duties thereunder and made without the assent of the other contracting party, discharges the contractual duty owing to him and destroys his right. The alteration is material also if it adversely affects a contracting party's legal relations with third persons. The wrongful party's alteration does not vary the innocent party's rights under the contract; but if a party to the contract, knowing of the alteration, asserts his rights under the contract, his duties and the wrongful party's rights and duties to him are revived as though no alteration had occurred. If a party manifests assent to the terms as changed by the other party, as to those parties the old contract is rescinded and the new changed contract takes its place. The authority to fill in a blank space in a contract may be express or implied, but the other party's fraudulent insertion of material matter in such space which is contrary to such express or implied authority discharges the contractual duty of the innocent party to perform to the wrongdoer.

Discharge of Joint Debtors. Joint promisors—i.e., joint obligors or debtors—as well as joint promisees—i.e., joint obligees or creditors—each are a unit with the element of survivorship. All joint promisees must sue and all joint promisors must be sued, unless one or more is dead, beyond the jurisdiction of the court, or discharged in bankruptcy, in which event the remainder of such joint promisees or promisors available, respectively, sue or are sued. Joint promisors may object to the nonjoinder of all available joint promisors in a suit brought against them, but failure to object causes a judgment to be binding against the ones sued; the remaining available joint promisors are discharged because there no longer is any claim against them, the claim having been merged in the judgment obtained. In some states there are joint debtor statutes which provide that judgment against less than all the available joint debtors does not extinguish the claim against the others not sued.[12] Death of a joint promisor causes the joint duty to survive in the remaining joint promisors; the estate of the deceased joint promisor no longer is bound by the joint promise, although in many states statutes are to the contrary. Death of the

---

[11] See above, pp. 10, 13 ff., 34 ff.

[12] As applicable to partnerships, see below, pp. 657–58.

last surviving joint promisor causes the joint duty to survive to his estate. Death of a joint promisee causes the joint right to survive to the remaining joint promisees. A promisee's discharge of *a* joint promisor discharges all the joint promisors, unless the discharge *reserves* rights against the other joint promisors, in which case the reservation operates as a promise not to sue that joint promisor, and the others are still liable. Full or partial performance or satisfaction of a contractual duty by less than all the joint promisors operates for the benefit of all the joint promisors and discharges the joint duty of all of them to the extent of such performance or satisfaction. This last is equally true if the promisors are several, or joint and several, as well as joint.

By Operation of Law

A contractual duty is discharged by the rendition of a *judgment*, an *arbitration award*, a *bankruptcy discharge*, the *statute of limitations*, and *excusable impossibility*. Each of these methods of discharge will be considered briefly in turn.

Judgment. The rendition of a judgment discharges the contractual duty and substitutes for the claim to performance of such duty a final, judicial pronouncement of the validity of such claim and the liquidated nature of such duty. The contractual duty is merged in the judgment.

Arbitration Award. Arbitration is the determination of a controversy in a nonjudicial proceeding by persons selected to decide the matter, pursuant to the agreement of the parties whose controversy is to be determined. The decision of the arbitrators is called an "award" which is enforceable in the courts. If the purpose of the arbitration is to determine whether there is a duty alleged to exist, an arbitration award discharges the duty found to exist, and the award itself is enforceable in the courts as a new cause of action. If the purpose is not to determine the existence of a contractual duty but solely to determine the liquidated amount due under such duty, then the duty is not merged in the arbitration award and the effect of the award is to fix the limit of the duty. The duty was never in dispute and is not discharged; it exists, limited in liquidated amount by the award, and may be sued on in the courts. In some of the states permitting contracts to arbitrate, such contracts must be in writing. The arbitration clauses included in a contract must not be unfair or unconscionable. An arbitration award is to be made in good faith, and if the arbitrator has not acted in good faith a court may set aside the arbitration award.

Bankruptcy Discharge. The Bankruptcy Code provides that in a bankruptcy proceeding the debtor bankrupt may be discharged from all provable claims, with certain exceptions. A discharge in bankruptcy discharges the debtor from the contractual duties inherent in such discharged claims.

Statute of Limitations. The statute of limitations is a statute which provides certain specified periods of time within which matured claims may be asserted by legal action. The periods of time vary among the states. Failure to act within the prescribed time bars *enforcement* of such a claim in the courts.[13] In effect, and for all practical purposes, the duties are discharged.

The statute of limitations begins to run as soon as a cause of action for an amount accrues. In open book accounts, the statute begins to run from the date the last item was entered in the account, unless the parties agree to the contrary. In some states the statute begins to run on each item from the date of entry of such item. In contracts for the sale of goods, the amount payable is due at the time the goods are delivered, unless the parties agree to the contrary,[14] and the statute begins to run at that time. In commercial paper, the statute begins to run from a date dependent upon whether it is a time or demand instrument. A cause of action against a maker or an acceptor accrues: in the case of a time instrument, on the day after maturity; in the case of a demand instrument, upon its date or, if no date is stated, on the date of issue.[15]

It should be noted that, by statute in many states, the running of the statute of limitations is halted or suspended: when a person with a cause of action is under legal disability to sue, e.g., an infant or insane person, at the time the cause of action accrues; during the imprisonment of a person with a cause of action, while the person against whom a cause of action has accrued is absent from the state or has absconded or concealed himself; until the person upon whom fraud has been perpetrated discovers the fraud or facts sufficient to put him on inquiry. Also, courts will suspend the running of the statute between citizens of states at war. The statute is "tolled" (resumes running) when the statutory bar to an action is removed or ended. This has been discussed previously.[16]

Excusable Impracticability (Impossibility). The existence or non-existence, or the occurrence or the non-occurrence, of particular circumstances is a basic assumption for making a contract. If an event occurs, the non-occurrence of which was a basic assumption on which a contract was made, making a party's performance impracticable without any fault on his part, he is discharged, unless he assumed the risk of the event's non-occurrence. "Impracticability" means that performance is either a *physical* impossibility or *impracticable* because of the extreme and unreasonable expense, difficulty, loss, or injury to one of the parties which may be involved. A promise which is impracticable of performance because of the *subjective* inability of the party with the duty to perform is no excuse for nonperformance, and his duty is not discharged. Impracticability may exist at the time the promise to perform is made, called "existing impracticability," or it may occur after the contract is made, called "supervening impracticability." If a promise is impracticable

[13] "Laches" is a non-statutory doctrine of equity that an equitable claim will not be enforced when the claimant has not been diligent in asserting it by an action. The purpose of the doctrine, like the legal equivalent the statute of limitations, is to bar the enforcement of stale claims.

[14] For the rules for sales of goods under the Code see below, pp. 218–19.

[15] See UCC 3–122(1).

[16] See above, pp. 63–65.

of performance *when made,* not because of the subjective inability of the party with the duty to perform but, rather, because of facts of which he does not know or has no reason to know, the promise does not create a duty of performance and it is not a contract. (A promises to sell, and B promises to buy, a certain chattel which, unknown to them, has been destroyed previously. There is no contract because of a mutual mistake of fact concerning the nonexistence of the chattel. Neither promise created a duty of performance.)[17] Supervening impracticability other than by the subjective inability of the party with the duty to perform discharges his contractual duty to perform, and consequently that of the other contracting party, if the impracticability: is not wrongfully caused by him; could not reasonably be foreseen by him at the time the contract was made; occurred before performance was overdue; occurred before he has breached the contract other than by an anticipatory breach; and if the risk of the supervening impracticability has not been assumed by him. Illustrations of discharge by supervening impracticability[18] are:

1. Supervening illegality of contractual performance by legal prohibition, or by legal prevention, of performance by the party with the duty to perform. This may occur by governmental executive order, by legislation, or by judicial or administrative decision.

2. In *personal service* contracts, the supervening death of the party with the duty to perform, or his supervening illness which makes his performance impossible or seriously harmful to him, such death or illness not having been wrongfully caused by him. In personal service contracts, it is implied that personal performance will be rendered if the party is alive and well. A test of whether or not a contract is for personal services is whether or not the duty of performance is delegable. In a contract of a personal character the duty is nondelegable without the obligee's assent.[19] (A, a building contractor, made a contract with B to build a house for B. No unusual or unique services were to be rendered by A. A died without rendering performance. A's duty to perform is not discharged because the contract was not of a personal character. A's personal services were not required; another capable building contractor could perform the contract.)

3. Supervening destruction or material impairment of the *requisite* subject matter of the contract or of the *requisite* means of performing the contract, making performance impossible by the party with the duty to perform, provided such destruction or impairment was not wrongfully caused by him. When the parties contemplate, or provide in their contract for, *specific* subject matter—e.g., *that* horse, *this* machine, or *that* building—or for a certain mode of performance—e.g., the arbitrator is to be A, or the product of *that* particular factory—the continued existence of such subject matter or mode of performance is *requisite* for performance. Destruction or material impairment thereof discharges the duty of the party to render performance.

4. Supervening nonexistence of certain facts other than requisite subject matter and requisite means of performance, making performance impossible by the

[17] See UCC 2–613(a). Also, see above, p. 23.

[18] See Restatement (Second) of Contracts 1980, secs. 281–84.

[19] See above, pp. 82–83.

party with the duty to perform, the parties having contemplated or provided in their contract for performance only on the continued existence of such facts, provided such nonexistence was not wrongfully caused by the party with the duty to perform. For example, a contract to ship goods from one country to a particular port in another country is made impossible of performance by an embargo or quarantine on the port of delivery; the party with the duty to perform is discharged. The continued existence of the fact that the port of delivery would be available has ceased.

Impracticability is an impediment to a party's performance. However, instead of a party not being able to perform because of impracticability, his principal purpose in making the contract may be substantially frustrated, without his fault, by the occurrence of a supervening event the non-occurrence of which was a basic assumption on which he made his contract. (A contracts to pay B for use of a seat space to view an athletic contest, which subsequently is canceled because of the illness of one of the teams. A's duty to pay B is discharged, and B is not liable to A for breach of contract.) If an event did not exist on the basic assumption of which a party made his agreement, the frustration of the basic purpose for making his agreement precludes the *creation* of any contractual duty to perform. An example is an agreement to sell goods which, at the time of the agreement and unknown to the parties, did not exist. Generally, the same rules for impracticability apply to frustration.

PROBLEMS

1. (a) A, 17 years of age, wanted to drive to work on a motorcycle instead of using a streetcar. B and A contracted for the sale of B's motorcycle to A in exchange for A's watch and $300. B delivered the motorcycle to A and A paid the $300 and delivered the watch to B. B immediately sold and delivered the watch to C, a good faith purchaser for value. Two years later the motorcycle was destroyed in an accident while being driven by A to his home, and A demanded the return of his watch and $300.
   (1) Can A enforce his demand?
   (2) Why?

   (b) Alex agreed with Bowers to relinquish a part of a debt due Alex from Bowers if Bowers would pay the balance. This was reduced to writing and signed by both. Is this a contract? Explain.
2. A sent B an offer by mail which provided that an acceptance was effective as such only when received by A. B mailed A an acceptance. A then mailed B a revocation. B received the revocation before A received the acceptance. Is there a contract between A and B?
3. In August 1980, X and Y duly made a legally valid written contract whereby X agreed to audit the books and accounts of Y for the calendar year 1981 for a fee fixed by this contract. At the time of the making of this contract and as a part of the negotiations leading up to it, X and Y orally agreed that said contract was to be effective only in the event that Y procured certain additional capital from Z prior to January 1, 1981. If Y is unable to procure such capital, is the written contract legally binding? (Former C.P.A. Examination question, dates changed)

4. In January 1980, A and B made a contract whereby A was to construct certain buildings for B by December 1, 1980, for which B would pay $100,000 by installments as the buildings were completed. In March, A unjustifiedly refused to construct the remainder of the buildings unless B promised to pay A an additional $10,000, which B promised to do if A would agree to complete the buildings by October 1; A so agreed. The buildings were completed by October 1, and B paid A the last installment of the agreed $100,000 but refused to pay the additional $10,000.
   (1) Is A entitled to the additional $10,000?
   (2) Why?
5. A, an accountant, sent B a bill for $1,000 for personal services. There had been no agreement as to the price to be paid. B, on receiving the bill, sent a letter to A questioning the reasonableness of the amount charged but did not dispute the service, enclosing a check for $500 which he stated was in full satisfaction of A's claim. A made no reply and deposited the check in the bank; it was paid. He subsequently sued B to recover the $500 as balance due. Is he entitled to recover? (Former C.P.A. Examination question)
6. D owes C five debts, two of which are barred by the statute of limitations. D pays C $100.
   (a) If D specified that the $100 was to be applied to a particular barred debt, is the remainder of that debt recoverable by C?
   (b) If D did not specify to which debt the $100 was to be applied, what may C do and how would it affect the barred debts?
   (c) If D had paid C $100 on C's promise to discharge the two barred debts totaling $500, is C's promise enforceable by D?
7. (a) A owed B $500. C promised A that, if A would lend $500 to C, C would discharge A's debt to B in 30 days by paying the $500 to B. A loaned $500 to C but C refused to pay B at the end of 30 days.
      (1) Does B have any right against C?
      (2) Why?
   (b) X borrowed $100 from Y and agreed with Y to pay it to Z at the end of 30 days as a gift from Y to Z. X refused to pay Z at the end of 30 days.
      (1) Does Z have any right against X?
      (2) Why?
   (c) R contracted with S to construct a building for S upon S's land adjoining T's land. Such a building would enhance materially the value of T's land; and T immediately made substantial improvements to his land, intending to sell it at a high price as soon as R had completed the building. R refuses to perform his contract.
      (1) Does T have any right against R?
      (2) Why?
8. In January 1980, Hitchcock, as manager of City Clinic having specific authority to conduct its affairs, engaged Jones, a C.P.A., to make an audit of the books of the clinic for the year ended December 31, 1979. At that time Jones stated he could begin the job soon after income tax time. On September 22, 1980, Hitchcock wrote Jones stating that he needed some figures and asking Jones to start the audit. Jones started the audit on October 7, 1980, and continued to work on it from time to time

until March 31, 1981. During this period he conferred with Hitchcock several times and furnished him with some preliminary figures. The last of these conferences took place on February 17, 1981. At such conferences no indication was given to Jones that there was concern about the delay in the completion of the audit. On March 31, 1981, Hitchcock notified Jones by letter that his engagement was terminated because delay in completion of the audit rendered it worthless at that late date. At this time Jones could have completed the audit within four days. Hitchcock, for the clinic, refused to pay Jones any fee.

Would Jones be entitled to any compensation? If so, on what grounds could he recover and how would the amount be determined? Explain fully. (Former C.P.A. Examination question, dates changed)

9. On July 25, 1980, A, as president of Boston Company, and with the approval of his board of directors, engaged C, a certified public accountant, to examine the financial statements of Boston Company as at July 31, 1980, and to render his report in time for the annual stockholders' meeting to be held on September 5, 1980. C proceeded at reasonable speed but on August 10 objected to A that the company's staff was so inefficient and uncooperative that it might be impossible to meet the deadline. A said: "Don't worry! I'll fix that." C proceeded, but the Boston Company staff showed no improvement. Notwithstanding C's reasonable efforts, the report was not ready until September 7. A, acting on behalf of Boston Company, refused to accept or to pay for the report since it no longer served its intended purpose. A maintains that delivery of the report by September 5 was a condition of the contract. What are C's rights? Explain fully. (Former C.P.A. Examination question, dates changed)

10. S and B executed a written contract which provided that S was to sell and convey, and B was to buy, certain land. Subsequently, S sold the land to C but later reacquired it in time to tender its conveyance to B in compliance with the terms of the contract. B knew of these transactions and refused the conveyance tendered by S.
    (a) May S enforce the contract against B?
    (b) Was B's silent inactivity a waiver?
    (c) Would it have made any difference if B had sued S for damages for breach of contract before S's reacquisition of the land?

11. D borrowed $20,000 from C, secured by a real property mortgage, repayable monthly with interest over a period of 10 years. A higher rate of interest would apply to delinquent monthly payments. Five years later, C complained to D that there had been too many delinquent payments and that he was having a difficult time computing two sets of interest. C demanded immediate payment of all delinquent monthly payments together with regular and delinquent interest. At D's request, C computed the total interest and principal due to date, and D then mortgaged one of his other buildings in order to obtain the agreed amount, D honestly believing the amount stated by C to be correct. One month after the money was paid by D to C, C found that he had forgotten to include in the amount the delinquent interest, amounting to $700. C demanded the $700, but D refused to pay it.

    You are the accountant for C and you have kept his books on an accrual basis in the past. How will you carry this item on C's books, and why?

SOME PREVIOUS C.P.A. LAW EXAMINATION QUESTIONS AND AUTHOR'S MODEL ANSWERS

NOVEMBER, 1979

Number 1

Select the **best** answer for each of the following items.

1. Cox Manufacturing repudiated its contract to sell 300 televisions to Ruddy Stores, Inc. What recourse does Ruddy Stores have?
   a. It can obtain specific performance by the seller.
   b. It can recover punitive damages.
   c. It must await the seller's performance for a commercially reasonable time after repudiation if it wishes to recover anything.
   d. It can "cover," that is, procure the goods elsewhere and recover any damages.

2. In the process of negotiating the sale of his manufacturing business to Grand, Sterling made certain untrue statements which Grand relied upon. Grand was induced to purchase the business for $10,000 more than its true value. Grand is **not** sure whether he should seek relief based upon misrepresentation or fraud. Which of the following is a correct statement?
   a. If Grand merely wishes to rescind the contract and get his money back, misrepresentation is his **best** recourse.
   b. In order to prevail under the fraud theory, Grand must show that Sterling intended for him to rely on the untrue statements; whereas he need *not* do so if he bases his action on misrepresentation.
   c. Both fraud and misrepresentation require Grand to prove that Sterling knew the statements were false.
   d. If Grand chooses fraud as his basis for relief, the statute of frauds applies.

3. Which of the following will **not** be sufficient to satisfy the consideration requirement for a contract?
   a. The offeree expends both time and money in studying and analyzing the offer.
   b. The offeree makes a promise which is a legal detriment to him.
   c. The offeree performs the act requested by the offeror.
   d. The offeree makes a promise which benefits the offeror.

4. Marsh and Lennon entered into an all inclusive written contract involving the purchase of a tract of land. Lennon claims that there was a contemporaneous oral agreement between the parties which called for the removal by Marsh of several large rocks on the land. Marsh relies upon the parol evidence rule to avoid having to remove the rocks. Which of the following is correct?
   a. The parol evidence rule does **not** apply to contemporaneous oral agreements.
   b. Since the statute of frauds was satisfied in respect to the contract for the purchase of the land, the parol evidence rule does **not** apply.
   c. Since the oral agreement does not contradict the terms of the written contract, the oral agreement is valid despite the parol evidence rule.
   d. The parol evidence rule applies and Lennon will be precluded from proving the oral promise in the absence of fraud.

7. Master Corporation, a radio and television manufacturer, invited Darling Discount Chain to examine several odd lots of discontinued models and make an offer for the entire lot. The odd lots were segregated from the regular inventory but inadvertently included 15 current models. Darling was unaware that Master did not intend to include the 15 current models in the group. Darling made Master an offer of $9,000 for the

entire lot, which represented a large discount from the normal sales price. Unaware of the error, Master accepted the offer. Master would **not** have accepted had it known of the inclusion of the 15 current models. Upon learning of the error, Master alleged mistake as a defense and refused to perform. Darling sued for breach of contract. Under the circumstances, what is the status of the contract?

a. There is **no** contract since Master did not intend to include the 15 current models in the group of radios to be sold.
b. The contract is voidable because of a unilateral mistake.
c. The contract is voidable because of a mutual mistake.
d. There is a valid and binding contract which includes the 15 current-model radios.

Answer

1. 1.d(282) 2.a(35,36–37,121) 3.a(44) 4.d(44) 7.d(41–42,202)

MAY, 1979

Number 1

Select the **best** answer for each of the following items.

9. Williams purchased a heating system from Radiant Heating, Inc., for his factory. Williams insisted that a clause be included in the contract calling for service on the heating system to begin **not** later than the next business day after Williams informed Radiant of a problem. This service was to be rendered free of charge during the first year of the contract and for a flat fee of $200 per year for the next two years thereafter. During the winter of the second year, the heating system broke down and Williams promptly notified Radiant of the situation. Due to other commitments, Radiant did **not** send a man over the next day. Williams phoned Radiant and was told that the $200 per year service charge was uneconomical and they could **not** get a man over there for several days. Williams in desperation promised to pay an additional $100 if Radiant would send a man over that day. Radiant did so and sent a bill for $100 to Williams. Is Williams legally required to pay this bill and why?

a. No, because the pre-existing legal duty rule applies to this situation.
b. No, because the statute of frauds wil' defeat Radiant's claim.
c. Yes, because Williams made the offer to pay the additional amount.
d. Yes, because the fact that it was uneconomical for Radiant to perform constitutes economic duress which freed Radiant from its obligation to provide the agreed-upon service.

17. Abacus Corporation sent Frame Company an offer by a telegram to buy its patent on a calculator. The Abacus telegram indicated that the offer would expire in ten days. The telegram was sent on February 1, 1979, and received on February 2, 1979, by Frame. On February 8, 1979, Abacus telephoned Frame and indicated they were withdrawing the offer. Frame telegraphed an acceptance on the 11th of February. Which of the following is correct?

a. The offer was an irrevocable offer, but Frame's acceptance was too late.
b. Abacus' withdrawal of the offer was ineffective because it was **not** in writing.
c. Since Frame used the same means of communication, acceptance was both timely and effective.
d. **No** contract arose since Abacus effectively revoked the offer on February 8, 1979.

Answer

1. 9.a(51) 17.d(23–24)

NOVEMBER, 1978

Number 1

Select the **best** answer for each of the following items.

27. Martin Stores, Inc., decided to sell a portion of its eight-acre property. Consequently, the president of Martin wrote several prospective buyers the following letter:

> Dear Sir: We are sending this notice to several prospective buyers because we are interested in selling four acres of our property located in downtown Metropolis. If you are interested, please communicate with me at the above address. Don't bother to reply unless you are thinking in terms of at least $100,000.
>
> James Martin, President

Under the circumstances, which of the following is correct?

a. The statute of frauds does **not** apply because the real property being sold is the division of an existing tract which had been properly recorded.
b. Markus, a prospective buyer, who telegraphed Martin that he would buy at $100,000 and forwarded a $100,000 surety bond to guarantee his performance, has validly accepted.
c. Martin must sell to the highest bidder.
d. Martin's communication did **not** constitute an offer to sell.

28. Fashion Swimming Pools, Inc., mailed a letter to Direct Distributors offering a three-year franchise dealership. The offer stated the terms in detail and at the bottom stated that "the offer would **not** be withdrawn prior to October 1, 1978." Under the circumstances, which of the following is correct?

a. The offer is an irrevocable option which can **not** be withdrawn prior to October 1, 1978.
b. A letter of acceptance from Direct to Fashion sent on October 1, 1978, but **not** received until October 2, 1978, would **not** create a valid contract.
c. The statute of frauds would **not** apply to the proposed contract.
d. The offer can **not** be assigned to another party if Direct chooses **not** to accept.

30. Exeter Industries, Inc., orally engaged Werglow as one of its district sales managers for an 18-month period commencing April 1, 1978. Werglow commenced work on that date and performed his duties in a highly competent manner for several months. On October 1, 1978, the company gave Werglow a notice of termination as of November 1, 1978, citing a downturn in the market for its products. Werglow sues seeking either specific performance or damages for breach of contract. Exeter pleads the statute of frauds and/or a justified dismissal due to the economic situation. What is the probable outcome of the lawsuit?

a. Werglow will prevail because the statute of frauds does **not** apply to contracts such as his.
b. Werglow will prevail because he has partially performed under the terms of the contract.
c. Werglow will lose because the reason for his termination was caused by economic factors beyond Exeter's control.
d. Werglow will lose because such a contract must be in writing and signed by a proper agent of Exeter.

Answer

1. 27.d(19–20) 28.d(19–20,26–27) 30.d(86)

Number 5

Part a. Clauson Enterprises, Inc., was considering adding a new product line to its existing lines. The decision was contingent upon its being assured of a supply of an electronic component for the product at a certain price and a positive market study which clearly justified the investment in the venture.

Clauson's president approached Migrane Electronics and explained the situation to Migrane's president. After much negotiation, Migrane agreed to grant Clauson an option to purchase 12,000 of the necessary electronic components at $1.75 each or at the prevailing market price, whichever was lower. Clauson prepared the option below incorporating their understanding.

Option Agreement
Clauson Enterprises/Migrane Electronics

Migrane Electronics hereby offers to sell Clauson Enterprises 12,000 miniature solid state electronic breakers at $1.75 each or at the existing market price at the time of delivery, whichever is lower, delivery to be made in 12 equal monthly installments beginning one month after the exercise of this option. This option is irrevocable for six months from January 1, 1978.

Clauson Enterprises agrees to deliver to Migrane its market survey for the product line in which the component would be used if it elects not to exercise the option.

Both parties signed the option agreement and Migrane's president signed Migrane's corporate name alongside the last sentence of the first paragraph. On May 1, 1978, Migrane notified Clauson that it was revoking its offer. The market price for the component had increased to $1.85. On May 15, 1978, Clauson notified Migrane that it accepted the offer and that if Migrane did not perform, it would be sued and held liable for damages. Migrane replied that the offer was not binding and was revoked before Clauson accepted. Furthermore, even if it were binding, it was good for only three months as a matter of law.

Upon receipt of Migrane's reply, Clauson instituted suit for damages.

Required:

Answer the following, setting forth reasons for any conclusions stated.

Who will prevail? Discuss all the issues and arguments raised by the fact situation.

Part c. Novack, an industrial designer, accepted an offer from Superior Design Corporation to become one of its designers. The contract was for three years and expressly provided that it was irrevocable by either party except for cause during that period of time. The contract was in writing and signed by both parties. After a year, Novack became dissatisfied with the agreed compensation which he was receiving. He had done a brilliant job and several larger corporations were attempting to lure him away.

Novack, therefore, demanded a substantial raise, and Superior agreed in writing to pay him an additional amount as a bonus at the end of the third year. Novack remained with Superior and performed the same duties he had agreed to perform at the time he initially accepted the position. At the end of the three years, Novack sought to collect the additional amount of money promised. Superior denied liability beyond the amount agreed to in the original contract.

Required:

Answer the following, setting forth reasons for any conclusions stated.

Can Novack recover the additional compensation from Superior?

Part d. The basic facts are the same as stated in **Part c** except that one of Superior's competitors, Dixon Corporation, successfully lured Novack away from Superior by offering a substantially higher salary. Dixon did this with full knowledge of the terms of the original three-year contract between Novack and Superior.

Required:

Answer the following, setting forth reasons for any conclusions stated.

1. Does Superior have any legal redress against Dixon?
2. Would Superior be successful if it seeks the equitable relief of specific performance (an order by the court compelling Novack to perform his contractual undertaking) for the remaining two years of the contract?

Answer

5. a. Clauson will prevail. Since the transaction contemplates a sale of goods, the Uniform Commercial Code is applicable. Under the Sales part of the Code, a firm offer is a signed written offer to buy or sell goods, made by a merchant, which gives assurance that it will be held open for a period not to exceed three months. Consideration is not required. Also, if the assurance term is on a form supplied by the offeree, the term must be separately signed by the offeror. Here, Migrane made a firm offer to Clauson, signing the assurance term in the written form prepared by Clauson. However, at the end of March the three months' period of the firm offer expired, even though Migrane's offer to sell was for six months.

Under the law of Contracts, an option is an irrevocable offer as prescribed in the option contract. The subsidiary offer to keep open the main offer to sell must be supported by consideration in order to be an option. Here, Clauson promised to deliver to Migrane its market survey if Clauson elected not to exercise its option to buy. Clauson's promise is a legal detriment to Clauson and consideration for Migrane's subsidiary offer to keep open its main offer to sell the 12,000 items to Clauson. Therefore, Migrane's six months offer to sell is an option which was irrevocable until June 30. Accordingly, Migrane's attempt to revoke the option on May 1 was ineffective, and Clauson's acceptance on May 15 was effective to create a contract for the sale of the goods under the Code. Migrane's refusal to perform is a repudiation and a breach of contract under the Code for which damages is a remedy. It should be noted that, since the contract is for the sale of goods for more than $500, it is within the Code's statute of frauds and enforceable because the contract was in writing. (pp. 25 ftn 12, 25–26, 202–3, 264, 278)

c. No. Under the law of Contracts, a promise is unenforceable as a contract unless it is supported by consideration. Consideration must be a legal detriment to the person rendering it. A legal detriment is the performance of something which the performing party was under no previous legal obligation to do. Here, Superior's promise to pay an additional amount of salary as a bonus to Novack if he would perform the remainder of his employment contract with Superior was not supported by consideration because Novack was already under a previous legal obligation so to perform. Since such performance is not a legal detriment to Novack, it is not consideration for Superior's promise to pay a bonus. Therefore, Superior's promise is not a contract and Superior is not liable on its promise. (pp. 00, 00–00)

d.1. Yes. Dixon has committed the tort of inducing breach of contract for which Dixon is liable to Superior for special damages. The tort occurs when one person, intentionally and by inducement, causes another person to breach his contract with a third person. Here, Dixon did this by intentionally inducing Novack to breach his contract with Superior. (p. 69, ftn. 52)

2. No. A decree of specific performance of personal service contracts will not be rendered primarily because of the U.S. Constitution's prohibition of involuntary servitude. Here, there is a personal service contract between Superior and Novack because it is impliedly nondelegable by Novack by reason of his special skill as an industrial designer. (p. 110)

NOVEMBER, 1975

Number 4

Part a. On June 1, 1975, Markum Realty, Inc., offered to sell one acre of land in an industrial park it owned to Johnson Enterprises, Inc. The offer was by mail and, in addition to the other usual terms, stated: "This offer will expire on July 2, 1975, unless acceptance is received by the offeror on or before said date."

Johnson decided to purchase the tract of land and on July 1, telegraphed its acceptance to Markum. The acceptance telegram was delayed due to the negligence of the telegraph company which had admitted that delivery was not made to Markum until July 3. Markum decided not to sell to Johnson because it had received a better offer, but it remained silent and did not notify Johnson of its decision.

When Johnson did not hear from Markum by July 11, its president called the president of Markum and inquired when Johnson might expect to receive the formalized copy of the contract the two companies had entered into. Markum's president responded that there was no contract.

Required:

1. Did a contract result from the above described dealings between Markum and Johnson? Discuss the legal implications of **each** communication between the parties in your explanation.
2. Assuming a contract did not arise, does Johnson have any legal recourse against the telegraph company? Explain.

Answer

4.a.1. No. A contract requires a manifestation of mutual assent consisting of an offer and an acceptance. When an offer expires in accordance with its terms, no acceptance can occur. Here, Markum's offer limited the time of acceptance to his receipt of Johnson's acceptance before July 2. Since Markum did not receive Johnson's acceptance until after that date, Markum's offer had expired and, there being no manifestation of mutual assent, therefore there was no contract. Johnson's telegraphic acceptance became a new offer which Markum never accepted, his silence not being an acceptance. The telegraph company's negligent delay is irrelevant to the dealings between the parties. (p. 22)

2. Yes. Negligence proximately causing harm subjects the negligent party to liability for such harm. Here, the telegraph company was negligent and, if Johnson suffered damage by being unable to form the contract with Markum, Johnson has a right of action against the telegraph company. (pp. 612–13)

Part Three:
Personal Property

A. Nature of Personal Property

Chapter 9

IN GENERAL

Property as a physical substance is a thing, which may be immovable or movable. Real property is a tangible, immovable thing (land); and personal property is a movable thing, which may be either a tangible movable called a "chattel" or "goods," or an intangible movable called a "chose in action." In a technical legal sense, property is an interest in a thing.

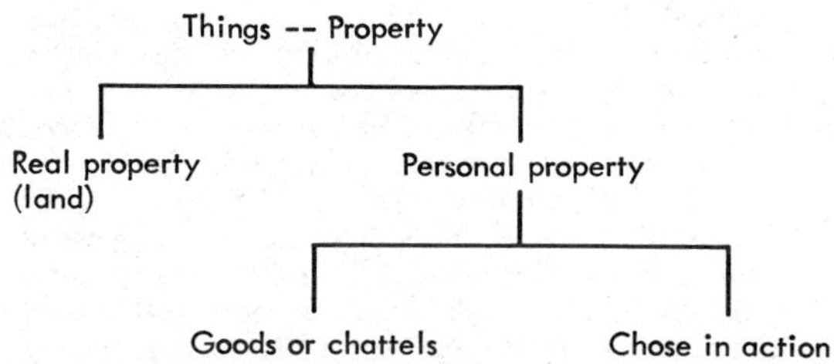

Things

Personal property is concerned with movable things. A "thing" may be an object which has corporeal or physical substance, like furniture, machinery, textiles, land. Such a thing is called a "tangible." Tangibles may be immovable, such as the surface and subsurface of the earth and that which is so annexed to it as to be a permanent part thereof (e.g., a building), usually described as "land." Tangibles also may be movable, as an automobile or furniture, usually described as "chattels" or "goods."[1] Goods and their trans-

[1] For the different definition of "goods" under the various Articles of the UCC, see 2–105,7–102(1)(f); and 9–105(1)(h).

fer by sale are governed by the Sales portion of the Code. Goods are tangible, movable things, but do not include money, investment securities, and things in action. Goods does include the unborn young of animals and growing crops. Oil, minerals, or a structure (e.g., building) affixed to land are land; but a contract for their sale, contemplating their severance from the land *by the seller* after the formation of the contract, causes them to be treated as goods *for the purpose of the contract.* However, *if the buyer is to make severance,* the transaction is considered to be a contract affecting land.[2] All things which are not tangible are incorporeal and are known as "intangibles," such as goodwill, a contract right, a trademark, a patent, or a copyright.[3] A thing in action—i.e., a right of action—is called a "chose in action" (e.g., the right contained in a check, promissory note, bill of exchange, a simple contract, bond, account receivable). An intangible may be included in a chattel which evidences the intangible, as a certificate of stock evidences a share in the corporation and its ownership, and a check evidences the right to money in accordance with the terms of the check. Thus, all things are either land (a tangible immovable), chattels (tangible movables), or intangibles (rights).

---

[2] See UCC 2–107, and below, p. 198.

[3] Under federal law, a **patent** is a grant by the federal government through its Patent Office to the inventor (and his heirs and assigns) of "any new and useful process, machine, manufacture, or composition of matter, or any new and useful improvement thereof," not previously patented or used, "of the right to exclude others from making, using, or selling the invention throughout the United States" for a nonrenewable period of 17 years.

Under federal law, a **copyright** is a grant by the federal government through its Register of Copyrights to the author of original works in a tangible medium of expression in the categories of: literary works; musical works, including accompanying words; dramatic works, including accompanying music; pantomimes and choreographic works; pictorial, graphic, and sculptured works; motion pictures and other audiovisual works; and sound recordings. Copyright protection does not extend to any idea, procedure, process, system, method of operation, concept, principle, or discovery contained in an original work of authorship. With certain exceptions, such as "fair use," the copyright owner has exclusive rights of use of the copyrighted work. For copyrighted works prior to 1978, the term is still 28 years with a renewable period of 47 years. Beginning with 1978, the term is for the author's life plus 50 years after his death, except that works made for hire and for anonymous and pseudonymous works the term is 75 years from publication or 100 years from creation, whichever is shorter. For a joint work by two or more authors not for hire, the term is for the life of the last surviving author plus 50 years after his death.

Goods often are identified by a **trademark**, which is a symbol, mark, device, or other designation which a person affixes to goods to identify them as being marketed by him. An interest in a trademark is acquired by the person who first uses it. Federal and state legislation provide for registration of trademarks (federal—Patent and Trademark Office), which assists the registrant to prove the time of his initial use. However, registration is not necessary to the acquisition of an interest in a trademark. The person with a trademark has the exclusive right to use it with respect to those goods which, by reason of the trademark, prospective customers would associate with the source identified by the trademark; and he has this exclusive right in those territorial areas in which he used it prior to anyone else. Registration is for renewable periods of 20 years.

The assignment of an interest in a patent, copyright, or trademark must be in writing, and the assignment of a trademark must also be acknowledged. Assignment is valid as between the assignor and the assignee, but it is void as against a subsequent bona fide purchaser for value unless it has been recorded. The assignment of a patent or trademark is recorded in the United States Patent and Trademark Office, and the assignment of a copyright is recorded with the Register of Copyright, both in Washington, D.C.

Property

A person may have an interest in some thing. Such an interest is "property." Customarily, the object of the interest is called property, but technically only the interest therein constitutes property; the thing itself is the object of property. (A's interest in possession of a chattel or of land is property. The chattel or land is the object of property.) An owner is the person who has such an interest, and "ownership" describes the interest as belonging to a person. The purpose of business transactions is the transfer of property—i.e., interests in things.

It should be noted carefully, however, that because the word "property" usually is used to describe a thing rather than an interest in a thing, *throughout this book the word "property" refers to a thing rather than to an interest in a thing, except when otherwise indicated.*

Classification. Property may be classified in various ways. It may be classified on the basis of its physical substance either as tangible property (e.g., land, chattels) or as intangible property (e.g., a chose in action). Classification may be made on the basis of ownership, "public property" being property owned by a nation, state, or political subdivision thereof, and "private property" being property owned by a private person. The broadest classification of property is "real property" and "personal property." In a strictly technical sense, the term "real property" describes a particular kind of interest in land, called a "freehold," which is an interest in land for a period of time the termination of which cannot be measured or computed exactly in terms of years, months, and days, and which is not terminable at the will of the transferor.[4] An interest in land which is not a freehold is a "chattel real." All chattels real and all interests in movables are "personal property." However, as indicated previously, the word "property" commonly is used to refer to a thing rather than to an interest in a thing, and so, unless otherwise indicated, *throughout this book "real property" refers to land while "personal property" refers to chattels and to intangible things.*

PROBLEMS

1. As to patents, trademarks, and copyrights:
   (a) (1) Can any interest in any of them be transferred?
   (2) Which?
   (3) How?
   (4) Is any record required?
   (5) Where? Explain.
   (b) What is the life of a (1) patent? (2) trademark? (3) copyright; and are any of them renewable? If so, which, and how long?
   (c) Of what value is this knowledge to the accountant? (Former C.P.A. Examination question)

---

[4] See below, p. 765 f.

SOME PREVIOUS C.P.A. LAW EXAMINATION QUESTIONS AND AUTHOR'S MODEL ANSWERS

NOVEMBER, 1979

Number 1

Select the **best** answer for each of the following items.

43. Gail Monet has decided to make certain gifts to her family. Her goal is to reduce her estate and income taxes. Which of the following need **not** be present in order for Monet to make valid gifts?

a. Monet must be competent to make the gifts in question.
b. Monet must have some purpose or motive other than, or in addition to, the mere saving of taxes.
c. There must be delivery of the gifts to the donees.
d. The gifts must be made voluntarily and with the requisite donative intent.

Answer

1. 43.b(141)

NOVEMBER, 1975

Number 5.a

3. If an investor acquires shares of stock in Boswell Realty Corporation, is his interest real or personal property? Explain.

Answer

5.a.3. Personal property. Personal property consists of movable things, whether tangible or intangible. A share of stock is an intangible unit of interest in a corporation, and not in the corporate real property which is owned by the corporation. (p. 137)

Part Three:
Personal Property

B. Acquisition of Personal Property

Chapter 10

IN GENERAL

Ownership of chattels is acquired in various ways: (1) *By occupancy*—acquiring possession of an unowned chattel with the intention of owning it. A chattel becomes unowned by abandonment. (2) *By finding*—a chattel is *lost* when it is located at a place where it was not put by the owner and which is unknown to him. A chattel is *mislaid* when it is located at a place where it was put by the owner but now forgotten by him. Loss or mislaying has no effect upon the owner's interests therein. The finder of a lost or mislaid chattel acquires ownership and the right to possession inferior only to the rightful owner, except that the establishment where a mislaid chattel is found has a temporary superior right to hold it for the rightful owner. The finder is an involuntary bailee with the duty to hold and preserve the property for the rightful owner. (3) *By gift*—unconditionally, or by *causa mortis*. (4) *By accession*—the increase in a chattel by what it produces or by the addition to it of another chattel so as to become a permanent part thereof. (5) *By confusion*—the intermingling of chattels of different owners so that the respective chattels of each are indistinguishable from the others. (6) *By satisfaction of a judgment for conversion*—unpermitted interference with another's possession of a chattel inconsistent with his right to its immediate possession and his right to control and dominion over the chattel. Conversion alone does not disturb the rightful owner's interest in a chattel, but his acquisition of a judgment and its satisfaction generally causes his title to transfer to the defendant tortfeasor.

Ownership of personal property may be acquired in various ways, such as by: occupancy, finding, gift, accession, confusion, satisfaction of a judgment for conversion, bailment,[1] sale,[2] bankruptcy,[3] will or intestacy,[4] trust,[5] a judgment *in rem*.[6] Only the first six will be considered at this time; the others are considered elsewhere in this book, at the places indicated.

By Occupancy

Occupancy is a method of acquiring ownership of a chattel which is *unowned* by acquiring possession of the property with the intention of owning it. Thus, wild animals (and fish) which are captured, dead or alive, belong to the captor. Should a captured animal escape and regain its wild state, it is again a wild animal owned by nobody. By the majority view and in the absence of statute to the contrary, a wild animal captured by a trespasser upon another person's land belongs to the landowner. The state has a public interest in wild animals within its boundaries and regulates their capture by game laws. Similarly, the federal government regulates interference with migratory birds.

Abandoned Chattels. A chattel becomes unowned by abandonment. A chattel which has been voluntarily relinquished by an owner without any intent to reclaim it and which has not been acquired by another person is abandoned personal property. Abandoned personal property is subject to acquisition by the first occupant—i.e., the person who first accomplishes its occupancy.

By Finding

Lost chattels and mislaid (misplaced) chattels are to be distinguished carefully from abandoned personal property and from each other. Abandoned personal property has been discarded intentionally and is unowned. Lost personal property describes a chattel located at a place where it was *not put* by the owner and which is *unknown* to the owner. Mislaid or misplaced personal property describes a chattel located at a place where it was put by the owner but now forgotten by him. (A placed her handbag upon a counter in a store as she examined some merchandise. She left the store forgetting to regain the handbag and she cannot remember where she left it. The property is mislaid but still belongs to A. If another customer accidentally had pushed the handbag upon the floor, or if A carelessly had dropped the bag upon the floor and was unaware of it, the property is lost.)

---

[1] Below, p. 157 ff.

[2] Below, p. 197 ff.

[3] Below, p. 514 ff.

[4] Below, p. 784 ff.

[5] Below, p. 798 ff.

[6] A judgment *in rem* affects the interests of all persons in some thing.

The loss or mislaying of personal property has *no effect upon the rightful owner's interests therein,* but it does have an effect upon the *finder's* interests therein. If the property is lost or mislaid the finder thereby acquires ownership of the property good as against everyone except the rightful owner. If lost, the finder has the right to its possession superior to everyone except the rightful owner. If mislaid, it is presumed that the rightful owner will return and reclaim the property, and the owner of the premises upon which the article was found has a right to its possession for a limited period of time, after which the finder has the right to its possession superior to everyone except the rightful owner. The finder of lost property and the owner of the premises upon which mislaid property has been found and who has possession of the property, have a legal obligation to hold the property for the rightful owner. They are in the position of an involuntary bailee[7] with a duty to exercise slight care for the preservation of the property. Often statutory provisions prescribe how the finder of lost property may perfect title to lost property in himself. If a finder knows the identity of the rightful owner, he has a duty to return the property; refusal to do so may constitute the tort of conversion and also a crime.

By Gift

A chattel may be acquired by gift. A gift is a voluntary transfer of ownership of a chattel by one person to another without consideration. It is essential to a gift that possession of the property be transferred from one person to another with the intent to transfer ownership therein to the donee, who accepts before revocation by the donor or by the donor's death. Possession need not be transferred to the donee but may be transferred to a third person for the donee; and if the donee already is in possession, a manifestation by the donor of intent thereby to make a gift to the donee is a gift. Also, if possession cannot be transferred because the property is not present or, if present, because of the article's size or weight, symbolical or constructive delivery may be made by delivery of the means of access to the property, as by the delivery of keys to the place where it is located.

A gift may be absolute or subject to a condition subsequent and may be either *inter vivos* or *causa mortis.* A gift *inter vivos* is a gift among living persons. A gift *causa mortis* is a gift among living persons in contemplation of impending death of the donor from a present illness or impending peril, subject to the condition subsequent that the donor's failure to die from *such* illness or peril shall revoke the gift.[8] Death of the donee prior to death of the donor revokes the gift. A gratuitous fraudulent transfer of personal property may be set aside by creditors of the donor, or by the trustee in bankruptcy under

---

[7] See below, p. 159.

[8] It should be noted carefully that the unofficial objective type answers to the uniform C.P.A. examination questions on gift *causa mortis* have consistently considered an intent to pass present title to the property as *not* being a required element in order to make such gift. The author respectfully disagrees.

certain circumstances.[9] A gift induced by fraud or undue influence is revocable by the donor.

By Accession

The increase in a chattel by what it produces or by the addition to it of another chattel so as to become a permanent part thereof is called "accession." The increase of animals by birth of their young and the increase in the value of chattels by labor or materials are illustrations of accession. There may be accession of real, as well as of personal, property, as by the erection of a building upon land, the building becoming a part of the land. Accession may change the identity of the original property.[10]

By Confusion

When the chattels of more than one owner are intermingled so that the respective chattels of each are indistinguishable from the others there is "confusion of goods." The storage of grain of various owners in the same enclosure or bin in a warehouse, and the mixture of oil of various owners in the same tank or other container, are examples of confusion. Fungible goods are the usual subject of confusion; they are goods of which any unit is, by nature or usage of trade, the equivalent of any other like unit,[11] such as oil or wine in a vat, grain in a bin, cotton or wool in a heap.

The legal effect of confusion depends upon whether confusion occurred by consent of the parties, by tortious conduct, by innocent mistake of fact, or by inevitable accident, and whether the proportionate share of each owner in the mass can be ascertained. Confusion by consent of the parties causes the owners to become owners or tenants in common of the mass and to have an undivided interest therein to the extent of the contribution of each; they share proportionately any damage or loss to the mass. A similar result occurs, by the majority view, when confusion is caused by an innocent mistake of fact. Confusion by tortious conduct may occur either intentionally or negligently. If intentionally, generally the property of the tortfeasor is forfeited and transferred to the innocent owner, unless the tortfeasor can prove that proportionate division of the mass can be made between them, in which case the owners are owners in common of the mass. In other words, as between the intentionally wrongful and the innocent owners the innocent owner shall not suffer, and the intentionally wrongful owner shall not profit, from the confusion. If confusion is caused by a party's negligence, while there is conflict, in general, the negligent party must sustain any loss caused by his negligent conduct. However, if the negligent party has a fiduciary obligation to other persons with respect to

---

[9] See below, p. 525.

[10] For priorities among security interests in accessions, see Secured Transactions, below, pp. 446–47.

[11] See UCC 1–201(17).

certain goods which he negligently confuses with his own, his negligence usually results in the forfeiture of his goods.

By Satisfaction of a Judgment for Conversion

Conversion is a tortious interference with another person's right to immediate possession of chattels and may be defined[12] as a person's unprivileged (unpermitted) act in interfering with possession of a chattel inconsistent with another person's right to its immediate possession and inconsistent with his right to control and dominion over the chattel. Conversion alone does not disturb a person's interests in a chattel. He has a right of action for repossession of the chattel, and he also has an alternative right of action against the tortfeasor for conversion of the chattel and may recover its value at the time of the latter's conversion. Rendition of a judgment for conversion and its satisfaction generallly causes the plaintiff's title to the property to be transferred to the defendant. In a few states rendition of the judgment alone, irrespective of its satisfaction, causes such a transfer. Generally, transfer relates back to the time of conversion by the defendant.

---

[12] See below, p. 166, ftn. 18, for a fuller discussion of conversion.

Chapter 11

THE TRANSFEREE GETS ONLY WHAT THE TRANSFEROR HAS RULE, WITH EXCEPTIONS

A person can transfer only what he has. Very important exceptions to this rule occur in the Code areas of Sales of goods, and negotiable paper consisting of Negotiable Documents of Title, Negotiable Instruments under Commercial Paper, and Investment Securities, where the transferor has the *power* to transfer more than what he has. Accordingly, the *transferee gets only what the transferor has or has power to transfer*, hereafter called the Transferee/Transferor rule with its "power" exceptions.

***Under the Code on Sales of goods*, the transferee/transferor rule applies. Exceptions illustrating the transferor's *power to transfer more than he has* are: estoppel; factors; voidable title transfers; and entrusting goods to a merchant who deals in goods of that kind. (1) *For Estoppel.* There must be a holding out of a material fact, and a material change of position in reasonable reliance on the holding out. (2) *Factors* generally are bailees in possession of goods with authority to sell them. By statute in many states, a purchaser of goods from a factor, without knowledge of the factor's violation of his authority, obtains the title of the person who entrusted the goods to the factor. (3) Under *voidable title transfers*, when goods have been delivered by a seller to a buyer who obtains a voidable title, the latter has the power to transfer a good non-voidable title to the goods to a "good faith purchaser for value." (4) For *entrusting goods to a merchant*, any entrusting of possession of goods to a merchant who deals in goods of that kind gives him power to transfer all rights of the entruster to a "buyer in ordinary course of business." Consideration, but not a past debt, is value for a buyer in ordinary course of business.**

Negotiable Paper under the Code

Negotiable Document of Title (UCC 7)	Negotiable Instrument (UCC 3)	Investment Security (UCC 8)
(Duly Negotiated Holder)	(Holder in Due Course)	(Bona Fide Purchaser)
Bills of lading and warehouse receipts for shipped or warehoused goods	Checks, drafts, negotiable promissory notes, and certificates of deposit	Certificates of stock or bonds
To order or to bearer (past debt is *not* value for the *purchase* of a document)	To order or to bearer (past debt *is* value)	Negotiable per se (past debt *is* value)

Under the Code on negotiable paper, **the transferee/transferor rule with its exceptions of the transferor's power apply. If the paper is not negotiable, the transferee gets only what his transferor has. However, if the paper is *negotiable,* not only would the transferee get what his transferor has but, also, if the negotiable paper were properly indorsed and delivered to a holder who takes it in good faith, for value, without notice of any defense against, or claim to, it on the part of any person, the holder would own the paper and all rights thereon to the goods if it is a *negotiable document of title,* to the payment of money if it is a *negotiable instrument,* and to the corporate shares if it is a certificate of stock as an *investment security.* For a document of title or an instrument to be negotiable it must have the key words of negotiability indicating that the goods are deliverable, or that the instrument is payable, "to order" of a named person or "to bearer." An investment security need not have these words; it is negotiable *per se.***

A document of title, **(e.g., a bill of lading or a warehouse receipt) evidences a receipt of *goods* for shipment or storage. *If a "negotiable document of title" is "duly negotiated" to a holder, he acquires the title to the document and to the goods represented by it.* It is duly negotiated if it is (1) a negotiable document of title (2) properly indorsed (if not a "bearer" document) and delivered (3) to a holder, who purchases it (4) for value (consideration; a past debt for the *purchase* of a document is not value for "duly negotiated") and (5) in good faith without notice of any defense against, or claim to, it on the part of any person, and (6) in the regular course of business or financing. If the negotiable document of title is not "duly negotiated," the transferee/transferor rule applies.**

An instrument **is a paper promising or ordering the payment of *money. If a "negotiable instrument" is negotiated to a "holder in due course," he takes the instrument free from all claims to it on the part of any person and all personal defenses of any party to the instrument with whom the holder has not dealt.* He is a holder in due course if he is a "holder" of a "negotiable instrument," and took it in due course by taking it: (1) for value (consideration and a past debt constitute value) (2) in good faith (3) without notice that the instrument is overdue or has been dishonored or of any defense against, or claim to, the**

instrument on the part of any person. If he is not a holder, or has not taken it in due course, the transferee/transferor rule applies.

An investment security **is concerned with** ***certificates of stock and bonds,*** **called "securities," which are negotiable** ***per se. A "bona fide purchaser" of a certificate of stock or bond investment security in addition to acquiring the rights of a purchaser also acquires the security free of any adverse claim.*** **He is a "bona fide purchaser" if the security is properly indorsed (if not a "bearer" security) and delivered to him as a holder, purchasing it for value (consideration and a past debt constitute value) and in good faith without notice of any adverse claim to the security.**

A "holder" is a person in possession of the negotiable paper which flows to him either originally or by indorsement. If the negotiable paper is issued to "bearer," no indorsement is required because the holder is the bearer and the paper flows to him. If the person to whom the paper flows indorses it with just his signature, the paper now flows to "bearer," and anyone who possesses it is a holder.

The Concept

An owner of personal property continues as its owner until he disposes of it or is deprived of it by law. If the owner transfers his ownership, he transfers to the transferee only the interest that he has in the property. Although the transferee gets only what his transferor has, there are very important exceptions to this rule when the transferor has the *power* to transfer more than he has. Accordingly, *the transferee gets only what the transferor has or has power to transfer,* hereafter called the Transferee/Transferor rule with its "power" exceptions. (O owns a horse. If O sells it to B, B gets O's title to the horse. Instead, if T steals the horse from O and sells it to B, a good faith purchaser for value,[1] B gets what T his transferor had and, since there was *no transfer* from O to T, T got nothing from O and neither did B, T's transferee. O still has title to the horse.)

This concept applies also under the Code on Sales of goods (Article 2), and also in the various areas concerned with negotiable paper, such as Negotiable

[1] The familiar term "bona fide purchaser for value" is a purchaser for value in good faith, without notice of any adverse claim. "Bona fide" means good faith. In the law of Sales under the Code, he is called a "good faith purchaser for value."

Under UCC 1–201: "(33) 'Purchaser' means a person who takes by purchase"; "(32) 'Purchase' includes taking by sale, discount, negotiation, mortgage, pledge, lien, issue or re-issue, gift or any other voluntary transaction creating an interest in property"; "(44) 'Value'. Except as otherwise provided with respect to negotiable instruments and bank collections (Sections 3–303, 4–208 and 4–209) a person gives 'value' for rights if he acquires them

(a) in return for a binding commitment to extend credit or for the extension of immediately available credit whether or not drawn upon and whether or not a charge-back is provided for in the event of difficulties in collection; or
(b) as security for or in total or partial satisfaction of a pre-existing claim; or
(c) by accepting delivery pursuant to a pre-existing contract for purchase; or
(d) generally, in return for any consideration sufficient to support a simple contract."

Documents of Title (Article 7), Commercial Paper (Article 3), and Investment Securities (Article 8). As each area is discussed in the order indicated, it is important to remember that the approach is: first, application of the rule that the transferee gets only what the transferor has; second, application of the transferor's power to transfer more than he has as an exception to this rule.

Goods Under the Code on Sales

The Transferee/Transferor Rule. Under the Code on Sales of goods "A purchaser of goods acquires all title which his transferor had or had power to transfer except that a purchaser of a limited interest acquires rights only to the extent of the interest purchased. . . ."[2] If the transferor does not have title to goods, his *power* to transfer a good title under certain circumstances becomes of utmost importance. *Except* for estoppel, Factors Acts, transfer of voidable title, and entrusting goods to a merchant, which will be discussed in that order, *only the owner of an interest can transfer that interest.* A person who is the owner of goods continues as such owner until he, or his authorized agent, transfers the title to the goods. A person who is not the owner of goods, and who has no authority to transfer title to such goods, can transfer no better title than the one he has. *The buyer gets no better title than the title of the seller.*

Transfer of Title by Estoppel. In our previous discussion of estoppel[3] we learned that when one person represents or "holds out" to another person a material fact and the other person changes his position materially to his prejudice in reasonable reliance on the holding out, the first person is prohibited in law or "estopped" to deny what he had asserted previously. *The owner of goods may be precluded, i.e., estopped, from setting up his title to such goods because of his conduct, which has misled an innocent person to purchase the goods.* (B asks O whether T is the owner of a certain horse in T's possession. O informs B that T is the owner, when in fact O is the owner. In reliance on the information received from O, B innocently purchased the horse from T. Although T did not have title to the horse or any authority to sell such horse and B would acquire only whatever title T had, nevertheless O has held out that T owned the horse and B has changed his position materially in reliance on the holding-out by purchasing the horse from T. T is the apparent owner and O, therefore, is estopped to set up his title as against B. If B had bought the horse from T *before* O had informed B that T was the owner, then, since B had not relied on O's statement, estoppel does not apply, and O retains title to the horse.)

Factors. A "factor" usually is a bailee in possession of goods with authority to sell them.[4] Under the laws in many of the states, called "Factors Acts," innocent persons who purchase goods from factors without knowledge of any

[2] UCC 2–403(1).

[3] See above, pp. 33–34.

[4] See below, p. 549.

violation of the authority of such factors obtain the title of the person who entrusted such goods to the factors.[5] Goods are sent to a factor "on consignment," signifying a bailment with authority to sell the goods, title remaining in the seller.[6]

Voidable Title Transfers. *When goods have been delivered by a seller under a transaction of purchase, the purchaser has the power to transfer a good title to the goods to a good faith purchaser for value.* It should be noted very carefully that the goods must be *delivered* only by the *initial seller* to the *initial purchaser.* A "voidable title" is a title which is subject to a power of avoidance, and the sale of a voidable title to a good faith purchaser for value without notice of such power of avoidance terminates such power as against such purchaser. (S fraudulently induces O to sell goods to S, creating a voidable contract voidable at O's election. O delivers the goods to S, who then sells and delivers them to B, a good faith purchaser for value without notice of the fraud. B has O's title to the goods, and O cannot assert any power of avoidance as against B.)[7] Exercise of the power of avoidance *before* a subsequent sale to a good faith purchaser for value revests the title in the person exercising such power of avoidance and, therefore, there is no voidable title to transfer. (S fraudulently induces O to sell and deliver a horse to S. O avoids the contract and *then* S sells and delivers the horse to B, a good faith purchaser for value. O has title to the horse because S has no voidable title to transfer. Note that, if O had delivered the horse to S who is a *merchant-dealer in horses,* B would acquire O's title to the horse under the rule concerned with entrusting goods to a merchant.[8] Note also that, if S is *not* a merchant-dealer in horses, if O had delivered the horse *and a bill of sale* to S and after avoidance S still possessed the horse *and* the bill of sale, S would be the apparent owner and title to the horse would be acquired by B.) It should be noted very carefully that a person with a voidable title has power to transfer a *good* title to a good faith purchaser for value. The Code[9] indicates the following ways by which a voidable title to goods may be created, although this does not preclude a power of avoidance arising by principles in other branches of the law (e.g., duress, coercion, undue influence in the law of Contracts):

1. The transferor was deceived as to the identity of the purchaser. (O, the owner, sold and delivered his horse to B, who misrepresented that he was C. B then sold and delivered the horse to D, a good faith purchaser for value. D now has title to the horse.)
2. The delivery was in exchange for a check, which is later dishonored. (O, the owner, sold and delivered his horse to B, who gave O a check for the purchase

[5] See Agency, below, p. 598.

[6] This is not the same as a "sale on approval" contemplating later transfer of title to the buyer, and it is not the same as a "sale or return" whereby title thereby passes by sale to the buyer with the option in the buyer to revest title in the seller. See below, pp. 215–16.

[7] An infant's voidable contract for the purchase of goods is similarly affected under the law of Contracts. See above, pp. 13–15.

[8] See below, pp. 149–50.

[9] UCC 2–403(1).

price. B sold and delivered the horse to C, a good faith purchaser for value. B's check subsequently was dishonored. C has title to the horse.)

3. It was agreed that the transaction was to be a "cash sale," i.e., simultaneous transfer of title and possession in exchange for the price immediately.
4. The delivery was procured through fraud punishable as larcenous under the criminal law.

Entrusting Goods to a Merchant Who Deals in Goods of That Kind. In the absence of statute to the contrary, the mere entrusting of possession of goods by one person to a non-merchant without authority to sell such goods does not of itself give to the non-merchant any power to transfer the entruster's title to the goods. By "entrusting" is meant *any* delivery of goods and *any* acquiescence in retention of possession by another.[10] (A rents his electric saw to B. B sells the saw to C. C does not acquire A's title to the saw.) The mere entrusting without authority to deal with the goods is not such a sufficient representation of ownership or of authority as to mislead third persons that such ownership or authority exists.[11] However, "any entrusting of possession of goods to a *merchant who deals in goods of that kind* gives him *power* to transfer all rights of the entruster to a *buyer in ordinary course of business*."[12] (Author's italics.) A merchant-dealer has apparent ownership of, and inherent agency power[13] to sell, the kind of goods in his possession in which he is dealing, and any entrusting of that kind of goods to him places him in a position to mislead persons who buy in ordinary course from him. " 'A buyer in ordinary course of business' means a person who in good faith and without knowledge that the sale to him is in violation of the ownership rights or security interest of a third party in the goods *buys in ordinary course from a person in the business of selling goods of that kind* but does not include a pawnbroker. All persons who sell minerals or the like (including oil and gas) at wellhead or minehead shall be deemed to be persons in the business of selling goods of that kind. 'Buying' may be for cash or by exchange of other property or on secured or unsecured credit and includes receiving goods or documents of title under a preexisting contract for sale but *does not include a transfer in bulk or as security for or in total or partial satisfaction of a money debt*." (Author's italics.)[14] (O entrusts his watch for repair to J, a jewelry store which sells and repairs watches. J's sale of the watch to B, a buyer in ordinary course of business, tranfers O's title to the watch to B, irrespective of whether J sells as the owner or as the agent of O.) (A buys an electric stove from D, a dealer in kitchen equipment, A to pick up the stove later. D sells and delivers the stove to B, a buyer in ordinary

[10] UCC 2–403(3): " 'Entrusting' includes any delivery and any acquiescence in retention of possession regardless of any condition expressed between the parties to the delivery or acquiescence and regardless of whether the procurement of the entrusting or the possessor's disposition of the goods have been such as to be larcenous under the criminal law."

[11] See Agency, below, pp. 597–98.

[12] UCC 2–403(2).

[13] See Agency, below, pp. 598–99.

[14] UCC 1–201 (9).

course of business. B has obtained A's title to the stove.) The rule extends even to a warehouseman of fungible goods, also in the business of buying and selling fungible goods, who unauthorizedly sells fungible goods entrusted to him for storage, even though a negotiable warehouse receipt is outstanding.[15] When other Articles of the Code are applicable to a transaction, they govern. Accordingly, the rights of other purchasers of goods and of lien creditors are governed by the Articles on Secured Transactions (Article 9), Bulk Transfers (Article 6) and Documents of Title (Article 7).

Negotiable Paper under the Code

The Transferee/Transferor Rule. We have just discussed the transferee/transferor rule with its exceptions reflecting the transferor's power to transfer more than he has as they relate to the sale of *goods* under the Code. The transferee/transferor rule with its exceptions also applies under the Code to *paper* representing goods shipped or stored (Documents of Title, Article 7), paper representing a promise or order to pay money (Commercial Paper, Article 3), and certificates of stock and bonds (Investment Securities, Article 8). An extremely important distinction is to be drawn between *negotiable* paper and *non-negotiable* paper. The reason is that there is much reluctance by a person to take paper *representing* goods, money, or corporate shares rather than to *receive* those goods, money, and shares when all he gets is what his transferor has. In order to encourage persons to take such paper, the Code provides that if the paper is *negotiable* not only would the transferee get what his transferor has but, also, if the negotiable paper were properly indorsed and delivered to a holder who takes it in good faith, for value, without notice of any defense against, or claim to, it on the part of any person, the holder would own the paper and all rights thereon to the goods, to the payment of money, or to the corporate shares. *This illustrates the transferor's power to transfer more than he has.* Such a holder has different names under Articles 7,3, and 8 because of the detailed differences of subject matter under those Articles. Under Article 7, he is a holder to whom the document of title has been "duly negotiated"; under Article 3, he is a "holder in due course"; and under Article 8, he is a "bona fide purchaser."

For a document of title or an instrument to be negotiable it must have the key words of negotiability indicating that it is payable, or the goods deliverable, "to order" of a named person or "to bearer." An investment security need not have these words; it is negotiable *per se* (of itself). Accordingly, the first question is whether the paper is negotiable, and the next question is has the negotiable document of title been "duly negotiated" to a holder, is the holder of a negotiable instrument a "holder in due course," and is the holder of an investment security a "bona fide purchaser." If the paper is not negotiable, or being negotiable the holder is not one of these three persons, then only the transferee/transferor rule applies.

---

[15] UCC 7–205. See below, pp. 176–77.

Negotiable Documents of Title. A document evidencing the receipt of goods for shipment issued by a person engaged in the business of transporting or forwarding goods is called a "bill of lading". A document evidencing the receipt of goods for storage issued by a person engaged in the business of storing goods for hire is called a "warehouse receipt." Inasmuch as these documents represent the goods shipped or stored and are a symbol of title to such goods, they are called "documents of title."

Documents of title may be either negotiable or non-negotiable. A document of title is negotiable: if, by its terms, the goods are to be delivered either *to the order* of a named person, or *to bearer;* or, where recognized in overseas trade, if it runs to a named person or assigns. Any other document is non-negotiable. A bill of lading which states that the goods are *consigned* to a named person is not made negotiable by a provision that the goods are to be delivered only against a written order signed by the same, or another, named person. Also, "Deliverable on proper indorsement and surrender of this receipt" does not cause the document to be negotiable, although such a provision is often included by bailees in their documents in order to ensure that they receive the non-negotiable document proving that delivery of the goods has been made. A document of title is either negotiable or non-negotiable at the time of its inception, and the indorsement of a non-negotiable document cannot thereby make it negotiable. A negotiable bill of lading often is called an "order bill."

Under the Code, "a transferee of a document, whether negotiable or non-negotiable, to whom the document has been delivered but not duly negotiated, acquires the title and rights which his transferor had or had actual authority to convey."[16] However, ". . . a holder to whom a negotiable document of title has been *duly negotiated* acquires thereby: (a) title to the document; (b) title to the goods. . . ."[17]

The negotiable document of title is "duly negotiated" if it is a:

1. Negotiable document of title,
2. Properly indorsed (if not a "bearer" document) and delivered,
3. To a holder, who *purchases* it,
4. For value (consideration; a past debt for the *purchase* of a document is not value for "duly negotiated"),
5. In good faith without notice of any defense against, or claim to, it on the part of any person, and
6. In regular course of business or financing.[18]

(S delivers goods to C, a carrier, for shipment to S in X city. C issues a bill of lading in favor of S. S indorses the bill of lading with his signature only, T steals it and sells it for value to M, a merchant, who takes it in good faith without notice of S's claim to the bill. Both S and M demand the goods from C. If the bill is non-negotiable, the transferee/transferor rule applies and M gets

---

[16] UCC 7–504(1).

[17] UCC 7–502(1)(a)(b). (Author's italics.)

[18] For explanation, see below, p. 189.

only what T has. Since T got nothing from S because there was no *transfer* from S to T, S prevails. If the bill were negotiable, since the bill was properly indorsed by S with his signature only, the bill was delivered to M irrespective of by whom, and M paid value and took the bill in good faith and without notice of S's claim to the bill, the bill was "duly negotiated" to M and he will get the goods from C.) A more detailed discussion will occur later in the chapter on Documents of Title.[19]

Negotiable Instruments. Article 3 of the Code on Commercial Paper is concerned with a certain kind of paper promising or ordering the payment of money, e.g., checks, promissory notes. It may be a "negotiable instrument," or a non-negotiable instrument. Under the Code, if a person is not a "holder in due course," the transferee/transferor rule applies and he takes the instrument subject to "all valid claims to it on the part of any person" and subject to "personal defenses" assertable against him.[20] If he is a holder in due course, "he takes the instrument free from (1) all claims to it on the part of any person, and (2) all defenses of any party to the instrument with whom the holder has not dealt. . . ."[21]

A person is a holder in due course if:

1. He is a holder.
2. He took the instrument in due course by taking it: (a) for value (consideration and a past debt constitute value), (b) in good faith, (c) without notice that the instrument is overdue or has been dishonored or of any defense against, or claim to, the instrument on the part of any person.[22]

(Dan draws a check on his bank payable to the order of Peter. Peter stole the check form Dan, indorsed it and sold it for value to Tom, who took it in good faith without notice of Dan's claim to the check. Dan ordered the bank not to pay the check, and Tom seeks to hold Dan liable on the check. Under the transferee/transferor rule, Tom got what Peter his transferor had which was nothing because there was no transfer from Dan to Peter, and Dan is not liable to Tom. However, the check is a negotiable instrument, Peter's indorsement of the check and its delivery to Tom made Tom a holder, and since Tom took the check for value, in good faith without notice of Dan's claim to the check, Tom is a holder in due course and Dan is liable to him on the check.) A more detailed discussion will occur later in the Part on Commercial Paper.[23]

Investment Securities. Article 8 of the Code on Investment Securities is concerned with certificates of stock and bonds, called "securities," which are negotiable *per se.* Under the Code, a "bona fide purchaser" is a "purchaser for

[19] See below, pp. 192–94.

[20] UCC 3–306.

[21] UCC 3–305(1)(2).

[22] UCC 3–302(1).

[23] See below, p. 336 ff.

value in good faith and without notice of any adverse claim who takes delivery of a certificated security in bearer form or in registered form issued or indorsed to him or in blank. . . ."[24] "A bona fide purchaser in addition to acquiring the rights of a purchaser also acquires the security free of any adverse claim. A purchaser of a limited interest acquires rights only to the extent of the interest purchased."[25] Here, similar to the above discussion, concerning a "duly negotiated" negotiable document of title to a holder and the "holder in due course" of a negotiable instrument, the investment security is negotiated to a "bona fide purchaser" if the security is properly indorsed (if not a "bearer" security) and delivered to a holder who purchases it for value[26] and in good faith without notice of any adverse claim to the security. (C corporation issues a certificate of stock in the name of S shareholder. S indorses the certificate with his signature only, T steals it and sells it for value to P, a purchaser who takes it in good faith without notice of S's claim to the certificate. Since the certificate was properly indorsed by S with his signature only, the certificate was delivered to P irrespective of by whom, and P paid value and took the certificate in good faith without notice of S's claim to the certificate, P is a "bona fide purchaser" and owns the certificate and the shares represented thereby.) A more detailed discussion will occur later in that portion of Corporations dealing with the transfer of shares of stock.[27]

It should be noted very carefully that, in all negotiable paper, the protected person, be he a holder to whom the negotiable document of title has been duly negotiated, a holder in due course, or a bona fide purchaser, *must be a "holder."* Under the Code a "'Holder' means a person who is in possession of a document of title or an instrument or investment security drawn, issued or indorsed to him or to his order or to bearer or in blank."[28] If the negotiable paper names a person to whom it flows initially, that person must indorse it so as to flow in turn to the next person who takes it, otherwise the latter is not a holder. (C's negotiable bill of lading names S as the consignee. S must indorse it so that it flows to B, his transferee, for B to be a holder. If T stole it and forged S's indorsement, since S has not indorsed it nobody subsequently can become a holder because the bill does not flow to him; it still flows to S. The same applies to a check payable to P who must indorse it for his transferee to become a holder of the check, and to an investment security which names S as the owner of the security who must indorse it for his transferee to be a holder of the security.) If the negotiable paper is issued to "bearer," no indorsement is required because the holder is the bearer and the paper flows to him. If the person to whom the paper initially flows indorses it with just his signature, the paper now flows to "bearer," and anyone who possesses it is a holder.

---

[24] UCC 8–302.

[25] UCC 8–301(2)(3).

[26] Consideration and past debt constitute value.

[27] See below, pp. 23–25.

[28] UCC 1–201(20).

PROBLEMS

1. B was on a business trip and, while packing his belongings in a hotel room where he was staying, he overlooked a brief case which he had left in the closet.
   (a) Who owns the brief case?
   (b) A maid found the brief case. As between the maid and the hotel, who is entitled to possession of the brief case?
2. (a) Is a promise to make a gift enforceable in law? (Give a legal reason to support your answer.) (Former C.P.A. Examination question)
   (b) What elements or factors must be found to make a transaction a gift of personal property? (Former C.P.A. Examination question)
   (c) H is ill in bed and knows he apparently is about to die from pneumonia. He handed to W, his wife, the keys to his safe deposit box in a bank located in a nearby city, telling her that the box contained H's valuables and that, inasmuch as he was about to die from pneumonia, W could have it all as hers, but if he recovered from the illness he wanted the valuables back.
      (1) Who owns the contents of the safe deposit box?
      (2) H recovered from pneumonia but died a few weeks later in an automobile accident. Who owns the contents of the safe deposit box?
3. A sold and delivered goods to B pursuant to B's fraudulent inducement. B sold and delivered the goods to C, a good faith purchaser for value without notice of B's fraud on A. A then discovers the fraud. Can A repossess the goods? Explain.
4. B stole goods from A and pledged them with C, who was innocent of the theft, as security for a loan. On B's failure to repay the loan, C sold the goods to D at public auction. Does A have any right to the goods? Explain.
5. O stored fungible goods in W's warehouse and obtained from W a negotiable warehouse receipt to the order of O. W buys and sells the same kind of fungible goods.
   (1) T stole the warehouse receipt from O, forged O's blank indorsement on the receipt and sold and delivered it for value to B, a purchaser innocent of the theft and a retailer of such goods. B tendered the receipt to W and, at the same time as O, demanded the goods from W. Who will prevail, and why?
   (2) O indorsed the receipt in blank, T stole it and sold and delivered it to B, a purchaser innocent of the theft in satisfaction of T's debt to B who is a retailer of such goods. B tendered the receipt to W and, at the same time as O, demanded the goods from W. Who will prevail and why?
   (3) W misrepresented that he owned the goods and unauthorizedly sold and delivered the goods for value to X, a retailer of such goods. The events in (2) above later having occurred, O and B now demand the goods from X. Who will prevail and why if X is a good faith purchaser of the goods for a past debt owing to him by W?

SOME PREVIOUS C.P.A. LAW EXAMINATION QUESTIONS AND AUTHOR'S MODEL ANSWERS

MAY, 1968

Number 8

a. You were requested by Charles to prepare a net worth statement for him as of December 31, 1967, which will be furnished to his bank. You must determine whether or not a truck having a fair market value of $20,000 should be included in Charles's net worth. Charles was in the trucking business as a sole proprietor during 1967. Filmore, Charles's uncle, looked upon Charles as his favorite nephew and wished to help Charles in business. Filmore decided to present Charles with a new truck which Charles needed but lacked the funds to purchase.

Filmore invited Charles to lunch and told him about the intent to make a gift of the truck to him. In fact, he told Charles he had hoped to give him the truck right after lunch, but delivery was not to be made to Filmore until the following week. To evidence his intent Filmore wrote the following on a piece of paper:

> "I hereby acknowledge my intent to make a gift of a new truck to my favorite nephew, Charles. Therefore, for good and valuable consideration, consisting of my love and respect for him, I irrevocably promise to deliver said truck to Charles as soon as I receive it.
>
> *Daniel Filmore.*"

Filmore had two waiters sign the paper as witnesses and gave it to Charles.

Filmore later learned that sometime before the luncheon Charles had been complaining to other relatives that "Uncle Filmore is a tightwad and a cheapskate." Consequently, Filmore refused to turn the new truck over to Charles.

Charles asserts that a valid *inter vivos* gift was made at the luncheon or, in the alternative, that his uncle was equally bound by the promise he made.

(1) What are the requirements necessary to establish a valid *inter vivos* gift?
(2) Did Filmore make a gift to Charles at the luncheon? Explain.
(3) Did Filmore make a legally binding contract with Charles for delivery of the truck? Explain.
(4) Assuming that the truck had actually been delivered to Filmore prior to the luncheon, that he turned the keys over to Charles at the luncheon and that Charles drove the truck back to his own place of business after the luncheon, would Charles be entitled to the truck? Explain.

b. Pierre, owner of Ritz Restaurant, Inc., had in his possession several valuable items which wealthy patrons had lost or left in the restaurant. The total value of these items was in excess of $5,000.

Ritz Restaurant's financial position was poor. Consequently, Pierre decided to pledge the items in question as collateral for a loan. He took the items to Friendly Finance Company and obtained a loan of $3,500 on the property pledged.

(1) What is the legal relationship and duty of Pierre of Ritz Restaurant, Inc. to the original owners of the property in question? Explain.
(2) As between the original owners of the property and Friendly Finance Company, who is entitled to the property? Explain.

Answer

8.a.(1) (a) A donor who is legally competent to make a gift.
(b) The donor's intent to make a gift and transfer ownership to the donee.
(c) Actual or symbolic delivery of the chattel by the donor to the donee or to a third person for the donee.
(d) Acceptance of the gift by the donee.
(e) No consideration is furnished to the donor.
(f) The gift must be irrevocable, except in the case of a gift *causa mortis*. (p. 141)

(2) No. It is necessary to a gift that the chattel be delivered by the donor. Here, Filmore did not deliver the truck. The paper executed by him at the luncheon was not a symbolic delivery of the truck; it was solely a promise to make a gift. (p. 141)

(3) No. A promise is unenforceable unless it is supported by consideration. Love and respect are not consideration. Since Filmore's promise requested nothing in exchange, there is no consideration and his promise is not a contract. (pp. 43, 49)

(4) Yes. Symbolic delivery of a chattel occurs by delivery of the means of access to the chattel. Here, Filmore's delivery of the keys to the truck to Charles constituted a delivery of the truck to Charles. Since the other elements necessary to make a gift are present, a gift of the truck has been made to Charles and he has title and the right to its possession. (p. 141)

8.b.(1) Pierre is an involuntary bailee. As a finder and involuntary bailee, he has the duty, imposed upon him by law, to hold the items for the rightful owners, and to exercise slight care for their preservation. He has no right to pledge the items.

(2) The original owners. Loss or mislaying of chattels by the owners does not deprive them of their title and paramount right to possession. While the finder acquires various interests in such chattels, such interests are subordinate to that of the owners. The same is true of the finder's transferee.

Part Three: Personal Property

C. Bailments

Chapter 12

NATURE AND SCOPE OF BAILMENTS

Special Note Regarding "Bailments." The AICPA list of legal areas for examination purposes does not specifically include the subject of "Bailments." However, the subject of Bailments is concerned not only with the storage and transportation of goods, but also with documents of title (bills of lading and warehouse receipts) issued for stored or shipped bailed goods, secured interests in bailed goods, the sale of bailed goods, and with insurable interests in bailed goods, all of which are frequent subjects of examination questions. Because of this impact of bailed goods in these various transactions, a brief discussion of the basics and background of bailments for better student comprehension is included here.

Bailment occurs by (1) delivery (2) of goods by a bailor to a bailee (3) pursuant to an agreement that the goods are to be returned to the bailor or pursuant to his direction in accordance with the bailment agreement. An "involuntary bailment" occurs when there is imposed by law a legal duty to care for goods possessed by a person who is not a bailee, e.g., a finder. "Ordinary" or "private" bailees are liable only for their *negligence* causing damage to bailed goods. There are three kinds of ordinary bailments—mutual-benefit bailment, sole benefit of the bailor, and sole benefit of the bailee. There are two kinds of "public" or "special" bailees—innkeepers and common carriers—both being *absolutely liable* for damage to the bailed goods, although there must be a shipper-carrier relationship between the common carrier and the shipper, which occurs when goods are delivered to the carrier for *immediate* shipment; if not for immediate shipment, there is only an ordinary mutual-benefit bailment with liability only for negligence. Liability of a pub-

lic bailee, whether absolute or for negligence, cannot be waived. Exceptions to absolute liability are for damage caused by an act of God, act of a public enemy, act of the shipper, inherent nature of the goods, or when goods are seized pursuant to legal process.

A bailee's right to possession and use of bailed goods is determined by the bailment agreement. Unless otherwise agreed, the bailee's duty is to deliver the goods to the bailor or pursuant to his direction, or to a person whose right to possession is superior to that of the bailor, and for misdelivery or deviation from permitted use he is absolutely liable for damages for breach of contract or for the tort of conversion. A lien is a legal right in the property of another as security for the performance of an obligation. A bailee has a specific, *possessory* lien on the bailed goods for services, labor, skill, or materials rendered to them, and his voluntary surrender of possession to the bailor terminates the lien.

A bailment terminates if: its agreed purpose is accomplished, the bailment period expires, the bailed goods are so damaged as to prevent accomplishment of the bailment's purpose, or the bailee materially breaches the bailment agreement.

SECTION I. BAILMENT DISTINGUISHED FROM OTHER LEGAL RELATIONSHIPS

A knowledge of the law of bailments is necessary in the marketing and storage of goods. It indicates the rights and the duties involved in the handling of goods for other persons. Bailments is concerned with goods and that the bailee, that is the person to whom the goods have been delivered, may be a person engaged in the business of transporting or storing goods, e.g., a carrier or warehouseman, or a person not in such a business, e.g., a bank holding securities to assure payment on a loan or a person to whom a truck or machinery has been rented. Documents of title, to be discussed later under Chapter 13, are issued by persons engaged in the business of transporting or storing goods, and such documents evidence that the holder is entitled to receive, hold, and dispose of such documents and the goods they cover. It is because of this difference in bailees that the subject of bailments is treated in two parts, Chapter 12 dealing with bailments without reference to documents of title, and Chapter 13 dealing with documents of title representing bailed goods for transportation or storage. Bailments without reference to documents of title do not come within the purview of the Code, but documents of title do, and, therefore, two fields of law are involved. This must be kept in mind because of the difference in meaning of similar terminology used in each field of law. For example, the words "goods" and "bailee" have different meanings in each field of law. Under Chapter 12, "goods" has a much broader meaning than under documents of title in Chapter 13, which is concerned with a limited kind of goods as a subject of documents of title. Similarly, "bailee" has a much broader meaning in Chapter 12 than under documents of title in Chapter 13, which is concerned with a more limited class of persons who are engaged in the business of transporting and storing goods and who issue documents of title for such goods.

Definition

Bailment is a legal relationship occurring when there is a delivery of goods by a bailor to a bailee pursuant to an agreement whereby the goods are to be returned to the bailor or pursuant to his direction in accordance with the bailment agreement. Leased equipment is an illustration. Consideration is not required because the bailment may be gratuitous. However, bailment duties may be implied by law without agreement or delivery, creating an *involuntary bailment.* For example, the law imposes a duty on the finder of lost or mislaid goods to hold such goods as an "involuntary bailee" for the benefit of the owner.[1] Delivery may be actual or constructive, as when goods are not capable of manual delivery because of their physical size.

Delivery of goods by a master to his servant for an agency purpose does not create a bailment, because the servant has "custody"[2] and not possession of the goods. The word "goods" generally means tangible movable things, called "chattels."[3] In the law of bailments, goods include money only when treated as a commodity and not as a medium of exchange, and also includes documents and instruments[4] whether representing goods (e.g., bills of lading and warehouse receipts representing goods) or representing intangibles (e.g., certificates of stock representing shares in a corporation, and negotiable and non-negotiable instruments representing rights of action, such as checks, promissory notes, insurance policies, and savings bank books). The bailment agreement may be informal and need not be in writing. However, an agreement *to make* a bailment is unenforceable unless it has the requisites of a contract.

Bailment Distinguished

A bailment should be distinguished from certain other legal terms:

1. A Present Sale and a Contract to Sell. A present sale[5] effects the present transfer of title, and a contract to sell[6] contemplates the future transfer of

[1] It should be noted carefully that the unofficial objective type answers to the uniform C.P.A. examination questions on bailments often have considered an involuntary bailment to be a bailment, meaning that it is a bailment by operation of law.

[2] "Custody is not the same as possession in connection with chattels. By custody is meant physical control over the chattel in order to care for it or to have charge of it for someone, without any claim to interests in the chattel adverse to another. An illustration is goods held by a servant for his master. By possession is meant physical control over the chattel together with a claimed interest in the chattel to retain physical control over it to the exclusion of others, in other words, a physical control with a property right to retain such physical control." Joseph L. Frascona, *Agency* (Englewood Cliffs, N.J.: Prentice-Hall, Inc.) 1964, p. 104.

[3] See above, p. 135.

[4] See American Law Institute, Restatement of Security, 1941, sec. 2.

[5] See below, p. 199.

[6] Ibid.

title; transfer of possession is not essential to either. A bailment is not concerned with the transfer of title, but rather with the transfer of possession and the property right to such possession. (A and B contract for the sale of oil to B, the oil to be delivered in drums returnable to A. B is to pay A $5 for each drum not delivered. This is a contract to sell oil and for the bailment of the drums. The provision for $5 fixes liquidated damages for the nondelivery of each drum.) If goods are delivered under an agreement whereby they are *exchanged* for the other goods, the transaction is one involving sale. If the goods delivered are to be *returned* even in a different form, the transaction is one of bailment.

2. *A Mortgage.* A mortgage[7] is a security device whereby one to whom an obligation is owing acquires the right of recourse to certain real property on the other's failure to perform his obligation. In the real property mortgage a transfer of possession is neither usual nor necessary. A bailment requires a transfer of possession of goods regardless of the purpose therefor.

3. *A Trust.* The creation of a trust[8] involves the transfer of title to property to be held and administered for the benefit of a person, called a beneficiary; transfer of possession is not necessary. In the creation of a bailment, transfer of possession is necessary.

4. *A Gift.* A gift[9] is effected only by the transfer of title together with an actual or symbolical transfer of possession.

5. *A Pledge, a Factor, a Warehouseman.* These all involve certain types of bailment and differ only in the purpose of their creation. A "pledge"[10] involves a bailment for the purpose of *security* for the performance of an obligation. A "factor"[11] is a person who is an agent usually in possession of goods with authority *to sell* them. A "warehouseman" is a person who, for compensation, has received possession for the purpose *of storage.*

SECTION II. CLASSIFICATION OF BAILMENTS

Bailments may be divided into two classes: *ordinary bailments,* often called "private bailments"; and bailments of a public character, often called "*special bailments.*" *Special bailees hold themselves out to serve the public generally to the limit of their facilities in the type of bailment transactions in which they are engaged.* Private bailees do not make such a holding out; they agree to carry goods for customers as they choose in each particular transaction. These two classes of bailment are distinguished from each other also by their different rights and duties.

---

[7] See below, pp. 461 ff.

[8] See below, p. 802.

[9] See above, pp. 141–42.

[10] See below, pp. 458–61.

[11] See below, p. 549.

Bailment

Public (Special)
1. Innkeeper
2. Common carrier
   a. Checked baggage
   b. Freight (if shipper-carrier relationship)

} Absolute liability with exceptions

Ordinary (Private)	Bailee's Duty of Care	Bailee's Liability
1. Mutual-benefit bailment	Reasonably careful person in position of the bailee	A bailee is liable only for his negligence for failing in his duty of care.
2. Gratuitous bailments: a. Sole benefit of bailor	Slight degree of care	
b. Sole benefit of bailee	Great degree of care	

Ordinary Bailments

Ordinary bailments are of three kinds: for the *sole benefit of the bailor;* for the *sole benefit of the bailee;* and for the *mutual benefit* of the bailor and the bailee. The first two types of bailment are called *"gratuitous bailments"*; the third is called a *"mutual-benefit bailment."* If the bailment agreement does not define the duties of the parties thereto, then the law implies a duty of care determined by the type of ordinary bailment. Whether the bailment is gratuitous or mutual-benefit is determined by the *intent of each of the parties regarding their primary expectation of benefit at the time of the formation of the bailment agreement*. If each *primarily* expects a benefit, it is a mutual-benefit bailment; otherwise it is a gratuitous bailment. The realization of benefit by either the bailor or the bailee, or both, is immaterial; the test is their expectation of benefit. (A bails a picture to B for exhibition at a fair. A is not to receive any monetary compensation therefor, but B will profit by charging admission to view the picture. At the time of the bailment, A expected a benefit in the form of greater notoriety as an artist, and B expected a financial benefit. This is a mutual-benefit bailment.) Gratuitous transportation of certain articles as a part of an overall agreement wherein the carrier expects a benefit does not create a gratuitous bailment of those articles; they are part of a mutual-benefit bailment. The fact that incidental benefit to one of the parties will occur does not make the bailment one of mutual benefit. It is the primary expectation of benefit which is important. (A bails goods to B subject to withdrawal by A as he desires from time to time. B accepts such goods as an accommodation to A and does not intend to receive a benefit thereby, although B derives an incidental benefit because B's position and reputation in the community will be enhanced by the bailment. It is a bailment for the sole benefit of the bailor.)

The bailee's duty of care in gratuitous bailments is *great* in the case of a bailment for the sole benefit of the bailee and *slight* in the case of a bailment for the sole benefit of the bailor. A mutual-benefit bailment imposes upon the bailee the care of *a reasonably careful person in the position of the bailee under the circumstances.* It is a question of fact for the jury whether the particular duty of care has been observed. Negligence is a failure to exercise that amount of care required under the circumstances, and what is negligence in one type of ordinary bailment would not be negligence in another type. A warehouseman is an ordinary bailee of a mutual-benefit bailment with a duty of ordinary, reasonable care even though warehousing is regulated by statute and often is considered to be a public duty. By the majority view, in the case of bailments without a public duty, a bailor and bailee generally may contract to relieve the bailee of a duty of care toward the bailed goods.[12] However, this does not permit the bailee so to act with respect to such goods as to abandon all care whatsoever and thereby negate the very purpose for which the bailment was made.

It is essential to a bailment that there be a transfer of possession of goods. A patron's deposit of clothing on a hanger provided by a restaurant or other establishment does not create a bailment, because *the establishment* never received possession of the clothing. The hanger is provided for the convenience of the patrons, and the clothing may be removed without the permission of the establishment. The patron's use of checking facilities made available by an establishment whereby the patron surrenders possession of clothing to an authorized attendant creates a bailment because possession has been transferred. Similarly, the parking of an automobile in a parking lot is a bailment, if control of the automobile is surrendered to an authorized attendant; when no control is assumed by the attendants and merely a space is designated in which the driver is to park, there is no bailment but merely a license to use the designated space.

Special Bailments

Innkeepers. Today, innkeepers are those who operate hotels, inns, motels, and taverns. Innkeepers hold themselves out to accommodate all proper transient persons, called "guests," with lodging or with lodging and meals. Inns, or "hotels" as they are called today, are distinguished from lodging, or boarding, houses which do not hold themselves out to serve the public generally; they are ordinary bailees. There is a conflict of authority regarding the duty of care to be exercised by innkeepers over the baggage of their guests. By the better view, the liability is the same as that of the common carrier of goods who has the absolute liability of an insurer, with certain exceptions. Statutes in many states permit the innkeeper to limit his liability to that of an ordinary bailee by providing a place for the safe custody of guests' valuables and by giving reasonable publicity of the availability of such facilities. A guest who does not avail himself of such facilities can hold the innkeeper liable only for failure to exercise the care required in a mutual-benefit bailment. The innkeeper is liable only for baggage of the guest, and not for goods for sale or exhibition.

[12] Under the Code this does not apply to warehousemen, see UCC 7–204, and below, p. 176; nor to private carriers, see UCC 7–309, and below, p. 182.

Common Carriers. A common carrier is a special bailee which holds itself out for hire to transport goods or persons; it is called a "common carrier of goods" or a "common carrier of persons," respectively. The common carrier holds itself out to serve all who apply for the available services to the limit of its facilities. A common carrier of goods is distinguished from a private carrier of goods which does not hold itself out to serve the public generally and which is an ordinary bailee. Examples of common carriers of goods or of persons are: railroads, taxicabs, airplanes, boats, ferries, express companies, and bus companies. The person named in a bill of lading[13] as the person from whom the goods have been received for shipment is called the "consignor," and the person named in a bill of lading to whom or to whose order the bill promises delivery is called a "consignee."[14]

While *a common carrier of goods is required by law to receive goods for transportation,*[15] nevertheless it is not required to receive for transportation goods which it is not equipped to carry, goods which are inherently dangerous, goods which have not been properly prepared for transportation, goods injurious to public health, or goods which cannot be transported legally.

SECTION III. LIABILITY OF A COMMON CARRIER OF GOODS

Absolute Liability of an Insurer

By state law for intrastate commerce in many states, and by federal law for interstate commerce, when goods have been delivered to a *common carrier* of goods for immediate shipment, a *shipper-carrier relationship* thereby is established, *imposing upon the carrier the absolute liability of an insurer, with certain exceptions.* The delivery of goods to the carrier not for immediate shipment does not create a shipper-carrier relationship; it creates an ordinary bailment. (A delivers goods to B, a common carrier, for shipment ten days later. On the fifth day part of the goods are destroyed without B's negligence, and on the twelfth day the remainder of the goods is destroyed without B's negligence. During the ten days the relationship is an ordinary mutual-benefit bailment, and, inasmuch as no negligence occurred, B is not liable for the loss. On the twelfth day the relationship was shipper-carrier because the goods were to be shipped on the tenth day and, B's liability being that of an insurer, B is liable for the loss occurring on the twelfth day.) If the common carrier transports goods outside its calling, or gratuitously, then it is a private carrier with the liability of an ordinary bailee. *The shipper-carrier relationship begins when a common carrier accepts goods for immediate shipment and ends when delivery is made as provided in the agreement between the shipper and the*

[13] For bill of lading see UCC 1–201(6), and below, p. 180 ff.

[14] UCC 7–102(b)(c).

[15] For the lien of such common carrier of goods, see below, p. 183 ff.

carrier. If the agreement provides for delivery *directly* to the consignee, then only an actual delivery to the consignee within a reasonable period of time, at a reasonable hour, on a proper day, constitutes delivery. Otherwise, delivery occurs either when the consignee or his agent for that purpose takes possession of the goods, or when the goods have been delivered at the depot or docks nearest to the destination point and a reasonable period of time has expired within which the consignee could have removed the goods after having received reasonable notice of their arrival. On the expiration of a reasonable period of time within which the consignee could have removed the goods, the shipper-carrier relationship ceases, the carrier becomes an ordinary bailee for the consignee, and the carrier may charge for storage thereafter. While the minority view does not require notice to be given to the consignee on the arrival of the goods, by the better view such notice must be given.

Often goods are transferred from one carrier to another in the process of carriage from the point of shipment to the point of delivery. The carrier who first receives the goods for shipment is called the *initial carrier;* the other carriers handling the goods are agents of the initial carrier and are called *connecting carriers.* The initial carrier is liable to the owner of the goods for loss of, or damage to, the shipped goods caused by a connecting carrier.

Exceptions to Absolute Liability of an Insurer. The law imposes the absolute liability of an insurer on a common carrier of goods because the carrier is in sole possession of the goods which it receives from the public generally and the shipper would experience great difficulty in proving fault on the part of the carrier through its agents. The following are five exceptions to the liability of a common carrier as an insurer:

1. Loss caused by an act of God.
2. Loss caused by an act of a public enemy.
3. Loss caused by an act of the shipper.
4. Loss caused by the inherent nature of the goods.
5. Loss of goods seized from the carrier pursuant to legal process.

Act of God. A common carrier is not liable for loss caused by an act of God. An act of God is an occurrence of nature, but in the law of bailments the phrase is used as an excuse from liability and means an occurrence of nature which reasonably could not have been foreseen by the carrier. Illustrations are tornadoes, hurricanes, lightning, earthquakes, unusual rains, and floods. If a human agency joins with an act of God in causing loss, the carrier is not excused. The act of God must be the sole cause of the loss in order to excuse the carrier's liability. When a carrier delays transportation of goods and loss occurs through an act of God, which loss would not have occurred but for the delay, most courts hold that the delay, although a human factor, did not create a risk of loss by an act of God and the carrier's liability for the delay does not extend to include such loss.[16] Loss caused by fire usually is not caused by an act

[16] See William L. Prosser, *Handbook of the Law of Torts,* 4th ed. (St. Paul: West Publishing Co., 1971), pp. 285–86.

of God because of the presence of a human agency; a fire caused by lightning or unforeseeable spontaneous combustion is caused by an act of God, and loss caused by such a fire is not borne by the carrier.

Act of Public Enemy. A common carrier is not liable for the loss caused by an act of a public enemy. By "public enemy" is meant an enemy of the United States, such as revolutionaries, or hostile military forces operating against the United States. Thieves, mobs, and rioters are not public enemies.

Act of Shipper. A common carrier is not liable for loss caused by an act of the shipper, irrespective of the shipper's negligence. (A ships horses accompanied by B, a caretaker employed by A, by C, a common carrier. B's lantern causes fire, injuring the horses while in transit. A is liable for the loss regardless of whether or not A or B was negligent.) Damage caused by the improper preparation of goods for shipment must be borne by the shipper, unless the common carrier knew, or reasonably should have known, of such defective preparation and negligently failed to correct the defect or to refuse to ship the goods.

Inherent Nature of the Goods. A common carrier is not liable for loss caused by the inherent nature of the goods, unless the carrier is aware of the nature of the goods and fails to take adequate precautions to preserve them during their transportation. The common carrier is under a duty to provide adequate facilities for the transportation of perishables of which the common carrier is aware.

Legal Process. A common carrier is not liable for the loss of goods seized from it pursuant to legal process—e.g., garnishment, execution, attachment. (A, a sheriff, seizes goods from B, a common carrier, in order to satisfy a judgment obtained by C against D, the owner of the goods. B is not liable for its inability to deliver the goods to D, or for any loss occurring after the goods have been taken from B by A.)

Reasonable Limitation of Liability. The right of a common carrier of goods reasonably to limit damages for the *amount* of liability in the case of loss of, or injury to, the transported goods with or without negligence on its part by contract with the shipper is discussed later under Documents of Title.[17]

The common carrier may issue reasonable rules and regulations for the operation of its business and may charge reasonable rates. Such rates usually are fixed by the federal government through the Interstate Commerce Commission for interstate transportation, and by state regulatory bodies for intrastate carriage. The common carrier cannot discriminate unfairly between shippers. A common carrier is permitted to fix its rates dependent upon the quantity, bulk, value, and special nature—e.g., explosives—of the goods transported. It may insist upon prepayment for the transportation of goods. Reasonable rates include a reasonable charge for storage in connection with shipments and *demurrage* charges for unreasonable retention of cars by customers, as well as transportation rates.

---

[17] See below, p. 182 ff.

Duties Regarding Baggage. While a common carrier *of persons* is not a bailee of its passengers because only goods are the subject of bailment, nevertheless, it has certain duties in connection with the transportation of its passengers and of their baggage.

The liability of a common carrier of persons for *checked baggage* being transported is the same as the absolute liability of a common carrier of goods in transporting goods, while its liability for *unchecked baggage* within the personal possession of the passenger is only for negligence because there is no bailment. A passenger must be permitted to bring a reasonable amount of baggage without charge. Baggage is that which is reasonably necessary for the convenience of the passenger for his personal use in making the journey, considering his station in life and the length, nature, and purpose of his journey. Thus, jewelry suitable to the condition in life of the passenger and intended for personal use on the journey is baggage; but it is not baggage when carried by a passenger for the use of another or for the purpose of business or sale. A lawyer's or accountant's brief case containing business papers in connection with the purpose of the journey is baggage; sample jewelry carried by a jewelry salesman is not baggage.

SECTION IV. THE RIGHT TO POSSESSION AND USE OF BAILED GOODS

The Right to Possession of Bailed Goods

The bailee's right to possession of bailed goods is determined by the bailment agreement. In the absence of agreement to the contrary, the bailee has the duty of delivering the goods to the bailor or pursuant to his direction. The bailee's misdelivery of the goods, whether innocent or intentional, subjects the bailee to liability to the bailor for damages for breach of the bailment contract or for damages for the tort of conversion,[18] unless the bailee made delivery

[18] "Conversion" is a tort (a civil, noncontractual wrong) and may be defined as a person's unprivileged (unpermitted) act in interfering with *possession* of a *chattel* inconsistent with another person's right to its *immediate possession* and inconsistent with his right to *control and dominion* over the chattel. The wrongdoer has converted the chattel to his own use. Interference is inconsistent with another person's control and dominion over a chattel when either:

1. A person intentionally and without privilege *dispossesses* another person of a chattel. (A steals goods from B and bails them to C. A has committed conversion.)
2. A person in possession of a chattel *refuses to surrender possession* of the chattel to another person who is entitled to its immediate possession and who has *demanded* its possession. (A steals goods from B and bails them to C. B demands the goods from C who refuses to deliver them to B. C has committed conversion.)
3. A person in possession of a chattel *uses* the chattel either without authority, or with authority pursuant to a bailment agreement but so excessively as to constitute a material breach of the bailment agreement. (A bails goods to B for B's use in a way specified in the bailment agreement. B's use of the goods in an entirely different way is a conversion.) Although unprivileged commingling of chattels by one person with those of another is a conversion, nevertheless by contract, custom and usage, as provided in UCC 7–207, a warehouseman may commingle fungible goods of the same kind and grade belonging to different persons.
4. A person *disposes* of (delivers) a chattel with the intent to transfer a *proprietary* interest in

pursuant to the authority of a person with a right to their immediate possession superior to that of the bailor. (F, a factor of B, is directed by B to redeliver the goods to B by Railway Express. F innocently delivers the goods to C, an impostor representing that he is from the express company. C absconds with the goods. F is liable to B for damages for breach of contract or for conversion.) In the absence of agreement to the contrary, the bailor has a right to recover possession of the goods.[19] In the foregoing illustration, B had such a right against C.

The bailee also has a right to immediate possession of the bailed goods, and he may institute an action to recover their possession from one unlawfully possessing them. Even the bailor cannot recover possession of goods from the bailee unless the bailment is terminable at will and the bailor terminates it, or the bailee has materially breached the bailment contract, thereby entitling the bailor to repossession of the goods. However, the bailor does have a right of action against third persons for their tortious damage to his reversionary interest in the goods.[20] (A bails goods to B for a term during which they are stolen by C, who permanently damages the goods. B has rights of action against C for repossession of the goods and for damage to his possessory interest in the goods caused by C's trespass. A has a right of action against C for the damage done to his reversionary interest in the goods. In the absence of agreement to the contrary, possession of the goods is to revert to A at the end of the bailment term, and A's interest in the return of the goods is called a "reversionary interest.") As between one unlawfully in possession and another who unlawfully obtains possession, the first person is entitled to immediate possession as against the second person and those who acquire possession through him. (A

---

the chattel. "Proprietary interest" means an interest which entitles the owner to possession permanently or for a period of time. (A bails goods to B for safekeeping, and B leases or sells and delivers them to C. B has committed conversion.) However, as an exception, a bailee who misdelivers the bailed chattel to a person other than the one entitled to immediate possession, whether or not pursuant to the bailment agreement, is liable to the person entitled to immediate possession only if the latter had made a previous demand upon the bailee for surrender of possession and the bailee's delivery was unprivileged. (A stole goods from B and bailed them to C, who was unaware of the theft. C's redelivery of the goods to A prior to any demand by B is not a conversion by C, even if C had learned of the theft.)

5. A person *acquires* possession of a chattel with the intent to obtain a *proprietary* interest in the chattel either for himself or for a third person. (A bails goods to B for safekeeping, and B leases or sells and delivers them to C. C is liable to A for conversion for wrongful *receipt* of the goods, and B is liable to A for conversion for wrongful *disposal* of the goods.) However, as an exception, a bailee who receives a chattel on behalf of the bailor and who, at the time of his receipt, is innocent that another person is entitled to the immediate possession of the chattel, is not liable for conversion. This situation frequently arises in connection with the bailment of stolen goods.

Damages for the tort of conversion is for the full value of the chattel, in effect imposing a forced sale of the chattel upon the wrongdoer. Generally, the value is measured by its market value at the time and place of conversion with interest from that time.

[19] The legal form of action to recover possession of specific chattels was called "Replevin."

[20] It should be noted that a bailee's negligence is not imputed to his bailor, while a master is liable for damages caused by the negligence of his servants while acting within the scope of their employment. See below, p. 609.

bails goods to B which C steals from B. D steals the goods from C. As between B and C or D, B is entitled to possession. As between C and D, C is entitled to possession.)

The bailee's failure to deliver the bailed goods to the bailor or pursuant to his direction subjects the bailee to liability except in the following instances:

1. In the case of carrier and warehouseman bailees, reference should be made to Documents of Title, discussed later.[21]
2. When the bailee has delivered the goods to a person whose right to their immediate possession is superior to that of the bailor. (A purchases goods from B under a contract voidable at the election of B. A bails the goods to C for a term. B avoids his contract with A and, at the end of the bailment term, *demands* possession of the goods from C. C must deliver the goods to B.)
3. When the goods have been damaged, destroyed, or lost by: an act of God; an act of a public enemy; an act of the shipper; the inherent nature of the goods; or seizure of the goods pursuant to legal process—e.g., garnishment, execution, or attachment—and the bailee gives the bailor prompt notice thereof.

A bailee acts at his peril when he delivers bailed goods to someone other than the bailor and not pursuant to the bailor's direction. If the recipient of the goods does not have a right to their immediate possession superior to the right of the bailor, the bailee is liable for such misdelivery. The bailee's primary duty is to deliver the goods to the bailor or pursuant to his direction. If the bailee is confronted by conflicting claims to possession asserted by the bailor and others, the bailee may avail himself of the remedy of *interpleader.* In a suit by the bailor against the bailee for refusal to redeliver possession of bailed goods at the end of the bailment term, the bailee may interplead, or bring in, any other party asserting the right to possession and make the goods available to the court for disposition on its determination of the one entitled to possession. The bailee itself may institute a proceeding joining the bailor and other parties who assert the right to possession of the goods. The Code provides for this right of interpleader on the part of a carrier or warehouseman.[22] A bailee is estopped to set up title in himself as adverse to the bailor because, by accepting the bailed goods, the bailee impliedly agrees that the bailor is entitled to the possession of the goods on the termination of the bailment term.

The Bailee's Right of Lien. A lien may be defined as a *legal right in the property of another as security for the performance of an obligation.* In the law of bailments this right of lien is a right to possession of the goods and a right to subject such goods to sale in payment for reasonable charges in connection with such goods; it is a security device. The lien may be provided for by contract or may be implied by law. At Common Law a lien was accorded when services rendered in connection with bailed goods enhanced the value of such goods. Today it is not necessary that the value of such goods be enhanced; an artisan's lien is prescribed by law when services, labor, skill, or

[21] See below, pp. 186–87.

[22] UCC 7–603.

material have been rendered in connection with bailed goods. A finder of goods who has incurred reasonable expense in connection with their preservation had a lien at Common Law only to the extent of the offer of reward if made, while by statute today a finder frequently has a lien for such expense.

Special bailees have liens on the goods in connection with which services have been rendered. An innkeeper has a lien on all the goods of its guests to the extent of reasonable charges for the accommodation furnished. Such a lien extends not only to baggage or luggage of the guest but to all goods that he may have. Similarly, a common carrier or a warehouseman has a lien as security for reasonable charges for goods transported, the storage of such goods, and for demurrage charges. These liens are *specific liens,* and not general liens,[23] in the sense that *these liens attach only to the specific goods to which services have been rendered.* For a common carrier, the lien extends to all parts of a shipment, and the surrender of one installment to the consignee permits the carrier to retain possession of the remaining installments as security for the amount owing for all the installments. Such a lien does not extend to goods which have been entrusted to the bailee without the consent of the real owner.[24]

The right of lien is terminated in the following ways: by payment of the charges owing; by improper refusal of a valid tender of payment; or by a voluntary surrender of possession by the bailee to the bailor.

The Bailee's Right to Use the Bailed Goods

The extent to which the bailee may make use of bailed goods depends upon the bailment agreement. In ordinary bailments the degree of use of the bailed goods by the bailee depends in turn upon the kind of bailment. In a mutual-benefit bailment except for carriage or storage, and in a bailment for the sole benefit of the bailee, generally the bailee may make use of the goods for his primary benefit, limited by the terms of the bailment agreement. In a bailment for the sole benefit of the bailor, generally the bailee has the implied authority to use the bailed goods for their preservation even though by such use the bailee may derive an incidental benefit. The bailee, however, may not derive a primary benefit. (A bails his race horse to B for the sole benefit of A. B has the implied authority to exercise the race horse in order to keep it in good condition. He may not, however, use the race horse primarily for his own benefit. The fact that B derives an incidental benefit by the pleasure he obtains from the use of the race horse does not change the nature of the bailment; it still is a bailment for the sole benefit of the bailor.)

In ordinary mutual-benefit bailments except for carriage or storage, the bailor has the duty of providing goods which are reasonably suitable and fit for

---

[23] For an extended discussion of specific and general liens, see below, p. 469.

[24] But see variations in a warehouseman's lien, below, pp. 178–79, and a carrier's lien, below, pp. 183–85.

use in accordance with the purpose of the bailment. Damage caused by the bailor's failure to observe such duty subjects the bailor to liability therefor. (A rents a defective tool to B to be used for a known particular purpose. The defect causes the tool to break and damage other property of B. A is liable to B for such damage.) The bailee has the obligation of making ordinary and incidental repairs to the goods, while the bailor has the obligation of making unusual and extraordinary repairs to such goods if such repairs were not necessitated by any fault of the bailee. In the absence of any provision to the contrary in the bailment agreement or by custom and usage, the bailee is under no duty to insure the bailed property. However, he may insure such property because he has an insurable interest in the property.[25]

Deviation. The bailee may not deviate or depart from the terms of the bailment agreement. If the bailment was created by contract, the bailee's deviation subjects him to liability for damages for breach of contract. In tort, the bailee is liable in conversion for: his use of the goods when the bailment agreement does not permit his use; or, if his use is permitted, his excessive use amounting to a material breach of contract. If his use is permitted and his excessive use does not amount to a material breach of contract, he is absolutely liable for any damage to the goods during such deviation or caused by such deviation irrespective of his negligence. By custom and usage and usually by contract, a warehouseman may commingle fungible goods of the same kind and grade belonging to different persons, such owners thereby becoming owners or tenants in common of the mass, each with an undivided interest therein to the extent of his contribution. Such commingling is not a deviation from the terms of the bailment agreement.

SECTION V. TERMINATION

A bailment may be terminated in accordance with the terms of the bailment agreement or by the conduct of the parties. The bailment agreement may provide for the accomplishment of a certain purpose, and on the accomplishment of this purpose the bailment is at an end. The bailment agreement may provide for the duration of the bailment in terms of a period of time, and on the expiration of such period of time the bailment terminates. It is implied in a bailment agreement that the bailment relationship will continue as long as there are bailed goods. If there is a total destruction or loss of the subject matter of the bailment, or if such subject matter is partially destroyed or so changed as to be unfit and unsuitable for the purpose for which it was bailed, the bailment is terminated.

The parties themselves, acting together or individually, may terminate the bailment agreement. When a bailment agreement is for an indefinite period of time, the bailment is one that is terminable at will. Either the bailor or the bailee may terminate such a bailment at any time. In a bailment that is not

[25] For concept of insurable interest in property, see below, p. 745.

terminable at will, the bailee may terminate the bailment by reason of his material failure to perform or because of his material deviation from the terms of the bailment agreement. If the bailment is a contract, breach of contract by the bailor or bailee subjects him to liability for such breach. The bailor cannot wrongfully terminate a mutual-benefit bailment without the bailee's consent when the bailee has an interest in the subject matter. (A bails a machine to B for one year. B is to pay a rental for such machine during that period. On the expiration of six months A attempts to terminate the bailment agreement and repossess the machine. A cannot terminate the bailment agreement by himself because the bailee has an interest in the possession of the machine for one year.) The bailor and the bailee mutually may agree to rescind the bailment agreement, in which case the bailment thereby is terminated.

Chapter 13

DOCUMENTS OF TITLE

A bill of lading and a warehouse receipt are documents of title for goods shipped or warehoused.

A *warehouseman* is an ordinary bailee of a mutual-benefit bailment, liable for loss or damage to the warehoused goods by failure of his duty to exercise reasonable care. This duty cannot be impaired by agreement. If he is in the business of buying and selling fungible goods and he unauthorizedly sells and delivers bailed fungible goods to a buyer in ordinary course of business, the buyer acquires title to such goods free from any claim under a warehouse receipt even if the receipt is negotiable. He is liable to a good faith purchaser for value of a *negotiable* receipt, issued with blanks and later unauthorizedly completed, as though completed authorizedly. If not negotiable, he is liable only according to its original tenor. He has a statutory specific possessory lien against the bailor and holders of the receipt on the goods covered by the receipt or on the proceeds thereof for his expenses and services rendered to the goods. However, the lien is not effective against a person who, before issuance of the receipt, has any legal interest in the goods and who had not consented to nor authorized such bailment nor is precluded by his conduct from asserting his interest in the bailed goods. The warehouseman's voluntary delivery of the goods or his unjustified refusal to deliver terminates his lien.

A *carrier* is either a public or ordinary bailee of goods for transportation which issues ordinary as well as *through* and *destination* bills of lading. Both a private and a common carrier have a duty to exercise reasonable care, and the common carrier is also absolutely liable as a shipper-carrier for the bailed goods. This duty of care and absolute liability cannot be impaired by agreement. If an unauthorized completion of blanks or other alteration is made on a bill issued by a *private* carrier, the carrier is liable only according to its original tenor. The *common carrier* has a statutory specific possessory lien on the goods and the proceeds thereof effective against the consignor or *any person* entitled

to the goods for its expenses and services rendered to the goods. If it is a *private carrier*, its rights of lien are the same as for a warehouseman, and the lien may be terminated in the same way.

Documents of title issued by the warehouseman or carrier bailee may be negotiable or non-negotiable, and the issuer is liable for any irregularities in such documents and for his wrongful conduct in their issue. The bailee's obligation is to deliver the goods only to the *holder* of a *negotiable* document on its *surrender* to the bailee, and to the *consignee* of a *non-negotiable* document in the absence of any knowledge of any previous transfer of it without the necessity of its surrender to the bailee. An innocent bailee is not liable in conversion for goods unauthorizedly bailed to him. *For the nature and the effect of negotiation and transfer of negotiable and non-negotiable documents of title, reference should be made to the summary headnote and to the text content of "Negotiable Paper under the Code."*[1] A claimant under a missing document may have to post a bond to protect the bailee in its delivery of the goods to the claimant.

In General

The subject of documents of title comes under Article 7 of the Uniform Commercial Code and is governed by its provisions.[2] On the receipt of bailed goods, carriers and warehousemen issue a writing which constitutes both a receipt for such goods and also a contract containing the terms on which such goods were received. The writing issued by a common carrier is called a "bill of lading," "evidencing the receipt of goods for shipment issued by a person engaged in the business of transporting or forwarding goods, and includes an airbill."[3] The writing issued by a warehouseman is called a "warehouse receipt," which is "a receipt issued by a person engaged in the business of storing goods for hire."[4] Bills of lading and warehouse receipts are called "documents of title"[5] because they represent the goods and are symbols of title to such goods. Under the Code:[6] a bailee is "the person who by a

[1] See above, pp. 145, 150–52.

[2] UCC 7–103: "To the extent that any treaty or statute of the United States, regulatory statute of this State or tariff, classification or regulation filed or issued pursuant thereto is applicable, the provisions of this Article are subject thereto."

[3] "'Airbill' means a document serving for air transportation as a bill of lading does for marine or rail transportation, and includes an air consignment note or air waybill." UCC 1–201(6).

[4] UCC 1–201(45).

[5] "'Document of title' includes bill of lading, dock warrant, dock receipt, warehouse receipt or order for the delivery of goods, and also any other document which in the regular course of business or financing is treated as adequately evidencing that the person in possession of it is entitled to receive, hold and dispose of the document and the goods it covers. To be a document of title a document must purport to be issued by or addressed to a bailee and purport to cover goods in the bailee's possession which are either identified or are fungible portions of an identified mass." UCC 1–201(15).

[6] UCC 7–102(1)(a)(b)(c)(f).

warehouse receipt, bill of lading or other document of title acknowledges possession of goods and contracts to deliver them"; a consignor is "the person named in a bill as the person from whom the goods have been received for shipment"; a consignee is "the person named in a bill to whom or to whose order the bill promises delivery"; and goods "means all things which are treated as movable for the purposes of a contract of storage or transportation."

FORM 1585 12-47—100M Sets

(Uniform Domestic Order Bill of Lading, adopted by Carriers in Official, Southern, Western and Illinois Classification Territories, March 15, 1922, as amended August 1, 1930, and June 15, 1941.) 1st SHEET

UNION PACIFIC

UNIFORM ORDER BILL OF LADING
ORIGINAL

Shipper's No.________
Agent's No.________

UNION PACIFIC RAILROAD COMPANY

RECEIVED, subject to the classifications and tariffs in effect on the date of the issue of this Bill of Lading,

at________________________________ 194____

from________________________________

the property described below, in apparent good order, except as noted (contents and condition of contents of packages unknown), marked, consigned, and destined as indicated below, which said company (the word company being understood throughout this contract as meaning any person or corporation in possession of the property under the contract) agrees to carry to its usual place of delivery at said destination, if on its own road or its own water line, otherwise to deliver to another carrier on the route to said destination. It is mutually agreed, as to each carrier of all or any of said property over all or any portion of said route to destination, and as to each party at any time interested in all or any of said property, that every service to be performed hereunder shall be subject to all the conditions not prohibited by law, whether printed or written, herein contained, including the conditions on back hereof, which are hereby agreed to by the shipper and accepted for himself and his assigns.

The surrender of this Original ORDER Bill of Lading properly indorsed shall be required before the delivery of the property. Inspection of property covered by this Bill of Lading will not be permitted unless provided by law or unless permission is indorsed on this Original Bill of Lading or given in writing by the shipper.

Consigned to **ORDER OF**____________________

Destination__________ State of__________ County of__________

Notify____________________

At__________ State of__________ County of__________

Route____________________

Delivering Carrier__________ Car Initial__________ Car No.__________

No. Packages	DESCRIPTION OF ARTICLES, SPECIAL MARKS AND EXCEPTIONS	*WEIGHT (Subject to Correction)	CLASS OR RATE	CHECK COLUMN	
					Subject to Section 7 of conditions, if this shipment is to be delivered to the consignee without recourse on the con-
					(The signature here acknowledges only the amount prepaid.)

*If the shipment moves between two ports by a carrier by water, the law requires that the bill of lading shall state whether it is "carrier's or shipper's weight."
NOTE—Where the rate is dependent on value, shippers are required to state specifically in writing the agreed or declared value of the property.
The agreed or declared value of the property is hereby specifically stated by the shipper to be not exceeding

per

Charges Advanced:

$________

__________Shipper. __________Agent

Per__________ Per__________

Permanent postoffice address of shipper__________

COURTESY, SAFETY AND RELIABLE SERVICE

Order Bill of Lading (*front*)

It is very important to distinguish between negotiable and non-negotiable documents of title because different rights and duties are associated with each. These will be discussed later.[7] The law of documents of title is concerned mainly with warehouse receipts and bills of lading. Accordingly, first special rules applicable only to warehouse receipts, then special rules applicable only to bills of lading, and finally rules applicable to both warehouse receipts and bills of lading will be discussed, in that order.

---

[7] See below, pp. 189–194. The difference between a negotiable and non-negotiable document of title has been discussed previously, above, p. 150.

Warehouse Receipts Only

Form. A warehouse receipt is issued by a warehouseman,[8] and it need not be in any particular form. A warehouse receipt should contain the following information, and the warehouseman is liable for damages caused by any omission to a person injured thereby:

(a) the location of the warehouse where the goods are stored;
(b) the date of issue of the receipt;
(c) the consecutive number of the receipt;
(d) a statement whether the goods received will be delivered to the bearer, to a specified person, or to a specified person or his order;
(e) the rate of storage and handling charges, except that where goods are stored under a field warehousing arrangement a statement of that fact is sufficient on a non-negotiable receipt;
(f) a description of the goods or of the packages containing them;
(g) the signature of the warehouseman, which may be made by his authorized agent;
(h) if the receipt is issued for goods of which the warehouseman is owner, either solely or jointly or in common with others, the fact of such ownership; and
(i) a statement of the amount of advances made and of liabilities incurred for which the warehouseman claims a lien or security interest. . . . If the precise amount of such advances made or of such liabilities incurred is, at the time of the issue of the receipt, unknown to the warehouseman or to his agent who issues it, a statement of the fact that advances have been made or liabilities incurred and the purpose thereof is sufficient.[9]

Additional terms may be inserted by the warehouseman in the receipt as long as they are not contrary to the provisions of the Code and they do not impair his obligation of delivery or his duty of care.

When a document of title other than a bill of lading is issued without the issuer[10] having received the goods or with a misdescription of the goods, the issuer is liable for damages caused by such non-receipt or misdescription to a party to the document or to a good faith purchaser for value of the document who relied upon the description of the goods in the document.[11] Of course, to

---

[8] However, a receipt issued by a non-warehouseman owner of goods (e.g., distilled spirits, agricultural commodities) under a statute requiring a bond against withdrawal or a license for the issuance of receipts in the nature of warehouse receipts has the same effect as a warehouse receipt.

[9] UCC 7–202(2).

[10] "'Issuer' means a bailee who issues a document except that in relation to an unaccepted delivery order it means the person who orders the possessor of goods to deliver. Issuer includes any person for whom an agent or employee purports to act in issuing a document if the agent or employee has real or apparent authority to issue documents, notwithstanding that the issuer received no goods or that the goods were misdescribed or that in any other respect the agent or employee violated his instructions." "'Delivery order' means a written order to deliver goods directed to a warehouseman, carrier or other person who in the ordinary course of business issues warehouse receipts or bills of lading." UCC 7–102 (g)(d).

[11] This is a reflection of the law of agency illustrating the application of inherent agency power subjecting a disclosed principal to liability for the unauthorized acts of his general agent. "Under the law of Agency, when a principal appoints another as a general agent in a position where, as a

the extent that the document conspicuously indicates that the issuer does not know whether any part or all of the goods in fact were received or conformed to the description, if such indication be true, or the party or purchaser otherwise has notice, the issuer is not liable for such non-receipt or misdescription of the goods. For example, the description may be in terms of marks or labels or kind, quantity or condition, or the receipt or description is qualified by "contents, condition and quality unknown," "said to contain," or the like.[12]

Duty of Care. A warehouseman is an ordinary bailee of a mutual-benefit bailment, even though a warehouseman may be licensed by statute and is called a "public warehouseman." As such, he has a duty to exercise the care of a reasonably careful person in the position of the bailee under the circumstances, and he is liable for damages for loss of, or injury to, the goods caused by his negligence in failing to exercise such care. *In the absence of state statute or judicial decision to the contrary, this duty of care of a warehouseman cannot be impaired by agreement.* However, damages for the *amount* of liability in the case of loss or damage by the warehouseman's failure to exercise such care may be limited by a term in the warehouse receipt or storage agreement, which must set forth a specific liability per article or item, or value per unit of weight, beyond which the warehouseman shall not be liable. However, on the bailor's written statement that the goods are of a greater value and his written request, made at the time of signing such storage agreement or within a reasonable time after receipt of the warehouse receipt, the warehouseman must increase his liability on part or all of the goods thereunder for which he may charge increased rates based on such increased valuation but not contrary to a lawful limitation of liability contained in the warehouseman's tariff, if any. The warehouse receipt or tariff may include reasonable provisions as to time and manner of presenting claims and instituting actions based on the bailment.

Any agreement to limit the warehouseman's liability for conversion[13] of bailed goods to his own use is contrary to public policy and, therefore, ineffective. However, it should be noted very carefully that, *if the warehouseman is also in the business of buying and selling fungible goods*[14] *and he unau-*

---

part of his regular employment, he is to issue commercial documents representing chattels or choses in action only when certain facts exist or on the occurrence of a certain event, such facts or event being within the peculiar knowledge of the general agent, if A [agent] issues such commercial documents unauthorizedly and they are purchased by innocent persons for value without notice of A's impropriety, P [principal] is bound by A's conduct as though A had acted authorizedly. Examples are: the agent of a common carrier or of a warehouseman with authority to issue bills of lading or warehouse receipts on receipt of goods for carriage or storage. . . ." (Author's brackets.) Joseph L. Frascona, *Agency* (Englewood Cliffs, N.J.: Prentice-Hall, Inc., 1964), pp. 66–67. Also, see below, pp. 593–94.

[12] UCC 7–203.

[13] For conversion, see above, p. 166, ftn. 18.

[14] Fungible goods are goods of which any unit is, by nature or usage of trade, the equivalent of any other like unit; for example, oil in a vat. However, goods which are not fungible shall be deemed fungible for the purposes of the Code to the extent that under a particular agreement or document unlike units are treated as equivalents. UCC 1–201(17).

thorizedly sells and delivers bailed fungible goods to a buyer in ordinary course of business,[15] *the buyer acquires title to such goods free from any claim under a warehouse receipt even if the receipt is negotiable.* This is consistent with that portion of the law of Sales, discussed before,[16] concerned with entrusting possession of goods to a merchant who deals in goods of that kind. The warehouseman would be liable for the conversion by unauthorized sale of such fungible goods.

Except for fungible goods and as otherwise provided in the warehouse receipt, a warehouseman must not commingle the goods represented by the various warehouse receipts outstanding, but he must keep separate the goods covered by each receipt so as to permit their identification and delivery at all times. Unless otherwise agreed, *fungible* goods may be commingled; they are owned in common by the various persons entitled to them. The warehouseman is liable to each owner of commingled goods for that owner's share. Should the warehouseman overissue warehouse receipts for commingled fungible goods, so that the mass of fungible goods is insufficient to meet all the receipts which the warehouseman has issued against it, the persons entitled to the mass include all holders to whom overissued receipts have been duly negotiated. In such an event, each owner is an owner in common of such mass to the extent of his pro rata share based on the proportion that the amount stated on his receipt bears to the mass. The warehouseman is liable to each owner for his respective deficiency.

A warehouse receipt may not reflect the warehouseman's intent because of its unauthorized alteration, either by its issuance with blanks and subsequent unauthorized completion, or by other unauthorized alteration. The extent of the warehouseman's liability to the holder of the altered receipt depends upon the negotiable or non-negotiable character of the receipt and the type of alteration. The warehouseman must be careful in issuing warehouse receipts, particularly negotiable receipts, so as to ensure that each warehouse receipt is complete and has no blanks. As between a warehouseman whose issued *negotiable* receipt has a *blank,* and a good faith purchaser for value without notice that the blank has been filled in without authority, the warehouseman will be held liable to such purchaser *who may treat the insertion as authorized.*[17] As between the warehouseman and such purchaser the risk falls on the warehouseman who, by leaving the blank and facilitating unauthorized completion, has misled the purchaser as to the correctness of the negotiable receipt and the warehouseman is estopped or precluded from asserting such unauthorized alteration by unauthorized completion of the blank.[18] Unauthorized completion of a *blank* on a *non-negotiable* warehouse receipt is disregarded as of no effect, and the receipt is enforceable against the issuer *according to its*

[15] As to who is a buyer in ordinary course of business, see above, p. 149.

[16] See above, pp. 149–50.

[17] But see below, p. 183, for a different effect if the document is a bill of lading.

[18] See below, p. 323, for similar reasoning when a material alteration of a negotiable instrument has been caused by the negligence of the drawer or maker.

original tenor. Any other unauthorized alteration on *any* warehouse receipt, whether negotiable or non-negotiable, is disregarded as of no effect, and the receipt is enforceable against the issuer *according to its original tenor.*

Warehouseman's Lien. ***Nature of the Lien.*** By Code provision *a warehouseman automatically acquires a statutory specific, possessory lien against the bailor on the goods covered by the warehouse receipt or on the proceeds thereof*[19] *in his possession,* "for charges for storage or transportation (including demurrage and terminal charges), insurance, labor, or charges present or future in relation to the goods, and for expenses necessary for preservation of the goods or reasonably incurred in their sale pursuant to law."[20] All persons take warehouse receipts subject to such lien. Should the warehouseman desire to increase the lien on such goods against the person on whose account the goods are held[21] to assure payment by such person of his liability for like charges and expenses for *other* goods, whether or not delivered to the warehouseman, then in order that holders of a *non-negotiable* warehouse receipt are put on notice of such a *general*[22] lien it is necessary that the warehouse receipt so state such lien for such additional charges and expenses. If the warehouse receipt is *negotiable,* as to persons to whom the receipt has been *negotiated*[23] the "warehouseman's lien is limited to charges in an amount or at a rate specified on the receipt or if no charges are so specified then to a reasonable charge for storage of the goods covered by the receipt subsequent to the date of the receipt."[24] Also, should the warehouseman desire to reserve a security interest against the bailor in the goods for a maximum amount for charges other than those just mentioned, the receipt must so state such security interest and the maximum amount. Thus, the warehouseman may have advanced a loan of money to the bailor apart from the warehousing transaction.[25]

A warehouseman's lien is not so broad as a carrier's lien, discussed later,[26] the extent of the increased breadth of the carrier's lien depending on whether or not the carrier was required by law to receive the goods for transportation. The above warehouseman's lien is, to the extent indicated, effective against the bailor and subsequent third persons holding the warehouse receipt. However, the effect of the lien on parties with an interest in the goods *prior* to the lien varies. (O owns goods which are stolen by T and bailed to W, a warehouseman. Or O has entrusted his goods to M, a merchant dealing in such

---

[19] The proceeds may result from a proper sale of the goods by the warehouseman.

[20] UCC 7–209(1).

[21] The person on whose account the goods are held may be the bailor or a purchaser of the warehouse receipt from the bailor.

[22] It is a general lien because it is on goods on which services for the additional charges have not been rendered.

[23] For negotiation, see below, pp. 187–89.

[24] UCC 7–209(1).

[25] See UCC 7–209, *Comment 2.*

[26] See below, pp. 183–85.

goods, with authority to sell the goods, and M unauthorizedly bailed them to W, a warehouseman.) The warehouseman's lien is not effective against a person who, *before* issuance of the receipt, had a legal interest or a perfected security interest[27] in the goods and who has not consented to nor authorized such bailment nor is precluded by his conduct from asserting his interest in the bailed goods.[28] Thus, in the first illustration given, T's theft of the goods from O and bailment to W created a lien effective as *against* T but ineffective as *against* O. O owns the goods and has not, by his conduct, jeopardized his interest in those goods and, therefore, W's lien is ineffective as to him.[29] However, his conduct may cause W's lien to be effective against him; the second illustration is an example. For conduct by a person prior to the bailment which causes the warehouseman's lien to be effective as against him, see later discussion.[30] Until the lien on the bailed goods is satisfied, the warehouseman is not obligated to deliver the goods. *His voluntary delivery of the goods or his unjustified refusal to deliver them terminates his lien on such goods.*

We have observed that the warehouseman's lien may be on the proceeds resulting from his proper sale of the bailed goods. Such sale terminates storage and may result from the exercise of the warehouseman's option to terminate storage under various circumstances, either for reasons other than non-payment of storage charges or because of non-payment of storage charges. First, termination of storage and sale other than for non-payment will be discussed and then sale in enforcement of the warehouseman's lien for non-payment.

Termination of Storage. *First,* the warehouseman may, on notifying the person on whose account the goods are held or any other person known to claim an interest in the goods, require that the goods be removed from the warehouse on the expiration of the period of storage fixed in the receipt, or, if there is no such fixed period, then within a period of time stated in the notification but which is not less than 30 days after the notification. Most warehousing is for an indefinite term, terminable by delivery of the goods to the bailor on his reasonable demand. If the goods are not removed before the expiration of such period, the warehouseman has the right to advertise and sell the goods in the same way as he would sell goods in the enforcement of his warehouseman's lien. The warehouseman's right to terminate storage includes a right to demand payment of storage charges, which demand may be included in the notification of termination of storage. *Second,* the warehouseman may, in good faith, believe that the goods are about to *deteriorate or decline in value to less than the amount of his lien within the above-described period for notification, advertisement and sale.* If he so believes, he may specify in the notification any reasonable shorter time for removal of the goods, and, on their non-

[27] For perfected security interest, see below, pp. 433–34.

[28] UCC 7–209(3), 7–503(1). But compare UCC 7–307(2).

[29] Compare the result if it were a carrier's lien instead of a warehouseman's lien. See below, pp. 183–84.

[30] See below, p. 191 ff.

removal, he may sell them. *Third,* if the warehouseman had no notice at the time of deposit of the goods with him of a quality or condition of such goods which makes them a hazard to other stored property, to the warehouse, or to persons, he may, without advertisement and on reasonable notification to all persons known to claim an interest in the goods, sell the goods at public or private sale. The warehouseman's right to removal of stored goods is, however, subject to state regulatory statutes and their implementing regulations. If sale occurs, the warehouseman may utilize so much of the proceeds as is sufficient to satisfy his lien and, if there are any proceeds remaining, he must hold the balance for delivery on the demand of any person to whom he would have been bound to deliver the goods.

Enforcement of the Lien. In addition to all other rights allowed by law to a creditor against his debtor, a warehouseman has a right to enforce his lien by sale of the bailed goods after giving proper notification. It is important to determine at the outset whether the goods to be sold are commercially stored, i.e., stored by a merchant in the course of his business, or non-commercially stored, i.e., principally by private owners of household goods. The warehouseman's sale of commercially stored goods is faster, more flexible and less detailed in its requirements. The rules for sale of each type of goods differ only in the kind and content of notification of the sale and in the need for advertisement in a sale of non-commercially stored goods. It should be noted very carefully that, *despite non-compliance by the warehouseman with the rules for sale, a good faith purchaser for value takes the goods free of any rights of persons against whom the lien was valid.* (O stored his goods with W, a warehouseman. On W's enforcement of his lien and sale to B, a good faith purchaser for value, B acquires a title to the goods valid against O. However, if T stole O's goods and stored them with W, a warehouseman innocent of the theft, who then enforced his lien and sold the goods to P, a good faith purchaser for value without notice of T's theft, P has a good title as against T but not as against O.[31]) However, the warehouseman is liable for damages caused by his failure to comply with requirements for sale and, in the case of wilful violation, he is liable for conversion.[32] The warehouseman may utilize so much of the proceeds as is sufficient to satisfy his lien and, if there are any proceeds remaining, he must hold the balance for delivery on demand to any person to whom he would have been bound to deliver the goods. The warehouseman may buy at any *public* sale.

Bills of Lading Only

Form. The bill of lading issued by a carrier may take a variety of forms depending upon its purpose with consequent differing liability thereunder. Only Through and Destination bills of lading will be considered here.

[31] Compare the result if it were a carrier's lien instead of a warehouseman's lien; see below, pp. 183–84. W is not liable to P for breach of warranty of title; see below, pp. 233–34.

[32] For discussion of conversion, see above, p. 166, ftn. 18.

Through Bills of Lading. The bill may be a through bill of lading, which is a bill embodying an undertaking to be performed in part by persons other than the issuer. Such persons may be the issuer's agents or connecting carriers.[33] (D delivers goods to R railroad for delivery to a point not served by R but served by S railroad. R may issue a through bill of lading because R undertook the duty of transporting the goods which will occur over its own lines and over lines owned by S.)

The Code does not require that a through bill be issued in such a case, but its issuance affects the rights and liabilities of the issuer (initial carrier), its agents and connecting carriers. When the issuer's agent or a connecting carrier receives the goods covered by a through bill of lading, such person holds the goods under the terms of the through bill and he has the issuer's obligation to perform thereunder while the goods are in his possession. Such person discharges his obligation under the document by his delivery of the goods to another such agent or connecting carrier pursuant to the document and he is not liable thereafter for subsequent breach under the document by such other person. Accordingly, the issuer is liable not only for *his* own breach of obligation under the document, but also for breach thereunder by his agent or *any* connecting carrier while the goods are in such person's possession if such person's breach would subject the latter to liability thereunder. In other words, the initial carrier has the liability of its agent or any connecting carrier for loss which occurred while the goods were in either's possession. *This liability of the issuer of the through bill for its agent or any connecting carrier cannot be varied by agreement;* although to the extent that the bill covers an undertaking to be performed overseas or in territory not contiguous to the continental United States or an undertaking including matters other than transportation, this liability may be varied by agreement. If the issuer has been held liable under the through bill for loss occurring while the goods were in the possession of such agent or connecting carrier, the issuer has a right to recover from such agent or connecting carrier the amount which the issuer has paid or may be required to pay for such breach, together with any expense reasonably incurred by the issuer in defending any action brought by anyone entitled to recover on the document therefor.

Destination Bills of Lading. High-speed carriers may cause the transported goods to arrive at the destination point before the arrival there of documents for such goods issued by the carrier when such goods were initially delivered to the carrier for transportation. This requires storage of such goods by the carrier until the documents are received by the consignee at the destination point and presented for such goods, and also impedes the consignee buyer and the financing agency used by him from the use of such goods and in financing their purchase. Accordingly, instead of the consignor obtaining a bill of lading from the carrier on delivery of goods to it for shipment, he may request the carrier to issue a bill of lading at destination or any other place and

[33] The carrier who first receives the goods for shipment is called the "initial carrier"; the other carriers handling the goods are called "connecting carriers."

to any person as indicated in the consignor's request. Such a bill of lading is called a "destination bill." A destination bill may be issued by a carrier in exchange for the surrender of an ordinary bill of lading, previously issued by the carrier on its receipt of goods for shipment, upon the request of anyone entitled as against the carrier to control the goods while in transit. The Code permits the carrier to issue a destination bill; but the carrier has no legal obligation to do so.

Diversion of Transported Goods. The carrier's obligation is to deliver the transported goods to the person or destination as indicated in its issued bill of lading; it is liable for misdelivery. However, unless the bill of lading otherwise provides, the carrier may divert the goods and thereby effect a reconsignment by delivering them otherwise than as stated in the bill in accordance with instructions from any one of certain persons entitled to control the goods while in transit. Such persons are:

(a) the holder of a negotiable bill; or
(b) the consignor on a non-negotiable bill notwithstanding contrary instructions from the consignee; or
(c) the consignee on a non-negotiable bill in the absence of contrary instructions from the consignor, if the goods have arrived at the billed destination or if the consignee is in possession of the bill; or
(d) the consignee on a non-negotiable bill if he is entitled as against the consignor to dispose of them.[34]

The carrier is not obligated to divert the goods as requested. But, under the Code, the carrier is protected from a charge of misdelivery for not delivering the goods to the person or at the destination indicated in the bill if it diverts the goods in accordance with instructions by the proper person under the conditions indicated. However, if a *negotiable* bill of lading is outstanding, the carrier should make a notation on the bill itself of such instructions for diversion; the carrier's failure to do so exposes it to liability to a person innocent of the reconsignment to whom the bill has been subsequently negotiated and who is entitled to hold the carrier according to the original terms on the bill.

Duty of Care. *A carrier, whether a common carrier or a private carrier, has a duty to exercise the care of a reasonably careful person in the position of the bailee under the circumstances,* and the carrier is liable for damages for loss of or injury to the goods caused by its failure to exercise such care. If the carrier is also a common carrier in intrastate commerce, as previously discussed,[35] state law in many states imposes an absolute liability upon the carrier while there is a shipper-carrier relationship. Federal law imposes absolute liability on a common carrier in interstate commerce. *In the absence of state statute or judicial decision to the contrary, the carrier's duty of care cannot be impaired by agreement.* However, the damages for the *amount* of liability in the case of loss or damage by the carrier's failure to exercise such care may be

[34] UCC 7–303(1).

[35] See above, pp. 163–64.

limited by a provision in the bill of lading "that the carrier's liability shall not exceed a value stated in the document if the carrier's rates are dependent upon value and the consignor by the carrier's tariff is afforded an opportunity to declare a higher value or a value as lawfully provided in the tariff, or where no tariff is filed he is otherwise advised of such opportunity."[36] However, any agreement to limit the carrier's liability for conversion[37] of bailed goods to his own use is contrary to public policy and, therefore, ineffective. The bill of lading or tariff may include reasonable provisions as to time and manner of presenting claims and instituting actions based on the shipment.

A bill of lading may not reflect the issuer's intent because of its unauthorized alteration, either by its issuance with blanks and subsequent unauthorized completion, or by other unauthorized alteration. The issuer must be careful in issuing bills of lading so as to ensure that each bill is complete and has no blanks. *An unauthorized alteration of any bill of lading, whether negotiable or non-negotiable and whether by unauthorized completion of a blank or otherwise, leaves the bill enforceable according to its original tenor.* It should be noted as discussed previously[38] that, in the case of unauthorized completion of a blank in a *negotiable warehouse receipt*, the warehouseman is liable at the election of a good faith purchaser for value without notice of the unauthorized completion as though such completion had been authorized.

Carrier's Lien. ***Nature of the Lien.*** *By Code provision a carrier automatically acquires a statutory specific, possessory lien on the goods covered by a bill of lading* "for charges subsequent to the date of its receipt of the goods for storage or transportation (including demurrage and terminal charges) and for expenses necessary for preservation of the goods incident to their transportation or reasonably incurred in their sale pursuant to law."[39] All persons take bills of lading subject to such lien. If the bill of lading is *negotiable,* then as to a purchaser for value the carrier's lien is limited to charges stated in the bill or the applicable tariffs, or if no charges are stated then to a reasonable charge.

The above carrier's lien on transported goods is effective against the consignor and subsequent third persons holding the bill of lading. However, the effect of the lien on parties with an interest in the goods *prior* to the lien depends upon whether or not the carrier was required by law to receive such goods for transportation and whether or not the carrier had notice of any lack of authority in the consignor to deliver the goods to the carrier for transportation. *When the carrier is required by law to receive such goods for transportation (common carrier), the lien is effective against the consignor or any person entitled to the goods, unless the carrier had notice that the consignor lacked authority to subject the goods to such charges and expenses.* It should be noted very carefully that such a lien is effective against an owner who never

---

[36] UCC 7–309(2).

[37] For conversion, see above, p. 166, ftn. 18.

[38] See above, p. 177.

[39] UCC 7–307(1).

consented to such transportation. (O owns goods which are stolen by T and delivered for transportation to C, a carrier who is required by law to receive such goods for transportation and who had no notice of the theft. C's lien is effective against both O and T.) Inasmuch as the carrier was legally required to receive and accept such goods for transportation, the consignor's mere possession is sufficient to justify the carrier's lien as effective not only against the consignor but also against persons with interests in the goods, provided the carrier had no notice of the consignor's lack of authority to subject the goods to such charges and expenses. *When the carrier is not required by law to receive such goods for transportation (private carrier), the lien is effective against the consignor and any person who permitted the bailor to have control or possession of the goods, unless the carrier had notice that the consignor lacked authority to subject the goods to such charges and expenses.* (O owns goods which are stolen by T and delivered for transportation to C, a carrier without notice of the theft and not legally required to receive and accept such goods. Or O delivers his goods to A to hold for him and A unauthorizedly delivers the goods for transportation to C, a carrier not legally required to receive and accept such goods. In the first illustration, C's lien is effective against T but is not effective against O. In the second illustration, whether or not C's lien is effective against O depends upon whether or not C had notice of A's lack of authority when the goods were delivered for transportation to C. If C did not have such notice, C's lien is effective against O; if C had such notice, C's lien is not effective against O.) *Until the lien on the bailed goods is satisfied, the carrier is not obligated to deliver the goods. The carrier's voluntary delivery of the goods or its unjustified refusal to deliver them terminates its lien on such goods.*

Enforcement of the Lien. In addition to all other rights allowed by law to a creditor against his debtor, a carrier has a right to enforce its lien by sale of the bailed goods after giving proper notification. The carrier may enforce its lien on the goods by public or private sale after *notifying* all persons known to claim an interest in the goods. Thus, notification here means proper *sending* of the notice; it is not necessary that the addressees *receive* such notice. It should be noted very carefully that, *despite non-compliance by the carrier with the rules for sale, a good faith purchaser for value takes the goods free of any rights of persons against whom the lien was valid.* (O delivered his goods for transportation to C, a carrier. On C's enforcement of its lien and sale to B, a good faith purchaser for value, B acquires a title to the goods valid against O. However, suppose T stole O's goods and delivered them for transportation to C, a carrier without notice of the theft. On C's enforcement of its lien and sale to B, a good faith purchaser for value without notice of the theft, B acquires a title to the goods valid against T; but whether or not B's title is valid against O depends upon whether or not C was legally required to receive and accept such goods for transportation. If C was so legally obligated, then B acquires title valid against O. If C was not so legally obligated, then B does not acquire a title valid against O.) Compare the result in these illustrations if a warehouseman's lien instead of a carrier's lien was involved, discussed previously.[40] However, the carrier is liable for damages caused by its failure to comply with requirements for sale and, in the case of wilful violation, it is liable for conversion.[41] The carrier may utilize so much of the proceeds as is sufficient to satisfy its lien and, if there are any proceeds remaining, it must hold the balance for delivery on demand to any person to whom it would have been bound to deliver the goods. The carrier may buy at any *public* sale.

Warehouse Receipts and Bills of Lading

Various Code rules are applicable equally to warehouse receipts and bills of lading. The issuance of such documents of title and their subsequent negotiation or transfer materially affect the rights and obligations of the issuer, bailee, and holders of the documents. First the general obligations of the issuer and bailee will be discussed, then the legal effects of the issuance, negotiation, and transfer of negotiable and non-negotiable documents of title, and finally missing documents of title.

General Obligations. ***Irregularities in the Issue of Documents of Title or Issuer's Conduct.*** *The issuer[42] of a document of title acquires the obligations imposed by the Code for such issuance and he cannot avoid them because of irregularities in the document, violation of the law by its issuance, or his own wrongful conduct.* The issuer cannot profit from his own wrong and use such wrong as a reason to escape obligation. The obligations of the issuer of a document of title are not affected by: non-compliance of the document with the requirements of the Code or any other statute or administrative regulation regarding its issue, form, or content; the issuer's violation of laws regulating the conduct of his business; ownership by the bailee of goods covered by the document at the time the document was issued; the issuer of a purported warehouse receipt not being a warehouseman at the time of its issuance.

Duplicate Document of Title or Overissue. The issuance of a duplicate document of title or the overissue of documents of title does not confer any right in the covered goods, except in the case of a lawfully issued bill of lading in a set of parts, overissue of documents for fungible goods,[43] and substitutes for lost, stolen or destroyed documents.[44] A duplicate document of title is an exact copy of another document of title outstanding. The issuance of a duplicate document of title should identify the document as a duplicate by conspicuous[45] notation of such fact on its face. Overissue occurs when a document of title is issued to cover goods already represented by an outstanding docu-

---

[40] See above, pp. 178–80.

[41] For conversion, see above, p. 166, ftn. 18.

[42] For meaning of issuer, see above, p. 175, ftn. 10.

[43] Discussed previously, above, p. 177.

[44] Discussed later, below, p. 195.

[45] See below, p. 319, ftn. 28.

ment of the *same* issuer. Two or more valid documents outstanding for the same goods at the same time but issued by *different* issuers do not constitute an overissue.[46] The issuer is liable for damages caused by his overissue or failure so to identify the document as a duplicate. It should be noted carefully that the issuer's liability for such damages is to *anyone*, which in the case of a non-negotiable document of title is an exception to the general rule that a transferee acquires only the rights of his transferor. (C issues a duplicate non-negotiable bill of lading without identification of its being a duplicate to A, who knows this. C is not liable to A. If A then transferred the duplicate to B, a good faith purchaser for value without notice of the document being a duplicate, while under the general rule B would get only what A had and, therefore, he could not hold C liable, nevertheless, by Code exception to the general rule here, B does not have to claim through A but may recover in his own right against C.)

Obligation to Deliver, Excuse. The bailee's obligation under the document is to deliver the goods covered by the document to a "person entitled under the document,"[47] provided such person complies with two conditions. If the document is *negotiable*, such person is the *holder*[48] of the document; if it is *non-negotiable*, such person is the one to whom delivery is to be made by the terms of, or pursuant to *written* instructions under, the document. *With respect to the first condition of such person,* if he has a right in the covered goods[49] and a *negotiable* document of title is outstanding, *he must surrender the document to the bailee* for cancelation or notation of partial deliveries. On his receipt of such negotiable document, the bailee must either cancel the document or conspicuously note the partial delivery thereon, and his failure to do so will make him liable to any innocent person to whom the document is duly negotiated.[50] *The bailee has no obligation to take up a non-negotiable document of title outstanding.* The obligation of the bailee of a non-negotiable document is to deliver the goods to the consignee, in the absence of knowledge of any previous transfer of the document. *With respect to the second condition of such person,* he must satisfy the bailee's lien where the bailee so requests or where the bailee is prohibited by law from delivering the goods until the charges are paid.

The bailee is excused from delivering the covered goods to a person entitled to the goods under the document if the bailee establishes any of the following:

---

[46] An illustration is a freight forwarder who combines its customers' small shipments into one carload shipment and issues a bill of lading to each customer for his small shipment, the common carrier issuing a bill of lading to the forwarder for the carload.

[47] UCC 7–403(1).

[48] See below, pp. 187–88.

[49] See below, pp. 190–91, when a document of title confers no right in the covered goods against a person who, before issuance of the document, had a legal interest or a perfected security interest in the goods.

[50] A bill of lading sometimes is called "spent" if the carrier had delivered the goods to a previous holder of the bill and the carrier had not taken up and canceled the bill.

1. Delivery of the goods to a person whose receipt was rightful as against the claimant. (O owns goods which are stolen by T and delivered for transportation to C, a carrier without notice of the theft. D is the consignee named in the bill of lading issued by C. O paid C the amount of the lien and demanded the goods from C. C's delivery of the goods to O excuses C from delivering them to D.)
2. Damage to, or delay, loss, or destruction of, the goods for which the bailee is not liable.
3. Previous sale or other disposition of the goods in lawful enforcement of the bailee's lien.[51]
4. Previous sale or other disposition of the goods in lawful termination of storage.[52]
5. The seller's exercise of his right of stoppage of delivery.[53]
6. Diversion, reconsignment or other disposition as provided under the Code[54] or tariff regulating this right.
7. The bailee has a personal defense against the claimant of the goods, as by a release, satisfaction, or any other fact.
8. Any other lawful excuse. This "may well protect a bailee who delivers pursuant to oral instructions of the person entitled, despite the requirement of 'written instructions' in the definition of 'person entitled under the document'."[55]

A bailee who in good faith has received goods and delivered or otherwise disposed of them according to the terms of the document of title or pursuant to the Documents of Title portion of the Code is not liable therefor. Good faith here includes observance of reasonable commercial standards, inasmuch as the bailee is a commercial warehouseman or carrier. It should be noted very carefully that such immunity from liability of the bailee applies "even though the person from whom he received the goods had no authority to procure the document or to dispose of the goods and even though the person to whom he delivered the goods had no authority to receive them"[56] but was a person entitled under the document. This is an exception to the Common Law liability for the tort of conversion[57] by an *innocent* bailee.

Negotiation and Transfer. ***In General.*** *Reference should be made at this time to "Negotiable Paper under the Code," discussed previously.*[58] Before getting into negotiation and transfer of documents of title, let us thoroughly understand the meaning of a very important word, "holder." A person is a holder of a document of title if two things are present. First, he must possess

---

[51] See above, for warehouseman, pp. 180; for carrier, pp. 184–85.

[52] See above, pp. 179–80.

[53] See below, pp. 275–77.

[54] See above, p. 182.

[55] Robert Braucher, "The Uniform Commercial Code—Documents of Title," in *Uniform Commercial Code Handbook* (Chicago: American Bar Association, 1964), p. 187.

[56] UCC 7–404.

[57] For conversion, see above, p. 166, ftn. 18.

[58] See above, pp. 150 ff.

the document; secondly, the document must flow to him either by its issuance or by indorsement. An indorsement is a person's signature made alone or with other words, on a document signed by the issuer. (S delivers goods to R railroad who signs and issues a document of title naming Frank Fay as the consignee. Frank Fay's signature in blank—without any additional words—on the document is an indorsement.) *The document flows to a person on its issuance:* to him ("to Frank Fay"); to his order ("to the order of Frank Fay"); to bearer ("to bearer") and he possesses the document; or in blank without designating any person or bearer and he possesses the document. *The document flows to him by indorsement:* to him ("to John Smith. [signed] Frank Fay"); to his order ("to the order of John Smith. [signed] Frank Fay"); to bearer ("to bearer. [signed] Frank Fay") and he possesses the document; or in blank, the indorsement not designating any person or bearer ("______. [signed] Frank Fay") and he possesses the document. A person may be a holder of a document whether it be negotiable or non-negotiable, and whether or not it is to order. This discussion of a holder should help in understanding its very compact definition under the Code:[59] "'Holder' means a person who is in possession of a document of title or an instrument or an investment security drawn, issued or indorsed to him or to his order or to bearer or in blank." *A document is negotiated or transferred to a holder when it is delivered to a person in such form that the transferee becomes a holder.* He has possession and the document flows to him by name, as bearer, or by the blank indorsement of the specified person to whom the document previously flowed.

A document of title is *negotiable* if, by its terms, the goods are to be delivered either *to the order of* a named person, or *to bearer.*[60] A negotiable document of title may be either negotiated or transferred without negotiation, while a non-negotiable document of title can only be transferred. The rights acquired under a *negotiable* document of title depend upon whether the document has been negotiated or transferred without negotiation. A negotiable document of title may run to the order of a named person or, by its original terms, it may run to bearer. When the negotiable document runs to the order of a named person, it can be negotiated only by that person's indorsement and delivery of the document. His indorsement may be in blank or to bearer in which case any person can negotiate the document by delivery alone; and similarly, a negotiable document originally issued to bearer may be negotiated by delivery alone. On the other hand, his indorsement may be to a specified person ("to John Smith. [signed] Frank Fay"), and the latter's indorsement and delivery of the document are necessary to further negotiation of the document. In the illustration given, John Smith will have to indorse the document before it can be further negotiated. When a negotiable document running to the order of a named person is delivered to him, the effect is the

---

[59] UCC 1–201(20).

[60] ". . . or where recognized in overseas trade, if it runs to a named person or assigns." UCC 7–104(1) (b).

same as if the document had been negotiated. In brief, *a negotiable document of title is negotiated when it is transferred in such form that the transferee becomes a holder. A negotiable document of title is "duly negotiated" when it is negotiated to a holder who purchases it in good faith, without notice of any defense against, or claim to, it on the part of any person, and for value.*[61] A person to whom a negotiable document of title has been "duly negotiated" will thereby acquire rights in the document greater than if it had merely been negotiated to him. There is an exception to "duly negotiated"; if the negotiation is not in the regular course of business or financing, or involves receiving the document in settlement or payment of a money obligation, the document cannot be considered to have been "duly negotiated." For example, the transferor of the document may not be the kind of person with whom it is reasonable to deal in that type of transaction; he is not a person in the trade. Or the transaction may be one in which a person would not engage without inquiry, as a purchase for resale at an unusually low price or the document itself manifests irregularity. While a pre-existing claim is value and the pledge of a negotiable document of title to *secure* a past debt is normal, nevertheless the *payment* of a debt with the document as commodity paper is not commercially regular. It should be noted in passing that the indorsement of a non-negotiable document neither makes it negotiable nor adds to the transferee's rights. Also, the naming in a negotiable bill of a person to be notified of the arrival of the goods does not limit the negotiability of the bill nor constitute notice to a purchaser thereof of any interest of such person in the goods.

Rights Acquired by Due Negotiation. A negotiable document of title stands in the place of the goods, and *the bailee cannot safely deliver the goods covered by the document to anyone as long as the negotiable document of title is outstanding.* It is a symbol of title to the goods. Except for those instances where a document of title to goods may be defeated, to be discussed later,[62] and except for the power of a warehouseman of fungible goods to transfer title to such goods to a buyer in ordinary course of business, discussed previously,[63] a holder of a negotiable document of title duly negotiated to him thereby acquires the following:

(a) title to the document;
(b) title to the goods;
(c) all rights accruing under the law of agency or estoppel, including rights to goods delivered to the bailee after the document was issued; and
(d) the direct obligation of the issuer to hold or deliver the goods according to the terms of the document free of any defense or claim by him except those arising under the terms of the document or under this Article. In the case of a [*negotiable*] *delivery order* the bailee's obligation accrues only upon acceptance and the obligation acquired by the holder is that the issuer and any

[61] For the meaning of value, see UCC 1–201(44), above, pp. 48–49.

[62] See the next two paragraphs.

[63] See above, pp. 176–77.

> indorser will procure the acceptance of the bailee. (Author's brackets and italics.)[64]

The Code particularizes *the following defenses and claims which the issuer cannot assert against the holder of a negotiable document of title duly negotiated to him,* (subject to those instances where a document of title to goods may be defeated). They are: any stoppage of the goods represented by the document;[65] the bailee's unauthorized surrender of the goods to some other person; the negotiation or any prior negotiation of the document was in breach of a duty; a person was deprived of possession of the document by misrepresentation, fraud, accident, mistake, duress, loss, theft, or conversion; a previous sale or other transfer of the goods or the document has been made to a third person.

We have just discussed the general rule that the holder of a negotiable document of title duly negotiated to him acquires title to the document and to the covered goods. But the rule is general because it is subject to certain instances where title to the covered goods may be defeated because of the more righteous and, therefore, superior position of a claimant *prior to such holder.* The desirability of encouraging persons to accept negotiable documents of title with assurance that a holder to whom it was duly negotiated will thereby acquire title to the goods conflicts, however, with a legal fundamental that *the owner of an interest in goods continues as the owner until by his conduct he deprives himself of such ownership either by his disposition of his interest or by his conduct precluding himself from asserting his ownership against such a holder.* Where the conduct of a prior party introduced the goods into the stream of commerce or carried them along that stream, as between him and the holder of the negotiable document duly negotiated to such holder, the latter prevails because of the prior party's conduct to the prejudice of such subsequent holder. However, if the prior party is not guilty of such conduct, then his interest in the covered goods should prevail over the holder of the negotiable document duly negotiated to such holder. (T steals O's goods and delivers them for transportation to C, a carrier who issues a negotiable bill of lading to T as consignee. T duly negotiates the document to H, a holder. O and H now demand the goods from C. O has title to the covered goods and he will prevail over H and against C.) Accordingly, the Code states that *the holder of a negotiable document of title duly negotiated to him acquires title to the document and to the covered goods, but title to the goods is subject to a prior claimant with either a legal interest or a perfected security interest*[66] *in the goods, unless certain conduct of the prior claimant with respect to possession of the goods has occurred.*[67] The nature of that conduct therefore becomes vitally important.

---

[64] UCC 7–502.

[65] For stoppage of delivery, see below, pp. 275–77.

[66] For perfected security interest, see below, 433–34.

[67] See UCC 7–502(1).

A person with a legal interest or a perfected security interest in goods *subsequently* covered by *any* document of title prevails over any rights acquired under such document, and the document confers no right in the goods *against such person unless the latter:* (a) *delivered or entrusted the goods or any document of title covering them to the bailor or his nominee* (1) *with actual or apparent authority to ship, store or sell them,*[68] *or* (2) *with power to obtain delivery under the Code provisions on Documents of Title,*[69] *or* (3) *with power of disposition under this Code generally,*[70] *or other statute or rule of law;*[71] *or* (b) *acquiesced in the procurement by the bailor or his nominee of any document of title.* This applies to non-negotiable, as well as to negotiable, documents of title.

Delivery orders and bills of lading issued by freight forwarders are documents of title, and title to the goods thereunder may be defeated. A delivery order is "a written order to deliver goods directed to a warehouseman, carrier or other person who in the ordinary course of business issues warehouse receipts or bills of lading."[72] For example, the holder of a bill of lading may issue a delivery order to the carrier to deliver the covered goods to another person named in the delivery order. On the bailee's acceptance of a delivery order, the delivery order has the same effect as a document of title issued by the bailee, the delivery order is for all practical purposes indistinguishable from a warehouse receipt, and *the bailee now holds the goods pursuant to the delivery order and not the document of title previously issued by the bailee.* A bailee who has issued a *negotiable* document of title outstanding should not accept a delivery order without the surrender of the negotiable document of title to him and either cancelling it or making a notation conspicuously thereon that partial delivery has been made; his failure to do so makes him liable to any person to whom the document is duly negotiated, as discussed previously.[73] The bailee's obligation accrues only on his acceptance of the delivery order, and the issuer and any previous indorsers of an unaccepted delivery order have an obligation to the holder of such order to procure the bailee's acceptance. Until the bailee accepts a delivery order, he is not bound thereon and has only the obligations of his contract with the depositor of the goods with him. *Title to goods based upon an unaccepted delivery order is subject to the rights of anyone to whom a negotiable warehouse receipt or bill of lading covering the goods has been duly negotiated. Also, the title to the goods covered by an unaccepted delivery order may be defeated as indicated in the next paragraph.* It should be noted carefully, with respect to bills of lading issued by freight forwarders, that *title to the goods covered by a bill of lading*

---

[68] For example, see Factors, above, pp. 147–48.

[69] See Obligation to Deliver, Excuse, above, pp. 186–87.

[70] See Voidable Title Transfers, above, pp. 148–49; Entrusting Goods to a Merchant Who Deals in Goods of That Kind, above, pp. 149–50; Goods Under the Code on Sales, above, p. 147–50.

[71] See Transfer of Title by Estoppel, above, p. 147.

[72] UCC 7–102(1) (d).

[73] See above, p. 186.

issued to a freight forwarder is subject to the rights of anyone to whom a negotiable bill issued by the freight forwarder is duly negotiated, although delivery by the carrier pursuant to its own bill of lading in accordance with the Code[74] discharges the carrier's obligation to deliver. This seems but fair inasmuch as the bailee's bill of lading issued to the freight forwarder gives notice on its face that a freight forwarder is involved, which fact gives notice that the freight forwarder may issue or may have already issued his own bills of lading for the same goods.

The rights of a "transferee" of a negotiable document of title may also be defeated. A negotiable document of title may be either negotiated or transferred, but a non-negotiable document of title may only be transferred. A negotiable document of title is negotiated by its delivery to a holder,[75] who is the person in possession of the document and to whom the document runs either originally or by indorsement. *Lack of a required indorsement on a negotiable document precludes negotiation and the person to whom the document was delivered is solely a transferee.* However, "the transferee of a negotiable document of title has a specifically enforceable right to have his transferor supply any necessary indorsement but the transfer becomes a negotiation only as of the time the indorsement is supplied."[76] A person is also a transferee of a negotiable document if, while it has been negotiated to him, it has not been "duly negotiated" to him.[77] *Thus, a transferee of a negotiable document of title is the person to whom the document has been delivered but not duly negotiated.* (T steals O's goods and delivers them for transportation to C, a carrier who issues a negotiable bill of lading to T as consignee. T delivers the bill for value to P, who is not aware of the theft. At this point P is a transferee. P then discovers the theft and obtains T's blank indorsement on the bill. P is a holder of the bill negotiated to him as of the time of T's indorsement and, since *at the time of negotiation* P knew of the theft, the bill has not been "duly negotiated" to him and he is still a transferee.) It is important to ascertain the status of the possessor of a document of title because, if he is only a *transferee,* his rights under the document are much narrower than those rights acquired by a holder of a negotiable document of title *duly negotiated* to such holder.

Rights Acquired in the Absence of Due Negotiation. A document of title can be only *transferred* if the document is non-negotiable or, if negotiable, it has not been properly indorsed. *A transferee of a document of title, whether negotiable or non-negotiable, acquires the title and rights which his transferor had or had actual authority to convey. With respect to non-negotiable documents of title, the transferee has the right to notify the bailee of the transfer of the document to him and thereby acquire whatever obligation the bailee*

---

[74] See above, p. 187.

[75] For holder, see above, pp. 187–88.

[76] UCC 7–506.

[77] UCC 7–504 (1). For negotiation, see above, 187–89; for due negotiation, see above, p. 189.

owed to the transferor of the bill immediately before notification. Before such notification is given to the bailee by the transferee or transferor, the transferee's rights under the non-negotiable document of title and his right to acquire the bailee's obligations to his transferor may be defeated by various persons. *First,* before notification to the bailee of the transfer to the transferee, the transferor's creditors may exercise their right to avoid the sale by the transferor, discussed later under Sales,[78] and thereby defeat the transferee's rights. *Second,* before notification to the bailee of the transfer to the transferee, the transferor may sell the goods to a buyer in ordinary course of business and the bailee either delivers the goods to such buyer or receives notification of such buyer's rights, thereby defeating the transferee's rights. *Third,* before notification to the bailee of the transfer to the transferee, the bailee may deal in good faith with the transferor, as by delivering the goods to him or otherwise, and thereby defeat the transferee's rights.

There are other instances in the case of non-negotiable documents of title where the consignee's rights under the document may be defeated either by the consignor or by the seller of shipped goods. The consignor of shipped goods under a non-negotiable bill of lading may divert the goods or otherwise change the shipping instructions, discussed previously,[79] which causes the bailee not to deliver the goods to the consignee, thereby defeating the consignee's rights against the bailee. Should the diverted or reshipped goods be delivered to a buyer in ordinary course of business, the consignee's title to the goods is thereby defeated, and the new buyer consignee acquires the title. The seller's exercise of his right to stoppage in transit or otherwise and the exercise of his legal remedies in the disposition of the goods thereby defeats the consignee's rights against the bailee and the consignee's rights against the goods. A bailee honoring the seller's instructions is entitled to be indemnified by the seller against any resulting loss or expense. However, it should be noted that the bailee cannot be compelled to deliver to creditors of the person who deposited with the bailee the goods covered by a *negotiable* document of title outstanding without the surrender, or the legal impounding, of such document. But there is an exception; a person with a legal interest or a perfected security interest in the goods who has not by his conduct caused the loss of his interest[80] has the right to such goods and, therefore, *his* creditors can reach such goods and obtain them from the carrier *without* having to surrender any document of title outstanding. Under the Code:

> Except where the document was originally issued upon delivery of the goods by a person who had no power to dispose of them, no lien attaches by virtue of any judicial process to goods in the possession of a bailee for which a *negotiable* document of title is outstanding unless the document be first surrendered to the bailee or its negotiation enjoined, and the bailee shall not be compelled to de-

[78] See below, pp. 228–29.

[79] See above, p. 182.

[80] For when conduct causes loss of interest, see above, pp. 190–91.

> liver the goods pursuant to process until the document is surrendered to him or impounded by the court. One who purchases the document for value without notice of the process or injunction takes free of the lien imposed by judicial process.[81] (Author's italics.)

Warranties. A person, other than a mere intermediary, who negotiates or transfers a document of title to a *purchaser for value* thereby makes various warranties with respect *to the goods* covered by the document and also with respect *to the document* itself, whether it be negotiable or non-negotiable. Unless otherwise agreed, his warranties are made *only* to his immediate purchaser. The transfer or negotiation of the document warrants the express and implied warranties made in selling goods under the Sales portion of the Code.[82] To the extent that the Sales portion of the Code permits disclaimer of any warranty, the parties may so provide in their agreement. In addition, unless otherwise agreed, the person negotiating or transferring the document makes *all* of the following warranties: that the document is genuine, i.e., "free of forgery or counterfeiting";[83] that he has no knowledge of any fact which would impair its validity or worth; that his negotiation or transfer is rightful with respect to the title to the document and the goods it represents; that his negotiation or transfer is fully effective with respect to the title to the document and the goods it represents. When the person negotiating or transferring a document of title is an intermediary entrusted with the document, he thereby makes by such negotiation or transfer limited warranties and only with respect to the document. Under the Code:[84] "A collecting bank[85] or other intermediary[86] known to be entrusted with documents on behalf of another or with collection of a draft or other claim against delivery of documents warrants by such delivery of the document *only its own good faith and authority.* This rule applies even though the intermediary has purchased or made advances against the claim or draft to be collected." (Author's italics.)

With respect to indorsements on a document of title, whether negotiable or non-negotiable, the purpose of an indorsement is to perfect the rights of the transferee under the document rather than to impose any obligation upon the indorser. Accordingly, "The indorsement of a document of title *issued by a bailee* does not make the indorser liable for any default by the bailee or by previous indorsers."[87] (Author's italics.) We have already seen[88] that among the

---

[81] UCC 7–602.

[82] See below, pp. 230–46.

[83] UCC 1–201(18).

[84] UCC 7–508.

[85] UCC 4–105(d): " 'Collecting bank' means any bank handling the item for collection except the payor bank."

[86] UCC 4–105(c): " 'Intermediary bank' means any bank to which an item is transferred in course of collection except the depositary or payor bank."

[87] UCC 7–505.

[88] See above, p. 191.

rights which a holder acquires under an *unaccepted negotiable delivery order*[89] duly negotiated to him is the obligation that the issuer and any indorser will procure the acceptance of the delivery order by the bailee. Once the bailee accepts the delivery order, the indorser has no further obligation under the delivery order.

Missing Documents of Title. A document of title may be missing because it has been lost, stolen, or destroyed. If a document of title has been lost, stolen, or destroyed, action may be taken either by the bailee or by a court. The bailee may, without court order, deliver the goods to a person claiming under a missing document of title, but by doing so the bailee becomes liable to any person injured thereby. Also, if the bailee does not act in good faith in making such delivery without court order, he becomes liable for conversion. He makes delivery in good faith without court order and is not liable for conversion if either the delivery was made in accordance with a filed classification or tariff, or, where no classification or tariff is filed, the claimant posts security with the bailee in an amount at least double the value of the goods at the time of posting to indemnify any person injured by the delivery who files a notice of claim within one year after the delivery. Alternatively, at the request of either the bailee or a claimant and on the applicant's proof that the document of title has been lost, stolen, or destroyed, a court may order either delivery of the goods or the issuance of a substitute document of title to the claimant. The bailee must comply with the court order and, therefore, he is not liable to anyone by his compliance. If the document was negotiable, the claimant must post security approved by the court to indemnify any person who may suffer loss as a result of non-surrender of the document. If the document was not negotiable, such security is not required, although the court may, in its discretion, order payment of the bailee's reasonable costs and counsel fees. It should be noted that, unless otherwise indicated, the above discussion applies to all documents of title, whether negotiable or non-negotiable.

PROBLEMS

1. A delivers goods to B, a common carrier, in X city for shipment to C in Y city with instructions that such goods are to be held at X for five days and then sent on their way. During the five days, part of the goods is damaged without any negligence by B. After the expiration of five days and while the goods are being transported by B, further damage occurs without any negligence by B. While the goods are being transported by D, a connecting carrier, more damage occurs.
   (1) Is B liable for such damage to the goods?
   (2) Why?
2. (a) A delivered his truck to B under an agreement whereby B was to have the use of the truck for six months for a specified rental charge payable in advance. At the end of three months, A needed the truck and demanded its possession from B, tendering the return of one-half the rent received by him. B refused to deliver

[89] For meaning of delivery order, see above, p. 191.

the truck to A, who forcibly repossessed the truck. What are the rights of the parties?

(b) X bailed goods to Y for one month for $100. Z stole the goods and damaged them. What are the rights of X and Y?

3. T stole goods from O and sold them to B, a good faith purchaser for value and without notice of the theft, and shipped them to B by C, a common carrier. T received from C a bill of lading drawn to the order of B and delivered it to B.

(1) If both O and B demand the goods from C, B tendering the bill to C, who is entitled to them? Why?

(2) May C assert a carrier's lien on the goods for the transportation charges? Why?

4. *See problem number 5, at the end of Chapter 11, above, p. 154.*

Part Three:
Personal Property
D. Sales

Chapter 14

FORMATION OF THE CONTRACT

In a "present sale" of goods, title passes at the time the sales contract is made. In a "contract to sell," title passes only in the future. *Title cannot pass until the goods are "existing and identified" to the contract.* If they are existing and identified when the contract is made, there can be a present sale or a contract to sell depending on the *intention* of the parties. If they are not, they are "future goods" and there can be only a contract to sell, except that a present sale or a contract to sell can occur if there is a sale of a part interest in existing and identified goods or of an undivided share in existing and identified bulk fungible goods.

An irrevocable *"firm offer"* under the Code does not require any consideration and is a *merchant's* signed written offer to buy or sell goods assuring that the offer will be kept open for no more than three months, or for a reasonable time not exceeding three months if no time is expressly stated. An offeree's *written confirmation* of an order for goods is an acceptance. An offeree's expression of acceptance is an acceptance of the terms offered, even though it states terms additional to or different from those offered, the additional terms being proposals for addition to the contract. *Between merchants,* the additional terms become part of the contract unless: the offer expressly limits acceptance to the terms of the offer; they *materially* alter it; or notification of objection to them has already been given or is given within a reasonable time after notice of them has been received. The parties may agree: in good faith and without consideration, to modify the agreement terms; to waive any of them; or to rescind the agreement. The contract as modified may come under the Statute of Frauds for the sale of goods. Rights to damages for breach and rights to proceeds for the assignor's performance are *always* assignable. Unless the cir-

cumstances indicate the contrary, a prohibition of assignment of "the contract" means that *only delegation is not permitted.* The assignee's acceptance of a delegation is a promise to perform creating a third party creditor beneficiary contract.

A contract for the sale of goods for the price of $500 or more is under the Code on Sales Statute of Frauds and is *unenforceable* unless there is a proper writing with three elements: (1) the writing indicates that a contract for the sale of goods has been made; (2) it is signed by the party against whom the contract is sought to be enforced or by his authorized agent; (3) it must specify a quantity of goods. The writing may consist of more than one writing either attached to, or referred to by, the signed writing. Four contracts are excluded from the Statute: (1) for non-resellable goods; (2) to the extent of part or all of the goods received and accepted by the buyer; (3) to the extent of the apportioned value of the goods for part or complete payment made by the buyer to the seller; (4) to the extent of the goods admitted by a party in court to have been the subject of a contract for sale.

Subject Matter

Code Coverage. The law of sales of goods is governed by Article 2 of the Uniform Commercial Code entitled "Sales," which is concerned only with *transactions for the sale of goods.* That Article does not apply to transactions involving goods which are intended to operate *only as security transactions;* such transactions are considered under Article 9 on Secured Transactions. Goods may be a part of a stock in trade of a business and, when transferred in bulk by sale or otherwise, Article 6 of the Uniform Commercial Code entitled "Bulk Transfers" is applicable in order to prevent commercial fraud. First Sales under Article 2, and then Bulk Transfers under Article 6, will be discussed.

Goods. "'Goods' means all things (including specially manufactured goods) which are movable at the time of identification to the contract for sale other than the money in which the price is to be paid, investment securities (Article 8) and things in action. 'Goods' also includes the unborn young of animals and growing crops and other identified things attached to realty as described in the section on goods to be severed from realty (Section 2–107)."[1] It should be noted carefully under UCC 2–107(1) that if the *seller* is to sever those enumerated items (oil, minerals, structure) related to the land, the contract is for the sale of goods and is under this Article of the Code; but if the *buyer* is to sever such items, the contract affects an interest in land, it is not a contract for the sale of goods under the Code, and it comes within that portion of the statute of frauds concerned with the transfer of an interest in land.[2]

---

[1] UCC 2–105(1). UCC 2–107.

[2] See above, pp. 88–89.

Subsection 2 of UCC 2–107 is concerned with different items related to the land (growing crops or other things attached to realty and capable of severance without material harm thereto and not included in subsection (1)) which may be severed by either the seller *or* the buyer, and a contract for their sale is for goods and is under the Code. Inasmuch as a third person may become a subsequent purchaser or creditor of the land innocent of the contract for sale of the goods related to the land and thereby adversely affect the original buyer's interest in the goods under his contract of purchase, the original buyer of goods to be severed from the realty may protect his interest in such goods from such subsequent impairment by recording his contract for sale against the land and thereby put all third persons on constructive notice of the contract. While money bargained for as a medium of exchange is not goods, it is goods if bargained for as a commodity.

The Code introduces the two new terms "lot" and "commercial unit." "Lot" means "a parcel or a single article which is the subject matter of a separate sale or delivery, whether or not it is sufficient to perform the contract."[3] For example, each chair in a contract for sale of 100 chairs is a lot; it is a single item. A "commercial unit" is "such a unit of goods as by commercial usage is a single whole for purposes of sale and division of which materially impairs its character or value on the market or use."[4] It may be a single unit, as a machine; a set of articles, as a suite of furniture or an assortment of sizes; a quantity, as a bale, gross, or carload; or any other unit treated in use or in the relevant market as a single whole.

Contracts for Sale

The transaction for the sale of goods is called a "contract for sale," which includes both a "present sale" of goods and a "contract to sell" goods at a future time. If the title to the goods passes from the seller to the buyer *at the time the contract is made,* the transaction is a *present sale.* In a *contract to sell,* the title does not pass at the time the contract is made but is to *pass in the future.* Inasmuch as the title to goods may be transferred as a gift, which does not come under the Code, the Code uses the term "sale" to mean the passing of title for a price.

Kinds of Goods

"Existing and Identified" and "Future" Goods. The kind of goods in a contract for sale is determined *as of the time the contract is made.* If the goods exist *and* are identified to the contract at that time, they are called "existing and identified goods"; if not, they are called "future goods." It is irrelevant whether the seller has the potentiality of performing his contract. The kind of

[3] UCC 2–105(5).

[4] UCC 2–105(6).

goods is important because *goods must be both existing and identified*[5] *to the contract before any interest in them can pass.* An exception is a contract for sale of a part interest in existing and identified goods, discussed immediately below. Accordingly, a *contract to sell* goods may be concerned with existing and identified goods, the title to which is to be transferred at a future time, or it may involve future goods. When the future goods are subsequently identified to the contract, only then can title to such goods pass to the buyer. A *present sale* of goods involves only existing and identified goods or a part interest in existing and identified goods. Although the intention of the buyer and seller governs, nevertheless there cannot be a present sale of future goods. Should the parties' language attempt to do this, the purported present sale operates as a contract to sell.[6]

Sale of Part Interest in Goods. As an exception to the rule that goods must be existing and identified before any interest in them can pass, *a present sale may occur of a part interest in existing and identified goods.* (S owns an automobile and contracted for the sale to B of a one-half share in such automobile. The automobile is existing and identified and, although the undivided share exists but is not identified, nevertheless there is a present sale to B of a one-half share in the automobile.)

Fungible Goods. Existing and identified goods which are *fungible* in nature and *in bulk* may also be the object of a present sale of an *undivided share* therein. " 'Fungible' with respect to goods or securities means goods or securities of which any unit is, by nature or usage of trade, the equivalent of any other like unit. Goods which are not fungible shall be deemed fungible for the purposes of this Act to the extent that under a particular agreement or document unlike units are treated as equivalents."[7] Oil or wine in a vat, grain in a bin, cotton or wool in a heap, are illustrative of fungible goods. However, while several bales of cotton, several barrels of butter, or several barrels of flour do not constitute fungible goods, nevertheless the parties may by their agreement specify that such goods shall be considered as fungible goods, in which case they will be so considered. "An undivided share in an identified bulk of fungible goods is sufficiently identified to be sold although the quantity of the bulk is not determined. Any agreed proportion of such a bulk or any quantity thereof agreed upon by number, weight or other measure may to the extent of the seller's interest in the bulk be sold to the buyer who then becomes an owner in common."[8] (B examines S's 1,000 gallon vat of wine. If B contracts with S for the sale of 500 gallons from that vat, there is a present sale of 500 gallons to B. However, if B contracts with S for the purchase of 500 gallons of wine like that in the vat, there is a contract to sell future goods because there

---

[5] For identification of goods, see below, pp. 225–26.

[6] UCC 2–105(2).

[7] UCC 1–201(17).

[8] UCC 2–105(4). For the transfer of title to fungible goods by a warehouseman even though covered by a negotiable warehouse receipt, see above, p. 150.

was no intent to sell an undivided share *of that* existing and identified wine but rather future wine *like that* in the vat.)

Contracts between Merchants

The Code recognizes the professional status of merchants and those who profess to be such or have the knowledge and skill of such. A merchant is "a person who deals in goods of the kind or otherwise by his occupation holds himself out as having knowledge or skill peculiar to the practices or goods involved in the transaction or to whom such knowledge or skill may be attributed by his employment of an agent or broker or other intermediary who by his occupation holds himself out as having such knowledge or skill. . . . 'Between merchants' means in any transaction with respect to which both parties are chargeable with the knowledge or skill of merchants."[9]

In order to establish clear and specific criteria among merchants in their dealings with each other, the Code expressly states certain rules applicable "between merchants" and "as against a merchant," wherever they are needed. *They apply only to merchants,* not to non-merchants. These rules may be conveniently grouped into three categories. The rules in the first category are concerned with normal, non-specialized business practices of merchants acting in a mercantile capacity.[10] The rules for the second category are concerned with the rights in goods which buyers may reasonably expect to acquire from merchant sellers and the rights of creditors in goods possessed by merchants.[11] The rules for the third category are concerned with a merchant's good faith, which means "honesty in fact and the observance of reasonable commercial standards of fair dealing in the trade."[12] They deal with responsibilities of merchant buyers to follow a seller's instructions, risk of loss, and adequate assurance of performance.[13]

[9] UCC 2–104(1) (3).

[10] UCC 2–201(2) is concerned with the Statute of Frauds; 2–205 with firm offers; 2–207(2) with the inclusion in a merchant's acceptance or written confirmation of terms additional to or different from those in the offer; 2–209(2) with clauses excluding modification or recission of a written agreement except by a signed writing.

[11] UCC 2–312(3) is concerned with the merchant seller's express warranty against infringement; 2–314(1) with the merchant seller's implied warranty of merchantability; 2–402(2) with the non-fraudulent legal effect of a merchant seller's retention in good faith of sold goods; 2–403(2) with the legal power of a merchant seller unauthorizedly to transfer to a buyer in ordinary course of business the rights in the goods of the person entrusting their possession to the merchant seller; 2–326(3) with the fixing of a transaction as a sale or return as to creditors of a merchant seller under certain conditions.

[12] UCC 2–103(b).

[13] UCC 2–327(1)(c) is concerned with the merchant buyer's obligation to follow reasonable instructions of the seller on the merchant buyer's election to return goods under a sale on approval; 2–603 with a merchant buyer's duties as to rightfully rejected goods; 2–605(1)(b) with waiver of a buyer's objections by failure to particularize defects in goods when the transaction is between merchants; 2–509(3) with a merchant seller's risk of loss in the absence of breach for goods, physical delivery of which is to be made at the merchant seller's place; 2–609(2) with the application of commercial standards in determining the reasonableness of grounds for insecurity and the adequacy of any assurance offered when the transaction is between merchants.

Offer and Acceptance

Manifested Intention of the Parties. A contract for sale of goods will result if the manifestations of the parties show agreement to make a binding transaction. Their manifestations may be expressed in any form, whether oral, written, or otherwise, irrespective of whether or not they are enforceable under the statute of frauds. Their *conduct* may be sufficient not only to create a contract but also to recognize the *prior* existence of a contract. A contract may be made even though the time of its creation is undetermined. For example, while the conduct of the parties may show that a contract was made, nevertheless their writings may not clearly indicate the exact time when they finished bargaining. Even though the parties have left some terms open, this does not preclude the formation of a contract for indefiniteness, as long as: (*1*) *the parties have intended to make a contract, and* (2) *there is a reasonably certain basis for giving an appropriate remedy.* Commercial standards provide the basis for filling in the missing terms and giving an appropriate remedy, and the Code provides for such standards, e.g., open price terms,[14] open delivery terms,[15] and open payment terms.[16] It should be noted, however, that the greater the number of terms left open the greater the likelihood that the parties did not intend to make a contract. Also, if the parties manifest an intent not to have a contract until the open terms become certain, then no contract is formed until this occurs. Auctions were considered under Contracts.[17]

The Offer. Under the law of Contracts, in the absence of statute to the contrary, a promise is unenforceable unless supported by consideration, and an oral or written promise to keep an offer open is unenforceable without such consideration. If consideration for the promise is present, the promise is enforceable as a contract to keep the offer open, and the offer is an option.[18] This is also the law under the Code, with one exception.[19] When a *signed written* offer to buy or sell goods, made by a *merchant,* by its terms gives assurance that it will be held open, the offer is called a "firm offer," which is enforceable without consideration. A merchant's *oral* offer, and a non-merchant's oral or written offer, is governed by the law of Contracts and requires consideration to be enforceable. Under the Code, the Common Law effect of the seal with respect to consideration is destroyed. However, a seal may still be used to authenticate a signature, or even to serve as a signature of a party who so intends it or if it is so provided by statute. The merchant's firm offer without consideration is irrevocable for the time stated therein, or if no time is stated then for a reasonable time, but in no event is it irrevocable for more than three months. If such offer states that it is for a longer time, it is irrevocable only for

[14] UCC 2–305.

[15] UCC 2–308.

[16] UCC 2–310.

[17] See above, p. 21.

[18] See above, p. 25.

[19] UCC 2–205.

three months. However, it can be renewed without consideration. Note that such offer is made *by* a merchant; it may be made *to* anyone. To protect a merchant from inadvertently signing an offer with an assurance that it will be held open *on a form supplied by the offeree,* the merchant offeror must *separately sign such assurance clause in the offer.* " 'Signed' includes any symbol executed or adopted by a party with present intention to authenticate a writing."[20] It should be noted that *anyone* may make a promise to keep an offer open which, if supported by consideration creates an option under the law of Contracts which is irrevocable for as long as the parties agree.

The Acceptance. When an offer clearly *prescribes* the *exclusive* manner or medium of acceptance, only the offeree's use of that manner or medium constitutes an acceptance. Under the Code, if the offer does not clearly *require* otherwise, an offer to make a contract shall be construed as inviting acceptance in any manner and by any medium reasonable in the circumstances.

The Code reflects commercial practice by providing that an order or other offer to buy goods for prompt or current shipment shall be construed as inviting acceptance *either* by a prompt promise to ship or by prompt or current shipment.[21] Shipment here does not include the *beginning of delivery* by the *seller's* own truck or by his messenger. The offeree seller may clearly manifest his intention to become bound by *beginning to render* the requested performance and, when this is a reasonable mode of acceptance, if he so notifies[22] the offeror buyer within a reasonable time, such beginning of performance is an acceptance. If the offeror buyer is not notified of acceptance within a reasonable time, he may treat the offer as having lapsed before acceptance. It should be noted that, inasmuch as the offeree seller's shipment of goods manifests his intention to close the bargain and accept the offer, his shipment of conforming *or non-conforming* goods is an acceptance, although shipment of non-conforming goods is also a breach of contract. The offeree seller may protect himself from having his defective shipment constitute an acceptance and a breach by seasonably notifying the offeror buyer that the shipment is an offer for the *accommodation* of the offeror buyer. In effect, the seller is making a counteroffer.

When the buyer and seller have closed the deal there is a contract. A definite and seasonable expression of acceptance or a *written confirmation* which is sent within a reasonable time operates as an acceptance. However, a party's written confirmation or expression of acceptance may state terms additional to, or different from, those offered or agreed upon; this does not stop the expression of acceptance or confirmation from being an acceptance, as long as it does

---

[20] UCC 1–201(39). Initialling is signing. A person's handwriting on his own stationery confirming his previous firm offer would probably be sufficient as a signature, as would a telegram even though the draft contained only a typewritten signature. See UCC 2–205, *Comment 2.*

[21] For a discussion of shipment, see below, pp. 249–50.

[22] UCC 1–201(26): "A person 'notifies' or 'gives' a notice or notification to another by taking such steps as may be reasonably required to inform the other in ordinary course whether or not such other actually comes to know of it."

not expressly make acceptance conditional on the other party's assent to the additional or different terms. For example, a party adds "Ship by Tuesday," "Rush," "Ship draft against bill of lading inspection allowed." The additional or different terms are construed as *proposals or offers for addition to the contract* and are available for acceptance or rejection by the offeree under the normal rules of the law of Contracts governing acceptance. However, *when the transaction is between merchants,* the additional terms *become part of the contract, unless:*

(a) the offer expressly limits acceptance to the terms of the offer;
(b) they materially alter it; or
(c) notification of objection to them has already been given or is given within a reasonable time after notice of them is received.[23]

The test of whether or not the additional terms *materially* alter the bargain between merchants is *whether they would result in unreasonable surprise or hardship if so incorporated in the contract without express awareness by the other party.* Examples of additional terms materially altering the contract are: "a clause negating such standard warranties as that of merchantability or fitness for a particular purpose in circumstances in which either warranty normally attaches; . . . a clause reserving to the seller the power to cancel upon the buyer's failure to meet any invoice when due; a clause requiring that complaints be made in a time materially shorter than customary or reasonable." Examples of additional terms not materially altering the contract are: "a clause fixing a reasonable time for complaints within customary limits, or in the case of a purchase for sub-sale, providing for inspection by the sub-purchaser; a clause providing for interest on overdue invoices or fixing the seller's standard credit terms where they are within the range of trade practice and do not limit any credit bargained for; . . . Where clauses on confirming forms sent by both parties conflict each party must be assumed to object to a clause of the other conflicting with one on the confirmation sent by himself. As a result the requirement that there be notice of objection . . . is satisfied and the conflicting terms do not become a part of the contract. The contract then consists of the terms originally expressly agreed to, terms on which the confirmations agree, and terms supplied by" the Code.[24]

There are occasions where the *conduct* of both parties recognizes the existence of a contract but their writings do not of themselves establish a contract. Inasmuch as the Code effects the manifested intent of the parties to have a contract, it provides that *a contract may be made by both parties' conduct recognizing the existence of such a contract.* When this occurs, the terms of the contract consist of those terms on which the writings of the parties agree, together with any supplementary terms incorporated under any other provisions of the Code.[25]

---

[23] UCC 2–207.

[24] UCC 2–207, *Comments 4, 5, 6.*

[25] UCC 2–207(3).

Interpretation. In order to interpret the meaning of an agreement which has resulted in a contract for sale of goods, various factors become important. The intent of the parties is best expressed by themselves: in the *express terms* of their agreement; by their conduct in the *course of performance* under the agreement; their *course of dealing;* and *usage of trade.* All of these are to be construed whenever reasonable as consistent with each other, but when such construction is unreasonable the express terms control course of performance, course of performance controls both a course of dealing and usage of trade, and course of dealing controls usage of trade.

During the course of performance under the agreement, the conduct of the parties will well reflect their understanding of whether or not such known "course of performance" is or is not in accord with their agreement, and if it is not in accord the performing party would reasonably expect the other party to object thereto. A course of performance involves repeated occasions of performance and not a single occasion. It is for this reason that the Code provides: "Where the contract for sale involves repeated occasions for performance by either party with knowledge of the nature of the performance and opportunity for objection to it by the other, any course of performance accepted or acquiesced in without objection shall be relevant to determine the meaning of the agreement."[26] It should be noted that a course of performance, and even conduct insufficient to constitute a course of performance, may not only assist in the interpretation of the meaning of an agreement, but it is also relevant to show a waiver or modification of a term in the agreement inconsistent with such course of performance or conduct. Where it is in doubt whether a course of performance is reflective of the meaning or is a modification of the agreement on the one hand, or is a waiver on the other, because of the greater flexibility of a waiver (e.g., ease of retraction)[27] and to guard against surprise or other hardship, the course of performance is construed as a waiver.

While a course of performance consists of a sequence of conduct by the parties *subsequent* to the formation of their agreement, in contrast a "course of dealing" is a sequence of their conduct *prior* to the formation of their agreement. Their course of dealing is helpful in the interpretation of their expressions and other conduct resulting in their agreement.

Parties speak in a language and in an environment which are a part of the circumstances bearing upon the meaning of their agreement. Commercial usage, or "usage of trade" as it is usually called, is a part of such circumstances. The Code reflects this by providing: "A usage of trade is any practice or method of dealing having such *regularity of observance* in a place, vocation or trade as to justify an expectation that it will be observed with respect to the transaction in question. . . . An applicable usage of trade in the place where any part of performance is to occur shall be used in interpreting the agreement as to that part of the performance. . . . A course of dealing between parties and

---

[26] UCC 2–208(1).

[27] See below, p. 206.

any usage of trade in the vocation or trade in which they are engaged or of which they are or should be aware give particular meaning to and supplement or qualify terms of an agreement."[28] (Author's italics.)

Modification, Rescission, Waiver. The parties make their own agreement resulting in a contract for sale of goods and, except as precluded by law, they may agree to whatever terms they please. They may agree to various terms, subsequently *agree*[29] to modify them, waive any of them, or rescind the agreement. Consideration is not required to make binding an agreement modifying their contract, nor is consideration required if the modification is by their course of performance. However, any such modification whether with or without consideration *must be in "good faith,"* which means "honesty in fact in the conduct or transaction concerned,"[30] and in the case of a merchant it means "honesty in fact and the observance of reasonable, commercial standards of fair dealing in the trade."[31] For example, a market shift may have occurred which would cause performance to result in a loss, or supervening unforeseen circumstances have caused performance to be commercially impracticable.

A contract for sale may be modified by agreement or by course of performance, irrespective of the form of the original agreement. The Code has special provisions to protect against misrepresentation that an oral agreement of modification has occurred. *First,* if the contract as modified comes within the statute of frauds as being a contract for the sale of goods for $500 or more, the agreement for modification itself comes within the statute and must be a proper, signed writing to be enforceable. If the modification agreement takes the contract *out* of the statute, it may be in any form. *Second,* a signed agreement which excludes its modification or rescission except by a signed writing cannot be otherwise modified or rescinded. However, when such exclusion is on a form *supplied by a merchant to a non-merchant,* the *clause* must be *separately signed* by the non-merchant; but as *between merchants,* such separate signing of the clause is not required.

It should be noted that if an attempt at modification or rescission is ineffective because of the statute of frauds or because of the prohibiting clause in the contract, nevertheless the new agreement may operate as a waiver. However, reflecting the law of Contracts, "a party who has made a waiver affecting an executory portion of the contract may retract the waiver by reasonable notification *received* by the other party that strict performance will be required of any term waived, unless the retraction would be unjust in view of a material change of position in reliance on the waiver."[32] (Author's italics.) A person *receives* a notice or notification when "it comes to his attention; or . . . it is

[28] UCC 1–205(2)–(5). It should be noted that "regularity of performance" is the test of trade usage, and not the old English concept of custom as of ancient or immemorial origin.

[29] Note that modification cannot occur unilaterally; it can occur only mutually by agreement.

[30] UCC 1–201(19).

[31] UCC 2–103(1)(b).

[32] UCC 2–209(5).

duly delivered at the place of business through which the contract was made or at any other place held out by him as the place for receipt of such communications."[33]

Delegation and Assignment. It is usual in commercial trade to have parties assign their rights under the contract and to delegate performance of their duties under the contract. Contract rights may be *assigned* but contract duties may only be *delegated;* responsibility for performance and for breach remains in the delegating party even though the person to whom the duty has been delegated may also be responsible for performance and breach under the contract. Inasmuch as the parties make their bargain and each relies on the other party's performance, by their agreement they may prohibit assignment or delegation, except that a prohibition of assignment in the agreement is inoperative to prevent a party's assignment of his *right to damages for breach of the whole contract or a right arising out of the assignor's due performance of his entire obligation* (e.g., the commercial account receivable). Delegation by a party cannot occur if the agreement precludes delegation or if the other party has a "substantial interest" in having his original promisor perform or control the acts required by the contract. By "substantial interest" is meant that the non-delegating party had bargained for performance *only by the original delegating promisor.* To resolve possible ambiguity, the Code establishes a rule of construction that, "*unless the circumstances indicate the contrary a prohibition of assignment of 'the contract' is to be construed as barring only the delegation to the assignee of the assignor's performance.*" (Author's italics.)[34] Another Code rule of construction is that a *general assignment* operates as *both* an assignment of rights *and,* unless the language of the agreement or circumstances indicate the contrary, a delegation of the performance of duties. For example, an assignment of "the contract" or of "all my rights under the contract" or similar general terms is a general assignment. An assignment of rights that are *no longer executory,* such as a right to damages for breach of the entire contract or of an account receivable, or an assignment of rights for the purpose of security are circumstances which indicate that there is no delegation of duties. If the person to whom delegation has been made *accepts* such delegation, *his acceptance constitutes a promise to perform those duties* thereby creating a third party creditor beneficiary contract[35] and making him, as well as the delegating party, liable to the other party for performance of the contract duties and for breach of contract therefor.

The non-delegating party may treat delegation as creating reasonable grounds for insecurity and he may, without prejudice to his rights against the delegating party, demand adequate assurance of due performance from the party to whom delegation has been made. This reflects the well-established legal principle that each contracting party has an obligation not to impair the

---

[33] UCC 1–201(26).

[34] UCC 2–210(3).

[35] See above, p. 83.

other's expectation of receiving due performance. "Between merchants the reasonableness of grounds for insecurity and the adequacy of any assurance offered shall be determined according to commercial standards."[36]

All rights of either the seller or the buyer can be assigned except where the assignment would *materially:*

1. Change the duty of the other party, or
2. Increase the burden or risk imposed on him by his contract, or
3. Impair his chance of obtaining return performance.

Form of the Transaction

Statute of Frauds. As discussed previously under the law of Contracts,[37] the statute of frauds in each state has for its purpose the prevention of effective fraudulent allegation that a contract exists, and the statute accomplishes this by requiring that certain kinds of contract therein enumerated are *unenforceable* unless proved in a specified way. The statute of frauds is really a general description of those statutory provisions in various areas of the law prescribing *proof* of various kinds of contract in order for such contracts to be enforceable. Under the Code, the various types of transactions included are: a contract for the sale of goods for the price of $500 or more (UCC 2–201); a contract for the sale of securities (UCC 8–319);[38] a security agreement for a non-possessory security interest, e.g., accounts receivable (UCC 9–203);[39] a contract for general intangibles, e.g., goodwill, royalty rights, rights to performance (UCC 9–106), and a contract for various types of security transaction (UCC 9–104)[40] for more than $5,000 are governed by UCC 1–206.[41]

Under UCC 2–201(1), a contract for the sale of goods for the price of $500 or more is unenforceable unless: *there is a writing sufficient to indicate that a contract for sale has been made between the parties; and the writing is signed by the party against whom enforcement of the contract is sought or by his authorized agent or broker.* Also, if a contract as subsequently modified by the parties[42] is for the sale of goods for $500 or more, the contract as well as the agreement of modification comes within the statute. It should be noted that, inasmuch as "sale or return" contracts[43] are relatively so infrequent, in order to prove such a contract the "or return" term of a contract for sale irrespective of sales price is treated as a separate contract for sale under the statute of frauds and is unenforceable unless proved as required by the statute.

---

[36] UCC 2–609(2).

[37] See above, pp. 85–86.

[38] See below, pp. 717–19.

[39] See below, p. 431.

[40] See below, pp. 422–23.

[41] See above, p. 86.

[42] See above, p. 206.

[43] See below, p. 215.

The Contract Price. Under the Sales Article of the Code, the statute of frauds provision is concerned only with goods with a sales price of $500 or more. It is the *contract price* of $500 or more that is important, and not the actual value of the goods. If a number of items are bought by the same buyer from the same seller at the same time, all the items are considered as forming part of one contract and a total price as being the contract price.

The Writing. The contract for sale itself may be in writing, or there may be an oral contract supported by a written memorandum indicating that the contract had been made and the memorandum has been signed by a party or his authorized agent or broker. The writing is proof only against a signatory. Accordingly, *the writing must be signed by the party against whom the contract is sought to be enforced.* If the seller is the signatory, the contract is enforceable against him by the buyer; if the buyer is the signatory, the contract is enforceable against him by the seller; if both buyer and seller are signatories, each may enforce the contract against the other. The validity of the contract is not questioned; it is solely a matter of *enforceability.* (A and B make an oral contract for the sale of goods for $1,000. There is a contract; but unless the contract is proved by a proper writing, it is unenforceable.)

It is not necessary that the writing required by the statute state all the terms of the agreement. The writing is not insufficient because it omits or incorrectly states a term of the agreement. For example, the price, the time and place of delivery, and warranties may all be omitted. The Code fills in these items by reflecting commercial understanding in its implementing sections; course of performance, course of dealing, and usage of trade become important in this respect. The Code is interested in sufficient proof that a contract has been made, and the person who signs a writing so indicating should be responsible for the contract which he has indicated is in effect. Irrespective of whether or not the items in the writing are correct, a party signed it, and it is evidence against him. He is bound only to the extent of the quantity of goods shown in the writing as the object of the contract. *All that is required is that the writing contain three things: it must indicate that a contract for sale of goods has been made; it must be signed by the party against whom the contract is sought to be enforced; and it must specify a quantity of goods.*

Commercial understanding *between merchants* is reflected in the Code,[44] which provides that *a merchant's written confirmation* of the contract for sale of goods which is sufficient to make the contract enforceable *against him* will also be sufficient as a writing of confirmation *against the merchant recipient if he received the writing within a reasonable time after the transaction was made, he had reason to know its contents, and he did not give to the sender written notice*[45] *of his objection to the contents within ten days after he received the written confirmation.* In short, *as between merchants,* one merchant has a duty to manifest his objection to another merchant's timely errone-

[44] UCC 2–201(2).

[45] For Notice, see UCC 1–201(26) above, p. 203, ftn. 22.

ous confirmation and his failure to do so soon is an admission that the confirmation is correct and he thereby makes it a written manifestation of his own.

The writing may be made at or after the time that the contract has been made, and it may be in any tangible form, (e.g., printing, typewriting, ink, pencil). It may be in the form of correspondence between the parties, (e.g., letters and telegrams), or it may be by will or negotiable instrument. The writing may be formal or informal and may be one writing or a series of related writings. If there is more than one writing, either all the writings must be attached to the signed writing or the signed writing must refer to all the other writings. (A writes to B complaining about B's failure to perform an oral contract within the statute of frauds and sets forth all the data regarding such contract. B's answering signed letter refers to A's letter and admits the formation of such a contract but refuses to perform it. B's signed letter refers to A's letter, and *the two letters constitute the writing* sufficient to satisfy the statute and to prove the oral contract. The contract is enforceable by A against B. If B were seeking to enforce the oral contract against A, *A's signed letter would be the writing.*)

The writing must be signed by the party against whom the contract is sought to be enforced. " 'Signed' includes any symbol executed or adopted by a party with present intention to authenticate a writing."[46] For example, the signature may be any writing, seal, stamp, or mark which a party intends to adopt as his own, whether or not made by him, and irrespective of whether or not he intended such signature to be on a writing to satisfy the statute of frauds. The signature may occur anywhere on the writing; and it is different from the word "subscribe," which means that the signature must occur at the bottom of the document. A party's agent or broker may sign the writing for him only if such agent or broker is so authorized. Such authorization is a matter of the law of Agency,[47] but briefly the authorization may be given by the party principal orally, in writing, by his other conduct (e.g., the agent's signing for the principal party in his presence and without his objection), by ratification, and by apparent authority. The agent may be a corporate employee[48] or a partner.[49] The agent need not disclose his principal's identity inasmuch as, under the law of Agency,[50] the principal can be held liable as a party to the contract when his identity becomes known to the other contracting party. In sales by auction,[51] by law the auctioneer is the agent of both seller and buyer to prepare and sign on their behalf a memorandum of sale immediately after the sale, which is a writing sufficient to satisfy the requirements of the statute of frauds.

---

[46] UCC 1–201(39).

[47] See below, pp. 550, 553–76.

[48] See below, pp. 562–63.

[49] See below, pp. 563, 651.

[50] See below, pp. 601–602.

[51] For Auction, see above, p. 21.

Transactions Excluded from the Statute of Frauds. The Code excepts four transactions concerning goods *from the statute of frauds provision under Sales*, but the other Sales sections of the Code apply to the transaction because goods are involved.

The first transaction excluded from the statute is concerned with non-resellable goods. A contract for services alone is not within this statute of frauds provision and is enforceable even though oral. A contract is not within the statute and is enforceable "if the goods are to be specially manufactured for the buyer and are not suitable for sale to others in the ordinary course of the seller's business and the seller, before notice of repudiation is received and under circumstances which reasonably indicate that the goods are for the buyer, has made either a substantial beginning of their manufacture or commitments for their procurement."[52] (A, a manufacturer of carriages, orally contracts with B to build B a carriage like the carriages A usually builds. It is a contract to sell and is within the statute. If the carriage were to be made especially for B according to certain specifications different from the type of carriage A ordinarily makes and sells, and A so made the carriage, the contract is for services, is not within the statute, and is enforceable even though orally made. An oral contract to make a suit of clothes which the tailor then begins to make involves the same principle. Similarly, an oral contract between A, a dentist, and B whereby A was to make for B's use an artificial denture and which A subsequently so made is not within the statute and is enforceable.)

The second transaction excluded from the statute is concerned with a contract for the sale of goods and the buyer has received and accepted part or all of the goods. The buyer's receipt and acceptance of goods is good proof that a contract for their sale was made and, accordingly, *only to the extent of such goods the buyer's receipt and acceptance of them causes the contract for their sale to be enforceable without a writing.* A buyer has receipt when he has acquired possession, personally or through his agent, with the assent of the seller. Delivery of the goods to a warehouseman or to anyone else, as requested by the buyer, is a delivery to the buyer through his agent. In the absence of agreement to the contrary, delivery to a carrier for shipment to the buyer is delivery to the buyer, the carrier being the buyer's agent to transport the goods. In these instances the buyer has possession. Unless the circumstances indicate that the seller is a bailee for the buyer, the seller's possession of the goods awaiting the buyer's acquisition is not a receipt by the buyer; the seller is not his agent to receive the goods. *The buyer's possession* of a negotiable document of title (e.g., negotiable bill of lading or negotiable warehouse receipt) drawn or indorsed in his favor, or the buyer's possession of a non-negotiable document of title in which the buyer is the consignee, is a receipt of the goods. The document of title is a symbol of the goods to which it refers. A buyer has accepted the goods when he expressly or impliedly so indicates. Acceptance is implied from the buyer's exercise of dominion over

[52] UCC 2–201(3)(a).

the goods, or his retention of such goods for an unreasonable period of time without informing the seller that he has rejected them. Acceptance usually occurs after receipt, but it can precede receipt. (B, the buyer, selects 100 rolls of cloth and asks S, the seller, to send them to him. S sends the goods by railroad. There is a receipt by B through the railroad as his agent, and there is an acceptance which occurred when B selected and assented to those 100 rolls.)

The third transaction excepted from the statute is concerned with a contract where the buyer has made part or complete payment which has been accepted by the seller. The buyer's payment and the seller's acceptance is good proof that a contract for the sale of goods was made and, accordingly, *only to the extent of the apportioned value of the seller's goods, the buyer's part or full payment of the price causes the contract for the sale of such goods to be enforceable without a writing.* The price need not be in money and may be anything other than money.[53] If the price is in terms of money, delivery of a check or negotiable promissory note which the seller accepts *is payment for the purpose of satisfying the statute,* although it is only *conditional payment as far as performance of a contract duty is concerned.* Part payment is sufficient, but a tender of payment is not. Payment may be made at any time. If payment is to be made by cancellation of an existing claim by the buyer against the seller, the time when payment is made depends upon the intention of the parties. If cancellation is to occur when the goods are received, then no payment is made until the goods are received. If cancellation is to occur immediately on the making of the contract, then payment occurs at that time.

The fourth transaction excepted from the statute is concerned with a contract for sale which a party admits in court, e.g., by his pleading, testimony, or otherwise, *was made by him.* Such admission in court is good proof that a contract for the sale of goods was made and, accordingly, *only to the extent of the goods admitted, a party's admission in court of a contract for the sale of goods is enforceable against him without a writing.*

Parol Evidence Rule. The parol evidence rule has been discussed previously under the law of Contracts.[54] The Code reflects this rule with modification. Terms which the parties have agreed upon in their confirmatory memoranda or final written agreement may not be *contradicted* by any prior oral or written agreement or by a contemporaneous oral agreement between such parties. However, such terms may be explained or supplemented by: course of performance, course of dealing, or usage of trade; and by consistent additional terms, unless the court finds the writing to have been intended as a complete and exclusive statement of the terms of the agreement. The writing may be reformed[55] by the court to reflect the previous intentions of the parties not properly expressed in the writing.

---

[53] See below, p. 217.

[54] See above, pp. 42–43.

[55] For Reformation, see above, p. 43.

Chapter 15

CONSTRUCTION OF THE CONTRACT

In a "sale on approval," the goods are delivered to the buyer but title and risk of loss remain with the seller until the buyer approves of the goods and thereby accepts them. In a "sale or return," the goods are delivered to the buyer, the title and risk of loss pass to the buyer, but the buyer may return the goods in lieu of paying the purchase price. Unless otherwise agreed: if the goods were delivered primarily *for use*, it is a sale on approval; if primarily *for resale*, it is a sale or return.

The purchase price may be money or any other property or services. If the parties intend to conclude a contract but do not fix the price, it is a reasonable price at the time and place where the goods were to be delivered to the buyer, unless otherwise agreed payment being due at that time and place subject to the buyer's right first to inspect the goods. The sales contract may be indefinite as to the quantity of goods and may provide that the quantity is measured by the seller's output or the buyer's requirements.

Unless otherwise agreed, delivery and payment are not made by installments. However, circumstances may indicate that it is not commercially feasible to deliver or to receive goods in a single lot, and either party may make or demand delivery in lots and the price, if it can be apportioned, may be demanded for each lot. Unless otherwise agreed, delivery is to be made at the seller's place of business or, if none, at his residence; but if the parties know that the goods are in some other place, then that place is the place of delivery. If the goods are possessed by a bailee in some other place, the seller's acquisition of the bailee's acknowledgement of the buyer's right to possession is a delivery to the buyer.

"C.O.D." means collect on delivery. "F.O.B." means free on board.

"F.A.S." means free alongside. "C.I.F." means cost, insurance, and freight. "C. & F." means cost and freight. Delivery "ex-ship" means the seller is to deliver the goods from a ship at the destination point; the reverse of "F.A.S." "No arrival, no sale" means the seller is not liable for the non-arrival of shipped goods.

Title can pass to existing and identified goods or to a part interest in such goods as the parties have expressly or impliedly intended. Unless otherwise expressly agreed, **if by the contract: (1) the seller is to *send* the goods to the buyer (F.O.B. shipping point), title passes to the buyer at the time and place of shipment; (2) the seller is to *deliver at destination* (F.O.B. destination point), title passes on tender of delivery there; (3) the seller is to make *delivery without moving the goods,* title passes at the time the contract is made, except that if the seller is to deliver a document of title, title passes at the time and place where he delivers such document. The seller's reservation of a security interest in the goods has no effect on the passing of title, and any attempted retention or reservation by the seller of title in identified goods shipped or delivered to the buyer is limited in effect to a reservation of a security interest in the goods. The form of the bill of lading and whether the seller or buyer is the consignee have no effect on the passing of title.**

For whether or not a good faith purchaser acquires title to identified goods, reference should be made to the summary headnote and to the text content of **"THE TRANSFEREE GETS ONLY WHAT THE TRANSFEROR HAS RULE, WITH EXCEPTIONS."[1]**

SECTION I. INTENTION OF THE PARTIES GOVERNS

The intention of the parties as expressed or implied in their sales agreement governs their transaction, except where it is contrary to law as prohibited by the Code. Many times the intention of the parties is not expressed on important factors involved in the particular transaction, or the legal import of the commercial terms used by them is not clearly understood. The Code prescribes certain rules for ascertaining the *implied intention* of the parties, and it clarifies the legal meaning and effect of commercial terms. All this is a matter of *construing* the agreement to reflect its meaning in light of the terminology used by the parties and the surrounding circumstances of course of performance, course of dealing, and usage of trade. First the general obligations of the contracting parties, open terms, shipment, and delivery will be considered, then title, creditors, and good faith purchasers.

---

[1] See above, pp. 144 ff.

SECTION II. GENERAL OBLIGATIONS, OPEN TERMS, SHIPMENT, AND DELIVERY

General Obligations

Generally. The Code seeks to observe carefully fair dealing in commercial transactions. It exacts good faith between parties dealing with each other which means honesty in fact and, in the case of a merchant, means also honesty in the observance of reasonable commercial standards of fair dealing in the trade. In dealing with each other, the seller has the obligation to transfer and deliver the goods and the buyer has the obligation to accept and pay for the goods in accordance with their contract, and they may provide for their risks and burdens as they wish unless prohibited by the Code as not reflective of fair dealing. *The Code's allocation of risks and burdens is so to provide only if the parties have not otherwise agreed.* When it is claimed by a party that the contract or a clause therein was unconscionable at the time the contract was made, as not reflecting fair dealing, the parties will be afforded reasonable opportunity to present evidence to assist the court to decide as a matter of law whether or not such contract or clause was unconscionable at the time it was made. The court, not the jury, may refuse to enforce the contract if it is permeated by unconscionability, it may delete the unconscionable clause and enforce the remainder of the contract, or it may so limit the application of an unconscionable clause as to avoid an unconscionable result.

Sale on Approval and Sale or Return. Two types of transaction are different from other transactions involving sale of goods; they are "sale on approval" and "sale or return." In these two transactions, the parties are agreeing that the buyer has a power to turn back the goods to the seller, not because of nonconformity of the goods to the contract but, rather, because of the particular nature of the contract. *In a sale on approval,* the goods are delivered to the buyer but *the seller retains the title and risk of loss* for such goods until the buyer gives his approval of the goods and thereby accepts them. *In a sale or return,* the goods are delivered to the buyer, *the title and risk of loss pass to the buyer,* but the buyer may return the goods to the seller in lieu of paying the purchase price. Although the parties determine which transaction it is, often it is difficult to determine which transaction is meant by the parties. *Unless otherwise agreed,* the kind of transaction is determined primarily by the purpose for which the goods are delivered: *if primarily for use, it is a sale on approval; if primarily for resale, it is a sale or return.* The reason for this test is that, by commercial practice, when a returnable power is included in the sales agreement consumers take the goods subject to their approval and merchants take goods for resale and return if not resold. The sale "on approval," or "on trial," or "on satisfaction," or any other words of like import, is a contract with an option to purchase if the goods are satisfactory to the buyer; as distinguished from a sale or return, in which title passes on delivery with an option in the buyer to return the goods if they are not satisfactory to him, or for any other agreed reason. The sale on approval is a bailment of the goods with an option to buy. In a sale or return, there is no bailment but rather a sale with the option to revest title to the goods in the seller.

In a sale on approval, if the buyer retains the goods without giving notice to the seller of his approval or acceptance, or of his rejection, within the agreed time in which the buyer is to return the goods, then such retention without any indication by the buyer beyond such period of time is the equivalent of approval or acceptance, and the title passes to the buyer. If no time has been specified within which the goods are to be returned to the seller, then on the expiration of a reasonable period of time the title passes to the buyer. Similarly, in a sale or return contract, the buyer may exercise his option of revesting title in the seller only by doing so within the agreed period of time, or within a reasonable period of time if no time has been fixed. On the expiration of such period of time, the option to revest the title in the seller can no longer be exercised. In a sale on approval, the buyer's use of the goods consistent with the purpose of trial is at the seller's risk and is not an acceptance; but the buyer's acceptance of any part of conforming goods is an acceptance of the whole. His return of the goods, *after due notification to the seller of his intention to do so,* is at the seller's risk and expense; but if he is a *merchant buyer,* he must follow any reasonable instructions of the seller. By contrast, in a sale or return the buyer has the option to return all *or* any commercial unit of the goods, and return is at the buyer's risk and expense. It should be noted that, inasmuch as it is most unusual for an ordinary contract for the sale of goods to include an "or return" clause, the Code stipulates: that *such clause* be treated as a separate contract for sale within the statute of frauds and unenforceable unless proved by a proper signed writing;[2] and that, when the sales agreement is in writing but the agreed "or return" provision is oral, such provision is contradictory of the written sales agreement and inadmissible in evidence under the parol evidence rule.[3]

Creditors' Rights. While the goods are in the buyer's possession, the buyer's creditors can resort only to the interest of the buyer in the goods, unless the buyer's business is such as to cause his creditors to be misled by the seller's delivery of the goods to the buyer. If it is a sale on approval, no title has passed to the buyer and, until he accepts the goods, the goods are not available to his creditors. If it is a sale or return, the buyer has the title to the goods and the goods are available to his creditors. *However, when the seller delivers goods for sale to a buyer-dealer who deals in goods of that kind and who maintains a place of business under a name other than that of the seller or person making such delivery, then, as to the buyer's creditors, the transaction is treated as a sale or return irrespective of the intentions of the parties, and the goods are available to the buyer's creditors.* In effect, if a seller delivers the goods for sale to such a buyer-dealer, he is estopped to assert *to the buyer's*

---

[2] See above, p. 208.

[3] See above, pp. 42–43.

creditors that it is anything other than a sale or return. This is true whether "on consignment," "on memorandum," or similar words of reservation of title in the seller are used. Of course, if the buyer's creditors are on notice of the interest of the seller in the goods, then, since they have not been misled by the seller's delivery of the goods to the buyer, the true nature of the transaction and the seller's interest in the goods prevail. Such notice to the buyer's creditors occurs when either: pursuant to local law, the seller posts a sign on the buyer's premises and thereby has his interests protected; the buyer or person conducting the business is generally known by his creditors to be substantially engaged in selling the goods of others (e.g., factor); or the seller gives notice of his security interest in the goods by proper filing.[4]

Open Terms

The Price. The parties determine by their agreement whether or not there is to be a contract for the sale of goods and also the price therefor. The price, that is the consideration, may be money or any other property or services. The price, in full or in part, may be bartered goods, services, or an interest in land. When all or part of the price is payable in an interest in land, the transfer of the goods and the seller's obligations with respect to them are subject to the Code's provisions on Sales, but not the transfer of the interest in land or the transferor's obligations in connection therewith. The agreement may specifically fix the price for the goods; however, *if the parties intend to conclude a contract for sale without determining the price, a contract is made even though there is indefiniteness concerning the price.* In such case, *the price is a reasonable price at the time and place where the goods were to be delivered to the buyer if:* nothing is said as to the price; or the price is left to be agreed by the parties and they fail to agree; or the price is to be fixed in terms of some agreed market or other standard as set or recorded by a third person or agency and it is not so set or recorded; or the price is to be determined by a particular person's judgment when there is no market standard for fixing the value or price for the goods and the third person does not so fix the price. An agreement to agree later on the price is perfectly reasonable, *as long as the parties intend to conclude a contract for sale at the time of their initial agreement.* If the parties agree that the price is to be fixed by the buyer or the seller, the price must be fixed by that party in good faith. When the price is to be fixed otherwise than by subsequent agreement of the parties but the buyer or the seller wrongfully prevents the fixing of such price, the other party may at his option treat the contract as cancelled or he himself may fix a reasonable price. Of course, *if the parties intend not to be bound unless the price be fixed or agreed* and the price is not fixed or agreed, there is no contract. When the price is payable in whole or in part in goods, each party is a seller of the goods which he is to transfer.

---

[4] See Property Security Transactions, below, pp. 435, 448 ff.

Output, Requirements, and Exclusive Dealings. ***Output, Requirements.*** It is common for the parties to an agreement for the sale of goods not to provide for a specific quantity of goods to be supplied by the seller to the buyer but, rather, to provide that the quantity of goods is measured by the seller's output or the buyer's requirements. For example, the buyer agrees to buy 60 percent of the seller's output. The indefiniteness of the quantity of goods does not preclude the agreement from resulting in a valid contract. In order to be on the safe side, the agreement may specify minimum or maximum amounts which may be tendered by the seller or demanded by the buyer. However, the parties may not feel that they can establish minimums or maximums and that the best that they can provide for is a stated estimate of the quantity to be furnished by the seller or demanded by the buyer, bearing in mind the seller's output and the buyer's requirements. If the agreement does not provide for a stated estimate, then the prior experience of the parties on output and requirements is to be examined in order to determine some reasonable limitation on the quantity that may be tendered by the seller or demanded by the buyer. An output or requirements agreement contemplates good faith by the parties according to commercial standards of fair dealing and contemplates reasonable expansion or contraction of production or requirements.

If the parties had made a stated estimate, reasonable variation in quantity is intended, as long as such variation is not unreasonably disproportionate to the stated estimate. Similarly, in the absence of a stated estimate, variation cannot be unreasonably disproportionate to the prior output or requirement experience of the parties. Improper demand by either party may be disregarded by the other party, who may insist that the contract be performed as agreed and also insist that, inasmuch as such improper demand constituted reasonable grounds for insecurity of performance by the demanding party, the latter furnish adequate assurance of due performance.[5]

Exclusive Dealings. In an exclusive dealing contract, the parties agree on a specified geographical territory in which the agent-buyer is to have the exclusive right to sell the principal-seller's goods. Whether or not the agreement results in a valid contract is determined by local law and, where applicable, by federal law. Unless the parties have agreed to the contrary, they have a duty to employ reasonable diligence and good faith in performing their contract, the principal-seller to use his best efforts to supply the goods and to refrain from supplying any other dealer or agent in the exclusive territory, and the agent-buyer to use his best efforts to promote the sale of his principal-seller's goods and to expand their market.

Payment. It is the duty of the seller to deliver the goods to the buyer, and it is the duty of the buyer to accept and pay for such goods as provided by their contract. Often the parties do not expressly provide in their agreement when and where payment is to be made by the buyer. *Unless otherwise agreed,*

[5] See below, pp. 265–67.

payment is due at the time and place at which the buyer is to receive the goods, even though the place of shipment is the place of delivery. When the seller has been authorized by the contract to *send* the goods to the buyer, the seller's delivery of the goods to the carrier or other suitable bailee constitutes a delivery to the buyer. However, inasmuch as this kind of a delivery is a special kind of delivery, the buyer is under no obligation to pay on the seller's delivery to the carrier; but after the goods have arrived *and* the buyer has had a reasonable opportunity to inspect the goods, then the buyer is under an obligation to make payment. *If, pursuant to the contract, the seller sends the goods to the buyer C.O.D. (collect on delivery) or the contract provides for payment against documents of title,*[6] *unless otherwise agreed the buyer is not entitled to inspect the goods before making payment.* When payment is to be made against documents of title, payment is due at the time and place at which the buyer is to receive the documents, regardless of where the goods are to be received. It should be noted that, *unless otherwise agreed, a seller who is authorized to send goods may ship them and reserve in himself a security interest in the goods by having the documents of title name the seller as the consignee.* Where the seller is required or authorized to ship the goods on credit, the credit period runs from the time of shipment. It is common commercial understanding that the dating of the invoice is recognized as a representation of the time of shipment, and postdating the invoice delays the starting of the credit period until the date on the invoice. If the seller delays sending the invoice to the buyer, inasmuch as the buyer will not have the opportunity of knowing when to pay, the credit period does not begin until the invoice has been sent to the buyer.

Shipment and Delivery

In General. We have already observed that an agreement for sale which is otherwise sufficiently definite to be a contract is not made invalid by the fact that it leaves particulars of performance to be specified by one of the parties. Any such specification, however, must be made in good faith and within limits set by commercial reasonableness. This applies also in connection with the shipment and delivery of goods. Unless otherwise agreed, specifications relating to assortment of goods are at the buyer's option and, except as otherwise provided by the Code,[7] specifications or arrangements relating to shipment are at the seller's option. Where such specification would materially affect the other party's performance and the specification is not seasonably[8] made, or where one party's cooperation is necessary to the agreed performance of the other but such cooperation is not seasonably forthcoming, the other party in

---

[6] In the case of payment against documents (e.g., bill of lading), *payment is required before inspection* by the buyer because the shipping documents usually are tendered while the goods are still in transit.

[7] See F.O.B. and F.A.S. shipments, below, pp. 221–22.

[8] See UCC 1–204(3)(2) for "seasonably."

addition to all other remedies for breach of contract "is excused for any resulting delay in his own performance; and he may also either proceed to perform in any reasonable manner or, after the time for a material part of his own performance, treat the failure to specify or to cooperate as a breach by failure to deliver or accept the goods."[9]

Delivery by Installments. *Delivery means voluntary transfer of possession* from one person to another and may be made by one person through his authorized agent to another person through the latter's authorized agent. The agreement of the parties may provide expressly or impliedly whether or not delivery or payment is to be made by installments; but in the absence of any such provision, the buyer is under no obligation to accept delivery, and the seller is under no obligation to accept payment, by installments. All the goods called for by the contract for sale must be tendered in a single delivery, and payment is due only on such tender. An example of an agreement implying that delivery may be made by several lots[10] instead of a single lot of goods is an agreement in which the seller is to deliver the goods as required by the buyer. A buyer may accept delivery of several lots rather than a single lot and thereby waive his right to refuse such delivery by lots; similarly, the seller's acceptance of payment by installments may waive his right to refuse payment by installments. However, circumstances may indicate that it is not commercially feasible to deliver or to receive the goods in a single lot and, when this occurs, either party has the right to make or demand delivery in lots and the price, if it can be apportioned, may be demanded for each lot.[11] Where such circumstances exist and a partial delivery is made the remaining goods must be delivered within a reasonable time and in a reasonable manner.

Place and Time of Delivery. ***Place.*** The agreement of the parties determines the place and time of delivery. Later discussion will consider delivery to be made by a carrier.[12] When goods are to be delivered other than by a carrier, "Unless otherwise agreed (a) the place for delivery of goods is the seller's place of business or if he has none his residence; but (b) in a contract for sale of identified goods which to the knowledge of the parties at the time of contracting are in some other place, that place is the place for their delivery; and (c) documents of title may be delivered through customary banking channels."[13] If the goods located in some other place are in the possession of a bailee, the seller has the additional obligation of obtaining the acknowledgment by the bailee of the buyer's right to possession in order to effect delivery to the buyer.

Time. The parties may agree on the time of delivery of goods either expressly, or impliedly by course of performance, course of dealing, usage of

[9] UCC 2–311(3)(a)(b).

[10] For Lot see above, p. 199.

[11] The buyer may be unable to store at one time all the goods ordered, e.g., brick, coal, cattle.

[12] See below, pp. 249 ff.

[13] UCC 2–308. But customary banking channels may be to the contrary, making tender unnecessary under (c).

trade, or the circumstances under which the agreement was made. Should one party propose a time limit, the other party's failure to reply may constitute an assent to such time limit.[14] *If the time for shipment, delivery, or any other action under the contract is not agreed to by the parties then, unless otherwise provided by the Code, the time is a reasonable time.* Acceptable commercial conduct in light of the nature, purpose, and circumstances determines what is a reasonable time. Failure to deliver or tender delivery within a reasonable time is a breach of contract. An unreasonably early demand for, or offer of, delivery is not a breach of contract but constitutes a manifestation of intent requesting the other party's assent, whose subsequent silence may constitute assent. If such demanding or offering party *insists* on such unreasonably early delivery, such insistence may constitute conduct amounting to a breach of contract or justify a request for adequate assurance of performance.[15] If both parties silently let a reasonable time go by, their conduct may enlarge such reasonable time.

When the contract is of a continuing nature, that is providing for successive performances but without agreement as to how long such performances are to continue, the contract continues for a reasonable time; however, unless otherwise agreed, either party may terminate[16] the contract at any time. However, the other party must *receive* reasonable notification of such termination. If the agreement of the parties had provided for termination on the happening of an agreed event, then no notification is required.

Shipping Terms. In commercial practice, various terms in connection with the shipment of goods have a well-defined meaning. While the parties to the transaction may vary this meaning and their intent governs, nevertheless, unless such variation is clearly indicated, the established meaning will prevail.

C.O.D. "C.O.D." means collect on delivery. In a C.O.D. shipment the carrier is the agent of the consignor seller for the purpose of collecting payment, and the carrier is *also* the agent of the consignee buyer for the purpose of transporting the goods. This contract term means that payment to the carrier must precede *transfer of possession* from the carrier to the consignee buyer; *it does not mean that such payment is to precede the transfer of title.*

F.O.B. "F.O.B." means free on board. F.O.B. is at a named place, and is a delivery term *indicating the extent of the consignor seller's obligation under the contract.* When the term is *F.O.B. the place of shipment,* the seller's obligation is to ship the goods at that place and bear the expense and risk of

[14] See above, p. 205.

[15] See below, pp. 265–67.

[16] UCC 2–106: "(3) 'Termination' occurs when either party pursuant to a power created by agreement or law puts an end to the contract *otherwise than for its breach.* On 'termination' all obligations which are still executory on both sides are discharged but any right based on prior breach or performance survives. (4) 'Cancellation' occurs when either party puts an end to the contract *for breach* by the other and its effect is the same as that of 'termination' except that the cancelling party also retains any remedy for breach of the whole contract or any unperformed balance." (Author's italics.)

putting them into the possession of the carrier. When the term is *F.O.B. the place of destination,* the seller's obligation is to transport the goods to that designated place and there tender delivery of the goods, such transportation being at the seller's expense and risk. When the goods are to be shipped *F.O.B. the place of shipment, or F.O.B. the place of destination, and, in addition, the term provides also for F.O.B. vessel, car or other vehicle,* the seller has the additional obligation of loading the goods on board at his own expense and risk. When the term is F.O.B. vessel: the seller has the obligation of obtaining a bill of lading in the proper form; and the buyer has the obligations of naming the vessel, seasonably giving any needed instructions for delivery including the loading berth of the vessel and in an appropriate case its name and sailing date, and unless otherwise agreed of making payment on the tender of the documents by the seller.

F.A.S. The term "F.A.S." means free alongside. *F.A.S. vessel* is at a named port and, is a delivery term *indicating the extent of the consignor seller's obligation under the contract.* The seller's obligations are: to deliver the goods alongside the vessel in the manner usual in that port or on a dock designated and provided by the buyer; and to obtain a receipt for the goods which he is to exchange for a bill of lading to be issued by the carrier. The buyer's obligations are: seasonably to give any needed instructions for delivery, including the loading berth of the vessel and in an appropriate case its name and sailing date, and, unless otherwise agreed, to make payment on the tender of the documents by the seller.

It should be noted that in all of the F.O.B. and F.A.S. terms just discussed, except for F.O.B. place of destination, should the buyer fail to provide the needed instructions, the seller may treat such failure as a failure of cooperation[17] and, at his option, move the goods in any reasonable manner preparatory to delivery or shipment. Also, under F.O.B. vessel or F.A.S., unless otherwise agreed, the seller may not tender nor the buyer demand delivery of the goods in substitution for the documents.

C.I.F. and C. & F. Terms. The term "C.I.F." means cost, insurance, and freight, signifying that the seller is to ship the goods and to pay for insurance thereon and the freight charges to the point of destination. *The lump sum sales price includes these charges.* The intention of the parties to a C.I.F. contract is that the buyer desires insurance because he does not wish to bear the risk of loss, which has shifted to the buyer under this type of contract, indicating that the intention is that title is to be transferred to the buyer on the seller's delivery of the goods to the carrier and on the seller's payment of the insurance and freight charges. Accordingly, the seller's compliance with the C.I.F. requirements in the contract causes the title to the goods to be transferred at the time of such compliance, even though the agreement has provided that the seller is to pay the freight to the point of destination. The term "C. & F." means cost and freight, signifying that the seller is to ship the goods and pay for the freight

---

[17] See above, pp. 219–20.

charges to the point of destination; insurance is not included in the lump sum sales price for these two charges.

Unless otherwise agreed, the term C.I.F. destination or its equivalent imposes upon the seller the following obligations at his own expense and risk:

> (a) put the goods into the possession of a carrier at the port for shipment and obtain a negotiable bill or bills of lading covering the entire transaction to the named destination.
> (b) load the goods and obtain a receipt from the carrier (which may be contained in the bill of lading) showing that the freight has been paid or provided for.
> (c) obtain a policy or certificate of insurance, including any war risk insurance, of a kind and on terms then current at the port of shipment in the usual amount, in the currency of the contract, shown to cover the same goods covered by the bill of lading and providing for payment of loss to the order of the buyer or for the account of whom it may concern; but the seller may add to the price the amount of the premium for any such war risk insurance.
> (d) prepare an invoice of the goods and procure any other documents required to effect shipment or to comply with the contract.
> (e) forward and tender with commercial promptness all the documents in due form and with any indorsement necessary to perfect the buyer's rights.[18]

Unless otherwise agreed, the buyer's obligations are: to bear the risk of loss after the goods have been delivered to the carrier; and to make payment to the seller against tender of the required documents, without any right to inspect the goods prior to such payment. The seller may not tender, nor the buyer demand, delivery of the goods in substitution for the documents. Unless otherwise agreed, C. & F. has the same effect and imposes upon the seller the same obligations and risk as a C.I.F. term except the obligation as to insurance, and imposes upon the buyer the same obligations and risks as a C.I.F. term.[19]

Delivery Ex-Ship. Delivery "ex-ship" means that the seller has the obligation of delivering the goods from a ship which has reached a place at the named port of destination where goods of the kind are usually discharged. Ex-ship is the reverse of F.A.S.[20] Unless otherwise agreed, the seller has the obligation of discharging all liens arising out of the carriage and of furnishing

[18] UCC 2–320(2).

[19] The parties to a C.I.F. or C. & F. contract may wish to modify the effect of these terms only to such an extent as to shift to the seller the risk of loss for ordinary deterioration, shrinkage and the like which may occur during transportation. If this is done, the other ingredients of the C.I.F. and C. & F. contracts are not disturbed by such modification, e.g., the risk of loss other than by such modification is still with the buyer. Under UCC 2–321(1): "Where the price is based on or is to be adjusted according to 'net landed weights', 'delivered weights', 'out turn' quantity or quality or the like, unless otherwise agreed the seller must reasonably estimate the price. The payment due on tender of the documents called for by the contract is the amount so estimated, but after final adjustment of the price a settlement must be made with commercial promptness." While payment is due on tender of the required documents without any right of prior inspection, nevertheless if the parties should otherwise agree that payment is to be made on or after arrival of the goods, the seller must before payment allow such preliminary inspection as is feasible; but if the goods are lost, delivery of the documents and payment are due when the goods *should* have arrived.

[20] See above, pp. 222 f.

the buyer with a direction to the ship thereby putting the carrier under a duty to deliver the goods; the seller bears the risk of loss until the goods leave the ship's tackle or are otherwise properly unloaded, at which time the risk of loss passes to the buyer.

No Arrival, No Sale. The seller who has the risk of loss during shipment may wish to avoid liability to the buyer for their non-arrival. The contract term "no arrival, no sale" accomplishes this intention of the parties. The seller still must properly ship conforming goods and if they arrive he must tender them on arrival to the buyer, but the seller assumes no obligation that the goods will arrive. However, the seller must not be the cause of their non-arrival; he has a duty not to interfere with the arrival of the goods. If, during shipment and without the fault of the seller, the goods experience partial loss, or have so deteriorated as no longer to conform to the contract, or arrive after the contract time, the buyer may treat the loss, deterioration, or late arrival as if there had been a casualty to identified goods,[21] i.e., either treat the contract as avoided or accept the goods with due allowance from the contract price for the loss, deterioration, or late arrival.

"Letter of Credit" and "Confirmed Credit." Often the sales contract may provide that the buyer is to furnish a letter of credit. A "letter of credit" or "banker's credit" is an irrevocable credit issued by a financing agency[22] of good repute and, where the shipment is overseas,[23] of good international repute. The buyer's failure seasonably to furnish the agreed letter of credit is a breach of the contract. If the buyer seasonably delivers to the seller a proper letter of credit, the letter of credit is conditional payment[24] and the buyer's obligation to pay the purchase price is suspended pending presentation of the letter of credit for honor. If the letter of credit is dishonored, the seller must seasonably notify the buyer that payment is to be made directly by the buyer to the seller. The term "confirmed credit" means that the credit must also carry the direct obligation of such a financing agency which does business in the seller's financial market.

SECTION III. TITLE, CREDITORS, AND GOOD FAITH PURCHASERS

Title

Property is an interest in a thing, and one kind of property is title. We have already seen[25] that *an interest in goods can pass from one person to another only when the goods exist and are identified to the contract,* with the exception of a sale of a part interest in goods. If the goods are existing and are

[21] See below, pp. 268 f.

[22] For the meaning of "financing agency," see UCC 2–104(2).

[23] For the meaning of "overseas," see UCC 2–323(3).

[24] See Contracts, above, p. 53.

[25] See above, p. 199.

identified to the contract, there can be either a present sale or a contract to sell depending upon the intention of the parties; while if the goods are future goods, there can be only a contract to sell and title cannot pass until the goods become existing and are identified to the contract. The intention of the parties as expressed in their agreement determines when the title to the goods is to be transferred, limited only by the legal requirement that title to goods can be transferred only when they are existing and identified to the contract. Often the parties do not clearly express their intention as to when title is to be transferred. The Code[26] prescribes certain legal rules which are to apply, reflecting the implied intention of the parties concerning passage of title. Inasmuch as ignorance of the law is no excuse, if the parties do not express their intention concerning passage of title, then they impliedly intend the legal rules to apply. *Accordingly, the approach in determining who has title to goods is: first, are the goods, or have the goods become, existing and identified to the contract; next, what is the expressed intent of the parties regarding the passage of title; and lastly, in the absence of expressed intent, how do the legal rules regarding the passage of title apply?* First, identification of existing goods to the contract will be discussed, and then the rules concerning passage of title in the absence of expressed intent by the parties.

Identification of Goods. *When particular existing goods are designated as the goods for a contract, such goods are then identified as the goods for that contract.* It is not relevant to identification whether the goods do or do not conform to the contract and that the buyer has a right to return or reject non-conforming goods. What is important is the identification of those particular goods to that contract. The parties by their agreement can determine how and when identification is to occur. In the absence of expressed intent, whether or not identification occurs depends upon the kind of goods involved *at the time the contract is made. If already existing goods are designated for the contract,* they are identified. *If the goods are future goods other than future crops and unborn animals,* they are identified when they are later designated by the seller as goods to which the contract refers. *Such designation may occur by shipping, marking, or otherwise designating such goods as the goods to which the contract refers. If the future goods are crops to be grown under a contract for the sale of crops to be harvested within twelve months or the next normal harvest season after the contract was made, whichever is longer,* identification occurs when the crops are planted or otherwise become growing crops. A crop of wool on an animal is a "growing" crop. *If the future goods are unborn animals to be born within twelve months after the contract was made,* identification occurs when the young are conceived. *If the goods are an undivided share of existing goods,* such as an undivided share in a fungible mass, identification of the existing goods or of the mass is sufficient to identify the share therein to be sold. It is not necessary to identification that the goods be in a deliverable state or that the seller has

[26] UCC 2–401.

not completed his contractual duties with respect to the goods; the seller bears the risk of loss for his non-completion of such duties even though the goods have been identified to the contract.

Identification of itself does not cause the title to pass to the buyer, although identification is one of the elements necessary for this to occur. However, identification does affect the rights of both the buyer and the seller. By identification, the buyer obtains a *special property* as well as an *insurable interest* in the goods. Generally, the buyer's special property consists of the buyer's right to recover the identified goods from the seller: on the seller's insolvency occurring within ten days after the buyer has made part or full payment;[27] or on the seller's repudiation or failure to deliver the identified goods.[28] Inasmuch as the buyer has such special property, he can insure the same against risk of loss; he has an insurable interest in the goods.[29] As for the seller, so long as he retains title to the goods or any security interest in the goods, he has property which he can insure against risk of loss; he too has an insurable interest in the goods. Identification of itself does not deprive the seller of his insurable interest in the goods, although it causes the buyer also to obtain an insurable interest in the goods. *It should be noted very carefully that, where the identification is by the seller alone, he may, until default or insolvency or notification to the buyer that the identification is final, revoke his identification and substitute other goods for those identified.*

Legal Rules for Passing of Title. There are only three limitations which the Code places on the transfer of title in a contract for the sale of goods, whether such transfer is by express agreement of the parties or otherwise:

1. *The goods must be existing and identified to the contract before title to them can pass,* with the exception of a sale of a part interest in existing and identified goods.[30]
2. *Title will pass to the buyer even though the seller reserves a security interest*[31] *in the goods.*
3. *Any attempted retention or reservation by the seller of title in identified goods shipped or delivered to the buyer is limited in effect to a reservation of a security interest in the goods.* Thus, if the goods are to be shipped, the transfer of title to the buyer is not affected by the fact that the goods were shipped with a reservation of a security interest in the seller, even though a document of title (e.g., bill of lading) is to be delivered at a time and place different from the goods, and despite any reservation of a security interest in the bill of lading.

Except as so prohibited by the Code, title to existing and identified goods passes from the seller to the buyer in any manner and on any conditions

[27] See below, p. 228.

[28] See below, p. 282.

[29] For insurable interests, see Insurance, below, pp. 745–46.

[30] See above, p. 200.

[31] UCC 1–201(37): "'Security interest' means an interest in personal property or fixtures which secures payment or performance of an obligation. . . ."

expressly agreed on by the parties. If the parties do not expressly agree on when title is to pass then, unless otherwise expressly agreed, under the Code[32] title will pass depending on whether the seller is to make a *physical delivery* of the goods or to make *delivery without moving the goods.*

If the seller is to make physical delivery of the goods then, unless otherwise expressly agreed, title passes when the seller completes his performance with respect to delivery of the goods pursuant to the contract. *If the contract requires or authorizes the seller to* send *the goods to the buyer but does not require him to* deliver them at destination, *title passes to the buyer at the time and place of shipment. But if the contract requires* delivery at destination, *title passes on tender of delivery*[33] *there.* For example, a purchase order providing for shipment "direct *to* (buyer's address)" without any other condition is merely a shipping direction, and title to the goods ordered passes *on their delivery to the carrier by the shipper.* However, while "delivery *at* (buyer's address)" without any other condition is also a shipping direction, title to the goods ordered passes only *on tender of the goods at the buyer's address.*

If the seller is to make delivery without moving the goods then, unless otherwise expressly agreed: *if the seller is to deliver a document of title, title passes at the time when and the place where he delivers such document; but if the goods are at the time of contracting already identified and no document is to be delivered, title passes at the time and place of contracting.* For example, the seller may have a bill of lading for goods being shipped to him and he contracts for the sale of such goods to the buyer, the agreement providing that the seller is to deliver the bill of lading to the buyer; title passes to the buyer when the seller delivers the bill of lading to the buyer at the proper time and place. Another example would be the buyer's contract to purchase and pick up a specific item in the seller's store; the title passes to the buyer at the time the contract is made.

In summary, goods must be existing and identified to the contract before title to them can pass in a contract for sale, with the exception of a sale of a part interest in existing and identified goods. The expressed intent of the parties concerning the transfer of title to goods when they are, or become, existing and identified to the contract for sale governs. *Except as prohibited by the Code, title to existing and identified goods passes to the buyer when, unless otherwise expressly agreed, the seller delivers the goods pursuant to the contract.* The reasoning is that the seller has finally committed himself with respect to the identified goods, and he is held to that commitment. If he is required or authorized to send the goods, then his commitment occurs when he has delivered the goods to the carrier. If the contract requires him to make delivery at destination, then his commitment occurs when he has done this. If no shipment is to occur, then his commitment is when he delivers the agreed document of title to the goods, or if no such document is to be delivered then his

[32] UCC 2–401.

[33] For tender of delivery, see below, pp. 249 ff.

commitment is at the time the contract is made. Under the Code, *any* attempt by the seller to vary this result by reservation of title (e.g., bill of lading with seller as consignee)[34] is ineffective and results only in the creation of a seller's security interest in the goods. It should be noted carefully that a buyer's justified revocation of acceptance,[35] or his justified or unjustified rejection or other refusal to receive or retain the goods,[36] or his setting the transfer aside pursuant to any principle under the law of Contracts[37] (e.g., fraud, duress, coercion, undue influence), revests title to the goods in the seller by operation of law, and such revesting is not itself a sale.

Rights of Seller's Creditors against Sold Goods

We have seen[38] that when existing goods are identified to the contract, the buyer acquires a special property in the goods consisting of the buyer's right to recover the identified goods from the seller under the conditions of the seller's insolvency or his repudiation or failure to deliver the identified goods. In the absence of the Code or state law to the contrary, the rights of *unsecured creditors* of the seller with respect to goods which have been identified to a contract for sale are subject to such buyer's rights. However, under the Code a creditor who has perfected his security interest has a right in the goods superior to that of the subsequent buyer.[39] If by state law where the goods are located retention of possession by the seller is fraudulent as to his creditors, the creditors may treat the sale or an identification of goods to a contract for sale as void.[40] However the Code modifies such state law to the extent that "retention of possession in good faith and current course of trade by a *merchant seller* for a commercially reasonable time after a sale or identification is not fraudulent." (Author's italics.)[41] However, "Where identification to the contract for delivery is made not in current course of trade but in satisfaction of or as security for a pre-existing claim for money, security or the like and is made under circumstances which under any rule of law of the state where the goods are situated"[42] would constitute the transaction a fraudulent transfer or voidable

[34] For this effect irrespective of form of bill of lading, see below, pp. 251–52.

[35] See below, pp. 251–52.

[36] See below, pp. 259–60.

[37] See above, pp. 34 ff.

[38] See above, p. 226.

[39] See below, pp. 433–34.

[40] Whether or not retention by the seller is fraudulent as a matter of law as to the seller's creditors varies among the states. In most states, such retention raises a presumption of fraud which is rebuttable, as by the buyer showing he has not had a reasonable period of time in which to remove the goods because of their bulk or other meritorious reason. In the minority of states, the presumption is conclusive and the sale is void as to creditors. In some states, retention is presumptively or conclusively fraudulent only as to subsequent creditors, i.e., creditors who become such subsequent to the sale; while in other states, the presumption applies to existing creditors, i.e., creditors who were such at the time of the sale, as well as to subsequent creditors.

[41] UCC 2–402(2).

[42] UCC 2–402(3)(b).

preference, the rights of the seller's creditors are preserved and are not impaired. If the retention is fraudulent in fact, i.e., made with an intent to hinder, delay, or defraud creditors, the sale is fraudulent as to the seller's creditors.

Good Faith Purchasers

The subject of good faith purchasers, involving the rule that "the transferee gets only what the transferor has, with exceptions," has been discussed previously[43] *at length, and reference should be made to that material at this time.*

---

[43] See above, pp. 146–50.

Chapter 16

WARRANTIES

Warranty is part of a contract for sale, unless lawfully otherwise agreed and in the absence of circumstances to the contrary. The five *express* warranties made by the seller are contractual warranties that the goods shall conform to the affirmation, promise, description, sample, or model. The two *implied* warranties are imposed by law and are: merchantability, made by a merchant-dealer; and fitness for a particular purpose, made by any seller. There are two separate warranties imposed by law: title, made by any seller; against infringement, made by a merchant-dealer. All these warranties may be cumulative.

The warranty of title by any seller is that: the title shall be good and its transfer rightful; and the goods shall be free of any lien not actually known to the buyer. It may be excluded or modified only by *specific language*, or by circumstances which give the buyer reason to *know* that the person selling does not claim title in himself or that he is purporting to sell only such right or title as he or a third person *may* have. *The warranty against infringement* by a merchant-dealer is that the goods shall be delivered free of any infringement of rights of third persons. It may be excluded or modified in any way.

The express warranties are made by the seller as a part of the basis for the bargain, and may be made subsequent to the contract for sale as a modification thereof and without consideration, as well as at the time the contract is made. Any express warranty does not cover any defect of which the buyer *knows* or *reasonably should know.* The buyer is not required to examine the goods. The seller's puffing, and his opinion without facts, is not an express warranty. It may be excluded or modified only by clear specific language or circumstances.

The implied warranty of merchantability by a merchant-dealer in goods of

the kind being sold is that the goods are of a quality comparable to that generally acceptable in that line of trade—fit for the *ordinary purposes* for which such goods are used. It may be excluded or modified by language specifically mentioning merchantability and, if in writing, it must be *conspicuous* therein. The buyer is aware that there are *no* implied warranties: if the goods are sold "as is" or "with all faults"; concerning defects which an examination ought to have revealed to him; if course of dealing, course of performance, or usage of trade would exclude them.

***The implied warranty of fitness for a particular purpose* by any seller is that the goods are fit for the seller's *known* purpose of that particular buyer, who must *rely* on the seller's skill or judgment. Purchase of goods by patent or trade name does not of itself exclude the warranty. It's exclusion or modification must be in *writing* and be *conspicuous* therein, may be in general language, and may otherwise be by the buyer's *awareness* of when there are no implied warranties as under the warranty of merchantability.**

The federal Magnuson-Moss Warranty—Federal Trade Commission Improvement Act is concerned only with full and limited written warranties on consumer products with varying sales prices. Its dual purpose is to require the inclusion of certain information in the warranties and to make proper disclosure of the warranties to consumers.

The enforceability of warranties is closely tied to product liability. The Common Law rule of privity continues in effect except as it is modified by the tort of negligence with its strict liability development and by the Code's precise limitation on privity specifying third party beneficiaries of express and implied warranties.

SECTION I. IN GENERAL

The Warranty

Meaning. The word "warranty" has a variety of meanings in the various branches of the law. In the law of Sales, a warranty is essentially a party's assurance of fact, either expressly or impliedly in an agreement, concerning a state of goods and resulting in a contractual obligation of performance. An example is a statement that certain goods are or shall be of a certain kind. The warranty obligation springs from *the bargain in the agreement of the parties and it is a part of the basis for such bargain,* unless the parties lawfully disclaim the presence of such warranty obligation as not being a part of their agreement. The warranty term may be expressly or impliedly agreed to as a part of their agreement. A warranty expressly agreed to is called an "express warranty," and a warranty impliedly agreed to is called an "implied warranty." However, the warranties of title and against infringement imposed by the Code are not classified as either express or implied and, therefore, are considered as separate warranties.[1]

[1] See UCC 2–312, *Comment 6.*

A warranty may occur at the time an agreement for the sale of goods is made, or subsequently as a modification of such prior agreement before the agreement is fully performed. As we have already seen,[2] a modification of a prior agreement may be made by a subsequent agreement or by course of performance, irrespective of the form of the original agreement, and *need not be supported by consideration* to be binding. (S and B contract for the sale of goods by S to B. Subsequently, S warrants the quality of the goods. S's warranty is in modification of the original agreement and becomes a part of the contract.)

Caveat Emptor. The Common Law doctrine of *caveat emptor* does not exist under the Code. At Common Law, the seller was not responsible for the quality or condition of the goods under a contract for their sale, unless he had given an express warranty concerning them. Where the buyer had an opportunity to examine the goods and there was no fraud by the seller, the buyer took the risk of ascertaining that the goods were of the quality or condition that he expected them to be. This was the rule of *caveat emptor,* meaning "let the buyer beware." Later, by judicial decision, then by the Uniform Sales Act, and now by the Code various warranties are imposed by law *in accord with the spirit of the bargain agreement* between the parties. Warranties imposed by law are sometimes called "imposed" warranties, examples of which are the two separate warranties of title and against infringement and the two implied warranties of merchantability and fitness for a particular purpose. Warranties arising expressly from the contract of the parties are sometimes called "contractual" warranties, examples of which are the five express warranties that goods will conform to an affirmation, promise, description, sample, or model.

	Contractual Warranties	*Imposed Warranties*
Express Warranties:	1. Goods shall conform to the affirmation. 2. Goods shall conform to the promise. 3. Goods shall conform to the description. 4. Goods shall conform to the sample. 5. Goods shall conform to the model.	
Implied Warranties:		1. Merchantability, by merchant-dealer. 2. Fitness for a particular purpose, by any seller.
Separate Warranties:		3. Title, by any seller. 4. Against infringement, by merchant-dealer.

First the separate warranties, the express warranties, then implied warranties, and finally enforceability of warranties will be discussed.

[2] See above, p. 206.

SECTION II. SEPARATE WARRANTIES

Warranties may be imposed by law as a part of the agreement of the parties. The Code imposes the two separate warranties of title and against infringement, as well as the two implied warranties of merchantability and fitness for a particular purpose. Only the two separate warranties will be discussed at this time.

Warranty of Title

Nature of the Warranty. The Code recognizes that, unless otherwise agreed and in the absence of circumstances to the contrary, the parties to a contract for the sale of goods intend to transfer title to the goods. The buyer wants, and in good faith expects, to acquire a good, valid, clean title to the goods free from any lien or encumbrance of which he has no knowledge at the time of contracting. The seller is held to know this. Accordingly, *unless otherwise agreed and in the absence of circumstances to the contrary, in every contract for the sale of goods there is the following warranty by the seller:*

(a) *The title conveyed shall be good, and its transfer rightful; and*
(b) *The goods shall be delivered free from any security interest or other lien or encumbrance of which the buyer at the time of contracting has no knowledge.*[3]

It should be noted carefully that, with respect to (b) above, *at the time the contract was made* the buyer must not have any *knowledge,* not merely notice,[4] of any lien or encumbrance on the goods. A buyer is on *constructive notice* of a recorded lien but, for the purpose of the warranty of title, he does not have *knowledge* of it and there is a breach of the seller's warranty of title. A contract for sale includes a present sale and a contract to sell, and this warranty occurs in either transaction. It is unimportant whether or not the seller has possession of the goods at the time of the contract for their sale. Quiet possession is a part of what is warranted under the warranty of title, and any disturbance of the buyer's quiet possession of the goods is evidence of breach of the warranty of title. Under the Code,[5] the Statute of Limitations begins to run on a breach of warranty of title when tender of delivery of the goods is made.

Exclusion or Modification. The warranty of title may be excluded or modified "only by *specific language* of the parties, or by *circumstances* which give the buyer reason to know that the person selling does not claim title in himself or that he is purporting to sell only such right or title as he or a third person may have." (Author's italics.)[6] A contract for the sale of goods "as is" or "with all faults" does not disclaim this warranty. *The language must specifically exclude or modify with respect to title.* For example, "We assume no respon-

[3] UCC 2–312 (1).

[4] For the difference between knowledge and notice, see UCC 1–201(25), pp. 325–26.

[5] UCC 2–725(2).

[6] UCC 2–312(2).

sibility that the title conveyed shall be good or its transfer rightful or that the goods shall be delivered free from any security interest or rightful claim of any third person by way of infringement or otherwise"[7] excludes the warranty of title as well as the express warranty against infringement. *The circumstance of persons selling goods by reason of their representative capacity does not impose a warranty of title by themselves personally.* Illustrations of such persons are: sheriff, auctioneer, one with a security interest, agent, executor, and broker. Such persons manifest to sell only what *they* have. Also, a contract for the sale of only what the *seller* has negates a warranty of title.

Warranty against Infringement

Nature of the Warranty. A buyer of goods *from a merchant-dealer in goods of that kind* expects the goods not to be an infringement on the rights of third persons, such as their patent or trademark. Such an infringement would mar the buyer's title. A non-merchant seller is not in a position to learn whether or not such an infringement exists, but a merchant-dealer of such goods is in business and should be held to this responsibility. Accordingly, *unless otherwise agreed, in a contract for the sale of goods by a seller who is a merchant-dealer in goods of the kind sold, there is a warranty by the seller that the goods shall be delivered free of any infringement or the like of rights of third persons.* However, if the buyer orders goods by furnishing specifications prepared by himself, the buyer now is assuring or warranting to the seller that goods of such specifications would not infringe the rights of third persons; there is then no warranty against infringement by the seller, and the buyer must indemnify the seller for any loss suffered by him for infringement by his compliance with the buyer's specifications. The Code does not specify any particular way of excluding or modifying this warranty other than the buyer furnishing specifications or by agreement to the contrary.

SECTION III. EXPRESS WARRANTIES

Warranties by Affirmation, Promise, Description, Sample, or Model

Nature of These Warranties. Warranty is reflection of what the buyer desires and, accordingly, *what the seller has agreed to sell.* The *bargain* of the parties determines what is being sold and, therefore, warranted by the seller. The Code cuts through formality and concentrates on the *bargain.* It is for this reason that the bargain begets the seller's warranty and that clear proof must be given of the exclusion or modification of a seller's warranty. The parties' agreement consists of their bargain as found in their language or by implication from other circumstances, including course of dealing, usage of trade, or

---

[7] William D. Hawkland, *Sales and Bulk Sales* (Philadelphia, Pa.: The American Law Institute, 1958), p. 49.

course of performance. When the seller expressly makes an affirmation or promise relating to the goods, gives a description of the goods, or uses a sample or model *as a part of the basis for the bargain,* this induces the buyer to rely on it in making the bargain, and the seller thereby has made five corresponding *express warranties* that:

1. The goods shall conform to the affirmation.
2. The goods shall conform to the promise.
3. The goods shall conform to the description.
4. The goods shall conform to the sample.
5. The goods shall conform to the model.

Form. It is not necessary that the seller use any special words, such as "warrant" or the often misused word "guarantee,"[8] or even that he intend to make an express warranty. Making the affirmation, promise, description, or using the sample or model as a basis for the bargain of itself assures and thereby warrants that performance in conformity will occur. An express warranty need not be in any special form, and it may be written or oral. "I promise the machine to be accurate" and "The machine is accurate" are express warranties. The first quotation is in the form of a promise. The second quotation is in the form of an affirmation of fact. An express warranty may be made for a future time, such as a promise that the machine will operate accurately for one year. The express warranty may occur in a present sale or in a contract to sell. The description need not be by language, but may be by a drawing, blueprint, map, design, or the like. Even a course of dealing of previous deliveries may expressly or impliedly constitute a description of quality. By "sample" is meant something drawn in good faith from a bulk, and by "model" is meant something illustrative but not drawn from a bulk. The affirmation, promise, description, sample, or model may be made at any time, and if made after the bargain it thereby becomes, *without any requirement of consideration,* a modification and part thereof. These five warranties are express warranties of quality and, since they were expressly made by the contract, are sometimes called "contractual warranties." In contrast, the separate warranties of title and against infringement and the implied warranties of merchantability and fitness for a particular purpose are imposed by law.

The seller's affirmation, promise, description, sample, or model establishes the respective corresponding warranty, and proof of reliance by the buyer on the seller's conduct is not required to establish such warranties. A seller's statement which becomes *part of the basis for the bargain* signifies that it *induced* the buyer to rely on such statement in entering into the bargain. *The seller's statement creates the warranty;* reliance on such statement by the buyer is *presumed,* and it is a *part of the bargain.* If the seller claims that none of these warranties exists, he must prove that his affirmation, promise, description, sample, or model was not a part of the bargain because the buyer did not

[8] See Suretyship, below, p. 481.

rely on it. If the seller can prove that the buyer knew that the seller's affirmation, promise, description, sample, or model is untrue, then it does not create a corresponding warranty in the bargain. The Code does not specifically state any requirement of inducement by the seller or reliance by the buyer on the seller's affirmation, promise, description, sample, or model; however, the Code's repeated use of the phrase "part of the basis for the bargain" is interpreted to presume such inducement and reliance. Reliance by the buyer occurs by his purchase of the goods, induced by the express warranty. The purpose of the express warranty is to induce the buyer to purchase the goods without making any examination of them, and the buyer's purchase without making any such examination in reliance on the express warranty excuses the buyer from sustaining the loss from any defects which such examination might have revealed. *An express warranty does not cover any defect of which the buyer knows, or reasonably should know.* The buyer's reliance must be a reasonable or justifiable reliance; he cannot reasonably rely on a seller's affirmation or promise of fact when he knows that such is false. A seller's express warranty may be general, such as that a horse is sound, and if the buyer knows that the horse is blind in one eye, the express warranty applies to the horse in every particular except the blindness in one eye.

Puffing. Courts permit sellers a great deal of latitude in praising and commending their wares, commonly called "puffing," in order to induce the buyer to purchase goods. Puffing and the use of words customarily used by honest traders and extravagant expressions regarding the goods that the buyer reasonably could understand to mean puffing do not constitute an express warranty. "The best car on the market" and "the best buy in toothpaste" are illustrations of puffing. Such puffing or sales talk is recognized by the public for what it is and, as really a representation of opinion only, it is not to be relied upon by a reasonable man *as a part of the basis for a bargain.*

Opinion. Under the Code, a statement purporting to be merely the seller's opinion or commendation of the goods, or the seller's affirmation merely of the value of the goods, does not create an express warranty.[9] A statement of value is a form of opinion, but a statement of the facts which determine the expressed value is an affirmation of fact and is an express warranty. "The goods are worth $100" is quite different from "The goods have a book value of $100"; the former is an expression of value and is not an express warranty, while the latter is a statement of fact and is an express warranty. "I have received two offers for this property at $500 each" is a statement of fact and is an express warranty; this is more than puffing. Similarly, a statement of the cost of the particular goods is a statement of fact and is an express warranty.

[9] Although the Code flatly so states, and the C.P.A. examiners have expected this as an answer, nevertheless mention should be made that a statement of opinion or of value may become an express warranty when the opinion or value is indicated *as a fact* and is made by an expert, or by someone who should know the correctness of the opinion or value, to a person who is *ignorant* of the correctness of the opinion or value. This could become a part of the basis for the bargain and an express warranty result.

Exclusion or Modification. Under the Code: "Words or conduct relevant to the creation of an express warranty and words or conduct tending to negate or limit warranty shall be construed wherever reasonable as consistent with each other; but subject to the provisions of this Article on parol or extrinsic evidence (Section 2–202)[10] negation or limitation is inoperative to the extent that such construction is unreasonable."[11] This Code provision seeks to protect the buyer and preserve the express warranties of conformity with affirmation, promise, description, sample, or model as a part of the basis for the bargain against a purported disclaimer that is not specific enough to dispel what the buyer bargained for. The disclaiming phrase excluding "all warranties express or implied" is not specific enough to exclude these express warranties.

SECTION IV. IMPLIED WARRANTIES

Again, *the basis of the bargain* of the parties reflecting what goods the buyer expects from the seller and, therefore, *what the seller undertakes to supply* determines the warranties of the seller assuring the buyer with respect to such goods. The parties may *expressly* agree on warranties of merchantability and fitness for a particular purpose resulting in these two *express warranties* of quality. However, under certain circumstances these warranties of quality are *implied by law* in a contract for the sale of goods and, for this reason, they are sometimes called "imposed" warranties. Under the Code,[12] the serving for value of food or drink to be consumed either on the premises or elsewhere is a sale and, therefore, such food or drink can be the subject of the warranties of merchantability and fitness for a particular purpose imposed by law.

The warranties of merchantability and fitness for a particular purpose are easily distinguished from each other by their content. Under a warranty of merchantability, the goods are warranted *by a merchant in a given line of trade to be of a quality comparable to that generally acceptable in that line of trade*—fit for the *ordinary* purposes for which such goods are used. Under a warranty of fitness for a particular purpose, the goods are warranted by the seller, whether a merchant or not, to be *fit for the known purpose of that particular buyer* who has relied on the seller's skill or judgment. The two warranties may exist at the same time, springing from the same transaction. First the implied warranty of merchantability and then the implied warranty of fitness for a particular purpose will be discussed.

Implied Warranty of Merchantability

Nature of the Warranty. *An implied warranty of merchantability is implied by law if the seller is a merchant-dealer in goods of the kind being sold*

[10] For the parol evidence rule, see above, p. 212.

[11] UCC 2–316(1).

[12] UCC 2–314(1).

under the contract for sale. The merchant-dealer may be a grower or manufacturer of the goods. The buyer may order the goods by description, or he may specifically designate the goods he desires. The warranty of merchantability applies to a contract for secondhand goods, although such goods are in a different category of what is fit for the *ordinary* purposes for which such goods are sold. "Ordinary purposes" does not include the unusual use by a supersensitive or allergic buyer.

The Code clearly states when goods are merchantable and provides a standard for performance in conformity with the warranty:

> (2) *Goods to be merchantable must be at least such as*
> (a) pass without objection in the trade under the contract description; and
> (b) in the case of fungible goods, are of fair average quality within the description; and
> (c) are fit for the *ordinary* purposes for which such goods are used; and
> (d) run, within the variations permitted by the agreement, of even kind, quality and quantity within each unit and among all units involved; and
> (e) are adequately contained, packaged, and labeled as the agreement may require; and
> (f) conform to the promises or affirmations of fact made on the container or label if any.[13] (Author's italics.)

Exclusion or Modification. The warranty of merchantability is commonly taken for granted, and its exclusion or modification in a contract for the sale of goods is so very unusual that it must be clearly brought to the buyer's attention and thereby prevent his unexpected and unbargained disclaimer.[14] It is for this reason that the Code provides that, in order to exclude or modify the warranty of merchantability or any part of it:

1. The language of exclusion or modification *must specifically mention merchantability.*
2. *If* the exclusion or modification is contained *in a writing,* it *must be conspicuous therein.* "A term or clause is conspicuous when it is so written that a reasonable person against whom it is to operate ought to have noticed it. A printed heading in capitals (as: NON-NEGOTIABLE BILL OF LADING) is conspicuous. Language in the body of a form is 'conspicuous' if it is in larger or other contrasting type or color. But in a telegram any stated term is 'conspicuous.' Whether a term or clause is 'conspicuous' or not is for decision by the court."[15]
3. If the *"fit for the ordinary purposes" part* of the warranty of merchantability is to be excluded or modified, the exclusion or modification *must be in writing and be conspicuous.*

---

[13] UCC 2–314(2).

[14] But see the federal Magnuson-Moss Warranty–Federal Trade Commission Improvement Act of 1975, below, pp. 241 ff., especially p. 242.

[15] UCC 1–201(10).

However, the circumstances surrounding the transaction may in themselves be sufficient to call the buyer's attention to the fact that no implied warranties are made or that a certain implied warranty is being excluded. Circumstances which do this and thereby exclude *any* implied warranty are:

1. The agreement is for the sale of goods "as is," "with all faults," or other similar language the common understanding of which has the same effect of calling to the buyer's attention that there is no such implied warranty.
2. Before entering into the contract: the buyer examined the goods, sample, or model as fully as he desired; or, after demand made by the seller to examine the goods fully, the buyer refused to do so. On such examination or refusal to examine, there is no implied warranty with regard to defects which an examination ought in the circumstances to have revealed to him.[16]
3. Course of dealing, course of performance, or usage of trade may exclude an implied warranty.
4. The buyer's conduct may exclude an implied warranty. For example, where the buyer gives precise and complete specifications as to the goods, there is no implied warranty because the buyer expects to get only what he has specifically ordered and not merchantable goods. However, the precise description of the goods is a part of the basis of the bargain and, therefore, creates an express warranty that the goods shall conform to the description.[17] Also, inasmuch as the Code in its consideration of warranties is trying to reflect the reasonable expectations of the parties, if the buyer knows of a defect in the goods rendering them unmerchantable, a warranty of merchantability will not be implied.

Implied Warranty of Fitness for a Particular Purpose

Nature of the Warranty. An implied warranty that goods are fit for a *particular* purpose is imposed by law if two things occur:

1. *The buyer requires the goods for a particular purpose and is relying on the seller's skill or judgment to select or furnish goods suitable for that purpose;* and
2. *At the time the contract is made, the seller has reason to know of such particular purpose and of the buyer's reliance.* The buyer need not inform the seller of the particular purpose and reliance, although he can do so; what is important is that the seller has reason so to know at the time the contract is made, whether he was told by the buyer or the circumstances reasonably should so indicate to him.

An implied warranty of fitness for a particular purpose may arise in connection with a present sale or a contract to sell. The seller may be anyone, whether

[16] The particular buyer's skill and the normal method of examination under the circumstances are important in order to determine whether, on examination, defects should have been revealed to the buyer.

[17] See the express warranty created by description, above, pp. 234–35.

or not a manufacturer or grower and whether a merchant or a non-merchant, and the buyer may purchase for his own use or for resale.

A particular purpose means that the purpose is different from the ordinary purpose for which such goods are used. It is for some peculiar use by this buyer. If the goods are for ordinary use, then there is no implied warranty of fitness for a particular purpose, but there is an implied warranty of merchantability, because that warranty is for ordinary use. Both the warranties of fitness for a particular purpose and of merchantability may occur from the same transaction, the ordinary and particular purposes being present. (S contracts with B to supply and deliver to B a heater, which S knows B intends to use to heat B's house. There is an implied warranty of merchantability that the heater will heat, and there is an implied warranty of fitness for a particular purpose that the heater will heat B's house. If S had no reason to know of B's particular purpose of heating his house, then only the implied warranty of merchantability exists.)

The buyer must rely on the seller's skill or judgment. The buyer's selection of particular goods is in reliance on his own skill and judgment and not on that of the seller. (A picked out a TV set in S's retail TV store and bought it. There is no warranty of fitness for a particular purpose, although the implied warranty of merchantability is present.) The buyer need not give a description of the goods to the seller, although he may and often does so. However, the buyer's description may be so detailed a specification as to the goods that the buyer is not relying on the seller's skill or judgment, and there is no warranty of fitness for a particular purpose, nor of merchantability either,[18] although there will be an express warranty by the seller that the goods will conform with the description.[19] The buyer's purchase of goods by patent or trade name does not *of itself* exclude the warranty of fitness for a particular purpose; it is only one fact among others as evidence to prove that the buyer has not relied on the seller's skill or judgment. However, the buyer's *insistence* on a particular brand of goods may be such that he no longer relies on the seller's skill or judgment in supplying him with goods suitable for his particular purpose, and there is no implied warranty of fitness for a particular purpose.

Exclusion or Modification. It should be noted carefully that there are two warranties concerned with fitness for *a* purpose. One is the implied warranty of *fitness for a particular purpose.* The other is the implied warranty of *merchantability* which assures that the goods will be *fit for ordinary purposes.*[20] The Code provisions concerning exclusion or modification deal equally with the implied warranty of fitness for a particular purpose and with *only that part of the warranty of merchantability concerned with fitness for ordinary purposes.*[21] Solely for the purpose of discussion under this paragraph heading, we

---

[18] See above, pp. 237–38.

[19] See above, pp. 234–35.

[20] See above, p. 237.

[21] See above, p. 237 and ftn. 14.

will describe these two warranties concerned with fitness as "the two fitness warranties." The two fitness warranties may be excluded or modified only in any of the following five ways:

1. Except for 2, 3, 4, and 5 below, exclusion or modification *must be in writing and be conspicuous therein.* The language of exclusion or modification need not specifically refer to the two fitness warranties, but *may be general language* excluding both warranties. For example, "There are no warranties which extend beyond the description on the face hereof"[22] excludes the two fitness warranties.

2,3,4,5. These are the same as the four items on page 239, above, in connection with exclusion or modification of the implied warranty of merchantability by the circumstances surrounding the transaction.

SECTION V. CUMULATION AND CONFLICT OF WARRANTIES

The intention of the contracting parties as disclosed by their agreement determines their respective contractual rights and obligations. Inasmuch as their contract is to be examined as a whole, reflecting all their intentions, if there is more than one warranty involved then *they are considered to be cumulative, and are to be construed as consistent with each other to the extent that this is possible.* If such construction is unreasonable, then recourse must be made to the intention of the parties to determine which of the conflicting warranties is to be dominant. The matter of the seller's good faith becomes important here. If the seller in good faith made warranties which subsequently are found to be inconsistent, then it must be determined which is to be dominant. However, if the seller has not acted in good faith and has misled the buyer by assuring him that the inconsistent warranties can be performed, then he is bound to perform *all* of them and he is estopped to assert their inconsistency. The Code establishes specific criteria to ascertain the intention of the parties as to which of inconsistent warranties is dominant:

(a) Exact or technical specifications displace an inconsistent sample or model or general language of description.
(b) A sample from an existing bulk displaces inconsistent general language of description.
(c) Express warranties displace inconsistent implied warranties other than an implied warranty of fitness for a particular purpose.[23]

SECTION VI. THE FEDERAL MAGNUSON-MOSS WARRANTY—FEDERAL TRADE COMMISSION IMPROVEMENT ACT OF 1975

This federal[24] warranty law on consumer product warranties is concerned only with *written* warranties concerning contracts for the sale of *consumer*

---

[22] UCC 2–316(2).

[23] UCC 2–317.

[24] 15 U.S.C. sections 2301–2312.

products in interstate commerce or affecting interstate commerce with a sales price of *more than $10*. The Act requires full and complete disclosure of terms and conditions in the written warranties. It deals primarily with two kinds of *written* warranties, namely "full" and "limited" warranties. If the seller (warrantor) designates the warranty as a "full warranty," he must, among other things, free of charge, repair the product if it fails to conform to the written warranty and, if this cannot be done, replace the product or refund the purchase price at the option of the consumer. Also, he cannot exclude or limit consequential damages for breach of any written or implied warranty on such product, unless such exclusion or limitation conspicuously appears on the face of the warranty. A limited warranty has limitations not included in the full warranty. The seller must make available to the consumer the written terms of the written warranty for his examination prior to the sale. Under the Act, the state implied warranties of merchantability and of fitness for a particular purpose cannot be disclaimed, thereby apparently superseding the Uniform Commercial Code which permits such disclaimers. The Act also provides that, if the sales price is more than $5, the written warranty *must* clearly and conspicuously disclose in a single document certain information, although the Federal Trade Commission Regulation raises the price to *more than $15:*

> "(a) Any warrantor warranting to a consumer by means of a written warranty a consumer product actually costing the consumer more than $15.00 shall clearly and conspicuously* [explained in bracketed paragraph below] disclose in a single document in simple and readily understood language, the following items of information: (1) The identity of the party or parties to whom the written warranty is extended, if the enforceability of the written warranty is limited to the original consumer purchaser or is otherwise limited to persons other than every consumer owner during the term of the warranty;
>
> (2) A clear description and identification of products, or parts, or characteristics, or components or properties covered by and where necessary for clarification, excluded from the warranty;
>
> (3) A statement of what the warrantor will do in the event of a defect, malfunction or failure to conform with the written warranty, including the items or services the warrantor will pay for or provide, and, where necessary for clarification, those which the warrantor will not pay for or provide;
>
> (4) The point in time or event on which the warranty term commences, if different from the purchase date, and the time period or other measurement of warranty duration;
>
> (5) A step-by-step explanation of the procedure which the consumer should follow in order to obtain performance of any warranty obligation, including the persons or class of persons authorized to perform warranty obligations. This includes the name(s) of the warrantor(s), together with: the mailing address(es) of the warrantor(s), and/or the name or title and the address of any employee or department of the warrantor responsible for the performance of warranty obligations, and/or a telephone number which consumers may use without charge to obtain information on warranty performance;

(6) Information respecting the availability of an informal dispute settlement mechanism elected by the warrantor in compliance with Part 703 of this subchapter;

(7) Any limitations on the duration of implied warranties, disclosed on the face of the warranty as provided in Section 108 of the Act, accompanied by the following statement:

> *Some states do not allow limitations on how long an implied warranty lasts, so the above limitation may not apply to you.*

(8) Any exclusions of or limitations on relief such as incidental or consequential damages, accompanied by the following statement, which may be combined with the statement required in sub-paragraph (7) above:

> *Some states do not allow the exclusion or limitation of incidental or consequential damages, so the above limitation or exclusion may not apply to you.*

(9) A statement in the following language:

> *This warranty gives you specific legal rights, and you may also have other rights which vary from state to state.*"

Under the FTC Regulation, a consumer product "means any tangible personal property which is distributed in commerce and which is normally used for personal, family, or household purposes (including any such property intended to be attached to or installed in any real property without regard to whether it is so attached or installed). Products which are purchased solely for commercial or industrial use are excluded solely for purposes of this Part."

* [The first FTC complaint issued under the Act in 1978 was against a television appliance dealer for violation of the FTC Regulation that any warranties offered be disclosed, properly labeled as full or limited, and made available for the consumer to read and compare before a purchase. The Commission's order of November 1979 required the dealer to take specific steps to comply with the Act. The steps included making certain disclosures about the written warranties and notifying customers of the availability of warranties by signs in the stores. If the dealer should choose to make warranties available by means of binders in the store, the binders must be displayed so that they will be noticed, and each binder must include copies of warranties for all products sold in the department where it is displayed.]

SECTION VII. ENFORCEABILITY OF WARRANTIES AND PRODUCT LIABILITY

At Common Law

The *Common Law* liability of a supplier of goods to a user of the goods was largely based upon the tort of negligence and was limited by *caveat emptor* (let the buyer beware). As time went on, a strong emphasis on warranties began to replace *caveat emptor.* Privity (immediate relationship) between the parties was required. A person's negligence directly and proximately causing harm to another person caused the negligent party to be liable to the injured party. In the area of warranties, the express and implied warranties made by a supplier to a user exposed the warrantor to liability for breach of his warranty. Today, the transition from a small personal relationship in business to that of a huge rather impersonal business community with large manufacturers and suppliers has prompted a change in the basic concept of privity, and, correspondingly, in the basis for liability by negligence and warranty. It is deemed too much to require privity of contract in *all* cases between the supplier (e.g., manufacturer, retailer) and the ultimate consumer in order that the latter can recover for injury sustained by a product defectively manufactured.

The Tort of Negligence

Not too long ago it was established by a leading case that, if a manufacturer negligently manufactured a chattel which he should realize, *if made negligently,* would involve an unreasonable risk of *substantial bodily harm* in its use for the purpose manufactured, he would be liable to a remote user for injury sustained caused by the defect in the product. No privity existed between the manufacturer and the injured user of the product. The manufacturer was liable for such unreasonable risk of harm caused by his negligence. However, today the courts, and some legislatures, have gone beyond this early development and, in many cases, e.g., defective food and drink, have held the supplier of the defective product absolutely liable on the basis of *strict liability* for certain defective products the defective nature of which caused injury to users, and often to other third persons, without any requirement of privity between the supplier and the ultimate user. This product liability is based on the tort of negligence and has been extended to strict liability as reflected in the Restatement (Second) of Torts:

> §402A. Special Liability of Seller of Product for Physical Harm to User or Consumer.
>
> (1) One who sells any product in a defective condition unreasonably dangerous to the user or consumer or to his property, is subject to liability for physical harm thereby caused to the ultimate user or consumer, or to his property, if
>
> (a) the seller is engaged in the business of selling such a product, and
>
> (b) it is expected to and does reach the user or consumer without substantial change in the condition in which it is sold.
>
> (2) The rule stated in Subsection (1) applies although
>
> (a) the seller has exercised all possible care in the preparation and sale of his product, and
>
> (b) the user or consumer has not bought the product from or entered into any contractual relation with the seller.

Warranties

Historically privity of contract was required as an essential factor for warranty between the two bargaining parties (e.g., seller and buyer) regarding the nature, quality, condition, and suitability of the goods involved in the transaction. This is true today, but with very important exceptions caused by both the huge expansion and growth of large business and the need for a change in public policy when the injury to a user from a defective product required a modification in the application of the privity rule. Courts have asserted that, in many cases, especially when the product's defect causes the product to become unreasonably dangerous (defective food, drink), a warranty is implied from the manufacturer to the remote consumer that there are no defects in the manufactured product. If a defect in a manufactured product is the proximate cause of injury to a user consumer, there is a breach of warranty and the manufacturer is liable on his warranty. The liability here is on the basis of *warranty, not negligence.* Realistically, this is an abandonment of the privity rule under the guise of the implied warranty, often called a warranty implied by law, in order to establish a relationship basis between the parties for liability to occur. Today, an injured user can sue for injury on the basis of negligence, strict liability, and breach of warranty at the same time.

The warranty accompanies the product through intermediate parties (e.g., wholesaler, retailer) to the ultimate consumer. UCC 2–318 reflects this extension of warranty to various persons by its three alternatives for state adoption, the first alternative being the one most widely adopted and the last one reflecting the trend of recent decisions and the Restatement (Second) of Torts, section 402A, quoted above. Only to this extent *under the Code* is the privity of contract rule broken. However, the Code does not preclude the enlargement or restriction of developing case law on the further invasion of the privity of contract rule, nor does the Code restrict or limit any right or remedy based on the tort of negligence. The Code limits its legislative invasion only to the extent indicated. The Code *compulsorily* makes only those persons indicated below in UCC 2–318 beneficiaries of a warranty; it does *not preclude* any other persons from being beneficiaries either by contractual provision of the parties or by the developing case law. For example, the parties may contract that the seller's warranties shall extend to third persons, who then can enforce such warranties directly against the seller as third party beneficiaries under the contract.[25]

UCC 2–318. Third Party Beneficiaries of Warranties Express or Implied
Note: *If this Act is introduced in the Congress of the United States this section should be omitted.* (*States to select one alternative.*)

Alternative A

A seller's warranty whether express or implied extends to any natural person who is in the family or household of his buyer or who is a guest in his home if it is reasonable to expect that such person may use, consume or be affected by the goods and who is injured in person by breach of the warranty. A seller may not exclude or limit the operation of this section.

---

[25] See Contracts, above, p. 74.

Alternative B

A seller's warranty whether express or implied extends to any natural person who may reasonably be expected to use, consume or be affected by the goods and who is injured in person by breach of the warranty. A seller may not exclude or limit the operation of this section.

Alternative C

A seller's warranty whether express or implied extends to any person who may reasonably be expected to use, consume or be affected by the goods and who is injured by breach of the warranty. A seller may not exclude or limit the operation of this section with respect to injury to the person of an individual to whom the warranty extends.

Notice that, under the Restatement and also under the UCC third alternative, liability extends not only to the user but also *to his property*. Also, notice that, reflecting public policy of unconscionability, the seller is precluded from excluding or limiting his liability to such beneficiaries of the warranty, any such waiver, disclaimer, or limitation in the warranty being void.

Chapter 17

PERFORMANCE AND BREACH OF CONTRACT

SECTION I. PERFORMANCE OF THE CONTRACT

The seller's obligation is to transfer and deliver goods or a bill of lading, and the buyer is to accept and pay for such goods, pursuant to their contract. Unless otherwise agreed, tender of delivery and tender of payment are concurrent conditions.

The contract may require *the seller to tender delivery* either by: (1) *physical delivery of the goods* by shipment—if to *send* the goods then F.O.B. shipping point by delivery to the carrier, if to *deliver* then F.O.B. destination point by tendering delivery of the goods or documents at destination; or (2) *delivery without moving the goods,* by the seller or, if the identified goods are in the possession of a bailee other than the seller, by either tendering a *negotiable* document, procuring the bailee's acknowledgement of the buyer's right to possession, or, subject to the buyer's objection, tendering a *non-negotiable* document or a written direction to the bailee to deliver the goods to the buyer. If the seller acquires a *negotiable* bill, he has a security interest in the goods, while if it is a *non-negotiable* bill he has a security interest of possession only if he is the consignee. A seller has the right to "cure" non-conformity before his time for performance under the contract has expired.

***The purchase price tendered by the buyer* may be money or any other property or services as provided in the contract for sale, payable at the time and place where the goods were to be delivered to the buyer. If the seller demands legal tender and refuses to accept the *buyer's* check as conditional payment for money, the buyer has a reasonable time to procure the legal tender. A negotiable instrument drawn, made, or accepted by a *bank* is proper**

payment. Unless otherwise agreed, the buyer has the right to inspect the goods before making payment or accepting them. This right is lost if the contract provides for delivery C.O.D., payment against documents, or C.I.F. without any payment "on or after arrival" clause. On the seller's insolvency within ten days after the buyer has made a payment for goods identified by the seller, the buyer can recover the goods provided he tenders any balance of the price remaining.

The seller bears the risk of loss to the goods until the buyer accepts the goods, or the seller completes his performance with respect to the delivery of the goods pursuant to the contract by making physical delivery or by making delivery without moving the goods, except that if the seller is a merchant the risk passes to the buyer only on his *receipt* of the goods. In a sale on approval, the risk passes to the buyer when he accepts the goods.

Each of the parties to a contract for the sale of goods has contractual rights and obligations to perform. Performance means complete performance; nonperformance means a failure of performance, whether in small or great degree. Performance or nonperformance by one party has an immediate legal effect on the rights and obligations of the other party. This chapter will discuss performance in the first section and nonperformance amounting to breach of contract in the second section.

Delivery and Payment

Obligations of the Parties. The seller's obligation is to transfer and deliver goods or a bill of lading, and the buyer's obligation is to accept and pay for such goods, in accordance with their contract. We have already seen[1] that the agreement of the parties determines their contractual rights and obligations and that an agreement consists of the bargain of the parties as expressly made, or as implied from other circumstances which include course of dealing, usage of trade, and course of performance. The Code fills in the omitted details of their bargain by reflecting commercial practice. The parties may agree that delivery of the goods or bill of lading by the seller and payment of the price by the buyer are to occur concurrently, or that payment is to precede or follow delivery. *Unless the parties otherwise agree, the seller's tender of delivery of the goods or bill of lading and the buyer's tender of payment of the price pursuant to the contract are concurrent conditions.* If the seller makes a conditional delivery to the buyer and demands payment, the buyer has no right with respect to the goods or document of title delivered to him until payment is made. Should the seller make conditional delivery and, on nonpayment by the buyer, fail to assert his right to repossession, the condition of payment is waived, it is a sale on credit, and the seller is merely a general creditor with no specific rights in the goods; although later discussion[2] will

[1] See above, p. 202.

[2] See below, p. 273.

indicate that the seller has ten days after such delivery in which to reclaim goods sold on credit to an insolvent buyer.

Effect of the Seller's Insolvency. The seller's insolvency materially affects the buyer's rights to identified goods. A person is insolvent "who either has ceased to pay his debts in the ordinary course of business or cannot pay his debts as they become due or is insolvent within the meaning of the federal bankruptcy law."[3] *After identification,* the buyer acquires a special property interest in the goods which includes the right to possession of the goods under certain conditions. If the *seller* identified goods to the contract and he becomes insolvent within ten days after the buyer has paid either the full purchase price or the first installment of the purchase price, the buyer has the right to recover the identified goods from the seller, provided that if the full purchase price has not been paid the buyer make and keep good a tender of the unpaid portion of the purchase price. If the *buyer* made the identification, in addition to the above the identified goods must conform to the contract. The reason for this special provision when the buyer has made the identification is to preclude the buyer from getting goods greatly superior in quality or quantity to that called for by the contract.

The remainder of this section will consist of a discussion of delivery by the seller, payment by the buyer, and risk of loss in that order.

Delivery by the Seller

Seller's Tender of Delivery. Delivery means voluntary transfer of possession from one person to another. It may be made by one person through his authorized agent to another person through the latter's authorized agent. As we have seen,[4] delivery is important in the transfer of title. *Tender of delivery* is also important in connection with the buyer's duty to pay the price. *Tender of delivery by the seller occurs when the seller puts and holds conforming goods at the buyer's disposition and gives to the buyer any notification reasonably necessary to enable the buyer to take delivery.*[5] Unless otherwise agreed, it is the buyer's obligation to furnish facilities reasonably suited to the receipt of the goods. The contract of the parties determines the manner, time, and place for tender. Unless otherwise agreed, delivery may be tendered or demanded only at a reasonable hour, and if the tender is to be made of goods rather than of documents of title the goods must be kept available for the period reasonably necessary to enable the buyer to take possession. The seller's obligation may be to make a physical delivery of the goods, to make delivery without moving the goods, or to deliver documents, and his tender of delivery will vary accordingly.

Physical Delivery—Shipment. If the seller is to make physical delivery of the goods, normally he is only to *"ship,"* i.e., *send,* the goods to the buyer,

[3] UCC 1–201(23).

[4] See above, p. 227.

[5] UCC 2–503(1).

although at times he is to *deliver them at a particular destination.* Each of these will be considered separately.

Under the Code,[6] when the seller is required or authorized to *send* the goods to the buyer then, unless otherwise agreed, in order to make a *tender of delivery* he must:

1. Put conforming goods in the possession of such a carrier and make such a contract for their transportation as may be reasonable having regard to the nature of the goods and other circumstances of the case; and
2. Obtain and promptly deliver or tender in due form any document which is necessary to enable the buyer to obtain possession of the goods or which is otherwise required by the agreement or by usage of trade; and
3. Promptly notify the buyer of the shipment.

The seller's failure to make a proper contract for the transportation of the goods as required in (1) above or to notify the buyer as in (3) above does not invalidate the seller's tender but, rather, is a ground for the buyer's rejection *only if material delay or loss ensues.* With respect to the seller's contract for transportation of the goods, if without the fault of either buyer or seller the agreed *manner of delivery* becomes commercially impracticable, as where there is a failure of facilities (e.g., the agreed berthing, loading, or unloading facilities fail), the Code permits *substituted performance* by the seller.[7] The seller has the obligation of making all necessary arrangements with the carrier which are reasonable under the circumstances, such as sending along any necessary help, refrigeration, watering of livestock. The seller's prompt notification to the buyer of shipment may be accomplished by the commercial practice of sending an invoice if it is an open credit shipment, or sending documents as provided in requirement (2). It should be noted that, unless otherwise agreed, since the seller has the right to demand payment on tender of delivery,[8] if the seller should so demand payment he must first permit the buyer to exercise his right to *inspect* the goods[9] so as not to impair his tender of delivery, unless the buyer's right of inspection has been precluded, such as by a C.I.F., C.O.D., or cash against documents contract.

If a seller is to *deliver goods at a particular destination,* he makes a *tender of delivery* if: he puts and holds conforming goods at the buyer's disposition at the destination; he gives to the buyer any notification reasonably required to enable the buyer to take delivery; and, if documents are involved, he tenders such documents as appropriate as indicated in the following two paragraphs where delivery occurs without moving the goods or the contract requires the seller to deliver documents.

Delivery without Moving the Goods. Where the goods are in the possession of a bailee (e.g., carrier, warehouseman, or other person not the seller),

---

[6] UCC 2–504.

[7] UCC 2–614; also see below, p. 268.

[8] See above, p. 249.

[9] See below, pp. 254–56.

under the Code[10] the seller may make a *tender of delivery* in the following ways:

1. The seller may tender to the buyer a *negotiable* document of title covering the goods.
2. The seller may procure acknowledgment by the bailee of the buyer's right to possession of the goods.
3. The seller may tender to the buyer a *non-negotiable* document of title, subject to the buyer's seasonable objection.
4. The seller may tender to the buyer a written direction to the bailee to deliver the goods to the buyer, subject to the buyer's seasonable objection.

The first two methods of tender are proper and valid; but the buyer need not accept the third and fourth methods of tender, although his failure seasonably to object causes them to be valid. In connection with the fourth method of tender, receipt by the bailee of notification of the buyer's rights fixes those rights as against the bailee and all third persons. In connection with the third and fourth methods of tender, until the buyer has had a reasonable time to present the document of title to the bailee, *the seller bears the risk of loss* of the goods and the risk of any failure by the bailee to honor the non-negotiable document of title or to obey the direction to the bailee to deliver the goods to the buyer; a refusal by the bailee to honor the document or to obey the direction nullifies the tender.

Seller Required to Deliver Documents. Although it is extremely unusual, where the contract *requires* the seller to deliver documents instead of delivering goods, the seller is required to tender all such documents in correct form, except that with respect to bills of lading in a set under certain circumstances only one part of the bill of lading need be tendered.[11] Tender of documents through customary banking channels is sufficient, and dishonor of a draft[12] (i.e., bill of exchange) accompanying the documents constitutes non-acceptance or rejection by the buyer.[13]

Seller's Shipment under Reservation; Form of Bill of Lading. When goods are shipped by the seller, he will obtain a bill of lading from the carrier. The form of the bill of lading is irrelevant to the transfer of title to existing and identified goods which occurs when the goods have been delivered by the seller pursuant to the contract, irrespective of the seller's reservation of a security interest in the goods.[14] *Any attempted retention or reservation by the seller of title in identified goods shipped or delivered to the buyer is limited in effect to a reservation of a security interest in the goods.* However, the form of the bill of lading does affect the nature of the interests therein of the seller and buyer and their transferees, and the obligation of the carrier.

---

[10] UCC 2–503.

[11] See UCC 2–323(2) and 7–304.

[12] See UCC 3–104(2)(a).

[13] UCC 2–503(5)(b).

[14] See above, p. 226.

The bill of lading may be negotiable or non-negotiable. Under the Code,[15] where the seller has identified goods to the contract by or before shipment and has procured a *negotiable bill of lading*, irrespective of who the consignee named therein is, *the seller thereby acquires a security interest in the goods.* This is so even though the bill of lading is to the order of a financing agency[16] or of the buyer, which indicates that, in addition to the seller's security interest in the goods, the seller has the expectation of transferring that interest to that consignee. If the bill of lading is *non-negotiable,* then: if the *seller or his nominee*[17] is the consignee, the seller's security interest is his *right to possession* of the goods as security; but if the *buyer* is the consignee, the seller has *no security interest in the goods* even though the seller retains possession of the bill of lading, and the buyer can rightfully obtain the goods from the carrier without surrendering any bill of lading to the carrier. As previously discussed,[18] the carrier's contract is to deliver possession of the goods to the consignee, or his known transferee, of a *non-negotiable* bill of lading without picking up the bill of lading; while if a *negotiable* bill of lading is outstanding, the carrier has the obligation of delivering the goods to the order of the consignee named in the bill, and the carrier cannot be compelled to deliver the goods to anyone without the surrender of the bill of lading. However, the seller consignee of a non-negotiable bill of lading still has the power, *as the unpaid seller of an insolvent buyer,* to stop the goods while they are in transit.[19] If the contract for sale provided that the seller had a right of payment against delivery of the goods, the seller could make an immediate demand for payment by the buyer and assert that his delivery of the goods to the carrier in exchange for a non-negotiable bill of lading *with the buyer as consignee* was a conditional delivery; but it should be noted carefully that, as previously discussed,[20] the buyer has the power to transfer title to the goods to a good faith purchaser for value or to a buyer in ordinary course of business, depending on the character of the latter's seller. It should be noted further that the shipping seller's reservation of a security interest in violation of the contract for sale is a breach of contract and is also an improper contract for transportation and, therefore, not a tender of delivery by the seller.[21] It should also be noted that a financing agency which has paid, or purchased for value, a draft which relates to a shipment of goods acquires to the extent of the payment or purchase: the rights of a holder of the draft;[22] the rights of a holder of any document of title securing the draft; the shipping seller's security rights in the goods (e.g., right

[15] UCC 2–505(1)(a).

[16] Ibid.

[17] The seller may find it convenient to have the goods sent to the order of his nominee, such as the bank extending credit to the seller or the financing agency to whom he intends to negotiate the bill of lading.

[18] See above, p. 186.

[19] See below, pp. 275–77.

[20] See above, pp. 148 ff.

[21] See above, pp. 249 ff.

[22] See Commercial Paper, below, pp. 344–47.

to stop the goods while in transit if the buyer becomes insolvent); and the shipping seller's right to have the buyer honor the draft. When the financing agency has in good faith honored or purchased the draft under the commitment to or authority from the buyer, the agency has a right of reimbursement from the buyer, and this right is not impaired by subsequent discovery of defects with reference to any relevant document which was apparently regular on its face.

Cure and Replacement. Sellers do not always tender or deliver conforming goods. *As long as the time for a seller's performance under his contract has not expired,* he may make other attempts to perform and cure the nonconformity. If the buyer rejects the seller's tender or delivery of nonconforming goods and the time for the seller's performance under the contract has *not expired,* the seller may make a delivery of conforming goods *provided he first seasonably notifies the buyer of his intention to cure his previous non-conforming tender or delivery.* If the buyer rejects a non-conforming tender *which the seller had reasonable grounds to believe would be acceptable,* and the time in which the seller was to perform *has expired,* nevertheless the seller may have a further reasonable time to substitute a conforming tender *provided he seasonably notifies the buyer of his intention to cure his previous non-conforming tender.*

Payment by the Buyer

Form of Payment. The price may be money or any other property or services, as previously discussed.[23] We have seen[24] that, unless the buyer and seller otherwise agree, the seller's tender of delivery and the buyer's tender of payment of the price pursuant to the contract are concurrent conditions. The parties may otherwise agree, as in a contract providing for credit to the buyer (which occurs in most commercial sales), in which case payment is to be made in accordance with such credit provision. Because tender of delivery and tender of payment are concurrent conditions unless otherwise agreed, and since the Code rules provide for the place of the seller's delivery if the parties have not otherwise agreed,[25] then the place and time of tender of payment by the buyer are determined by those Code provisions unless otherwise agreed.

Tender of payment is sufficient if made in the medium and manner agreed to by the parties. *Unless otherwise agreed, tender of payment is sufficient when made by any means or in any manner current in the ordinary course of business, which includes legal tender.*[26] However, unless otherwise agreed,

---

[23] See above, p. 217.

[24] See above, p. 248.

[25] See above, p. 220.

[26] Legal tender statutes prescribe the particular kind of money which an obligee is required to accept in discharge of an obligation. The term "money" includes, but is not limited to, legal tender. UCC 1–201(24): "'Money' means a medium of exchange authorized or adopted by a domestic or foreign government as a part of its currency."

the seller has the right to payment in legal tender if he so desires to assert it. Because the buyer may be surprised at the time of the seller's performance by the seller's rightful demand for legal tender when the buyer may have contemplated payment in another manner, as by check, if the seller demands payment in legal tender he must also give any extension of time reasonably necessary for the buyer to procure it. The check[27] is a very widely used device to make payments and, if accepted by the seller, it is *conditional payment*, meaning that the check is accepted on the condition that it is paid. The buyer's contractual obligation to pay is not performed unless the check is honored. Meanwhile, the buyer's contractual obligation to pay the purchase price is suspended until the check's dishonor when duly presented for payment;[28] such dishonor nullifies the conditional payment by check. The seller's acceptance of a *credit* instrument from the buyer, such as the buyer's promissory note or his post-dated check, constitutes a delivery *on credit* as far as third parties are concerned, although as between the buyer and the seller the buyer's dishonor of the instrument affects the buyer's solvency and the seller's remedies therefor.[29] It should be noted carefully that we have considered only the *buyer's* check. Under the Code, if a *bank* is drawer, maker or acceptor of the instrument delivered by the buyer to the seller in payment, the buyer has made full payment and his contractual obligation is discharged.[30] The reason is that such primary obligation of the *bank* is currently accepted in ordinary business as full payment.

It should also be noted that the seller may have obtained documents for goods shipped and may wish to draw a draft (i.e., bill of exchange) on the drawee (the person who is ordered to pay the instrument, e.g., buyer, financing agency financing the transaction) so as to be paid the purchase price on delivery of the documents to the drawee. Unless otherwise agreed, if the draft is payable *more than three days after presentment*, then the seller is to deliver the documents to the drawee on his "acceptance" (the drawee's signed engagement to honor the draft as presented)[31] of the draft; but if the draft is payable *earlier*, the drawee is to receive the documents only on the drawee's payment.

Buyer's Right of Inspection. The buyer should have a reasonable opportunity to examine the goods being purchased in order to determine whether they conform to the contract and whether he should make payment, unless the contract precludes it. Accordingly, under the Code,[32] *unless otherwise agreed, where goods are tendered or delivered or identified to the contract for sale, the buyer has a right before payment or acceptance to inspect them. He has this right even though:* the seller sent the goods under reservation of a security interest and tenders documents of title; the goods are sent under a C.I.F.

[27] For definition of check, see below, p. 304.

[28] See Commercial Paper, below, pp. 373 ff.

[29] See below, p. 272.

[30] UCC 3–802(1), see below, p. 384.

[31] See UCC 3–410(1), below, p. 360.

[32] UCC 2–513.

contract which, however, *provides for payment on or after arrival*, although if the goods are lost delivery of the documents and payment are due when the goods should have arrived; the contract provides for payment against documents, *but also provides for payment due only after the goods become available for inspection.* Also, where there is casualty to identified goods resulting in partial loss to such goods or such deterioration in the goods as to cause them to become non-conforming, the buyer may demand an inspection.[33] However, *unless otherwise agreed, the buyer has no right of inspection if the contract provides:* for delivery C.O.D. or any other like terms; for payment against documents of title; for C.I.F. without any payment "on or after arrival" clause.

Unless otherwise agreed, the buyer's right is to inspect the goods at any reasonable place and time and in any reasonable manner. When the seller is required or authorized to send the goods to the buyer, the inspection may be after their arrival. The parties may, by their agreement, fix a place or method of inspection, and such place or method shall be presumed to be exclusive. If compliance with the agreed place or method of inspection becomes impossible, the intention of the parties becomes important. If the intention of the parties was that such compliance as agreed was an indispensable condition of the contract, then the contract is avoided. However, if this is not the intention of the parties, then the inspection shall be at any reasonable place and in any reasonable manner. The buyer bears the expense of inspection; however, if the goods are non-conforming and are rejected by the buyer, he may recover such expense from the seller. Where the contract requires the buyer to make payment before inspection, the buyer's payment does not constitute an acceptance of the goods or impair his right to inspect or any of his remedies. Under such a contract, the fact that the goods are non-conforming does not excuse the buyer from making the required payment, with two exceptions; the buyer is to pay first and, if the goods are non-conforming, litigate later. This is the intention of the parties, and it is to be observed. However, the buyer is not required to make payment preceding inspection under such a contract if: the non-conformity of the goods appears without inspection; or, despite tender of the required documents, the circumstances would justify injunction against honor under UCC 5–114.

As can be expected, there are times when the parties disagree concerning the conformity or condition of the goods. In order to further the adjustment of any claim or dispute between them, the Code provides:

1. Either party on reasonable notification to the other and for the purpose of ascertaining the facts and preserving evidence has the right to inspect, test and sample the goods including such of them as may be in the possession or control of the other; and
2. The parties may agree to a third party inspection or survey to determine the conformity or condition of the goods and may agree that the findings shall be binding upon them in any subsequent litigation or adjustment.[34]

---

[33] UCC 2–613.

[34] UCC 2–515.

This provision lays the basis for amicable non-judicial adjustment, as by arbitration or otherwise.

Risk of Loss

The parties to the contract determine who shall bear the risk of loss to the goods. If their agreement does not make provision for risk of loss, the Code provides that who bears the risk of loss depends primarily on whether or not there is a breach of contract by the seller or buyer.

Without Breach of Contract. *If there is no breach* then, unless otherwise agreed, *the risk of loss is on the seller until he completes his performance with respect to delivery of the goods pursuant to the contract by making physical delivery or by making delivery without moving the goods,* except for "3" below:

1. Where the contract requires or authorizes the seller to *ship the goods by carrier:* if he is merely to *send* the goods, *the risk of loss passes to the buyer when the goods are duly delivered*[35] *to the carrier even though the shipment is under reservation;*[36] but if the contract requires the seller to *deliver the goods at a particular destination, the risk of loss passes to the buyer when delivery is tendered*[37] *to the buyer.*
2. Where the goods are *held by a bailee (not the seller) to be delivered without being moved, the risk of loss passes to the buyer:* on the buyer's *receipt* of a *negotiable* document of title covering the goods; or on *acknowledgment by the bailee* of the buyer's right to possession of the goods; or after the buyer's *receipt* of a *non-negotiable* document of title or other written direction to the bailee to deliver, *unless the buyer seasonably objects.*[38]
3. *In any case not within (1) or (2) above,* the risk of loss passes to the buyer on his *receipt* of the goods *if the seller is a merchant;* otherwise the risk passes to the buyer on *tender of delivery.* This seems fair since the *merchant* possesses and controls the goods at his establishment and usually carries insurance on his inventory, while the buyer will probably not carry insurance to cover goods not in his possession or control.

It should be noted that, as previously discussed,[39] in a sale on approval the risk of loss does not pass to the buyer until he accepts the goods. It should be noted further that if the seller is selling goods shipped prior to his contract with the buyer, as by the seller purchasing the goods already shipped by someone else, when the seller identifies such goods to the contract and the shipment of which is in conformity with the seller's contract with the buyer,

[35] To be "duly delivered," the goods must be delivered to the carrier and a contract made for their transportation as may be reasonable, having regard to the nature of the goods and other circumstances of the case; and the seller must obtain a suitable document to enable the seller to tender delivery to the buyer. For tender of delivery, see above, pp. 249 ff.

[36] For shipment under reservation, see above, p. 226.

[37] For tender delivery at destination, see above, pp. 249 ff.

[38] See above, pp. 250–51.

[39] See above, pp. 215–16.

the risk of loss then passes to the buyer *from that point* and not retroactively to the point of the initial shipment of such goods. The party who has caused loss to the goods should bear such risk of loss.

With Breach of Contract. *Until the seller performs the contract or the buyer accepts the goods, the seller bears the risk of loss; thereafter it shifts to the buyer.* If the seller's tender or delivery of the goods is non-conforming and the buyer has a right of rejection,[40] the seller bears the risk of loss until his cure of such improper tender or delivery[41] or until the buyer accepts the goods. However, where the buyer has accepted the goods but later rightfully revokes[42] his acceptance he may, to the extent that his effective insurance does not cover such loss, shift the risk of loss back to the seller as of the time the contract was made. Similarly, if the seller is still in possession of conforming goods identified to the contract and the buyer breaches the contract (e.g., repudiation) before the risk of loss passes to the buyer the seller may, to the extent that his effective insurance does not cover such loss, shift the risk of loss to the buyer for a commercially seasonable time. This means that the seller, provided he acts promptly, may procure insurance coverage to the extent of his non-coverage at the buyer's expense; any delay by the seller will cause him to waive his right so to act, and any subsequent loss to the extent of deficiency in his effective insurance coverage will be borne by the seller.

SECTION II. BREACH OF CONTRACT

Except for special Code provisions, the seller's *improper delivery* by failure of the goods, or tender of delivery, in any respect to conform to the contract is a breach of contract, and the buyer may reject all the goods, accept all the goods, or accept part and reject the rest. The buyer may rightfully reject the goods only within a reasonable time after their delivery or tender and only if he seasonably notifies the seller of his rejection. His wrongful rejection is a breach of contract. A buyer can rightfully reject a wrongful delivery of an *installment* by the delivery of non-conforming goods only if the non-conformity *substantially* impairs the value of that installment *and* the seller cannot "cure" the non-conformity. If the non-conformity installment substantially impairs the value of the *whole contract*, the whole contract is breached. A rightfully rejecting buyer has an obligation of "salvage" of the rejected goods.

The buyer may *waive* a seller's breach of contract by: his failure to particularize in his rejection defects ascertainable by him on a reasonable inspection; or his express or implied acceptance of non-conforming goods. The buyer's failure to reject the goods after he has had a reasonable opportunity to inspect them, or his conduct inconsistent with the seller's ownership of the

[40] See below, p. 259.

[41] See above, p. 253.

[42] As to when revocation of acceptance may occur, see below, pp. 263–64.

goods, is an implied acceptance. The buyer also may waive a seller's breach of the *whole* of an installment contract. A rejection precludes a subsequent acceptance and, with certain exceptions, an acceptance cannot be revoked. Parties have a right to adequate assurance of performance, and a repudiation and anticipatory repudiation are a breach of contract. However, when delivery or payment cannot be made in the agreed *manner*, "substituted performance" may be made under certain conditions.

Nonperformance may be excused and the contract avoided without liability by each of the parties to the other if, before risk of loss passes to the buyer, the identified goods are totally destroyed without the fault of either seller or buyer. If the loss is not total, the buyer can accept the partially destroyed or deteriorated goods with proper price adjustment. Except for the seller's assumption of a greater obligation under the contract and for his duty to make substituted performance, the seller's delay in delivery or non-delivery caused by the failure of presupposed conditions is not a breach of contract.

In General

Under the law of Contracts,[43] nonperformance of a contractual duty may or may not be a breach of contract, depending on whether or not such nonperformance is wrongful. A breach of contract is a wrongful nonperformance of a contractual duty. Failure to render performance when due without any legal justification or excuse for such nonperformance is wrongful and is a breach of contract. Repudiation when performance is due is a breach of contract; anticipatory repudiation before performance is due is an anticipatory breach of contract, which may be retracted under certain conditions.[44] The Code provisions on breach of contract in the law of Sales reflect in large part the law of Contracts, with adjustment to the sales transaction.

Under the Code,[45] the obligation of the seller is to transfer and deliver, and the obligation of the buyer is to accept and pay, in accordance with the contract. Improper delivery by the seller's failure to supply goods or to tender delivery in conformity with the contract,[46] or his failure to deliver the goods[47] constitutes a breach of contract. Wrongful rejection of goods by the buyer,[48] his wrongful revocation of his previous acceptance of the goods,[49] or his failure to make a payment when due on or before delivery[50] constitutes a breach of contract. Repudiation and anticipatory repudiation by either party is a breach

[43] See Contracts, above, pp. 104 ff.

[44] See above, p. 105.

[45] UCC 2–301.

[46] UCC 2–601.

[47] UCC 2–711 (1).

[48] UCC 2–703.

[49] UCC 2–703.

[50] UCC 2–703.

of contract,[51] and failure to furnish specifications for performance or to cooperate in performance by either party may be treated by the other as a breach of contract, already discussed.[52] Most of these breaches will be discussed later under Remedies.[53] The seller's nonperformance may be excused under certain circumstances[54] or may be waived by the buyer.[55] First improper delivery by the seller's failure to supply goods or to tender delivery in conformity with the contract, then repudiation, then substituted performance, and finally excused nonperformance will be discussed.

Improper Delivery

Under the Code,[56] and subject to special Code provisions on breach in installment contracts,[57] contractual limitations of remedy,[58] and the seller's right to cure improper tender or delivery,[59] *if the goods or tender of delivery fail in any respect to conform to the contract, the buyer has the following rights: reject all the goods; accept all the goods; accept any commercial unit*[60] *or units and reject the rest.* Once a cause for rejection arises, the buyer acquires a remedy therefor, and the buyer's acceptance of a non-conforming tender or delivery does not deprive him of such remedy.[61] The buyer's right of rejection must be exercised in a certain manner, especially if he is a merchant; it is limited in installment contracts; it entails salvage of the rejected goods by the buyer; and it may be waived by the buyer's waiver of the breach of contract for wrongful delivery. These aspects of rejection will be discussed in that order.

Rightful Rejection. ***Manner and Effect.*** This discussion is confined to the buyer's rightful rejection. Should his rejection be wrongful, it would constitute a breach of contract with resulting legal rights and remedies in the seller.[62] The buyer may either reject or accept goods for nonconformity with the contract. Unless the buyer acts diligently to reject, his inactivity may constitute both a waiver of his right of rejection and an acceptance of the goods. The buyer may rightfully reject goods only in a proper manner and his subsequent conduct must not be inconsistent with his rejection. *The buyer may reject goods only within a reasonable time after their delivery or tender,*

[51] UCC 2–609, 610.

[52] UCC 2–311 (3), see above, p. 219.

[53] See below, pp. 271 ff.

[54] See below, pp. 268–69.

[55] See below, p. 261.

[56] UCC 2–601.

[57] See below, p. 260.

[58] See below, p. 285.

[59] See above, p. 253.

[60] For definition of commercial unit, see above, p. 199.

[61] Remedies are discussed in Chapter 18 below, pp. 271 ff.

[62] See below, pp. 272 ff.

and only if he seasonably notifies the seller of such rejection. What is a reasonable time depends on the circumstances and is directly affected by the buyer's right of inspection.[63] While the parties may expressly agree on the time for inspection or rejection, if such contractual provision is unconscionable because it does not afford the buyer a reasonable time to discover defects, the provision is void. Except for the buyer's limited obligation of salvage of the rightfully rejected goods, especially if he is a merchant, *the buyer has only two obligations with respect to rightfully rejected goods:*

1. He must not exercise ownership with respect to any commercial unit.
2. He must hold the goods with reasonable care at the seller's disposition for a time sufficient to permit the seller to remove them, if before rejection the buyer obtained physical possession of the goods in which he has no security interest.[64]

He is in effect an involuntary bailee for the seller. If negotiations are in process between the parties, of course the above discussion is appropriately limited or modified accordingly.

Installment Contracts. Often wrongful delivery occurs in connection with installment contracts. A contract which requires or authorizes delivery of goods in separate lots to be separately accepted is an installment contract. The parties cannot change this legal effect, even if the contract contains a clause "each delivery is a separate contract" or equivalent wording. Non-conformity by reason of a defect in *required documents* creates a right of rejection in the buyer; but if *goods* are non-conforming, the goods cannot be rightfully rejected unless the non-conformity *substantially* impairs the value of that installment *and* the non-conformity *cannot be cured* by the seller. However, if the non-conformity does not constitute a breach of the whole contract and if the seller gives adequate assurance of its cure,[65] the buyer *must* accept that installment. The reason for this is that the seller has the right to cure for improper delivery, and if the seller gives adequate assurance the entire contract can be saved. If the non-conformity or default in one or more installments substantially impairs the value of the *whole contract*, the whole contract is breached, although it may be reinstated by the aggrieved party's waiver of such breach. The test of substantial impairment of value is *whether material inconvenience or injustice will result to the aggrieved party by the non-conforming installment.* Waiver of the breach of the *whole contract* by the aggrieved party occurs by: his acceptance of a non-conforming installment without seasonably notifying the other party of cancellation; his bringing an action with respect only to past installments; or his demand of performance as to future installments. An installment agreement which expressly or impliedly requires accurate conformity in quality as a condition to acceptance in effect establishes the criterion of what is a substantial impairment of value impossible to cure.

[63] See above, pp. 254 ff.

[64] For the buyer's security interest in rejected goods, see below, p. 284.

[65] The seller's allowance against the price for a non-conforming installment often is a cure.

Salvage. Under the Code,[66] the rightfully rejecting buyer has a limited obligation of salvage of the rejected goods, especially if he is a merchant.

When the rightfully rejecting buyer is a *merchant,* under the Code,[67] he has the following two obligations, in addition to the two indicated above, subject to his security interest in the goods, *if the seller has no agent or place of business at the market where rejection occurred:*

1. The merchant buyer has a duty after rejection of goods in his possession or control to *follow any reasonable instructions received from the seller with respect to the goods.*
2. *In the absence of such instructions from the seller and if the goods are perishable or threaten to decline in value speedily,* the merchant buyer has the duty to *make reasonable efforts to sell them for the seller's account.*

Under (1), to be reasonable, the seller's instructions must, on the buyer's demand, include indemnity for expenses. Under (2), on such sale by the merchant buyer, he has a right of reimbursement from the seller or out of the proceeds for reasonable expenses of caring for and selling the goods, and if the expenses include no selling commission then to such commission as is usual in the trade or if there is none to a reasonable sum not exceeding 10 percent on the gross proceeds. The merchant buyer is held only to good faith, and good faith conduct is neither acceptance on his part, conversion, nor the basis for any action for damages for errors in judgment.

When the buyer, *whether or not a merchant,* has rightfully rejected goods and the seller has given no instructions to him within a reasonable time after notification of rejection, the buyer has three options *which he may exercise if he wishes;* except, as indicated immediately above, if the buyer is a merchant and the goods are perishable he must make a reasonable effort to sell them for the seller's account. The options are: to store the rejected goods on the seller's account; to reship them to the seller; or to resell them for the seller's account, with reimbursement as in the case of a merchant buyer's sale of perishables. The buyer's exercise of an option is not an acceptance or conversion of the goods, and it does not impair his right of rejection.

Waiver of Breach by Buyer. ***In General.*** Either party may waive a breach of contract. The waiver may be without consideration and may be oral, by estoppel, or in case of a disputed or alleged breach it must be in writing and signed and delivered by the aggrieved party to the other party. Course of performance is relevant to show a waiver of a contract term inconsistent with such course of performance,[68] although course of performance involves repeated occasions as contrasted with estoppel, which involves a single occasion. Our discussion will be concerned primarily with waiver on the single occasions of the buyer's failure to particularize defects and his acceptance of non-conforming goods, which will be discussed in that order. It should be noted however that, although the Code provides that in certain instances the

[66] UCC 2–603.

[67] UCC 2–603.

[68] See above, p. 205.

buyer's remedies for defects survive his acceptance without being expressly claimed as long as he *notifies* the seller of such defects,[69] the Code also provides that, to be on the safe side, "A party who with explicit reservation of rights performs or promises performance or assents to performance in a manner demanded or offered by the other party does not thereby prejudice the rights reserved. Such words as 'without prejudice,' 'under protest' or the like are sufficient."[70] A waiver of a breach of an executory contract may be retracted by reasonable notification *received* by the other party that strict performance will be required of any term waived, unless the retraction would be unjust in view of the other party's material change of position in reliance on the waiver. Unless a contrary intention by the parties clearly appears, expressions of "cancellation" or "rescission" of the contract or the like are not construed as a waiver, renunciation, or discharge of any claim in damages for an antecedent breach.

Buyer's Failure to Particularize Defects. When the buyer has an opportunity to inspect the tendered *goods* to see if they are conforming, or to inspect tendered *documents* relating to the goods against which payment is required in order to see if the documents are correct on their face, the buyer may either reject or accept the goods, and he may pay or refuse to make payment against the documents.

In the case of goods, when both the seller and buyer are *not merchants,* if the buyer rejects the goods and the seller if seasonably notified by the buyer could have cured the defect,[71] then the buyer *must state in his rejection* particular defects *which he could have ascertained by reasonable inspection. If the buyer does not so particularize in his rejection such defects ascertainable by him, he is estopped to assert such ascertainable defects as a justification for his rejection or to establish breach of contract by the seller. The buyer has waived his right to resort to such defects.* If the defects were *not ascertainable* by the buyer on a *reasonable inspection,* there is no waiver by the buyer with respect to such non-ascertainable defects. However, if both the seller and buyer are *merchants,* after rejection the *merchant seller must make a written request* for a full and written statement of all defects on which the merchant buyer proposes to rely and, if the merchant buyer does not so comply with the seller's written request, *to the extent of particular defects ascertainable by him after a reasonable examination the merchant buyer is estopped to assert such defects as a justification for his rejection or to establish breach of contract by the seller.*

Where payment is required against documents, the buyer has the opportunity to inspect such documents to see if they are correct on their face, and *the buyer's payment without reservation of rights is an acceptance of such documents and he is estopped from recovering such payment because of the defects apparent on the face of the documents.* His acceptance of the documents

[69] See below, p. 263.

[70] UCC 1–207.

[71] For cure, see above, p. 253.

does not constitute an acceptance of the goods nor does it impair his remedies for improper delivery of the goods by the seller.

Acceptance of Goods. The buyer has the obligation of accepting a proper delivery of goods conforming with the contract. *Acceptance is a manifestation of assent to become the owner of the identified goods* and may be made expressly, or impliedly as by his conduct or silence when he is to speak. The acceptance may be conditional on the conditions indicated in the acceptance; it may be qualified; and it may extend to part rather than all the tendered goods, except that acceptance cannot be a part of a commercial unit[72] and a purported acceptance of a part of any commercial unit is an acceptance of that entire unit. The buyer *expressly* accepts the goods if, after he has had a reasonable opportunity to inspect the goods, he signifies to the seller that the goods are conforming or that he will take or retain them in spite of their non-conformity. Express words of acceptance are not required. Payment for the goods is a circumstance to prove acceptance, but it is not conclusive by itself. *The buyer must either accept or reject the goods, and his failure to effectively reject them after he has had a reasonable opportunity to inspect them constitutes an acceptance.* The buyer's conduct inconsistent with the seller's ownership is an acceptance. For example, the buyer's testing of an *unreasonable* quantity of the goods to determine their conformity with the contract is an acceptance of the goods. To the same effect is the buyer's use of the goods or his sale of the goods to another, although the buyer's conduct pursuant to his rights and duties concerning salvage[73] do not constitute acceptance or the tort of conversion. The buyer's act inconsistent with the seller's ownership of the goods but which is wrongful against the seller may, at the seller's option, be ratified by the seller and treated as an acceptance. It should be noted that, *once the buyer has effectively rejected the goods, he cannot thereafter accept them,* unless the seller has re-tendered the goods or has indicated that he is holding the tender open. Also, *once the buyer has accepted the goods he cannot revoke his acceptance,* except under the following circumstances, all of which he must meticulously observe:

1. The goods must be non-conforming.
2. Such non-conformity must substantially impair their value to the buyer.
3. The buyer accepted the goods on the reasonable assumption that their non-conformity would be cured, and they have not been seasonably cured; or he has accepted the goods without discovery of such non-conformity, his acceptance having been reasonably induced either by the difficulty of discovery before acceptance or by the seller's assurances.
4. Revocation must occur within a reasonable time after the buyer discovers or should have discovered the ground for it.
5. Revocation must occur before any substantial change occurs in the condition of the goods which is not caused by their own defects.
6. Revocation is not effective until the buyer notifies the seller of it.

[72] For commercial unit, see above, p. 199.

[73] See above, p. 261.

While the agreement of the parties may limit the time for notification by the buyer, such provision must be in good faith and not unconscionable. Also, the buyer's revocation of his acceptance may be with respect to all the goods or to a lot or commercial unit. A buyer who has so revoked his acceptance has the same rights and duties with regard to the goods as if he had rejected them.[74] Reference should be made to previous discussion[75] concerning rightful rejection in installment contracts where breach of the whole contract could be waived by conduct of the aggrieved party in accepting a non-conforming installment.

While the buyer's acceptance of goods with knowledge of non-conformity precludes rejection and is non-revocable except under the conditions just discussed, *such acceptance does not of itself impair other remedies for non-conformity.* However, the buyer has the burden of establishing a breach of contract with respect to the goods accepted. When the buyer accepts a tender of delivery, within a reasonable time after he discovers or should have discovered any breach, he must notify the seller of the breach; his failure to do so is a waiver barring him from any remedy for such breach. Also, where the buyer accepts a tender of delivery, the seller has breached his warranty against infringement,[76] and the buyer is sued as a result of such breach, the buyer must notify the seller within a reasonable time after he receives notice of the litigation; his failure to do so is a waiver barring him from any remedy against the seller for liability established by such litigation.[77] It should be noted in passing that the buyer has a duty to pay at the contract rate for any goods he accepts. Partial acceptance requires reasonable partial apportionment of the price if this can be accomplished.

Repudiation

Meaning. Repudiation[78] by a party of his duty to perform under his contract is wrongful and a breach of contract. Repudiation is a manifestation of an intention not to render substantial performance of a contractual duty. It may be made expressly, or impliedly from voluntary conduct which causes substantial performance to be either actually or apparently impracticable. Unjustified repudiation may occur at the time when the duty is to be performed, and also prior to such time in which case it is called "anticipatory repudiation."

Anticipatory Repudiation. Under the Code law of Sales,[79] an anticipatory repudiation is characterized as *a party's repudiation of the contract with*

---

[74] See above, p. 259.

[75] See above, p. 260.

[76] See above, p. 234.

[77] See UCC 2–607(5) for the effect of seller participation or non-participation in a third party suit against the buyer for breach of warranty or other obligation for which the seller is answerable over to the buyer.

[78] See Contracts, above, p. 104.

[79] UCC 2–610.

respect to a performance not yet due, the loss of which will substantially impair the value of the contract to the other. Two things must occur: a party's repudiation of performance not yet due; and the loss of such performance will substantially impair the value of the contract to the other party. First, repudiation occurs by a party's expression, by statement or conduct, which either renders performance impracticable or clearly indicates his intention not to perform the contract.While a party's demand for more than the contract provides is not in itself a repudiation, nevertheless if the demand reasonably indicates the demanding party's intention not to perform except on the condition that the other party perform in excess of what the contract provides, then such demand is a repudiation. The substantial impairment must be to the value of the contract *to the aggrieved party,* not to a reasonable man; this is a subjective test. Substantial impairment occurs if the aggrieved party will experience material inconvenience or injustice by having to wait and receive a tender of what is not repudiated.

When an anticipatory repudiation has occurred, the aggrieved party may do one of four things.

First, he may, for a commercially reasonable time, await performance by the repudiating party. His inactivity and silence do not mislead the repudiating party. But he must not wait beyond a commercially reasonable time because, by doing so, he will not be able to recover resulting damages which he could have avoided on the expiration of the reasonable time; on breach, the aggrieved party has a duty to reduce or mitigate the damage caused by the repudiating party's breach.

Second, he may resort to any remedy for breach even though he has notified the repudiating party that he would await the latter's performance and has urged retraction of the repudiation. His notification and urging of retraction do not prejudice his rights.

Third, in addition to the first two courses of action, he may suspend his own performance. The anticipatory repudiation exposes the aggrieved party to a risk of nonperformance which he had not contemplated previously and, therefore, in all fairness to him he need not continue to perform his contractual promise if he so wishes.

Fourth, if he is the seller he may decide not to suspend his own performance but, in addition to the first two courses of action, exercise his seller's right to identify goods to the contract notwithstanding the breach or to salvage unfinished goods.[80]

Right to Adequate Assurance of Performance. Parties make a contract to obtain the performance agreed upon, and if one party's performance becomes reasonably uncertain to the other party, the latter should not be subjected to the hardship of continuing his performance while such uncertainty exists. If the initial willingness or ability of one party to perform *reasonably* appears to the other party to be *materially* reduced, reasonable uncertainty of perfor-

---

[80] See below, p. 274.

mance exists causing understandable concern as to whether or not the due performance which was expected will occur and as to what should be done to minimize damage in the event due performance does not occur. The Code recognizes the well-established legal principle that *each contracting party has an obligation not to impair the other's expectation of receiving due performance*, and it provides: "*When reasonable grounds for insecurity arise with respect to the performance of either party the other may in writing demand adequate assurance of due performance and until he receives such assurance may if commercially reasonable suspend any performance for which he has not already received the agreed return.*"[81]

Various elements are involved in this right to adequate assurance of due performance.

First, the concerned party's expectation of receiving due performance must be impaired; he no longer has security of expectation. His insecurity must be based on reasonable grounds and be in conformance with his obligation to act in good faith; it must not be arbitrary or capricious. *As between merchants*, which is where this right becomes exceedingly important, the reasonableness of grounds for insecurity is determined according to commercial standards. Under commercial standards, insecurity may arise in various ways, only a few of which will be briefly considered. Anticipatory repudiation is a reasonable ground for insecurity. The ground for insecurity may arise because of the nature of the sales contract. For example, word to the buyer from a reliable source that the seller has shipped, or intends to ship, defective goods is a reasonable ground for the buyer's insecurity; although it should be noted that, if the contract was C.I.F. or cash against documents, the buyer must perform his contractual obligation to make payment before inspection of the goods, inasmuch as the risk of receiving defective goods after payment was assumed by the buyer and cannot be avoided on the ground of insecurity. The ground for insecurity need not arise from the sales contract or even be related to it, but it may be based on other transactions. Examples are: the seller's insecurity caused by the buyer's failure to pay on other purchases from the same seller; the buyer's insecurity caused by hearing that the seller is supplying similar goods to other persons under their contracts and that such goods are defective. Another ground for insecurity is a party's repetition of occasions, such as breach of contract, which caused insecurity on those occasions. Similarly, a sudden expansion in the buyer's use of credit is a reasonable ground for the seller's insecurity. Rumors, even though false, of financial instability of a party to the sales contract are a reasonable ground for insecurity.

Second, what is adequate assurance of due performance depends objectively upon all the circumstances and upon the good faith of a reasonable man in the position of the aggrieved party, not on the *subjective* good faith of the aggrieved party; except that, as between merchants, the adequacy of assurance offered is determined according to commercial standards. A banker's good

[81] UCC 2–609(1).

credit report on the party from whom assurance is due is usually adequate to dispel insecurity for suspected financial instability.

Third, when one party has reasonable ground for insecurity of due performance by the other, he *may* make a *written* demand for adequate assurance of due performance by the other. He need not make a demand, but if he does it must be in writing.

Fourth, until the aggrieved party receives adequate assurance of due performance from the other he may, if commercially reasonable, suspend any performance for which he has not already received the agreed return and also suspend preparation for such performance.

It should be noted very carefully that, if the demand for assurance is not pursuant to a reasonable ground for insecurity and therefore is unjustified, the aggrieved party's suspension of performance itself constitutes a reasonable ground for the *other party's* insecurity and justifies the *latter's* demand for assurance and *his* suspension of performance. Also, the demanding party must not have already received what was due for that performance or part of performance which he intends to suspend; he has no insecurity for such performance inasmuch as he has already been paid therefor. However, acceptance of any improper delivery or payment by the aggrieved party does not prejudice his right to demand adequate assurance of future performance.

The party upon whom a justified demand has been made for adequate assurance of due performance has *a reasonable time not to exceed 30 days* after his *receipt* of the demand in which to provide such assurance, and his failure so to provide is a *repudiation* of the contract and a breach thereof. However, this, as well as any other, anticipatory repudiation may be retracted by the repudiating party, provided it is done before his performance is due and provided the aggrieved party has not indicated since the repudiation that he considers the repudiation as final. The aggrieved party's cancellation[82] or material change of position in reliance on the repudiation indicates that he considered the repudiation as final. Tender of assurance or of performance to the aggrieved party after such cancellation or material change of position is ineffectual to restore the aggrieved party's duty of performance under the contract; the latter's duty is discharged. Timely retraction of the repudiation may be made by any method which clearly indicates to the aggrieved party that the repudiating party intends to perform. However, to be effective, the retraction must include the adequate assurance of due performance justifiably demanded by the aggrieved party. An effective retraction restores the repudiating party to his status immediately prior to his repudiation. However, the repudiating party cannot profit from his own wrong and, therefore, his effective retraction of itself does not extend the time for his performance, although the *aggrieved* party receives due excuse and allowance for any delay caused by the repudiation.

---

[82] Cancellation is the ending of a contract by one party because of the other party's breach. See above, p. 221, ftn. 16, for the distinction between cancellation and termination.

Substituted Performance

When the parties cannot make delivery or payment *in the agreed manner*, substituted performance is permissible under certain conditions. It should be noted initially that, in the cases of casualty to identified goods[83] and failure of presupposed conditions,[84] discussed later, the failure or impracticability of performance is concerned with a basic assumption of the contract and goes to the essence of the contract, causing excuse and complete avoidance of the contract. In contrast, failure or impracticability to deliver or make payment *in the agreed manner* do not go to the essence of the contract, and an available commercially reasonable substitute must be made and the contract preserved.

If without the fault of either buyer or seller the agreed manner of delivery becomes commercially impracticable but a commercially reasonable substitute is available, the seller must tender and the buyer must accept such substitute. Failure of agreed facilities, such as berthing, loading or unloading, or unavailability of an agreed type of carrier are illustrations of such commercial impracticability. The seller and buyer have no choice; the seller must tender and the buyer must accept an available commercially reasonable substitute. For example, when the contract provided for shipment of grain F.O.B. a named vessel place of shipment and the event of war compelled cancellation of shipment by that vessel, substituted delivery at the warehouse on the ship line's loading dock could be legitimately demanded by the buyer or tendered by the seller.

When the agreed *means or manner of payment* fails because of domestic of foreign governmental regulation, the effect depends upon whether or not the goods have already been delivered. If the goods have not been delivered, the seller may refuse delivery by withholding the goods or stopping their delivery en route; but if the buyer provides a means or manner of payment which is commercially a substantial equivalent of what was agreed to in the contract, the seller must accept the same and deliver the goods as agreed with reasonable allowance for any delay caused by the substitution of the equivalent manner or means of payment. If the goods were delivered before the governmental regulation and the regulation is not discriminatory, oppressive, or predatory (i.e., destructive), the buyer may tender and the seller must accept payment by the means or in the manner provided by the regulation; the buyer's obligation is discharged by such payment.

Excused Nonperformance

Casualty to Identified Goods. *When the goods are identified at the time the contract for their sale is made and, before the risk of loss passes to the buyer,*[85] *the goods suffered casualty (i.e., destruction) without the fault of*

[83] See below, pp. 268–69.

[84] See below, p. 269.

[85] For risk of loss, see above, pp. 256 ff.

either party, the effect of such casualty depends upon whether or not the loss is total. If the loss is total, the contract is avoided without any liability of either party to the other. If the loss is partial, or the goods have so deteriorated as no longer to conform to the contract, the buyer no longer has any obligation to perform unless he wishes to avail himself of the option to accept such goods. He can demand the opportunity to inspect the goods and at his option either treat the contract as avoided or accept the goods. If he accepts the goods, he is liable to the seller for the contract price less due allowance for the deficiency in quantity or deterioration, but with no other right against the seller. If the buyer has paid the full price to the seller in advance, the buyer's election to accept the goods entitles him to a reimbursement for the due allowance. It is irrelevant whether or not the contract is divisible. It should be noted that the identified goods may have so suffered before the contract was made without the knowledge of the parties as well as subsequent to the making of the contract. The above discussion is applicable, before the risk of loss passes to the buyer, in the case of a "no arrival, no sale" contract, when the seller has the obligation to ship conforming goods but he assumes no obligation that the goods will arrive, although he is not to interfere with their arrival.[86] The buyer has the above same option in the event of partial loss or deterioration of the goods, or their late arrival.

Failure of Presupposed Conditions. We have seen previously[87] under substituted performance that where, without the fault of either party, the agreed manner of delivery becomes commercially impracticable but a commercially reasonable *substitute is available*, the substitute must be tendered and accepted. We have also seen[88] under casualty to identified goods that the seller is *excused* to the extent of casualty to goods identified when the contract was made, the casualty having occurred without fault of either party and before the risk of loss has passed to the buyer. However, circumstances may arise which were *not previously contemplated* by the parties at the time their contract was made and a non-occurrence of which was a *basic assumption* on which the contract was made, making it *commercially impracticable to perform the contract as agreed* because of delay in delivery or non-delivery. Since the underlying basis for the contract is affected, the failure of delivery should not be a breach of contract and the seller should be *excused* for such delay or non-delivery. Accordingly, under the Code,[89] unless the seller has assumed a greater obligation under his contract and except for the duty to make substituted performance, *the seller's delay in delivery or non-delivery whether in whole or in part is not a breach of contract if performance as agreed has become commercially impracticable because of unforeseen supervening circumstances not within the contemplation of the parties at the time their*

[86] See above, p. 224.

[87] See above, p. 268.

[88] See above, p. 269.

[89] UCC 2–615.

contract was made and the non-occurrence of which was a basic assumption at such time. There are two conditions to the seller not being held to a breach for such failure to make delivery as agreed. *First,* inasmuch as the excused seller should fulfill his contract to the extent that the supervening contingency permits, if only a part of the seller's capacity to perform is affected he *must allocate* production and deliveries among his customers in a fair and reasonable manner. He may at his option include among such customers his regular customers not then under contract as well as his own requirements for further manufacture in such allocation. His regular customers may be relying on making spot orders for supplies as they are needed. *Second,* the seller *must notify* the buyer seasonably of such delay in delivery or non-delivery and, when allocation of production and deliveries is being made, of the estimated quota that will be available for the buyer. Such unforeseen supervening circumstances are of great variety in business. While increased cost or the rise or fall of prices in the market place are not of themselves excuses for the seller's nonperformance, nevertheless they could be if the circumstances causing them were unforeseen and their non-occurrence was a basic assumption of the contract.[90] It should be noted carefully that, if the agreed performance has become commercially impracticable, resulting in the seller's delay of delivery or non-delivery caused by an applicable foreign or domestic governmental regulation or order, whether or not later proved to be invalid, with which compliance has been made in good faith, the seller is similarly excused for such delay or non-delivery under the conditions discussed above and there is no breach of contract on his part.

While the seller is excused for his delay in delivery or non-delivery because of the failure of the presupposed conditions, the buyer is also affected by such failure of presupposed conditions. After the buyer has *received* the seller's notification of a material or indefinite delay in delivery or of a justified allocation, *the buyer may notify the seller in writing* that, with respect to the delivery in the seller's notice or with respect to the contract as a whole if such delivery substantially impairs the value of the whole contract: the contract is modified to the extent that the buyer acquiesces in the delay and agrees to take his available quota in substitution; or the contract is terminated and discharged as to any unexecuted portion thereof. The buyer's failure so to notify the seller within a reasonable time not exceeding 30 days after the buyer's *receipt* of the seller's notice causes the contract to be terminated and discharged as to any unexecuted portion thereof. Any contractual provision which seeks to vary the buyer's right so to notify the seller is void.

---

[90] For illustrations, see UCC 2–615, *Comments 4, 5.*

Chapter 18

REMEDIES

SECTION I. SELLER'S REMEDIES

The seller's remedy on the *buyer's insolvency* depends upon whether or not the goods have been delivered to the buyer. If *undelivered* goods, the seller may refuse delivery except for cash, or stop delivery of the goods in transit. *If delivered goods*, when the seller discovers that the buyer has received goods on credit while insolvent, he can reclaim the goods within ten days after the buyer's receipt of the goods, or at any time if the buyer had misrepresented his solvency in writing to the seller within three months before delivery.

The seller has various remedies on the buyer's breach of contract. (*1*) *Cancellation* of the contract. (*2*) *Withhold delivery* of the goods. (*3*) *Identify conforming goods* in his possession or control to the contract, or *salvage unfinished goods* either by finishing them and identifying them to the contract or cease manufacture and resell them for salvage value. (*4*) *Stoppage of delivery in transit* or otherwise. When the seller has a right to withhold or claim the goods, as the consignor he may stop delivery of the goods *while they are still in the bailee's possession* by notifying the bailee in sufficiently reasonable time for the bailee to prevent such delivery to the buyer. If a *negotiable* document is outstanding, the bailee can disobey such notification to stop delivery until surrender of the document to him. (*5*) *Resale* of the goods. The seller retains any profit on the resale. He can bid if it is a public (auction) sale. (*6*) *Seller's damages for non-acceptance or repudiation* by the buyer. (*7*) *Action for the price*, with certain limitations. (*8*) *Seller's incidental damages* for expense reasonably incurred by the seller as a result of the buyer's breach.

Each of the parties to a contract for the sale of goods acquires rights and obligations of performance. The seller's obligation is to transfer and deliver the goods, and the buyer's obligation is to accept the goods and pay for them, in accordance with their contract. Each party has a right to the other party's performance of his obligation and, on his nonperformance, a right to pursue remedies for relief. "Right" includes "remedy," which means "any remedial right to which an aggrieved party is entitled with or without resort to a tribunal."[1] Most of the remedies of the seller or buyer are the result of breach of contract, although each party has certain remedies in the event of the other party's insolvency even though no breach of contract has occurred. The remedies provided by the Sales portion of the Code do not exclude or impair any other remedies for breach of any obligation or promise which is collateral or ancillary to a contract for the sale of goods. Thus, action may be brought on a dishonored check to pay for goods purchased and against a surety on the contract for sale. The seller's remedies will be discussed in Section I, the buyer's remedies in Section II, and miscellaneous remedies in Section III.

In General

The seller's remedies arise either as the result of the buyer's insolvency or as the result of the buyer's breach of contract by his wrongful rejection, wrongful revocation of acceptance of goods, failure to make payment when due on or before delivery, or repudiation with respect to a part or the whole of the contract. First the seller's remedies on the buyer's insolvency will be discussed, and then his other remedies occasioned by the buyer's breach of contract.

Remedies on the Buyer's Insolvency

Prospective failure of consideration[2] occurs by the buyer's insolvency. "A person is 'insolvent' who either has ceased to pay his debts in the ordinary course of business or cannot pay his debts as they become due or is insolvent within the meaning of the federal bankruptcy law."[3] It is manifestly unfair for the buyer to hold the seller to his contractual obligation *to deliver* goods to the buyer when the buyer does not appear to be able to pay the price for such goods. Also, if the buyer misrepresents to the seller that he is solvent and the seller then *delivers* goods to the buyer, it would be unfair to permit the buyer to profit from his fraud and deny to the seller a reasonable opportunity to repossess such goods subject, of course, to the rights of intervening third parties. The buyer's misrepresentation of solvency may be made expressly, or impliedly by his receipt of goods while insolvent.

---

[1] UCC 1–201(34)(36).

[2] See Contracts above, pp. 99–100.

[3] UCC 1–201(23). For the meaning of insolvency under the bankruptcy law, see below, p. 520.

The Code precludes this injustice and deals with the seller's remedies with respect to goods not yet delivered and goods already delivered to an insolvent buyer.

Undelivered Goods. *As to goods not yet delivered to the buyer, when the seller discovers the buyer to be insolvent he has two remedies: refuse delivery except for cash, including payment for all goods theretofor delivered under the contract; and stop delivery of goods in transit or otherwise,* discussed later.[4] The seller's right so to withhold delivery exists irrespective of whether the buyer or seller has title to the goods.

Delivered Goods. *As to goods delivered to the buyer, when the seller discovers that the buyer has received goods on credit while insolvent, he has a right to reclaim the delivered goods: upon demand made within ten days after the buyer's receipt of such goods; or at any time if the buyer has misrepresented his solvency in writing to the seller within three months before such delivery.* If the seller knew of the buyer's insolvency at the time of a delivery, the seller has no remedy to reclaim the goods delivered with such knowledge. It should be noted carefully that the seller's right is to *reclaim* the goods; a demand for their repossession is sufficient, and physical repossession is not required. However, until the seller obtains physical repossession, his right to repossession is subject to the risk of intervening rights of third parties. We have already discussed: the good faith purchaser for value from a buyer with a voidable title;[5] the buyer in ordinary course of business from a merchant entrusted with possession of goods;[6] the lien creditors[7] of the buyer on consignment sales.[8] Inasmuch as the reclaiming creditor is given this preferential treatment over other creditors of the buyer, the seller's successful reclamation of goods excludes all other remedies with respect to such goods.

Remedies on the Buyer's Breach of Contract

In General. The seller acquires remedies also as a result of the buyer's breach of contract. Under the Code,[9] *where the buyer wrongfully rejects*[10] *or wrongfully revokes acceptance*[11] *of goods, or fails to make a payment due on or before delivery,*[12] *or repudiates with respect to a part or the whole of the*

---

[4] See below, p. 275.

[5] See above, pp. 148–49.

[6] See above, pp. 149–50.

[7] UCC 9–301(3): "A 'lien creditor' means a creditor who has acquired a lien on the property involved by attachment, levy or the like and includes an assignee for benefit of creditors from the time of assignment, and a trustee in bankruptcy from the date of the filing of the petition or a receiver in equity from the time of appointment. . . ."

[8] See above, pp. 216–17.

[9] UCC 2–703.

[10] See above, p. 259.

[11] See above, p. 263.

[12] See above, p. 255.

contract,[13] *then with respect to any goods directly affected and, if the breach is of the whole contract,*[14] *then also with respect to the whole undelivered balance, the aggrieved seller has the following remedies:* cancellation; withhold delivery of such goods; identify goods to the contract or salvage unfinished goods; stoppage of delivery in transit or otherwise; resale; recover damages for non-acceptance or repudiation; action for the price in a proper case; incidental damages. These remedies will be discussed in that order.

The Code provides that a *"person in the position of a seller"* acquires certain rights of that seller so as to protect himself with respect to the goods and the seller's rights against the buyer on the buyer's insolvency or breach. He may withhold delivery, stop the goods in transit or otherwise, resell, and recover incidental damages. *A person in the position of a seller includes anyone who holds a security interest or other right in the goods similar to that of a seller.* He may be an agent who has authorizedly paid or become responsible for the price of goods on behalf of his principal and, therefore, has rights of reimbursement or indemnity against his principal;[15] and he may be a financing agency.[16]

Cancellation. The seller may cancel the contract. By cancellation a party puts an end to the contract because of the other's breach, all obligations which are still executory on both sides are discharged, and the cancelling party retains any remedy for breach of the whole contract or any unperformed balance.

Withhold Delivery. The buyer's breach of contract creates a right in the seller, or a person in the position of a seller, to withhold delivery of goods directly affected by the breach or, in the case of a breach of the whole contract, the whole undelivered balance of the goods. Withholding of delivery does not of itself cancel the contract; the parties may subsequently, in good faith, adjust their differences and the goods be delivered.

Identify Goods to the Contract or Salvage Unfinished Goods. On the buyer's breach of contract, the aggrieved seller may also deal with the goods so as to place him in the best position to recover the contract price and at the same time minimize the loss caused by the buyer's breach. What he may do depends upon whether or not the goods are finished and conforming to the contract.

Conforming Goods. *When the goods conform to the contract, the seller may identify to the contract conforming goods not already identified if, at the time he learned of the breach, they are in his possession or control.* In this way, on identification of conforming goods to the contract: the seller has a right of resale of the goods;[17] if resale is not practicable, the seller has a right to bring an action for the price of the goods.[18]

---

[13] For anticipatory breach, see above, pp. 264–65.

[14] As to when a breach of the whole contract occurs, see above, p. 260.

[15] See Agency, below, p. 579.

[16] For definition see UCC 2–104(2). For its rights, see UCC 2–506.

[17] See below, pp. 277.

[18] See below, p. 279.

Unfinished Goods. *When the goods are unfinished, the seller may, in the exercise of reasonable commercial judgment for the purposes of avoiding and minimizing loss*[19] *either: complete the manufacture of the unfinished goods and then wholly identify them to the contract,* thereby putting the seller in the same position as when he identified conforming goods to the contract, as discussed above; *cease manufacture and resell for scrap or salvage value the unfinished goods which have demonstrably been intended for the particular contract; or proceed in any other reasonable manner.*

Stoppage of Delivery in Transit or Otherwise. The seller, or a person in the position of a seller,[20] acquires the right to stop delivery of the goods to the buyer under the contract for their sale under certain conditions and with certain limitations on the quantity of goods which can be stopped.

When Created. *The seller's remedy of stopping delivery arises on the following occasions: when the seller discovers the buyer's insolvency; the buyer's repudiation; the buyer's failure to make payment when due before delivery; when, for any other reason, the seller has a right to withhold or claim the goods.* We have already discussed the various remedies which the seller may assert when the buyer becomes insolvent,[21] one of these remedies being the right to stop delivery. But the buyer's insolvency is only one of these occasions when the right to stop delivery arises. The quantity of goods which may be stopped depends upon the kind of occasion creating the right to stop delivery. *When the seller discovers the buyer to be insolvent,* he may stop delivery of goods in the possession of a carrier or other bailee, *regardless* of the quantity of goods involved. *When the buyer repudiates or fails to make a payment due before delivery, or if for any other reason the seller has a right to withhold or claim the goods,* he may stop delivery of *only* carload, truckload, planeload or larger shipments of express or freight. The reason for the difference in the quantity of goods that may be stopped is that stoppage in transit may impose a great burden on the carrier if it included small shipments, and so the right to stop for other than insolvency is limited in quantity to large shipments. If this fact should be of concern to the seller, he can agree to ship goods in smaller shipments C.O.D.

How Exercised. In order that the seller may exercise this right of stoppage of delivery, he must do two things.

First, the seller must stop delivery to the buyer while the goods are still in the possession of the carrier or other bailee. To the extent that goods have been delivered to the buyer by the carrier or other bailee, the seller has no right of stoppage of delivery with respect to such goods. *Delivery is made to the buyer,* and the seller's right of stoppage of delivery cannot be exercised, if: the buyer has *received* the goods; *the non-carrier bailee has acknowledged to the*

[19] For example, in the seller's reasonable commercial judgment, completion of manufacture of the goods would bring a better resale price resulting in an overall reduction in loss which would otherwise occur by a resale for salvage.

[20] See above, p. 274.

[21] See above, p. 272.

buyer that he holds the goods for the buyer; *the carrier has acknowledged to the buyer* that he holds the goods for the buyer *by reshipment or as a warehouseman;* or a *negotiable* document of title (e.g., negotiable bill of lading or negotiable warehouse receipt) covering the goods has been *negotiated to the buyer.*[22] The buyer receives the goods either directly, or by his designated representative such as a subpurchaser to whom the seller has directly shipped the goods at the buyer's direction without the goods ever having been delivered directly to the buyer. The bailee's acknowledgment that the goods are held by him for the buyer causes the goods to have been delivered to the buyer through the bailee, who now holds the goods as the buyer's agent authorized to accept delivery. However, such an acknowledgment by a carrier must be by reshipment[23] or by agreement to hold the goods as a warehouseman for the buyer. Attachment or levy of execution upon the goods initiated by creditors of the buyer prior to the delivery of such goods to the buyer does not interrupt the status of the goods while in transit, nor is such action by the buyer's creditors effective when the goods are in the possession of a bailee other than a carrier who has not made acknowledgment to the buyer; the seller's right of stoppage of delivery is not cut off. In contrast, only the seller or a person in the position of the seller can exercise the right of stoppage of delivery.

Second, in order to stop delivery, the seller must so notify the bailee as to enable the bailee by reasonable diligence to prevent delivery of the goods. After such notification, the bailee must hold and deliver the goods according to the directions of the seller, who is liable to the bailee for any ensuing charges or damages. If a *negotiable* document of title has been issued for the goods, *the bailee is not obliged to obey a notification to stop delivery until surrender of the document.* The reason for this is that, since the bailee's agreement is to deliver the goods to the *order of* the consignee, the bailee has the obligation to hold the goods subject to such order, and should the negotiable document of title be *duly negotiated to a holder,* the latter would acquire title to the document and the bailee would be liable to him for the goods covered by the document.[24] If the carrier has issued a *non-negotiable* bill of lading, the carrier is obligated to obey the notification to stop delivery only when the notification is issued by the *consignor.* The carrier's contract is only with the consignor, and the carrier's obligation with respect to the goods is to him. It should be noted very carefully that, *as between the seller and the buyer,* the seller has the right to stop delivery of the goods, irrespective of whether or not the carrier is obligated to obey the stop order when a negotiable or a non-negotiable bill of lading is outstanding. So, if the carrier obeys the stop order, the buyer cannot complain; but the seller will be liable to the carrier for any ensuing charges or damages for following the seller's orders.[25]

---

[22] See above, pp. 187 ff.

[23] Diverting a shipment is not a reshipment if it is merely incidental to the original contract of shipment.

[24] See above, pp. 189–90.

[25] UCC 2–705(3)(b).

Effect. Once delivery has been stopped, the seller is in the same position as though he had never made delivery to the carrier or other bailee for the buyer, and he re-acquires his seller's rights in the goods as though he had never made such delivery. Stoppage of delivery is not of itself a cancellation of the contract; the parties may subsequently, in good faith, adjust their differences and the goods be delivered. If the seller's stoppage of delivery is wrongful, it is a breach of contract on his part.

Resale. *On the buyer's breach of contract, the aggrieved seller or a person in the position of a seller*[26] *may resell the goods directly affected, or the whole undelivered balance of the goods if the whole contract is breached.* The remedy of resale is predicated on the seller acting in good faith and in a way that is commercially reasonable.

How. Unless otherwise agreed, resale may be by public or private sale, including sale by way of one or more contracts to sell or of identification to an existing contract of the seller. A public sale means a sale by auction. The resale must be reasonably identified as referring to the broken contract. *The resale may be at any time and place and on any terms, but every aspect of the resale, including the method, manner, time, place, and terms must be commercially reasonable,* which also includes a resale within a reasonable time after the buyer's breach. Should the buyer demand an inspection pursuant to his right in connection with preserving evidence of goods in dispute,[27] the time may be extended appropriately. The resale may be as a unit or in parcels. In the event of an anticipatory breach, the goods may not be in existence nor any or all of them have been identified to the contract before the breach. *After the breach, the seller may exercise his right to identify conforming goods to the contract*[28] *and then resell them at a public sale.* Only identified goods may be sold at a public sale; however, if there is a recognized market for a public sale of futures in goods of the kind involved, then the unidentified goods can be sold as future goods at the public sale. *Where the resale is at a private sale,* the seller must give to the buyer reasonable notification of *his intention* to resell; the notice need not indicate the time and place of the resale.

Special additional rules govern a resale by public sale. The seller must give the buyer reasonable notice of the time and place of the public resale, except in the case of goods which are perishable or threaten to decline in value speedily, in which event no notice need be given. Such notice enables the buyer to attend and bid and, also, to induce others to do so. If the goods are not to be within the view of those attending the sale, the notification of sale must state the place where the goods are located and provide for their reasonable inspection by prospective bidders. *The seller may buy at the public resale.* After all, his power to sell is given by law, he sells in his own behalf, his opportunity to bid tends to increase the resale price, and he is selling as best he can to reduce the loss he may sustain and to mitigate the buyer's damages.

---

[26] See above, p. 274.

[27] See above, pp. 254.

[28] See above, p. 274.

The seller is to resell only at a usual place or market for public sale if one is reasonably available, which is a place where prospective bidders may reasonably be expected to attend.[29]

Effect. A good faith purchaser for value at a resale takes the goods free of any rights of the original buyer, even though the seller fails to comply with one or more of the legal requirements for resale. *The seller retains any profit on the resale.* However, if the person reselling is a person in the position of a seller, he may not keep any excess over his security interest and must account to the seller for such excess. The reason for resale by a person with a security interest is to obtain cash in satisfaction therefor, and this having been accomplished he has been made whole and should not be able to benefit any further. Where the resale is made in good faith and in a commercially reasonable manner, the seller may recover the difference between the resale price and the contract price together with any incidental damages allowed under the Code, but less expenses saved in consequence of the buyer's breach. When the seller has not conducted the resale properly, the measure of his damages is changed to that measure employed for non-acceptance or repudiation, which will now be discussed.

Seller's Damages for Non-acceptance or Repudiation. The buyer's obligation is to accept and pay for the goods. On the buyer's breach of contract by his non-acceptance of a proper tender of delivery or by repudiation, the seller has a right to damages therefor. The measure of damages is the difference between the market price[30] at the time and place of tender and the unpaid contract price together with any incidental damages,[31] but less expenses saved in consequence of the buyer's breach. If this measure of damages is "inadequate to put the seller in as good a position as performance would have done then the measure of damages is the profit (including reasonable overhead) which the seller would have made from full performance by the buyer, together with any incidental damages . . . , due allowance for costs reasonably incurred and due credit for payments or proceeds of resale."[32] The Code permits the recovery of lost profits in all appropriate cases. For example, if the seller is a dealer in goods similar to that contracted for and the market price is equal to or above the contract price, the seller's resale of the refused goods would not cause loss to him thereby, but it deprives the seller of making another sale of similar merchandise to the purchaser who bought the refused goods, with a consequent loss of profit from the other possible sale. The buyer's breach has depleted the seller's sales from two to one, and the loss of profit from the lost sale should be a part of the seller's damages.

---

[29] See UCC 2–706, *Comment 9.*

[30] In the absence of a current market price at the time and place of tender, proof of a substitute market may be made under UCC 2–723, 724. See below, pp. 288–89.

[31] See below, p. 279.

[32] UCC 2–708(2).

Action for the Price. *When the buyer fails to pay the price as it becomes due,*[33] *the seller may recover the contract price together with any incidental damages for:*

1. *Goods which have been accepted*[34] by the buyer and the acceptance has not been justifiably revoked.[35]
2. *Conforming goods* lost or damaged within a commercially reasonable time after risk of their loss has passed to the buyer.[36]
3. *Goods identified to the contract*[37] but which the seller is unable *after reasonable effort to resell at a reasonable price,* or the circumstances reasonably indicate that such effort will be unavailing.

It should be noted carefully that, *in the case of goods identified to the contract, the seller has a primary remedy of resale previously discussed,*[38] *and he must resort to it in order to be made whole before he can bring an action for the price of the identified goods. This requirement does not exist with respect to accepted goods and to conforming goods lost or damaged as indicated above.* It is irrelevant whether or not the title to the goods has passed to the buyer. If the seller *properly* sues for the price and still has in his possession or control goods identified to the contract, he must hold such goods for the buyer; but he has the privilege, but not the obligation, at any time after suit but prior to the collection of the judgment against the buyer to resell them for the price if a resale becomes possible. If such a resale occurs after suit and before collection of the judgment, the net proceeds therefrom must be credited to the buyer and payment of the judgment entitles the buyer to any goods not resold. The fact that the seller may not come within the above three occasions when he may sue for the price does not mean that he does not have any other remedies. After the buyer has wrongfully rejected or revoked acceptance of the goods or has failed to make a payment due or has repudiated, a seller who is held not entitled to the price shall nevertheless be awarded damages for non-acceptance or repudiation, previously discussed.[39]

Seller's Incidental Damages. The seller is entitled to reimbursement from the buyer for expenses which he has reasonably incurred as a result of the buyer's breach, called "incidental damages." Incidental damages to the aggrieved seller include "any commercially reasonable charges, expenses or commissions incurred in stopping delivery, in the transportation, care, and custody of goods after the buyer's breach, in connection with return or resale of

---

[33] See above, pp. 248–49.

[34] See above, p. 263.

[35] See above, pp. 259–60.

[36] For risk of loss, see above, pp. 256–57.

[37] For goods identified to the contract without breach, see above, p. 225, and notwithstanding breach, see above, pp. 274–75.

[38] See above, p. 277 f.

[39] See above, p. 278.

the goods or otherwise resulting from the breach."[40] The seller is not precluded by the Code from obtaining "consequential damages," although such damages are more frequently sustained by the buyer rather than by the seller and, for that reason, consequential damages are discussed later under the buyer's remedies.[41]

SECTION II. BUYER'S REMEDIES

The buyer's remedy on the seller's insolvency is in the preceding headnote summary for Chapter 17, Section I.[42] The buyer has various remedies on the seller's breach of contract. (*1*) *Cancellation* of the contract. (2) *Recovery of the purchase price paid.* (3) *Cover*, by making in good faith and without unreasonable delay any reasonable purchase of, or contract to purchase goods in substitution for, those due from the seller. (4) *Buyer's damages for non-delivery or repudiation* by the seller. (5) *Accept the goods and obtain damages.* (6) *Accept the goods and deduct damages from the price.* (7) *Specific performance*, when the goods are *unique;* or *replevin* to obtain possession of specific goods if the buyer cannot or will not be able to effect "cover," or if the goods were shipped under reservation of a security interest in the goods and payment to satisfy it has been made or tendered. (8) *Resale* of the goods, the same as an aggrieved seller, as security for reimbursement for payments made on the price and for expenses incurred; except that the buyer cannot keep any profit from the resale. (9) *Buyer's incidental damages* for expense reasonably incurred by the buyer as a result of the seller's breach; and, in a proper case, *consequential damages* for loss to the buyer which the seller reasonably could foresee would be a consequence of his failure to perform.

In General

The obligation of the seller is to transfer and deliver the goods in accordance with his contract. The buyer has various remedies against the seller or against the goods which arise either as the result of the seller's insolvency or as the result of the seller's breach of contract. First the buyer's remedy on the seller's insolvency will be briefly restated, and then his other remedies occasioned by the seller's breach of contract will be discussed.

Remedy on the Seller's Insolvency

We have already discussed the buyer's right to goods on the seller's insolvency,[43] and we have seen that, after the seller has identified goods to the

[40] UCC 2–710.

[41] See below, p. 284.

[42] See above, p. 248.

[43] See above, p. 249.

contract and the seller becomes insolvent within ten days after the buyer has made a payment, the buyer has the right to recover from the seller the goods identified to the contract; but if the buyer, instead of the seller, identified the goods to the contract, the goods must also be conforming.

Remedies on the Seller's Breach of Contract

In General. The buyer acquires remedies also as a result of the seller's breach of contract. Under the Code,[44] when the seller fails to make delivery[45] of repudiates,[46] or the buyer rightfully rejects[47] or justifiably revokes acceptance,[48] then with respect to any goods involved, and with respect to the remaining unperformed part of the contract if the breach goes to the whole contract,[49] the aggrieved buyer has the following remedies: cancellation; recovery of the purchase price paid; and either cover and damages, or damages for non-delivery or repudiation. If the buyer receives non-conforming goods, the buyer may accept such goods and recover damages for non-conformity of tender. If the seller has breached the contract in any way, the buyer may accept the goods and deduct damages from the price due. If the seller fails to make delivery or repudiates, the buyer also has the remedies of specific performance or replevin in a proper case. On rightful rejection or justifiable revocation of acceptance, the buyer has the right of resale. The buyer also has remedies for incidental damages and, in a proper case, for consequential damages resulting from the seller's breach. These remedies will be discussed briefly in that order. However, *it should be recalled at the outset the seller has the right to cure his improper tender or delivery under certain conditions,*[50] *and the effect of cure of non-conformity in installment contracts.*[51]

Cancellation. The buyer may cancel the contract. By cancellation a party puts an end to the contract because of the other's breach, all obligations which are still executory on both sides are discharged, and the cancelling party retains any remedy for breach of the whole contract or of any unperformed balance.

Recovery of the Purchase Price Paid. Irrespective of whether or not the buyer cancels the contract, the buyer also has the right to recover so much of the purchase price as has been paid, together with damages as indicated in connection with either cover or non-delivery or repudiation, depending on which is applicable.

---

[44] UCC 2–711.

[45] For delivery by the seller, see above, pp. 249 ff.

[46] For anticipatory breach, see above, pp. 264 f.

[47] See above, p. 259.

[48] See above, p. 264.

[49] As to when a breach of the whole contract occurs, see above, p. 260.

[50] See above, p. 253.

[51] See above, p. 260.

Cover. On the seller's failure to deliver or repudiation, or the buyer's rightful rejection or justifiable revocation of acceptance, then with respect to any goods involved, and with respect to the whole if the breach goes to the whole contract, the buyer may "cover," and his failure to cover does not bar him from any other remedy. *The buyer covers by making in good faith and without unreasonable delay any reasonable purchase of, or contract to purchase, goods in substitution for those due from the seller.* While the buyer is not required to cover and it is a matter of whether he wishes to avail himself of this remedy, nevertheless its exercise is important to the subjects of: consequential damages,[52] where recovery is limited to what could not reasonably have been prevented by cover; and replevin of identified goods,[53] where the buyer is unable to effect cover for such goods. The buyer may recover from the seller as damages the difference between the cost of cover and the contract price together with any incidental or consequential damages, but less expenses saved in consequence of the seller's breach.

Buyer's Damages for Non-Delivery or Repudiation. The seller's obligation is to transfer and deliver the goods. On the seller's breach of contract by his failure to make delivery or repudiation, the buyer has a right to damages therefor. The measure of damages is the difference between the market price[54] *at the time when the buyer learned of the breach* and the contract price together with any incidental and consequential damages,[55] but less expenses saved in consequence of the seller's breach. The place where the market price is to be determined *normally is the place of tender;*[56] but if the buyer has rightfully rejected or justifiably revoked his acceptance after arrival of the goods, the place where the market price is determined is *the place of arrival.* It should be noted that this right to damages for non-delivery or repudiation is alternative to the buyer's right to cover, just discussed, and cannot be utilized to the extent that the buyer has exercised cover.

Accept the Goods and Obtain Damages. We have already considered the buyer's acceptance of goods with proper notification to the seller of non-conformity of tender,[57] and we have seen that his failure to notify the seller would bar his right to reject and to recover damages for non-conformity. If the buyer has accepted and given proper notice of non-conformity of tender, and the time for revocation of acceptance has gone by, the damages which the buyer may recover depend upon whether or not it is a breach of warranty case. If it is not a breach of warranty, the buyer may recover as damages the loss resulting in the ordinary course of events from the seller's breach as determined in *any manner which is reasonable* and, in a proper case, any incidental

[52] See below, p. 284.

[53] See below, p. 283.

[54] In the absence of a current market price at the time and place of tender, proof of a substitute market may be made under UCC 2–723, 724. See below, pp. 288–89.

[55] See below, p. 284.

[56] See above, p. 249.

[57] See above, p. 264.

and consequential damages. If it is a breach of warranty, the measure of the buyer's damages is *the difference at the time and place of acceptance between the value of the goods accepted and the value they would have had if they had been as warranted,* unless special circumstances show proximate damages of a different amount, and in a proper case any incidental and consequential damages.

Accept the Goods and Deduct Damages from the Price. If the buyer who has accepted the goods and properly notified the seller of the non-conforming tender has not yet paid the purchase price in full, he may recoup and not have to sue the seller to recover the purchase price, as just discussed. The buyer, on notifying the seller of his intention to do so, may deduct all or any part of the damages resulting from any breach of the contract from any part of the price still due under the same contract. It should be noted carefully that no general set-off is permitted here. The buyer may deduct from the purchase price of *that contract* the damages resulting from the seller's breach of *that contract.*

Specific Performance or Replevin. The buyer has two remedies available to him whereby he can proceed directly against the goods, namely specific performance of the contract and replevin for the goods. These will be considered briefly in turn.

Specific Performance. Specific performance means that, pursuant to court decree, the contract is to be performed as provided therein. It is an injunction to achieve as nearly as possible the contract effect. *The buyer may obtain a decree of specific performance only when the goods are unique or in other proper circumstances; the decree may include such terms and conditions as to payment of the price, damages, or other relief as the court may deem just.*[58] The goods may be existing or future goods. Uniqueness may be because of value, or because of irreplaceability in that such goods are one of a kind or unobtainable in the open market—often as the result of a special source of the goods, e.g., as a result of output and requirements contracts.

Replevin. Replevin is a form of action to recover possession of specific goods. The right of replevin here is different from the buyer's right to recover possession of identified goods in the event of the *seller's insolvency,* previously discussed.[59] *Here, replevin is the buyer's right to sue for possession of goods: if after reasonable effort he is unable to effect cover for such goods, or the circumstances reasonably indicate that such effort would be unavailing; or if the goods have been shipped under reservation and satisfaction of the security interest in them has been made or tendered.* If a negotiable document of title representing the goods is outstanding, the buyer's right of replevin is directed to the document and not to the goods. It should be noted very carefully that, with respect to goods not shipped, the buyer cannot resort to replevin unless he has not been able to effect cover or the circumstances reasonably appear to preclude cover.

---

[58] See above, p. 109.

[59] See above, p. 249.

Resale. *When the buyer has rightfully rejected or justifiably revoked his acceptance, he has a security interest in goods in his possession or control for any payments made on their price and any expenses reasonably incurred in their inspection, receipt, transportation, care, and custody, and in order to recover such payments and expenses he has the right to hold such goods and resell them in like manner as an aggrieved seller.*[60] It should be noted that the buyer may not keep any profit which results from the resale; the profit goes to the seller. Also, payment includes not only cash but also acceptance of a draft or other time negotiable instrument, or the signing of a negotiable note.

Buyer's Incidental and Consequential Damages. The buyer is entitled to incidental damages and, in a proper case, consequential damages resulting from the seller's breach of contract.

Incidental Damages. "Incidental damages resulting from the seller's breach include expenses reasonably incurred in inspection, receipt, transportation and care and custody of goods rightfully rejected, any commercially reasonable charges, expenses or commissions in connection with effecting cover and any other reasonable expense incident to the delay or other breach."[61]

Consequential Damages. It is but fair that the seller should be liable for loss which he reasonably could foresee would be a consequence of his failure to perform. This is particularly true in warranties. "One who warrants goods to possess a certain quality is held to an extensive liability for consequential damages for breach of the warranty. The nature of the warranty often gives notice to the seller of the probable consequences of a breach. He can more readily foresee injurious consequences from a breach of his obligation than an ordinary contractor."[62] However, the buyer has a duty to minimize damages, and his right of cover is one method of doing so. Accordingly, under UCC 2–715(2): "Consequential damages resulting from the seller's breach include (a) any loss resulting from general or particular requirements and needs of which the seller at the time of contracting had reason to know and which could not reasonably be prevented by cover or otherwise; and (b) injury to person or property proximately resulting from any breach of warranty." A commonly occurring illustration of a buyer's consequential damages resulting from the seller's breach is the buyer's injury from the loss of a profitable resale of goods caused by the seller's failure to deliver them, provided the seller had reason to know at the time of contracting that the buyer was contemplating such resale, and provided also that the buyer could not reasonably have prevented the loss by cover or otherwise.

---

[60] See above, pp. 277 ff.

[61] UCC 2–715(1).

[62] Samuel Williston, *The Law Governing Sales of Goods*, rev. ed. (New York: Baker, Voorhis & Co., 1948), Vol. III, sec. 614.

SECTION III. MISCELLANEOUS REMEDIES

Remedies of buyer and seller are affected by contractual provisions, made in good faith and without unconscionability, for the liquidation or limitation of damages and return of deposit, and for modification or limitation of remedies in the event of breach by either party. The damages fixed must not be a penalty, although reasonable forfeitures can be imposed by the seller on the buyer's payments. Standards of reasonableness and unconscionability are established by the Code. In a contract for sale for consumer goods, it is unconscionable to limit consequential damages for injury to the person. Rights accrued by an aggrieved party for a previous breach are retained by him even though the contract is "cancelled" or "rescinded," unless a contrary intention is clearly expressed, as a cancellation of a contract "without reservation of rights." An aggrieved party has various remedies for a contract induced by fraud or material misrepresentation. A contracting party with an interest in the goods has a right against third parties who have damaged that interest. In certain instances, the market price may be determined to be a measure of damages. The Statute of Limitations for breach of a contract for sale of goods is four years after the cause of action has accrued, which may be shortened by agreement to not less than one year but not extended beyond the four-year period. A cause of action accrues when the breach occurs, and a breach of warranty occurs when tender of delivery is made except that for a breach of warranty for *future* performance of the goods the cause of action accrues when the breach is, or should be, discovered.

Various miscellaneous remedies applicable to both parties to a contract for the sale of goods are covered in sections 2–718 through 2–725 of the Code. They deal with contractual provisions for damages and remedies, the effect of certain terms on remedies, remedies for fraud, remedies against third parties for injury to goods, determination of market price as a measure of damages, and a uniform Statute of Limitations applicable to contracts for the sale of goods. These will be considered briefly in turn. However, it should be recalled at this point that remedies for breach of any obligation or promise collateral or ancillary to a contract for the sale of goods are not impaired by the Sales part of the Code.

Contractual Provisions for Damages and Remedies

The parties may provide in their contract for the liquidation or limitation of damages and return of deposit, and for modification or limitation of remedies, *as long as such contractual provisions are made in good faith*[63] *and are not*

---

[63] UCC 1–201(19), 1–203, 2–103(1)(b).

unconscionable.[64] Every contract or duty under the Code imposes an obligation of good faith in its performance or enforcement.

Liquidation or Limitation of Damages; Deposits. The parties' agreement may make provision for the liquidation of damages in the event of breach by either party. In this way certainty of reasonable compensation for loss caused by wrongful conduct is accomplished when it is difficult to determine the extent of such loss. The amount must not be a penalty to deter such conduct but, rather, it must be reasonably compensatory. *The liquidated amount must be reasonable in light of the anticipated or actual harm caused by the breach, the difficulties of proof of loss, and the inconvenience or nonfeasibility of otherwise obtaining an adequate remedy.* A provision fixing unreasonably large liquidated damages is void as a penalty, and a provision fixing unreasonably small liquidated damages is unconscionable and void.

When the buyer has made a payment or payments, either as a deposit or on the purchase price, and the seller justifiably withholds delivery of goods because of the buyer's breach, only a *reasonable* forfeiture can be imposed by the seller on the buyer. If their agreement provides for reasonable liquidated damages, then the seller is to make restitution to the buyer of any amount by which the sum of the buyer's payments exceeds the liquidated damages. If their agreement does not provide for reasonable liquidated damages, then the seller is to make restitution to the buyer of any amount by which the sum of the buyer's payments exceeds 20 percent of the total performance for which the buyer is obligated under the contract, or $500, whichever is smaller. However, the amount which the seller is obligated to refund to the buyer is subject to offset, or certain deductions which the seller may assert. He may deduct the amount of damages which he may properly claim under the Code, apart from the liquidated damages provided in their agreement. Also, he may deduct the amount or value of any benefits received by the buyer directly or indirectly by reason of the contract. If the buyer's payment was in the form of goods, the amount of such payment is the reasonable value of such goods or the proceeds from their resale in good faith and commercial reasonableness by the seller; except that if the seller has notice of the buyer's breach *before* such resale, his resale is governed by the rules applicable to an aggrieved seller's remedy of resale on the buyer's breach,[65] the seller is not required to resell the goods which he received as payment from the buyer, and in the absence of resale the reasonable value of the goods will determine the amount of the buyer's payment and the excess to be refunded by the seller to the buyer.

Modification or Limitation of Remedies. The parties' agreement may also provide for remedies additional to, in substitution for, or in restriction of those remedies provided under the Code, and the parties may agree to limit or alter the measure of damages recoverable under the Code, *as long as such provisions are in good faith and are not unconscionable.* The parties should expect

---

[64] See UCC 2–302.

[65] See above, pp. 277 ff.

that each should have minimum adequate remedies available for breach of contractual obligation. Contractual provision limiting the buyer's remedies to return of the goods and repayment of the price or to repair and replacement of non-conforming goods or parts are reasonable provisions. When additional or substitutive remedies are provided, as a rule of construction it is deemed that such remedies are cumulative and optional rather than exclusive, unless a remedy is *expressly* agreed to be exclusive, in which case it is the sole remedy. Where circumstances cause an exclusive or limited remedy to fail of its essential purpose, the remedy or remedies available under the Code may be utilized.

The parties may limit or exclude consequential damages, unless the limitation or exclusion is unconscionable. *In the case of consumer goods,* which are goods used or bought for use primarily for personal, family, or household purposes, *it is prima facie unconscionable to limit consequential damages for injury to the person.* Limitation of consequential damages for commercial loss is not unconscionable. It should be recalled that remedies for breach of warranty can be limited and the seller can disclaim warranties, except that a seller cannot exclude or limit his liability to certain third party beneficiaries of his warranties.[66]

Effect of Certain Terms on Remedies

When an antecedent breach has occurred, rights accrue to the aggrieved party. Such rights are not to be impaired lightly and intended impairment must be clearly indicated. Such terms as "cancellation" or "rescission" or the like merely discharge contractual duty of *future* performance, but not of rights arising from previous nonperformance. As a rule of construction, "Unless the contrary intention clearly appears, expressions of 'cancellation' or 'rescission' of the contract or the like shall not be construed as a renunciation or discharge of any claim in damages for an antecedent breach."[67] A cancellation of a contract stating that it is "without reservation of rights" clearly renounces such rights.

Remedies for Fraud

Material misrepresentation or fraud in a contract for the sale of goods creates certain remedies in the aggrieved party, such as rescission or rightful rejection, but the existence of such remedies should not deprive the aggrieved party of those remedies available in non-fraudulent breach cases. Under the Code,[68] remedies for material misrepresentation or fraud include all remedies available under the Sales part of the Code for non-fraudulent breach. Neither

---

[66] See above, p. 245.

[67] UCC 2–720.

[68] UCC 2–721.

rescission nor a claim for rescission of the contract for sale, nor rejection nor return of the goods shall bar, or be deemed inconsistent with, a claim for damages or other remedy.

Remedies against Third Parties for Injury to Goods

A contracting party with an interest in the goods has a right against third parties who have damaged such interest. He is the real party in interest. Prior to identification of the goods to the contract, only the seller has an interest in the goods and only he can recover against wrongful third persons for injury to that interest. After identification of the goods to the contract, usually both the seller and buyer have interests in the goods which may be injured by a third person. The interest may be the title to the goods, a security interest or a special property interest or an insurable interest in the goods. If the goods have been destroyed or converted[69] by a third person, the contracting party who bears the risk of loss under the contract for sale or who has assumed that risk after the injury occurred has the right to institute suit against the third person. The seller and buyer may agree that one of them may sue for the benefit of both or either of them as their interests may appear, or for the benefit of whom it may concern. If the parties have not so agreed and, at the time of injury, the party plaintiff did not bear the risk of loss as against the other party to the contract for sale, the plaintiff's suit or settlement is, subject to his own interest, as a fiduciary for the other party to the contract.

Determination of Market Price as a Measure of Damages

We have previously discussed the time and place when the market price is determined in connection with damages obtainable by the seller for non-acceptance or repudiation,[70] and damages obtainable by the buyer for non-delivery or repudiation.[71] However, if there has been an *anticipatory* repudiation and trial occurs before the time when performance was due for some or all of the goods, inasmuch as the market price cannot be ascertained at the time performance is due, damages based on the market price are determined according to the market price of the goods prevailing at the time when the aggrieved party learned of the repudiation. If evidence of the price prevailing at the times and places on the occasion of breach by the seller or buyer, whether anticipatory or not, is not readily available, "the price prevailing within any reasonable time before or after the time described or at any other place which in commercial judgment or under usage of trade would serve as a reasonable substitute for the one described may be used, making any proper allowance for the cost of transporting the goods to or from such other place."[72]

---

[69] For conversion, see above, p. 166, ftn. 18.

[70] See above, p. 278.

[71] See above, p. 282.

[72] UCC 2-723(2).

When evidence of a relevant price prevailing at a time or place other than the one described in the Sales portion of the Code is offered by one of the parties, the evidence is not admissible unless and until the offering party has given to the other party such notice as the court finds sufficient to prevent unfair surprise.

In order to provide for the admissibility into evidence of market quotations, but without prescribing the weight to be given to such quotations, UCC 2–724 provides: "Whenever the prevailing price or value of any goods regularly bought and sold in any established commodity market is in issue, reports in official publications or trade journals or in newspapers or periodicals of general circulation published as the reports of such market shall be admissible in evidence. The circumstances of the preparation of such a report may be shown to affect its weight but not its admissibility."

Statute of Limitations

Because the statutes of limitations for actions for breach of contract for the sale of goods differ in the various states, the Code has provided for a uniform Statute of Limitations. *An action for breach of contract for sale must be commenced within four years after the cause of action has accrued.* By their original agreement, the parties may shorten the period to not less than one year, but may not extend it beyond four years. When an action is timely commenced but has been so terminated that the plaintiff can institute another action for a remedy for the same breach, he may commence the new action after the expiration of the time within which he could originally sue but only within six months after the termination of the first action. However, if the termination of the first action resulted from the plaintiff's voluntary discontinuance or from dismissal for failure or neglect to prosecute, then the plaintiff is limited solely to the time in which he originally could institute an action.

A cause of action accrues when the breach occurs, regardless of the aggrieved party's lack of knowledge of the breach. However, *a breach of warranty occurs when tender of delivery is made;* but where a warranty explicitly extends to *future* performance of the goods and discovery of the breach must await the time of such performance, the cause of action accrues when the breach *is, or should have been, discovered.*

Chapter 19

BULK TRANSFERS

A bulk transfer is any transfer in bulk and not in the ordinary course of the transferor's business of a major part of inventory of an enterprise whose principal business is the sale of merchandise from stock, including the manufacturer of what it sells. Special Code provisions govern a bulk transfer by auction. A bulk transfer is ineffective as to the transferor's creditors unless *proper notice* of the proposed transfer is given to such creditors so that they can protect themselves by proper legal action. A list of such creditors and their addresses together with the amount of their claims is to be furnished by the transferor to the transferee who, at least 10 days before the transferee takes possession of the goods or pays for them, whichever first occurs, is to give proper notice of the proposed transfer and the names and addresses of the transferor and transferee, personally or by registered or certified mail, to all the listed creditors and other persons known to the transferee to hold or assert claims against the transferor. Errors or omissions in the list of which the transferee has no knowledge do not cause the transfer to be ineffective. In a bulk transfer for new consideration, the proceeds are to be made available by the transferee to be applied to the transferor's debts.

Conduct of a debtor which is not usual and which is not ordinarily associated with honest dealing is subject to the suspicion of fraud on creditors if creditors' rights are involved. Such conduct is often called a "badge of fraud," creating a presumption of a fraudulent conveyance. An illustration is a bulk transfer, dealt with in Article 6 of the Uniform Commercial Code. An example of commercial fraud serves to indicate the need for this Code provision: the merchant with debts sells out his stock in trade for less than its worth and pays his creditors only part of what he owes them, or he sells it for any price and disappears without paying anything to his creditors. While this is a form of fraudulent conveyance, no provision is made in the Uniform Fraudulent Conveyance Act for any requirement of advance notice to the seller's creditors of the proposed sale so that they could investigate and decide whether to prevent the proposed sale from taking place, or to impound the sale proceeds and thereby protect themselves. *The requirement of adequate notice is the primary purpose of the Code's provisions covering bulk transfers.* While red tape and delay along with danger to an innocent purchaser are occasioned by the Code's provisions, nevertheless the necessary protection to creditors justifies such restrictions on certain kinds of bulk transfers. For a transfer to come within the Code's provisions on bulk transfers, it must be a *particular kind of transfer* in a *particular kind of enterprise* or business. Each of these will be considered in turn.

The Transfer

A bulk transfer is any transfer in bulk and not in the ordinary course of the transferor's business of a major part of the materials, supplies, merchandise, or other inventory of an enterprise covered by the Code. Goods are "'inventory' if they are held by a person who holds them for sale or lease or to be furnished under contracts of service or if he has so furnished them, or if they are raw materials, work in process or materials used or consumed in a business."[1] Equipment is not inventory; it is goods which are used or bought for use primarily in business, including farming or a profession, and which are not inventory, farm products, or consumer goods.[2] While a transfer of equipment is not of itself a bulk transfer, nevertheless a transfer of a substantial part of equipment of an enterprise included in the Code *in connection with* a bulk transfer of inventory is a bulk transfer. Since transfers of investment securities, money, accounts receivable, chattel paper, negotiable instruments, and things in action generally are not believed to carry any major bulk sales risk, they are not included in the bulk transfer covered by this portion of the Code. The Code enumerates certain types of transfers which come within the definition of a bulk transfer but which are specifically *excluded* from the provisions on bulk transfers because the major bulk sales risk to creditors is not present:

(1) Those made to give security for the performance of an obligation;
(2) General assignments for the benefit of all the creditors of the transferor, and subsequent transfers by the assignee thereunder;
(3) Transfers in settlement or realization of a lien or other security interest;
(4) Sales by executors, administrators, receivers, trustees in bankruptcy, or any public officer under judicial process;

[1] UCC 9–109(4).

[2] UCC 9–109(1): [Goods are] "'consumer goods' if they are used or bought for use primarily for personal, family or household purposes."

(5) Sales made in the course of judicial or administrative proceedings for the dissolution or reorganization of a corporation and of which notice is sent to the creditors of the corporation pursuant to order of the court or administrative agency;
(6) Transfers to a person maintaining a known place of business in this State who becomes bound to pay the debts of the transferor in full and gives public notice of that fact, and who is solvent after becoming so bound;
(7) A transfer to a new business enterprise organized to take over and continue the business, if public notice of the transaction is given and the new enterprise assumes the debts of the transferor and he receives nothing from the transaction except an interest in the new enterprise junior to the claims of creditors;
(8) Transfers of property which is exempt from execution.[3]

The Enterprise

The enterprise covered by the Code is one whose principal business is the sale of merchandise from stock, including one who manufactures what it sells. Such an enterprise does not include farming, contracting, professional services, nor businesses whose principal business is the sale of services and not merchandise. For example, restaurants and hotels are not included within such an enterprise.

Notice to Transferor's Creditors

A bulk transfer under the Code is ineffective as to every creditor of the transferor unless the transferee complies with the Code's provisions for notice to such creditors. First, the transferee is to obtain from the transferor a written list, signed and either sworn to or affirmed by the transferor or his agent, containing the names and business addresses of all existing creditors of the transferor, with the amounts owed when known, together with the names of all persons who, the transferor knows, assert claims against him, even though such claims are disputed.[4] It should be noted *very* carefully that: "*Responsibility for the completeness and accuracy of the list of creditors rests on the transferor, and the transfer is not rendered ineffective by errors or omissions therein unless the transferee is shown to have had knowledge.*"[5] (Author's italics.) *Second,* the transferor and transferee are to prepare a schedule sufficient to identify the property to be transferred. *Third,* the transferee is to preserve the list and schedule for six months after the transfer has been made and permit any creditor of the transferor at all reasonable hours to inspect either or both and to copy therefrom, or he is to file the list and schedule if, and

[3] UCC 6–103.

[4] UCC 6–104(2): "If the transferor is the obligor of an outstanding issue of bonds, debentures or the like as to which there is an indenture trustee, the list of creditors need include only the name and address of the indenture trustee and the aggregate outstanding principal amount of the issue."

[5] UCC 6–104(3).

at the place, prescribed by state law. *Fourth, except in the case of a bulk transfer made by auction sale, at least 10 days before the transferee takes possession of the goods or pays for them, whichever happens first, the transferee is to give proper notice by personal delivery or by registered or certified mail to all persons shown on the list of creditors furnished by the transferor and to all other persons who are known to the transferee to hold or assert claims against the transferor.*[6] Creditors who are entitled to receive such notice are those who were creditors of the transferor *before* the bulk transfer and *before* the required notice to creditors was given. Those who became creditors thereafter are not entitled to such notice.

Under the Code:

> (1) The notice to creditors . . . shall state:
> (a) that a baulk transfer is about to be made; and
> (b) the names and business addresses of the transferor and transferee, and all other business names and addresses used by the transferor within three years last past so far as known to the transferee; and
> (c) whether or not all the debts of the transferor are to be paid in full as they fall due as a result of the transaction, and if so, the address to which creditors should send their bills.
> (2) If the debts of the transferor are not to be paid in full as they fall due or if the transferee is in doubt on that point then the notice shall state further:
> (a) the location and general description of the property to be transferred and the estimated total of the transferor's debts;
> (b) the address where the schedule of property and list of creditors . . . may be inspected;
> (c) whether the transfer is to pay existing debts and if so the amount of such debts and to whom owing;
> (d) whether the transfer is for new consideration and if so the amount of such consideration and the time and place of payment.[7]

When new consideration becomes payable under a bulk sale, the transferee must assure that it will be made available to pay the debts of the transferor as shown on the list furnished to him by the transferor or which are filed as stated in the transferee's notice within 30 days after its mailing.

It should be noted very carefully that, while a transferee's title to the property sold is defective because of *his* non-compliance with the Code's requirements, nevertheless *a good faith purchaser for value from such transferee without notice of such non-compliance takes the property free of such defect and acquires good title to the property.*

Special Code provisions govern a bulk transfer by sale at auction because of the presence of an auctioneer[8] and the uncertainty of the identity of the trans-

[6] The Code suggests additional provisions for those states which wish to impose additional duties on the transferee to assure that payment of new consideration will be applied to pay creditors of the transferor. See UCC 6–106, 6–107(2)(e), 6–108(3)(c), 6–109(2).

[7] UCC 6–107.

[8] UCC 6–108(3): "The person or persons other than the transferor who direct, control or are responsible for the auction are collectively called the 'auctioneer.'"

feree, both of which facts require modification relative to the giving of notice and the effectiveness of the auction sale. Neither the price nor the transferee purchaser will be known until an auction sale has occurred. Also, the obligation to give notice to the transferor's creditors cannot be imposed on bidders at the auction, and the auction sale must be effective. Accordingly, the Code requires an auctioneer: to obtain from the transferor the list of creditors described in "first" above; to assist the transferor in the preparation of the schedule of property described in "second" above; to preserve the list and schedule and make them available as described in "third" above; and at least ten days before the auction occurs to give notice by personal delivery or by registered mail to all persons shown on the list of creditors furnished by the transferor and to all other persons who are known to the auctioneer to hold or assert claims against the transferor. *Failure of the auctioneer to perform any of these duties does not affect the validity of the sale or the title of the purchaser.* If the auctioneer did not know that the auction was a bulk sale, he is not liable to anyone for his non-compliance with the above four requirements. However, if he knew that it was a bulk sale, he is liable for his non-compliance to the transferor's creditors as a class for the sums owing to them by the transferor up to but not exceeding the net proceeds of the auction.

It should be noted in passing that the Code establishes a short-term Statute of Limitations of six months within which action may be brought or levy made after the date when the transferee took possession of the goods because of his non-compliance with the Code's requirements. However, if the transfer was concealed, action and levy may occur within six months after discovery of the concealed transfer.

PROBLEMS

1. A orally contracted with B to sell B certain goods for $10,000. A tendered the goods, which B unjustifiedly refused to accept. A wrote a letter to B reciting the terms of the contract and inquiring the reasons for B's refusal. B's answering letter to A acknowledged receipt of A's letter and stated: "The goods which were the subject of the contract we made, as recited in your letter, no longer are desired by me."
   (1) Can A maintain an action against B for damages for non-acceptance of the goods?
   (2) Why?
2. A and B contracted whereby A agreed to sell and B agreed to buy two specific lots of merchandise, title to the first lot to be transferred together with delivery to B at the time the contract was made, and title to the second lot to be transferred together with delivery to B 30 days after the date of the contract—at which time B was to make payment for both lots. At the time the contract was made, the first lot had been partially destroyed without the knowledge of the parties, subsequent to such contract but prior to the expiration of 30 days and prior to payment by B, the second lot was partially destroyed without the fault of A or B. What are the rights of the parties?

3. A delivered two machines to B, pursuant to an agreement between them whereby B was to try out the machines for a week to see if they were satisfactory and then either to keep one or both and pay A $500 for each one kept by B or to return to A what he did not want.
   (1) During the week, damage was caused to one machine by B's negligence and, before the end of the week, this machine was returned to A. On the expiration of two weeks after receiving the machines, B tendered the return of the second machine, which A refused to accept. What are the rights of the parties?
   (2) In the absence of (1), what are the rights of B's creditors against the two machines during the one-week period? Explain.
   (3) In the absence of (1), what would be the legal effect of B's sale as owner and delivery of the two machines to C, a good faith purchaser for value during the one-week period? Explain.
   (4) In the absence of (1), A delivered five additional machines to B for repair. What would be the legal effect of B's sale as owner and delivery of three of these machines to X, a good faith purchaser in satisfaction of a past debt owed by B to X? Explain.
4. A orders goods by description from B, such goods to be sent to A, which goods B delivers to a bailee for shipment to A.
   (1) Where is the title to the goods? Explain.
   (2) If, pursuant to the contract, the goods are to be sent C.O.D., where is the title? Explain.
   (3) If the bailee is a railroad and B obtains a bill of lading to B's order, where is the title to the goods? Explain.
   (4) If the bailee is a railroad and B obtains a straight bill of lading in favor of A, where is the title to the goods? Explain.
   (5) If B, pursuant to the contract, shipped the goods F.O.B. destination, how does this affect the transfer of title? Explain.
5. *See problems numbered 3 and 4 at the end of Chapter 11, above p. 154.*
6. What is the effect of a seller's delivery to a buyer of:
   (1) A quantity of goods less than that provided in the contract?
   (2) A quantity of goods greater than that provided in the contract?
7. X selected and purchased a washing machine from Y, a retailer of home appliances. The machine was delivered to X, who discovered that it was defective and would not function. What may X do?
8. A ordered goods by description from B to be sent to A, payment to be made in 30 days. B sent such goods to A by C, a carrier, from whom B obtained a negotiable bill of lading to the order of A and which was delivered to A. A sold, indorsed in blank, and delivered the bill of lading to D, a good faith purchaser for value. A became insolvent while the goods were being transported by C. Does B have any right to reacquire possession of the goods? Explain.
9. A and B are merchants who, over the telephone, made an oral contract for the sale of goods by A to B for $10,000, delivery in two weeks when B would pick up the goods at A's store. A immediately sent a letter to B confirming the transaction which B received the next day. Two weeks later, B refused to pick up the goods or to acknowledge the transaction. Can A enforce the contract against B? Explain.
10. S, a merchant, offered in a signed writing to sell certain goods to R for $1,000, the writing stating that the offer would be kept open for two months. After one month,

R placed a written order with S for the goods on the terms stated in S's written offer. S refused to perform.

(1) Can R enforce a contract against S? Explain.
(2) Would it make any difference if the period of S's offer was five months and R placed his order with S at the end of four months? Explain.
(3) Would it make any difference if S's offer was oral rather than in writing? Explain.
(4) Would it make any difference if the form of written offer signed by S had been supplied by R? Explain.

11. X's letter offered to buy ten horses from Z for a total purchase price of $20,000. Z's reply letter of acceptance contained additional and different terms.
(1) Explain the legal effect of Z's additional and different terms.
(2) Would it make any difference if X and Z were merchants? Explain.

12. A and B contracted for the sale of certain equipment by A to B over a period of six months.
(1) If A assigned "the contract" to C, who accepted it, what is the legal effect of such assignment?
(2) What is the effect of a clause in the contract between A and B "prohibiting assignment of the contract"?

13. As between the seller and the buyer, who bears the risk of loss to the goods when:
(1) The transaction is F.O.B. point of shipment?
(2) The transaction is F.O.B. destination?
(3) The goods are to be picked up by the buyer at the seller's establishment?
(4) The goods are held by a bailee and are to remain with the bailee after sale?

14. A and B contract for the sale of goods to be shipped by A to B. Before the date of A's performance, B wrote to A that he would not accept delivery. A then telephoned B and told him that, in light of B's letter, the contract was cancelled and he would sell the goods to C, a competitor of B. The next day, while A and C were negotiating for the sale of the goods by A to C, B telephoned A and told him he had changed his mind and that he would go through with the contract and accept the goods when delivered. A refused to deliver the goods to B and, instead, sold and delivered them to C. Is A liable to B? Explain.

SOME PREVIOUS C.P.A. LAW EXAMINATION QUESTIONS AND AUTHOR'S MODEL ANSWERS

NOVEMBER, 1979

Number 1

Select the **best** answers for each of the following items.

8. A salesman for A & C Company called upon the purchasing agent for Major Enterprises, Inc., and offered to sell Major 1,500 screwdriver sets at $1.60 each. Major's purchasing agent accepted and the following day sent A & C a purchase order which bore Major's name and address at the top and also had the purchasing agent's name and title stamped at the bottom with his initials. The purchase order recited the agreement reached orally the prior day. Subsequently, Major decided it did **not** want the screwdriver sets since it was overstocked in that item. Major thereupon repudiated the contract and asserted the statute of frauds as a defense. Under the circumstances, which of the following is correct?

a. The statute of frauds does **not** apply to this transaction since performance is to be completed within one year from the date of the making of the contract.
b. Major will lose but only if its purchasing agent's authority to make the contract was in writing.
c. The fact that an authorized agent of A & C did **not** sign the purchase order prevents its use by A & C against Major to satisfy the statute of frauds.
d. The purchase order is sufficient to satisfy the statute of frauds even though the purchasing agent never signed it in full.

9. Lally sent Queen Supply Company, Inc., a telegram ordering $700 of general merchandise. Lally's telegram indicated that immediate shipment was necessary. That same day Queen delivered the goods to the Red Freight Company. The shipment was delayed due to a breakdown of the truck which was transporting the goods. When the merchandise did **not** arrive as promptly as expected, Lally notified Queen that it revoked the offer and was purchasing the goods elsewhere. Queen indicated to Lally that the merchandise had been shipped the same day Lally had ordered it and Lally's revocation was **not** good. Which of the following statements **best** describes the transaction?
a. The statute of frauds will be a defense on any action by Queen to enforce the contract.
b. Prompt shipment of the merchandise by Queen constituted an acceptance.
c. Lally's revocation of the offer was effective since Lally had **not** received a notice of acceptance.
d. Lally's order was an offer to Queen to enter into a bilateral contract which could be accepted only by a promise.

11. Which of the following omissions will prevent a writing from satisfying the statute of frauds with respect to the sale of goods?
a. It does **not** indicate that a sale has occurred.
b. It is **not** signed by both the buyer and seller.
c. The time and place of delivery are **not** indicated.
d. The payment terms are **not** contained in the writing.

13. On March 11, Vizar Sales Corporation telegraphed Watson Company:

> "Will sell 1,000 cases of coffee for $28 a case for delivery at our place of business on April 15. You may pick them up at our loading platform."

Watson telegraphed its acceptance on March 12. On March 20, coffee prices rose to $30 a case. Vizar telegraphed Watson on March 21 that it repudiated the sale and would **not** make delivery. The telegram was received by Watson on March 22 when the price was $32; Watson could have covered at that price but chose not to do so. On April 15 the coffee was selling at $35 a case. Watson tendered $28,000 to Vizar and indicated it was ready to take delivery. Vizar refused to deliver. What relief, if any, is Watson entitled to?
a. Specific performance, because it made a valid tender of performance.
b. Nothing, because it failed to cover.
c. Damages of $4,000 (the difference between the contract price and the fair market value at the time Watson learned of the breach).
d. Damages of $7,000 (the difference between the contract price and the fair market value at the time delivery should have been made).

Answer

1. 8.d(208, 209, 210) 9.b.(203) 11.a.(208) 13.c.(209)

MAY, 1979

Number 1

Select the **best** answers for each of the following items.

39. Duval Liquor Wholesales, Inc., stored its inventory of goods in the Reliable Warehouse Company. Duval's shipments would arrive by truck and be deposited with Reliable who would in turn issue negotiable warehouse receipts to Duval. Duval would resell the liquor by transferring the negotiable warehouse receipts to the buyer who was responsible for transporting it to his place of business. In one of the sales of liquor to a retailer, the liquor was badly damaged and a question has arisen as to who has the risk of loss, Duval or the retailer. If the contract is silent on this point, when did the risk of loss pass to the retailer?
   a. When the goods have been placed on the warehouseman's delivery dock awaiting pick up by the retailer.
   b. When the goods have been identified to the contract.
   c. On his receipt of the negotiable warehouse receipts covering the goods.
   d. When the goods have been properly loaded upon the retailer's carrier.

44. Major Steel Manufacturing, Inc., signed a contract on October 2, 1978, with the Hard Coal & Coke Company for its annual supply of coal for three years commencing on June 1, 1979, at a price to be determined by taking the average monthly retail price per ton, less a ten cent per ton quantity discount. On March 15, 1979, Major discovered that it had made a bad bargain and that it could readily fulfill its requirements elsewhere at a much greater discount. Major is seeking to avoid its obligation. Which of the following is correct?
   a. The pricing term is too indefinite and uncertain hence there is **no** contract.
   b. Since the amount of coal required is unknown at the time of the making of the contract, the contract is too indefinite and uncertain to be valid.
   c. Major is obligated to take its normal annual coal requirements from Hard or respond in damages.
   d. There is **no** contract since Major could conceivably require **no** coal during the years in question.

Answer

1. 39.c(256) 44.c(218)

NOVEMBER, 1978

Number 1

Select the **best** answers for each of the following items.

31. Franklin purchased 100 sets of bed frames from Tully Manufacturing, Inc. Franklin made substantial prepayments on the purchase price. Tully is insolvent and the goods have **not** been delivered as promised. Franklin wants the bed frames. Under the circumstances, which of the following will prevent Franklin from obtaining the bed frames?
   a. The fact that he can obtain a judgment for damages.
   b. The fact that he was **not** aware of Tully's insolvency at the time he purchased the bed frames.
   c. The fact that the goods have **not** been identified to his contract.
   d. The fact that he did **not** pay the full price at the time of the purchase even though he has made a tender of the balance and holds it available to Tully upon delivery.

35. Gordon purchased 100 automatic sprinklers from Thompson, a jobber. Conrad was the rightful owner of the sprinklers which had been stolen from his warehouse. He had the sheriff repossess them and has asserted his ownership of them. Gordon's bill of sale specifically indicated that it made *no* implied warranties. The bill of sale did *not* contain any warranties of title. Which of the following is correct based on the above facts?

a. The title warranties have been effectively negated.
b. It is *not* possible to disclaim the title warranties.
c. Gordon's best course of action is to assert his superior title to the sprinklers since he is a good faith purchaser for value.
d. Thompson is liable in that he warranted that the title conveyed was good and his transfer rightful.

Answer

1. 31.c(249) 35.d(233–34)

MAY, 1975

Number 3

Select the **best** answers for each of the following items.

37. On February 1, 1975, Barron Explosives received an order from Super Construction, Inc., for 200 cases of dynamite at $25 per case with terms of 2/10, net/30, for delivery within two months, FOB seller's warehouse. The order was duly accepted in writing by Barron. Barron found that it could not perform, and therefore, it assigned the contract to a nearby competitor, Demerest Explosives. Demerest promised Barron it would perform on the Super contract and expressly released Barron from any responsibility. Demerest subsequently defaulted and has refused to deliver.

a. Barron's delegation of its duty to perform to Demerest Explosives constitutes an anticipatory breach of contract.
b. Super Construction need **not** perform since the assignment of the contract materially alters its burden of performing.
c. Super Construction can immediately proceed against Barron upon default by Demerest.
d. Super Construction has recourse only against Barron.

38. Haworth Discount Stores mailed its order to Eagle Recordings, Inc., for 100 eight-track cassette recordings of "Swan Songs" by the Paginations at $5.50 per cassette. Eagle promptly wired its acceptance, delivery to take place within two weeks from date of Haworth's order and terms of net 30 days. Before delivery was made by Eagle, the retail price of this recording by the Paginations fell to $4.95. Haworth Discount informed Eagle of this and pleaded with Eagle, "Because we have been good customers give us a break by either reducing the price to $4.95 so we can break-even or by allowing us to cancel the order." Eagle's sales manager called Haworth the next day and informed them that the price would be $4.95 per cassette, not the price that appeared on the original invoice.

The modification of the initial Haworth-Eagle contract

a. Fails due to lack of consideration.
b. Need **not** satisfy the Statute of Frauds.
c. Must be written and signed by the parties to be valid if **no** consideration is given by the party seeking to rely upon the modification.

d. Is voidable by Eagle at any time prior to shipment of the 100 cassettes.

39. A merchant made the following offer: "I offer you 100 cases of No. 3 macaroni at $13.50 per case. This offer is irrevocable for ten days." In which of the following situations would the offer be irrevocable because it is a "firm offer" or option contract under the Uniform Commercial Code?

a. The offer was made orally and admitted to in court by the seller.
b. The offer was written and signed by the seller.
c. The offer was written and signed by the seller, but the second sentence read: "Acceptance must be made within ten days."
d. Like all previous contracts for macaroni between the offeror and offeree, the offer was made by telephone.

43. On February 1, 1975, Colonial Industries ordered 10,000 feet of two-inch pipe in 20-foot lengths from the Eire Steel Company. Delivery was to be made on or before March 15, time being of the essence, FOB buyer's loading platform, cash on delivery. Eire Steel accepted the order. On February 15, Eire informed Colonial that its biggest customer had just purchased and taken delivery of its entire stock of two-inch pipe and that it would be impossible for Eire to deliver the pipe until May 15, at the earliest. Colonial demanded that Eire perform as agreed; Eire apologized but reiterated its prior position that it was now impossible for them to perform until the middle of May.

a. Eire's action of February 15 constituted an anticipatory repudiation of the contract.
b. Colonial must "cover" (procure the same or similar goods elsewhere) within a reasonable time in order to determine the damages recoverable.
c. If Colonial waits for performance by Eire and tenders the amount due on March 15, it can recover damages of the difference between the contract price and the market value on March 15.
d. Because Eire had sold and delivered all its supply of two-inch pipe, it can successfully plead impossibility of performance in order to avoid liability.

Answer

3. 37.c(207) 38.b(208) 39.b(202–3) 43.a(264–65)

Part Three:
Personal Property

E. Commercial Paper

Chapter 20

INTRODUCTION

The purpose of having a *negotiable* instrument is for a transferee to become a "holder in due course" and thereby acquire greater rights on the instrument than a transferee. There are four negotiable instruments, which may be used in a variety of ways: draft, check, negotiable promissory note, certificate of deposit. A "drawer" draws a draft or check on a "drawee"; a "maker" makes a note or certificate of deposit. A "holder" is one who holds the instrument which flows to him either initially as a payee or bearer, or by proper indorsement. A holder of an instrument taken for value, in good faith, and without notice that it is overdue or has been dishonored or of any defense against, or claim to, it on the part of anyone is a "holder in due course." Parties "primarily liable" are the maker and the acceptor-drawee who are absolutely liable on the instrument. Parties "secondarily liable" are the drawer and the indorser whose liability depends on certain conditions, and who have recourse against parties primarily liable.

Historical Background

The law of negotiable instruments had its beginnings in the customs of merchants in commercial transactions, called the "Law Merchant,"[1] several centuries ago. The Law Merchant developed apart from the early Common Law and included commercial paper, which includes negotiable and non-negotiable instruments. First, the Uniform Negotiable Instruments Act in

[1] See above, p. 48, ftn. 41.

1896 and now, today, the Uniform Commercial Code codifies the Law Merchant regarding *negotiable instruments* in the United States. The Code repealed the Uniform Negotiable Instruments Act.

Article 3 of the Code is entitled "Commercial Paper" and is concerned with four *negotiable instruments:* the draft (formerly called "bill of exchange"), the check, the certificate of deposit, and the promissory note. Bonds, documents of title (e.g., bills of lading, warehouse receipts), and money are excluded from Article 3.[2] However, Article 3 also applies to any instrument whose terms do not preclude transfer and which would be negotiable except for the fact that it is not payable to order or to bearer; *but, because it is not negotiable, no one can be a holder in due course of such an instrument.* Since the rights acquired by a holder in due course are much greater than those acquired by one not a holder in due course, and since the instrument must be negotiable in order for a person to become a holder in due course of the instrument, it is understandable why the status of a holder in due course is so desirable and at the heart of Article 3, and why it is of the utmost importance to determine whether an instrument is negotiable. It is for this reason that, under the Code and throughout this E portion of Part Three of the book, unless otherwise indicated *the word "instrument" means a negotiable instrument.*

It should be noted that the Law Merchant is not dead and, under the Code,[3] unless displaced by the Code, it supplements the Code. It should be noted also that bank deposits and collections are included under Article 4 and letters of credit are included under Article 5 of the Code. Some sections of Article 4 are discussed later in Chapter 27 of this part of the book. Inasmuch as negotiable instruments are the subject of collection by banks and are also used as collateral under Article 9 of the Code on Secured Transactions, Article 3 on Commercial Paper will apply to negotiable instruments as involved under Articles 4 and 9, unless inconsistent therewith, in which case Articles 4 and 9 will prevail, because they are concerned with the *use* of such instruments.[4]

Purpose of Negotiable Instruments

Reference should be made at this time to "Negotiable Paper under the Code," briefly discussed previously.[5] A "negotiable instrument" is a formal writing containing a contractual obligation or chose in action, payable in money, and with certain unusual effects on its transfer. The purpose of the negotiable instrument is to provide a simple, easy method of transferring a credit device or substitute for money, assuring to the holder of the instrument

[2] Bonds are included in Investment Securities under Article 8, and documents of title are included in Article 7. Traders may acquire bonds knowing that bonds are negotiable *per se* and, as bona fide purchasers for value, their ownership and status will not be adversely affected by the fact that the bonds are overdue or that default has occurred.

[3] UCC 1–103.

[4] UCC 3–103(2).

[5] See above, pp. 150 f.

that he has an absolute right to receive the money as indicated on the instrument. The transfer of tangible property and the assignment of a chose in action[6] at Common Law caused the transferee to acquire no better title to the property than that of the transferor[7] and the assignee to acquire no better title to the chose in action than the assignor had.[8] However, by the Law Merchant, the delivery of a properly indorsed negotiable instrument to a good faith purchaser for value, without notice of any defect of title or infirmity in the instrument (called a "holder in due course"), transferred to such purchaser a valid title to the negotiable instrument and to the claim or chose in action represented thereby. In other words, such a transfer of a negotiable instrument cut off all equities or claims to the instrument, and the transferee obtained a valid title. (B steals A's horse and sells it to C, a good faith purchaser for value without notice of the theft. The transferee, C, obtained only what his transferor, B, had, and since A never had made any transfer to B, then A may regain his horse. C would have a right of action against B for breach of express warranty of title.[9] The same effect would result if S fraudulently induced R to buy goods from S and S assigned to T his claim against R for the purchase price. S's fraud caused his contract with R to be voidable by R, and the assignee, T, acquired only what his assignor, S, had. R may avoid the contract, and T cannot enforce his claim against R. T would have a right of action against S for breach of implied warranty.[10] However, if P fraudulently induced D to draw a check payable to the order of P which P indorsed with solely his signature on the back of the check, and X stole the check from P and sold and delivered it to Z, who is a good faith purchaser for value without notice of the theft, Z would have title to the instrument which P could not regain and which D would have to pay.) Such protection to the transferee of the negotiable instrument, resulting in ready acceptance of such an instrument by merchants, was the objective of the Law Merchant.

In order to achieve this result the instrument had to be negotiable and the transferee had to obtain the instrument under circumstances making him a "holder in due course." *Basically, a study of negotiable instruments is a study of the character of the instrument to determine whether it is negotiable, and a determination of the character of the transferee to determine whether he is a holder in due course.* Article 3 is concerned basically with negotiable instruments and its provisions generally deal with: the formal requisites of negotiable instruments; the negotiation of such instruments; the holder in due course; the liabilities of the parties on such an instrument; the presentment of such instrument for payment or acceptance, notice of dishonor and protest; and the discharge of the parties from liability on the instrument. The subject of

[6] For a discussion of "chose in action," see above, p. 136.

[7] See above, p. 146.

[8] See above, p. 81.

[9] See Sales, above, pp. 233–34.

[10] See above, p. 82 for implied warranties in an assignment.

Commercial Paper will be discussed in this order after a brief, preliminary examination of the kinds of negotiable instrument and of the parties thereto.

Classification

There are four kinds of negotiable instrument: the draft (formerly called "bill of exchange"), the check, the certificate of deposit, and the promissory note. Examples of these instruments follow on pages 305–6. They are distinguishable from each other in the following ways: the draft is a written order drawn by one person and directing another person to pay to the order of the person indicated in the draft or to bearer; the check is a draft of a special kind in which the order is directed to a bank and the instrument is payable on demand; the certificate of deposit is a bank's written acknowledgment of a receipt of money and its promise to repay it; and the note is a written promise other than a certificate of deposit by one person to pay to the order of the person indicated in the note or to bearer.

The above four negotiable instruments are used in a variety of ways and, because of this, particular names often are given to such instruments indicating the use to which they have been put.

Bank Draft. A check drawn by a bank on another bank commonly is called a "bank draft."

Cashier's Check. A "cashier's check" is a check drawn by a bank on itself and payable to the order of the person named as payee in the cashier's check.

Traveller's Check. What is called a "traveller's check" is a check on which there is no payee's name at the time of its issuance, the person drawing the instrument and the person required to pay it often being the same person, the latter having accepted (i.e., assenting to pay it) the instrument in advance. When the instrument is not drawn on a bank it is a draft and not a check. The purchaser of the instrument signs his name on the instrument at the time of its issuance to him, and when he wishes to cash it he writes the name of the payee in the space provided and he signs the instrument.

Certified Check. A "certified check" is a check which has been accepted by the bank on which it is drawn.

Banker's Acceptance. A "banker's acceptance" is a draft which has been drawn on a bank and which has been accepted by that bank.

Letter of Credit. A "letter of credit" is not a negotiable instrument; however, it is considered at this time in order to distinguish it from a negotiable instrument. Generally, it is a written promise or authorization to honor drafts or other demands for payment to be drawn on the promissor by the person named and pursuant to the terms stated therein.[11]

Trade Acceptance. A "trade acceptance" is a draft which is drawn by a seller on the buyer to whom he has sold goods and which is accepted by the buyer.

---

[11] See UCC 5–103(1)(a) and 2–325(3).

NO PROTEST
Return at once if not paid. Do not hold for convenience of parties.
DETACH THIS TICKET BEFORE PRESENTING

$ ______ CHICAGO, ______ 19__

AT ______ SIGHT

PAY TO AMERICAN NATIONAL BANK AND TRUST COMPANY OR ORDER
of Chicago

______ DOLLARS
WITH EXCHANGE

VALUE RECEIVED AND CHARGE THE SAME TO ACCOUNT OF

TO (Name of Buyer) } (Signature of Seller)

FORM 68

Draft

MEMO ______ 82-19/1070

RUTH DONALDSON
1818 RIDGE ROAD

No. 1152

April 19 1980

PAY TO THE ORDER OF Francis Poore $100.00

One Hundred xx/xx DOLLARS

FIRST NATIONAL BANK
P.O. BOX 59 ■ BOULDER, COLORADO 80302

Ruth Donaldson

⑆1070⑉0019⑆ 12⑉3456100⑈

Check

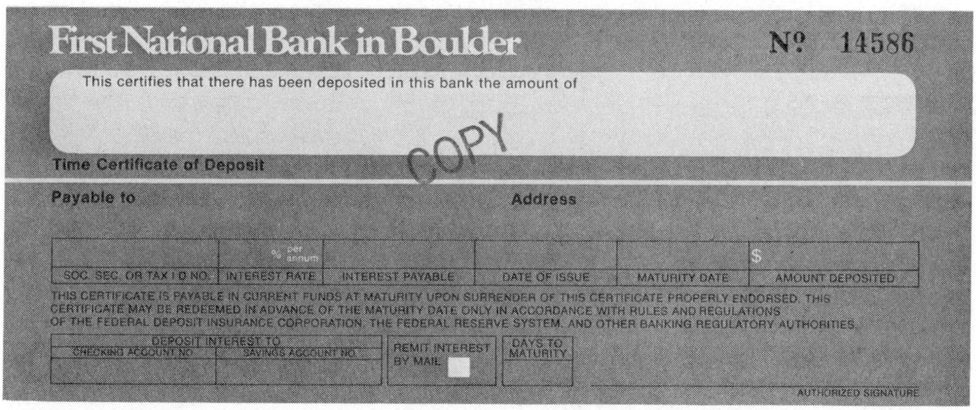

First National Bank in Boulder No. 14586

This certifies that there has been deposited in this bank the amount of

Time Certificate of Deposit COPY

Payable to Address

SOC. SEC. OR TAX I.D NO.	INTEREST RATE (% per annum)	INTEREST PAYABLE	DATE OF ISSUE	MATURITY DATE	AMOUNT DEPOSITED ($)

THIS CERTIFICATE IS PAYABLE IN CURRENT FUNDS AT MATURITY UPON SURRENDER OF THIS CERTIFICATE PROPERLY ENDORSED. THIS CERTIFICATE MAY BE REDEEMED IN ADVANCE OF THE MATURITY DATE ONLY IN ACCORDANCE WITH RULES AND REGULATIONS OF THE FEDERAL DEPOSIT INSURANCE CORPORATION. THE FEDERAL RESERVE SYSTEM, AND OTHER BANKING REGULATORY AUTHORITIES.

DEPOSIT INTEREST TO		REMIT INTEREST BY MAIL	DAYS TO MATURITY
CHECKING ACCOUNT NO.	SAVINGS ACCOUNT NO.		

AUTHORIZED SIGNATURE

Certificate of Deposit

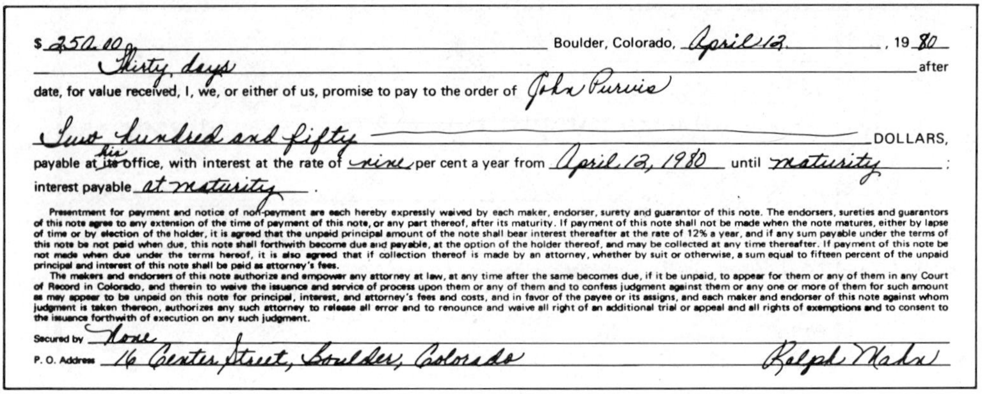

$ 250.00 Boulder, Colorado, April 12, 1980

Thirty days after date, for value received, I, we, or either of us, promise to pay to the order of John Purvis

Two hundred and fifty DOLLARS,

payable at ~~its~~ his office, with interest at the rate of nine per cent a year from April 12, 1980 until maturity;

interest payable at maturity.

Presentment for payment and notice of non-payment are each hereby expressly waived by each maker, endorser, surety and guarantor of this note. The endorsers, sureties and guarantors of this note agree to any extension of the time of payment of this note, or any part thereof, after its maturity. If payment of this note shall not be made when the note matures, either by lapse of time or by election of the holder, it is agreed that the unpaid principal amount of the note shall bear interest thereafter at the rate of 12% a year, and if any sum payable under the terms of this note be not paid when due, this note shall forthwith become due and payable, at the option of the holder thereof, and may be collected at any time thereafter. If payment of this note be not made when due under the terms hereof, it is also agreed that if collection thereof is made by an attorney, whether by suit or otherwise, a sum equal to fifteen percent of the unpaid principal and interest of this note shall be paid as attorney's fees.

The makers and endorsers of this note authorize and empower any attorney at law, at any time after the same becomes due, if it be unpaid, to appear for them or any of them in any Court of Record in Colorado, and therein to waive the issuance and service of process upon them or any of them and to confess judgment against them or any one or more of them for such amount as may appear to be unpaid on this note for principal, interest, and attorney's fees and costs, and in favor of the payee or its assigns, and each maker and endorser of this note against whom judgment is taken thereon, authorizes any such attorney to release all error and to renounce and waive all right of an additional trial or appeal and all rights of exemptions and to consent to the issuance forthwith of execution on any such judgment.

Secured by None

P. O. Address 16 Center Street, Boulder, Colorado Ralph Mahn

Promissory Note

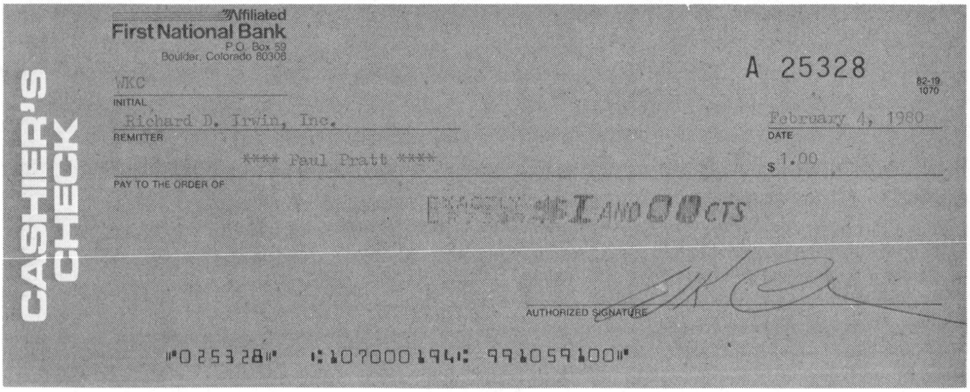

Affiliated First National Bank
P.O. Box 59
Boulder, Colorado 80306

CASHIER'S CHECK

A 25328

82-19
1070

WKC
INITIAL

Richard D. Irwin, Inc.
REMITTER

February 4, 1980
DATE

PAY TO THE ORDER OF **** Paul Pratt **** $ 1.00

EXACTLY $1 AND 00 CTS

AUTHORIZED SIGNATURE

⑈025328⑈ ⑆107000194⑆ 991059100⑈

Cashier's Check

American National Bank
and Trust Company of Chicago

RICHARD D. IRWIN, INC.
1818 RIDGE ROAD
HOMEWOOD, ILL. 60430

45859

August 25, 1980

2-77
710

PAY EXACTLY $15,731.23 DOLLARS $15,731.23

TO THE ORDER OF
KINGSPORT PRESS INC.
P. O. BOX 10072
CHURCH STREET STATION
NEW YORK, NEW YORK 10249

RICHARD D. IRWIN, INC.
AUTHORIZED SIGNATURE

CERTIFIED
PAYABLE ONLY AS ORIGINALLY DRAWN AND WHEN PROPERLY ENDORSED
$15731.23
AMERICAN NATIONAL BANK AND TRUST COMPANY OF CHICAGO 2-77
AUG 25 1980
AUTHORIZED SIGNATURE
DO NOT DESTROY

⑈045859⑈ ⑆07100077⑆ 03 45⑈ 60

Certified Check

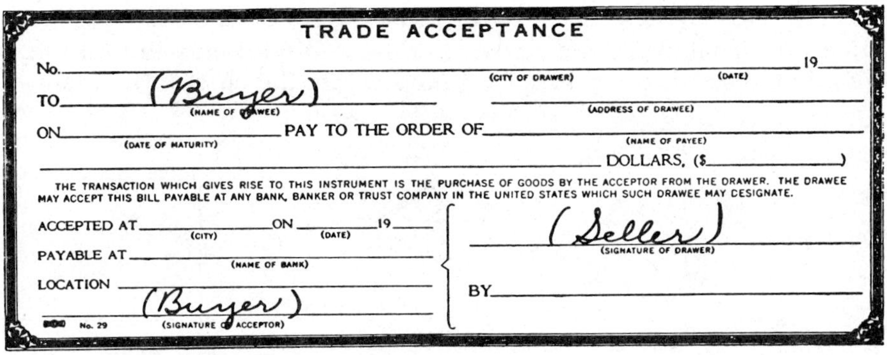

TRADE ACCEPTANCE

No.________ ____________________ 19____
(CITY OF DRAWER) (DATE)

TO (Buyer) ____________________
(NAME OF DRAWEE) (ADDRESS OF DRAWEE)

ON________ PAY TO THE ORDER OF____________________
(DATE OF MATURITY) (NAME OF PAYEE)

____________________ DOLLARS, ($________)

THE TRANSACTION WHICH GIVES RISE TO THIS INSTRUMENT IS THE PURCHASE OF GOODS BY THE ACCEPTOR FROM THE DRAWER. THE DRAWEE MAY ACCEPT THIS BILL PAYABLE AT ANY BANK, BANKER OR TRUST COMPANY IN THE UNITED STATES WHICH SUCH DRAWEE MAY DESIGNATE.

ACCEPTED AT________ ON________ 19____
(CITY) (DATE)

PAYABLE AT____________________
(NAME OF BANK)

LOCATION____________________

(Buyer)
(SIGNATURE OF ACCEPTOR)

No. 29

(Seller)
(SIGNATURE OF DRAWER)

BY____________________

Trade Acceptance

Parties

The parties to an instrument have definite names in order to facilitate immediate comprehension of their status.

Maker. A "maker" is the person who executes or makes a certificate of deposit or a note and who thereby promises to pay the same. When two or more persons execute a certificate of deposit or note, each is called a "co-maker."

Drawer. A "drawer" is the person who executes or draws a draft or a check ordering the drawee to pay the same.

Drawee. A "drawee" is the person on whom a draft or a check is drawn and who is ordered to pay the same.

Payee. A "payee" is the person to whose order an instrument is originally written.

Bearer. A "bearer" is the person in possession of an instrument which is either payable to bearer or indorsed in blank.

Indorser. An "indorser" is the person who places his signature on an instrument other than as a maker, drawer, or acceptor and who does not indicate any intention to be bound in any other capacity.

Indorsee. An "indorsee" is the person to whom an indorser by his indorsement makes the instrument payable.

Acceptor. An "acceptor" is the drawee who has properly manifested his written assent to the order of the drawer and thereby agreed to pay the draft.

Holder. A "holder" is the payee or indorsee of an instrument who is in possession thereof, or who is a bearer. In short, he is within the tenor of the instrument and is in possession of it.

Holder in Due Course. A "holder in due course" is a special kind of holder. He is a person who became a holder of an instrument for value, in good faith, and without notice that it is overdue or has been dishonored or of any defense against, or claim to, it on the part of any person.

Several of these parties are visually presented in the previous illustrations of instruments. On the check Ruth Donaldson is the drawer, First National

Bank is the drawee, the Francis Poore is the payee. On the certified check the American National Bank and Trust Company of Chicago, and on the trade acceptance the buyer drawee, is the acceptor. On the note Ralph Mahn is the

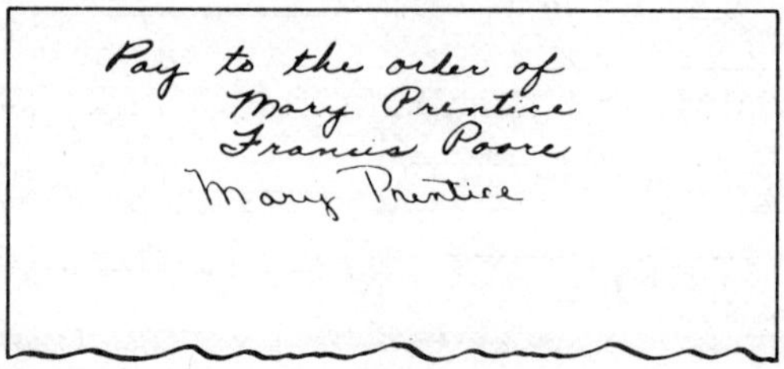

maker and John Purvis is the payee. The following indorsements on the back of the check, now possessed by Frank Fay, visually present the remaining parties. In the illustration above, Mary Prentice is an indorsee by reason of the indorsement of Francis Poore who now is an indorser, and Mary Prentice's subsequent signature is a blank indorsement (signature without any accompanying words) causing her to be an indorser. The last indorsement being in blank, the instrument is now payable to bearer. Since Frank Fay possesses the bearer instrument he is the bearer and, thus, a holder.

Drafts and checks are order instruments "Pay," while notes and certificates of deposit are promissory instruments "I promise to pay."

Note, C/D		*Draft, Check*	
M ↖ |) P	presented for payment	D—E | ↗ P	presented for payment

Primary and Secondary Liability. The parties to an instrument may be classified in accordance with their liability as parties primarily liable and parties secondarily liable. The person *primarily liable* on an instrument is the person who, by the terms of the instrument, is absolutely required to pay the same. All other parties are liable on the instrument on a condition, and they are *secondarily liable.* On a certificate of deposit or a note the *maker* is the party primarily liable. On a draft or a check the *acceptor* (*accepting drawee*) is the party primarily liable. Until the drawee of a draft or a check accepts the same he is not liable on the instrument; he is under no contractual obligation to the holder to pay the instrument. On acceptance, the acceptor becomes absolutely liable on the instrument. The drawer and indorsers are secondarily liable on an instrument, and they are called "secondary" parties.[12] It is important to note the distinction between parties primarily and secondarily liable, inasmuch as parties secondarily liable have recourse against parties primarily liable for whatever loss they have sustained on the instrument.

[12] UCC 3–102(1)(d).

Chapter 21

FORMAL REQUISITES OF NEGOTIABLE INSTRUMENTS

The negotiable character of an instrument is always determined by *what appears on the face of the instrument alone;* legality affecting the liability of parties thereon is irrelevant to negotiability. There are five requisites for a negotiable instrument. (*1*) *A writing signed by the maker or drawer.* Only persons whose signatures are on an instrument are liable thereon. A person is liable for his negligence which substantially contributes to his unauthorized signature. A signature may be in any form which the person intended as his signature. The drawer's or maker's signature can appear anywhere on the instrument and, except when appearing in the lower right-hand corner on the face, it must be indicated as that of the drawer or maker, otherwise the signature is an indorsement. A representative is not liable for his signature on the instrument if he indicates his representative capacity and the identity of his principal. Authority to sign is not required to be in writing. (*2*) *Unconditional promise or order to pay.* A promise is an undertaking to pay, and the word "promise" is not required. An order requires, it is imperative, as "Pay." An authorization is not an order, but "please pay" is a courteous order. The promise or order on its face must be payable unconditionally, absolutely, and not be uncertain or subject to any condition. (*3*) *Sum certain in money.* Any governmental currency is money. It must be certain from the face of the instrument. In a few instances the Code makes certain otherwise uncertain provisions, e.g., "attorney's fees." Whether or not it is legal to charge the interest rate indicated on the instrument is irrelevant to its being a sum certain and to negotiability. "With interest" without a rate means at the judgment rate. Words control figures. (*4*) *Payable on demand or at a definite time.* If no time is stated, it is on demand. Payment is definite only if it can be determined from

the face of the instrument. An undated instrument payable "thirty days after date" does not state a definite time. An instrument payable only upon an act or event uncertain as to time of occurrence is not payable at a definite time. (5) *Payable to order or to bearer*. An *order* instrument must be payable *initially* to the *order* of a specified person as the payee; to a specified person's "assigns" is satisfactory. A *bearer* instrument must *initially* not specify any payee. "Pay to the order of——" is an incomplete order instrument. An instrument payable to order and indorsed in blank *becomes* a bearer instrument and if then specially indorsed it *becomes* to order.

The negotiability of an instrument is not affected if it is undated, antedated or postdated, with one exception. An undated instrument is incomplete, and if the date is not essential to the instrument it is negotiable and enforceable; but if the date is essential, then it is neither negotiable nor enforceable until subsequently dated. An instrument ambiguous in its appearance as a draft or note may be treated as either by the holder. When conflicting, handwritten terms control typewritten or printed terms, and typewritten terms control printed terms. The unauthorized completion of an incomplete instrument makes the instrument effective as completed. Unauthorized completion may be a material alteration assertable as a defense to liability, but the instrument is now complete on its face. An instrument describing the named payee in any other manner than a particular or general kind of fiduciary for a specified person or purpose is payable to the payee unconditionally. Negotiability is not affected by the fact that there is a separate agreement apart from the instrument but part of the same transaction; but if the instrument *states* that it is *subject to* the separate agreement, the instrument is not negotiable. An instrument "payable through" a bank designates that bank as a collecting bank but not authorized to pay the instrument. The time when a cause of action accrues against the parties on an instrument depends upon whether the parties are primarily or secondarily liable and whether it is a demand or time instrument. Unless the instrument states otherwise, interest will run on an instrument and at the judgment rate.

SECTION I. SPECIFIC REQUISITES

For All Negotiable Instruments

The same specific requisites apply to all four negotiable instruments, whether a draft, check, certificate of deposit, or note, except that, inasmuch as these instruments differ in purpose, the specific requisites for each differ only to the following extent: the draft contains an *order* on a drawee to pay; the check is a draft drawn *on a bank* and payable *on demand;* and the certificate of deposit and the note contain a *promise* to pay.

The specific requisites of a negotiable instrument are:

1. A writing signed by the maker or drawer containing
2. An unconditional promise or order to pay (and no other promise, order, obligation, or power given by the maker or drawer except as authorized by Article 3)
3. A sum certain in money
4. Payable on demand or at a definite time
5. Payable to order or to bearer.[1]

The fifth requisite contains the key words of negotiability; without them the writing is merely a contract, assignable without the effects of negotiability, and there cannot be a holder in due course of a non-negotiable instrument.

It is of the utmost importance to remember that *the negotiable character of an instrument is always to be determined by what appears on the face of the instrument alone.*

For Particular Negotiable Instruments

Draft. A draft must comply with the above requisites except for the deletion of the word "maker" in the first requisite and the word "promise" in the second requisite. Under the Code,[2] an instrument which complies with the above requisites is a "draft" ("bill of exchange") if it is an order.

Check. A check must comply with the same requisites as a draft, indicated above; and, in addition, the instrument must be drawn on a bank and payable on demand. Its purpose is immediate collection. Under the Code,[3] an instrument which complies with the above requisities is a "check" if it is a draft drawn on a bank and payable on demand.

Certificate of Deposit. A certificate of deposit must comply with the above requisites except for the deletion of "drawer" in the first requisite and "order" in the second requisite. Under the Code,[4] an instrument which complies with the above requisites is a "certificate of deposit" if it is an acknowledgment by a bank of receipt of money with an engagement to repay it.

Note. A negotiable promissory note must comply with the above requisites except for the deletion of "drawer" in the first requisite and "order" in the second requisite. Under the Code,[5] an instrument which complies with the above requisites is a "note" if it is a promise other than a certificate of deposit.

SECTION II. INTERPRETATION OF FORMAL REQUISITES

General Rule of Form

It is not essential to a negotiable instrument that the specific language in the first paragraph of this section be used. It is sufficient if the words used in the

[1] UCC 3–104(1).
[2] UCC 3–104(2)(a).
[3] UCC 3–104(2)(b).
[4] UCC 3–104(2)(c).
[5] UCC 3–104(2)(d).

writing are a *clear equivalent* of those specific words. The words "I undertake" instead of "I promise," or "Pay to holder" instead of "Pay to bearer," would be clear equivalents and not prevent negotiability.[6]

Writing Signed by Maker or Drawer

An instrument must be in writing; it may be written in pencil or ink, and may be "printing, typing, or any other intentional reduction to tangible form."[7] An instrument must be signed by the maker or drawer. *Only persons whose signatures are on an instrument are liable thereon.* An undisclosed principal whose signature is not on an instrument is not liable thereon.[8] It should be noted very carefully that, under the Code,[9] a person is liable for his negligence which substantially contributes to material alteration of the instrument or to the making of his unauthorized signature, e.g., a person's negligence is not properly caring for a signature stamp or other similar device. He is precluded from asserting the alteration or lack of authority against a holder in due course or against a drawee or other payor who pays the instrument in good faith and in accordance with the reasonable commercial standards of the drawee's or payor's business.

The maker's or drawer's signature may appear anywhere on the instrument and need not be in any particular form. A maker's or drawer's signature usually appears on the face of the instrument in the lower right-hand portion thereof. The signature may be placed anywhere on the instrument, so long as it is indicated as being the signature of the person as a maker or as a drawer. A maker or drawer is not required to "subscribe" to the instrument; the signature does not have to be at the end of the instrument. The signature may be written, printed, engraved, or stamped; may be made with pencil or pen; and may be made in a trade name, assumed name, or by mark (e.g., an "X" or a thumb print), *so long as the intent of the maker or drawer is to make it his signature.* The signature may even appear in the body of the instrument, as "I, Frank Fay, promise to pay," etc.

A negotiable instrument may be signed by one or more persons or by their authorized agents. The signature may be by two or more persons acting jointly, severally, jointly and severally, or by an incorporated or an unincorporated association. *An agent's authority to sign a negotiable instrument on behalf of his principal is not required to be in writing.* The same is true of an agent's signature on behalf of any other party to the instrument. An authorized agent

[6] Electronic Funds Transfer systems used by banks utilize various paper forms on which the cardholder causes to be imprinted his card code number when making a transaction for the transfer of funds on deposit at the bank. The transaction receipt retained by the bank is deemed to be, as to cash advances, a check under the Code for the limited purpose of determining the liability of the parties thereunder, and the cardholder's code number thereon to be his signature.

[7] UCC 1–201(46).

[8] See Agency, below, pp. 601–2, 587.

[9] UCC 3–406. See below, p. 356.

who signs a negotiable instrument, indicating his representative capacity *and* disclosing the identity of his principal, is not liable as a party to the instrument. However, under the Code, an authorized representative who signs his own name to an instrument is, except as otherwise established between the immediate parties, "personally obligated if the instrument names the person represented but does not show that the representative signed in a representative capacity, or if the instrument does not name the person represented but does show that the representative signed in a representative capacity."[10] For example, if the instrument is signed

Peters
Anderson

it can be shown *only as between Peters and Anderson* that Peters was the principal and Anderson the agent signing for him. In litigation between the immediate parties, e.g., Peters and Anderson, the parol evidence rule permits the introduction of parol evidence to prove a signature as having been made by an agent in a representative capacity.

Unconditional Promise or Order to Pay

An instrument must contain an unconditional promise or order to pay the amount of money indicated in the instrument. First the promise or order and then the unconditional character will be considered.

The Promise or Order. The promise or order must be stated expressly on the face of the negotiable instrument. The exact terms of "promise" or "order" are not required; any words of like import are sufficient if they can be interpreted as manifesting an intent to promise or to order payment.

The Promise. Under the Code,[11] a promise is an undertaking to pay and must be more than an acknowledgment of an obligation. An acknowledgment of a debt, in the form of an I.O.U. or a due bill or otherwise, may raise an implied promise imposing a contractual obligation under the law of Contracts, but such expressions are insufficient as a promise which is requisite for a negotiable instrument. However, under judicial decisions prior to the Code, an acknowledgment of a debt accompanied by such words as "payable on demand" or similar words which could be interpreted as indicating an intent to pay such debt, constituted a promise sufficient for a negotiable instrument. Similarly, instruments containing words of the following nature contain an express promise sufficient for a negotiable instrument: "due John Jones on demand," "due John Jones or bearer," "I.O.U. $100 payable on demand," "I.O.U. $100 payable 30 days from date." It would seem that this would still be the result under the Code.

---

[10] UCC 3–403(2)(b).

[11] UCC 3–102(1)(c).

The Order. An order to pay directs and requires payment; it is imperative. Under the Code,[12] an order is a direction to pay and must be more than an authorization or request. An authorization to the addressee to pay an instrument is not an order, because it does not *require* the addressee to pay. An order to pay is not qualified by words of courtesy such as "please" or "kindly." However, "I wish you would pay" is not an order. A draft or check does not contain the word "order" in directing the drawee to pay, as "I order you to pay"; instead, the word "pay" is used to order the drawee to make such payment. In the phrase "pay to the order of," the word "pay" is the order or direction to the drawee, while the words "order of" relate to the payee and mean that the drawee is to pay as the payee may direct. The order must identify the person to pay with reasonable certainty, and it may be addressed to one or more such persons jointly or in the alternative but *not in succession.* Often, a firm may have accounts with more than one bank in the same city or different cities, and for commercial convenience it should be able to issue checks with various drawees, e.g., to pay indebtedness and dividends to corporate shareholders. However, drawees in succession is prohibited so that the payee should not be required to make more than one presentment for payment.[13]

Unconditional. The promise or order must be payable absolutely, unqualifiedly, and in any event; there must not be any uncertainty regarding such payment at the time indicated by the instrument. Whether or not the promise or order is unconditional is determined *solely from the instrument itself;* any separate agreement apart from the instrument does not affect its negotiability. However, if the instrument states that it is subject to, or governed by, any other agreement, it is conditional on that agreement and, therefore, it is non-negotiable. Thus, a note which promises to pay *subject to* the conditions as stated in the mortgage security for the note is non-negotiable, because the promise is conditional on such mortgage terms. Similarly, a promise to pay *subject to* the terms of a particular contract is conditional, and performance is dependent on such contract terms. However, the promise or order is unconditional if the instrument: "states its consideration, whether performed or promised, or the transaction which gave rise to the instrument, or that the promise or order is made or the instrument matures in accordance with or 'as per' such transaction."[14] For example, the instrument may refer to, or state that it arises out of, a separate agreement, or it may refer to a separate agreement for rights as to prepayment or acceleration; or it may state that it is drawn under a letter of credit. Similarly, the promise or order is unconditional if the instrument states that it is secured, whether by mortgage, reservation of title, or otherwise. To the same effect, the instrument may indicate the source or fund from which *reimbursement* of the money is to be made, e.g., as by *debiting* a particular

[12] UCC 3–102(1)(b).

[13] See below, p. 377, indicating that presentment may be made to any one of various drawees.

[14] UCC 3–105(1)(b).

reimbursing account, or by specifying a particular sinking fund, road tolls, or special taxes as a source of *reimbursement.*

But, with two exceptions, a promise or order to pay *only out of* a particular source or fund limits the promise to that source or fund and makes it conditional on sufficient money being in that source or fund. Thus, a promise to pay "on account of" or "as per" a particular contract does not promise to pay out of a particular fund, but a promise to pay out of the *proceeds* of such contract is conditional. *The first exception* to the rule that a promise or order to pay only out of a particular fund or source is conditional precluding negotiability is when the promise or order is contained in an instrument issued by a government or governmental agency or unit. This exception is intended not to disappoint the public in its acquisition of such instruments in reliance on their negotiability. *The second exception* is an instrument which limits payment only out of the entire assets of a partnership, unincorporated association, trust, or estate by, or on behalf of, which the instrument is issued.

Sum Certain in Money

The instrument to be negotiable must promise or order to pay a sum certain in money. First money, and then a sum certain, will be discussed.

Money. A negotiable instrument cannot be made payable in anything but money at the time the instrument is made. By money is meant a medium of exchange authorized or adopted by a domestic or foreign government as a part of its currency.[15] Money is not limited to legal tender. The unusual instruments payable in "current funds" or in "currency" are payable in money. Under the Code: "A promise or order to pay a sum stated in a foreign currency is for a sum certain in money and, unless a different medium of payment is specified in the instrument, may be satisfied by payment of that number of dollars which the stated foreign currency will purchase at the buying sight rate for that currency on the day on which the instrument is payable or, if payable on demand, on the day of demand. If such an instrument specifies a foreign currency as the medium of payment the instrument is payable in that currency."[16] Fluctuation in the exchange value of foreign currency does not affect the sum as being certain in money.

Sum Certain. The money payable under a negotiable instrument must be a sum certain in amount *as determined from the instrument, including any necessary computation which can be made from the instrument itself.* A promise to pay taxes, and a promise to pay income if earned, are not negotiable because of uncertainty in amounts; the promise to pay income if earned also is not an unconditional promise because payment of income is not absolute but is subject to the condition that income is earned. Although the principal sum payable is certain in amount, nevertheless, *additional provisions in the in-*

[15] UCC 1–201(24).

[16] UCC 3–107(2).

strument may cause uncertainty in connection with interest to be paid, discounts or additions, acceleration or extension[17] clauses, payment in exchange, or collection costs and attorney's fees on default in payment of principal or interest. The Code[18] removes from these additional provisions this uncertainty in amount by providing that the sum payable is certain *in such instances.* Thus, provisions for the payment of collection costs and attorney's fees upon default in the payment of principal or interest give to the instrument greater security, enhance its attractiveness, and encourage more ready negotiation. Also, the sum payable is certain even though the instrument provides for a stated discount or addition of money if the instrument is paid before or after the date fixed for payment, as long as the computation can be made from the instrument itself. Similarly, the amount may be payable with exchange or less exchange, whether at a fixed rate or at the current rate.

A sum payable with interest is certain in amount. The interest may be computed easily when payment is to be made. A promise that, on default in payment at maturity, a different rate of interest will be paid before or after default or a specified date does not affect the certainty of the sum to be paid. However, it should be noted carefully that, if such interest is to be increased and begin from the date of the instrument or a specified date before maturity rather than solely from the date of maturity, the increased rate from such date is a sum certain, although by local law such antedating of increased interest may be illegal as a forfeiture. *The Code's rules regarding a sum certain are concerned only with the negotiability of an instrument and are not intended to validate any term which is otherwise illegal,* e.g., as constituting usury under state law. The instrument may provide for a *stated* interest; or it may provide for payment "with interest" without specifying the rate, in which event interest is at the *judgment rate*[19] at the place of payment from the date of the instrument, or if it is undated from the date of its issue.[20]

Under the Code, *words control figures except that if the words are ambiguous figures control.* Thus, where the sum payable is expressed in words and also in figures and there is a discrepancy between the two, the sum denoted by the words is the sum payable; but if the words are ambiguous, then the figures control and fix the amount payable.

A sum, whether principal or interest, payable in stated installments is certain in amount. The sum payable is certain although the instrument contains an acceleration clause providing that the whole amount shall mature and become due on the default of an installment of principal or of interest, or providing that the instrument as one of a series of instruments is subject to acceleration on default of one of the instruments in the series.

---

[17] Extension is discussed later under "Definite Time," below, pp. 317 f.

[18] UCC 3–106.

[19] For contracts other than commercial paper which provide for interest but do not specify the rate, the legal rate applies. See above, p. 109.

[20] UCC 3–102: "'Issue' means the first delivery of an instrument to a holder or a remitter."

Payable on Demand or at a Definite Time

A negotiable instrument must be payable at a time certain to arrive, otherwise the instrument would not circulate freely. The time is certain when it is payable on demand or at a definite time.

On Demand. An instrument is payable on demand when it so states, when it is payable at sight or on presentation, or when no time for payment is stated on the instrument.

Definite Time. If not payable on demand, the instrument must be payable at a definite time in order to be negotiable. *The time of payment is definite if it can be determined from the face of the instrument.* An instrument which is not dated but which is payable "thirty days after date" is not payable at a definite time because the time of payment cannot be determined from the face of the instrument. However, such an instrument is an incomplete instrument and, when completed later with a date, will state a definite time. Similarly, an instrument which by its terms is otherwise payable only upon an act or event *uncertain as to time of occurrence* is not payable at a definite time even though the act or event later occurred.[21] Examples are: a post-obituary promise payable on the death of a specified person; a promise to pay on the completion of a specified building; a promise to pay a specified person on his attainment of a stated age; and a promise to pay on the marriage of a specified person.[22] The occurrence of the particular event does not make definite the time when payment is to be made and, therefore, the instrument is not negotiable.

An instrument is payable at a definite time if, by its terms, it is payable:

(a) on or before a *stated date* or at a fixed period after a *stated date;* or
(b) at a fixed period after sight; or
(c) at a *definite* time subject to any *acceleration;* or
(d) at a *definite* time subject *to extension* at the option of the *holder,* or *to extension* to a further *definite* time at the option of *the maker or acceptor or automatically upon or after a specified act or event.*[23] (Author's italics.)

Often the maker or drawer may wish to have the opportunity to pay before the stated date and the insertion of "on or before" the stated date states a definite time when the instrument is payable under (a) above.

Acceleration and Extension Clauses. Acceleration and extension clauses under (c) and (d) above are basically the same in that they vary the time of payment from the stated time. A note payable in two years but providing that the maker may pay it after one year involves *acceleration* in payment time. A note payable in two years but providing that the maker may extend the time of payment one year involves an *extension* in payment time. It should be noted

[21] UCC 3–109(2).

[22] It should be observed that an acceleration clause might be so used as to accomplish what is otherwise prohibited, e.g., acceleration to a specific point of time in the event of death, nonpayment of taxes, etc., if as a matter of judicial interpretation such a clause is not deemed to constitute an evasion of pertinent Code provisions.

[23] UCC 3–109(1).

carefully that, in any event, the instrument must state a definite time which is subject to such acceleration or extension. The instrument may provide for acceleration at the option of the maker, the holder, or automatically upon the occurrence of an event. The possibility of abuse of an acceleration term by whim and caprice does not affect the definite time and the negotiable character of the instrument.[24]

While a definite time is subject to *any* acceleration, it should be noted carefully that this is not true of an *extension* of a definite time. Every holder of an instrument has the legal right to extend the definite time when it is payable, and the Code merely recognizes this right. However, a holder may not exercise his option to extend an instrument over the objection of a maker or acceptor or other party who properly tenders full payment[25] when the instrument is due.[26] The extension clause at the option of the holder need not indicate a time limit. However, if the extension is at the option of the maker, acceptor, or automatically upon or after a specified act or event, then the clause must indicate a definite time limit to such extension or the time of payment would be uncertain and the instrument not be negotiable. Unless otherwise specified, consent to extension authorizes a single extension for not longer than the original period. A consent to extension, expressed in the instrument, is binding on secondary parties and accommodation makers.[27] An illustration of such an extension clause is "The makers and indorsers of this note consent that it may be extended without notice to them."

Payable to Order or to Bearer

A negotiable instrument must contain words of negotiability. The usual words are "to order" and "to bearer."

To Order. An instrument is payable to order when it specifies a person therein with reasonable certainty as the payee and makes the instrument payable to the payee's order. The phraseology may be either "to the order of" the payee, or to the payee "or his order"—e.g., "pay to the order of John Jones," and "pay to John Jones or his order." An instrument payable to a specified payee without containing the words "order of" or their equivalent is not a negotiable instrument payable to order, with two exceptions. The first exception is an instrument payable "to the assigns" of a specified payee, without using the words "to the order"; the instrument is payable to order. The second

[24] UCC 1–208 deals with abuse in the exercise of an acceleration term in a *time* instrument: "A term providing that one party or his successor in interest may accelerate payment or performance or require collateral or additional collateral 'at will' or 'when he deems himself insecure' or in words of similar import shall be construed to mean that he shall have power to do so only if he in good faith believes that the prospect of payment or performance is impaired. The burden of establishing lack of good faith is on the party against whom the power has been exercised."

[25] For tender payment, see below, p. 389.

[26] UCC 3–118(f).

[27] Ibid.

exception is an instrument which has conspicuously[28] designated on its face that the instrument is "exchange" or the like and names a payee; the instrument is payable to order, reflecting international usage.

An instrument payable to order may be made payable to the order of:

1. The maker or drawer.
2. The drawee.
3. A payee who is not a maker, drawer or drawee.
4. Two or more payees together or in the alternative. The Code does not use the word "jointly" here; this is deliberately done so as to preclude any possible implication of a right of survivorship, unless otherwise expressly indicated on the instrument. An instrument payable to "A and B" is payable to A and B as tenants in common, without any right of survivorship. An instrument payable to "A or B" is payable to either of them. An instrument payable to "A and/or B" is payable to either A or B or to both of them together as tenants in common.
5. An estate, trust or fund, in which case it is payable to the order of the representative of such estate, trust or fund or his successors. It is not necessary that the reasonably identified payee be a legal entity. "The Community Chest" or "The Community Fund" are sufficient to identify the payee.
6. An office, or an officer by his title as such, in which case it is payable to the principal, but the incumbent of the office or his successors may act as if he or they were the holder.[29] For example, an instrument payable to the order of the "Italian Consulate" or to the order of the "Treasurer of the City of Denver" is payable to the incumbent of that office or his successors.
7. A partnership or unincorporated association, in which case it is payable to the partnership or association and may be indorsed or transferred by any person thereto authorized. The payee is not required to have a legal entity. The instrument may be payable to the order of a partnership or a labor union. The authorized representative of the partnership or association payee may indorse or transfer the instrument in the name of such partnership or association payee.[30]

When an instrument is made payable both to order and to bearer, it is payable to order; however, if the bearer words are handwritten or typed, the instrument is payable to bearer. Normally, people specifying a payee on an instrument mean to make the instrument payable to the order of that payee and not to bearer, even though the printed words "or bearer" appear on the instrument—which words the signer may not have noticed. Accordingly, only if a person writes or types "or bearer" is such construed to signify that he intended to have it payable to bearer and not to order. Thus, an instrument

---

[28] UCC 1–201(10): " 'Conspicuous': A term or clause is conspicuous when it is so written that a reasonable person against whom it is to operate ought to have noticed it. A printed heading in capitals (as: NON-NEGOTIABLE BILL OF LADING) is conspicuous. Language in the body of a form is 'conspicuous' if it is in larger or other contrasting type or color. But in a telegram any stated term is 'conspicuous.' Whether a term or clause is 'conspicuous' or not is for decision by the court."

[29] For a discussion of instruments payable to a named payee with the addition of words describing him, see below, pp. 324 f.

[30] See UCC 3–110(1).

reading "Pay to the order of Frank Fay or bearer" is payable to the order of Frank Fay, unless the words "or bearer" are handwritten or typed, in which case the instrument is payable to bearer.

To Bearer. An instrument not payable to order must be payable to bearer in order to be negotiable. While an order instrument must specify a payee with reasonable certainty, a bearer instrument does not specify any particular payee. An instrument is payable to bearer only when, *by its terms,* it is payable to either: bearer or to the order of bearer; or a named person or bearer; or "cash" or to the order of "cash"; or any other indication which does not purport to designate a specific payee.[31] Thus, an instrument reading "Pay to the order of ——" is not a bearer instrument but, rather, an incomplete order instrument. Similarly, the fact that the instrument is made payable to the order of a specified unnamed officer of a specified association, such officer not existing, does not cause the instrument to be payable to bearer; it is an order instrument. It should be noted carefully that an *instrument payable to order and indorsed in blank becomes payable to bearer and continues to be a bearer instrument until it is specially indorsed, at which time it no longer is a bearer instrument.*[32]

Terms and Omissions Not Affecting Negotiability

Date, Antedating, Postdating. Where an instrument or any signature thereon is dated, the date is presumed to be correct. The negotiability of an instrument is not affected by the fact that it is undated, antedated or postdated.

Undated. The lack of a date on an instrument causes the instrument to be incomplete, but the date may or may not be *essential* to the instrument. If the date is not essential, the instrument is not incomplete in any *necessary* respect and it is negotiable and enforceable, e.g., an undated check. If the date is essential, the instrument is incomplete in a necessary respect and, therefore, is neither negotiable nor enforceable until subsequently dated. For example, an undated instrument payable "thirty days after date" is incomplete in a necessary respect and, therefore, is incomplete, non-negotiable, and unenforceable.

Antedating and Postdating. If an instrument is signed January 5 but dated January 3 it is antedated, and if dated January 7 it is postdated. Whether or not such antedating or postdating is made for a fraudulent or illegal purpose is a matter of defense, but does not affect the negotiability of the instrument, which is *determined from its face.* Thus, a note signed and delivered January 5, 1980, promising to pay interest at 12 percent per annum on a loan then made and payable January 4, 1981, as stated on the instrument, but which is antedated to January 5, 1979, may be illegal and void as evidencing an usurious loan, but the instrument on its face states a definite time when it is payable and it is negotiable *on its face.* Where an instrument is antedated or postdated, the

[31] UCC 3–111.

[32] See below, p. 333.

time when it is payable is determined by the stated date if the instrument is payable on demand, or at a fixed period after date. The person to whom an antedated or postdated instrument is delivered acquires the title thereto as of the date of such delivery.

Seal. An instrument otherwise negotiable is negotiable even though it is under seal.

Omission of Stated Consideration and Where Drawn or Payable. The negotiability of an instrument is not affected by the omission of a statement of any consideration or of the place where the instrument is drawn or payable.

Collateral. The negotiability of an instrument is not affected by a statement that collateral has been given to secure obligations either on the instrument or otherwise of an obligor on the instrument, or that in case of default on those obligations the holder may realize on, or dispose of, the collateral. Also, the instrument may state a promise or power to maintain or protect collateral, or to give additional collateral—e.g., the holder is "to pay taxes" on the collateral of the note. Often, instruments containing the latter terms will provide for acceleration in the event of non-compliance with such terms, which is permissible as discussed previously under definite time.[33]

Confession of Judgment. The negotiability of an instrument is not affected by a term authorizing a confession of judgment[34] on the instrument if it is not paid when due. Whether or not such a confession of judgment is legal is irrelevant to the matter of the instrument being negotiable. A note with such a term is called a "cognovit note."

Waiver of Statutory Benefits. The negotiability of an instrument is not affected by a term purporting to waive the benefit of any law intended for the advantage or protection of any obligor. Again, whether or not such a waiver is legal is irrelevant to the matter of the instrument being negotiable.

Indorsement of Full Satisfaction. The negotiability of an instrument is not affected by a term in a draft providing that the payee by indorsing or cashing it acknowledges full satisfaction of an obligation of the drawer.

Draft in a Set of Parts. The negotiability of an instrument is not affected by a statement in a draft drawn in a set of parts to the effect that the order is effective only if no other part has been honored.

Construction of Ambiguous Terms

The Code establishes fixed rules for construing ambiguous terms in an instrument in order to encourage freer circulation of an instrument without the

---

[33] See above, p. 318, ftn. 24.

[34] By confession of judgment is meant a person's consent to the jurisdiction of a court and to a judgment against him without the trial of any issues between the parties. Under U3C, sec. 3.306: "Authorization to Confess Judgment Prohibited. A consumer may not authorize any person to confess judgment on a claim arising out of a consumer credit transaction. An authorization in violation of this section is void."

necessity of having to resort to the parol evidence rule for protection. Several have been discussed.[35]

Draft or Note? When the appearance of an instrument, as by phrasing or by form, is such that there is doubt whether the instrument is a draft or a note, the holder may treat it as either at his election. *The instrument must be ambiguous in its appearance;* an instrument unambiguous in its appearance but lacking in essential requisites may not be treated as another instrument at the election of the holder. For example, an instrument in the form of a draft but with the drawee omitted thereon cannot be treated as a draft or a note; it is an incomplete instrument and neither negotiable nor enforceable until subsequently completed. Holders are on notice of the omission and of the apparent intent to make the instrument a draft. The purported draft without a drawee does not contain an express unconditional *promise* to pay and cannot be a note and, inasmuch as it does not have a *drawee,* it cannot be a draft. A draft drawn on the drawer is effective as a note, e.g., a draft drawn by a corporation on its treasurer; the drawer is liable as the maker.

Conflicting Handwritten, Typewritten, and Printed Terms. Handwritten terms control typewritten and printed terms, and typewritten terms control printed terms.

Co-signers. Often two or more persons sign in the same capacity, e.g., as co-makers. When co-signers indicate their capacity, it is in that capacity that they are liable to all subsequent parties on the instrument. However, unless they indicate otherwise, are they jointly, severally, or jointly and severally liable thereon? Under the Code, unless the instrument otherwise specifies, two or more persons who sign as maker, acceptor, drawer, or indorser and *as a part of the same transaction* are jointly and severally liable thereon. Such liability is not altered if the instrument contains the words "I promise to pay." This rule of construction applies only where the parties sign in the same capacity as a part of the same transaction. Successive indorsers do not sign as a part of the same transaction and, therefore, are liable only severally.

Incomplete Instruments

Whether or not a paper is, or may become, a negotiable instrument is determined at the time it is signed. If the *contents* of the paper at the time of signing do not indicate that it was *intended* to be, or to become, a negotiable instrument, it cannot then or later be or become a negotiable instrument. For example, a blank paper with a signature is not, and after being filled in subsequently cannot become, a negotiable instrument. However, a person can, apart from the Code rule, authorize another to fill in a negotiable instrument on the blank paper above the first person's signature and thereby cause such

[35] Conflicting words and figures, above, p. 316; judgment rate of interest applicable to an instrument providing for interest without specifying the rate, above, p. 316; and consent to an extension of time when an instrument is payable, and the holder's exercise of his option to extend, above, p. 318.

paper to become a negotiable instrument. This would then be a matter of proving such authority under the law of Agency. If a writing is complete but one of the requisites for a negotiable instrument is missing and there is no blank or space for insertion of the missing requisite, it is not an incomplete instrument; it is not meant to be a negotiable instrument at all.

When a paper whose contents at the time of signing show that it is intended to become an instrument is signed while still incomplete in any necessary respect, it is an incomplete instrument under the Code and cannot be enforced until subsequently completed.[36] If the omission is not of a necessary element, e.g., the instrument is not dated and does not require it to make the time definite when the instrument is payable, the instrument is negotiable, as previously discussed under definite time[37] and undated instruments.[38] The date of issue of an instrument is not essential, unless it is necessary to fix the date when the instrument is payable, in which event the omitted date is a necessary element and the instrument is incomplete. An illustration is an instrument payable at a fixed time after such date, e.g., an undated instrument payable "thirty days after date." However, the omission may be of an essential element, one which is necessary to a complete instrument, e.g., the promise or order, the amount payable, a specified payee. When a blank is left for the insertion of a time when the instrument is payable, a necessary element is missing and the instrument is incomplete; but where it is clear that no time is intended to be stated, the instrument is complete and is payable on demand.[39]

The authorized completion of an incomplete instrument makes the instrument effective as completed. The unauthorized completion of an incomplete instrument may be a material alteration and, as later discussed,[40] such lack of authority can be asserted as a defense against anyone except a holder in due course, or holder or transferee properly claiming through a holder in due course, who may enforce the instrument as completed even though the instrument was never delivered by the maker or drawer. The completion of an instrument is presumed authorizedly done, and the burden of establishing that any completion is unauthorized is on the party so asserting.

Miscellaneous

Instruments Payable to Two or More Persons. An instrument may be made payable to the order of two or more persons; this occurs frequently. If the instrument is payable in the alternative, e.g., "A or B," it is payable to any one of them, and it may be negotiated or enforced by any one of them who has possession of it. However, if the instrument is not payable in the alternative,

---

[36] UCC 3–115(1).

[37] See above, pp. 317 f.

[38] See above, pp. 320 f.

[39] See above, p. 317.

[40] See below, pp. 356–57.

e.g., "A and B," it is payable to all of them, and it may be negotiated or enforced only by all of them. An instrument payable to "A and/or B" is payable in the alternative to A or B and it is also payable to A and B together; it may be negotiated or enforced by either of them or by all of them.

Named Payee with Description. We have seen from previous discussion[41] that an instrument may be made payable to the order of a named officer by his title. When an instrument is made payable to a named person with the addition of words describing him, such words may describe him as a particular kind of a fiduciary, as a general kind of fiduciary, and in any other manner. The kind of description is important for the purposes of determining who the payee is, who may act as the holder, and the effect of such person's indorsement with respect to subsequent parties.

Particular Kind of Fiduciary. If the words describe the named person as an agent or officer of a specified person, the instrument is payable to his specified principal. However, the agent or officer may act as if he were the holder. Illustrations are: "John Smith, President of Utopia Corporation"; "Frank Fay, Mayor of the City of Boulder"; and "Joseph Kane, agent of Neil Duncan." It is commercially understood in such cases that the instrument was made to be paid to the principal and that the agent was named only to convenience the principal, so that the named agent could cash the instrument for him. It should be noted carefully that an instrument made payable to a person as agent or officer without specifying the principal, e.g., "John Jones, agent," does not come within the Code rule, and it is payable to him as payee and not to his principal.

General Kind of Fiduciary. If the words describe the named person as a fiduciary, other than an agent or officer, for a specified person or purpose, the instrument is payable to the payee and may be negotiated or enforced by him. Illustrations are: "Frank Smith, Trustee of Franklin Trust"; "James King, Administrator of the Estate of Roland Calhoun"; and "Charles Dunn, Executor of the Will of Fanny Kellogg." Of course, the payee is liable for breach of his fiduciary obligation, and, while subsequent holders of the instrument are on notice of the payee's fiduciary character, they are not precluded from becoming holders in due course unless they have notice of his breach of fiduciary obligation. It should be noted carefully that an instrument made payable to a person without specifying the interest or purpose for which he is a fiduciary does not come within the Code rule, and the instrument is payable to him as payee for all purposes as far as subsequent third parties dealing with the instrument are concerned.

Any Other Manner. If the words describe the named person in any other manner than a particular or general kind of fiduciary for a specified person or purpose, it is payable to the payee unconditionally, and the additional words are without effect on subsequent parties. Illustrations are: "Joseph Lang, Attorney"; "Bernard Jones, agent"; "Mary King, 945 Spring Street"; "Charles

---

[41] See above, p. 319.

Doe, Treasurer." Whether or not the payee meets the description is irrelevant as far as third parties are concerned.

Other Writings Affecting an Instrument. Several writings may be executed as a part of the same transaction, such as a note and a security agreement providing for a security interest in connection with the sale of goods or the lending of money (e.g., a note secured by a real property mortgage). Under the familiar law of Contracts, the writings are to be read and construed together as a part of the agreement. However, what is the effect of an additional writing on the negotiability of an instrument in the same transaction, and on the original parties to the instrument and subsequent transferees thereof? First the effect of an additional writing on the negotiability of an instrument, both of which are executed as a part of the same transaction, will be discussed and then the effect of the additional writing on the rights and obligations of the original parties and subsequent transferees of the instrument.

The mere fact that there is a separate agreement, apart from the instrument but part of the same transaction, does not of itself affect the negotiability of the instrument. The negotiability of an instrument is determined only by what appears on its face, and a purchaser without notice of a separate writing is not affected by it. An instrument which states that it is subject to or governed by any other agreement is not negotiable; however, if the instrument just refers to a separate agreement or states that it arises out of such an agreement, it is negotiable.

As between the original parties to the instrument and subsequent transferees thereof, the terms of the instrument may be modified or affected by the additional writing, except to the extent that a transferee is a holder in due course without notice of any limitation of his rights on the instrument. A purchaser of the instrument may or may not know of the additional writing and may or may not know of the terms of such additional writing. If he takes the instrument without knowledge of the additional writing, he may become a holder in due course. If he takes the instrument with knowledge of the additional writing but without notice of any defense or claim arising from the terms of such additional writing, he may become a holder in due course; but if he has notice of any such defense or claim, he cannot be a holder in due course. If he takes the instrument with knowledge of the additional writing and with notice of a limitation in the additional writing, such limitation not itself giving notice of any present defense or claim (e.g., a limitation that the note shall be extended one year under certain conditions), he can be a holder in due course although he takes the instrument subject to such limitation. In the latter case, if he has no notice of such limitation at the time he took the instrument, he does not take the instrument subject to such limitation.

> A person has "notice" of a fact when
> (a) he has actual knowledge of it; or
> (b) he has received a notice or notification of it; or
> (c) from all the facts and circumstances known to him at the time in question he has reason to know that it exists.

> A person "knows" or has "knowledge" of a fact when he has actual knowledge of it. "Discover" or "learn" or a word or phrase of similar import refers to knowledge rather than to reason to know. The time and circumstances under which a notice or notification may cease to be effective are not determined by this Act.[42]

Instruments "Payable through" a Bank. Often a firm will issue instruments "payable through" a bank specified in the instrument. An instrument which states that it is "payable through" a bank or the like designates that bank as a collecting bank to make presentment but does not of itself authorize the bank to pay the instrument.[43] The through bank is not a drawee and is not authorized or directed to pay the instrument.

Instruments Payable at a Bank. There is a strong difference of view among the various states concerning the effect of a note or acceptance payable at a bank. The commercial and banking practice of New York and its surrounding states causes such states to treat such a note or an acceptance as the equivalent of a draft on the bank, ordering it to pay the instrument when it falls due and without consultation out of the account of the maker or acceptor. Western and southern states treat such a note or acceptance as merely designating a place of payment, the bank to notify the maker or acceptor of presentment of the instrument and to ask for instructions; the instrument is not, of itself, an order or authorization to the bank to pay it.

Accrual of Cause of Action

Maker and Acceptor. These parties are *primarily liable* on the instrument and a cause of action accrues against them: on *time* instruments, on the day after maturity; on *demand* instruments, on the date stated on the instrument or, if no date is stated, on the date of issue.[44] *No demand for payment is required of the maker and acceptor* because, being primarily liable on the instrument, presentment of the instrument to them for payment is not necessary in order to cause them to be liable thereon. However, an *exception* is made in the case of the maker obligor of *a certificate of deposit.* Because certificates of deposit are taken with the expectation of holding them for a considerable time, whether they are demand or time certificates, and with the bank's expectation that the holder will demand payment when he wants it, a cause of action accrues against the obligor *only upon demand,* which can be made only after the maturity date in the case of a time certificate of deposit.

Drawer and Indorser. The drawer of a draft, including a check, and an indorser on any instrument are parties *secondarily* liable. Under their contract on an instrument,[45] they engaged to pay the instrument on its dishonor and on any necessary notice of dishonor or protest. These are the conditions which

---

[42] UCC 1–201(25).

[43] UCC 3–120.

[44] For date of issue, see above, p. 316, ftn. 20.

[45] See below, pp. 363–65.

must occur before they can be charged with payment on the instrument. A notice of dishonor to the drawer or an indorser is a demand for payment. Accordingly, a cause of action accrues against them when the instrument is dishonored *and* a demand upon them has been made. However, if no notice of dishonor or protest is necessary, e.g., it has been waived or excused, after dishonor a demand for payment is not necessary, and the holder of the instrument has an immediate right of recourse against them, the cause of action accruing solely on dishonor of the instrument. It should be noted that, as discussed later,[46] neither presentment, nor notice of dishonor, nor protest is necessary in order to charge an indorser who has indorsed an instrument after maturity.

Interest. The terms of an instrument determine the interest to be paid thereon. As previously discussed,[47] if an instrument provides for interest but does not specify the rate or time when it runs, the judgment rate applies from the date of the instrument or, if the instrument is undated, from the date of issue. However, if the instrument is silent on the matter of interest, unless the instrument otherwise provides, interest at the judgment rate runs from the date of the accrual of a cause of action, with one exception. The exception is that on a demand instrument the interest runs only from the date of actual demand.

---

[46] See below, p. 375.

[47] See above, p. 316.

Chapter 22

NEGOTIATION

A negotiable instrument is "negotiated" when it is *delivered* to a *holder*, who is either a payee, indorsee, or bearer. The transfer of an instrument to a person not a holder causes the transferee to acquire only the rights of his transferor. Non-negotiable paper can be only transferred. A delivery is presumed to have occurred if the instrument is held by a holder, and if he is a holder in due course the personal defense of a non-delivery to a prior party (e.g., theft), cannot be asserted against him. Also, lack of intent not to transfer a property interest in the instrument by delivery by one prior party to another cannot be asserted against a holder in due course.

An indorsement is a signature of a person other than a maker, drawer, or an acceptor made alone or with written words by an "indorser." Unless the instrument clearly indicates that a signature is made in some other capacity, it is an indorsement. An indorsement must transfer the entire instrument or any unpaid residue thereof to be effective as a negotiation. An indorsement is required of the payee or indorsee, or his authorized agent, in order to further negotiate the instrument. An indorsement is effective as such irrespective of its legal consequences. If the payee's name is misspelled or improperly designated by a name other than his own, he may indorse in such name or his own or, preferably, both. There are three kinds of indorsement. (*1*) "*Special indorsement.*" This indorsement specifies the person to whom, or to whose order, it makes the instrument payable, and the latter's indorsement is necessary for a further negotiation. (2) "*Indorsement in blank.*" This indorsement is a signature with no accompanying words and does not specify any indorsee. It causes the instrument to be payable to bearer, and it then can be negotiated solely by delivery. (3) "*Restrictive indorsement.*" No indorsement can destroy

the negotiable character of an instrument nor prohibit its further negotiation or transfer, and any such prohibitory indorsement is a restrictive indorsement. The transferee of a restrictively indorsed instrument for collection, *other than an intermediary bank,* must pay or otherwise perform consistently with the indorsement. A prior party's reacquisition of the instrument causes intervening parties to be discharged as against the reacquiring party and as against subsequent holders not holders in due course.

SECTION I. GENERAL CONCEPT

An instrument is a contract which is revocable and of no effect until it has been issued by delivery to the first holder. Once issued, it may be negotiated by the holder to another holder, who may negotiate it to other holders. Negotiation includes issue, which is the first negotiation of the instrument.

Definition

"Negotiation" consists of the delivery of an instrument to a person who thereby becomes a *holder.* A "holder" is a person who has possession of an instrument and who is within the tenor thereof either as the payee, indorsee, or bearer. An "indorsee" is a person to whom an instrument has been indorsed. Accordingly, in every negotiation an instrument is delivered to either a payee, indorsee, or bearer. Inasmuch as instruments are most frequently made payable to the order of a payee rather than to bearer, the subsequent negotiation by the payee of an instrument requires delivery *and* his indorsement. First delivery and then indorsement will be considered, after distinguishing negotiation from transfer.

Distinguished from Transfer

A careful distinction should be made between the words "negotiation" and "transfer." Commercial paper may be *transferred* by its *delivery* to a transferee. Non-negotiable paper can only be *transferred.* Only *negotiable paper*—e.g., negotiable document of title under UCC 7, investment security under UCC 8, and negotiable instrument under UCC 3—can be *negotiated.* If a negotiable instrument is transferred *without the transferee becoming a holder,* it has not been *negotiated* and the transferee, like an assignee, acquires only the rights of his transferor, which may be subject to some defense precluding payment of the instrument. However, if *the transferee becomes a holder,* then the negotiable instrument has been *negotiated* to the holder. The holder may, either as a holder in due course or by properly claiming through a previous holder who was a holder in due course, acquire the right to payment on the instrument, and what are often called "personal defenses" may not be asserted against him.

SECTION II. DELIVERY

Requirement and Presumption of Delivery

Until a negotiable instrument is delivered with the intent to transfer the rights in the instrument, the instrument is of no effect *between the immediate parties*. When a *holder* possesses an instrument, a valid delivery is presumed to have been made to him unless the defendant establishes otherwise. However, as later discussed,[1] the personal defense of non-delivery cannot be asserted against a holder in due course. (D makes a check or note payable to the order of P, which is stolen by P. As between D and P, D can prove that he never delivered the instrument to P and that P never obtained any property rights in the instrument because of such non-delivery, and D would thereby avoid liability to P on the instrument. If P had indorsed and delivered the instrument to H, a holder in due course, D would be liable to H because the personal defense of non-delivery cannot be asserted against a holder in due course. As between D and H, D made the instrument and took the risk of its being negotiated without his consent to a holder in due course.)

Intent to Transfer Title by Delivery

As between the immediate parties to a delivery, the transferor may prove that the parties did not intend that the property in the instrument was to be transferred by such delivery, but as against a subsequent holder in due course, such a personal defense cannot be established. (M made a note payable to the order of P and delivered it to P on condition that P deliver certain goods to M before the note matured. P did not deliver the goods. As between M and P, M may prove that delivery was made with the intention of making M liable on the instrument only when P had delivered the goods, and that M is not liable thereon to P. If P had indorsed and delivered the instrument to H, a holder in due course, M would be liable to H.)

SECTION III. INDORSEMENT

Nature of Indorsement

An "indorsement" is a *signature*[2] of a person other than as maker, drawer, or acceptor, made alone or with written words qualifying the effect of such signature, and made on the instrument itself or on a paper so firmly affixed thereto as to become a part thereof. Such affixed paper is called an "allonge." The person making the indorsement is the "indorser" and, if the indorsement is made to a specified person, such specified person is the "indorsee." An indorsement of

[1] See below, p. 350.

[2] For a discussion of what constitutes a signature, see above, pp. 312 f.

an instrument which is delivered so as to constitute a negotiation has a twofold effect: title to the instrument is transferred to the holder, and liability is imposed on the indorser according to the terms of his indorsement, discussed later.[3] *Unless the instrument clearly indicates that a signature is made in some other capacity, it is an indorsement.* The character of a signature on an instrument is to be determined solely from the face of the instrument itself.[4]

Words often accompany an indorsing signature and are a part of the indorsement. While they may qualify the legal *effect* of the indorsement, they do not qualify the nature of a *signature itself as an indorsement.* Thus, words of assignment (e.g., "I hereby assign all my right, title and interest in the within note"), condition (e.g., "Pay A on the completion of the building"), waiver (e.g., "I waive notice of dishonor and protest"), guaranty (e.g., "I guarantee payment"), limitation or disclaimer of liability ("without recourse") and the like accompanying an indorsement do not affect its character as an indorsement.[5] The liability of the indorser on the instrument may be affected by additional words, but his signature is an indorsement.

An indorsement is effective for negotiation only when it transfers the entire instrument or any unpaid residue thereof. If the indorsement purports to be of less, it operates only as a partial *assignment* and is not effective for negotiation. Consequently, no subsequent person can become a holder. An illustration of such an indorsement is "Pay John Jones one-half." The reason for this is that the maker or drawer would be subjected to a multiplicity of actions on the instrument by more than one person in the event of the dishonor of the instrument, which was a risk that the obligor did not intend to assume. The splitting of a cause of action is prohibited.

When Indorsement Required

Only the person to whom the instrument is payable, either as payee or indorsee, is required to indorse the instrument in order to transfer title to it to a holder. An instrument payable to bearer requires no indorsement, and title is transferred by delivery of the instrument with the intent thereby to transfer title to such instrument. However, the transfer of title to an instrument payable to the order of a specified person either as a payee or indorsee requires the indorsement of such person and the delivery of the instrument with the intent thereby to transfer title to such instrument. If an instrument is delivered *for value* with such an intent but without a proper indorsement, the transferee has the right to obtain the transferor's indorsement[6] in order to effect a negotiation of the instrument to him. An accommodation party may be an indorser, as well as a maker, drawer, or drawee, but such accommodation indorsement is not

[3] See below, pp. 364–65.

[4] However, a signature in the lower right hand corner of an instrument is recognized as indicating an intent to sign as the maker or the drawer of the instrument.

[5] UCC 3–202(4).

[6] See above, pp. 330 f.

necessary to transfer title to the instrument and is placed on the instrument solely for the purpose of giving additional security to the instrument by subjecting the accommodation indorser to liability thereon in the event the instrument should be dishonored.

The Indorser

An instrument payable to the order of a specified person must be indorsed by such person,[7] and an instrument indorsed to a specified person must be indorsed by such indorsee. When an instrument is made payable to the order of two or more persons jointly—e.g., "A and B"—the instrument must be indorsed by all such payees, unless one of them is authorized to sign for the others. The signature of an indorser, or any party to the instrument, may be made by an authorized agent; authority to do so is not required to be in writing or in any particular form. As discussed previously,[8] an instrument made payable to a named person with the addition of words describing him as agent or officer of a specified person is payable to his principal, but the agent or officer may act as if he were the holder. Thus, an instrument payable to the order of, or indorsed to, a "cashier" of a specified bank or corporation is deemed payable to the bank or corporation, but the instrument may be negotiated by the indorsement either of the cashier or of the bank or corporation.

An indorsement is effective as such even though rescindable, even if it imposes no liability on the indorser, and even if its character causes the transaction itself to be rescindable or void. *It is an indorsement,* quite distinct from legal remedies and other legal effect. Thus, the indorsement of an infant or a corporation acting *ultra vires*[9] is effective to transfer the title to the instrument, regardless of whether or not such indorsement imposes any liability upon the indorser. An instrument, whether a note or draft, payable to the order of the maker or drawer must be indorsed by the payee maker or drawer. The indorsement does not enlarge the maker's or drawer's liability on the instrument but is merely a step in the negotiation of the instrument, effected by the delivery of the instrument so indorsed to a holder. Further, negotiation is effective to transfer the instrument although the negotiation is: (1) made by an infant, a corporation exceeding its powers, or any other person without capacity; or (2) obtained by fraud, duress or mistake of any kind; or (3) part of an illegal transaction; or (4) made in breach of duty.[10] Except as against a subsequent holder in due course, the negotiation by items (1) through (4) is, in an appropriate case, subject to rescission, the declaration of a constructive trust, or any other remedy permitted by law.

---

[7] For impostors and negligence contributing to unauthorized signatures, see below, pp. 35–56.

[8] See above, p. 319.

[9] See below, pp. 703 f.

[10] UCC 3–207(1).

It often occurs that the payee's name is misspelled or improperly designated by a name other than his own. He may indorse in such name or his own, or both. While the indorsement of such a payee in the misspelled or improperly described name, or in his own true name, will transfer his interest in the instrument and can be negotiated by subsequent delivery, nevertheless this is not commercially desirable. The proper and desirable form of indorsement consists of indorsements in both names, and a person paying or giving value for the instrument has a right to require this.

Kinds of Indorsement

There are three kinds of indorsement: special, in blank, and restrictive.[11] None of these destroys the negotiable character of an instrument. An instrument which is negotiable continues to be negotiable; it continues to be negotiable even after maturity.

Special Indorsement. A special indorsement is an indorsement specifying the person to whom, or to whose order, it makes the instrument payable—e.g., "Pay A," or "Pay to the order of A." *Any* instrument specially indorsed becomes payable to the order of the special indorsee and may be further negotiated only by his indorsement. For example, if an instrument payable to the order of A is indorsed in blank by A, the instrument thereby becomes payable to bearer and may be negotiated by A's delivery of the instrument to B. If B indorses the instrument "Pay to C (signed) B," the instrument is no longer a bearer instrument, and C's indorsement is necessary for its further negotiation. The owner of an instrument has the right to direct its subsequent payment as he wishes, as long as his direction is not violative of the Code. The rule applies to an instrument originally issued payable to bearer, which may be specially indorsed and thereby no longer be a bearer instrument. For example, an instrument drawn "Pay to bearer" is indorsed by A, the holder, "Pay to B." B's indorsement is necessary for further negotiation of the instrument.

Indorsement in Blank. An indorsement which does not specify any particular indorsee is an indorsement in blank or "blank indorsement." Such an indorsement causes the instrument to be payable to bearer, and it then may be negotiated solely by delivery; however, should a special indorsement be made subsequently, the instrument ceases to be a bearer instrument. The holder may convert a blank indorsement into a special indorsement by writing above the signature of the indorser in blank any contract consistent with the character of the indorsement. This is commonly done by the holder inserting words above the blank indorsement making the instrument payable to him or to his order. For example, an instrument drawn payable to the order of A is indorsed by A in blank "Pay to B." However, the insertion of words above the blank indorsement which unauthorizedly vary the contract of the blank indorser constitutes a material alteration of the blank indorsement, and, if made with a

[11] For what is often called a "qualified indorsement," see below, pp. 364, 367.

fraudulent purpose, thereby discharges the blank indorser from liability on the instrument, except as to a subsequent holder in due course. Illustrations are: "Without recourse" and "Protest waived."

Restrictive Indorsement. Often indorsements are accompanied by words which seek to prohibit further transfer or negotiation of the instrument. Under the Code this cannot be done. Such an indorsement is called a "restrictive indorsement." An indorsement is restrictive if the additional words: are conditional; purport to prohibit further transfer of the instrument; include the words "for collection," "for deposit." "pay any bank," or like terms signifying a purpose of deposit or collection; or otherwise state that the indorsement is for the benefit or use of the indorser or of another person.[12] Examples are: conditional, "Pay A on his twenty-first birthday"; prohibiting further transfer, "Pay A only"; for benefit or use, "Pay A for the benefit of B," which is a trust indorsement, A being a trustee for B.

A restrictive indorsement has various legal effects.

First, as already indicated, a restrictive indorsement cannot prevent further transfer or negotiation of the instrument. Because of this, the indorsee or any holder from him can become a holder in due course.

Second, a restrictive indorsement does not, of itself, give notice to subsequent parties of any defense or claim of the indorser.

Third, an intermediary blank,[13] or a payor bank[14] which is not the depositary bank,[15] is neither given notice nor otherwise affected by a restrictive indorsement of any person except the bank's immediate transferor or the person presenting the instrument for payment. This is because many of these banks ordinarily handle instruments, particularly checks, in great bulk and they do not have an opportunity to consider the effect of restrictive indorsements. With the exceptions indicated, such banks may disregard any restrictive indorsement.

Fourth, when the indorsement is conditional or includes the words "for collection," "for deposit," "pay any bank," or like terms signifying a purpose of deposit or collection, any transferee except an intermediary bank must pay or apply any value given by him for or on the security of the instrument consistently with the indorsement, and to the extent that he does so he becomes a holder for value. In addition, if he otherwise complies with the requirements of being a holder in due course, he is a holder in due course.

Fifth, the first taker under an indorsement for the benefit or use of the indorser or of another person must pay or apply any value given by him for or on the security of the instrument consistently with the indorsement, and to the

[12] UCC 3–205.

[13] UCC 4–105(c): " 'Intermediary bank' means any bank to which an item is transferred in course of collection except the depositary or payor bank."

[14] UCC 4–105(b): " 'Payor bank' means a bank by which an item is payable as drawn or accepted."

[15] UCC 4–105(a): " 'Depositary bank' means the first bank to which an item is transferred for collection even though it is also the payor bank."

extent that he does so he becomes a holder for value. In addition, such taker is a holder in due course if he otherwise complies with the requirements on what constitutes a holder in due course. A *later* holder for value is neither given notice nor otherwise affected by such restrictive indorsement, unless he has *knowledge* that a fiduciary or other person has negotiated the instrument in any transaction for his own benefit or otherwise in breach of duty.

Reacquisition

An instrument may be returned to, or reacquired by, a prior party. For example, M's note to P may be subsequently negotiated by P to A, A to B, and finally B to P. It is unimportant whether the instrument is negotiated or just transferred to the prior party; he does not have to be a holder on reacquisition. When such reacquisition occurs, intervening parties are discharged *as against the reacquiring party* and as against subsequent holders who are *not holders in due course*. Thus, in the above illustration, A and B are discharged from liability to P on the instrument. Otherwise, P would have an action against B and A who, in turn, would have an action back against P on the instrument. Such a discharge by reacquisition precludes such circuity of action. However, intervening parties are not discharged as against a holder in due course subsequent to the reacquiring party if he should reissue or further negotiate the instrument. In the above illustration, if P should negotiate the note to X, a holder in due course, A and B would still be secondarily liable on the instrument *to X*. P may prevent this and discharge the liability of A and B to X by *cancelling* the indorsements of A and B. The reacquiring party owns the instrument and has the right to relieve any indorser from liability on the instrument and, therefore, he has the right to cancel intervening indorsements. However, he must be careful not to cancel any indorsement necessary to his title.

Chapter 23

THE HOLDER IN DUE COURSE

SECTION I. REQUISITES

A holder in due course is (1) a *holder* of a *negotiable* instrument, who takes the instrument (2) *in due course* by taking it (a) for value, (b) in good faith, and (c) without *notice* that the instrument is overdue or has been previously dishonored or of any defense to it or claim to it on the part of any person. However, if such a person fulfilling these requisites takes the instrument not in due course of trade, e.g., by purchasing it at a judicial sale or under judicial process or in taking over an estate or as a part of a bulk transaction not in the transferor's regular course of business, he is not a holder in due course.

The status of a holder in due course is determined as of the time the instrument was negotiated to him as the holder. The person asserting that he is a holder has the burden of proving it. When he claims under a signature, it is presumed to be genuine or authorized until it is questioned when he then has the burden of establishing it. A holder is presumed to be a holder in due course until a defense is asserted against him when he then has the burden of proving that he, or some person through whom he claims, is a holder in due course.

The holder in due course must take the instrument for value; consideration and a past debt are value. A promise to give value is not value, unless he gives a negotiable instrument or makes an irrevocable commitment to a third person. A holder in due course purchaser of a limited interest in an instrument becomes a holder in due course only to the extent of the interest purchased.

Good faith means honesty in fact, and is subjective in that the holder did not know facts at the time he took the instrument *causing him to believe* that

any person had a defense against, or a claim to, the instrument; not what *should have* caused him so to believe. However, if, from the facts and circumstances at the time he took the instrument he has *reason to know* a fact, then he has *notice* of such fact, and if the fact is that the instrument is overdue or has been previously dishonored or that a person has a defense against or a claim to the instrument, then he is not a holder in due course. He can have *good faith*, but if he *has notice* of the above facts he cannot be a holder in due course. Taking a demand instrument, i.e., draft or check, more than a reasonable time after its issue is taking with notice that it is overdue. A reasonable time for a check drawn and payable within the United States is presumed to be 30 days.

A distinction must be drawn between a holder and a holder in due course because the rights of each, and the rights which each may transfer, differ greatly. A holder in due course is a *holder* to whom an instrument has been *negotiated* under circumstances which make him so *innocent* a purchaser for *value* as to merit his obtaining complete title to the instrument subject to no claims by anyone, and subject to no so-called "personal defenses" by anyone a party thereto with whom he has not dealt. The elements constituting a holder in due course are very simple:

1. He is a holder of the instrument.
2. He takes the instrument:

   in due course
   - (a) for value,
   - (b) in good faith,
   - (c) without notice that the instrument is overdue or, has been dishonored or of any defense against, or claim to, the instrument on the part of any person.

A payee may be a holder in due course.

However, it should be carefully noted at the outset that, although a person satisfies the above requisites, under the Code he cannot become a holder in due course of an instrument:

(a) *by* purchase of it at judicial sale or by taking it under legal process; or
(b) *by* acquiring it in taking over an estate; or
(c) *by* purchasing it as part of a bulk transaction not in regular course of business of the transferor.[1] (Author's italics.[2])

The reason is that, in these particular circumstances, he has taken the instrument under unusual circumstances not in due course of trade, indicating that he is merely a successor in interest to the prior holder and, therefore, should acquire only the rights of his transferor. Note that he cannot become a holder

---

[1] Examples of (c) are the purchase for value of the assets in bulk by: a bank of another bank which is in financial trouble; a new partnership with a new partner of the old partnership; or a reorganized or consolidated corporation of its predecessor.

[2] UCC 3–302(3).

in due course *by* acquiring the instrument in such a manner, but he can be a holder in due course if his transferor was, or could claim through a prior transferor as, a holder in due course.

The above requisites for becoming a holder in due course will be considered in the order stated.

Holder

A holder of an instrument is a person in possession of the instrument which is issued or indorsed to his order, to bearer, or in blank.[3] The payee can be a holder. The forged indorsement of a specified person to whom the instrument is payable, either as payee or indorsee, precludes any person subsequent to the forgery from being a holder.[4] There is a gap in the chain of indorsements, and the person in possession is not within the tenor of the instrument; it has never been properly indorsed to him. The person asserting that he is a holder has the burden of proving it.

When a person is a holder of an instrument, he may recover on the instrument as a holder in due course, unless the defendant establishes a defense. The burden of going forward and proving that the holder is a holder in due course is satisfied by proof of the status of being a holder. Until a defense is raised, there is no issue of whether or not he is a holder in due course. After it is shown that a defense exists, a person claiming the rights of a holder in due course has the burden of establishing that he, or some person under whom he claims, is in all respects a holder in due course. (D drew a check to the order of P for $1,000 and delivered it to P on P's promise to deliver certain goods to D. P negotiated the check to H and never delivered the goods to D. H sues D for payment of the check. H proves he is a holder. D proves failure of consideration for the check by P's non-delivery of the promised goods. H *now* has the burden of going forward and proving that he is a holder in due course and, if he so proves, D must pay H.) The holder can prove either that he is a holder in dur course, or that he acquired the rights of a prior holder in due course.

For Value

For a holder to acquire the status of a holder in due course, he must take the instrument for value. The Code distinguishes between "value" and "consideration." *Value is either: what a person parts with* (*consideration*), e.g., the payee pays money, surrenders a claim, gives a negotiable instrument or makes an irrevocable commitment to a third person in exchange for the instrument which he thereby acquires; *or an antecedent claim,* whether or not the claim is due, e.g., M gives P his note as security for an antecedent debt owing to P. The

---

[3] UCC 1–201(20).

[4] William E. Britton, *Handbook of the Law of Bills and Notes* (St. Paul: West Publishing Co., 1961), sec. 139.

presence of value by the holder justifies, in exchange, his acquisition of an interest in an instrument. *For a person to have a contractual obligation to perform his promise,* either: someone must have furnished *consideration,* i.e., *what the promisor requested* and which the party rendering it was under no previous legal obligation to do; or there is an *antecedent claim* against the promisor or anyone else supporting the promise. (M promises to pay P $100 if P will sell and deliver certain goods to M. P sells and delivers the goods to M, and M's promise now is a contract with an obligation to pay. P's sale and delivery of the goods to M was what M's promise requested and, when performed by P, is the consideration for M's promise. If M gave P his note for such goods, and P never delivered the goods, M's promise on the note is not a contractual obligation to pay and such defense may be asserted against P, but not against a holder in due course or a transferee or holder under the shelter of a holder in due course.) So when we say "value," we are thinking of *what a holder paid* (or an antecedent claim) in order to see if he is a holder in due course with his superior status. When we say "consideration," we are thinking of *what an obligor or an instrument has requested and whether it was rendered* (or an antecedent claim); if it was not rendered, he has a personal defense of failure of consideration. Usually the value and the consideration in a transaction are the same thing. (M's note to the order of P is for the purchase price of goods to be sold and delivered by P to M. P cannot become a holder in due course until he gives value, i.e., he sells and delivers the goods to M. M cannot be held liable to P on M's promise to pay in the note until the consideration, namely the sale and delivery of the goods to M, has occurred. If M delivered his note to P, who never delivered the goods to M but, rather, negotiated the note to H, a holder in due course for $100, H is a holder in due course having paid value, and M has a personal defense of failure of consideration assertable against P but not against H.) Thus, under the Code, a holder takes the instrument for value:

(a) to the extent that the agreed consideration has been performed or that he acquires a security interest in or a lien on the instrument otherwise than by legal process; or
(b) when he takes the instrument in payment of or as security for an antecedent claim against any person whether or not the claim is due; or
(c) when he gives a negotiable instrument for it or makes an irrevocable commitment to a third person.[5]

Examples of a holder taking an instrument under the above circumstances may be helpful. The following two illustrations are concerned with (a) above. (1) D draws and delivers to P a check in payment for the goods sold and delivered to him by P; P took the instrument for value, namely the goods, which he delivered as the agreed consideration. (2) M made a note to P who pledged it to B bank as security for a loan then made to P; B has a security

[5] UCC 3–303.

interest in, and lien on, the instrument for the money loaned to P. If, in the latter illustration, B had instead levied execution and thereby acquired the note from P, B would not have taken the instrument for value. The following illustration is concerned with (b) above. The debtor, D, owes C bank money, which debt is due and unpaid, and D delivers to C, either as security for the debt or in payment therefor, a note made by M to D. In either case, the antecedent debt serves as the basis for the use of the instrument for payment or security, and C takes M's note for value. The following two illustrations are concerned with (c) above. (1) P delivers to B a note, previously made by M to P, in exchange for B's check drawn by B to the order of P; P took the check for value, namely, M's note. (2) D is in debt to C and S later becomes a surety for such debt, D delivering to S D's check as compensation for S becoming a surety. S took D's check for value, namely, S's irrevocable commitment to C to be liable as a surety for D.

It should be noted carefully that under (a), the holder must actually render the consideration for there to be value. An executory promise to give value is not itself value, except as indicated in (c) above. *Performance* of the executory promise is value. It is for this reason that a bank's credit to a depositor's account of an item to be collected *without a right to draw against it until collected*[6] is, in effect, a promise by the bank to pay the amount to the depositor and, as such, the promise does not constitute value; only to the extent that the depositor actually withdraws some or all of the amount of the credit is there value and the bank becomes to that extent a holder for value. It should be noted that, if the bank takes the item in partial or complete satisfaction of an antecedent debt, the bank becomes a holder for value for the full amount of the item. In determining when the depositor has drawn on the credit established by the bank in connection with a collectible item, under the Code the "first money in is the first money out."[7]

A holder in due course purchaser of a limited interest in an instrument becomes a holder in due course only to the extent of the interest purchased. (C lends D $1,000 and receives D's note for that amount, secured by D's pledge of M's note payable to D for $5,000 which D indorsed in blank and delivered to C. D had fraudulently induced M to issue his note to D, of which C was innocent. C is a holder in due course of the M note only to the extent of D's debt to C. On maturity of both notes and on D's default on his note to C, C can overcome M's personal defense of fraud on his note to D and recover from M *only the amount of D's debt to C*, because C is a holder in due course for value only to that extent. Anything beyond that amount on M's note is subject to M's defense thereon.)

---

[6] If the depositor has the right of immediate withdrawal before collection, see below, p. 400, and UCC 4–208(1), 209 for collecting bank's security interest.

[7] See UCC 4–208, and below, pp. 400 f.

In Good Faith

The holder must take the instrument in good faith. Under the Code, " 'Good faith' means honesty in fact in the conduct or transaction concerned."[8] The test of good faith is a *subjective* one—did the holder know facts at the time he took the instrument which *caused him to believe* that any defense against, or claim to, the instrument existed on the part of any person? If he did, then he took the instrument dishonestly and not in good faith, but rather in bad faith. Good faith is the converse of bad faith. It is the holder's state of mind which is the measure of good faith, and not what the facts and circumstances *should have* caused him to believe. Persons differ in their astuteness and have different beliefs based upon the same facts and circumstances. What may be bad faith for one holder may not be bad faith for another holder. An instrument is taken in good faith when *in fact* it is taken honestly, whether or not it is taken negligently or imprudently. Mere knowledge of suspicious circumstances is not bad faith per se, i.e., in and of itself, although it is evidence of bad faith. Bad faith must be proved as a fact and is a question of fact for the jury. The purchase of an instrument at a heavy discount is evidence of bad faith, but is not bad faith per se. If the holder can prove that he made all reasonable inquiry prior to his purchase of the instrument in order to determine whether anything was wrong with the instrument or with the title of the person negotiating it to him, there would be no bad faith.

Without Notice of Certain Facts

A holder may have taken the instrument in good faith but still not be a holder in due course because the Code also requires that he take the instrument *without notice:* (1) that the instrument was overdue; (2) that it has been dishonored; (3) of any defense against, or claim to, it on the part of any person. Notice of such facts, therefore, becomes extremely important in determining whether a holder is a holder in due course. Under the Code,[9] a person has notice of a fact when: (1) he has actual knowledge of it; or (2) he has received a notice or notification of it; or (3) from all the facts and circumstances known to him at the time in question, he has reason to know that it exists.

It should be noted carefully that, just as the status of a good faith purchaser for value is determined at the time of the purchase and not subsequent to such purchase, so *the status of a holder in due course is determined as of the time the instrument was negotiated to him as the holder.* One who is a holder in due course does not lose such status because of his *subsequent* notice of facts which would have precluded him from being a holder in due course if he had had such notice at the time the instrument was negotiated to him. If an instru-

[8] UCC 1–201(19).

[9] UCC 1–201(25).

ment is negotiated to a holder who pays part of the value agreed upon and, in all other respects, is a holder in due course, he is a holder in due course only to the extent of what he has paid, and he can recover only that amount. Should he obtain notice of a defense against, or claim to, the instrument on the part of any person prior to his payment of the remaining amount, he is not a holder in due course as to such additional payment. (A note for a face amount of $200 is negotiated to H for $150, H paying $100 down and the remaining $50 to be paid in 30 days. Prior to the expiration of the 30 days H learns of a defense against the instrument. H is a holder in due course only for the amount of $100.) If an instrument subject to defenses is pledged as security for value extended by the pledgee, and the pledgee is a holder in due course, he is a holder in due course with a lien on the instrument for the face amount of the instrument to the extent necessary to satisfy the obligation.

Notice that Instrument Is Overdue. The purchaser has notice that an instrument is overdue if he has reason to know any of the following:

1. That any part of the principal amount is overdue.
2. That there is an uncured default in payment of another instrument of the same series.
3. That the instrument has been accelerated.
4. That he is taking a demand instrument after demand has been made.
5. That he is taking a demand instrument more than a reasonable length of time after its issue. A reasonable time for a check drawn and payable within the states and territories of the United States and the District of Columbia is presumed to be 30 days.[10]

Notice of a Claim or Defense. The holder must take the instrument without notice of any defense against, or claim to, the instrument on the part of any person. The purchaser of the instrument has notice of a claim or defense if:

1. *On its face,* the instrument is so incomplete, bears such visible evidence of forgery or alteration, or is otherwise so irregular as to call into question its validity, terms or ownership or to create an ambiguity as to the party to pay. (The irregularity indicates to the purchaser that something is *wrong.*)[11]
2. The purchaser has notice that the obligation of any party is voidable in whole or in part.
3. The purchaser has notice that all parties on the instrument have been discharged.[12]

The purchaser has notice of a claim against the instrument when he has *knowledge* that a fiduciary has negotiated the instrument in payment of, or as security for, his own debt or in any transaction for his own benefit or otherwise in breach of duty.

---

[10] See UCC 3–304(3), but see UCC 3–503(2) and below, p. 377, regarding a 30 day reasonable time for *presentment* of an uncertified check.

[11] Minor erasures or a change in date indicating that an obvious error had been made, e.g., June 6, "1979" changed to "1980," would not normally constitute notice of a claim or defense.

[12] See UCC 3–304(1).

Facts Not Constituting Notice of Claim or Defense. Knowledge of the following facts does not of itself give the purchaser notice of a claim or defense:[13]

1. That the instrument is antedated or postdated.
2. That the instrument was issued or negotiated in return for an executory promise or accompanied by a separate agreement, unless the purchaser has notice that a defense or claim has arisen from the terms thereof.
3. That any party has signed for accommodation.
4. That an incomplete instrument has been completed, unless the purchaser has notice of any improper completion. Any person in possession of an instrument has prima facie authority to complete the instrument by filling in the blanks thereon.[14]
5. That any person negotiating the instrument is, or was, a fiduciary. The purchaser's payment to the fiduciary for the instrument is not in itself notice of impropriety or breach of fiduciary obligation.
6. That there has been default in payment of interest on the instrument or in the payment of any other instrument, except one of the same series. This is a reflection of banking and commercial practice recognizing the great frequency of delayed interest payments.

It should be noted that the filing or recording of a document does not of itself constitute notice within the provisions of the Commercial Paper portion of the Code to a person who would otherwise be a holder in due course. Also, to be effective, notice must be received at such time and in such manner as to give a reasonable opportunity to act on it. Thus, a notice to a corporation president one minute before the treasurer paid for the purchase of a promissory note is ineffective to prevent the corporation from becoming a holder in due course.[15]

SECTION II. RIGHTS AND DEFENSES

A transferee or holder who is not a holder in due course acquires only the rights of his transferor[16] with one exception, and is subject to all valid claims to the instrument by any person and to personal and real defenses of a party defending against liability on the instrument. *A holder in due course is subject only to real defenses.*

Defenses may be either: (1) *real defenses,* which attack the inherent validity or continuing existence of an instrument *as a contract binding on the defending party;* or (2) *personal defenses,* which seek to *avoid* the instrument and liability thereon. *Real defenses may be asserted against everyone including a holder in due course.* They are: infancy; lack of capacity; that kind of duress or illegality which precludes the formation of a contract; fraud in the procure-

[13] See UCC 3–304(4).

[14] See UCC 3–406 and 3–407; and below, pp. 356–57.

[15] See UCC 1–201(27) regarding notice to an organization.

[16] See above, Negotiable Paper under the Code, pp. 150 ff.

ment; and a discharge in insolvency proceedings. *Personal defenses may be asserted against everyone except a holder in due course and a transferee or holder claiming through a holder in due course, except a transferee or holder who has himself been a party to any fraud or illegality affecting the instrument or who, as a transferee or holder prior to the holder in due course, had notice of a defense or claim against it.* They are: valid claims to the instrument; all defenses of any party which are available in a contract action; want or failure of consideration; nonperformance of a condition precedent; nondelivery; delivery for a special purpose; and the defense that the person with the instrument or a person through whom he holds the instrument acquired it by theft, or that payment or satisfaction to such holder would be inconsistent with the terms of a restrictive indorsement.

Rights

The rights of parties seeking to enforce an instrument vary according to their status. First, the rights of a person who is not a holder in due course will be discussed, and then, the rights of a holder in due course.

Person Not a Holder in Due Course. A transferee, and a holder who is not a holder in due course, individually have certain rights solely because of the status of each, and both together with all other persons have certain rights because they are not holders in due course. The rights of these persons will be discussed in that order.

Transferee. A transferee of an instrument *payable to the order of* his transferor and delivered unindorsed to the transferee *for value* acquires the title to the instrument and has the specifically enforceable equitable right to have the instrument *unqualifiedly indorsed* by his transferor,[17] unless the transferor and the transferee have agreed to the contrary. Until such transferor indorses, the transferee is not a holder because he is not within the tenor of the instrument, i.e., he is not a payee, an indorsee, or bearer. Negotiation is completed and takes effect by such indorsement, and the time for determining whether the transferee is a holder in due course is when he becomes a holder, which is when the negotiation is completed. (An instrument is delivered unindorsed by the payee to H for value, without notice of a defense against the instrument. However, at the time H obtains the payee's subsequent indorsement, H has notice of the defense. H is not a holder in due course.) The transferee must prove that he is the lawful owner of the instrument, and until negotiation takes effect there is no presumption that he is the owner of the instrument.

When the transferee proves the transfer, he is entitled to the presumption of ownership of the instrument and of the rights of a holder of it. Until then he has rights similar to those of an assignee of a chose in action or of a nonnegotiable instrument, namely *only the rights of his transferor subject to whatever defenses were available against his transferor on the instrument.* If

[17] See above, p. 331.

his transferor was a holder in due course, the transferee has the rights of a holder in due course, with one very important exception. *A transferee who has himself been a party to any fraud or illegality affecting the instrument, or who as a prior holder had notice of a defense or claim against it, cannot improve his position by taking from a later holder in due course.*[18] (P fraudulently induced M to make an instrument payable to the order of P. If P negotiates the instrument to H, a holder in due course who delivers it to X who has notice of the fraud, X is not a holder in due course but, as the transferee of H, he acquires H's rights on the instrument free of M's defense of fraud. If P had repurchased the instrument from H, he would not acquire H's rights as a holder in due course free of M's defense of fraud but, instead, he would take the instrument subject to the defense. If P had negotiated the instrument to A, who had notice of the fraud, A then negotiated the instrument to H, a holder in due course, and H then resold the instrument to A, A would not acquire H's rights as a holder in due course free of M's defense of fraud but, instead, he would take the instrument subject to the defense. In the last illustration, if A had no notice of the fraud when the instrument had been negotiated to him as a holder but, before he had delivered the instrument to H, he had such notice, the same result would follow.)

It should be noted that the transfer of a limited interest in the instrument (e.g., a security interest in the instrument), passes only the transferor's rights in the instrument to the extent of such interest. If the interest transferred is a security interest, then the transaction comes under Article 9 of the Code on Secured Transactions.[19]

Holder. A person may be a holder but fail to comply with the requisites of being a holder in due course. (P fraudulently induces M to make and deliver his note to P, who then negotiates the note to H, indorsee, as a gift. P was a holder, but because of his fraud he was not a holder in due course. Also, H is a holder, since he is an indorsee, but he is not a holder in due course because he did not take the note for value.) As previously discussed,[20] until a defense is raised by the defendant, there is no issue of whether or not a holder is a holder in due course and, therefore, payment is to be made to him. *After* it is shown that a defense exists, a person claiming the rights of a holder in due course has the burden of establishing that he, or some person under whom he claims, is in all respects a holder in due course.

The holder of an instrument, whether or not he is the owner (e.g., finder of a bearer instrument is holder but not owner), may transfer or negotiate the instrument,[21] and he has the right to recover on the instrument unless the defendant establishes a defense.[22] To the extent that a party liable on the

---

[18] UCC 3–201.

[19] See below, p. 422.

[20] See above, p. 338.

[21] UCC 3–301.

[22] UCC 3–307(2).

instrument makes payment or satisfaction to the holder, the liability of such party is discharged, with three exceptions, later discussed.[23] If an instrument has been transferred to a holder, the holder is also a transferee within the tenor of the instrument and, as such, he has the right of a transferee and acquires the rights of his transferor, as discussed above under the rights of a transferee. A holder may improve his position by taking the instrument from a prior holder in due course, subject to the limitations already discussed under the rights of a transferee.

By operation of law the holder's rights and title to an instrument may vest in another. The death of the holder causes the title to vest in the legal representative of his estate. The bankruptcy of the holder causes the title to vest in the trustee in bankruptcy. When there is more than one payee as tenants in common, the death of one payee causes his title to vest in the representative of his estate.

Any Person Not a Holder in Due Course. All persons not holders in due course acquire an instrument subject to all valid claims to it by any person and subject to the so-called "personal defenses" and "real defenses," to be discussed shortly.[24] If the person acquiring the instrument is a transferee, and *a holder can be a transferee,* the transferee acquires the rights of his transferor. This means that, with the limitations discussed previously under the rights of a transferee,[25] the latter can improve his position and acquire the rights of a previous holder in due course. (P fraudulently induces M to make and deliver his note to P, who negotiates the note to H, a holder in due course. H then negotiates the note to B, a purchaser for value, with notice that the note is overdue. B is not a holder in due course, because he took the note with notice that it was overdue. However, B acquires the rights of his transferor, H, and since H is a holder in due course B therefore acquires the rights of a holder in due course, even though he himself is not a holder in due course.)

We have learned that a holder has a right to recover on the instrument unless the defendant establishes a defense. *The obligor's contract on an instrument is to pay the holder of the instrument.* If other persons have claims to the instrument, that is not the concern of the obligor whose obligation is to perform his contract on the instrument. It is for this reason that the obligor is neither required nor permitted to assert any such claim adverse to the holder and, with certain exceptions,[26] he is discharged to the extent of payment to the holder. Besides, the obligor may not be certain of the validity of the adverse claim and not wish to take the risk or time to refuse payment of the instrument.

[23] The three exceptions are: an adverse claimant to the instrument either posts indemnity or restrains payment by legal process, or payment in bad faith involving theft of the instrument by the holder or one through whom the holder claims, or payment to the holder not in accordance with the restrictively indorsed instrument possessed by the holder. These are discussed below, pp. 387–88.

[24] See below, pp. 347–52.

[25] See above, pp. 344–45.

[26] See above, ftn. 23, and below, pp. 387–88.

Accordingly, for the protection of both the obligor and the holder, under the Code,[27] *the claim of any third person to the instrument is not otherwise available as a defense to any party liable thereon, unless the third person himself defends the action for such party.* (D drew a check to the order of P and delivered it to P. A fraudulently induced P to negotiate the check to A, who then negotiated it to H, a holder, after maturity. D cannot assert against H P's defense of fraud against A, and D must pay H on the check.)

Holder in Due Course. A holder in due course has the right to enforce the instrument according to its terms at the time it was negotiated to him. He takes the instrument free from all *claims* to it by any person, free from the so-called "*personal defenses,*" but subject only to the so-called "real defenses," about to be discussed. In contract, a holder and a transferee take the instrument subject to all valid claims to it by any person, subject to all personal defenses except as the holder or transferee acquires the rights of a previous holder in due course, and subject to real defenses available on the instrument against their respective transferors.

Defenses

Although the Code does not use the terms "real defense" and "personal defense," under the prior law these terms were used extensively, "personal defenses" to describe those defenses which were effective against everyone except a holder in due course or a transferee or holder properly claiming through a holder in due course, and "real defenses" to describe those defenses which were effective against everyone, including a holder in due course. There is no reason to believe that the courts will not continue to use these terms in this context, and they are used here for that purpose. A negotiation of an instrument to a holder in due course cuts off personal defenses but not real defenses. Accordingly, it becomes very important to distinguish between real and personal defenses.

Real or absolute defenses are readily distinguishable from personal defenses, which include Common Law as well as equitable defenses. Defenses which successfully attack the inherent validity or continuing existence of an instrument *as a contract binding on the defending party* are real defenses. Personal defenses do not question the inherent validity or continuing existence of the instrument as a contract binding on the defending party but, rather, seek to *avoid* the instrument and liability thereon. First real defenses will be discussed and then personal defenses.

Real Defenses. Under the Code,[28] to the extent that a holder is a holder in due course, he takes the instrument free from all claims to it on the part of any person, and free from all defenses of any party to the instrument with whom the holder has not dealt, except the following real defenses: incapacity, in the

[27] UCC 3–306(d).

[28] UCC 3–305.

case of the limited incapacity of an infant to the extent that infancy is a defense to a simple contract, or because of no capacity to contract at all; such duress or illegality of the transaction as precludes the creation of a contractual obligation; fraud in the procurement; discharge in insolvency proceedings. Also a material alteration of a negotiable instrument is, with certain exceptions, a real defense. These will be considered in turn, except for material alteration, which is considered later.[29]

Incapacity—Limited Capacity and Lack of Capacity. The Code distinguishes between the *limited capacity* of an infant to make a contract and *lack of capacity* of a person to make any contract.

1. Infancy. *To the extent that infancy is a defense to a simple contract,* it is a real defense by an infant party to an instrument, personal only to him, and assertable against everyone, including a holder in due course. An infant has a limited capacity to contract and, therefore, may issue an instrument; but should the infant exercise his power of avoidance, he no longer is liable as a party on the instrument. The law of a particular state may impose conditions upon an infant in the exercise of his power of avoidance, e.g., he is to return the consideration as a condition precedent to avoidance, or preclude the infant from exercising such right, e.g., estoppel as by his misrepresentation of his age. It is for this reason that, only to the extent that an infant may assert infancy as a defense to the contract on the instrument, infancy is a real defense. The law of the local state governs.

2. Lack of Capacity. *Lack of capacity to contract precludes the creation of a contract* and, therefore, of a contractual obligation on an instrument. Lack of capacity is a real defense assertable against a holder in due course. Local state law governs in determining the existence of such lack of capacity. Thus, a corporation[30] and a nontrading partnership[31] without authority to issue negotiable instruments are not bound by their issue of such instrument; their defenses are real. However, although they have no contractual liability on an instrument, nevertheless title to the instrument can pass through them to a subsequent holder in due course.

Duress Precluding Contract. Duress may either preclude the formation of a contract or render a contract voidable at the election of the wronged party.[32] *To the extent that duress precludes the formation of a contract,* the party upon whom duress has been imposed has no contractual liability and, therefore, is not liable as a party to an instrument. Such duress is a real defense, assertable against everyone, including a holder in due course. Local state law governs the effect of duress. Duress which may render a contract voidable at the election of the wronged party is a personal defense and is not assertable against a holder in due course.

---

[29] See below, pp. 356 ff. UCC 9–206 prohibits waiver by buyer or lessee, as against an assignee, of real defenses in a security agreement for consumer goods; see below, p. 432.

[30] See below, pp. 701, 703.

[31] See below, p. 652.

[32] See Contracts, above, pp. 38–39.

Illegality Precluding Contract. An agreement is illegal when its formation or performance is contrary to law by being opposed to statute, or to public policy as declared by the courts.[33] While, generally, illegal agreements are void by either statute or judicial decision and create no contractual obligation, nevertheless in some instances illegality causes an agreement to be voidable and not void. Although the issuance of an instrument or the transaction giving rise to the instrument may be illegal, nevertheless, they are not void unless made void by statute or judicial decision. Accordingly, mere illegality in connection with the issuance of an instrument is a personal defense, not assertable against a holder in due course; but if, *by law, the illegality nullifies or precludes any contractual obligation on the instrument,*[34] the illegality is a real defense and assertable against everyone, including a holder in due course. The effect of illegality is a matter of local state law—e.g., a state statute declaring void an instrument given in settlement of a gambling debt.

Fraud in the Procurement. Fraud may either preclude the formation of a contract or render a contract voidable at the election of the person wronged, depending on the type of fraud which occurs.[35] *Fraud in the procurement* (also called "fraud in the factum," "fraud in the execution," "fraud in the inception," or "fraud in the essence") *precludes the formation of a contract.* The Code describes fraud in the procurement as "such misrepresentation as has induced the party to sign the instrument with neither knowledge nor reasonable opportunity to obtain knowledge of its character or its essential terms."[36] (P misrepresents to M that a paper is a receipt when, in fact, it is a form of note. M, with neither knowledge nor reasonable opportunity to obtain knowledge of the character of the paper or its essential terms, signs the paper. M is not liable on any contractual obligation on the instrument.) Fraud in the procurement is a real defense assertable against everyone, including a holder in due course. In contrast, fraud in the inducement (also called "fraud in the treaty") causes the resulting contract to be voidable at the election of the party wronged and is a personal defense assertable against everyone except a holder in due course or a transferee or holder properly claiming through a holder in due course. (P intentionally misrepresented his financial solvency to M and induced M to enter into a contract to buy goods from P. M made a note payable to the order of P for the purchase price. M may avoid the sales contract and assert the fraud as a personal defense against P on the note.) It should be noted that *when the word "fraud" is used without qualification, it signifies fraud in the inducement.*

---

[33] See Contracts, above, pp. 68–69.

[34] Under U3C sec. 3.307: "Certain Negotiable Instruments Prohibited. With respect to a consumer credit sale or consumer lease, (except a sale or lease primarily for an agricultural purpose,) the creditor may not take a negotiable instrument other than a check dated not later than ten days after its issuance as evidence of the obligation of the consumer." Sec. 3.404 permits claims and defenses to be asserted against a holder in due course of other than a check.

[35] See Contracts, above, pp. 35–36.

[36] UCC 3–305(2)(c).

Discharge in Insolvency Proceedings.[37] The discharge in bankruptcy or other insolvency proceedings of a party to an instrument terminates his contractual obligation thereon and, therefore, is a real defense assertable against everyone including a holder in due course.

The discharge of a party *other than* in bankruptcy or other insolvency proceedings is a *personal defense* which is assertable against anyone except a holder in due course without notice of such discharge at the time he took the instrument. As indicated previously,[38] a purchaser of an instrument has notice of a claim or defense if he has notice that *all* the parties on the instrument have been discharged, but notice of the discharge of one person on the instrument (e.g., by cancellation of an indorsement) does not prevent him from becoming a holder in due course nor from recovering against all other parties to the instrument except for the cancelled indorser of whom he has notice.

Personal Defenses. *Personal defenses may be asserted against everyone except a holder in due course and a transferee or holder claiming through a holder in due course, except a transferee or holder who has himself been a party to any fraud or illegality affecting the instrument or who, as* transferee *or holder prior to the holder in due course, had notice of a defense or claim against it.*[39] All defenses which are not real are personal. The Code succinctly sums up the rights of one not a holder in due course, indicating the nature of the personal defenses assertable against him:

> Unless he has the rights of a holder in due course any person takes the instrument subject to
> (a) all valid claims to it on the part of any person; and
> (b) all defenses of any party which would be available in an action on a simple contract; and
> (c) the defenses of want or failure of consideration, nonperformance of any condition precedent, non-delivery, or delivery for a special purpose (Section 3–408); and
> (d) the defense that he or a person through whom he holds the instrument acquired it by theft, or that payment or satisfaction to such holder would be inconsistent with the terms of a restrictive indorsement. The claim of any third person to the instrument is not otherwise available as a defense to any party liable thereon unless the third person himself defends the action for such party.[40]

[37] UCC 1–201(22): "'Insolvency proceedings' includes any assignment for the benefit of creditors or other proceedings intended to liquidate or rehabilitate the estate of the person involved."

[38] See above, p. 342.

[39] See above, p. 345. But see U3C sec. 3.404 and below, p. 432, ftn. 44. Also, effective May 14, 1976, the Federal Trade Commission has announced that, pursuant to its authority to preserve consumers' claims and defenses, any holder of a consumer credit contract (which includes a holder in due course) is subject to all claims and defenses which the debtor could assert against the seller of goods or services, where the purchase price is not over $25,000. This rule does not apply to: sales for industrial or commercial uses; transactions by legal entities other than natural persons; purchase of realty, commodities, securities, farm equipment, or services of public utilities; nor consumer goods or services where the purchase price is more than $25,000.

[40] UCC 3–306.

It may be helpful to give an explanation or illustrations of the items indicated above. *Under (a) above,* there are included claims of legal title and any other rightful claims against the instrument or its proceeds. *Under (b) above,* the person who takes the instrument takes it as though it were non-negotiable and, therefore, acquires only the rights of his transferor. Defenses available against his transferor are also available against him. (P fraudulently induced M to issue his note to P, who indorsed it in blank and delivered it to H after maturity. H is not a holder in due course because he took the instrument after maturity and also without value. H cannot improve his position by claiming through P as a holder in due course, because P is not a holder in due course by reason of his lack of good faith and notice of M's defense on the instrument for fraud. Since H got what P, his transferor, had, and P is subject to M's personal defense of fraud, H takes the instrument subject to that defense also.) *Under (c) above,* want of consideration exists when an instrument is given without any expectation of consideration in return. (D draws and delivers to his son a check for $2 as a gift. D may assert want of consideration as a personal defense against his son on the check.) Failure of consideration exists when the consideration bargained for is not received. (D draws and delivers to P a check in payment of the purchase price for goods sold and to be delivered by P to D, which goods are never delivered to D. D may assert failure of consideration as a personal defense against P on the check.) An illustration of nonperformance of a condition precedent is M's issuance of his note payable to P in payment of the purchase price of property bought by M from P on approval, the note to be returned to M if M did not elect to take the property. If M did not elect to take the property, the condition precedent for M's note has not occurred, and M can assert non-purchase of the property as a personal defense against P on the note. An illustration of non-delivery is where D drew a check to the order of P, lost it, and P found it. D may assert non-delivery as a personal defense against P on the check. An illustration of delivery for a special purpose is where D drew a check to the order of P, delivered it to S, D's secretary, and asked her to hold it. Instead, S delivered the check to P. D has a personal defense of unauthorized delivery against P on the instrument. *Item (d)* indicates that, with two exceptions, a defendant party liable on an instrument cannot assert as a defense the claim of a third person to the instrument unless the third person himself defends the action for the defendant party. The first exception is that the defendant may assert as a defense that the holder claimant, or a person through whom he holds the instrument, acquired it by theft from a third person. "The exception made in the case of theft is based on the policy which refuses to aid a proved thief to recover, and refuses to aid him indirectly by permitting his transferee to recover unless the transferee is a holder in due course." (D's check to the order of P and delivered to P is indorsed by P in blank and stolen by A. D stops payment on the check, and A sues to enforce the check against D. While A is a holder, nevertheless D can assert P's defense that the check belongs to P. If A had negotiated the check to B after maturity thereby precluding B from being a holder in due course, D could also assert the defense against B. But if A had negotiated the check to H, a holder in due course, H would take the check free of such defense. If H had negotiated the check to C after maturity thereby precluding C from being a holder in due course, nevertheless C would acquire H's rights and, therefore, take the check free of the defense.) The second exception is that payment or satisfaction to such holder would be inconsistent with the terms of a restrictive indorsement.[41]

Establishing Signatures and Burden of Proof. Under the Code,[42] when a party brings an action to recover on an instrument, each signature thereon is admitted as effective, unless specifically denied in the pleadings. When the effectiveness of a signature is put in issue, the party claiming under the signature has the burden of establishing it. He is assisted in his burden by a legal presumption that a signature is presumed to be genuine or authorized, except where the action is to enforce the obligation of a purported signer who has died or become incompetent before proof is required. When signatures on an instrument have been admitted or established, production of the instrument by the holder entitles him to recover on the instrument unless the defendant establishes a defense. After it is shown that a defense exists, a person claiming the rights of a holder in due course has the burden of establishing that he or some person under whom he claims is a holder in due course.

---

[41] See above, pp. 334–35.

[42] UCC 3-307.

Chapter 24

LIABILITY OF PARTIES

SECTION I. IN GENERAL

No person is liable on a negotiable instrument unless his signature appears thereon; see the summary headnote on signature.[1] An unauthorized signature operates as the signature of the unauthorized signer in favor of any person who, in good faith, pays the instrument or takes it for value. The person whose name was unauthorizedly signed may *ratify* the unauthorized signature, or be precluded from denying the signature as his, as by *estoppel*. When an instrument is issued to a payee who is *not intended by the issuer* to have any interest in the instrument, it must be indorsed in the payee's name which may be done by *any person* in the payee's name. A party who, by his *negligence*, substantially contributes to the making of an unauthorized signature or to a material alteration of the instrument is *estopped* from asserting the alteration or lack of authority against a holder in due course or against the payor of the instrument paid properly and in good faith.

An instrument is materially altered when the alteration changes the *contract* of any party to the instrument *in any respect*. An alteration is fraudulent if made intentionally to alter unjustly a contractual obligation. *If an alteration is not both fraudulent and material*, and irrespective of by whom made, except as against a subsequent holder in due course it does *not* discharge any party to the instrument, which may be enforced according to its *original tenor* or, as to incomplete instruments, according to the authority given. *If an alteration is both fraudulent and material and is made by a holder*, except as against a subsequent holder in due course it *discharges* any party to the instrument

[1] See above, p. 309.

whose contract is thereby changed, unless that party assents or is precluded (estopped) from asserting the defense. However, a subsequent holder in due course may, in all cases, enforce the instrument according to its *original tenor*, and an incomplete instrument as unauthorizedly completed.

Signature Required

An instrument is a formal contract, and no person is liable *on the instrument* unless his signature appears thereon. "'Signed' includes any symbol executed or adopted by a party with present intention to authenticate a writing."[2] An allonge[3] with an indorsement is part of the instrument to which it is affixed. A principal is not liable *on an instrument* signed by his agent without the principal's name appearing on the instrument, irrespective of whether or not the payee knew of the principal's identity. However, a person not liable on an instrument because his signature does not appear thereon may have liability arising from circumstances outside of the instrument. For example, a person may be liable on an obligation pursuant to which the instrument was issued—e.g., the buyer is liable on his contract of purchase even though he did not sign the instrument executed by someone else to pay the purchase price. Or, a person may be liable for payment of the instrument by estoppel—e.g., D erroneously tells H that a signature on the instrument is D's, and H justifiably then purchases the instrument from P, causing D to be estopped to deny that it is his signature. Local state law governs any requirement and method of authentication of a signature on an instrument—e.g., witnessing or acknowledging a signature by mark (X).

The signature on an instrument determines the status of the signing party and, therefore, the extent of his liability. The face of the instrument alone determines the character of a signature thereon and, *unless the instrument clearly indicates that a signature is made in some other capacity, it is an indorsement.* Parol evidence is not admissible to prove such a signature in any other capacity, except as local law permits for the purpose of reformation. A signature in the lower right-hand corner of an instrument is recognized as indicating an intent to sign as the maker or drawer of the instrument.

A person's signature on an instrument may be made by another person, either with or without authority to do so. A signature may be made by an authorized representative, whether an agent or other representative (e.g., corporate officer, trustee, executor). The representative's authority so to sign may be established as in other cases of representation. *The authority need not be in writing,* and no particular form of appointment is necessary in order to establish such authority. An authorized representative who signs his own name to the instrument is personally obligated on the instrument as a party thereto, unless the instrument names the person represented *and* shows that the rep-

---

[2] UCC 1–201(39).

[3] See above, p. 330.

resentative signed in a representative capacity, in which case the representative is not obligated on the instrument; either one without the other is insufficient to relieve the representative from being personally obligated on the instrument. Thus, if Arthur Anderson is the authorized representative and Peter Pan is the principal, what would be the legal effect of the following signatures appearing on an instrument:

(1) "Arthur Anderson";
(2) "Arthur Anderson, agent";
(3) "Peter Pan";
(4) "Peter Pan
Arthur Anderson";
(5) "Peter Pan by Arthur Anderson, agent"?

The representative is personally obligated on the instrument in (1), (2), and (4), but not in (3) and (5). The principal is bound on the instrument in (3), (4), and (5). Except as otherwise established, the name of an organization preceded or followed by the name and office of an authorized individual is a signature made in a representative capacity. For example, "Peter Pan Corporation by Arthur Anderson, President," or "Arthur Anderson, President, Peter Pan Corporation."

An *unauthorized* signature is wholly inoperative as that of the person whose name is signed. "'Unauthorized' signature or indorsement means one made without actual, implied or apparent authority and includes a forgery."[4] However, *the unauthorized signature operates as the signature of the unauthorized signer in favor of any person who, in good faith, pays the instrument or takes it for value.* (P forged M's signature as maker of a note payable to the order of P, indorsed it in blank and delivered it to H, who took it for value in good faith without notice of the forgery. The purported signature of M is treated as the signature of P, who is liable as a maker to H on the instrument.) *The person whose name was unauthorizedly signed may ratify the unauthorized signature or, by reason of negligence*[5] *estoppel, be precluded from denying the signature as his.* Ratification may be expressed, or implied from the conduct of the ratifying party, as by his retention of what he received from the transaction with knowledge of the unauthorized signature. The law of Agency on ratification is applicable.[6] Ratification of the signature is retroactive in effect, authenticating the signature at the time it was made as though it had been authorized. Ratification causes the ratifying party to be bound by such signature as though authorizedly made and, since the signature on the instrument is now that of the ratifying party and not of the unauthorized signer, the latter is no longer liable *on the instrument.* However, ratification does not relieve the unauthorized signer from criminal liability, particularly if it is a forgery, nor does it relieve him of civil liability for loss caused to the ratifying

[4] UCC 1–201(43).

[5] See above, p. 312, and UCC 3–406.

[6] See below, pp. 569 ff.

party. Estoppel occurs when the person whose name was unauthorizedly signed represents to another person that the signature is genuine and the latter, in reliance thereon, subsequently purchased the instrument.

An instrument may be issued to a payee who is intended not to have any interest in the instrument. The person who intends that the payee is not to have any interest in the instrument may be: the maker or drawer; one signing for them; the agent of the maker or drawer who supplied the name of the payee to the latter who signed the instrument; or any impostor who, impersonating as the payee face to face with the maker or drawer or by the use of the mails, persuaded the maker or drawer to issue the instrument to him or his confederate in the name of the payee. Since the instrument on its face is payable to the order of a named payee, it is not payable to bearer and, therefore, must be indorsed in the payee's name so that the chain of continuity from maker or drawer through the payee as indorser is not broken. Since the payee is not intended to have any interest in the instrument, an indorsement by him is not required but may be made by *any person* in the name of such payee. Although such an indorsement and delivery of the instrument is effective to negotiate the instrument, the local state criminal law is not affected thereby, and prosecution for any crime involved may occur.

The Code imposes a duty of care upon anyone handling an instrument not to act *negligently* and thereby *substantially contribute* to a material alteration of the instrument or to the making of an unauthorized signature. The negligent party is not made liable in tort but, instead, is precluded or estopped from asserting the alteration or lack of authority against a holder in due course or against a drawee or other payor who pays the instrument in good faith and in accordance with the reasonable commercial standards of the drawee's or payor's business. The party must be *negligent,* and his negligence must *substantially contribute* to the *material alteration* of the instrument or the making of an *unauthorized signature.* Negligence is a question of fact for the jury, or the judge if there is no jury. The negligence must afford an opportunity of which advantage may be taken. Leaving spaces in the body of an instrument so that words or figures could be inserted has been held to be such negligence. Other examples are: a drawer's negligence in caring for a signing device (e.g., stamp or signature machine), or in negligently mailing a check to a wrong person with a name similar to that of the payee.

Alteration

It is very important to understand the effect of an alteration of an instrument under the Code.[7] The alteration may be material or not material. *It is material if it thereby changes the contract of any party to the instrument in any respect.* Illustrations are a change in: the number or relations of the parties; an incomplete instrument, by completing it otherwise than as authorized; the

[7] UCC 3–407.

writing as signed, by adding to it or by removing any part of it. *If an alteration is both fraudulent and material* and is made *by a holder,* except as against a subsequent holder in due course *it discharges* any party to the instrument whose contract is thereby changed, unless that party assents or is precluded from asserting the defense. If an alteration is *not* both fraudulent and material, and *irrespective of by whom made,* except as against a subsequent holder in due course it does *not* discharge any party to the instrument, which may be enforced according to its original tenor or, as to incomplete instruments, according to the authority given. *In contrast, a subsequent holder in due course may, in all cases, enforce the instrument according to its original tenor, except that if an incomplete instrument has been unauthorizedly completed he may enforce it as completed.*[8]

Several aspects of alteration should be particularly noted. *For discharge of a party to occur, the alteration must be both fraudulent and material.* By fraudulent is meant intentionally altering unjustly a contractual obligation. Generally, a change made with a benevolent motive, or of benefit *to the obligor* on the instrument, or with an honest belief that it was authorized, is not fraudulent. The material and fraudulent alteration must be made by the *holder* (personally or through his agent), and not by a meddler who is a stranger to the instrument, in order for a discharge to occur. Only the party on the instrument whose contract thereon is changed by a holder's fraudulent and material alteration can assert the defense of discharge; the defense is only his and cannot be asserted by anyone else. It should be noted in passing that a purchaser who takes a materially altered instrument with notice of such,[9] takes with notice of a defense against the instrument and cannot be a holder in due course.

SECTION II. CONTRACTUAL OBLIGATIONS OF PARTIES TO AN INSTRUMENT

The maker and acceptor are parties "primarily liable" and are absolutely required to pay the instrument, but they may assert personal or real defenses. Neither demand nor presentment for payment is necessary to make them liable. They engage that they will pay the instrument according to its tenor at the time the maker signed it or on its acceptance, or as later completed either authorizedly or unauthorizedly, and they admit as against all subsequent parties the existence of the payee and his then capacity to indorse. An acceptor is the drawee whose acceptance occurs by his signed engagement on the draft to

---

[8] Paralleling the protection given to a subsequent holder in due course, UCC 4–401(2) provides: "A bank which in good faith makes payment to a holder may charge the indicated account of its customer according to

(a) the original tenor of his altered item; or

(b) the tenor of his completed item, even though the bank knows the item has been completed unless the bank has notice that the completion was improper." For the effect of a drawer's negligence on a paying drawee bank, see above, p. 312.

[9] For notice of defense, see above, p. 342.

honor the draft as presented; the acceptor's signature without additional words is sufficient. If a *holder* obtains an acceptance, the drawer and all prior indorsers are discharged. A bank's certification of a check is an acceptance; and a holder is entitled to have any draft other than a check honored by acceptance in accordance with its terms. An acceptance of a previously altered instrument is of the instrument as altered.

Payment or acceptance of an instrument is *final* in favor of a holder in due course, a transferee with the rights of a holder in due course, or a person who has, in good faith, changed his position in reliance on the payment, with two exceptions: (1) the warranties made by the person obtaining payment or acceptance; (2) the right of a payor bank which has not made "final payment" to recover a payment improperly paid if it returns the item or sends notice of dishonor within the limited time provided by the Code. The maker and acceptor are estopped to assert forgery of the maker's or drawer's signatures, and the acceptor is estopped to assert insufficiency of the drawer's funds.

The drawer and indorser are parties "secondarily liable" on an instrument. *The drawer engages* that (1) upon dishonor of the draft and (2) any necessary notice of dishonor or protest, he will pay the amount of the draft to the holder or to any indorser who takes it up. He admits as against the drawee and all subsequent parties the existence of the payee and his then capacity to indorse. *The indorser engages* that, unless the indorsement otherwise specifies, (1) upon dishonor of the instrument and (2) any necessary notice of dishonor and protest, he will pay the instrument according to its tenor at the time of his indorsement to any holder or to any subsequent indorser who takes it up. Unless they otherwise agree, indorsers are liable to each other in the order in which they indorse. An indorser can disclaim or qualify his liability as an indorser on the instrument only by specifying the disclaimer in the indorsement itself, as by the words "without recourse," often called a "qualified indorsement." An accommodation party is one who signs the instrument in any capacity for the purpose of lending his name as a surety to another party to it. He is liable only if value has been given before the instrument is due by the person who took the instrument. He is not liable to the party accommodated. When words of guaranty accompany an indorsement, presentment, notice of dishonor, and protest are not necessary to make the guarantor liable on the instrument. A "guaranty of payment" is different from a "guaranty of collection."

An instrument is a contract and the parties thereto have certain contractual obligations thereon and make various warranties on its presentment for payment or acceptance and on its transfer. This Section will consider their contractual obligations, and Section III will consider their warranties. First parties primarily liable will be considered, then parties secondarily liable, followed by the accommodation party and lastly by the guarantor.

Parties Primarily Liable

In General. Parties on a negotiable instrument who, by the terms thereof, are absolutely required to pay it are parties primarily liable; all other parties on the instrument are secondarily liable. "Absolutely" liable means "unconditionally" liable, as distinguished from the conditional liability of parties secondarily liable. The absolute liability of parties primarily liable does not mean that real and personal defenses are unavailable to them; such defenses may be asserted by them. *The only parties who are primarily liable are a maker of a note and an acceptor of a draft or a check.*

Neither demand nor presentment for payment is necessary in order to charge a party primarily liable on the instrument. The liability of the maker is fixed and absolute the moment the instrument is issued and that of the acceptor is fixed and absolute the moment he accepts the instrument. If the party primarily liable tenders the full amount to a holder when or after it is due and such tender is improperly refused, the familiar effect of an improper refusal of a valid tender of payment prevails: the debt is not discharged; costs of collection on the instrument are borne by the party wrongfully refusing the tender; interest stops running on the instrument from that date; and the lien on the collateral security for payment of the instrument is discharged. Under the Code, "Where the maker or acceptor of an instrument payable otherwise than on demand is able and ready to pay at every place of payment specified in the instrument when it is due, it is equivalent to tender."[10] It should be observed that, for this rule to apply, the instrument must be payable at a specified place. If the instrument is payable at more than one specified place, the maker or acceptor must be able and ready to pay the instrument at each of such specified places.

Maker. As a party primarily liable on the note made by him, *the maker engages that he will pay the note according to its tenor at the time he signed it, or as later completed either authorizedly[11] or unauthorizedly,[12] and he admits as against all subsequent parties the existence of the payee and his then capacity to indorse the note.* The maker, therefore, is estopped to assert against a subsequent party that the purported signature of the payee is not that of the payee because he does not exist, and that the payee was an infant who avoided his indorsement or a foreign corporation which could not contract by its indorsement because it did not comply with state statutes for the regulation of foreign corporations doing business in that state. However, if the issuance of the note is void (not voidable) for illegality, the real defense of illegality may be asserted by the maker against all subsequent parties, including a holder in due course.

---

[10] UCC 3–604(3).

[11] For incomplete instruments, see above, pp. 322–23.

[12] See alteration, above, pp. 356–57.

Acceptor. *No person is liable on an instrument until his signature appears thereon.*[13] A check or other draft does not of itself operate as an assignment of any funds in the hands of the drawee available for its payment, and the drawee is not liable on the instrument until he accepts it. *Acceptance is the drawee's signed engagement to honor the draft as presented.* It *must* be written on the draft, and may consist of his signature alone.[14] Writing "Accepted" on the instrument is not necessary, but if written it is ineffective until accompanied by the drawee's signature. Where the draft is payable at a fixed period after sight (e.g., payable "30 days after sight"), if the acceptor fails to date his acceptance the holder may complete it by supplying a date in good faith. The reason for this is that such an undated acceptance is incomplete until dated. The acceptance may be anywhere on the draft, either front or back, although it is usually written vertically across the face of the instrument. It is not an acceptance if accompanied by words refusing to honor the draft as presented. A draft may be accepted although it has not been signed by the drawer, or is otherwise incomplete, or is overdue, or has been dishonored. An acceptance becomes operative when completed by delivery or notification to the holder or pursuant to his instructions. This is an exception to the rule that an obligation on the instrument is effective only on delivery. Usually the instrument is forwarded to the drawee for his acceptance; sometimes, instead, the holder relies on a separate written obligation (e.g., letter of credit), which cannot be an acceptance because the drawee's signature is on it and not on the instrument itself.

Certification of a check is acceptance. Where a *holder* procures certification, the drawer and all prior indorsers are discharged. It should be noted carefully that if, instead of the holder, the *drawer* procures the certification, the drawer is not discharged from liability on the instrument. Also, if an indorsement is placed on the instrument after certification, the indorsement is effective as such. Unless otherwise agreed, a bank has no obligation on the check to certify it; it is a demand instrument calling for payment rather than acceptance, and also, until it is accepted, the drawee has no obligation thereon. However, the bank may be liable for breach of a contract separate from the check, made with a person (e.g., the drawer, holder, or any other person) that the bank would certify the check.

A holder is entitled to have the draft honored by being accepted in accordance with the terms of the draft. While a draft not honored as presented is dishonored, nevertheless, if the drawee's proffered acceptance in any manner varies the terms of the draft, the holder has an election. He may treat the draft as dishonored, in which case the drawee is entitled to have his acceptance cancelled. Or, he may assent to the proffered acceptance varying the terms of the draft, in which case each drawer and indorser who does not *affirmatively* assent is discharged from liability on the draft. There is no implied assent by

[13] UCC 3–401(1).

[14] UCC 3–410(3).

the silence of such a drawer and indorser; their assent must be made expressly in order to preclude such discharge. Illustrations of a proffered acceptance which varies the terms of the draft are when the proffered acceptance: is to pay part only of the amount for which the draft is drawn; qualifies the time as expressed in the draft in which it is to be paid after acceptance; is by some one or more of the drawees but not all of them; is payable on the fulfillment of a condition not expressed in the draft. The terms of the draft are not varied by an acceptance to pay at any particular bank or place in the United States, but they are varied if the acceptance states that the draft is to be paid *only* at such bank or place.

As a party primarily liable on the instrument (draft or check) accepted by him, *the acceptor engages that he will pay the instrument according to its tenor at the time of his acceptance, or as later completed either authorizedly*[15] *or unauthorizedly,*[16] *and he admits as against all subsequent parties the existence of the payee and his then capacity to indorse the instrument.* If the instrument was altered *prior* to acceptance, the acceptance applies to the instrument as altered and not to its original tenor.[17] The effect of alteration of the instrument *after* an acceptance is governed by the rules on alteration.[18] The acceptor, therefore, is estopped to assert against a subsequent party that the purported signature of the payee is not that of the payee because he does not exist, and that the payee was an infant who avoided his indorsement or a foreign corporation which could not contract by its indorsement because it did not comply with state statutes for the regulation of foreign corporations doing business in that state. However, if the issuance of the instrument is void (not voidable) for illegality, the real defense of illegality may be asserted by the acceptor against all subsequent parties, including a holder in due course.

Finality of Payment or Acceptance. *Payment or acceptance of an instrument is final in favor of a holder in due course, a transferee with the rights of a holder in due course, or a person who has, in good faith, changed his position in reliance on the payment, with two exceptions.* First, the rule is subject to the warranties made by a person who obtains payment or acceptance, discussed later.[19] Second, the rule is subject to the right of a payor bank, which has not made final payment,[20] to recover a payment improperly paid if it returns the item or sends notice of dishonor within the limited time provided in UCC 4–301. Thus, under this rule of finality of payment or acceptance, if the drawee accepts or pays an instrument on which the drawer's signature was forged, the acceptor is bound by his acceptance and the drawee cannot recover the money paid. A paying maker and a paying or accepting drawee are respon-

[15] See above, p. 323.

[16] See above, pp. 356–57.

[17] For warranty of no material alteration of an instrument prior to acceptance, made by the person obtaining acceptance, see below, pp. 371–72.

[18] See above, pp. 356 ff.

[19] See below, pp. 370 ff.

[20] See UCC 4–213.

sible; they are in a better position to determine the genuineness of the maker's or drawer's signature than anyone else, and they should bear the loss for such payment or acceptance. In the case of a paying maker, he certainly ought to recognize his own signature, and in the case of a paying or accepting drawee, he has the drawer's signature available to him for examination. Similarly, if an instrument is accepted or paid by a drawee when the funds of the drawer are insufficient, the acceptor is liable on his acceptance and is *estopped* to assert insufficiency of the drawer's funds as a defense to payment, nor can the drawee recover the money paid. By accepting the instrument the acceptor, and by paying on the instrument the drawee, admit that the drawer's funds are sufficient to permit payment of the instrument, and they are estopped from later denying such sufficiency. They are responsible for knowing the state of the drawer's account with them before the instrument is accepted or before the money is paid. It should be noted carefully that finality of payment and acceptance applies only to a holder in due course; a transferee, under the shelter of a holder in due course, who has the rights of a holder in due course; and a person who has, in good faith, changed his position in reliance on the payment. A holder who is neither a holder in due course nor under the shelter of a holder in due course and *who has not given value*, loses nothing by being denied any right to enforce the acceptance or by being compelled to return the money paid. He should not profit at the expense of the drawee.

Conversion of the Instrument. An instrument is property belonging to the holder and, like other chattels, is subject to conversion by a wrongdoer. The tort of conversion has been discussed at length previously,[21] but briefly it involves interference with possession of a chattel inconsistent with another person's right to its immediate possession and inconsistent with his right to control and dominion over the chattel. The Code lists, but does not limit conversion to,[22] three ways by which an instrument may be converted:

(a) a drawee to whom it is delivered for acceptance refuses to return it on demand; or
(b) any person to whom it is delivered for payment refuses on demand either to pay or to return it; or
(c) it is paid on a forged indorsement.[23]

Several aspects should be noted particularly. Since an instrument is voluntarily delivered for payment or acceptance, its detention by the recipient is not wrongful until demand has been made, either expressly or impliedly, for its return. By "refuses" is meant an *intentional* failure to return the instrument, and does not include a *negligent* failure to do so although the refusing party may be liable for the tort of negligence. Also, in an action for conversion under any of the above three ways *against the drawee*, the drawee's liability *is* the face amount of the instrument; as *against anyone else*, the measure of liability

[21] See above, p. 166, ftn. 18.

[22] See UCC 1–103.

[23] UCC 3–419(1).

is *presumed* to be the face amount of the instrument.[24] The reason for the presumption as against anyone other than the drawee is that evidence may show that the obligation on the instrument is of no value or worth less than the face amount, as by a condition of insolvency. As an exception to the conversion rule, a representative, including a depositary[25] or collecting[26] bank, who has in good faith and in accordance with the reasonable commercial standards applicable to the business of such representative dealt with an instrument or its proceeds on behalf of one who was not the true owner, is not liable in conversion or otherwise to the true owner beyond the amount of any proceeds remaining in his hands.[27] Refusal by the representative to turn over the proceeds still in his possession to the true owner is a conversion of such proceeds. If the representative still has possession of the instrument, he can be compelled to turn it over to the true owner. An intermediary[28] bank, or a payor bank which is not a depositary bank, is not liable in conversion *solely* by reason of the fact that proceeds of an item indorsed restrictively are not paid or applied consistently with the restrictive indorsement of an indorser other than its immediate transferor.[29]

Parties Secondarily Liable

The drawer and indorsers are secondarily liable on an instrument and, therefore, are called "secondary parties."[30] They are liable on a condition and have recourse against parties primarily liable thereon for whatever loss they have sustained on the instrument. Each will be considered briefly.

Drawer. As a party secondarily liable on the instrument, *the drawer engages that, upon dishonor of the draft and any necessary notice of dishonor or protest, he will pay the amount of the draft to the holder or to any indorser who takes it up.*[31] (D draws a check on E payable to P, who negotiates it to H. On H's presentment of the check to E for payment it is dishonored. D is liable to H as holder of the instrument. If H had recovered from P on his indorsement, D would be liable to P as an indorser.) The drawer may disclaim this liability by drawing the instrument without recourse. *By drawing an instrument, the drawer admits as against all subsequent parties, including the drawee, the existence of the payee and his then capacity to indorse.* It should be noted very carefully that the drawer's liability on the instrument is condi-

[24] UCC 3–419(2).

[25] UCC 4–105(a): "'Depositary bank' means the first bank to which an item is transferred for collection even though it is also the payor bank."

[26] UCC 4–105(d): "'Collecting bank' means any bank handling the item for collection except the payor bank."

[27] UCC 3–419(3).

[28] UCC 4–105(c): "'Intermediary bank' means any bank to which an item is transferred in course of collection except the depositary or payor bank."

[29] See UCC 3–205, 3–206, and above, pp. 334–35.

[30] UCC 3–102(1)(d).

[31] UCC 3–413(2).

tional upon dishonor of the instrument and any necessary notice of dishonor or protest. *Failure* to give necessary notice of dishonor or protest discharges the drawer *from liability on the instrument.* However, as discussed later,[32] unexcused *delay* in giving such notice of dishonor discharges the drawer *only to the extent of loss sustained by him through the drawee's supervening insolvency during the delay.* The drawer, therefore, is estopped to assert against a subsequent party that the purported signature of the payee is not that of the payee because he does not exist, and that the payee was an infant who avoided his indorsement or a foreign corporation which could not contract by its indorsement because it did not comply with state statutes for the regulation of foreign corporations doing business in that state. However, if the drawing of the instrument is void (not voidable) for illegality, the real defense of illegality may be asserted by the drawer against all subsequent parties, including a holder in due course.

Indorser. Every indorser is a party secondarily liable on the instrument and engages that, unless the indorsement otherwise specifies, *upon dishonor of the instrument and any necessary notice of dishonor and protest he will pay the instrument according to its tenor at the time of his indorsement to the holder or to any subsequent indorser who takes it up,* even though the indorser who takes it up was not obligated to do so. (M issues a note payable to P, who indorses and delivers it to A, who negotiates it to H. The note is dishonored. Since P and A are indorsers and H is the holder, H can recover from A or P, and if H recovers from A then A in turn can recover from P.) It should be noted very carefully that, similar to acceptance of a draft, the indorser conditionally engages to pay the instrument *according to its tenor at the time of his indorsement.* If the instrument was altered *prior* to an indorsement, that indorsement applies to the instrument as altered and not to its original tenor. The effect of alteration of the instrument *after* an indorsement is governed by the rules on alteration, previously discussed.[33] Unless they otherwise agree, indorsers are liable to each other in the order in which they indorse.

An indorser can disclaim, or qualify, his contractual liability as an indorser on the instrument only by *specifying the disclaimer in the indorsement itself;* the disclaimer cannot be proved by parol evidence. Such an indorsement often is called a "qualified indorsement" because it qualifies the indorser's liability on the instrument. The liability of an unqualified indorser is very different from that of an assignor who merely assigns what he has and is not liable for the value thereof. An indorsement *assigning* the title to the instrument limits the indorser's liability and does not preclude either the further negotiation of the instrument or subsequent holders from being holders in due course. "Without recourse" or words of similar import clearly indicate that the indorser merely assigns the title to the instrument and that no recourse is to be made against the indorser for non-payment of the instrument. Prior to the Code there was

---

[32] See below, p. 376.

[33] See above, pp. 356–57.

conflict but, by the majority view, words of assignment in an indorsement did not qualify the indorsement and were mere surplusage; the intent to qualify an indorser's liability had not been sufficiently expressed. An example is an indorsement, "I hereby assign this instrument." The Code does not seem to have resolved this controversy. Qualified indorsements usually are made by persons acting in a representative capacity, such as attorneys, trustees, and executors, so as to exclude personal liability.

Accommodation Party

An accommodation party is one who signs the instrument in any capacity for the purpose of lending his name to another party to it. He may be an accommodation maker, acceptor, drawer, or indorser. (H will extend credit to P to purchase goods only if M signs a note to pay the price. M issues a note to the order of P, who negotiates it to H. M is an accommodation maker for P. If M had wanted to purchase the goods from H but needed P's signature on the note as security, M's issuance of the note to the order of P, who negotiated it to H, causes P to be an accommodation indorser for M.) An accommodation party is a surety for the party accommodated, and his signature is placed on the instrument solely for the purpose of giving additional security to the instrument by subjecting the accommodation party to liability thereon in the event that the instrument should be dishonored. It is immaterial whether or not the accommodating party has received value therefor, i.e., whether he is a paid or a gratuitous surety. It is important, however, that *value be given before the instrument is due by the person who took the instrument,* irrespective of whether he gave value before or after the accommodation party signed the instrument. Only when this occurs is the accommodation party liable on the instrument in the capacity that he signed, even though the taker knew of the accommodation. Except as against a holder in due course without notice of the accommodation, parol evidence that a party signed for accommodation is admissible to give the accommodation party the benefit of discharges dependent on his character as such. It should be noted that an indorsement which shows that it is not in the chain of title is notice of its accommodation character. (M issues his note payable to P to pay for goods sold by P to M. The note made and delivered to P has A's blank indorsement on the back. P indorses the note in blank and delivers it to H. P and H are on notice by the first indorsement of A that A is an accommodation indorser for M.)

An accommodation party is not liable to the party accommodated, and if he pays the instrument he has a right of recourse on the instrument against such party. (M is an accommodation maker for P on a note held by H. The note is dishonored and H recovers on it against P. P cannot recover on the note against M, who accommodated P. If H had recovered from M instead of P on the note, M has a right of recourse on the note against P.)[34]

[34] M is a surety for P and his right of recourse is based on the rights of reimbursement and subrogation under the law of Suretyship, see below, pp. 501 ff, 504 ff.

Guarantor

The addition of words of guaranty to a signature on an instrument has a meaning and effect varying as such words. If words of guaranty accompany an indorsement, they do not affect its character as an indorsement.[35] When words of guaranty are used, presentment, notice of dishonor and protest are not necessary to charge the user; he has waived them as a condition to liability on the instrument. Inasmuch as a sole maker or sole acceptor on an instrument is primarily and absolutely liable on the instrument, words of guaranty added to the signature of either do not affect his liability thereon. However, words of guaranty added to the signature of one of two or more makers or acceptors create a presumption that the signature is for the accommodation of others. When words of guaranty accompanying a signature do not otherwise specify (e.g., "Guaranteed"), they guarantee payment of the instrument. A guaranty of payment (e.g., "payment guaranteed" or equivalent words) added to a signature means that the signer engages that if the instrument is not paid when due he will pay it according to its tenor without resort by the holder to any other party. But a guaranty of collection (e.g., "collection guaranteed" or equivalent words) added to a signature means that the signer engages that, if the instrument is not paid when due, he will pay it according to its tenor only: (1) after the holder has reduced his claim against the maker or acceptor to judgment and execution has been returned unsatisfied; or (2) after the maker or acceptor has become insolvent or it is otherwise apparent that it is useless to proceed against him. Any guaranty written on the instrument is enforceable notwithstanding any statute of frauds.

SECTION III. WARRANTIES ON PRESENTMENT AND TRANSFER OF AN INSTRUMENT

The Code imposes certain warranties on transfer, and on obtaining payment or acceptance, of a negotiable instrument which may be disclaimed by agreement between the *immediate* parties. An indorsement "Without recourse" disclaims only an indorser's warranty that no defense of any party is good against him.

***Five warranties on transfer of a negotiable instrument* are made at the time of such transfer by any person who *transfers* an instrument and *receives consideration.* They are made by an *indorser* to his *immediate* transferee and to any subsequent *holder* who takes the instrument in good faith, but if the transfer is *without indorsement* they are made by the transferor only to his *immediate* transferee. (1) Warranty of title or authority. (2) Warranty of signatures as genuine or authorized. (3) Warranty against material alteration. (4) Warranty of no good defense by any party against him. (5) Warranty of no *knowledge* of insolvency proceedings against the maker, acceptor, or the drawer of an unaccepted instrument.**

---

[35] UCC 3–202(4).

Three warranties on obtaining payment or acceptance **are made at the time of such payment or acceptance by the person who obtains payment or acceptance to the person who in good faith so paid or accepted. If any warranty is breached the payment or acceptance is not final and the payment may be recovered or the acceptance rescinded. (1) Warranty of title or authority. (2) Warranty of no knowledge of unauthorized signature of maker or drawer. This warranty does not apply to a holder in due course, except that if he subsequently learns of such an unauthorized signature and, in bad faith, presents the instrument and obtains payment or acceptance the warranty then applies to him. (3) Warranty of no material alteration. This warranty does not apply to a holder in due course, except that if he subsequently learns of a material alteration and, in bad faith, presents the instrument and obtains payment or acceptance the warranty then applies to him.**

The Code provides for warranties in connection with commercial paper and distinguishes warranties on transfer of an instrument from warranties on presentment resulting in payment or acceptance of an instrument. These warranties will be considered in that order after a brief examination of principles applicable to all of these warranties.

In General

Initially it should be observed that these warranties are important to all parties who have dealt with the instrument. The warranties are concerned with: title to the instrument; the genuineness of signatures and authority to sign for another; material alteration; and defenses to liability on the instrument. Some of these warranties are applicable to parties who have transferred the instrument merely by delivery without their signature appearing thereon, e.g., the transfer of a bearer instrument. Unless disclaimer of warranty is prohibited by law, warranties may be disclaimed by the parties to a transaction. Under the law on Commercial Paper, the warranties imposed by the Code may be disclaimed by the *immediate parties as between themselves*, e.g., the payee *orally* disclaiming warranties to the maker on taking the maker's note from him; but a disclaimer of warranties *by an indorser* is ineffective unless the words of disclaimer *specifically* accompany, or appear in the form of, his indorsement on the instrument. For example, the payee's indorsement on a note "Without recourse. (signed) John Jones" is effective to disclaim certain warranties which the payee would otherwise be held to as an indorser of the instrument. When there is reliance in good faith on a warranty, various remedies become available for breach of warranty, e.g., rescission of the transaction and an action for damages. Lastly, the liability on these warranties of a selling agent or broker (but not an agent for collection), representing another, who transfers an instrument or obtains payment or acceptance of it depends upon whether or not he has disclosed his status. If he has, he warrants only his good faith and authority; if he has not, the warranties apply to him.

Warranties on Transfer

In General. The warranties on transfer are *in addition* to contractual liability on the instrument, previously discussed.[36] It may be that a holder may prefer to rescind or bring action immediately for breach of contract rather than wait until the instrument becomes due and then assert his rights against parties secondarily liable on the instrument. Or, if the holder is unable to enforce such secondary liability, as by his having failed to comply with the requisites of presentment, notice of dishonor or protest, or because of a qualified indorsement or lack of an indorsement, the remedies for breach of warranty are his only source of relief.

Unless otherwise properly disclaimed, there are five warranties (discussed below) given by *any* person who *transfers* an instrument and *receives consideration.* It should be noted carefully that the transferor's warranty must be supported by consideration.[37] Also, the transfer may be by negotiation or by assignment. *If the transfer is by indorsement,* the transferor makes these warranties to his *immediate transferee* and to any subsequent *holder* who takes the instrument *in good faith. If the transfer is without indorsement,* the transferor makes these warranties *only to his immediate transferee.* (M makes a note payable to P and delivers it to P. P indorses it in blank and delivers it to A, who indorses it in blank and delivers it to B, who delivers it without indorsement to C, who delivers it without indorsement to H, who takes it in good faith. P's warranties are to A, B, C, and H. A's warranties are to B, C, and H. B's warranties are only to C, and C's warranties are only to H.)

Warranty of Title or Authority. *The transferor of an instrument for consideration received warrants that (1) he has good title to the instrument or is authorized to obtain payment or acceptance on behalf of one who has a good title, and (2) the transfer is otherwise rightful.* A transferee expects to acquire a good title to the instrument from his transferor, safe against the claim of any true owner and, when he presents the instrument for payment or is paid, safe against any defense that he lacks good title and will not be paid or a claim that he must refund the money. The transfer of an instrument with a forged required indorsement in the chain of title precludes any subsequent transferee from acquiring title to the instrument and, therefore, there is a breach of warranty of title by the transferor. It should be noted that the transferor of a bearer instrument found or stolen by him is the bearer but he does not have title, and while his transfer of the instrument to a holder in due course is a breach of warranty of title, nevertheless the holder in due course does acquire title. The holder in due course may wish to rescind the transfer rather than risk the inconvenience of having to sue to enforce the instrument, or defending against a claim to the instrument, and establishing that he is a holder in due course in order to overcome the claim or defense.

---

[36] See above, pp. 359–67.

[37] For consideration, see above, pp. 338–39.

Warranty of Signatures as Genuine or Authorized. *The transferor of an instrument for consideration received warrants that all signatures are genuine or authorized.* "Genuine" means free of forgery or counterfeiting.[38] An "unauthorized" signature means one made without actual, implied, or apparent authority, and includes a forgery.[39] The transfer of an instrument with a forged required signature in the chain of title is a breach of warranty of genuine signature and also a breach of warranty of title. A transferee expects to acquire not only title to the instrument but also freedom from concern that he may not be able to hold a purported party on the instrument secondarily liable, and that he may become liable for breach of warranty of genuine signature if he transfers the instrument to his transferee.

Warranty against Material Alteration. *The transferor of an instrument for consideration received warrants that the instrument has not been materially altered.* A transferee expects to acquire an instrument without a material alteration thereon, which would either limit the liability of previous parties on the instrument who became such prior to such alteration or discharge them entirely.

Warranty of No Good Defense. *The transferor of an instrument for consideration received warrants that no defense of any party is good against him.* A transferee expects to acquire an instrument capable of being enforced. While this warranty may be breached and, nevertheless, the transferee become a holder in due course so that personal defenses are cut off against him as a holder in due course, he may not wish to take on a lawsuit in order to enforce the instrument and have to establish his status as a holder in due course. It should be noted very carefully that a transfer "without recourse" changes this warranty of the transferor to be a warranty that he has *no knowledge* of any defense of any party good against him. As previously discussed,[40] the words "without recourse" in an indorsement also effectively disclaim the *contractual* obligation of that indorser on the instrument.

Warranty of No Knowledge of Insolvency Proceedings. *The transferor of an instrument for consideration received warrants that he has no knowledge of any insolvency proceeding instituted with respect to the maker, acceptor, or the drawer of an unaccepted instrument.* The transferor of an instrument does not warrant the credit risk or solvency of any party on the instrument; this is a matter for the buyer of the instrument to determine for himself. However, the Code imposes a duty upon a transferor of an instrument who knows that such insolvency proceedings have been instituted to disclose this information to his transferee prior to such transfer. The transferor's concealment of this very important fact is a fraud on the transferee buyer. A transferee of an instrument expects to acquire an instrument which will be paid when due. The institution of insolvency proceedings against one of the parties expected to pay

[38] UCC 1–201(18).

[39] UCC 1–201(43).

[40] See above, p. 364.

the instrument puts such payment in jeopardy; also, should the transferee in turn transfer the instrument, there is a greater risk that he may be held to his secondary liability on the instrument if dishonored.

Warranties on Obtaining Payment or Acceptance

We have already observed[41] that, with two exceptions, *payment or acceptance of an instrument is final in favor of a holder in due course* (or a transferee with rights of a holder in due course), *or a person who has in good faith changed his position in reliance on the payment.* The two exceptions are concerned with recovery of bank payments under Article 4 of the Code on Bank Deposits and Collections[42] and with liability for breach of *warranty on presentment* for payment or acceptance, now about to be discussed.

When an instrument is presented for payment or acceptance, the person who obtains payment or acceptance, and any prior transferor, makes three warranties. If any of these warranties is breached, the payment or acceptance is not final and the payment may be recovered or the acceptance rescinded. These warranties are: warranty of title or authority to obtain payment or acceptance; warranty of no knowledge of unauthorized signature of maker or drawer; warranty of no material alteration. It is expected that the person presenting an instrument for payment or acceptance does so in good faith that he is the owner of the instrument, that he has no knowledge that the signature of the maker or drawer is unauthorized, and that the instrument has not been materially altered. The holder in due course so acts and, because of his superior status, these warranties are applicable to him to a very limited extent. These warranties are imposed upon any person who obtained payment or acceptance, and any prior transferor, for the benefit of the person who *in good faith* paid or accepted. If payment or acceptance was not made in good faith, they were made without reliance on the presentment as being in good faith and, therefore, there is no breach of these warranties.

Warranty of Title or Authority. *Only the person with good title to the instrument, or his authorized representative, has the right to obtain payment or acceptance of the instrument.* While the drawee can verify the drawer's signature by comparing the drawer's signature on the instrument with that in his records, the drawee usually has no opportunity to verify the *indorsements* on the instrument. It is for this reason that the party who pays or accepts an instrument does not thereby admit the genuineness of the indorsements thereon and, if they are not genuine, can recover the money paid to the person presenting the instrument or rescind his acceptance. The party who presented the instrument did not have good title. *In effect, therefore, this warranty by the presenting party includes the genuineness of the required indorsements.* (D drew a check on E bank payable to the order of

[41] See above, pp. 361–62.

[42] See UCC 4–301 and 4–213.

P. A stole the check from P, forged P's blank indorsement and delivered it for value to H who took the check in good faith. H presented the check to E, who paid it in good faith. H has breached his warranty of title, E may recover the money from H, who does not have good title to the instrument, and D is still liable to P, the owner of the check even though P does not have possession of the check. If, before E had demanded repayment or attempted to rescind his acceptance, H had meanwhile, in good faith, changed his position in reliance on the payment, under the rule of finality of payment E could not recover the money from H.)

Warranty of No Knowledge of Unauthorized Signature of Maker or Drawer. Any person who obtains payment or acceptance, and any prior transferor, warrants to a person who in good faith pays or accepts that he has *no knowledge that the signature of the maker or drawer is unauthorized,* with certain limitations as to a holder in due course. It should be noted that in the warranty of title or authority the warranty included that *all required indorsements were genuine,* while this warranty is that the presenting party has *no knowledge* that the signature of the maker or drawer is unauthorized and not genuine.

A holder in due course had no notice of any defense to the instrument *at the time he took the instrument as a holder,* but he may learn of the unauthorized signature of the maker or drawer of the instrument *thereafter and before presenting the instrument for payment or acceptance.* If this should occur, since he has not acted in good faith the warranty should apply to him and the maker recover the money or the acceptor rescind his acceptance. However, if this did not occur, then the warranty should not apply to him and recovery be denied the maker or rescission be denied the acceptor. The reason for this result is that the maker ought to recognize his own signature, and the drawee is in a superior position to verify the drawer's signature with a copy in his possession. If payment or acceptance is made mistakenly by them, as between them and the holder in due course who acted *in good faith,* they must bear the loss.[43]

Warranty of No Material Alteration. Any person who obtains payment or acceptance, and any prior transferor, warrants to a person who in good faith pays or accepts that *the instrument has not been materially altered,* with certain limitations as to a holder in due course. The paying or accepting party is not obliged to be contractually liable for other than the tenor of the instrument as originally drawn and can recover money paid or rescind an acceptance for more than that amount on a materially altered instrument, except as to a holder in due course of an instrument materially altered *by unauthorized completion.*[44]

A holder in due course had no notice of any defense to the instrument *at the time he took the instrument as a holder,* but he may learn of the material

[43] UCC 3–417(1)(b).

[44] See above, p. 357.

alteration *thereafter and before presenting the instrument for payment.* If this should occur, since he has not acted in good faith the warranty should apply to him with respect to the maker or drawer of the altered note or draft, and to the acceptor of the altered draft, and the paying party recover the money and the acceptor rescind his acceptance. However, if this did not occur, then the warranty should not apply to him and recovery be denied to the paying party, and rescission be denied to the acceptor even though the acceptance provided "payable as originally drawn" or equivalent terms. If legal effect were given to such words in the acceptance, they would defeat the entire purpose of making an acceptance, which is to obtain a definite obligation of the drawee to honor a definite instrument.

Chapter 25

PRESENTMENT, NOTICE OF DISHONOR, AND PROTEST

Presentment for acceptance or payment is not necessary to fix the liability of primary parties but, unless excused or waived, *it is necessary for secondary parties* because their obligation is that (1) upon dishonor and (2) any necessary notice of dishonor and protest, they will pay the instrument to the holder or to any subsequent indorsers who take it up. The *demand* for payment or acceptance is a presentment and is made by, or on behalf of, the holder.

Presentment for acceptance is necessary to charge the drawer and indorsers of a *draft* when it so provides, or it is payable elsewhere than at the drawee's residence or place of business, or its date of payment depends upon such presentment. *Presentment for payment is necessary to charge* any indorser, any drawer, and the acceptor of a draft and the maker of a note *payable at a bank.* The *time for presentment for acceptance* depends upon whether the instrument is payable at, or a fixed period after, a stated date; it is payable at sight; or otherwise. The *time for presentment for payment* depends upon whether the instrument is payable at a stated date, it is an accelerated instrument, or otherwise. An uncertified check drawn and payable within the U.S. and which is not a draft drawn by a bank must be presented: 30 days after date or issue, whichever is later, with respect to the drawer's liability; and seven days after his indorsement, with respect to an indorser's liability. If the instrument is *presented for acceptance,* acceptance may be deferred until the close of the next business day. If *presented for payment,* payment must be made no later than the close of business on that day.

Unjustified refusal of a demand for acceptance or payment, or acceptance or payment is not made when presentment is excused, *dishonors* the instrument. *Notice of dishonor* is necessary to charge any indorser, any drawer, and the

acceptor of a draft and the maker of a note *payable at a bank.* Notice is given by or on behalf of the holder or by an indorser who has himself received notice, although it may be given by any party who may be compelled to pay the instrument. Notice operates for the benefit of all parties who have rights on the instrument against the party notified. Notice by a person other than a bank must be given before midnight of the third business day after dishonor or receipt of notice of dishonor. A bank must give notice before its midnight deadline.

***Protest* of dishonor is necessary only for a draft which, on its face, appears to be drawn or payable outside of the U.S., called a "foreign" or "international" draft. Protest is necessary to charge the drawer and indorsers of the draft, and is in addition to presentment, dishonor, and notice of dishonor. It is a certificate of dishonor issued by a proper official.**

***Presentment, notice of dishonor, and protest* may be *waived* by the party to be charged. If the waiver is embodied in the instrument, it is binding on all parties; if written above the signature of an indorser, it binds him only. Presentment, notice of dishonor and protest are *entirely excused* if: waived, the party to be charged has no reason to expect or right to require that the instrument be accepted or paid, or they cannot be made with reasonable diligence; additionally, only for presentment, the maker, acceptor or drawee of the instrument is dead or in insolvency proceedings, or acceptance or payment is refused for other than lack of proper presentment. *Delay* is excused under certain conditions. *Failure* to make necessary presentment, notice of dishonor, and protest causes the discharge of: the indorsers fully; and the drawer, acceptor of a draft and maker of a note payable at a bank, only to the extent that he has been deprived of funds under certain conditions.**

SECTION I. REQUIREMENTS AND LEGAL EFFECT

Purpose

Presentment is *a demand for acceptance or payment* made upon the maker, acceptor, drawee or other payor by, or on behalf of, the holder. Presentment is *not* necessary in order to fix the liability of the *maker or acceptor as a party primarily liable* on the instrument; his absolute contractual obligation is to pay the instrument according to its tenor.[1] However, the contractual obligation of the *drawer and indorser as secondary parties* on an instrument is that *upon dishonor and any necessary notice of dishonor and protest* he will pay the instrument to the holder or to any subsequent indorser who takes it up. It becomes important, therefore, whether presentment for acceptance or pay-

[1] UCC 3–122(2) makes an exception and *requires* demand by presentment of a *demand or time certificate of deposit* on or after the date of maturity in order for a cause of action to accrue against the obligor thereon at the time of such demand.

ment, notice of dishonor, and protest are necessary in order to charge secondary parties, i.e., hold them liable on the instrument. First we will consider when presentment for acceptance and payment, notice of dishonor, and protest are necessary; then, in order, the elements of presentment for acceptance and payment, notice of dishonor, protest, evidence of dishonor, and notice of dishonor, and finally when presentment, notice of dishonor, and protest are waived or excused.

When Necessary

Presentment, notice of dishonor, and protest are necessary in certain instances and not in others. When they are not necessary, the secondary parties remain liable on the instrument for the statute of limitations period, just as do primary parties. Presentment, notice of dishonor, and protest are not necessary in order to charge an indorser who has indorsed an instrument after maturity.

Presentment for Acceptance or Payment. ***Presentment for Acceptance.*** Unless excused,[2] presentment for acceptance is *necessary* in order to charge the drawer and indorsers of a *draft* where the draft: (1) so provides; or (2) is payable elsewhere than at the residence or place of business of the drawee; or (3) its date of payment depends upon such presentment, e.g., a draft payable after sight. A holder *may*, at his option, present for acceptance *any other* draft payable at a stated date.

Presentment for Payment. Unless excused,[3] presentment for payment is *necessary* in order to charge: (1) any indorser; (2) any drawer; (3) the acceptor of a draft payable *at a bank;* (4) the maker of a note payable *at a bank.* Presentment for payment is *not necessary* in order to charge an acceptor of a draft or maker of a note payable other than at a bank.

Failure to Present when Necessary. Where, without excuse, any necessary presentment is delayed beyond the time when it is due, the following parties are discharged fully, with one limitation: (1) any indorsers; (2) any drawer; (3) the acceptor of a draft payable at a bank; (4) the maker of a note payable at a bank. The limitation applies to the last three parties, each of whom is discharged *only to the extent that he has been deprived of funds if:* (1) he maintained with the drawee or payor bank sufficient funds to cover payment of the instrument; (2) the drawee or payor bank became insolvent during the delay causing the party to be deprived of such funds; *and* (3) the party makes a written assignment to the holder of his rights against the drawee or payor bank in respect of such funds. The holder's delay caused such loss of funds, and the party is discharged, but only to the extent of such loss.

Notice of Dishonor. Unless excused,[4] notice of dishonor is *necessary* in order to charge: (1) any indorser; (2) any drawer; (3) the acceptor of a draft

[2] See below, pp. 382–83.

[3] Ibid.

[4] Ibid.

payable *at a bank;* or (4) a maker of a note payable *at a bank.* Where, without excuse, any necessary notice of dishonor is delayed beyond the time when it is due, any indorser is discharged fully; and the drawer, the acceptor of a draft payable at a bank, and the maker of a note payable at a bank are discharged *only to the extent of the deprived funds as indicated in the preceding paragraph.*

Protest. Unless excused,[5] protest of any dishonor is *necessary* in order to charge the drawer and indorsers of any draft which *on its face* appears to be *drawn or payable outside of the states and territories of the United States and the District of Columbia.* This is an "international" or "foreign" draft and, because protest of any dishonor of such a draft is generally required by foreign law, the necessity of protest under the Code is retained. For his convenience, a holder *may,* at his option, make protest of any dishonor of *any other* instrument and, in the case of a foreign draft, may on insolvency of the acceptor before maturity make protest for better security.[6] Where, without excuse, a necessary protest is delayed beyond the time when it is due, any drawer or indorser is *completely discharged.*

Presentment

Time When Made. If the instrument states a time when presentment is to be made, that time governs. The times for presentment for acceptance and payment differ.

Presentment for Acceptance. Unless a different time is expressed in the instrument, the time for presentment for acceptance is determined as follows:

1. *Instrument payable at, or a fixed period after, a stated date.* Any presentment for acceptance must be made on or before the date it is payable.
2. *Instrument payable after sight.* It must either be presented for acceptance or negotiated within a reasonable time after date, or issue, whichever is later.
3. *Any other instrument.* With respect to the liability of any *secondary party,* presentment for acceptance is due within a reasonable time after such party becomes liable thereon.

Presentment for Payment. Unless a different time is expressed in the instrument, the time for presentment for payment is determined as follows:

1. *Instrument payable at stated date.* Presentment for payment is due on that date.
2. *Accelerated instrument.* Presentment for payment is due within a reasonable time after the acceleration.
3. *Any other instrument.* With respect to the liability of any *secondary party,* presentment for payment is due within a reasonable time after such party becomes liable thereon.[7]

---

[5] Ibid.

[6] UCC 3–501(3).

[7] See UCC 3–503(1).

Reasonable Time. A reasonable time for presentment is determined by the nature of the instrument, any usage of banking or trade, and the facts of the particular case. If the instrument is an *uncertified check which is drawn and payable within the United States and which is not a draft drawn by a bank,* the following are presumed to be reasonable periods within which to present for payment or to initiate bank collection:

1. With respect to the liability of the *drawer, 30 days after date, or issue, whichever is later.*[8]
2. With respect to the liability of an *indorser, seven days after his indorsement.*

Time of Day and Day. Presentment to be sufficient must be made at a reasonable hour and, if at a bank, during its banking day. Where any presentment is due on a day which is not a full business day for either the person making presentment or the party to pay or accept, presentment is due on the next following day that is a full business day for both parties.

How Made. ***The Demand.*** Presentment is a *demand* for payment or acceptance. The demand itself is presentment, and the instrument *need not be exhibited,* although the party to whom presentment is made may properly require its exhibition. A demand is made *by,* or on behalf *of,* the holder. Presentment may be made *to:* (1) any one of two or more makers, acceptors, drawees, or other payors, irrespective of whether or not they are partners or one has authority to act for the other; or (2) any person who has authority to make or refuse the acceptance or payment.

Method and Place.[9] Presentment may be made in the following ways and places:

1. By mail, in which event the time of presentment is determined by the time of receipt of the mail.
2. Through a clearing house, in which event the time of presentment is the time when it reaches the obligor.
3. At the place of acceptance or payment specified in the instrument, or if there be none at the place of business or residence of the party to accept or pay. If neither the party to accept or pay, nor anyone authorized to act for him, is present or accessible at such place, presentment is excused.

---

[8] See above, p. 342, in connection with notice to a purchaser that after 30 days a check is overdue, precluding him from becoming a holder in due course.

[9] UCC 4–210. "**Presentment by Notice of Item Not Payable by, Through or at a Bank; Liability of Secondary Parties.** (1) Unless otherwise instructed, a collecting bank may present an item not payable by, through or at a bank by sending to the party to accept or pay a written notice that the bank holds the item for acceptance or payment. The notice must be sent in time to be received on or before the day when presentment is due and the bank must meet any requirement of the party to accept or pay under Section 3–505 by the close of the bank's next banking day after it knows of the requirement.

"(2) Where presentment is made by notice and neither honor nor request for compliance with a requirement under Section 3–505 is received by the close of business on the day after maturity or in the case of demand items by the close of business on the third banking day after notice was sent, the presenting bank may treat the item as dishonored and charge any secondary party by sending him notice of the facts."

A draft accepted, or a note made payable, at a bank in the United States *must* be presented at such bank.

Rights of Party to Whom Presentment Is Made. Presentment is merely a demand for acceptance or payment. While refusal of the demand dishonors the instrument, nevertheless the party to whom presentment is made has the right to protect himself from making improper payment or acceptance by making reasonable demands upon the presenting party without thereby dishonoring the instrument. The Code[10] permits him to require the presenting party: to exhibit the instrument; reasonably to identify himself and prove his authority if he is acting for another; to produce the instrument at the proper place, which is that specified in the instrument or, if not so specified, at any place reasonable under the circumstances;[11] to sign a receipt on the instrument for partial or full payment; to surrender the instrument if full payment is made. The party to whom presentment is made must not demand more than is permitted by the Code nor be unreasonable in connection with any permitted demand. For example, if he knows the presenting party, it would be unreasonable for him to require identification by the presenting party. If the demand by the party to whom presentment has been made is unreasonable, the instrument is thereby dishonored. The presenting party's failure to comply with a reasonable demand invalidates the presentment. However, the time for presentment is extended for a reasonable time in which the presenting party may comply with the demand. The time for acceptance or payment runs from the time of such compliance. If the presenting party should fail to comply with the demand within a reasonable time, the effect is as though a presentment had never been made.

Time Allowed for Acceptance or Payment. The party to whom presentment is made must act promptly in deciding whether or not to accept or pay the instrument. The short times allowed for acceptance and payment differ. *If the instrument is presented for acceptance,* the party to whom presentment is made may, without dishonor, defer acceptance until the close of the next business day following presentment. The holder also may, in a good faith effort to obtain acceptance and without either dishonor of the instrument or discharge of secondary parties, allow postponement of acceptance for an additional business day. *If the instrument is presented for payment,* payment of the instrument may be deferred without dishonor pending reasonable examination to determine whether it is properly payable; but, with two exceptions, payment must be made in any event before the close of business on the day of presentment. The first exception is that payment may be made at any earlier time if agreed to by the party to pay. Under the second exception, a longer time

---

[10] UCC 3–505.

[11] UCC 4–204(3): "Presentment may be made by a presenting bank at a place where the payor bank has requested that presentment be made."

may be allowed for payment in the case of documentary drafts[12] drawn under a letter of credit.[13]

Dishonor. Dishonor of an instrument may occur when presentment is necessary or optional, or when presentment is excused. *When a necessary or optional presentment is duly made,* the instrument is dishonored if: due acceptance or payment is refused or cannot be obtained within the prescribed time; or, in the case of bank collections, the instrument is seasonably returned by the midnight deadline.[14] *When presentment is excused,*[15] the instrument is dishon-

---

[12] UCC 4–104(1)(f): " 'Documentary draft' means any negotiable or non-negotiable draft with accompanying documents, securities or other papers to be delivered against honor of the draft."

[13] See UCC 5–112, 5–114.

[14] UCC 4–301. "**Deferred Posting; Recovery of Payment by Return of Items; Time of Dishonor.** (1) Where an authorized settlement for a demand item (other than a documentary draft) received by a payor bank otherwise than for immediate payment over the counter has been made before midnight of the banking day of receipt the payor bank may revoke the settlement and recover any payment if before it has made final payment (subsection (1) of Section 4–213) and before its midnight deadline it

(a) returns the item; or

(b) sends written notice of dishonor or nonpayment if the item is held for protest or is otherwise unavailable for return.

"(2) If a demand item is received by a payor bank for credit on its books it may return such item or send notice of dishonor and may revoke any credit given or recover the amount thereof withdrawn by its customer, if it acts within the time limit and in the manner specified in the preceding subsection.

"(3) Unless previous notice of dishonor has been sent an item is dishonored at the time when for purposes of dishonor it is returned or notice sent in accordance with this section.

"(4) An item is returned:

(a) as to an item received through a clearing house, when it is delivered to the presenting or last collecting bank or to the clearing house or is sent or delivered in accordance with its rules; or

(b) in all other cases, when it is sent or delivered to the bank's customer or transferor or pursuant to his instructions.

UCC 4–302. "**Payor Bank's Responsibility for Late Return of Item.** In the absence of a valid defense such as breach of a presentment warranty (subsection (1) of Section 4–207), settlement effected or the like, if an item is presented on and received by a payor bank the bank is accountable for the amount of

(a) a demand item other than a documentary draft whether properly payable or not if the bank, in any case where it is not also the depositary bank, retains the item beyond midnight of the banking day of receipt without settling for it or, regardless of whether it is also the depositary bank, does not pay or return the item or send notice of dishonor until after its midnight deadline; or

(b) any other properly payable item unless within the time allowed for acceptance or payment of that item the bank either accepts or pays the item or returns it and accompanying documents."

UCC 4–213: "(1) An item is finally paid by a payor bank when the bank has done any of the following, whichever happens first:

(a) paid the item in cash; or

(b) settled for the item without reserving a right to revoke the settlement and without having such right under statute, clearing house rule or agreement; or

(c) completed the process of posting the item to the indicated account of the drawer, maker or other person to be charged therewith; or

(d) made a provisional settlement for the item and failed to revoke the settlement in the time and manner permitted by statute, clearing house rule or agreement.

Upon a final payment under subparagraphs (b), (c), or (d) the payor bank shall be accountable for the amount of the item."

[15] See below, pp. 382–83.

ored if it is not duly accepted or paid. The return of an instrument for lack of proper indorsement is not a dishonor.

We have seen previously[16] that a bank may certify a check before returning it for lack of a proper indorsement; by doing so, the drawer is discharged. A draft or an indorsement thereon may provide a stated time within which re-presentment of the instrument may be made in the event the draft is dishonored by non-acceptance if a time draft or by non-payment if a sight draft. The holder of a draft with such a provision may, at his option, waive the dishonor and present it again within the stated time without affecting the liability of any secondary party who is bound by the provision.

We have seen[17] that the contractual obligations of a drawer of a draft and, unless the indorsement otherwise specifies, of every indorser on an instrument is that, upon dishonor of the instrument and any necessary notice of dishonor and protest, he will pay the amount of the instrument to the holder or to any subsequent indorser who takes it up. Thus on dishonor of an instrument and subject to any necessary notice of dishonor and protest,[18] the holder has an immediate right of recourse against the drawer and indorsers. It should be recalled that, as previously discussed,[19] a cause of action against a drawer of a draft or an indorser of any instrument accrues *upon demand* following dishonor of the instrument. *Notice of dishonor is a demand.*

Notice of Dishonor

By Whom. Usually notice of dishonor is given by the holder or by an indorser who has himself received notice. Notice of dishonor may be given by any party who may be compelled to pay the instrument to any party who may be liable on the instrument. Thus, notice may be given by, or on behalf of, the holder or any party who has himself received notice. In addition, an agent or bank in whose hands the instrument is dishonored may give notice to his principal or customer or to another agent or bank from which the instrument was received. Notice operates for the benefit of all parties who have rights on the instrument against the party notified. Thus, it is sufficient if a party is notified of dishonor *once;* his liability is fixed and so he need not receive additional notice. (D draws a check on E payable to P and delivers it to P, who indorses it in blank and delivers it to A. A indorses it in blank and delivers it to B, who indorses it in blank and delivers it to H. H presents it to E for payment, and it is dishonored. H gives notice of dishonor to B, A, P, and D. It is not necessary for B to give A, P, and D notice again. Their liability is fixed as secondary parties by H's previous notice of dishonor to them.)

Time. Any necessary notice given by a person other than a bank must be given *before midnight of the third business day after dishonor or receipt of*

---

[16] See above, p. 360.

[17] See above, p. 363.

[18] See above, pp. 375–76.

[19] See above, pp. 326–27.

notice of dishonor. (The drawer of a check is D, and the indorsers in order are P and A. H is the holder. On dishonor, H gives A notice of dishonor. A must give notice of dishonor to P and D before midnight of the third business day after *he* received notice of dishonor from H. If A gives notice of dishonor only to P, P in turn must give notice of dishonor to D before midnight on the third business day after *he* received notice of dishonor from A.) A bank must give any necessary notice of dishonor before its midnight deadline.[20]

Method. Notice may be given in any reasonable manner. It may be oral or written and in any terms which identify the instrument and state that it has been dishonored. A misdescription which does not mislead the party notified does not cause the notice to be insufficient. Sending the instrument bearing a stamp, ticket, or writing stating that acceptance or payment has been refused, or sending a notice of debit with respect to the instrument, is sufficient. Written notice is given when *sent,* although it may not be received.

To Whom. We have just observed that an agent or bank in whose hands the instrument is dishonored may give notice of dishonor as indicated. Notice to one partner is notice to each partner, although the firm may have been dissolved. When any party is in insolvency proceedings instituted after the issue of the instrument, notice may be given either to the party or to the representative of his estate. When any party is dead or incompetent, notice may be sent to his last-known address or given to his personal representative.

Protest

Protest of dishonor is necessary only for a draft which, *on its face,* appears to be drawn or payable outside of the states and territories of the United States and the District of Columbia. Such a draft is sometimes called a "foreign" or "international" draft.[21] Unless excused,[22] protest of any dishonor is necessary in order to charge the drawer and indorsers of such a draft. The purpose of protest is to preserve proof of presentment and dishonor in a form recognized and given credence universally. Protest is required *in addition* to presentment, dishonor, and notice of dishonor as a condition precedent to the exercise of the holder's right of recourse against the drawer and indorsers.

A protest is a certificate of dishonor made under the hand and seal of a United States consul or by a vice-consul or a notary public or other person authorized to certify dishonor by the law of the place where dishonor occurs. It may be made upon information satisfactory to such person, and he need not certify as to his own knowledge. The protest need not be in any particular form, but it must: (1) identify the instrument; (2) certify either that due presentment has been made or the reason why it is excused; and (3) certify that the instrument has been dishonored by non-acceptance or non-payment. The pro-

[20] See below, p. 397, ftn. 14.

[21] See UCC 3–701.

[22] See below, pp. 382–83.

test need not be annexed to the instrument, and it may be forwarded separately. Protest usually certifies, although it is not required to do so, that notice of dishonor has been given to all parties or to specified parties. Usually, protest is forwarded together with the notice of dishonor and, with one exception, necessary protest is due at the time that notice of dishonor is due. Under the exception, if, before protest is due, an instrument has been noted for protest by the officer to make protest, the protest may be made at any time thereafter as of the date of the noting. It should be observed that, where protest is not necessary but merely optional with the holder, it may be made at any time before it is used as evidence.

Evidence of Dishonor and Notice of Dishonor

There are three kinds of evidence which are admissible to prove dishonor and notice of dishonor. Each kind creates a presumption of dishonor and notice of dishonor if shown therein. The obligor can overcome the presumption by evidence that dishonor did not occur, that notice of dishonor was not given, and that protest is not valid. The first kind of evidence is the protest itself; it is authentic. The second kind of evidence is the purported stamp or writing of the drawee, payor bank or presenting bank on the instrument or accompanying it stating that acceptance or payment has been refused for reasons consistent with dishonor. The following reasons are satisfactory evidence of dishonor: "Not sufficient funds"; "Account garnished"; "No account"; "Payment stopped." The third kind of evidence is any book or record of the drawee, payor bank, or any collecting bank kept in the usual course of business which shows dishonor, even though there is no evidence of who made the entry.

Waiver and Excuse

Under certain circumstances *delay* in presentment, notice of dishonor, or protest is *excused*, and in other circumstances presentment, notice of dishonor, or protest are *entirely excused*. In some instances they are *waived*. First their waiver will be considered and then their excuse.

Waiver. Where a waiver of presentment or notice of dishonor or protest is embodied in the instrument itself, it is binding on all parties; but where it is written above the signature of an indorser it binds him only. *A waiver of protest is also a waiver of presentment and of notice of dishonor,* even though the protest is not required, e.g., "protest waived" on an instrument.

Excuse. ***Delay Excused.***[23] *Delay* in making presentment, notice of dishonor, or protest is excused when the party to make it is without notice that the instrument is due, or the delay is caused by circumstances beyond his control and he exercises reasonable diligence after the cause of the delay ceases to operate. Illustrations are where the instrument has been accelerated without

---

[23] UCC 3–511(1).

his knowledge, or demand has been made by a prior holder immediately before his purchase.

Entirely Excused.[24] *Presentment or notice of dishonor or protest,* as the case may be, *is entirely excused* under the following circumstances:

1. The party to be charged has expressly or impliedly waived presentment or notice of dishonor or protest. The waiver may be oral or in writing and may be made either before or after it is due.
2. The party to be charged has no reason to expect, or right to require, that the instrument be accepted or paid. Illustrations are: he himself has dishonored the instrument, or countermanded payment as by a stop order on the drawee bank on a check; the drawee of a check has no funds or insufficient funds of the drawer party to be charged.
3. Presentment or protest cannot be made or notice of dishonor given by the exercise of reasonable diligence. For example, after the exercise of reasonable diligence presentment for payment cannot be made because the maker's whereabouts cannot be ascertained.

Presentment is also *entirely excused* when: (1) the maker, acceptor or drawee of any instrument, except a documentary draft, is dead or in insolvency proceedings instituted after the issue of the instrument; or (2) acceptance or payment is refused but not for want of proper presentment. The reason for (1) is that, in such instances, immediate payment or acceptance is impossible or unlikely so that the holder cannot reasonably be expected to make presentment. He is permitted, instead, to have his *immediate* recourse against the drawer or indorser. The reason for (2) is that, since the purpose of presentment is to ascertain whether or not the maker, acceptor, or drawee will pay or accept the instrument, respectively, if a refusal to do so is given without a presentment having been made, then there is no sense in requiring presentment for a purpose which has already been refused.

If a draft has been previously dishonored by non-acceptance, later presentment for payment, notice of dishonor, and protest for non-payment are excused entirely. However, if the previous dishonor by non-acceptance is followed by an acceptance, then necessary presentment for payment, notice of dishonor, and protest for non-payment are not excused.

---

[24] UCC 3–511(2)(3).

Chapter 26

DISCHARGE

A party to a negotiable instrument may be discharged from his liability thereon in various ways, such as those provided by the Code, by any act or agreement effecting a discharge for the payment of money under the law of Contracts, and by statute. No discharge of any party other than a discharge in insolvency proceedings is effective as against a subsequent holder in due course unless he has notice thereof when he takes the instrument.

Any party, under the Code, may be discharged from his liability *on the instrument* in the following ways: (*1*) ***Payment or Satisfaction.*** His payment or satisfaction to the holder discharges him, except: (a) if he knows of another person's claim to the instrument, and the claimant has either posted indemnity or obtained an injunction in an action involving the holder and the claimant enjoining payment or satisfaction; or (b) if he paid in bad faith to a holder who acquired the instrument by theft or who (unless having the rights of a holder in due course) holds through one who so acquired it; or (c) if the payor is other than an intermediary bank or a payor bank and pays or satisfies an instrument restrictively indorsed in a manner not consistent with the terms of such restrictive indorsement. (*2*) ***Tender of Payment.*** A holder's improper refusal of a valid tender of full payment causes the party who tendered to be discharged *only to the extent* of all subsequent liability for interest, costs, and attorney's fees; he is still liable for the face amount of the instrument. Also, such refusal wholly discharges any party on the instrument who has a right of recourse against the tendering party. (*3*) ***Cancellation and Renunciation.*** The holder's cancellation on the instrument of a party's liability, or his renunciation of his rights by his signed and delivered writing or by surrender of the instrument to the party to be discharged, does not require consideration. (*4*) ***Impairment of Right of***

Recourse or of Collateral. **The holder's release or agreement not to sue, without reservation of rights, any person against whom a party on the instrument has recourse without the latter's consent discharges the latter. Also, to the extent that, without the consent of a party on the instrument, the holder impairs any collateral for the instrument given by or on behalf of such party or of any person against whom such party has a right of recourse, such party is discharged. (5)** ***Reacquisition of the Instrument by a Prior Party.*** **This was previously discussed.[1] (6)** ***Fraudulent and Material Alteration.*** **This was previously discussed.[2] (7)** ***Certification of a Check.*** **This was previously discussed.[3] (8)** ***Acceptance Varying a Draft.*** **If on the holder's presentment of a draft for acceptance the drawee's proffered acceptance varies the terms of the draft and the holder assents thereto, the drawer and indorsers are discharged. (9)** ***Unexcused Delay in Presentment or Notice of Dishonor or Protest.*** **This was discussed previously.[4]**

Under the law of Contracts, **any party is discharged from his liability on a negotiable instrument to another party by any act or agreement with such party which would discharge a simple contract for the payment of money, e.g., accord and satisfaction, novation.**

The loss, destruction, or theft of an instrument does not, of itself, discharge the obligations thereon, and the owner may recover from any party liable on the instrument, although he may be required to provide security to indemnify the defendant against loss by reason of further claims on the instrument.

Any party, as distinct from *all parties,* on an instrument may be discharged from liability thereon in various ways. The instrument is a paper evidencing the contractual obligations of the parties thereon; it is not the liability itself and, therefore, cannot as such be discharged. Often an instrument is given in payment of an obligation. It is usually said that a check or other instrument given in payment of an obligation is "conditional payment," meaning that the underlying obligation for which the instrument is given is not thereby discharged but, rather, cannot be enforced by suit until the instrument is due. Does the instrument discharge the underlying obligation for which it was issued, or is it solely conditional payment suspending enforcement of the underlying obligation until the due date of the instrument? The agreement of the parties governs, and in the absence of agreement the effect will depend upon the type of instrument given. *Unless otherwise agreed, where an instrument is taken for an underlying obligation, the obligation is completely discharged if a bank is drawer, maker or acceptor of the instrument, and there is no recourse on the instrument against the underlying obligor.* Thus, the debt-

[1] See summary headnote, above, p. 329.

[2] See summary headnote, above, pp. 353–54.

[3] See summary headnote, above, p. 358.

[4] See summary headnote, above, p. 374.

or's delivery to the creditor of a cashier's check with the creditor as payee and not indorsed by the debtor causes the debtor to be discharged immediately from his underlying obligation. Since his signature is not on the cashier's check, he is not liable thereon. However, usually the debtor will give his own check or other instrument in payment. *Unless otherwise agreed, where an instrument is taken for an underlying obligation in any case other than that stated in italics above, the underlying obligation is suspended completely until the instrument is due or, if it is payable on demand, until its presentment.* If the instrument is dishonored, action may be taken on *either* the instrument or the obligation; discharge of the underlying obligor on the instrument also discharges him on the obligation. It should be recalled that, as discussed previously,[5] if the *holder* of a check causes it to be certified, the drawer as well as all prior indorsers on the check are thereby discharged.

It should be noted that the taking in good faith of a check does not of itself so extend the time on the original obligation as to discharge a surety, as long as the check is not postdated. This is in accord with the law of Suretyship.[6] The check is taken as a means of immediate payment; the 30-day period for presentment, previously discussed,[7] does not affect the surety's liability.

First the discharge from liability of *any party* on an instrument will be discussed and then the discharge of *all parties* from liability on an instrument.

Discharge of Any Party on an Instrument

Any party may be discharged from his liability on an instrument in any of the following ways:

1. Payment or satisfaction.
2. Tender of payment.
3. Cancellation or renunciation.
4. Impairment of right of recourse or of collateral.
5. Reacquisition of the instrument by a prior party (previously discussed).[8]
6. Fraudulent and material alteration (previously discussed).[9]
7. Certification of a check (previously discussed).[10]
8. Acceptance varying a draft (previously discussed).[11]
9. Unexcused delay in presentment or notice of dishonor or protest (previously discussed).[12]

Any party is also discharged from his liability on an instrument to another party by any other act or agreement with such party which would discharge his

[5] See above, p. 360.

[6] See below, pp. 496 f.

[7] See above, p. 377.

[8] See above, p. 335.

[9] See above, pp. 356–57.

[10] See above, pp. 360 ff.

[11] Ibid.

[12] See above, p. 375.

simple contract for the payment of money. Discharge may also occur by additional ways provided by statute (e.g., federal bankruptcy discharge) and state statutes concerning negotiable instruments negotiated in furtherance of gambling transactions; the Code is not intended to preclude discharge arising apart from it.

Before considering these various methods of discharging a party from liability on an instrument, it should be recalled very carefully that *no discharge of any party other than a discharge in insolvency proceedings is effective against a subsequent holder in due course unless he has notice thereof when he takes the instrument.* Any such discharge of a party is a personal defense which is cut off, and cannot be asserted, against a holder in due course who took the instrument without notice of any defense to the instrument.[13] He takes the instrument free of all defenses of any party to the instrument with whom he has not dealt,[14] with certain exceptions, one of which is any discharge other than a discharge in insolvency proceedings of which the holder has notice when he took the instrument. (H is a holder in due course of a note made by M. When H took the note he knew that A, one of the indorsers, had been released from liability on the note. On dishonor of the instrument, H cannot recover against A, but he can recover against the other indorsers and M on the note.)

Payment or Satisfaction. We have seen[15] that the holder of an instrument, whether or not he is the owner, has the right to recover on the instrument unless the defendant establishes a defense. *The liability of any party to the instrument is discharged to the extent of his payment or satisfaction to the holder, with three exceptions.*

First Exception. If the payment or satisfaction is made to the holder *with knowledge* of a claim of another person to the instrument, *the payor is discharged by such payment or satisfaction unless, prior to such payment or satisfaction, the adverse claimant either:* supplies indemnity deemed adequate by the payor; or enjoins payment or satisfaction by court order in an action in which the adverse claimant and the holder are parties.[16] On notification of an adverse claim to the instrument, the payor usually is unable to ascertain whether or not the adverse claim is valid. The paying obligor's contractual obligation on the instrument is to pay the holder of the instrument, and he should not be inconvenienced because of a dispute between two other parties unless the adverse claimant either posts indemnity or restrains payment or satisfaction by legal process.

Second Exception. A party who, in *bad faith,* pays or satisfies the holder who acquired the instrument *by theft or who* (unless having the rights of a holder in due course) *holds through one who so acquired it, is not discharged from liability on the instrument.* The policy of the law here refuses to aid a

---

[13] See above, pp. 342 f., 350.

[14] See above, p. 337.

[15] See above, p. 338.

[16] UCC 3-803.

thief directly, or indirectly by aiding his transferee, unless the latter is a holder in due course or a holder or transferee claiming through a holder in due course with his rights. (M's note to the order of P and delivered to P is indorsed by P in blank and stolen by A. A presented the note to M, who paid it, and P sues M on the note. While A is the holder, nevertheless, whether or not M is discharged depends upon whether M paid A in bad faith, knowing that A was a thief. If M paid in *bad faith,* he is not discharged; if M paid in *good faith,* he is discharged. If A had negotiated the note to B after maturity, thereby precluding B from being a holder in due course, whether or not M's payment to B would discharge M from liability on the note again depends on M's good or bad faith. However, if A had negotiated the note to H, a holder in due course, M's payment to H would discharge M, irrespective of whether or not he paid in bad faith. H would take the note free of the defense of theft. If H had negotiated the note to C after maturity, thereby precluding C from being a holder in due course, M's payment to C would discharge M from liability on the note. C would acquire H's rights and, therefore, take the note free of the defense of theft.)

Third Exception. A party, *other than* an intermediary bank[17] or a payor bank which is not a depositary bank,[18] who pays or satisfies the holder of an instrument which has been restrictively indorsed *in a manner not consistent with the terms of such restrictive indorsement, is not discharged from liability on the instrument.* The effect of restrictive indorsements has been discussed previously.[19] (M is the maker of a note restrictively indorsed by P, the payee, to A, an indorsee for collection. If M pays A, M is discharged since, by his indorsement, P desired such payment to occur and it has occurred consistent with such indorsement. However, if M had credited *A's personal account,* M has not paid consistently with such indorsement, and he is not discharged.) *If the indorsee, or transferee of the indorsee, of a restrictively indorsed note is a holder in due course, then the maker's payment to him discharges the maker from liability on the note.* With respect to banks, *an intermediary bank or a payor bank which is not the depositary bank is neither given notice nor otherwise affected by a restrictive indorsement of any person except the bank's immediate transferor or the person presenting the instrument for payment.* (D is the drawer of a check on E bank restrictively indorsed for deposit by P, the payee, and delivered by P to X for safekeeping. X deposited the check with A bank. A forwarded it for collection to B bank, who obtained collection from E. E paid B, who paid A, and X then withdrew the money from his account with A. P can recover on the check from A, which is a depositary bank not paying consistently with the terms of the restrictive indorsement—for the deposit to *P's* account. B is an intermediary bank and E is a payor bank which is not the depositary bank, and so they are not liable to P.) The depositary bank is bound

[17] See below, p. 395.

[18] Ibid.

[19] See above, p. 334.

by all prior indorsements and, if the instrument is restrictively indorsed, becomes a holder in due course if payment is made to the holder consistently with the restrictive indorsement.

Two additional points should be noted carefully. First, if the holder *accepts* any other satisfaction instead of payment of the instrument, the party rendering such satisfaction is discharged from liability on the instrument. Second, payment or satisfaction may be made with the *consent of the holder* by *any* person, including a stranger to the instrument. Surrender of the instrument to such a person gives him the rights of a transferee.[20]

Tender of Payment. Any party making tender of full payment to a holder when or after it is due is discharged *only to the extent* of all subsequent liability for interest, costs, and attorney's fees. He is still liable on the instrument for the face amount thereof up to the time of tender. He has made the money available to the holder and should not be penalized because the money is not accepted. *The holder's refusal of such tender wholly discharges any party who has a right of recourse against the party making the tender.* (M is the maker of a note, P is the payee, and the order of blank indorsements is P, A, B. H is the holder. On the due date P tenders the full amount of the note to H, who refuses it. B and A are completely discharged from liability on the instrument, and P is discharged to the extent of all subsequent liability for interest, costs, and attorney's fees. B and A would have had recourse against P in the event that they had to pay the note on dishonor. They should not now continue to be liable to H on the note when the proffered full payment by P was made available to H.) Where the maker or acceptor of an instrument payable otherwise than on demand is able and ready to pay at every place of payment specified in the instrument when it is due, it is equivalent to tender.

Cancellation and Renunciation. The *holder* may discharge any party from his liability on the instrument, without any requirement of consideration, by cancellation or renunciation. Neither cancellation nor renunciation affects the title to the instrument as long as the holder does not surrender it. *Cancellation is made by the holder in any manner apparent on the face of the instrument or the indorsement,* as by *intentionally cancelling* the instrument or the party's signature by destruction or mutilation, or by *striking out* the party's signature. *Renunciation occurs by the holder renouncing his rights by a writing signed and delivered, or by the surrender of the instrument, to the party to be discharged.*

Impairment of Recourse or of Collateral. Under the law of Suretyship, the creditor's release of the principal debtor discharges the debt and, since there is no debt for which there can be security, the surety as security for such debt is also discharged and the lien on any property as security is also terminated. If the creditor releases the principal debtor but *reserves his rights against the surety,* his release is construed as a covenant not to sue the principal debtor and, since the principal debtor is not discharged, the surety is not discharged

[20] See above, pp. 343 f.

and has rights against the principal debtor in the event that the creditor enforces his suretyship obligation on the principal debtor's default. To the extent that the principal debtor's contract with the creditor is modified by the creditor without the consent of the surety so as to create a possibility that the surety's risk will be increased thereby, the surety is thereby discharged. A common illustration is the creditor's binding agreement with the principal debtor extending the time of payment by the principal debtor to the creditor without the surety's consent and without reserving the creditor's rights against the surety. Also, to the extent that the creditor, *with knowledge of the suretyship relationship,* surrenders or impairs the security, the creditor makes it unavailable to the surety for recourse in the event that the creditor enforces his suretyship obligation on the principal debtor's default and causes the surety to be discharged *to the extent of such surrender or impairment.* All this is discussed later under Suretyship.[21] If the surety *consents* to these actions of the creditor, he is not discharged.

The Code reflects these elements of suretyship in connection with a party's discharge in Commercial Paper. Thus, the holder of an instrument may, without a party's consent, by his conduct toward another party on the instrument or a person off the instrument cause the discharge of the party on the instrument. (M is the maker of a note with P as the payee, who negotiated it to A, who indorsed it in blank and delivered it to B, who indorsed it in blank and delivered it to H. (a) Without the consent of P, A, and B, H released M. P, A, and B are discharged, *because they have been deprived of recourse against M.* (b) Without the consent of A and B, H released P. A and B are discharged *because they have been deprived of recourse against P.* (c) Without the consent of A and B, H released P, *reserving his rights* against A and B, and H promptly notified A and B. Nobody is discharged on the note, although H cannot recover against P on the note. (d) H releases P, A, and B, knowing that M is an accommodation maker. Not only are P, A, and B discharged, but M is discharged also *because he has been deprived of recourse against P* in the event M should be held liable on the note. If H did not know of M's accommodation status, M would not be discharged.) Consent by parties on the instrument to such conduct by a holder which would otherwise constitute suretyship defenses against the holder may be given in advance or after such conduct, although it very frequently is written on the instrument itself and is binding on the parties subject to it. No consideration is required for such consent.

We can now better understand the Code's provision on impairment of recourse or of collateral concerning complete discharge:

(1) The holder discharges any party to the instrument to the extent that without such party's consent the holder
  (a) *without express reservation of rights* releases or agrees not to sue any person against whom the party has *to the knowledge of the holder* a right of recourse or agrees to suspend the right to enforce against such person

[21] See below, pp. 492–98.

the instrument or collateral or otherwise discharges such person, except that failure or delay in effecting any required presentment, protest or notice of dishonor with respect to any such person does not discharge any party as to whom presentment, protest or notice of dishonor is effective or unnecessary; or

(b) unjustifiably impairs any collateral for the instrument given by or on behalf of the party or any person against whom he has a right of recourse.

(2) By *express* reservation of rights against a party with a right of recourse the holder preserves

(a) all his rights against such party as of the time when the instrument was originally due; and

(b) the right of the party to pay the instrument as of that time; and

(c) all rights of such party to recourse against others.[22] (Author's italics.)

Perhaps a brief comment would be helpful with respect to the provision in (1) (a) above regarding presentment, protest, or notice of dishonor. The failure of a holder to make necessary presentment or protest or to give notice of dishonor discharges liability *to him* by the party who was entitled to have such occur, but it has no effect on the other parties to the instrument. (M is the maker of a note with P as the payee, indorsed in order by P, A, and B. H, the holder, gives only A necessary notice of dishonor. B and P are discharged from their secondary liability *to H* as indorsers under their engagement that they would be liable only if necessary notice of dishonor was given to them.[23] A can give P notice of dishonor within the proper time[24] and thereby recover from P—as well as from M as a party primarily liable—on the instrument.)

By Any Other Act or Agreement. Any party is also discharged from his liability on an instrument to another party by any other act or agreement with such party which would discharge a simple contract for the payment of money. This includes accord and satisfaction, novation, mutual rescission, and the other methods of discharge discussed previously under "Contracts."[25]

Although discharge by payment means that money has been paid, it is commonplace to refer to discharge by payment when, instead of the payment of money, new instruments are issued to the creditor discharging the obligation of a party or parties liable on the old instrument. Actually, such new instruments are forms of accord and satisfaction or of novation, and discharge is occurring by that method. It is important to determine when newly issued instruments do, and do not, effect a discharge of the obligation of a party or parties liable on the old instrument. Most of the cases are concerned with promissory notes. The agreement of the parties controls, and if the new note is issued solely as *security* for the old note, there is no accord and satisfaction or novation and the obligation of a party or parties liable on the old note is not discharged. When, pursuant to agreement, the new note is issued to the credi-

[22] UCC 3–606.

[23] See above, p. 364.

[24] See above, pp. 380–81.

[25] See above, pp. 114 ff.

tor as a *renewal* of the old note which the creditor is to *retain* along with the new note, in the absence of agreement to the contrary and by the majority view it is presumed that the obligation of a party or parties liable on the old note is not discharged. However, if the renewal note is issued to the creditor *in exchange* for the surrender of the old note, in the absence of agreement to the contrary it is presumed that the obligation of a party or parties liable on the old note thereby is discharged.

Discharge of All Parties on an Instrument

All the parties to an instrument are discharged when no party is left with rights against any other party on the paper. As stated previously, the instrument is a paper evidencing the contractual obligations of the parties thereon; it is not the liability itself and, therefore, cannot as such be discharged. Accordingly, under the Code[26] the liability of all parties is discharged when any party who has himself no right of action or recourse on the instrument (e.g., maker, drawer) either: (1) reacquires the instrument in his own right; or (2) is discharged under any provision of the Article on Commercial Paper, except as otherwise provided with respect to discharge for impairment of recourse or of collateral. The instrument still exists and may be reissued or renegotiated. If it subsequently is taken by a holder in due course, we have seen[27] that no discharge of any party on an instrument other than a discharge in insolvency proceedings is effective against a subsequent holder in due course unless he has notice thereof when he takes the instrument.

Lost, Destroyed, or Stolen Instruments

The loss, destruction, or theft of an instrument does not, of itself, discharge the obligations of the parties thereon, and the owner may recover on the instrument. Under the Code,[28] the owner of an instrument which is lost, whether by destruction, theft, or otherwise, may maintain an action in his own name and recover from any party liable thereon upon due proof of (1) his ownership, (2) the facts which prevent his production of the instrument, and (3) its terms. The court *may* require security indemnifying the defendant against loss by reason of further claims on the instrument. The circumstances may be such, as by lapse of considerable time, that there is so little doubt about destruction of the instrument and about its ownership that the court may not require any indemnity. The matter is left to judicial discretion.

---

[26] UCC 3–601(3).

[27] See above, p. 350.

[28] UCC 3–804.

Chapter 27

THE RELATIONSHIP BETWEEN A PAYOR BANK AND ITS CUSTOMER

Banks are "depositary," "payor," "intermediary," "collecting," "presenting," or "remitting." Unless otherwise agreed, a collecting bank is an agent or subagent of the owner of the item being collected, and any settlement for the item before it becomes final is provisional. The agreement between a bank and its customer cannot disclaim a bank's liability for its own lack of good faith or failure to exercise ordinary care, nor can it limit the measure of damages for such lack or failure, nor can the agreement establish unreasonable standards by which such responsibility is to be measured. A collecting bank has the duty to exercise ordinary care in the collection process, and it acts seasonably if it takes proper action before its midnight deadline following receipt of an item, notice, or payment.

The relationship between a bank and its customer for funds in the customer's account is debtor-creditor. A bank is not liable *on a check* until its signature appears thereon. A deposit of money is available for withdrawal as of right at the opening of the bank's next banking day following receipt of the deposit, but is subject to any right of the bank to apply it to any obligation of the customer. A bank is not required to certify a check. Unless an item states that the payee's indorsement is required, a depositary collecting bank may supply an indorsement of a customer which is necessary to title. Both the customer and a collecting bank make warranties under the Code with respect to a collection item.

A collecting bank can become a holder in due course by giving value for an item. When a collecting bank acquires a security interest in a collection item, it has given "value" and if the bank complies with the other Code requirements it can become a holder in due course. The text should be examined to

see how a bank can acquire such a security interest. Credits first given are first withdrawn.

A bank drawee may charge against its customer's account any item which is otherwise properly payable from that account, even though the charge creates an overdraft which the bank has no obligation to pay. The bank is to pay only the *holder* of an item. When an item by a customer has been altered by unauthorized completion or otherwise, a bank which makes payment in good faith to a holder may charge its customer's account according to: the original tenor of his altered item; or the tenor of his completed item, even though the bank knows the item has been completed as long as the bank does not have notice that the completion was improper. A payor bank is liable to its customer for damages proximately caused by its wrongful dishonor of its customer's item. A customer has the right to order his bank to stop payment of any item payable from his account, but the bank must have a reasonable opportunity to act on the order. An oral order is binding on the bank for 14 calendar days, and a written order for six months. A bank's right to subrogation on improper payment causes the bank to acquire the rights of the person to whom payment is made as against the customer, and the rights of the customer against the person paid. A bank has no obligation to its customer having a checking account to pay his uncertified check if presented more than six months after its date, although it may pay it in good faith.

Death or incompetence of a customer does not revoke the authority of a payor or collecting bank to accept, pay, collect an item or to account for proceeds of its collection until the bank *knows* of such death or adjudication of incompetence and has a reasonable opportunity to act on it. However, even with knowledge of its customer's death, a bank may, for *ten days after the date of death*, pay or certify checks drawn on or prior to that date, unless ordered to stop payment by a person claiming an interest in the account.

The customer has a duty to discover and report an unauthorized signature and an alteration of any item. After the bank's periodic statement of the customer's account and the items have been made available to the customer, he must discover and report to the bank: his unauthorized signature or any alteration on an item within one year thereafter; and any unauthorized indorsement within three years thereafter.

Code Articles 4 and 5

Article 3 of the Code is concerned with Commercial Paper, Article 4 with Bank Deposits and Collections, and Article 5 with Letters of Credit. Although various provisions in Articles 4 and 5 tie in with Commercial Paper either directly or indirectly, nevertheless because of the specialized nature of these two Articles they are treated separately under the Code. Because of their specialized nature and because, with the exception of Part 4 of Article 4, they are not of such pressing importance with respect to the function of this book as to merit analysis here, these two Articles will not be discussed. However, because Part 4 of Article 4 deals with the relationship between payor bank and its customer and it is very closely aligned with Commercial Paper, it will be considered briefly here.

It should be noted initially that, to the extent that items[1] in Article 4 are also within the scope of Articles 3 on Commercial Paper and 8 on Investment Securities, they are subject to those Articles. In the event of conflict, the provisions of Article 8 govern over 4, and those in Article 4 govern over 3.[2] Also, the liability of a bank for action or non-action with respect to any item handled by it for purposes of presentment, payment, or collection is governed by the *law of the place where the bank is located.* In the case of action or non-action by or at a branch or separate office of a bank, its liability is governed by *the law of the place where the branch or separate office is located.*[3]

Kinds of Bank

It is important to understand the various kinds of bank which may be involved with an item which the customer has deposited with his bank for collection. Under the Code.

(a) "Depositary bank" means the first bank to which an item is transferred for collection even though it is also the payor bank;
(b) "Payor bank" means a bank by which an item is payable as drawn or accepted;
(c) "Intermediary bank" means any bank to which an item is transferred in course of collection except the depositary or payor bank;
(d) "Collecting bank" means any bank handling the item for collection except the payor bank;
(e) "Presenting bank" means any bank presenting an item except a payor bank;
(f) "Remitting bank" means any payor or intermediary bank remitting for an item.[4]

Legal Status of Bank and Customer Relationship

In General. The relationship between the bank and its customer is the result of their agreement. Their agreement is usually in the form of the signature card on which the customer agrees to be bound by the rules of the bank, which are usually stated on the deposit receipt or on a separate paper or card. Under the Code,[5] *unless a contrary intent clearly appears, and prior to the time that a settlement given by a collecting bank for an item is or becomes*

[1] UCC 4–104(1)(g): " 'Item' means any instrument for the payment of money even though it is not negotiable but does not include money."

[2] UCC 4–102.

[3] UCC 4–102.

[4] UCC 4–105.

[5] UCC 4–201.

final,[6] *the bank is an agent or subagent of the owner of the item, and any settlement given for the item is provisional.* This applies regardless of the form of indorsement or lack of indorsement, and even though credit given for the item is subject to immediate withdrawal as of right or is in fact withdrawn.

Bank's Duty of Care in the Collection Process. The bank and the customer each has a duty of care with respect to the other. Under the Code,[7] *the effect of the provisions under Article 4 may be varied by agreement, except that no agreement can disclaim a bank's responsibility for its own lack of good faith*[8] *or failure to exercise ordinary care, nor can it limit the measure of damages for such lack or failure.* However, the parties may by agreement determine the standards by which such responsibility is to be measured if such standards are not manifestly unreasonable. Inasmuch as the agreement between the bank and customer is in light of banking activity, there is included in their agreement, whether or not specifically assented to by all parties interested in the items handled, Federal Reserve regulations and operating letters, clearing house[9] rules, and the like. Action or non-action approved by Article 4 or pursuant to Federal Reserve regulations or operating letters constitutes the exercise of ordinary care and, in the absence of special instructions, action or non-action consistent with clearing house rules and the like or with a general banking usage not disapproved by Article 4 prima facie constitutes the exercise of ordinary care. The measure of damages for failure to exercise ordinary care in handling an item is the amount of the item reduced by an amount which could not have been realized by the use of ordinary care, and where there is bad faith it includes other damages, if any, suffered by the party as a proximate consequence.[10]

A collecting bank has the duty to exercise ordinary care in the collection process. However, except for its duty of care in the selection of properly qualified intermediary banks and giving to them proper instructions, the bank is not liable for the insolvency, neglect, misconduct, mistake, or default of another bank or person, or for loss or destruction of an item in transit or in the possession of others. A collecting bank must use ordinary care in: (1) presenting an item or sending it for presentment;[11] (2) sending notice of dishonor or nonpayment, or returning an item other than a documentary draft[12] to the bank's transferor, after learning that the item has not been paid or accepted, as the case may be; settling[13] for an item when the bank receives final settlement;

[6] UCC 4–211(3), 4–212, 4–213.

[7] UCC 4–103.

[8] UCC 1–201(19): " 'Good faith' means honesty in fact in the conduct or transaction concerned."

[9] UCC 4–104(1)(d): " 'Clearing house' means any association of banks or other payors regularly clearing items."

[10] UCC 4–103(5).

[11] As previously discussed, above, p. 378, presentment may be made by a presenting bank at a place where the payor bank has requested that presentment be made.

[12] See above, p. 378.

[13] UCC 4–104(1)(j): " 'Settle' means to pay in cash, by clearing house settlement, in a charge or credit or by remittance, or otherwise as instructed. A settlement may be either provisional or final."

making or providing for any necessary protest; and notifying its transferor of any loss or delay in transit within a reasonable time after discovery thereof. A collecting bank acts seasonably if it takes proper action before its midnight deadline[14] following receipt of an item, notice, or payment. Taking proper action within a reasonably longer time may be seasonable, but the bank has the burden of so establishing.

Delays will occur in the collection process. Under the Code,[15] unless otherwise instructed, a collecting bank in a good faith effort to secure payment may, in the case of specific items and with or without the approval of any person involved, waive, modify or extend time limits imposed or permitted by Article 4 for a period not in excess of an additional banking day without discharge of secondary parties and without liability to its transferor or any prior party. Delay by a collecting bank or payor bank beyond time limits prescribed or permitted by Article 4, or by instructions, is excused if caused by interruption of communication facilities, suspension of payments by another bank, or emergency conditions or other circumstances beyond the control of the bank, provided it exercises such diligence as the circumstances require.

In order to establish ground rules among collecting banks as to the source of authority of each in the collection process, the Code provides[16] that, subject to Code provision in Articles 3 and 4 on conversion of instruments[17] and restrictive indorsements,[18] *only a collecting bank's transferor* can give instructions which affect the bank or constitute notice to it; a collecting bank is not liable to prior parties for any action taken pursuant to such instructions or in accordance with any agreement with its transferor.

Deposits and Issuance of Checks

In General. When the customer makes a deposit of cash, or he has deposited checks drawn by others for collection and his account has been credited on their final settlement, the relationship between the bank and the customer is debtor-creditor. The money deposited or collected became a part of the bank's funds. The customer's issuance of a check is not an assignment of funds in the bank, and the holder of the check has no recourse against the bank. *Until the bank's signature appears on the check, it is not liable thereon.*[19] The bank's obligation is to *its customer* for violation of its contract to pay pursuant to the customer's order. The holder's only recourse is against the parties liable on the instrument issued by the customer. A deposit of money in a bank is final when made but, subject to any right of the bank to apply the deposit to any

[14] UCC 4–104(1)(h): "'Midnight deadline' with respect to a bank is midnight on its next banking day following the banking day on which it receives the relevant item or notice or from which the time for taking action commences to run, whichever is later."

[15] UCC 4–108.

[16] UCC 4–203.

[17] See above, pp. 362–63.

[18] See above, p. 334, and below, p. 398.

[19] See above, pp. 354, 360.

obligation of the customer, the deposit becomes available for withdrawal as of right at the opening of the bank's next banking day following receipt of the deposit.

While the bank is not required to certify a check,[20] banks are usually willing to certify, at the customer's request, checks drawn by him. They are not so willing to do so at the request of a *holder* of a check. By certification of a check, the bank has accepted the instrument and now is a party primarily liable thereon. There are many occasions (as when a relatively large amount of money is involved) when the parties to a transaction feel that a certified check is more desirable than an uncertified check with the risk of its dishonor. When certification of a check is procured by the *holder,* the drawer and all indorsers are discharged; when procured by the *drawer,* only the indorsers are discharged, the drawer remaining secondarily liable on the instrument.

Often a customer may not have indorsed an item to be deposited in his account at the bank. A depositary bank which has taken an item for collection may supply an indorsement of the customer which is necessary to title, unless the item contains the words "payee's indorsement required" or the like. *In the absence of such a requirement, a statement placed on the item by the depositary bank to the effect that the item was deposited by a customer or credited to his account is effective as the customer's indorsement.* As discussed previously,[21] an intermediary bank, or payor bank which is not a depositary bank, is neither given notice nor otherwise affected by a restrictive indorsement of any person except the bank's immediate transferor.

Warranties of Customer and Collecting Bank Concerning Items. We previously discussed[22] under Commercial Paper the warranties made by a person who obtains payment or acceptance of an instrument, and any prior transferor, to a person who in good faith pays or accepts the instrument, and those made to his transferee by a person who transfers an instrument and receives consideration and, if the transfer is by indorsement, those made to any subsequent holder who takes the instrument in good faith. Under the Code,[23] in general,

---

[20] See above, p. 360.

[21] See above, p. 334.

[22] See above, pp. 368–72.

[23] UCC 4–207. " '**Warranties of Customer and Collecting Bank on Transfer or Presentment of Items; Time for Claims.** (1) Each customer or collecting bank who obtains payment or acceptance of an item and each prior customer and collecting bank warrants to the payor bank or other payor who in good faith pays or accepts the item that

(a) he has a good title to the item or is authorized to obtain payment or acceptance on behalf of one who has a good title; and

(b) he has no knowledge that the signature of the maker or drawer is unauthorized, except that this warranty is not given by any customer or collecting bank that is a holder in due course and acts in good faith

(i) to a maker with respect to the maker's own signature; or

(ii) to a drawer with respect to the drawer's own signature, whether or not the drawer is also the drawee; or

(iii) to an acceptor of an item if the holder in due course took the item after the acceptance or obtainied the acceptance without knowledge that the drawer's signature was unauthorized; and identical warranties are made by: each customer or collecting bank who obtains payment or acceptance of an item, and each prior customer and collecting bank, to the payor bank or other payor who in good faith pays or accepts the item; and by each customer and collecting bank who transfers an item and receives a settlement or other consideration for it made to his transferee and to any subsequent collecting bank who takes the item in good faith. *Reference should be made to the previous discussion under Commercial Paper.*

However there are a few differences from the warranty provisions under Commercial Paper. First, in the warranties on transfer, the distinction between transfer without indorsement to a transferee and with indorsement to a subsequent holder does not exist here. Second, no qualification is made here for any warranty "without recourse" nor for a selling agent or broker. However, there are included here some things not under the warranty provisions under Commercial Paper. Each customer and collecting bank transferring an item and receiving a settlement or other consideration engages that, upon dishonor and any necessary notice of dishonor and protest, he will take up the item. Also, these warranties by customer and collecting bank on payment or acceptance and on transfer arise notwithstanding the absence of indorsement or words of guaranty or warranty in the transfer or presentment, and a collecting bank remains liable for their breach despite remittance to its transferor. Damages for breach of such warranties or engagement to honor shall not ex-

---

(c) the item has not been materially altered, except that this warranty is not given by any customer or collecting bank that is a holder in due course and acts in good faith

(i) to the maker of a note; or

(ii) to the drawer of a draft whether or not the drawer is also the drawee; or

(iii) to the acceptor of an item with respect to an alteration made prior to the acceptance if the holder in due course took the item after the acceptance, even though the acceptance provided 'payable as originally drawn' or equivalent terms; or

(iv) to the acceptor of an item with respect to an alteration made after the acceptance.

"(2) Each customer and collecting bank who transfers an item and receives a settlement or other consideration for it warrants to his transferee and to any subsequent collecting bank who takes the item in good faith that

(a) he has a good title to the item or is authorized to obtain payment or acceptance on behalf of one who has a good title and the transfer is otherwise rightful; and

(b) all signatures are genuine or authorized, and

(c) the item has not been materially altered; and

(d) no defense of any party is good against him; and

(e) he has no knowledge of any insolvency proceeding instituted with respect to the maker or acceptor or the drawer of an unaccepted item.

In addition each customer and collecting bank so transferring an item and receiving a settlement or other consideration engages that upon dishonor and any necessary notice of dishonor and protest he will take up the item.

"(3) The warranties and the engagement to honor set forth in the two preceding subsections arise notwithstanding the absence of indorsement or words of guaranty or warranty in the transfer or presentment and a collecting bank remains liable for their breach despite remittance to its transferor. Damages for breach of such warranties or engagement to honor shall not exceed the consideration received by the customer or collecting bank responsible plus finance charges and expenses related to the item, if any.

"(4) Unless a claim for breach of warranty under this section is made within a reasonable time after the person claiming learns of the breach, the person liable is discharged to the extent of any loss caused by the delay in making claim."

ceed the consideration received by the customer or collecting bank responsible plus finance charges and expenses (e.g., ordinary collection expenses) related to the item, if any. Lastly, unless a claim for breach of warranty is made within a reasonable time after the person claiming learns of the breach, the person liable is discharged to the extent of any loss caused by the delay in making claim.

Bank As a Holder in Due Course. A bank may become a holder in due course if it complies with the requirements for such status.[24] One of the ways that the Code says a bank has given value for an item is the extent that the bank has a security interest in such item.

Security Interest of Collecting Bank in Items, Accompanying Documents, and Proceeds. The Code specifies when a collecting bank has a security interest in an item and any accompanying documents or the proceeds of either, how the security interest is spread over various items, and for self-liquidation of the bank's security interest:

(1) A bank has a security interest in an item and any accompanying documents or the proceeds of either
 (a) in case of an item deposited in an account to the extent to which credit given for the item has been withdrawn or applied;
 (b) in case of an item for which it has given credit available for withdrawal as of right, to the extent of the credit given whether or not the credit is drawn upon and whether or not there is a right of chargeback; or
 (c) if it makes an advance on or against the item.[25]

(2) When credit which has been given for several items received at one time or pursuant to a single agreement is withdrawn or applied in part the security interest remains upon all the items, any accompanying documents or the proceeds of either. For the purpose of this section, credits first given are first withdrawn.

(3) Receipt by a collecting bank of a final settlement for an item is a realization on its security interest in the item, accompanying documents and proceeds. To the extent and so long as the bank does not receive final settlement for the item or give up possession of the item or accompanying documents for purposes other than collection, the security interest continues and is subject to the provisions of Article 9 except that
 (a) no security agreement is necessary to make the security interest enforceable (subsection (1)(a) of Section 9–203); and
 (b) no filing is required to perfect the security interest; and
 (c) the security interest has priority over conflicting perfected security interests in the item, accompanying documents or proceeds.[26]

When Bank May Charge Customer's Account. A draft, including a check, is an order to make payment and, as against its customer, *a bank drawee may*

---

[24] See above, p. 336.

[25] A bank's general mercantile lien or right of set-off is not nullified by subsection (1). See below, p. 469, "General Liens."

[26] UCC 4–208.

charge against his account any item which is otherwise properly payable from that account, even though the charge creates an overdraft. The draft implies a promise to reimburse the bank for an overdraft. The bank has no obligation to pay an overdraft, although banks generally do extend this courtesy to some of their customers depending upon various factors—e.g., the size of the overdraft and the credit standing of the customer.

The item drawn by the customer and paid by the bank may have been altered by unauthorized completion or otherwise. We have seen[27] that: a holder's fraudulent, material alteration of an instrument discharges any party on the instrument whose contract thereon is changed without his assent; and any other alteration does not discharge any party but, rather, the instrument may be enforced according to its original tenor, or as to incomplete instruments unauthorizedly completed enforced according to the authority given. Also, if the altered instrument is negotiated to a holder in due course, he may enforce the instrument according to its original tenor if it was complete when issued, and as completed if it was incomplete when issued and subsequently unauthorizedly completed. As between the customer drawer and bank drawee, should the drawer be discharged by the fraudulent, material alteration and the bank be unable to charge the customer's account and have to look to the holder who has been paid? Under the Code,[28] *a bank which, in good faith, makes payment to a holder may charge the indicated account of its customer according to: (1) the original tenor of his altered item; or (2) the tenor of his completed item, even though the bank knows the item has been completed as long as the bank does not have notice that the completion was improper.*

Bank's Liability to Customer for Wrongful Dishonor. The obligation of the bank is to honor an item of its customer if the item is in proper form, e.g., properly indorsed, and sufficient funds of the customer are available on deposit. *In the event the payor bank wrongfully dishonors an item, it is liable to its customer for damages proximately caused by such wrongful dishonor.* If the wrongful dishonor occurs through the bank's *mistake,* the bank's liability is limited to *actual* damages which are proved. The actual damages may include *consequential* damages, such as damages for the arrest or prosecution of the customer or damages for injury to his reputation, provided the damages are proximately caused by the wrongful dishonor. Proximate cause is a question of fact and not of law.

Customer's Right to Stop Payment. A *customer* sometimes has occasion to stop the payment of an item which he has drawn. For example, he may have made a mistake in its amount or issuance, or the party to whom he issued the item has defrauded him or failed to render the agreed consideration. While having the bank stop payment on the item is an inconvenience to the bank, nevertheless this is a service which the bank must render to its customer. Accordingly, *a customer has the right to order his bank to stop payment of*

[27] See above, pp. 356–57.

[28] UCC 4–401(2).

any item payable from his account. However, the order must be received by the bank at such a time and in such a manner as to give the bank a reasonable opportunity to act on it before it has taken any of the following action on the item which would preclude the stop payment order from being effective:

(a) accepted or certified the item;
(b) paid the item in cash;
(c) settled for the item without reserving a right to revoke the settlement and without having such right under statute, clearing house rule or agreement;
(d) completed the process of posting the item to the indicated account of the drawer, maker or other person to be charged therewith or otherwise has evidenced by examination of such indicated account and by action its decision to pay the item; or
(e) become accountable for the amount of the item under subsection (1)(d) of Section 4–213[29] and Section 4–302[30] dealing with the payor bank's responsibility for late return of items.[31]

Only the customer can stop payment, with the exception of an interested party stopping the bank from paying after the customer's death.[32]

Usually the order to stop payment will be given hastily, and normally it is done over the telephone. Because of the haste, the oral stop payment order should exist for only a short time and then be put in writing to be effective for a longer time and also for the protection of both the customer and the bank. Accordingly, under the Code,[33] *an oral order is binding upon the bank only for 14 calendar days, unless confirmed in writing within that period. A written order is effective for only six months, unless renewed in writing.*

The bank's payment in violation of a valid stop payment order is improper and subjects the bank to liability for loss resulting therefrom. It is inevitable that mistakes will be made by a bank in failing to comply with a stop payment order, but this is a part of the overhead expense in the operation of the banking

---

[29] "(1) An item is finally paid by a payor bank when the bank has done any of the following, whichever happens first:

(d) made a provisional settlement for the item and failed to revoke the settlement in the time and manner permitted by statute, clearing house rule or agreement." UCC 4–213.

[30] UCC 4–302. "**Payor Bank's Responsibility for Late Return of Item.** In the absence of a valid defense such as breach of a presentment warranty (subsection (1) of Section 4–207), settlement effected or the like, if an item is presented on and received by a payor bank the bank is accountable for the amount of

(a) a demand item other than a documentary draft whether properly payable or not if the bank, in any case where it is not also the depositary bank, retains the item beyond midnight of the banking day of receipt without settling for it or, regardless of whether it is also the depositary bank, does not pay or return the item or send notice of dishonor until after its midnight deadline; or

(b) any other properly payable item unless within the time allowed for acceptance or payment of that item the bank either accepts or pays the item or returns it and accompanying documents."

[31] UCC 4–303(1).

[32] See below, p. 404.

[33] UCC 4–403(2).

business. We have already seen[34] that no agreement between bank and customer can disclaim the bank's responsibility for its own failure to exercise ordinary care nor can it limit the measure of damages for such failure. The customer has the burden of establishing the fact, and amount, of loss resulting from the payment of an item contrary to a binding stop payment order. However, the bank has a right of subrogation to prevent unjust enrichment by the bank's payment, now to be discussed.

Stop payment *at the request of a customer debtor* cannot be made on the drawer bank of a cashier's check, nor of any other instrument on which the bank is the maker or acceptor, because under UCC 3–802(1) the payee creditor loses its right against its debtor when a cashier's check is taken in payment of an underlying debt. The bank cannot refuse payment on the instrument.

Payor Bank's Right to Subrogation on Improper Payment. The effect of the stop payment order is to retain in the customer's account the amount of the item. Should the bank fail to comply with a stop payment order, it will have to reimburse the customer's account. However, the bank must be able to be made whole to the extent possible; it cannot profit from the occasion. Thus, the bank has: a right of subrogation; a possible defense that the customer, by conduct in recognizing the bank's payment, has ratified such payment over the stop payment order; the right to recover money paid under a mistake.

The bank's right of subrogation places the bank in a position to have the rights of the person to whom payment is made as against the customer, and the rights of the customer against the person paid. If the person paid is a holder in due course and the customer's defenses are not assertable against him, the bank, by being subrogated to the rights of the holder in due course, can charge the customer. Often customers erroneously believe that all that need be done to avoid liability on an item is to stop payment thereon. (D draws a check on E payable to P for goods that P intentionally never delivers to D. D issues a stop payment order to E. P negotiates the check to H, a holder in due course, who presents the check to E, who dishonors it. H can recover against D on the check because the personal defenses of P's fraud and failure of consideration are cut off as to a holder in due course. If E had wrongfully paid the check over the stop payment order, E would be subrogated to H's rights on the instrument and, therefore, would be able to recover the money from D, its customer.) Accordingly, under the Code:[35]

> If a payor bank has paid an item over the stop payment order of the drawer or maker or otherwise under circumstances giving a basis for objection by the drawer or maker, to prevent unjust enrichment and only to the extent necessary to prevent loss to the bank by reason of its payment of the item, the payor bank shall be subrogated to the rights
>
> (a) of any holder in due course on the item against the drawer or maker; and

[34] See above, p. 396.

[35] UCC 4–407.

(b) of the payee or any other holder of the item against the drawer or maker either on the item or under the transaction out of which the item arose;[36] and

(c) of the drawer or maker against the payee or any other holder of the item with respect to the transaction out of which the item arose.[37]

Payment of Stale Checks. By banking and commercial practice, checks outstanding for a period of more than six months are considered stale. Prior to the Code, while banks could pay such checks, by many state statutes they were not compelled to do so. Reflecting this practice and concern, under the Code[38] *a bank is under no obligation to its customer having a checking account to pay his uncertified check if presented more than six months after its date.* However, the bank may, if it wishes and provided it acts *in good faith,* pay the stale check and charge the customer's account therefor. For example, the drawee bank knows that its drawer corporate customer will want to have its outstanding dividend checks paid even though they are presented more than six months after date. Certified checks are excluded because the customer's account has been charged on certification and the certified check is now a primary obligation of the bank to the holder.

Death or Incompetence of Customer. Although under the law of Agency[39] the supervening death or adjudication of incompetency of the principal immediately and without notice terminates the agency relationship, the unique position of a bank payor or a collecting bank justifies a modification in the law based on the bank's knowledge of such state of facts in connection with its authority to pay or collect items. The very large volume of items handled in the collection process and the bank's difficulty in learning of the death or adjudication of incompetence of its customer make a change in the law necessary. *Accordingly, neither death nor incompetence of a customer revokes the authority of a payor or collecting bank to accept, pay, collect an item or to account for proceeds of its collection until the bank knows of such death or adjudication of incompetence and has a reasonable opportunity to act on it.* Also, such authority is not affected by the customer's incompetency at the time the item is issued or its collection undertaken if the bank does not know of an adjudication of incompetence. It should be noted carefully that only actual knowledge, and not constructive notice, is the criterion.

Under the Code *a bank, even with knowledge of its customer's death, may, for ten days after the date of death, pay or certify checks drawn on or prior to*

---

[36] D (drawer) receives nonconforming goods bought from P (payee) and telephones a stop payment order to E (D's drawee bank) not to pay D's check to P in payment for such goods. D keeps the goods. E mistakenly pays P on the check and charges D's account. Since P has a right against D for a part of the purchase price of the goods retained by D, E is subrogated to P's claim against D therefor.

[37] In the illustration in ftn. 36 above, if D had rejected the goods and returned them to P, since D has a right to recover from P the purchase price paid to him, E would be subrogated to D's right and could recover the money from P.

[38] UCC 4–404.

[39] See below, p. 617.

that date, unless ordered to stop payment by a person claiming an interest in the account. Examples of a person claiming an interest in the account are a surviving relative or creditor of the decedent, or the person named in the decedent's will as executor or legatee even though the will has not yet been admitted to probate.

It should be noted in passing that the gift of a check is not a gift of the amount indicated on the check until the drawee has paid or certified the check, and should the drawer die before payment or certification, the gift is *incomplete* and the holder has no claim against either the drawee or the estate of the drawer. The protection given to a bank who pays without knowledge of the death of its drawer customer or within ten days after death with knowledge thereof is solely to relieve the payor bank of liability for such payments; it has no effect upon the validity of the claims of recipients of payment nor upon the right of an executor or administrator of the decedent's estate to reclaim money paid to the holders.

Customer's Duty to Discover and Report Unauthorized Signature or Alteration. Generally a bank makes available to its customers a periodic statement of account accompanied by items, e.g., cancelled checks, paid in good faith in support of the charges against their accounts. This may be done either by: sending the statement and items to the customer; or holding the statement and items available to the customer pursuant to his request or instructions; or otherwise in a reasonable manner making them available to the customer. *The customer has a duty to exercise reasonable care and promptness to examine the statement and items to discover his unauthorized signature or any alteration on any item, and to notify the bank promptly after discovery thereof.* The customer's failure so to comply with his duty of reasonable care, promptness, and notification has a twofold effect. *First,* the customer is precluded or estopped from asserting against the bank his unauthorized signature or any alteration if the bank establishes that it suffered a loss by reason of the customer's failure. It should be noted that the bank has the burden of establishing both the customer's failure and that it suffered loss by reason thereof in order to preclude the customer. *Second,* if the statement and an item with *an* unauthorized signature or alteration are made available to the customer, the customer does not notify the bank of such unauthorized signature or alteration within a reasonable period not exceeding 14 calendar days, and before notification concerning the item the bank in good faith pays *another* item unauthorizedly signed or altered by the *same wrongdoer,* the customer is precluded from asserting such *additional* unauthorized signature or alteration against the bank. Again, the bank has the burden of establishing the customer's failure to comply with his duty of reasonable care, promptness, and notification. However, even if the bank proves such failure by the customer, the customer is not precluded in the above two instances if the customer establishes lack of ordinary care on the part of the bank in paying the item or items. Examples of the latter are: the bank's payment or acceptance of an item which has been altered and which alteration the bank *could have detected* by the exercise of ordinary care in the examination of the item; and the bank's payment or acceptance of an item on which the *customer's signature has been forged.* The customer has the burden of proving the bank's lack of ordinary care.

Irrespective of care or lack of care of either the customer or the bank, the customer has a limited time within which to assert a claim against the bank for payment of an item with his unauthorized signature, alteration, or unauthorized indorsement, after which time he is precluded from asserting such claim. After the statement and item are made available to the customer, he must discover and report: *his unauthorized signature or any alteration* on the face or back of the item *within one year thereafter; any unauthorized indorsement within three years thereafter.* The reason for the difference in times is that it will probably take a longer time for the customer to learn of a forged indorsement. Reference should be made to previous discussion[40] concerning negligence that contributed to an alteration or unauthorized signature, which is a protection to the bank against its customer.

A payor bank cannot waive its defense or fail to assert a defense to the prejudice of a collecting bank. Accordingly, under the Code, "If under this section a payor bank has a valid defense against a claim of a customer upon or resulting from payment of an item and waives or fails upon request to assert the defense the bank may not assert against any collecting bank or other prior party presenting or transferring the item a claim based upon the unauthorized signature or alteration giving rise to the customer's claim."[41]

PROBLEMS

1. (a) What is the effect of the following provisions in an otherwise negotiable promissory note, and explain why:
   (1) The writing promised to pay "$1,000 or, at the holder's election, to deliver 100 shares of common stock of X corporation."
   (2) The writing promised to pay $10,000 in installments of $1,000 each and provided that, on default in the payment of an installment, the whole amount would become due at the holder's option.
   (3) The writing promised to pay interest but did not state the amount or percentage.
   (4) The writing provided that, on default, the interest should be increased from 4 percent to 6 percent, the increased rate to be retroactively effective as from the date of the instrument.
   (5) The writing provided for collection costs and attorney's fees if the instrument were dishonored.

   (b) How are the following ambiguities in a negotiable instrument resolved:
   (1) Where the sum payable is expressed in words and also in figures and there is a discrepancy between the two.

[40] See above, p. 356.

[41] UCC 4–406(5).

(2) Where the instrument provides for the payment of interest, without specifying the date from which interest is to run.
(3) Where the instrument is not dated.
(4) Where there is a conflict between the handwritten, typewritten, and printed provisions.

2. (a) A negotiable promissory note in the amount of $1,000 payable to the order of "A and B," who were not related to each other in any way, was indorsed by A to C for $500 and to D for $500.
(1) What was the effect of this indorsement?
(2) Why?
(b) A check was payable to the order of "John Jarson," an infant whose proper name is "John Larson." The infant indorsed the check "John Larson" and delivered it to another person, who subsequently negotiated it to a holder in due course. The infant then disaffirmed all liability on the instrument.
(1) What was the effect of the infant's indorsement?
(2) Why?
3. B sold goods to A for $200, taking A's negotiable promissory note in payment, with the agreement that B would deliver the goods immediately. B sold and indorsed the note to C, an innocent party, for $100, of which $50 was paid in cash and $50 was to be paid in ten days. B did not deliver the goods, for which the note had been given, before the ten days expired, and A so informed C. C sued A for $200 on the note.
(1) Can C recover?
(2) Why? (Former C.P.A. Examination question)
4. P fraudulently induced D to issue his check to P, who two days later indorsed it in blank and delivered it for value to A, who knew of the fraud. Two weeks later, A indorsed the check in blank and delivered it for value to H, who took it in good faith without notice of the fraud. A week later, H in good faith negotiated the check to A for value. Can A enforce the check against D? Explain.
5. M issued a negotiable promissory note to the order of P who changed the face amount of the note from $1,000 to $10,000. Before maturity P indorsed the note in blank and delivered the note for value to H, who did not know of, and reasonably could not discern, the change in amount. The note was dishonored subsequently.
(1) Does H have any right against M on the note?
(2) Why?
(3) Would the result have been any different if, instead of P's changing the face amount of the note, M had issued the note with the amount blank and instructed P to fill in the amount for $1,000, but P filled it in for $10,000? Explain.
6. A stole goods from B, misrepresented to M that A was B, sold and delivered the goods to M, and received from M a negotiable promissory note payable to the order of B. Before maturity of the note, A forged B's signature as an indorsement in blank and sold and delivered the note for value to C, who was innocent of what had occurred previously. The note was dishonored subsequently.
(1) Does C have any right against M on the note?
(2) Why?
7. P was general manager of M's large firm. It was part of P's job to prepare the payroll list every week with the names of the firm's employees and the weekly compensation due each employee. Unknown to M, over a period of months P

included in the payroll list the names of many former employees, and M innocently prepared and signed checks for them drawn on E bank, delivering the checks to P for distribution among the employees each week. P forged the blank indorsements of the former employee payees on the checks and cashed them through the various banks where P had checking accounts. M now discovers the facts.

(1) Can M compel E to recredit his account for the checks drawn to such former employees and paid by E?
(2) Explain.

8. (a) Allen, without receiving any consideration, and for the accommodation of Brown, signs a negotiable promissory note payable to the order of Brown, who indorses and delivers it for value to Cox before due. When Cox took the note he knew that Allen received no value and was only an accommodation party. Brown is irresponsible, and Cox sues Allen on the instrument.
   (1) Can Cox recover from Allen? Explain.
   (2) If Cox had released Brown from liability on the note, could Cox now recover from Allen on the note? Explain.

   (b) Amos, who was 17 years old, gave a negotiable promissory note in payment for goods to Blue, who indorses it to Coty for value before maturity. The note is not paid at maturity. Coty sues Amos and Blue. Both Amos and Blue set up the infancy of Amos as a defense. Can Coty recover from Amos, or Blue, or both, or neither? Explain. (Former C.P.A. Examination question)

9. On January 9, 1981, D issued to the order of P a check drawn on E in the amount of $1,000. On the same day the check was negotiated by P to A; and on January 19 it was negotiated to B, who immediately presented it to E for payment. The check was dishonored for insufficient funds, the account never having had more than $200 on deposit. Notice of dishonor was given immediately to P and A.
   (1) Does B have any rights against D, P, or A?
   (2) Why?

10. P forged D's signature as drawer to a check on E bank payable to the order of P. P indorsed the check in blank and sold and delivered it for value to H who was unaware of the forgery. Later that day, H telephoned D and, after accurately describing the check to D, he asked D if it was a check signed and issued by D. D said "Yes, and I will stand behind it." Two days later, D stopped payment on the check, which was dishonored when presented for payment the next day by H to E. Can H recover the amount of the check from:
    (1) D? Explain.
    (2) P? Explain.

11. M is the maker of a negotiable promissory note and P is the payee holder. A stole the note from P, forged P's blank indorsement, indorsed the note in blank, and sold and delivered it for value to H, who took the note in good faith and without notice of the theft and forgery. At maturity, H presented the note to M, who paid it in good faith without notice of the theft and forgery.
    (1) Does P have any rights against M on the note? Explain.
    (2) Does M have any rights against H? Explain.

12. Allen drew his check to the order of Burt upon the Yanktown Bank. Burt duly presented the check at the bank for payment. Though the bank at the time had funds of Allen more than sufficient to pay the check, it refused to pay it. Can Burt maintain an action against the bank? (Former C.P.A. Examination question)

13. On a Monday afternoon X signed a check for $7,000 and delivered it to P, the payee, as a gift. On the next day, X was killed in an accident. The bank learned of X's death that day. Two weeks later, P cashed the check at the bank on which it was drawn, P not knowing of X's death.
    (1) Can X's estate recover from the bank the amount of the check?
    (2) Can the legal representative of X's estate recover the amount of the check from P? Explain.
14. On the maturity date of his negotiable promissory note, M paid the note to H, the holder but not a holder in due course. Is M discharged from liability on the note, indorsed in blank by P, the payee, if:
    (1) The note had been stolen from P by A who then negotiated the note to H? Explain.
    (2) If A, the thief, had negotiated the note to B, a holder in due course, who later negotiated it to H? Explain.
15. A certified public accountant who had completed his professional work for an out-of-town corporate client delivered his report to the president of the corporation in the latter's office. The president thereupon told him that the corporation's check for his fee would be given to him in half an hour and that the accountant could have it certified on his way to the railroad station, or, if the accountant preferred, a check already certified would be given to him in three quarters of an hour. Disregarding entirely all matters of personal convenience, which offer should the accountant accept? (Former C.P.A. Examination question.)

SOME PREVIOUS C.P.A. LAW EXAMINATION QUESTIONS AND AUTHOR'S MODEL ANSWERS

NOVEMBER, 1979

Number 3

Part a. Glasco Machinery and Manufacturing, Inc., sells industrial machinery to various customers on credit terms of 20 percent down and three-month promissory notes for the balance.

Glasco was experiencing severe financial difficulty and desperately needed a loan for working capital and to stave off persistent creditors. Its bank insisted upon security for any loan it might make. Glasco agreed to pledge $25,000 of its customer's promissory notes as collateral for a $20,000 demand loan. The notes pledged included some which Glasco knew had been received on sales of defective machinery and several notes which Glasco's president forged in anticipation of future shipments to customers.

After a short time Glasco's president saw that detection was inevitable, withdrew all funds in the bank, and absconded with the cash. The bank is seeking to enforce payment of the notes against the various parties.

Required:

Answer the following, setting forth reasons for any conclusions stated.

Discuss the bank's rights, if any, to collection on the various promissory notes.

Part b. Grover had an $80 check payable to the order of Parker that Parker had indorsed in blank. The check was drawn by Madison on State Bank. Grover deftly raised the amount to $800 and cashed it at Friendly Check Cashing Company. Friendly promptly presented it at State Bank where it was dishonored as an overdraft. Grover has been apprehended by the police and is awaiting trial. He has no known assets.

Friendly is seeking collection on the instrument against any or all of the other parties involved.

Required:

Answer the following, setting forth reasons for any conclusions stated.

Will Friendly recover against Madison, State Bank, or Parker?

Part c. Horn Audio purchased some audio components from Samuels Sounds. The high quality audio components were to be used by Horn in its expensive customized sound systems to be sold to its customers. Samuels fraudulently substituted a large number of reconditioned audio components for the new ones that Horn was shown and believed he had purchased. In payment of the purchase, Horn executed and delivered the following instrument to Samuels:

> January 8, 1979
>
> For value received, Horn Audio promises to pay Three Thousand Dollars ($3,000.00) to the order of Samuels Sounds, two weeks after their receipt and out of the proceeds from the resale of the audio components this day purchased from Samuels Sounds and used as major components in the customized sound systems sold to our customers.
>
> John Horn
>
> Horn Audio

Samuels transferred the instrument to Wilmont for value by signing it on the back and delivering it to him. Wilmont had no knowledge of the fraudulent substitution of the audio components by Samuels. Several months later, Wilmont presented the instrument to the maker for payment. Horn refused to pay the instrument alleging fraud and breach of warranty. Furthermore, Horn stated that all the audio components were returned to Samuels immediately upon discovery of the facts. Wilmont has commenced legal action against Horn on the instrument.

Required:

Answer the following, setting forth reasons for any conclusions stated.

Will Wilmont prevail in his legal action against Horn on the instrument?

Answer

3.a. It is assumed that the promissory notes transferred to the bank were properly indorsed by Glasco, as is normally done, so that the bank becomes a holder of them.

Under the Uniform Commercial Code on Commercial Paper, no person is liable on a negotiable instrument unless his signature appears thereon. Forgery is a real defense assertable against everyone, including a holder in due course. Here, the customers whose signatures as makers were forged on the notes are not liable thereon, and therefore the bank cannot hold them liable. However, an unauthorized signature operates as the signature of the unauthorized signer in favor of any person who, in good faith, takes the forged instrument for value. Therefore, Glasco's president is liable to the bank as the maker of the forged notes.

The other notes signed by Glasco's customers were of two kinds. Some were for goods from Glasco concerning which the customers had no complaint, and some were for machinery which was defective. The customer makers on the first kind of notes will be liable to the bank because they have no defenses to payment.

With respect to the second kind of notes for defective machinery, the customer makers have personal defenses which may be asserted against anyone except a holder in due course. The defective machinery causes a breach of contract and of warranty as well as a failure of consideration, which are personal defenses not assertable against a holder in due course. Therefore, these customer makers also will be liable to the bank if it is a holder in due course.

A holder in due course must have given value, and is such only to the extent of such value. A bank gives value for an item to the extent that the bank acquires a security interest in the item. Here, the bank loaned $20,000 to Glasco and thereby acquired a security interest to that extent in the $25,000 of notes taken as collateral. Therefore, the bank has given value of $20,000, is a holder in due course of the notes in that amount, and can recover on all the notes to that extent.

While there may be some question of whether the bank's security interest in each item is limited to 80 percent of that item, nevertheless the Code appears to indicate that, since the bank's security interest is over all the items, any item may be enforced to the full face amount of the item as long as the total amount recovered on all the items is not more than the 80 percent or $20,000. (pp. 338, 354, 355, 350, 400)

b. Friendly will recover $80 against either Madison or Parker, nothing against State Bank. Under the Code, a fraudulent material alteration of a negotiable instrument by a holder discharges any party to the instrument whose contract is thereby changed, except as to a subsequent holder in due course to whom they are liable for the original tenor of the instrument. Here, Parker's blank indorsement made the check payable to bearer and, since Grover possessed it, he was the bearer holder. Grover's intentionally raising the check's amount changed the contract liability of Madison and Parker on the check—and is a fraudulent material alteration. Apparently Friendly is a holder in due course. Therefore, Madison as drawer and Parker as indorser are liable to Friendly for $80 on dishonor of the check. Parker is not liable to Friendly for any breach of warranty of no alteration because the alteration occurred subsequent to his transfer of the check to Grover. State Bank is not liable to Friendly because it has no relationship with Friendly, and it had not accepted the check, since no person is liable on a negotiable instrument unless his signature appears thereon. (pp. 356–57, 360, 363–65)

c. No. Under the Code, if an instrument is not negotiable, no subsequent person can be a holder in due course, and the assignee transferee acquires only what his assignor transferor has. In order to be a negotiable promissory note, an instrument must contain an unconditional promise to pay on demand or at a definite time. Here, the instrument's promise to pay is conditional on Horn's receipt of the goods from Samuels and payment is to be made out of a particular fund, namely out of the proceeds from resale of the goods. Also, the money is not payable at a definite time, payment to be made when Horn receives such proceeds. If Horn's defenses of fraud and breach of warranty are true, since they can be asserted against Samuels, they can be asserted against his transferee, Wilmont. (pp. 145, 303, 315, 317)

MAY, 1979

Number 1

Select the **best** answers for each of the following items.

25. Martindale Retail Fish Stores, Inc., purchased a large quantity of fish from the Seashore Fish Wholesalers. The exact amount was **not** ascertainable at the moment, and Martindale, rather than waiting for the exact amount, gave Seashore a check which was blank as to the amount. Seashore promised **not** to fill in any amount until it had talked to Martindale's purchasing agent and had the amount approved. Seashore disregarded this agreement and filled in an amount that was $300 in excess of the correct price. The instrument was promptly negotiated to Clambake & Company, one of Seashore's persistent creditors, in payment of an account due. Martindale promptly stopped payment. For what amount will Martindale be liable to Clambake? Why?

a. Nothing because Martindale can assert the real defense of material alteration.
b. Nothing because Clambake did not give value and the stop order is effective against it.
c. Only the correct amount because the wrongful filling in of the check for the $300 excess amount was illegal.
d. The full amount because the check is in the hands of a holder in due course.

26. Filbert Corporation has in its possession an instrument which Groves, the maker, assured Filbert was negotiable. The instrument contains several clauses which are **not** typically contained in such an instrument and Filbert is **not** familiar with their legal effect. Which of the following will adversely affect the negotiability of the instrument?

a. A promise to maintain collateral and to provide additional collateral if the value of existing collateral decreases.
b. A term authorizing the confession of judgment on the instrument if **not** paid when due.
c. A statement to the effect that the instrument arises out of the November 1, 1978, sale of goods by Filbert to Groves.
d. A statement that it is payable only out of the proceeds from the resale of the goods sold by Filbert to Groves on November 1, 1978.

27. Mitchell sold his ranch to Campbell. Campbell tendered his uncertified check for $35,000 at the closing. Mitchell objected and asserted that the check had to be certified. An examination of the contract revealed that the usual certification requirement had been omitted. Mitchell begrudgingly accepted the check after a phone call to the bank confirmed that "the check is good." He promptly proceeded to Campbell's bank and requested that it be certified in that he needed a certified check for a closing the following day in connection with the purchase of another property. Regarding Mitchell's request for certification, which of the following is correct?

a. The bank is legally obligated to certify the check.
b. If the bank did certify the check, it constituted an acceptance and released Campbell.
c. The bank's oral statement that "the check is good" constituted an implied certification.
d. Once a check has been properly certified, further negotiation is prohibited.

29. Archer has in his possession a bearer negotiable instrument. He took it by negotiation from Perth who had stolen it from Cox's office along with cash and other property. The robbery of Cox's office had received appropriate coverage in the local papers in the area in which both Archer and Cox reside. Archer did **not** know that Perth had stolen

the instrument when he purchased it at a 20 percent discount. Cox refuses to pay and Archer has commenced legal action asserting that he is a holder in due course. Which of the following statements is correct?

a. Even if all other requisites are satisfied, Archer's title is defective in that there was **no** delivery by Cox of the instrument.
b. Archer is a holder in due course and will prevail.
c. Archer is prevented from qualifying as a holder in due course because there had been general notice published in the community about the robbery.
d. The discount in and of itself prevents Archer from qualifying as a holder in due course or at least prevents him from so qualifying as to the 20 percent.

30. Path stole a check made out to the order of Marks. Path forged the name of Marks on the back and made the instrument payable to himself. He then negotiated the check to Harrison for cash by signing his own name on the back of the instrument in Harrison's presence. Harrison was unaware of any of the facts surrounding the theft or forged indorsement and presented the check for payment. Central County Bank, the drawee bank, paid it. Disregarding Path, which of the following will bear the loss?

a. The drawer of the check payable to Marks.
b. Central County Bank.
c. Marks.
d. Harrison.

31. Troy fraudulently induced Casper to make a negotiable instrument payable to the order of Troy in exchange for goods he never intended to deliver. Troy negotiated it to Gorden, who took with notice of the fraud. Gorden in turn negotiated it to Wagner, a holder in due course. Wagner presented it for payment to Casper, who refused to honor it. Wagner contacted Gorden who agreed to reacquire the instrument by negotiation from Wagner. Which of the following statements is correct?

a. Casper would have been liable if Wagner had pursued his rights on the negotiable instrument.
b. Gorden was initially a holder in due course as a result of the negotiation to him from Troy.
c. Casper is liable to all parties except Troy in that it was his fault that the instrument was issued to Troy.
d. Gorden can assert the rights of his prior holder in due course, Wagner, as a result of the repurchase.

32. Franco & Sons, Inc., was engaged in the furniture manufacturing business. One of its bi-weekly paychecks was payable to Stein, who negotiated it to White in payment of a gambling debt. White proceeded to raise the amount of the check from $300 to $800 and negotiated it to Carson, a holder in due course, for cash. Upon presentment by Carson at the drawee bank, the teller detected the raising of the amount and contacted Franco who stopped payment on the check. Franco refuses to pay Carson. Carson is seeking to recover the $800. Under the circumstances, which of the following is a correct statement?

a. Franco is liable, but only for $300.
b. Franco is liable for the $800.
c. Stein is liable for the $800.
d. Franco has **no** liability to Carson.

Answer

1. 25.d(356–57, 323) 26.d(315) 27.b(360) 29.b(341–42, 350) 30.d(368, 398–99) 31.a(350) 32.a(356–57)

MAY, 1978

Number 2

Part a. Your CPA firm was engaged to audit the Meglo Corporation. During the audit you examined the following instrument:

> April 2, 1977
>
> Charles Noreen
> 21 West 21st Street
> St. Louis, Missouri
>
> I, Charles Noreen, do hereby promise to pay to Roger Smith, Two Thousand Dollars ($2,000) one year from date, with 8 percent interest upon due presentment.
>
> FOR: Payment for used IBM typewriters.
>
> Charles Noreen

Meglo purchased the instrument from Smith on April 10, 1977, for $1,700. Meglo received the instrument with Smith's signature and the words "Pay to the order of Meglo Corporation" on the back. Upon maturity, Meglo presented the instrument to Noreen, who refused to pay. Noreen alleged that the typewriters were defective and did not satisfy certain warranties given in connection with the purchase of the used IBM typewriters which were guaranteed for one year. Noreen had promptly notified Smith of this fact and had told him he would not pay the full amount due.

Required:

Answer the following, setting forth reasons for any conclusions stated.

1. Is the instrument in question negotiable commercial paper?
2. Assuming that the instrument is negotiable, does Meglo qualify as a holder in due course entitled to collect the full $2,000?
3. Assuming that the instrument is negotiable, is Noreen's defense valid against a holder in due course?
4. Assuming that the instrument is nonnegotiable, what is the legal effect of the transfer by Smith to Meglo?

Part b. Marvin Farber cashed a check for Harold Kern which was made to the order of Charles Walker by Marglow Investments & Securities. The check had the following indorsements on the back:

1. Charles Walker
2. without recourse
   Doris Williamson
3. Pay to the order of Harold Kern
   Jack Dixon
4. Pay to the order of Marvin Faber

Kern neglected to sign his indorsement when he gave the check to Farber, and Farber did not notice this until the following day. Before Farber could locate Kern and obtain his signature. Farber learned that Walker had fraudulently obtained the check from Marglow (the drawer). Farber finally located Kern and obtained his signature. Farber promptly indorsed the check in blank and cashed it at National Bank. National Bank presented the check for payment through normal banking channels, but it was dishonored by Marglow's bank pursuant to a valid stop order. National Bank contacted Farber and informed him of the situation. Farber repaid the amount and the check was returned to him with National Bank's blank indorsement on the back.

Required:

Answer the following, setting forth reasons for any conclusions stated.

1. Identify the type of indorsement and indicate the liability for each indorsement numbered 1, 2, and 3 above.
2. Will Farber prevail in a legal action seeking payment of the check by Marglow?

Answer

2.a.1. No. Under the Uniform Commercial Code on Commercial Paper, for an instrument to be negotiable it must be payable to order or to bearer. Here, the note does not contain these words of negotiability and, therefore, it is a nonnegotiable promissory note. (p. 311)

2. Yes. For a holder to be a holder in due course he must take the negotiable instrument in good faith. The purchase of the instrument at a discount is evidence of bad faith, but it is not bad faith per se. Here, Meglo's purchase of the note at a discount of $300 is not sufficient, without other facts, to prove bad faith on Meglo's part. Therefore, since all other requisites for being a holder in due course are present, Meglo is a holder in due course entitled to collect the full $2,000. (p. 341)

3. No. Personal defenses cannot be asserted against a holder in due course. Failure of consideration is a personal defense. Here, Noreen's assertion of defective typewriters in breach of warranty is a personal defense and, therefore, it cannot be asserted against a holder in due course, here Meglo. (p. 350)

4. Since the note is nonnegotiable, Meglo cannot be a holder in due course. Only a negotiable instrument can be negotiated to a holder in due course. Therefore, Noreen's personal defense can be asserted against Meglo who cannot recover the face amount of the note. However, Meglo is an assignee of Smith's contract claim against Noreen and, therefore, he acquires Smith's rights. Since Smith had a right to recover from Noreen the contract price less damage for breach of warranty, therefore Meglo has this same right against Noreen. (pp. 350, 81)

b.1. *Walker Indorsement.* Blank indorsement. An indorsement which does not specify any particular indorsee is a blank indorsement; it is only a signature with no accompanying words. Under the Code, every indorser is a party secondarily liable on the instrument and engages that, unless the indorsement otherwise specifies, upon dishonor of the instrument and any necessary notice of dishonor he will pay the instrument according to its tenor at the time of his indorsement to the holder or to any subsequent indorser who takes it. Walker has this contractual liability on the check. Also, on his transfer of the check for consideration he gives the warranties of title, that the signatures are genuine, that there is no material alteration of the instrument, that there is no good defense against him, and that he has no knowledge of any insolvency proceedings against the drawer, Marglow. (pp. 333, 368–70)

Williamson Indorsement. Qualified indorsement. This indorsement disclaims or qualifies the indorser's contractual liability on the instrument. The indorser merely assigns the title to the instrument and no recourse can be made against him for non-payment of the instrument. He gives the same warranties stated above, except that he warrants that he has no knowledge of any defense good against him. (pp. 364, 368–70)

Dixon Indorsement. Special indorsement. This indorsement specifies the person to whom, or to whose order, it makes the instrument payable. The instrument is now payable to the order of the special indorsee and may be further negotiated only by his indorsement. The same liability and warranties as in the Walker indorsement apply here. (pp. 333, 368–70)

2.b. Yes, if either Kern, Dixon, or Williamson was a holder in due course. Farber is not a holder in due course. Under the Code, the status of a holder in due course is determined as of the time the instrument was negotiated to him as a holder. Here, Farber did not become a holder until he obtained Kern's indorsement, at which time Farber knew of Walker's fraud. Thus, Farber did not take the check in good faith and without notice of Marglow's personal defense of fraud. Personal defenses may be asserted against anyone except a holder in due course or a holder claiming through a holder in due course, except that a holder who, prior to the holder in due course, had notice of a defense against the instrument cannot improve his position by claiming through a holder in due course. Here, Farber can claim through the prior indorsers except Walker, who is not a holder in due course because of his fraud, and except the bank because Farber was a holder but not a holder in due course prior to the bank's indorsement. (pp. 341, 350)

Part Four: Security

A. Property Security Transactions

Chapter 28

CONSENSUAL PROPERTY SECURITY TRANSACTIONS

SECTION I. CONCEPT OF SECURITY

"Security" is a creditor's interest in specific property, or in the obligation of a third person, as assurance for the performance of the debtor's obligation. Property security transactions may be *consensual*, e.g., Article 9 of the Code covering only personal property, and the real property mortgage, or *nonconsensual*, e.g., Common Law and statutory liens.

Purpose of Security

The word "security" has a broad, general, well-recognized meaning; it also has a narrow, technical meaning under Article 8 of the Uniform Commercial Code on Investment Securities. Under Article 8 of the Code, security is an "investment security," an instrument traded on the securities markets, e.g., a certificate of stock or bond, discussed later.[1] Throughout this book, except in the portion on Investment Securities under the transfer of corporate shares in the law of corporations, such an instrument is described by its full name as an "investment security." In the broad, general, and well-recognized sense *the word "security" is the name for the creditor's interest in specific property, or in the obligation of a third person, as assurance for the performance of the debtor's obligation.* The purpose of security for the performance of an obligation, whether for the payment of a debt or otherwise, is to provide a specific

[1] See below, p. 717 f.

source from which the creditor or obligee will obtain performance of the obligation, or payment for loss sustained by the obligee, in the event of the obligor's failure to perform. Essentially, the purpose is to obtain *priority* over other obligees of the obligor in resorting to a particular source. (A delivers his horse to B as security for B's loan of money to A. B has security against which he has the prior right to resort in the event of A's default.) A "secured creditor" has security for the obligation owing to him, while an "unsecured creditor" has no such security. The security may be in the form of property or in the form of a third person's contract to perform the debtor's obligation in the event of his default, called "suretyship." Accordingly, the entire subject of Security will be divided into two parts, namely Property Security Transactions and Suretyship, and will be considered in that order.

Kinds of Property Security Transaction

Property security transactions may be consensual or nonconsensual. In consensual transactions the parties *agree* to create the security for an obligation, as A's delivery of a horse as security for a loan. In nonconsensual transactions the parties *do not agree* to any property as security for the performance of an obligation, but by statute or Common Law, a security interest in specific property is created, e.g., the right of a mechanic to retain an automobile that he has repaired at the request of the owner as security for the payment of such repairs. When the lien is created by statute, it is called a "statutory lien." Consensual property security transactions may involve personal or real property. Accordingly, in this chapter, Section II will consider secured transactions involving personal property and fixtures, Section III will consider the real property mortgage; Chapter 29 will consider nonconsensual property security transactions.

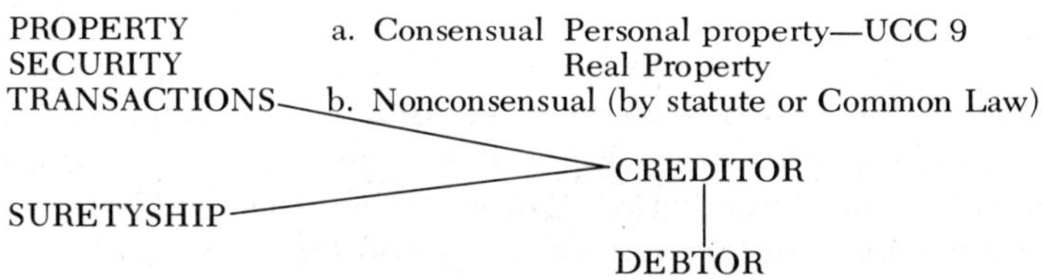

SECTION II. PERSONAL PROPERTY AND FIXTURES

The "security agreement" creates or provides for a "security interest," which is an interest in personal property or fixtures which secures payment or performance of an obligation. Security interests arising under the Article on Sales are under Article 9. A "debtor" is the obligor and the "secured party" the obligee, and when an account is assigned for security the assignee becomes the "secured party," the assignor becomes the "debtor" as to the assignee, and the

original debtor becomes an "account debtor." A "purchase money security interest" is a particular kind of security interest. The Code provides for "perfection of a security interest," meaning compliance with the Article's provisions by proper filing, with exceptions, in order to obtain *maximum priority* for a security interest in collateral against third persons.

"Collateral" is tangible or intangible personal property subject to a security interest. *Tangible* personal property is "goods," the *nature and use* of which determines its kind: (*1*) *Consumer goods*—used or bought for use primarily for personal, family or household purposes. (2) *Equipment*—used or bought for use primarily in business or by a debtor nonprofit organization or governmental subdivision or agency. (3) *Inventory*—held for sale or lease or to be furnished under contracts of service, or raw materials, work in process or materials used or consumed in a business. (*4*) *Farm products*—crops or livestock or supplies used or produced in farming operations, or products of crops or livestock in their unmanufactured states, *and* if they are in the possession of a debtor engaged in farming operations. "Fixtures" are goods which become so related to particular real estate that an interest in them arises under real estate law. Ordinary building materials incorporated into the real estate are not fixtures. *Intangible* personal property is a right. *It may be represented by indispensable paper,* e.g., documents (of title), instruments (negotiable instruments or investment securities), and chattel paper (a writing evidencing both a monetary obligation and a security interest in or a lease of specific goods). Rights not so evidenced are "accounts" (the usual account receivable) and "general intangibles," e.g., rights to performance, patents, copyrights. A security interest may be acquired in after-acquired collateral.

The state where collateral is located has jurisdiction to determine its legal status and whether or not it is subject to a security interest. *With respect to accounts, general intangibles (other than uncertificated securities), and mobile goods:* the law of the jurisdiction *where the debtor is located* will govern the perfection and the effect of perfection or non-perfection of a security interest with regard to accounts, general intangibles, and mobile goods of a type which are normally used in more than one jurisdiction if such goods are equipment or inventory because of their being leased or held for lease by the debtor to others. *With respect to documents, instruments, and ordinary goods:* when tangible collateral subject to a security interest perfected in one state comes into a second state, the status of perfection with respect to such collateral is determined by various rules. (1) The state where perfection of collateral was attempted determines whether or not perfection occurred. If a security interest was perfected there, it continues in any state where the collateral later is located, except that the law of the latter state governs for 30 days in the case of a purchase money security interest in goods which the parties creating the security interest intended to be permanently located in the latter state. (2) The perfected security interest created in the first state continues in the state where the collateral subsequently is located for four months, and also thereafter if, within the four-month period, it is perfected in the latter state. Failure to perfect within that period causes the secured party's interest to be unperfected, and any later perfection by him dates from such time. If goods are covered by a certificate of title issued by a state which requires indication on the certificate of any security interest in the goods as a condition of perfection, the law of the state which issued the certificate governs, until removal of the goods from that state and the expiration of a four-month period in another state. Three things are necessary to perfect a security interest, irrespective of the order of their occurrence: (1) *creation of the security interest*, either by a security agreement or the secured party has possession of the collateral; (2) *attachment of the security interest to collateral*, in which the debtor has rights and for which security interest the secured party has given value; and (3) the security interest must be *perfected* either by filing of a financing statement or by the secured party acquiring possession of the collateral. *With certain exceptions, perfection of a security interest can be made only by filing a financing statement.* Some exceptions when filing is not necessary to perfection are: (1) *Possession* of the collateral by the secured party—this is notice to all persons of a security interest therein. (2) *A temporary perfection* for 21 days of a security interest *in instruments* (*other than certificated securities*) *and negotiable documents* from the time the security interest attached, the collateral normally being possessed by the debtor so as to obtain proceeds from their disposition to repay the secured party on the debtor's obligation. (3) A *temporary perfection* for ten days of a security interest in *the proceeds* resulting from the disposition of collateral, beginning from the day the debtor received such proceeds. (4) A *purchase money security interest in consumer goods.* (5) The security interest of a collecting bank in items, accompanying documents and proceeds therefrom, *a security interest in securities,* or a security interest arising solely under the Article on Sales as long as the debtor does not lawfully possess the collateral. The Code permits a secured party to have a "floating lien" on a shifting stock of goods of the debtor.

With respect to purchasers of goods subject to a security interest, if sold *with the authority* of the secured party, then the purchaser takes free of the security interest. If sold *without such authority*, the purchaser takes *subject to* the security interest, unless he is *a buyer in ordinary course of business,* other than a person buying farm products from a person engaged in farming operations, who *takes free* of the security interest created by his seller even though the security interest is perfected and even though the buyer knows of its existence. But the purchaser of *consumer goods* subject to a security interest *perfected by filing* takes *subject to* the security interest; if perfection occurred in *any other way*, and the buyer purchased without knowledge of the security interest, for value, and for his own personal, family, or household purposes, he takes free of the security interest.

With respect to purchasers of chattel paper and negotiable paper, the buyer from a debtor seller of *chattel paper* subject to a perfected security interest *by permissive* filing (temporary protection) takes *subject to* the security interest, unless he gives new value, takes possession in the ordinary course of his business and without knowledge that the specific paper is subject to a security interest, in which event he *has priority* over the security interest perfected by permissive filing. If the purchase is of *negotiable paper,* the holder in due course of a negotiable instrument, the duly negotiated holder of a negotiable document of title, and the bona fide purchaser of an investment security prevail over an earlier perfected security interest.

Priorities among conflicting security interests are established by the Code. Because of the detail and complexity involved, reference should be made to the text.[2]

Accounts are assignable and security interests perfected in them, and any term in the agreement between an account debtor and an assignor prohibiting such assignment or creation of a security agreement is void. With certain limitations, their agreement may validly provide that the account debtor will not assert against an assignee of the secured party assignor defenses which the account debtor may have against the assignor. They may also modify their contract or make a substitute contract without the consent of the assignee, under certain conditions. Unless the assignee *demands* payment by the account debtor, the latter may properly make payment to the assignor.

The financing statement is *filed* and must contain the names and addresses of the debtor and secured party, an itemization or description of the collateral, and be signed by the debtor. Under certain conditions, only the secured party's signature is required. Filing occurs by presentation of the financing statement to the filing officer and tender of the filing fee, or by the latter's acceptance of the financing statement. The filing is effective for five years, and can be extended for another five years by filing of a "continuation statement" within six months prior to the expiration of the five year period. A "termination statement" signed by the secured party and properly filed terminates the perfection of the security interest.

On the debtor's default: the secured party's rights are to sue and obtain judgment and execution sale, collection, take possession of the collateral, and dispose of the collateral; the debtor has the right to redeem the collateral. The secured party is liable for loss caused to the debtor by his failure to comply with his duties after the debtor's default.

A pledge is the security interest in goods, and in the indispensable paper and the intangible it represents, created by a bailment for the purpose of security. It is a consensual *possessory* lien with the power to sell the property on default, the pledgor retaining the title and the pledgee the security interest. Filing is not necessary for perfection as long as the pledgor does not lawfully have possession of the property. The pledgee's voluntary surrender of the property to the pledgor terminates the pledge. The pledgee still has possession in "field storage warehousing."

---

[2] See below, pp. 442 ff.

Introduction

In General. Article 9 of the Uniform Commercial Code on Secured Transactions is concerned with all *consensual* security interests in *personal property and fixtures,* with a few exceptions. It simplifies and unifies in a single structure security devices dealing with such property, removing many of the complexities in security financing which have grown up during a long period of time in a vastly expanding economy. *There is only one security device,* namely the "security agreement," which is "an agreement which creates or provides for a security interest."[3] A "security interest" is "an interest in personal property or fixtures which secures payment or performance of an obligation. . . . The term also includes any interest of a *buyer* of accounts or chattel paper which is subject to Article 9."[4] *The Article applies to any transaction (regardless of its form) which is intended to create a security interest in personal property or fixtures, and also to sales of accounts or chattel paper.* It should be noted very carefully that the Article applies to security interests created by a contract which *intended* to create such security interest, as well as to *sales* of accounts and chattel paper. Accordingly, *statutory* liens are excluded from the Article, except for a provision with respect to priorities, discussed later.[5] A security interest in property is a *"lien," which is a legal right in the property of another as security for the performance of an obligation.* Some liens are possessory, in that they include the right to possess specific property, e.g., the pledge;[6] while other liens are non-possessory, in that they do not include such right to possession, e.g., the security interest in an automobile possessed by the owner. The fact that the security interest is in an obligation itself secured by a transaction or interest to which the Article does not apply does not exclude such security interest from the Article.[7]

Various types of transaction are excluded from the Article because primarily they are not security transactions, and also because they are either the subject of federal statute or of such local social concern that they are more properly within the purview of state statute rather than a uniform law. The Article does not apply:

(a) to a security interest subject to any statute of the United States to the extent that such statute governs the rights of parties to and third parties affected by transactions in particular types of property; or
(b) to a landlord's lien; or

---

[3] UCC 9–105(1)(h). The term "security agreement" replaces various terms, such as "chattel mortgage," "conditional sale," "trust receipt," "assignment of accounts receivable."

[4] UCC 1–201(37).

[5] See below, p. 443.

[6] See below, pp. 458 ff.

[7] While a note secured by a mortgage on real property is a security interest not under the Code when the transaction occurred, nevertheless the mortgagee's pledge of the mortgagor's note as security for a loan made to the mortgagee creates a security interest in the note and is under Article 9.

(c) to a lien given by statute or other rule of law for services or materials except as provided in Section 9–310 on priority of such liens; or
(d) to a transfer of a claim for wages, salary or other compensation of an employee; or
(e) to a transfer by a government or governmental subdivision or agency; or
(f) to a sale of accounts or chattel paper as part of a sale of the business out of which they arose, or an assignment of accounts or chattel paper which is for the purpose of collection only, or a transfer of a right to payment under a contract to an assignee who is also to do the performance under the contract or a transfer of a single account to an assignee in whole or partial satisfaction of a preexisting indebtedness; or
(g) to a transfer of an interest or claim in or under any policy or insurance, except as provided with respect to proceeds (Section 9–306) and priorities in proceeds (Section 9–312); or
(h) to a right represented by a judgment (other than a judgment taken on a right to payment which was collateral); or
(i) to any right of set-off; or
(j) except to the extent that provision is made for fixtures in Section 9–313, to the creation or transfer of an interest in or lien on real estate, including a lease or rents thereunder; or
(k) to a transfer in whole or in part of any claim arising out of tort; or
(l) to a transfer of an interest in any deposit account (subsection (1) of Section 9–105), except as provided with respect to proceeds (Section 9–306) and priorities in proceeds (Section 9–312).[8]

Security interests arise under the Sales portion of the Code, e.g., the seller may reserve a security interest in shipped goods, and they come within the purview of Article 9. However, they are exempted from certain provisions of the Article under certain conditions. While a security interest arising *solely* under the Sales portion of the Code is under Article 9, nevertheless to the extent that, and so long as, the debtor does not have or does not lawfully obtain *possession* of the goods: no security agreement is necessary to make the security interest enforceable; no filing is required to perfect the security interest; and the rights of the secured party on default by the debtor are governed by the Sales portion of the Code.[9] However, if the debtor lawfully obtains *possession* of the goods under a sales transaction, the secured party must comply with the provisions of Article 9 in order to obtain security protection thereunder against third parties. It should be noted in passing that the creation of a security interest is not a bulk transfer under the Bulk Transfers portion of the Code.[10]

Terminology. It is important to understand the terminology employed by the Article. Some basic terms will be considered at this time. The "security agreement" and "security interest" terms have already been defined. The parties to the security agreement are the "debtor" and the "secured party." A

---

[8] UCC 9–104.

[9] UCC 9–113.

[10] See above, pp. 290 ff.

debtor is "the person who owes payment or other performance of the obligation secured, whether or not he owns or has rights in the collateral, and includes the seller of accounts or chattel paper."[11] A secured party is "a lender, seller or other person in whose favor there is a security interest, including a person to whom accounts or chattel paper have been sold."[12] By the security agreement, the secured party acquires a security interest in "collateral," which is "the property subject to a security interest, and includes accounts and chattel paper which have been sold."[13] An "account debtor" is "the person who is obligated on an account, chattel paper or general intangible."[14] A security interest is called a "purchase money security interest" *to the extent that it is:* taken or retained by the seller of the collateral to secure all or part of its price; or taken by a person who, by making advances or incurring an obligation, gives value to enable the debtor to acquire rights in or the use of collateral if such value is in fact so used. It should be noted very carefully that *a security interest taken as security for, or in satisfaction of, a preexisting claim or antecedent debt does not qualify as a purchase money security interest.*

The Collateral

Tangibles and Intangibles. The security interest is in personal property or fixtures under Article 9, which are called "collateral." *Collateral means the property subject to a security interest, and includes accounts and chattel paper which have been sold.* Collateral consists of tangible and intangible personal property. First tangibles consisting of goods and fixtures will be discussed, then intangibles consisting of those represented by indispensable paper and those not evidenced by any instrument or document, and lastly after-acquired collateral.

Tangibles—Goods, Fixtures. Tangible personal property consists of goods. *Goods includes all things which are movable at the time the security interest attaches or which are fixtures.* Goods includes the unborn young of animals, growing crops, and standing timber which is to be cut or removed under a conveyance or contract for sale. *Goods does not include money, documents, instruments, chattel paper, accounts, general intangibles, or minerals, oil, gas, or the like before extraction.* There are four classes of goods, namely, consumer goods, equipment, farm products, and inventory. While most of the Article's sections apply to all kinds of goods, there are some sections which have rules applicable only to a particular kind of goods. It is very important

[11] UCC 9–105(1)(d); (continued): "Where the debtor and the owner of the collateral are not the same person, the term 'debtor' means the owner of the collateral in any provision of the Article dealing with the collateral, the obligor in any provision dealing with the obligation, and may include both where the context so requires."

[12] UCC 9–105(1)(m); (continued): "When the holders of obligations issued under an indenture of trust, equipment trust agreement or the like are represented by a trustee or other person, the representative is the secured party."

[13] UCC 9–105(1)(c).

[14] UCC 9–105(1)(a).

that the *nature* and *use* of these different kinds of goods be understood inasmuch as failure to comply with the particular sections applicable to each of them may preclude the perfection[15] of a security interest in them. Goods are *consumer goods* "if they are used or bought for use primarily for personal, family or household purposes."[16] For example, a refrigerator used in a home is consumer goods. Goods are *equipment* "if they are used or bought for use primarily in business (including farming or a profession) or by a debtor who is a nonprofit organization or a governmental subdivision or agency or if the goods are not included in the definitions of inventory, farm products or consumer goods."[17] For example, a refrigerator used in a store to hold perishable foods for sale is equipment. Goods are *inventory* "if they are held by a person who holds them for sale or lease or to be furnished under contracts of service or if he has so furnished them, or if they are raw materials, work in process or materials used or consumed in a business. Inventory of a person is not to be classified as his equipment."[18] For example, a refrigerator for sale in a kitchen appliance store is inventory. Difficulty in distinguishing goods as inventory rather than equipment can be resolved by applying the principal test, are the goods held for immediate or ultimate sale? If they are, they are inventory. Goods are *farm products* "if they are crops or livestock or supplies used or produced in farming operations or if they are products of crops or livestock in their unmanufactured states (such as ginned cotton, wool-clip, maple syrup, milk and eggs), *and* if they are *in the possession of a debtor engaged in* raising, fattening, grazing or other *farming operations*. If goods are farm products they are neither equipment nor inventory."[19] (Author's italics.) When farm products are put into the process of manufacturing which is not so closely connected with farming as to remain farm products they cease to be farm products; and if, after manufacturing they are held for sale, they become inventory.

Under the Article, security interests may be acquired in fixtures. The Article defines a fixture in very broad terms as goods which "become so related to particular real estate that an interest in them arises under real estate law,"[20] *with the legal effect that interests in the goods as chattels become subordinate to real estate interests*—except for priorities of interests in the fixture as established by the Code. It is for this reason that the Code provides for "fixture filing," i.e., *recording* in real estate records (where real estate mortgages are filed or recorded) in order to acquire priority against real estate interests. The Article leaves to local law the determination of when a chattel becomes a fixture because of its integral incorporation into the real estate, except that the Article precludes ordinary building materials incorporated into an improve-

---

[15] By perfection is meant compliance with the Article's provisions in order to obtain maximum priority for a security interest in collateral as against third persons. See below, pp. 433–34.

[16] UCC 9–109(1).

[17] UCC 9–109(2).

[18] UCC 9–109(4).

[19] UCC 9–109(3).

[20] UCC 9–313(1)(a).

ment on land from becoming fixtures. Glass, lumber, bricks, tile, cement, and metal work are examples of such a kind of building materials.[21]

Intangibles. Intangible personal property consists of intangibles represented by indispensable paper, and intangibles not evidenced by any instrument or chattel paper. *Intangibles are rights.* Intangibles may be represented by indispensable paper, i.e., paper the possession of which is essential to the enjoyment, transfer, or enforcement of the intangible. Such *indispensable paper consists of documents, instruments, and chattel paper.* By *document* is meant a document of title, which is a document "which in the regular course of business or financing is treated as adequately evidencing that the person in possession of it is entitled to receive, hold and dispose of the document and the goods it covers."[22] Examples are bills of lading and warehouse receipts, previously discussed under Documents of Title.[23] By *instrument* is meant a negotiable instrument[24] or an investment security[25] "or any other writing which evidences a right to the payment of money and is not itself a security agreement or lease and is of a type which is in ordinary course of business transferred by delivery with any necessary indorsement or assignment."[26] Examples of a negotiable instrument are checks, negotiable promissory notes, and drafts; and examples of a security investment are certificates of stock and bonds. By *chattel paper* is meant "a writing or writings which evidence both a monetary obligation and a security interest in or a lease of specific goods. . . . When a transaction is evidenced both by such a security agreement or a lease and by an instrument or a series of instruments, the group of writings taken together constitutes chattel paper."[27] For example, the former conditional sales contract, whereby the buyer acquires a refrigerator but the seller reserves a security interest in the refrigerator, evidences both the buyer's debt to the seller of the balance of the unpaid purchase price and also that the seller has a security interest in the refrigerator to assure payment of the debt. The conditional sales contract is the security agreement and, should the seller wish to borrow money on the contract and his security interest in the refrigerator, he may refinance by using the contract representing his security interest in the refrigerator as security for his refinancing. The conditional sales contract is the chattel paper and the collateral for such refinancing.

Intangibles may not be evidenced by any instrument or document. Such intangibles are accounts and general intangibles. An account is "any right to payment for *goods sold or leased* or for *services rendered* which is not evidenced by an instrument or chattel paper, whether or not it has been earned by performance."[28] (Author's italics.) This is the usual account receivable. (S

[21] See UCC 9–313(1)(2); and below, pp. 445–46, 766.

[22] UCC 1–201(15).

[23] See above, pp. 172 ff.

[24] See above, p. 310.

[25] See below, p. 717.

[26] UCC 9–105(1)(i).

[27] UCC 9–105(1)(b).

[28] UCC 9–106.

orally sells and *delivers* goods to B for $100 on 30 days' credit. S has an account receivable of $100.) General intangibles "means any personal property (including things in action) *other than* goods, accounts, chattel paper, documents, instruments, and money."[29] (Author's italics.) Examples are goodwill, rights to performance, patents, and copyrights. General intangibles is a catchall term including miscellaneous types of right included in the Article but not included in account or the rights represented by instruments, documents, and chattel paper. An illustration may help to clarify some of these terms. A retailer in refrigerators sells one to a drugstore in which to store perishables, the retailer taking a purchase money security interest contract (conditional sales contract). The contract is a "security agreement," the drug store is the "debtor," and the refrigerator is "equipment" and the "collateral." The retailer borrows from a bank and uses the contract as security for the loan. Inasmuch as the contract evidences both a monetary obligation and a security interest in the refrigerator, it is "chattel paper." Thus, prior to the loan transaction the drugstore was the "debtor" and the retailer the "secured party." After the loan transaction, the drugstore became the "account debtor," the retailer became the "debtor" *as to the bank*, and the bank became the "secured party" of both the retailer and the drugstore.

It should be noted that the collateral subject to a security interest may be owned by a person other than the debtor. The Article fixes the legal status of such owner, unless otherwise agreed, with respect to his right to receive from the secured party any surplus resulting after the claim of the secured party has been enforced and satisfied, the owner not being liable for the debt or for any deficiency after resale of the collateral.[30]

After-Acquired Collateral. The secured party may wish to acquire a security interest in personal property to be later acquired by the debtor.[31] It becomes very important whether such a security interest is acquired as security for an antecedent debt or as security for new value given, because if no new value is given the acquisition of the additional security interest may have an important effect in federal bankruptcy[32] or state insolvency proceedings as a voidable preference. The Article specifies that a security interest in after-acquired collateral is acquired for new value and not as security for an antecedent debt if two things occur. *First,* the secured party must give new value, which occurs if he makes an advance, incurs an obligation, releases a perfected security interest, or otherwise gives new value. *Second,* the debtor acquires rights in the after-acquired collateral either in the ordinary course of his business, or under a contract of purchase made pursuant to the security agreement within a reasonable time after new value is given. A purchase money security interest is also new value.[33]

---

[29] Ibid.

[30] UCC 9–112.

[31] See below, pp. 443 f., for details regarding after-acquired property clause coverage.

[32] See below, p. 526.

[33] For the definition of value, see above, p. 146, ftn. 1.

Conflict of Laws Rules concerning Perfection of Security Interests in Multiple State Transactions. The state where the collateral is located has jurisdiction over it and has legal power to declare not only its legal status, but also whether perfection of a security interest in the collateral has occurred and the legal effect of perfection or non-perfection of a security interest in the collateral. The state in which the collateral is located must, however, consider comity with other state jurisdictions with respect to *tangible* collateral which has come from another jurisdiction and with respect to the location of *intangible* collateral, such as an account or general intangible. While the Article's provisions apply as the law of the state in which the collateral is located, nevertheless special rules in the Article apply to: accounts, general intangibles, and mobile goods; documents, instruments, and ordinary goods; certificate of title; chattel paper; minerals; and uncertificated securities. Before considering each of these in the order indicated, it should be recognized at the outset that the Article's provisions apply to rights, obligations, and remedies regardless of the location of title to the collateral, whether it is in the secured party or in the debtor.

Accounts, General Intangibles, and Mobile Goods. Each state has laws for the *filing* of assignment of accounts so that creditors of the debtor-assignor in each particular state will have constructive notice of such assignment and of the security interest in the account. There are similar state laws for general intangibles and mobile goods. The Article has special rules with respect to accounts, general intangibles (other than uncertificated securities), and mobile goods of a type which are *normally* used in *more than one jurisdiction* (such as motor vehicles, trailers, rolling stock, airplanes, shipping containers, road building and construction machinery, and commercial harvesting machinery, and the like) if such goods are classified as equipment or classified as inventory by reason of their being leased or held for lease by the debtor to others, and are not covered by *a certificate of title*. The place where creditors of a debtor will most probably look to see if he has made an assignment and thereby created a security interest in his accounts, and the place where creditors of a debtor will most probably look to see if any other creditors have perfected a security interest in the debtor's general intangibles or such mobile goods, is the place where the debtor is located. Accordingly, *the Article provides that the law of the jurisdiction where the debtor is located will govern the perfection and the effect of perfection or nonperfection of a security interest with regard to accounts, general intangibles, and mobile goods of a type which are normally used in more than one jurisdiction if such goods are classified as equipment or classified as inventory by reason of their being leased or held for lease by the debtor to others.* The debtor is considered to be located at "his place of business if he has one, at his chief executive office if he has more than one place of business, otherwise at his residence."[34]

Documents, Instruments, and Ordinary Goods. Tangible collateral may be subject to a security interest before *coming into a state*. The state into

[34] UCC 9–103(3)(d).

which the collateral has come has jurisdiction to determine its legal status. Several rules under the Article[35] become pertinent. *First,* for the purpose of determining whether perfection of a security interest has occurred, and the legal effect of perfection or non-perfection of a security interest, of collateral consisting of documents, instruments, and ordinary goods, the governing law is that of the jurisdiction *where the collateral was located at the time when the last act necessary to such alleged perfection or non-perfection has occurred.* It is the law of the place of the collateral's location *at that time* which governs. Thus, with respect to a refrigerator located in state A where a financing statement is filed, the law of state A governs the perfection of the security interest in the refrigerator, and any security interest so perfected in state A will continue to be effective in state B into which the refrigerator is brought subsequently. *Second,* if a *purchase money security interest in goods* is created, and the parties creating such security interest understood at the time that the security interest *attached* that the goods would be kept *permanently* in another jurisdiction, then the law of the latter jurisdiction governs from the time the security interest attaches until 30 days after the debtor receives possession of the goods. If a filing and perfection occur in the latter jurisdiction, and the goods arrive in that jurisdiction within the 30-day period, the perfection continues to be effective without any interruption. Thus, in the refrigerator illustration just mentioned, if at the time the security interest attached to the refrigerator the debtor-owner of the refrigerator and the secured party knew that the debtor-owner planned to move his residence to state B, and the debtor-owner brought the refrigerator into state B within 30 days after the security interest attached to the refrigerator, then the law of state B governs the perfection and the effect of perfection or non-perfection of the security interest. *Third,* if the security interest was already perfected under the law of the jurisdiction from which the collateral was removed before being brought into the state where the collateral now is, the security interest continues perfected in the state where the collateral now is for *four months* and also thereafter, if within the four-month period it is perfected in the state where the collateral now is. However, if the period of perfection effectiveness in the state from which the collateral comes is less than four months, then the security interest becomes unperfected at the end of that shorter period, rather than at the end of a four-month period. Thus, secured parties from other jurisdictions have a reasonable time in which to trace the collateral subject to their security interest, and purchasers in the state into which the collateral has come can deal with the debtor-owner of the collateral with assurance that, on the expiration of the reasonable time, there is no perfected security interest in the collateral. On the expiration of the four-month period, the secured party's security interest is treated as unperfected, and it then becomes subject to defeat by those persons who will have priority in the collateral over an unperfected security interest therein, as determined by the law of the state in which the

[35] UCC 9–103(1).

collateral is located. However if, *within* the four-month period, the secured party perfects his security interest anew in the state where the collateral is now located, his original perfected security interest continues through the new perfection, without gap in time. While the security interest may be perfected in the state where the property is located *after* the expiration of the four-month perod, nevertheless perfection dates from the time of perfection in the state where the collateral is located. It should be noted that these rules concerned with collateral subject to a security interest being brought into a state do *not* apply to collateral moved from one filing district to another *within the same state,* but only to collateral being brought *into* the state from another jurisdiction.

Certificate of Title to Goods. If the goods are covered by a certificate of title issued under a statute of a jurisdiction which requires indication on the certificate of title of any security interest in the goods as a condition of perfection, then the perfection and the effect of perfection or non-perfection are governed by *the law of the jurisdiction which issued the certificate.* An automobile certificate of title is a good example. However, if the goods are removed from that jurisdiction, then the law of that jurisdiction no longer governs after the four months or the surrender of the certificate, and the goods are no longer covered by the certificate. For further details, see UCC 9–103(2)(c)(d).

Chattel Paper. Security interests in chattel paper may be possessory or non-possessory. If the security interest is possessory, the rules under "Documents, Instruments, and Ordinary Goods" apply. If the security interest is non-possessory, the rules under "Accounts, General Intangibles, and Mobile Goods" apply.

Minerals. *The law of the jurisdiction where the wellhead or minehead is located* governs the "perfection and the effect of perfection or non-perfection of a security interest which is created by a debtor who has an interest in minerals or the like (including oil and gas) before extraction and which attaches thereto as extracted, or which attaches to an account resulting from the sale thereof at the wellhead or minehead."[36]

Creation and Attachment of a Security Interest

There are three steps to perfection of a security interest: (1) the security interest must be created; (2) it must attach to collateral; and lastly (3) it must be perfected either by the filing of a financing statement[37] or by the secured party acquiring possession of the collateral, as required by the Article. However, some security interests may be perfected without compliance with the third step, from which they are exempted, e.g., a purchase money security interest in consumer goods.[38] These three steps will be considered in that order.

[36] UCC 9–103(5).

[37] For the formal requisites of a financing statement, see below, pp. 449–51.

[38] See below, p. 436.

Creation. ***Possessory and Non-Possessory Security Interests.*** Except for those security interests arising under the Code in connection with a collecting bank[39] and under Sales,[40] *a security interest will not be recognized as enforceable against the debtor or third parties with respect to the collateral, and it does not attach to collateral, unless either the collateral is in the possession of the secured party or the debtor has signed a security agreement.* A security agreement is an agreement which creates or provides for a security interest. It need only be in writing, signed by the debtor, and contain a description of the collateral or kinds of collateral. Any description of personal property (or real property) is sufficient, whether or not it is specific, as long as it reasonably identifies what is described. However, if the security interest covers crops, growing or to be grown, or timber to be cut, a description of the land is to be included in the security agreement. These are the simple formal requisites of the security agreement, although in commercial practice it may generally include much more information. These formal requisites constitute a statute of frauds with respect to security agreements. The Article does not intend to invalidate *regulatory* statutes, particularly in the field of consumer finance (e.g., small loan acts, retail installment acts, and the like) *which will prevail over the Article's provisions*, except as they provide for filing, default, etc., in which case the Article governs. Thus, an enforceable security interest may be either possessory, or non-possessory and created by a security agreement.

Validity. A non-possessory security interest is not invalid or fraudulent as to creditors because the debtor has unfettered dominion or control over the collateral.[41] The former requirement by judicial decision of policing the conduct of the debtor is no longer required as a matter of law, although the debtor and secured party may, for business reasons, agree to strict accountability, etc., by the debtor. Thus, the "floating lien" or floating charge or lien on a shifting stock of goods is validated by the Article. Unless otherwise agreed, the debtor may use, commingle, or dispose of all or part of the collateral (including returned or repossessed goods); collect or compromise accounts or chattel paper; accept the return of goods or make repossessions; use, commingle, or dispose of the proceeds; and do all this without accounting for the proceeds or replacing the collateral.[42] When the security interest is possessory, perfection of the security interest depends upon possession of the collateral by the secured party or by a bailee (e.g., a field storage warehouseman),[43] and the freedom of the debtor is limited only by the necessity that the collateral remain in the possession of the secured party or a bailee.

---

[39] See above, p. 400.

[40] See above, pp. 422 f.

[41] UCC 9-205.

[42] Ibid.

[43] For definition of pledge, see below, pp. 458 f. Under the increasingly prevalent device of field storage warehousing, the pledgor does not have possession of the pledged chattels which are warehoused convenient to the pledgor's temporary and limited use from time to time, and the pledgee has sufficient control and possession of the chattels so that third persons have notice of the pledgee's interest therein.

Also, with certain limitations, the validity of a security agreement is not affected by a provision therein that the buyer or lessee will not assert against an assignee of the seller or lessor secured party defenses which the buyer or lessee may have against the seller or lessor. Such a waiver of defenses is enforceable by an assignee for value, in good faith and without notice of a claim or defense. There are three limitations on the validity of such a waiver. *First,* the waiver is valid as to buyers and lessees of *consumer* goods only if no statute or judicial decision establishes a different rule. There is much controversy concerning the validity of such waivers in the consumer goods field,[44] and the Article takes no position in that area. *Second,* defenses which could be asserted against a holder in due course of a negotiable instrument[45] and thereby cancel the obligation of the buyer or lessee may not be waived by the buyer or lessee in a security agreement and, as to such defenses, the waiver clause is illegal and void. *Third,* purchase money security transactions are sales of goods and the Sales portion of the Code governs the sale and any disclaimer, limitation, or modification of the seller's warranties.[46]

Duties of the Secured Party. The secured party may acquire possession of collateral as a pledgee before the debtor's default, or he may take possession of the collateral after the debtor's default. In either case, *the secured party's possession of the collateral imposes upon him a duty of reasonable care in the custody and preservation of the collateral. The duty of care imposed by the Article cannot be disclaimed by agreement between the parties,*[47] although they may agree on reasonable standards as to what shall constitute reasonable care. The secured party's failure to exercise reasonable care will subject him to liability for any loss caused thereby, but he does not lose his security interest.

It is but reasonable for the debtor to verify the status of his account with the secured party. The Article recognizes a right in the debtor to make a written demand of the secured party for a statement of account or of collateral and imposes a duty on the secured party reasonably to comply with such demand. The secured party must comply with such request within two weeks after its receipt. The secured party's failure without reasonable excuse to comply with such request makes him liable for any loss caused *to the debtor thereby;* and also, if the debtor has properly included in his request a good faith statement of the obligation or a list of the collateral or both, the secured party may claim a security interest *only as shown in the statement against persons misled by his failure to comply.* A debtor is entitled to such a statement from the secured party without charge once every six months. The secured party may require payment of a charge not exceeding $10 for each additional statement furnished. Unless otherwise agreed, when a secured party knows that collateral is

---

[44] U3C sec. 3.404. "Assignee Subject to Claims and Defenses . . . (4) An agreement may not limit or waive the claims or defenses of a consumer under this section." See Federal Trade Commission rule, above, p. 350, ftn. 39.

[45] UCC 3–305(2). See above, pp. 347–50.

[46] See above, pp. 230 ff.

[47] UCC 1–102(3).

owned by a person who is not the debtor, the owner of the collateral has the same right as the debtor to receive the above statements from the secured party.

Attachment of the Security Interest. A security interest is created by the security agreement and is effective according to its terms. However, the security interest must attach to collateral in order to be an interest therein and for the secured party to acquire rights in the collateral *as against the debtor.*

In the absence of explicit agreement to the contrary postponing the time of attaching, *a security interest attaches to collateral when three things occur, irrespective of the order of their occurrence: (1) there is a security agreement that the security interest attach, or the collateral is in the possession of the secured party pursuant to agreement; (2) value has been given; and (3) the debtor has rights in the collateral.* The interest of a secured party is in what is owned by the debtor in collateral, and until the debtor acquires rights in the collateral the security interest cannot attach to the collateral to the extent of such rights of the debtor. The value to be given is generally consideration sufficient to support a simple contract or an antecedent or preexisting debt.[48] The security agreement may provide that a security interest will attach to collateral not yet owned by the debtor. A security agreement may contain an after-acquired property clause by providing that collateral, *whenever acquired,* with one exception, shall secure all obligations covered by the security agreement. This, when combined with the debtor's right to use and deal freely with the collateral in his possession and proceeds therefrom, validates the floating lien or floating charge or lien on a shifting stock of goods. The obligations covered by a security agreement may include future advances or other value whether or not the advances or value are given pursuant to commitment. However, the security interest in future advances may be subordinated to a conflicting purchase money security interest in the same collateral.[49] The one exception to "whenever acquired" is that no security interest attaches under an after-acquired property clause to consumer goods, other than accession,[50] when given as additional security *unless the debtor acquires rights in them within ten days after the secured party gives value.*

Perfection of the Security Interest

Meaning. We have seen that a security interest attaches when the collateral becomes subject to the security interest. The reason for a secured party perfecting his security interest is to obtain the maximum priority for his security interest in collateral which cannot be defeated in insolvency proceedings or, in general,[51] by other creditors of, or innocent transferees for value from, the

---

[48] For "value" under UCC 1–201(4), see above, p. 146, ftn. 1.

[49] See below, pp. 443–44.

[50] For accessions, see below, pp. 446–47.

[51] Some interests have priority even over perfected security interests. See UCC 9–312, and also below, pp. 442 ff.

debtor. *A security interest is perfected when the security interest has attached and the secured party has complied with all of the Article's requirements for perfection of the security interest.* The order of occurrence is unimportant. Thus, if the various steps required for perfection occur before the security interest attaches to the collateral, the security interest is perfected when it attaches. For example, the financing statement may have been filed before value has been given or before the debtor has acquired rights in the collateral; the later giving of value or the debtor's subsequent acquisition of rights in the collateral causes the security interest to attach and the security interest to become perfected at that time. *If a security interest is perfected in one way and subsequently, without an intermediate period when it is unperfected, it is perfected in another way under the Article, it is perfected continuously from the time of its original perfection.* Failure to perfect a security interest causes it to be subordinate to the rights of certain persons who have a limited priority over the unperfected security interest. They are:

(a) persons entitled to priority under Section 9–312;[52]
(b) a person who becomes a lien creditor[53] before the security interest is perfected;
(c) in the case of goods, instruments, documents, and chattel paper, a person who is not a secured party and who is a transferee in bulk[54] or other buyer not in ordinary course of business[55] or is a buyer of farm products in ordinary course of business, to the extent that he gives value and receives delivery of the collateral without knowledge of the security interest and before it is perfected;
(d) in the case of accounts and general intangibles, a person who is not a secured party and who is a transferee to the extent that he gives value without knowledge of the security interest and before it is perfected.[56]

It should be noted very carefully that a *purchase money security interest*, discussed previously,[57] relates to the time when the security interest attaches and has a limited priority over rights during the intervening period between the time of the filing of a financing statement and when the security interest attaches. Thus, if the secured party of a purchase money security interest files his financing statement before or within *ten days after the debtor receives possession of the collateral*, the secured party takes priority over only the rights of a transferee in bulk or of a lien creditor which arise between the time the security interest attaches and the time of filing.[58]

---

[52] See below, pp. 442 ff.

[53] UCC 9–301(3): "A 'lien creditor' means a creditor who has acquired a lien on the property involved by attachment, levy or the like and includes an assignee for benefit of creditors from the time of assignment, and a trustee in bankruptcy from the date of the filing of the petition or a receiver in equity from the time of appointment."

[54] A transferee in bulk is not in the ordinary course of business. For bulk transfer, see above, p. 290.

[55] For "buyer in ordinary course of business" under UCC 1–201(9) see above, pp. 149 f.

[56] UCC 9–301(1).

[57] See above, p. 424.

[58] UCC 9–301(2).

Methods of Perfecting. ***Filing Required.*** The filing of a financing statement[59] is the basic requirement of the Article in order to perfect a security interest. *Unless otherwise provided by the Article, perfection of a security interest can be made only by filing.*

Filing Not Required. There are eight various transactions which are exempted from the Article's requirement of filing a financing statement in order to perfect a security interest in collateral.

First, possession by the secured party of goods, instruments (other than certificated securities), money, negotiable documents, chattel paper, or letters and advices of credit[60] *perfects his security interest in such collateral without filing.* It should be noted very carefully that not all kinds of collateral are included. Accounts and general intangibles are excluded. This method of perfection by possession reflects the Common Law of pledge, the secured party's possession of the collateral being notice to all persons of an interest therein, so that filing to give notice of such security interest thus becomes unnecessary. Possession of the collateral may be by the secured party himself or by his agent on his behalf. The security interest is perfected by possession from the time possession is taken and continues only so long as possession is retained, except as otherwise provided in the Article. However, if the collateral, except for goods covered by a negotiable document, is in the possession of a bailee, the secured party is deemed to have possession from the time the bailee receives notification of the secured party's interest in the collateral and, therefore, the time of perfection of the secured interest is when the bailee receives such notification. It is no longer necessary for a bailee to inform the secured party or acknowledge that he holds the collateral for the secured party. Perfection by the secured party's possession of the particular collateral does not preclude perfection before or after possession in any other way permitted by the Article.

Second, a security interest in instruments (other than certificated securities) or negotiable documents is perfected without filing or the taking of possession of such instruments or negotiable documents for a period of 21 days from the time it attaches to the extent that it arises for new value given under a written security agreement. This is a temporary perfection which expires at the end of the 21-day period unless perfected as required by the Article within that period, in which event the security interest continues uninterruptedly from the time of its original perfection at the beginning of the 21-day period.

Third, a secured party's perfected security interest in collateral continues as a perfected security interest in the proceeds resulting from disposition of the collateral. However, if the proceeds are received by the debtor, the security interest continues to be perfected for only ten days after the debtor's receipt of the proceeds, when perfection then ceases unless the proceeds from the original collateral are identifiable cash proceeds, or the security interest

[59] For the formal requisites of a financing statement, see below, pp. 449–51.

[60] See UCC 5–116(2)(a).

in the proceeds is perfected by filing a financing statement or by acquiring possession of the proceeds before the expiration of the ten-day period.[61]

Fourth, a purchase money security interest in consumer goods is perfected without filing; but filing is required for a motor vehicle required to be registered, and for fixtures for priority over conflicting interests in fixtures. *This is the only transaction where filing is not required when the goods subject to the security interest are in the debtor's possession.*

Fifth, while a filing is necessary to perfect a security interest in accounts, nevertheless no filing is necessary to perfect a security interest on the assignment of accounts which does not transfer, either alone or in conjunction with other assignments to the same assignee, a significant part of the outstanding accounts of the assignor. This is meant to cover casual or isolated assignments; however, any person who regularly takes assignments of any debtor's accounts should file. It should be recalled that the Article does not apply "to a sale of accounts or chattel paper as part of a sale of the business out of which they arose, or an assignment of accounts or chattel paper which is for the purpose of collection only, or a transfer of a right to payment under a contract to an assignee who is also to do the performance under the contract, or a transfer of a single account to an assignee in whole or partial satisfaction of a pre-existing indebtedness."[62]

Sixth, no filing is required in order to perfect a security interest of a collecting bank in items, accompanying documents and proceeds therefrom,[63] *a security interest in securities, or a security interest arising solely under the Article on Sales as long as the debtor does not have or lawfully obtain possession of the goods.*[64]

Seventh, no filing is required for a security interest created by an assignment of a beneficial interest in a trust or a decedent's estate.[65]

Eighth, also no filing is required for an assignment for the benefit of all the creditors of the assignor, and subsequent transfers by the assignee thereunder. This obviously is not a financing transaction.[66]

Often the secured party will assign his perfected security interest. Since the security interest has been perfected and is effective against the *debtor's* creditors and transferees, it continues to be so perfected in the hands of the assignee and no filing is required in order to continue the perfected status of the security interest against creditors of, and transferees from, the *original debtor.* However, if the assignment was intended as security from the assignor to the assignee, or it was a sale of accounts or chattel paper,[67] the assignee will

[61] For further discussion of perfecting a security interest in proceeds, see below, pp. 438–39.

[62] UCC 9–104(f). See above, p. 423.

[63] UCC 4–208.

[64] UCC 9–113.

[65] UCC 9–302(1)(c).

[66] UCC 9–302(1)(g).

[67] Under UCC 9–102(1)(b) the Article applies to any sale of accounts or chattel paper.

have to comply with the requirements of the Article in order to perfect his security interest in the collateral against the *assignor's* creditors and transferees.

The filing provisions of the Article are not necessary to perfect a security interest in property subject to: a federal statute or treaty which provides for a national or international registration, or a national or international certificate of title, or which specifies a place of filing different from that specified in this Article for filing of the security interest; a certificate of title statute of another jurisdiction requiring indication of a security interest on the certificate as a condition of perfection.[68]

The Article makes special provisions for the perfection of a security interest in instruments, documents, and goods covered by documents, and also for a secured party's rights on disposition of collateral. These will be considered in that order.

Perfection of Security Interest in Instruments, Documents, and Goods Covered by Documents. We have seen that a security interest in instruments, negotiable documents, and chattel paper may be perfected by possession in the secured party. However, a security interest in *negotiable documents and chattel paper* may also be perfected by *filing;* but, except for temporary perfection, a security interest *in instruments* (other than instruments which constitute part of chattel paper) and money can be perfected *only* by the secured party taking *possession* of the instruments and money, except for the proceeds of collateral which is discussed later.[69] In normal commercial practice, the secured party has possession of instruments and negotiable documents, and their possession is sufficient to alert creditors and transferees of the debtor of the existence of a security interest therein. However, chattel paper often is assigned and possession is left in the hands of the assignor for the purpose of collection, in which case the assignee can perfect his security interest against the assignor's creditors and transferees by filing a financing statement.

A distinction is drawn between *negotiable* and *non-negotiable* documents because title to the covered goods is deemed tied into a negotiable document, but not into a non-negotiable document. Inasmuch as the way to deal with goods covered by a *negotiable document* is through the negotiable document, perfection of a security interest in the document is automatically perfection of a security interest in the covered goods. Also, any other security interest perfected in the covered goods while a negotiable document is outstanding is subject to the perfected security interest in the negotiable document. If goods are in the possession of a bailee who has *not issued a negotiable document* therefor, a security interest in the goods is perfected by either of three ways: issuance of a document in the name of the secured party (e.g., as consignee of a *straight* bill of lading or as the person to whom delivery would be made under a *non-negotiable* warehouse receipt); the bailee's receipt of notification of the

---

[68] UCC 9–302(3)(a).

[69] See below, pp. 438–40.

secured party's interest in the goods, which is the equivalent of the secured party's obtaining possession of the goods; or by filing as to the goods.

The Article also recognizes that commercial practice often requires the temporary surrender of the possession of goods, documents, and instruments to the debtor. For example, the goods or documents representing the goods may be made available to the debtor for the purpose of ultimate sale or exchange or for the purpose of dealing with them in a manner preliminary to their sale or exchange, such as loading, unloading, storing, shipping, transshipping, manufacturing, processing; and an instrument may be delivered to the debtor for the purpose of ultimate sale or exchange or of presentation, collection, renewal, or registration of transfer. Accordingly, the Article provides for *temporary perfection without filing by, or possession in, the secured party.* In the case of a *non-perfected* security interest in *instruments,* or *negotiable documents,* the secured interest is perfected without filing or the taking of possession for a period of 21 days from the time it attaches to the extent that it arises for *new value* given under a written security agreement. In the case of *an already perfected security interest* in *goods, negotiable document, or instrument* in the possession of a bailee who has not issued a negotiable document therefor, the security interest remains perfected for a period of 21 days without filing *only if* the secured party makes available to the debtor the goods or documents, or he delivers the instrument to the debtor, for any of the purposes as respectively indicated immediately above. On the expiration of the 21-day period in the last two paragraphs, the temporary perfection is ended unless, meanwhile, the security interest has been perfected as otherwise provided by the Article.

Disposition of Collateral. The collateral or proceeds may be disposed of by sale, exchange, collection, or otherwise, and whatever is received therefrom is called "proceeds." When the proceeds are in the form of money, checks, deposit accounts, and the like, it is called "cash proceeds"; all other proceeds are "non-cash proceeds." *A filing as to collateral is now considered to be an automatic filing as to the proceeds from such collateral;* no further indication need be given on the financing statement in order to accomplish this automatic effect. Except as the Article otherwise provides, when collateral is disposed of without authority from the secured party, the latter's security interest continues in the collateral and also in any *identifiable* proceeds therefrom, including collections received by the debtor. However, if the secured party authorized such disposition of the collateral, his security interest in the collateral is terminated but his security interest continues in the *identifiable* proceeds therefrom. In other words, if the secured party can trace the proceeds, his security interest in them survives. If the security interest of the secured party in the original collateral was perfected, then the security interest in the proceeds therefrom is a continuously perfected security interest. However, if the proceeds are received by the debtor, the security interest continues to be perfected *for only ten days after the debtor's receipt of the proceeds,* when perfection then ceases, unless the proceeds from the original collateral are identifiable cash proceeds, or the security interest in the proceeds is perfected by filing a financing statement or by acquiring possession of the proceeds before the expiration of the ten-day period, as discussed previously.[70] It should be observed carefully that, although a perfected security interest in collateral continues therein when unauthorizedly disposed of, some purchasers of such collateral take free of the security interest. This is discussed later.[71]

The institution of insolvency proceedings[72] does not affect the secured party's security interest in proceeds, and a secured party with a perfected security interest in proceeds has a perfected security interest:

> (a) in *identifiable non-cash proceeds and in separate deposit accounts containing only proceeds;*
> (b) in *identifiable cash proceeds in the form of money* which is *neither* commingled with other money nor deposited in a deposit account prior to insolvency proceedings;
> (c) in *identifiable cash proceeds in the form of checks and the like* which are *not* deposited in a deposit account prior to the insolvency proceedings; and
> (d) in all *cash and deposit accounts* of the debtor, *in which proceeds have been commingled with other funds,* but the perfected security interest under this paragraph (d) is
>
> (i) subject to any right of set-off; and
> (ii) limited to an amount not greater than the amount of any cash proceeds received by the debtor within ten days before the institution of the insolvency proceedings less the sum of
> (I) the payments to the secured party on account of cash proceeds received by the debtor during such period and
> (II) the cash proceeds received by the debtor during such period to which the secured party is entitled under paragraphs (a) through (c) of this subsection (4).[73] (Author's italics.)

When previously sold collateral is returned to the debtor seller, questions arise as to who have security interests in the collateral and of priorities among secured parties. If a sale of goods results in an account or chattel paper which is transferred by the seller to a secured party, and if the goods are returned to, or are repossessed by, the seller or the secured party, various rules determine the priorities of competing secured parties to the goods. *First,* the goods may have been collateral for the seller's debt at the time of the sale, and the secured party is still unpaid at the time of their return to, or repossession by, the seller.

---

[70] See above, p. 435–36.

[71] See below, pp. 440–42.

[72] UCC 1–201(22), (23): "'Insolvency proceedings' includes any assignment for the benefit of creditors or other proceedings intended to liquidate or rehabilitate the estate of the person involved. A person is 'insolvent' who either has ceased to pay his debts in the ordinary course of business or cannot pay his debts as they become due or is insolvent within the meaning of the federal bankruptcy law."

[73] UCC 9–306(4).

In this event, as between the debtor and the secured party, the original security interest attaches again to the goods and continues as a perfected security interest if it was perfected at the time when the goods were sold. Whether or not the security interest continues to be perfected after reattachment depends upon the method used to perfect it originally. If it was originally perfected by a filing which is still effective, nothing further is required to continue the perfected status; however, in any other case, the secured party must take possession of the returned or repossessed goods or must file a financing statement. *Second,* the seller of goods that are subject to a security interest of a secured party may sell such goods to a buyer who executes chattel paper in favor of the seller. The seller transfers the chattel paper as security for the seller's debt to the transferee. When the goods are returned to, or repossessed by, the seller, the unpaid transferee of chattel paper has a security interest in the goods *against the transferor.* However, his security interest is subordinate to the security interest of the original secured party, except as the transferee is entitled to priority as a purchaser of the chattel paper under certain conditions, discussed later.[74] *Third,* the seller of goods, which are subject to a security interest of a secured party, may sell such goods to a buyer who now owes part or all of the purchase price. The seller transfers the "account" as security for the seller's debt to the transferee. When the goods are returned to, or repossessed by, the seller, the unpaid transferee *of the account* has a security interest in the goods *against the transferor.* However, such security interest is subordinate to the security interest of the original secured party. It should be noted very carefully that the security interest of an unpaid transferee of chattel paper or of an account must be perfected in order to protect it against creditors of the transferor and purchasers of the returned or repossessed goods.

Rights of Third Parties. Often there is conflict between a secured party on the one hand and a purchaser of the collateral on the other hand, and also between secured parties in the same collateral. First, purchasers of collateral will be discussed and then priorities among conflicting security interests.

Purchasers of Collateral. We have already seen that certain purchasers of collateral take free of an *unperfected* security interest therein.[75] Here we are concerned with whether, and to what extent, if any, purchasers take free of *perfected* security interests in the collateral purchased. The collateral purchased may be the goods themselves, or other collateral such as chattel paper, negotiable instruments, negotiable documents, and investment securities. These will be discussed briefly in that order.

Goods subject to a perfected security interest may be sold with or without the authority[76] of the secured party. If sold with authority, the purchaser takes the goods free of the security interest. *If sold without authority, only a buyer*

---

[74] See below, pp. 441 f.

[75] See above, p. 434.

[76] Under the Article "authority" means consent. Under the law of Agency, authority is an agent's power to act in accord with his principal's manifestation to him. See Agency, below, p. 554.

in ordinary course of business,[77] *other than a person buying farm products from a person engaged in farming operations, takes free of a security interest created by his seller even though the security interest is perfected and even though the buyer knows of its existence.* Such a buyer purchases *inventory* from a merchant.[78] Also, such a buyer purchases in good faith and without knowledge that the sale to him is *in violation* of the ownership rights or security interest of a third party in the goods. A buyer's knowledge of a security interest does not mean that he knows that the *sale* is in violation of the security agreement. (For example, if a secured party files a financing statement of a security interest in inventory consisting of refrigerators in the dealer's showroom, and a buyer in ordinary course of business purchases one of the refrigerators knowing that it is subject to a security interest, the buyer takes the refrigerator free of the security interest.) However, in the case of *consumer goods* the manner of perfecting the security interest, the buyer's knowledge of the security interest at the time of the sale, and the purpose of the purchase become important. *If the secured party has filed a financing statement before the sale,* the buyer takes *subject to* the security interest. *If perfection occurred in any other way and* the buyer purchased without knowledge of the security interest, for value and for his own personal, family, or household purposes, the buyer takes free of the security interest. Although a secured party with a purchase money security interest in consumer goods need not file a financing statement in order to perfect the security interest,[79] nevertheless he should do so in order that all *buyers* will take subject to his security interest. Conflicting security interests in fixtures are discussed later.[80]

The purchase may be of chattel paper or of negotiable paper. First let us consider chattel paper. The security interest in chattel paper of a secured party may be a specific interest acquired by his giving new value against the paper or merely a claim to proceeds therefrom. We have seen that possession of chattel paper by the secured party perfects his security interest without filing.[81] He may also perfect his security interest in the chattel paper by permissive filing,[82] which he may wish to do if he permits the chattel paper to be possessed by the debtor. Commercial practice varies as to whether the debtor seller who acquires chattel paper from the buyer will be permitted by the secured party to retain possession of the chattel paper and make collections thereon from the buyer. If chattel paper is permitted to remain in the debtor-seller's possession, purchasers of such chattel paper would take subject to a prior perfected security interest, except for a certain kind of purchaser who

[77] See above, pp. 149 f.

[78] For the effect of entrusting goods to a merchant who sells them to a buyer in ordinary course of business, see above, pp. 149 f.

[79] See above, p. 436.

[80] See below, pp. 445–46.

[81] See above, p. 435.

[82] See above, p. 438.

would have priority. If the purchaser of chattel paper gives *new value* and *takes possession* of it in the ordinary course of *his* business and *without knowledge* that the specific paper is subject to a security interest, he has priority over a security interest which has been perfected by permissive filing or has temporary perfection. If such a purchaser of chattel paper *has knowledge* that the specific paper is subject to a security interest, nevertheless he has priority over a security interest in chattel paper which is *claimed merely as proceeds of inventory* subject to a security interest.

The purchase may be of negotiable paper, namely a negotiable instrument,[83] a negotiable document of title,[84] or an investment security.[85] We have already discussed the paramount position of certain purchasers of such negotiable paper, and nothing in the Article limits the rights of a holder in due course of a negotiable instrument,[86] a holder to whom a negotiable document of title has been duly negotiated,[87] or a bona fide purchaser of an investment security.[88] Such holders or purchasers take priority over an earlier security interest, even though perfected, and filing under the Article does not constitute notice of the security interest to them.

Priorities among Conflicting Security Interests. We have already considered priorities in mentioning the security interest of collecting banks in items being collected, accompanying documents and proceeds,[89] and in discussing: the rights to which an unperfected security interest is subordinate;[90] goods covered by documents;[91] proceeds and repossessions;[92] buyers of goods;[93] possessory against non-possessory interests in chattel paper or negotiable instruments;[94] and security interests in negotiable instruments, negotiable documents of title, and investment securities, immediately above. We will now consider: (1) priorities between perfected security interests and liens by operation of law; (2) conflicting security interests in crops; (3) the priority of a purchase money security interest; (4) priorities in cases for which the Article has not otherwise provided; (5) security interests in fixtures as against interests in real estate; (6) security interests in accessions as against interests in goods, and conflicting security interests where goods lose their identity or become part of a product; and (7) contractual subordination.

---

[83] See above, p. 310.

[84] See above, p. 151.

[85] See below, p. 718.

[86] UCC 3–305, and see Commercial Paper, above, p. 336.

[87] UCC 7–501, and see Documents of Title, above, p. 190.

[88] UCC 8–301, and see Investment Securities, below, pp. 723 ff.

[89] See above, pp. 400, 437.

[90] See above, p. 434.

[91] See above, pp. 437–38.

[92] See above, pp. 438–40.

[93] See above, pp. 440–41.

[94] See above, pp. 441–42.

1. Often there is conflict for priority between *earlier perfected security interests and later Common Law or statutory liens* for materials and services rendered to the collateral, called an artisan's lien at Common Law. Inasmuch as such materials and services rendered in the ordinary course of business are intended to preserve or enhance the value of the collateral, it is but just that the liens for them should have priority, unless state public policy by statute is to the contrary. Accordingly, under the Article, when a person *in the ordinary course of his business* furnishes services or materials with respect to goods subject to a security interest, a lien upon goods *in the possession of such person* given by statute or rule of law for such materials or services takes priority over a perfected security interest; however a state statute to the contrary on this will prevail over the Article.

It is not unusual for a debtor to have an interest, whether legal title or an equity, in collateral. Previous conflicts as to whether the security agreement legally could prohibit the debtor's transfer of his rights in the collateral and whether the debtor's creditors could proceed by judicial process against his rights, such as by attachment, levy, or garnishment, are resolved in favor of voluntary and involuntary alienability of the debtor's rights in the collateral. Accordingly, *the debtor's rights in collateral may be voluntarily or involuntarily transferred notwithstanding a provision in the security agreement prohibiting any transfer or making the transfer constitute a default.*

2. Conflict between *security interests in crops* as the result of a *current* crop production loan is resolved on the length of time of such loan relative to the time when the collateral became growing crops. A perfected security interest in crops securing obligations *due more than six months before* the crops became growing crops by planting or otherwise is subordinate to a later perfected security interest in the crops which (1) is for new value (2) to enable the debtor to produce the crops during the production season and (3) *given not more than three months before* the crops became growing crops by planting or otherwise. Such later security interest has priority even though the secured party giving new value had knowledge of the earlier security interest. Reference should be made to previous discussion concerning the extent to which a security interest attaches to collateral other than crops under an after-acquired property clause.[95]

3. Conflicts of priority often arise in the same collateral between *purchase money security interests* and non-purchase money security interests, which are interests arising mainly under after-acquired property clauses. Under certain conditions the purchase money security interest will have priority. It should be recalled that, while a security agreement may provide that collateral, whenever acquired, shall secure all obligations covered by the security agreement, nevertheless no security interest attaches under an after-acquired property clause to consumer goods, other than accessories, when given as

---

[95] See above, p. 433.

additional security unless the debtor acquires rights in them *within ten days after the secured party gives value.*[96] The rules for priority distinguish between purchase money security interests in non-inventory collateral and in inventory collateral. *With respect to non-inventory collateral,* a purchase money security interest in non-inventory collateral has priority over a conflicting security interest in the same collateral or its proceeds if the purchase money security interest is perfected (by filing or temporarily[97]) *at the time the debtor receives possession* of the collateral *or within ten days thereafter.*[98] *With respect to inventory collateral,* a perfected purchase money security interest in inventory collateral has priority over a conflicting security interest in the same collateral and also has priority in identifiable cash proceeds received on or before the delivery of the inventory to a buyer only if the following conditions occur:

(1) The purchase money security interest is *perfected at the time the debtor receives possession* of the collateral inventory.
(2) The holder of the purchase money security interest has given written notice of his purchase money security interest to any secured party whose security interest is *known* to him, or to a secured party who has *filed* a financing statement covering the same items or type of inventory either *before* the purchase money secured party filed his financing statement, or *before* the beginning of the 21-day period where the purchase money security interest is temporarily perfected without filing or possession.
(3) The secured party with the non-purchase money security interest has *received* such written notice within five years *before* the debtor has received *possession* of the inventory covered by the purchase money security interest.
(4) Such notice states that the person giving the notice has or expects to acquire a purchase money security interest in inventory of the debtor, describing such inventory by item or type.

4. Unless otherwise provided by specific rules, the Article establishes catchall provisions for the resolution of conflicting security interests in the same collateral in all other cases. The date of filing or perfection with respect to the collateral is also the date of filing or perfection as to its proceeds: "If future advances are made while a security interest is perfected by filing or the taking of possession, the security interest has the same priority . . . with respect to the future advances as it does with respect to the first advance. If a commitment is made before or while the security interest is so perfected, the security interest has the same priority with respect to advances made pursuant thereto. In other cases a perfected security interest has priority from the date the advance is made."[99]

[96] Ibid.

[97] For a temporary perfected interest in goods covered by documents, see above, p. 438.

[98] UCC 9–312(4).

[99] UCC 9–312(7).

5. Security interests may be acquired in fixtures, which are goods that "become so related to particular real estate that an interest in them arises under real estate law,"[100] *with the legal effect that interests in the goods as chattels become subordinate to real estate interests.* The concept of fixtures and the law applicable have been discussed previously.[101] For the purpose of financing interests in goods, the exact character and legal status become very important. Some goods are not affixed to realty and thus they retain their character and legal status as chattels; some goods become construction materials and, when affixed to realty, become such an integral part of the realty as to lose their character and legal status as chattels for the purpose of chattel financing; and other goods, although affixed to the realty, retain their character and legal status as chattels and become fixtures for the purpose of chattel financing. Inasmuch as state real estate law can create an encumbrance or lien on fixtures, when this occurs a conflict may be created regarding priority of security interests in such fixtures.

Security interests may be created in goods before they become fixtures as well as after they become fixtures. *Priority in time of filing, or recording of a real estate interest, governs the priority of dominance of a particular interest here.*[102] Thus, a perfected security interest in fixtures has priority over a conflicting interest of an encumbrancer or owner of the real estate where the security interest is perfected by a "fixture filing"[103] before the interest of the encumbrancer or owner is of record, the debtor has an interest of record in the real estate or is in possession of the real estate, and the security interest has priority over any conflicting interest of a predecessor in title of the encumbrancer or owner. However, if the security interest in the fixture is a *purchase money security interest,* the interest of the encumbrancer or owner arises before the goods become fixtures, the debtor has an interest of record in the real estate or is in possession of the real estate, and the security interest is perfected by a fixture filing *before* the goods become fixtures or *within ten days thereafter,* then the perfected security interest in the fixtures has priority. This priority of the purchase money security interest in fixtures is subordinate, however, to a construction mortgage recorded before the goods become fixtures if the goods become fixtures before the completion of the construction. To the extent that a mortgage is given to refinance a construction mortgage, the mortgage has the same priority as that of the construction mortgage. If the fixtures are readily removable factory or office machines or are readily removable replacements of domestic appliances which are consumer goods, and the security interest in the goods is perfected by any method permitted by the Article before the goods become fixtures, the security interest in the fixtures has priority. Also, the security interest in a fixture perfected by any method

---

[100] UCC 9–313(1)(a).

[101] See above, p. 425. For a further discussion, see below, p. 766.

[102] UCC 9–313(4).

[103] See above, p. 425.

permitted by the Article has priority over a conflicting interest in real estate which was obtained by legal or equitable proceedings after the security interest in the fixtures was perfected. Of course, if the encumbrancer or owner has consented in writing to the security interest in fixtures or has disclaimed an interest in the goods as fixtures, or if the debtor has a right to remove the goods as against the encumbrancer or owner, the security interest in fixtures, irrespective of whether or not perfected, has priority. If the debtor's right to remove the goods terminates, the priority of the security interest in fixtures continues for a reasonable time. *In all other instances of conflicting security interests in fixtures, the security interest in fixtures is subordinate to the conflicting interest of an encumbrancer or owner of the real estate who is not the debtor.* A secured party with priority over the claims of all persons who have interests in the real estate may, on default, remove his collateral from the real estate. However, he has a duty to reimburse any encumbrancer or owner of the real estate who is not the debtor, and who has not otherwise agreed, for the cost of repair of any physical injury, but not for any diminution in the value of the real estate caused by the absence of the goods removed or by necessity for replacing them. A person entitled to reimbursement may refuse permission to remove the fixture until the secured party gives adequate security for the performance of his obligation of reimbursement.

6. Accession to goods subject to a security interest is a normal, everyday occurrence. Accession means augmentation, addition. In the law of secured transactions, *accession means goods which have been so added to other goods as to become a permanent part thereof*—for example, the addition of component parts into a machine, as a new muffler in an automobile, a new generator in a power plant, a new engine in a truck. A security interest may attach to goods before or after they become accessions. A security interest in goods *either before or after* they become accessions is *subordinate* to the interests of the following persons who acquired their interests *after* the security interest in the accessions was acquired, *without knowledge* of the security interest, and *before it was perfected:* a subsequent purchaser for value of any interest in the whole; a creditor with a lien on the whole subsequently obtained by judicial proceedings; a creditor with a prior perfected security interest in the whole to the extent that he makes subsequent advances.

Except as just indicated, a security interest in goods which attaches *before* they are installed in or affixed to other goods takes priority as to the goods installed or affixed over the claims of all persons to the whole. However, if the accession has become part of a product or mass and is so manufactured, processed, assembled, or commingled that *its identity is lost in the product or mass:* the security interest continues in the product or mass; and the security interest ranks equally without priority with other security interests in the product or mass according to the ratio that the cost of the goods to which each interest originally attached bears to the cost of the total product or mass. If a financing statement covering the accession also covered the product into which it was manufactured, processed, or assembled, while the security interest continues in the product or mass, nevertheless no separate security interest in that part of the accession which has been manufactured, processed, or assembled into the product may be claimed.

Also *except as just indicated,* a security interest which attaches to accessions *after* they become part of a whole is valid and takes priority against all persons subsequently acquiring interests in the whole, except that it is invalid as against any person with an interest in the whole at the time the security interest attached to the accession who has not *in writing consented* to the security interest or disclaimed an interest in the accession as part of the whole. A purchaser of the whole at a foreclosure sale other than the holder of a perfected security interest purchasing at his own foreclosure sale is a subsequent purchaser of an interest in the whole, just discussed. A secured party with priority over the claims of all persons who have interests in the whole may, on default, remove his collateral from the whole. However, he has a duty to reimburse any encumbrancer or owner of the whole who is not the debtor and who has not otherwise agreed for the cost of repair of any physical injury, but not for any diminution in the value of the whole caused by the absence of the accessions removed or by any necessity for replacing them. A person entitled to reimbursement may refuse permission to remove the accession until the secured party gives adequate security for the performance of his obligation of reimbursement.

7. It should be noted that the owner of a security interest with a priority may waive, and agree to waive, such priority either completely, or partially by *subordinating* it to a particular claim or interest. It should be noted further that a secured party is not vicariously liable in contract or tort for the debtor's acts or omissions merely because of the existence of the security interest or because the secured party authorized (consented) the debtor to dispose of or use the collateral.

Assignment of Accounts. *The law under the Code favors freely the assignment of accounts and the creation of a security interest in a general intangible for money due or to become due.* A term is ineffective in any contract between an account debtor and an assignor if the term prohibits assignment of an account or prohibits creation of a security interest in a general intangible for money due or to become due, or requires the account debtor's consent to such assignment or security interest.[104] *With certain limitations, as discussed previously,*[105] an account debtor's security agreement may validly provide that the account debtor will not assert against an assignee of the secured party assignor *defenses which the account debtor may have against the assignor.* If the account debtor has not agreed to waive his defenses, the rights of an assignee are subject to all the terms of the contract between the account debtor and assignor and any defense or claim arising therefrom, and any other defense or claim of the account debtor against the assignor which accrues

[104] See UCC 9–318.

[105] See above, p. 432; and U3C, sec. 3.404(4).

before the account debtor receives notification of the assignment. The account debtor and secured party assignor may modify their contract or make a substitute contract without the consent of the assignee, even though the account debtor has notice of the assignment, under certain conditions. Such modification or substitution is effective against an assignee who acquires corresponding rights under the modified or substituted contract. *First*, the contract between the account debtor and secured party assignor must not prohibit such modification or substitution. Although no such prohibition is present, the contract between the *assignor and the assignee* may properly provide that such modification or substitution is a breach of contract by the assignor. If modification or substitution is made in violation of a contract prohibition against it, such modification or substitution may be binding on the parties to it but it is not effective as to the assignee. *Second*, such modification or substitution is *effective* against an assignee only if the assignor has *not already fully earned* the right to part or full payment by his performance of his contract with the account debtor. To the extent that the assignor *has earned* the right to part or full payment, such modification or substitution is *ineffective* against the assignee. This occurs when the work or goods have been rendered by the assignor in accordance with the contract and payment then becomes due. *Third*, such modification or substitution must be made in good faith and in accordance with reasonable commercial standards.

The account debtor's contractual obligation is to pay the assignor the amount due or to become due. The account debtor's receipt of notice that the amount due or to become due has been assigned does not, of itself, vary his obligation; *the account debtor must also receive notice that payment is to be made to the assignee. On his receipt of such notice of assignment and that payment is to be made to the assignee, the account debtor's obligation is to make payment only to the assignee.*[106] The notice must reasonably identify the rights assigned, or it is ineffective. The account debtor has the right to request that the assignee furnish him with reasonable proof that the assignment has been made. The assignee has the duty to comply with such request, and his failure so to comply permits the account debtor to make payment to the assignor.

Filing. ***Purpose.*** The purpose of filing a financing statement is to give public notice of a security interest in collateral. A filing as to collateral is now considered to be automatic filing as to the proceeds from such collateral. As we have already seen,[107] filing is required in order to perfect a security interest, with several exceptions.

Place. The Article[108] provides for local filing, which is usually in the Office of the County Clerk and Recorder, and for central filing, which is usually in the Office of the Secretary of State. Provision is also made for double filing, both local and central. Inasmuch as it was not expected that uniformity among

[106] UCC 9–318(3). Also see U3C sec. 3.204.

[107] See above, pp. 435 ff. Also, see UCC 9–302.

[108] UCC 9–401.

the various states could be attained as to the place of filing, three alternatives are presented by the Article. *One* is central filing for all transactions except for timber to be cut, minerals or the like (including oil and gas) and an account resulting from their sale after extraction at the wellhead or minehead, and fixtures, which is local filing. The *second* is local filing for transactions of essentially local concern, including fixtures, and central filing for all other transactions. The *third* is the same as the second except that it provides for double filing in the case of a debtor who has only one, or no, place of business in the state. A filing which has been made in good faith, but in an improper place or not in all of the places required, is effective insofar as it was properly filed and it is also effective for the collateral covered by the financing statement against any person who knows the contents of such financing statement. The Article provides two alternatives in the case of a change in the county of the debtor's residence, place of business, or location of the collateral or its use. *One alternative* does not require any new filing in the county to which the collateral has been removed; the place of the original proper filing continues effective. Under the *second alternative*, the original filing is effective for four months after the change, but is ineffective thereafter unless a copy of the financing statement signed by the secured party is filed in the new county *within* the four-month period, in which case perfection continues uninterruptedly from the data of the original filing. Under the second alternative, perfection in the new county *after* the expiration of the four-month period dates from the time of such perfection in the new county. The rules with respect to collateral brought into the state from another jurisdiction have been discussed previously.[109] The residence of an organization is its place of business if it has one, or its chief executive office if it has more than one place of business.

The Financing Statement. The document filed in order to perfect a security interest is called a "financing statement." Financing statement means the original financing statement and any amendments thereto, except that if the amendment adds collateral it is effective as to the added collateral only from the filing date of the amendment. A financing statement substantially complying with the Article's requirements is effective even though it contains minor errors which are not seriously misleading. A financing statement is sufficient if it: (1) gives the names of the debtor and the secured party, (2) is signed by the debtor (and the secured party where required by state law), (3) gives an address of the secured party from which information concerning the security interest may be obtained, (4) gives a mailing address of the debtor, (5) contains a statement indicating the types, or describing the items, of collateral. When the financing statement covers crops growing or to be grown, the statement must also contain a description of the real estate concerned. When the financing statement covers timber to be cut, minerals or the like (including oil and gas) or an account resulting from their sale after extraction at the wellhead or minehead, or fixtures, the statement must also show that it covers this type of collateral, must recite that it is to be filed for record in the real estate records,

[109] See above, pp. 428–30.

and must contain a description of the real estate. If the debtor does not have an interest of record in the real estate, the financing statement must show the name of the record owner. A copy of the security agreement is sufficient as a financing statement if it contains the above information and is *signed by the debtor* (or both parties where required by state law). A reproduction of a security agreement or a financing statement is sufficient as a financing statement if the security agreement so provides or if the original has been filed in the same state where the reproduction is being filed.

The reason for the required filing of the financing statement is to give notice to everyone of its contents. It is "constructive notice." It can be readily understood, therefore, why this system of filing such a simple and uncomplicated document is called "notice filing." The financing statement merely indicates that the secured party has an interest in the collateral described, and anyone who desires details may obtain them by inquiry from the parties at their addresses as shown on the financing statement. It should be noted that the financing statement is not required to be witnessed or acknowledged. A suggested form of financing statement is provided by the Article.[110] When the filing is concerned with a security interest in collateral which is already subject to a security interest in another jurisdiction and the collateral is now located in the state of filing, or when the debtor's location is changed to the latter state, the financing statement must state that the collateral was brought into the state or that the debtor's location was changed to the state under such circumstances. When the filing is concerned with a security interest in proceeds[111] and the security interest in the original collateral was perfected, the financing statement must describe the original collateral. In the two cases described in the two preceding sentences, or if the financing statement is to perfect a security interest in collateral as to which the filing has lapsed, or if collateral is acquired after a change of name, identity or corporate structure of the debtor, the financing statement is deemed sufficient if it is *signed only by the secured party instead of the debtor* and is otherwise in compliance with the Article's requirements. When the name, identity, or corporate structure of a debtor is so changed that a filed financing statement becomes seriously misleading, the filing is not effective to perfect a security interest in collateral acquired by the debtor more than four months after the change, unless a new appropriate financing statement is filed before the expiration of that time. It should be noted carefully that the Article now permits a mortgage of real estate which describes goods which are, or are to become, fixtures to be effective as a financing statement filed as a fixture filing if the goods are described by item and type, the mortgage complies with the requirements for a financing statement, and the mortgage is duly recorded.

A reservation of title under a lease or consignment of goods is not a security interest, unless intended to be such.[112] If it is so intended, the lessor or con-

[110] UCC 9–402(3).

[111] For proceeds, see above, pp. 435–36, 439.

[112] UCC 1–201(37).

signor may file a financing statement using the terms "consignor," "consignee," "lessor," and "lessee," instead of "secured party" and "debtor," and the security interest of the lessor or consignor which attaches to the goods is perfected by such filing.

Method and Duration of Filing. Filing occurs by presentation for filing of a financing statement and tender of the filing fee, or by acceptance of the financing statement by the filing officer. *Constructive notice of the filing runs from the time of presentation of the financing statement and tender of the filing fee.*

The filing period is for five years, except for a real estate mortgage effective as a fixture filing, and it is effective from the date the financing statement was filed. The effectiveness of a filed financing statement lapses on the expiration of such five-year period, unless a continuation statement is filed prior to the lapse. Upon such lapse, the security interest becomes unperfected, unless it is perfected without filing. Upon unperfection by such lapse, the security interest is deemed to have been unperfected as against a person who became a purchaser or lien creditor *before* lapse. Upon timely filing of the continuation statement, the effectiveness of the original statement is *continued* for five years after the last date to which the filing was effective, whereupon it lapses unless another continuation statement is filed prior to such lapse. Succeeding continuation statements may be filed in the same manner to continue the effectiveness of the original statement. A continuation statement may be filed by the secured party within six months prior to the expiration of the five-year period. A continuation statement must identify the original statement by file number, state the original statement is still effective, and be signed by the secured party except that a continuation statement signed by a person other than the secured party of record must be accompanied by a separate written statement of assignment signed by the secured party of record. A filing officer marks each statement with a file number and with the date and hour of filing, indexes the statements according to the name of the debtor, notes in the index the file number and the address of the debtor given in the statement, and holds the statement for public inspection. A financing statement filed as a fixture filing, or covering timber to be cut, minerals or the like (including oil and gas) and an account resulting from their sale after extraction at the wellhead or minehead, is indexed under the names of the debtor and any owner of record shown in the financing statement in the same fashion as if he were the mortgagor in a mortgage of the real estate described and, where the state law provides for indexing of mortgages under the name of the mortgagee, under the name of the secured party as if he were the mortgagee thereunder.

Termination Statement. A procedure is established under the Article for giving public notice that the secured obligation is discharged and the financing transaction is terminated. This is done by means of a termination statement. The termination statement simply states that the secured party no longer claims a security interest under the financing statement which is identified by file number, and it is signed by the secured party. A termination statement signed by a person other than the secured party of record must include or be accompanied by the assignment or a statement by the secured party of record that he has assigned the security interest to the signer of the termination statement. *When a financing statement covers consumer goods,* and there is no outstanding secured obligation and no commitment to make advances, incur obligations or otherwise give value, *within one month* or within *ten days following written demand by the debtor* the secured party *must file with each filing officer* with whom the financing statement was filed a termination statement to the effect that he no longer claims a security interest under the financing statement, identified by file number. *If the financing statement covers other than consumer goods,* whenever there is no outstanding secured obligation and no commitment to make advances, incur obligations or otherwise give value, the debtor *may* make a *written demand* on the secured party for a statement that he no longer claims a security interest under the financing statement. The secured party must comply with the latter request *within ten days after demand, by sending to the debtor* a termination statement for each filing officer with whom the financing statement was filed. Failure by the secured party to send such termination statements or to file them as prescribed, makes him liable to the debtor for $100 and, in addition, for any loss caused to the debtor by such failure. On presentation of the termination statement to the filing officer, he notes it in the index.

Assignment of Security Interest. The secured party may assign all or a part of his security interest in collateral either before or after filing the financing statement. However, to be effective against persons *other than the secured party,* the assignment should be made a matter of record. If the assignment is made *before* filing, the financing statement may disclose the amount of the security interest in the collateral described in the statement by an indication in the statement of the name and address of the assignee or by the assignment itself or a copy thereof on the face or back of the statement. The assignment may occur *after* filing, and it is made a matter of record by the filing, in the place where the original financing statement was filed, of a separate written statement of assignment signed by the secured party of record and setting forth the name of the secured party of record and the debtor, the file number and the date of filing of the financing statement, the name and address of the assignee, and a description of the collateral assigned. A copy of the assignment is sufficient as a separate statement if it complies with the preceding sentence. An assignment of record of a security interest in a fixture contained in a mortgage effective as a fixture filing may be made only by an assignment of a mortgage as prescribed by state law other than Code provision.

Release of Collateral. A secured party of record may, by his signed statement, release all or part of any collateral described in a filed financing statement. The statement of release is sufficient if it contains a description of the collateral being released, the name and address of the debtor, the name and address of the secured party, and the file number of the financing statement.

Information from the Filing Officer. If the person filing any financing statement, termination statement, statement of assignment, or statement of release furnishes the filing officer a copy thereof, on request the filing officer will note upon the copy the file number and date and hour of the filing of the original and deliver or send the copy to such person. Upon the request of any person, the filing officer will issue his certificate showing whether there is on file on the date and hour stated therein, any presently effective financing statement naming a particular debtor and any statement of assignment thereof and, if there is, giving the date and hour of filing of each such statement and the names and addresses of each secured party therein.

Default

In General. The rights of a secured party in the collateral after the debtor's default is the heart of a security transaction. Such rights, duties, and remedies distinguish a secured creditor from an unsecured or general creditor. When a debtor is in default under a security agreement, the secured party and also the debtor have various rights, remedies, and duties. The secured party has the rights and remedies provided by the Article and, unless contrary to the Article, those provided in the security agreement. The secured party's rights are cumulative, and he may exercise any of them. The secured party may reduce his claim to judgment and have it satisfied. The secured party in possession of the collateral has various rights, remedies, and duties, already discussed.[113] After default, the debtor also has the rights and duties provided by the Article, those provided in the security agreement and, as already discussed,[114] those where the secured party is in possession of the collateral. The Article provides that the parties may not waive or vary certain rights of the debtor and duties of the secured party under some of the sections on default, but does permit waiver or variation in connection with compulsory disposition of collateral and redemption of collateral. However, where waiver or variance is prohibited, the parties may, by agreement, determine the *standards* by which the fulfillment of these rights and duties is to be measured if such standards are not manifestly unreasonable. It should be noted that, if the security agreement covers both real and personal property, the secured party may proceed under the Article provisions on default as to the personal property or he may proceed as to both the real and the personal property in accordance with his rights and remedies in respect of the real property (outside the Code), in which case the default provisions do not apply.

The following rights and duties will be discussed in the order indicated: the secured party's rights to judgment and execution sale; the secured party's collection rights; the secured party's right to take possession after default; the

[113] See above, pp. 432–33.

[114] Ibid.

secured party's right to dispose of collateral after default; the debtor's right to redeem collateral; the secured party's liability for failure to comply with the Article's requirements.

Judgment and Execution Sale. On the debtor's default, the secured party may bring an action against the debtor, reduce his claim to judgment, and foreclose[115] or otherwise enforce the security interest by any available judicial procedure. If the collateral is documents, the secured party may proceed either as to the documents or as to the goods covered thereby. When a secured party has reduced his claim to judgment and levy is made upon the collateral by virtue of execution based upon the judgment, the resulting lien upon the collateral relates back to the date of the perfection of the security interest in such collateral. A judicial sale, pursuant to such execution, is a foreclosure of the security interest by judicial procedure within the meaning of the Article, and the secured party may purchase at the sale and thereafter hold the collateral free of any other requirements of the Article.

Collection Rights of the Secured Party. Among the advantages to an assignee in financing by assignment of intangibles (accounts, general intangibles, chattel paper, instruments) is the fact that the collateral is a highly liquid asset, may be utilized with a minimum of interference with the operation of the debtor's business, and does not have the complexities on default inherent in other kinds of financing. The security agreement may provide for either direct collection, where payment is made *directly* by the account debtor to the assignee of the collateral, called "notification financing" because the account debtor is to receive notice of the assignment of his obligation and is to pay to the assignee, or indirect collection, where payment is made *indirectly* by the account debtor to the assignor and by the assignor to the assignee, called "non-notification financing." If the security arrangement is non-notification financing, on default the secured party acquires the same rights as in notification financing, namely to notify an account debtor or the obligor on an instrument to make payment to him whether or not the assignor was theretofor making collections on the collateral, and also to take control of any proceeds[116] to which he is entitled.

There are two forms of account financing concerned with the credit risk: one in which the assignee assumes the credit risk without any right of recourse or charge-back against the assignor if the account is uncollectible; the other in which the assignee does not assume the credit risk and has a right of full or limited recourse or charge-back if the account is uncollectible. (S sells goods to B and sells and assigns B's chattel paper to C. B defaults on his contract of purchase and has insufficient assets to pay C's claim against him. If the assignment provided for charge-back, C could charge back to S and recover the deficiency from S. If it did not provide for charge-back, C could not recover the deficiency from S.) A secured party who by agreement is entitled to charge

---

[115] By foreclosure is meant the termination of the debtor's right to redeem the collateral.

[116] For a discussion of proceeds, see above, pp. 435–36, 439.

back uncollected collateral or otherwise to full or limited recourse against the debtor and who undertakes to collect from the account debtors or obligors must proceed in a *commercially reasonable manner* and may deduct his reasonable expenses of realization from the collections. Dumping accounts receivable, which would increase a possible deficiency claim or reduce a possible surplus, is not commercially reasonable. *If the security agreement secures an indebtedness* (collateral assigned as security for a loan), the secured party must account to the debtor[117] for any surplus, and, unless otherwise agreed, the debtor is liable for any deficiency. But, *if the underlying transaction was a true sale* of accounts or chattel paper, the debtor is not entitled to any surplus and is not liable for any deficiency unless the security agreement so provides.

Secured Party's Right to Take Possession after Default. Unless otherwise agreed, on default a secured party has the right to take possession of the collateral. Of course, if the secured transaction was possessory, i.e., a pledge in which the secured party had possession under the security agreement before default, he has no problem about acquiring possession on default. In taking possession on default, a secured party may proceed without judicial process if this can be done without breach of the peace, or he may proceed by action.[118] However, removal of the collateral from the debtor's premises may not be economically feasible or practicable. For example, the collateral may be heavy equipment in the debtor's plant or storage, and removal would be very expensive if not impracticable. For this reason, if the collateral is equipment, a secured party may repossess the equipment without removing it from the debtor's premises, render it unusable, and dispose of collateral on the debtor's premises. Also, the collateral possessed by the debtor may be in different places and be difficult or expensive for the secured party to gather it together in one place. For this reason, *if the security agreement so provides,* the secured party may require the debtor to assemble the collateral and make it available to the secured party at a place to be designated by the secured party which is reasonably convenient to both parties. The secured party must act in a *commercially reasonable manner* inasmuch as every aspect of the exercise of the secured party's right to disposition of the collateral must be in a commercially reasonable manner.

Secured Party's Right to Dispose of Collateral after Default. After default, a secured party may sell, lease, or otherwise dispose of any or all of the collateral in its then condition or following any commercially reasonable preparation or processing. Any sale of *goods* is subject to the Code provisions on Sales, previously discussed.[119]

> (3) Disposition of the collateral may be by public or private proceedings and may be made by way of one or more contracts. Sale or other disposition may be as a

---

[117] See above, p. 432–33, for secured party's duties when he knows that the collateral is owned by a person who is not the debtor.

[118] Replevin is the form of action to recover possession of specific chattels.

[119] See above, pp. 277–78, for a discussion of the seller's right of resale.

> unit or in parcels and at any time and place and on any terms but every aspect of the disposition including the method, manner, time, place and terms *must be commercially reasonable.*[120] Unless collateral is perishable or threatens to decline speedily in value or is of a type customarily sold on a recognized market, reasonable notification of the time and place of any public sale or reasonable notification of the time after which any private sale or other intended disposition is to be made shall be sent by the secured party to the debtor, if he has not signed after default a statement renouncing or modifying his right to notification of sale. In the case of *consumer goods* no other notification need be sent. *In other cases* notification shall be sent to any other secured party from whom the secured party has received (before sending his notification to the debtor or before the debtor's renunciation of his rights) written notice of a claim of an interest in the collateral. The secured party may buy at any public sale and if the collateral is of a type customarily sold in a recognized market or is of a type which is the subject of widely distributed standard price quotations he may buy at private sale.[121] (Author's italics.)

The proceeds of the disposition must be distributed in a prescribed order of priority.[122]

When collateral is disposed of by a secured party after default, the disposition transfers to a purchaser for value all of the debtor's rights in such collateral, discharges the security interest under which it was made and any subordinate security interest or lien. *The purchaser takes free of all such rights and interests even though the secured party failed to comply with the requirements of the Article for disposition or of any judicial proceedings as long as the purchaser acted in good faith.* The purchaser acted in good faith at a *public sale* if he had no knowledge of any defects in the sale and he did not buy in collusion with the secured party, other bidders, or the person conducting the sale. A person who is liable to a secured party under a guaranty, indorsement, repurchase agreement, or the like, and who receives a transfer of collateral from the secured party or is subrogated to his rights, has thereafter the rights and duties of the secured party. Such a transfer of collateral is not a sale or disposition of the collateral under the Article.[123]

On the debtor's default, the secured party is not required to take possession of the collateral subject to the security interest. However, if the secured party does take possession, he may make disposition of it or, under certain conditions, retain it in satisfaction of the secured obligation. *When the transaction involves consumer goods:* if the secured party has either a purchase money security interest in such goods, or has a non-purchase money security interest in such goods to secure a loan; the debtor has paid 60 percent of the cash price or 60 percent of the loan, respectively; and the debtor has not, after default, signed a statement renouncing or modifying his rights under the Default part

[120] For what is commercially reasonable, see below, p. 458.

[121] UCC 9–504(3).

[122] UCC 9–504(1).

[123] UCC 9–504(5).

of the Article, the secured party *must* make disposition of the collateral within 90 days after he takes possession of the collateral. His failure so to dispose of the collateral subjects him to liability for conversion of the collateral at the option of the debtor. *In any other case involving consumer goods or any other collateral,* the secured party in possession of the collateral is not required to sell it but may retain it in satisfaction of the secured obligation. However, in order to do so, he must send a written notice of his intention to the debtor if the debtor has not, after default, signed a statement renouncing or modifying his rights in this connection. *If consumer goods are involved, no other notice* need be given; but *in the case of other kinds of goods,* the secured party *must send notice* to any other secured party from whom he has received (before sending his notice to the debtor or before the debtor's renunciation of his rights) *written* notice of a claim of an interest in the collateral. If the secured party does *not* receive written objection from a person entitled to receive notification within 21 days *after the notice was sent,* the secured party may retain the collateral in satisfaction of the debtor's obligation. However, if he receives such written objection, then he *must* dispose of the collateral.

Debtor's Right to Redeem Collateral. Except in the case of consumer goods, just discussed, and apart from the requirement that all aspects of the secured party's disposition of the collateral on the debtor's default must be in a commercially reasonable manner, the Article does not require the secured party who has possession to dispose of the collateral within a prescribed period of time. Meanwhile, the debtor,[124] or any other secured party, has a right to redeem after the debtor's default. Redemption may be made (1) after the debtor's default, (2) before the secured party has disposed of the collateral or entered into a contract for its disposition, and (3) before the obligation has been discharged by the secured party's retention of possession in satisfaction of the secured obligation. Unless otherwise agreed in writing after the debtor's default, redemption of the collateral may be made by tendering fulfillment of all obligations secured by the collateral as well as the expenses reasonably incurred by the secured party in retaking, holding, and preparing the collateral for disposition, in arranging for the sale and, to the extent provided in the agreement and not prohibited by law, his reasonable attorney's fees and legal expenses.

Secured Party's Liability for Failure to Comply with the Article. As we have seen in previous discussion under Default, the buyer's default on his secured obligation imposes various duties on the secured party. If it is established that the secured party is not complying with such duties, he may be restrained by court order. Disposition of the collateral may be ordered or restrained. If disposition has occurred, the debtor or any person entitled to notification[125] or whose security interest has been made known to the secured

[124] See above, p. 432–33, for secured party's duties when he knows that the collateral is owned by a person who is not the debtor.

[125] Ibid.

party prior to the disposition, has a right to recover from the secured party any loss caused by a failure to comply with the provisions of the Article. If the collateral is consumer goods, the debtor has a right to recover in any event an amount not less than the credit service charge plus 10 percent of the principal amount of the debt or the time price differential plus 10 percent of the cash price.[126]

The Article[127] establishes criteria of disposition of collateral in a commercially reasonable manner. A secured party has sold collateral in a commercially reasonable manner if:

1. He sells the collateral in the usual manner in any recognized market therefor.
2. He sells at the price current in such market at the time of his sale.
3. He has otherwise sold in conformity with reasonable commercial practices among dealers in the type of property sold.

Any other disposition in compliance with these criteria is commercially reasonable. A disposition which has been approved in any judicial proceeding or by any bona fide creditors' committee or representative of creditors is conclusively commercially reasonable. The fact that a better price could have been obtained by a sale at a different time or in a different method from that selected by the secured party is not of itself sufficient to establish that the sale was not made in a commercially reasonable manner.

Pledge

Although pledge as a security interest is included under the Secured Transactions portion of the Code, nevertheless its distinctiveness and wide application in business transactions justify a closer examination of its elements.

Definition. A bailment of goods, or of indispensable paper representing intangibles, as security for the performance of an obligation creates a right in the bailee to retain possession of such goods or indispensable paper as security and, on default of the obligation, to deal with the property in a certain way—e.g., sell it and apply the proceeds on the obligation in default. The security interest so created is a property interest in the bailed goods, and in both the indispensable paper and in the intangible it represents. *This security interest in goods, and in the indispensable paper and the intangible it represents, created by a bailment of such goods or indispensable paper for the purpose of security, is called a "pledge" or "pawn."* The person creating the pledge is the "pledgor," and the person acquiring the pledge is the "pledgee." Indispensable paper representing intangibles has been discussed previously.[128]

In the absence of agreement to the contrary and unless the pledgee has waived it, the security interest is also in the increase or profits occurring from

[126] UCC 9–507(1).

[127] UCC 9–507(2).

[128] See above, p. 426.

the bailed property, such as interest or dividends on bailed investment securities, i.e., certificates of stock or bonds,[129] and the young born of bailed animals. It is for this reason that, in the absence of agreement to the contrary, the pledgee has the privilege, in order conveniently to obtain such increase or profits from bailed investment securities when he is entitled to it, to cause the pledged investment securities to be registered in his own name.[130] The pledgee's failure so to register is evidence of a waiver of this privilege, permitting the pledgor to retain the increase or profits which he receives. The pledgee must account to the pledgor for any such increase or profits received by him and is to apply it in accordance with the pledge agreement.

A pledge is one of various types of lien. A lien may be defined as a legal right in the property of another as security for the performance of an obligation. Some liens include the right to possess specific property—e.g., the pledge—while other liens do not include such right to possession—e.g., security interest in an automobile still in the debtor's possession. The lien of pledge also includes the power to sell on default of the obligation for which it is security. A "lienor" is the person who has a lien, while a "lienee" is the person against whose property there is a lien.

Delivery. It is of the essence of pledge that a bailment, involving a delivery of goods or indispensable paper, occur with the intent to make such a security for the performance of an obligation.

Delivery may be actual or symbolical. Actual delivery may occur by the pledgor's physical delivery of the property to the pledgee, by the pledgee's retention of property previously in his possession, or by a third person already in possession of property for the pledgor continuing in such possession for the benefit of the pledgee pursuant to the bailment agreement *and after having been notified so to do.* (A holds goods of B. B and C agree to a pledge of such goods to C. A pledge is effected when A is notified by B or C of such bailment agreement.) Another illustration of the latter requirement of notice is where a straight bill of lading or a non-negotiable warehouse receipt has been delivered by one person to another, and the carrier or warehouseman, on being notified of such delivery, retains possession of the bailed goods for the benefit of the holder of the document. Notification to the carrier or warehouseman is necessary in order to create such a pledge in the case of a non-negotiable document of title because, as between the consignee of a non-negotiable document of title and the bailee, the consignee has the right to acquire possession of such goods without production of the document.[131] A transferee of such a document must notify the carrier or warehouseman of such transfer to him in order to acquire the bailee's obligation to hold the goods for him.[132]

Symbolical delivery occurs by delivery of the means by which access may

[129] See below, pp. 717 f.

[130] See below, p. 715.

[131] See above, p. 186.

[132] Pp. 186 f.

be made to the particular property—e.g., delivery of keys to a strongbox thereby accomplishing delivery of the contents thereof—or by the pledgee's manifested assumption of control over identified goods which can be moved only with difficulty—e.g., bulky goods, as metal in a heap.

Pledgee's Right to Possession. A contract *of* pledge is not required to be in writing, and the terms of the contract determine the rights of the parties thereto. In the absence of agreement certain rights are created and certain duties are imposed by law.[133] The pledgee has the right to retain possession of the pledged property until the obligation for which the pledge occurred has been performed. The pledgee may bring an action against the pledgor who has wrongfully dispossessed the pledgee or who refuses to return to the pledgee the pledged property *temporarily* returned to the possession of the pledgor. Such action may be for damages for breach of contract, replevin for recovery of the property, or conversion of the property to the extent of the value of the pledgee's interest therein. Similarly, the pledgee may bring an action against third persons who wrongfully have acquired possession of the property without the consent of the pledgee. Such action may be in replevin for repossession of the property, in trespass for damage to the pledgee's interest in the property, or in conversion for the value of the property (which includes trespassory damage to the pledgor's reversionary interest in the property).

Where the pledgor transfers his interest in pledged property to a third person the transferee acquires the pledgor's interest in the property but the transferee's interest is subject to the interest of the pledgee unless the transferee is a:

(a) good faith purchaser for value from a pledgor who is in possession with the consent of the pledgee and the purchaser has relied upon the pledgor's possession,[134] or
(b) holder in due course of a negotiable instrument[135] or a holder to whom a negotiable document of title has been duly negotiated.[136]

A pledgee can assign his *claim* against the pledgor and, inasmuch as the pledge follows the claim, the pledge can be assigned also. The pledgee has the duty of care of a reasonably careful man required of a bailee in a mutual-benefit bailment and has a right of reimbursement against the pledgor for reasonable expense incurred in the care, maintenance, and preservation of the property. The pledgee's security interest in the property has priority over the claims of all other creditors of the pledgor.

Pledgor's Rights in the Property. The pledgor retains title to the pledged property and may sell such property subject to the pledge of the pledgee. When a purchaser authorizes a broker to purchase securities on margin, the

[133] The pledgee's rights on the debtor's default have already been discussed. See above, pp. 453 ff., and UCC 9–501. For the pledgee's duties, see above, pp. 432 f.

[134] See above, pp. 431, 434. But note carefully p. 438.

[135] See above, pp. 337, 347.

[136] See above, pp. 189 ff.

broker's purchase of such securities causes the purchaser to obtain title thereto and to be a pledgor of the securities to the pledgee, who may have these securities (and other securities pledged as security for the securities purchased on margin) registered in the pledgee's name to facilitate their sale on the pledgor's default on his obligation; also, the pledgee may sell and repledge such securities to secure advances made by him. The pledgor has a cause of action against the pledgee for loss caused to the pledged property by the negligent or wilful misconduct of the pledgee, and a cause of action against the pledgee in conversion for the value of his interest if the pledgee has used the pledged property other than for its care and preservation. The pledgor also has a cause of action against third persons for their wrongful trespassory damage to the pledgor's reversionary interest in the pledged property, unless the pledgee already has obtained a judgment against the third person therefor.

Termination. A pledge is dependent upon the pledgee's *right* of retention of possession of the pledged property. The pledgee's voluntary surrender of the pledged property to the pledgor terminates the pledge, but a pledge is not terminated by delivery of the property to the pledgor for a temporary and limited purpose, such as for the purpose of ultimate sale or exchange or for the purpose of dealing with the property in a manner preliminary to its sale or exchange.[137] Under the increasingly prevalent device of *field storage warehousing*, the pledgor does not have possession of the pledged goods which are warehoused convenient to the pledgor's temporary and limited use from time to time, and the pledgee has sufficient control and possession of the goods so that third persons have notice of the pledgee's interest therein. The pledge is not disturbed by the wrongful dispossession of the pledgee without his authority, and the pledgee can recover possession of the pledged property. Performance of the obligation for which the property has been pledged, as well as tender of such performance, terminates the pledge. A pledgee's improper refusal or failure to return the pledged property to the pledgor constitutes a conversion which terminates the pledge. Similarly, the pledgee's unauthorized use of the pledged property constitutes a conversion and terminates the pledge.

SECTION III. THE REAL PROPERTY MORTGAGE

A real property mortgage is the non-possessory interest in real property for the purpose of securing the performance of an obligation owing to the mortgagee. The transfer of the claim is accompanied by the mortgage security. A "trust deed" is in effect a mortgage. The real property mortgage contract is within the Statute of Frauds and is unenforceable without a proper writing. A mortgage which is valid between the mortgagor and mortgagee is *void* as to all *innocent* third persons unless it has been *recorded* in the proper place.

---

[137] Note carefully pp. 437–38, above.

Most states are "lien" states, the mortgage being solely a non-possessory security interest and lien on the property, the mortgagor having the title and the mortgagee the lien. Some states are "title" states, the title being in the mortgagee subject to defeasance by the mortgagor's performance of his obligation. In lien states, on the mortgagor's default and subsequent forced sale of the property by foreclosure sale—cutting off the mortgagor's equitable right to redeem the title to the property—the proceeds are applied to the indebtedness and legal costs, any surplus going to the mortgagor. A statutory right to redeem extends the time to redeem for a short period of time after expiration of the equity of redemption. The most prevalent type of foreclosure is by "suit for foreclosure and sale." Many mortgage contracts provide for sale pursuant to a power in the mortgagee or by the trustee in a trust deed. Marshaling of assets applies in a foreclosure.

The mortgagor's conveyance of the property does not relieve him of his obligation, and the transferee acquires the title subject to the mortgage. If the transferee contractually assumes the mortgagor's obligation, there is a third party creditor beneficiary contract and, as between the mortgagor and the transferee, the mortgagor is a surety for the transferee.

Nature

The real property mortgage is a widely used credit device. *It is the non-possessory interest in real property transferred by one called the "mortgagor" to another called the "mortgagee" for the purpose of securing the performance of an obligation owing to the mortgagee,* usually the payment of money. It is a lien[138] on the property, with no right to possession of such property, but with a right to have such property sold on default of the obligation and to use the proceeds to satisfy the creditor's claim. *A mortgage is the security for the claim* and, on transfer of the claim, accompanies such claim. It is easily distinguishable from the pledge, which is predicated on possession of the pledged movable property; the mortgage does not usually include possession and is on real property. A "purchase-money mortgage" is a mortgage on real property given by the purchaser to the seller at the time of the conveyance of the property to the purchaser as security for the unpaid portion of the purchase price. A contract to give a mortgage does not create a mortgage but creates an equitable lien on specific property, and the creditor has the right to enforce such contract specifically. A mortgage on specific property with an after-acquired property clause, whereby the mortgagor agrees that the mortgagee will have a mortgage on any future property acquired by the mortgagor, does not create a mortgage on such future property until it has been

[138] A "lien" is a legal right in the property of another as security for the performance of an obligation. A "lienor" is the person who has a lien, while a "lienee" is the person against whose property there is a lien.

acquired and, in that event, the mortgagee has an equitable mortgage or lien on such after-acquired property.

Deeds as Mortgages

Any such conveyance of property for the above-described purpose is a mortgage of such property. A trust deed or "deed of trust," whereby a debtor party conveys title to the property to a trustee to hold such title as security for the performance of the debtor's obligation to a creditor, is in effect a mortgage, and such is its status. The temptation to creditors to insist on receiving title to property as security and, on default of the debtor, to keep such title—thereby masking the transaction as a transfer of title rather than a mortgage—and defeat the debtor's right to redeem, causes the courts to make an exception to the parol evidence rule so that the true nature of the transaction may be proved, the conveyance treated as a mortgage, and injustice prevented.

The Contract of Mortgage

The contract creating a real property mortgage, often called "the mortgage," is within that provision of the Statute of Frauds providing that a contract to transfer, buy, or pay for an interest in land is unenforceable unless it is in writing, or there is a note or memorandum in writing of the contract signed by the party to be charged or by his authorized agent.[139] A contract of mortgage does not create a mortgage until it has been delivered by the mortgagor to the mortgagee and the mortgagee has accepted it. A contract of mortgage contains the names of the parties, the consideration, words of conveyance, a description of the property mortgaged, any covenants which may be involved, a defeasance clause, and the signature under seal of the mortgagor. In most states the seal does not have its common law effect, and its absence does not affect the validity of the mortgage.

Notice to Third Persons

As between the mortgagor and the mortgagee, the latter has a mortgage, but as between the mortgagee and third persons ignorant of the mortgage, no mortgage appears to be outstanding against the property[140] of the mortgagor, who has title to the mortgaged property and is in possession thereof. A sale of the property by the mortgagor to an innocent third person, or a levy on such property by an innocent creditor of the mortgagor, is valid, and the interest of such a party is superior to the mortgage of the mortgagee. The reason for this result is that the failure of the mortgagee to give notice of such mortgage to third persons would make it possible to defraud such third persons in their

[139] See above, pp. 88 f.

[140] For security interests in fixtures, see above, pp. 425, 445–46.

innocent dealings with the mortgagor. Today, *statutes provide that a mortgage which is valid as between the mortgagor and the mortgagee is void as to all innocent third persons unless it has been recorded in the proper place,* which is usually in the county clerk's office in the county where the property is located. Prompt recording by the mortgagee is essential in order to protect the mortgage as against innocent creditors and innocent third persons who subsequently may deal with the mortgagor. Third persons who are *on notice* of such mortgage, whether by reason of the recording or otherwise, and who subsequently acquire any interests in the mortgaged property, acquire interests which are subject to the priority of the mortgage.

The Right to Redeem

The Common Law Right of Redemption. At Common Law a contract of mortgage conveyed title to the property to the mortgagee, subject to the common law right of the mortgagor to perform his obligation *when due* and thereby to reacquire the title to the property. This is called the "title theory" of mortgages because the title passed to the mortgagee, subject to the condition subsequent of defeasance by the mortgagor's performance of his obligation. Immediately on the mortgagor's default, the mortgagee kept the title absolutely and the mortgagor no longer had any right to redeem. The mortgagor's default caused undue hardship to the mortgagor when the value of the mortgaged property was in excess of the obligation secured by the mortgage.

The Equitable Right of Redemption. In order to remedy this injustice, there was created the equitable "lien theory" of mortgages. Under this lien theory, the contract of mortgage, although stating that it conveyed title to the mortgagee subject to defeasance by the mortgagor's performance, was construed as conveying solely a security interest in the property which constituted a lien without the right to possession but with the right in the mortgagee to proceed against the property on the mortgagor's default. The mortgagor retained the title and possession of the property. On the mortgagor's default, inasmuch as the mortgagee acquired solely a security interest in the mortgaged property, on the foreclosure sale of the property, which cut off or "foreclosed" the mortgagor's equitable right to redeem the unencumbered title to the property, the proceeds were applied in satisfaction of the obligation secured by the mortgage and to legal costs, and any surplus remaining belonged to the mortgagor. Today the majority of states are lien states with respect to real property mortgages.

The Statutory Right of Redemption. The last broad step in the development of the right of redemption occurred when, by statute, the mortgagor was accorded the right to redeem within a statutory short period of time *after his equity of redemption had expired* by foreclosure sale. The time in which to redeem after foreclosure sale usually is six months to a year.

Exercise of the Right to Redeem. Either the mortgagor or any person claiming through the mortgagor—e.g., an assignee of the right of redemption, the legal representative of the deceased mortgagor, or a judgment creditor of the mortgagor—may exercise the mortgagor's right of redemption, as provided by statute. The person exercising the equity of redemption before sale must pay to the mortgagee the mortgage obligation, the interest thereon, and the expenses incurred by the mortgagee, including costs. After sale, the person redeeming must pay to the purchaser at the sale, or to the sheriff or other proper public official, the price at which the property was sold and, on such payment, a certificate of redemption or its equivalent is issued to the mortgagor, which he may record, thereby giving notice that the title has been redeemed. The effect of redemption after sale is to nullify such sale and to revest in the mortgagor the title to the property, subject to the liens thereon at the time of the sale.

Foreclosure

The mortgage is enforceable after the mortgagor has defaulted in the performance of his obligation. Default occurs when the mortgagor has failed to perform his obligation for which the mortgage is security, or to perform some other obligation contained in the mortgage contract—e.g., to pay taxes on the mortgaged property or to insure the same. A mortgage contract may provide that, on the mortgagor's default in the payment of principal or interest, the whole principal shall become due; such provision is an acceleration clause.

Kinds of Foreclosure. Statutes in the various states prescribe how foreclosure may be accomplished. There are four statutory methods: by entry and by writ of entry; by strict foreclosure; by suit for foreclosure and sale; and by foreclosure by sale pursuant to a power of sale. The first two methods apply to mortgages in only a few states. Foreclosure by entry and by writ of entry are substantially the same, foreclosure being accomplished after the mortgagor's default by entering into possession of the property; after the expiration of the statutory period of time, the mortgagee obtains absolute title.

Strict Foreclosure. Strict foreclosure occurs on the mortgagor's default by the decree of foreclosure providing that, if the mortgagor does not perform his obligation within a specified period of time after such default, the mortgagee acquires absolute title to the property. Because of the harshness of strict foreclosure, this method of foreclosure is used infrequently, except when the mortgaged property is worth less than the mortgage obligation, the mortgagee is willing to accept the property in satisfaction of the mortgage obligation, or the mortgagor is insolvent. Strict foreclosure is prohibited in some states.

Suit for Foreclosure and Sale. The usual method of foreclosure is by suit for foreclosure and sale. On the mortgagor's default of his obligation the mortgagee institutes a proceeding in a court of equity, or a court with similar powers, asking for an adjudication and judgment for the amount due and for a decree directing the sale of the mortgaged property. Notice of the proposed sale is given to the public and to all interested parties whose rights will be affected by the foreclosure. The court may order the sale of only part of the mortgaged property if it appears that the proceeds therefrom would be sufficient to satisfy the mortgagee's claim. The property is sold at public auction to the highest bidder, and the mortgagee may bid at such sale. All other liens on the property inferior to the mortgage being foreclosed are extinguished by such sale, except to the extent that they have a right to share in any surplus remaining after the mortgagee's claim has been satisfied. If the sale has been conducted properly by the official responsible therefor, the sale will be confirmed by the court, the court will issue a deed to the property in favor of the purchaser, and the proceeds will be applied in the following order of priority: to pay the expense of sale and court costs; to satisfy the mortgage debt; and to satisfy other creditors of the mortgagor having liens on the mortgaged property; any surplus remaining belongs to the mortgagor. If the proceeds are insufficient to satisfy the mortgagee's claim, a deficiency judgment for the amount still owing is rendered in favor of the mortgagee. Where, by statute, the right of redemption may be exercised within a specified period of time after the foreclosure sale, a deed to the property is not delivered to the purchaser at the sale until the expiration of such period of time. It often occurs that there are various liens on property with varying priorities. In the event of foreclosure by an inferior lien—e.g., a second mortgage—the property is sold subject to all liens superior to the lien being foreclosed—e.g., a first mortgage.

Sale Pursuant to a Power. In order to avoid the expense of a judicial proceeding by suit for foreclosure and sale, mortgage contracts frequently provide that the mortgagee has a power of sale in the event of default by the mortgagor. Although such a provision is prohibited in some states, nevertheless, it is valid in most. This is a power coupled with an interest in the subject matter and, therefore, is irrevocable by the mortgagor or by the death of the mortgagor or mortgagee. In the absence of the usual statute requiring public sale under a power of sale, the mortgagee may sell at a public or private sale. In the absence of the mortgagor's express consent or statutory sanction, the mortgagee may not purchase the property at the sale. The proceeds of the sale are held in trust by the mortgagee and, after deducting what is necessary in order to satisfy his claim against the mortgagor, he must account to the mortgagor for any surplus. If the proceeds are insufficient to satisfy the mortgagee's claim, he may bring an action against the mortgagor for the deficiency and obtain a judgment therefor. Similarly, if a trust deed has been issued by a mortgagor, on the latter's default the trustee can sell the mortgaged property without any judicial proceeding.

Marshaling of Assets. The equitable doctrine of marshaling of assets is applicable in the foreclosure of mortgages. This doctrine applies when there are two classes of creditors, one class having recourse to more than one asset while the other class has recourse to only some but not all of those assets. Under the doctrine, *creditors are to resort first to those assets not available to other creditors and then to the other assets available to the other creditors.* Thus, when a creditor holds a first mortgage on two parcels of the debtor's land and another creditor holds a second mortgage on one of those two parcels, on the debtor's default on his debt to the first mortgagee the second mortgagee can compel the first mortgagee seeking to foreclose to proceed first against the parcel unencumbered by the second mortgage.

Rights and Duties of the Mortgagor

The mortgagor and the mortgagee have various rights and duties in connection with the mortgage. The mortgagor has the right to exercise his equity of redemption within the prescribed period of time. Inasmuch as the mortgagor retains title in most states, he may convey title to the property *subject to* the mortgage and, similarly, a creditor of the mortgagor may levy upon and sell the mortgaged property subject to the mortgage. The mortgagor is liable for the mortgage debt, and the property is subject to the mortgage. Accordingly, any transfer of the property by the mortgagor does not cause the transferee to become personally liable on the mortgagor's debt. The transferee acquires the mortgagor's title to the property *subject to* the mortgage of the mortgagee. However, if the transferee *assumes* payment of the mortgagor's obligation, a change occurs in the relationship between the mortgagor and the transferee and in the relationship between the transferee and the mortgagee. The mortgagor cannot escape liability on his obligation by transferring the property to another and, accordingly, the mortgagor remains liable to the mortgagee thereon. However, as between the mortgagor and the assuming transferee, the transferee is ultimately liable for the performance of the mortgagor's obligation, and the mortgagor becomes a surety for the transferee.[141] By contracting to assume the mortgagor's obligation, the transferee becomes personally liable to the mortgagee, who is a third party creditor beneficiary[142] of the contract between the mortgagor and the transferee, and the mortgagee may enforce the contract against the transferee. Although the mortagor is liable for the payment of taxes on the mortgaged property, if the mortgagor fails to make such payment, the mortgagee may do so and add such expense to the mortgage debt. Regardless of whether the mortgagor or the mortgagee is in possession of the mortgaged property, the one in possession may not waste such property, and he must exercise reasonable care in its preservation. The mortgagee has a right of reimbursement against the mortgagor for expenses reasonably incurred in the preservation of the mortgaged property.

[141] See below, pp. 484–85.

[142] See above, pp. 75 ff.

Chapter 29

NONCONSENSUAL PROPERTY SECURITY TRANSACTIONS

Common Law **liens are** ***possessory,*** **consisting of:** ***specific liens,*** **only on the specific property for services rendered to such property (e.g., artisan's lien, common carrier's lien); and** ***general liens,*** **on property other than that on which services have been rendered (e.g., mercantile liens). The creditor's** ***voluntary*** **surrender of possession to the debtor extinguishes the lien, and the debtor's subsequent return of possession to the creditor does not reestablish the lien. The creditor's improper refusal of a valid tender of payment terminates the lien. Common Law liens are nonconsensual, although parties today often expressly provide for them in their agreement. New liens are created by statute—e.g., mechanics' lien on real property, and landlord's and finder's liens.**

SECTION I. COMMON LAW LIENS

Nature

At Common Law various liens[1] on personal property could be acquired without the consent of the owner of such property, but not on real property. Common law liens were called "possessory liens" because the liens consisted

[1] A "lien" is a legal right in the property of another as security for the performance of an obligation. A "lienor" is the person who has a lien, while a "lienee" is the person against whose property there is a lien.

only of the right to possess the property; they contained no power to foreclose or to sell such property. In the latter respect, common law liens differed from the pledge, which also existed at Common Law as a lien. Such liens were accorded to those persons engaged in a public calling, for the improvement of another's property at his request, and pursuant to mercantile custom.

Specific Liens

The innkeeper, common carrier, and public warehouseman were engaged in businesses of a public calling and, because they had the duty of serving the public generally, the law accorded to them a lien on the property which they served. The innkeeper had an innkeeper's lien on the goods of each guest as security for the payment of the cost of lodging. The common carrier had a carrier's lien on the goods transported and stored in connection with such transportation for the charges therefor. Similarly, the public warehouseman had a warehouseman's lien on the goods stored with him as security for the payment of storage charges. A lien was accorded to persons who improved the property of another at the latter's request. The lien on such property, called an "artisan's lien," was security for the payment of proper charges therefor. These liens are *specific liens* because they are only on the *specific* property for services rendered *to such property*. The lien did not extend to other property of the debtor in the creditor's possession on which services had not been rendered. (A delivers a bureau to B for repair and later delivers a chair to B for repair. After making such repairs, B has a lien on the chair for the repairs made to it, and a separate lien on the bureau for the repairs made to it. If B delivers the bureau to A without receiving payment, B does not have a lien on the chair for the cost of repairs to the bureau and to the chair. B has a common law artisan's lien on the chair only for the repairs made to it. B's delivery of the bureau to A caused B to lose his lien on the bureau.)

General Liens

A *general lien* is a lien on property other than that on which services have been rendered. A general lien will not be created except either by express agreement between the parties concerned or by mercantile custom. Mercantile liens are general liens arising from mercantile custom. An illustration of a mercantile lien which is a general lien is a banker's lien on the funds and securities of a depositor as security for a debt of the depositor to the bank. However, the delivery of property to another for a special purpose excluding a lien thereon as inconsistent with such purpose, precludes any lien from attaching to such property. The deposit of money in a trust account, or the delivery of securities or other property in trust, does not permit the creation of a lien on such property in favor of the person in possession as security for a debt owing by the person who has delivered such property.

Extinguishment of Liens

Common law liens carry only the *right to possess* the *particular property;* they are possessory liens and exist only so long as the creditor retains the *right* to possession. The creditor's loss of possession without his consent or authority, as by theft, does not terminate the lien, and he has the right to reacquire possession. The creditor's voluntary relinquishment of possession to the debtor for a temporary and limited purpose,[2] or pursuant to the debtor's fraudulent inducement to part with such possession, does not terminate the lien. The creditor's voluntary surrender of possession to the debtor extinguishes the lien, and the debtor's subsequent return of possession to the creditor does not re-establish the lien. Payment of the debt owing to the creditor, or a valid tender of such payment, discharges the lien and, on the creditor's refusal to return possession to the debtor, the debtor may bring an action in replevin for such possession or an action in conversion for the reasonable value of the property.

SECTION II. STATUTORY LIENS

Today statutes in the various states have expressly included many of the common law liens and have created new liens. The Code provides for carriers' liens and warehousemen's liens.[3] Some of the new liens refer to personal property—e.g., landlord's liens and finder's liens—and some refer to real property, the most important of which are the mechanics' liens.

Mechanics' Liens

Mechanics' liens are accorded to those persons who, pursuant to contract with the owner of real property or his agents or independent contractors, have rendered labor, services, or material for the improvement of such property; the lien is security for payment for such labor, services, or material. Contractors, subcontractors, laborers, and material-men benefit from such a lien. In some states the lienor—i.e., the one who has the lien—has a lien on the property only to the extent of what is owing by the owner to the contractor, while in other states the lien extends to the real property regardless of the amount owing by the owner to the contractor. In order to establish their liens, lienors must file a notice of lien within a specified period of time after the last of such labor, services, or materials has been furnished. Such liens must be foreclosed within a specified period of time or the lien is lost. Foreclosure proceedings are the same as for foreclosure of a real estate mortgage. The mechanic's lien does not disturb prior liens on the property, but such prior liens are usually superior only to the extent of the value of the property in its unimproved state.

---

[2] Note carefully p. 438 above.

[3] UCC 7–307, 7–209. See above, pp. 183 ff. and 178 ff.

The mechanics' lien usually has priority to the extent that improvement has been made, if this can be ascertained.

PROBLEMS

1. Explain what is meant by the following terms under Article 9 on Secured Transactions under the Uniform Commercial Code:
   (a) Security agreement.
   (b) Security interest.
   (c) Secured party.
   (d) Collateral.
   (e) Purchase money security interest.
   (f) Chattel paper.
   (g) Perfection of a security interest.
2. Is Article 9 on Secured Transactions under the Code applicable to:
   (a) Statutory liens? Explain.
   (b) A pledged note secured by a real property mortgage? Explain.
   (c) Accounts and chattel paper? Explain.
   (d) A security interest arising under the Sales portion of the Code? Explain.
3. (a) Explain the meaning of each of the four classes of goods under Article 9 on Secured Transactions under the Code.
   (b) Without explaining, indicate the class of goods of each of the following:
      (1) Refrigerator in a home.
      (2) Refrigerator for fish in a retail fish business.
      (3) Refrigerator for sale by a retailer of electrical appliances.
      (4) Cattle raised for sale.
      (5) Materials used up or consumed in a business.
4. Sam sold and delivered goods to Bob for $1,000. Under Article 9 on Secured Transactions under the Code, does Sam have an "account" against Bob? Explain.
5. Name the three things which must occur for each of the following:
   (a) Perfection of a security interest.
   (b) A security interest to attach to collateral.
6. If a secured party with a perfected security interest assigns it, how does such assignment affect the perfected security interest?
7. Select the **best** answer for each of the following items:
   (a) Marcus purchased a Zomar 21-inch color television set from Hart Appliance, Inc. Marcus made a down payment of $100 and signed a negotiable promissory note and a security agreement. Hart Appliance did not file a financing statement covering the sale to Marcus.
      (1) Hart's failure to file the financing statement will allow subsequent creditors of Marcus to defeat Hart's security interest in the television set.
      (2) The sale of the television set by Marcus to a neighbor without disclosure of Hart's security interest in the set will result in the security interest being valid against the neighbor.
      (3) In order to perfect its security interest against any parties who subsequently assert rights against the television set, Hart must file the financing statement.

(4) The transaction would be treated as the sale of a consumer good, subject to a purchase-money security interest in Hart.

(b) Forward Motor, Inc., is a franchised automobile dealer for National Motors. National provides the financing of the purchase of its automobiles by Forward. It sells Forward 25 to 50 automobiles at a time and takes back promissory notes, a security agreement, and a financing statement on each sale. The financing statement covering this revolving inventory has been duly filed.

(1) Each automobile sold to Forward must be described and the serial number listed on the financing statement.

(2) Sales by Forward to bona fide purchasers for value in the ordinary course of business will be subject to the rights of National.

(3) No filing is required against the creditors of Forward since the automobiles are "consumer goods" in its hands.

(4) As against the creditors of Forward, National has a valid "floating lien" against the automobiles and the proceeds from their sale.

(c) Waldo Washing Machine Co. sold a Zippo Super Suds washing machine to Franklin. Waldo took a promissory note, a security agreement, and a financing statement. Waldo filed only the financing statement. The financing statement is invalid if

(1) Not filed within five days from the time of execution.

(2) Not signed by two witnesses and appropriately notarized.

(3) Not signed by the debtor.

(4) The property involved is a "consumer good."

(d) Baker Loan Company made secured loans to Smith, Jack, and Roe. Smith gave Baker a security interest in his household furniture. Jack delivered Baker his rare-coin collection as a pledge. Roe's loan is evidenced by his promissory note, payable over three years in monthly payments and secured by a security interest in the inventory of Roe's Clothing Store, a sole proprietorship owned by Roe. Proper security agreements were made and financing statements were duly executed and filed with respect to all of these transactions on the dates of the transactions.

(1) A filing of a financing statement was not required to perfect the security interest in Smith's household furniture.

(2) Baker's security interest in Jack's coin collection was perfected before a financing statement was filed.

(3) On filing a financing statement covering Roe's inventory, Baker's security interest therein was perfected for a maximum period of one year.

(4) The financing statement for Roe's inventory must include an itemization and valuation of the inventory if the financing statement is to be valid. (Former C.P.A. Examination question)

8. B contracts with S to buy a refrigerator from S, B to pay for the same in installments.

(a) What is the effect of a clause in the contract prohibiting S from assigning this account against B?

(b) If S had defrauded B in the transaction, may B assert such fraud against X, S's assignee of the account? Explain.

(c) If S assigns the account to E, may B and S subsequently modify the terms of the sales contract without E's consent? Explain.

(d) If S delivers the refrigerator to B, S then assigns the account to Z who notifies B of the assignment, and B then makes an installment payment to S, does Z have a right against B for payment to Z of that installment? Explain.

9. (a) What is the purpose and nature of a financing statement?
   (b) Explain fully how the length of the filing period is determined.
   (c) What is the purpose and nature of a continuation statement?
   (d) If a security interest is assigned, explain fully what the assignee should do in order to make it effective against persons other than the secured party assignor.
10. A delivered his automobile for repair to B, an automobile repair shop. B redelivered the automobile to A without collecting the $100 charges due for the repairs. One month later A again delivered his automobile to B for additional repairs amounting to $50. A tendered $50 to B, but B now refuses to redeliver the automobile to A until A has paid the $150 repair charges.
   (a) Does B have a right to retain possession of the automobile?
   (b) Why?
11. (a) Allen delivered silver to Burt, a jeweler, to be made into a medallion. Burt was to receive $50 for his work, 30 days after the delivery of the medallion. After the completion of the medallion Burt refused to deliver it except upon the payment of the $50, claiming a workman's lien. Was Burt justified in his refusal?
   (b) Allen delivered woolen cloth to Williams to be made into ladies' suits, agreeing to pay him $20 for each suit. After the suits were finished and before they had been paid for, Fredericks levied upon them under a judgment recovered against Williams. Was the levy good? (Former C.P.A. Examination question)

SOME PREVIOUS C.P.A. LAW EXAMINATION QUESTIONS AND AUTHOR'S MODEL ANSWERS

NOVEMBER, 1979

Number 1

Select the **best** answers for each of the following items.

22. Williamson purchased from Dilworth Hardware a new lathe for his home workshop for cash. Two weeks later, Williamson was called by the Easy Loan Company. Easy explained to Williamson that it had been financing Dilworth's purchases from the manufacturers and that to protect its interest it had obtained a perfected security interest in Dilworth's entire inventory of hardware and power tools, including the lathe which Williamson bought. Easy further explained that Dilworth had defaulted on a payment due to Easy, and Easy intended to assert its security interest in the lathe and repossess it unless Williamson was willing to make payment of $200 for a release of Easy's security interest. If Williamson refuses to make the payment, which of the following statements is correct?

   a. Williamson will **not** take free of Easy's security interest if he was aware of said interest at the time he purchased the lathe.
   b. Even if Williamson had both actual notice and constructive notice via recordation of Easy's interest, he will prevail if Easy seeks to repossess the lathe.
   c. Easy's security interest in the lathe in question is invalid against all parties unless its filing specifically described and designated the particular lathe Williamson purchased.

d. Williamson must pay the $200 or the lathe can be validly repossessed and sold to satisfy the amount Dilworth owes Easy and any excess paid to Williamson.

23. Two Uniform Commercial Code concepts relating to secured transactions are "attachment" and "perfection." Which of the following is correct in connection with the similarities and differences between these two concepts?

a. They are mutually exclusive and wholly independent of each other.
b. Satisfaction of one automatically satisfies the other.
c. Attachment relates primarily to the rights against the debtor and perfection relates primarily to the rights against third parties.
d. It is **not** possible to have a simultaneous attachment and perfection.

24. Which of the following requirements is **not** necessary in order to have a security interest attach?

a. There must be a proper filing.
b. The debtor must have rights in the collateral.
c. Value must be given by the creditor.
d. Either the creditor must take possession or the debtor must sign a security agreement which describes the collateral.

25. In respect to obtaining a purchase money security interest, which of the following requirements must be met?

a. The property sold may only be consumer goods.
b. Only a seller may obtain a purchase money security interest.
c. Such a security interest must be filed in all cases to be perfected.
d. Credit advanced to the buyer must be used to obtain the property which serves as the collateral.

26. Vista Motor Sales, a corporation engaged in selling motor vehicles at retail, borrowed money from Sunshine Finance Company and gave Sunshine a properly executed security agreement in its present and future inventory and in the proceeds therefrom to secure the loan. Sunshine's security interest was duly perfected under the laws of the state where Vista does business and maintains its entire inventory. Thereafter, Vista sold a new pickup truck from its inventory to Archer and received Archer's certified check in payment of the full price. Under the circumstances, which of the following is correct?

a. Sunshine must file an amendment to the financing statement every time Vista receives a substantial number of additional vehicles from the manufacturer if Sunshine is to obtain a valid security interest in subsequently delivered inventory.
b. Sunshine's security interest in the certified check Vista received is perfected against Vista's other creditors.
c. Unless Sunshine specifically included proceeds in the financing statement it filed, it has **no** rights to them.
d. The term "proceeds" does **not** include used cars received by Vista since they will be resold.

39. Lantz sold his moving and warehouse business, including all the personal and real property used therein, to Mallen Van Lines, Inc. The real property was encumbered by a duly-recorded $300,000 first mortgage upon which Lantz was personally liable. Mallen acquired the property subject to the mortgage but did **not** assume the mortgage. Two years later, when the outstanding mortgage was $260,000, Mallen decided to abandon the business location because it had become unprofitable and the value of the real property was less than the outstanding mortgage. Mallen moved to another loca-

tion and refused to pay the installments due on the mortgage. What is the legal status of the parties in regard to the mortgage?

a. Mallen breached its contract with Lantz when it abandoned the location and defaulted on the mortgage.
b. Mallen took the real property free of the mortgage.
c. If Lantz pays off the mortgage, he will be able to successfully sue Mallen because Lantz is subrogated to the mortgagee's rights against Mallen.
d. Lantz must satisfy the mortgage debt in the event that foreclosure yields an amount less than the unpaid balance.

40. Carter wished to obtain additional working capital for his construction company. His bankers indicated that they would be willing to lend the company $50,000 if the bank could obtain a first mortgage on the real property belonging to the business. Carter reluctantly acquiesced and mortgaged all his real property to secure repayment of the loan. Unknown to the bank, one portion of the real property was already mortgaged to Johnson for $30,000, but Johnson had neglected to record the mortgage. The bank promptly recorded its mortgage. Which of the following is correct regarding the rights of the parties?

a. Johnson's failure to record makes the mortgage invalid against Carter.
b. The bank's mortgage will have a priority over Johnson's mortgage.
c. Both mortgagees would share the proceeds from any foreclosure on a pro rata basis.
d. The bank will be deemed to have notice of Johnson's mortgage and will take subject to the mortgage.

Answer

1. 22.b(440) 23.c(433, 434) 24.a(433) 25.d(424)
26.b(438) 39.d(467) 40.b(464)

MAY, 1979

Number 1

Select the **best** answers for each of the following items.

14. Wilcox Laboratories, Ltd., manufactures medical equipment for sale to medical institutions and retailers. Wilcox also sells directly to consumers in its wholly-owned retail outlets. Wilcox has created a subsidiary, Wilcox Finance Corporation, for the purpose of financing the purchase of its products by the various customers. In which of the following situations does Wilcox Finance **not** have to file a financing statement to perfect its security interest against competing creditors in the equipment sold by Wilcox?

a. Sales made to medical institutions.
b. Sales made to consumers who purchase for their own personal use.
c. Sales made to retailers who in turn sell to buyers in the ordinary course of business.
d. Sales made to any buyer when the equipment becomes a fixture.

15. Kelmore Appliances, Inc., sells various brand name appliances at discount prices. Kelmore maintains a large inventory which it obtains from various manufacturers on credit. These manufacturer-creditors have all filed and taken secured interests in the appliances and proceeds therefrom which they have sold to Klemore on credit. Kelmore in turn sells to hundreds of ultimate consumers; some pay cash but most buy on credit. Kelmore takes a security interest but does **not** file a financing statement for credit sales. Which of the following is correct?

a. The appliances in Kelmore's hands are consumer goods.
b. Since Kelmore takes a purchase money security interest in the consumer goods sold, its security interest is perfected upon attachment.
c. The appliance manufacturers can enforce their secured interests against the appliances in the hands of the purchasers who paid cash for them.
d. A subsequent sale by one of Kelmore's customers to a bona fide purchaser will be subject to Kelmore's secured interest.

20. Bigelow manufactures mopeds and sells them through franchised dealers who are authorized to resell them to the ultimate consumer or return them. Bigelow delivers the mopeds on consignment to these retailers. The consignment agreement clearly states that the agreement is intended to create a security interest for Bigelow in the mopeds delivered on consignment. Bigelow wishes to protect itself against the other creditors of and purchasers from the retailers who might assert rights against the mopeds. Under the circumstances, Bigelow

a. Must file a financing statement and give notice to certain creditors in order to perfect his security interest.
b. Will have rights against purchasers in the ordinary course of business who were aware of the fact that Bigelow had filed.
c. Need take no further action to protect himself, since the consignment is a sale or return and title is reserved in Bigelow.
d. Will have a perfected security interest in the mopeds upon attachment.

21. Johnson loaned money to Visual, Inc., a struggling growth company, and sought to obtain a security interest in negotiable stock certificates which are traded on a local exchange. To perfect his interest against Visual's other creditors, Johnson

a. Need do nothing further in that his security interest was perfected upon attachment.
b. May file or take possession of the stock certificates.
c. Must take possession of the stock certificates.
d. Must file and give the other creditors notice of his contemplated security interest.

Answer

1. 14.b(436) 15.b(436, 433)
   20.a(444) 21.c(435, 426)

MAY, 1977

Number 7

Part b. You have been assigned by the CPA firm of Stanford, Cox & Walsh to audit the accounts of Super Appliances, Inc., a retail discount chain. Super sells almost exclusively to retail customers in the ordinary course of business. It typically requires 25 percent as a down payment and takes a promissory note and a signed security agreement for the balance. However, if the purchase price of the appliance or appliances purchased by the customer exceeds $500, it arranges with a local financing company, Friendly Finance, to have credit extended to the customer. In such cases, Friendly supplies the 75 percent financing and takes a promissory note and a signed security agreement. A financing statement is neither obtained nor recorded by Super or Friendly.

Required:

Answer the following, setting forth reasons for any conclusions stated.

1. Does Super or Friendly have a "purchase-money security interest" in respect to the appliances sold to Super's customers?

2. What is the legal importance of the distinction between a "purchase-money security interest" and the usual nonpossessory security interest?

Answer

7.b.1. Both Super and Friendly have purchase money security interests here. Under the Uniform Commercial Code, a security interest is a purchase money security interest to the extent that it is taken or retained by the seller of the collateral to secure all or part of its price, or taken by a person who by making advances gives value to enable the debtor to acquire rights in the collateral if such value is so used. Therefore, Super as the seller, and Friendly as the lender making advances so used, have purchase money security interests in the collateral. (p. 424)

2. Under the Code, perfection of a security interest can be made only by filing a financing statement, with certain exceptions. One exception is when the seller or lender has possession of the collateral, in which case perfection occurs by reason of such possession and filing is unnecessary. Thus, a seller or lender with a security interest in collateral but not having possession of the collateral has a nonpossessory security interest which can be perfected and be effective as a priority against third parties only by filing a financing statement. Another exception to the filing requirement is that a purchase money security interest in consumer goods is perfected without filing, and it is effective as a priority against other creditors of the debtor; however, it is not effective as a priority against a subsequent buyer of the collateral without knowledge of the security interest, for value, and for his own personal, family, or household purposes, and he takes free of the security interest. (pp. 435, 436, 441)

Part Four:
Security

B. Suretyship

Chapter 30

NATURE OF SURETYSHIP

SECTION I. GENERAL

Suretyship is a legal relationship in which (1) the "surety" and the "principal debtor" are obligated to perform the *same* obligation for a "creditor" (2) who is entitled to only *one* performance (3) and as between the surety and the principal debtor the latter is to perform and is *ultimately* liable therefor. *Suretyship* has three persons, the contract contemplates loss caused by default or wrong of the principal debtor, and since the surety (other than a *strict* surety) promises to the creditor to answer for the debt, default, or miscarriages of the principal debtor his contract is within the Statute of Frauds. In contrast, in *indemnity* there are two persons, the indemnitor will pay the indemnitee for loss he sustains regardless of the liability of any third person therefor, and the indemnitor's contract is not within the Statute of Frauds.

Background

Suretyship arose because of the need for shifting risks in the doing of business—the desire for security against loss from nonperformance of an obligation owing.[1] (D desires to purchase goods on credit from C, who requires some security that D will pay for such goods if they are sold to him. S agrees that, if C sells such goods to D and D does not pay therefor, S will make such payment. Pursuant to this agreement C sells the goods to D. C's risk of loss from D's nonperformance of his obligation is now shifted to S. C now has two

[1] See above, pp. 417–18.

persons to whom he may resort for performance of D's obligation.) In the illustration, S is called the surety, D is called the principal debtor, and C is called the creditor. The surety undertakes to perform specific *obligations of a third person,* then existing or which may occur in the future, owing to the creditor on the default of such third person. It is readily apparent that suretyship is both a credit device to the principal debtor and a risk-bearing device to the creditor. Suretyship is widely used in business today as a security device.

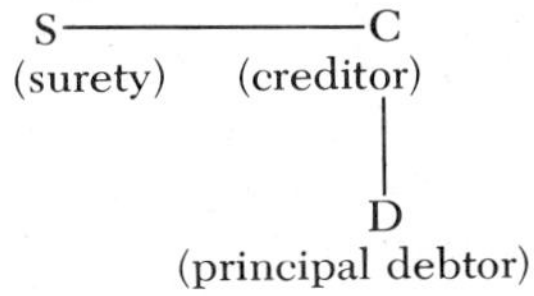

Definition

"Suretyship" is a particular kind of legal relationship involving three parties, used for the purpose of security. It may be defined as *a relationship in which one person called a "surety" and another person called a "principal debtor" are obligated to perform the same obligation to a person called a "creditor" who is entitled to only one performance, and as between the surety and principal debtor the latter is to perform the obligation and is ultimately liable therefor.* (S contracts with C that, if C will extend credit to D, S will pay the amount owing by D on D's default. Both D and S are under the same obligation to pay C the amount, although S's obligation is not performable until D defaults, while D's obligation is performable on the day the debt matures. C is entitled to but one payment. As between S and D, D is to pay and will be ultimately liable to S for S's payment to C on the obligation; it is for this reason that D is called a *principal* debtor.) Essentially, a surety makes his credit or his property available to the creditor for the benefit of the principal debtor.

Suretyship is the relation among the three parties of surety, creditor, and principal debtor, and is created by the suretyship contract. The suretyship contract may include all three parties, only the surety and the creditor (which is a very common occurrence), or only the surety and the principal debtor for the benefit of the creditor. The consent or knowledge of the principal debtor is not necessary to the suretyship contract between the surety and the creditor. The suretyship contract relates to the obligation of the principal debtor, and although the obligation of the principal debtor, as well as the obligation of the surety under the suretyship contract, usually is a contract obligation, it may be an obligation arising from a tort. (S contracts with C that D's obligation to pay the damage D caused to C's property will be performed.) Further, the respective obligations of the surety and of the principal debtor may not be coextensive. (S contracts with C to pay for all the merchandise that D purchases from C not in excess of $10,000 on D's failure to make such payment. D purchases merchandise costing $15,000 from C. D is liable to C for $15,000 while S is liable only to the extent of $10,000 if D defaults.) The surety's obligation is fixed by the suretyship contract, and the obligation of the principal debtor is fixed by his contract or tort.

Contract of Indemnity Distinguished

A contract of suretyship should be distinguished carefully from a contract of indemnity because the Statute of Frauds is applicable to a suretyship contract (except a contract for strict suretyship) but not to an indemnity contract.[2] An important difference is that the indemnity contract does not promise to answer for the *debt, default, or miscarriages of the promisee's* (creditor's) *obligor* (principal debtor), while a suretyship contract (except a contract for strict suretyship) does. A contract of indemnity is made by an indemnitor with an indemnitee whereby the indemnitor assures the indemnitee that any loss he sustains will be paid by the indemnitor, *regardless of the liability of any third person therefor.* Such a contract contemplates loss for which third persons may not be involved or liable; a contract of suretyship contemplates loss caused by the *default* or *wrongs* of the promisee's obligor. (A contracts with B to pay B for any damage B sustains by the use of B's automobile. B damages his automobile. This is a contract of indemnity and A is liable to B for such damage.) (X contracts with Y whereby X is to pay Y for any defalcations of his employees; or X contracts with Y whereby X is to pay Y for any defaults of customers of Y in paying their debts. These are contracts of suretyship and X is liable to Y for such defalcations or defaults.) A contract of indemnity may later give rise to a suretyship relation. (A contracts with B to pay B for any damage B sustains by the use of B's automobile. This is a contract of indemnity. C wrongfully damages B's automobile thereby causing C to be liable to B. A and C are liable on the same obligation to B for which C is ultimately liable. The relation is suretyship, A being the surety, B the creditor, and C the principal debtor.)

SECTION II. CLASSIFICATION

The following types of suretyship reflect the different obligations of the surety to the creditor. (*1*) *Strict suretyship.* The surety is a *co-debtor* with the principal debtor. (2) *Absolute guaranty.* A guarantor is a surety whose obligation is to perform on the principal debtor's nonperformance, as distinguished from a strict surety who is a co-debtor. In an absolute guaranty, the guarantor's obligation is to perform absolutely on the *principal debtor's default.* (3) *Conditional guaranty.* The guarantor's contract is to perform *on a condition* in addition to the principal debtor's default. Time is not a condition. The guaranty of

[2] This is the reason why, in the absence of statute to the contrary, life and fire insurance contracts being for indemnity are not within the Statute of Frauds. See below, p. 749.

collection guarantees payment *if* the obligation is *uncollectible,* meaning the creditor's judgment against the principal debtor on his default cannot be satisfied by levy of execution and the guarantor is so notified by the creditor. (4) *Continuing guaranty.* This guaranty contemplates a series of transactions and undertakes to guarantee their payment or collection. (5) *Unlimited guaranty.* This guaranty is unlimited in time *and* amount. (6) *Limited guaranty.* This guaranty is limited in time *or* amount. (7) *General guaranty.* This guaranty is made to the public generally. (8) *Special guaranty.* This guaranty is made to a designated person or persons.

The terms of the suretyship contract between the surety and the creditor determine the obligation of the surety. Because the nature of the surety's obligation varies according to the terms of each particular contract, specific names are given to various types of suretyship contract, which are classified according to the nature of the surety's obligation. The following classifications will be discussed: strict surety, absolute guaranty, conditional guaranty, continuing guaranty, unlimited guaranty, limited guaranty, general guaranty, special guaranty, and the position of a general indorser on a negotiable instrument.

Strict Suretyship

A "strict surety" is a surety who is a *co-debtor* with the principal debtor for the same obligation owing to the creditor. He is a surety because: he and the principal debtor are liable to the creditor for the same obligation; the creditor is entitled to only one performance of the obligation; and as between the surety and the principal debtor the latter is ultimately liable for performance of the obligation. It is the nature of the surety's obligation as a co-debtor which characterizes this special type of suretyship and distinguishes it from all others, where the obligation of the surety is so very different. For example, S and M are co-makers of a promissory note, S being a surety for M. Since S and M are co-debtors on the note, S is a strict surety.

Guaranty

Guaranty is a type of suretyship in which the surety is called a "guarantor," the suretyship contract is called a "guaranty," and the person to whom the guaranty is made is called a "guarantee," and in which the verb "guarantee" is used. Guaranty differs from strict suretyship in the nature of the surety's obligation. The strict surety has a primary liability to the creditor in that his obligation is to perform as co-debtor the same obligation as the principal debtor. In contrast, the guarantor has a liability secondary or collateral to the obligation of the principal debtor; the guarantor's obligation is to perform the principal debtor's obligation only when the principal debtor has defaulted or when something else has occurred—e.g., the creditor cannot make collection on the principal debtor's obligation. Further, the contract of strict suretyship is not, while the contract of guaranty is, within the Statute of Frauds.

Guaranty and warranty often are used interchangeably but they should be distinguished because of their different meanings. A warranty is a promise or affirmation of fact relating to certain property which induces the buyer to purchase such property—e.g., warranties of title or quality; a guaranty is not concerned with the attributes of property but, rather, with security for performance of an obligation. A warranty involves two, while a guaranty involves three, persons. A warranty is not necessarily, while a guaranty is, within the Statute of Frauds.

Absolute Guaranty. An "absolute guaranty" is an absolute or unconditional contract to perform another's obligation *on his default.* A common example is the *guaranty of payment* whereby the guarantor guarantees payment to the creditor *when* the principal debtor fails to pay him; "I guarantee payment of the within obligation" are words indicating such a guaranty. Such a guaranty is enforceable only on the principal debtor's default. A promise performable only after the lapse of a certain period of time is an absolute promise. There are no conditions to its immediate performance; the law does not consider a lapse of time as a condition.

Conditional Guaranty. A guaranty which is not absolute is conditional. Any contract of guaranty which undertakes to perform the obligation, usually to pay a debt, of the principal debtor on a contingency or a condition is a conditional guaranty. It is a contract to pay "*if.*" A common illustration is the *guaranty of collection,* which undertakes to pay the debt of the principal debtor if the creditor is unable to collect it. The liability of a guarantor of collection is contingent and is not enforceable until the creditor has exercised due diligence in collecting the debt and the result has been no recovery or incomplete recovery thereof. The creditor must bring an action against the principal debtor promptly, obtain a judgment, attempt to levy execution, the writ of execution must be returned unsatisfied, and the creditor must notify the guarantor within a reasonable time of his failure to effect collection.

Continuing Guaranty. A "continuing guaranty" contemplates a series of transactions and undertakes to guarantee their payment or collection. "I guarantee payment for all of the merchandise A may buy from you" is an illustration of a continuing guaranty contemplating a series of purchases of merchandise. "I'll be responsible and answer for all the horses bought by A up to $10,000" is a continuing guaranty, effective so long as A's purchases of horses do not exceed $10,000. If A's purchases reach $10,000 and then A pays $5,000 of the debt, the guaranty continues in effect up to the original amount of $10,000.

Unlimited Guaranty. An "unlimited guaranty" is a guaranty unlimited in time and in amount. "I guarantee payment for all the goods A buys from you" is an illustration.

Limited Guaranty. A "limited guaranty" is a guaranty limited in time or amount. "I guarantee payment for all the goods A buys from you up to $10,000," and "I guarantee payment for all the goods A buys from you from January 2 through June 30, 1981," are illustrations. Similarly, a guarantor may limit his liability to particular property, as by his pledging securities with the creditor for the principal debtor's obligation or by his lending the securities to the principal debtor so that he may pledge them as security for credit extended to him.

General Guaranty. A "general guaranty" is a guaranty made to the public generally and is not addressed to any particular person. A guaranty addressed to all the merchants of a particular area—e.g., a city—is a general guaranty.

Special Guaranty. A "special guaranty" is a guaranty addressed to a designated person or persons, and only such person or persons may rely on the guaranty. A general or special guaranty is, in effect, a letter of credit which is acted upon by the addressee. A guaranty may be of one or more of the several guaranties just discussed. "John Jones. I guarantee payment of all the merchandise you may sell to John Smith not in excess of $10,000 (signed) John Doe" if relied on by John Jones, is an absolute, continuing, limited, special guaranty. The various types of guaranty are named for the particular suretyship obligation involved.

Indorser on a Negotiable Instrument. An indorser is a special kind of guarantor, and his liabilities as such are fixed by the Commercial Paper portion of the Code. Unless the indorsement otherwise specifies, an indorser on a negotiable instrument is a secondary party liable thereon, engaging that upon dishonor and any necessary notice of dishonor and protest he will pay the instrument. On his payment of the instrument, he has a right against the maker or acceptor of the instrument for whom he was a guarantor, and a right against those secondary parties liable on the instrument prior to him on their guaranty to him. The liability of an indorser developed mostly under the Law Merchant rather than under the Common Law and an indorser's guaranty, therefore, differs from that of other guaranties under the law of Suretyship.

SECTION III. THE SURETYSHIP CONTRACT

The suretyship contract is normally between the surety and the creditor, although it may be made by a debtor with another person who contractually assumes the debtor's obligation thereby creating a third party creditor beneficiary contract for the benefit of the creditor and also a suretyship relationship in which, as between the debtor and the assuming party, the debtor becomes a surety for the assuming party as the new debtor.

The contract requires an offer and acceptance and consideration. A surety's continuing offer of suretyship is accepted each time compliance with the offer is made resulting in a suretyship contract or contracts. An offer of suretyship is revocable by the surety offeror, or it may terminate by operation of law, (e.g.,

death of the surety offeror, or the creditor offeree). The surety's offer may be for a bilateral or a unilateral contract and, if the latter, the creditor offeree is not required to notify the offeror of his acceptance by his performance unless the offeree has reason to know that the offeror will not learn of such performance within a reasonable time and in the ordinary course of affairs, in which event he has a duty to notify the offeror within a reasonable time. Failure so to notify discharges the offeror of his contractual duty to perform as a surety.

The contract of a strict surety is not, and that of a guarantor is, within that portion of the Statute of Frauds that a promise to answer for the debt, default or miscarriages of another is unenforceable without a proper writing. For the suretyship contract to come within the statute *all* of the three following things must occur: (1) the surety's promise must be *made to the creditor;* (2) the surety's promise must be made primarily for the *principal debtor's benefit,* but the promise of a paid surety is within the statute if the only consideration is a premium of insurance; and (3) the surety must *not assume* the principal debtor's obligation and thereby become a strict surety not promising to the creditor to answer for the debtor's default.

General

The suretyship contract *between the surety and the creditor* may be made at the same time as the contract between the principal debtor and the creditor, and both obligations may be contained in the same instrument or in different instruments. (In one writing, S contracts as an absolute guarantor, C contracts to sell goods to D, and D contracts to buy the goods from C. Or, S and C may contract in one writing and C and D may contract in another writing.) The two obligations may occur at different times. (D contracts to purchase goods from C, and subsequently S contracts with C as an absolute guarantor for D.) A contract between the surety and the principal debtor for the benefit of the creditor may create the suretyship relation, but the creditor is not affected by the suretyship relation until he has *knowledge* of it.[3] (S owns land which he has mortgaged to C. S contracts with D whereby the land is sold to D and D assumes payment of the mortgage debt. C is a third party creditor beneficiary of the contract and, inasmuch as S and D are both liable to C on the same obligation for which one payment may be made, there is a suretyship relation. *As between S and D,* D now is the principal debtor and S is his surety. If S is required to pay the debt, S has a right of reimbursement against D. If mortgaged land is sold to the purchaser subject to the mortgage, but the purchaser *does not assume* the mortgage, the land is still subject to the same obligation as is the mortgagor; the purchaser being liable *only to the extent of the land for the same obligation as the mortgagor,* the relation of suretyship is

[3] See the legal effect of the creditor's lack of such knowledge when he surrenders or impairs the security, below, p. 497.

created in which, *as between the purchaser and the mortgagor,* the purchaser is a surety to the extent of the land and the mortgagor is the principal debtor. If the mortgage is foreclosed and the land sold, the previous purchaser whose land was sold is entitled to reimbursement from the mortgagor.)

Surety as a Party

Any person with capacity to contract may contract to become a surety.

Manifestation of Mutual Assent

A suretyship contract is governed by the law of Contracts, except as otherwise modified by the law of Suretyship; reference should be made to the law of Contracts regarding the formation of contracts.[4] Accordingly, manifestation of mutual assent, which is concerned with offer and acceptance, is governed by the law of Contracts.

Offer. Only the offeree can accept the offer to contract as a surety. (S offers to C to become a surety for D. Only C can accept S's offer.) A continuing offer of suretyship may be made, and each compliance with the offer in reliance thereon constitutes an acceptance creating a contract; if more than one acceptance occurs, then more than one contract is formed. (G offers to guarantee to C the payment by D for all merchandise bought by D from C. In reliance on G's offer, C sells goods to D on three different occasions. There are three contracts of suretyship between G and C. G's offer is an offer of a continuing guaranty of payment, unlimited in amount, addressed to C.)

An offer is revocable by the offeror, or it may terminate by operation of law, at any time prior to acceptance. Revocation by the offeror is ineffective until the offeree has actually received notice of such revocation. An offer may be terminated by operation of law—e.g., death of the offeror—and no notice to the offeree of such termination is required. In the case of a continuing offer of suretyship, the acceptances which have already occurred created contracts of suretyship, but an effective revocation of the continuing offer precludes any future acceptances. Any attempt to accept subsequent to an effective revocation of the offer is of no effect because there is no offer to accept.

Acceptance. An offer to contract as a surety may be unilateral or bilateral. If the offer is for a bilateral contract of suretyship, acceptance must be made as required by the offer. Unless the offer provides to the contrary, acceptance by the use of the same means of communication as used for the transmission of the offer, or whatever channel is customarily used for transactions of that nature at the place where the offer is received, is proper and effective to create a contract, even though the acceptance is never received by the offeror.[5] If the offer

---

[4] See Contracts, Chapter 3, pp. 12 ff.

[5] For the general rule of the acceptable channel of communicating an acceptance when the offer does not expressly prescribe it, see above, p. 31.

is for a unilateral contract of suretyship, the offeree is not required to give the offeror notice of his acceptance, unless the offeree has reason to know that the offeror will not receive notice of acceptance with reasonable promptness in the ordinary course of affairs, in which case, by the majority view, the offeree has the duty to notify the offeror of performance of the unilateral act requested within a reasonable time thereafter.[6] Failure to notify the offeror when required does not affect the formation of the unilateral contract, which occurred when the act requested was performed, but it does *discharge* the offeror from the duty of performing under the contract. (G offers to guarantee to C the payment by D for all merchandise bought by D from C. On each occasion when C extends credit to D for purchases in reliance on the offer, C has the duty of informing G of such purchases within a reasonable time after each purchase. Failure to do so discharges G from liability as a guarantor on each such contract.)

Consideration

A suretyship contract requires consideration. The focal point of attention is the consideration requested by the offer to contract as a surety. If that consideration is rendered, and the other elements of a contract are present, a contract of suretyship is formed. If the offer requests an act—e.g., extension of credit to the principal debtor or the formation of a contract between the principal debtor and the creditor—the performance of the act creates a unilateral contract.

The suretyship contract may occur at the same time as the principal debtor's obligation is created, or subsequently. (G, D, and C all contract together that C will sell goods to D on credit, D will buy such goods, and G guarantees to C payment by D for such purchases. C's contract with D is the consideration for G's promise to guarantee, thereby creating a contract between G and C. G's promise does not become enforceable until C extends credit to D who defaults in payment therefor.) If the suretyship contract occurs subsequently, consideration must be present. (C advanced credit to D. G subsequently promises C to guarantee payment of the debt by D. G's promise is unenforceable—i.e., there is no contract—because no consideration is present. If C had paid G for his promise, then a suretyship contract would have been formed.)

Legally Valid Transaction

The requirement under the law of Contracts that the transaction be legally valid is applicable to contracts of suretyship.

Statute of Frauds

A common provision in the Statute of Frauds in effect throughout the various states is that *a promise to answer for the debt, default, or miscarriages of*

---

[6] See above, p. 33.

another person (construed to mean the promisee's obligor) *is unenforceable unless the contract is in writing or there is a note or memorandum in writing of the contract signed by the party to be charged or by his lawfully authorized agent.*[7]

Contracts of Strict Surety and Guarantor. The suretyship contract of a *strict surety is not,* while that of a *guarantor is,* within the Statute of Frauds. The suretyship contract of a strict surety is not within the statute because the strict surety does not promise to answer for the obligation of *another.* The strict surety has *assumed* the principal debtor's obligation as his own and is a *co-debtor* with the principal debtor on the same obligation owing to the creditor. In contrast, the suretyship contract of a guarantor is within the statute because it undertakes to answer for the *principal debtor's obligation.*

Promisee Must Be Creditor. It should be observed very carefully that the statute has been construed to refer only to such promises *made to the person to whom the principal debtor's obligation is owing*—namely, the creditor. (For consideration G *orally* promises X to guarantee payment to C of D's debt to C. G's promise is not within the statute because the promisee is not the person to whom D's obligation is owing; C's promise is enforceable. If G's oral promise had been made to C, the promise would be within the statute and unenforceable.) A promise *to the principal debtor* to guarantee payment of his obligation to his creditor is not within the statute, although it creates a suretyship relation if it is supported by consideration. (G orally contracts with D to guarantee payment by D of his obligation owing to C. The contract is not within the Statute of Frauds and is enforceable; however, G is liable to C as a third party creditor beneficiary[8] of the contract between G and D and, therefore, the relation of suretyship exists.) A promise of suretyship is not within the statute if no principal obligation is owing to the promisee. (G contracts with C whereby C is to deliver goods to G, the cost is to be charged to D, and G guarantees payment by D. G has no authority to order these goods on D's account and inasmuch as D is under no obligation to C, G's promise is not within the Statute of Frauds.)

Simultaneous Promises for Benefit of One Promisor. If promises are made by two or more persons to the same promisee for the same obligation in return for consideration for the sole benefit of only one of the promisors, *the promise of the one not benefited is within the Statute of Frauds, unless the promises were made jointly or unless the promisee did not have knowledge that the consideration was for the sole benefit of only one promisor.* The reason for this is that when only one of two promisors receives a benefit the other is deemed to be a surety for him. However, if the promises are joint only, and not joint and several or several, the promises can be treated only as a unit and, inasmuch as *both* promises are not made for the purpose of being sureties, neither

[7] See discussion above, pp. 87 ff. The statute makes the contract unenforceable and not void, although in a few states the statute is construed as making the agreement void.

[8] See above, pp. 76 ff.

promise is within the statute. If the promises are not joint and are for the benefit on only one promisor and the promisee has no reason for knowing that the benefit is for only one of them, the promisee should not be subjected to possible loss in not being able to enforce the contract because of his ignorance of their true relationship. The promisee's delivery of goods or benefits to one of the promisors is not notice to him that the benefit is to inure to only one of them.

Promise of Suretyship Primarily for Principal Debtor's Benefit. The promise to answer for another's obligation is a benefit to the principal debtor and, therefore, is within the Statute of Frauds. If the promise appears to be of suretyship and for another's benefit, but really is for the *primary* benefit of the promisor in that the consideration for his promise is primarily for himself, the promise is not within the statute.[9] The fact that the promisor derives an incidental benefit from the consideration rendered by the promisee does not bring it within the main purpose rule. (S and C are creditors of D. C is about to attach D's property. S is afraid that such attachment will ruin D and thereby jeopardize S's collection of the debt owing to him by D, and S *orally* promises C that if C will not attach the property for one month, S will guarantee payment of D's debt to C if D does not pay by that time. C, in reliance on S's promise, forbears from attaching the property. S's promise is not within the statute and is enforceable because it was made solely for his own benefit and not for D's benefit. If S were not a creditor of D and had made the promise as a friend of D, S's promise would be within the statute and, being oral, would be unenforceable.) The promise of a del credere agent—i.e., a factor who for consideration in the form of a higher commission guarantees to his principal that the purchaser of goods from the agent will pay for the same—is not within the statute because his promise is made primarily for his own benefit.[10] However, the promise of a *paid surety* is within the Statute of Frauds if the only consideration received by the *surety* is a premium of insurance that the principal debtor's obligation will be performed. The reason for this exception to the "main purpose" rule is that the purpose of the statute was to include this type of promise irrespective of premium benefit to the promisor *surety*. The distinction between a paid *surety* and a paid *indemnitor* should be noted carefully again.[11]

[9] See above, p. 88.

[10] See below, p. 549.

[11] See above, p. 480.

Chapter 31

DEFENSES OF THE SURETY

On the principal debtor's default, the creditor has the right to proceed, at his election, against the principal debtor or the surety according to the suretyship contract, or both, or against the property security, except that in the case of a guaranty of collection the creditor must attempt to collect before proceeding against the surety. Payment by the principal debtor to the creditor must be applied as directed by the principal debtor, except that if the creditor *knows* that the funds were provided by the surety then he must apply the payment *only* on the debt on which the surety is bound. If the principal debtor does not indicate to which of the various obligations owing to the creditor a payment is to be applied, the creditor may apply it to any of them.

The surety has various defenses available to him assertable against the creditor—his own, and also those of the principal debtor except the principal debtor's bankruptcy discharge, his infancy or insanity, and set-off of personal debts, all of which *are personal to the debtor. With regard to the surety's partial defenses,* the following defenses discharge the surety partially only to the extent of loss of security or prejudice caused by the creditor's wrongful conduct: (1) The creditor's surrender or negligent or wilfull impairment of the security, with knowledge of the suretyship relationship, causing discharge to the extent of the security surrendered or so impaired. (2) The creditor's release of a co-surety, without reservation of rights against the remaining co-sureties, causing the co-sureties not released to be discharged to the extent of the contributive share of the released co-surety at the time of their performance of their suretyship obligations. (3) In a guaranty of collection, the creditor's failure to act with reasonable promptness to enforce collection which caused him not to effect collection discharges the surety to that extent, and the creditor's

failure to give notice to the surety of the creditor's inability to effect collection thereby prejudicing the surety's position discharges the surety to that extent. *All other defenses of the surety are complete defenses.*

***With regard to the surety's complete defenses,* the following defenses discharge the surety completely: (1) Performance of the principal debtor's obligation. (2) The surety's lack of capacity to contract. (3) Discharge by operation of law, e.g., *impracticability* of performance by the principal debtor, the surety's bankruptcy discharge. (4) The creditor's conduct by: (*a*) his releasing the principal debtor without reservation of rights against the surety; (*b*) his improper refusal of a performance by the principal debtor or the surety with knowledge of the suretyship relationship; (*c*) his fraud or duress on the principal debtor; (*d*) his fraud on the surety by his actual fraud, or by his failure to disclose material facts which increase the surety's risk *prior* to the suretyship contract or, only in a continuing suretyship, *after* the suretyship contract; (*e*) modification of the principal debtor's contract by the creditor and the principal debtor without the surety's consent if the modification *both increases the possibility of the surety's risk and is binding on the modifying parties;* (*f*) his unexcused failure of consideration; (*g*) his fraudulent, material alteration of the contract with the principal debtor without the surety's assent.**

The surety can set off against the creditor *any* claim of the surety against the creditor and, with the principal debtor's assent, *any* claim of the principal debtor against the creditor.

SECTION I. RIGHTS OF THE CREDITOR

Against the Surety

The creditor has the right to proceed against the surety on his obligation when the surety's promise is enforceable according to its terms. The strict surety's promise is enforceable on the due date of the obligation, while the enforcement of the guarantor's promise is dependent on the type of guaranty—the absolute guaranty being enforceable on default by the principal debtor and the conditional guaranty being enforceable on the occurrence of the condition (e.g., a guaranty of collection is enforceable after the creditor has exercised reasonable diligence in his unsuccessful attempt to effect collection from the principal debtor). *When the principal debtor has defaulted on his obligation, the creditor has the right, at his election, to proceed: against the principal debtor, or against the surety when the surety's obligation is enforceable according to its terms, or both; or against the property held as security for performance of the principal debtor's obligation.* The principal debtor's waiver or extension of the Statute of Limitations in favor of the creditor on the principal debtor's obligation has no effect on the statute as running on the creditor's claim against the surety on his obligation; and similarly, such waiver or extension by the surety does not affect the principal debtor's obligation to the creditor. The creditor is not required to give to the surety notice of the principal debtor's default, except when the suretyship contract provides to the contrary, although the creditor must give a guarantor of collection reasonable notice of his failure to collect on the principal debtor's obligation. The creditor may delay in taking any action after the principal debtor's default, except that in the case of a guaranty of collection the creditor is required to exercise reasonable diligence in attempting to make collection. Except for such guaranty of collection, the creditor is not unlike any other creditor with a right against his surety debtor which he may assert when and if he wishes to do so.

Against the Security

A creditor has a security interest in any property delivered to the creditor or to the surety[1] as security for performance of the principal debtor's obligation. *On the principal debtor's default, the creditor can proceed against such security or, at his election, proceed against the surety.* The creditor has the right to recover on the obligation owing to him, without delay, and is not required to resort to the security. However, if by doing so the surety will suffer undue hardship, *and* if postponement of the creditor's right to proceed against the surety before resorting to the security will not prejudice the creditor, the surety may obtain a court decree compelling the creditor to resort first to the security. The reason that, except in such case of undue hardship to the surety, the surety cannot compel the creditor to proceed *first* against the security as an application of the doctrine of marshaling of assets is that the surety can protect himself by paying the creditor's claim against the debtor on which the surety is bound and thus become subrogated to the creditor's rights in such security, which he then can use to reimburse himself for what he has paid to the creditor.

Application of Payment by Principal Debtor to Creditor

Payment by the principal debtor to the creditor on his obligation is applied to such obligation. If the principal debtor has obligations to the creditor other than the one on which the surety is bound, such payment is to be applied on the particular obligation *as indicated by the principal debtor.* If the principal debtor does not indicate, then the creditor may, at his election, apply it to any of the obligations within a reasonable time after he has received such payment. If neither the principal debtor nor the creditor indicates his intention as to how the payment is to be applied, it will be applied in the manner most favorable to the creditor, unless such application would be inequitable under the circumstances (e.g., application of the doctrine of marshaling of assets if

[1] See equitable subrogation, below, pp. 504–5.

other persons are affected by the application of the payment). The source of the funds for such payment is unimportant, except that *if the funds originate from the surety* as security for performance of the principal debtor's obligation and *the creditor knows this,* then such payment must be applied to the obligation on which the surety is bound *regardless* of the principal debtor's instructions to the creditor to the contrary.

SECTION II. DEFENSES AVAILABLE TO THE SURETY

Defenses in General

The principal debtor and the surety each may have defenses to the creditor's claims on their respective obligations. *Some of the defenses available to the principal debtor are personal only to him, while the others are available to the surety as well as to the principal debtor.* The surety has, in addition to defenses which are not personal to the principal debtor, defenses which are available only to the surety. Some of the defenses available to the surety completely discharge him from his obligation, while others discharge him only to the extent of the loss he has sustained or to the extent that he has been prejudiced. First the defenses available to the principal debtor, and then the defenses available to the surety, will be enumerated briefly; then the defenses which completely discharge the surety will be examined, and finally the defenses partially discharging the surety will be considered.

Defenses Available to Principal Debtor. The defenses available *to the principal debtor against the creditor* on the principal debtor's obligation are as follows: (1) discharge of the principal debtor by performance of his obligation; (2) tender of performance of the principal debtor's obligation by either the principal debtor or the surety; (3) the creditor's release of the principal debtor from his obligation; (4) fraud or duress perpetrated by the creditor on the principal debtor; (5) by operation of law; (6) material nonperformance of the creditor's promise not justified by any conduct of the principal debtor; (7) the creditor's fraudulent, material alteration of the written contract between him and the principal debtor; (8) the principal debtor's power of avoidance because of his infancy or insanity; (9) and set-off of personal debts. *Only the principal debtor's discharge in bankruptcy—i.e., by operation of law—and the last two defenses are personal to him and may be exercised solely by him.*

Defenses Available to Surety. Defenses *available to the surety against the claim of the creditor* on the surety's obligation, *as well as those defenses available to the principal debtor and not personal to him,* are as follows: the surety's power of avoidance because of his infancy; by operation of law; the creditor's nondisclosure of material facts bearing on the surety's risk and unknown to the surety; modification of the principal debtor's contract by the principal debtor and the creditor without the consent of the surety; the creditor's surrender or impairment of security received from the principal debtor;

the creditor's release of a co-surety without the other surety's consent; inability of the creditor to make collection because of his delay in enforcing a guaranty of collection; and failure of the creditor to give a guarantor of collection reasonable notice of the creditor's inability to effect collection, to the prejudice of the guarantor.

Complete Defenses

Those defenses which completely discharge the surety may occur by performance of the principal debtor's obligation, by reason of the surety's lack of capacity or limited capacity to contract, by operation of law, and by the conduct of the creditor.

Performance of Principal Debtor's Obligation. Performance of the principal debtor's obligation, either by the principal debtor or by someone on his behalf, discharges the principal debtor and the surety.

Surety's Capacity to Contract. A person who has no capacity to contract cannot be a party to a suretyship contract. An infant has limited capacity to contract and may become a surety; however, he may avoid liability as a surety by exercising his power to avoid the contract.

Operation of Law. The surety is completely discharged if the Statute of Limitations has run against the creditor on the surety's obligation or the surety has been discharged in bankruptcy. Impracticability of performance[2] by the principal debtor or illegality of such performance also completely discharges the surety, in the absence of a contrary provision in the contract between the surety and the creditor.

Conduct of Creditor. Most of the instances where the surety is completely discharged occur by reason of the conduct of the creditor. Several of these instances will be considered.

Release of Principal Debtor. The creditor's release of the principal debtor from his obligation discharges the surety, unless the creditor has *reserved* his rights against the surety or the surety *consents* to such release. The principal debtor's obligation has been terminated, and there is no reason for any further liability of the surety as security for the performance of the terminated obligation. An additional reason for the surety's discharge is that such release deprives the surety of the creditor's right against the principal debtor, to which the surety would have been subrogated on his performance of his suretyship obligation to the creditor. When the principal debtor has been discharged from his obligation under a composition agreement, the surety on such obligation is discharged because the creditor has voluntarily agreed to the discharge of the principal debtor. However, such release does not extinguish the creditor's interest in any security which the surety may be holding for performance of the principal debtor's obligation. It may have been because of such security that the creditor released the principal debtor.

---

[2] See above, pp. 123–25.

It should be noted that, should a surety be discharged by reason of performance by the principal debtor or on his behalf and subsequently the creditor is legally compelled to surrender what he has received from the principal debtor, on such surrender the surety's suretyship obligation is revived. An illustration is an insolvent principal debtor's payment to his creditor, set aside subsequently as a voidable preference in a bankruptcy or an insolvency proceeding against the principal debtor, and the creditor is compelled to return such preference; on the creditor's return of such preference the surety's suretyship obligation is revived.

The creditor's *reservation* of his rights against the surety is construed as *a covenant not to sue the principal debtor,* and the *principal debtor is not discharged* from the performance of his obligation to the creditor. The effect of this is that, on the creditor's recovery against the surety on his suretyship obligation, the surety acquires the rights of reimbursement, and of subrogation to whatever security the creditor may have, for performance of the principal debtor's obligation. If it were not for such reservation of rights, the creditor's release of the principal debtor would discharge the principal debtor and would deprive the surety of his rights of reimbursement and of subrogation because the principal debtor is no longer liable on any obligation and, therefore, the surety is discharged.

Improper Refusal of Proper Tender. The creditor's improper refusal of a proper tender of performance of the principal obligation by the principal debtor or by the surety, *with knowledge of the suretyship relation,* discharges the surety. (S and D contract with C for the purchase of goods for $900. C does not know that S is a surety for D. When D tendered $900 on the due date, C mistakenly refused the money. Neither S nor D is discharged for the debt.)

Creditor's Fraud or Duress on Principal Debtor. When the creditor has perpetrated fraud or duress on the principal debtor in inducing him to become obligated to the creditor, the principal debtor's defense of such fraud or duress is, by the majority view, also available to the surety. The surety may assert the defense regardless of whether or not the principal debtor has done so. The creditor may not profit from his fraud by obtaining the obligation of a surety as security for a voidable obligation of the principal debtor. The principal debtor may waive the fraud or duress and then the defense is not available to the surety.

Creditor's Fraud on Surety. The creditor's fraudulent inducement of the surety to become such causes the contract of suretyship to be voidable at the surety's election. *Prior to formation of the suretyship contract,* the creditor has a *duty to disclose* to the surety all material facts which increase the surety's risk, which are known to the creditor, which the creditor reasonably believes are unknown to the surety, and which are unknown to the surety. The creditor's failure to observe this duty is a fraud on the surety. *After the suretyship contract is formed,* the creditor has no duty to inform the surety of material facts of which he learns subsequently, unless the contract of suretyship provides to the contrary, or the contract of suretyship is terminable by the surety at any time as in the usual type of fidelity bond, or if it is a continuing suretyship. *In a continuing suretyship* the surety makes a continuing offer to contract as a surety, and the creditor has a *duty to make disclosure* to the surety, inasmuch as the latter's liability will be increased by his ignorance of such material facts. *Fidelity bonds* usually provide for termination of the bond on the occurrence of conditions indicated therein, and the creditor's failure to make proper disclosure to the surety of facts which would permit the surety to terminate his bond discharges the surety from liability thereon. (S contracts with C, an employer, as surety for C against the defalcations of his employees. X, an employee of C, embezzles money from C, who does not inform S, who is ignorant of what has occurred. X again embezzles money from C. S is not liable for the second embezzlement.)

Although a principal debtor's exercise of his power of avoidance of his obligation on the ground of his infancy does not discharge the surety, except to the extent of the consideration returned by the principal debtor to the creditor, however, if the creditor knew of such infancy at the time the suretyship contract was made and he reasonably believed that the surety was unaware of it at that time, *the creditor had a duty to disclose this material fact of infancy to the surety at that time.* The creditor's failure so to disclose is a fraud on the surety and causes the suretyship contract to be *voidable at the election of the surety.* Nondisclosure of the principal debtor's infancy increases the surety's risk of performance because of the increased possibility of the principal debtor's default on his obligation by the exercise of his power to disaffirm the obligation.

Modification of Principal Debtor's Contract. Whether or not modification of the principal debtor's contract by the principal debtor and the creditor without the surety's consent will result in discharging the surety depends upon such modification. *If the modification (1) increases the possibility of the surety's risk and (2) is binding on the modifying parties, the surety is discharged.* Each of these will be considered in turn.

If the modification can be only beneficial to the surety, by the majority view the surety is not discharged; however, *if there is any possibility that the surety's risk will be increased, the surety is discharged. A contract* between the creditor and the principal debtor for the reduction of the rate of interest payable on the obligation does not discharge the surety because there is no possibility that the surety's risk will be increased and also because, in effect, it constitutes a reduction of the indebtedness. The substitution of a new obligation of the principal debtor to the creditor, or a material change in the principal debtor's obligation, discharges the surety. The surety never agreed to be liable for such a modified obligation of the principal debtor. While there is conflict, by the better view[3] a paid surety is not discharged if his risk is increased slightly; he is discharged only to the extent of any loss caused to him by the modification of the principal debtor's contract. The basis for this exception is

[3] Restatement of Security, 1941, sec. 128.

that the paid surety should anticipate small changes affecting his risk slightly and take this into consideration in fixing his premiums.

If the creditor makes a *binding agreement* with the principal debtor extending the time of payment by the principal debtor, without the surety's consent and without reserving his rights against the surety in the agreement, the surety is discharged.[4] The surety is discharged because of the possibility of an increase in the surety's risk. The surety is deprived of his privilege, at the time his obligation to the creditor matures, to perform the obligation himself and thereby become entitled to reimbursement by the principal debtor and become subrogated to the creditor's rights against the principal debtor *immediately.* The binding agreement between the creditor and the principal debtor postpones this right of the surety, which is prejudicial to the surety, adversely affecting his risk. *Unless the extension agreement is binding, the obligation of the principal debtor is not modified.* The agreement must be supported by consideration.[5] The creditor's *gratuitous* promise to extend the time of payment is not enforceable for want of consideration, and the surety is not discharged. If the surety consents to a *binding* extension agreement between the creditor and the debtor, the surety's express or implied promise to continue to be bound is enforceable without consideration as an exception to the consideration rule.[6] Although there is conflict, by the better view[7] a paid surety is discharged only to the extent that he has been prejudiced by such extension of time. The discharge of a nonpaid surety by such an extension agreement does not disturb the creditor's interest in security held by the surety for performance of the principal debtor's obligation.

Creditor's Material Nonperformance. Unexcused failure of consideration by the creditor—i.e., material nonperformance without justification[8]—discharges the principal debtor's obligation to perform and thereby increases the risk of the principal debtor's nonperformance of his obligation and increases the surety's risk of loss on the suretyship contract. It is for this reason that the surety is discharged completely. However, should the principal debtor elect to treat the creditor's material nonperformance as an immaterial nonperformance or to waive it, the surety's risk has not been increased and, therefore, the surety is not discharged.

Creditor's Fraudulent, Material Alteration of Written Contract. As discussed previously in Contracts,[9] a fraudulent material alteration of a written contract discharges such contract. The alteration must be made to the instrument containing the contractual obligation. When this is done by the creditor, the surety is discharged as well as the principal debtor.

---

[4] For the application of this rule to commercial paper, see above, pp. 389–90.

[5] For extension of an interest-bearing obligation *as a contract,* see above, p. 52.

[6] See above, p. 66. Also, see above, p. 390.

[7] Restatement of Security, 1941, sec. 129.

[8] See above, p. 98.

[9] See above, pp. 121 f.

Partial Defenses

The creditor's conduct may cause a *reduction in the security available* to the surety or *otherwise prejudice the surety's position* in the event of the principal debtor's default, justifying the surety's discharge *only to the extent of such loss of security or prejudice.* A few of the ways by which the surety's partial discharge may occur will be examined briefly.

Creditor's Surrender or Impairment of Security. A creditor who *has knowledge* of the suretyship relation and who surrenders to the principal debtor, or negligently or wilfully impairs the value of, security received from the principal debtor thereby causes the surety to be discharged *to the extent of the security surrendered or so impaired by the creditor.* Should the creditor subsequently proceed against the surety on the surety's obligation, the surety would be deprived of the opportunity to have recourse against the security so surrendered or impaired and, rather than cause the surety to suffer to such extent, the surety is *partially discharged.*

Creditor's Release of Co-Surety. Unless the creditor reserves his rights against the remaining co-sureties, the creditor's release of one of two or more co-sureties causes the co-sureties not released to be deprived of the contributive share of the released co-surety in the event of the principal debtor's nonperformance of his obligation, and the co-sureties not released are *discharged to the extent of such contributive share at the time of their performance of their obligations.* The contributive share of the released co-surety is measured as of the time when the co-sureties not released are entitled to such contributive share, which occurs at the time they are compelled to perform their suretyship obligations. If the released co-surety is insolvent or unavailable *at that time,* the remaining co-sureties are not discharged to any extent.

Creditor's Conduct if Guaranty of Collection. A guarantor of collection engages that the principal debtor's obligation is *collectible* and, if not, that he will pay it. Before the guarantor's promise is enforceable the creditor has two duties to perform. *He must act with reasonable promptness to enforce collection* of the obligation of the principal debtor and, *on failure to effect collection, he must give to the guarantor notice of such failure within a reasonable time thereafter.* The guarantor is discharged *to the extent* that the creditor's failure to act promptly to enforce collection caused him not to effect collection, and the guarantor is also discharged *to the extent* that he has been prejudiced by the creditor's failure to give notice to the guarantor of the creditor's inability to effect collection.

It should be noted carefully that, if the guaranty of collection is on *commercial paper,* under the Code:

> "Collection guaranteed" or equivalent words added to a signature mean that the signer engages that if the instrument is not paid when due he will pay it according to its tenor, but only after the holder has reduced his claim against the maker or acceptor to judgment and execution has been returned unsatisfied, or

after the maker or acceptor has become insolvent or it is otherwise apparent that it is useless to proceed against him.[10]

Surety's Right of Set-Off. A surety has the right to set off against the creditor any claims against the creditor which are available *to the surety* whether or not arising out of the suretyship transaction. A claim *of the principal debtor* against the creditor is *personal* to the debtor and is not available to the surety unless the principal debtor has assented thereto.

---

[10] UCC 3–416(2); also see above, p. 366.

Chapter 32

REMEDIES OF THE SURETY

A surety's "right of exoneration" is his right to a court order to compel the principal debtor, to the extent that he can, to perform his express or implied enforceable *promise to the surety* that he would perform his obligation to the creditor and thereby prevent loss and inconvenience to the surety who has not yet performed his now enforceable suretyship obligation on the principal debtor's default. This right is assertable also by a surety against a co-surety to the extent that he became such at the request of the co-surety.

A surety's "right of reimbursement" is to receive from the principal debtor, on his default, whatever reasonable outlay the surety has made pursuant to his suretyship obligation to the creditor. The surety cannot profit at the expense of the principal debtor. The surety *must* assert against the creditor's claim any defense *of the principal debtor;* he does not have to assert his own defenses. A principal debtor has a duty to disclose, *only to a surety whom he requested to be such,* those of his defenses which are also available to the surety; but he has no duty to disclose his discharge of his obligation to the creditor.

A surety's "right of subrogation" is to occupy the creditor's position, on discharge of the principal debtor's obligation to his creditor, to the extent that the surety contributed to such discharge by his performance of his suretyship contract. The *creditor's* "right of equitable subrogation" entitles him to any security deposited by the principal debtor with the surety.

A surety's "right of contribution" occurs when he has performed his suretyship obligation to the extent that he has paid more than his proportionate share of the principal debtor's obligation on his default and thereby acquires a right against his co-sureties for their respective contributive shares for such excess. Generally, co-sureties are entitled to share proportionately in any security

received by a co-surety from the principal debtor after he became a co-surety. In the absence of a contract among co-sureties, the contributive share of each co-surety is determined according to his maximum liability under his suretyship contract. If the maximum liability is the same for each co-surety, the liability of each co-surety to the one who has paid the entire amount is measured by dividing such amount paid by the number of solvent and available co-sureties. If the maximum amount is different, the contributive share of each co-surety is determined by the proportion that his maximum liability under his contract bears to the total of the maximum liability of them all. The conduct by a co-surety adversely affecting his co-sureties may affect his right of contribution against them.

SECTION I. EXONERATION

When the principal debtor has failed to perform his obligation and the surety's obligation becomes enforceable, the surety has various remedies: exoneration, reimbursement, subrogation, and contribution. Exoneration is a remedy available to the surety *before* the surety has performed his obligation. Reimbursement is a remedy available to the surety *after* the surety has performed *part* or *all* of his obligation. Subrogation is a remedy available to the surety *after* the surety has performed his obligation *completely.* Contribution is a remedy available to the surety against a co-surety *after* the surety has paid more than his proportionate share of the principal debtor's obligation. These remedies will be considered in turn.

Nature

A surety's right of exoneration is an equitable right *springing from the principal debtor's duty to the surety* to perform his obligation to the creditor and thereby spare the surety loss and inconvenience in the performance of his suretyship obligation. The principal debtor's duty originates in his promise *to the surety* to perform his obligation to the creditor and, in the event of his nonperformance, to make the surety whole for the surety's performance of his suretyship obligation. The principal debtor's promise may be *express* and contained in a contract between the principal debtor and the surety, or may be *implied* from the principal debtor's *request* to the surety. Accordingly, on the principal debtor's nonperformance of his obligation to the creditor and when the surety's obligation *becomes enforceable,* the surety has the right to be exonerated from the performance of his suretyship obligation by obtaining a court decree compelling the principal debtor to perform in accordance with his promise to the surety. The surety's right to such equitable relief is called the "right of exoneration."

Exercise

The surety may assert this right before, or at the same time as, the creditor seeks recovery against the surety on his suretyship contract. Although *a surety cannot obstruct the right of the creditor to recover against him,* nevertheless, the surety can join the principal debtor as a party to the action by the creditor and *have the principal debtor compelled to perform his obligation to the extent that he can do so.* If the principal debtor has a defense to the performance of his obligation to the creditor, the surety has no right of exoneration. If the surety has a defense to the creditor's claim—e.g., the Statute of Limitations bars enforcement of the creditor's claim—then since the surety is not exposed to any loss the surety has no right of exoneration.

Co-sureties who become such *at the request of each other* owe to each other the duty to contribute their respective shares of the liability imposed upon them by the principal debtor's nonperformance of his obligation. A surety has the right of exoneration to the extent of the contributive share of each co-surety when the suretyship obligation matures and is enforceable against him. He need not wait until the creditor seeks to enforce his obligation.

SECTION II. REIMBURSEMENT OR INDEMNITY

The terms "reimbursement" and "indemnity" often are used interchangeably as describing a right which one person, the surety, has against another, the principal debtor, for the surety's performance of his obligation by his partial or complete performance of the principal debtor's obligation. Inasmuch as the surety's right of indemnity against the principal debtor is limited to reimbursement for the expenditure of the surety in the performance of his obligation, the term "reimbursement" will be used.

Nature

A surety has the right to receive from the principal debtor, on the latter's failure to perform his obligation, whatever reasonable outlay the surety has made pursuant to his suretyship obligation to the creditor. This right is the surety's "right of reimbursement." Such outlay may reduce or discharge the principal debtor's obligation to the creditor and, although the surety may make such outlay prior to, as well as after, the date when the principal debtor's obligation is enforceable, *the surety has no right of reimbursement until the principal debtor's obligation matures.*[1] (D's contract with C provides for D's payment on a certain date. S, surety for D, pays D's obligation to C prior to that date. S has no right of reimbursement against D until the date when D was to perform. The Statute of Limitations does not begin to run on the surety's right of

[1] Restatement of Restitution, 1937, sec. 77.

reimbursement against the principal debtor until the surety acquires such right.) The surety need not pay the principal debtor's obligation in full in order to acquire a right of reimbursement against him; *an outlay which reduces the principal debtor's obligation gives rise to the surety's right of reimbursement.* If the surety's outlay does not reduce or discharge the principal debtor's obligation to the creditor but was reasonably made while acting as a surety, the surety has a right of reimbursement for this outlay also.

Extent

The *extent* of a surety's right of reimbursement depends upon whether or not the surety became such *at the principal debtor's request* because the surety's right of reimbursement originates in the principal debtor's duty to reimburse the surety. *If the principal debtor requested the surety to be such* then, either because the surety's right of reimbursement is expressed in the contract or is implied in the contract from the principal debtor's request of the surety to be such, *the surety has a contract right of reimbursement for his reasonable outlay, whether or not it reduced the principal debtor's obligation to the creditor.* The surety reasonably may have defended an action brought by the creditor against the surety on the surety's obligation for the principal debtor's failure to perform his obligation, which action the principal debtor has refused to defend. The surety has the right to be reimbursed by the principal debtor for the expense of his reasonable defense of such action, as well as for his payment to the creditor discharging the principal debtor's obligation to him. If the surety has become such by contract with the creditor *without the consent of the principal debtor,* the surety is entitled equitably to his outlay *only to the extent that it discharged or reduced the principal debtor's obligation to the creditor* because only to that extent has the principal debtor become *unjustly enriched at the surety's expense.* It is essential to the right of reimbursement that the outlay be made by a person under a suretyship obligation for performance of the principal debtor's obligation; a person who is not under a suretyship obligation and who makes such outlay is a volunteer with no right of reimbursement against the principal debtor.

Surety Cannot Profit. *The surety cannot profit from the suretyship relation at the expense of the principal debtor.* The purpose of a surety is security for the performance of the principal debtor's obligation, and the purpose of the surety's right of reimbursement against the principal debtor is to make whole the surety for his reasonable outlay on the principal debtor's behalf. If the surety settles with the creditor for less than the obligation of the principal debtor who is thereby *discharged,* the surety has a right of reimbursement only for his reasonable outlay, consisting of the amount paid by the surety to the creditor and the surety's reasonable settlement expenses, if any. If the surety elects to perform the specific obligation of the principal debtor on the latter's failure to perform, the surety cannot profit from such performance. (S is surety for D's performance of his contract with C to construct a building. On D's failure to do so, S completes the building and, pursuant to the contract between C and D, S receives from C an amount thereunder greater than S's expense in making such completion. S must account to D for the excess. If S had received an amount less than his expense in constructing the building, S would have a right of reimbursement for such deficiency.)

Effect of Defenses

When defenses against the creditor's claim are available to the principal debtor, to the surety, or to both, the possibility of a surety's right of reimbursement is seriously affected. A surety is not required to assert his *own* defense to the creditor's claim against him on his suretyship obligation, and the principal debtor cannot require the surety to assert such defense. The surety's failure to assert such a defense does not affect his right of reimbursement. (S is surety for D's payment to C. The Statute of Limitations runs on C's claim against S but not on C's claim against D. S pays C. S has a right of reimbursement against D.) However, a surety cannot disregard a defense of the *principal debtor* because, to the extent of such defense, the principal debtor is not liable to the creditor and the surety has no right of reimbursement to that extent.

In the above illustration, if the Statute of Limitations had run on C's claim against D but not on C's claim against S, S's failure to assert D's defense and S's payment to C do not cause S to acquire any right of reimbursement against D. The surety is security for performance of the principal debtor's obligation and, on the surety's performance of his obligation, he has a right of reimbursement *only to the extent that he has performed the principal debtor's obligation.* (S, without D's consent, became a surety on D's obligation to pay C $1,000. D has a partial defense to C's claim to the extent of $400 of which S is ignorant. S pays C $1,000 on D's default. S has a right of reimbursement against D only to the extent of $600. D has been unjustly enriched only to the extent of $600, for which S has the right of reimbursement.) If the surety knows of defenses of the principal debtor which are also available to the surety, the surety should assert them in any claim made by the creditor against the surety. If the surety is ignorant of such defenses and performs his suretyship obligation to the creditor, the surety has no right of reimbursement against the principal debtor to the extent of such defenses, unless the principal debtor has failed in his duty to disclose such defenses to the surety.

Principal Debtor's Duty of Disclosure. A principal debtor has the duty to disclose, *only to a surety whom he has requested to be such,* those defenses of the principal debtor which are also available to the surety; he has no duty to inform the surety of the principal debtor's discharge from his obligation to the creditor. Should the principal debtor fail in his duty to make such disclosure to the surety and the surety perform his obligation to the creditor ignorant of such defenses, the surety has a right of reimbursement therefor against the principal debtor. A defense against the creditor which is personal to the principal debtor[2] cannot be asserted by the surety, but defenses not personal to the principal debtor and which are available to the surety may be asserted by the surety against the creditor. If the surety knows of defenses of the principal debtor which are available to the surety, the surety may assert them and give the principal debtor an opportunity to defend against the claim asserted by the creditor in an action against the surety; should the principal debtor refuse to defend the action and the surety satisfies a judgment obtained by the creditor against the surety, the latter has a right of reimbursement therefor.

SECTION III. SUBROGATION

Nature

A surety's recovery on his right of reimbursement against the principal debtor is assisted materially by the right of subrogation, which arises *when the principal debtor's obligation to the creditor is discharged.* To the extent that the surety has contributed to such discharge by performance of his suretyship obligation, the surety acquires an equitable right to occupy the creditor's position immediately on such discharge of the principal debtor. This right is available to the surety by operation of law, independent of any contract, although it may be provided for by contract. The surety is subrogated to: (1) the creditor's rights against the principal debtor; (2) the creditor's interests in property held as security for performance of the principal debtor's obligation; (3) the creditor's rights against third persons who are also liable to the creditor on the principal debtor's obligation; and (4) to the creditor's rights against co-sureties and security held by them for the principal debtor's nonperformance of his obligation. If the creditor has a preferred claim against the principal debtor, the surety acquires the creditor's preference of such claim. If the creditor's claim is a secured claim, the surety acquires the security for such claim. *The surety's right to be placed in the creditor's position on the discharge of the principal debtor's obligation to the creditor to the extent that the surety's property has been used to satisfy the creditor's claim and to effect such discharge,* is called the surety's "right of subrogation."

Equitable Subrogation Distinguished

The surety's right of subrogation should be distinguished carefully from the creditor's right of equitable subrogation. On the principal debtor's default the creditor has the right to resort to any security which has been deposited by the debtor *with the surety.* The creditor is subrogated to the surety's right against the property of the principal debtor. This right of the creditor to reach such

[2] For the principal debtor's personal defenses, see above, pp. 492 f.

security is called the "right of equitable subrogation." Until the principal debtor's default, the surety has the obligation to preserve the security.

Proof of Claim When Debtor is Bankrupt

When the principal debtor is adjudicated bankrupt, the creditor's claim must be proved against the principal debtor's estate within a specified period of time if it is to be allowed. If the creditor does not prove his claim within such time and the principal debtor is discharged from his provable debt, the creditor no longer has any claim against the principal debtor. However, the creditor can recover from the surety for the principal debtor on his suretyship obligation to the creditor. *The principal debtor's discharge in bankruptcy is a defense personal to the principal debtor and is not available to the surety, who remains liable to the creditor on his suretyship obligation.* On payment to the creditor, the surety has no right of reimbursement against the discharged principal debtor, and he is not subrogated to any right of the creditor, because the principal debtor's obligation has been discharged. In order to avoid such loss to the surety by the creditor's failure to prove his claim against the principal debtor's estate, the Bankruptcy Code provides that *where the creditor does not prove his claim the surety may prove it in the creditor's name.* Now the creditor will receive some payment on the principal debtor's obligation, and the surety is liable to the creditor only for the deficiency. Should the surety prove the creditor's claim in the creditor's name and then pay the creditor on the principal debtor's obligation, to the extent of such payment the surety is subrogated to the creditor's claim.

SECTION IV. CONTRIBUTION

Nature

Co-sureties are sureties for performance of the same obligation of a principal debtor and may contract together, or on different contracts, as co-sureties. *When a surety has performed his suretyship obligation to the extent that he has paid more than his proportionate share of the principal debtor's obligation on the principal debtor's default, he has a right against his co-sureties on their suretyship obligations for their respective contributive shares for such excess.* Such right is called the "right of contribution." The Statute of Limitations begins to run against a surety's right of contribution as soon as the surety acquires such right. A surety's right of contribution does not arise until the principal debtor has defaulted, the surety has paid more than his proportionate share of the principal debtor's obligation, and the obligations of the co-sureties have matured. A surety's negotiable promissory note made by the surety and delivered to the creditor, who accepts it in discharge of the creditor's claim against the surety, has the effect of payment and creates an immediate right of contribution in the surety against his co-sureties.

Duty to Disclose Defenses

Co-sureties who have become such *with the consent of each other* have the duty to disclose to each other whatever defenses they may have against the creditor. Failure to disclose such defenses to a surety who paid the creditor in ignorance of them subjects the co-sureties to liability for their contributive shares. If such defenses are disclosed, the paying surety must assert such defenses against the creditor or the paying surety will not have any right of contribution to the extent of such defenses. Co-sureties who have become such *without the consent of each other* have no duty to disclose to each other defenses available to them.

Amount of Contributive Share

The amount contributed by each co-surety depends on whether or not the co-sureties became such by mutual assent. *If there is mutual assent,* then the co-sureties share in all expenses incurred by a particular surety, regardless of whether or not the surety's expense reduced or discharged the liability of each co-surety—e.g., cost of reasonably defending an action brought against one surety by the creditor. *If there is no mutual assent* among the co-sureties, then the contributive share of each co-surety is limited *only to the extent that his respective liability to the creditor has been reduced or discharged.* Inasmuch as the right of contribution is an equitable right, contribution is to be made among the *available, solvent co-sureties.* (S_1 discharges D's obligation by paying C $1,000. There are five co-sureties. S_1 has a right of contribution against his four co-sureties for $200 each. If S_2 is insolvent, S_3 is outside the state, and S_4 is an infant who has avoided his suretyship contract, S_1 has a right of contribution against S_5 for $500.) Co-sureties may not profit at the expense of each other and must share the loss caused to any of them and, accordingly, if one of them has settled and discharged the creditor's claim against the principal debtor *and* the co-sureties for less than the amount due the creditor, the co-sureties are liable only for their respective contributive shares of such reduced payment. Once final settlement has been determined among co-sureties and their respective contributions made, if one of them should be reimbursed subsequently by the principal debtor or any person on his behalf, the other former co-sureties have no right to share in such reimbursed amount.

When one of several co-sureties has security or other benefit for the performance of the principal debtor's obligation, whether or not his co-sureties have any proportionate rights in such security depends upon the reason for delivery of the security, the agreement if any among the co-sureties, the consent of the other co-sureties, who gave the security, and when the security was given. Also, the extent of the right of contribution of the co-surety who has the security against his co-sureties depends upon what he did with the security. Any agreement among the co-sureties regarding such security is, of course, determinative of their rights. In the absence of agreement to the contrary, however, various equitable principles control. As a general rule, co-sureties are entitled to share proportionately in any security or other benefit received by a co-surety from the principal debtor in assurance of the latter's performance on which they are co-sureties. The reason for this principle is that the resources of the principal debtor are assets to which the co-sureties would have recourse if and when they were entitled to proceed against the principal debtor on his default, and any diminution of such resources of a co-surety as security for his own suretyship obligation, without the consent of the other co-sureties, would be inequitable to the other co-sureties and a breach of good faith on the part of such co-surety receiving the security. If such security should emanate from a third person or from another co-surety, the reason for the rule ceases to exist and the other co-sureties have no right to participate in the security. The general rule that all co-sureties share proportionately in the security received from the principal debtor applies only when the recipient of the security is a co-surety. Therefore, if the recipient receives such security for his sole benefit at or before the time he became a co-surety, the general rule does not apply. Also, when the various co-sureties have paid their respective contributive shares and thereby become independent creditors of the principal debtor, their relationship of co-suretyship ceases, and any subsequent reimbursement by the principal debtor to one of them for his sole benefit does not enure to the benefit of the others.

A co-surety who receives security from the principal debtor, in which, under the general rule stated above, his co-sureties have rights proportionate to their liability on the principal debtor's default, has a right of contribution against his co-sureties when he has paid more than his proportionate share of the principal debtor's obligation on the latter's default, irrespective of such security. His right of contribution has matured and he can enforce it; but he may do so only if he shares the security with his co-sureties and accounts to them therefor. The extent of his right of contribution is reduced proportionately by his impairment or surrender of the security and by the amount he has received from its proper and careful disposal. His right of contribution is affected further by his expense incurred in connection with the creation, preservation, or enforcement of such security, which entitles him to reimbursement therefor, and by income which he has received from the security, which reduces what he otherwise should receive.

Co-sureties are liable to each other for their contributive shares according to whether there is a contract among them providing for such liability or, in the absence of such a contract, by the terms of their respective contracts of suretyship. *In the absence of a contract among them, the contributive share of each co-surety is determined according to his maximum liability under his suretyship contract. When the co-sureties are all liable for the same maximum amount,* the liability of each co-surety to the one who has paid the entire amount is measured by dividing such amount paid by the number of co-sureties who are *solvent and available.* (If there are four co-sureties, each liable for a maximum amount of $1,000, and one pays the creditor the $1,000 owing by the principal debtor to the creditor in discharge of the liability of the principal debtor and the co-sureties, each of the three other co-sureties is liable to the payor for \$250.) *When the co-sureties are not liable in the same maximum amount* on their respective suretyship contracts, the contributive share of each co-surety is determined by the proportion that his maximum liability under his contract bears to the total of the maximum liability of all of them. (S_1's liability on his suretyship contract is \$10,000, S_2's is \$15,000, and S_3's is \$20,000. S_1 paid the entire debt of the principal debtor amounting to \$9,000. S_1's share is 10,000/45,000 of \$9,000—namely, \$2,000. S_2's share is 15,000/45,000 of \$9,000—namely \$3,000. S_3's share is 20,000/45,000 of \$9,000—namely, \$4,000. Accordingly, S_1 has a right of contribution of \$3,000 from S_2 and \$4,000 from S_3.)

Contribution Affected by a Surety's Conduct

Just as a creditor's conduct may affect his right of recovery against a surety, so the conduct of a surety may affect his right of contribution against his co-sureties after he has paid more than his proportionate share of the principal debtor's obligation. A surety's *binding* agreement with the principal debtor to extend the time within which he may make reimbursement discharges the nonpaid co-sureties from their duty to make contribution, unless the paying surety reserves his rights against the co-sureties. A paid surety is discharged only to the extent that he has been prejudiced by such extension of time. If the paying surety releases the principal debtor from his duty to make reimbursement, or surrenders or impairs the security which he has for the performance of the principal debtor's obligation, the co-sureties are discharged from their duty to make contribution *to the extent that such release, surrender, or impairment is in excess of the proportionate share of the payor.* The reason for such partial discharge of the co-sureties is that, on payment of their respective contributive shares, they become subrogated to the paying surety's right of reimbursement against the principal debtor or against the particular security and, to the extent that such right of reimbursement from the principal debtor or from the security has been reduced, the co-sureties are discharged.

PROBLEMS

1. (a) What is suretyship?
   (b) Distinguish a contract of suretyship from a contract of indemnity, and indicate why this distinction is important.
   (c) S orally contracted with C to be liable with D on D's debt to C.
      (1) Is the contract enforceable?
      (2) Why?
   (d) Distinguish a guaranty from a warranty.
2. A promised B that, if B sold goods to C and C did not pay therefor, then A would pay B. D also promised B that, if B sold goods to C and B could not recover the money from C, then D would pay B. In reliance on these promises B sold goods to C, who failed to pay for them.

(1) Does B have any rights against A and D?
(2) Why?

3. A mortgaged his land to B as security for payment of A's mortgage debt to B. A then sold and conveyed the land to C.
   (1) If C purchased the land subject to the mortgage, explain the relationship among the parties.
   (2) If C purchased the land and assumed the mortgage, explain the relationship among the parties.
4. A, in one state, promised B, in another state, that he would be liable for all of C's purchases of merchandise from B up to $10,000 if C did not pay therefor. In reliance thereon B sold merchandise to C on three different occasions, the purchase price totaling $15,000. A did not know of such sales by B to C. A died. C paid B $10,000 on the debt. B was ignorant of A's death and sold $5,000 of additional merchandise to C. C then failed to pay the $10,000 owing to B.
   (1) Does B have any right against A's estate?
   (2) Why?
5. A guaranteed payment by B to C for merchandise to be sold by C to B on credit, in reliance on which C sold merchandise to B. B gave C his negotiable promissory note for the purchase price, payable in 90 days at 6 percent interest per anum.
   (1) If B defaulted on his note, what would be the effect on A's liability of an agreement between B and C for the extension of time within which B could pay the debt? Why?
   (2) What would be the effect on A's liability of a contract between B and C to reduce the interest rate from 6 percent to 5 percent? Why?
   (3) What would be the effect on A's liability of C's release of B from the debt? Why?
6. Allen was the guarantor for the payment of rent by Burt under a lease from Carr. The lease was for two years. There was a clause in the lease to the effect that at the expiration of the lease the lessee had the privilege to renew upon 30 days' notice or, if he remained in possession after the expiration, it was agreed that the lease was to continue for two years more. There was a default in the payment of rent for the extended time and Carr sues Allen on the guaranty. Allen contends that he was liable only for the term of the lease and not for the extended term. Who should receive judgment, Allen or Carr? On what principle? (Former C.P.A. Examination question)
7. A surety company duly guaranteed the honesty of X's cashier. Thereafter, the cashier embezzled X's funds, which X discovered, but X did not discharge the cashier nor did X notify the surety company. Still later, the cashier committed a further embezzlement, whereupon X discharged him and notified the surety company. Is the surety company liable to X for either part or both of these thefts? (Former C.P.A. Examination question)
8. Allen and Bell are co-sureties on a debt of Covey to Dixon for $12,000. Covey fails to pay. Allen is compelled to pay Dixon $8,000 in partial payment of the debt. Allen sues Bell, his co-surety, for $4,000 contribution. Can Allen recover $4,000 from Bell? State your reason. (Former C.P.A. Examination question)
9. (a) S is surety on one of D's obligations to C. D paid C but did not specify to which of his obligations the payment was to be applied.
   (1) May C apply the payment to obligations of D other than the one on which S is a surety?

(2) If S had advanced the money to D which he had paid to C, would this affect the answer to (1) above?

(b) C knew, and reasonably believed that S did not know, that D was an infant at the time S became bound as a surety for performance of D's obligation to C. S did not know of D's infancy at that time. Do these facts affect S's suretyship obligation to C?

(c) How is a surety's obligation affected by the creditor's surrender to the principal debtor of security held by the creditor as assurance of performance by the principal debtor?

(d) S_1, S_2, S_3, and S_4 are co-sureties on an obligation owing by D to C. C released S_1 from his suretyship obligation to C. How are the suretyship obligations of S_2, S_3, and S_4 affected by such release?

10. S had a contract with D to make repairs and additions to S's house, in which S was residing. D purchased lumber from C, as he needed it for the work on S's house. D was in arrears on payments for the lumber and C refused to extend further credit to D. S orally promised C that, if C would continue to extend credit to D, S would guarantee payment by D. In reliance thereon, S extended further credit to D who, after purchasing more lumber from C for S's house, defaulted in making any further payments to C. Can C recover from S as a surety the money owing by D to C for lumber purchased by D and used in S's house? Explain.

SOME PREVIOUS C.P.A. LAW EXAMINATION QUESTIONS AND AUTHOR'S MODEL ANSWERS

NOVEMBER, 1979

Number 4

Part a. The King Surety Company, Inc., wrote a performance bond for Allie Stores, Inc., covering the construction of a department store. Rapid Construction Company, the department store contractor, is a general contractor and is simultaneously working on several buildings. Until the entire building is completed, the bond contained a provision that obligated Allie to withhold 20 percent of the progress payments to be made to Rapid at various stages of completion. After approximately two-thirds of the project had been satisfactorily completed, Rapid pleaded with Allie to release the 20 percent withheld to date. Rapid indicated that he was having a cash flow problem and unless funds were released to satisfy the demands of suppliers, workmen, and other creditors, there would be a significant delay in the completion date of the department store. Rapid claimed that if the 20 percent withheld were released, the project could be completed on schedule. Allie released the amounts withheld. Two weeks later Rapid abandoned the project, citing as its reason rising cost which made the contract unprofitable. Allie has notified King of the facts and demands that either King complete the project or respond in damages. King denies liability on the surety bond.

Required:

Answer the following, setting forth reasons for any conclusions stated.

Who will prevail?

Part b. Barclay Surety, Inc., is the surety on a construction contract that the Gilmore Construction Company made with Shadow Realty, Inc. By the terms of the surety obligation, Barclay is not only bound to Shadow, but also is bound to satisfy materialmen and laborers in connection with the contract. Gilmore defaulted, and Barclay elected to complete the project and pay all claims and obligations in connection with the contract, including all unpaid materialmen and laborers' claims against Gilmore. The total cost to complete exceeded the construction contract payments Barclay received from Shadow. Some of the materialmen who were satisfied had either liens or security interests against Gilmore. Gilmore has filed a voluntary bankruptcy petition.

Required:

Answer the following, setting forth reasons for any conclusions stated.
What rights does Barclay have as a result of the above facts?

Answer

4.a. King will prevail. Under the law of Suretyship, if the creditor and the principal debtor modify their contract without the consent of the surety, the surety is discharged on its suretyship contract. The modification must both increase the possibility of the surety's risk in the performance of its suretyship contract, and be binding on the modifying parties. Here, the contract between Allie and Rapid was modified, and the modification was binding on them by Allie's release to Rapid of the 20 percent of the progress payments before Rapid's completion of construction. Under Allie's contract with Rapid and under King's bond, the 20 percent was to be withheld until after Rapid's completion of construction. The purpose for withholding the 20 percent was to induce Rapid to complete the construction in order to receive the withheld 20 percent. Allie's release of the 20 percent before completion increased the possibility of King's risk as a surety in that Rapid now would not be induced to complete the construction since he has been paid in full and King would have to perform its bond. Therefore, the modification discharged King as a surety. (pp. 495–96)

b. Barclay as a surety has rights of reimbursement and subrogation against Gilmore which Barclay may file as claims in Gilmore's bankruptcy. When a surety performs its contract on the nonperformance of the principal debtor, the surety has a right of reimbursement against the principal debtor for its reasonable expense in discharging the principal debtor's obligation to the creditor. Here, by Barclay's completion of the construction contract on Gilmore's failure to do so, Barclay acquired a right to be reimbursed by Gilmore for Barclay's construction expense. Also, since Barclay paid the laborers and the materialmen with liens and security interests and thereby discharged Gilmore's obligations to them, Barclay is subrogated to their rights, liens, and security interests. Since Gilmore is in bankruptcy, Barclay has the right to file its claims against Gilmore for what Barclay is entitled to by his rights of reimbursement and subrogation. Under the Bankruptcy Code, since laborers as wage earners have certain priority to their claims, Barclay's claims would have these priorities. Also, Barclay would file claims as a secured creditor with claims for the materialmen's liens and security interests. (pp. 501, 504, 528, 523)

MAY, 1979

Number 1

Select the **best** answer for the following item.

1. Martinson borrowed $50,000 from Wisdom Finance Company. The loan was evidenced by a nonnegotiable promissory note secured by a first mortgage on Martinson's

ranch. One of the terms of the note required acceleration of repayment in the event that Wisdom "deemed itself insecure." When the value of the property declined, Wisdom notified Martinson that pursuant to the terms of the note, it "deemed itself insecure" and demanded that either additional collateral or an acceptable surety be provided. Martinson arranged for Clark, a personal friend, to act as surety on the loan. Clark signed the note as an indorser and Wisdom agreed in writing **not** to accelerate repayment of the loan during the life of the debt. Martinson has defaulted. Which of the following is a correct statement:

a. Clark's promise is **not** supported by consideration, hence is unenforceable.
b. Clark is a guarantor of collection and his obligation is conditioned upon Wisdom's first proceeding against Martinson.
c. Release of the mortgage by Wisdom would release Clark to the extent of the value of the property.
d. Wisdom must first foreclose the mortgage before it can proceed against Clark.

Answer

1. 1.c(497)

NOVEMBER, 1978

Number 1

Select the **best** answers for each of the following items.

20. Maxwell was the head cashier of the Amalgamated Merchants Bank. The Excelsior Surety Company bonded Maxwell for $200,000. An internal audit revealed a $1,000 embezzlement by Maxwell. Maxwell persuaded the bank **not** to report him, and he promised to pay the money back within ten days. The bank acquiesced and neither the police nor Excelsior was informed of the theft. Maxwell shortly thereafter embezzled $75,000 and fled. Excelsior refuses to pay. Is Excelsior liable? Why?

a. Excelsior is liable since the combined total of the embezzlements is less than the face amount of the surety bond.
b. Excelsior is liable for $75,000, but **not** the $1,000 since a separate arrangement was agreed to by Amalgamated with Maxwell.
c. Excelsior is liable since it is a compensated surety and as such assumed the risk.
d. Excelsior is **not** liable since the failure to give notice of the first embezzlement is a valid defense.

21. Adams, Baker, and Carter are co-sureties on a $250,000 loan by the Wilson National Bank to Marathon Motors, Inc. Adams is a surety for the full amount of the debt; Baker's obligation is limited to $100,000; and Carter has agreed to pay $50,000 upon default. In the event of default by Marathon on the entire $250,000 loan, what is the liability of Adams, Baker, and Carter?

a. Baker is liable for the first $100,000; Carter, the next $50,000; and Adams, the balance.
b. Baker and Adams are each liable for $100,000 and Carter for $50,000.
c. If both Baker and Carter know of Adams' obligation for the full amount, then they are **not** liable unless Adams can **not** satisfy the debt.
d. Adams is liable for $156,250; Baker, $62,500; and Carter, $31,250.

24. Ace Corporation loaned $10,000 to King Enterprises, Inc., one of its best customers. The loan was for three years and was evidenced by a note duly executed by King's president on behalf of the corporation. In addition, Walsh and Paxton, King's principal

shareholders, had orally guaranteed the repayment of the loan. With respect to Walsh and Paxton, which of the following is a correct statement?

a. Unless otherwise indicated, each guaranteed $5,000 of the loan.
b. They will be denied the usual surety defenses.
c. They are co-sureties and, as such, their surety undertaking must be in a signed writing.
d. Some additional consideration, independent of the making of the loan by Ace, must pass directly to Walsh and Paxton.

Answer

1. 20.d(495) 21.d(507–8) 24.c(486–87)

NOVEMBER, 1977

Number 2

Select the **best** answers for each of the following items.

19. Franks is a surety on a $5,000 debt owed by Smith to Jones. Jones also holds as collateral property worth $4,000 belonging to Smith. Under these circumstances, which of the following statements is true?

a. Franks has the right to the property immediately upon default.
b. Jones need **not** first proceed against the collateral in order to hold Franks liable.
c. Jones may return the collateral to Smith at any time prior to default without impairing his rights against Franks.
d. Jones must file a financing statement in order to perfect his rights in the collateral he holds.

27. The typical conditional guarantor of collection is

a. Liable only upon the creditor's establishing that the debtor has fled the jurisdiction.
b. Liable upon the creditor establishing that he has had a judgment returned unsatisfied.
c. **Not** entitled to the usual defenses asserted by other typical types of sureties.
d. **Not** entitled to the right of subrogation.

Answer

2. 19.b(491) 27.b(482)

Part Five: Bankruptcy

Chapter 33

BACKGROUND AND ADMINISTRATIVE STRUCTURE OF THE BANKRUPTCY REFORM ACT (CODE) OF 1978

SECTION I. CREDITORS' RIGHTS IN GENERAL

Bankruptcy is a specialized branch of the law concerned with the rights and duties of debtors and creditors. Before beginning a discussion of bankruptcy a brief survey of creditors' rights in general should be made, in order to become familiar with the underlying concepts of the debtor-creditor relationship and the methods of enforcing creditors' rights.

Property Available to Creditors

All property of a debtor, except as otherwise provided by statute, is available to his creditors for utilization in satisfaction of their claims when such claims are in the form of judgments. Such property may be legal or equitable and includes real and personal property. By statute in the various states, certain property is exempted and is made unavailable to creditors, such as a homestead and a certain portion of a debtor's salary.

Fraudulent Conveyances. Should the debtor attempt to make any of his property unavailable to his creditors, the latter may utilize various legal remedies which preclude the successful conclusion of such an attempt and which permit recovery of property fraudulently conveyed or transferred. In most states, a conveyance or transfer of property by a debtor without a fair consideration in exchange creates a presumption of fraud on existing creditors, rebuttable by the debtor's proof that sufficient assets remain available to satisfy the claims of his creditors. If insufficient assets remain available, the debtor is insolvent because, under the Uniform Fraudulent Conveyance Act, sec. 2(1),

". . . the present fair salable value of his assets is less than the amount that will be required to pay his probable liability on his existing debts as they become absolute and matured. . . ."

Ordinary Creditors' Remedies

The process by which a creditor may enforce his debtor's obligation and utilize the debtor's assets in satisfaction of his claim is fixed by statute in each state. The creditor cannot simply seize his debtor's property; he must follow the method outlined by the statute.

Execution. The creditor usually first brings an action[1] against his debtor and reduces his claim to a judgment. After a judgment has been obtained, the creditor is called a "judgment creditor" and the debtor is called a "judgment debtor." If the *judgment* debtor does not satisfy the judgment, the judgment creditor has a right to obtain a "writ of execution" issued by the court through the clerk of court directing the sheriff (or marshal, if a federal court) to levy upon and seize so much of the *tangible* property of the judgment debtor as is necessary in order to satisfy the judgment, sell it at public sale, deliver to the judgment creditor, or to the court where so required, the proceeds in an amount sufficient to satisfy the judgment, and deliver the surplus to the judgment debtor. It is usually provided that docketing of the judgment causes the judgment to become a lien on any real property of the judgment debtor located in the particular county in which the judgment has been docketed, thereby precluding the subsequent creation of any interest in such property superior to the lien of the judgment creditor. Such property is available for sale under the writ of execution. The judgment debtor usually has a statutory right of redemption (right to redeem) in real property so sold, which must be exercised within the period of time specified by the statute.

Garnishment after Judgment. The writ of execution normally cannot reach debts owed by third persons to the *judgment* debtor or chattels of the judgment debtor lawfully possessed by third persons. Generally, in the absence of statute to the contrary, such assets of the judgment debtor are not available in satisfaction of the judgment until the writ of execution has been returned unsatisfied to the issuing court, and an affidavit has been made to the effect that no other property of the judgment debtor is deemed available to satisfy the judgment and designating third persons who are believed to be indebted to the judgment debtor or who are in possession of his chattels. An order is issued by the court through the clerk of court directing the third person, called a "garnishee," to appear in court and to answer questions regarding such indebtedness or property. If, after examination of the garnishee, it is found that he owes money to the judgment debtor or is in possession of the judgment

[1] "*Lis pendens*" means that a suit is pending. A notice of *lis pendens* is a warning to all persons that the property involved in the suit is subject to a judgment affecting it. The *lis pendens* is made a matter of public record by filing in the official public place of record.

debtor's chattels in which the garnishee has no property interest, the court may order that such money or chattels be made available for use in satisfaction of the judgment. The judgment creditor is proceeding against the *interest owned by the judgment debtor* and cannot obtain more than such interest. Accordingly, if the judgment debtor's interest is a debt owing by the garnishee to the judgment debtor and if the garnishee has a claim or "set-off" against such debt, the judgment creditor can garnish such debt less the set-off. Or if the garnishee has a possessory lien (a right to possession) on a chattel of the judgment debtor as security for a claim of the garnishee against the judgment debtor, the judgment creditor may garnish the chattel subject to the lien of the garnishee.

Attachment. Attachment is an extraordinary remedy and is statutory. Its purpose is to cause property of a specified person or persons to be levied upon and seized *before judgment* is rendered in favor of the plaintiff and to utilize such property to satisfy the anticipated judgment when rendered. The plaintiff is required to post a bond to protect the defendant debtor from loss he may sustain by being deprived of the use of his property pending trial and for court costs in the event that the plaintiff is unsuccessful in his action. The grounds for attachment are enumerated by statute and are, generally: that the defendant debtor is a nonresident of the state or is a foreign corporation; or that he is concealing himself, or that he has been absent from the state for a prescribed period of time, so that service of process cannot be made upon him; or that his whereabouts have been unknown for a prescribed period of time; or that he has made, or is about to make, a fraudulent conveyance; or that he has concealed, or is about to conceal, his property; or that he has removed, or is about to remove, his property from the state.

Attachment is begun by an affidavit of the plaintiff which states his cause of action against the defendant—e.g., the indebtedness by the defendant to the plaintiff—and which states a legal ground for attachment. On the filing of the affidavit and bond, the court issues a writ of attachment directing the proper public officer, usually the sheriff or constable (or marshal, if a federal court), to levy upon and to seize the defendant debtor's property to the extent necessary to satisfy the plaintiff's demand. If the plaintiff is successful in the action, the property is sold and the proceeds used to satisfy the plaintiff's judgment. Attachment process must be in accordance with procedural "due process of law" and, when a public official, (e.g., sheriff), is utilized, must be preceded by notice and hearing so that the debtor defendant will have the opportunity to appear and to be heard before his property is seized.

Garnishment under Attachment. Garnishment *before judgment* is a statutory remedy. Its function is to reach before judgment property of the debtor not available under a writ of attachment. When garnishment is used as a species or type of attachment, it is subject to the same requirements as for attachment and, in general, has the same effect.

Special Statutory Limitations on Garnishment. One federal law and one uniform state law impose limitations on garnishment before and after judgment.

Federal Consumer Credit Protection Act (1968). Section 303(a) provides for the maximum part of the aggregate disposable earnings of an individual for any workweek which may be subjected to garnishment. It may not exceed "(1) 25 per centum of his disposable earnings for that week, or (2) the amount by which his disposable earnings for that week exceed *thirty* times the Federal minimum hourly wage prescribed by section 6(a)(1) of the Fair Labor Standards Act of 1938 in effect at the time the earnings are payable, whichever is less. . . ." (Author's italics.) Section 304(a) prohibits an employer from discharging "any employee by reason of the fact that his earnings have been subjected to garnishment for any *one* indebtedness" (Author's italics). Section 305 provides that the Secretary of Labor, who is charged with enforcement of this law, may by regulation exempt from the provisions of section 303(a) "garnishments issued under the laws of any State if he determines that the laws of that State provide restrictions on garnishment which are substantially similar to those provided in section 303(a)." Section 307 provides that this law "does not annul, alter, or affect, or exempt any person from complying with, the laws of any State (1) prohibiting garnishments or providing for more limited garnishments than are allowed under this title, or (2) prohibiting the discharge of any employee by reason of the fact that his earnings have been subjected to garnishment for more than one indebtedness."

Uniform Consumer Credit Code (1974). Section 5.104 prohibits a creditor from garnishment of a consumer's unpaid earnings *before obtaining a judgment* for a debt *arising from a consumer credit* transaction. Section 5.105 provides for the maximum part of the aggregate disposable earnings of an individual for any workweek which may be subjected to garnishment to enforce payment of a *judgment* arising from a *consumer credit transaction.* It may not exceed the lesser of "(2)(a) 25 percent of his disposable earnings for that week, or (b) the amount by which his disposable earnings for that week exceed *forty* times the Federal minimum hourly wage. . . ." (Author's italics.) Section 5.106 prohibits an employer from discharging an employee "for the reason that a creditor of the employee has subjected or attempted to subject unpaid earnings of the employee to garnishment or like proceedings directed to the employer for the purpose of paying a judgment arising from a consumer credit transaction. Section 5.106 prohibits employment discharge for *any* such garnishment, whether one or more.

SECTION II. BACKGROUND AND ADMINISTRATIVE STRUCTURE OF THE BANKRUPTCY CODE

Background

The rigors of business competition and economic fluctuation have their effect in causing some businessmen to succumb, financially. While creditors have their usual remedies,[2] nevertheless, society is strongly of the opinion that

---

[2] See above, pp. 515 ff.

these remedies alone are insufficient under such circumstances to assist creditors and failing debtors adequately. The Bankruptcy Code is an additional recourse available to creditors to ensure *equitable distribution of all the debtor's nonexempt assets among themselves, except for secured creditors and creditors with claims with priority status;* and it also is a boon to honest debtors, making it possible for them *to begin anew unencumbered by many debts.* In essence, this is the purpose of the Bankruptcy Code today.

Under the United States Constitution, Article I, section 8(4), Congress has the sole power to establish ". . . uniform Laws on the subject of Bankruptcies throughout the United States"; the states do not have this power. Congress passed and repealed four bankruptcy laws before the fifth law was passed in 1978.

Administrative Structure

Only Congress has the constitutional power to enact a bankruptcy law. The *substantive* provisions of the new (fifth) Bankruptcy Act (U.S. Code Title 11), now being called the *Bankruptcy Code* to distinguish it from the former Act, became effective October 1, 1979, and the provisions for the establishment of the new *United States Bankruptcy Court* as an *adjunct* of the federal District Court becomes effective April 1, 1984. During the transition period, the current bankruptcy courts continue *under* the federal District Courts. The currently sitting bankruptcy judges (*no longer are they called Referees*) will continue in office, exercise all the powers and jurisdiction of the new courts to come into existence in 1984 with a few exceptions, and apply the Code's substantive provisions. The judges serve for 14-year terms. Appeals from the bankruptcy court go to the District Court in the district of the bankruptcy court, or to a panel of bankruptcy judges if established by a Circuit Council, or to the U.S. Circuit Court of Appeals if the parties agree.

Title 11 has eight chapters. Chapters 1 "General Provisions," 3 "Case Administration," and 5 "Creditors, the Debtor, and the Estate" are, basically, procedural chapters. Chapters 7 "Liquidation," 9 "Adjustment of Debts of a Municipality," 11 "Reorganization," and 13 "Adjustment of Debts of an Individual With Regular Income" are operational chapters. Chapter 7 on Liquidation replaces the Act's provisions concerned with "straight bankruptcy" involving collection, liquidation, distribution of the debtor's estate, and the debtor's discharge. Under the Code, *the term "debtor" replaces the term "bankrupt."* Chapters 9, 11, und 13 replace the Act's previous provisions concerned with various compositions or arrangements and provide for full or part payment to creditors. Chapter 15 is concerned with United States Trustees.

An important change by the Code is the *separation of the administrative and judicial functions,* formerly performed by bankruptcy judges, by having trustees in bankruptcy do the administrative work and the judges do the judicial work. The Code is trying an experiment, ending April 1, 1984, by providing for *United States Trustees,* appointed by the Attorney General of the United States who will appoint one U.S. Trustee in each of a group of ten districts. The U.S. Trustee will create a panel of private trustees in bankruptcy to serve as trustees under the Code. This experimental program supplements the trustee system existing prior to the Code and continuing in the districts not included in the experiment. Present trustees represent the debtor's estate, can sue and be sued, and are removable by the bankruptcy court for cause; a U.S. Trustee is removable by the Attorney General for cause. The trustee may employ various professional persons to assist him, (e.g., accountants), provided they are disinterested persons who do not hold or represent an interest adverse to the estate, and do not represent a creditor in the case.

The Code provides for a *uniform percentage adjustment of each dollar amount in Title 11, based on cost of living changes,* on the recommendation of the Judicial Council of judges.

Chapter 34

LIQUIDATION UNDER CHAPTER 7

SECTION I. THE PETITION

A bankruptcy case commences with the filing of a petition. A debtor is a person that resides in the United States, or has a domicile, a place of business, or property in the United States, or a municipality. *Under Chapter 7,* any such person may be a debtor except a railroad, bank, insurance company, savings and loan association, or building and loan association. The debtor need not be insolvent. *Insolvent* means: if the debtor is *not a partnership,* the debtor's debts are greater than his assets, exclusive of property exempted or fraudulently transferred; if the debtor *is a partnership,* the partnership's debts are greater than all of the partnership's property, exclusive of property fraudulently transferred, *and* the sum of the excess of the value of each general partner's separate property, exclusive of property exempted, over such partner's separate debts.

In a voluntary case, the petition is filed by the debtor, and *now may be filed jointly by husband and wife.* The commencement of a voluntary case constitutes an *order for relief,* which is the equivalent of an adjudication of bankruptcy under the Act.

In an involuntary case, any person may be a debtor except those excluded above under a voluntary case and, in addition, a farmer and a charitable corporation. *A farmer is a person who received more than 80 percent of his gross income during the previous year from a farming operation* owned or operated by such person. A person includes an individual, partnership, and corporation, but not a governmental unit. If there are 12 or more creditors, at least 3 with noncontingent, unsecured claims totaling at least *$5,000* may file a petition. If there are fewer than 12 creditors, 1 or more of such creditors whose claim or claims equal at least *$5,000* may file a petition. The Act had $500. Also different from the Act, *there is no requirement of the debtor committing an act of bankruptcy.* If the debtor does not file an answer to the petition, the court will order the relief requested in the petition. If the debtor files an answer, after trial the court will order relief only if: the debtor is generally not paying his debts as they become due (equity insolvency test); or, *within 120 days before the date the petition was filed,* a custodian was appointed and took possession of the debtor's property. If the court dismisses the petition without the consent of all the petitioners and the debtor, *the court may grant judgment in favor of the debtor for costs, his attorney's fee, and damages including punitive damages if the petition was filed in bad faith.*

SECTION II. AUTOMATIC STAY AND ADEQUATE PROTECTION

The filing of a voluntary or involuntary petition operates as an *automatic stay,* effective against everyone, of: the commencement or continuation of judicial, administrative, or other proceedings against the debtor; the enforcement against the debtor or property of the estate of a judgment obtained before the case began; any act to obtain such property, to create or enforce a lien against such property, to collect on a claim against the debtor which arose before the case began. Among the exclusions from the stay are criminal proceedings against the debtor, collection of alimony and support, certain governmental unit proceedings to enforce police or regulatory powers. The Code provides for *adequate protection* to the interests of parties whose property interests will be adversely affected by the stay if it is to be continued. The protection may be provided by: payments by the trustee to the party needing protection equal to the decrease in the value of his property interest; additional or replacement collateral to affect any decrease in the value of the party's property interest; and other proper relief. This applies mainly to secured creditors with their property interests.

SECTION III. THE TRUSTEE

After the commencement of an involuntary case but before an order for relief, the court, at the request of a party in interest, or if necessary to preserve or prevent loss to the property of the estate, may appoint an *interim trustee* to take possession of such property and to operate the debtor's business. *The Code does not provide for a receiver. Before* the order for relief, *the debtor may regain possession* of the property by filing a sufficient *bond.* Promptly after the order for relief the court must appoint an interim trustee, whose appointment expires with the appointment of a *permanent trustee.* The duties of a trustee are to: collect the property of the estate, reduce it to cash, and expeditiously close up the estate; be accountable for all property received; investigate the affairs of the debtor; examine, and object to, improper claims; if advisable, oppose the debtor's discharge; furnish information to a requesting party in interest; report to the court regarding the debtor's business operated by the trustee pursuant to court order; and make and file a final report and final account with the court.

SECTION IV. CREDITORS

Meeting of Creditors

The court will order the first meeting of creditors within a reasonable time after the order for relief, which under the Bankruptcy Rules is not less than 10 nor more than 30 days after adjudication of bankruptcy. *The court may not preside at, and may not attend, any meeting of creditors. This is new.* The debtor must appear and submit to examination under oath. The creditors may elect a trustee and, if one is not elected, then the interim trustee serves as trustee in the case. The creditors may also elect a creditors' committee of creditors with unsecured claims to consult with the trustee and make recommendations to him.

Creditors' Claims

The Code broadens the meaning of "claims" which includes *all* legal obligations of the debtor, no matter how remote or contingent. A claim is: *any right to payment*, whether or not reduced to judgment, liquidated or unliquidated, fixed or contingent, matured or unmatured, disputed or undisputed, legal, secured or unsecured; *any right to an equitable remedy to performance.* Proof of a claim may be filed by: a creditor; an equity security holder; and, if a creditor does not file a timely proof of his claim, such claim may be filed by an entity that is liable to such creditor with the debtor or that has secured such creditor, or by the debtor or trustee. Under the Bankruptcy Rules, claims must be proved within six months after the first meeting of creditors.

A filed claim is deemed allowed unless objected to by a party in interest. Following are some exceptions to allowance:

(1) a claim unenforceable against the debtor for *any* reason (e.g., usury, fraud, failure of consideration, unconscionability);
(2) to the extent that the claim is for unmatured interest as of the date of the petition;
(3) to the extent that the claim may be offset against a debt owing to the debtor;
(4) to the extent that a property tax claim for tax due exceeds the value of the estate in such property;
(5) to the extent that the claim of an *insider* (a new term—one who has a close relationship with the debtor) or attorney exceeds the reasonable value of such services;

(6) a claim for a debt that is unmatured on the date of the filing of the petition and is excepted from discharge (post-petition claims for alimony, maintenance or support—these are payable from the debtor's post-petition property);
(7) to the extent that a landlord's claim for damages resulting from the termination of a lease exceeds the rent reserved by the lease for the greater of one year, or 15 percent, not to exceed three years, of the remaining term of such lease plus any unpaid rent due under the lease, at the time of filing of the petition or when the landlord regained possession of the leased property whichever is earlier;
(8) to the extent that a claim for damages resulting from the termination of an employment contract exceeds the compensation provided by such contract for one year plus the unpaid compensation due under such contract, at the time of filing the petition or the date of termination, whichever is earlier.

If a claim is contingent or unliquidated, or is a right to an equitable remedy for breach of performance giving rise to a right to payment (e.g., specific performance), the court may estimate its value for the purpose of allowance. If a creditor's allowed claim is secured by a lien on property in which the estate has an interest or which is subject to set-off, *it is a secured claim to the extent of the value of the creditor's interest in the estate's interest in the property or to the extent of the amount subject to set-off, and is an unsecured claim to the extent that the value of the creditor's interest in the estate's interest in the property or the amount subject to set-off is less than the amount of the allowed claim.*

Debtor's Duties

The debtor has various duties among which are the following: (1) file a list of creditors, a schedule of assets and liabilities, and a statement of his financial affairs; (2) if there is a trustee, cooperate with him and surrender to him all property of the estate and any recorded information, including books, documents, records and papers relating to such property; (3) appear at the court hearing concerning his discharge; (4) submit to examination at the first and subsequent meetings of his creditors.

SECTION V. PROPERTY OF THE ESTATE

The commencement of a bankruptcy case creates an *estate* comprised of the following property, wherever located.

All Legal and Equitable Interests

All legal and equitable interests of the debtor in property *as of the commencement of the case* are a part of the estate. This does not include: any power (e.g., a power of appointment) that the debtor may only exercise solely for the benefit of an entity other than the debtor; or a restriction on the transfer of a beneficial interest of the debtor in a trust that is enforceable under applicable nonbankruptcy law (e.g., income limitations of a spendthrift trust). Once the estate is created, no property interests remain in the debtor. However, except for the latter exclusion, restrictions on the transfer of property of the debtor are *invalidated* in order that *all* property interests of the debtor will become the property of the estate. *This provision that all property of the debtor constitutes a part of the estate is new.* However, after the property comes into the estate, then the debtor is permitted to exempt it, and the court will have jurisdiction to determine what property may be exempted and what remains as property of the estate. Trust property held by the debtor in trust for another, while becoming part of the estate, will be held in trust for the beneficiary.

The estate also includes property that the debtor acquires or becomes entitled to acquire *within 180 days after the filing of the petition:* by bequest, devise, or inheritance; as a result of a property settlement agreement with the debtor's spouse, or of a divorce decree; as the beneficiary of a life insurance policy or of a death benefit plan. Also in the estate are proceeds, product, offspring, rents, and profits of or from property of the estate, except such as are earnings from services performed by an *individual* debtor after the commencement of the case.

Community Property

All interests of the debtor and the debtor's spouse in community property, subject to certain limitations, are a part of the estate. *This is new.*

Interests Recovered by the Trustee

Any interest that the trustee recovers under the following are a part of the estate:

(1) *Turnover by anyone other than a custodian* of property of the estate which the trustee may use, sell, or lease, under certain conditions. However, it should be noted carefully that a person, without notice or knowledge of the commencement of a case is not liable for transferring property of the estate, or paying a debt owing to the debtor, in good faith to someone other than the trustee, the effect being the same as if the case had not been commenced.
(2) *Turnover by a custodian* of the debtor's property unless the court decides to leave it in the custodian's possession.
(3) Property or its value resulting from *voidable transfers* avoided by the trustee and obtained from either the transferee or one for whose benefit the transfer was made, or any immediate or mediate transferee of such initial transferee. But a good faith transferee from whom the trustee can recover

has a lien on the property recovered to the extent of the lesser of the cost of any improvement the transferee makes in the transferred property and the increase in the value of the property as a result of the improvement. However, the trustee cannot recover from: a transferee that took for value, including satisfaction or securing of a present or antecedent debt, in good faith, and without knowledge of the voidability of the transfer avoided; or any immediate or mediate good faith transferee of such transferee.

The trustee has the use of the Code's (and Act's) so-called strong arm clause giving to the trustee the rights of a *judgment creditor and a lien creditor* enabling the trustee to exercise any state law power of avoidance, and *the new right of being a bona fide purchaser of real property from the debtor enabling the trustee to avoid transfer of real property interests which were not properly recorded for security protection.* Also, the trustee has the power to utilize an unsecured creditor's power of avoidance under state law. The trustee also has the power to avoid certain statutory liens on the debtor's property, particularly those which are not perfected or enforceable against a bona fide purchaser. The trustee has the power to avoid fraudulent transfers and obligations made within one year before the petition was filed: with the intent to hinder, delay, or defraud past or future creditors; or for less than a reasonably equivalent value if the debtor was then insolvent or became insolvent as a result of such transfer. The trustee also can avoid transfers which occurred *after* the petition was filed when the transfer was: unauthorized; or was authorized either when the debtor was still conducting his business, or by a person in good faith without notice or knowledge of the commencement of the case. Further, the estate has the benefit of defenses available to the debtor (e.g., Statute of Limitations, Statute of Frauds). Also, generally, if the trustee does not assume or reject an executory contract or unexpired lease of the debtor within 60 days after the order for relief, or within such additional time as the court, for cause, within such 60-day period, fixes, then such contract or lease is deemed rejected.

A creditor has the well recognized right of set-off between himself and the debtor of claims which arose *before* the commencement of the case, except to the extent that: the creditor's claim is disallowed; the creditor acquired the claim from other than the debtor after commencement of the case or after 90 days before the date the petition was filed and while the debtor was insolvent; or the debt owed to the creditor was incurred after 90 days before the date the petition was filed, while the debtor was insolvent and for the purpose of obtaining a right of set-off against the debtor. *With respect to set-off,* the debtor is presumed to have been insolvent on and during the 90 days preceding the date of the filing of the petition.

The Code materially changes the old law with respect to partnerships by providing that, if there is a deficiency of property of the estate to pay in full all claims allowed in a case concerning a partnership, then *each general partner in such partnership is liable to the trustee for the full amount of such defi-*

ciency. Prior to the Code, the individual creditors of a general partner had first priority against the partner's assets before partnership creditors under the equitable doctrine of marshaling of assets. However, the trustee must, to the extent practicable, *first* seek to recover the deficiency from any general partner that is *not* a debtor in a bankruptcy case.

Voidable Preferences

Section 547 of the Code carefully defines the terms "inventory," "new value," and "receivable"; it also specifies when a debt for a tax is incurred—when the tax is last payable, including an extension, without penalty. The trustee may avoid a preferential transfer of the debtor's property if five conditions occur:

(1) the transfer was made to or for the benefit of a creditor;
(2) for or on account of an antecedent debt owed by the debtor before such transfer was made;
(3) made while the debtor was insolvent;
(4) *made on or within 90 days before the date of the filing of the petition* (or between 90 days and one year before the date of the filing of the petition if the creditor at the time of transfer was an insider and had reasonable cause to believe the debtor was insolvent at the time of such transfer); and
(5) the transfer enables the creditor to whom or for whose benefit it was made to receive a greater percentage of his claim than he would have received under the distributive provisions of the Code.

Two new changes in the old law occur here. First, the transferee no longer is required to have reasonable cause to believe that the debtor was insolvent at the time of transfer. Second, the period involved is 90 days instead of four months before the date of the filing of the petition.

However, there are six kinds of transfer when the trustee cannot avoid. He cannot avoid a transfer:

(1) to the extent that the transfer was intended by the parties to be a contemporaneous exchange for new value and, in fact, was substantially contemporaneous (e.g., payment by check);
(2) to the extent that the transfer was: in payment of a *debt incurred* in the ordinary course of business or financial affairs of the parties, made not later than 45 days after the debt was incurred, made in the ordinary course of business or financial affairs of the parties, and made according to ordinary business terms (e.g., payment of monthly telephone bills);
(3) of a purchase money security interest which secured new value and is perfected before ten days after the security interest attaches;
(4) to or for the benefit of a creditor to the extent that, after the transfer, the creditor gave new value unsecured;
(5) of a perfected security interest in inventory or receivables or the proceeds

of either, to the extent that the secured creditor does not improve his position during the 90-day period before the filing of the petition (e.g., protection for the floating lien creditor); and

(6) that is the fixing of a nonavoidable statutory lien.

Exemptions

An individual debtor may exempt certain property from the property of the estate *by choosing either the exemption available under state law or exemptions under the Code, except that state law may not authorize such a choice and require the debtor to use the state exemptions.* It is not improper for a debtor to convert nonexempted property into exempt property before a petition is filed. The debtor must choose federal or state exemption, he cannot have some of each, and he must file a list of the property which he claims as exempt. If there is a joint debtor case (e.g., husband and wife), each debtor must file separately. Property exempt under the federal law is not liable during or after the case for any debt of the debtor that arose before the commencement of the case, except claims for alimony, maintenance or support, and taxes excepted from discharge, and valid liens.

The following 11 categories of property are exempt under *federal law:*

(1) the debtor's equity in a homestead not to exceed $7,500 used by the debtor or a dependent as a residence;
(2) the debtor's equity in one automobile not to exceed $1,200;
(3) household furnishings, household goods, wearing apparel, appliances, books, animals, crops, or musical instruments held primarily for the personal, family, or household use of the debtor or dependent up to a maximum of $200 in value for *each item;*
(4) the debtor's equity up to $500 in personal jewelry;
(5) any other property up to a value of $400, plus any unused amount of the homestead exemption in (1) above;
(6) implements, professional books, tools of the debtor's trade, up to $750 in value;
(7) any unmatured life insurance contract owned by the debtor, other than credit life insurance;
(8) up to $4,000 loan value in a life insurance policy owned by the debtor;
(9) professionally prescribed health aids for the debtor or a dependent;
(10) various *state and federal benefits* including social security, unemployment compensation, local public assistance benefit, veterans' benefit, disability, illness, and unemployment benefits; and *private benefits* including stock bonus, pension, profit-sharing and other plans, and alimony, support, and maintenance, to the extent reasonably necessary for the support of the debtor or dependent;
(11) the debtor's right to receive certain types of compensation for losses, such as crime victim's reparation payments; wrongful death benefits from a

dependent's death and life insurance proceeds under a dependent's policy to the extent reasonable for the support of the debtor or dependent; payment for actual personal bodily injury of the debtor or dependent up to $7,500; payment in compensation of loss of future earnings to the extent reasonably necessary for the support of the debtor or dependent.

The debtor's waiver of his exemptions in favor of an unsecured creditor is unenforceable. Also, the debtor can avoid a judicial lien on any property to the extent that the lien impairs an exemption, and can avoid a nonpossessory, nonpurchase-money security interest in the property indicated in (3), (6), and (9) above.

SECTION VI. DISTRIBUTION OF PROPERTY OF THE ESTATE

After the trustee has collected, and usually liquidated (reduced to cash), the debtor's assets, the nonexempt estate property is distributed in payment of allowable claims. The Code establishes the following priority among the allowable claims, subject to section 510 which provides for the court's equitable power of subordination of allowed claims or interests:

(1) Administrative expenses and certain fees and charges for administering and preserving the estate.
(2) In an involuntary case, expenses arising in the ordinary course of the debtor's business or financial affairs after commencement of the case but before the earlier of the appointment of a trustee or the order of relief.
(3) Unsecured claims for wages, salaries, or commissions earned by an individual within 90 days before the date the petition was filed or the date of the cessation of the debtor's business, whichever occurs first, to the extent of *$2,000* for each individual.
(4) Unsecured claims for contributions to employee benefit plans arising from services rendered within 180 days before the petition was filed or the date of the cessation of the debtor's business, whichever occurs first, but only for each plan to the extent of $2,000 per employee less the amount paid to such employees for wage claims and paid to other employee benefit plans.
(5) Unsecured claims up to $900 of individuals who, before commencement of the case, deposited money for the purchase of consumer goods or services that were never delivered or provided.
(6) Unsecured tax claims of governmental units (federal, state, municipal, etc.) with priority in the order listed.

After the priority claims have been paid, whatever property is left is first distributed among the unsecured creditors in payment of their allowed claims on a pro rata basis, and any surplus goes to the debtor.

SECTION VII. DISCHARGE

When the estate has been distributed the court considers the matter of granting the debtor a discharge releasing him from his debts, and the court holds a hearing for that purpose. The court is required to grant the debtor a discharge unless *one* of several conditions occurs, in which case a discharge will not be granted.

When No Discharge

A discharge will not be granted if any *one* of the following instances occurs:

(1) *The debtor is not an individual,* which includes a deceased debtor. *Only an individual can be discharged under the Code, not corporations or partnerships. This is new.*
(2) The debtor, with intent to hinder, delay, or defraud a creditor or an officer of the estate charged with custody of property, has transferred, removed, destroyed, mutilated, or concealed, or has permitted to be transferred, removed, destroyed, mutilated, or concealed: property of the debtor within one year *before* the date the petition was filed; or property of the estate *after* the date the petition was filed.
(3) The debtor has concealed, destroyed, mutilated, falsified, or failed to keep or preserve any recorded information, including books, documents, records, and papers, from which the debtor's financial condition or business transactions might be ascertained, unless such act or failure to act was justified under all the circumstances of the case.
(4) The debtor knowingly and fraudulently in, or in connection with, the case: made a false oath or account; presented or used a false claim; gave, offered, received, or attempted to obtain money, property, or advantage, or promise of money, property, or advantage, for acting or forebearing to act; or withheld from an officer of the estate entitled to possession, any recorded information, including books, documents, records, and papers, relating to the debtor's property or financial affairs.
(5) The debtor has failed to explain satisfactorily, before determination of denial of discharge, any loss of assets or deficiency of assets to meet the debtor's liabilities.
(6) The debtor has refused to obey any lawful order of the court, or he has refused to testify after he had been granted immunity or after improperly claiming the privilege against self-incrimination.
(7) The debtor has committed an act specified in (2), (3), (4), (5), or (6) above, on or within one year before the petition was filed, or during the case, in connection with another case concerning an insider.
(8) The debtor has been granted a discharge in a previous case commenced within six years before the petition was filed in the present case.
(9) The court approves a written waiver of discharge executed by the debtor after the order of relief.

No longer does a debtor's materially false written statement respecting his financial condition constitute a basis for denying a discharge.

The discharge voids any judgment with respect to any debt discharged irrespective of whether or not the discharge of the debt was waived, and constitutes an injunction prohibiting any effort to collect debts. A discharge can be revoked, before the later of one year after the discharge was granted or the date the case was closed, if the discharge was obtained through the debtor's fraud, or the debtor acquired property of the estate and fraudulently failed to report or deliver it to the trustee, or failed to obey a lawful order of the court or to testify.

Debts Not Discharged

While a discharge of an individual debtor relieves him of many of his debts, there are some debts from which he is not discharged and for which he is still liable. There is *no* discharge for a debt:

(1) For certain taxes, such as taxes entitled to a priority, and taxes for which the debtor made a fraudulent return or failed to file a return.
(2) For obtaining money, property, or services, or an extension, renewal, or refinance of credit, by: false pretenses, a false representation, or actual fraud respecting the debtor's or an insider's financial condition; or using a written statement that is materially false respecting the financial condition of the debtor or insider on which the creditor has reasonably relied, made with the intent to deceive.
(3) Neither listed nor scheduled, but known to the debtor, in time for the creditor to protect his rights, unless the creditor had notice or actual knowledge of the case in time for timely filing.
(4) For fraud or defalcation while acting in a fiduciary capacity, embezzlement, or larceny.
(5) For alimony, maintenance, and support.
(6) For willful and malicious injury caused by the debtor to another person or his property.
(7) For a fine, penalty, or forfeiture owed to a governmental unit including tax penalties if the underlying tax for which a penalty was imposed is also nondischargeable.
(8) For educational loans by a government unit or a nonprofit institution of higher learning.
(9) From a previous bankruptcy case in which the debtor was denied a discharge for other than the six-year rule.

SECTION VIII. REAFFIRMATION

The Code changes the old law under which a debtor could easily reaffirm (reassume) a dischargeable debt from which he was discharged without the necessity of prior judicial advice. In order to prevent abuse by creditors refusing to do business with a discharged debtor unless he agreed to reaffirm the discharged debt, the Code establishes certain controls before reaffirmation can occur.

There must be a hearing by the court who must inform the debtor: that an agreement to reaffirm is not required under the Code or nonbankruptcy law; and of the legal effect and consequences of such an agreement and of a default under such an agreement. A reaffirmation agreement between the debtor and creditor concerning a dischargeable debt must be made *before* the granting of a discharge and *may be rescinded by the debtor within 30 days* after the agreement became enforceable. If the debt is a *consumer debt not secured by the debtor's real property, the court must approve of the agreement* either: as not imposing an undue hardship on the debtor or dependent and in the best interest of the debtor; or as entered into in good faith and either in settlement of litigation concerning exceptions to discharge, or as providing for redemption by the debtor of his exempted property subject to a lien securing a dischargeable consumer debt by paying the holder of the lien the amount of the allowed secured claim. If a discharge *has* been granted, and if at a hearing on discharge the debtor indicates a desire to make an agreement of affirmation, the above remarks apply.

Chapter 35

ADJUSTMENT OF DEBTS OF AN INDIVIDUAL WITH REGULAR INCOME UNDER CHAPTER 13

This chapter replaces the old Chapter 13 on wage earners' plans with the purpose of allowing individuals with regular income to adjust their debts and make full or *part* payment out of future earnings. Chapter 13 is, at only an *individual's* election, an alternative to straight bankruptcy under Chapter 7 on Liquidation, and is a voluntary proceeding. A debtor under Chapter 13 can be only an individual, but not a stockbroker or a commodity broker, with regular income that owes noncontingent, liquidated, *unsecured* debts of less than $100,000 and noncontingent, liquidated, *secured* debts of less than $350,000. *Such an individual with spouse with debts in the aggregate of these figures may be such a debtor.*

The case is begun with the filing of a petition by the debtor with the bankruptcy court. The filing acts as an order for relief and operates as an automatic stay of most collection enforcement proceedings against the debtor as in Chapter 7 on straight bankruptcy. *The debtor may elect to convert the case from a Chapter 13 to a Chapter 7 or 11 case at any time, but cannot be compelled to do so.* A trustee is appointed by the court and has similar duties as in a Chapter 7 case, and if the debtor is engaged in a business the trustee has also investigative powers. A debtor that is self-employed and incurs trade credit in the production of income from such employment is engaged in business. Such a debtor may operate his business, and have the rights and duties of a trustee free from interference by the trustee, except that the trustee has the duty to advise the debtor on other than legal matters and assist him in performing the plan.

The Plan

Only the debtor can file a repayment plan, usually with a petition. The plan *must:* (a) provide for the submission of all or such portion of future earnings or other future income of the debtor to the supervision and control of the trustee as is necessary for the execution of the plan; (b) provide for the *full payment,* in deferred cash payments, of all *claims entitled to priority under Chapter 7;* and (c) if the plan classifies claims, provide the same treatment for each claim within a particular class. The plan *may* include many other items permitted by the Code, including modification of the rights of holders of secured and unsecured claims except claims wholly secured by real estate mortgages, cure or waive any default, propose payments on unsecured claims concurrently with payments on any secured claim or any other class of unsecured claims. *The plan may not provide for payments over a period longer than three years, unless the court, for cause, approves a longer period but not more than for a total of five years.* The debtor may modify the plan at any time before confirmation. Generally, the trustee may assume or reject an executory contract or unexpired lease of the debtor at anytime before the confirmation of the plan.

Confirmation

The court holds a hearing on the plan when objections can be made. The court *must* confirm the plan if: it complies with the Code's provisions; it has been proposed in good faith; the value, as of the effective data of the plan, of property to be distributed under the plan on account of *each* allowed *unsecured* claim is not less than the amount that would be paid on such claim if the estate of the debtor were liquidated under Chapter 7 on Liquidation on such date; it has been accepted by the holder of *each* allowed *secured* claim provided for by the plan, or where the holder of such secured claim is to receive value not less than the amount of the allowed secured claim, or where the debtor surrenders to the holder the collateral securing any such allowed secured claim; the debtor will be able to make all payments under the plan and to comply with the plan; and the requisite fees and charges have been paid. *The Code changes the old law by not requiring the plan's acceptance by unsecured creditors.* If the plan is confirmed, its provisions bind the debtor and each creditor, whether or not the claim of such creditor is provided for in the plan, and whether or not such creditor has objected to, accepted, or rejected the plan. Unless otherwise provided in the plan or the confirming order, *the confirmation vests all of the property of the estate in the debtor free and clear of any claim or interest of any creditor provided for by the plan.* Priority of payment on claims is in accordance with the priority in Chapter 7, and if there is a trustee he shares in the first priority.

Discharge

After completion by the debtor of all payments under the confirmed plan, the court must grant the debtor a discharge of all debts provided for by the plan or disallowed as under Chapter 7, except debts for alimony, maintenance, or support, and certain long term debts particularly provided for in the plan.

Chapter 36

REORGANIZATION UNDER CHAPTER 11

Before the Plan

Chapter 11 consolidates Chapters X, XI, and XII of the old law. The case may be voluntary or involuntary, and the same provisions under Chapter 7 on Liquidation are generally applicable. *Only a debtor under Chapter 7,* except a stockbroker or a commodity broker, *and a railroad may be a debtor.* Although Chapter 11 is concerned mainly with a business, *individuals are eligible as debtors.* Chapter 11 is a *desirable alternate* to straight bankruptcy for a business that desires to reorganize and adjust its liabilities, and thereby preserve the business as a going concern, avoid a Chapter 7 liquidation, and avoid the extensive expense of state receiverships.

A voluntary or involuntary petition is filed commencing the case. After the order for relief the court must appoint a committee of creditors holding unsecured loans. The court may also, on the request of a party in interest, appoint additional committees of creditors or of equity security holders. These committees represent the various creditors and act on their behalf, are the main bodies participating in the negotiations for a plan of reorganization, and supervise both the debtor in possession of the property in the estate and the trustee. These committees may request the appointment of a trustee or an examiner if not already appointed.

If a trustee is not appointed, then *the debtor remains in possession of the property and has all the rights, powers, and duties of a trustee* except for the investigative powers of a trustee which may be performed by an examiner if one is appointed. The trustee's duties are similar to those of a trustee under a Chapter 7 case, plus: file with the court, if the debtor has not done so, the list of creditors, schedule of assets and liabilities, and a statement of the debtor's affairs; investigate and report on all aspects of the debtor's business; and file a plan of reorganization, file a report of why the trustee will not file a plan, or recommend conversion of the case to a case under Chapter 7 or 13 or dismissal of the case. *Unless the court orders otherwise, the debtor's business can continue to be operated.* The debtor may convert a Chapter 11 case to a Chapter 7 case unless the debtor is not in possession, the case was begun initially as an involuntary case, or the case was converted to a Chapter 11 case on other than the debtor's request. The court, after request by a party in interest and a hearing, for cause generally may convert the case to a Chapter 7 case or may dismiss the case whichever is for the best interests of creditors and the estate.

The Plan

Once a petition is filed, *only the debtor in possession may file a plan for 120 days after the order for relief.* However, if a trustee is appointed, or if the debtor does not file a plan within the 120 days, or if the debtor does timely file a plan but it is not approved by each class of creditors whose claims are impaired under the plan within 180 days after the date of the order for relief, then any party in interest may file a plan, including the debtor, the trustee, a creditors' committee and others. The plan must:

(1) designate classes of claims;
(2) specify any class of claims or interests that are not impaired under the plan;
(3) specify the treatment of any class of claims or interests that is impaired under the plan;
(4) provide the same treatment for each claim or interest of a particular plan;
(5) provide adequate means for the plan's execution.

The plan must prohibit the issuance of nonvoting shares, and if voting shares are issued the plan must provide for an appropriate distribution of voting power among the various classes of shares. Generally, the trustee may assume or reject an executory contract or unexpired lease of the debtor at any time before the confirmation of the plan.

Confirmation

The plan or a summary of the plan, together with a *written disclosure statement* approved, after notice and hearing by the court as containing *adequate information,* must be transmitted to each holder of a claim or interest for acceptance or rejection. Adequate information means "information of a kind, and in sufficient detail, as far as is reasonably practicable in light of the nature and history of the debtor and the condition of the debtor's books and records, that would enable a hypothetical reasonable investor typical of holders of claims or interests of the relevant class to make an informed judgment about the plan." A class of interests has accepted a plan if at least *two thirds in amount* of the *allowed interests of the class* held by holders voted for the plan. The Code changes the old law and does not require a *majority* of such *holders*. After a confirmation hearing, the court must confirm the plan if it complies with Chapter 11 and the court finds it fair and equitable, even though a class of claims or interests has not accepted the plan. Once the plan has been confirmed by the court, it binds all parties involved, and, unless it provides otherwise, all property of the estate vests in the debtor free and clear of all claims and interests.

Discharge

The debtor is discharged of all claims and interests not protected by the plan.

[Chapter 9 is entitled Adjustments of Debts of a Municipality Under Chapter 9. That chapter applies to municipalities which are insolvent or unable to pay their debts as they mature, and are not prohibited by State law from a voluntary proceeding under Chapter 9. Appropriate provisions in the other chapters are applicable. This chapter will not be considered; however, reference to it may be made in 11 United States Code, secs. 901–946.]

PROBLEMS

1. (a) In general, what is the purpose of the Bankruptcy Code?
   (b) What is the name of the official who presides over bankruptcy matters?
   (c) To what legal forum may an appeal be made from a decision of the bankruptcy court?
   (d) Who may be a trustee in bankruptcy?
2. Under Chapter 7 on Liquidation:
   (a) How does a bankruptcy case commence?
   (b) Who are not debtors in a voluntary case?
   (c) When is a partnership insolvent?
   (d) What is an order for relief?
   (e) Who may file an involuntary petition in bankruptcy?
   (f) What are the acts of bankruptcy?
   (g) What is meant by an automatic stay?
   (h) To what extent does the bankruptcy judge preside over a meeting of creditors?
   (i) Within what period of time must a claim be proved?
   (j) What is a voidable preference?
   (k) Do individual creditors have any choice of federal or state exemptions?
   (l) Does the debtor's estate include secured claims?
   (m) Who can obtain a discharge?
3. Under Chapter 13 on Adjustments of Debts of an Individual With Regular Income:
   (a) Who may be a debtor?
   (b) Who files a repayment plan?
   (c) What must the plan include?
   (d) To what extent do unsecured creditors have an opportunity to accept the plan?
   (e) On confirmation of the plan, what happens to the property of the estate?

4. Under Chapter 11 on Reorganization
   (a) Who may be a debtor?
   (b) Why is Chapter 11 a desirable alternative to straight bankruptcy?
   (c) Who files the plan?

SOME PREVIOUS C.P.A. LAW EXAMINATION QUESTIONS AND AUTHOR'S MODEL ANSWERS

NOVEMBER, 1979

Number 1

Select the **best** answer for the following item.

15. Jon and Frank Clarke are equal partners in the partnership of Clarke & Clarke. Both Jon Clarke and the partnership are bankrupt. Jon Clarke personally has $150,000 of liabilities and $100,000 of assets. The partnership's liabilities are $450,000 and its assets total $250,000. Frank Clarke, the other partner, is solvent with $800,000 of assets and $150,000 of liabilities. What are the rights of the various creditors of Jon Clarke, Frank Clarke, and the partnership?
   a. Jon Clarke must divide his assets equally among his personal creditors and firm creditors.
   b. Frank Clarke will be liable in full for the $200,000 partnership deficit.
   c. Jon Clarke's personal creditors can recover the $50,000 deficit owed to them from Frank Clarke.
   d. Frank Clarke is liable only for $100,000, his equal share of the partnership deficit.

Answer

1. 15.b(525–26)

4. Part b. Barclay Surety, Inc., is the surety on a construction contract that the Gilmore Construction Company made with Shadow Realty, Inc. By the terms of the surety obligation, Barclay is not only bound to Shadow, but also is bound to satisfy materialmen and laborers in connection with the contract. Gilmore defaulted, and Barclay elected to complete the project and pay all claims and obligations in connection with the contract, including all unpaid materialmen and laborers' claims against Gilmore. The total cost to complete exceeded the construction contract payments Barclay received from Shadow. Some of the materialmen who were satisfied had either liens or security interests against Gilmore. Gilmore has filed a voluntary bankruptcy petition.

Required:

Answer the following, setting forth reasons for any conclusions stated.
What rights does Barclay have as a result of the above facts?

Answer

4.b. Barclay as a surety has rights of reimbursement and subrogation against Gilmore which Barclay may file as claims in Gilmore's bankruptcy. When a surety performs its contract on the nonperformance of the principal debtor, the surety has a right of reimbursement against the principal debtor for its reasonable expense in discharging the principal debtor's obligation to the creditor. Here, by Barclay's completion of the construction contract on Gilmore's failure to do so, Barclay acquired a right to be reimbursed by Gilmore for Barclay's construction expense. Also, since Barclay paid the laborers and the materialmen with liens and security interests and thereby discharged Gilmore's obligations to them, Barclay is subrogated to their rights, liens, and security interests. Since Gilmore is in bankruptcy, Barclay has the right to file its claims against Gilmore for what Barclay is entitled to by his rights of reimbursement and subrogation. Under the Bankruptcy Code, since laborers as wage earners have certain priority to their claims, Barclay's claims would have these priorities. Also, Barclay would file claims as a secured creditor with claims for the materialmen's liens and security interests. (pp. 501, 504, 528, 523)

Part Six:
Agency*

Chapter 37

CONCEPT OF AGENCY

Agency is a legal relationship between two persons who (1) agree that one (agent) is to act on behalf of the other (principal) (2) subject to the latter's control. A "trust" differs in that the trustee has title to the trust property, he makes contracts in his own name, and the trust is not revocable by the trustee. A "lien" differs in that the lienor does not act on behalf of the obligor and he has a vested power. Marriage or consanguinity does not of itself create agency. A "bailment" differs in that the bailee has goods and does not necessarily hold them on behalf of the bailor nor subject to his control. An "independent contractor" differs in that he contracts to render an agreed result to his "employer," does not act on the employer's behalf, and is not subject to his employer's control.

The subject of agency is concerned with the legal effect of the acts of one person who represents another. It is an old legal maxim that he who acts through another acts himself. The law of Agency developed for the most part during the 19th century, influenced in large part by the great expansion in business and in business organization. Today the law of Agency is to be found everywhere in business, whether the businesses are large or small. The discussion of agency will consider: the concept of agency; how a person can become a representative to act on behalf of another; the extent of the representative's authority to act; the effect of the representative's acts; and, finally, the termination of the agency.

* Substantial portions of this Part on 'Agency' are reproduced from the author's book, *Agency*. © 1964 by Prentice-Hall, Inc. By permission of the publisher.

Definition

"Agency" is a legal relationship between two persons who agree that one is to act on behalf of the other, subject to the latter's control. The party manifesting consent to have the other act on his behalf is called a "principal," and the party who consents to act on his behalf is called an "agent." (P asks A to sell P's horse, and A consents to do so. P is a principal, and A is an agent.) *The two focal elements of agency are: the agreement that one is to act on behalf of another; and the principal's right of control over the agent's acts.* The agent's consent to the principal's manifestation must be given as required in such manifestation. The manifestation may require a written or oral consent to be communicated to the principal, or performance of the act requested in reliance on the manifestation. (P writes A asking him to sell P's horse. A, in reliance thereon, sells P's horse. A has consented to the manifestation, and agency has been created. If A, ignorant of P's writing, had sold P's horse for P, the sale would not be binding on P because there was no agency. P's manifestation had not been communicated to A, and A had not consented thereto in reliance thereon.) The principal's right to control performance of the agency is essential, and without it agency cannot exist. *A person is responsible only for the instruments he employs and over which he has the right of control.*

Agency Distinguished

Agency should be distinguished from other legal relationships which are similar to, but different from, agency.

Trust. A "trust" is similar to agency in that a person called a "trustee" acts on behalf of a person called a "beneficiary." They differ in that the trustee has title to the property held in trust, while the agent usually does not have title to any property; the trustee does not have authority to make his beneficiary a party to a contract with anyone, while an agent usually has authority to bind his principal by contract; the trustee acts in his own name as trustee, while the agent usually acts in the name of his principal; and the trust is not revocable by the trustee, while an agency usually is revocable by the agent or the principal.

Lien. A person having a *lien*—i.e., *a legal right in the property of another as security for the performance of an obligation*—has certain powers exercisable on default of the obligation secured. The existence of the powers inherent in a seller's lien, a pledge, or a mortgage, which are exercisable on the obligor's default, does not constitute an agency relationship between an obligor and obligee because neither the seller, pledgee, nor mortgagee is to act on behalf of the obligor, but rather on his own behalf. In agency the agent acts on behalf of his principal. A "lienor" is the person who has a lien, while a "lienee" is the person against whose property there is a lien.

Family Relationships. It is sometimes said that the purchase of necessaries by a spouse or an infant subjects the other spouse or the parent to liability for the purchase because there is authority implied by law to make such purchase and the person bound is a principal. This is not an agency relationship because the person liable has not manifested consent to another's acting for him; and the obligation to pay for the reasonable value, rather than the contract price, of such purchases is based on a quasi-contractual liability imposed by law. Similarly, the liability imposed on an owner of an automobile for damage caused to third persons and to their property by the negligence of one to whom the owner has entrusted the automobile for his own pleasure, usually a member of the owner's family, is based on statute and not on any agency relationship. *Marriage or consanguinity does not of itself create agency.* The elements of the definition of agency must be present.

Bailment. When goods are delivered to an agent with authority to dispose of the goods as directed by the principal, the agent is a bailee with authority to sell. Bailment differs from agency in that a bailment may be solely for the purpose of holding goods for the bailor with no duty to act otherwise for the bailor (e.g., warehouseman), while in agency the agent has a duty of loyalty and obedience to his principal.

Independent Contractor Compared

An independent contractor is not an agent. He is a person who contracts to render an agreed performance for another, called an "employer," does not act on his employer's behalf, has no authority to deal with third persons or to affect the employer's contractual relations with third persons, and whose manner of performance is not subject to any right of control by the employer. Builders, engineers, public accountants, plumbers, electricians, masons, carpenters, and supervisors of construction are illustrations of an independent contractor. The independent contractor exercises some independent calling, usually supplies his own labor and materials, and often is paid in a lump sum or on a cost-plus basis. He contracts to render an end result. Generally,[1] the employer is not liable to third persons for the acts of the independent contractor employed. Franchisees are independent contractors.

While ordinarily it is easy to distinguish an independent contractor from a servant because of the *lack of a fiduciary relationship* and *no right of control*, nevertheless, at times it is difficult to distinguish between them. In a way, the independent contractor and the servant produce an end result, but the principal's right of control differs. A plumber or electrician usually is an independent contractor, but the principal's right of control over his performance may be such that he has the status of a servant to the person for whom he is doing the job. The terms of their agreement and the surrounding circumstances must be considered in determining the relationship. One's right to object to materials to be used or to supervise performance through the architect does not

[1] While an employer generally is not liable for the wrongful conduct of an independent contractor working for him, nevertheless, there are exceptions when the employer is liable, as when the work is intrinsically dangerous or the responsibility is nondelegable from the employer to the independent contractor.

disturb the status of an independent contractor. However, the right to authorize the purchase of certain materials or to employ certain labor, together with employment by the day, probably would cause the relationship to be one of master and servant. Household employees are servants, and skilled employees are servants of their employers although they may be independent contractors as to third persons because, as to such third persons, the principal's legal stature is present through his servant. An example of the latter is a plumber who is a skilled servant of the firm employing him, but an independent contractor to the third person for whom he is rendering service.

Chapter 38

CREATION OF AGENCY

Any natural or juristic person who has legal capacity to authorize another to act for him and can be contractually bound can be a principal. Anyone physically and mentally able to act can be an agent. An infant agent or principal has a power to avoid his contracts. When an agent has interests adverse to his principal which are unknown to the principal and to which he has not consented, the principal may avoid the contract *between them,* but he cannot avoid his contract made by the agent binding him to a third person unless the latter knew of such adversity of interest when the contract was made.

When the principal has the right to control, or has control over, the *physical conduct* of his agent, the agent is a "servant" and the principal is a "master" liable for the *tortious physical harm* caused by the servant to third persons while acting within the scope of his "employment." A "general agent" has *continuity of service,* while a "special agent" is authorized to conduct a single transaction or a series of transactions not involving continuity of service. Some independent contractors when employed become special or "professional" agents for that employment, e.g., lawyers, auctioneers, brokers, factors, while others remain such, e.g., C.P.A., doctors. An auctioneer is the agent of the person making the sale, and also the agent of both the buyer and the seller to sign a memorandum of the sale. A "del credere" agent is a factor who sells goods on credit and, for a higher commission, guarantees payment by the buyer, but his guaranty is not within the Statute of Frauds.

Agency may be created by contract, or gratuitously, but not by ratification or estoppel. The law of Contracts determines whether an *agency* contract is within the Statute of Frauds, except that an *agency contract* to convey an interest in land must be in writing to be enforceable. The burden of proving an agency is on him who asserts such agency. An illegal agency agreement is of no legal effect between the principal and agent.

SECTION I. PARTIES

Principal

The principal and the agent are the only parties to an agency. A principal may be any person who has legal capacity to authorize another to act for him and who has legal capacity to be bound by the authorized transaction between the agent and the third person. *A person can do through another whatever he can do himself.*[1] If the principal enters into a contract of agency with his agent, the principal must have legal capacity to contract. If the principal authorizes one to act as his agent without any contract of agency, the principal need have only the legal capacity to authorize an agent to act for him. *Persons with limited capacity may be principals,* such as infants and the insane; but if the agency is one of contract, then such contract is *voidable at the election of the principal and the law of Contracts applies.* In some states an infant cannot act through someone else, and his attempt to do so is legally void. Partnerships and corporations, if acting within the scope of their authority, and joint, joint and several, and several, persons, may be principals and may be agents.

Agent

Anyone may be an agent, except a person who physically or mentally cannot act.[2] The agent usually does not become a party to the transaction which he negotiates between his principal and a third person, so that there is no problem of his legal capacity to act for himself. *An infant may be an agent.* A husband and wife may act as agent or principal for each other, but not because of their marital relationship. A person with interests adverse to another may, nevertheless, act as an agent for the other, although he has a duty to inform the other of his adverse interest. If the agent does not disclose his adverse interest, then the remedies available to the principal depend upon the nature of the transaction. If the transaction is *solely between the principal and the agent,* it is voidable at the election of the principal. (P authorizes A to buy certain securities on the market. A had the same securities and sold them to P at the market price without informing P. The transaction between P and A is voidable by P.) If the agent does not disclose to his principal that he represents a third person whose interests are adverse to the principal, the principal may avoid the transaction *with the third person, only if such third person knew of such adverse interests at the time of the transaction;* but if the third person did not have such knowledge, the transaction is not voidable by the principal against the third person.[3] If the agent discloses to his principal his adverse

[1] But see "Illegality," below, pp. 551 f.

[2] An act is a person's affirmative physical manifestation of his will. Every act, therefore, is voluntary.

[3] See the example on p. 582.

interest and the principal consents to it, or the agent discloses to his principal and to the third person the adverse interests of the principal and the third person, both of whom the agent is representing, and the principal and third person consent to his representation of both, then neither the third person nor the principal may avoid the transaction.

Master and Servant. The law of Agency has developed greatly from its beginnings in the law of "Master and Servant," as it was called prior to the 19th century, when the word "agent" rarely occurred. Brokers, factors, and attorneys at law were called by those names and were not known as "special agents" as they are today. Beginning with the 19th century, it was recognized that there were two types of person acting for others, "servants" who performed manual services and "agents" who dealt in business transactions for others, they being distinguished from each other by their functions. Inasmuch as both types of person acted for others, it was later realized that the same rules with respect to their creation, operation, and the legal effect of their relationship with others should apply to both "servant" and "agent." These terms were consolidated, and today the word "agent" includes these two types of person with such functions, and the same rules of agency apply to each, with one extremely important difference, *the effect of control.*

Control. Under the law, one who has control or the right to control an activity becomes subject to liability for the improper exercise of control over that activity. Since an agent's *conduct* is subject to the principal's control, the principal is subject to liability for the agent's conduct while acting on behalf of his principal. However, the principal has a varying degree of control over the conduct of his agents; *he has the right to control the physical conduct or movements of some agents but not of others. Only to the extent that the principal has control over, or the right to control, the physical conduct of his agent should the principal be liable for such physical conduct. Accordingly, solely in order to distinguish the two types of agent over whose physical conduct the principal does or does not have the right of control and for which he is or is not liable, the term "servant" has been retained to indicate the agent whose physical conduct is subject to the principal's control.* The person served by the servant is called a "master." Accordingly, we can define a *servant* as an agent employed to render services for his master and whose physical *conduct* in the rendition of such services is controlled, or is subject to the right to control, by the master. A *master* may be defined as a principal who has employed an agent to render services on his behalf and who controls or has the right to control the agent's *physical conduct* in the rendition of such services. *Unless otherwise indicated, everything that is said in this book about principal and agent applies also to master and servant.*

Liability. The master's liability for the conduct of the servant is the same as the principal's liability for the conduct of a non-servant agent, only *in addition,* the master is liable for the *tortious physical harm* caused by the servant to third persons while the servant is acting within the "scope of his employment," and in certain special instances when he is acting outside the scope of his employment.[4] Also, the master being an employer and the servant being an employee, certain duties and immunities are imposed because of this relation. Today, the term "employee" as generally used in statutes[5] and in court decisions means a servant, although some statutes[6] are interpreted to give the term "employee" a wider meaning.

Distinguished. As we have observed, an agent may be a servant or a non-servant agent. If we look to the closeness of the relationship between the agent and his principal, we can more readily determine whether or not he is a servant.[7] Since a servant renders services, sells his time, and his *physical* conduct is subject to his master's control, he is an integral part of the establishment; although he need not necessarily be physically located at the business plant or office, he generally is. A non-servant agent is not a part of the establishment and his *physical* movements or conduct are not subject to control by the business, although he assists in its operations. For example, the business manager and other officers of a business, store salesmen along with the typists, secretaries, and other such non-officer personnel are servants. A travelling salesman may or may not be a servant. Many cases are concerned with the independent contractor, the question to be resolved being whether the independent contractor has become a servant, thereby subjecting his master to liability by his conduct. Where a railroad company's contract with a construction company provided that the latter was to construct a temporary place for war materials in the railroad's yards and that, among other details for performance of the work, the railroad's superintendent was to select the time and place of loading and approve of purchases and costs, the court held that the construction company was not an independent contractor but, rather, a servant of the railroad and that the railroad was liable for injuries to employees of the construction company, even though the contract provided that the construction company was an independent contractor for performance of the work.[8]

General and Special Agents. Agents may be classified as "special agents" and "general agents." The distinction is important because of the difference in their authority, apparent authority, the liability of the principal for their conduct, and the termination of their authority and apparent authority. They may

[4] See below, p. 609.

[5] For example, Employer's Liability Acts, Workmen's Compensation Acts, social security, and unemployment insurance.

[6] For example, minimum wage and fair labor statutes.

[7] "The relation of master and servant is indicated by the following factors: an agreement for close supervision or *de facto* close supervision of the servant's work; work which does not require the services of one highly educated or skilled; the supplying of tools by the employer; payment by hour or month; employment over a considerable period of time with regular hours; full time employment by one employer; employment in a specific area over a fixed route; the fact that the work is part of the regular business of the employer; the fact that the community regards those doing such work as servants; the belief by the parties that there is a master and servant relation; an agreement that the work cannot be delegated." Restatement (Second) of Agency, 1958, sec. 220, *Comment h.*

[8] *Cimorelli* v. *N.Y. Central Railroad Co.*, 148 F. 2d 575, 577 (1945).

be distinguished by their *continuity of service*. "(1) A general agent is an agent authorized to conduct a series of transactions involving a continuity of service. (2) A special agent is an agent authorized to conduct a single transaction or a series of transactions not involving continuity of service."[9] As the number of transactions to be performed, the number of persons to be dealt with, and the time required to perform the job increase, the agent tends to become a general agent. *Most general agents are servants,* such as sales clerks and managers of businesses. An agent employed to deliver a truck is a special agent, although he may also be the sales clerk and therefore a *general agent to sell the store's merchandise.* Look to see whether there is *a continuity of service with respect to the particular transaction he is to perform.* It is often said erroneously that a general agent has wide general discretion, while a special agent does not. Each job to be performed has its own degree of discretion, but this has nothing to do with continuity of service. An agent authorized to purchase a truck, or a broker or an attorney, as special agents, may have more discretion than a sales clerk general agent. Sometimes a professional independent contractor, such as a broker, factor, auctioneer, or attorney at law, who is employed as a special agent, is called a "professional agent."

Four common types of special agent are attorneys at law, auctioneers, brokers, and factors. *They are independent contractors, but when employed they become special agents for that employment only.* While they exercise discretion in the manner of their performance, nevertheless, the principal has the right to give them lawful directions which they are under a duty to obey; and they have the authority to affect the principal's contractual relations in their dealings with third persons.

Attorney at Law. An attorney at law is a lawyer licensed by a state to engage in legal proceedings and legal functions. The word "attorney" means "agent" or "representative." An "attorney in fact" is not a lawyer but is one who has authority to perform acts of a nonlegal nature, his authority being in writing and called a "letter of attorney" or "power of attorney"; although, in a larger sense, attorney in fact includes all such persons with authority irrespective of whether or not the authority is in writing.

Auctioneer. An auctioneer is a person authorized or licensed by law to sell property for another at a public sale. He is the agent of the person making the sale and *has authority to accept bids and to sell for cash.* On the acceptance of a bid, unless the parties indicate to the contrary, *he is the agent of the buyer and of the seller to sign a memorandum of the sale.* In the absence of any express authority to the contrary, an auctioneer has *implied authority* to fix the terms of the sale, to receive the price, to deliver possession of the property to the buyer on receiving the price, and to sue the buyer for the price in his own name. He also has *apparent authority* to do this. An auctioneer has *no implied or apparent authority to:* sell at a private sale; sell on credit; delegate his authority to another; deliver possession to the buyer before he has received

[9] Restatement (Second) of Agency, 1958, sec. 3.

payment; give an express warranty regarding the property; modify or cancel the sales contract.

Broker. A broker is a person engaged in the *negotiation* of contracts for the sale of property on behalf of others. He usually does not have possession of the property and does not act in his own name but rather in the name of the person he is representing. Examples are stockbrokers, insurance brokers, and real estate brokers.

Factor. A factor is a person who is authorized to buy goods or to sell goods in his possession, on behalf of another, and who buys or sells, usually in his own name, for a commission called a "factorage." He is often called a "commission merchant" or "commission agent." He has a lien on the goods or proceeds for his compensation. *A del credere agent is a factor who sells goods on credit and, for a higher commission, guarantees to his principal performance of the sales contract by the buyer.* Such a promise is made primarily for the benefit of the del credere agent (promisor) and not for the benefit of the buyer (debtor) and is not within the Statute of Frauds.[10] The del credere agent is liable to his principal on the guaranty.

SECTION II. METHOD

Appointment

By Contract and Gratuitously. Agency is a consensual and voluntary relationship between principal and agent. Agency may be created by appointment in two ways: by a contract, which is the usual method; and without a contract—e.g., gratuitous agency. If agency is created without a contract, then the law of Contracts does not apply, except to the extent of promissory estoppel.[11] Agency usually is created by a contract between the agent and the principal, and the law of Contracts applies in the formation, interpretation, and enforcement of such a contract. Just as in contracts the offeror's manifestation is tested by what a person in the offeree's position reasonably could understand from it, *so in the law of Agency the principal's manifestation is tested by what a person in the agent's position reasonably could understand the principal's expression to mean.* If the agent reasonably can understand that the principal's manifestation indicated an intent to authorize the agent, and the agent assents thereto, then the relationship of agency exists. If the principal's manifestation indicates an intent to have a contract of agency, then there is no agency until a contract is formed between the agent and the principal.

Application of Estoppel and Ratification

Inasmuch as estoppel and ratification have, to a large extent, the same *effect* as the creation and operation of agency by appointment and by contract, it is

---

[10] See above, pp. 88 f., and above, p. 488.

[11] See above, pp. 66 f.

often said that an agency may be created by ratification and by estoppel. Although they do not create agency *because there has been no manifestation of consent by a principal to an agent to act on behalf of the principal,* nevertheless, the frequency of the assertion that they are methods of creating agency requires their mention at this point. The application and effect of estoppel[12] and ratification[13] will not be considered at this time but rather under the discussion of authority in the next chapter.

SECTION III. FORM

The principal's manifestation creating the agency may be in writing, oral, or by any other conduct, unless required to be in a certain form by law. The principal's *silence* may be a manifestation of authority if it is usual for one in the principal's position to speak and dissent to unauthorized acts and the principal does not manifest dissent, causing the agent reasonably to believe that he is authorized. An illustration of silence creating authority is a prior course of unauthorized action by a person to which the principal did not object.

In Writing

It is often said that if the authorized act that is to be performed must be in writing or under seal, then, for the act to have any legal effect, the authority must be of the same stature or formality as the act to be performed. This is not true, generally. The Statute of Frauds provides that, to be enforceable, a contract to transfer, buy, or pay for an interest in land, and a contract not performable within one year after the making thereof, must be in writing, or a note or memorandum thereof must be in writing. Most states require the authority to sell, i.e., *to convey an interest in, land* to be in writing to the enforceable. Inasmuch as most real estate brokers usually have only the authority to find a person who is ready, willing, and able to buy, the broker's authority does not have to be in writing. By statute in some states, the authority of an agent to execute a contract not performable within one year from the making thereof must be in writing. The Code[14] provides that a person may sign a negotiable instrument by his authorized agent and does not require such authority to be in writing. An agent's execution of a sealed instrument on behalf of the principal, made outside of the principal's presence, is of no legal effect unless the agent is authorized by a sealed writing, or a statute removes the Common Law effect of a seal.

---

[12] See below, pp. 567–68.

[13] See below, pp. 568–76.

[14] UCC 3–403(1).

SECTION IV. PROOF

The burden of proving an agency is on him who asserts or alleges such agency; it may be the principal, the agent, or the third person. An agent may testify as to facts in order to prove or disprove agency. For example, the agent may testify as to the words spoken to him by the principal; these are facts proving agency. If the agency is by written authority, then the writing is the best evidence of the agency. An agent's statements of his authority or of the extent of his authority, made prior to a trial, are admissible against the agent to show that he purported to act as an agent for a principal or that he purported to act for himself. However, such statements are inadmissible as proof of agency unless it is shown that the agent had authority to make such statements. The agent's statement that "P authorized me to tell you" is not admissible by itself to prove agency; but if it can be shown that the principal informed the third person that the agent would tell him of the agent's authority, then the agent's statement is admissible to prove agency.

SECTION V. ILLEGALITY

An agency agreement must be legally valid in its formation and in its purpose and is subject, generally, to the principles of the law of Contracts regarding illegality. Agency agreements which are contrary to statute or to public policy as declared by the courts are illegal. Statutes provide that certain acts are of such a personal character that their performance cannot be delegated to someone else. Illustrations are the right to vote in a public election, the execution of an affidavit, and the essential duties to be performed by the holder of a public office. Statutes provide that only specific persons may perform particular acts. Illustrations are a broker in real estate transactions, an attorney at law for the practice of law, and a doctor for the practice of medicine; these people must be licensed in order to perform the acts essential to their profession. Illustrations of agency agreements contrary to public policy as declared by the courts are agency agreements to restrain trade unreasonably or to commit a crime or a tort.

While generally an illegal agency agreement is of no legal effect, there are instances where it does have a legal effect. *As between the principal and the agent,* the legal effect of the agency agreement is determined by the law of Contracts, previously discussed,[15] to which reference should be made at this time. *As between the principal and the third person,* the agent's performance of the illegal agreement may cause the principal, as well as the agent, to be responsible criminally for the agent's commission of the crime and to be liable civilly for the agent's commission of the tort, contemplated by the agency agreement. Generally, a principal is not responsible for the criminal acts of his

[15] See above, pp. 68 ff.

agent. However, a principal who authorizes, participates in, aids, procures, or approves of the commission of a crime by his agent is responsible therefor. Also, by statute in specific instances criminal responsibility may be imposed vicariously upon the principal for his agent's criminal acts, e.g., the agent's violation of pure food laws.

Chapter 39

AUTHORITY

SECTION 1. ACTUAL AUTHORITY

Authority is the power of an agent to affect his principal's legal relations by acting in accordance with the principal's manifestation of consent *to him*, which is tested by what a person in the position of the agent reasonably can understand such manifestation to mean. The agent's actual authority may be "express authority," or "implied authority," which is what the agent reasonably can believe he is to do in order to carry out the express authority. If the agent's authority is to disclose to third persons that he is an agent for the principal, the principal's manifestation through the agent's disclosure to third persons creates apparent authority. If the agent unauthorizedly so manifests to third persons, the principal is not manifesting through the agent and apparent authority is not created.

Implied authority may be incidental authority, by custom and usage, by course of dealing, or by emergency. An agent's authority *"to sell" personal property* implies that, if the agent has *possession* of such property, he is to transfer title thereto, further implying that he can contract in the principal's name and deliver the property in exchange for the purchase price; if he *does not have possession*, his implied authority is to produce a willing buyer. If his authority is to sell *real property* and is *in writing*, his implied authority is to transfer title; if not in writing, it is to produce a willing buyer. Authority to sell implies authority to sell only for cash, except that a factor has implied authority to sell also on credit. Authority to sell does not imply authority to modify or rescind a completed transaction. An agent's authority *"to buy" personal property* implies authority to buy for cash only if the principal has advanced the

money to the agent; otherwise, his implied authority is to buy only on the principal's credit.

With regard to additional implied authority: (1) To borrow money, not implied readily. (2) To receive payment, means to receive only full payment when due, in cash or by check as conditional payment, and to give receipts therefor. (3) *To issue* commercial paper, not implied readily; but authority to borrow implies authority to issue necessary negotiable instruments in the principal's name for the amount authorizedly borrowed. Authority to *indorse* commercial paper, not implied readily, unless for deposits in the principal's account. *But if there is authority to issue or indorse negotiable instruments, the agent's wrongful use of such authority subjects the principal to liability only to a holder in due course and to holders properly claiming through him.* (4) Authority to manage a business implies authority to do what is reasonably required to operate the business. (5) To delegate and to appoint others. There is no implied authority *to delegate authority,* unless the agent's discretion, special skill or judgment is not required for his performance. An agent's authority to appoint *other agents* of the principal is implied when the agent's position, the business, or other circumstances reasonably so require, and the other agent becomes an agent of the principal of the appointing agent. A subagent is a person authorizedly appointed by an agent for whose conduct the agent agrees with the principal to be primarily liable; he has two principals—the appointing agent, and the latter's principal. Pursuant to authority, only a servant can appoint a subservant, both the master and the servant being liable for the tortious physical harm to third persons committed by the subservant while acting within the scope of his employment, but for which harm the servant is primarily liable.

Interpretation

Agency is essentially a matter of authority. *Authority is the power of an agent to affect his principal's legal relations by acting in accordance with the principal's manifestation of consent to him.*[1] The nature and extent of authority is a matter of interpretation of the principal's manifestations. The rules of interpretation in the law of Contracts are applicable to the law of Agency. *What can a person in the position of the agent reasonably understand the principal's manifestation to him to mean?* Authority is created by a principal's manifestation, made and communicated to an agent, which the agent reasonably can understand to mean that he is empowered to act on the principal's behalf and is subject to the principal's control in accordance with such manifestation. Authority is his power to act in accordance with such interpretation. The authority of the agent is to affect the principal's relations with third persons. It is the principal's manifested intent to authorize another, and not the

[1] Restatement (Second) of Agency, 1958, sec. 7.

principal's unexpressed intent, which is important. As in the law of Contracts, an offer can be accepted only by the offeree's knowledge of the offer and his assent thereto, so in the law of Agency the agent's act must be in reliance on, and in compliance with, the principal's manifestation of authority. (P sends A written authority to buy a horse for P. A buys the horse for P without knowledge of the written authority. There was no agency because P's manifestation had not been received by A and A had not consented to it. A had no authority to make such purchase for P because he was not acting in reliance on, and in compliance with, the written authority.)

The principal's manifestation of a desire for agency must be communicated to the agent and the agent's consent given in order to create the agency. The principal's manifestation usually indicates what the agent is to do, which is the agent's authority or power to act for his principal. Subsequent manifestations by the principal may direct how performance is to occur and these constitute authority also. Authority is power to act as directed and in reliance thereon, and acts not so done are not authorized.

Express and Implied Authority

The authority received by the agent is called *"actual authority"* because that is the authority he actually has. The authority specifically expressed in the principal's manifestation is called *"express authority."* Often, the performance of the express authority requires the agent to do something not included in the express authority. It is implied from the principal's manifestation that the agent has authority to do that which is reasonably required to perform the express authority, and such is called *"implied authority"* or *"inferred authority."* "Implied authority" and "inferred authority" are different ways of expressing the same authority; the manifestation implies, and the agent infers from the manifestation, such authority. *Implied authority is that authority which the agent reasonably may understand is implied from the principal's manifestation of express authority in light of the circumstances under which the manifestation was made.* Implied authority is in furtherance, and is not in contradiction, of such express authority, except in the case of implied authority by emergency,[2] or for the protection of the agent's security interest.[3] Accordingly, actual authority is that express and implied authority deriving from the principal's manifestation as reasonably interpreted by the agent.

General Implied Authority. Unless his express authority indicates to the contrary, an agent generally has implied authority to act primarily and only on behalf of his principal. In dealing with third persons, A normally would be expected to disclose that he is an agent, who his principal is, and to disclose the extent and proof of his authority, unless P has expressly or impliedly indicated otherwise to him; accordingly, A has implied authority to do these

---

[2] See below, pp. 557, 583.

[3] See below, p. 583.

things. "The authorized disclosure would not, however, include statements of matters commonly not revealed to third persons, such as the maximum price authorized to be paid for a specified article or conditions to which the principal is willing to accede, but which he hopes will not be required."[4] *Since A is authorized to disclose that he has authority, his disclosure is therefore a manifestation by P to T creating apparent authority.* It should be noted carefully that A's authority is to act on behalf of P and that his implied authority is to disclose that he has authority to act for P and that he is acting for P; however, *if A does not intend to act for P he has no implied authority to disclose that he has authority to act in the particular transaction, because he is not acting for P.* For example, P authorizes A to borrow money from T for P. A, intending to act for P, has implied authority to represent to T that he is P's agent to borrow for P, and the subsequently accomplished loan binds P. However, if A intended to borrow the money in P's name and to keep it for himself, A has neither authority to borrow in P's name nor implied authority to represent to T that he is P's agent to borrow for P; *A's unauthorized disclosure of authority does not create apparent authority.*[5]

There are other instances of general implied authority commonly occurring in business. Ordinarily, previously hired employees may assume that they are authorized to continue to do what they have been doing and new employees may assume that they have the authority of their predecessors, in the absence of P's manifestation or circumstances to the contrary. Usually, directions to a general agent are construed as suggestions or advice and not as limitations on his authority, and directions to a servant are construed usually as limitations on his authority. Unless indicated to the contrary, the manifestations of two or more principals to an agent to act for them jointly does not imply authority to act for them severally. For example, if X and Y are partners in a partnership that owns land, X and Y individually also owning separate pieces of land, their joint authority to A to sell "their land" implies authority to sell only their partnership land.

Extent of Implied Authority

Generally, unless the principal has expressed an intent to the contrary, an agent has implied authority: to disclose the indicia of his authority; to act only for the benefit of his principal; to act jointly if he is jointly authorized with others; to act as an agent only so long as his authority exists; to disclose the identity of his principal; and to interpret his express authority in light of what is incidental to such express authority, of custom and usage, of previous course of dealing between him and his principal, of an emergency, and of what he reasonably can interpret the principal's manifestation to mean. In general, it

---

[4] Restatement (Second) of Agency, 1958, sec. 46, *Comment a.*

[5] However, this is one of the instances of inherent agency power, discussed on pages 595–96, when liability would be imposed upon P by A's unauthorized borrowing.

may be said that there are the following kinds of implied authority: incidental, by custom and usage, by course of dealing, and by emergency.

Incidental Authority. *Incidental authority* is implied authority to do that which is incidental to the performance of what has been expressly authorized. An agent authorized in writing to sell land has incidental authority to sign a contract for the sale and to sign a deed; a manager of a store has the incidental authority to hire salesmen; and authority to sell includes the incidental authority to receive payment in cash. A general agent has broad incidental authority, while a special agent has a narrow incidental authority. The nature and extent of incidental authority will vary with the circumstances.

By Custom and Usage. A principal is presumed to know the custom and usage[6] in his own locality and that custom and usage prevail in other communities and throughout the United States. Accordingly, his manifestation, as interpreted under the circumstances, implies authority to comply with custom and usage which are not contrary to the express authority in carrying out such express authority. Custom and usage do not enlarge nor limit the express authority, but authority is implied to comply with such custom and usage as is reasonably necessary to the performance of the express authority.

By Course of Dealing. *Silence implies authority only when there is a duty to speak and the principal's silence reasonably leads one to believe that the principal intends assent by such silence.* Authority to perform one act does not imply authority to continue to perform similar acts, but, as the number of similar acts authorized increases, authority reasonably may be implied that similar acts are to be performed in the future. Accordingly, authority to do an act may be implied by course of dealing.

By Emergency. An agent has implied authority by emergency, sometimes called "by necessity," to act as he believes reasonably necessary under the circumstances *in the event of an emergency exposing the principal to loss,* provided the agent reasonably believes: that the emergency was caused by an event not anticipated by the principal; that it is impracticable or impossible under the circumstances for him to communicate the fact to his principal; that action contrary to, or in excess of, his actual authority is necessary to protect his principal's interests; and that his principal under the circumstances would have authorized him so to act. (P in California ships oranges to A, his factor, to sell in New York. While the oranges are in transit, the market price drops severely in New York and sale of P's oranges there will result in loss to P. A cannot communicate with P. A reroutes the oranges for sale in Philadelphia where the market price is higher. A had implied authority by emergency so to reroute reasonably under the circumstances.)

Specific Instances. It may be helpful to discuss briefly some specific instances of implied authority in common transactions and forms of business.

---

[6] Usage is an habitual or customary practice. Generally, the words "custom" and "usage" are used synonymously. The circumstances surrounding a transaction are considered in interpreting the manifestations which occurred. Custom and usage are a part of the circumstances. For "usage of trade" under the Code, see UCC 1–205(2).

Authority cannot be implied contrary to the express authority, except in the case of implied authority by emergency, or for the protection of the agent's security interest.[7]

Authority to Buy or Sell. The express authority "to buy" or "to sell" is ambiguous, requiring interpretation under the circumstances. Such authority may mean to find a willing buyer or seller, or to make a contract to buy or to sell, or to transfer or receive title. *When the agent's authority is to sell personal property,* it is usual for him to have possession of such property if he is to transfer title to it. Therefore, *if the agent with authority to sell personal property has possession of such property, his implied authority is to transfer title to the property; without such possession, his implied authority is merely to solicit orders for the purchase of the property and obtain willing buyers. When the agent's authority is to sell land,* inasmuch as authority to convey land is required to be in writing under the Statute of Frauds,[8] *if the agent's authority to sell land is in writing and does not indicate otherwise, his implied authority is to transfer title to the land; if not in writing, his implied authority is to produce a willing buyer.*

It is important to determine whether the implied authority of an agent is to produce a willing buyer or seller, or whether his authority is to transfer or acquire title. *When the agent's express or implied authority is to transfer title to the principal's property, or to acquire title to property on behalf of the principal, the agent has the following implied authority:* to fix the terms of the sale or purchase; to make or receive the warranties usually given or which are required in connection with such transaction; to execute the necessary papers in connection with such transaction; to pay or to receive payment; and to deliver or to receive possession of the subject matter or documents of title. *If the authority is to produce a willing buyer or seller, authority is implied:* to describe the subject matter of the transaction; to explain the principal's terms; and to solicit offers to buy or sell. Authority to purchase implies authority to purchase at a private or public sale, while authority to sell implies authority to sell only at a private sale.

Usually the manifestation of express authority to buy or sell indicates the price. *Unless the circumstances surrounding the manifestation of such authority indicate to the contrary, the agent has implied authority to sell or buy at a price most favorable to the principal but not in excess of the express authority.* (P authorizes A to purchase a certain horse for $100. A has the implied authority to purchase the horse for $90.) The agent's knowledge that his principal has a fixed price policy is an illustration of circumstances which preclude any implied authority to deviate from the fixed price. In the absence of any indicated price in the authority to buy or sell, there is implied authority to buy or sell at the market price or, if there is no market price, at a reasonable price.

---

[7] See below, p. 583.

[8] See above, p. 550.

An agent with authority to sell personal property, but who does not have possession of such property, has no implied authority to receive the purchase price; if he is in possession, he has the implied authority to receive the purchase price. An agent with authority to buy personal property but with no authority to receive possession of such property has no implied authority to pay the purchase price.

Authority to sell implies authority to sell only for cash, except that a factor has implied authority to sell also on credit; however, authority to sell on credit usually implies authority also to sell for cash, unless the circumstances preclude such an implication. *Authority to buy implies authority to buy for cash only if the principal has advanced the money to the agent; otherwise, authority is implied to buy only on the principal's credit.*

Authority to buy or sell implies authority to give or receive only those warranties usually accompanying such a transaction, either in connection with the subject matter of the transaction or in connection with the credit of the principal if it is a sale to the principal on credit. Although there is a conflict of authority on whether or not there is implied authority to give a warranty of quality, most courts hold that such authority may be implied.

Authority to buy or sell does not imply authority to modify or rescind a completed transaction; except that an agent with authority to buy has implied authority to have the contract corrected to state the terms properly, and to return the purchase price if the agent has made material misrepresentations to the seller with or without the principal's authority.

It should be noted that, in the absence of agreement to the contrary, authority to act for two or more principals jointly does not include authority to act for them severally. (A and B authorize C to sell their land. C sells A's land. C has no authority to do this inasmuch as his authority is to represent *them* and not *each* separately.) (A and B authorize C to sign a contract for them with D. C signs a contract for A with D. C does not have authority to represent A; his authority is to represent A and B.)

Authority to Borrow. An agent's authority to borrow in his principal's name is *not implied readily.* Such authority is implied only when performance of the express authority otherwise cannot occur, or it is implied by emergency. Authority to borrow implies the pledging of the principal's credit only to the extent reasonably required under the circumstances.

Authority to Receive Payment. Authority to receive payment may be implied from the express authority if the circumstances permit. Such *authority to receive payment implies authority to receive only full payment when due, in cash, and to give receipts and other necessary papers in exchange therefor.* Today as a general practice checks are given and received only as conditional payment and, should they be dishonored, the debtor is liable on the original debt. *An agent to receive payment has implied authority to receive a check, bank draft, certified check, or a Post Office money order as conditional payment* and, should such an instrument be to the agent's order and paid, such payment to the agent is payment to the principal.

Authority regarding Commercial Paper. Authority *to issue* negotiable instruments usually is not incidental to performance of the authorized acts and, therefore, it is *not implied readily*. Authority to borrow implies authority to issue negotiable instruments in the name of the principal for the amount authorized to be borrowed. When the agent's position in the management of a principal's business is such that it is absolutely necessary to the operation of such business that the agent issue commercial paper, he has implied authority to draw on the principal's bank account for such purposes. Such authority may be implied also by emergency only when it is necessary to avoid any extremely substantial loss to his principal. Authority *to indorse* commercial paper in the name of a principal is *not implied readily*, except for deposits in the principal's account, in which case it is readily implied.

Where there is implied authority to issue or indorse negotiable instruments, the agent's wrongful use of such implied authority subjects the principal to liability only to a "holder in due course."[9] and to holders who properly claim through him, as though the agent had acted properly.

This is as good a place as any to emphasize the rule, to be discussed later,[10] that when an agent with authority to contract in P's name and for P's benefit acts for his own benefit or for other *improper purpose*, P is subject to liability to third persons who are innocent of A's improper purpose. P gave A the authority and placed A in a position where third persons could trust to P's selection of a reliable agent and, therefore, P assumes the risk of liability to innocent third persons for A's conduct with an improper purpose.

Authority to Manage a Business. Authority to manage a business implies authority to do what is reasonably required to operate the business, such as to employ help, to buy or sell depending on the nature of the business, and to obtain supplies and equipment. Similarly, authority to manage or take care of property implies authority to do what is reasonably required in order to preserve and maintain such property.

Authority to Delegate and to Appoint Others. An agent may not delegate authority to perform his authorized acts if he has no implied authority to do so. An agent has a fiduciary duty to act on behalf of his principal, and, usually, he has discretion, special skill, or judgment in the performance of the expressly authorized act. For this reason authority to perform, usually being of a *personal character*, cannot be delegated by the agent to someone else. However, delegation to a subagent of the authority to perform all or an incidental part of the authorized act is permitted as an *exception to the rule if the agent's discretion, special skill, or judgment is not required for such performance*, such as performance of an act of a mechanical or ministerial character. (P authorizes A, a real estate broker, to procure a willing purchaser of P's land, or to sell the land at a fixed price. A's discretion, special skill, or judgment is not required to perform the authorized act, and A may delegate the authority to perform to B.

[9] See UCC 3–302, and above, p. 336.

[10] See below, pp. 596–97.

If P had authorized A to sell the land, leaving to A the discretion of fixing the price or selling at the best price obtainable, authority to delegate performance would not be implied.) Authority to buy or sell is not impliedly delegable, and authority to settle claims is not impliedly delegable to an arbitrator, because the agent's discretion, special skill, or judgment is involved in the performance of such authorized acts. When the agent's discretion, special skill, or judgment is required for the performance of the authorized act, the agreement between the agent and the principal is a personal agreement, and *the legal principles governing assignments in the law of Contracts are applicable regarding non-delegation of duties in personal contracts.*[11] First the appointment of other agents will be discussed, then the appointment of subagents, and finally the appointment of subservants.

1. Appointment of Other Agents. Unless otherwise manifested by P, authority is implied to appoint *other* agents of P if A's business position or operation of the business reasonably so requires or such authority is implied by usage or emergency. Thus, the general manager of a store has implied authority to hire sales and other necessary personnel for operation of the store. A bank that has received from a depositor a check for collection from a bank in another locality has implied authority to appoint a bank in the other locality as the depositor's agent for collection and to forward the check to it. There are many cases involving perishables in which it has been held that A had implied authority to appoint other agents for P to help preserve the perishables in an emergency.

It should be noted carefully that when an agent appoints *another agent* pursuant to his authority, the other agent is *solely the agent of P* and is not the agent of the appointing agent. The diagram would be:

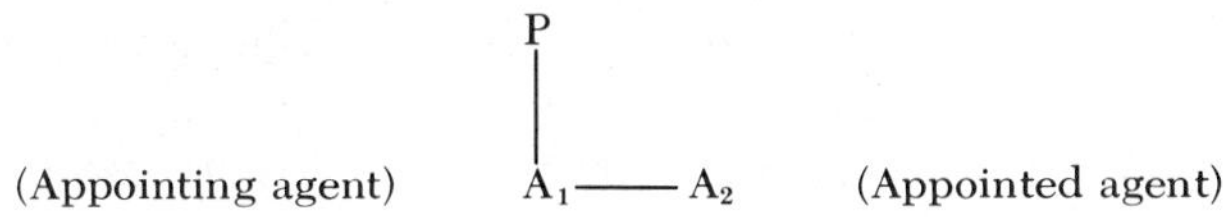

The fact that the appointed agent is subject to the orders of the appointing agent, as a salesman appointed by the general manager of a store takes orders from the latter, does not cause the appointed agent to be a subagent of the appointing agent. *The authorized appointment of another agent places the latter in the same relationship with P as though P had made the appointment himself.* The appointing agent or the appointee, or both, may be non-servant agents or servants. Since the appointee is not an agent of the appointing agent, *the latter is not responsible to P for the appointee's conduct.* Should A *unauthorizedly* appoint another agent for P, the appointee does not become the agent of P, who is not liable for the appointee's acts; the appointing agent is in the position of being a principal toward the appointed agent, and the latter

[11] See above, p. 83.

has the power to subject the appointing agent to liability as a principal with third persons.

*2. **Appointment of Subagents.*** We have seen that the authorized appointment of *another agent* causes the appointee to be *solely the agent of P.* However, if an agent's authority is to conduct a transaction or perform an act himself or *have another person do it for P,* if the agent appoints another to do it for P, *the appointee to be the agent of the appointing agent and the appointing agent to be responsible to P* for the conduct of the appointee, then the appointee is a *subagent.* He is "sub," under the appointing agent; and because the appointee is an agent of the appointing agent, the latter is a principal as to the appointee and responsible for his conduct. *The appointee has two principals, the appointing agent's principal and the appointing agent himself.* The Restatement of Agency defines a subagent as "a person appointed by an agent empowered to do so, to perform functions undertaken by the agent for the principal, *but for whose conduct the agent agrees with the principal to be primarily responsible.*"[12] (Author's italics.) The diagram would be:

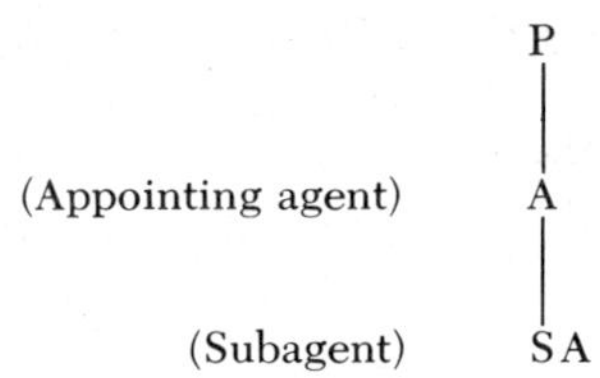

For example, the bank teller who has the responsibility for collecting notes for depositors is the servant agent of the bank principal and the subagent for the depositors as principals. An insurance company's general agent, responsible for a specified territory with authority to open offices within that territory and who appoints insurance agents in such offices, causes such appointees to be subagents—agents under the general agent and working as agents for the company in selling insurance.

Unless otherwise manifested by P, authority is implied to an agent, who is to conduct a transaction for P, to appoint a subagent to do so *only if A reasonably can believe that P is willing for A to have someone else do it. A reasonably can so believe if:* A is an organization, such as a corporation or a partnership, which acts through its employees; it is either impracticable or illegal for A to perform; or usage or emergency so permits. Thus, an agent with authority to act for P may not be licensed by law so to act and would have to appoint licensed subagents to perform, such as a lawyer to sue, an auctioneer to auction, or a real estate broker to sell land. Also, it is usual for brokers, attorneys at law, and factors to have implied authority to act through their employees as subagents of the principal. It should be noted carefully that, should an agent *unau-*

[12] Restatement (Second) of Agency, 1958, sec. 5(1).

thorizedly appoint a subagent of P, the appointee does not become a subagent of P and P is not liable for his acts; the appointing agent is in the position of being a principal toward the subagent, and the latter has the power to subject the appointing agent to liability as a principal to third persons.

*3. **Appointment of Subservants.*** We have learned that an agent may be either a servant or a non-servant agent, such as a professional special agent (e.g., broker, attorney at law, factor). *While an agent may appoint a subagent, only a servant can appoint a subservant.* As discussed previously,[13] the only reason for distinguishing a servant from a non-servant agent is that the *master* controls or has the right to control the *physical conduct* of the servant agent and, therefore, he is subject to liability to third persons for the physical acts of the servant. Since the *principal* does not have such control, he is not liable for the physical conduct of his non-servant agent. *Thus, the servants of a non-servant agent are not servants of the principal.* When, pursuant to authority, a servant appoints another servant to perform the first servant's duties for his master, *the master and first servant to control the physical conduct of the appointed servant,* the appointee is both a servant of the first servant and a subservant of the master, *for whose conduct the first servant is responsible to the master*. In other words, the appointee has two masters, the appointing servant and the latter's master. The Restatement of Agency defines a subservant as "a person appointed by a servant empowered to do so, to perform functions undertaken by the servant for the master and subject to the control as to his physical conduct both by the master and by the servant, *but for whose conduct the servant agrees with the principal* [*master*] *to be primarily responsible*."[14] (Author's italics and brackets.) The diagram would be:

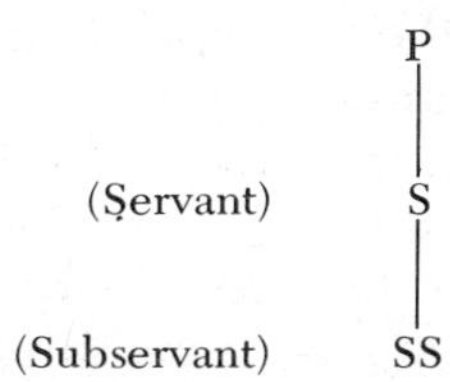

When a servant is paid by the job and is authorized to employ his own assistants who, it is agreed between the master and the servant, are to be subject to the control of the servant and subject to the superior control of the master, such assistants are subservants. For example, where a company's branch manager has authority to hire, pay, and control his employees, the company having the right to control both the manager and the employees, such employees are subservants with the power to subject the company and the manager to liability for their conduct, but for which the manager is ulti-

[13] See above, pp. 546–47.

[14] Restatement (Second) of Agency, 1958, sec. 5(2).

mately liable to the company as an indemnitor. *If the company did not retain the right to control the manager's employees, they would be the servants solely of the manager and only the manager would be liable for their physical conduct.* They would be subagents but not subservants of the company. *It is the element of control over physical conduct that is the key to servant status and concomitant liability.* If a company master wants control over the servants of an employee servant, then the company must pay the price in terms of risk of loss therefor.

The section which follows considers the subject of apparent authority. *The above discussion of the extent of implied authority is applicable to apparent authority, in determining the extent of such apparent authority.* Information available to the agent and not to the third person may cause the agent's implied authority to be different from his apparent authority. (P appoints A as general manager of P's large retail store, but without authority to hire sales personnel. T knows that A is the general manager of P's store. While A has no *implied* authority to hire sales personnel, nevertheless, since T reasonably can believe that A as general manager has authority to hire sales personnel, A has *apparent* authority to do so.)

SECTION II. APPARENT AUTHORITY

The principal's manifestation *to a third person* that someone is his agent causes the latter to be an "apparent agent" with "apparent authority" to act for the principal with the same effect as though he were an agent. The extent of apparent authority is tested by what a person in the position of the third person reasonably could understand the principal's manifestation *to him* to mean. If the *same* principal's manifestation of authority is made to both the agent and the third person, the agent's actual authority and his apparent authority will be the same and, therefore, *the previous discussion of the extent of implied authority is equally applicable to the extent of apparent authority.* If the principal's manifestations to the agent and to the third person differ, to the extent of such difference the actual authority and the apparent authority differ.

The principal's manifestation to the third person may be made: directly to the third person; by the principal's appointment of a general agent whose status is known to the third person, such status being the manifestation to the third person; by the principal's silence with knowledge that someone is misrepresenting himself as his agent with authority to the third person, such silence under such circumstances being the manifestation to the third person; and by the agent's authorized disclosure of his agency and authority to the third person, the agent's disclosure being the manifestation to the third person. The agent's misrepresentation of his authority, or his disclosure of his authority for an improper purpose and not on the principal's behalf, is unauthorized and, not being the principal's manifestation, does not create apparent authority.

Interpretation

A person is responsible for the reasonable interpretation put upon his utterances and acts by persons to whom they have been directed. In the law of Contracts if a person in the position of an addressee reasonably could interpret the manifestation made to him as an expression of an intent to contract with him, the manifestation is an offer to him which he may accept and thereby form a contract. Similarly, *in the law of Agency if the addressee reasonably can interpret the manifestation made to him as an expression of an intent to have him act on behalf of the utterer and subject to the latter's control, and he consents thereto, agency has been created.* The extent of the *agent's* authority again is the *agent's* reasonable interpretation of the principal's manifestation made *to him.* If a person's manifestation is made to a *third person* which the *third person* reasonably can interpret as creating an agency in, and as conferring authority on, another, the latter is an "*apparent agent*" with "*apparent authority*" to act on behalf of the first person as his "apparent principal." *The third person may rely justifiably on the manifestation of the apparent principal and deal with the apparent agent with the same effect as though agency and actual authority existed.* (P informs T that A is his agent with certain authority. A has apparent authority to act as P's agent to the extent as manifested by P to T.) Apparent authority often is called "ostensible authority."

Principles Applicable

The principles applicable to the creation, interpretation, and operation of agency and authority are equally applicable to apparent agency and apparent authority. Just as an agent's reasonable interpretation of the principal's manifestation to him is the measure of his authority, so *the third person's reasonable interpretation of the principal's manifestation to him is the measure of the apparent authority of the apparent agent.* Similarly, to the third person the manifestation of the apparent principal may *imply* authority in the apparent agent. (P tells T that A is authorized to sell P's horse in A's possession. T reasonably can believe that A has implied authority to deliver the horse to T and to receive payment at the time of the sale.)

Apparent authority exists whether or not there is any actual authority. (P tells T that A has authority to sell P's horse. P tells A that he is authorized to sell the horse for $100. A has apparent authority to sell the horse at a reasonable price. If P had told T that A could sell only for $100, the extent of the actual and apparent authority would have been the same.) It is the apparent principal's manifestation to the third person, not the principal's manifestation to his agent, which is the source of apparent authority.

An apparent principal's manifestation to a third person may be made orally, in writing, or by other conduct. If the manifestation is in writing intended for the third person's examination, and the third person knows this, apparent authority is limited by the contents of the writing. The manifestation may be made by the appointment of a general agent whose status is known to the third person. (P appoints A as general manager of P's store. P has held A out to the public as a general manager, and this manifestation creates apparent authority to act as a general manager with all the authority implied from that position.) Just as silence at times may be interpreted reasonably by a person as a manifestation of intent to authorize him to perform as an agent, so a third person may interpret silence as creating apparent authority. (In P's presence and hearing, A represents to T that he has authority to sell P's horse, when he had no such authority, and the horse is sold to T by A acting on P's behalf. P remained silent. A had *apparent authority* to sell P's horse. P's silence *under the circumstances,* when he reasonably should speak, is a manifestation *to T* that A had authority to sell the horse. Note that A also had *authority* here because A reasonably could so believe from P's manifestation of silence *to A* under the circumstances.)

It should be noted very carefully that A's disclosure of his agency and authority to T pursuant to his express or implied authority to do so on P's behalf creates apparent authority to the extent of such disclosure. However, A's misrepresentation of his authority, or his disclosure of authority for an improper purpose and not on P's behalf, is unauthorized and does not create apparent authority. P is not manifesting through A when the latter occurs.

Sequential Approach to Establish P's Contractual Liability for A's Conduct

I. By Authority	*II. By Apparent Authority*	*III. Ratification*	*IV. Application of Estoppel*
1. Has P manifested *to* A that he is to act as P's agent, and has A assented?	1. Has P manifested *to T* that A is P's agent?	1. P's manifestation of consent to a previous transaction by A, which	1. Applies only if P is not bound by authority, apparent authority, or ratification.
2. The extent of A's authority: *a.* Express authority *b.* Implied authority	2. The extent of A's apparent authority.	2. was unauthorized and *did not bind P,** and	2. *P's holding out to T of other than authority,* and
3. Has A acted within the scope of his authority? If yes, P is bound.	3. Has A acted within the scope of his apparent authority? If yes, P is bound.	3. in which A *purported* to be an agent acting for P	3. *T's material change of position in reliance on the holding out.*
		4. P ratified *before T withdrew* from the transaction	

* (This is why apparent authority must first be examined.)

SECTION III. APPLICATION OF ESTOPPEL

A person's manifestation *to another* may be that someone is his agent, or it may not have anything to do with agency. In the first instance there is apparent authority, while in the second instance there may be estoppel if reliance occurs. Estoppel consists of (1) a manifestation, called a "holding out," *of other than authority*, and (2) a material change of position in reasonable reliance on the holding out. Estoppel does not create agency, because the manifestation is not made to an agent but instead is made to the third person, and the manifestation has nothing to do with authority.

In General

Estoppel is a principle of law which prevents a person from asserting the reverse of what he has represented previously if, meanwhile, the addressee has changed his position materially in reasonable reliance on the previous representation.[15] (T asks P if the signature on a certain check is P's signature. P says it is, when in fact it is not his signature. T then buys the check and pays for it. P refuses to honor the check on the ground that it was not signed by him. P is liable on the check and is estopped to deny the signature as his own.) In the above illustration of forgery, P did not manifest to T that *A had authority to sign for P;* if he had, then, instead of estoppel, apparent authority would be present. (T asks P if A is *authorized to sign* a check for P, and P says A is authorized. A signs a check for P and delivers it to T, who delivers value to A for it. P is bound because A had *apparent authority*. Estoppel does not apply.)

If an apparent principal is bound by the apparent authority of his apparent agent, there is no room for the use of the principle of estoppel. The utterer (apparent principal) is bound without the use of estoppel. It should be observed that, while reliance on *apparent authority binds the apparent principal* (through his apparent agent) *and the third person to the transaction as parties thereto*, the application of estoppel does not do this. By estoppel the third person can enforce the transaction against the utterer, but the utterer may not enforce the transaction against the third person. Thus, when the circumstances permit application of the principle of apparent authority, this principle becomes more desirable than the principle of estoppel, which then becomes inapplicable.

The Holding Out

Estoppel occurs when two elements are present: a holding out to another of something other than authority; and a material change of position by the other in reasonable reliance on the holding out. P's holding out, which is manifestation, may be in any form. It may be oral, in writing, and even silence

[15] See above, pp. 33–34.

under circumstances in which P has reason to know that A is misrepresenting that he owns property belonging to P, and P does not take reasonable steps to notify T of the facts. (P knows that A is stating to T that A owns certain goods, which actually belong to P. P does nothing and T buys the goods and pays A the purchase price. There is no authority because P has not manifested to A that he has authority, and there is no apparent authority because P has not manifested to T that A has authority. P is estopped to deny that A owns the goods and loses his interest in the goods to T.) This is but another illustration of the fundamental principle discussed previously[16] that silence under circumstances when a person has a duty to speak and dissent is an assent to the transaction that occurs, and responsibility is imposed for such silence.

Material Change of Position in Reliance

While a third person need only rely on the apparent authority, in estoppel a third person must change his position materially in reliance on the holding out so that it would be to his detriment or damage to permit the utterer to deny the truth of his previous assertion. The third person's making a contract with A is reliance but is not a material change of position. (P informs T that A is authorized to sell P's horse, P knowing A has no such authority. T relies on P's statement and contracts with A to buy P's horse. Immediately after the contract was made but before anything was done thereunder T learned that A did not have authority to sell the horse. Under the principle of apparent authority, T's reliance was sufficient and P is bound by the contract.) In the illustration given in the last paragraph, T's purchase of the goods and payment of the purchase price was a *material change of position* in reliance on the holding out, resulting in estoppel.

It is of the utmost importance to determine initially whether P's manifestation to T is of *authority. If it is,* there is *apparent authority; if not,* then P's manifestation is a "*holding out*" and we then look to see if there is a material change of position in reliance on the holding out resulting in estoppel.

SECTION IV. APPLICATION OF RATIFICATION

Ratification *relates back* to authenticate what previously occurred, and does not create agency because there is no manifestation by a principal to another that he is *to act* as an agent. Ratification is a person's manifestation of consent to a previously *unauthorized* act *not binding* on him, made by one who purported to act on the first person's behalf as his agent, or by one who rendered *services* purporting or intending to act on the first person's behalf, which has an effect as though such act were previously authorized by the first person.

To have ratification: (1) The previous transaction must not have been binding on the ratifying party *by actual or apparent authority.* (2) Authority must

[16] See above, p. 550.

have been previously possible. (3) The one acting unauthorizedly must have purported to the third person *that he was an agent* for the ratifying party, or that he was rendering services purporting or intending to do so on the behalf of the ratifying party. Ratification may be of the ratifying party's forged signature. (4) The ratifying party must manifest his consent to the unauthorized transaction; no communication to anyone is required. His manifestation of consent may be made *expressly,* or *impliedly* by: (*a*) His *silence with knowledge* of the unauthorized transaction under circumstances in which he would be expected to repudiate the transaction and dissent to it. (*b*) His *receipt* of the benefits of the unauthorized transaction *with knowledge of all the facts.* (*c*) His *retention* of the benefits of the unauthorized transaction with *knowledge of all the facts,* and before he has changed his position so greatly that it would be inequitable for him to return what he received and consider such non-return as a ratification. (*d*) His *assertions in a legal action* made *with knowledge of all the facts* which constitute a manifestation of consent to the transaction. By the most authoritative view, the ratifying party's ignorance of a material fact when he *expressly* manifested his consent does not preclude ratification, but he may *avoid the unauthorized transaction* if, meanwhile, the third party has not changed his position in reliance on the ratification. (5) Ratification must occur before the third person manifests his withdrawal from the transaction. (6) The entire transaction must be ratified, not just a part thereof. (7) The situation must not have so changed in the meanwhile as to make it inequitable to permit ratification to occur.

Definition

Often a person, A, professes to act on behalf of another, P, but, because of his lack of authority so to act, the other is not bound by such act. However, the other may wish to be bound by such act to the third person, T, with whom A had dealt on P's behalf. In order to give effect to what both parties desire without having to go through the throes of making a new contract, the law permits the alleged principal to consent to the transaction and thereby to cause the transaction to be binding upon both parties as of the time the transaction occurred, as though it had been authorized. When this occurs it is called "ratification." *Accordingly, ratification may be defined as a person's manifestation of consent to a previously unauthorized act not binding on him, made either by one who purported to act on the first person's behalf as his agent or by one who rendered services purporting or intending to act on the first person's behalf, which has an effect as though such act were previously authorized by the first person.* (A unauthorizedly, and in P's name, sells P's horse to T. P later learns of the sale and tells T that he approves of the transaction. P and T are bound to each other by contract as of the time when A originally acted.) The word "affirmance" is used in this book when discussing ratification to indicate P's manifestation of consent to the unauthorized act on P's behalf.

Ratification is not authority, because authority is the power *to act* in compliance with the principal's manifestation, while ratification is concerned with an unauthorized act which has *already occurred.* However, ratification has the effect of authority and relates back to the time of the occurrence of the transaction. The elements of ratification will be discussed separately.

Previous Transaction Not Otherwise Binding on Ratifying Party

The purpose of ratification is to overcome the effect of a transaction not authorized. If the transaction *bound* the principal either because of actual or apparent authority, or otherwise, ratification cannot occur.

Authority Previously Possible

Inasmuch as *ratification relates back to the time of the occurrence of the transaction,* the principles applicable to the creation of agency and of authority are applicable to ratification. A transaction which could not have been authorized at the time of its occurrence because of incapacity of the parties, illegality, or other reason precludes ratification. A person cannot ratify an act that he could not have authorized at the time of its occurrence because he was not in existence at that time. (For example, when promoters of a corporation to be formed make a contract in the corporation's name with a third person, on its creation, the corporation cannot ratify the contract.)[17] An exception is made in the case of legal representatives, whose appointments are made effective as of a previous time; they may ratify acts that they could have authorized if they had been appointed at the earlier time. Examples are trustees in bankruptcy, executors and administrators, and assignees. Ratification by a person with limited capacity—e.g., an infant—subjects the ratification to possible avoidance by such person subsequently. Only the principal on whose behalf the agent purported to act may ratify the transaction. A transaction which was illegal at the time of its occurrence cannot be ratified, but a transaction which was legal at the time of its occurrence and subsequently became illegal may be ratified, provided the statute making such transaction illegal is not retroactive.

Purporting to Act for the Principal

Ratification is to authenticate the transaction. Ratification gives legal effect to the intentions of the parties to an unauthorized consensual transaction not binding on them by binding the parties to each other. They intended to deal with each other, T at the time the unauthorized transaction occurred when A

---

[17] While the courts are in conflict on this phase of agency and corporate law, nevertheless, the legal concepts of adoption, novation, and continuing offer are employed by dissenting courts to accomplish the same result as ratification. See below, pp. 698–99.

purported to be acting for P, and P when he subsequently manifested his consent to the transaction. *P's affirmance gives to T what he desired, namely P as a party to the transaction with T. If A had not purported to be acting on P's behalf, T would not have intended to deal with P but rather with A.* (A, without authority and in P's name, sold P's goods to T. P affirmed the sale. P is bound to T. If A had misrepresented to T that the goods belonged *to* A, the contract would have been between A and T since T intended to deal only with A and, inasmuch as *A had not purported to act for P, P cannot ratify the sale.*) It would be contrary to T's manifested intent to permit P, a party with whom T did not intend to contract, to make himself a party to an unauthorized transaction in which A did not purport to act for anyone but himself.[18] It is the manifested intent of the parties that is being furthered by ratification so as to achieve the effect of an agreement, usually a contract, properly entered into by the manifesting parties. A's motive is of no importance; what is important are the manifested intentions of P and T to make and agreement between themselves, although indirectly through A.

"Purporting" here is a professing or manifesting by A that he is acting on behalf *of another.* It is not necessary for A to identify P to T, although he usually does. A need only indicate that he is acting for another and then, unless otherwise indicated by T, T's intent is to deal with that other person as represented to him by A. If A identifies P to T, then P is the person with whom T wished to deal. If A describes P without identifying him, for example as "my principal" or "the abutting landowner," then affirmance can be made only by the person complying with that description. If the description applies equally to two or more persons, then it seems but logical that affirmance can be made only by the one on whose behalf A intended to act. A need not even indicate that he is authorized, although A is impliedly so warranting unless he has otherwise indicated,[19] nor need T even believe that A has authority so to act. For example, A may tell T that he is not sure that he is authorized so to act, or that he is not authorized but that P will probably affirm A's conduct in acting on P's behalf in dealing with T. *It is T's intent to deal with P that controls;* if T intends to deal with P through A, even though T may believe A is not authorized so to act and can merely hope that P will affirm, the law deems T's intent to deal with P sufficient for the purpose of ratification.

Forgery. *The Restatement of Agency permits ratification of any simulated signature by the person whose signature it has been purported to be.* The Code also permits ratification of a forged signature on negotiable paper. Liability for a forged signature may be imposed by estoppel. (A forged P's signature to a check. P told T that it was his signature and T, in reliance thereon,

[18] It is for this reason that an undisclosed principal cannot ratify the unauthorized act of his agent not binding on him and thereby become bound as a party to the contract; A does not purport to represent anyone but himself. However, he may be liable to the third person for restitution of the reasonable value of what he has received. See Restatement (Second) of Agency, 1958, sec. 104, *Comment d.*

[19] For A's express and implied warranties of authority, see below, pp. 611–12.

took the check in exchange for merchandise then sold to A. P is estopped to deny the signature as his and he is liable on the check.)

A's Rendition of Services. Thus far we have been discussing consensual transactions with third persons, conduced by A when A has purported to T that he was acting on P's behalf. However, there are situations not involving a consensual transaction with third persons when A is rendering *services* intending them to be on P's behalf and either purporting or not purporting to third persons that he is acting on P's behalf in rendering such services. (P has a retail store. A, without P's authority, takes and drives P's truck, delivering P's merchandise to customers to whom sales have been made. A drives negligently and injures T.) Some courts have extended the rationale of ratification and have permitted P to affirm A's conduct, thereby causing the relationship between P and A to be master and servant with consequent liability on P for the tortious physical conduct of his servant, A, while acting within the scope of his employment. It should be noted carefully that A must be rendering *services,* and *either* intending *or* purporting to be acting on P's behalf in the rendition of such services for ratification to be possible. Thus, in this type of case, P may be liable to T even though A did not purport to T that he was acting on behalf of P. In the example given, P may affirm A's conduct and thereby become liable to T for A's negligence.

The Principal's Consent

The principal must consent to the previous unauthorized transaction in order for ratification to occur. His manifestation of consent is proof of his intent to consent to the transaction, and may be in writing, oral, or implied from his conduct. *The form of his consent must be the same as that required in order to create an agency to engage in that transaction.* An *oral* consent to an agent's contract to sell the principal's land is ineffective as a ratification. The principal's expression or conduct must manifest his intent to make the transaction his own.

P's manifestation of consent is not required to be communicated to anyone in order for it to be effective in producing a ratification. All that is required is that P manifest an intent to make the transaction his own or to adopt another's conduct; the *manifestation is merely proof of P's intent.* (P, with knowledge of A_1's unauthorized conduct in making a contract in P's name with T, tells A_2 to inform A_1 that A_1 did a good job. P has manifested consent and the transaction is ratified.) However, if T without knowledge of P's affirmance changes his position so that it would be inequitable to permit ratification, T may avoid P's subsequent affirmance.

There are various ways by which P may manifest his consent. Although P's affirmance may be oral, written, or any other conduct of his indicating his consent, inasmuch as ratification relates back to the time of A's unauthorized act, if it was required that authority to do the unauthorized act be made with a specified formality (e.g., under seal or in writing), then P's manifestation of consent must also be in that form. *P's conduct other than an express manifestation may imply consent.*

P's *Silence* with Knowledge. *P's silence with knowledge of an unauthorized transaction under circumstances in which P would be expected to repudiate the unauthorized transaction and dissent to it* may be an affirmance resulting in ratification. (P learns of A's previous unauthorized contract to purchase goods in P's name and does nothing. P's silence is an affirmance resulting in ratification.) (A unauthorizedly makes a contract in P's name and either A or T telegraphs P to inquire if it is all right. P does not reply; his silence is an affirmance resulting in ratification.)

P's *Receipt* of Benefits with Knowledge. *P's receipt of the benefits of an unauthorized transaction with knowledge of all the facts, and not for any reason other than the transaction itself,* is an affirmance, even though P received the benefits under a mistake of law. Thus, if A has authority to contract in P's name with T, A unauthorizedly included additional terms in the contract not binding on P, and A receives the benefits of the contract, which he then turns over to P, who knows of all the facts, P's *receipt of such benefits with knowledge* is an affirmance resulting in ratification of the transaction. (P authorizes A to sell merchandise to T for $100. A unauthorizedly sells the merchandise to T for $80 and delivers the money to P, who knows all the facts. P's *receipt of the money with knowledge* is an affirmance resulting in ratification.) If P should receive the benefits with knowledge of all the facts but at the same time *repudiate* the unauthorized transaction, T has an election either to treat the transaction as ratified or to rescind it. On the other hand, P's receipt of the benefits of the unauthorized transaction with knowledge of all the facts but for a reason other than the transaction itself, for example, belief that he is entitled to such benefits irrespective of the unauthorized transaction, is not an affirmance, irrespective of whether or not he is right in his belief. (P is fraudulently induced by X to sell his horse to T, a good faith purchaser for value, who thereby obtains title to the horse. A, unauthorizedly and in P's name, purchases the horse from T and delivers it to P, who knows all the facts but believes that the horse is still his because of the fraud. P's receipt is not an affirmance because he claimed the horse not by reason of A's unauthorized transaction but, rather, because he believed he had never lost title to the horse because of the fraud.) Obviously, if P is actually entitled to such benefits irrespective of the unauthorized transaction, of course, his receipt of them is not an affirmance. (A_1 steals P's goods and sells them as the owner to T. A_2 without authority and in P's name, purchases the goods from T and delivers them to P, who knows all the facts. P's receipt is not an affirmance because he never lost title to the goods.) If P should receive benefits from an unauthorized transaction without knowledge of the facts, there is no affirmance, unless P assumes the risk of his lack of knowledge and receives the benefits not caring what the facts are.

P's *Retention* of Benefits with Knowledge. *P's retention of the benefits of an unauthorized transaction with knowledge of all the facts and before P has* *changed his position and not for any reason other than the transaction itself* is an affirmance. In the previous paragraph we considered P's *receipt with knowledge* as an affirmance. Here, we are concerned with P's *retention with knowledge* as an affirmance, *P not having knowledge when he received the benefits.* If P has received the benefits and later learns of all the facts, he is then in the same position as when a principal receives the benefits with knowledge of all the facts, and the rules applicable in the latter instance as discussed previously apply with respect to retention with knowledge. The difference occurs if P has changed his position *before* learning of all the facts. If P has so changed his position *without* knowledge of all the facts so that it would be inequitable to require P to return what he has innocently received from the unauthorized transaction, then P will not be required to return what he has received and his retention is not an affirmance, although P may be liable to T restitutionally for that which T has parted with and P has received.

P's change of position before learning of all the facts precluding retention as an affirmance may occur in a variety of ways: P may, as a good faith purchaser for value, obtain title to the property unauthorizedly acquired by A in P's name; P may have so mixed the property with P's own property or something else as to make the original property inseparable or no longer individually distinguishable; or P's own situation may have so changed as to make it inequitable to require P to return what he has received from the unauthorized transaction. (A, husband, unauthorizedly and in the name of his wife, P, purchased from T an automobile on P's credit. A delivered the automobile to P *as a gift,* P not knowing the facts. P continued to drive the automobile *after* she had learned of what A had done. P has affirmed the transaction and is liable to T for the same.) (A unauthorizedly and in P's name purchased building materials from T and delivered them to P's workmen who included them in the building construction. After the building was built, P learned all of the facts. P's retention of the materials is not an affirmance, and no ratification results.) (A unauthorizedly took P's goods and, stating that the goods were his own, sold them to T who paid by giving to A his check payable to A's order. A indorsed the check in blank and delivered it to P in exchange for cash in the face amount of the check. P then learned of all the facts. P's retention of the check is not an affirmance and no ratification results, because P validly obtained title to the check as a holder in due course when he innocently purchased it from A.) (A, a special agent, with authority to sell P's corporate shares, unauthorizedly agrees with a purchaser, T, that, at T's election, P will repurchase the shares after a lapse of three years at a higher amount per share. A delivers the purchase price to P who, without knowledge of the unauthorized additional terms, places the money in the business. If T exercises his option at the end of three years, P's retention of the money is not an affirmance and no ratification results.)

P's Assertions in a Legal Action. *P's assertion of a claim or a defense in a legal action, based upon A's unauthorized transaction in P's name as though it were authorized, made with knowledge of the facts,* is an affirmance. (A, unauthorizedly and in the name of P, an ice manufacturer, made a contract to sell ice to T. P, without knowledge of the facts, delivered only some of the ice to T. T sued P for damages for breach of contract and P, with knowledge of what A had done, asserted a counterclaim for the price of the ice already delivered to T. P has affirmed and is liable on the contract for its breach by P.) P's assertion of a claim or a defense in an action with T or A, P not believing T's statement that A has unauthorizedly inserted additional terms in the agreement between T and A in P's name, is not an affirmance of the unauthorized additional terms.

P's Ignorance of Material Facts. There is a wide difference of view among the courts as to whether or not P's ignorance of a material fact precludes his *express* affirmance.[20] The Restatement of Agency holds to what is probably the minority but the preferred view that ignorance of a material fact involved in an unauthorized transaction made by A in P's name does not preclude P's affirmance and resulting ratification. However, since P's ignorance existed also at the time of the unauthorized transaction, the transaction is thereafter *voidable by P provided T, meanwhile, has not changed his position in reliance on the ratification.* (P authorizes A to sell P's goods, which A does in P's name but unauthorizedly misrepresents the goods to T_1, the buyer. A tells P of the sale without informing P of the misrepresentation, and P innocently affirms the transaction. Later P learns of the misrepresentation. P can rescind his affirmance. However, if T_1 had innocently resold the goods to T_2 prior to P's attempted rescission of his affirmance, P cannot rescind his affirmance because of T_1's change of position.)[21] *A fact is material if it would so substantially affect the existence or extent of the liabilities of the parties to a transaction as to be important to a reasonable person's decision of whether or not to become a party to the transaction or to affirm previous conduct.*[22] Of course, if P assumes the risk of his ignorance of material facts and consents to an unauthorized transaction in his name, not caring to investigate when, in the light of his knowledge, a normally prudent man would make inquiry, then P's affirmance cannot be avoided for ignorance of material facts. (P authorizes A to sell P's goods, which A does in P's name but unauthorizedly misrepresenting the goods to T, the buyer. P is informed of the transaction and, ignorant of the details of the transaction including the misrepresentation, P states that he will stand by A in *whatever he has done.* P cannot avoid his affirmance.) P's affirmance with ignorance of the material fact of *T's* fraud or duress in inducing A to make the unauthorized transaction in P's name is voidable by P. Also, T's inducement of P's affirmance by fraud or duress causes the affirmance to be voidable by P.

---

[20] See extensive *Reporter's Notes*, Restatement (Second) of Agency, 1958, Appendix, sec. 91.

[21] Under UCC 2–403, when the seller of goods has a voidable title that has not been avoided at the time the goods are sold to a good faith purchaser for value, the latter acquires the title free of the power of avoidance.

[22] See above, p. 31.

Third Person's Withdrawal Precludes Ratification

Lack of authority on the part of the purported agent causes the transaction *not to be binding on the third person.* The third person is then in a position similar to that of an offeror who may withdraw his offer at any time prior to acceptance. Accordingly, *the third person may manifest his withdrawal from the transaction at any time prior to ratification.* Once ratification occurs, the transaction has the same effect as though it had been authorized previously. *The third person's manifestation of withdrawal may be any expression or conduct which reasonably can be understood as indicating his intent not to continue with the transaction,* and it is effective as a withdrawal regardless of his reason and regardless of his knowledge or ignorance of the purported agent's lack of authority. The commencement of an action by the third person against the agent for damages for breach of warranty implies his intent to withdraw. If, prior to any attempt to withdraw, the principal first repudiates the transaction and then ratifies the transaction, the third person cannot withdraw, unless the third person had acted in reliance on the repudiation prior to the attempted ratification.[23]

Ratification of Entire Transaction

Ratification is of the *entire* transaction and cannot be confined to a part of such transaction. If there are several *independent* unauthorized transactions, the principal may ratify one or several but need not ratify all.

Change of Situation

The situation subsequent to the occurrence of the unauthorized transaction may so change as to make it *inequitable* to permit ratification to occur. (A, without authority and purporting to act on behalf of P, sold P's valuable race horse to T, the price to be paid in 30 days. Three days thereafter the horse died without the fault of anyone. P will not be permitted to ratify the transaction.) A common illustration is the attempt of the owner of a building, after a fire has occurred, to ratify the issuance of a fire insurance policy on such building obtained previously by a person without authority and purporting to act on behalf of the owner.

---

[23] See "Anticipatory Breach," above, pp. 105 ff.

Chapter 40

OPERATION OF AGENCY

SECTION I. DUTIES AND LIABILITIES BETWEEN PRINCIPAL AND AGENT

The principal has the duty to compensate his agent for performance in accordance with the terms of his contractual agency. A request by the principal for services by the agent implies a promise to pay therefor, and ratification of an unauthorized act may create a duty to compensate the agent. When payments have been made by an agent pursuant to his authority, the principal has a duty to *reimburse* the agent. He also has the duty to *indemnify* the agent for his expense or loss incurred without his fault and while acting within the scope of his authority. He is liable to the agent for breach of the agency contract. If the agent has acted adversely to his principal without his knowledge and consent, or if the agent has acted for more than one principal with adverse interests in the same transaction and without their knowledge or consent, the principal has no duty to compensate the agent for his services. The agent has a specific possessory lien on the principal's property in the agent's possession as security for reimbursement or indemnity for expense incurred in connection with that property under the terms of the agency. A master's duties to his servant for personal injury while employed are, to a large extent, fixed by workmen's compensation statutes.

The agent has a fiduciary duty of *loyalty* to his principal. He has a duty to disclose to his principal adverse interests of himself and third persons whom he represents, and to notify his principal of all material facts. Notice to the agent with authority or apparent authority to receive such notice is notice to his principal, unless a third person knows, or has reason to know, that the agent would not communicate such information to his principal. The agent has a

duty not to disclose confidential agency information to the principal's disadvantage. An agent has the duty *to obey* reasonable instructions of his principal, and he is absolutely liable for loss caused to his principal by his disobedience. An agent may justifiably disobey such instructions: (1) When authority is implied by emergency. (2) When the agent has a security interest in the principal's property and obedience would endanger such security interest, e.g., the agent's lien as security for his right of reimbursement. The agent has the duties: to exercise reasonable care; to account to his principal for all money and property he has received and which belong to his principal—he cannot secretly profit from his agency; and to perform his agency contract.

The duties of the parties to an agency are determined, expressly or impliedly, by the terms of the appointment of agency. In the absence of any manifested intent to the contrary, the law fixes certain duties between the principal and the agent. Duties on the part of either reflect correlative rights of the other.

Principal to Agent

A principal has, essentially, four duties to his agent: compensation, reimbursement, indemnity, and performance according to the terms of the agency. These will be considered in turn.

Compensation. Unless the terms of the agency are to the contrary, a principal is under an obligation to compensate his agent for performance in accordance with the terms of the agency. A gratuitious agency creates no obligation of compensation. *If there is no express contract of agency, rendition of performance by an agent at the request of his principal implies a promise on the part of the principal to pay the reasonable value of such services.* A request for performance is implied by a person's knowing acceptance of performance which he reasonably can understand was rendered with the expectation of compensation, such as where payment is usual, especially in a business or profession. In the absence of anything to the contrary, performance rendered by near relatives does not imply any expectation of compensation. *Ratification of an unauthorized act may create a duty to compensate the agent,* because ratification relates back to the time when the unauthorized act was performed and validates such act as though it had been authorized.

Compensation is due when the agent has performed under the terms of the agency and is in such amount as agreed therein. *If the amount of compensation has not been specified under the terms of the agency, then the market rate prevails, or, if there is no market rate, then a reasonable rate.* Unless provided to the contrary, a drawing account, in effect, is a salary and is not a loan or advance. A salesman on commission with a drawing account has no obligation to return or to pay for what he draws.

P's Competition with A. It is important to distinguish between an exclusive agency and an exclusive sale. Unless otherwise agreed, an *exclusive agency* to deal with particular property is generally interpreted as *precluding P from employing another agent* but not precluding P from competing with A to accomplish the particular result, although an exclusive agency to sell a manufacturer's or dealer's product in a specified locality generally is interpreted to preclude P's competition. An *exclusive sale contract* generally is interpreted to mean that A *has the exclusive power to sell.* All of this is a reflection of the larger rule that unless otherwise provided, P's contract to compensate for A's accomplishment of a particular result does not preclude P from competing with A either personally or through another agent.

Indemnity and Reimbursement. The word "indemnity" connotes a legal assurance by one person to another of payment to the other for his appropriate expense and loss sustained. Part of this duty of indemnity is concerned with payment to the other for *authorized payments* that he has made out of his own pocket, which we will call "reimbursement." Payment to the other for *expense and loss* sustained by the other *as a result of acting within the scope of his authority,* we will call "indemnity." These terms will be used in this sense.

Reimbursement. Unless otherwise agreed, P has a duty to pay A for payments made by A *pursuant to his authority.* A's right to such payment is called the "right of reimbursement." If such expenditures were made at the *actual request of the principal,* there is express authority to make such expenditures; if such expenditures are incurred in *performing an authorized act reasonably requiring such expenditures,* a request to make the same *is implied,* creating *implied authority* to make such expenditures. Authority to perform an act requiring travel by the agent implies authority to incur reasonable travel expense. However, if A's *compensation* depends upon his accomplishing a particular result, such as a broker with authority to sell land, unless otherwise agreed, P has no duty to reimburse A for the expense he incurs in endeavoring to accomplish the result, such as if in his search for potential purchasers he incurs advertising expense in listing the land for sale and expense in driving potential purchasers to the land. A cannot make a profit by reimbursement; he is made whole.

Indemnity. Unless otherwise agreed and in the absence of statute to the contrary, P has a duty to compensate A for expense and loss sustained *without A's fault while acting within the scope of his authority.* Thus, a right of indemnity arises from A's payment on contracts that he authorizedly made for P, as by becoming a party to the contract and becoming liable thereon. If such performance is not obviously illegal, and the agent is ignorant of the illegality, the principal has the duty to indemnify his agent for any loss or damage caused thereby. If such performance is obviously illegal, then there is no such obligation on the part of the principal.

Performance. Either P or A has the power to terminate agency at any time because the relation exists only by the *continuing* consent of P and A. There is a duty on the part of the principal, as well as on the part of the agent, not to breach a contract of agency. If the agreement is terminable at will, the agency agreement may be terminated with impunity, although the principal is liable for compensation due at the time of the termination. If the agency is one of contract, the principal has no right to terminate such contract except for cause—e.g., the agent's violation of his duty thereunder. *Should a principal breach a contract of agency, the law of Contracts is applicable.* Immediately on such breach, the agent has three remedies. *First,* he may sue for damages for breach of contract immediately on the occurrence of such breach. *Second,* if it is an anticipatory breach, he may bring an action for damages immediately, or he may wait until the arrival of the time when the principal was under a duty to perform under the contract and then sue for damages. If he waits until such time, he has a duty to mitigate, and not to enhance, damages and he must make a reasonable effort to secure similar employment elsewhere. His *third* remedy is to rescind the contract and to assert his right to restitution for the reasonable value of the services he has rendered, less what he has been paid already under the contract.

The principal is not liable for damage proximately caused by his justifiable termination, although the agent may be able to obtain restitution for the reasonable value of the services he has rendered, less the damage caused to the principal by his wrongful conduct. Similarly, when termination occurs by operation of law, such as by the death of the principal or agent, there is no right of action for any damage caused by such termination inasmuch as it is not a breach of contract, although compensation may be due for services already rendered under such a contract.

If the agent has acted adversely to his principal in the transaction without the knowledge and consent of his principal, or *if the agent has acted for more than one principal with adverse interests* in the same transaction and *without* the knowledge and consent of both, the agent has *no right to compensation for such services rendered. If the principal* had *knowledge* of the agent's adverse interests and had consented to the agent's performance of the authorized act, or if both the principals with adverse interests had *knowledge* of the circumstances and had *consented* thereto, the agent then *has a right of compensation* for the services he has rendered to the *consenting* principal. An agent has a duty of loyalty and may not profit from his disloyalty in performance of the agency.

Unless otherwise agreed, an agent has a *possessory lien by law* on the principal's property in the agent's possession *as security for reimbursement and indemnity* for expense or loss incurred in connection with that property under the terms of the agency. The lien is a *specific lien* and not a general lien (except that factors, bankers, and attorneys at law also have a general lien) and applies *only to the particular property on which the expenditures were made;* it is not a lien on all of the principal's property. An attorney at law has such a lien on his client's papers to secure the payment of fees owing in connection with those papers. Similarly, a factor has a lien on the principal's goods in his possession for advances made, or expenses incurred, in connection with such goods. Agents who, pursuant to authority, buy goods on behalf of the principal and advance their own money or pledge their own credit in connection with such purchases, have a *security interest* in such goods and a right to retain such goods in their possession. The lien cannot be exercised by the sale of such property, except in the case of a factor's lien, when sale may be made on default as provided by law. *The privilege of the lien is to retain the property until the debt has been paid.*

An agent who, pursuant to authority, has purchased goods for his principal in his own name and has paid for such purchase and shipped the goods to the principal, may retain a security interest in such goods and cause the issuance of a bill of lading in favor of himself. Should conditions occur which create a seller's right of stoppage in transit,[1] such an agent may exercise this same right in furtherance of his right of lien.

When Relationship Is Master and Servant. When the agency relationship is one of master and servant,[2] the master's duties to his servant for personal injury while employed are, to a large extent, fixed by statute.[3]

It should be noted that, *in the absence of agreement to the contrary, the inventions and discoveries of a servant employee belong to him,* irrespective of whether they were made before, during, or after the termination of his employment. However, if an employee *on his employer's time or by the use of his employer's facilities and materials* invents or discovers a new process, inasmuch as the time, facilities, or materials involved *were at the employer's expense,* the employer acquires, in the absence of agreement to the contrary, a *limited shop right* to the use of such invention or discovery without any obligation to pay the employee therefor. In effect, the employer's right is a free, nonexclusive, irrevocable, nonassignable license to use the invention or discovery under the equitable principle called the "shop right" doctrine.

Agent to Principal

The duties of an agent to his principal may be described as: to be loyal to his principal; to give obedience in complying with the terms of the agency; to exercise reasonable care in performance of the agency; to account to his principal for what he has received under such agency; and to perform his agency obligations.

Loyalty. An agent has a *fiduciary* duty of loyalty and trust toward his principal because he is authorized to act on his principal's behalf and is trusted by him. An agent may act for another whose interests are *not adverse* to that of his principal in the performance of the agency. A carrier of goods sent C.O.D. is the agent of the consignee for the purpose of transportation and is also the

---

[1] An unpaid seller's right of stoppage in transit is the right to stop and regain possession of goods while they are in transit to the buyer if the buyer is insolvent. See above, pp. 275 ff.

[2] For a discussion of servant, see above, pp. 546 ff.

[3] For a discussion of Workmen's Compensation Statutes, see below, pp. 855 f.

agent of the consignor for the purpose of collecting the purchase price. An agent authorized to produce a buyer ready, willing, and able to purchase may also act as the agent of a willing buyer in procuring a sale to him;[4] there is *no discretion in* A which he can use to the disadvantage of either P or T. In each of these two instances the two principals do not have adverse interests; the consignee is interested in transportation and the consignor is interested in payment, while the seller of the property is interested only in the procurement of a willing buyer and the willing buyer is interested in obtaining the property, respectively.

An agent with interests adverse to his principal, and an agent representing a *third person with interests adverse to those of his principal,* may be, and act as, an agent, but he has a *duty to disclose the facts to his principal and to such third person.* (P authorizes A to sell P's land on a *commission basis.* T authorizes A to purchase such land on a *commission basis.* P is interested in selling his land at as high a figure as possible and has entrusted this *discretion* to A. T is interested in purchasing the land for as low a price as possible and has entrusted this *discretion* to A. *P and T have adverse interests* and A should not represent both without their mutual knowledge and consent. If A acts representing both, without their mutual knowledge and consent, the transactions between *P and* A and between *A and T* are voidable at the election of P or T and, if avoided, A is *not entitled to compensation.*)[5] An agent may act for himself in dealing with his principal regarding the subject matter of the agency only with his principal's knowledge and consent. Without the principal's knowledge and consent the transaction is voidable at the election of the principal, regardless of the benefit or loss derived by the principal from the transaction.

The agent has a duty to notify his principal of all material facts of which he has notice in connection with the agency. He should notify his principal of the adverse interests of himself or of other agents of the principal, or of threatened loss to the principal's interests. *Notice to the agent with authority or apparent authority to receive such notice is notice to his principal, unless a third person knows, or has reason to know, that the agent would not communicate such information to his principal.* An agent would not be expected to communicate information to his principal under the following circumstances: when the agent is under a duty to another not to disclose the information to his principal; when the agent is known to be acting adversely to his principal, either on his own or on another's behalf; and when information is given by a third person to an agent, both of whom collude to defraud the principal. An agent has the duty

[4] In the law governing real estate brokers, adversity of interest has been defined generally to include representing the buyer as well as the seller in the same transaction; also, it is unethical and illegal by statute in many states for a broker to represent both the buyer and the seller without their knowledge of, and consent to, this fact.

[5] As between *P and T,* if P and T are ignorant of such adverse interests, neither can avoid against the other, although each may avoid against A; while if either P or T is not ignorant of such adverse interests, the innocent party may avoid against the knowing party. See above, pp. 545 f.

not to disclose during, or after termination of, the agency *confidential information* which he acquired during such agency when such disclosure would be to the principal's disadvantage or prejudice. After the agency has been terminated, the agent may use the names of customers and methods of operation of the principal's business as he remembers them; but he cannot make use of such information if he obtained the information in violation of his agency.

Obedience. An agent has the duty of obeying all reasonable instructions of his principal in the performance of the agency. *The agent is absolutely liable for loss proximately caused to his principal by his disobedience.* Selling goods for less than the authorized price; selling for credit when authorized to sell only for cash, resulting in loss caused by the debtor's default; and the agent's failure to comply with instructions to sell at the market price, believing that the market will go up in price when the market in fact goes down, causing loss to the principal, are illustrations of disobedience causing loss for which the agent is liable to the principal. The good faith of the agent, intending and purporting to act on behalf of the principal, is no excuse. *The principal's ratification of the unauthorized act discharges the agent from the liability for loss caused to the principal by his disobedience.*

An agent may justifiably disobey his principal's instructions in only two instances. The first is where authority to disobey is implied by emergency. The second is where the agent has a security interest in the principal's property and obedience of the principal's instructions would endanger such security interest. An agent who has *authorizedly* advanced money on the security of the principal's property in the agent's possession may justifiably disobey the principal's instruction to sell the property, as such sale would endanger the agent's security interest.

Reasonable Care. *An agent has the duty to exercise the care of a reasonable, prudent person in the position of the agent,* in the performance of the agency, and is liable to the principal for any loss proximately caused by his negligence in failing to exercise such care. An agent professing to have abilities or special skill has the duty of care of a person with such abilities or special skill. *Liability is imposed upon the agent only for his negligence.* An agent with authority to insure has the duty of exercising reasonable care in the selection of a competent insurance company, and he is not liable for loss caused to his principal by subsequent insolvency of such a company if the agent has used reasonable care in its selection. A collection agent is not liable for his failure to effect collections, provided he was not negligent in his efforts to make such collections. An agent with authority to sell on credit is not liable for loss caused to the principal by the debtor's default if the agent has exercised reasonable care in selling to a financially responsible buyer. An agent also has the duty to exercise reasonable care in his conduct toward, and transactions with, third persons in the performance of the agency so as not to subject his principal to liability for his torts.

To Account. *An agent is under a duty to account to his principal for all money and property which he has received and which belong to his principal.*

He may not secretly profit from his agency, and, in the absence of agreement to the contrary, *any* profit he acquires as a result of any transaction in which he has engaged on behalf of his principal, and *any* profitable use of the principal's property or of confidential information received during the course of the agency, he holds *in trust* for the principal. The agent is under a duty to keep the funds and property of his principal separate from his own, and failure to do so may result in liability for any loss caused to the principal. If the principal's funds are intermingled with the funds of the agent in a bank account, and the bank should fail, the agent is liable for any loss which the principal suffers by such failure. Similarly, if the agent mixes the principal's property with his own so that separation is impossible, the principal is entitled to the entire mass.

Performance. An agent has a duty to perform a contract of agency, but no duty to perform an agency of a noncontractual nature. However, once an agent begins performance of a noncontractual agency and the principal relies on his acts, the principle of equitable estoppel[6] applies and the agent is liable to the principal for damages caused by the agent's nonperformance or his negligent performance. If the agent breaches a contractual agency, the agent is liable for damages for breach of contract. The agent is also liable in conversion for the reasonable value of the principal's goods if they are used by the agent in a manner or for a purpose not authorized. Further, the principal may have a right of action in replevin for repossession of the goods while they are still in the possession of the agent.

SECTION II. DUTIES AND LIABILITIES BETWEEN PRINCIPAL AND THIRD PERSON

***When a principal is disclosed*, unless the agent and the third person have contracted otherwise, only the principal and the third person are parties to a contract authorizedly made by his agent, with three exceptions when only the agent and the third person are the contracting parties: (1) The contract is under seal and the principal is not described as a party thereto. (2) The contract is in the form of a negotiable instrument and the principal's name does not appear thereon. However, the principal is a party to the contract under which the negotiable instrument was issued. (3) The oral or written *contract specifically excludes* the principal as a party. The manner of the agent's signature is important in determining who are the parties to a written contract.**

Third persons have the duty to ascertain agency and authority. A principal's manifestation of agency and authority, made directly or authorizedly through his agent, satisfies such duty. If authority is dependent upon the occurrence of a contingency the knowledge or occurrence of which is peculiarly only that of

[6] Under the principle of equitable estoppel, one person whose voluntary conduct causes another person materially to change his position in reliance thereon precludes the first person from asserting rights which he otherwise might have; e.g., when, under a gratuitous agency, the agent begins to perform and the principal relies on such beginning of performance, the agent is estopped to assert as against the principal that there is no contract between them.

the agent, the third person may rely on the agent's representation regarding the occurrence of the contingency. If a principal's express authority is subject to limitations secret between the principal and his agent, such limitations are not binding on a third person ignorant of them. If the agent's authority is in a writing which is known by the third person, the third person is under a duty to examine the writing; but if the third person is unaware of the writing and it was intended not to be made available to him, then he is not limited by its contents.

Public policy through judicial decisions employing the following "*special principles of agency*" has caused liability to be imposed upon a *disclosed principal* for the *unauthorized acts* of his agent in *certain instances* on the basis of "*inherent agency power,*" *even though apparent authority at times is also present:* (1) The agent as an unauthorized party to the authorized contract. When the agent makes the authorized contract, but unauthorizedly makes himself rather than his principal a party thereto, the principal, as well as the agent, is bound as a contracting party. (2) The agent's negligent ascertainment of facts for authority. When the agent has authority only if certain facts exist, and he reasonably but negligently determines such facts to exist, then the agent has authority and the principal is bound as though such facts did exist. (3) Unauthorized amount or separable part of contract. If the only difference between the unauthorized contract and the contract as it would be if it were authorizedly made is in the amount involved or in the exclusion or inclusion of a separable part, the principal is bound on the contract as it was authorized to be made, provided that, before the principal changes his position in reliance on the unauthorized contract, the third person manifests assent to the contract as it was authorized to be made. (4) The third person's reliance on the agent's unauthorized representations pursuant to the principal's invitation. When the principal *invites* the third person to *rely* on the agent's representations as to when he has authority to act for the principal, if the agent's representations are unauthorizedly made and the third person innocently and reasonably *relies on them,* the principal is bound as though such representations were authorized. (5) Certain unauthorized acts of *general agents.* When a general agent is in a position where it is within his peculiar knowledge when certain things are to be done, or his position indicates that certain transactions are made incidental to such status, the principal is bound to innocent third persons by the agent's unauthorized conduct in doing those things and engaging in such transactions as though the agent were so authorized. (6) Unauthorized untruthful misrepresentations of what the agent has been authorized to represent truthfully. When an agent with authority to make a contract for his principal, and with actual or apparent authority to make representations with respect to *incidents* in connection with the contract, makes untrue representations to an innocent third person *with respect to such incidents* in connection with an authorized contract made for his principal with such third person, the principal is bound on the contract with the third person as though the agent was authorized to make such representations. (7) Authorized conduct with an improper purpose

by the agent. When an agent makes an authorized contract with a third person in his principal's name but *for an improper purpose* by the agent, the principal is bound as a party to the contract as though the agent had acted for a proper purpose. (8) The agent's unauthorized acts with chattels, documents, and instruments entrusted to him by his principal. Whether or not the principal is bound by the agent's unauthorized conduct depends upon the authority given to the agent and to whom the item was entrusted. Reference should be made to the text for the many situations in this connection.[7] (9) The agent's unauthorized acts in the payment or collection of debts. In such cases, the principal usually is bound by the mistakes and unauthorized misrepresentations of his agent to third persons in connection with such payments or collections.

When a contract is made by an agent *pursuant to his authority* for his *undisclosed principal*, the parties to the contract are the agent, the third person, and the undisclosed principal who is imposed by law as a party unless the contract was under seal or a negotiable instrument, or the contract specifically excluded him. The principal and the agent are *severally liable* to the third person on the contract, who is not required to elect between them; but he may elect either expressly, or impliedly by obtaining a *judgment* against the principal or, *with knowledge of the principal's identity*, obtain a *judgment* against the agent. The principal takes the contract as it existed before the third person learned of the principal's identity, in effect as an assignee of rights and an assumer of duties thereunder. The legal rules applicable to disclosed principals, insofar as they can be applied with the same legal effect, govern the liabilities of the undisclosed principal in his relations with the third person with whom the agent has dealt. When the agent has acted *unauthorizedly*, in certain instances the undisclosed principal is liable to the third person on the basis of inherent agency power. Reference should be made to the above discussion under disclosed principals and inherent agency power, numbers (3), (5), (6), (7), (8). Also, if the undisclosed principal entrusts to the agent title to something, the agent has the *power* to transfer the legal title to an innocent third person who pays value or changes his position in reliance thereon. Reference should be made to the text[8] for defenses available to the principal and third person against each other.

The master is liable for loss or harm caused to third persons by the *tortious physical acts of his servants* while acting within the scope of their employment. The principal also is liable to innocent third persons for *non-physical torts of his non-servant agent* while acting within the scope of the agent's authority, apparent authority, or in connection with a transaction of the kind authorized.

A principal's manifestations expose him to liability for the authorized acts of his agent and for the unauthorized acts of his apparent agent. Third persons

[7] See below, pp. 597–600.

[8] See below, pp. 606–609.

expose themselves to liability by their dealings with an agent or an apparent agent. *This liability between principal and third persons may be in contract or in tort.* First their duties and liabilities in contract will be discussed and then their duties and liabilities in tort.

Contracts

A discussion of the contractual duties and liabilities of a principal and third person will be divided into two parts—namely, when the principal is disclosed or partially disclosed, and when the principal is undisclosed. Under each part will be discussed the effect of the authorized and unauthorized acts of an agent or apparent agent.

Disclosed Principal. *In the absence of a manifested intent by the principal to the contrary, an agent has implied authority to disclose his agency and the identity of his principal, unless such disclosure would adversely affect the interests of his principal, in which case such authority is not implied.* However, agents with or without authority often do not disclose their agency, or if they do disclose their agency they do not disclose the identity of their principals. Whether or not a principal is *disclosed, partially disclosed,* or *undisclosed* depends on the knowledge of the third person at the time of the transaction between the agent and such third person. If the third person knows, or reasonably should know, that the agent is acting as an agent for a principal known to such third person, the principal is a *disclosed principal.* If the third person knows, or reasonably should know, that the agent is, or may be acting as, an agent for a principal but he does not know the principal's identity, the principal is a *partially disclosed principal.* If the third person does not know, or reasonably should not know, that the agent is an agent acting for a principal, the principal is an *undisclosed principal.* Unless otherwise indicated, use of the term "disclosed principal" includes a partially disclosed principal.

Parties. A disclosed principal may become a party to a contract by the authorized act of his agent. *It is for the agent and the third person to decide who are the parties to the contract;* whether the contract is between the principal and the third person, between the agent and the third person, or between the principal and agent and the third person. Inasmuch as the principal has been disclosed, it is implied that the third person desires the principal, and not the agent, as a party to the contract, unless the agent and the third person manifest an intent to the contrary. An agent and his *partially disclosed principal* are parties to the contract.

A disclosed principal is presumed to be a party to every contract authorizedly made by his agent and a third person, whether or not the principal is described therein, with the following three exceptions when he is not a party:

1. If the contract is *under seal* in a state where the Common Law effect of the seal exists and the principal is not described as a party thereto.
2. If the contract is in the form of a *negotiable instrument* and the principal's name does not appear thereon. Although the principal is not a party *to the*

negotiable instrument he is a party *to the contract under which the negotiable instrument was issued.* However, if the principal's name appears anywhere on the instrument, evidence is admissible to show that the intent of the agent and third person was to include the principal as a party to the contract.

3. If *the contract,* whether written or oral, *specifically* excludes the principal as a party. The contract definitely must exclude the principal as a party. If the contract is signed by the agent indicating his status as agent but not identifying his principal, while the agent and the third person are parties to the contract, nevertheless, such a contract does not *specifically* exclude the principal as a party, and evidence may be introduced to prove the intent of the agent and the third person to have the principal as a party.

The parties to a contract may be the disclosed principal and third person, the agent and third person, or all three. *Unless an intent is manifested to the contrary, only the disclosed principal and the third person are parties to the contract.*

Although, as discussed thus far in this section, extrinsic evidence may be utilized to prove that a disclosed principal is a party to a simple written contract, nevertheless, *on the face of the contract,* that is, by the appearance and wording, is P a party? If the written instrument or a series of written instruments when considered as a whole indicate that an agent was acting as such for a principal *disclosed in the instrument,* then, unless the parties have manifested to the contrary therein, the instrument is considered that of the principal and not of the agent. All printing and other writing on the instrument, the heading, salutation, body, signature, etc., the language used, and the form of the instrument, are considered in order to interpret who were meant to be the parties. Thus, checks with P's name printed on them and containing blanks to be filled in, and stationery with P's name printed on it, when filled in and signed by an agent, are considered to be that of P. If the signature on the instrument contains both P's name and A's name, indicating that he is an agent of P, the instrument is interpreted to be that of P and not of A. The signature may be: "P, by A"; "P, by A, agent"; "A, agent for P"; "P, by A, President." *But if the instrument without P's name thereon is signed simply "A, agent" then, unless otherwise manifested in the instrument, on the face of the instrument A is a party to the instrument;* although, as stated above, extrinsic evidence is admissible to prove that P is also a party, or that P and not A was to be the party to the contract. If the contract is not in writing, and in the absence of manifestation therein to the contrary, the known fact that A is acting for the disclosed principal is enough to cause the contract to be between P and T, without A being a party. An agent should be careful to sign an instrument clearly to preclude his being a party thereto by having the signature contain P's name and A's name, followed by his office or status.

Although a note or memorandum of a transaction within the Statute of Frauds is not a contract, nevertheless, the above principles apply, and the authorized signature by an agent acting on behalf of his principal, but not identifying the principal in the note or memorandum, is binding upon the principal as though he had signed such note or memorandum himself.

Liability by Actual and Apparent Authority. Agency is a method of becoming a party to a contract through the authorized act of another. *If the agent's contractual act on behalf of his principal is unauthorized, the principal is not a party to the contract and is not bound thereby, unless the principal has created apparent authority and the agent's acts were within the scope of such apparent authority.* If an apparent agent acts within the scope of his apparent authority, his acts have the same effect in binding his apparent principal to a third person relying on such apparent authority as though the apparent agent had been authorized and had acted within the scope of his actual authority.

A principal may create apparent authority by his manifestation made *to third persons.* The principal may make such manifestation to a third person himself or he may place his agent in a position where the principal knows, or reasonably should know, that the agent will represent him to third persons. *Appointment of a general agent creates apparent authority in the agent to do what a person in such position apparently has the authority to do. A limitation on his actual authority does not affect his apparent authority if the third person does not know, or reasonably should not know, of such limitation.* (P appoints A general manager of his store but instructs A that he has no authority to hire personnel or to purchase goods for the store. A, purporting to act as P's agent, contracts with T for the purchase of goods for the store, and hires S as a salesman. P is bound as a party to the contracts with T and S because of A's apparent authority and the reliance of T and S thereon. While A had no implied authority so to act because of P's instructions, yet he had apparent authority so to act because T and S reasonably can interpret *A's position as implying such authority.*) The principal's limitation may be on his agent's express or implied authority, but if the principal manifests to a third person that another has authority, such other is an apparent agent with apparent authority. The above example illustrates the principal's limitation on an agent's implied authority.

Duty of Third Persons to Ascertain Agency and Authority. *It is the duty of third persons to ascertain the existence, nature, and extent of an agent's authority.* Third persons deal at their peril with a person who purports to be an agent of someone. Third persons cannot rely solely on the agent's statements of authority. Authority originates in the principal, and a third person must make sure that such authority has been given by the principal. Where a principal manifests to a third person that another is his agent, the principal's manifestation creates apparent authority, making it unnecessary for the third person to make further inquiry regarding such authority.

If authority is dependent upon the occurrence of a contingency, a third person has the duty to ascertain whether or not such contingency has occurred, *unless knowledge of such occurrence is peculiarly that of the agent and the third person cannot ascertain easily,* if at all, whether the contingency has occurred, in which case the third person justifiably may rely on the agent's representation regarding the occurrence of the contingency. (T knows that P has authorized A to sell goods shipped to P by X, but A is to sell such goods only on the arrival of the ship. A represents to T that the ship has arrived. T cannot rely on A's statement but must ascertain such arrival for himself.) If the agent of a common carrier unauthorizedly and wrongfully issues a negotiable bill of lading without first having received the goods for which the bill was issued, a third person without knowledge of the carrier's nonreceipt of the goods may rely on the agent's representation by his issuance of such bill that the goods have been received by the carrier because the third person cannot ascertain this fact for himself. Another illustration is a bank cashier's certification of a check when the drawer has insufficient funds.

A principal may give an agent express authority subject to certain limitations which are to remain secret as between the principal and agent. While the agent's express authority is narrowed by the secret limitations, nevertheless, *the secret limitations are not binding on a third person who is ignorant of them because he cannot ascertain them for himself.* (P authorized A to sell P's chattel for not less than $100 but not to reveal this price limitation. A sells the chattel in P's name for $90 to T, who does not know of P's instructions. P is bound by the sale.) The principal, by his conduct, has held out his agent as having authority without such secret limitations, and such conduct in conjunction with A's representation to T that A is acting for P creates apparent authority in the agent not limited by the secret instructions. The express and apparent authority differ, and the principal is bound by the third person's reliance on the apparent authority.

When an agent's authority is in writing and this is known to the third person, or if the agent's authority to be legally effective and to create an agency must be in writing or under seal, *the agent's actual and apparent authority is limited by the authority as expressed in the writing* or the writing under seal. The third person is under a duty to examine what is in writing or under seal, as that is the only manifestation from the principal on which the third person may rely. *If the writing is not meant to be available for examination by third persons, then the third persons are not limited by the contents of such writing.*

When a third person is on notice that the acts or interests of a purported agent are adverse to the interests of the principal whom he purports to represent, the third person is under a duty to examine and question whether or not the agent has the authority he alleges he has. Under such circumstances, many courts hold that there is a presumption that no agency exists.

Notice. Notice to an agent is notice to his principal if the agent had actual or apparent authority to receive such notice or, in the case of an undisclosed principal, if the agent had acted within his powers until the principal is disclosed. If a third person knows, or reasonably should know, that the agent would not communicate such information to his principal, notice to the agent is not notice to his principal.[9]

Liabilities of P and T for A's Unauthorized Conduct. Thus far we have considered the liabilities of a disclosed or partially disclosed principal and a

---

[9] See above, p. 582.

third person as parties to contracts *authorizedly* and purportedly made by A for P. Many times in business transactions, the agent varies from his authority and, because of the social desirability of imposing liability upon P rather than upon an innocent T *in certain particular instances only,* A's unauthorized conduct in such situations is binding upon a disclosed or partially disclosed principal with the same effect between P and T as though A were authorized so to act. *Liability is imposed upon the disclosed or partially disclosed P not because of A's authority but because of apparent authority or because of A's inherent power, springing from the agency relation alone.* These instances are very important in business because they provide to P judicial guidelines of his potential liability for *A's unauthorized* conduct, on the basis of which P can pattern his business organization and conduct more clearly and provide for adequate insurance protection against such liability.

There is no problem about apparent authority, the rules discussed previously with respect to whether or not a disclosed or partially disclosed P is a party to a contract being equally applicable to apparent principals and with the same effect as when the agent is authorized. *The discussion that follows concerning the effect of unauthorized conduct on the part of A applies to both disclosed and partially disclosed principals as well as to apparent principals. In many of the following instances where liability has been imposed upon P for A's unauthorized conduct, apparent authority has been present and P could be bound on that basis. When apparent authority is not present, the rules in the following instances apply to bind P irrespective of any apparent authority. For the most part, these rules are illustrations of inherent agency power,* which binds P in the absence of authority and apparent authority, although many courts inappropriately apply the rule of apparent authority instead of these rules.[10] As time goes on, more of the courts will utilize these rules, not previously crystallized and established as such, as reflective of the trend of decisions in order to attain the results desired.

Special principles of agency apply inherent agency power subjecting disclosed and partially disclosed principals to liability for A's unauthorized conduct. It should be recalled that an agent's power to affect his principal's legal relations by acting *in accord* with the principal's manifestation to the agent is called "authority." The power of an agent to affect his principal's legal relations *without acting in accord* with P's manifestation to the agent is called "inherent agency power."[11] Some of these special principles will be discussed.

1. Unauthorized Party to the Authorized Contract. A may have been authorized to make the contract in P's name and A *makes the authorized contract but in A's, instead of P's, name.* The contract, nevertheless, is binding on P (as well as A) because, as discussed previously,[12] when P is a disclosed or partially

---

[10] See Judge Learned Hand's comment in *Kidd* v. *Thomas A. Edison, Inc.,* 239 F. 405 (D.C.N.Y. 1917), affirmed 242 F. 923 (2d Cir.).

[11] See Restatement (Second) of Agency, 1958, sec. 8A.

[12] See above, p. 587.

disclosed principal, he is presumed to be a party to the contract, unless the contract is under seal, a negotiable instrument or it specifically excludes him. If A's authority was to make the contract in A's name and not to disclose his agency or P's identity and A *makes the authorized contract but discloses his agency or P's identity,* since P got essentially what he desired, namely the contract, even though his existence was disclosed, he is bound as a presumed party to it.

2. A's Negligent Ascertainment of Facts for Authority. When A has authority only if certain facts exist, *if A reasonably but negligently determines that such facts exist,* then A has authority and P is bound as though such facts did exist. If A is unreasonable, then A does not have authority.

3. Unauthorized Amount or Separable Part of Contract. Although an unauthorized contract made by A does not bind his disclosed or partially disclosed principal, nevertheless, *if the only difference between the unauthorized contract and the contract as it would be if it were authorizedly made is in the amount involved or in the exclusion or inclusion of a separable part, P is bound on the contract as it was authorized to be made, provided that, before P changes his position in reliance on the unauthorized contract, T manifests assent to the contract as it was authorized to be made.* (P authorizes A to sell P's land without warranties. A, in P's name, sells the land to T_1 with warranties. If P, on learning of what A has done, sells the land to T_2, P is not bound on the unauthorized contract with T_1. If, before P has sold the land to T_2, T_1 tendered P the money and offered to take the land *without any warranties,* P is bound to T_1.) It seems most equitable that T should be able to hold P to what he authorized A to do if the unauthorized part is easily and clearly separable and if P has not yet done anything to prejudice his position in reliance on the unauthorized transaction. Thus, by various cases: where A's authority was to guarantee payment of $22,000 and A unauthorizedly, in the same contract by a separate clause, guaranteed $40,000 more, T could hold P for $22,000; where A's authority was to borrow at 7 percent interest and A unauthorizedly borrowed at 8 percent, T could hold P to the loan at 7 percent; where A made a contract unauthorizedly adding a settlement clause, T could enforce the contract if he did not insist on the settlement clause; where A's authority was to borrow $75 and he unauthorizedly borrowed $150, T could enforce the loan against P for only $75, since A could have borrowed on two separate items of $75 each.

4. T's Reliance on A's Unauthorized Representations Pursuant to P's Invitation. A disclosed or partially disclosed principal is not bound by A's false representations of the existence and extent of his authority or the facts on which it depends. (P authorized A to buy certain corporate stocks when the market price reaches a certain point, and P tells this to T. A misrepresents to T that the market price has reached the specified point and T, relying on A's statement as being true, makes a contract with P through A to sell P the stock. P is not bound. *It should be noted carefully that P did not invite T to rely upon*

A's statement as to when the specified point had been reached.) Nevertheless, there are occasions when P's conduct so causes T reasonably to rely on A's representations that P is bound by them even though made unauthorizedly, of which T does not have notice. Three such occasions will be discussed.

First, when P manifests to T that A is P's agent with *authority to disclose the terms* on which he is authorized to deal with T and *P invites T to rely on A's statement regarding such terms,* if A discloses terms that are not authorized and of which T has no notice of their being unauthorized, P is bound by such terms. (P hires A as a sales clerk in P's store. T asks A what the price of a sweater is and A misreads the cyphered price on the sweater and sells it for a slightly lower price than marked. P is bound. *T can rely on A's statement of the price.*) This seems but fair, since P has invited T to rely on A's statement of the terms.

Second, if P manifests to T that A is P's agent with *authority to begin on the occurrence of a specified event and P invites T to deal with* A, not when the event occurs, but *when A tells T that the event has occurred,* T is justified in reasonably relying on A's statement that the event has occurred and P is bound even if A was untruthful. (P informs T that when the road gravel bed has been levelled by A, P's foreman, A will inform T and order the concrete for the roadbed from T. A tells T that the roadbed has been levelled and, in P's name, orders the concrete from T, who *reasonably relies on A's statement* which, unknown to T, is untrue. P is bound to T.)

Third, if P manifests to T that A is his *general agent with authority to make a contract in P's name when a particular event occurs, its occurrence being within the peculiar knowledge of* A, then if A misrepresents to T that the event has occurred and T reasonably relies on A's statement and contracts with A for P, P is bound to T. A's *general agency status,* indicating that he is a part of P's business establishment and conducting multiple transactions, is more readily to be relied upon by T in this type of situation than that of a special agent, although P can manifest to T regarding a special agent instead of a general agent with the same result, as, for example, where P's special accreditation of A[13] to T is to buy a particular machine and T can *rely on A's statement* that A has not as yet bought such a machine.

5. *Certain Unauthorized Acts of General Agents.* This element of general agency status is very important in T's dealing with A for P because it connotes reliability and trust placed in A by P, on which T may justifiably rely and, *in certain instances,* it causes P to be bound to T even though A has acted unauthorizedly. In addition to the last instance stated in the above paragraph, there are other occasions reflecting this concept. Three such occasions will be discussed.

First, when P appoints A *as a general agent in a position where, as a part of his regular employment, he is to issue commercial documents representing*

---

[13] See below, pp. 619–20.

chattels or choses in action[14] *only when certain facts exist or on the occurrence of a certain event, such facts or event being within the peculiar knowledge of the general agent,* if A issues such commercial documents unauthorizedly and they are *purchased by innocent persons for value without notice of A's impropriety,* P is bound by A's conduct as though A had acted authorizedly. Examples are: the agent of a common carrier or of a warehouseman with authority to issue bills of lading or warehouse receipts on receipt of goods for carriage or storage; a corporate stock transfer agent with authority to issue new certificates of stock in place of cancelled certificates; and a cashier of a bank with authority to certify checks of depositors who have sufficient funds in their accounts to pay for such checks when they are presented for payment. Should the agent issue a bill of lading or a warehouse receipt without receiving the goods or the cashier certify the check when the drawer of the check does not have an account with the bank or, if he is a depositor, there are insufficient funds in his account, P as the common carrier, warehouseman, or bank is liable to an innocent purchaser for value of the bill of lading, warehouse receipt, or certified check as though A were authorized so to act.

Second, when P employs A *as a general agent in a position where it is usual for A to issue (to sign and deliver) negotiable instruments,* should A issue a negotiable instrument for an unauthorized purpose and *the instrument be acquired by a holder in due course,*[15] P is liable to him on the instrument as though A had acted authorizedly.[16] This often occurs in trading partnerships, where a partner unauthorizedly issues a firm check for his private purpose. (A, of the *trading* partnership consisting of A, B, and C, and engaged in retail men's clothing, buys a wrist watch for his own use and unauthorizedly draws a check in the partnership name payable to V, the vendor. Although the partnership, P, is not liable to V on the check if V is deemed on notice of A's unauthorized act, if V purchases supplies from H and negotiates the check to H in payment, H not having notice of A's unauthorized conduct, the partnership, P, is liable to H on the check.)

The importance of this rule to businessmen cannot be overemphasized, and adequate office administration and insurance coverage should be considered. Under this rule, a general agent in such a position has the *power to issue* a check in P's name to the order of a person not intended to have any interest in the instrument and by indorsing the check in the payee's name to cause it to be cashed, the principal being none the wiser until the fateful day when he discovers the fraud of his agent. *Under the law of Agency, the knowledge of the agent here is the knowledge of his principal.* The Code[17] reflects this and

[14] By "commercial documents representing chattels or choses in action" are meant documents that carry with them the owner's interests in things or rights, which are transferred by transfer of the document. Examples are bills of lading and warehouse receipts for goods, and certificates of stock for corporate shares.

[15] For holder in due course, see above, p. 336.

[16] See UCC 3–305.

[17] See UCC 3–405, and above, p. 356.

provides that when an instrument is drawn and signed by the general agent for his maker or drawer principal, naming as payee a person not intended to have any interest in the instrument, an indorsement by *any* person in the name of the named payee is effective and the instrument can be negotiated to a holder in due course who can enforce the instrument against the maker or drawer principal. It should be noted carefully that the same result occurs when a general agent without authority or inherent agency power *to issue* a negotiable instrument *prepares for P's signature* a negotiable instrument naming as payee a person not intended by the agent, and therefore by his principal, to have any interest[18] in the instrument, and the principal innocently signs the instrument. Such conduct by the agent has caused the so-called "padded payroll cases."

Third, a general agent with authority to conduct transactions subjects his disclosed principal to liability to a third person for his unauthorized acts on his principal's behalf, which usually accompany or are incidental to such transactions, if the third person reasonably believes that the agent is authorized to do them and has no notice that he is not so authorized.[19] This is one of the most important illustrations of inherent agency power binding P for the unauthorized acts of A, his general agent. This often occurs when P places A in a position of managing the business of P, a disclosed or partially disclosed principal, and A deals with third persons contrary to A's authority but in conformity with what is usual in such business, T not having notice of the impropriety of A's conduct. (P appoints A as *the manager of P's textile manufacturing business with authority to buy raw materials* only from T_1. A buys raw materials from T_2, who has no notice of A's lack of authority to deal with him. P is bound to T_2. If T_2 did not know of A's status as manager, A would *not have apparent authority* and P is bound to T_2 only by reason of this *special agency power.* If T_2 *knew* of A's status as manager, then A would have *apparent authority* so to act and P could be bound to T_2 on the basis of *either* inherent agency power or apparent authority.) Although it is true that in many of the cases apparent authority is present and they can be decided on that basis, *there are many other cases where A's status as a general agent is not known to T and P's liability can be predicated only on the basis of this inherent agency power rule;* many courts, however, still reach the same result by inappropriately asserting that P is liable on the basis of apparent authority when apparent authority is not present. It should be noted very carefully that it is the *status of a general agent under the circumstances indicated in the rule* here that is important, *irrespective of whether or not T knows of such status* in his dealing with A.

Although the above rule illustrates inherent agency power in connection with general agents, it should be remembered that *inherent agency power*

---

[18] Ibid.

[19] See Restatement (Second) of Agency, 1958, sec. 161, and Appendix, *Reporter's Notes,* sec. 161.

exists also in connection with special agents. Thus far we have discussed inherent agency power rules that, unless indicated as applicable only to general agents, apply equally to all agents irrespective of whether they are general or special agents. *The following discussion, unless otherwise indicated, applies to special and general agents.* It should be noted that a general agent, because of his position, has broad inherent agency power to bind P in instances where a special agent cannot do this. The special agent, generally, is pretty much limited to authority and apparent authority to bind P, although as we have seen and will see the special agent as well as the general agent can, in certain instances, bind P by inherent agency power.

Illustrative of the force of inherent agency power are the following two particular instances concerned with unauthorized representations made by A and A's improper purposes or motives.

6. Unauthorized Untruthful Misrepresentations of What A Has Been Authorized to Represent Truthfully. When a disclosed or partially disclosed P authorizes A *to make a contract and A has authority or apparent authority to make true representations other than of his authority with respect to incidents in connection with the contract,* if A should make untrue representations with respect to such *incidents* in connection with the authorized contract and T is not on notice of A's lack of authority or of their untruthful nature, P is liable to T *in an action on the contract or for its rescission* for such representations *as though A were authorized so to represent.* (P appoints A as his sales clerk in P's store. A misrepresents the cotton and wool content of an article and sells it to T, who reasonably relies on A's untruthful statement without notice of its falsity. T can rescind the contract or sue P for breach of contract.) Misrepresentations by a bank cashier to a customer purchaser of discounted notes of the financial condition of the makers, by an automobile salesman to a customer purchaser of an automobile concerning the parts of the automobile, and by a salesman of securities to a customer purchaser concerning the assets, liabilities, and personnel management of a corporation whose securities are bought by the customer, are other examples of situations where P is liable for A's misrepresentations and T, the customer, can rescind or sue P for breach of the contract.

7. Authorized Conduct with an Improper Purpose by A. When a disclosed or partially disclosed P authorizes A to make a contract for P's benefit and A *makes the authorized contract in P's name but for an improper purpose,* as for the benefit of A or someone other than P, and T is not on notice of A's improper purpose, *P is liable on the contract as though A had acted for an authorized purpose.* It is P's responsibility to select agents to contract for him on whose fiduciary sense of loyalty he can rely. *Third persons cannot question the purposes or motives of an agent* and, unless they have notice from the circumstances that A's purpose is, improperly, not to act for P's benefit, as between T and P it is P who must be bound by A's conduct for an improper purpose as though A's purpose had been proper. (P authorizes A, in P's name and for P's benefit, to borrow money from T. A does so with the intent to embezzle the funds. P is bound to T.) *It should be noted very carefully that, although A has apparent authority to state to T that he has authority to do that which he was authorized to do for P's benefit, he does not have apparent authority to state to T that he has authority when he does not intend to act for P's benefit.*[20] In the example given, A's improper purpose *precluded any apparent authority* to state that he had authority to borrow. *Thus, when A's improper purpose is present, if P has not manifested to T that A has authority, there cannot be authority or apparent authority, and P's liability to T is based solely on inherent agency power.* The impact of this rule on business transactions is extremely important. Thus, an agent with authority to issue and to indorse checks in P's name and for P's benefit has *power* to do so for his own purposes, causing P to be liable on the signature to a holder in due course and permitting P's bank innocently to rely on the signature to a negotiable instrument and charge P's account for the same. The door of legal liability is wide open for P by the authorized acts of his agent performed for an improper purpose.

8. A's Unauthorized Acts with Chattels, Documents, and Instruments Entrusted to Him by P. When P entrusts to A a chattel, a commercial document representing a chattel (e.g., document of title) or a chose in action (e.g., certificate of stock), a negotiable instrument, or a document with blank spaces, and A acts unauthorizedly in connection with it, whether or not P is bound by A's unauthorized conduct depends on the authority given by P to A and to whom the item was entrusted. Seven situations will be discussed.

First, if P entrusts to A possession of a chattel, other than a commercial document representing a chattel or chose in action, but with no authority to affect P's interest in the chattel, A's unauthorized act to transfer P's interest in the chattel does not bind P, *in the absence of statute to the contrary.* Thus, the bailment[21] of a chattel without authority in the bailee agent to sell it, or to display it for sale, or otherwise to affect P's interest in it, does not subject P to liability or loss of interest in the bailed chattel by the bailee agent's unauthorized conduct with the goods. Examples are: the garage to whom P has delivered his automobile for repair or storage has no power to sell or encumber P's automobile; the bailee of hogs or cattle for fattening them or having them on the ranch for feed has no power to sell them. Mere entrusting of possession of a chattel without authority to deal with it is not such a sufficient representation of ownership or authority over it as to cause P to be deprived of an interest in it by a bailee's unauthorized disposition of it. Even if the bailee has authority to use the chattel, such as to demonstrate it to induce persons to purchase an article similar to it, the bailee cannot unauthorizedly deprive P of his interest in it. However, the Code, Section 2–403(2), provides: "Any entrusting

[20] See above, p. 566.

[21] Bailment is a legal relationship that occurs when chattels or goods are delivered by one person, called a bailor, to another person, called a bailee, pursuant to an agreement whereby the goods are to be returned to the bailor or pursuant to his direction in accordance with the bailment agreement.

of possession of goods to a merchant who deals in goods of that kind gives him power to transfer all rights of the entruster to a buyer in ordinary course of business." (P delivers his watch for repair to A, a jeweler, who repairs and sells watches. A sells the watch unauthorizedly and in P's name to T, an innocent customer. Under the Code, T obtains P's title.)

Second, if P entrusts to A possession of a chattel, other than a commercial document representing a chattel or chose in action, with authority to deal with it in a specified manner, A's unauthorized act dealing with the chattel *in a different manner than authorized* does not affect P's interest in the chattel, *in the absence of statute to the contrary.* By statute in many states, called *Factors Acts,* it is provided, generally, that P's delivery of chattels to a mercantile agent for disposition of a particular interest therein *empowers* the agent to dispose of *any* interest of P in the chattel, whether or not it is the interest authorized by P, to a good faith purchaser for value in the regular course of trade. Thus, consignees and factors have power *to pledge* goods delivered to them *for sale.* Accordingly, it is of utmost importance that the statutes in each state be consulted to determine the extent of inherent agency power in A to act unauthorizedly and thereby to affect P's interests in chattels entrusted to A. For example: P entrusts an automobile to A, an automobile dealer, to sell and A, in P's name, creates a security interest in it, such interest is ineffective as to P; P delivers a watch to A, a watch dealer, to sell it, and A in P's name exchanges it for a ring, the exchange is ineffective as to P. In these examples, many current statutes would cause P to lose the interest in the chattel unauthorizedly disposed of by A.

Third, if P entrusts to P possession of a chattel, other than a commercial document representing a chattel or chose in action, with authority to deal with it in a specified manner, and A deals with it in the same manner as authorized but not in accord with other parts of his authority, P's interests in the chattel are affected if T reasonably believes A to be authorized so to act and T pays value. Thus, P's authority to A to sell, pledge, or otherwise deal with a chattel at a specified price and on other terms *empowers* A to do these things at a different price and on different terms and thereby affects P's interests in the chattel.

Fourth, if P entrusts to *a dealer* possession of a chattel *with authority to exhibit it for sale or to sell it but only with P's consent, or to other than a specified person, or for a specified price,* and A sells the chattel, in accord with normal business practice but not in accord with the conditions in his authority, to T, who reasonably believed A to be authorized so to act, P is bound by the transaction as though A were authorized so to act. The Code, Section 2–403(2), quoted previously[22] is applicable. (P delivers a horse to A, *a horse dealer,* with authority to find a willing purchaser and to inform P. A unauthorizedly sells the horse to T, who reasonably believes that A has authority to do so. P is bound to

---

[22] See above, p. 597.

T. If P had delivered the horse to A for sale for $1,000 and A had sold it to T for $900, P would be bound to T, both by his "dealer" rule and also by the *third rule* in the above paragraph.) *More than one of these rules may apply concurrently to a particular transaction.*

Fifth, if P entrusts to A possession of a commercial document representing a chattel or chose in action, which is in such form that its possessor is commonly regarded as having a power to dispose of it, and P gives to A a limited authority to deal with the document, A's unauthorized disposal of the document to an innocent purchaser without notice of A's lack of authority causes P's interests in the document to be thereby affected. A commercial document was described previously.[23] (P delivers a warehouse receipt to A with authority to obtain the goods in the warehouse and to store them elsewhere. A, in P's name, unauthorizedly sold the warehouse receipt to T, an innocent purchaser without notice of A's lack of authority. Whether or not T obtains title to the warehouse receipt depends upon its form. If the warehouse receipt is in favor of P and P indorsed it in blank, T gets title to it. If the warehouse receipt has not been properly indorsed by P, then P still has title to it.)[24]

Sixth, if P entrusts to A possession of a negotiable instrument not payable to bearer and not indorsed to A, and A unauthorizedly transfers the instrument or collects the claim on it, P's interests in the instrument are not affected. Although the Code[25] provides that a holder in due course of a negotiable instrument takes it free from all claims, with exceptions not material here, in order to be a holder in due course the instrument must be properly indorsed so as to read in favor of the possessor. For example, a check payable to the order of P, the payee, may be indorsed: by P in blank with just his signature, thereby making the instrument payable to bearer; or by P in favor of X, who on receiving it in good faith and for value can enforce it. Until the instrument has been indorsed by the payee in blank or in favor of the possessor, it cannot be *negotiated* further and, since all persons are on notice of this, the rule described above concerning negotiable instruments precludes any unauthorized person from affecting the interests of the person in whose favor the instrument reads. (P has a check payable to his order, and he entrusts it to A to hold for him. A cannot collect it or dispose of it unauthorizedly and thereby affect P's interest in the check.) It should be noted that apparent authority to collect on the instrument or to dispose of it may be created by the appointment of A to a position in P's business where he would have apparent authority so to act, as, for example, by appointment as general manager in charge of an investment business, or by authorization on previous occasions so to act, and third persons have notice of this fact but not of the limitation on A's authority.

Seventh, if P entrusts to A a document executed by P and containing blanks with authority to complete the blanks in a particular manner and A com-

[23] See above, p. 594, ftn. 14.

[24] In connection with the preceding first through fifth rules, see Restatement (Second) of Agency, 1958, Appendix, *Reporter's Notes*, sec. 174.

[25] UCC 3–305.

pletes the blanks in an unauthorized manner and, in P's name, transfers the document to T, an innocent purchaser for value, P is liable on the document only if T had no notice that the document had blanks when delivered to A. P has placed within A's power the opportunity to mislead innocent third persons that the document was completed properly and, accordingly, P exposes himself to possible liability by entrusting such a document to A. This rule is in accord with the Code where the maker of a negotiable instrument with blanks that are unauthorizedly filled in by another is liable to a holder in due course of the instrument.[26] It should be noted that this rule applies to non-negotiable, as well as to negotiable, documents. Also, *if A were a general agent he would come under not only this rule but also under the rule discussed previously[27] concerning the unauthorized acts of a general agent incidental to transactions that he is authorized to conduct.*

9. A's Unauthorized Acts in the Payment or Collection of Debts. Often an agent authorized to pay debts of his principal or to collect debts due to his principal acts unauthorizedly, either mistakenly or deliberately. *If P authorizes A to pay P's debt and A does so but in a mistaken amount, P is bound to the creditor by A's conduct as though A were authorized so to act.* Although restitutional remedies may become available for overpayment by P, depending on the innocence of the creditor and his change of position, P is bound by A's act. If P authorizes A to inform the debtor of what he owes to P when the creditor ordinarily computes the amount, A's unauthorized misrepresentation to the debtor of a larger amount owing, which the debtor pays to A, binds P to T as though A were authorized so to act. (A, pursuant to authority from P, a gas utility, reads a gas meter and informs T, the gas user, of the amount owing, unauthorizedly stating a larger amount than what is actually due, which T pays, A keeping the excess over the correct amount due. P is bound to T, who may obtain restitution of the excess amount from P.) *This rule applies to situations where P usually obtains and computes the amount due and often employs an agent to do this.* The rule does not usually apply in the case of fixed amounts owing under a contract and, P's collecting agency not normally being directed to state such amounts to the debtor, P is not bound by A's unauthorized erroneous representation to the debtor. *If A were a general agent under these rules, he would come under not only these rules but also under the rule discussed previously[28] concerning the unauthorized acts of a general agent incidental to transactions that he is authorized to conduct.*

Defenses. Rights and duties between the contracting parties may be in existence at the time the contract is made, may arise out of the transaction, or may occur subsequent to the contract's formation. Whether or not they can be asserted as between P and T depends upon the time of their occurrence. Each of these will be considered in turn.

---

[26] See UCC 3–115, 3–407, and above, pp. 323, 356–57.

[27] See above, p. 595.

[28] See above, p. 595.

1. Defenses Existing When Contract Is Made. Rights and liabilities between the disclosed or partially disclosed principal and A and between T and A, *existing at the time a contract is made* binding P and T, do not affect the rights and liabilities of P and T with respect to each other, unless otherwise agreed. (P authorizes A to *sell* a typewriter to T for $500, which A does in P's name. If A owed T $100 at the time the contract was made, T cannot set off against P the $100 claim that T has against A; T owes P $500. Similarly, if A's authority had been to *buy* the typewriter for $500 and T owed A $100 at the time the contract was made, P could not set off against T the $100 claim that A has against T; P owes T $500.)

2. Defenses Arising out of the Transaction. However, all defenses *arising out of the transaction between A and T* are available to the contracting parties, *except that defenses which are personal to A*, such as infancy, bankruptcy discharge, and set-off of personal debts owing to A, are not available to P. Thus fraud, duress, or coercion perpetrated by T on P through A or upon P by collusion between A and T, may be asserted by P as a defense against T; and, similarly, if such has been perpetrated by A on T, then T can assert it as a defense against P. If P is not a party to the contract, either because he has been specifically excluded or the contract is under seal or in the form of a negotiable instrument and P's name does not appear therein, then, since the contract cannot be enforced by T or P against the other, such defenses are unavailable to them against each other.

3. Defenses Arising After the Contract Is Made. When T is paid what is owing to him by P, T's claim against P is discharged. This is obviously true if A and P are joint contracting parties on the contract with T, because payment by one joint contracting party, such as A, discharging the debt, operates to discharge all the joint contracting parties on the debt to T. This raises the matter of indemnity as between A and P, previously discussed.[29] P's settlement with A for expenses authorizedly incurred by A in P's name for which P is liable to T, but for which expenses P indemnifies A without notice that A has not paid T, does not relieve P of his liability to T for such expenses, unless P has relied on T's conduct misleading P that A's account with T has been paid by A and which conduct by T has not been fraudulently induced by A. The courts are not in accord here, except that they are in accord *when T misleads P and P relies thereon without any inducing misrepresentations by A to T.* (A authorizedly ships P's goods and obtains a paid receipt from the railroad without having paid for the transportation charges. A misrepresents to P that A has paid the charges and delivers the railroad paid receipt to P, and P in reasonable reliance thereon pays A the amount of such charges. *P is no longer liable to T* for such charges. *If A had fraudulently induced the railroad to issue the receipt*, P is still liable to the railroad for such charges.)

The Undisclosed Principal. An undisclosed principal is a principal of whose existence T is unaware. As previously defined,[30] if T has no notice that

[29] See above, p. 579.

[30] See above, p. 587.

A is acting for a principal, the principal is undisclosed. Often P wishes A to act for P without disclosing his agency status. This section will discuss, in the following order: the parties to a contract made for an undisclosed principal; T's election when he later learns of P's identity; the liabilities between P and T; and, finally, the defenses of P and T against the claim of the other.

Parties. Inasmuch as P is undisclosed, any contract made by A with T would have only A and T as the parties thereto. Although P is not a party to the contract, he obtains the benefit of the contract authorizedly made by A, who holds the contract on P's behalf; also, T's assets are available to A and, through A, to P for T's breach of the contract, while only A's assets are available to T for A's breach. Because of this imbalance, *the courts have caused P to become liable as a party to any contract authorizedly, and in some instances unauthorizedly,*[31] *made by A for an undisclosed P from which P is not excluded either by the contract being under seal or in the form of a negotiable instrument, or by the contract specifically excluding P or any undisclosed principal as a party to it.*[32] *By law, therefore, P is made a contracting party,* quite contrary to the law of Contracts where only the manifested intentions of the parties determine who are the parties to the contract. In effect, therefore, *T has two rights, one against A and one against P.* It is not unusual outside of the law of Contracts for one person to have two rights, one against each of two different persons originating from one transaction; for example, a pedestrian negligently struck by A, P's truck driver, authorizedly delivering merchandise for P, has a claim against A as the wrongdoer and a claim against P as a master responsible for the torts of his servants while acting within the scope of their employment. If, as indicated previously, P is excluded from the contract, then the law will not impose P as a party upon the contracting parties, A and T, who emphatically do not desire P as a party to the contract. P is bound by A's exercise of his authority, and the previous discussion of authority[33] is applicable here. *Apparent authority is inapplicable to a discussion of undisclosed principals because A is not an apparent agent for any principal.*

T's Election. T's discovery of P's identity is of legal importance in two ways. First, thereafter, in T's dealings with A, T is dealing with A on behalf of a disclosed principal and the previous discussion concerning disclosed and partially disclosed principals[34] is applicable. Second, T can continue to look to P and A *as severally liable* on the contract *or make a choice between them,* the choice being irrevocable and discharging the party not selected. Since P and A are severally liable to T, *T is not required to make any choice between them.* If T elects to choose between them, *he can make a choice in only one way. After T learns of P's identity, if T obtains a judgment against either P or A for breach of contract,* the party against whom the judgment was *not* obtained is

[31] See below, pp. 603–6.

[32] See above, pp. 587–88.

[33] See above, pp. 553–76.

[34] See above, pp. 587–601.

discharged from liability on the contract. Although there is conflict, by the majority view, satisfaction of a judgment is not necessary to the election; by the minority view, satisfaction is necessary, thereby permitting two judgments by T against A and P, respectively, in order to satisfy T's claim on the contract. If T obtains judgment against A *before* he learns of P's identity, T has not made an election and he can still obtain a judgment against P to the extent that T's claim has not yet been satisfied against A on that judgment; the courts are in accord on this. T's *commencement* of an action against P or A is not election by T.

After T learns of P's identity, T does not make an election thereby discharging P by continuing to look only to A for performance of the contract. For example, T's billing A for payment or T's proving his claim in bankruptcy against A's bankrupt estate after T learns of P's identity do not cause T to lose his right against P on the contract.

Liabilities between P and T. We have found that, when an agent acts within the scope of his authority, the agent's conduct binds his principal. If the agent's authority was to make a contract for his disclosed or partially disclosed principal with a third person and the agent does this, his principal is bound to the third person as parties to the contract. The fact that P is an undisclosed principal does not preclude his becoming a party to the contract by operation of law.[35] This being so, *the legal rules applicable to disclosed and partially disclosed principals, insofar as they can be applied with the same legal effect, should govern the liabilities of the undisclosed principal in his relations with third persons with whom his agent has dealt.*

The discussion thus far about undisclosed principals has been concerned with whether an undisclosed principal can be a party to the contract *authorizedly* made by his agent. Since he can be a party, then his liability on the contract is like that of the disclosed or partially disclosed principal on contracts *authorizedly* made for them. However, so that the rights and liabilities of the undisclosed P and T may be equitably balanced against each other, with respect to such rights and liabilities P is put in the position substantially of an assignee. *P takes the contract as it existed before T learned of P's identity.* There is no real problem in fixing the rights and liabilities of P and T as of that time if the contract between them was *authorizedly* made. However, the same problem posed for disclosed and partially disclosed principals is posed for undisclosed principals, namely, to what extent is the undisclosed P bound by A's *unauthorized* conduct? The following discussion will consider this problem.

The liability of the undisclosed principal for the *unauthorized* acts of his agent is an example of *inherent agency power.* Some of the instances where such liability is imposed will be discussed.

1. Unauthorized Acts of General Agents. With respect to *general agents,* the previous discussion of a general agent's unauthorized conduct on behalf of

---

[35] See above, p. 602.

a disclosed or partially disclosed principal[36] is applicable here. Briefly, *a general agent with authority to conduct transactions subjects his undisclosed P to liability to a third person for his unauthorized acts on P's behalf, which usually accompany or are incidental to such transactions, if the third person reasonably believes that the agent is authorized to do them and has no notice that he is not so authorized.* This often occurs when the undisclosed P places his agent in charge of P's business as the apparent owner of it and A acts contrary to his authority but in conformity with what is usual in such business. (P authorizes A to manage P's men's retail clothing store and to represent that it belongs to A, but not to pay more than $40 for suits for resale. A buys suits for $50 from T, a clothing manufacturer who does not know of A's status as an agent and believes A to be the owner. P is liable to T for the sale.) However, P's liability is limited to the assets of the business and to the benefits P received.

There are many other situations where, whether the agent be a general agent or a special agent, an undisclosed P is liable for A's unauthorized conduct. These situations will be discussed briefly.

2. *Unauthorized Untruthful Misrepresentations of What A Has Been Authorized to Represent Truthfully.* An undisclosed P is liable in an action on the contract or for its rescission not only for A's authorized representations in connection with the authorized contract, but also for *A's unauthorized representations with respect to incidents in connection with the otherwise authorized contract if A had authority to make true representations with respect to such incidents and T has no reason to know that such representations are untrue.* (A is P's agent with authority to sell P's goods in A's name but not to expressly warrant the goods. A sells the goods with an express warranty to T, who believes that A owns the goods and who relies on A's express warranty. P is bound to T on the sale and on the warranty.)

3. *Authorized Conduct with an Improper Purpose by A.* Unlike the case of disclosed and partially disclosed principals where P is liable for A's authorized act for an improper purpose,[37] *an undisclosed P is not liable for A's making the authorized contract without an intent to act for P.* (P authorizes A to buy goods from T. A makes a contract with T to buy the goods but with the intent to resell the goods as his own and to keep the proceeds for himself. T does not know of A's agency nor of A's intent. P is not bound on the contract with T.) However, if *A intends to act for P but he has an improper motive,* such as the purchase by A, an apparent store owner, of inferior goods so as to disparage P's reputation, P is bound by A's conduct. The mere fact of agency is not enough to justify an inherent agency power in A to make P liable for A's conduct when *A does not intend to act for P,* although inherent agency power is present to make P liable for *A's improper motive.*

---

[36] See above, pp. 593–96.

[37] See above, p. 597.

4. *Unauthorized Nondisclosure of P. A's unauthorized nondisclosure of the existence or identity of his P causes P to be liable on the otherwise authorized contract with T, if T has no reason to know of P's existence and if P is not excluded as a party to the contract* because the contract either is under seal, in the form of a negotiable instrument, or it specifically excludes P. As indicated later,[38] the fact that P did not seek to conceal his existence affects T's right of set-off against P's enforcement of the contract against T.

5. *Unauthorized Amount or Separable Part of Contract.* The same rule[39] applies to an undisclosed principal as to a disclosed or partially disclosed principal that, although an unauthorized contract made by A does not bind his undisclosed P, nevertheless, *if the only difference between the unauthorized contract and the contract as it would be if it were authorizedly made is in the amount involved or in the exclusion or inclusion of a separate part, P is bound on the contract as it was authorized to be made, provided that, before P changes his position in reliance on the unauthorized contract, T manifests assent to the contract as it was authorized to be made.* (P authorizes A to sell P's goods in A's name as the owner for $1,000. A makes a contract in his own name to sell the goods to T for $850. P informs T that A was acting for him, but unauthorizedly as to the price, and P refuses to deliver the goods to T. T may assent to the contract for $1,000 and hold P liable for damages for breach of the contract. If P should change his position in reliance on the contract made by A, as by selling the goods to another before T assents to the contract, the contract cannot be enforced by T against P.)

6. *A's Unauthorized Acts with Chattels, Documents, and Instruments Entrusted to Him by P.* Generally, the same rules apply to an undisclosed principal as to a disclosed or partially disclosed principal with respect to A's unauthorized acts with chattels and instruments entrusted to him by P, as previously discussed,[40] and reference should be made to that material for explanation, examples, and the impact of statutes. Those rules, changed to fit the undisclosed principal, are as follows:

First, if P entrusts to A possession of a chattel, other than a commercial document representing a chattel or chose in action, but with no authority to affect P's interest in the chattel, A's unauthorized transaction with respect to the chattel with T, who believes A to be the owner of the chattel, does not bind P, *in the absence of statute to the contrary.*

Second, if P entrusts to A possession of a chattel, other than a commercial document representing a chattel or chose in action, with authority to deal with it in a specified manner, A's unauthorized act dealing with the chattel *in a different manner than authorized* does not affect P's interest in the chattel, *in the absence of statute to the contrary.*

---

[38] See below, p. 607.

[39] See above, p. 592.

[40] See above, pp. 597–600.

Third, if P entrusts to A possession of a chattel, other than a commercial document representing a chattel or chose in action, with authority to deal with it in a specified manner and A deals with it in the usual and ordinary course of business *in the same manner as authorized but not in accord with other parts of his authority,* P's interests in the chattels are affected if T reasonably believes A to be the owner and T pays value.

Fourth, if P entrusts to a dealer possession of a chattel with authority to exhibit it for sale or to sell it but only with P's consent, or to other than a specified person, or for a specified price, and A sold the chattel, in accord with normal business practice but *not in accord with the conditions in his authority,* to T who reasonably believed A to be the owner, P is bound by the transaction as though A were the owner.

Fifth, if P entrusts to A possession of a commercial document representing a chattel or chose in action, which is in such form that its possessor is commonly regarded as having a power to dispose of it, and P gives to A a limited authority to deal with the document, A's unauthorized disposal of the document to an innocent purchaser who believes that A is the owner causes P's interests in the document to be thereby affected.

7. A's Unauthorized Transfer of Title Entrusted to Him by P. If an undisclosed P entrusts to A title to something, A has power to transfer the title to T who has no notice of P's interests and who either pays value or changes his position in reliance thereon. A becomes a trustee of the legal title; and a good faith purchaser for value of the title, whether from A or from A's transferee who has notice of A's lack of authority, acquires the title. (A, pursuant to his authority and acting on behalf of his undisclosed P, purchases a horse from T_1 in A's name. P tells A to hold the horse and the bill of sale in A's name. A, unauthorizedly and in his own name, sells the horse to T_2, who paid the purchase price to A and who believes that A is the owner without notice of A's lack of authority. T_2 owns the horse.) A's transfer of the title to T, who knows of A's violation of his authority or who is a donee who has not changed his position in reliance on A's ownership without notice of A's lack of authority, can be set aside. The title may be to intangibles, such as accounts receivable, as well as to land and chattels.

Defenses. P and T can enforce against each other the contract made by A only if P is a party to it. If P is not a party to the contract because he was excluded from it, either because the contract was under seal or in the form of a negotiable instrument or it specifically excluded him as a party, then neither P nor T can enforce the contract against each other. Various situations affect P's and T's defenses.

1. Multiple Ps. If A is authorized by multiple undisclosed Ps *individually* to make a contract on their behalf and A, without their consent, combines all their orders into one contract, the undisclosed Ps are not parties to the contract with T.[41] However, since A holds the combined contract in trust for the Ps

[41] The same result is applicable to disclosed principals.

individually, all the Ps can, as the beneficial owners of the contract between A and T, combine and sue T on the contract.

2. *Misrepresentation that P Is Not a Principal.* Although an undisclosed P is a party to the contract made by A with T, *if A misrepresents to T that he is not acting for a principal, A or P having notice that T would not have dealt with P,* and thereby induces T to make the contract, *the contract is voidable by T. The mere fact that A did not disclose to T that he was acting for an undisclosed P does not of itself cause the contract to be voidable.* It is well known that agents often represent undisclosed principals and there is *no duty to disclose* the agency status, unless such status is material to T and A or P knows this; then the duty to disclose arises. Although there is conflict, this is the great majority view and tendency among the courts.

3. *Set-Off.* Whether or not P has authorized A to misrepresent to T about P's existence determines to what extent T may set off against P any claim that T had against A before T learned of P's existence. *If A's authority was to conceal P's existence,* then P gets only what A could enforce against T and, therefore, *T can set off against P any claim T had against A before T learned of P's existence. If A's authority was to disclose P and A did not do so,* then, since P did not want T to be misled as to whom he was dealing with, *T cannot set off against P any claim T has against A, unless P has entrusted the chattels to A and thereby misled T to extend credit to A on the basis of such chattels.* (A, pursuant to authority for his undisclosed P, made a contract in his own name to sell P's horse to T for $600. A owed T $100 at the time the contract was made. When P sued T on the contract, T could set off $100 against P's claim of $600. If P had authorized A to disclose P's identity and A did not do so, then T cannot so set off against P. If P had authorized A to disclose P's identity and had delivered the horse to A and A did not disclose P's identity, T can set off against P.) The reason for the distinctions here is that, although P is an undisclosed principal and should be bound by A's inherent agency power, there should be a limit to such power where P is trying to be forthright with T. Thus, if P intends to be disclosed, then only binding P on the contract should be enough and T cannot set off against P T's claim against A; but if P intends to conceal his existence or entrusts chattels to A, thereby more forcibly inducing T to deal with A as not representing anyone, then the full force of the inherent agency power is employed, and T can set off against P T's claim against A.

4. *A's Knowledge and Notice.* Before T knows of the existence of an undisclosed P, T is dealing only with A and A is, with P's knowledge, dealing with T. *Before P's existence is known to T, P is charged with knowledge or notice acquired by himself or through* A, and this may affect P's liability to T; *after P's existence is disclosed,* P becomes a disclosed or partially disclosed principal from that point on and *the rules concerning notice to the principal through his agent become applicable.*[42]

5. *A's Conduct after Contract's Formation.* If A had made a contract bind-

[42] See above, pp. 582–83, 590.

ing on his undisclosed P, A has the *power* to perform or to receive performance or to rescind the contract, or to modify the contract if the modified contract would have been binding upon P initially. After P's existence is known to T, from that point on A has only the power of an agent for a disclosed or partially disclosed P.[43]

6. *P's Contract Rights Similar to Those of Assignee.* *The undisclosed P's position in the enforcement of the contract made by A and binding P as a party is substantially that of an assignee. P takes the contract as it exists before T learns of P's identity.* T has all the defenses that he would have had if the transaction had been made by P instead of by A. Thus, if A had not performed the contract or had practiced fraud, duress, or coercion on T, *these defenses could be asserted by T against P* in his action to enforce the contract against T. Similarly, *P has all the defenses arising out of the transaction that A had against T, and which are not personal to A.*

A's personal defenses are infancy, bankruptcy discharge, and set-off against T in the absence of contract provision to the contrary. (A, an infant, pursuant to authority from his undisclosed P, made a contract with T. When T tries to enforce the contract against P, P could not assert A's infancy as a defense and thereby avoid the contract.)

T should not be exposed to a greater obligation than that provided for by the contract and, therefore, performance or tender of performance by P is proper unless it is substantially different from that which the contract requires, in which event there is nonperformance by P and A. *If the contract called for the rendition of personal services by A, since the contract is of a personal nature A's contractual duties are nondelegable and P cannot render the performance required by the contract.* (A, pursuant to authority from his undisclosed P, made a contract with T to sell P's land with a warranty deed to T. P tendered his own waranty deed to the land. P has not performed.) *If A has performed or tendered performance of his contractual obligation, P can enforce the contract against T irrespective of A's personal service already rendered or tendered.* Similarly, P can compel T to perform the contract to P instead of to A, unless *T's services to be rendered to A are personal* in nature or performance by T to P would impose upon T a performance substantially different from that required by the contract. (Under the terms of the contract for the sale of goods by T to A, who is acting authorizedly for an undisclosed P, *T extends credit to A personally.* A becomes insolvent. P cannot enforce the contract against T.)

7. *P's Discharge by T's Conduct.* P can assert the following as good defenses to an action by T on the contract made by A and binding P, his undisclosed principal, as a party to it:

First, T's Election to Hold A on the Contract. As discussed previously,[44] after T learns of P's identity, if T should obtain a judgment against A for breach of contract, by the majority view P is discharged from liability on the contract.

---

[43] See above, pp. 587–600.

[44] See above, pp. 602–3.

Second, Satisfaction of T's Claim against A. Satisfaction of T's claim against A discharges P as well as A from further liability to T on the contract. Since P's liability is based on A's contract with T, if the contract out of which T's claim arose is discharged, then there is no further basis for P's liability to T. Satisfaction may occur by: performance of the contract; mutual agreement between T and A discharging the contract, such as by mutual rescission, accord and satisfaction, novation, release; and by satisfaction of a judgment obtained by T against A.

Third, P's settlement of Accounts with A in Reliance on T's Misleading Conduct. P's settlement of accounts with A on the contract with T, without notice that the contract has not been performed but made in reliance on T's conduct misleading P that the contract has been discharged, T's conduct not having been fraudulently induced by A, discharges P from liability on the contract with T. This was discussed previously in connection with contracts of disclosed and partially disclosed principals.[45]

Torts

By Servants. The master is liable for loss or harm caused to third persons by the *tortious physical acts of his servants while acting within the scope of their employment,* but, generally, not while they are acting outside the scope of their employment. Whether or not a servant was acting within the scope of his employment is a question of fact. The purpose and nature of the servant's act, and the time, place, and manner of its performance all are considered in determining whether or not the act was performed within the scope of the employment. *A servant is acting within the scope of his employment if he is performing acts of the same kind as he was authorized to perform, not unreasonably outside the time or area when such performance was to occur, and with the purpose of serving his master.* Slight deviations in the manner of performance or in the time or place of such performance do not cause such performance to be outside the scope of the servant's authority. (P authorizes S to serve food up until 2:00 P.M. S serves food until 2:07 P.M. S was acting within the scope of his employment.) A servant's unauthorized use of equipment different from that authorized, but not substantially different, is conduct occurring within the scope of the servant's employment. Loss or damage caused to third persons by a servant's negligent use of equipment entrusted to him while acting within the scope of his employment subjects his master to liability therefor. *A servant acting with an intent not to serve his master is not acting within the scope of his employment.* The reason why a master is liable for loss or damage caused by the tortious physical acts of the servant while acting within the scope of his employment is that the master has a right of control over the physical acts of such servant and should be responsible for the acts of such servants.

---

[45] See above, p. 601.

By Non-Servant Agents. Inasmuch as *the principal has no right of control over the physical acts of non-servant agents,* as distinguished from servants, the principal is not liable for loss or damage caused by the tortious physical acts of such agents, unless they were acting as authorized by the principal and the principal had a duty to use care in the performance of such acts. *Misrepresentations made by an agent with authority, apparent authority, or in connection with a transaction of the kind authorized, which a third person reasonably believes to be true and made with authority, causes the principal to be liable for such misrepresentations.* (P appoints A as general manager of P's store. A gossips with B and slanders C. P is not liable to C for the slander. If A had fraudulently induced B, a customer, to buy goods by making intentional misrepresentations regarding the goods, P would be liable to B for the tort of deceit.[46] B could also rescind the transaction.)

Non-physical torts committed by an agent within the scope of his apparent authority subject the principal to liability therefor. (P appoints A, his agent, to send out bills to P's customers each month and to collect on the same. A pads a bill to C, a customer, who pays such bill, and A keeps the padded excess. P is liable for A's tort in obtaining the excess amounts.) A principal is not liable for torts of apparent agents or servants unless third persons rely on the apparent authority and are injured by torts committed by the apparent agent or servant occurring during such reliance. (P appoints A as manager of P's store, but A is *not* to demonstrate machines for sale, although it is incidental to the duties of a manager to do so. A demonstrates a machine to B, a customer. During the demonstration B is injured by the negligent demonstration. P is liable, as B has relied on A as acting within his apparent authority as manager of the store.) It is for this reason that an undisclosed principal is not liable for the non-physical torts resulting in loss or damage caused by his agent acting as apparent owner of a business; the principal being undisclosed there is no apparent authority.

SECTION III. DUTIES AND LIABILITIES BETWEEN AGENT AND THIRD PERSON

An agent who is a party to a contract with a third person, whether or not his principal is also a party, is liable for contractual nonperformance. A person who expressly or impliedly purports to act as an agent, expressly or impliedly warrants that he has authority so to act and is liable for breach of express or implied warranty of authority. An agent who commits a tort, whether within or without the scope of his authority, is liable to the third person for such tort perpetrated on him, regardless of whether or not the principal also is liable for the tort. An agent is liable to third persons for damage caused to them by his *active misconduct,* called "misfeasance," but not for his *failure to act,* called "nonfeasance." Once an agent *begins* to perform he has a duty to act reasonably, and his negligence proximately causing harm to third persons causes

[46] See above, p. 34; ftn. 28.

him to be liable to them for his "misfeasance." An agent with a duty to exercise control over other agents has a duty to exercise due care, and an agent for an undisclosed principal is liable for the torts of such other agents as though he were a principal.

Contracts

As discussed previously,[47] an agent may become a party to a contract with a third person, or with the third person and his principal. In the absence of agreement to the contrary, a person making or purporting to make a contract with a third person as an agent for a fully disclosed principal is not a party to the contract, while he is a party to the contract if his principal is partially disclosed. An agent acting for an undisclosed principal but purporting to contract for himself is a party to the contract with the third person. An agent is not a party to a contract under seal in a state where the Common Law effect of the seal exists if he is not described as a party thereto; nor is he a party to a contract in the form of a negotiable instrument on which his name does not appear. A person who purports to make a contract for a nonexistent principal, such nonexistence being known to the third person who is the other party to the contract, makes the agent a party to the contract with the third person. (A, acting as a promoter for a corporation to be formed, enters into a contract in the name of such unborn corporation with T, who knows of the nonexistence of the corporation. The contract is between A and T.) An agent who is not a party to the contract cannot maintain an action thereon in the name, and on behalf, of his principal; but if he is a party he can sue thereon in his own name on behalf of his principal. Factors often are parties to the contract along with the principal and the third person and can sue thereon in their own names.

A person who purports to act as an agent *impliedly warrants that he has authority so to act* and is liable for breach of such warranty, regardless of his good faith, to a third person reasonably believing him to have such authority. If the agent *intentionally deceived* a third person as to his authority, the agent is liable also in *tort for deceit. The principal's ratification of the agent's unauthorized acts discharges the agent from liability for breach of warranty or misrepresentation.* If an agent's disclosed principal has limited capacity to make the contract, the agent is not liable for damage caused to the third person by his principal's failure to perform the contract, unless the agent knows of the third person's ignorance of such limited capacity and he does not inform the third person, or the agent expressly warrants in the contract that the principal has full capacity to make the contract. *An agent does not impliedly warrant that his principal has full capacity to contract, but, if the agent knows of the third person's ignorance of his principal's limited capacity to contract, he is under a duty to disclose this fact to the third person.* When the agent fails in his duty to disclose such fact in his dealings with a third person, there is an

[47] See above, pp. 587–88.

implied warranty by law that the agent's principal has full capacity to contract and the agent is liable to the third person for damages for breach of such implied warranty if the principal should disaffirm the transaction.

Defenses. When an agent is a party to a contract with a principal and a third person, the agent may assert those defenses created by the contract and also his personal defenses against the third person. As a surety for his principal, the agent has the defenses available to a surety, which have been discussed previously under Suretyship.[48] An illustration of such a defense is performance by the principal which discharges the contract and discharges the agent from any liability thereon. If the agent and principal are not jointly liable on the contract, the third person has contract rights against each, and a judgment obtained by the third person against either one does not discharge the other unless the judgment is satisfied. When the principal is undisclosed and the third person, with subsequent knowledge of the principal's identity, obtains judgment against the principal, by the majority view, the agent is discharged by the third person's election to hold the principal liable for performance of the contract.

The third person may assert against an agent who is suing on the contract in his own name on behalf of his principal all the defenses which he could have asserted against the principal if the latter were the plaintiff. The third person can set off all claims he could have set off against the principal. The third person also may assert as a defense that the agent had no authority to bind the principal and did not bind him to any contract with the third person.

Torts

An agent who commits a tort, whether within or without the scope of his authority, is liable to the third person for such tort perpetrated upon him, regardless of whether or not the principal also is liable for the tort. (A, P's truck driver, negligently injures T while driving the truck delivering P's merchandise. A is liable as the wrongdoer, and P is liable for A's physical tort while acting within the scope of his employment as P's servant.) Similarly, *a third person is liable to an agent for torts committed against the agent,* regardless of whether or not the agent was acting within or without the scope of his authority. Some of the common torts committed by agents are deceit, negligence, and conversion.

Although an agent is liable to third persons for damage caused to them *by his active misconduct, commonly called "misfeasance,"* nevertheless, *an agent generally is not liable to third persons for his failure to act, commonly called "nonfeasance."* The reason for this result is that a person who acts has a duty to act reasonably, while a person without any duty to act violates no duty by his inaction, and he commits no wrong. Although an agent has a duty to his principal to perform his contract of agency, generally an agent has no duty to

---

[48] See above, pp. 492 ff.

third persons so to perform. However, *once an agent begins to perform he has a duty to act reasonably.* Also, if an agent undertakes with his principal to perform an act which he should realize, under the circumstances, is necessary to the safety of a third person or his property, thereby causing the third person or the principal to rely upon performance by the agent, a duty is imposed upon the agent to exercise reasonable care to perform his undertaking. The agent's failure to take affirmative action in accordance with his duty subjects him to liability for damage proximately caused thereby.

An agent who has the duty to exercise control over the acts of other agents or servants of his principal must exercise due care in performing his duty, and he is liable for his negligence in not exercising such care. If he exercises reasonable care and other agents or servants commit torts on third persons, *causing injury to them,* the agent is not liable; only the principal is liable to the third persons. However, if the principal is *undisclosed* to the other agents or servants, *the agent* with authority to supervise the other agents or servants is *liable for their torts as though he were a principal; this does not exclude the undisclosed principal from liability* therefor if the tort occurred during the performance of authorized acts.

Chapter 41

TERMINATION OF AGENCY

SECTION I. TERMINATION OF ACTUAL AUTHORITY

The principal and agent may terminate the agency in various ways. (1) By the express or implied terms of the agency. (2) By mutual rescission. (3) By the principal's revocation, or the agent's renunciation, of the agency. A party's revocation or renunciation to be effective must be actually received by the other party, or he must know facts causing him reasonably to believe that the agency has been revoked or renounced. By so-called "irrevocable agency," the authority or power to act is irrevocable if: (1) *the authority is given as security* in exchange for *consideration given by the agent or powerholder* as a part of the agency *contract;* or (2) *the authority is coupled with an interest in the subject matter* by the principal's *transfer of a property interest* to the agent or powerholder. Both may be present.

The agency may terminate also by operation of law by the death, insanity, or bankruptcy of the principal or agent, or by a change of law causing the agency or its performance to be illegal, or by destruction of the subject matter which is the object of the agency.

Agency may be terminated by the act of the parties or by operation of law. *Apparent agency* may be terminated by notice to third persons of the cessation of actual authority. The termination of actual and apparent authority will be discussed in turn.

By Act of the Parties

Express or Implied Terms of the Agency. *The relationship of agency terminates when the agency agreement expressly or impliedly so provides.* The agreement *may specify* that, on the accomplishment of the object to be performed, on the expiration of a certain period of time, on the occurrence of a particular event, or at the will of either party if it is an agency terminable at will, the agency is to terminate. It is implied that, *if the agreement does not specify when it is to terminate, the agency is meant to terminate on the expiration of a reasonable period of time under the circumstances. Conditions may so change as impliedly to cause the agency to terminate.* If the agent reasonably can believe from the change in conditions that the principal no longer would desire the agency to continue, the agency is terminated.

Mutual Rescission. Agency, by definition, is created by mutual consent and is a continuing, legal relationship until such mutuality of consent is terminated. The principal and agent consented to the creation of the agency, and it is their right to agree to rescind the agency.

Revocation or Renunciation. Either the principal or the agent individually may terminate the agency. *The principal's withdrawal of his consent is called "revocation," and the agent's withdrawal of his consent is called "renunciation."* The principal has the power *to revoke* an agency although his wrongful termination of a contract of agency subjects him to liability to the agent for damages for breach thereof. Similarly, the agent may *renounce* the agency and, if the agency is one of contract, the agent exposes himself to liability to his principal for damages for breach thereof. *Any provision in the agency contract that the contract is irrevocable does not prevent revocation or renunciation of the contract, but merely indicates that breach of the contract will impose liability therefor.* Unless otherwise agreed, a party's revocation or renunciation must be *actually received* by the other party either from the one revoking or renouncing, or by his knowledge of facts which would lead him reasonably to believe that the agency has been revoked or renounced. Revocation or renunciation is effective as such only if the addressee reasonably could understand such manifestation to be a revocation or renunciation. Agency under seal may be revoked by parol. Revocation or renunciation of the agency for cause does not constitute a breach and does not impose liability for termination.

"Irrevocable Agency." It is often said that there are two so-called exceptions to the rule that agency is revocable, namely, *authority given as security* (*consideration* is given by the powerholder), and *authority coupled with an interest in the subject matter* (*title* is transferred to the powerholder). These two instances do not involve authority but, rather, they are non-agency *power* situations. Authority may be revoked or renounced, as discussed previously, and on its termination all agency power, all inherent agency power, and agency itself are terminated. With these distinctions in mind, let us examine these two types of power.

1. *Authority Given as Security.* If the principal *contracts* (not merely agrees) with his agent, whereby the agent renders the performance requested by the principal who, in return, *promises authority to the agent as security for the principal's performance of an obligation* (often payment of his indebtedness) to the agent, such authority is irrevocable. *It is the fact that the principal's promise of authority to secure performance of his obligation is supported by consideration which causes the contract to be made and the authority to be irrevocable.* (P and A *contract* whereby A lends $1,000 to P, who agrees to repay the same on a certain date and, *as security for the payment of such debt, P authorizes* A to sell P's horse if P defaults on such payment. P does not deliver the horse to A. P's promise of authority for the purpose of security to A is supported by *consideration,* namely A's loan to P, and such authority therefore is irrevocable.) If the principal's promise of authority to A for the purpose of security is not supported by consideration, there is no contract but merely an agreement, and P's promise is unenforceable and revocable. (P owes A $1,000. P authorizes A to sell P's horse for $2,000, to retain $1,000 in satisfaction of the debt and to account to P for the balance. P does not deliver the horse to A. P's promise of authority is not supported by consideration and, therefore, it is revocable.) This irrevocable authority is called *authority given as security.* Authority given as security is irrevocable during the lifetime of the principal and, although there is conflict among the courts, by the better view it is also irrevocable on the death of the principal. At Common Law there was a failure to distinguish between a security power and the fiduciary power contained in authority. The death of the principal does not terminate any authority here because there is no agency nor authority but, instead, a security power and the powerholder as such is not an agent for the purpose of the power.

It should be noted carefully that while an agent may have an interest in performing his authority and thereby earn the agreed compensation for such performance (e.g., a commission for the sale of merchandise), nevertheless, such an interest is not sufficient to cause the authority to be irrevocable, even if the principal agreed not to revoke such authority. This authority is not given as *security.* This interest of the agent in compensation solely *for the excercise of authority* is a normal part of agency and, for the principal's failure to perform, the agent has the remedy of an action for breach of contract.

2. *Authority Coupled with an Interest in the Subject Matter.* If the principal *transfers to his agent a property interest* (e.g., title) in the principal's property *to secure performance of the principal's obligation* owing by the principal to the agent, *together with authority* to dispose of such property on the principal's default on his obligation, the agent's *authority is coupled with an interest in the subject matter* (the principal's property) and is irrevocable by the principal and by his death. *No contract is required* between the principal and the agent with respect to such authority. All that is necessary is such *transfer* and such *authority* for the purpose of *security.* (P owes A $1,000. P *delivers* to A *title* to P's horse with authority to sell the horse for $2,000 on P's

default, to retain $1,000 in satisfaction of the debt, and to account to P for the remainder. The authority to sell on default is coupled with an interest in the subject matter, namely, the title to the property, and is irrevocable by P or by P's death.)

Authority coupled with an interest in the subject matter is irrevocable by the principal's death because the agent may proceed against the property in his own name. *It is unimportant whether or not consideration is given for the property security interest, as long as the property security interest is created.*

By Operation of Law

Death. Inasmuch as the agency relation is consensual and *personal in character,* the death of the principal or of the agent *terminates the agency,* unless the agency is so-called irrevocable. *Notice* to the surviving agent or principal is *not required.* Termination in this matter *does not constitute a breach of any agency contract,* and the estate of the decedent is not liable for damages for such termination. The death of one or more joint principals or joint agents has the same effect. Although P's death immediately terminates authority without notice, under the Code business convenience and necessity require that, *in certain cases,* A should still have a *power* to bind P's estate when A, without notice of P's death, does what he was authorized to do. Thus the Code provides that the death or incompetence of a customer does not revoke the bank's authority to accept, pay, or collect items issued by the principal depositor, or to account for proceeds of collection on them, until the bank *knows* of the fact of death or of an adjudication of incompetence and has reasonable opportunity to act on it. The Code also provides that, *even with knowledge, a bank may for ten days after the date of death* pay or certify checks drawn on or prior to that date, unless ordered to stop by a person claiming an interest in the account.[1]

Insanity. Insanity of the principal or of the agent terminates the agency, unless the agency is so-called irrevocable. Notice to the principal or the agent of the other's insanity is not required. The insanity of one or more joint principals or joint agents has the same effect.

Bankruptcy. The effect of *the principal's bankruptcy* upon the agent's authority depends upon the transactions in which the agent is to engage, except that so-called irrevocable agency is not affected by such bankruptcy. On bankruptcy, a trustee in bankruptcy is appointed and the bankrupt's *nonexempt property* passes to him for distribution among the bankrupt's creditors. With respect to such *nonexempt property,* the agent's authority is terminated without any notice to the agent. *With respect to exempt property* and with respect to an agent's authority to bind the principal personally, the agent's authority does not terminate *until he receives notice* of the principal's bankruptcy. On receiving such notice, if the agent reasonably can believe from

---

[1] See above, pp. 404–5.

such a *change in the principal's financial condition* that the principal no longer would desire the agency to continue, the agency impliedly is terminated, as stated previously.[2] *Usually the bankruptcy of the agent* also will terminate the agency, although if his bankruptcy will not in any way affect his performance of authorized acts, his bankruptcy does not terminate the agency.

Change of Law. Generally, a change of law causing the agency to be illegal, or causing performance of the act authorized to be illegal and entirely ineffective, terminates the agent's authority without notice to the agent.

Destruction of Subject Matter. Generally, the loss or destruction of the particular subject matter which is the object of the agency terminates the agent's authority without notice to the agent.

The above discussion of termination of authority either by the acts of P and A or by the occurrence of subsequent events applies to the termination of the authority of subagents (which includes subservants), making allowance for their "sub" status. This, since subagency involves relations between P and A as a result of P's manifestation of consent to A, between A and SA (subagent) as a result of A's manifestation of consent to SA, and between P and SA as a result of P's manifestation of consent to SA through A, the withdrawal of either P's consent to A or A's consent to SA terminates the subagency. However, SA may still have apparent authority to bind P or A. *Accordingly, termination of the relation between P and A or between A and SA terminates the subagency but not necessarily SA's apparent authority.* When notice of termination is not required for termination of authority, SA's authority ceases immediately without notice; when such notice is required, notice to SA accomplishes this result, but if the notification of P's termination of his relation to A is received only by A, SA's authority does not terminate until A has had a reasonable time to communicate the notice of termination to SA.

SECTION II. TERMINATION OF APPARENT AUTHORITY

Apparent authority may be terminated: (*1*) *by notice* of cessation of actual authority given to third persons to whom the agent has apparent authority, depending on whether the agent is a general or special agent; (2) *by operation of law*, when no such notice is required, which occurs by the supervening death of the principal or agent, or by supervening impossibility by change of law or destruction of the subject matter object of the agency.

The third person must receive *actual notice of termination of authority* if: (1) he previously had *extended credit* to the principal, or *received credit* from the principal, through a *general agent;* or (2) the agent was a *special agent*(a) who was a *specially accredited* agent to the person, or (b) who had *begun to deal* with the third person which was known to the principal, or (c) who had exhibited to the third person the principal's *written indicia of authority.* Reasonable notice of termination of authority is to be given: to third persons to

[2] See above, p. 615.

whom the principal has manifested that they would be justified in relying on the statement of a general or special agent as to when, on the occurrence of a specified event, his authority is to terminate; and to all other third persons to whom the agent has apparent authority, except that *no notice* is required when the apparent authority is of special agents other than the three just mentioned.

Notice to T, When Required

Apparent authority is created by P's manifestation to T that A has authority to act as P's agent. Apparent authority is A's power to affect P's legal relations with T by acting in accordance with P's manifestation to T just as though A were P's agent. Since apparent authority is concerned with T's belief from P's manifestation to him that A has authority to act as P's agent, termination of apparent authority does not occur until T no longer reasonably has this belief. The supervening death or loss of capacity of P or A,[3] or supervening impossibility by change of law or *destruction of subject matter,*[4] *terminates authority and apparent authority immediately and without notice to anyone.* However, with these three exceptions, termination of authority does not of itself terminate apparent authority. Termination of apparent authority can occur only by proper notice to T. *It is only to those third persons to whom the agent has apparent authority that the principal must give notice of the termination of the agency in order to terminate such apparent authority.*

General and Special Agents. ***General Agents.*** Because general agents are authorized to conduct a series of transactions involving a continuity of service, it is considered a reasonable interpretation of a principal's appointment of a general agent that third persons are to continue to deal with a general agent until notified to the contrary or until lapse of time should cause third persons to realize that authority has been terminated. *Accordingly, unless otherwise manifested by P to T, notice to T is required in order to terminate the apparent authority of a general agent.*

Special Agents. However, in the case of a special agent, who is authorized to conduct a single transaction or a series of transactions not involving continuity of service, it is considered a reasonable interpretation of a principal's appointment of a special agent that third persons should realize that his authority may terminate without notice to third persons. *Accordingly, unless otherwise manifested by P to T, termination of authority of a special agent immediately terminates his apparent authority, without notice to T, with four exceptions when apparent authority exists and, unless otherwise manifested by P, when notice to T is required.* The exceptions follow.

1. A *specially accredited agent* is an agent whom P has indicated to T has been specially selected to deal with T and whose authority T reasonably can

---

[3] See above, p. 617.

[4] See above, p. 618.

believe is to continue unless P notifies T of its modification or termination. A general, as well as a special, agent may be a specially accredited agent; consequently, *unless otherwise manifested by P, notice to T is required to terminate the authority of a specially accredited agent.*

2. *A has begun to deal with T, of which P has notice.* T can reasonably expect that if, with P's knowledge, A is dealing with T on P's behalf as his agent, P would notify T of the termination of A's authority. It is deemed but reasonable that P should be required to respect T's expectation. The agent may be a special or a general agent. So, *unless otherwise manifested by P, notice to T is required to terminate the authority of an agent who, known to P, has begun to deal with T.*

3. *When P entrusts to A written authority intended for exhibition to third persons, as to third persons to whom the writing is exhibited and who do not know of termination of A's authority, the apparent authority of A cannot be terminated without notice to them of such termination.* The agent may be a special or a general agent.

4. *When P manifests to T that A's authority terminates on the occurrence of a specified event and that A has authority to represent when the event has occurred, T is justified in relying on the truth of A's statement concerning the occurrence or non-occurrence of the specified event, and the occurrence of the event without notice to T does not terminate A's apparent authority.* P's manifestation to T that A has authority to represent when the event has occurred may be made expressly, or may be made impliedly when knowledge of the event's occurrence is peculiarly, but not necessarily exclusively, within the knowledge of a general agent or when it is within the exclusive knowledge of a special agent. (P authorizes A to buy a horse and P tells T_1 that A has such authority and that A is coming over to look at T_1's horse. A, authorizedly and in P's name, buys a horse from T_2, without the knowledge of P and T_1. A then looks at T_1's horse, misrepresents to T_1 that he had not yet purchased a horse for P, and contracts in P's name with T_1 for the purchase of his horse, T_1 reasonably believing A. P is bound to T_1 A is *a special agent with exclusive knowledge of the occurrence of the event of the purchase of a horse and with apparent authority to represent its non-occurrence to T_1*.) (P appoints A as *general manager* of P's retail men's clothing store with instructions that he is not to have more than 500 shirts in stock for sale at any time, a fact which T, a shirt manufacturer, knows. A has 350 shirts in stock, but he tells T that there are only 200 shirts in stock. T reasonably believes A and he contracts with A in P's name to sell to P 300 more shirts. P is bound to T. A is a general agent.)

Kinds of Notice to T

Two kinds of notice are involved in the termination of apparent authority, namely *actual notice* and *reasonable notice*. The kind of notice of termination of authority that T is to receive in order to terminate apparent authority depends upon the *kind of agent* and *prior credit transactions* between T and P through A.

Actual Notice. *T must receive actual notice of termination of authority in all of the following cases,* the last three of which have just been discussed:

1. When T previously has either *extended credit* to P, or *received credit* from P, through A in reliance on P's manifestation of A's *continuing* authority.
2. A is a specially accredited agent to T.
3. A has begun to deal with T, of which P has notice.
4. A has exhibited to T, who reasonably can rely on A's exhibit, P's written indicia of authority, which P has entrusted to A.

Actual notice to T occurs when:

1. P has actually told T, or
2. A reasonable period of time has elapsed after P's written notice of termination of authority has been delivered by P either:
   a. To T personally, or
   b. To a person with authority or apparent authority to receive communications for T either:
      (1) At T's place of business, or
      (2) At the place that T has designated as one where his business communications are received, or
      (3) At "a place which in view of the business customs or relations between the parties is reasonably believed to be the place for the receipt of such communications by" T.[5]

Reasonable Notice. *All other third persons to whom A has apparent authority are entitled to reasonable notice by either:* "(a) advertising the fact in a newspaper of general circulation in the place where the agency is regularly carried on; or (b) giving publicity by some other method reasonably adapted to give the information to such third person."[6] Of course, if they receive actual notice of termination this would be sufficient notice also. Those third persons as to whom A has apparent authority and who are entitled to receive such reasonable notice are: those who have dealt previously with P through A on a *cash basis;* and those who have never dealt previously with P through A but who *knew* of A's authority either directly from P or through A's reputation as P's agent, *irrespective of whether they learned of A's apparent authority either before or after the termination of A's authority.* It should be noted that, after A's authority has been terminated, A does not have authority to represent to third persons with whom A is dealing for the *first* time that he has authority, and such wrongful misrepresentation by A to T does not thereby create apparent authority.

---

[5] Restatement (Second) of Agency, 1958, sec. 136(1)(b)(iv).

[6] Ibid., sec. 136(3)(a)(b).

It should be noted that the previous discussion of the termination of an agent's apparent authority applies also to the termination of the apparent authority of a subagent, which includes a subservant.

PROBLEMS

1. (a) P wrote to A authorizing him to purchase a truck. A, without knowledge of P's written authorization and without any other authority from P, represented to T that he was authorized by P to purchase a truck; and he purchased a truck from T in P's name. T did not know of P's written authorization. P refused to accept the truck and refused to pay for it.
   (1) Is P liable to T for such purchase? Why?
   (2) Is A liable to T for such purchase? Why?

   (b) P orally authorized A to mortgage P's land. Although he didn't tell A, P had meant that A was to mortgage only X land; instead, A executed and delivered to T a mortgage on P's Y land. P refused to recognize the mortgage as valid.
   (1) Is the mortgage valid?
   (2) Why?

2. A certified public accountant was making a balance sheet audit of a coal dealer's business and the accountant, at his own expense, engaged an engineer to survey coal piles and to report to the accountant the quantity in each pile. The engineer in the due performance of his work purchased necessary supplies for which he did not pay. Has the vendor of these supplies an enforceable claim against the accountant? (Former C.P.A. Examination question)

3. (a) P authorized A to sell and transfer title to 1,000 barrels of oil in P's possession. A, in P's name, sold the oil to T, who paid A the purchase price. A absconded with the proceeds. P refused to deliver the oil to T until T had paid P the purchase price.
   (1) Has T a right to possession of the oil without paying P the purchase price?
   (2) Why?

   (b) P authorized A to sell and transfer title to certain goods. After A, in P's name, had sold such goods to T, A and T agreed to rescind the sale. P refused to recognize the rescission, tendered the goods, and demanded the purchase price.
   (1) Was the rescission binding on P?
   (2) Why?

   (c) P delivered goods to A and authorized him to sell them. A, in P's name, sold the goods to T and received T's check for the purchase price.
   (1) Is the transaction binding on P?
   (2) Why?

4. Jones, an orange grower, ships oranges to his factor in New York. Twenty hours before they are due to arrive the factor learns that in New York, due to excessive arrivals, oranges will not bring enough to satisfy freight charges, but if diverted to a factor in Philadelphia, they will bring a much larger price at no greater freight cost. He cannot communicate with Jones in time to make the change. The factor reroutes the oranges to Philadelphia, where they are destroyed by flood.
   (1) Did the factor have authority to reroute the shipment of oranges?
   (2) Is he liable for the loss?
   (3) Explain. (Former C.P.A. Examination question)

5. P authorized A to purchase two used tractors at the lowest possible price. A delegated to B the authority to purchase one tractor, and B purchased a tractor from T in P's name. A agreed to purchase another tractor from X at an agreed price; and A authorized C to sign the contract in P's name, which C did. P disclaims any liability for both purchases for lack of authority and refuses to accept the tractors.
   (1) Who is bound by these transactions?
   (2) Why?

6. P appointed A general manager of P's large department store and informed him that he had no authority to buy goods for sale in the store nor any authority to sell any goods himself. A fired B, a salesman, and employed C to take B's place. In P's presence, A made an excellent sale of merchandise to D, P remaining silent throughout the transaction. A also purchased merchandise from E and in P's name for sale in the store. Only P and A knew of P's limitation on A's authority.
   (1) Is P bound by these transactions?
   (2) Why?

7. (a) P authorized A in writing to sell and transfer title to certain merchandise for $10,000 and directed A to show the writing to anyone interested in the purchase. P told T that A had authority to sell the merchandise and that A's authority was contained in a writing possessed by A and available for T's examination. T did not examine the writing and, ignorant of A's limitation of authority to sell only for $10,000, purchased the merchandise from A for $9,000. P refused to accept the $9,000 and refused to deliver the merchandise, claiming that the transaction was not binding upon him.
      (1) Is P bound?
      (2) Why?
   (b) In the above problem, would the result have been any different if P had directed A not to disclose the $10,000 limitation and T had been ignorant of the written authorization and of its $10,000 limitation? Why?

8. A misappropriated merchandise from P's warehouse and, representing that the merchandise belonged to A, sold and delivered it to T—intending to pocket the proceeds payable in 30 days. T did not know that the merchandise belonged to P until P informed T that he ratified the transaction and demanded the purchase price at the end of the 30 days. T then informed P of his withdrawal from the transaction and tendered the return of the merchandise, which P refused.
   (1) Does P have a right against T for the purchase price?
   (2) Why?

9. A traveling salesman, authorized to contract to sell certain securities at par, reported to his principal that he had contracted to sell a large quantity at 1 percent below par. The principal withheld action upon the report for one month and then notified the vendee that the contract was repudiated. Is the principal bound by the contract? (Former C.P.A. Examination question)

10. (a) P authorized A to travel to X, examine two dozen typewriters for sale, and—if satisfactory to A—to purchase them for cash. A paid the travel charges and advanced the purchase price for the typewriters, which were delivered to A. P demands the typewriters, which A refuses to deliver until the travel costs and advance of purchase price have been paid.
      (1) May A so refuse?
      (2) Why?

(b) P authorized A to obtain a ready, willing, and able purchaser of P's land for $10,000, A to receive a 5 percent commission for doing so. T offered A a 5 percent commission if A could get P to sell his land to T for $10,000. T is such a ready, willing, and able purchaser, whom A introduced to P as willing to buy the land for $10,000. Just before the sale was about to be made P learned of the agreement for a commission between A and T, and P refused to sell the land to T.
   (1) Does A have a right against P for the commission promised him by P?
   (2) Why?

11. An infant, 17 years of age, authorized his agent to purchase certain bonds, the agent knowing the infancy of his principal. The agent purchased the bonds, disclosing the name of his principal but not disclosing the fact of infancy. The vendor did not know that the principal was an infant, and the agent had every reason to believe that the vendor was ignorant of this fact. Upon reaching the age 18, the infant disaffirmed the purchase, returned the bonds and all interest received thereon, and was reimbursed for the purchase price. Is the agent legally responsible to the vendor? (Former C.P.A. Examination question)

12. (a) P authorized A to purchase a particular lot of goods if it was satisfactory to A and to resell it at the highest price possible. A examined the lot, purchased it in his own name and with his own funds, sold it at a profit, and kept the proceeds. A misrepresented to P that the lot was unsatisfactory to A. P later learned of A's acts.
   (1) Does P have any right against A?
   (2) Why?

   (b) P authorized A to purchase certain goods at a specified price. A learns that the goods are deteriorating in quality but, without telling P of such deterioration, bought the goods. P did not know of the deterioration until he received the goods and thereby suffered loss.
   (1) Is A liable to P for such loss?
   (2) Why?

13. P authorized A, an infant, to purchase on 30 days credit certain goods from T but not to disclose P's identity to T. T refused to sell the goods to A if he was representing P and A misrepresented that he was purchasing the goods for himself. Relying on this, T subsequently sold the goods to A on 30 days credit, taking A's negotiable promissory note therefor. On A's failure to pay the note when due, T sued A on the note and obtained judgment. A has no assets. T then learned of P's identity and demanded the purchase price from him.
   (1) Is P liable to T for the purchase price?
   (2) Why?

14. P owed A $5,000 and delivered his horse to A with authority to sell the horse, retain $5,000 in satisfaction of the debt, and to pay P the remainder. P died and E, the executor of P's estate, demanded the return of the horse from A. A refused to deliver the horse to E.
   (1) Does E have a right to possession of the horse?
   (2) Why?

15. P authorized A, his purchasing agent employee, to buy merchandise for P's store when A considered such purchases necessary. A, in P's name, made various purchases from different wholesalers, including T, over a period of years. P always

paid for such purchases. P sent A a letter revoking A's authority; but, after the letter was sent and before A had received it, A purchased merchandise from T for P. P also had sent a letter to T stating that A's authority had been revoked; but T never received the letter, nor did T know of such revocation. After A had received P's letter, A made a second purchase from T in P's name and absconded with the goods.

(1) Is P bound by A's first purchase from T? Why?
(2) Is P bound by A's second purchase from T? Why?
(3) What should P do immediately?

16. An agent sent an order in the name of his principal, by mail the day before the death of the principal, to a merchant with whom he had a general arrangement for goods to be supplied on order during the year. The merchant, who was ignorant of the principal's death, filled the order within a reasonable time. The principal's executor refused to pay for the goods. Can the merchant recover? (Former C.P.A. Examination question)

17. A drew a check payable to his own order, forged P's signature to it, and indorsed and sold it to T, who was innocent of the forgery. T subsequently telephoned P and asked him whether the signature on the check was his and whether A was P's agent to buy goods for P. P mistakenly believed it was his signature and that A was his agent and answered "Yes," when in fact A was not his agent. A then contracted in P's name with T for the purchase of goods for the reasonable value of $1,000 and A drew a check to T's order for the purchase price, signing it in P's name by A.

(1) Is P liable to T on the forged check?
(2) Is P liable to T on the contract for the purchase of the goods from T?
(3) Is P liable to T on the check for the purchase price?

18. P innocently purchased stolen goods belonging to O. P's agent, A, without notice of the theft and pursuant to his authority, sold the goods to B. A paid O $500 in reasonable compromise of O's claim against A for conversion of the goods. Does A have any right against P for $500?

SOME PREVIOUS C.P.A. LAW EXAMINATION QUESTIONS AND AUTHOR'S MODEL ANSWERS

NOVEMBER, 1979

Number 1

Select the **best** answers for each of the following items.

31. Magnus Real Estate Developers, Inc., wanted to acquire certain tracts of land in Marshall Township in order to build a shopping center complex. To accomplish this goal, Magnus engaged Dexter, a sophisticated real estate dealer, to represent them in the purchase of the necessary land without revealing the existence of the agency. Dexter began to slowly but steadily acquire the requisite land. However, Dexter made the mistake of purchasing one tract outside the description of the land needed. Which of the following is correct under these circumstances?

a. The use of an agent by Magnus, an undisclosed principal, is manifestly illegal.
b. Either Magnus or Dexter may be held liable on the contracts for the land, including the land that was **not** within the scope of the proposed shopping center.
c. An undisclosed principal such as Magnus can have **no** liability under the contract since the third party believed he was dealing with Dexter as a principal.

d. An agent for an undisclosed principal assumes **no** liability as long as he registers his relationship to the principal with the clerk of the proper county having jurisdiction.

33. Wanamaker, Inc., engaged Anderson as its agent to purchase original oil paintings for resale by Wanamaker. Anderson's express authority was specifically limited to a maximum purchase price of $25,000 for any collection provided it contained a minimum of five oil paintings. Anderson purchased a seven-picture collection on Wanamaker's behalf for $30,000. Based upon these facts, which of the following is a correct legal conclusion?

a. The express limitation on Anderson's authority negates any apparent authority.
b. Wanamaker can **not** ratify the contract since Anderson's actions were clearly in violation of his contract.
c. If Wanamaker rightfully disaffirms the unauthorized contract, Anderson is personally liable to the seller.
d. Neither Wanamaker **nor** Anderson is liable on the contract since the seller was obligated to ascertain Anderson's authority.

Answer

1. 31.b(603–4) 33.c(611)

MAY, 1979

Number 1

Select the **best** answer for the following item.

40. Dolby was employed as an agent for the Ace Used Car Company to purchase newer model used cars. His authority was limited by a $3,000 maximum price for any car. A wholesaler showed him a 1938 classic car which was selling for $5,000. The wholesaler knew that Ace only dealt in newer model used cars and that Dolby had never paid more than $3,000 for any car. Dolby bought the car for Ace, convinced that it was worth at least $7,000. When he reported this to Williams, Ace's owner, Williams was furious but he nevertheless authorized processing of the automobile for resale. Williams also began pricing the car with antique car dealers who indicated that the current value of the car was $4,800. Williams called the wholesaler, told him that Dolby had exceeded his authority, that he was returning the car, and that he was demanding repayment of the purchase price. What is the wholesaler's **best** defense in the event of a lawsuit?

a. Dolby had apparent authority to purchase the car.
b. Dolby's purchase was effectively ratified by Ace.
c. Dolby had express authority to purchase the car.
d. Dolby had implied authority to purchase the car.

Answer

1. 40.b(573)

MAY, 1978

Number 1

Select the **best** answer for each of the following items.

2. Halliday engaged Fox as her agent. It was mutually agreed that Fox would **not** disclose that he was acting as Halliday's agent. Instead he was to deal with prospective

customers as if he were a principal acting on his own behalf. This he did and made several contracts for Halliday. Assuming Halliday, Fox, or the customer seeks to avoid liability on one of the contracts involved, which of the following statements is correct?

a. The third party may choose to hold either Fox or Halliday liable.
b. The third party can avoid liability because he believed he was dealing with Fox as a principal.
c. Halliday must ratify the Fox contracts in order to be held liable.
d. Fox has **no** liability once he discloses that Halliday was the real principal.

4. Winter is a sales agent for Magnum Enterprises. Winter has assumed an obligation to indemnify Magnum if any of Winter's customers fail to pay. Under these circumstances, which of the following is correct?

a. Winter's engagement must be in writing regardless of its duration.
b. Upon default, Magnum must first proceed against the delinquent purchaser-debtor.
c. The above facts describe a *del credere* agency relationship and Winter will be liable in the event his customers fail to pay Magnum.
d. There is **no** fiduciary relationship on either Winter's or Magnum's part.

10. Futterman operated a cotton factory and employed Marra as a general purchasing agent to travel through the southern states to purchase cotton. Futterman telegraphed Marra instructions from day to day as to the price to be paid for cotton. Marra entered a cotton district in which she had not previously done business and represented that she was purchasing cotton for Futterman. Although directed by Futterman to pay no more than 25 cents a pound, Marra bought cotton from Anderson at 30 cents a pound, which was the prevailing offering price at that time. Futterman refused to take the cotton. Under these circumstances, which of the following is correct?

a. The negation of actual authority to make the purchase effectively eliminates any liability for Futterman.
b. Futterman is **not** liable on the contract.
c. Marra has **no** potential liability.
d. Futterman is liable on the contract.

Answer

1. 2.a(602–3) 4.c(549) 10.d(595)

MAY, 1977

Number 2

Select the **best** answer for the following item.

23. Star Corporation dismissed Moon, its purchasing agent. Star published a notice in appropriate trade journals which stated: "This is to notify all parties concerned that Moon is no longer employed by Star Corporation, and the corporation assumes no further responsibility for his acts." Moon called on several of Star's suppliers with whom he had previously dealt, and when he found one who was unaware of his dismissal, he placed a substantial order for merchandise to be delivered to a warehouse in which Moon rented space. Star had rented space in the warehouse in the past when its storage facilities were crowded. Moon also called on several suppliers with whom Star had never dealt and made purchases from them on open account in the name of Star. The merchandise purchased by Moon was delivered to the warehouse. Moon then

sold all the merchandise and absconded with the money. Which of the following most accurately describes the legal implications of this situation?

a. Moon had apparent authority to make contracts on Star's behalf with suppliers with whom Moon was currently dealing as Star's agent if they had **no** actual knowledge of his dismissal.
b. The suppliers who previously had **no** dealings with Star can enforce the contracts against Star if the suppliers had **no** actual knowledge of Moon's lack of authority.
c. Star is liable on the Moon contracts to all suppliers who had dealt with Moon in the past as Star's agent and who have **not** received personal notice, even though they had read the published notice.
d. Constructive notice by publication in the appropriate trade journals is an effective notice to all third parties regardless of whether they had previously dealt with Moon or read the notice.

Answer

2. 23.a(622, 564–65)

Part Seven:
Business Organizations

A. Partnerships

Chapter 42

NATURE OF PARTNERSHIP

The "general partnership" is governed by the Uniform Partnership Act and is an association of two or more persons (1) to carry on (2) as co-owners (3) a business for profit. It is distinguished from: (1) *a corporation* in its creation, as a legal entity, and in its liability, operation, and duration; (2) *a business trust* in which the owners of interests in property transfer such interests to trustees to manage the business or enterprise; (3) *a joint venture* in purpose and duration; and (4) from two unusual types of partnership—(a) *the limited partnership* with general and limited ("special") partners, governed by the Uniform Limited Partnership Act, and (b) *the joint-stock company* in which the members have transferable shares and the management is concentrated in representatives of the members. A partner may be either: ostensible, secret, dormant, nominal, retiring, incoming, surviving, continuing, general, and limited in a limited partnership.

SECTION I. GENERAL CONCEPT

A Form of Business Organization

Partnership is a very old form of business organization. To a large extent the law governing partnerships is in the statutory form of the Uniform Partnership Act, hereinafter referred to as the U.P.A.

A choice of sole proprietorship, corporation, or partnership as a form of business organization depends upon the business needs and purposes of the particular enterprise in which the organization is to engage. Each has its advantages and disadvantages, and some of the factors which are considered in making this choice are: the expense and complexity of creation, method of operation, credit, liability, risk of loss, and duration.

Definition

Under U.P.A., sec. 6, A *general partnership is "an association of two or more persons to carry on as co-owners a business for profit."* The word "partnership" designates a legal relationship of persons called "partners," or "co-partners" as they are sometimes termed. There is considerable dispute as to whether or not a partnership is a legal entity separate and distinct from its members. For some purposes it is, and for others it is not, a legal entity. A partnership consists of persons in a certain relationship and, under U.P.A., a partnership is an entity, as for the purpose of holding property. However, under U.P.A., a partnership also comprises the members thereof, as is indicated by their respective liabilities.

SECTION II. THE GENERAL PARTNERSHIP DISTINGUISHED FROM OTHER FORMS OF BUSINESS ORGANIZATION

Corporation

A partnership may be distinguished from a corporation in its creation, as a legal entity, and in its liability, operation, and duration. A partnership is formed by the voluntary agreement between the partners, while a corporation is formed only pursuant to statutory authority. A partnership is a legal entity in some respects and not in others and, in the absence of statute to the contrary, can sue and be sued only in the names of the individual partners. A corporation is a legal entity, separate and distinct from the shareholders, and can sue and be sued only in the corporate name. Each and every partner is liable for the partnership debts, while the shareholders are not liable for the corporate debts. A partnership acts through its partners, while a corporation acts through its elected or appointed officials. Partners control a partnership, while shareholders have an exceedingly small degree of control over the corporation. The death, bankruptcy, or withdrawal of a partner, or the admission of a new partner, dissolves the partnership, while such occurrences with reference to a shareholder or a director have no effect on the continuance of the corporation.

Business Trust

A business trust is a form of association created by owners of interests in property transferring such interests to trustees in exchange for certificates of interests or shares in the property, the trustees to manage the business or enterprise. There is a split of the legal and equitable title to property. Whether or not a business trust is a partnership depends upon the right of control which the certificate holders have over the trustees in the management of the business. If the certificate holders have no control, it cannot be a partnership; if they do have control, it is a partnership. *Usually a business trust is not a partnership.* Partners have full control in the management of the business, while in a business trust the certificate holders do not have any control. Partners are liable for partnership obligations, while in a business trust the certificate holders have no liability to creditors of the business. The death, bankruptcy, or withdrawal of a partner dissolves a partnership, while such occurrences do not affect the continuance of a business trust. A business trust has many of the characteristics of a corporation and it attempts to acquire the benefits of a partnership and of a corporation. It is sometimes referred to as a "Massachusetts Trust."

Joint Venture

A joint venture, or joint adventure, is a form of business organization which is not called a partnership but, because of its similarity to a "general" or an "ordinary" partnership, many of the principles of partnership law are applied to it. *Joint venture differs from a general partnership in its purpose and duration.* The joint venture usually is formed for a single undertaking which does not require the full attention of the members thereof. A general partnership may be formed for a single undertaking, but this is unusual. Inasmuch as the members of a joint venture *have control* over their activities they are liable for the debts of the joint venture. Members of a joint venture usually have very limited powers to affect the contractual relations of each other, and there is no mutual agency as in a general partnership. An example of a joint venture is where two parties agree to sell their individual properties together for the highest price.

Unusual Types of Partnership

The general partnership should be distinguished from certain unusual types of association which are essentially partnerships but which are not called such, except for the "limited partnership." Only the limited partnership and joint stock company will be considered briefly here.

Limited Partnership. Limited partnership is a form of partnership. It exists only by compliance with statutory authority. With a few exceptions it has all the characteristics of a general partnership. Limited partners *cannot participate in the management and control* of the partnership and, consequently, are not individually liable for partnership obligations. The death, bankruptcy, or withdrawal of a limited partner in no way affects the continuance of the limited partnership, unless no limited partner remains in the partnership. The subject of limited partnership will be considered separately later.[1]

---

[1] See below, pp. 666–73.

Joint-Stock Company. A joint-stock company is a form of partnership in which the members have shares in the company which are transferable without affecting the continued existence of the company. Authority to manage the company's affairs is concentrated in the representatives of the members of the company, but because the members have *power to control* the conduct of their representatives, they are personally liable for the debts of the company. A joint-stock company has many of the characteristics of a corporation.[2]

Classification of Partners

In a general partnership the partners may be classified as: ostensible, secret, dormant, nominal, retiring, incoming, surviving, or continuing. In a limited partnership the partners are classified as general or limited.

Secret Partner. A secret partner is a partner who actively participates in the business but is not known to the public as a partner.

Dormant Partner. A dormant partner is a partner who is not known to the public as such and who does not actively participate in the partnership business.

Ostensible Partner. An ostensible partner, sometimes called a "public" partner, is a person, who holds himself out, or permits others to hold him out, publicly as a partner, whether or not he actually is a partner. He usually engages actively in the partnership business. If he does not take an active part in the business, he is sometimes called a "silent" partner.

Nominal Partner. A nominal partner is not a partner at all but is a person who holds himself out, or permits others to hold him out, as a partner. He is sometimes called an "ostensible" partner.

Retiring Partner. A retiring partner is a partner who leaves a partnership.

Incoming Partner. An incoming partner is a partner who has come into an existing partnership.

Surviving Partner. A surviving partner is a partner surviving after the death of another partner.

Continuing Partner. A continuing partner is a partner continuing the business after the partnership has been dissolved.

General and Limited Partners. A limited partnership has one or more general partners and one or more limited partners. A general partner is an ordinary partner, as in a general partnership, while a limited partner is a partner with no control in the management of the partnership and who is not personally liable for the limited partnership obligations. A limited partner is sometimes called a "special" partner.

---

[2] See below, p. 681; ftn. 1.

Chapter 43

CREATION OF PARTNERSHIP

Under the U.P.A., any individual, partnership, corporation, and any other association *can* be a partner. In a majority of states a corporation *may* be a partner. Two or more persons must expressly or impliedly agree (1) to carry on (2) as co-owners (3) a business for profit. A person can *be liable as a partner* by estoppel, but he is not a partner unless he agrees to these three elements. The law of Contracts determines if a partnership agreement is within the Statute of Frauds.

A "business" is every trade, occupation, or profession, and it is "carried on" when it is being conducted in a continuing manner. Co-ownership must be of a business, not of property. *The receipt by a person of a share of the profits of a business is prima facie evidence that he is a partner* in the business, but no such inference is drawn if such profits were received in payment: (1) as a debt by installments or otherwise; (2) as wages of an employee or rent to a landlord; (3) as an annuity to a widow or representative of a deceased partner; (4) as interest on a loan, though the amount of payment vary with the profits of the business; or (5) as the consideration for the sale of a good-will of a business or other property by installments or otherwise. If to these five instances there is added the element of control in the management of the business, there is an inference of partnership.

SECTION I. PARTIES

The parties to a partnership enter into an agreement, and the law of Contracts is applicable in determining those who may be parties to a partnership agreement. All persons who have capacity to contract may be partners. Under U.P.A., sec. 2, a person "includes individuals, partnerships, corporations, and other associations." Infants, insane persons except those adjudicated to be insane, married women, and aliens who are not enemy aliens may be partners. Infant or insane partners have the power of avoidance or rescission as they do in contract. Rescission may occur also for fraud and material misrepresentation practiced by one partner on another in inducing him to become a partner. A corporation has capacity to contract and, therefore, can be a partner, but it may not become a partner unless the corporation has been expressly authorized to do so by statute or by charter. In a majority of states a corporation may be a partner.

SECTION II. METHOD, FORM, AND ILLEGALITY

Method

Partnership is a voluntary business association of persons formed pursuant to an agreement. The agreement manifests their intention and, *if it contains those elements requisite to the formation of a partnership, the legal relationship of partnership has been created.* Just as the manifestations of the parties had a particular significance in the law of Contracts and of Agency in creating those legal relationships, so is it true in the law of partnership. The agreement of the parties may expressly or impliedly create a partnership.

Express Agreement. The agreement of the parties is usually a contract, although not necessarily so, expressly providing for the formation of a partnership. It usually is in writing and is called "articles of partnership." An agreement of the parties contemplating the formation of a partnership and using the terms "partnership" and "partners" does not of itself create a partnership. Partnership is a legal relationship which exists *if the elements of a partnership exist;* the parties' intention to create a partnership and the use of the words "partnership" and "partners" are not sufficient in themselves to create a partnership. *A partnership is an association of two or more persons to carry on as co-owners a business for profit.* It is a question of law whether or not the agreement creates a partnership. A partnership may occur even if the agreement between the parties expressly excludes their relationship as partners.

Implied Agreement. The manifestation of the parties is the basis for a determination of whether or not a partnership has been formed. When the parties do not manifest any express intent to create a partnership, their manifestation in the form of a written or oral expression or other conduct must be interpreted to determine their intentions and whether or not a partnership exists. *If their manifestations comply with the requisites of partnership, then it is implied that their intention was to create a partnership and a partnership is formed.* The test of partnership is whether or not the elements in the definition of partnership exist.

Application of Estoppel. A partnership is formed by agreement among the parties and only those parties are partners. A person cannot become a partner in any other way and, therefore, *a person cannot become a "partner by estoppel,"* U.P.A., sec. 7 (1), provides, "Except as provided by section 16 persons who are not partners as to each other are not partners as to third persons." Section 16 deals with estoppel and provides for the *liability* of one who is estopped to deny that he is a partner. If a person holds himself out, or consents to another holding him out, as a partner to a third person, when he is not a partner, and the third person changes his position materially by *extending credit* to the purported partnership in reasonable reliance on the holding out, he is a nominal partner and cannot deny later that a partnership exists of which he is a member. Although it is commonly said that the person so holding out is a "partner by estoppel," he actually is not a partner because he is not a party to the agreement. However, as far as third persons are concerned, *he is liable to third persons as a partner.* A person who holds himself out as a partner may be enjoined from continuing to do so.

For the principle of estoppel to apply there must be: a holding out of one's status as a partner; *and* a material change of position *only by extending credit* to the purported partnership in reliance on the holding out. (A permits B to represent to C that A and B are partners, when they are not partners. D, unaware of the holding out, advances credit to the purported partnership of A and B. A is not estopped to deny that he is a partner. If C had extended credit in reliance on B's representation, A would be estopped.) The holding out may occur by a writing, words, or other conduct to which he consents, made by the purported partner or by someone else. Generally, a person who learns that he has been held out by another as a partner has a duty to dispel the impression of his status as a partner. His silence with knowledge, coupled with a duty to speak, is the equivalent of consent to the holding out. He must take reasonable steps to do this depending upon the circumstances of such holding out; usually publication in the proper newspapers in the proper place is sufficient to dispel the impression of partnership. Under U.P.A., sec. 16(1), if the holding out was made in a *public manner,* the person so held out as a partner is liable to third persons who subsequently dealt with the purported partnership on credit, regardless of whether or not such third persons had knowledge of the holding out or representation.

Form

No particular form of partnership agreement is necessary, although it is most desirable to have the agreement in writing so as to preclude future uncertainty regarding the terms thereof. Some provisions of the partnership agreement may come within the Statute of Frauds under the law of Contracts and, if so, they are unenforceable unless they have complied with requirements of the Statute. A partnership agreement not to be performed within one year from the making thereof is within the Statute. A partnership agreement *to transfer* an interest in real property to a partner also *is* within the Statute, although a partnership agreement *to engage* in the real estate business is *not* within the Statute. Generally, a promise made by an incoming partner to assume previous partnership obligations is not within the Statute inasmuch as it is made to the partner *debtors*[1]—namely, the partners in the existing partnership, and not to the *creditors* of the partnership. However, it should be noted that such a promise creates a third party creditor beneficiary contract which is enforceable by the creditor.[2]

The articles of partnership usually contain the following information: names of the partners; purpose of the partnership; name of the partnership; duration of the partnership; location of the partnership business; the capitalization or contributions of the partners; how the profits and losses are to be shared; a system of accounts and provision for the time when the partnership books are to be closed and the individual partners' accounts credited or debited; salary and withdrawals of each partner; the amount of time which each partner is to devote to the business; duties and authority of each partner; restrictions on the authority of each partner; and the method and priority of distribution of assets among the partners on dissolution. Sometimes a partnership has bylaws to implement the articles of partnership.

A partnership may use any name it wishes, provided it complies with whatever statute is in effect regarding such names. Some statutes provide that a person who is not a partner may not have his name in the partnership name; or that "& Co." must not be used to mislead the public into believing that the business is a corporation, but this phrase may be used to indicate that there are partners in the partnership other than the one whose name appears in the partnership name. Statutes usually require that partnerships must record a certificate indicating the name of the partnership, its location, the names of the partners and their addresses, and other information. If the statute is not complied with regarding the recording of such a certificate, the partnership will not be permitted to sue.

Illegality

The law of Contracts applies in connection with the legality of partnership agreements and, if the agreement is contrary to statute or to public policy as declared by the courts in its purpose or formation, it is illegal and the agreement is void. No partnership results from an illegal agreement, unless the illegal matter can be separated from the legal matter, in which event the partnership exists only for the legal purposes. If the agreement is illegal, the courts usually leave the parties where they find them and give no relief to any party to the agreement. *The partnership just does not exist.* (A and B agree to

[1] See above, pp. 87–88. Also present are: the promisor's *assumption* of the debt; and the promise made for the benefit of the incoming partner promisor and not *primarily for the debtors.*

[2] See above, pp. 76 ff.

be a partnership to carry on a business unlawful by statute, e.g., to commit a crime. There is no partnership for this purpose.)

SECTION III. THE PURPOSE OF THE ASSOCIATION

A partnership occurs when there is a voluntary association for the purpose of (1) *carrying on* (2) *as co-owners* (3) *a business for profit.* There is no partnership until the parties by their agreement expressly or impliedly intend to become partners. An agreement to become partners at a *future time* does not create a partnership at the time the agreement is formed. *Partnership occurs at the moment when the parties by their agreement intend their status to be that of partners.*

Carrying on a Business for Profit

It is essential to a partnership that the parties be *carrying on a business for profit.* By "business" is meant the carrying on of a series of commercial transactions as an enterprise. U.P.A., sec. 2, describes business as including "every trade, occupation, or profession." A business in the mercantile sense is carried on for the purpose of making a profit and is to be distinguished from fraternal or other nonprofit associations which are not partnerships. Although members of nonprofit associations are not partners, nevertheless, they may expose themselves to liability under the law of Agency if they authorize others to affect their contractual relations with third persons. A business is *"carried on" when it is being conducted in a continuing manner.*

Co-owners of a Business for Profit

Partners are *co-owners* of a *business* for profit. Co-ownership of property does not, of itself, create a partnership, but it is a factor for consideration in connection with other circumstances in determining whether or not a partnership exists. U.P.A., sec. 7(2), lists various forms of co-ownership of *property* which, in themselves, are insufficient to establish a partnership. Joint tenancy, tenancy in common, tenancy by the entirety, joint property, common property, and part ownership in property do not make a *business for profit* and, even though the co-owners share in the profits made from the use of their property, there is no partnership. Co-ownership of property is not necessary for a partnership; partners may own property individually which they have contributed to the partnership only for use in the partnership business. If to the fact of co-ownership of property is added the right to share in gross returns, this also is insufficient evidence to establish co-ownership of the business, although it is some evidence of such.

Co-ownership of a business means that the parties have a *mutual interest* in carrying on the business for profit. Co-ownership of property, control over the management of the business, and the sharing of losses constitute evidence to prove co-ownership of the business. However, the *sharing of profits* is sufficiently *strong* evidence to prove *co-ownership* of a business and, accordingly, under U.P.A., sec. 7(4), "The receipt by a person of a share of the profits of a business is prima facie evidence that he is a partner in the business." However, no such inference may be drawn if the person receiving such profits has no *mutual interest* in the carrying on of the business. There is no mutual interest and, therefore, no inference if "such profits were received in payment: (a) As a debt by installments or otherwise, (b) As wages of an employee or rent to a landlord, (c) As an annuity to a widow or representative of a deceased partner, (d) As interest on a loan, though the amount vary with the profits of the business, (e) As the consideration for the sale of a good-will of a business or other property by installments or otherwise." If, in these instances when the *receipt of profits alone* does not create co-ownership, there is added the element of control in the management of the business, the two factors of *sharing in the profits and the right of control* constitute sufficiently strong evidence to prove co-ownership of the business and to make such person a partner. Each of the above instances will be considered briefly.

Payment of a Debt. A *creditor* has no mutual interest in the carrying on of the business; his interest is solely in the profits for the purpose of *paying his debt.* Often creditors agree to run a failing business in order to produce enough partnership profit to pay their claims. Such creditors are not partners inasmuch as they have no mutual interest in the carrying on of the business; their interest is in the payment of their claims, they do not own the property interest in the business, and they merely operate the business on behalf of the debtor. Profits earned by the partnership business carried on by the creditors belong to the partnership, although such profits are to be made available to the creditors.

Wages or Rents. The payment of *wages* to an employee, or of *rents* to a landlord, out of profits does not create that co-ownership of the business necessary to a partnership and, therefore, wage earners are not partners with their employers and landlords are not partners with their tenants. The fact that their wages or rents may vary as the profits vary is irrelevant. A wage earner may, in addition to his share in the profits as compensation, have the right to exercise control over the management of the business, which makes him a co-owner of the business and, therefore, a partner. A landlord who shares in the *gross receipts from the use of land or chattels* is not a co-owner of the business to which such property is put. *The rental of land for a percentage of the crops does not make the landlord a partner.*

Annuity to Widow or Representative of a Deceased Partner. On the death of a partner it is often agreed between the remaining partners and the widow or representative of the estate of the decedent that the business will be continued by the surviving partners and a share in the profits will be paid to the widow or representative *in lieu of liquidation and payment of the decedent's interest in the partnership.* Such payments are in the form of an *annuity,* but the recipient is not a co-owner of the business and is not a partner therein.

Should the recipient of such payment have the right to participate in the control of the management, then the combination of the receipt of profits and the right of control in the management of the business creates co-ownership of the business and, therefore, the recipient is a partner.

Interest on a Loan. A person advancing a loan to a business, the interest on which is to be paid out of the profits, is an *investor* and is not a co-owner of the business. He has no mutual interest in the carrying on of the business for profit; he is concerned solely with the acquisition of *interest on the loan* from the profits. Often investors wish to supervise the management of the business with little, if any, control therein. Supervision, and no affirmative control, over the business does not make the investor a co-owner of the business. However, an investor's degree of control over the business may be such that, in conjunction with his receipt of a share of the profits, it is sufficient to make him a co-owner of the business and, therefore, a partner.

Consideration for Sale of Partnership Property. The terms of sale of tangible or intangible (e.g., good-will) property of a business may provide that the *sales price* is to be paid by a share in the profits. This interest in the profits is insufficient to make the seller a co-owner of the business. There is no *mutual interest* in the carrying on of the business for profit.

Chapter 44

PARTNERSHIP PROPERTY

The *assets* of a partnership are: (1) the partnership property; and (2) the contributions of the partners necessary for the payment of all the partnership liabilities. The property acquired by a partnership, usually by contribution of property by the partners or by the use of partnership funds in the purchase of property, is partnership property. Title may be in the name of one or more partners individually who then hold it in trust for the partnership, or it may be in the partnership name. *Partnership personal property* may be transferred by any partner with actual or apparent authority. With respect to *partnership real property*, title in the partnership name can be conveyed only in the partnership name and title in the name of one or more of the partners individually can be conveyed by them in their own names, not recoverable by the partnership if the conveying partner or partners had actual or apparent authority so to convey, or the property has been conveyed to a bona fide purchaser for value without notice of their lack of authority.

Each partner's right in specific partnership property is to possess the property for partnership purposes; he is a "tenant in partnership." A decedent partner's interest in *partnership personal property* passes to the surviving partners for partnership purposes, but his interest in *partnership real property in the partnership name* is considered as personal property for the purpose of winding up partnership affairs and passes to the surviving partners for this purpose. If legal title to partnership real property *is in the name of a decedent partner*, it vests in his heirs or devisees who hold it in trust for the partnership. All partnership property remaining after partnership obligations have been satisfied is personal property for the purpose of distribution.

SECTION I. NATURE AND ACQUISITION OF PARTNERSHIP PROPERTY

Nature

The *assets* of a partnership are the *partnership property*, and the *contributions of the partners* necessary for the payment of all the partnership liabilities. The partnership property consists of all that real or personal property acquired by the partnership at the time of its formation or subsequently, regardless of the method of acquisition. Such property may be an original or subsequent contribution by the partners, or it may be property created by the use of partnership property or of property belonging to the partners. The property may be intangible, such as the firm's interest in an insurance policy taken out by the firm on the life of a partner, the premiums having been paid by the firm. A partnership may have the right to use certain property which is still owned individually by the partners.

Acquisition

Partnership property usually is acquired by contributions of such property by the partners or by the use of partnership funds in the purchase of such property. Under U.P.A., sec. 8(2), "Unless the contrary intention appears, property acquired with partnership funds is partnership property." The intention of the parties determines the ownership of the property. (A and B are partners who agree to buy a horse from partnership funds, such horse to be a part of B's share in the profits, or as an advance to B. The horse is the property of B. If the horse had been purchased without such agreement, it would be partnership property.) When property is purchased by individual partners out of their own funds the property is owned by the individual partners, unless the bill of sale, deed of the property, or agreement between the parties indicates to the contrary. Similarly, if partners owning property as tenants in common use such property in the partnership business, such property still belongs to the individual partners as tenants in common, the partnership having merely the right of use.

SECTION II. TITLE TO PARTNERSHIP PROPERTY

Title to partnership property may be in the name of one or more partners, individually, who hold the same for the partnership and, under U.P.A, such property may be held in the partnership name, regardless of whether it is real or personal property. The extent of a partnership's interest in real property is entire, as though the partnership were a legal person; even words of inheritance are unnecessary.

Transfer of Partnership Property

Personal property of the partnership may be transferred by any partner with actual or apparent authority to do so. The manner of conveying real property of the partnership depends upon the terms of the conveyance to the partnership. Title in the name of the partnership can be conveyed only in the partnership name. Any partner can convey the title to *real property in the partnership name* by executing a *conveyance in the partnership name.* However, the partnership can recover the property, unless either the conveying partner had actual or apparent authority so to convey, or the property subsequently was conveyed to a bona fide purchaser for value without notice of the partner's lack of authority, in which case the partnership cannot recover the property. A partner's execution of a *conveyance of real property in his own name* when the *real property is in the name of the partnership,* passes equitable title to the grantee if it is within the actual or apparent authority of the partner. Since the grantee can, in a court with equity powers, compel the partnership to convey the legal title, the grantee has what is called "equitable title." If the real property of the partnership is *in the name of one or more but not all of the partners individually,* and the record does not disclose the interest of the partnership, only such partners have legal title to the property and they can convey title to the property by a conveyance in their own names. However, the partnership can recover the property, unless either the conveying partners had actual or apparent authority so to convey, or the grantee or his assignee is a bona fide purchaser for value without knowledge of the partner's lack of authority, in which case the partnership cannot recover the property. If the real property of the partnership is in the names of all of the partners individually, only the partners have legal title to the property and a conveyance executed by all of them passes all their rights in the property.

Individual Partner's Interest Therein

A partner has a property right in the specific property of the partnership and is a co-owner of such property with the other partners. He is called a "tenant in partnership." A tenancy in partnership is very different from a tenancy in common, joint tenancy, and other interests in real property held by more than one person. The partner's right in specific partnership property cannot be transferred by him unless all the other partners join in such transfer of the same property; it is not subject to legal process—e.g., attachment or execution—by his *personal* creditors; and it is not subject to dower or curtesy, which are common law interests of surviving spouses in real property. *Each partner has a right to possess specific partnership property for partnership purposes, unless the partners agree to the contrary.*

A decedent partner's interest in partnership *personal property* passes to the surviving partners or partner or, if there are none, to the legal representative of his estate, who possesses the property solely for partnership purposes. Although a decedent's interest in *real property* descends to his heirs, this is not so in the case of a decedent partner's interest in *specific partnership real property held in the partnership name.* Such interest in real property is considered in equity as *personal property* for the purpose of liquidating the partnership assets and of winding up the partnership affairs and passes to the surviving partners for such purpose. The principle of equity converting partnership realty into personalty for partnership purposes is called the "doctrine of equitable conversion." All partnership property remaining after partnership obligations have been satisfied is *personal property for the purpose of distribution.* If partnership real property is held in the name of a decedent partner then, inasmuch as he had legal title in trust for the partnership, the legal title vests in his *heirs or devisees,* who hold the same *in trust* for the partnership.

Chapter 45

RIGHTS AND DUTIES OF PARTNERS AMONG THEMSELVES

Unless otherwise agreed, the U.P.A. prescribes certain rights and duties of partners. All partners have equal rights in partnership management and operation; ordinary matters are decided by a majority of the partners, but unanimity is required to act contrary to the partnership agreement and dissenting partners are not bound. A partner has a right of reimbursement and indemnity for expenditures or losses reasonably incurred while acting authorizedly, and a right of contribution from other partners for his payment of partnership obligations in excess of his share. A partner has no right to additional compensation for his services to the partnership, except for winding up partnership affairs on the death of a partner. Partners share in profits and surplus equally, and they share in all losses as profits are shared. Unanimity is required for the admission of a new partner. Partnership books are to be kept at the principal place of the partnership business with the right of inspection and reproduction by partners. A "partnership at will" occurs if partnership business is continued after the expiration of the agreed partnership time for doing business. A partner is not entitled to a formal accounting prior to dissolution, with certain exceptions. A partner may assign his interest in the partnership without thereby dissolving the partnership, unless he also ceases to be engaged in the carrying on of the partnership business. An individual partner's unpaid judgment creditor may obtain a court "charging order" against that partner's interest in the partnership.

A partner is liable to the partnership for partnership loss caused by his failure to perform his partnership duties. As a fiduciary for the partnership: all profits and benefits acquired by him while acting for the partnership he holds in trust for the partnership; and he must make full disclosure to the other

partners of all transactions in connection with partnership business. Generally, one partner cannot sue another partner at law until there has been a complete settlement of partnership affairs and a balance struck, with certain exceptions.

SECTION I. RIGHTS

Articles of partnership usually specify the rights and duties of the various partners in connection with the carrying on of the partnership business. When the parties fail to make such express provision, it is implied that their intention is to comply with ordinary mercantile rules in effect. The rules to be discussed apply unless the parties have provided to the contrary in their agreement. First the rights, then the duties, and then the enforcement of such rights and duties of the partners, will be discussed.

In Partnership Operation

Management of Partnership. *Unless the partners agree to the contrary*, all partners have *equal rights in the management and operation of the partnership business,* regardless of the nature and extent of the partners' contributions.

Majority Vote. U.P.A., sec. 18(h), provides, "Any difference arising as to ordinary matters connected with the partnership business may be decided by a majority of the partners; but no act in contravention of any agreement between the partners may be done rightfully without the consent of all the partners." Majority rule applies to the *ordinary,* internal affairs of the partnership. "It is clear, however, that no majority however large can, against the dissent of the minority, change the essential nature or extent of the partnership business as originally agreed upon, as, for example, to alter or amend the articles, reduce or increase the capital, embark upon a new business, change its agreed location, alter the share of a partner, admit a new member, and the like. If they attempt to do so, the dissenting partners will not be bound."[1]

Reimbursement and Indemnity. A partner has the right to be reimbursed and indemnified for any expenditures or losses which he reasonably incurred while acting within his authority in carrying on the business in a proper way. A partner has a right of contribution from other partners to the extent that he has paid more than his share of the partnership obligations. A partner has no right of reimbursement or indemnity for expenditure or loss caused by the partner's negligence or bad faith.

Compensation. *Unless the partners agree to the contrary, a partner is not entitled to any additional compensation for his services rendered to the partnership.* His right to share in the profits is deemed to be adequate com-

---

[1] Floyd R. Mechem, *Elements of the Law of Partnership*, 2d ed. (Chicago: Callaghan & Co., 1920), sec. 281.

pensation. If the illness of one partner causes the other partners to carry a heavier load in operating the partnership business, such partners are not entitled to any extra compensation. Many partnership agreements, however, provide for special duties to be performed by a partner and specify that he is to receive compensation therefor. A partner may be the manager of the partnership business and obtain, in addition to his share in the profits, a specified salary for his services as manager. Although at one time a surviving partner was not entitled to any compensation for his services in *winding up the partnership affairs, nevertheless, today, in the absence of any agreement to the contrary, a surviving partner is entitled to compensation for such services.*

Advances. Advances by partners which are not additions to their capital contributions are loans to the partnership. Advances cannot be made contrary to the partnership agreement. In the absence of agreement to the contrary, the partner making such advance is entitled to interest thereon from the date such advance was made and is entitled to be repaid such advance when due. If the partnership assets are insufficient to make such repayment, then all the partners have a duty to contribute to the extent of their respective shares of such deficiency.

Capital. Property contributed by partners for use and risk in the carrying on of the partnership business is capital. On dissolution, or as otherwise agreed by the partners, after partnership liabilities have been satisfied, each partner's capital contribution is to be returned to the partner. In the absence of agreement to the contrary, a partner is not entitled to interest on such capital except from the date when repayment should have been made.

Profit and Loss. *In the absence of agreement to the contrary,* partners have the right to *share in partnership profits and surplus equally,* and have the duty to *share in partnership losses,* whether capital or otherwise, *in the same ratio as they share the profits.* (A contributed $10,000, B contributed $7,000, and C contributed $4,000 to the partnership business, making a total capital investment of $21,000. On dissolution the firm suffered a loss of $15,000. A, B, and C each are to contribute $5,000 toward this loss. Therefore, A receives $5,000 and B receives $2,000 as the remainder of their capital contributions, and C contributes $1,000 to make up his deficiency.) Although the capital contributions vary, nevertheless, *in the absence of agreement to the contrary, losses are shared as profits are shared.* Whether the profits are to be retained in the business as additions to the capital contribution of each partner, or are to be made available for distribution, depends upon the terms of the partnership agreement.

New Partners. A partnership is a voluntary association and, in the absence of agreement to the contrary, a person cannot become a member of a partnership without the consent of *all* the partners.

Partnership Books. Unless the partners agree to the contrary, partnership books are to be kept at the principal place of the partnership business, and the partners have a right to inspect and make copies of such books at all times.

Continuation of Partnership. A partnership may continue in business even though the agreed time of its duration has expired and, if there is no express agreement regarding such continuance, it is a *partnership at will.* A continuation of a partnership business by the partners without liquidation or settlement is prima facie evidence that the partnership is being continued. The rights and duties of the partners remain the same as they were at the time when the partnership was to have expired by its terms.

Accounting. A formal account of partnership affairs is inconvenient and costly and, inasmuch as the partnership accounts are available for examination by the partners, *a partner is not entitled to a formal account prior to dissolution,* with certain exceptions. As exceptions, a partner has a right to an accounting without dissolution: when he has been wrongfully excluded from participation in the partnership business; when the partnership agreement so provides; when a partner has acquired secret profits from his participation in the partnership business and has not accounted to the partnership for them; and whenever other circumstances are such that it would be just and reasonable to require an accounting.[2]

Property Rights

Under U.P.A., sec. 24, a partner has three property rights: "(1) his rights in specific partnership property, (2) his interest in the partnership, and (3) his right to participate in the management." A partner's rights in specific partnership property and his right to participate in the management of the partnership business have been discussed already.[3] *A partner's interest in the partnership consists of his interest in profits and surplus,* and this property right is personal property. Of these three property rights, *a partner individually may assign only one*—namely *his interest in the partnership. Such assignment does not dissolve the partnership,* but if the partner also ceases to be engaged in the carrying on of the partnership business then the partnership is dissolved. The assignee acquires only the assigning partner's rights to surplus and profits to the extent as provided in the assignment. On dissolution the assignee has the right to the assigning partner's interest in the partnership and the right to an accounting from the date of the last accounting agreed to by all the partners.

Charging Order. An unpaid judgment creditor of an individual partner may obtain a court order charging the debtor partner's interest in the partnership and directing that the payment of surplus and other moneys due the debtor partner by the partnership be paid to a receiver, appointed by the court for this purpose. Payments made to the receiver are, in turn, paid to the judgment creditor until the judgment has been satisfied. The interest charged may be redeemed by the debtor partner at any time prior to foreclosure, and foreclosure and sale of the debtor partner's interest in the partnership does not cause the partnership to be dissolved.

---

[2] 7 *Uniform Laws Annotated,* Uniform Partnership Act, 1914, sec. 22.

[3] See above, pp. 642–43, 645 ff.

SECTION II. DUTIES

To Perform Partnership Agreement

A partner has the duty to comply with the partnership agreement, which usually provides specific duties for various partners. A partner's *failure to observe and perform* his partnership duties subjects him to liability for loss caused to the partnership by such failure. The cost of employing others, whether partners or not, to perform the delinquent partner's duties is borne by such delinquent partner. Conduct by a partner *in violation* of his partnership duties causing loss to the partnership subjects him to liability for such loss.

Good Faith

A partner is a fiduciary and owes his complete loyalty to the partnership. He has a duty to act for the best interests of the partnership and not for himself alone. A partner cannot retain for himself, and he must account to the partnership for, any benefit or profit which he has acquired in any transaction performed in connection with the partnership. All profits and benefits so acquired belong to the partnership, and the partner holds them *in trust for the partnership*. Each partner has a duty to make *full disclosure* to the other partners of all transactions in connection with the partnership business. Dealings between a partner and the partnership without such full disclosure are voidable at the election of the partnership.

Unless the partners agree to the contrary, each partner has the duty of devoting his entire attention, time, skill, and efforts to the partnership business. However, a partner may engage in a noncompeting business elsewhere so long as the small amount of time required by the other business and the nature of the other business are not to the prejudice of the partnership business. Articles of partnership usually provide for the amount of time which partners are to devote to the partnership business and also provide that partners are not to engage in any other business competing with the partnership. A partner's devotion of excessive time elsewhere and his participation in a business competing with the partnership not only are grounds for dissolution, but the partner must account to his partnership for the benefits he received thereby and turn them over to the partnership. These same duties apply to a representative of a deceased partner winding up the partnership affairs.

Care and Skill

Each partner has the duty to exercise reasonable care and skill in transacting the partnership business, and he is liable personally to the partnership for loss proximately caused by his failure to do so. He is not liable for loss caused by his honest mistakes and errors of judgment. A partner who is also at fault in the same matter cannot complain to his co-partner at fault.

Keep Accounts

Each partner has the duty to keep a record of the partnership transactions in which he has engaged. Usually the duty of keeping accounts for the entire partnership is entrusted to one of the partners. Each partner has the right to examine any partnership transaction engaged in by any other partner.

Disclosure of Partnership Information

Each partner has a duty to disclose partnership information when demanded by other partners. He also has the duty to make voluntary disclosure of important partnership matters and to consult with his other partners.

SECTION III. REMEDIES

The proper legal forum for the settlement of disputes regarding partnership affairs is the equity court or a court with equity powers. The disputes may be between a partnership and a partner, or may be among partners. Such disputes are resolved in connection with an accounting or dissolution of the partnership. At law, in the absence of a statute to the contrary, a partnership cannot sue, nor be sued by, a partner because inasmuch as a partnership sues and is sued in the names of the partners, in effect the partnership would be suing, or would be sued by, itself; nor can a partnership sue another partnership when both partnerships have a partner in common. There are exceptions to this rule which permit such actions when the subject matter is not related to partnership affairs or when nothing remains to be done but to pay an amount owing on liquidation of partnership affairs.

Chapter 46

AUTHORITY AND APPARENT AUTHORITY OF PARTNERS

Each partner is a general agent of the partnership, and his actual and apparent authority is to carry on the partnership business in the usual way of that particular partnership and of partnerships similar to it. The law of Agency is applicable. Express authority is in the partnership agreement. A "trading partnership" engages in buying and selling property; a "nontrading partnership" engages in selling services. *In a trading partnership,* partners have implied and apparent authority to buy and sell property, to borrow money in the partnership name, and to execute and indorse negotiable instruments in the partnership name in order to carry on the partnership business. But if a partner in a trading partnership unauthorizedly issues or indorses partnership negotiable instruments in the partnership name, the partnership will not be bound except to a holder in due course and holders properly claiming through a holder in due course. Partners in a nontrading partnership do not have such implied and apparent authority, except by necessity and by custom and usage. Partners in both trading and nontrading partnerships have implied and apparent authority to: employ personnel reasonably necessary to carry on the partnership business; pay the firm's debts out of partnership funds; mortgage partnership property to provide security for partnership obligations; settle and compromise claims for and against the partnership, and receive payments due the partnership; and make admissions and representations in connection with partnership affairs in carrying on the partnership business. One or more but less than all the partners do not have implied or apparent authority to: (1) do any act which would make it impossible to carry on the ordinary business of the partnership, such as assign the partnership property in trust for creditors or on the assignee's promise to pay the partnership debts, or to dispose of the

good-will of the business; (2) confess a judgment; (3) submit a partnership claim or liability to arbitration or reference; (4) make the partnership a surety for another's obligation, unless such is implied by the nature of the partnership business; or (5) use partnership funds to buy corporate capital stock.

SECTION I. ACTUAL AUTHORITY

Each partner is an agent of the partnership *for the purpose of carrying on the partnership business in the usual way of that particular partnership and of partnerships similar to the particular partnership.* Every partner has such actual authority, express and implied, unless the partnership agreement provides to the contrary, and he also has such apparent authority by reason of his status as a partner. Each partner is both a principal of, and an agent for, the other partners. *The principles of the law of Agency are applicable.*

Express Authority

A partner's express authority to act for the partnership is found in the partnership agreement, which is the manifestation of the partners concerning their relationship.

Implied Authority

Unless the partnership agreement provides to the contrary, the nature and extent of a partner's implied authority depends upon the character of the partnership business. For the purpose of determining the character of a business, partnerships are classified as "trading partnerships" and "nontrading partnerships." *A trading partnership is one which is engaged in the business of buying and selling property; a nontrading partnership is engaged in selling services.* A partnership engaged in the manufacture or retailing of goods is an example of a trading partnership. A partnership of public accountants, lawyers, or doctors is an illustration of a professional nontrading partnership.

The implied and apparent authority of a partner to buy and sell, to borrow money, and to execute and indorse negotiable instruments on behalf of the partnership is different in trading and nontrading partnerships. The implied and apparent authority of a partner to employ personnel, to pay partnership debts, to mortgage partnership property, to settle and compromise claims for and against the partnership, to receive payment of obligations owing to the partnership, to receive partnership information and to make representations on behalf of the partnership generally is the same in trading and nontrading partnerships. Such implied and apparent authority of partners in trading and nontrading partnerships will be discussed briefly.

To Buy and Sell. Partners in a *trading partnership* have implied authority *to buy and sell property in which the partnership business is engaged,* and to make contracts therefor, when it is reasonably necessary to do so in order to carry on the partnership business. A partner does not have implied authority to sell property other than the property in which the partnership is engaged. Partners in a nontrading partnership may have implied authority by necessity, or by custom and usage in that or similar partnerships, to purchase property reasonably necessary for use in the partnership business. The authority of an accountant to purchase working papers for his public accounting firm, and the authority of a lawyer to purchase law books for his firm, is implied by necessity.

To Borrow Money. A partner in a *trading partnership* has implied authority *to borrow money in the name of the partnership,* if it is reasonably necessary *in order to carry on the partnership business.* The amount borrowed must be reasonable for the purpose. A partner in a nontrading partnership does not have this implied authority, except when implied by necessity or by custom and usage.

Regarding Negotiable Instruments. A partner in a *trading partnership has implied and apparent authority to execute and indorse negotiable instruments in the partnership name,* if such is reasonably necessary *in order to carry on the partnership business.* Should a partner so act when it was not reasonably necessary in order to carry on the partnership business, the partnership is *not bound* by such action *unless the instrument has been negotiated to a "holder in due course."*[1] *The partnership is bound to the holder in due course and to holders who properly claim through him.*[2] A partner in a nontrading partnership does not have this implied and apparent authority, except when implied by necessity or by custom and usage. The execution or indorsement of a negotiable instrument in the partnership name by a partner with *no* implied or apparent authority is not binding on the partnership, even as to a holder in due course.

Regarding Personnel. A partner has implied authority to employ personnel whose services are reasonably necessary in order to carry on the partnership business. He has implied authority to make reasonable contracts for a reasonable salary.

To Pay Partnership Debts. A partner has implied authority to pay the firm's debts and to satisfy the firm's obligations out of partnership funds. However, a partner has no implied authority to use partnership funds or property to pay or secure his personal debts.

To Mortgage. A partner has implied authority to mortgage the partnership property, whether or not the property is for sale in the partnership business, in order to provide security for partnership obligations or to borrow, when expressly or impliedly authorized, on behalf of the partnership.

To Settle, Compromise, and Receive Payment. A partner has implied authority to settle and compromise claims for and against the partnership. A

---

[1] See UCC 3-302, and above, pp. 336-37, 593-94.

[2] See above, pp. 344-34, 350.

partner also has implied authority to receive payments due the partnership and to execute proper papers, such as receipts, in connection therewith.

To Receive Partnership Information. A partner has implied authority to receive partnership notices, and such notice and his knowledge is notice to, and knowledge of, the partnership. U.P.A., sec. 12, provides, "Notice to any partner of any matter relating to partnership affairs, and the knowledge of the partner acting in the particular matter, acquired while a partner or then present to his mind, and the knowledge of any other partner who reasonably could and should have communicated it to the acting partner, operate as notice to or knowledge of the partnership, except in the case of a fraud on the partnership committed by or with the consent of that partner."

To Make Representations. A partner has implied authority to make admissions and representations in connection with partnership affairs if it is for the purpose of carrying on the partnership business in the usual way. Such admissions or representations are, in effect, those of the partnership.

Authority Not Implied. A partner does not have implied authority to perform certain acts in the partnership name *because they are not for the carrying on of the partnership business in the usual way.* U.P.A., sec. 9(3), enumerates instances when there is no such implied authority:

> (3) Unless authorized by the other partners or unless they have abandoned the business, one or more but less than all the partners have no authority to:
> (a) Assign the partnership property in trust for creditors or on the assignee's promise to pay the debts of the partnership,
> (b) Dispose of the good-will of the business,
> (c) Do any other act which would make it impossible to carry on the ordinary business of a partnership,
> (d) Confess a judgment,
> (e) Submit a partnership claim or liability to arbitration or reference.

The first three instances illustrate lack of implied authority to prevent the partnership business from continuing to function. The last two instances illustrate a lack of implied authority to delegate the performance of an act which requires the partner's special skill, judgment, or discretion. In addition to these instances, a partner does not have implied authority to make the partnership a surety or guarantor of another's obligation, although the partnership business may be such that this authority is implied. An illustration is a partnership engaged in the business of buying and selling securities, where signatures to such securities would have to be guaranteed. A partner does not have implied authority to use partnership funds for the purchase of corporate capital stock, although, again, the partnership business may be such that this authority is implied. A partner does not have implied authority to do business gratuitously on behalf of the partnership, although he can do so on his own behalf; a partnership business is carried on for profit.

SECTION II. APPARENT AUTHORITY

Regardless of whether or not a partner has actual authority, a partner has *apparent authority to carry on the partnership business in the usual way.* Transactions between a partner without actual authority but with apparent authority for the apparent purpose of carrying on the partnership business, and a third person who reasonably believes that the partner has such authority and enters the transaction in reliance thereon, are binding on the partnership. Under U.P.A., sec. 9(1):

> Every partner is an agent of the partnership for the purpose of its business, and the act of every partner, including the execution in the partnership name of any instrument, for apparently carrying on in the usual way the business of the partnership of which he is a member binds the partnership, unless the partner so acting has in fact no authority to act for the partnership in the particular matter, and the person with whom he is dealing has knowledge of the fact that he has no such authority.

Without any actual or apparent authority a partner cannot bind the partnership in transactions with third persons. A partner has no apparent authority to buy horses for a jewelry business; to buy a refrigerator for a clothing business; to borrow an obviously unreasonable amount; or to employ personnel at an obviously unreasonable salary. A partner has no apparent authority to act on behalf of a partnership if the third person is aware of the partner's adverse interest to the partnership. A partner with actual authority to act in the partnership name, but with no apparent authority, binds the partnership if he acts in accordance with his actual authority.

Chapter 47

PARTNERSHIP LIABILITY

A partnership is liable to third persons as a principal for its agent's conduct under the law of Agency. Since the partnership consists of the partners, the liability is also the liability of the partners, who are liable jointly and severally for partnership torts and only jointly for partnership contracts. An infant partner can avoid his partnership contract, but his capital contribution is available to partnership creditors and, in most states, it is available also to the claims of his co-partners. An incoming partner is liable for partnership obligations incurred prior to his admission, but such liability is satisfied only out of partnership *property*. The estate of a decedent partner is liable for partnership obligations after his individual creditors have been provided for.

Partners may be sued severally when they are so liable, but only collectively if jointly liable. If joint, an action against the partnership must join all available solvent partners, who must be served personally with process. On judgment, the claim against the partnership is merged in the judgment, and partners not served may not later be sued unless the action was brought in a "joint debtor statute" state. A judgment creditor of a partnership may satisfy his judgment only out of the property of the partnership and of the judgment debtors personally served, and in most states he does not have to resort first to partnership property. However, the equitable doctrine of "marshaling of assets" applies in cases of an equitable nature, e.g., judicial distribution of partnership property, but not with respect to partnership in bankruptcy courts under the Bankruptcy Code.

SECTION I. NATURE OF LIABILITY

Liability of Partnership

Partnership liability begins at the moment the partnership is formed. The partnership is liable for all contracts made on its behalf by partners with actual or apparent authority. The partnership is also liable for damage caused to third persons by the *torts of partners* while carrying on the partnership business in the usual way and, under the law of Agency, for the *torts of its employees* while acting within the scope of their employment. Negligence and fraud are frequent sources of partnership liability. Wilful torts usually are outside the scope or ordinary course of the partnership business, but not necessarily so. The person's intent, whether to act for himself or for the partnership, is an important factor. Acts by partners overzealous in their devotion to partnership affairs do not cause such acts to be out of the ordinary course of partnership business. U.P.A., sec. 14, provides, "The partnership is bound to make good the loss: (1) Where one partner acting within the scope of his apparent authority receives money or property of a third person and misapplies it; and (b) Where the partnership in the course of its business receives money or property of a third person and the money or property so received is misapplied by any partner while it is in the custody of the partnership."

Liability of Partners

The partnership consists of the partners within it, and the liability of the partnership is a liability of the partners. *Partners are liable jointly and severally for partnership torts and only jointly for partnership contracts.* Although in some states liability is made joint and several and, in some instances, specifically includes partnerships, some courts refuse to interpret general statutes to this effect as applying to partnerships. An agreement between the partners providing for their respective shares of partnership liability is binding on the partners but the agreement is not binding on third persons, even though they have knowledge of such provisions. (Partners A and B agree that A alone will be liable for all partnership contracts. This agreement is not binding on C, a partnership creditor, who can hold A and B liable personally on his contract with the partnership.)

An infant partner has the power to avoid his partnership contract, just as he can any other contract, and thereby avoid personal liability to his co-partners and to partnership creditors, in the absence of statute to the contrary. However, in weighing between the equities of an infant and those of a third person who has dealt with the partnership relying on the availability of its joint property and who has become a creditor of a partnership, the courts recognize the superiority of such creditor's equities and cause the infant's capital contribution to be available to such creditor. In most states the infant partner's capital contribution is made available also to the claims of those of his co-partners who have not fraudulently induced the infant to become a partner.

Under U.P.A., secs. 17 and 36, specific provision is made for the liability of an incoming partner, liability of the estate of a deceased partner, the effect of dissolution on a partner's liability, and for the discharge of a partner's liability. *An incoming partner is liable for partnership obligations incurred prior to his admission, but such liability shall be satisfied only out of partnership property.* Partnership creditors may not resort to his personal estate to satisfy such liability. The estate of a *decedent partner* is liable for partnership obligations *after his individual creditors have been provided for.* Dissolution of the partnership does not discharge the partners from their liability for partnership obligations. On dissolution, a novation may occur between the partnership creditor, the partners continuing the partnership business, and the particular partner who is to be discharged. *Release by a partnership creditor of a partner from a partnership obligation for which he is jointly liable discharges all the partners jointly liable.* However, a partnership creditor may contract not to sue a partner on a partnership obligation, *reserving his rights against the other partners;* this does not affect the joint liability of the other partners for the partnership obligation.

SECTION II. ENFORCEMENT OF PARTNERSHIP LIABILITY

Nature of Action

Partners who are liable severally, or jointly and severally, may be sued individually. However, when the partnership obligation is joint, in the absence of a statute to the contrary, a partnership can be sued and can sue only in the names of its partners. In many states a partnership can be sued and can sue in its firm name. An action against a partnership must join all the partners, and all available solvent partners must be served *personally* with process. Partners being sued may object to the nonjoinder of all the available solvent partners. Should no objection be made to the nonjoinder of all such partners, a judgment obtained against the partnership is effective only against the partnership property and against the property of those partners who were served personally with process or who appeared in the action. The claim against the partnership is merged in the judgment. Accordingly, no action may be brought subsequently against the other partners not joined in the previous action. "When the contract is joint, and not joint and several, the entire cause of action is merged in the judgment. The joint liability of the parties not sued with those against whom the judgment is recovered, being extinguished, their entire liability is gone. They cannot be sued separately, for they have incurred no several obligation; they cannot be sued jointly with the others, because judgment has already been recovered against the latter, who would otherwise be subjected to two suits for the same cause."[1] In some states this rule is changed by statute,

[1] *Mason* v. *Eldred,* 6 Wall. 231, 238 (U.S. 1867).

sometimes called "joint debtor statutes," which provide that when service is made on some of the parties jointly liable and judgment is obtained against them, the cause of action against the parties not served and who have not appeared is not merged in the judgment, and they may be sued subsequently on the original cause of action. (In state X, C is an unpaid creditor of the partnership of A and B. C sued the partnership, served process only on A, and obtained a judgment. Since the partnership property and A's assets are insufficient to satisfy C's judgment, C now wishes to sue B. He cannot do so, unless X is a joint debtor state, in which event he can.)

Satisfaction of Judgment

A judgment creditor of a partnership may satisfy his judgment only out of the property of the partnership and of the judgment debtors who were served personally with process in the action or who appeared therein. The judgment creditor of a partnership may obtain a writ of execution against the partnership property and the property of the partners who were so served. In some states he cannot proceed against the property of the individual partners until he has exhausted the partnership property in satisfaction of the judgment. In contrast with a judgment creditor of a partnership, a judgment creditor of an individual partner for his individual obligations first must resort to the property of the individual partner, and then he may charge[2] the individual partner's interest in the partnership.

Marshaling of Assets. *At law*, in the absence of a statute to the contrary, *a judgment creditor of a partnership has the right to satisfy his judgment out of an individual partner's estate without first resorting to partnership property*, thereby depriving such individual partner's creditors of that property in satisfaction of their claims. The rule is different in courts of equity, or courts with equity powers in cases of an equitable nature, where the doctrine of "marshaling of assets" is applied. Under this doctrine, each individual partner's estate is made available first to his individual creditors, and any surplus remaining is made available to partnership creditors; while partnership property is made available first to partnership creditors, and any surplus remaining is distributed among the partners and, as a part of an individual partner's estate, is made available to the creditors of each of the individual partners. U.P.A., sec. 40(h), provides, "When partnership property and the individual properties of the partners are in possession of a court *for distribution*, partnership creditors shall have priority on partnership property and separate creditors on individual property, saving the rights of lien or secured creditors as heretofore." (Author's italics.) Secured creditors, of course, have priority over all other creditors to the security on their obligations.

The new Bankruptcy Code materially changes the old law with respect to partnerships by providing that, if there is a deficiency of property of the estate

---

[2] See Charging Order, above, p. 647.

to pay in full all claims allowed in a case concerning a partnership, then *each general partner in such partnership is liable to the trustee for the full amount of such deficiency.* Prior to the Code, the individual creditors of a general partner had first priority against the partner's assets before partnership creditors under the equitable doctrine of marshaling of assets. However, the trustee must, to the extent practicable, *first* seek to recover the deficiency from any general partner that is *not* a debtor in a bankruptcy case.

Chapter 48

DISSOLUTION AND WINDING UP

Interruption in the "carrying on" of the partnership *dissolves* the partnership; after "winding up" partnership affairs, its entity is terminated. D T
WU

Dissolution may occur: by act of the partners, a wrongful partner being liable for breach of the partnership contract; and by operation of law, e.g., death or bankruptcy of a partner, or by court decree, e.g., for incapacity or misconduct of a partner, operation only at a loss, equitable necessity, and by a partner's assignee under certain circumstances.

Dissolution terminates the authority of the partners to act for the partnership except that, to the extent necessary to wind up partnership affairs, partners who have not wrongfully caused dissolution, or the legal representative of the last surviving partner not bankrupt, have implied authority to wind up. But, as to third persons aware of the partnership but ignorant of the dissolution, partners have apparent authority to carry on and, as to such persons unaware of the ineligibility of certain partners to wind up, apparent authority to wind up. Apparent authority to carry on may be terminated by *actual notice* of dissolution to third persons who *extended credit* to the partnership, and by *reasonable notice* to *other* third persons who knew of the partnership.

Winding up is the liquidation of partnership assets and settlement of partnership affairs; new business is not to be taken on. If, after dissolution, the partnership business is carried on without liquidation, creditors of the dissolved partnership are creditors of those carrying on the partnership business. "Continuation" or "buy-out" agreements provide for valuation and settlement of a partner's interest without liquidation and for continuance of the partnership business. Partners have the right to an accounting, and the priority of

payment of partnership liabilities is: (1) those owing to creditors other than partners; (2) those owing to partners other than for capital and profits; (3) those owing to partners in respect of capital; (4) those owing to partners in respect of profits. Partnership liabilities are satisfied first from partnership property, and then by contributions by the individual partners in the ratio that they share profits, unless otherwise agreed.

SECTION I. CAUSES OF DISSOLUTION

A partnership is formed for the purpose of *carrying on* as co-owners a business for profit. When a partner ceases to be associated in the *carrying on* of a partnership business, the partnership is *dissolved.* Dissolution does not terminate the partnership, however, and it continues in existence until its affairs have been settled. The settling of such affairs is called the "winding up" of the partnership. *The winding up begins with dissolution and ends with termination of the partnership.* The three terms of "dissolution," "winding up," and "termination" should not be confused.

Dissolution may occur by the act of the partners, by operation of law, and by the decree of a court ordering dissolution; they will be discussed in this order.

By Act of Partners

Dissolution usually occurs by the acts of the partners. When dissolution occurs without violation of the partnership agreement, there is no breach of contract and, therefore, no liability for such dissolution. If the partnership is terminable at will, any partner may dissolve the partnership at any time. If the partnership was formed for a particular period or for the accomplishment of a particular objective and such time has expired or the objective has been accomplished, the partnership dissolves by the terms of the partnership agreement. All the partners created the partnership and it is their privilege to dissolve the partnership; however, those partners who have assigned their interests in the partnership or whose interests have become subject to a charging order have no voice in the decision of the remaining partners to dissolve. A partnership agreement may specify causes for the expulsion of a partner and, in accordance with such provisions, a partner may be expelled for cause and the partnership dissolved thereby. *A partnership agreement is not irrevocable* and the partnership may be dissolved by the wrongful act of a partner at any time. Such partner is liable for damages for breach of contract and may be sued at law or his account charged therefor. *The admission of an incoming partner dissolves the partnership and creates a new partnership.*

By Operation of Law

A partnership is dissolved immediately and automatically by the death of a partner, the bankruptcy of a partner or of the partnership, and by a change of law causing the partnership to be illegal. A partner's death interrupts the relationship of the association in *carrying on* the partnership business. The bankruptcy of a partner deprives him of association in the *carrying on* of the partnership business. If the partnership itself becomes bankrupt, the partnership property is transferred to the trustee in bankruptcy, and the partnership business cannot be *carried on* any longer by the partners. A partnership may become involuntarily bankrupt. It also may become voluntarily bankrupt, but probably only on the petition of all the general partners. If fewer than all the general partners petition, then the partnership can become involuntarily bankrupt.

By Court Decree. A judicial determination is necessary in many instances to determine whether or not the circumstances are such that, on the application of a partner, the partnership should be dissolved. A court of equity, or a court with equity powers, has jurisdiction over such proceedings. If the circumstances are such that the *carrying on* of the partnership business is *seriously prejudiced*, the court has discretion to decree dissolution. Grounds for dissolution by decree of a court are as follows:

Incapacity of Partner. A partner may be adjudicated to be insane, he may be of unsound mind without any adjudication of insanity, or for some other reason he may be incapable of performing his part of the partnership agreement. However, such incapacity may be temporary or partial and, in the discretion of the court, the carrying on of the partnership business may not be affected for the time being and dissolution be denied.

Misconduct of Partner. A partner's misconduct, either in the carrying on of the partnership business or otherwise, may so prejudice or make impracticable the carrying on of the partnership business as to justify dissolution of the partnership. Bitter disagreements, or a rupture in working relationship, among the partners seriously affecting the carrying on of the partnership business justify dissolution; ordinary disputes among the partners are usually insufficient. Petition for dissolution may be made by any partner except the delinquent partner.

Operation Only at a Loss. The purpose of a partnership is to earn profits and, if it can operate only at a loss, the partnership may be ordered dissolved.

Equitable Necessity. Circumstances may exist which equitably justify dissolution. An illustration is the occurrence of fraud in the creation of the partnership.

By Partner's Assignee under Certain Circumstances. An assignee of a partner's interest in the partnership may obtain a decree of dissolution at any time if the partnership was terminable at will or on the expiration of the agreed duration of the partnership either in time or in objective.

SECTION II. EFFECT OF DISSOLUTION

Dissolution does not terminate the partnership but causes its affairs to be settled preliminary to its termination. Dissolution has an important effect on the authority of the partners, has a limited effect on the liability of the partners as among themselves, and involves rights and powers in connection with the winding up of the partnership business. These effects will be considered in turn.

Authority of Partners

Dissolution operates to terminate the authority of the partners to act on behalf of the partnership, except to the extent necessary in order to wind up the partnership affairs. In the absence of agreement to the contrary, partners who have not wrongfully caused dissolution of the partnership or the legal representative of the last surviving partner, not bankrupt, have implied authority to participate in the winding up of the partnership; in a proper case a court has power to wind up a partnership on application by a proper party. *Partners, nevertheless, have apparent authority to carry on the partnership business with third persons who knew of the partnership prior to dissolution but who are unaware of such dissolution,* and all partners have apparent authority to wind up the partnership affairs in dealing with third persons who are unaware of the ineligibility of certain partners to engage in the winding up. Accordingly, *proper notice must be given to third persons in order to terminate the apparent authority of partners.*[1]

The apparent authority of partners to carry on the partnership business may be terminated by giving proper notice of the dissolution to third persons who *knew of the partnership* prior to dissolution but had *no knowledge or notice of such dissolution.* If such third persons *had extended credit to the partnership prior to dissolution,* they are to be given *actual notice,* i.e., they are to *actually receive* notice of dissolution; sending such notice is not enough. If such third persons *had not extended credit to the partnership prior to dissolution,* they are to be given *general notice,* as by newspaper publication or otherwise in the place or places where the partnership business was carried on. Similar notice to such third persons must be given regarding the ineligibility of certain partners to participate in the winding up of the partnership business. *In the event that such notice is not given or otherwise received by such third persons, the partnership will be bound by the acts of the partners pursuant to their apparent authority to carry on the partnership business or to wind up a dissolved partnership.* However, under U.P.A., sec. 35(3), a partnership is not liable to third persons for the unauthorized act of a partner after dissolution if notice of dissolution has not been given to such third persons, "(a) Where the partnership is dissolved because it is unlawful to carry on the business, unless the act is appropriate for winding up partnership affairs; or (b) Where *the* partner has become bankrupt; . . ." (Author's italics.)

---

[1] If a dormant partner retires, no such notice is necessary to third persons who did not know that he was a partner; but notice must be given to those who knew he was a partner. See Alan R. Bromberg, *Crane and Bromberg on Partnership* (St. Paul, Minn.: West Publishing Co., 1968), p. 466.

When dissolution occurs because of a partner's misconduct, those partners who have not wrongfully caused dissolution may continue the business in the same name, subject to proper provision for security for, or payment to the wrongful partner of, the value of his partnership interest less any damage to the partnership caused by his breach of the partnership agreement.

Liability of Partners

Dissolution does not affect the liability of partners to third persons for partnership obligations, but it does affect the liabilities of the partners among themselves. Where dissolution has occurred by the act of a partner or by the death or bankruptcy of a partner but a partner, not having knowledge of the dissolution caused by the partner's act or not having knowledge or notice of the dissolution caused by a partner's death or bankruptcy, makes a binding transaction on behalf of the partnership, each of the partners has an obligation to contribute his share of any liability caused by such transaction.

Although a change in partnership personnel causes dissolution of the partnership, nevertheless, the partnership business may be carried on without liquidation of the partnership affairs. Under U.P.A., sec. 41, extensive provision is made for protection of the creditors of the dissolved partnership in the event the partnership business is continued without liquidation. Under the conditions in this section creditors of the dissolved partnership are also creditors of the person or partnership carrying on the partnership business. When a partnership is dissolved by a partner's death or retirement and the partnership business is continued without the settlement of accounts between the partnership and the retiring partner or the legal representative of the deceased partner, such partner or representative of a deceased partner has the right to an accounting of the value of the partner's interest in the partnership at the time of dissolution and the partner or representative is entitled to such interest as a creditor of the person or partnership continuing the business. The continued use of the surname of a deceased or retired partner does not of itself make the estate of the decedent or the retired partner liable for partnership obligations.

SECTION III. WINDING UP

Nature and Authority

The winding up of a partnership business involves the liquidation of partnership assets and the settlement of partnership affairs with partnership creditors and among the partners themselves, and precludes taking on new business for the partnership. U.P.A., sec. 35(1)(a), provides that a partner has authority to perform ". . . any act appropriate for winding up partnership affairs or completing transactions unfinished at dissolution. . . ." The partners have the authority to liquidate the assets, receive payment of debts due the partnership and to execute proper receipts therefor, pay the partnership debts, distribute to the various partners their interests in the partnership, and to do any other appropriate acts in effecting the winding up of the partnership affairs. In the absence of agreement to the contrary, partners who have not wrongfully caused dissolution of the partnership or the legal representative of the last surviving partner, not bankrupt, have implied authority to wind up the partnership affairs.

On dissolution, each partner has the right, with exceptions, to have the partnership business liquidated, his interest in the partnership determined, and to be paid in cash, unless otherwise provided in the partnership agreement. Such an agreement, often called a "continuation," "buy and sell," or "buy-out" agreement, may fairly provide for valuation and settlement of the decedent, disabled, or withdrawing partner's interest without liquidation, and for continuance of the partnership business by the remaining partners who would keep the partnership property.

Rights of Partners. Every partner has a right to an accounting for his interest in the dissolved partnership, to receive the advances he has made to the partnership and his capital contribution, and to participate in the surplus and profits as against the partners winding up the partnership affairs or as a creditor of the partnership continuing the business.

Distribution. The settlement of accounts between the partners *after dissolution,* in the absence of agreement to the contrary, is governed by U.P.A., sec. 40. Under section 40(b):

> The liabilities of the partnership shall rank in order of payment, as follows:
> I. Those owing to creditors other than partners,
> II. Those owing to partners other than for capital and profits,
> III. Those owing to partners in respect of capital,
> IV. Those owing to partners in respect of profits.

Partnership liabilities are satisfied *first by resorting to the partnership property* and *then to the contributions by the individual partners* in the ratio that they share profits, unless they have provided to the contrary. The estate of a decedent partner is liable for contribution of his share to such liabilities. The estate of a bankrupt partner is liable first to the trustee in bankruptcy.[2] If any partner has paid more than his share of such liabilities, he is entitled to contribution from the remaining partners for such excess.

---

[2] See above, p. 526, and below, pp. 525–26.

Chapter 49

LIMITED PARTNERSHIP

A limited partnership is a partnership of one or more general partners and one or more limited partners formed in compliance with the Uniform Limited Partnership Act. Limited partners are not liable for partnership obligations, but they are liable *to* the partnership for their capital contributions. The limited partnership comes into existence when a certificate of limited partnership, is filed in the proper place in a state. Exact compliance, or substantial compliance in good faith, with the U.L.P.A. is necessary to its existence.

Three very important items for a limited partner are: (1) his capital contribution may be only cash or other property, but not services; (2) his surname may not appear in the partnership name, unless it is the same as that of a general partner, or was included in the partnership name before he became a limited partner; (3) he may not participate in the control (management) of the partnership business. Death, or the assignment of a partnership interest, of a limited partner does not dissolve the partnership. Specific U.L.P.A. provisions govern rights of a limited partner, his compensation, withdrawal or reduction of his contribution, and his loans to and other business transactions with the partnership.[1] He has no authority to act for the partnership. On partnership dissolution, the assets are distributed in the following priority of liabilities: (1) those to creditors, in the order of priority as provided by law, except those to limited partners on account of their contributions, and to general partners; (2) those to limited partners in respect to their share of the profits and other compensation by way of income on their contributions; (3) those to limited partners in respect to the capital of their contributions; (4) those to general

[1] See below, pp. 669–70.

partners other than for capital and profits; (5) those to general partners in respect to profits; (6) those to general partners in respect to capital. The U.L.P.A. requires the certificate of limited partnership to be cancelled or amended in certain instances.[2]

SECTION I. PURPOSE

The purpose of a limited partnership is to have an association of partners, one or more of whom will not be liable for partnership obligations, and one or more of whom will be so liable. Those not so liable are "limited partners," inasmuch as they are liable only *to* the partnership and only *for* their contribution of cash or other property in accordance with their partnership agreement. The general partners are liable for the partnership obligations and may be contributing solely their skill and services. Statutes exist in all the states permitting the formation of a limited partnership. The Uniform Limited Partnership Act of 1916 has been adopted in almost all of the states. Comments will be made here on a few of the more salient provisions. Throughout this chapter, references to the Uniform Limited Partnership Act will carry the abbreviation of U.L.P.A.

SECTION II. LIMITED PARTNERSHIP DISTINGUISHED FROM GENERAL PARTNERSHIP

Definition

A "limited partnership" is a partnership of one or more general partners and one or more limited partners formed in compliance with U.L.P.A. There are only two kinds of partner in a limited partnership, namely, general partners who are the same as partners in a general partnership, and limited partners who have limited liability and interests in the limited partnership. Limited partners are sometimes called "special partners."

Formation

A limited partnership exists only by virtue of its compliance with the statute creating it. Failure to comply with the statute often results in the association becoming a general partnership. Under U.L.P.A., sec. 2, the partners must sign and swear to a certificate containing detailed information regarding: the name, character, and location of the principal place of business; the names and addresses of each of the limited and general partners, their status as such being indicated; the cash or other property contributed by each limited partner; how each limited partner is to share in the profits of the

[2] See below, pp. 671–72.

partnership; and other information. This certificate must be filed in the proper place as provided in each state. *A limited partnership may be formed by exact compliance with the statutory requisites regarding the details of the certificate, or by substantial compliance in good faith with such requirements.* Under U.L.P.A., sec. 11: A person who has contributed to the capital of a business conducted by a person or partnership erroneously believing that he has become a limited partner in a limited partnership, is not, by reason of his exercise of the rights of a limited partner, a general partner with the person or in the partnership carrying on the business, or bound by the obligations of such person or partnership; provided that on ascertaining the mistake he promptly renounces his interest in the profits of the business, or other compensation by way of income.

Contributions

A limited partner's contribution to the partnership may be only cash or other property, but not services. A general partner may contribute to the limited partnership just as he could to any general partnership. Under the U.L.P.A., sec. 12:

> (1) A person may be a general partner and a limited partner in the same partnership at the same time.
>
> (2) A person who is a general, and also at the same time a limited, partner shall have all the rights and powers and be subject to all the restrictions of a general partner; except that, in respect to his contribution, he shall have the rights against the other members which he would have had if he were not also a general partner.

Partnership Name

A limited partner's surname may not appear in the name of the partnership unless it is the same name as that of a general partner, or his name was included in the partnership name before he became a limited partner. Failure of a limited partner to comply with this requirement exposes him to liability as a *general partner* to partnership creditors who have extended credit to the partnership without knowing that he was not a general partner.

Participation in Management

A limited partner may not participate in the control of the limited partnership, and if he does participate he is liable as a general partner to partnership creditors. Only the *general partners* of the limited partnership may participate in the management or control of the partnership business.

Death, Assignment, New Partners

The partnership is not dissolved by the death of a limited partner, by a limited partner's assignment of his interest in the partnership, or by the admission of a new limited partner. In the latter instance, the certificate of limited partnership must be amended in order to include the information regarding the new limited partner. All partners must sign the amendment for admission of a new partner. However, the retirement, death, or insanity of a general partner dissolves the partnership unless the partnership is continued by the remaining general partners pursuant to the terms of the certificate or with the consent of all the partners.

Rights of Limited Partner

A limited partner's interest in the partnership is personal property. Under U.L.P.A., sec. 10:

> (1) A limited partner shall have the same rights as a general partner to
> (a) Have the partnership books kept at the principal place of business of the partnership, and at all times to inspect and copy any of them.
> (b) Have on demand true and full information of all things affecting the partnership, and a formal account of partnership affairs whenever circumstances render it just and reasonable, and
> (c) Have dissolution and winding up by decree of court.
> (2) A limited partner shall have the right to receive a share of the profits or other compensation by way of income, and to the return of his contribution as provided in sections 15 and 16.

Compensation of Limited Partner. Under U.L.P.A., sec. 15:

> A limited partner may receive from the partnership the share of the profits or the compensation by way of income stipulated for in the certificate; provided, that after such payment is made, whether from the property of the partnership or that of a general partner, the partnership assets are in excess of all liabilities of the partnership except liabilities to limited partners on account of their contributions and to general partners.

Withdrawal or Reduction of Limited Partner's Contribution. Under U.L.P.A., sec. 16:

> (1) A limited partner shall not receive from a general partner or out of partnership property any part of his contribution until
> (a) All liabilities of the partnership, except liabilities to general partners and to limited partners on account of their contributions, have been paid or there remains property of the partnership sufficient to pay them,
> (b) The consent of all members is had, unless the return of the contribution may be rightfully demanded under the provisions of paragraph (2), and
> (c) The certificate is cancelled or so amended as to set forth the withdrawal or reduction.
> (2) Subject to the provisions of paragraph (1) a limited partner may rightfully demand the return of his contribution
> (a) On the dissolution of a partnership, or
> (b) When the date specified in the certificate for its return has arrived, or
> (c) After he has given six months' notice in writing to all other members, if no

time is specified in the certificate either for the return of the contribution or for the dissolution of the partnership.

(3) In the absence of any statement in the certificate to the contrary or the consent of all members, a limited partner, irrespective of the nature of his contribution, has only the right to demand and receive cash in return for his contribution.

(4) A limited partner may have the partnership dissolved and its affairs wound up when

(a) He rightfully but unsuccessfully demands the return of his contribution, or

(b) The other liabilities of the partnership have not been paid, or the partnership property is insufficient for their payment as required by paragraph (1a) and the limited partner would otherwise be entitled to the return of his contribution.

Loans and Other Business Transactions with Limited Partner. Under U.L.P.A., sec. 13:

(1) A limited partner also may loan money to and transact other business with the partnership, and, unless he is also a general partner, receive on account of resulting claims against the partnership, with general creditors, a pro rata share of the assets. No limited partner shall in respect to any such claim

(a) Receive or hold as collateral security any partnership property, or

(b) Receive from a general partner or the partnership any payment, conveyance, or release from liability, if at the time the assets of the partnership are not sufficient to discharge partnership liabilities to persons not claiming as general or limited partners.

(2) The receiving of collateral security, or a payment, conveyance, or release in violation of the provisions of paragraph (1) is a fraud on the creditors of the partnership.

Liability of Limited Partner

Limited partners as such are not bound by the obligations of the partnership. Under U.L.P.A., sec. 17:

(1) A limited partner is liable to the partnership

(a) For the difference between his contribution as actually made and that stated in the certificate as having been made, and

(b) For any unpaid contribution which he agreed in the certificate to make in the future at the time and on the conditions stated in the certificate.

(2) A limited partner holds as trustee for the partnership

(a) Specific property stated in the certificate as contributed by him, but which was not contributed or which has been wrongfully returned, and

(b) Money or other property wrongfully paid or conveyed to him on account of his contribution.

(3) The liabilities of a limited partner as set forth in this section can be waived or compromised only by the consent of all members; but a waiver or compromise shall not affect the right of a creditor of a partnership who extended credit or whose claim arose after the filing and before a cancellation or amendment of the certificate, to enforce such liabilities.

(4) When a contributor has rightfully received the return in whole or in part of the capital of his contribution, he is nevertheless liable to the partnership for any sum, not in excess of such return with interest, necessary to discharge its liabilities to all creditors who extended credit or whose claims arose before such return.

Authority

In general, the authority of a general partner is the same as that of a partner in a general partnership. A limited partner does not have any authority to act on behalf of the partnership.

Litigation

A limited partner is not required to be a party in actions for or against the limited partnership, unless the limited partner is asserting a right against the partnership or the partnership is asserting a right against the limited partner. Only the general partners are proper parties.

Distribution

On dissolution of a limited partnership the assets are distributed among various persons in the following priority of liabilities, as provided under U.L.P.A., sec. 23:

(a) Those to creditors, in the order of priority as provided by law, except those to limited partners on account of their contributions, and to general partners,
(b) Those to limited partners in respect to their share of the profits and other compensation by way of income on their contributions.
(c) Those to limited partners in respect to the capital of their contributions,
(d) Those to general partners other than for capital and profits,
(e) Those to general partners in respect to profits,
(f) Those to general partners in respect to capital.

Cancellation or Amendment of Certificate

U.L.P.A. requires that the certificate of limited partnership be cancelled or amended in certain specified instances. Under sec. 24:

(1) The certificate shall be cancelled when the partnership is dissolved or all limited partners cease to be such.

(2) A certificate shall be amended when
  (a) There is a change in the name of the partnership or in the amount or character of the contribution of any limited partner,
  (b) A person is substituted as a limited partner,
  (c) An additional limited partner is admitted,
  (d) A person is admitted as a general partner,

(e) A general partner retires, dies or becomes insane, and the business is continued under section 20,
(f) There is a change in the character of the business of the partnership,
(g) There is a false or erroneous statement in the certificate,
(h) There is a change in the time as stated in the certificate for the dissolution of the partnership or for the return of a contribution,
(i) A time is fixed for the dissolution of the partnership, or the return of a contribution, no time having been specified in the certificate, or
(j) The members desire to make a change in any other statement in the certificate in order that it shall accurately represent the agreement between them.

SECTION III. (Revised) UNIFORM LIMITED PARTNERSHIP ACT (1976)

The American Institute of Certified Public Accountants has not recognized for purpose of coverage on the Uniform CPA Examination, as of the date of the publication of this book, the revised Uniform Limited Partnership Act of 1976 because of the limited opportunity for its adoption by a large number of states. However, to provide for the contingency of the AICPA's recognition of the revised Act before another edition of this book, some of the salient features of the revised Act are indicated here.

1. The name of the limited partnership must include the words "limited partnership."
2. The partnership must have and maintain a registered agent in the state where it is doing business so that service of process may be made on the partnership by serving the agent. Certain specified partnership records must be kept in the agent's office.
3. The certificate of limited partnership must be filed in the office of the Secretary of State in the state where the partnership is doing business.
4. The capital contribution of a limited partner may be the performance of services, cash, or property.
5. If a limited partner actively participates in the control of the partnership business he shall be liable only to those persons who transact business with the partnership knowing of the participation in such control.
6. Because of much concern and resulting litigation involving what does and does not constitute participation in the control of the partnership business by a limited partner, the revised Act specifies the following as *not constituting participation in such control:*

   a. Being a contractor for, or an agent of, the partnership.
   b. Consulting with and advising a partner with respect to the business.
   c. Acting as a surety for the partnership.
   d. Approving or disapproving of an amendment to the partnership agreement.
   e. Voting on various matters, such as dissolution; winding up; the transfer of all or substantially all of the assets, of the occurrence of debt, other than

in the ordinary course of the business; change in the nature of the business; and removal of a general partner.

As is readily apparent, the revised Act has made substantial changes in the previous law on limited partnerships. For details, the revised Act should be carefully examined.

PROBLEMS

1. Two men were legally engaged in an unincorporated business under the duly recorded assumed name of The Atlantic Company without any written agreement, and it became necessary to determine whether they were partners. One had invested cash in the business and the other had lent his credit to it and had assisted in the management of it. What documents would you examine and for what other facts would you inquire as apt to have significant bearing on the question? (Former C.P.A. Examination question)
2. (a) A owns a small business and pays a share of the profits to B and C, his employees, as compensation for their services and pays a share of the profits to D, his landlord, as rent. Such compensation and rent fluctuate as the profits fluctuate.
   (1) Is this a partnership?
   (2) Why?
   (b) X, Y, and Z are creditors of A, whose business is failing. They all agree that X, Y, and Z are to help A to operate the business and X, Y, and Z are to share in the profits until their claims are satisfied.
   (1) Is this a partnership?
   (2) Why?
3. (a) The real and personal property of the partnership of A and B is held in the name of A. A conveyed part of the partnership realty to C in violation of the partnership agreement. C conveyed it to D, a bona fide purchaser for value without notice of such violation. Can the partnership reacquire the title to the property? Why?
   (b) X, Y, and Z are partners, the firm property being held in the firm name.
   (1) C, a judgment creditor of X, caused a levy of execution on the partnership property. Could such property be sold to satisfy the judgment? Why?
   (2) Y died leaving a widow. Who is entitled to the partnership realty and personalty? Why?
4. In a partnership of A, B, and C:
   (a) A and B purchased merchandise for the carrying on of the partnership business in the usual way over the objection of C who refused to be bound by the purchase. Is C, together with A and B, liable for the purchase? Why?
   (b) Do A and B have the right to amend the Articles of Partnership over C's objection? Why?
   (c) C became ill, temporarily causing A and B to do extra work in operating the partnership business. Are A and B entitled to compensation for such additional work? Why?
5. (a) A contributed $5,000, B $10,000, and C $15,000 to the partnership of ABC, but no provision was made in the partnership agreement for the sharing of profits and losses. At the end of the year the firm had a loss of $6,000.

(1) How will the loss be shared?
(2) Why?

(b) When does a partner have a right to a formal accounting of partnership affairs prior to dissolution?

6. A, B, and C were partners under a written agreement made in 1975 that it should continue for 10 years. During 1980 C being indebted to X sold and conveyed his interest in the partnership to X. A and B paid X $5,000 as C's share of the profits for the year 1980, but refused X permission to inspect the books or to come into the managing office of the partnership. X brings an action setting forth the above facts and asks for an accounting and an order to inspect the books and to participate in the management of the partnership business.
   (1) Does C's action dissolve the partnership?
   (2) To what is X entitled with respect to (a) partnership profits, (b) inspection of partnership books, (c) accounting by the partnership, and (d) participation in the partnership management?
   (3) In case of a dissolution, to what is X entitled with respect to C's interest and accounting? (Former C.P.A. Examination question, dates changed)

7. On May 2, 1980, the three partners in the firm of A, B, & C signed a dissolution agreement whereby the firm's affairs were to be liquidated as of the following June 30. On May 15, B without the knowledge or consent of A or C procured for himself a five-year lease of the premises occupied by the firm to run from the following July 1, and on July 1 B sold this lease at a profit. Have A and C a legal right to share in B's profit? (Former C.P.A. Examination question, date changed)

8. It was provided in the partnership agreement between A, B, and C, that A would not be liable for partnership obligations. An employee of the firm negligently injured X while driving the firm truck on firm business. The firm failed to perform a contractual obligation owing to Y. Subsequently D was admitted to the partnership.
   (a) Are the partners who are liable for the claims of X and Y liable jointly, severally, or jointly and severally? Explain.
   (b) Is A liable for the claims of X and Y? Why?
   (c) Is D liable for the claims of X and Y? Why?
   (d) If X and Y obtained judgments on their claims, how may such judgments be satisfied?
   (e) If the partners liable have individual creditors:
      (1) Does this fact affect X and Y in the satisfaction of their judgments? Why?
      (2) Would it make any difference if the firm of A, B, C, and D were dissolved subsequent to the judgments obtained by X and Y but prior to any attempt to satisfy such judgments, and distribution is being made by a court? Why?

9. Jock and Kilroy, partners, took Lee in as a partner. At the time of Lee's admittance, the partnership liabilities were $10,000. One year after Lee's admittance the liabilities were $15,000 and the assets $6,000. The partners decided then to dissolve. What is the liability of each partner under the Uniform Partnership Act? (Former C.P.A. Examination question)

10. The copartnership articles of Alden and Bruer stipulated that Alden should furnish all the capital and that Bruer should manage the business but without any liability for firm debts. Connors, knowing of these provisions, sold goods on credit to the firm.

(1) Who is liable? Alden, or Bruer, or both Alden and Bruer?
(2) What would your answer be if the copartnership articles further stipulated that Bruer was a limited partner? (Former C.P.A. Examination question)

11. A, B, and C are partners in a retail rug business which has just been dissolved pursuant to mutual agreement. While the firm was being wound up, A purchased additional rugs from D who had never heard of the firm previously, from E who had known of the firm previously but had never dealt with it, and from F who had dealt with the firm previously. All of A's transactions were in the firm name and neither D, E, nor F knew of the dissolution.
(1) Is the firm bound by these transactions?
(2) Why?

12. X, Y, and Z are partners. X contributed $10,000, Y $20,000, and Z $30,000 to the partnership. X had loaned the firm $5,000; the firm owes R, a creditor, $7,000; and the firm has assets of $94,000 at the time of dissolution. In the absence of any provisions in the partnership agreement for the sharing of profits and losses and for distribution of the partnership's assets on dissolution, how should assets be distributed and in what priority?

13. X and Y are partners. Z is an incoming partner who orally promises X and Y to assume the partnership obligations existing prior to his entry into the partnership. Is Z's promise enforceable? Explain.

SOME PREVIOUS C.P.A. LAW EXAMINATION QUESTIONS AND AUTHOR'S MODEL ANSWERS

NOVEMBER, 1979

Number 1

Select the **best** answers for each of the following items.

17. Which of the following will **not** result in a dissolution of a partnership?
  a. The bankruptcy of a partner as long as the partnership itself remains solvent.
  b. The death of a partner as long as his will provides that his executor shall become a partner in his place.
  c. The wrongful withdrawal of a partner in contravention of the agreement between the partners.
  d. The assignment by a partner of his entire partnership interest.

Item 18 is based on the following information:

Teal and Olvera were partners of the T & O Real Estate Investment Company. They decided to seek more capital in order to expand their participation in the booming real estate business in the area. They obtained five individuals to invest $100,000 each in their venture as limited partners.

18. Assuming the limited partnership agreement is silent on the point, which of the following acts may Teal and Olvera engage in without the written consent of all limited partners?
  a. Admit an additional person as a general partner.
  b. Continue the partnership business upon the death or retirement of a general partner.
  c. Invest the entire amount ($500,000) of contributions by the limited partners in a single venture.

d. Admit additional limited partners from time to time in order to obtain additional working capital.

30. Which of the following is a correct statement concerning the similarities of a limited partnership and a corporation?
   a. Shareholders and limited partners may both participate in the management of the business and retain limited liability.
   b. Both are recognized for federal income tax purposes as taxable entities.
   c. Both can only be created pursuant to a statute and each must file a copy of their respective certificates with the proper state authorities.
   d. Both provide insulation from personal liability for all of the owners of the business.

Answer

1. 17.d(647) 18.c.(671, 651) 30.c.(667–68, 688, 692)

Number 5

Part a. Marcall is a limited partner of Guarcross, a limited partnership, and is suing a CPA firm which was retained by the limited partnership to perform auditing and tax return preparation services. Guarcross was formed for the purpose of investing in a diversified portfolio of risk capital securities. The partnership agreement included the following provisions:

> The initial capital contribution of each limited partner shall not be less than \$250,000; no partner may withdraw any part of his interest in the partnership, except at the end of any fiscal year upon giving written notice of such intention not less than 30 days prior to the end of such year; the books and records of the partnership shall be audited as of the end of the fiscal year by a certified public accountant designated by the general partners; and proper and complete books of account shall be kept and shall be open to inspection by any of the partners or his or her accredited representative.

Marcall's claim of malpractice against the CPA firm centers on the firm's alleged failure to comment, in its audit report, on the withdrawal by the general partners of \$2,000,000 of their \$2,600,000 capital investment based on back-dated notices, and the lumping together of the \$2,000,000 withdrawals with \$49,000 in withdrawals by limited partners so that a reader of the financial statement would not be likely to realize that the two general partners had withdrawn a major portion of their investments.

The CPA firm's contention is that its contract was made with the limited partnership, not its partners. It further contends that since the CPA firm had no privity of contract with the third party limited partners, the limited partners have no right of action for negligence.

Required:

Answer the following, setting forth reasons for any conclusions stated.

Discuss the various theories Marcall would rely upon in order to prevail in a lawsuit against the CPA firm.

Answer

5.a. One theory is that, while the contract between the firm and the limited partnership was apparently only between those two parties, nevertheless the partnership is not necessarily a legal entity separate and distinct from its members. The partnership consists of all the partners and as such each of them is a party to the contract. Under the Uniform Limited Partnership Act, a limited partnership is a partnership of one or more general partners and one or more limited partners. The general partners acted for themselves and as agents for the limited partners in making all of them parties to the contract with the CPA firm. Accordingly, Marcall as a limited partner can claim to be a party to the contract and can bring the lawsuit.

Another theory is that, if the limited partner is not considered to be a party to the contract with the firm, the CPA firm is liable to the limited partner as a third person for its simple negligence constituting malpractice. Although there is no privity of contract between the accountant and third persons and, therefore, no duty of care owing by him to third persons, nevertheless there is an exception. Only if the accountant has reason to believe that his accounting services which he has rendered to his client will be made available by his client to third persons will a legal duty of care be imposed upon him. If he knows the specific identity of the third person and that he intends to rely upon the accountant's professional opinion, then he has the duty to exercise reasonable care, and he is liable for his ordinary negligence which proximately causes damage to the third person. Since the CPA firm knew of Marcall as a limited partner who would rely on the firm's services rendered to the limited partnership, then the firm will be liable to Marcall for any loss.

A third theory is that the CPA firm was guilty of actual or constructive fraud in their services and, therefore, liable to Marcall for any consequent loss. (pp. 667, 630, 819)

MAY, 1979

Number 4

Part a. Strom, Lane, and Grundig formed a partnership on July 1, 1974, and selected "Big M Associates" as their partnership name. The partnership agreement specified a fixed duration of ten years for the partnership. Business went well for the partnership for several years and it established an excellent reputation in the business community. In 1978, Strom, much to his amazement, learned that Grundig was padding his expense accounts by substantial amounts each month and taking secret kickbacks from certain customers for price concessions and favored service. Strom informed Lane of these facts and they decided to seek an accounting of Grundig, a dissolution of the firm by ousting Grundig, and the subsequent continuation of the firm by themselves under the name, "Big M Associates."

Required:

Answer the following, setting forth reasons for any conclusions stated.

1. Were there any filing requirements to be satisfied upon the initial creation of the partnership?

2. What will be the basis for the accounting and dissolution and should such actions be successful?

3. Can Strom and Lane obtain the right to continue to use the firm name if they prevail?

Part b. Palmer is a member of a partnership. His personal finances are in a state of disarray, although he is not bankrupt. He recently defaulted on a personal loan from the Aggressive Finance Company. Aggressive indicated that if he did not pay within one month, it would obtain a judgment against him and levy against all his property including his share of partnership property and any interest he had in the partnership. Both Palmer and the partnership are concerned about the effects of this unfortunate situation upon Palmer and the partnership.

Required:

Answer the following, setting forth reasons for any conclusions stated.

1. Has a dissolution of the partnership occurred?
2. What rights will Aggressive have against the partnership or Palmer concerning Palmer's share of partnership property or his interest in the partnership?
3. Could Palmer legally assign his interest in the partnership as security for a loan with which to pay off Aggressive?

Answer

4.a.1. Nothing had to be filed in order to create the partnership. While a partnership may use any name it wishes, even an assumed or fictitious name which does not contain the names of any of the partners, statutes usually require that partnerships must record a certificate indicating the name of the partnership, its location, the names of the partners and their addresses, and other information. If the statute is not complied with, the partnership will not be permitted to sue.

2. The basis for an accounting and dissolution is the wrongful conduct of Grundig in violating his fiduciary duty as a partner.

Under the Uniform Partnership Act, a partner is a fiduciary for the partnership, and as such he has a duty to act for the best interests of the partnership and not for himself alone. He cannot retain for himself, and he must account to the partnership for, any benefit or profit which he has acquired in any transaction performed in connection with the partnership. He holds the profit in trust for the partnership. A partner has a right to a formal accounting when another partner has acquired such secret profits and has not accounted to the partnership for them. Here, Grundig's conduct in keeping the secret profits is a breach of his fiduciary duty and justifies the other partners' request for a formal accounting.

Under the Act, a partnership may be dissolved by court decree on the application of a partner because of the misconduct of another partner which may so prejudice or make impracticable the carrying on of the partnership business as to justify dissolution. Here, Grundig's misconduct by violation of his fiduciary duty in continuously keeping secret profits, and by exposing the partnership to liability for possible illegal price discrimination in violation of the antitrust laws, justifies dissolution.

3. Yes, if Strom and Lane comply with the Act, which permits the partners who have not wrongfully caused dissolution to continue the business in the same name, subject to proper provision for security for, or payment to the wrongful partner of, the value of his partnership interest less any damage to the partnership caused by his breach of the partnership agreement. This is the case here. (pp. 636, 662, 647, 661, 662, 648)

b.1. No. Under the Act, the bankruptcy of a partner dissolves the partnership. Here, although Palmer is having financial difficulties he is not yet a bankrupt. Failure to pay his debts does not of itself make him a bankrupt. Therefore, the partnership is not dissolved.

2. Aggressive will not have any rights against the partnership or its property. Aggressive is not a creditor of the partnership but only of Palmer, a partner. However, under the Act, a partner has a personal property right, namely his interest in the partnership which is his interest in profits and surplus. A partner's unpaid judgment creditor may obtain a court charging order against the debtor partner's partnership interest directing that the payment of surplus and other moneys due the partner by the partnership be paid to a receiver appointed by the court who is to pay the judgment creditor.

3. Yes. Under the Act, a partner may assign his interest in the partnership, in the absence of partnership agreement to the contrary. Such an assignment does not dissolve the partnership, and the assignee does not thereby become a partner. Since a partner's interest is personal property, it may be assigned by the partner as security for a loan made to him. (pp. 662, 641, 647)

Part Seven:
Business Organizations
B. Corporations

Chapter 50

A FORM OF BUSINESS ORGANIZATION

A corporation is an association of persons carrying on an enterprise or activity and clothed with a legal personality by compliance with a statute creating it. Its advantages are: a method of raising substantial capital; perpetual existence; ease of transfer of corporate interest; centralization of management; its legal entity; and no investor shareholder liability for corporate obligations. Courts will not go beyond the corporate legal entity unless it has an improper or illegal purpose.

Corporations may be public or private, stock or nonstock, domestic or foreign. Public corporations are created and controlled by a state or the federal government, while private corporations are composed of and controlled by private persons with no governmental functions or duties. The Subchapter S or "tax option" corporation has a maximum of ten natural persons with an exception having the corporate form with its corporate advantages but avoiding double taxation. A corporation is a "domestic corporation" in the state of its incorporation and a "foreign corporation" in another state. A foreign corporation has the right to do *interstate* business *through* a state without the state's permission; but permission is required to do *intrastate* business *in* that state, subject to reasonable state limitations on doing business there. A foreign corporation is "doing business" in a state when it is carrying on an enterprise in a substantial and continuous manner. The "long arm" of the state extends its jurisdiction over a foreign corporation, even though it may not be "doing business" therein, for its acts in the state where the corporation has certain minimum contacts with the state and suit would not offend traditional notions of fair play and substantial justice.

SECTION I. A LEGAL ENTITY

Definition

A "corporation" may be defined as *an association of persons carrying on an enterprise or activity and clothed with a legal personality by compliance with a statute creating it.* The business corporation, as distinguished from other types of corporation, developed in response to a need for a form of business organization with certain attributes not available in any other form of business organization. The great expansion of business in the last 175 years has accelerated the growth and development of the corporation. Today corporations are everywhere, and participation in business requires a knowledge of this form of business organization.

Desirability

The choice of sole proprietorship, partnership,[1] or corporation as the form of business organization depends upon which is best suited to the needs of the particular enterprise or activity. Among the outstanding advantages of the corporate form are: method of raising substantial capital; perpetual existence; ease of transfer of corporate interest; centralization of management; its legal entity; and no investor shareholder liability for corporate obligations. Its chief disadvantages are: the expense in its creation and maintenance; the burden of double taxation, first by the corporation and then by the shareholder on his income received as dividends; and the inconvenience of governmental supervision.

Perpetual Existence. A corporation may, unless it is provided in the charter to the contrary, continue perpetually. Unlike partnership, it is not dissolved by a change in the relation among the associates, caused by one of them ceasing to be associated in the carrying-on of the business. Perpetual existence makes for business stability; and, in the case of large business organizations, it is the only form of organization suitable.

Transferability of Interest. Shares or interests in the corporation are transferable easily without affecting the continuation of the organization's existence. This facilitates the acquisition of corporate capital.

[1] Although the general characteristics of a joint-stock association were discussed previously (see above, p. 632) under Partnerships, its resemblance to and its distinction from a corporation should be noted here. The joint-stock association resembles a corporation in the following respects: (1) it can have perpetual existence; (2) it issues shares of stock which are transferable; and (3) it is operated by directors and officers of the association. It differs from a corporation in the following respects: (1) it is created by agreement among its members, while a corporation is created by state statute; (2) property of the association is acquired and conveyed only in the names of its members individually, while acquisition and conveyance is in the corporate name; (3) it can sue and be sued only in the names of its members, while the corporate name is used in corporations; (4) its members are personally liable for the association's debts, while the shareholders of a corporation are not liable for corporate obligations; and (5) it may be dissolved without state approval, while corporate dissolution requires state approval.

Centralization of Management. The management and control of the corporation is concentrated or centralized in a small group, the board of directors, who are fiduciaries of the property of the corporation for the benefit of the shareholders and who owe a duty to the corporate creditors not to dissipate the corporate property.

Legal Entity. *The corporation is a juristic person, separate and distinct from its shareholders;* holds property in the corporate name; is sued and sues in the corporate name; and does business in the corporate name. A corporation retains its separate legal entity and personality even though one person may be the sole owner of all the shares in the corporation. (A wrongfully acquires possession of corporate property without corporate consent, and B, a sole shareholder, seeks to dispossess A of the property. B cannot succeed because the property belongs to the corporation.) Under the corporate form of organization a shareholder has no right to participate in its management and operation and is not liable for the obligations of the corporation. The shareholder has a limited amount of control but not such as to impose liability upon him for corporate obligations. This fact is of great importance in the acquisition of corporate capital.

Disregard of Legal Entity

Courts do not go beyond the corporate entity as an association of persons with a legal personality unless the association is formed, or is being conducted, for an improper or illegal purpose. Courts will not permit utilization of the legal cloak of a corporate entity to permit the perpetration of fraud or illegality and will disregard the corporate form and hold the individuals in the association liable personally. (X corporation is engaged in the manufacture of beer and is controlled by the same shareholders who control B corporation, which is engaged in the solicitation of freight for railroads. B did not solicit freight from businesses other than X and obtained so-called commissions from the railroad on the freight routed to them. In effect, the purported commissions were rebates going to X in violation of federal law, and such practice is illegal. Courts would look beyond the corporate entity because of the illegal purpose and operation of B corporation.)

SECTION II. CLASSIFICATION OF CORPORATIONS

Corporations may be classified as profit and nonprofit, in accordance with their purpose; as private, public, and quasi-public, depending upon the interests to be served; as stock and nonstock, if the corporation is divided into shares of interest; and as domestic and foreign, depending upon the place of incorporation. For convenience of discussion, corporations will be classified as public and private, stock and nonstock, and domestic and foreign.

Public Corporations

Public corporations are corporations created and controlled by a state or the federal government to administer governmental functions. The Federal Deposit Insurance Corporation is an illustration of a federal corporation, and a municipal corporation is an illustration of a state corporation. Municipal corporations are political subdivisions of a state which are incorporated for the better administration of governmental functions. Incorporated cities and towns are illustrations of municipal corporations. The term "quasi-corporation" often is used to describe local governmental bodies, such as counties and school districts; it is not a corporation but, inasmuch as it has some corporate functions and attributes, it is treated like a corporation. A "quasi-public corporation" is commonly known as a "public-service corporation." It is not organized by the federal or state government and is not for any governmental purpose; but it provides services in which the public has an interest and, for this reason, is subject to greater governmental regulation than private corporations. Electric light corporations, gas corporations, railroad corporations, and water corporations are illustrations of public-service corporations. They operate by virtue of a franchise from the state and have special powers.

Private Corporations

Private corporations are composed of, and controlled by, private persons with no governmental functions or duties. They may be conducted for profit or be nonprofit. The private business corporation is organized for the purpose of engaging in business for profit and often is called a "business corporation." Nonprofit corporations are not engaged in business with the purpose of making a profit but exist for the mutual benefit of the members. If they are formed for charitable or benevolent purposes they are often called "eleemosynary." Hospitals, educational institutions, and fraternal organizations are illustrations of nonprofit corporations. The principles of the law of Agency apply in the operation of nonprofit corporations, and those consenting to action to be taken by the association or corporation are bound as principals for such authorized acts. The Subchapter S or "tax option" corporation has the advantage of having the corporate form with its corporate advantages but avoiding double taxation. This corporation files an information tax return as do partnerships which allocates the corporate income among the shareholders for inclusion in their individual tax returns, irrespective of whether or not the corporate income has been distributed to the shareholders. Prior to 1977, this type of corporation was limited to a maximum of ten natural persons as shareholders. Beginning with 1977, if the corporation has had tax option status for a period of five consecutive taxable years, it may have a maximum of 15 shareholders if, during the five-year period, such increase is by reason of the additional shareholders acquiring the stock through inheritance. Also, shareholders may now be a grantor trust, a voting trust with each beneficiary treated as a shareholder, and any trust receiving stock under a will (but only for a 60-day period beginning with the day the stock is transferred under the will). The Subchapter S corporation has special advantages and disadvantages. The "professional service corporation" is formed by professional people who render professional services, (e.g., doctors, lawyers, public accountants), mainly for tax or pension program advantages.

Stock and Nonstock Corporations

A stock corporation is one in which the interests in the corporation are divided into shares of stock representing rights of participation in the limited control of the corporation, in its surplus or profits, and in the distribution of assets on dissolution. *Such shares are evidenced by certificates of stock.* The stock corporation is the form of corporate organization utilized by business. A nonstock corporation is a corporation in which the rights and liabilities of the members are determined by the corporation agreement without the creation of any shares of interest. Fraternal organizations are illustrations of nonstock corporations.

Domestic and Foreign Corporations

Domestic Corporations. A corporation is a domestic corporation in the state in which it was formed; in all other states and countries it is a foreign corporation. A corporation is a person and is a citizen of the state in which it was created. The use of the word "person" in statutes and constitutions is construed to include corporations, unless the statute or constitution provides to the contrary. Accordingly, corporations are included in the use of the term "person" in the Fifth and Fourteenth Amendments to the United States Constitution, respectively, which provide: ". . . nor shall any person . . . be deprived of life, liberty, or property, without due process of law; . . . ," and ". . . nor shall any State deprive any person of life, liberty, or property, without due process of law; nor deny to any person within its jurisdiction the equal protection of the laws." A corporation is not entitled to the equal protection of the laws, however, until it has been permitted to do business in the particular state. Corporations are not included within the term "citizen" as used in Article 4, section 2, and the Fourteenth Amendment to the Constitution of the United States which provide, respectively, that citizens of each state shall be entitled to all the privileges and immunities of citizens in the several states, and that no state shall make or enforce any law which shall abridge the privileges or immunities of citizens of the United States.

Foreign Corporations. A foreign corporation has the right to do *interstate* business *through* a state without permission from that state. However, a foreign corporation requires state permission to do *intrastate* business *in* a state subject to its compliance with reasonable statutory restrictions and regulations on their doing business therein. It is unconstitutional for states to enact unreasonable and arbitrary discriminatory legislation against foreign corporations.

In general, such regulations have as their purpose the protection of those resident persons who may deal with such foreign corporations. Statutes usually provide that: a copy of the foreign corporation's articles of incorporation is to be filed with the Secretary of State; a filing and license fee is to be paid; the name and registered office address of the corporation's registered agent for the service of process should be indicated; the proposed location of its office in the state and the names and addresses of its directors are to be disclosed; and it is not unusual for the state to require security of some kind. Failure to comply with these requirements has an effect which varies among the states. The corporation may be ejected, civil liability or criminal punishment may be imposed on its members severally, the corporation may be deprived of the right to use the state courts for suit on its contracts, its contracts may be declared to be void, and the shareholders may be exposed to liability for corporate debts.

"Doing Business." There is much uncertainty regarding the meaning of the phrase "doing business" in a state by foreign corporations. A *corporation is doing business in a state when it is carrying on an enterprise in a substantial and continuous manner*, as contrasted with isolated or casual transactions. The following corporate conduct in a state does not constitute "doing business" in that state: obtaining orders for goods by mail or by the corporation's representatives when such orders must be accepted by the corporation outside of the state in order to make them contracts binding on the corporation; engaging in acts which are concerned with the internal management of the corporation, such as holding corporate meetings and transferring corporate stock; the performance of a single transaction completed within a short period of time without intent of continuity. However, the installation of permanent corporate facilities in a state has been held to be doing business in that state. Under section 106 of the Model Business Corporation Act as amended in 1977, hereinafter called MBCA, the following activities by a foreign corporation are not considered to be transacting business in a state:

(a) Maintaining or defending any action or suit or any administrative or arbitration proceeding, or effecting the settlement thereof or the settlement of claims or disputes.

(b) Holding meetings of its directors or shareholders or carrying on other activities concerning its internal affairs.

(c) Maintaining bank accounts.

(d) Maintaining offices or agencies for the transfer, exchange and registration of its securities, or appointing and maintaining trustees or depositaries with relation to its securities.

(e) Effecting sales through independent contractors.

(f) Soliciting or procuring orders, whether by mail or through employees or agents or otherwise, where such orders require acceptance without this State before becoming binding contracts.

(g) Creating as borrower or lender, or acquiring, indebtedness or mortgages or other security interests in real or personal property.

(h) Securing or collecting debts or enforcing any rights in property securing the same.

(i) Transacting any business in interstate commerce.

(j) Conducting an isolated transaction completed within a period of 30 days and not in the course of a number of repeated transactions of like nature.

Corporate Acts Subject to State Court Jurisdiction. While a foreign corporation doing business in a state can be compelled by that state to qualify formally as a foreign corporation doing *intrastate* business therein, and to establish a registered office and a registered agent for the service of process and notice for failure of which the Secretary of State shall be the substitute, there is the question of whether the state has *in personam* (personal) jurisdiction over a foreign corporation *not* doing business in the state for a corporate *act* within the state. For example, a foreign corporation outside the state sent a contract to a resident in the state for his execution and return to the foreign corporation. Irrespective of whether or not a foreign corporation is "doing business" within a state, the United States Supreme Court has held[2] that the state acted within the federal due process and interstate commerce clauses when it asserted *in personam* jurisdiction over a foreign corporation for its acts in the state where the corporation has certain *minimum contacts* with the state and suit would not offend "traditional notions of fair play and substantial justice." The foreign corporation obtains a benefit from the state's protection and may not complain about the reasonable burden imposed upon it by being amenable to the jurisdiction of the state's courts for its acts within the state. As a consequence, many state statutes not extend the "long arm" of the state's jurisdiction over a foreign corporation for acts imputable to it within the state without having to rely on the concept of the corporation "doing business" therein;[3] although many states still rely on the "doing business" test as the basis of state *in personam* jurisdiction in an action against a foreign corporation for an activity within the state. Today, it can be said that a state has *in personam* jurisdiction over a foreign corporation for any activity within a state even though the corporation may not be doing business therein.

---

[2] *International Shoe Co.* v. *State of Washington,* 326 U.S. 310, 66 S.Ct. 154, 90 L.Ed. 95, 161 ALR 1057 (1945); *McGee* v. *International Life Insurance Co.,* 355 U.S. 220, 78 S.Ct. 199, 2 L.Ed.2d 223 (1957).

[3] See 26 Corp. Journal 75 (1970). Also see U3C, sec. 1.203.

Chapter 51

FORMATION OF THE CORPORATION

A "*de jure*" corporation is formed by complete or substantial compliance with all the state's mandatory statutory requirements. The Articles of Incorporation become the corporation's "charter" when accepted by the state. Incorporators who sign the articles are required in most states to be natural persons not infants, although only one person is necessary under the MBCA. The corporation is initially capitalized by the issuance of "shares," which are units of proprietary interests in the corporation owned by "shareholders" or "stockholders." "Stated capital" or "capital stock" is the sum of: the par value of all issued par value shares; the amount of the consideration received by the corporation for all issued no-par shares, except what has been allocated to capital surplus; and other amounts transferred to stated capital, whether for the issue of shares as a share dividend or otherwise as permitted by law. The articles are filed in a state office for approval as a charter, and a copy of the charter often is to be filed in the county where the corporation's principal place of business is located. A "*de facto*" corporation has not so completely or substantially complied with the mandatory requirements, but exists if there is: (1) a valid statute under which it could have become a *de jure* corporation; (2) an honest attempt to comply with the statutory provisions for incorporation; (3) colorable compliance with the statute; and (4) corporate user. Estoppel to deny an association of persons as a corporation occurs when there is a holding out of corporate status and a material change of position in reliance thereon.

A corporation is capitalized by the issuance of its shares of stock and by borrowing on its credit and issuing bonds and debentures therefor. Shares are evidenced by a "certificate of stock," and may be purchased for money, labor or services, or property actually received by the corporation, for a "fair value"

in most states and a "true value" in other states. Shares may be common or preferred, par value or no-par value. Preferred stock may be cumulative or non-comulative. Par value stock has a certain minimum nominal price issue. No-par stock has no nominal value indicated on the face of the certificate and may be issued for any consideration. There are also "authorized," "issued" or "outstanding," and "unissued" shares as well as "treasury stock." A "preincorporation subscription" is generally an offer to purchase shares in a corporation to be formed and is accepted by the corporation *by the act of its incorporation;* generally in the absence of statute to the contrary it may be revoked at any time before incorporation, although under the MBCA it is irrevocable for six months. A "postincorporation subscription" is generally an acceptance of the corporation's offer to sell the corporation's shares. A bond is a corporate secured promissory note, and may be "income," "collateral," "participating" or "profit-sharing." A debenture generally is a corporate unsecured promissory note.

"Promoters" undertake, further, originate, and organize the formation of a corporation, and have a fiduciary duty to act on behalf of the corporation and of the incoming shareholders. A promoter is a party to any preincorporation contracts made with third persons. On incorporation, the corporation is not automatically a party to such contracts, but if it wishes it may become bound by their terms by: "adoption;" "novation," which is the method most commonly used; "continuing offer;" and the not recommended method of "ratification." In the absence of statute to the contrary, a corporation is not liable for incorporation expense; in most states, an express corporate promise to pay is necessalary. Unless the promoter makes a proper disclosure of material facts of the transaction in which he sold to the corporation property *he acquired as a promoter*, he cannot retain the benefits and must return them to the corporation. He must either: (1) fully disclose to an independent board of directors for their approval; (2) fully disclose to all the original subscribers of corporate shares; (3) fully disclose to the existing shareholders at a shareholders meeting and obtain their ratification by a majority vote; or (4) subscribe to all of the shares involved in the corporate transaction.

SECTION I. INCORPORATION REQUIREMENTS

Incorporation may occur solely pursuant to federal or state law. At one time corporations were created individually by legislative enactment. The great increase in the number of corporations being formed, the desire to standardize incorporation procedure, and the inconvenience of separate legislative enactment for the creation of each corporation caused the states to formulate general corporation laws, and corporations were formed by complying with such laws. The issuance of a charter by a state to the incorporators pursuant to their request creates a contract between the state and the corporation which, under the United States Constitution, is irrevocable by the state except for cause through the proper exercise of its police power or except as the terms of such contract permit. In order to utilize the latter exception, state statutes usually contain a provision reserving to the state the power to repeal, amend, or modify its corporate law, such provision constituting a part of the contract between the state and the corporation.

Mandatory and Directory Requirements

As a condition precedent to the formation of a corporation, it is necessary for the incorporators to comply with the statutory requirements. Some of the statutory provisions are *mandatory* and some are *directory*. *Corporate existence is dependent upon substantial compliance with the mandatory provisions of the statutes.* Directory provisions are not essential to the formation of a corporation, and noncompliance with such provisions is an irregularity not affecting the formation of a corporation. Careful examination of the general corporation laws is necessary in order to determine the legislative intent regarding the mandatory or directory character of statutory provisions. In general, these mandatory provisions may be described as the preparation of articles of incorporation or of an application for incorporation, and the filing of such articles or application and the payment of fees in connection therewith as required by the statute. These two factors will now be considered.

Articles of Incorporation. The articles of incorporation constitute a proposal to incorporate and, when properly filed, are an acceptance of the state's offer to incorporate; on creation of the corporation, they form a contract between the corporation and the subscribing shareholders and also between the corporation and the state. The state's written approval of such articles of incorporation makes them a charter and creates the corporation. The state's approval also is necessary for amendment of the charter and amendment is governed by statute. The terms of the charter consist of the provisions contained therein and, whether expressly or impliedly indicated, the laws of the state. Statutes prescribe in detail the data to be included in such articles of incorporation and an examination will be made of these requirements.

Name. A corporate name is necessary to identify the corporate entity. In general, any name may be chosen, subject to legal restriction. Such restriction may be in statutory form requiring, as does the MBCA, the use of "Corporation," "Incorporated," or "Inc." to appear at the end of the corporate name so that the public can recognize the corporate nature of the organization. In some instances "Company" or "Co." are permitted at the end of the corporate name. Because certain types of corporation are governed by special statute—e.g., insurance and banking corporations—statutes usually provide that the following words are not permitted to be included in the corporate name of the corporation other than such special corporations: "bank," "trust," "safe deposit," "savings," "insurance," "guaranty," "title," "casualty," "benefit," and "cooperative." Use may not be made of names which all persons may lawfully use, such as geographical names; and names the same as, or deceptively similar to, those of other corporations or unincorporated associations may not be used. The reasons for the latter are to prevent unfair competition and to protect the goodwill of the names used by other businesses.

Object. The object of the corporation must be expressly stated. A corporation may be formed for any lawful object in which a natural person could engage, provided it is expressly permitted by a valid statute and is not contrary to law. The object of the corporation must be clearly stated in the articles of incorporation in order to determine whether or not it is sanctioned by statute and to determine the extent of the express corporate authority. If part of the object or purpose is unauthorized and part is authorized, the corporation may be formed for the authorized object and the unauthorized object will be surplusage and of no effect. Generally, a corporation may have more than one object and diverse objects if permitted by statute.

Duration. Generally, statutes require the duration of the corporation to be expressed in the articles of incorporation. A corporation has perpetual existence, unless the statute or the articles of incorporation provides to the contrary.

Place of Business. Statutes usually require the articles of incorporation to give the location of the principal office or place of business of the corporation.

Incorporators. Incorporators are those persons who sign the articles of incorporation. The charter is issued by the state to the incorporators authorizing them to do business as a corporation. Most statutes provide for a minimum number of incorporators, usually three. Under the MBCA, one or more persons, or a domestic or foreign corporation, may be an incorporator. Usually the statutes require the incorporators to be natural persons, and in many states a certain number of the incorporators must be either citizens or residents of the United States or of the state of incorporation. Inasmuch as incorporation is contractual in nature, the incorporators must have legal capacity to contract. In most states infants, however, cannot be incorporators. Married women may be incorporators. Unless a statute expressly authorizes a corporation to be an incorporator, the corporation is incapable; usually corporations are excluded. Often incorporators are dummies in the sense that they represent other people and, on incorporation, transfer their shares to others; in this way corporations can, in effect, create other corporations. The names and addresses of the incorporators must be stated in the articles of incorporation. A "closed corporation" exists when the shares of stock are held by a limited number of persons; and if such persons are members of the same family, there is a "family corporation."

Capitalization. In order to discuss capitalization, various terms should be defined. The Model Business Corporation Act,[1] section 2, provides:

> (d) "Shares" means the units into which the proprietary interests in a corporation are divided.
>
> (e) "Subscriber" means one who subscribes for shares in a corporation, whether before or after incorporation.

---

[1] Model Business Corporation Act, amended (1977).

(f) "Shareholder" means one who is a holder of record of shares in a corporation.

(j) "Stated capital"[2] means, at any particular time, the sum of (1) the par value of all shares of the corporation having a par value that have been issued, (2) the amount of the consideration received by the corporation for all shares of the corporation without par value that have been issued, except such part of the consideration therefor as may have been allocated to capital surplus in a manner permitted by law, and (3) such amounts not included in clauses (1) and (2) of this paragraph as have been transferred to stated capital of the corporation, whether upon the issue of shares as a share dividend or otherwise, minus all reductions from such sum as have been effected in a manner permitted by law.[3]

(k) "Surplus" means the excess of the net assets of a corporation over its stated capital.

(l) "Earned surplus" means the portion of the surplus of a corporation equal to the balance of its net profits, income, gains and losses from the date of incorporation, or from the latest date when a deficit was eliminated by an application of its capital surplus or stated capital or otherwise, after deducting subsequent distributions to shareholders and transfers to stated capital and capital surplus to the extent such distributions and transfers are made out of earned surplus. Earned surplus shall include also any portion of surplus allocated to earned surplus in mergers, consolidations or acquisitions of all or substantially all of the outstanding shares or of the property and assets of another corporation, domestic or foreign.

(m) "Capital surplus" means the entire surplus of a corporation other than its earned surplus. [The surplus, if any, created by or arising out of a reduction of the stated capital of a corporation shall be capital surplus. The capital surplus of a corporation may be increased from time to time by resolution of the board of directors directing that all or a part of the earned surplus of the corporation be transferred to capital surplus. A corporation may, by resolution of its board of directors, apply any part or all of its capital surplus to the reduction or elimination of any deficit arising from losses, however incurred, but only after first eliminating the earned surplus, if any, of the corporation by applying such losses against earned surplus and only to the extent that such losses exceed the earned surplus, if any. Each such application of capital surplus shall, to the extent thereof, effect a reduction of capital surplus.]

(n) "Insolvent" means inability of a corporation to pay its debts as they become due in the usual course of its business.

Statutes require that the articles of incorporation state: the authorized total amount of the capital stock; the number of shares into which it is to be divided; the different classes of stock and the number of shares in each class; the relative rights and preferences of each class of stock; and the names and addresses of all the original subscribers to the capital stock, with the amounts subscribed indicated opposite each name.

---

[2] The term "stated capital" has, in general, the same meaning as the commonly used term "capital stock."

[3] Also, see below, p. 697. Debentures are debt and are not stock and, therefore, are not part of stated capital.

Directors and Officers. In those states where a certain amount of organization is required as a condition precedent to incorporation, it is sometimes required that the names of the members of the first board of directors and the officers be stated. In those states where no such preincorporation organization is required, such names are not to be stated in the articles of incorporation.

Execution. Statutes require that the articles of incorporation be signed and sealed by the incorporators and, in some instances, that the original subscribers sign such articles. Although each signature is to be accompanied by a seal of the signatory, nevertheless, this requirement is usually deemed to be directory. Usually statutes require that such signatures be acknowledged before one authorized to administer oaths.

Filing and Recording. The articles of incorporation are to be filed in the office of a state official, usually the Secretary of State. If the articles are satisfactory, the Secretary files and records such articles and issues a certificate of incorporation together with an indorsement of approval on copies of the articles, called the charter. Often a copy of the charter is then filed in the county where the corporation's principal place of business is located, usually in the office of the county clerk. A fee for such filings is to be paid by the incorporators. *The filing or recording of a corporate charter is not notice to third persons of the contents thereof but is made for convenient reference when desired.*

A corporation must have and maintain a registered agent with a registered office so that service of process and notices may be directed to that office and agent. If a registered agent is not appointed, then the Secretary of State shall be such agent and have such office.

SECTION II. DEFECTIVE INCORPORATION

De Facto Corporations

A corporation which has complied completely or substantially with all the mandatory statutory requirements for its creation is a "de jure corporation." It has been held that the omission of the incorporators to seal the articles of incorporation was unimportant and that substantial compliance with the statutory requirements had occurred. The status of a *de jure* corporation cannot be questioned by anyone.

However, frequently incorporators fail to comply, completely or substantially, with the mandatory statutory provisions. In such an event, the status of the incorporators may be either a "*de facto* corporation" or a partnership. Courts have attempted to avoid the harshness of exposing incorporators to liability as partners when they have honestly tried but failed to comply substantially with the mandatory statutory requirements of incorporation, and have created the *de facto* doctrine. Under this doctrine, an association of incorporators may be recognized as, in effect, having all the attributes, rights, and liabilities of a corporation, subject to the power of the state in a direct proceeding, called a "quo warranto" proceeding, to question the existence of the purported corporation and to enjoin its continuance as such. For all practical purposes, therefore, a *de facto* corporation has the same status in business as a *de jure* corporation, except for the right of the state to question its existence.[4] In order for a *de facto* corporation to exist four things are necessary:

1. A valid statute under which such association could have become a *de jure* corporation.
2. An honest attempt to comply with the statutory provisions concerning incorporation. The attempt must be an honest one, bona fide; an intent not to comply with the statute precludes the creation of a *de facto* corporation.
3. Colorable compliance with the statute. This does not mean that substantial compliance with the mandatory provisions is necessary; if this were so, the association would have become a *de jure* corporation. However, if compliance with a mandatory provision is absolutely essential to the creation of a corporation, noncompliance with such a provision does not create a *de jure* or a *de facto* corporation.
4. Corporate user. If the associates have not begun to carry on any corporate business, no harm will come to them if their status as a *de facto* corporation is denied. However, if they have used the corporate entity in carrying on corporate business, harm will result and, accordingly, a *de facto* status is accorded to them. The extent of what is required for corporate user varies among the states. Generally, the courts do not require much evidence of corporate user, as long as some transactions or acts have occurred in the corporate name.

Application of Estoppel

When third persons innocently *deal* with an association as a corporation, the members of which innocently believe that they have a corporate status, in the absence of a statute to the contrary most courts hold that both the association and such third persons are estopped to deny the status of the association as a corporation for the purpose of that particular deal or transaction, regardless of whether or not the association is a *de facto* corporation. However, a person who knows that the association is not a corporation cannot estop the other party from denying that the association is a corporation, because there has been no material change of position in reasonable reliance upon the misrepresentation made to him and, accordingly, third persons or members of the association who know that no corporation exists cannot assert estoppel. (A, B, and C represent to D that they are a corporation and induce D to contract with them as a corporation. If A, B, and C, and also D, are unaware that there is no corporation *de jure* or *de facto*, all are estopped to deny that there is a corporation. If only D knew that there was no corporation, A, B, and C are not estopped to deny

[4] It should be noted that a "*de facto* officer" or a "*de facto* director" does not mean that he is an officer or a director of a *de facto* corporation. He is holding such office colorably as legally elected to it but, because of some irregularity, he has not been regularly so elected and, therefore, he is not a *de jure* officer or director.

that there is a corporation; if only A, B, and C so knew, D is not estopped to deny that there is a corporation.) The application of the principle of estoppel does not make the association a corporation, although it is commonly called a "corporation by estoppel;" it precludes a denial of corporate status in the *particular transaction* which has occurred.

Liability of Members of an Association Not a *De Jure* Corporation

A *de facto* corporation has the status of a *de jure* corporation in the carrying on of its business, and the members are liable only for their subscriptions for the purchase of corporate shares. When the association is not a *de facto* corporation and corporate estoppel is applicable, by the majority view the members of the association are not liable individually; only the association is liable as a corporation. However, if the third person is not estopped to deny the corporate status of the association—e.g., fraud perpetrated on the third person by members of an association holding out that they are a corporation—then the members of the association are liable as partners in most jurisdictions. Other courts hold either: that those members representing the association as a corporation are liable for damages for breach of implied warranty of authority, under the principles of the law of Agency when there is no principal and no authority; or that those members actively participating in dealings with third persons as representatives of a corporation are individually liable, and that innocent passive members are not liable individually. When a statute expressly imposes personal liability on members of a defectively formed association holding itself out as a corporation, the principle of estoppel is inapplicable and the members are liable as provided by the statute.

SECTION III. CAPITALIZATION

In many states, perhaps a majority, it is not required that any minimum amount of capital be acquired either prior to incorporation or subsequent to incorporation but before doing business. A corporation is capitalized—i.e., financed—by the issuance of membership shares in the corporation[5] and by borrowing on the credit of the corporation and issuing bonds and debentures therefor. First the issuance of shares of stock and then the issuance of bonds will be considered.

Issuance of Shares

A *share of stock* is intangible personal property consisting of a person's share or interest in the corporation and is owned by a "shareholder" or "stock-

[5] For the securities laws regulating the sale and transfer of corporate securities, see below, pp. 828–34.

holder." The share of stock is also a contract between the corporation and the shareholder. A *certificate of stock* is a writing issued by the corporation through its proper officer evidencing that the person named in such certificate is the registered owner of such shares. It contains: the name of the corporation; the state of incorporation; the name of the person to whom issued; the number and class of shares represented by the certificate; the par value of each share or a statement that the shares are without par value; and the signature of the corporation through its proper officers. *Shares may be purchased for money, labor or services, or property actually received by the corporation.* Such labor or services, or property, must have a fair value, although in the minority of states they must have a true value—i.e., a cash value equal to the value placed upon such labor or services or property.[6]

The consideration received by the corporation on the issuance of par value shares constitutes stated capital to the extent of the par value of the issued shares, and any excess of consideration is capital surplus. If no-par value shares are issued, the consideration received by the corporation also constitutes stated capital except for that part of the consideration which the corporation has allocated to capital surplus no later than 60 days after the issuance of the no-par value shares. The corporation has a lien on those shares which have not been paid for fully.[7]

Kinds of Shares. Shares of stock may be classified basically as either common or preferred, or par value or no-par value. *Common shares or common stock* contain the ordinary rights of a shareholder to participate to a small degree in the control of the corporation, in the surplus and profits, and in the distribution of corporate assets on dissolution. *Preferred stock* is stock which has some preference over the common stock, such as: preference in the payment of dividends; a fixed cumulative or noncumulative dividend; or a preferential priority on distribution of corporate assets on dissolution. *Par value stock* has a certain minimum nominal price issue, such price or "par value" fixing the pro rata interest of the share in the corporation. The par value of a share does not reflect the true value of such share but furnishes the basis for the extent of contribution to, and participation in, the corporation. *No-par stock* has no nominal or par value indicated on the face of the certificate of such stock, and it may be issued for such consideration as is determined by the board of directors or the shareholders, as provided by statute or charter.

"Authorized shares" are those shares which the corporation is authorized to issue under its charter. Until the shares have been issued they are called "unissued shares;" once issued they are called "issued" or "outstanding" shares. The issued shares reacquired by a corporation are called "treasury stock," which may be resold by the board of directors for any price. Treasury shares are still issued shares.

---

[6] For a discussion of the two tests of the value of services or property exchanged for shares, see below, p. 729.

[7] See UCC 8–103, and below, pp. 722 f.

Subscriptions. Persons may indicate their desire to purchase shares by subscribing for the purchase of such shares by indicating on a subscription list the number of shares each subscriber desires to purchase. A subscription agreement to purchase shares is to be distinguished from an underwriting agreement wherein a person, called an "underwriter," contracts that he will purchase the shares which he is unable to sell to the public. A subscription agreement is also distinguishable from a "stock warrant" which is not a share of stock but is an agreement on the part of the corporation to permit the holder of the stock warrant to subscribe to shares of stock. By the majority view a subscription agreement is not within the Statute of Frauds, unless the subscription agreement is not to be performed within a year from the making thereof, and may be in any form whatsoever. However, today by statute in some states subscription agreements are required to be in writing.

Preincorporation Subscriptions. Subscriptions may be made before incorporation, called "preincorporation subscriptions," or may be made after the corporation has been formed, called "postincorporation subscriptions." Preincorporation subscriptions are usually in the nature of continuing offers to purchase by subscribers and being subject to the law of Contracts, may be withdrawn or expire—e.g., by the subscriber's death—at any time before such subscription has been accepted by the corporation. Restrictions on withdrawal are imposed in some states. Under the MBCA, a subscription is irrevocable for six months unless otherwise provided by the subscription agreement or all the subscribers consent to the revocation of the subscriptions. By statute in many states, the persons who subscribe to the articles of incorporation automatically become shareholders upon incorporation.[8] Generally, express conditions in preincorporation subscriptions render the agreement void. In some states only the express condition is void and the remainder of the subscription agreement is valid. However, noncompliance with the offer contained in the subscription agreement, as by the formation of a different kind of corporation than that provided for in the subscription agreement, precludes enforcement of the subscriber's promise to purchase, inasmuch as his offer has never been accepted. Similarly, if the articles of incorporation which were made prior to the subscription were substantially changed subsequent to such subscription, the subscriber's offer cannot be enforced.

Postincorporation Subscriptions. A postincorporation subscription in response to a corporate offer to sell shares creates a contract immediately, making the subscriber a shareholder. However, infrequently the postincorporation subscription is not made in response to a corporate offer and is an offer to the corporation; a contract occurs only when the corporation subsequently accepts such subscription and, on such acceptance, the subscriber becomes a shareholder. Issuance of a certificate and payment for such shares are not conditions precedent[9] to the subscriber becoming a shareholder if a contract has been

---

[8] In some states the corporation is to act affirmatively to accept preincorporation subscription offers.

[9] See above, p. 95.

formed. A distinction is drawn at times between a subscription and a contract to purchase shares. Under a contract to purchase shares the purchaser does not become a shareholder until a certificate of stock has been issued to him. The problem is one of interpretation of the agreement to determine whether the intention of the parties was to subscribe or to purchase. Postincorporation subscriptions may have express conditions and, until such conditions are satisfied, the subscriber is under no liability if such conditions were conditions precedent. If the condition is a condition subsequent,[10] the subscriber becomes a shareholder when the contract is formed and has a right of action for damages against the corporation for breach of contract. Where there is doubt whether the conditional subscription contained a condition precedent or a condition subsequent, the subscription is construed as a condition subsequent.

Issuance of Bonds

The capitalization or financial structure of a corporation is dependent upon its issuance of bonds and debentures, as well as capital stock.[11] When a corporation borrows on its credit it usually executes two instruments, a bond and a mortgage. The bond, essentially, is the corporate promise to pay the indebtedness, and is secured by the mortgage. The mortgage is a lien on corporate property as security for performance of the bond. The mortgagee is a trustee holding the lien for the benefit of the bondholders, who are creditors. A "debenture" is an unsecured written corporate promise, often called a bond because, while it is not secured by any specific property, it is backed by the general credit of the corporation. A "convertible bond" is a bond with the privilege of its conversion into shares of stock at the option of the bondholder. An "income bond" is a bond on which the interest is payable only if earned and out of such earnings and after the interest on prior mortgages has been paid during a specified period. A "collateral trust bond" is a bond which is secured by miscellaneous pledged securities (e.g., stocks, bonds) owned by the issuing corporation. A "participating bond," also called a "profit-sharing bond," is a bond with a fixed rate of interest and with the right to participate with shareholders in corporate earnings to the extent as provided in the bond. The interest on a participating bond is a fixed charge and must be paid irrespective of earnings, and differs in this respect from the income bond.

SECTION IV. PROMOTION

The Promoter

"Promoters" are persons who undertake, further, originate, and organize the formation of a corporation. They have a *fiduciary duty to act on behalf of*

---

[10] See above, pp. 95–96.

[11] Corporate bonds are included under Article 8, Investment Securities, of the Code rather than under Commercial Paper.

the corporation and of the incoming shareholders. The fiduciary duties of agents, in general, are applicable to promoters. Promoters organize corporations with the expectation of receiving promotion profits of some kind.

Preincorporation Contracts

Promoters may enter into preincorporation contracts of various kinds on behalf of the corporation. *The promoter is a party to such contracts,* inasmuch as the unborn corporation is incapable of being a party, and is liable on such contracts, unless the parties provide to the contrary. Illustrative contracts are employment contracts, brokerage contracts, and purchase options on property to be used by the corporation when it comes into existence. The principles of the law of Contracts are applicable to these preincorporation contracts. If a preincorporation agreement contemplates perpetration of a fraud on the corporation when formed, the agreement is illegal and void. (P, promoter, agrees with V, vendor, that V is to sell certain property to the corporation and, on such sale, V is to pay P a commission or a part of the sales price without informing the corporation of such compensation to P. Such an agreement is void.) A promoter's contract with a third person may provide that, on the creation of the corporation, the corporation is to undertake the performance of the contract and, for corporate failure to do so, the promoter is to be discharged from any liability on such contract. As a party to a preincorporation contract, the promoter may enforce such contract against the other party thereto and, in turn, may be sued thereon by the other party, unless the contract provides to the contrary.

Theories of Corporate Liability. The creation of a corporation does not automatically make it a party to a preincorporation contract created by a promoter on its behalf, nor is the corporation liable for its performance. However, a corporation may become bound *by the terms* of a promoter's preincorporation contract, but there is much difference of judicial opinion as to how this result may be accomplished. Adoption, novation, continuing offer, and ratification are the theories utilized in order to accomplish this result. *Adoption* occurs when the corporation undertakes to perform the promoter's contract. Adoption does not discharge the promoter from any liability under the terms of the contract, and the corporation thereby does not become a party to the contract. If the promoter assigns the contract to the corporation, the promoter still is liable as a party to the contract and the corporation thereby does not become a party to it, although by assuming performance of the contract the corporation thereby becomes obligated to render such performance to the third person as a third party beneficiary of the contract[12] between the promoter and the corporation. *Novation* is the method most frequently used in order to discharge the promoter from any liability under the preincorporation contract and, by the new contract, to substitute the corporation as a party to the same terms as those

[12] For third party creditor beneficiary contracts, see above, p. 76.

in the preincorporation contract. The *continuing offer* theory is that a preincorporation agreement, such as a subscription agreement, is a continuing offer to the corporation and, when accepted by the corporation, a contract is formed between such offerors and the corporation. A corporation cannot *ratify* a preincorporation contract because it was not in existence at the time the contract was made and had no legal capacity to make such a contract.[13]

In the absence of statutory provision to the contrary, a corporation is not liable for the expenses of its incorporation. Statutes in some states provide that corporations have a quasi-contractual obligation to pay for the reasonable value of such incorporation services. In most states, only an express corporate promise to pay for a promoter's organizational expense will be enforced.

Fraudulent Promotion

A promoter has a fiduciary duty to the corporation to be created to act solely on its behalf and for its benefit. A promoter who derives benefit by defruading the corporation or by making secret profits can be compelled to disgorge such benefits and secret profits. Promoters often acquire property or options prior to incorporation which, subsequent to incorporation, are sold to the corporation at an inflated price, resulting in a profit to the promoter. Unless the promoter has made full disclosure of the material facts of such a transaction, he cannot retain the benefits and he may be compelled to deliver them to the corporation. Such property having been acquired by him as a promoter on behalf of the corporation, the promoter cannot profit therefrom without the consent of the corporation. If the promoter acquires property prior to his becoming a promoter, he may sell such property to the corporation without any duty of disclosure and he may make a fair and reasonable profit from such sale. For a promoter to retain the profits made from the sale of property to the corporation which he acquired while a promoter, he must do one of four things:

1. Make full disclosure to an independent board of directors not under the control of the promoter. Should the board of directors approve of the transaction, then the contract is binding on the corporation and on the promoter, who may retain his profits.
2. Make full disclosure to all the original subscribers of corporate shares.
3. Make full disclosure to the existing shareholders at a shareholders' meeting and obtain ratification of the transaction by a majority vote at such meeting.
4. Subscribe to all of the shares involved in the corporate transaction. Inasmuch as the corporation really consists of the shareholders, if all the shareholders have knowledge of the transaction there is no secret profit and the promoter or promoters may retain such profits. Subsequent purchasers of the corporate stock purchase at their own risk; they have the burden of ascertaining the value of the property being purchased.

---

[13] For ratification in the law of Agency, authority must have been previously possible; see above, p. 570.

Chapter 52

OPERATION OF THE CORPORATION

All corporate express authority derives from statute and the charter. A corporation's implied authority is to do what is reasonably incidental to the carrying on of the corporate business and what is usual in similar corporations, and includes: (1) to enact bylaws, prepared by shareholders unless delegated to the board of directors by statute or charter; (2) to have property; (3) to reacquire its own corporate stock; (4) to make contracts; (5) to borrow money on corporate credit; (6) to issue and indorse negotiable instruments, but if not issued for a corporate purpose the corporation is not bound, except to a holder in due course and to holders who properly claim through him; (7) to issue corporate bonds. It has no implied authority to act as a surety or guarantor, unless it is reasonably incidental to the corporate business, nor to be a partner unless permitted by statute or charter, which is permissible in most states today. When a corporation acts *ultra vires,* generally the courts will: (1) not enforce an *executory ultra vires* contract; (2) not interfere in an *executed ultra vires* contract; (3) enforce a *partially executed ultra vires* contract in an action brought by the party who performed his side of the contract. Under certain conditions, a corporate officer has a right to be indemnified for expenses incurred by him in a successful defense in a civil or criminal proceeding. A corporation is liable for damage caused by torts committed during the authorized performance of an *ultra vires* corporate transaction.

Although shareholders own the corporation, they are not liable for corporate obligations. They act only at corporate meetings and their action binds the corporation. Generally, notice is not required for regular meetings, but usually it is required for special meetings. Meetings must be held in the state of incorporation, unless statute is to the contrary. A quorum is necessary to begin

the meeting, but thereafter a quorum is not necessary to continue and take action at the meeting. Only shareholders registered on the corporate books may vote personally or by proxy, which is revocable unless coupled with an interest in the share. Treasury shares have no vote nor are they counted as part of the voting power. Unless charter or statute is to the contrary, each share has one vote. Shareholders elect directors, and cumulative voting is permitted in most states whereby a shareholder has a number of votes equal to the number of directors to be elected, multiplied by the number of his shares, distributable among the candidates as desired by the shareholder. In a "voting trust" title to the shares is in the trustees with the right to vote, and trust certificates are held by the trust members. Unless statute, charter, or bylaw is to the contrary: a majority of the shares voting at a meeting is required; but unanimous consent of all shareholders is required to make fundamental changes in the corporate business or structure.

Only the board of directors has the authority to act for the corporation as its policy-making body, which is derived from statute, charter, and bylaws. The board establishes corporate policy and, while it has the authority to manage the corporation, it delegates this authority to its appointed corporate officers. A director cannot vote by proxy. Generally, a director need not be a shareholder. For meetings of the board, generally a majority of the board is a quorum, and a majority vote of the quorum is required. The board is a fiduciary for the corporation, and because each director, as well as each corporate officer, has a fiduciary duty to the corporation he must make full disclosure of all material facts in his dealings on his own behalf with the corporation. Unless charter or bylaw is to the contrary, and in the absence of a contract to pay for his services, a director is not entitled to compensation for his services as a director. A corporation is liable as a principal for the torts of its agents while acting within the scope of their authority, and to a limited extent for crimes committed by it.

SECTION I. CORPORATE AUTHORITY

Actual Authority

Express Authority. *Corporate authority is the lawful power of a corporation to affect its legal relations with third persons.* A corporation is a creature of statute and derives its authority to exist and to act from statute. The corporate charter is the state's assent to the creation of the corporation and contains the authority to act pursuant to the corporate object indicated therein. Accordingly, *all corporate authority derives from statute and from the charter.* Corporate authority may be express or implied, the *express authority being indicated in the charter and the statute,* and the implied authority consisting of that reasonably required for carrying out the express authority. Corporate transactions made pursuant to corporate express or implied authority are binding on the corporation.

Implied Authority. *A corporation has implied authority to do those acts which are reasonably incidental to the carrying on of the corporate business and to do that which is usual in similar corporations.* A corporation has certain implied authority, in the absence of any statutory or charter provision or circumstances to the contrary, which will be discussed briefly.

Perpetual Succession. A corporation has implied authority to continue to do business during the period for which the corporation has been formed. If there is no fixed period, then the corporation has implied authority to continue for an indefinite period of time.

Corporate Name. A corporation has implied authority to sue and to be sued in the corporate name, and to acquire, hold, and transfer property in the corporate name.

Corporate Seal. Most states do not require a corporation to have a corporate seal; and, in the absence of statute to the contrary, a corporation has implied authority not to use a corporate seal, except when it is required of a natural person, in which case it may use or adopt any seal as its own for the purpose of the transaction.

Bylaws. A corporation has implied authority to enact bylaws for the implementation of its charter and the regulation of its corporate internal affairs. The power to make bylaws rests primarily in the shareholders, unless delegated to the board of directors by statute or charter. Under the MBCA, the initial bylaws must be adopted by the board of directors, and can be amended or repealed by the board unless the power is reserved to the shareholders by the articles of incorporation.

Property. A corporation has implied authority to acquire, hold, and dispose of real or personal property reasonably incidental to carrying on the corporate business. It has implied authority to sell its property to satisy, and to mortgage or pledge its property as security for, corporate obligations.

Stock. In most states corporations have implied authority to reacquire their own corporate stock, unless such reacquisition would be unfair to shareholders or to corporate creditors. By statute in most states corporations are permitted to acquire stock in other corporations provided it is incidental to carrying on the corporate business and, in many of these states, the acquired stock must be in corporations with objects similar to that of the acquiring corporation. In those states which do not have such statutory permission, most of them do not imply any corporate authority to acquire stock in other corporations unless such stock was acquired incidentally. An illustration of the latter is where a corporation takes the corporate stock of another corporation as security for debts due to the corporation, and, on default, the corporation thereby acquires such stock.

Make Contracts. A corporation has implied authority to make contracts in order to carry out its express and implied authority.

Borrow Money. A corporation has implied authority to borrow on the credit of the corporation if it is reasonably incidental to carrying on the corporate business.

Negotiable Instruments. A corporation, especially a trading corporation, has implied authority to issue and indorse negotiable instruments when it is *reasonably incidental* to carrying on the corporate business. If a corporation issues a negotiable instrument but such an instrument is not issued for a corporate purpose, *the corporation is not bound by the issuance of such an instrument unless the instrument is held by a "holder in due course."*[1] *The corporation is bound to the holder in due course and to holders who properly claim through him.*[2] A corporation does not have implied authority to act as an accommodation indorser on a negotiable instrument for a noncorporate purpose but, inasmuch as the corporation has implied authority to indorse negotiable instruments for a corporate purpose, *the corporation is bound on such an instrument only to a holder in due course and to holders who properly claim through him.* The corporation is not bound to a third person who knew that the corporation had acted in excess of its implied authority at the time such instrument was negotiated to him.

Bonds. Inasmuch as a corporation has implied authority to borrow on corporate credit and to pay corporate debts, it has implied authority to issue bonds, which are secured promises to pay the debt incurred.

Suretyship and Guaranty. A corporation has no implied authority to act as a surety or guarantor unless it is reasonably incidental to the corporate business.

Partnership. Unless the statute expressly permits, a corporation has no power and no implied or apparent authority to become a member of a partnership. The fixing of policy and the management of the corporation by the board of directors would be subject to interference by the other members of the partnership and, in this way, the board of directors and shareholders could lose control over the corporation. For this reason there is no such implied authority. Further, the liability of shareholders is limited to the purchase price of their shares. *Today, in a majority of states and under the MBCA a corporation may be a partner.*

Charitable Contributions. A corporation has no implied authority to make contributions to charity; however, there is a tendency on the part of the courts to countenance the expenditure of corporate funds when such expenditures are incidental to employee betterment, as for the erection of hospitals or lodging for employees.

Ultra Vires

The acts of a corporation within the scope of its authority are called *intra vires* acts; if the acts are outside the scope of the corporate authority, they are called *ultra vires* acts. A corporation is bound by *intra vires* acts, but there is conflict regarding the liability of a corporation for *ultra vires* acts. The courts

---

[1] See UCC 3–302, and above, pp. 336, 594–95.

[2] See above, pp. 346, 350.

will not enforce an *executory ultra vires* contract and will not interfere in an *ultra vires executed* contract but will leave the parties as it finds them. A majority of the courts will enforce an *ultra vires* contract which has been *partially executed*—i.e., it has been executed on one side but not on the other—*in an action brought by the party who has fully performed his side of the contract.* (C corporation makes an *ultra vires* contract with A to supply A with iron rails. C supplied the iron rails to A and A refused to pay the contract price. C may enforce the contract against A.) The reason for the enforcement of *partially executed ultra vires* contracts is that injustice otherwise would result. Shareholders may enjoin the threatened commission of an *ultra vires* act, and creditors may object on the ground that their security is being jeopardized.

Just as *ultra vires* is no defense to an action on a contract which has been partially executed by the plaintiff, so *ultra vires* is no defense and a corporation is liable for damage caused by *torts* committed during the authorized performance of an *ultra vires* corporate transaction. (C corporation without authority hired a truck to engage in the trucking business. While the truck was being driven in performance of an *ultra vires* corporate transaction, the driver negligently injured a pedestrian. The corporation is liable to the pedestrian for the tort of its driver during the performance of the *ultra vires* transaction.) Any other result would be obviously unjust.

SECTION II. CORPORATE MANAGEMENT

A corporation is an association of shareholders with a legal interest in the corporation and it operates on behalf of all of such shareholders. *A corporation is a juridical person and can act only through its agents. The shareholders have the right, at a legal shareholders' meeting, to elect directors to the board of directors.* The board of directors establishes corporate policy and manages the corporation. Although the *shareholders are the owners of the corporation,* nevertheless, they may not participate *directly* in the establishment of corporate policy and in managing the corporation. Shareholders have *indirect* control by their right to elect directors and to ratify voidable corporate transactions. Shareholders may act only at legal corporate meetings.

Corporate Meetings

The action taken by shareholders at corporate meetings is binding on the corporation. Such meetings must be legal in the sense that they have been properly held; otherwise action taken at such meetings is of no effect.

Time. The time when regular meetings, and the occasion when special meetings, are to occur are fixed by statute, charter, or bylaws. Notice of regular meetings usually is not required. However, *notice usually is required for special meetings.* The charter or bylaws usually contain special provisions regarding the number of shareholders or the percentage of the voting power which is necessary to require a special meeting. Notice of such special meeting must indicate the date, time, place, and nature of the business to be transacted, and must be given within a reasonable period of time prior to such meeting.

Under the MBCA, a shareholder or a director may, in a signed writing, waive his entitlement to a required notice. The waiver may be made before or after the time stated therein, and it is the equivalent of the giving of such notice. Also, action which may be taken at a shareholders' meeting may be taken without such a meeting with the same effect as though a meeting had taken place by a written consent indicating the action taken signed by all the shareholders entitled to vote on the subject matter.

Place. In the absence of statute, charter, or bylaw to the contrary, the corporate meetings must be held within the state of incorporation. The exact place of the meeting either is specified in the charter or bylaws, or is left to the discretion of the board of directors. Under the MBCA, if no place is fixed the place will be the registered office of the corporation.

Quorum. *A quorum is that number of persons required to be present at a meeting in order to transact business.* A quorum of the shareholders is necessary in order to have a corporate meeting. At Common Law and in the absence of statute to the contrary, any number of shareholders, not less than two, who appear at the meeting constitute a quorum. Today, by statute, charter, or bylaws, a quorum is determined by specific provision, often by a percentage of the voting power or a specific number of the holders of corporate shares. Under the MBCA, unless otherwise provided by the charter, a majority of the shares entitled to vote is a quorum. *Once a quorum is present and a corporate meeting begun, the meeting can continue and transact corporate business even though less than a quorum is present* because some of the shareholders have left the meeting.

Voting. *Only those shareholders registered on the corporate books as of the date when such books were closed in anticipation of the corporate meeting have the right to vote at such meeting.* A shareholder who has pledged his stock certificate and shares has the right to vote, in the absence of agreement to the contrary. *Shares held by the issuing corporation*—e.g., treasury shares—*have no voting rights and are not counted as part of the voting power.* At Common Law a shareholder had to appear personally in order to vote. Today, by statute, charter, or bylaws, shareholders have the right to authorize other persons to vote for them and in their stead. Such authorization is called a "proxy," which is in the form of an informal writing. A proxy can be given only by the legal owner of corporate shares. *A proxy is revocable, regardless of the terms therein, unless coupled with an interest in the share.* Revocation may be express or implied; the transfer of shares implies revocation of the proxy. The word "proxy" is used also to describe the person who has written authority to vote for a shareholder.

Unless there is charter or statutory provision to the contrary, each share has one vote. Statutes in most states permit cumulative voting *solely in connection with the election of the directors.* The charter or bylaws may permit cumulative voting. *The purpose of cumulative voting is to enable minority shareholders to obtain representation on the board of directors.* Under the cumulative voting method, *a shareholder has a number of votes equal to the number of directors to be elected, multiplied by the number of shares which he has, which he may distribute among the candidates as he wishes.* For example, if four directors are to be elected and a shareholder has 100 shares, he has four hundred votes, which he may distribute among the candidates as he wishes; he may cast all the votes for one candidate. (Three directors are to be elected. A has 90 shares and B has 40 shares. By ordinary voting, A would elect all three directors by casting 90 votes for each of his three nominees. B would be unable to elect any director because his 40 votes for his nominee would be insufficient. By cumulative voting, A would have 270 votes which he would use by casting 90 for each of his three nominees. B would have 120 votes and would cast them all for his nominee. A would elect two directors and B would elect one director.) In some states, cumulative voting is mandatory by law.

Voting Trusts. A shareholder may participate in a voting trust without any requirement of corporate authority. A voting trust is created by the transfer of shares by shareholders to a trustee or trustees for the purpose of voting all such shares in a block and thereby retaining control of corporate management. The title to the corporate shares is transferred to trustees, who then have the right to vote such shares at corporate meetings and who hold such shares in trust for the members of the voting trust. The trustees issue to such members voting trust certificates which are transferable in the same manner as certificates of stock. Voting trusts are valid in the majority of states provided they are not contrary to statute or public policy. If the purpose of the voting trust is to avoid the antitrust laws, or to perpetrate a fraud on the minority shareholders, or is for an unreasonable length of time, the voting trust is void.

Majority Rule. In the absence of statute, charter, or bylaws to the contrary, a majority of the shares voting at a legal corporate meeting is the will of the meeting, if the transactions are within the scope of the corporate business. The majority cannot make fundamental changes in the corporate business, such as a change in the capital stock, the nature of the corporate business, or the charter. *Fundamental changes in the corporate structure require the unanimous consent of all the shareholders, unless statute, charter, or bylaws provide to the contrary.* Usually it is provided that a specified large percentage of the holders of shares of corporate stock is required for fundamental changes. The majority may not exploit the corporation or oppress the minority shareholders. The majority may not, over the opposition of the minority, carry out *ultra vires* transactions.

Board of Directors

All corporate authority to act on behalf of a corporation is centered in the corporate board of directors. The board of directors is the policy making body of the corporation. *The authority of the board of directors is derived from statute, charter, and bylaws.* The acts of the board of directors within the scope of its corporate authority are binding on the corporation. *The board of directors has the primary function of establishing corporate policy and managing the corporation. The board of directors does not have the authority to make fundamental changes in the corporate structure without the consent of the shareholders*—e.g., dissolve the corporation, amend the charter, increase or decrease capital stock, sell the corporate assets, merge or consolidate the corporation with other corporations.

Eligibility. The number, qualifications, term of office, and method of election of directors are governed by statute, charter, and bylaws. In the absence of any provision to the contrary, anyone, including infants and persons who are not shareholders, may become directors.

Duty and Standard of Care. The board of directors is a fiduciary with the duty to act on behalf of the corporation, and also, by the minority but preferred view, on behalf of the shareholders. Directors have a duty to exercise that degree of care and diligence which an ordinary prudent director reasonably could be expected to exercise in a like position under similar circumstances. A director is not liable for honest errors of judgment in the exercise of his discretion on behalf of the corporation.

Meetings. *The directors may act only as a board at a legal meeting.* Usually notice of a regular meeting is not required to be given, but notice of a special meeting must be given unless it is impossible or impracticable or otherwise useless to give such notice. Failure to give proper notice causes the meeting to be illegal, and business transacted at such a meeting is not the act of the board of directors. *A majority of the board of directors constitutes a quorum, in the absence of statute, charter, or bylaws to the contrary. A vacancy* on the board is *counted* in determining the existence of a quorum. A majority vote of the quorum is the will of the board. Meetings of the board of directors may be held within or outside of the state of incorporation, in the absence of statute, charter, or bylaw to the contrary.

Dealings between Director and Corporation. A director who has a personal interest in the action to be taken by the board of directors should not participate in a vote on the matter because of the conflict of his *fiduciary duty* to the corporation and his *own self-interest.* If his presence is necessary for a quorum of the board, or if his vote is necessary in order to pass a resolution regarding the transaction, his participation makes the action taken *voidable* at the election of the corporation. By the majority view, although a director with a personal interest is disqualified from participating in any action by the board regarding the particular transaction in which he is interested, nevertheless, if his presence was not necessary to constitute a quorum and his vote was not necessary for passage of the resolution, the action taken by the board is valid. *A director dealing with the corporation on his own behalf has a fiduciary duty to make full disclosure of all material facts pertinent to the transaction,* and his failure to do so renders the transaction *voidable* at the election of the corporation. Action taken at an improperly held meeting of the board of directors may be ratified subsequently by a proper meeting of the board. The shareholders at a corporate meeting also may ratify improper action by the board of directors if such action was within the authority of the board but was not exercised properly. Under the MBCA, unless the shareholders have so authorized, a corporation may not lend money to its directors and employees unless the board of directors decides that such a loan would benefit the corporation.

Compensation. A director is not entitled to compensation for his services rendered to the corporation as a director in the absence of any provision in the charter or bylaws to the contrary or in the absence of a contract for such services. The shareholders at a corporate meeting, or the board of directors if specifically authorized may pass a resolution awarding compensation for such services. Should a director perform special services either outside of the ordinary services to be rendered as a director or as an officer of the corporation, a corporate promise is implied by law to pay for the reasonable value of such services. An officer who is also a director may receive a salary for his services as an officer, but may not receive any for his ordinary services as a director. The compensation of corporate officers is fixed by the board of directors.

Delegation. The board of directors has implied, if not express, authority to delegate to others some of its authority and discretion to manage and carry on the corporate business. Such authority is delegated to officers of the corporation who are elected by the board of directors. While the board of directors may delegate much of its authority, it may not delegate the authority to supervise and control the operation and management of the corporation. It is for this reason that *a director may not vote by proxy at a meeting of the board of directors* because he has no express or implied authority to delegate his special skill, judgment, and discretion, which he has a duty to exercise at a meeting of the board. The board of directors is the fountainhead of corporate authority, and it may delegate such authority not only to corporate officers but also to committees of directors, in order to accomplish some of the many duties of the board. As long as the board of directors retains the right to supervise and control all activities, whether on the part of its committees or by corporate officers, the board has not exceeded its express or implied authority so to delegate its authority.

Corporate Officers

Corporate bylaws usually provide expressly for the number of *corporate officers to be appointed by the board of directors,* their qualifications and terms of office, and their duties. Corporate officers usually consist of a president, one or more vice-presidents, a secretary, a treasurer, and a cashier if the corporation is a bank. Under the MBCA, the same person may hold two or more offices, except he cannot be both the president and the secretary. The authority of corporate officers is limited to that given to it by the board of directors and by the charter and bylaws. Their function is to operate the corporate business within the scope of their authority. *Corporate officers are agents of the corporation, and the principles of the law of Agency are applicable to their actions.* As *fiduciaries*, corporate officers have the duty to act on behalf of the corporation. Corporate officers have the duty to exercise the diligence and care which a reasonable, prudent person in their position would exercise under the circumstances. They are not liable for honest errors of judgment in the exercise of their discretion. Their compensation usually is determined by the board of directors at a directors' meeting, although the bylaws may fix their compensation.

Corporate Torts and Crimes

A corporation is liable, just like any other principal, for damage caused by the torts of its agents while acting within the scope of their authority. The corporation is liable for such torts even though they were committed during the course of an *ultra vires* transaction, so long as the agent was acting within the scope of the authority accorded to him. Similarly, criminal responsibility may be imputed to a corporation for the crime committed by its agents while acting within the scope of the authority given to them. Whether the corporation may be guilty of a criminal offense depends upon the expressed intention of the legislature in the state statutes. Corporations do not come within the purview of those criminal statutes which provide punishments which are inapplicable to corporations, such as imprisonment, or which prescribe elements of the crime which are inapplicable to corporations, such as murder which involves the killing of one human being by another human being. *Generally, criminal statutes apply to corporations as well as to natural persons, unless the statute expressly or impliedly excludes corporations.* Inasmuch as injunctions may be issued against corporations, it follows that corporations may be punished for civil or criminal contempt of court, as that is the only way that the injunctions may be enforced.

The federal Foreign Corrupt Practices Act of 1977 imposes: civil and criminal penalties upon corporations, their directors and officers, and other persons who violate the Act's requirements for strict record-keeping and internal accounting control requirements; abstention from certain foreign corrupt practices; and greater detailed disclosure in the filing of periodic and other reports with the Securities and Exchange Commission. Reference should be made to a later discussion of this subject.[3]

Indemnification of Officers, Directors, Employees, and Agents

Under the Model Business Corporation Act, to the extent that a corporate officer has successfully defended himself in certain types of civil or criminal proceedings, the corporation must indemnify him against expenses, which

[3] See below, pp. 831–34.

include attorney's fees, actually and reasonably incurred by him in connection with such proceedings. The proceedings include those in which he is a party by reason of his being an officer of the corporation or as one who was serving at the request of the corporation, and he had acted in good faith and in a manner he reasonably believed to be in the best interests of the corporation, and, in a criminal case, he had no reason to believe his conduct was unlawful.

Chapter 53

SHAREHOLDERS' RIGHTS AND LIABILITIES

Shares contain various rights, exercisable by the owner shareholder. (1) He has the right to *vote* at corporate meetings, and only the shareholders can vote on proposed fundamental changes in the corporate structure. (2) He has the right to *share in dividends,* which may be in cash, stock, scrip, or other property. A dividend is "declared" when (a) the board of directors has passed a resolution approving of a dividend and (b) such dividend has been announced, the shareholders then becoming general creditors of the corporation; funds need not be set aside but, if they are, they are a trust fund for participating shareholders. A dividend may be revoked under certain circumstances. Courts are reluctant to interfere in the internal management of the corporation or to interfere with the discretion of the board of directors, but it will compel declaration of a dividend if the board has abused its discretion. Cash and property dividends can be declared only out of surplus or "net profits," which may be earned or capital surplus, but cannot be declared out of unrealized appreciation. (3) He has a "*pre-emptive right*" to subscribe to an increase in the capital stock to the proportionate extent of his corporate holdings by a *newly authorized* issue of stock. (4) He has a right to *proportionate distribution* of corporate assets *on dissolution.* (5) He has a right to *inspect the corporate books* at reasonable times and a proper place for a proper purpose. (6) He has a right to *transfer his certificate and its shares,* limited only by any restriction on transfer *conspicuously* noted on the certificate.

Under UCC Article 8 on Investment Securities, a certificate of stock is an investment security negotiable *per se.* A contract for the sale of a certificate of stock and its shares is within the Statute of Frauds and is unenforceable unless proved in one of five ways: (a) a proper signed writing; (b) to the extent of the

delivery of a certificate of stock and its acceptance; (c) to the extent of a payment made; (d) a written confirmation of the contract sufficient against the maker and, if not objected to within ten days after receipt, effective against the recipient; (e) admission in a legal proceeding. The corporation cannot make registration on its books a condition to *transfer of title* to a certificate and its shares, but it can require such registration for the purpose of voting and dividends. A certificate and the shares represented thereby can be transferred only if: (a) the certificate is in registered form or has been specially indorsed, the appropriate person's indorsement, either special or in blank, must be made on the certificate or on a separate document; and (b) the certificate so indorsed, or the certificate and the separate document with the indorsement, must be delivered. The purchaser of a certificate has a right to have any necessary indorsement supplied. A corporation's lien on the certificate or its shares must be noted conspicuously on the certificate. The purchaser of a certificate acquires his transferor's rights in the certificate and its shares which his transferor had or had authority to transfer, except that he cannot claim through a "bona fide purchaser" if he participated in any fraud or illegality affecting the security, or he was a prior holder with an adverse claim. *A "bona fide purchaser" acquires the rights of a purchaser and also the certificate and the shares represented thereby free of any adverse claims.* He "is a purchaser for value, in good faith and without notice of any adverse claim who takes delivery of a security in bearer form or of one in registered form issued to him or indorsed to him or in blank." He must be a "holder"—he possesses the certificate, and it flows to him either originally or by indorsement. Various warranties are made by presentment for registration and on the transfer of a certificate of stock, and a corporation has certain rights and duties in connection with a certificate outstanding, for which reference should be made to the text.[1]

A wrong to a shareholder or to the corporation creates a right to legal relief. *When a wrong is done to a shareholder* by the corporation or a director or the board of directors, he has a right of action in his own name against whosoever caused his injury. If more than one shareholder has been so individually injured, one shareholder may bring a "class" or "representative" suit on behalf of all such wronged shareholders. *When a wrong is done to the corporation*, only the corporation as a legal entity may sue therefor. However, a complaining shareholder may, on behalf of the corporation, institute an action if he first exhausts his internal corporate remedies by: (1) requesting the board of directors to take proper action for the wrong done to the corporation, unless he can show this would be futile; and (2) requesting the shareholders at a corporate meeting to take proper action for such wrong, unless he can show this would be futile.

A shareholder is not liable for corporate obligations, but he is liable to the corporation for his unpaid subscription contracts for corporate shares, which corporate right is an asset available to corporate creditors after their resort to

[1] See below, p. 726.

corporate assets. Corporate creditors can recover from shareholders of watered stock the deficiency in value for par value shares issued to them. Such shareholders cannot avoid their liability by transferring such watered shares to a "bona fide purchaser," who is not liable for the previous watering and deficiency. Treasury shares may be sold at any price and such sale is not a watering.

SECTION I. SHAREHOLDERS' RIGHTS

Owners of shares have various rights as shareholders in the corporation. Among these rights are the following: the right to vote at corporate meetings; the right to share in the profits of the corporation; pre-emptive rights; the right to share in the surplus (i.e., net corporate assets) on dissolution of the corporation; the right to inspect corporate books; rights in connection with certificates of stock and transfer of stock; and the right legally to enjoin improper corporate action. These rights will be examined briefly in turn.

Right to Vote

A shareholder has the right to attend corporate meetings and to vote at such meetings, unless his shares are nonvoting shares. *Only the shareholders, and not the board of directors, may vote at corporate meetings on proposed fundamental changes in the corporate structure.* The right to vote is a source of great protection to shareholders and gives to such shareholders a limited degree of control over the corporation.

Right to Dividends

Shareholders have the right to participate in corporate profits in the form of dividends in the proportion that their holdings bear to the number of shares outstanding which are also entitled so to participate. The corporate profits or surplus set aside for, or distributed to, shareholders by a corporation pursuant to a declaration of its board of directors is called a "dividend." Dividends may be in the form of cash, stock dividend, or other property—e.g., securities of other corporations, personal or real property, scrip. One of the usual preferences of preferred stock is priority in dividends. Preferred stock may be *cumulative* in that a certain amount of dividends is to be paid each year and to accumulate over the years, with priority over dividends to be paid to holders of common stock; and it may be *noncumulative* so that the holders of preferred stock are entitled only to a priority of dividends declared each year. Dividends on preferred shares are impliedly cumulative. Preferred stock also may be participating or nonparticipating. *Participating preferred stock* is that stock which is entitled to participate along with the common stock in any surplus available for dividends remaining after dividends have been paid on the preferred stock. *Nonparticipating preferred stock* is that stock which cannot so participate in such surplus.

Declaration of Dividends and Effect. Dividends are distributed only within the discretion of the board of directors. *A dividend is declared when the board of directors has passed a resolution approving of a dividend and such dividend has been announced.* The shareholders become *general creditors* of the corporation and, should the corporation subsequently become insolvent prior to distribution of dividends, the shareholders would be general creditors of the corporation to the extent of the dividends due them. *It is not necessary that funds be set aside in order to make the dividend effective.* However, once funds have been set aside for the purpose of paying such dividends, such funds represent *a trust fund in favor of the shareholders,* and corporate creditors cannot proceed against such funds.

Whether or not a declaration of dividends is revocable by the corporation, through its board of directors, depends upon the nature of the dividend. If it is a *cash dividend,* it is *irrevocable* because a debtor-creditor relationship has been created between the corporation and the shareholders, with exceptions. The *ultra vires* declaration of an illegal cash dividend is revocable, as when there is no corporate surplus from which a dividend could be paid. The declaration of an *interim dividend,* which is a payment on account of the next forthcoming dividend, *may be revoked at any time before it becomes payable* where adverse change in corporate circumstances makes it advisable to do so. Where a resolution has been passed approving of a dividend and it has not been made public or communicated to the shareholders and no fund therefor has been set aside, the resolution may be rescinded. The declaration of a *stock dividend* does not create a debtor-creditor relationship, and, accordingly, it is *revocable* at any time prior to issuance of such stock. The declaration of a dividend payable in *scrip certificates,* which are convertible into cash, stock, or interest-bearing obligations, *may be revoked before the scrip is issued* if adverse change in corporate circumstances makes it advisable to do so, even though enough surplus remains to satisfy the dividend.

Equitable Relief. *Courts are very reluctant to interfere in the internal management of the corporation or to interfere with the discretion of the board of directors.* However, if the board of directors has *abused* its discretion in not declaring dividends when it should have done so, the shareholders may obtain a court decree compelling the corporation through the board of directors to declare and distribute dividends. It is not an abuse of discretion to set aside reasonable funds for reasonable corporate expansion and for adequate safety margins. Courts will not compel a corporation to borrow money in order to pay dividends.

Effective Date. *A proper declaration of dividends is irrevocable, and the dividends belong to the holders of the shares at the time such dividend is effective.* A dividend may be declared on one day, effective on another day, and payable on still another day. However, a corporation *ignorant* of a transfer of shares prior to the effective date is protected if it distributes dividends to the owner of the shares who is *registered on the books of the corporation on the effective date.* Dividends are payable to a pledgee of shares of stock, if the pledgee is registered on the corporate books or the corporation otherwise has notice of such pledge, and such dividend is to be applied by the pledgee in reduction of the pledgor's debt, in the absence of pledge agreement to the contrary.

Source of Dividends. In almost all states cash and property dividends can be payable only out of surplus, often called "net profits," and are not payable out of capital because the return of capital to shareholders would prejudice corporate creditors. *Excess of net assets over stated capital (capital stock) is surplus, which may be either earned surplus or capital surplus*—e.g., paid-in surplus consisting of the consideration paid for par value shares in excess of such par value or of that portion of the amount received as consideration for no-par value shares not allocated to capital stock. However, *unrealized appreciation of the value of fixed assets is not, and realized appreciation thereof is, surplus available for distribution as cash dividends in almost all states.* In some states a *stock* dividend may be declared out of a surplus from such unrealized appreciation, because no assets are being withdrawn from the corporation and creditors are not prejudiced. The illegal distribution of dividends out of capital is recoverable by the corporation, *except as against shareholders innocent of the illegality who may retain the dividends received by them.* However, if the corporation is *insolvent* at the time of such illegal distribution, *even innocent shareholders must return the dividends received by them.* The directors who voted the illegal dividend are liable personally to the corporation therefor.

Under the MBCA, stated capital includes the sum of the par value of issued corporate shares having par value, together with the consideration received by the corporation for all its issued no-par value shares except for that part of the consideration which the corporation has allocated to capital surplus no later than 60 days after the issuance of the no-par value shares.

A board of directors may declare and the corporation pay dividends in cash, its own treasury shares, or both, out of corporate unreserved and unrestricted earned surplus, except when the corporation is insolvent or when it is contrary to its articles of incorporation. The corporate stated capital is not affected. Dividends may be declared and paid in the corporation's own authorized but unissued shares out of unreserved and unrestricted surplus. However, if the dividend is payable in its own shares having a par value such shares shall be issued at not less than the par value and there shall be transferred to stated capital at the time such dividend is paid an amount of surplus equal to the aggregate par value of the shares to be issued as a dividend.

A split-up of the issued shares of any class into a greater number of shares of the same class without increasing the stated capital of the corporation may be made. This is not construed to be a share dividend. The split-up will cause an increase in the number of shares issued and outstanding, each share with an equal reduced par value. In order to accomplish the split-up, the articles of incorporation will have to be amended to permit it.

Under the Internal Revenue Code, a dividend payment in cash is ordinary income and is taxable, subject to a $100 dividend exclusion to a noncorporate shareholder or an 85 percent dividend received deduction to a corporate shareholder. Generally, stock dividends and stock splits are exempt from taxation. The shareholder recipients must allocate the cost basis for the shares originally owned to the number of shares owned after the stock dividend or stock split.

The Internal Revenue Code deals with unreasonable accumulation of earnings and profits. It allows a $150,000 credit against the amounts permitted to be accumulated. An accumulation of earnings and profits together with little dividends may be unreasonable, depending on the facts of the particular case. If the dividend were considered little and the accumulation large, a corporation's expansion plans would be a factor in establishing a bona fide business purpose showing the accumulation not to be unreasonable.

Pre-emptive Rights

At Common Law *a shareholder had the right to subscribe to an increase in the capital stock of the corporation to the proportionate extent of his holdings in the corporation.* This right is called a "pre-emptive right" and exists today in the absence of statute, charter, or bylaw to the contrary. This right exists only in connection with a *newly authorized* issue of stock, and it does not apply to the corporate sale of shares previously issued and reacquired by the corporation (treasury stock) or to unissued shares from an existing authorized issue. The purpose of this right is to permit shareholders to retain their relative interest in the corporation.

Rights on Dissolution

Each shareholder has the right, on corporate dissolution, to receive his proportionate share of corporate assets remaining after corporate obligations have been satisfied. Usually the remaining assets are liquidated and distribution is made in money. Distribution may also be made in securities or in kind. If the corporation is in reorganization proceedings, whether under the Bankruptcy Code or not, the expense of a sale may not be necessary in order to determine the value of the corporate property and the value of the shares owned by dissenting shareholders.

Inspection of Corporate Books

Shareholders are the owners of the corporation and have a right to be informed regarding the corporate business. Shareholders, and their representatives, have the right to examine the corporate books and to make copies thereof provided it is exercised at *reasonable times, at the proper place, and for a proper purpose.* Similarly, shareholders have the right to request and receive corporate information from officers and directors of the corporation, especially in connection with dealings between shareholders and such officers, directors, or the corporation.

A corporation should keep essential corporate books and records, whether or not required by statute. Such books and records are:

1. Charter.
2. Bylaws.
3. Minute books of the meetings of the board of directors and of the shareholders.
4. Subscription book.
5. Subscribers ledger.
6. Stock certificate book.
7. Stockholders ledger.

Corporate books and records are admissible in evidence if it is shown that they have been kept in the regular course of business and are properly authenticated. They represent prima facie evidence of their contents and the corporate transactions contained therein. For the admission of such records into evidence the following steps must be taken: (1) identification of the records by their custodian; (2) proof that the entries were made in the regular course of business; (3) proof that the entries were made at or near the time the transactions occurred; (4) proof that the entrant had personal knowledge of the facts recorded, or the date were furnished to him by those who had personal knowledge; (5) testimony regarding the entries must be given by the entrant, or, if he be dead, outside the state, or unavailable, then the official custodian must testify that such entries were made in the regular course of business.

Transfer of Shares

In General. ***Certificate of Stock under the Code.*** *Reference should be made at this time to "Negotiable Paper under the Code,"* briefly discussed previously.[2] Article 8[3] of the Uniform Commercial Code governs the transfer

[2] See above, pp. 150–53.

[3] The American Institute of Certified Public Accountants has not recognized for purposes of coverage on the Uniform CPA Examination, as of the date of the publication of this book, the 1977 Amendment of Article 8 on Investment Securities of the Uniform Commercial Code. However, a brief comment is in order here. The new 1978 Official Text of the Uniform Commercial Code incorporates the 1977 amendment of Article 8 on "Investment Securities" with its impact on Article 9 "Secured Transactions". Basically, investment "securities" now may be of two kinds rather than just one. Those securities represented by certificates or other instruments, previously just called "securities", are now called "certificated securities". Those securities not so represented are now recognized by the amendment as "uncertificated securities". The purpose of the amendment is to extend to uncertificated securities much of the same coverage as was previously extended, and now continued, to certificated securities. "An 'uncertificated security' is a share, participation, or other interest in property or an enterprise of the issuer or an obligation of the issuer which is (i) not represented by an instrument and the transfer of which is registered upon

of *investment securities,* called "security" for short under the Article. A security includes certificates of stock, stock warrants, bonds, and anything which securities markets are likely to regard as suitable for trading.[4] Money is not included in the term security. A security, and therefore *a certificate of stock, is an instrument of a negotiable character,*[5] and a "bona fide purchaser" of a security will acquire more rights under the security than would a mere "purchaser" of a security, a transferree of a chattel, or an assignee of a contract right. *A bona fide purchaser "is a purchaser for value in good faith and without notice of any adverse claim who takes delivery of a security in bearer form or of one in registered form issued to him or indorsed to him or in blank."*[6] A certificate of stock "is in 'bearer form' when it runs to bearer according to its terms and not by reason of any indorsement."[7] A certificate of stock is in "registered form" when it runs to a person named therein.

Statute of Frauds. *A contract for the sale of a certificate of stock and the shares represented thereby, irrespective of the price, is within the Statute of Frauds* and is *unenforceable* unless proved in any *one* of five ways. To the extent possible, the statute of frauds provisions under Article 8 are similar to the statute of frauds provisions under the Sales portion of the Code. Reference should be made to the full discussion there[8] in amplification of the requirements of the statute of frauds provisions discussed briefly here under Article 8. The *first* way is a *writing* indicating that (1) a contract had been made for the sale (2) of a stated number of shares of a particular stock (3) at a defined or stated price, and the writing has been *signed* by the party against whom enforcement of the contract is sought or by his authorized agent or broker. *Second, delivery* of a certificate of stock has been made and accepted, but the contract is enforceable only to the extent of the certificate so delivered. *Third,* a *payment* has been made, but the contract is enforceable only to the extent of such payment. *Fourth,* within a reasonable time after the contract was made, a *written confirmation* of the contract made by one of the parties to the contract, sufficient against the sender under *"first"* above, was received by the other party, who then failed to send a written objection to its contents within 10 days after his receipt. The recipient has a duty to manifest his objection to the sender's timely erroneous confirmation, and his failure to do so soon is an

---

books maintained for that purpose by or on behalf of the issuer; (ii) of a type commonly dealt in on security exchanges or markets; and (iii) either one of a class or series or by its terms divisible into a class or series of shares, participations, interests, or obligations." An example is stock of a closely-held corporation when no instrument representing the stock interest has been issued.

[4] "The validity of a security and the rights and duties of the issuer with respect to registration of transfer are governed by the law (including the conflict of laws rules) of the jurisdiction of organization of the issuer." UCC 8–106.

[5] A security is even called a "negotiable instrument" under this portion of the Code, although a security as a particular kind of negotiable instrument is governed only by Article 8, and not by Article 3, which is concerned with Commercial Paper—negotiable instruments payable in money.

[6] UCC 8–302. (Author's italics.)

[7] UCC 8–102(1)(d).

[8] See above, pp. 208–12.

admission that the confirmation is correct and he thereby makes it a written manifestation *of his own. Fifth,* the party against whom enforcement is sought *admits* in his pleading, testimony or otherwise in court that a contract was made for sale for a stated number of shares of a particular stock at a defined or stated price.

Restrictions on Transfer. An issuing corporation usually requires that the transfer of shares be recorded on the corporate books in order that the corporation may treat the registered owner as the owner of such shares for the purpose of dividends, voting at corporate meetings, and as liable for calls and assessments on the shares. However, *the corporation cannot require such registration as a condition precedent to the transfer of title to the certificate of stock or to the shares represented thereby.* Any lawful corporate restriction on the transfer of a certificate or the shares represented thereby must be *noted conspicuously*[9] *on the certificate* in order to be effective notice as to everyone except a person with actual knowledge of it, who obviously does not require such additional notice. The corporate bylaws or the contract for sale of such shares may provide that the corporation or other shareholders shall have a pre-emptive or prior right to the purchase of corporate shares; this is a reasonable and permissible restriction on the transfer of such shares, provided it is noted conspicuously on the certificate. The requirement of conspicuous notation is to provide notice of the restriction, and this can be accomplished without the notation stating the full text of the restriction. The Code law on restrictions deals only with restrictions *imposed by the corporation issuing the stock certificate.*

Method of Transfer. A certificate of stock and the shares represented thereby can be transferred only when two things occur. *First,* if the certificate is in registered form or has been specially indorsed, the "appropriate person's" indorsement, either special or in blank, must be made on the certificate or on a separate document. *Secondly,* the certificate so indorsed, or the certificate and the separate document with the indorsement, must be delivered. First indorsement and then delivery will be discussed.

Indorsement. An indorsement is a person's signature made alone or with other words on the issued certificate of stock or on a separate document. The indorsement may be complete or partial and is effective to the extent of the indorsement. If the certificate of stock is in registered form, an indorsement of the certificate is made when an appropriate person signs on it or on a separate document an assignment or transfer of the certificate or the shares represented thereby or a power so to assign or transfer, or when the signature of such person is written without more upon the back of the certificate. If the certificate is in bearer form, no indorsement is required, but if the certificate is indorsed the indorsement does not otherwise affect any right to registration which the holder may possess. An indorsement may be in blank or special. An indorsement in blank consists only of the signature of the person signing; it

[9] For conspicuously, see above, p. 319, ftn. 28.

includes an indorsement to bearer. A special indorsement specifies the person to whom the certificate is to be transferred, or who has power to transfer it ("to John Smith. [signed] Frank Fay"). A holder[10] may convert a blank indorsement into a special indorsement, as by the insertion of the name of a person above the blank indorsement. The indorsement must be made by an "appropriate person," who is:

> (a) the person specified by the security or by special indorsement to be entitled to the security; or
> (b) where the person so specified is described as fiduciary but is no longer serving in the described capacity,—either that person or his successor; or
> (c) where the security or indorsement so specifies more than one person as fiduciaries and one or more are no longer serving in the described capacity,—the remaining fiduciary or fiduciaries, whether or not a successor has been appointed or qualified; or
> (d) where the person so specified is an individual and is without capacity to act by virtue of death, incompetence, infancy or otherwise,—his executor, administrator, guardian or like fiduciary; or
> (e) where the security or indorsement so specifies more than one person as tenants by the entirety or with right of survivorship and by reason of death all cannot sign,—the survivor or survivors; or
> (f) a person having power to sign under applicable law or controlling instrument; or
> (g) to the extent that any of the foregoing persons may act through an agent,—his authorized agent.[11]

The purchaser of a certificate of stock has a specifically enforceable right to have any necessary indorsement supplied. Unless otherwise agreed, the transferor of the certificate must, on due demand, supply his purchaser "with any proof of his authority to transfer or with any other requisite which may be necessary to obtain registration of the transfer of the security but if the transfer is not for value a transferor need not do so unless the purchaser furnishes the necessary expenses. Failure to comply with a demand made within a reasonable time gives the purchaser the right to reject or rescind the transfer."[12] *Each signature in a necessary indorsement is presumed genuine* (i.e., free of forgery or counterfeiting) *or authorized, but if the effectiveness of a signature is put in issue, then the burden of establishing it is on the party claiming under the signature.* When an indorsement is admitted or established, production of the certificate entitles the holder to recover on it unless the defendant establishes a defense or a defect going to the validity of the certificate, in which event the plaintiff has the burden of establishing that he or some person under whom he claims is a person against whom the defense or defect is ineffective.[13] It should

---

[10] UCC 1–201(20): " 'Holder' means a person who is in possession of a document of title or an instrument or an investment security drawn, issued or indorsed to him or to his order or to bearer or in blank."

[11] UCC 8–308(3).

[12] UCC 8–316.

[13] UCC 8–105.

be noted very carefully that "Failure of a fiduciary to comply with a controlling instrument or with the law of the state having jurisdiction of the fiduciary relationship, including any law requiring the fiduciary to obtain court approval of the transfer, does not render his indorsement unauthorized for the purposes of this Article."[14] When an indorsement is unauthorized,[15] unless the owner has ratified the unauthorized indorsement or is otherwise *precluded* from asserting its ineffectiveness:

(a) he may assert its ineffectiveness against the issuer or any purchaser other than a purchaser for value and without notice of adverse claims who has in good faith received a new, reissued or re-registered security on registration of transfer; and
(b) an issuer who registers the transfer of a security upon the unauthorized indorsement is subject to liability for improper registration (Section 8–404).[16]

(T steals O's certificate of stock issued by C in registered form in O's name, forges O's blank indorsement on the certificate, and sells and delivers it to P, a purchaser for value in good faith without notice of O's adverse claim. O can reclaim the certificate from P. However, if P had delivered the certificate to C in exchange for a new certificate on registration of transfer, O could not reclaim the new certificate and would have only a right to damages against C.) Unless otherwise agreed, the indorser by his indorsement assumes no obligation that the certificate will be honored by the issuing corporation.

Delivery. If a sale of a certificate of stock and the shares represented thereby is made other than through brokers, then, unless otherwise agreed, the transferor of a certificate under a contract for sale has a duty to deliver the certificate by placing it, *in a form to be negotiated by the purchaser,* in the possession of the purchaser or of a person designated by him or, at the purchaser's request, by causing an acknowledgment to be made to the purchaser that it is held for him.[17] Delivery to a purchaser occurs when:

(a) he or a person designated by him acquires possession of a security; or
(b) his broker acquires possession of a security specially indorsed to or issued in the name of the purchaser; or
(c) his broker sends him confirmation of the purchase and also by book entry or otherwise identifies a specific security in the broker's possession as belonging to the purchaser; or
(d) with respect to an identified security to be delivered while still in the possession of a third person when that person acknowledges that he holds for the purchaser; or
(e) appropriate entries on the books of a clearing corporation are made under Section 8–320.[18]

---

[14] UCC 8–308(7).

[15] UCC 1–201(43): " 'Unauthorized' signature or indorsement means one made without actual, implied or apparent authority and includes a forgery." Unless a required indorsement is valid, a purchaser is not a bona fide purchaser. See above, p. 718.

[16] UCC 8–311.

[17] UCC 8–314(2).

[18] UCC 8–313(1).

Effect of Transfer. The purchaser of a certificate of stock and the shares represented thereby acquires rights against the corporation which issued the certificate and against his transferor. Each will be considered briefly in turn.

Purchaser's Rights against the Issuing Corporation. The issuing corporation has a duty, under certain conditions,[19] on request to register transfer of a certificate of stock which is in registered form and properly indorsed and which has been presented to it. If the certificate presented for transfer was *issued with an unauthorized*[20] *signature,* such signature is *ineffective, with one exception.* If the unauthorized signature was made by a person with *inherent agency power,*[21] as to a purchase for value in good faith without notice of the lack of authority such signature is effective and binding on the issuing corporation as though it were validly made. When the certificate contains the signatures necessary to its issue or transfer but is *incomplete in any other respect, any person may complete it by filling in the blanks as authorized; and if the blanks are incorrectly filled in, the certificate as completed is enforceable by a purchaser who took it for value and without notice of such incorrectness.* However, if completion of the blank for an incorrect number of shares resulted in an *overissue* of the corporate shares, meaning that the corporation will have issued a number of shares in excess of the amount which the corporation has corporate power to issue, *the corporation cannot be compelled to issue a certificate for such excess.* Although the person with a certificate which, if enforced against the issuing corporation, would result in an overissue cannot compel such overissue, nevertheless *he may compel the corporation to purchase and deliver an identical certificate for the proper number of shares* on the surrender of the original certificate, if the identical certificate does not constitute an overissue and is reasonably available for purchase; *or* if such an identical certificate is not so available for purchase, *he may recover from the corporation the price he or the last purchaser for value paid for the original certificate with interest from the date of his demand. Improper alteration of a complete certificate,* even though done fraudulently, *is ineffective, and the certificate remains enforceable only according to its original terms.* All the terms of the certificate must be stated on the certificate; however, the terms of the certificate include not only those stated on the certificate but also those made part of the certificate by reference to other instruments and records and which are not in conflict with the stated terms on the certificate.[22] "Such a reference does not of itself charge a purchaser for value with notice of a defect going to the validity of the security even though the security expressly states that a person accepting it admits such notice."[23] *A lien on a certificate of stock*

[19] UCC 8–401.

[20] For meaning of unauthorized, see above, p. 721, ftn. 15.

[21] The unauthorized signing is done by a person entrusted with the signing, preparation, or responsible handling of the certificate. See UCC 8–205; also Agency, above, pp. 593–94.

[22] The certificate may refer to another instrument, indenture, or document or to a constitution, statute, ordinance, rule, regulation, order, or the like.

[23] UCC 8–202(1).

or the shares represented thereby in favor of the issuing corporation must be noted conspicuously on the certificate in order to give notice of such lien to purchasers of the certificate and, therefore, to be effective as to them. If a certificate is required to be presented or surrendered for exchange, the purchase of the certificate more than two years[24] after the date when such surrender or presentation was to be made causes the purchaser, by law, to have notice of any defect in its issue or defense of the issuing corporation. *The issuing corporation's defense of non-delivery and conditional delivery,* as by theft or unauthorized delivery by the person to whom the certificate was entrusted, *of a certificate effective against the corporation, is ineffective against a purchaser for value without notice of the particular defense.*

Purchaser's Rights against Adverse Claims. The status of a purchaser of a certificate of stock and the shares represented thereby determines to what extent adverse claims to the certificate and such shares may be asserted against him. An adverse claim "includes a claim that a transfer was or would be wrongful or that a particular adverse person is the owner of or has an interest in the security."[25] *A purchaser is different from a bona fide purchaser for value, and the rights acquired by each differ.* Upon delivery of a certificate to a *purchaser,* he acquires the rights in the certificate and the shares represented thereby *which his transferor had or had authority to convey, with one exception.* The exception is that "a purchaser who has himself been a party to any fraud or illegality affecting the security or who as a prior holder had notice of an adverse claim cannot improve his position by taking from a later bona fide purchaser."[26] *In contrast with a purchaser, a bona fide purchaser acquires both the rights of a purchaser and also the certificate and the shares represented thereby free of any adverse claim.* It should be recalled carefully that, under Article 8 of the Code, a bona fide purchaser "is a purchaser for value in good faith and without notice of any adverse claim who takes delivery of a security in bearer form or of one in registered form issued to him or indorsed to him or in blank."[27] Accordingly, *a purchaser cannot be a bona fide purchaser if the delivered certificate does not have a necessary indorsement;* but when the purchaser does acquire that necessary indorsement, the transfer is *then* complete as of that time and, *as to all persons other than his transferor,* whether or not he is a bona fide purchaser is determined as of that time. However, *as between the transferor and the purchaser,* the transfer is complete upon delivery, although the purchaser has a specifically enforceable right to have any necessary indorsement supplied. (O owns a certificate of stock in registered form in O's name. (1) T steals the certificate, forges O's blank indorsement on the certificate, and sells and delivers it to P, a purchaser for value in good faith without notice of the theft and forgery. Since O's re-

---

[24] Under UCC 8–203(1)(a) the time is reduced to one year under certain circumstances.

[25] UCC 8–301(1).

[26] Ibid.

[27] UCC 8–302.

quired indorsement has not occurred, P is not a bona fide purchaser. (2) If O indorsed the certificate in blank and T stole, sold, and delivered the certificate to P, a purchaser for value in good faith without notice of the theft, P is a bona fide purchaser. However, if P then sold and delivered the certificate to R for value, R having notice of the theft, while R's notice precludes him from being a bona fide purchaser, nevertheless, as P's transferee, R acquires whatever rights P had, which was a valid title to the certificate and to the shares represented thereby. (3) A fraudulently induced O to indorse the certificate in blank and deliver it to A, who then sold and delivered it to P, a bona fide purchaser, who in turn later resold the certificate to A. Since A knew of O's adverse claim at the time he purchased the certificate from P he is not a bona fide purchaser; and since he was a party to the fraud on O, he cannot assert against O that he has O's title to the certificate. A cannot claim title through P.)

Whether or not the owner of a certificate of stock may recover possession of the certificate and title to the shares represented thereby after a transfer which is wrongful as to him, depends upon why the transfer was wrongful, the owner's conduct with respect to the wrongful transfer, and the status of the person presently in possession of the certificate. *If the transfer was wrongful because of an unauthorized indorsement,* the owner may recover the original certificate or new certificate from *anyone,* unless the owner has *ratified* the unauthorized indorsement, the owner is otherwise *precluded* from asserting its ineffectiveness,[28] or the other person is a purchaser for value without notice of adverse claims who has in good faith *received a new, reissued or re-registered certificate on registration of transfer.*[29] *If the transfer is wrongful for any reason other than an unauthorized indorsement,* the owner may, as against anyone *except a bona fide purchaser,* reclaim possession of the *original or new certificate* or obtain damages. The right to obtain or reclaim possession of a certificate may be specifically enforced and its transfer enjoined and the security impounded pending the litigation.

A *purchaser who has notice*[30] *of an adverse claim at the time a certificate is transferred to him cannot be a bona fide purchaser of such certificate.* The notice may come from the certificate itself as well as from circumstances apart from the certificate. If the certificate, whether in bearer or registered form, has been indorsed for a purpose not involving transfer, as "for surrender," a purchaser (including a broker for the seller or buyer but excluding an intermediary bank) of the certificate is on notice of an adverse claim. Similarly, such a purchaser has notice of an adverse claim if a certificate in bearer form has on it an unambiguous statement that it is the property of a person other than the transferor. The mere writing of a name on a certificate is not such a

---

[28] UCC 8–405(1).

[29] See UCC 8–315, 8–311. The issuing corporation is liable to the rightful owner of the original certificate and must issue an identical certificate to him unless such issuance would result in an overissue.

[30] For the meaning of "notice," see above, pp. 325–26.

statement.[31] If a certificate is required to be presented or surrendered for exchange, the purchase of the certificate *more than one year*[32] after the date when such surrender or presentation was to be made causes the purchaser, by law, to have *notice of adverse claims.*

Warranties on Presentment and Transfer. The Code specifies in detail the warranties made by a person on presentation of a certificate to the issuing corporation for registration of transfer, by a purchaser for value without notice of adverse claims who receives a certificate from the corporation, by a person transferring a certificate to a purchaser for value, by an intermediary, by a pledgee or other holder for security, and by a broker.

> (1) A person who presents a security for registration of transfer or for payment or exchange warrants to the issuer that he is entitled to the registration, payment or exchange. But a purchaser for value without notice of adverse claims who receives a new, reissued or re-registered security on registration of transfer warrants only that he has no knowledge of any unauthorized signature (Section 8–311) in a necessary indorsement.
>
> (2) A person by transferring a security to a purchaser for value warrants only that
> (a) his transfer is effective and rightful; and
> (b) the security is genuine and has not been materially altered; and
> (c) he knows no fact which might impair the validity of the security.
>
> (3) Where a security is delivered by an intermediary known to be entrusted with delivery of the security on behalf of another or with collection of a draft or other claim against such delivery, the intermediary by such delivery warrants only his own good faith and authority even though he has purchased or made advances against the claim to be collected against the delivery.
>
> (4) A pledgee or other holder for security who redelivers the security received, or after payment and on order of the debtor delivers that security to a third person makes only the warranties of an intermediary under subsection (3).
>
> (5) A broker gives to his customer and to the issuer and a purchaser the warranties provided in this section and has the rights and privileges of a purchaser under this section. The warranties of and in favor of the broker acting as an agent are in addition to applicable warranties given by and in favor of his customer.[33]

It should be noted carefully that, under the second sentence of the first paragraph quoted, the purchaser for value without notice of adverse claims warrants to "knowledge" as distinguished from "notice," which affords him real protection against a claim of forged indorsement.

---

[31] UCC 8–304(1)(b). Also, the "fact that the purchaser (including a broker for the seller or buyer) has notice that the security is held for a third person or is registered in the name of or indorsed by a fiduciary does not create a duty of inquiry into the rightfulness of the transfer or constitute notice of adverse claims. If, however, the purchaser (excluding an intermediary bank) has knowledge that the proceeds are being used or that the transaction is for the individual benefit of the fiduciary or otherwise in breach of duty, the purchaser is charged with notice of adverse claims." UCC 8–304(2).

[32] Under UCC 8–305(b) the time is reduced to six months under certain circumstances.

[33] UCC 8–306.

Effect of Certificate Outstanding. *Once a certificate of stock is issued and outstanding, no attachment or levy may be made upon the certificate or the shares represented by such certificate unless either:* the certificate is actually seized by the officer making the attachment or levy; the certificate is surrendered to the corporation which issued it; or the transfer of the certificate by the holder is enjoined by court order. *Also, the corporation cannot be compelled to issue a new certificate of stock for such shares unless the certificate outstanding is surrendered to the corporation.*

If a certificate has been lost, apparently destroyed or stolen, the status of such certificate and of a new certificate in its place, the rights and liabilities of the owner of the old certificate and the purchasers of the original and new certificates are materially affected. When an owner claims that a certificate has been lost, destroyed, or wrongfully taken, the issuing corporation *must* issue a new certificate in place of the original certificate if the owner complies with the following conditions: the owner must request a new certificate before the corporation has notice that the certificate has been acquired by a bona fide purchaser; the owner files with the corporation a sufficient indemnity bond; and the owner satisfies any other reasonable requirements imposed by the corporation. A court may compel a corporation wrongfully refusing to issue a new certificate to do so. If a new certificate is issued and a bona fide purchaser of the *original* certificate presents it for registration of transfer, *the corporation must register the transfer,* unless such registration would result in an overissue, in which event the corporation's liability is that previously discussed under overissue.[34] However, the owner of a certificate which has been lost, apparently destroyed or wrongfully taken has a *duty to notify the issuing corporation of that fact within a reasonable time after he has notice of it.* If the corporation, without notice of an adverse claim and without violation of its duty to inquire into adverse claims, registers a transfer of a properly indorsed certificate before receiving notice from the owner of its loss, destruction or wrongful taking and after a reasonable time has expired in which the owner could have notified the corporation, the owner is *precluded* from asserting any claim against the corporation for so registering and from asserting any claim to a new certificate from the corporation.

Right to Sue

A share of stock represents a contract between the corporation and the shareholder. Shareholders have the right to redress for loss caused by impairment of the value of their shares by wrongful conduct. *When a shareholder sustains injury individually,* as distinct from injury sustained by all shareholders because of a wrong done to the corporation, *the individual shareholder has a right of action against the wrongdoer.* The injury has been personal to the shareholder. *The shareholder has the right to institute an action in his*

[34] See above, p. 722.

own name against the corporation or the director or directors who caused such injury. An individual shareholder has a right of action against the corporation for breach of the contractual relation and may either enforce the contract or bring an action for damage caused thereby, in the following illustrative instances: improper refusal to declare dividends; refusal to permit a shareholder to exercise his right to vote at corporate meetings; refusal to permit a shareholder to make a proper inspection of corporate books; and refusal to permit a shareholder to exercise his pre-emptive right. *In dealings between a shareholder and a director of a corporation,* misrepresentation, or in a minority of states non-disclosure, of material facts by the director to the shareholder causing loss to the shareholder creates a right of action in such shareholder *against such director* for the loss caused by the dirrctor's wrongful conduct. If more than one shareholder has been *individually injured* by wrongful conduct, *one* of such shareholders may institute an action on behalf of all the other injured shareholders; this is called *a class or representative suit.* A class or representative suit also may be instituted by one shareholder on behalf of all the other shareholders if the wrong has been done *to the corporation;* however, in this instance, shareholders cannot sue in their own names, but can sue *derivatively on behalf of the corporation.*

Derivative Suits. *When a wrong has been done to the corporation, only the corporation as a legal entity may bring an action therefor.* Individual shareholders may not sue in their own names as they could in actions where they were individually wronged and injured. The right of action is that of the corporation, which may be asserted by the board of directors. Inasmuch as the corporation consists of all the shareholders in it, the shareholders should have an opportunity to consider the matter. Injuries caused to the corporation by mismanagement or wrongful conduct on the part of the board of directors is an illustration of a corporate injury with a corporate right of action for damages therefor. *Courts are very reluctant to interfere in the internal management of a corporation and to interfere with the discretion of those who are responsible for such management. However, if a wrong has been caused to the corporation and there is an abuse of discretion or wrongful conduct in not asserting a proper claim for such wrong, the courts will interfere and grant relief.*

A complaining shareholder first must exhaust his internal corporate remedies before he may, on behalf of the corporation, institute an action for a wrong done to the corporation.[35] The shareholder must request the board of directors to take proper action or show cause why it would be futile to make a request of the board of directors. If a majority of the board of directors is involved in the particular wrong or is prejudiced, recourse need not be made to the board of directors. Similarly, the minority shareholders must request the

[35] The corporation becomes a nominal party defendant to the action and, since the shareholders are suing on behalf of the corporation, the proceeds of a successful action generally inure to the corporation's benefit. In some instances the proceeds inure to the benefit of shareholders. See note, *Individual Pro Rata Recovery in Stockholders' Derivative Suits,* 69 Harv. L. Rev. 1314 (1956).

shareholders at a corporate meeting to take proper action regarding the wrong to the corporation, unless such recourse is futile. An illustration of such futility would be that a majority of the shareholders is involved in the wrong or is prejudiced in the matter, or that such biased shareholders have a sufficient number of shares to control corporate meetings in general. *A shareholder's suit on behalf of the corporation is defective unless such internal corporate remedies have been exhausted or resort to them excused.* Although there is conflict, by what appears to be the preferable view, a shareholder is disqualified from instituting such a suit unless he was a shareholder at the time the wrongful transacton occurred or he became a shareholder subsequently by operation of law. Shareholders who acquiesced in the particular wrong also are disqualified from instituting a shareholder's suit therefor.

SECTION II. SHAREHOLDERS' LIABILITIES

The corporate entity, being separate and distinct from the shareholders, precludes shareholder liability for corporate obligations, whether in contract or tort. Whatever shareholder liability exists is predicated, essentially, on the shares issued to him or his contracts made for the acquisition of shares. Shareholders are exposed to liability as partners in the event of a defectively organized corporation which does not have a *de jure* or a *de facto* status and when the doctrine of estoppel is inapplicable. Also, in the case of illegal dividends, those shareholders are liable for the return of such dividends who received such dividends with notice of the illegality or who received dividends declared by an insolvent corporation. Corporate creditors may enforce the above instances of shareholder liability.

Subscription Liability

Shareholders are liable *to the corporation* for the unpaid portion of their subscription contracts for corporate shares. The right to such payments is a corporate asset. *Corporate creditors* may not proceed against shareholders for such unpaid subscription price until they have first exhausted their legal remedies in resorting to other corporate assets. It is only then that creditors, by a creditors' bill in equity or in a court with equity powers, may proceed against such shareholders. In most states subscriptions fraudulently induced are voidable at the election of the shareholders who, on avoidance, are not liable to corporate creditors on such subscriptions.

Watered Stock

Corporate creditors can proceed against the *corporate assets* and, through a creditors' bill, proceed against shareholders for *their liability to the corporation.* However, if shares are issued to a shareholder gratuitously, called "bonus stock" or "bonus shares," there is no shareholder liability *to the corpo-*

ration and there is, therefore, no such corporate asset available to corporate creditors. Similarly, if shares are issued to shareholders for labor or services, or for property, at a known overvaluation, the asset available *to the corporation,* and therefore to the corporate creditor, is solely the property exchanged for the shares. *However, such shareholders may be liable to corporate creditors for fraud on them.*[36]

Methods of Watering. The capital stock and, therefore, the value of the shares may be diluted or watered, from which the phrase "watered stock" originates. *Shares may be watered in the following ways:* issuance of shares in exchange for services or property which are knowingly overvalued and worth less than the par value of the shares; shares issued for payment in money less than the par value; shares issued as stock dividends without transfer of any surplus to capital; shares issued as a bonus either to induce the purchase of preferred shares or bonds, or gratuitously. *The capital stock is watered to the extent the shares are issued for less than their par value.* This is unfair to creditors who rely on the corporate assets, including capital contributions by shareholders on their shares, from which the creditors' claims are to be satisfied. In many states an exception is made in the case of a corporation in financial difficulties, which may issue par value shares below the par value for the highest price it can obtain in order to rehabilitate the corporation's financial position.

Tests of Value. There are two tests of the value of services or property exchanged for shares, the *"good-faith" rule* which prevails in the majority of states, and the *"true-value" rule* which prevails in the minority of states. Under the good-faith rule, the value is adequate if it was fixed by the corporation through its board of directors in good faith and without fraud, and the shareholders are not liable for any deficiency between the value fixed in good faith and the actual value of the services or property. Overvalue, by itself, is insufficient to make the value inadequate. Under the true-value rule, good faith is disregarded and the actual value of the services or property is the test. If the actual value is less than the par value of the shares received in exchange for such services or property, the shareholders of such shares are liable to corporate creditors for the deficiency in making full payment. Under state blue-sky laws, state boards or commissions are set up to determine the adequacy of the consideration to be exchanged for the issuance of shares and to permit such issuance only when the value is adequate. Under the federal Securities Act, the Securities and Exchange Commission has the function of determining the relative adequacy of the consideration to be exchanged for the shares to be issued and requires full disclosure of all material facts.

Watering, a Wrong to Corporate Creditors. The issuance of watered shares is a wrong to corporate creditors in that the represented capital is not available as a part of the assets to satisfy the creditors' claims. Corporate creditors may recover from the shareholders of watered stock the deficiency in value for the

---

[36] See below, p. 730.

par value shares issued to them. Each shareholder is liable to corporate creditors only to the extent of his pro rata portion of the amount due such creditors, but not in excess of the deficient amount due on such shares. Creditors first must proceed against corporate assets and, if such assets are insufficient to satisfy their claims, creditors may then proceed in equity or in a court with equity powers under a creditors' bill against the shareholders of the watered shares. The amounts owing by shareholders under subscription contracts with the corporation are available to creditors as a corporate asset. Any further liability of the shareholders is to the creditors and not to the corporation, by reason of their wrong perpetrated on such creditors. Inasmuch as the right to recover from shareholders of watered shares belongs to the corporate creditors and is not a corporate asset, the receiver or trustee in bankruptcy of an insolvent corporation cannot assert this right.

The corporation and the shareholders of the watered shares have committed the tort of fraud or deceit on corporate creditors by misrepresenting to such creditors that the capital stock outstanding represents an amount of capital paid, or agreed to be paid, to the corporation. *In order for a creditor to recover for fraud, it is necessary for him to show that he has relied upon such misrepresentation.* It is deemed that reliance has occurred if the creditor became such *subsequent* to such misrepresentation; however, if a subsequent creditor has knowledge of the misrepresentaion at the time he became a creditor, there is no reliance on the misrepresentation and he cannot recover. Accordingly, *only subsequent creditors without notice may recover from shareholders of watered shares; prior creditors, and subsequent creditors with notice of such misrepresentation, cannot recover, but some states permit recovery.*

Nonliability of Certain Shareholders. The shareholder to whom watered shares have been issued may not avoid his liability to corporate creditors by transferring such shares to a bona fide purchaser. *Bona fide purchasers of watered shares for value in good faith and without notice of their watered character are not liable for the previous watering and deficiency.* Shareholders of treasury stock and shareholders of no-par shares have no liability except for the *agreed* purchase price of their shares. *Treasury shares may be sold at any price and need not be sold for the par value.*

Chapter 54

CORPORATE DISSOLUTION AND WINDING UP

A corporation can be dissolved only by law, which terminates the corporate entity and the corporate property then belongs to the shareholders subject to the rights of corporate creditors. Dissolution may occur by: (*1*) *Expiration* of the corporate charter. (*2*) *Legislative repeal* of the corporate charter. (*3*) *Surrender* of the corporate charter—in most states a large majority of the voting power is required for a voluntary dissolution. (*4*) *Involuntary dissolution by forfeiture* of the corporate charter—a court will decree dissolution only for cause. (*5*) *Involuntary dissolution by court decree on the request of minority shareholders*, e.g., the corporation cannot be operated except at a loss, or serious mismanagement. (*6*) "*Merger*," which occurs when one corporation is absorbed by another corporation, or by "*consolidation*," which occurs when various corporations are unified and absorbed into a newly created corporation; corporate assent must be by the board of directors and a large majority of the shareholders; creditors of the merged or consolidated corporation are creditors of the remaining or new corporation; dissenting shareholders can have their shares appraised.

A corporation is an entity created by law and can be dissolved only by law. Insolvency of a corporation, lack of corporate assets, or temporary cessation of corporate activities does not constitute a dissolution of the corporation. Liquidation of the corporate assets and distribution to creditors and shareholders does not dissolve the corporation. Dissolution means termination of the corporate entity by legal authority, and may occur by: expiration of the corporate charter; legislative repeal of the corporate charter; surrender of the corporate charter; forfeiture of the corporate charter; order of a court of equity, or a court with equity powers, in some instances; the merger or consolidation. Each of these will be considered briefly in turn.

Expiration of Corporate Charter

A corporation has the right, as a legal entity, to continue uninterruptedly for its duration as provided in the corporate charter. It is not usual today to incorporate for a fixed term but when this occurs the corporation automatically dissolves on the expiration of such term and no further action is required.

Legislative Repeal of Corporate Charter

A corporate charter issued by a state constitutes authority for the creation of the corporation for the purposes indicated therein and *is a contract between the state and the corporation.* The United States Constitution, Article I, section 10, provides that no state shall pass any law impairing the obligation of contract. Accordingly, a state may not alter or repeal the corporate charter without the consent of the corporation. Today most states reserve the right to alter or repeal corporate charters; however, under the Fourteenth Amendment to the United States Constitution, no state shall deprive any person of property without due process of law. There is no violation of the due process clause if the state validly exercises its police power and legislatively repeals or modifies the corporate charter.

Surrender of Corporate Charter

Inasmuch as a corporate charter is issued on the application of persons desiring to incorporate, the state of incorporation will dissolve such corporation on the application of the shareholders. In the absence of a statute to the contrary, the consent of all the shareholders is required for corporate dissolution, unless the corporation is insolvent; in the event of corporate insolvency a majority of the voting power and, in some states, merely a vote of the board of directors, is sufficient to constitute corporate action. Today, statutes in the various states specify what is necessary for voluntary dissolution. In most states a large majority of the voting power—e.g., two-thirds—is required. If the corporation has been adjudicated bankrupt, then a majority of the voting power and the resolution of the board of directors are sufficient to constitute corporate action. In a few states only the resolution of the board of directors is sufficient. Although corporate insolvency by itself does not constitute dissolution, yet in some states by statute it does.

Involuntary Dissolution by Forfeiture of Corporate Charter

The state of incorporation has the right, through its attorney general, to institute quo warranto proceedings requesting a court decree to dissolve a corporation. *A court will decree dissolution only for cause.* Improper corporate acts—e.g., fraud—seriously affecting the public constitute sufficient cause. *Ultra vires* acts by themselves usually are insufficient for forfeiture, although the state may either: through quo warranto proceedings oust the corporation from further exercise of the unauthorized powers; or, by suit in a court with equity powers, obtain an injunction against the *ultra vires* act. Dissolution lies within the court's discretion, and a court may decree dissolution or it may permit the corporation to continue in existence but punish it by fine and enjoin continuance of such wrongful conduct. A state statute may provide for automatic forfeiture of a corporate charter by a corporation's noncompliance with statutory requirements, such as by nonpayment of taxes or failure to make corporate reports. Automatic forfeiture and dissolution by such noncompliance does not occur unless the statute expressly permits. Under the MBCA, involuntary dissolution will occur if the corporation has failed for 30 days to appoint and maintain a registered agent, or has failed for 30 days after change of its registered office or registered agent to file in the office of the Secretary of State a statement of such change.

Involuntary Dissolution by Court Decree on Request of Minority Shareholders

Today, by statute in many states, courts of equity or courts with equity powers are given the authority to dissolve and wind up a corporation at the request of minority shareholders under certain circumstances. Courts of equity or courts with equity powers will grant such relief when there is fraud or serious mismanagement by the board of directors or the majority of shareholders; an additional ground is that the corporation cannot be operated except at a loss.

Merger or Consolidation

A corporation may sell its assets and discontinue doing any business as a corporation without thereby causing corporate dissolution, although usually a dissolution occurs soon thereafter. By statute today a prosperous corporation may sell all of its corporate assets and business on approval by the board of directors and a large majority of the voting shareholders, and a failing corporation may make such sale on approval by the board of directors and a majority of the voting shareholders. Such assets and business usually are sold to another corporation in exchange for the other corporation's shares of stock. Dissenting shareholders may cause their shares to be appraised and receive payment in cash for their fair value. Today, reorganization of a failing corporation usually is administered under the Bankruptcy Code.[1] Such a sale must not be contrary to the corporate charter or to public policy or law, and it must not be in fraud of corporate creditors.

---

[1] See above, pp. 535–37.

Often such sale is a part of a merger or consolidation of corporations. *In a merger one corporation is absorbed by another corporation, while in a consolidation various corporations are unified and are absorbed into a newly created corporation.* Statutes provide for merger and consolidation and, on their occurrence, *the old corporation is dissolved.* Statutes require that corporate assent to merger or consolidation be given by the board of directors and by a large majority of the holders of outstanding voting shares. *Creditors of the merged or consolidated corporation are creditors of the remaining or new corporation, respectively,* unless the transfer of such corporate assets and business constitutes a fraudulent conveyance, in which case the creditors can set aside such conveyance. It is not often that dissenting shareholders take advantage of statutory provision for appraisal of the fair value of their old shares, because of the considerable expense involved in an appraisal proceeding.

Effect of Corporate Dissolution

Dissolution terminates the corporate entity, and the corporate property then belongs to the shareholders subject to the rights of corporate creditors. Dissolution may occur before or after winding up of the corporate affairs. Winding up consists of liquidating the corporate assets and making distribution first to corporate creditors and then to shareholders. By statute in a few states winding up must precede dissolution. If dissolution precedes winding up, by statute in many states the members of the former corporation may sue and be sued as a corporate entity *solely* for the purpose of winding up the corporate affairs. To this extent the corporate personality continues in existence until the board of directors as trustees for corporate creditors and shareholders has wound up the corporation. If winding up proceedings are under judicial supervision, the court may appoint a receiver for this purpose.

PROBLEMS

1. (a) A, B, and C subscribed to purchase shares of stock in a corporation to be formed. Prior to incorporation A died and B informed the promoter and other interested persons of the withdrawal of B's subscription. The corporation was formed and it demanded of A's estate, of B, and of C payment of the amounts of their respective subscriptions. All refused to make any payment and C informed the corporation that he thereby withdrew his subscription.
   (1) Are A's estate, B, and C liable to the corporation for their respective subscription amounts?
   (2) Why?
   (b) If the corporation was formed for a purpose different from that described in the subscription agreement, would the liability of any of the parties have been affected thereby? Why?
   (c) Would the result have been any different in "(a)" above if the subscriptions had been made after the corporation had been formed? Why?

2. A, B, and C were promoters engaged in the formation of X corporation and they acquired land and machinery for $50,000 expecting to sell this property to X at a profit. The corporation was created and the property sold to it for $150,000.
   (1) Can the corporation compel the promoters to return $100,000 to the corporation?
   (2) Why?
3. (a) A contracted to sell to X corporation 100 shares of stock in X corporation and 100 shares of stock in Y corporation. X was engaged in the manufacture of refrigerators and Y was an automobile manufacturer. A refused to perform the contract.
   (1) Can X enforce the contract?
   (2) Why?
   (b) P, president of R corporation engaged in the retailing of home appliances, had authority to issue corporate checks for corporate purposes. Without authority, P purchased an automobile for himself and issued a check in R's name for the purchase price.
   (1) Is R liable on the check?
   (2) Why?
4. (a) A corporation engaged in mining contracted with B corporation to manufacture and sell to it a specified quantity of explosives, which A was not authorized to do by its charter. A manufactured and delivered the explosives to B, who subsequently refused to pay for it on the ground that A had acted *ultra vires*.
   (1) Can A enforce the contract against B?
   (2) Why?
   (b) P, a pedestrian, was negligently injured by one of A's trucks hauling explosives manufactured by A under its contract with B in "(a)" above.
   (1) Is A liable for such injury?
   (2) Why?
5. The officers of a manufacturing corporation, by authority of the directors, indorsed, in the corporate name, a note for the accommodation of an allied corporation. The note was discounted by a bank on the faith of the indorsement, and with knowledge that it was indorsed for accommodation.
   (1) May the corporation do this? Why?
   (2) Was the bank a holder in due course? Why?
   (3) May the bank recover upon the indorsement? Why?
   (Former C.P.A. Examination question)
6. (a) D, a director of X corporation, learned of facts which would cause certain corporate property to become very valuable if the facts were known. D did not disclose this information to other directors who were ignorant of it and contracted with the corporation for his purchase of the property. The other directors then learned the facts and refused to transfer the property to D.
   (1) Is the contract enforceable against X?
   (2) Why?
   (b) A director has a personal interest in action to be taken by the board of directors.
   (1) Should he vote on the matter?
   (2) Why?
7. You are called upon to audit the books of a corporation for 1980 and you find, among other things, the following: The corporation is on a calendar-year basis. In De-

cember, the corporation paid to each of its five directors a salary of $2,000 and to the treasurer, who was not a director, $12,000, for their services during 1980 as such officials.

(1) Were these payments proper as to (a) the directors, and (b) as to the treasurer? Why?

(2) Where would you look for authority to make these payments? (Former C.P.A. Examination question, dates changed)

8. (a) X corporation had a large surplus at the end of its first year of operation which the directors reasonably believed should be used for expansion of the corporate plant.
   (1) Can the shareholders compel the board of directors to declare a dividend?
   (2) Why?

   (b) A corporate board of directors declared a dividend.
   (1) What is the status of the shareholders?
   (2) If specific funds for the payment of such dividend had been set aside solely for this purpose, could corporate creditors proceed against such funds? Why?
   (3) Is a proper declaration of corporate dividends revocable?
   (4) If the corporation had notice that a share of stock had been pledged, is the dividend to be paid to the pledgor or to the pledgee?

9. A corporation has realized an operating profit and has a balance in its surplus account, but because of additions to fixed capital assets it has no cash beyond its requirements for working capital.
   (a) Can this corporation legally declare a dividend (not a liquidating one)?
   (b) On the assumption that such a dividend can legally be declared, how can payment of it be arranged? (Former C.P.A. Examination question)

10. A certified public accountant, in his examination of a wholly owned subsidiary corporation, finds that its board of directors has declared a dividend in excess of the amount of surplus at the beginning of the year plus the net profit for the year, and that this dividend has been paid to the parent corporation. What should the accountant do with respect to this situation? (Former C.P.A. Examination question)

11. X corporation issued its shares of stock as a bonus to its shareholders. May corporate creditors recover the par value of such shares? Explain fully.

12. (a) B fraudulently induced A to deliver to him A's certificate of stock representing 1,000 shares in X corporation. B forged A's signature in blank on the certificate and sold and delivered it to C, a purchaser for value without notice of B's fraud and forgery. C delivered the certificate to X who issued a new certificate of stock to C for 1,000 shares in X.
   (1) Does A have any rights?
   (2) Why?

   (b) O is the owner of a certificate of stock representing 9,000 shares in Z corporation, the certificate being indorsed in blank by O. T stole the certificate from O and delivered it to C in satisfaction of T's debt to C. C did not know of the theft.
   (1) Does O have a right to the certificate?
   (2) Why?

13. P, the president of a corporation engaged in selling machinery, had authority to issue corporate checks for corporate purposes. P purchased furniture for his home and drew a corporate check, which he delivered to V, the vendor, in payment of the purchase price.

(1) Is the corporation liable to V on the check?
(2) If V negotiated the check to H, a holder in due course without notice of P's wrongful conduct, is the corporation liable to H on the check?
(3) If H negotiated the check to R who knew of P's wrongful conduct, is the corporation liable on the check to R?

14. (a) Explain when a shareholder has a right to sue:
(1) In his own name against the corporation or a director. Give an illustration of an instance.
(2) Derivatively on behalf of the corporation.
(b) What is meant by the phrase watered stock, and how, in general, does this watering occur?
(c) To what extent, if any, are shareholders of watered stock liable to corporate creditors?

SOME PREVIOUS C.P.A. LAW EXAMINATION QUESTIONS AND AUTHOR'S MODEL ANSWERS

NOVEMBER, 1979

Number 2

Part a. Fairfax Corporation was created on April 2, 1979. Its initial capitalization consisted of (1) 5,000 shares of no-par voting common stock which it sold to subscribers at $20 a share; (2) 1,000 shares of cumulative, non-voting, 8 percent, $100 par value, preferred stock which it sold at $100 per share; and (3) 2,000 20-year debentures with a face value of $1,000 each, interest at 10 percent, which it sold at a 5 percent discount. All securities were sold for cash during April 1979. At a meeting on May 15, 1979, the board of directors voted to increase the capital surplus of the corporation by transferring to capital surplus $19 per share of the $20 per share originally credited to stated capital upon the sale of the no-par common stock.

Required:

Answer the following, setting forth reasons for any conclusions stated.

What is the stated capital of the Fairfax Corporation as of May 16, 1979?

Part b. The directors of Despard & Company, Inc., are considering several alternatives to their usual declaration of a cash dividend. The cost of borrowing money has become prohibitive and the directors would prefer to retain the cash to further the corporation's expansion plans. The following possibilities have been suggested:

- A dividend to each shareholder consisting of 60 percent treasury stock and 40 percent cash.
- A stock dividend declared and paid in its own authorized and unissued $1.00 par value common shares.
- A 2-for-1 split-up of the issued shares of the $1.00 par value common shares. Par value would be changed from $1.00 to $0.50.

Required:

Answer the following, setting forth reasons for any conclusions stated.

1. Separately analyze and discuss the legal impact of each of these possibilities from the standpoint of the corporate requirements (ignore accounting entries) that must be met and the effect that each would have upon the stated capital of the corporation.

2. What are the federal income tax effects or implications to the shareholder as to each of the above possibilities?

3. What is the federal income tax consequence if the corporation continuously elects **not** to pay any cash dividends?

Part c. The United States Justice Department commenced a criminal action against Sky Manufacturing Corporation and its president, Masterson, for conspiring to fix prices on the sale of certain heavy industrial machinery. Both the corporation and Masterson denied the allegations. After a lengthy trial, the jury found that although a conspiracy did exist among certain manufacturers, neither Sky nor Masterson were parties to the illegal conspiracy. The cost to the corporation to defend the action against it was $500,000. Masterson's individual legal fees and expenses amounted to $250,000 of which Sky has paid $50,000 directly. Masterson seeks indemnification for the remaining $200,000.

Heinz, a dissenting shareholder of Sky, advised the board of directors that payment by the corporation of any of Masterson's expenses was improper. In the event no action is taken to recover the $50,000 already advanced, Heinz will commence a shareholder derivative action against Masterson. Furthermore, unless the board unequivocally promoses **not** to indemnify Masterson for the unpaid balance of his legal expenses, Heinz will seek injunctive relief.

Required:

Answer the following, setting forth reasons for any conclusions stated.

What rights and limitations apply to Sky's payment of Masterson's legal fees and expenses in defending the criminal action brought against him?

Answer

2.a. $105,000. Under the Model Business Corporation Act, stated capital includes the sum of the par value of issued corporate shares having par value, together with the consideration received by the corporation for all its issued no-par value shares except for that part of the consideration which the corporation has allocated to capital surplus no later than 60 days after the issuance of the no-par value shares. Here, the $100,000 representing the 1,000 $100 par value shares of preferred stock is stated capital. Also, within 60 days after April 2 when the no-par value shares were issued, the corporation allocated to surplus $19 of each of the issued $20 no-par value shares and, therefore, the remaining $1 for each of the 5,000 shares is stated capital, equalling $5,000. The total of these two amounts represents Fairfax corporate stated capital of $105,000. The debentures are debt and are not stock and, therefore, are not part of stated capital. (p. 691)

b.1. Under the Model Business Corporation Act, a board of directors may declare and the corporation pay dividends in cash, its own treasury shares, or both, out of corporate unreserved and unrestricted earned surplus, except when the corporation is insolvent or when it is contrary to its articles of incorporation. No problems exist here regarding such power and its limitations. The corporate stated capital is not affected.

Dividends may be declared and paid in the corporation's own authorized but unissued shares out of unreserved and unrestricted surplus. However, if the dividend is payable in its own shares having a par value, as here, such shares shall be issued at not less than the par value, and there shall be transferred to stated capital at the time such dividend is paid an amount of surplus equal to the aggregate par value of the shares to be issued as a dividend.

A split-up of the issued shares of any class into a greater number of shares of the same class without increasing the stated capital of the corporation may be made. This is not construed to be a share dividend. The split-up will cause an increase in the number of shares issued and outstanding, each share with an equal reduced par value. In order to accomplish the split-up, the articles of incorporation will have to be amended to permit it. (pp. 713–15)

2. Under the Internal Revenue Code, the 40 percent dividend payment in cash is ordinary income and is taxable, subject to a $100 dividend exclusion to a noncorporate shareholder or an 85 percent dividend received deduction to a corporate shareholder. The stock dividends and stock splits are exempt from taxation in the present case. The shareholder recipients must allocate the cost basis for the shares originally owned to the number of shares owned after the stock dividend or stock split.
3. The Internal Revenue Code deals with unreasonable accumulation of earnings and profits. It allows a $150,000 credit against the amounts permitted to be accumulated. An accumulation of earnings and profits together with little dividends may be unreasonable, depending on the facts of the particular case. If the dividend here were considered little and the accumulation large, the corporation's plans would be a factor in establishing a bona fide business purpose showing the accumulation not to be unreasonable.

c. Sky has properly paid Masterson $50,000 toward his attorney's fees and other legal expenses, and it must indemnify him for the balance of $200,000. Under the Model Business Corporation Act, to the extent that a corporate officer has successfully defended himself in certain types of civil or criminal proceedings, the corporation must indemnify him against expenses, which include attorney's fees, actually and reasonably incurred by him in connection with such proceedings. The proceedings include those in which he is a party by reason of his being an officer of the corporation or as one who was serving at the request of the corporation, and he had acted in good faith and in a manner he reasonably believed to be in the best interests of the corporation, and, in a criminal case, he had no reason to believe his conduct was unlawful. Here, Masterson successfully defended himself, had apparently acted in good faith believing his conduct lawful, and apparently his expenses were reasonable. Therefore, he was entitled to corporate indemnification of $250,000. (p. 579 refer to the law of Agency and, since the corporate officer is a corporate agent, the concept of corporate indemnification is consistent with the law of Agency.)

NOVEMBER, 1978

Number 1

Select the **best** answer to the following item.

15. Watson entered into an agreement to purchase 1,000 shares of the Marvel Corporation, a corporation to be organized in the near future. Watson has since had second thoughts about investing in Marvel. Under the circumstances, which of the following is correct?

a. A written notice of withdrawal of his agreement to purchase the shares will be valid as long as it is received prior to incorporation.

b. A simple transfer of the agreement to another party will entirely eliminate his liability to purchase the shares of stock.
c. Watson may **not** revoke the agreement for a period of six months in the absence of special circumstances.
d. Watson may avoid liability on his agreement if he can obtain the consent of the majority of other individuals committed to purchase shares to release him.

Answer

1. 15.c(696)

MAY, 1978

Number 4

Part b. Duval is the chairman of the board and president of Monolith Industries, Inc. He is also the largest individual shareholder, owning 40 percent of the shares outstanding. The corporation is publicly held, and there is a dissenting minority. In addition to his position with Monolith, Duval owns 85 percent of Variance Enterprises, a corporation created under the laws of the Bahamas. During 1977 Carlton, the president of Apex Industries, Inc., approached Duval and suggested that a tax-free merger of Monolith and Apex made good sense to him and that he was prepared to recommend such a course of action to the Apex board and to the shareholders. Duval studied the proposal and decided that Apex was a most desirable candidate for acquisition. Duval informed the president of Variance about the overture, told him it was a real bargain, and suggested that Variance pick it up for cash and notes. Not hearing from Duval or Monolith, Carlton accepted an offer from Variance and the business was sold to Variance. Several dissenting shareholders of Monolith learned the facts surrounding the Variance acquisition and have engaged counsel to represent them. The Variance acquisition of Apex proved to be highly profitable.

Required:

Answer the following, setting forth reasons for any conclusions stated.

Discuss the rights of the dissenting Monolith shareholders and the probable outcome of a legal action by them.

Answer

4.b. The dissenting Monolith shareholders have two possible alternative rights.

One is to bring a derivative shareholder suit in the name of Monolith and on its behalf to set aside the acquisition contract between Variance and Apex, and award to Monolith the business and profits acquired by Variance from the time of the acquisition. Corporate officers are agents of the corporation and, as such, they are fiduciaries with the duty to act on behalf of the corporation. Here, Duval, as chairman of the board and president of Monolith, had a fiduciary duty to bring to the board and the shareholders of Monolith the opportunity of acquiring Apex. This he did not do but, instead, he furthered his own interests by having Variance, in which he had an 85 percent ownership, acquire Apex. The acquisition has become highly profitable.

Another possible right is for the dissenting shareholders to bring the derivative suit directly against Duval for damages for loss to Monolith caused by Duval's breach of his fiduciary duty to Monolith. He cannot secretly profit from his agency, as he did here in shifting the acquisition opportunity to Variance in which he had 85 percent ownership.

However, complaining shareholders must first exhaust their internal corporate remedies before they may institute a derivative action for a wrong done to the corporation. They must request the board of directors to take proper action, unless this would be futile. If this is unsuccessful or futile, they must make the same request of the shareholders at a shareholders meeting, unless this would be futile. The problem does not indicate facts which suggest such futility in either case. (pp. 708–9, 727–28)

Part Eight: Insurance

Chapter 55

THE INSURANCE CONTRACT

Insurance is a method of *indemnity against loss* by widespread assumption of the risk of loss by many persons pursuant to a contract. Loss by the indemnitee "insured" will be paid by the indemnitor "insurer" regardless of fault by anyone. Insurance companies may be stock, mutual, or mixed.

The insured must have an "*insurable interest*" in the subject matter insured. A person has an insurable interest in property or life when he will benefit by the continued existence, or suffer loss by the destruction, of such property or life. The following persons have *an insurable interest in property:* (1) mortgagor and mortgagee in the mortgaged property; (2) tenant in rented property; (3) partner in partnership property; (4) bailee in bailed property; (5) stockholder in corporate property; (6) a person with a legal or equitable interest in property; (7) a secured creditor in security. An *insurable interest in life* is determined by the relationship between the insured and the person whose life is insured. Blood, marital, and commercial relationships create such an insurable interest in life, as: (1) parents and children; (2) brothers and sisters; (3) husband and wife; (4) business associates in the lives of each other, "key personnel;" (5) a creditor's interest in the life of his debtor; (6) the insured in his own life. The insured must have an insurable interest *in property at the time of loss, and in life insurance at the time the insurance contract was made.*

The contract of insurance usually is called a "policy." In a contract for property insurance, the insurer's promise to insure and the insured's promise to pay the premium are consideration for each other; while for life insurance, the insurer promises to insure the insured who promises to pay only the first premium—he does not promise to pay any other premiums, but the insurer is to insure only as long as the insured pays his premiums. The insurer's accep-

tance of a check as conditional payment for the premium is a waiver of its right to receive only money. The contract must be for a legally valid transaction. Usually the contract terms provide that the policy is effective only on its actual or constructive delivery and payment of the first premium. An insurance "binder" is a written memorandum of an oral, temporary contract of *property* insurance evidencing such contract pending consideration and issuance of a formal policy. *Innocent* material misrepresentation by *nondisclosure* does not make the contract voidable, but if *fraudulent* it is voidable. Material misrepresentation *other than by concealment* causes the contract to be voidable, except that misrepresentation of age in a life insurance policy does not make it voidable and the premium paid buys only the insurance coverage at the correct age. A breach of warranty by the insured justifies rescission of the contract by the insurer. Both a warranty and a representation are statements of fact, the warranty being *in* the contract and the truth of which is a condition to the insurer's liability, the representation not being in the contract but made to induce making the contract. Contracts of insurance are not within the Statute of Frauds, unless otherwise provided by statute—which often provides for standard forms of policies. The insurer may waive its defense to recovery on a contract or its right to rescind the contract. Misrepresentation of a material fact made with knowledge of its falsity which induces the other contracting party to materially change his position in innocent reliance thereon estops the utterer from denying what he previously asserted.

SECTION I. NATURE OF INSURANCE

Concept of Insurance

The subject of insurance is concerned with the shifting of risk of loss. Risk is the likelihood of the occurrence or nonoccurence of a specified event. Risk of loss is inherent in business, and it is socially desirable to effect the transfer of risk of loss, except where it is contrary to public policy. Insurance is a risk-bearing device whereby risk of loss is shifted from one person and spread among many. It is a method of *indemnity against loss* by widespread assumption of the risk of loss by many persons. It is in this respect that insurance is distinguished from a wager, which is contrary to public policy in most states. By means of insurance, persons seek to shift the risk of loss occurring by chance, while in a wager persons seek to make a profit by chance. By insurance loss is avoided, while by a wager gain and loss are created. By insurance an existing risk of loss is shifted, while immediately before a wager is made there is no risk of loss to shift, and the risk of loss is created by the wager itself.

Insurance Contract

Although the risk of loss may be shifted by operation of law—e.g., workmen's compensation statutes—ordinarily *insurance is created by contract.* A contract of insurance is a contract whereby one party for a consideration called a "premium" assumes the risk of loss borne by another party and agrees to indemnify the latter for loss caused by a specified contingency, the assumed risk to be distributed among a group of persons. There are many forms of the insurance contract varying according to the risk assumed, such as life, fire, marine, health, accident, and a host of others. First an examination of the fundamental principles underlying the concept of the insurance contract as a contract of indemnity, and then an examination of fire and life insurance, will be made.

As a Contract of Indemnity. While the subject of insurance includes both contracts of indemnity and contracts of suretyship, *throughout this discussion of insurance and unless otherwise indicated only insurance as a contract of indemnity will be considered.* When the insurer is a surety the rules of suretyship apply; these rules have been discussed previously[1] and a contract of indemnity was distinguished from a contract of suretyship.[2] Briefly, in a contract of indemnity the indemnitor assures the indemnitee that any loss he sustains will be paid by the indemnitor, *regardless of the liability of any third person therefor*—e.g., fire insurance and life insurance contracts. While in a suretyship contract the surety engages to be *liable for the fault of a third person*—e.g., S's contract with C assuring him that if C will extend credit to D and D doesn't pay, S will pay C.

SECTION II. FORMATION OF THE INSURANCE CONTRACT

Parties

The principles of the law of Contracts are applicable to the insurance contract, commonly called a "policy." One of the essential elements in the formation of an insurance contract is that the parties have capacity to contract. The party who assumes the risk is called the "insurer," and the party whose risk has been assumed is called the "insured" or "assured." Although natural persons may, in the absence of statute to the contrary, act as insurers, nevertheless, most insurers are corporations.

Insurance companies may be stock, mutual, or mixed. A stock company has capital which is divided into shares of stock; the shareholders have no relation to the insured. Mutual companies do not issue shares of stock, and the members thereof are both insurers and the insured, the company contracting to indemnify each member. In mutual companies a fixed advanced premium is

[1] See above, pp. 479–88.

[2] See above, p. 480.

paid and a fund is accumulated to indemnify for loss sustained; profits are shared by the members. Mixed companies have characteristics of both the stock and mutual companies, a small amount of stock being issued entitling shareholders to dividends thereon, and all policyholders becoming members with beneficial interests as in a mutual company.

Infants have limited capacity to contract[3] and, except as otherwise provided by statute, they may be parties to contracts of life insurance and may exercise their power to avoid such contracts. While there is conflict, by the majority view if an infant is the insured, on his disaffirmance of his life insurance contract he may recover all premiums paid by him; the insurance contract is not one for necessaries. Statutes in many states permit infants above a specified age to procure life insurance with certain specified persons as beneficiaries (e.g., mother, father, brother, sister) but deprive infants of power to avoid such insurance contracts. In most instances a parent, rather than the infant, procures the contract of life insurance on the infant's life and the parent then is both the insured and the contracting party with the insurer.

Insurable Interest

An insurance contract is concerned with the assumption of a risk of loss. *A person who is exposed to a risk of loss has an insurable interest in the object of the risk. It is essential that the insured have an insurable interest in the subject matter insured;* otherwise there is no contract of insurance and the transaction is a wager. *A person has an insurable interest in property or life when he will benefit by the continued existence, or suffer loss by the destruction, of such property or life.*

A person has an *insurable interest in property* if he will *suffer pecuniary loss by its destruction or impairment, or benefit from its preservation.* Examples of persons with an insurable interest in particular property are: mortgagor and mortgagee in the mortgaged property, tenant in the rented property, partner in the partnership property, bailee in the bailed property, stockholder in the corporate property, and a person with a legal or equitable title in property. A secured creditor has an insurable interest in the security to the extent of the obligation owing to him, while a general creditor does not have an insurable interest in his debtor's property, although he does have an insurable interest in his debtor's life. Risk of *pecuniary* loss fixes the insurable interest.

Inasmuch as it is impossible to determine the value of a person's life, precluding any estimation of the loss caused by his death, the test of the risk of pecuniary loss in a determination of insurable interest cannot be applied to life insurance. Accordingly, an *insurable interest in life* is determined by the relationship existing between the insured and the person whose life is insured. *If the relationship is such that the insured has a reasonable expectation of deriving a benefit by the continuance of the life insured or of suffering loss*

[3] See above, pp. 13 ff.

by its termination, the insured has an insurable interest in the life insured. Blood, marital, and commercial relationships in which this expectation of benefit or loss is present create an insurable interest. Examples of a person who has an insurable interest in the life of another are: parents and children; brothers and sisters; husband and wife; business associates in the lives of each other—e.g., partners and officers or directors of a corporation or other "key personnel"; and a creditor's interest in the life of his debtor. It is obvious that a person has an insurable interest in his own life.

There are three important distinctions to be observed between an insurable interest in property and an insurable interest in life. *First,* an insurable interest in property is predicated upon some legal or equitable interest in property, the impairment or destruction of which will cause pecuniary loss; while an insurable interest in life is not predicated necessarily upon any legal or equitable interest in life or upon pecuniary loss by termination of that life. *Second,* in property insurance the insured must have an insurable interest only *at the time of loss,*[4] provided the parties to the contract intend that the insurer's risk is to attach to property of the insured then, or subsequently to be, acquired, although there is much apparently obsolete dicta and a minority view which requires that the insured have an insurable interest also at the time the contract was made.[5] In life insurance the insured must have an insurable interest in the life insured only *at the time the contract of insurance was made. Third,* recovery on property insurance is limited to the extent of pecuniary loss to the insurable interest, while recovery on life insurance is for the face value of the policy.

Consideration

A *contract of insurance requires consideration.* The money paid by the insured, pursuant to the terms of the insurance contract, is called a "premium." In a contract for property insurance the insurer's promise to insure and the insured's promise to pay premiums, or his payment of premiums, constitute consideration for each other.

The consideration is different in a life insurance contract. *The insurer promises to insure the insured who promises to pay only the first premium; he does not promise to pay any other premiums.* The contract of life insurance does not exist until the insured has paid, or has promised to pay, the first premium and the insurer has agreed to insure the insured. *The insurer is bound to keep the insurance contract alive as long as the premiums are paid* and, on the nonpayment of a premium when due, the contract of insurance is discharged. It is really a contract subject to discharge by the occurrence of a condition

[4] In marine insurance, the insured must have an insurable interest at the time the contract of insurance is made and, by the majority view, at the time of loss, except for "lost or not lost" insurance coverage when no insurable interest is required.

[5] William R. Vance, *Handbook on the Law of Insurance,* 3d ed., Buist M. Anderson (St. Paul : West Publishing Co., 1951), sec. 30.

subsequent—namely, failure to pay the premiums when due. *The insured is not liable for his failure to pay any premiums after the first premium.*

The payment of premiums is to be made as specified in the contract of insurance. Usually such premiums are required to be paid in money, but the insurer may expressly or impliedly waive such right and accept payment by check. The insurer's acceptance of a check in conditional payment of premiums is a waiver of its right to receive only money. Similarly, the insurer may waive its right to receive payment at the place indicated in the contract.

Legally Valid Transaction

The contract of insurance must be for a legally valid transaction. Noncompliance by the insurer with statutory requirements has a varying effect among the states. In most states such agreements to insure are void. In states where such an agreement is not expressly made void, the contract is not enforceable by the insurer, but it is enforceable by the insured. An agreement to insure for loss caused by the wilful commission of a crime or a tort is void.

Manifestation of Mutual Assent

Offer and acceptance constituting a manifestation of mutual assent is essential to a contract of insurance. Usually an offer is made by the person desiring insurance on an application form provided by the particular insurer and addressed to the insurer. On the insurer's acceptance of such application, the contract of insurance is created. *Usually by the terms of the insurance policy representing the contract of the parties, the policy becomes effective only on its delivery and payment of the first premium.* However, this may be varied by the terms included in the application, there is no contract of insurance until the insured accepts the policy according to its terms. *Delivery of a life insurance policy may be actual or constructive.* While most jurisdictions would hold that delivery of the policy by the insurer *to the broker* would be a constructive delivery to the insured, *a constructive delivery to the insured exists when the policy is mailed to the insured.* Pending consideration by the insurer of an application for property insurance and pending issuance of a formal policy, often the insurer through its agent will make a temporary oral contract of property insurance evidenced by a written memorandum of the contract, called a "binder."[6]

Misrepresentation. *Material misrepresentation,* whether fraudulent or innocent, in the inducement of a contract of insurance causes the contract to be *voidable* at the election of the party to whom the misrepresentation was made.

[6] An insurance binder is a written memorandum of an oral, temporary contract of property insurance, issued by the insurer to evidence such contract pending consideration and issuance of a formal policy.

A misrepresentation is material when knowledge of the fact misrepresented would have been likely to have influenced the conduct of a reasonable man. The problem of material misrepresentation usually arises in connection with false statements made by the applicant for insurance on the application form. If the applicant's misrepresentation is material, the contract represented by the policy is voidable at the election of the insurer. Courts more readily interpret intentional misrepresentations of fact as material than they do misrepresentations of fact which were made innocently. Although formerly *a misrepresentation of age in a life insurance policy* caused the policy to be voidable by the insurer, *today in most states the policy is not voidable on this ground and payment is made by the insurer on death in an amount of what coverage the premium paid would provide for the person on the basis of his correct age.*

Warranties. *A breach of the warranty by the insured justifies rescission of the contract by the insurer.* It is important, therefore, to distinguish between representations and warranties. A *representation is a statement of fact made to induce formation of the insurance contract and is not included in the contract. A warranty is a statement of fact contained in the contract, or included therein by reference, the truth of which is a condition to the insurer's liability under the contract.* Inasmuch as the law abhors forfeitures, *statements of fact made by the insured are interpreted as representations rather than as warranties, unless the parties clearly indicate that such statements constitute warranties.* Warranties, therefore, are distinguished from representations in the following ways: warranties are part of a contract and essential to it, while representations are not part of the contract and are made to induce formation of the contract; warranties always are material to the contract, while representations may or may not be material; breach of warranty by the insured justifies the insurer in rescinding the contract and declaring it forfeited, while the representation must be false and must be material in order to create the power to avoid or rescind the contract.

Concealment. In the law of Contracts, failures to disclose material facts in violation of a duty to make such disclosure constitutes a material misrepresentation, regardless of whether such nondisclosure was intentional or innocent, and any contract so made is voidable at the election of the party to whom such disclosure should have been made. If such nondisclosure was intentional, it constitutes fraud; if it was innocent, it constitutes solely a material misrepresentation. In the law of Insurance, innocent material misrepresentation by nondisclosure is insufficient as a ground for rescission of the contract. *The concealment, or nondisclosure, must have been fraudulent in order to justify rescission;* except in the case of marine insurance where, following the law of England, innocent material misrepresentation is sufficient. *An applicant for a contract of insurance has a duty to make disclosure of all material facts to the insurer,* and fraudulent concealment of material facts causes the contract induced thereby to be voidable at the election of the insurer.

Statute of Frauds

The Statute of Frauds is inapplicable to contracts of insurance, unless otherwise provided by statute. It is not a contract to answer for the debt, default, or miscarriages of another; it is a contract of indemnity,[7] to pay for loss. Further, a contract of insurance is not within that part of the Statute of Frauds which provides for contracts which are not to be performed within the space of one year from the making thereof; the contract is *performable* within the space of one year should the insured event occur within that time. Although oral contracts of insurance are enforceable in the absence of statute to the contrary, nevertheless, most contracts of insurance are in writing. Often statutes provide for standard forms of insurance policies.

Waiver and Estoppel

Waiver and estoppel often are confused; their distinction is important in determining the rights of the parties, inasmuch as waiver and estoppel mean different things.

Waiver. *A waiver is the insurer's manifestation of intent to give up a known defense to recovery on the contract of insurance or to give up its right to rescind the contract.* An illustration is the insurer's *acceptance* of a premium with knowledge that the insurance contract has been materially breached by the insured. Although the *act* of an insurer in recognizing the insurance contract as still in force even though there has been a breach of condition or warranty justifying its forfeiture constitutes a waiver of such defense, the insurer's *silence* after he has acquired knowledge of such fact justifying forfeiture of the policy does not of itself constitute a waiver of such forfeiture, unless *there was a duty to speak when he learned of such fact.* The insurer's silence with knowledge that *premiums have not been paid* does not waive the insurer's right to declare the contract forfeited, unless the insurer has waived such right by a previous course of dealings between the parties. *If the ground of forfeiture is other than for nonpayment of premiums* and the insurer learns of such fact prior to the occurrence of the insured event, the insurer has the *duty* to notify the insured of his exercise of his right of forfeiture within a reasonable period of time after he has acquired knowledge of such fact; his failure to give such notice constitutes a *waiver* of such forfeiture.[8] Waivers made prior to, or at the time of, the formation of the contract of insurance are inadmissible as evidence because of the parol evidence rule. Waivers which occur *after* the contract of insurance has been formed are admissible in evidence. Any right acquired by the contract may be waived, unless such waiver would be contrary to public policy. An illustration is an insurer's inability to waive the legal requirement that the insured have an insurable interest.

---

[7] See above, pp. 743–44.

[8] Vance, *op. cit.*, p. 493.

Estoppel. *Estoppel occurs when a material fact has been misrepresented with knowledge of its falsity in order to induce reliance thereon, and the addressee reasonably relies thereon by changing his position materially;* the utterer is estopped to deny what he previously had asserted. The insurer's representation that a contract of insurance is enforceable when the insurer knows of a defense to the enforcement of the policy, if relied on by the applicant, estops the insurer from asserting his defense subsequently. It is essential to estoppel that the addressee of the misrepresentation be ignorant of the falsity thereof and reasonably rely thereon.

Chapter 56

OPERATION OF THE INSURANCE CONTRACT

A fire insurance contract insures against property loss proximately caused by a hostile fire, and is a personal contract. There are valued, open, blanket, specific, and floating policies. A fire is hostile when it is burning in a place where it was not intended to burn. Fire proximately causes loss if it is a substantial factor in causing such loss, e.g., loss by fire smoke, falling walls, water extinguishing the fire, theft of property being rescued. The insurer is liable for loss irrespective of the insured's negligence, but not if intentionally caused by him. If the loss is *total*, then under an *open policy* the loss is the actual cash value up to the maximum of the policy; under a *valued policy* the loss is the fixed amount in the policy. If the loss is *partial*, the loss is the cost of repair, "*replacement cost*." The insurer has a right of subrogation. Under a coinsurance clause, if the insured does not insure his property up to a certain percentage of its fair value, the insured shares with the insurer in the risk of loss to the extent of the deficiency between the face amount of the policy and the amount of insurance that should have been carried on the property. Policies also carry a pro rata clause, and provide for notice and proof of loss for failure of which by the insured no forfeiture occurs unless the policy expressly so provides. The insured must have an insurable interest *only at the time of loss* in order to recover on the policy. The policy may contain a "loss payable" or "open mortgage" clause, or it may contain a "standard" or "union" mortgage clause, in both the mortgagee being a third party creditor beneficiary of the contract. Subrogation exists when a mortgagee is the insured, but not for accident or life insurance. The contract is not assignable *before loss* without the

insurer's consent, but a claim for loss under the contract is assignable without such consent.

A life insurance contract is to pay a specified amount on death of the insured. There are "ordinary" or "straight" life, "limited payment" life, "term," "endowment," and "split-dollar" life insurance policies. Policies exclude insurer liability in very few instances. An "incontestable" clause provides that after the expiration of a certain period of time the policy is incontestable, except as otherwise provided therein. The policy *beneficiary* is not required to have an insurable interest in the life insured; but the *insured* had to have an insurable interest *only at the time the contract was made.* If the right to change the beneficiary has not been reserved by the insured, the beneficiary has a vested interest in the policy and the beneficiary's consent is necessary for the insured to terminate the beneficiary's rights under the policy or to assign the policy. If the right was reserved, the insured can terminate the beneficiary's rights and assign the policy without such consent. Although the right is reserved, nevertheless almost all states have exempted all or part of the proceeds from life insurance contracts as unavailable to creditors or a trustee in bankruptcy. State statutes provide for distribution of policy proceeds when premiums were paid with embezzled funds or by an insolvent husband. An insured may cancel or surrender a policy, but the insurer cannot do so as long as premiums are paid. The reserve fund available on policy surrender is a "cash surrender value."

SECTION I. NATURE OF FIRE AND LIFE INSURANCE

Fire Insurance

A fire insurance contract is a contract of indemnity, insuring against property loss proximately caused by a hostile fire. The character of the insured is a material consideration in determining the risk of the insurer and, accordingly, *a contract of fire insurance is a personal contract.*

There are various kinds of fire insurance contract, each kind varying according to the risk assumed. Among the more common types of fire insurance contract are valued and open policies, blanket and specific policies, and floating policies. In a *valued policy* a specific value is placed upon the insured property so that, in the event of its total destruction or loss, the extent of such loss is fixed and cannot be questioned by the parties. An *open policy* does not specify the value of the insured property but establishes a fixed maximum liability of the insurer for loss or damage to such property. The value of the property is left open for determination at the time of loss. The total destruction of the insured property under an open policy, in the absence of statute or contract provision to the contrary, does not entitle the insured to the maximum amount as fixed by the policy. It can be shown that the loss was less than the maximum amount of the policy. In a *blanket policy* several items of property are insured with a fixed maximum over-all liability for loss or damage to the property, but the value of each item and the maximum liability of the insurer on each item are not specified. A *specific policy* specifically indicates the maximum liability of the insurer on each item. In a *floating policy* the insured property is of such a nature that it is constantly changing and is transitory—e.g., a merchant's stock in trade—and the policy applies to the particular property as it comes within the terms of the policy.

Life Insurance

Technically, a contract of life insurance is not a contract of indemnity because it is impossible to determine the value or extent of the particular loss of life. *It is a contract to pay a specified amount in the event the life insured is terminated.* The insurer builds up a reserve from each premium paid by the insured in order to accumulate the amount payable on the maturity of the policy and, for that reason, a life insurance contract often is considered as a form of investment. The life insured may be either that of the insured, or that of a person other than the insured if the insured has an insurable interest therein at the time the insurance contract is made.

There are various kinds of life insurance contract, the most common of which are: ordinary life, limited payment life, term, and endowment insurance contracts. *Ordinary life insurance,* or "whole" or "straight" life insurance as it is often called, provides for a fixed payment to the beneficiary of the contract at the time of the termination of the life insured in return for the payment of premiums during the entire lifetime of the life insured. *Limited payment life insurance* provides for a limited number of payments of premiums during a specified period and, after having made such payments, the insured is protected for the rest of the life insured, as well as the period during which such payments were made. *Term insurance* provides for a fixed premium for a specified term during which term only is the insurer liable for the termination of the life insured. There usually is no accumulation of any reserve. In term insurance the insurer is subjected to a risk of loss which may or may not happen during the period of the term, as contrasted with ordinary life and limited payment life insurance when the insured event—namely the termination of the life insured—is certain to happen during the life of the policy. *Endowment insurance* provides for the payment of fixed premiums for a specified period of time and, on the expiration of such time, a fixed amount is to be paid to the insured or to his beneficiary. The sum is payable at a fixed period of time if the insured is still alive or, on his death, at the time of his death. This form of policy represents a combination of term and annuity insurance. "Split-dollar" life insurance should be mentioned. This usually means a life insurance contract where the insured's employer pays that portion of the premium which is equal to the policy's cash surrender value, the employer's interest in the policy proceeds being limited to this amount.

SECTION II. RIGHTS AND LIABILITIES UNDER THE INSURANCE CONTRACT

Fire Insurance

The liability of the insurer is determined by the occurrence of the insured event and the terms of the policy fixing the extent of such liability. *In a fire insurance contract the insured event is the destruction or impairment of property proximately caused by a hostile fire.* By fire is meant actual ignition. It is the fire which must begin the chain of causation leading to loss, although the actual loss may not be by direct contact with the fire. The fire must be hostile and not friendly. *A fire is hostile when it is burning in a place where it was not intended to burn.* A fire in a fireplace where it was intended to burn is a friendly fire, but if it should extend beyond the fireplace to where it was not intended it becomes a hostile fire. Fire proximately causes loss if it is a *substantial factor in causing such loss.* Loss caused by actual contact of the insured property with the hostile fire, by smoke from the fire, by falling walls caused by the fire, by the use of water in extinguishing the fire, or by the occurrence of theft of the insured property while being rescued from the fire, is proximately caused by the fire. The insurer is not liable for loss specifically excluded by the terms of the policy. *The insurer is liable for loss irrespective of the negligence of the insured, but he is not liable for loss intentionally caused by the insured.*

Extent of Insurer's Liability. The extent of the insurer's liability for property loss is determined by the terms of the insurance contract.[1] This involves a determination of whether the loss was total or partial, the measure of the loss, and whether the policy has any coinsurance or pro rata provisions. Loss is total or partial; it is *total* if there is nothing left to use in the restoration of the property to the purpose for which it was used at the time of the loss; otherwise it is *partial. If there is a total loss, the policy should be examined to see whether or not it is a valued or open insurance policy. If it is a valued policy,* then the insurer must pay the *fixed amount* as specified in the policy. *If it is an open policy,* then the extent of the *actual loss* must be determined, and the insurer is liable for such loss not in excess of the maximum amount as specified in the policy. *If it is a total loss under an open policy,* the measure of the loss is the *actual cash value of the insured property* at the time of the loss. If it is a partial loss, the measure of the loss is the cost of repair in order to restore the

---

[1] It should be noted that, in one form or another, a policy of fire insurance may provide that any change in the interest, title, or possession of the subject matter insured which *increases the risk to the insurer* terminates the policy of fire insurance. There is conflict concerning the effect of a partner's transfer of his partnership interest when the partners are jointly insured. Generally, in the absence of contract provision to the contrary: a partner's transfer of his interest in the partnership (i.e., his interest in profits and surplus) to another partner or to one not a partner, does not affect insurance; a partner's retirement from the partnership does not affect the insurance; but *the admission of a new partner terminates the insurance.*

property to its original condition—i.e., *replacement cost.* In order to protect the insurer against an unfair valuation of loss and against unfair proofs of loss, fire insurance policies usually provide that the insurer has the option to restore the damaged property to its condition at the time of the loss. It should be noted in passing that the insurer of property is *subrogated* to the insured's rights against a wrongdoer who caused damage to, or loss of, the insured property for which the insurer has paid under the policy.

Coinsurance Clause. Because fires usually do not result in a total loss of the property, owners insure their property for less than its full value. In order to induce owners to insure their property against loss by fire for a higher percentage of the property's value, coinsurance clauses are often included in fire insurance contracts. *The theory of coinsurance is that if the insured does not insure his property up to a certain percentage of its fair value, the insured shares with the insurer in the risk of loss to the extent of the deficiency between the face amount of the policy and the amount of insurance which should have been carried on the property.* (The coinsurance clause in a fire insurance policy provided that the owner was to carry insurance for 80 percent of the fair value of the property. The property was worth $10,000 at the time of loss to such property of $4,000. The owner had a fire insurance policy on the property for $6,000. To the extent that the owner failed to carry insurance in the amount of 80 percent of the fair value of the property, the insured is to participate in such loss.

$$\frac{\$6{,}000\text{ (policy)}}{\$8{,}000\text{ (80\% of \$10,000)}} \times \$4{,}000\text{ [loss]} = \$3{,}000\text{ [owner's recovery]}.$$

He has shared in the loss to the extent of his failure to carry insurance to the extent of 80 percent of the fair value of the property.) A coinsurance clause in a fire insurance policy is not applicable to total losses. A coinsurance clause is implied by law in marine insurance policies.

Pro Rata Clause. Fire insurance contracts often contain a pro rata clause which provides that, if there is more than one insurer on the same risk, any loss will be apportioned among them in the ratio that the amount of insurance issued by each insurer bears to the total amount of the insurance on the risk, and each is liable to the insured for his pro rata share of such loss.

Notice and Proof of Loss. The requirement in fire insurance contracts for notice of loss and proof of loss is a condition subsequent after the insurer's liability for loss has become fixed by the occurrence of loss. *Because the law does not favor forfeitures unless the parties specifically so provide in their contract, failure to give the notice or proof of loss as required by the contract does not cause the contract to be forfeited, unless there is an express contract provision to the contrary.* If the policy provides for an immediate notice of loss, the word "immediate" is interpreted to mean a reasonable period of time after the loss has occurred by the exercise of due diligence. Such notice of loss must indicate the nature and extent of such loss. The purpose of notice of loss is to inform the insurer of the loss so that he may protect the property from further loss; and the purpose of proof of loss is to inform the insurer of the extent of his liability on such loss and to give him an opportunity to ascertain the correctness of the loss alleged. *In most courts, the requirement of notice and proof of loss is not considered to be a condition subsequent causing forfeiture for their nonobservance.* This discussion of notice and proof of loss is applicable equally to life insurance.

Beneficial Interests. *The insured* of a fire insurance policy is entitled to the proceeds on the occurrence of loss, provided he has an insurable interest in the property insured *at the time of the loss.* On the issuance of a mortgage it is usual to provide that the mortgagor must insure the mortgaged property for the benefit of the mortgagor and the mortgagee. *Fire insurance policies contain one of two types of mortgage clause.* Under the type which designates the mortgagee as the payee as his interest may appear, sometimes called an "open mortgage" or "loss payable" clause, the mortgagee is merely a beneficiary of the policy; he is not a party to the insurance contract and the continuance of his interest in the policy depends upon the performance or default of the mortgagor insured. Under the other type, often known as a "standard" or "union" mortgage clause, a contract is created between the insurer and the mortgagee whereby the policy will not lapse by reason of the mortgagor's default but the mortgagee can pay the premium; most courts hold the mortgagee is under no obligation so to pay, while other courts hold the mortgagee is obligated so to pay, the premium. *In both types of mortgage clause, the mortgagee is a third party creditor beneficiary of the insurance contract and he can recover on the same.*[2] Fire insurance policies with a mortgage clause usually provide that, in the event of loss, the proceeds will be applied first to the mortgagee in satisfaction of the mortgage debt and any surplus will be paid to the owner of the property. *If the policy does not provide for payment to the mortgagee, the mortgagee has no interest in the policy;* however, the mortgagee may become a judgment creditor and then be able to reach the proceeds owing to the mortgagor under the policy. *If the mortgagee carries fire insurance on the mortgaged premises, the insurer's payment to the mortgagee for loss that has occurred subrogates the insurer to the mortgagee's claim against the mortgagor. The right of subrogation does not exist in accident or life insurance.*

Assignment. Whether or not a fire insurance *contract* is assignable depends upon the terms of the contract and when, and to whom, assignment is to be made. Assignment may occur before or after loss covered by the policy has occurred. Because a fire insurance contract is a *personal contract* between the insurer and the insured, whether or not it is assignable *before loss* depends upon to whom assignment is to be made. Assignment *before loss* cannot be made to a purchaser of the entire insurable interest of the insured in the

[2] See above, pp. 75 ff.

subject matter covered by the contract without the consent of the insurer. *Consent by the insurer creates a novation,* the new contract having the insurer and the assignee (thereafter he is the insured) as parties and containing the same terms as the old contract. Assignment before loss *for the purpose of security* to an assignee with an insurable interest in the property insured (e.g., assignment of the contract to a mortgagee of the insured property) may be made without the consent of the insurer, as long as the insured retains an insurable interest in the property insured. *After loss,* the contract *claim* for the loss may be assigned without the consent of the insurer, just as any other chose in action may be assigned.

If the fire insurance contract is assigned and the insurer does not consent to the assignment when such consent is required, the insured is entitled to a refund of the unearned premium, the insurer retaining the customary short rate of insurance premium for the period during which the insurance was in effect. It is for this reason that vendors of insured property acquire the consent of the insurer to the assignment of the policy to the vendee, so that the lower rate of insurance for the longer period of time will result in a more favorable adjustment in the purchase price in favor of the vendor when the sale takes place.

Cancellation. Fire insurance policies usually provide for a few days' advance notice of the intention of a party to cancel the policy. Such notice may be waived by either party. On cancellation, the unearned portion of the premium paid is to be returned to the insured after the insurer has retained the customary short rate of insurance premium.

Life Insurance

The liability of the insurer is determined by the termination of the life insured and by the terms of the policy fixing the extent of the insurer's liability. Life insurance contracts exclude insurer liability for termination of the life insured in but few instances, such as: death caused by the commission of a crime; death caused by, or while in, military service in time of war; execution as punishment by the state or federal government; suicide within the period of time specified in the policy; and death caused by an airplane in which one is a passenger under the circumstances specified in the contract. The occurrence of death during the commission of a crime, or while in military service during time of war (if the contract excludes death *caused by,* but does not exclude death *while in,* military service), but not caused by *such* fact does not exempt the insurer from such liability under the policy for such death. Life insurance policies usually exclude liability for death caused by suicide within a specified period of time. Such suicide clauses are interpreted by most courts to mean that the insurer is liable if the person was insane at the time of such suicide; suicide while insane is a risk not excluded from the policy. In the absence of any clause in a policy excluding liability for death by suicide, in most states suicide is included as one of the insurer's risks. It should be noted in passing that *subrogation is inapplicable to life insurance because no accurate valuation can be placed on human life.*

Incontestable Clause. It is usual for life insurance policies to include an *incontestable clause* which provides that after the expiration of a certain period of time the policy is incontestable, except as otherwise provided therein. The purpose of such a clause is to induce people to acquire life insurance policies and thereby be relieved of the fear that the policy will be avoided on the termination of the life insured or that payment thereon will be contested. Unless the defense of suicide is expressly reserved and excepted from the incontestable clause, such clause includes suicide. Defenses which are not excluded by the incontestable clause are: those so stated in the policy; lack of an insurable interest on the part of the insured; failure to give proof of loss as provided in the policy; and the loss was a risk excepted from the terms of the policy.

Beneficiary. The beneficiary of a life insurance contract may be the insured or some other person. *The beneficiary is not required to have an insurable interest in the life insured if the insured had an insurable interest at the time the contract was made;* it is not necessary that the insured's insurable interest exist at the time of the policy's maturity. A common example is the issuance of life insurance to a partnership or a corporation on the life of a partner or of an officer or director in the corporation and, at the time of death, the insured did not have his previous business status. A *beneficiary has a vested interest in a life insurance policy if the insured has not reserved the right to change the beneficiary.* However, if such right has been reserved, the beneficiary is an expectant beneficiary whose rights under the contract may be terminated at the will of the insured.

Assignment. *Unlike a fire insurance contract, a life insurance contract is assignable without the consent of the insurer.* If the beneficiary is the insured or his estate, or if the beneficiary is a third person and the insured has reserved the right to change the beneficiary, such insurance contract may be assigned without any difficulty. However, if the beneficiary is a third person and the insured has not reserved the right to change the beneficiary, the beneficiary has a vested interest in the insurance contract which cannot be assigned without his consent. In the absence of statute to the contrary, *a beneficiary with a vested interest in the insurance contract may assign his interest.* An assignment of the insurance contract or of an interest therein must be accomplished as provided by the terms of the insurance contract. Life insurance contracts usually provide that the insurer is not affected by an assignment of the insurance contract until the insurer receives notice of the assignment.

Creditors. Creditors of the insured may, on obtaining judgment, resort to the assets of the insured in satisfaction of their claims. *The insured's interest in a life insurance contract is an asset.* However, under the law of Insurance, if the beneficiary is a third person and the insured has reserved the right to change the beneficiary, by state statute the creditors cannot reach this power or right and cannot cause the beneficiary to be changed so that the proceeds of the policy will be made available to them. *Almost all states by statute have exempted all or part of the proceeds from life insurance contracts as unavailable to creditors.* If the right to change the beneficiary has not been reserved, there is no interest of the debtor in the policy available to the creditors. The insured's fraudulent transfer of his interest in a life insurance policy may be set aside by his creditors, just as any other transfer fraudulent as to creditors.

When premiums are paid by the insured from embezzled funds, there is a constructive trust[3] *of the proceeds of the policy in favor of the person from whom the funds were embezzled.* However, the extent of the interest of such person depends upon whether all the premiums were paid with such embezzled funds or whether the first premium at least was paid by the insured without embezzled funds. In the former instance, the beneficiary is a constructive trustee of the proceeds in favor of the person from whom such funds were embezzled. In the latter instance, there is conflict on whether there is a constructive trust of the proceeds only to the extent of the amount embezzled (with interest) and used to pay the premiums, or to the extent that the embezzled money contributed to the proceeds of the policy. *By statute in most of the states, the proceeds of a life insurance policy in a reasonable amount on which the premiums were paid by an involvent debtor husband, the beneficiary being the insured's wife or children, are exempt from his creditors, unless there was actual fraud on the part of the insured.* If actual fraud is shown, then the creditors have an interest in the proceeds of the policy to the extent of the amount of the premiums paid while insolvent or such premiums and interest thereon.

Cancellation. *Although the insured may cancel or surrender the policy, nevertheless, the insurer cannot do so.* On the surrender of a life insurance policy, there is a reserve fund which has been accumulated from the premiums paid on the policy. The surrender value of the policy is determined by this reserve less a handling charge. Such surrender value is often called the "cash surrender value." In order to avoid forfeiture of policies for nonpayment of premiums, many policies include clauses which provide for the utilization of the cash surrender value to purchase paid-up insurance, or extended insurance (which is term insurance) in the same amount as the original policy for a period of time dependent upon the amount of the cash surrender value.

PROBLEMS

1. (a) A mortgaged his realty to B as security for the payment of A's debt to B.
   (1) Does B have an insurable interest in the mortgaged property? Why?
   (2) Does B have an insurable interest in the rest of A's property? Why?
   (3) Does B have an insurable interest in A's life? Why?

   (b) X, Y, and Z are partners. The partnership applied for and obtained life insurance on the life of Y, the policy naming the partnership as beneficiary. Later Y with-

---
[3] See below, p. 800.

drew from the partnership but X and Z continued as partners and maintained the policy of insurance until Y's death.
(1) Does the partnership have a right to the proceeds of the policy on Y's death?
(2) Why?

2. (a) A insured his house against loss by fire, naming himself as beneficiary. A's house was mortgaged to B as security for the payment of A's debt to B. A sold the house to C and assigned his fire insurance policy to C without the consent of the insurance company. Subsequently, the house was damaged by fire.
(1) Who has a right to enforce the policy?
(2) Why?
(b) Would the result have been any different if the sale and assignment had taken place subsequent to the fire? Why?
3. A fraudulently misrepresented to B Insurance Company that he had an insurable interest in certain property and obtained a policy of fire insurance on the property from B. B subsequently learned of the fraud but continued to receive the payment of premiums from A. The property was destroyed by fire.
(a) Is B liable to A on the policy?
(b) Why?
4. A has a policy of fire insurance on his property for $10,000. The policy contained an 80 percent coinsurance clause. A's property was worth $20,000 at the time it was damaged by fire to the extent of $8,000.
(a) How much can A recover under the policy?
(b) Explain your answer.
5. A obtained a policy of insurance on his life in which someone other than the insured or his estate was named as the beneficiary.
(a) Does A have the right to assign such policy? Why?
(b) Does a creditor of A have a right to resort to the policy in order to satisfy his claim? Why?
(c) If A had embezzled funds from B and used them to pay premiums on the policy and then A had died, does B have any right to the proceeds? Why?
(d) If A had paid premiums on the policy while he was insolvent, do A's creditors have any rights against the proceeds of the policy on A's death? Why?
(e) Can A or the insurer cancel or surrender the policy? Why?

SOME PREVIOUS C.P.A. LAW EXAMINATION QUESTIONS AND AUTHOR'S MODEL ANSWERS

NOVEMBER, 1979

Number 1

Select the **best** answers for each of the following items.

12. Charleston, Inc., had its warehouse destroyed by fire. Charleston's property was insured against fire loss by the Conglomerate Insurance Company. An investigation by Conglomerate revealed that the fire had been caused by a disgruntled employee whom Charleston had suspended for one month due to insubordination. Charleston seeks to hold its insurer liable for the $200,000 loss of its warehouse. Which of the following is correct insofar as the dispute between Charleston and the Conglomerate Insurance Company?

a. Since the loss was due to the deliberate destruction by one of Charleston's employees, recovery will be denied.
b. Conglomerate must pay Charleston, but it will be subrogated to Conglomerate's rights against the wrongdoing employee.
c. The fact that the employee has been suspended for one month precludes recovery against Conglomerate.
d. Arson is excluded from the coverage of most fire insurance policies, and therefore Conglomerate is **not** liable.

38. Glick was the owner of a factory valued at $100,000. He procured a fire insurance policy on the building for $40,000 from Safety Insurance Company, Inc. The policy contained an 80 percent coinsurance clause. The property was totally destroyed by fire. How much will Glick recover from the insurance company?
a. $20,000.
b. $32,000.
c. $40,000.
d. Glick will recover nothing because he did **not** meet the coinsurance requirements.

45. The usual fire insurance policy does **not**
a. Have to meet the insurable interest test if this requirement is waived by the parties.
b. Provide for subrogation of the insurer to the insured's rights upon payment of the amount of the loss covered by the policy.
c. Cover losses caused by the negligence of the insured's agent.
d. Permit assignment of the policy prior to loss without the consent of the insurer.

Answer

1. 12.b(755, 609) 38.c(755) 45.d(756–57)

MAY, 1979

Number 1

Select the **best** answer for each of the following items.

2. Wilson obtained a fire insurance policy on his dairy farm from the Columbus Insurance Company. The policy was for $80,000, which was the value of the property. The policy was the standard fire insurance policy sold throughout the United States. A fire occurred late one night and caused a $10,000 loss. Which of the following will prevent Wilson from recovering the full amount of his loss from Columbus Insurance?
a. The coinsurance clause.
b. Wilson had a similar policy with another insurance company for $40,000.
c. The fact that 50 percent of the loss was caused by smoke and water damage.
d. The fact that his negligence was the primary cause of the fire.

3. Dobbins insured his life for $100,000, naming his wife as beneficiary. After the policy had been in effect for ten years and had a cash surrender value in excess of $15,000, Dobbins assigned the policy to Suburban National Bank to secure a $20,000 loan. A copy of the assignment was filed with Suburban at its home office. Dobbins has died and his widow and Suburban are seeking to recover on the $100,000 life insurance policy. Which of the following is correct?
a. Suburban's recovery is limited to the amount of the loan outstanding plus interest.

b. The assignment to Suburban was void without the beneficiary's consent.
c. Suburban will be denied recovery due to a lack of an insurable interest.
d. The widow had a vested interest in the insurance policy in question.

4. DuBary and Young were business partners. They agreed that each would insure the life of the other for his own benefit (cross insurance). On the application for insurance, DuBary stated that he had never had any heart trouble when, in fact, he had suffered a mild heart attack some years before. Young's policy on DuBary's life contained a two-year incontestability clause. Three years later, after the partnership had been dissolved but while the policy on his life was still in force, DuBary was killed when his car was struck by a car negligently driven by Peters. The insurer has refused to pay the policy proceeds to Young, asserting that Young at the time DuBary died had **no** insurable interest in DuBary's life and that DuBary's misrepresentation voided the policy. Which of the following statements is correct?
a. The misrepresentation in the application is a bar to recovery.
b. If DuBary and Young were never partners, recovery will be denied.
c. Dissolution of the partnership eliminated any possible insurable interest and is a bar to recovery.
d. If the insurance company has to pay, it will be subrogated to DuBary's rights against Peters.

Answer

1. 2.b(755) 3.a(745, 746) 4.b(746)

MAY, 1978

Number 1

Select the **best** answer for each of the following items.

14. Wexford Furniture, Inc., is in the retail furniture business and has stores located in principal cities in the United States. Its designers created a unique cocktail table. After obtaining prices and schedules, Wexford ordered 2,000 tables to be made to its design and specifications for sale as a part of its annual spring sales promotion campaign. Which of the following represents the earliest time Wexford will have an insurable interest in the tables?
a. At the time the goods are in Wexford's possession.
b. Upon shipment of conforming goods by the seller.
c. When the goods are marked or otherwise designated by the seller as the goods to which the contract refers.
d. At the time the contract is made.

18. Marlo is seeking to collect on a property insurance policy covering certain described property which was destroyed. The insurer has denied recovery based upon Marlo's alleged lack of an insurable interest in the property. In which of the situations described below will the insurance company prevail?
a. The insured property does **not** belong to Marlo, but instead to a corporation which he controls.
b. Marlo is **not** the owner of the insured property but a mere long-term lessee.
c. The insured property belongs to a general trade debtor of Marlo and the debt is unsecured.
d. The property had been willed to Marlo's father for life and, upon his father's death, to Marlo as the remainderman.

20. Peters leased a restaurant from Brady with all furnishings and fixtures for a period of five years with an option to renew for two additional years. Peters made several structural improvements and modifications to the interior of the building. He obtained a fire insurance policy for his own benefit insuring his interest in the property for $25,000. The restaurant was totally destroyed by an accidental fire. Peters seeks recovery from his insurer. Subject to policy limits, which of the following is correct?

a. Peters is entitled to recover damages to the extent of the value of his leasehold interest.
b. Peters is entitled to recover for lost profits due to the fire even though the policy is silent on the point.
c. Peters must first seek redress from the owner before he is entitled to recover.
d. Peters will **not** recover because he lacks the requisite insurable interest in the property.

Answer

1. 14.c(745, 200, 226–27) 18.c(745–46) 20.a(745)

Part Nine:
Real Property

Chapter 57

NATURE AND TRANSFER OF INTERESTS IN LAND

SECTION I. NATURE OF INTERESTS IN LAND

Interests in land are either "real property" which is an interest in land called a "freehold," or a "chattel real" which is personal property. A "fixture" is a chattel so annexed to the land as to be a permanent part thereof but still retains its legal status as a chattel for the purpose of being subject to a security interest. All interests in land are classified as to whether or not they are "estates in land." Estates in land are either "freehold" or nonfreehold. The usual inheritable freehold estate is an "estate in fee simple," which is the largest estate in land, the owner having title to all property in the land. The two noninheritable freehold estates are life estates: (1) an estate for the life of the owner of the estate, called "life tenant" (2) an estate *pur autre vie,* which is for the life or lives of a person or persons other than, or in addition to, the life tenant.

Nonfreehold estates are "tenancies," which are for years, at will, from period to period, or at sufferance. The estate for years is an estate for a fixed period of time; it is created by a "lease," which determines the rights and duties of the lessor and lessee. Unless a statute or the lease provides to the contrary, the lessee is to make ordinary repairs and keep the premises in good condition. He is to pay the rent for failure of which the lessor can dispossess him; the lessor's breach of covenant for quiet enjoyment discharges the lessee from his duty to pay the rent. Unless the lease otherwise provides, the lessee may assign or sublet—in assignment, the lessee transfers his entire lease term to the assignee, while in a sublease, the lessee transfers to the sublessee a part of his term and the lessee has a "reversion" for the remainder of the term. No

rights or duties exist between the lessor and the sublessee, who is a tenant of the lessee. An estate for years may be terminated in various ways—e.g., expiration, forfeiture as provided in the lease, occurrence of a contingency, or surrender by the lessee. The tenant lessee may be physically ousted by the landlord by an "actual eviction," or nonphysically ousted by a "constructive eviction" by the landlord's conduct making continuance of the tenancy undesirable, difficult, uncomfortable, or unpleasant.

Some interests in land which are not estates in land are: easements; covenants running with the land; natural rights of a landowner; and liens on land (real property mortgages). An easement is different from a license which is not an interest in land but, rather, a permission to use or possess land. A "covenant" is a promise, and a "real covenant" is an obligation for the benefit of specific land and runs with the land. A landowner's "natural right" is that adjoining land be used in a natural way so as not to interfere with his right of enjoyment of his land. In a tenancy at will, the lessee has possession with the lessor's consent, and the tenancy is terminable at the will of the lessor or lessee. A tenancy from period to period has no definite duration of time and the rent is to be paid from one period to another. A tenancy at sufferance is created by a tenant holding over after termination of his previous tenancy without the consent of the landlord.

Concept of Property

Interests. The different concepts of the word "property," to which reference should be made at this time, have been discussed previously.[1] Usually, the word "property" is used in the sense of describing some thing, such as a tangible thing (e.g., land, chattels) or an intangible thing (e.g., a right, as a contract right). For example, a person may claim that a horse is his property, meaning that the horse is property. Technically, property describes an interest in some thing; the thing is the object of property. For example, a person may claim that he has title to a horse, meaning that he owns the full or general interest in the horse. Under this concept of property, an owner of property is a person who has an interest in some thing. Because the word "property" usually is used to describe a thing rather than an interest in a thing, throughout this book the word "property" refers to a thing rather than to an interest in a thing, except when otherwise indicated. In the law of Real Property, however, *the word "property" is used in its technical sense as an interest in land,* and, accordingly, it is used in this sense *throughout this chapter.*

The broadest classification of property is "real property" and "personal property." *The term "real property" describes a particular kind of interest in land called a "freehold,"* which is an interest in land for a period of time the termination of which cannot be measured or computed exactly in terms of

---

[1] See above, p. 137.

years, months, and days, and which is not terminable at the will of the transferor.[2] *An interest in land which is not a freehold is called a "chattel real,"* e.g., a tenant's interest in land by reason of his lease. *All chattels real and all interests in movables*—i.e., tangible things other than land and intangible things—*are called "personal property."*

Land. Land means the surface of the earth (whether soil or water) and that which is affixed to it permanently, that which is below it, and the space above it, in the absence of staute or judicial decision to the contrary.

Fixtures. *A fixture is a chattel which has been so annexed to the land that it becomes a permanent part thereof* but still retains its character and legal status as a chattel for the purpose of chattel financing.[3] Local state law governs, except that under Article 9 of the UCC ordinary building materials incorporated into an improvement on land do not become fixtures. Whether or not a chattel is a fixture is determined generally by the following tests: Is the chattel so physically attached to the land or of such a nature as an improvement that it is permanently a part of the land, and removal of the fixture would materially damage the land or a structure which is a part thereof; and is it the intention of the annexor, i.e., the party affixing the chattel, that it is to be a permanent part of the land? If the tenant annexes a chattel to the land and its removal would not substantially damage the land or destroy the chattel, generally as between the tenant and the landlord the chattel is not permanently annexed to the land and is not a fixture. *This type of chattel formerly was called a "trade fixture" and, like a "domestic fixture," is removable by the tenant.* Inasmuch as fixtures constitute a part of the land, they are not removable by the tenant without the consent of the landlord; and their improper removal damages the reversion of the landlord. If the duration of the lease is definite, the tenant must exercise whatever right he has to remove fixtures before the expiration of the term but no later than his surrender of possession of the premises. If the duration of the lease is indefinite, the tenant has a reasonable time after its termination in which to remove the fixtures. The landlord may cause fixtures to become chattels by his severance of them from the land. Until such severance, they are a part of the land, except that a contract for their sale contemplates severance and, *for the purpose of the contract,* they are considered as personal property.[4]

Estates in Land

Interests in land are distinguished from each other by whether or not they are estates in land. An estate in land is an interest in land which is, or may become, possessory and which is measured by duration of time.[5] Some inter-

---

[2] Restatement of Property, 1936, sec. 8.

[3] See above, pp. 425, 445 f.

[4] See above, pp. 135–36.

[5] See Restatement of Property, 1936, sec. 9.

ests in land are estates in land, while others are not. First those interests in land which are estates in land, and then a few common illustrations of interests in land which are not estates in land, will be considered.

Interests Which Are Estates in Land. Interests in land which are estates in land vary, principally, as to their duration. A freehold estate is for a period of time the termination of which cannot be measured or computed exactly in terms of years, months, and days, and it is not terminable at the will of the transferor. An estate less than a freehold exists for an ascertainable period of time or is terminable at the will of the transferor.

Freehold Estates. Freehold estates may be divided into those estates which pass to the owner's heirs or devisees,[6] called "estates of inheritance," and those estates which are not inheritable. The usual type of inheritable freehold estate is the "estate in fee simple." There are two kinds of freehold estates which are *not inheritable.* One is *an estate for the life of the owner of the estate* who is called a "life tenant." (A owns land and conveys the land to B for the life of B.) The other is *an estate "pur autre vie,"* which is for the life or lives of a person or persons other than, or in addition to, the life tenant. (A owns land and conveys the land to B for the life of C and D, or A conveys the land to B for the life of B and C.) A life estate, whether for the life of the tenant or *pur autre vie,* may be created in two ways. One way is by the act of the owner of the land—e.g., his delivery of a deed to the grantee, in which case it is called a "conventional life estate." Another way is by operation of law—e.g., the estates of dower and of curtesy, in which case it is called a "legal life estate." An estate of dower is the widow's life estate in a portion of the land of her deceased husband. An estate of curtesy is the surviving husband's life estate in the land of his deceased wife. Today, by statute, dower and curtesy are largely abolished and, in their place, provision is made for statutory interests of husband and wife in each other's estates.

Nonfreehold Estates. Estates less than a freehold estate are often called "tenancies." Such tenancies may be an estate or tenancy for years, a tenancy at will (meaning that it is terminable at the will of the landlord or of the tenant), a tenancy from period to period, or a tenancy at sufferance.

Some Interests Which Are Not Estates in Land. Easements, covenants running with the land, natural rights of a landowner, and liens on land (e.g., real property mortgages) are illustrations of interests in land which are not estates in land. A brief discussion of the first three of these interests may be helpful.

Easements. An easement is a person's interest in another's land without any right of profit in such land. The land with the interest is called the "domi-

[6] "Devisees" are those persons to whom a freehold estate in land passes on the death of the owner as provided in the decedent owner's will. "Heirs" has two meanings. The older meaning refers to those persons to whom a freehold estate in land passes directly on the death of the owner by operation of law and not by the decedent owner's will. Today, under statutes of descent and distribution in connection with decedents' estates, "heirs" refers to those persons to whom property, whether real or personal, passes on the death of the owner by operation of law and not by the decedent owner's will.

nant tenement," and the land subject to the easement is called the "servient tenement." An example is a right of way over the servient tenement as a means of access to, and egress from, the dominant tenement. *An easement is a right inherent in ownership of the dominant tenement and passes with the dominant tenement on the transfer of such ownership.* A purchaser of the servient tenement becomes the owner thereof subject to the easement. An easement is distinguishable from a *license,* which is *a permission to use or possess land but which is not an interest in the land and which is revocable at any time by the landowner,* who is called a "licensor;" the person to whom the license has been given is called the "licensee." If the license is coupled with an interest, it is irrevocable—e.g., a license to deposit chattels upon the licensor's land gives to the licensee the irrevocable right to enter upon the land and remove the chattels. The license is a privilege personal to the licensee; it cannot be assigned by him, and it is not inheritable.

An easement may be created in various ways. An easement may be created expressly or impliedly[7] by the owner of the servient tenement. It may be created also by "prescription," which is the name given to the acquisition of an incorporeal hereditament—i.e., an intangible inheritable interest in land—by open and continuous possession and use of land under a claim of right to such for a statutory period of time.

An easement may be terminated in various ways: the cessation of the purpose of the easement; the merger of the ownership of the dominant and servient tenements; the release of the easement by the owner of the dominant tenement to the owner of the servient tenement; abandonment of the easement; prescription by the use of the servient tenement adversely to the easement; conveyance of the dominant tenement without a reservation of the easement, because an easement appurtenant to land cannot be separated from the dominant tenement; and purchase of the servient tenement without the purchaser's actual notice, or constructive notice by recording, of the easement.

Covenants Running with the Land. A "covenant" was *a promise* under seal at Common Law; but today, because the Common Law effect of the seal does not exist in most of the states, it also may be a promise not under seal. A "real covenant" is a covenant running with the land and is an obligation for the benefit of specific land which becomes one of the rights of ownership of that land and inures to each subsequent landowner; it runs with the land. For

---

[7] *An easement by necessity* is an illustration of an implied easement. The circumstances under which a conveyance of one piece of land out of another piece of land may be such as to create the implicaton that the former owner's right of use of both pieces of land as a unit was intended to continue in the conveyee who may exercise such right of user in the land not conveyed to the extent justified by the circumstances. Public policy favoring land utilization is the most important factor causing implication of an easement by necessity when land cannot be used effectively without such easement. Only as the conveyance expressly denies such an implication is the easement precluded. (O possesses a parcel of land contiguous to a highway and he conveys a part of the land to A, retaining a piece of the land completely enclosing the portion conveyed to A. Nothing in the deed refers to easements. A has an easement by necessity over O's land in order to reach the highway.)

example, a clause in a deed provides that the premises shall not be used for a specified purpose. There must be privity of estate between the convenantor and the covenantee—e.g., mortgagor and mortgagee of the land under a mortgage creating an easement. A "personal covenant" is not concerned with land and is personal as between the covenantor and the covenantee. Examples of a personal covenant are the lessee's covenants to pay rent and to repair.

Natural Rights. A landowner has the right to have adjoining property used in a natural way so as not to interfere with his right of enjoyment of his land. Such a right is called a "natural right." He has no right to the passage of air or light, nor the right to a view; but he does have the right to have the air which comes to him be unpolluted. He also has the right to make reasonable use of water flowing on, through, or along the borders of, his land—such rights being relative to the rights of riparian owners. A landowner has the right to have his land remain in its natural state and to have lateral support by adjoining land, called the right to "lateral support."

Rights of Each Estate

Estate in Fee Simple. The owner of an estate in fee simple has all the property (often called "title") in the land. It is the largest and most comprehensive estate in land, and the owner may use and dispose of it as he wishes, provided he does not act contrary to law. The owner's property is subject to the rights of the state, which may sell it for unpaid taxes or which may exercise its right of eminent domain and thereby acquire the land for public use.

Life Estates. The life estates of curtesy and dower, created by operation of law, were described previously. Other life estates may be created by grant (i.e., by deed), or they may be created by will (i.e., by devise). The life tenant has the exclusive right to possession of the land and may institute possessory actions for interference with his right to exclusive possession. He is entitled to make reasonable use of the land and to retain the profits therefrom. However, he cannot injure the inheritance by the commission of "waste," which is the result of unreasonable use of the land. Timber on the land may be used for the repair and improvement of the property on the land and for firewood. The life tenant is entitled to the crops growing upon the land. *He also has the right to assign all or any part of his estate.* A life estate is an asset of the life tenant; and *his creditors may proceed against it,* sell it, and apply the proceeds in satisfaction of their claims. The life tenant has the duty of paying current taxes and his share of taxes for permanent improvements to the land, and he also has the duty to pay interest on encumbrances on the land. The life tenant is not required to make improvements to the property; but he is required, at his own expense, to make ordinary repairs to the property.

Estate for Years. *An estate for years is an estate for any fixed period of time,* the beginning and ending of which must be specified and certain—e.g., an estate for five years. The estate may be for one day or for 100 years, as long as it has a specified beginning and ending. An estate for years is created by a conveyance called a "lease," which creates the relationship of lessor and lessee, or landlord and tenant. The interest of the lessee is for the duration of the estate; thereafter, possession reverts to the lessor, whose interest in the residue on termination of the estate is called a "reversion." If, after the termination of a preceding estate, the residue of an estate returns to the grantor, the interest in such an estate is a reversion; however, if the interest passes to someone other than the grantor, it is called a "remainder" and the owner of the remainder is called a "remainderman."

An estate for years is created by a "lease." "Lease" is an *inter vivos* conveyance of an estate in land, usually for years, for a term less than that held by the lessor, and is also referred to as the contract for such conveyance. An ordinary lease contains the names of the parties, a description of the premises, the estate term, provisions for the payment of rent, covenants and conditions, and the signatures of the parties; in states where the Common Law effect of the seal continues, the signatures must be under seal. A lease may be oral or in writing but, inasmuch as it conveys an interest in land, by statute in the various states a lease of an interest in land for more than a specified minimum period of time is within the Statute of Frauds, requiring a written contract of lease or a note or memorandum of the lease in writing signed by the party to be charged.

Rights and Duties—Possession and Enjoyment. *The rights and duties of the lessor and lessee are determined by the lease.* A lessee has the right to exclusive possession and quiet enjoyment of the premises. *A provision in the lease that a party is to do or to refrain from doing something is a covenant,* and a lessor impliedly covenants that he has title to the premises and that the lessee will have quiet enjoyment of them. Under the covenant of quiet enjoyment, the lessee has the right of noninterference with his possession by the lessor during the lessee's estate and by any third persons with title paramount to that of the lessor. The lessor does not undertake the duty to prevent interference with the lessee's possession by third persons who do not have a title paramount to the lessor. The lessee has the right to institute possessory actions for interference with his possession, and the lessor has the right to damages from third persons for their damage to his reversion. The lessor has the right to enter upon the premises in order to determine whether or not waste by the lessee has occurred and also for the purpose of making repairs.

The lessee takes the premises as he finds them, in the absence of an express covenant to the contrary. On the expiration of the term, the lessee's duty is to return such premises in the same condition as they were received, except for reasonable wear and tear. He is liable for use of the premises in an unreasonable manner causing waste. The lessor has the duty to inform the lessee of hidden dangers on the premises of which the lessor knows, or reasonably should know, at the time of the lease. His failure to do so, which causes harm or loss to the lessee, subjects the lessor to liability therefor.

Repairs. Most states reflect the Common Law rule that, unless the lease provides to the contrary, the lessee has the duty to make ordinary repairs to the premises and to keep them in good condition so that he may return them to the lessor in the same condition as when he received them. The lessor does not have the duty to make such repairs, unless he covenants to the contrary;[8] and he is not liable to third persons for injuries caused to them because of the lessee's negligence in failing to keep the premises in proper repair. If the lessor has convenanted to make repairs, he is then liable to third persons for any injuries to them caused by his failure to make proper repairs. If the lessor retains control over any part of the premises, whether used by the lessor or by both the lessor and the lessee, the lessor has the duty of repair for such part and he is liable for injury caused by his failure to do so. If the lessor has covenanted to make repairs and has failed to do so, the lessee may: make such repairs and assert a right of reimbursement against the lessor; sue the lessor for damages caused by such failure; or, if such failure is substantial, he may treat the lessor's neglect as an eviction discharging the lessee from his duties under the lease. In the absence of a provision to the contrary in the lease, neither the lessor nor the lessee has the duty to make improvements on the premises, and the *lessor is to pay the taxes on the premises.*

Rent. The lessee covenants in a lease to pay a specified rent for the use and possession of the leased premises. The lessor's breach of his covenant of quiet enjoyment discharges the lessee from his duty to pay rent. The lessee's failure to pay the rent when due is a breach of covenant creating a right in the lessor to dispossess the lessee.

Assignment and Subletting. The lessee may assign his interest in the lease or sublet the premises, unless the lease expressly prohibits such assignment or sublease, and the lessor may assign his reversion. *By an assignment the lessee transfers his entire term to the assignee, while in a sublease the lessee transfers to the sublessee a part of his term* and the lessee has a reversion for the remainder of the term. Each assignee of the lessor and the lessee, respectively, acquires the rights and duties of his assignor and may enforce the covenants running with the land and conditions of the lease. An involuntary assignment of the lease may occur by operation of law—e.g., the bankruptcy or death of the lessee. The trustee in bankruptcy acquires the rights of the lessee and, an estate for years being personal property, the legal representative of the decedent lessee's estate acquires the benefit of the lease. Neither the lessor nor the lessee by assignment may avoid liability to each other under the lease. A prohibition against assignment of the lease does not prohibit subletting unless it, too, is expressly prohibited. Similarly, a prohibition against subletting of the lease does not prohibit assignment unless it, too, is expressly prohibited. The sublessee is a tenant of the lessee and has no contractual obligations to the

---

[8] By statute in some states the Common Law rule is changed and, unless the lease provides to the contrary, the lessor has this duty, for failure of which the tenant has the right to withhold rent.

lessor, unless a novation[9] has occurred. No rights or duties are owing between the lessor and the sublessee. However, subletting does not release the lessee from his duties to the lessor nor is the lessor precluded from asserting his rights—e.g., the lessor may dispossess or evict the sublessee for nonpayment of rent due and unpaid by the lessee.

Termination. An estate for years may be terminated in a variety of ways. The expiration of the term terminates the estate. If the lease expressly provides for forfeiture for breach of a specified covenant or condition, then the occurrence of such breach terminates the term by forfeiture. The lease may provide for termination of the estate on the occurrence of a contingency—e.g., the death of a particular person or the bankruptcy of the lessee. The lessee's surrender of his lease to the remainderman or to the owner of the reversion, which is accepted by such person, terminates the lease. The termination of the lessor's term terminates the lease, inasmuch as the lessor cannot create a term greater than that which he has. However, if the lessor owns the premises, his subsequent mortgage or conveyance of the premises has no effect on the previous lease and is subject to the term of the lease. Neither the death of the lessor nor of the lessee terminates the lease, unless the lease provides to the contrary. The reversion is acquired by the heirs or devisees of the lessor as real property if it is an inheritable estate, or by the legal representative of the lessor's estate as personal property if it is not an inheritable estate; and the residue of the term is acquired by the legal representative of the lessee's estate as personal property. By statute in many states the rule of the Common Law has been changed, and the accidental destruction of the premises without the fault of the lessee gives to the lessee the right to surrender or abandon the lease.

An *actual eviction* is the *physical ouster* of the tenant by the landlord from full or partial possession of the rented premises. A *constructive eviction* is the nonphysical ouster of the tenant by the landlord by means of conditions controlled by the landlord which make continuance of the tenancy undesirable, difficult, uncomfortable, or unpleasant, and otherwise contrary to the purpose for which the lease was acquired.

Tenancy at Will. A tenancy at will is an estate in which the lessee acquires possession of land with the consent of the lessor, terminable at the will of the lessor or the lessee and which is not for any specified or certain period of time. The lessee is called a "tenant at will" because he is a tenant only so long as it is the will of the lessor. A tenancy at will may be terminated by the lessor or the lessee at any time. (A conveys land to B "to hold at the will of A." Either A or B may terminate the tenancy.) The tenant at will has the right to the reasonable use and occupation of the premises. In the absence of statute, no notice of termination of a tenancy at will is necessary. The death of either the lessor or the lessee terminates such tenancy.

Tenancy from Period to Period. A tenancy from period to period is an estate with no definite duration of time and in which rent is agreed to be paid

---

[9] For a discussion of novation, see above, pp. 119–20.

from one period to another. It may exist from year to year, month to month, day to day, or any other period to period of time. It commonly is a tenancy from year to year because, usually, the rent is payable from year to year; however, it may be payable from month to month or day to day. (A owns land and leases it to B for one year. At the end of the year, B continues in possession of the land *with A's consent* but without any agreement as to the duration of B's occupancy. B is a tenant from year to year.) A tenancy from period to period is terminable by the lessor or by the lessee *giving to the other proper notice of his intent to terminate the estate;* state statutes usually prescribe the manner and time of such notice.

Tenancy at Sufferance. A tenancy at sufferance is an estate which is created by a tenant holding over after the termination of his previous tenancy *without the consent of the lessor.* It differs from a tenancy at will because no consent of the lessor is required in a tenancy at sufferance. The landlord has the option to treat the tenant either as a trespasser or as a tenant from period to period on the terms of the previous tenancy which has terminated.

SECTION II. TRANSFER OF OWNERSHIP

When an estate in land is owned by only one person, it is owned in "severalty." Ownership by "joint tenancy" means that the joint tenants as owners have a unity of interest, title, time, and possession in the property, with the right of survivorship. Ownership by "tenancy in common" means the tenants as owners have a unity of possession and each tenant owns a separate estate, as "in severalty." Ownership by "tenancy by entirety" means the tenants as owners are husband and wife who, otherwise, would be the same as joint tenants. "Community property" is property held by husband and wife which they acquired during their marriage by their joint efforts, as distinct from property which each had before marriage and property acquired by each after marriage by other than their joint efforts which continues after marriage as the separate property of each.

Ownership of land may be transferred pursuant to an agreement between the living parties by the grantor's delivery of a deed to the grantee who accepts it, thereby effecting a conveyance of the real property valid as between the parties but void as to all innocent third persons unless properly recorded. An abstract of title describes the history of ownership of the real property. The most commonly used deed of conveyance is the "deed poll," which is executed only by the grantor; a "deed indenture" is executed by the grantor and the grantee. Three types of deed poll are: (1) "quitclaim" deed, which conveys whatever title the grantor has and contains no covenants by the grantor; (2) "bargain and sale" deed, which conveys title for a valuable consideration and contains no covenants or warranties by the grantor; (3) "warranty" deed, which conveys title and contains the following covenant and warranties by the grantor: (a) the grantor has title, (b) he has theright to convey the estate, (c) the

estate is free of encumbrances, except as otherwise stated in the deed, (d) the grantee shall have quiet enjoyment, (e) the grantor will warrant and defend the title. Ownership of land may also be transferred by: (*1*) *will or intestacy* on death, the property going to the decedent owner's "devisee" by will and his "heirs" by intestacy; (2) "*adverse possession*," by actual, exclusive, and continuous possession of land under claim of right adverse to the true owner in an open and notorious manner for the statutory period of time; (*3*) *judicial process;* (*4*) "*eminent domain*" through condemnation proceedings by which the state exercises its power to appropriate land from private persons for public use on payment of proper compensation therefor.

Land may be owned, and ownership of it may be transferred, in various ways. First the various forms of ownership, and then some methods of transferring ownership, will be discussed.

Forms of Ownership

Land (also chattels and intangibles) may be owned in severalty, or concurrently with other persons by joint tenancy, tenancy in common, tenancy by entirety, or as community property. These will be considered briefly.[10]

Severalty. When an estate in land is owned by one person alone, it is owned in "severalty."

Joint Tenancy. Joint tenancy is a form of ownership of one estate in land by two or more persons as a unit and as one tenant. The persons or tenants in such a tenancy are called "joint tenants." *They have a unity of interest, title, time, and possession;* that is, they have an interest of the same duration which vested in them at the same time, and they all share in undivided possession. (A owns land and delivers to B and C a deed conveying the land "to B and C as joint tenants and not as tenants in common.") During their existence, joint tenants share the profits, use, and possession of the land. *The outstanding characteristic of joint tenancy is the right of survivorship*, so that on the death of a joint tenant the estate survives *as a unit* to the remaining joint tenants until only one tenant survives; and, on the latter's death, the estate passes either to his heirs or devisees if it is an inheritable estate, or to the legal representative of his estate if it is not inheritable. The destruction of one of the four unities of joint tenancy destroys the tenancy. Thus, the conveyance by one of three joint tenants of his interest to a fourth person has the following effect:

[10] It should be noted in passing that the need for co-ownership of housing in a multi-unit structure or plan of buildings with community living has been reflected in the co-operative plan of owning real estate and in the condominium. In the *co-operative*, the property is usually owned by a corporation with unit owners having stock or a membership and a lease of units. In the *condominium*, each member owns a unit in fee and is a tenant in common with the other members of the commonly used areas. State horizontal property acts regulate the legal status of the condominium.

the joint tenancy among the three joint tenants is terminated; the other two joint tenants continue to hold their interest by joint tenancy; and the fourth person becomes a tenant in common with the two joint tenants. If one of two joint tenants conveys his interest to a third person, the joint tenancy is terminated and the other former joint tenant and the third person become "tenants in common" in possession of the land. Inasmuch as the Common Law reason favoring joint tenancy as a form of ownership does not exist today, by legislation and by judicial decision *a conveyance or devise of an estate in land to two or more persons is construed, generally, to be a tenancy in common and not a joint tenancy, in the absence of a manifested intent to the contrary.* By statute, some states have abolished the right of survivorship and some states have abolished joint tenancy as a form of ownership.

Tenancy in Common. Tenancy in common is a form of ownership by more than one person who own various estates in the same land (e.g., one has a fee simple, another has a life estate), all of the tenants having a unity of possession. Each tenant owns a separate estate, but all the tenants have an undivided interest in the possession of the same land. The unity of interest, title, and time required for a joint tenancy is not required for a tenancy in common. Each tenant in common has the same interest as a tenant in severalty, except for the interest of possession which they all share. Conveyance by one tenant in common of his estate causes his grantee to become a tenant in common with his former tenants in common. There is no element of survivorship in a tenancy in common as there is in a joint tenancy, and, on the death of a tenant in common, the decedent's share in possession passes to his heirs or devisees, or to the legal representative of his estate, depending on whether or not his estate is inheritable. Inasmuch as each tenant has an undivided share in the possession, the tenancy is terminable either: by partition, whereby each tenant in common acquires the right to possess a separate portion of the land, each tenant becoming an owner in severalty; or by uniting all the interests in possession in one person, who thereby becomes an owner in severalty.

Tenancy by Entirety. Tenancy by entirety is a form of ownership by husband and wife who, but for their marital relationship, would be joint tenants. The Common Law concept of husband and wife as one person in law caused a conveyance or devise to them while they are husband and wife to vest the entire estate in them as one person. All the characteristics of a joint tenancy are present, except that the conveyance of either spouse alone to a third person cannot deprive the other spouse of the right of survivorship. A judgment creditor of one spouse alone cannot reach the judgment debtor's interest in the tenancy, but a judgment creditor of both spouses can reach their combined interests in the tenancy. Tenancy by entirety can be terminated by divorce or annulment of the marriage, which causes the parties to be either joint tenants or tenants in common; partition then is possible. Today, some states by statute have abolished tenancy by entirety as a form of ownership.

Community Property. The marital relationship has created another form of ownership by statute in several southwestern and western states, called "community property." This concept of ownership originated in the civil law and, as modified by the Common Law and by statute, exists today in those states and, in part, in the federal system of income taxation as applied to husband and wife. Under this concept, the property of spouses is either community property or the separate property of each. Husband and wife have a community of interest in property acquired during their marriage by their joint efforts, in the income and profits from that property, and in property exchanged for it, whether real or personal property. Such property is called "community property." Property acquired after marriage is presumed to be community property, unless shown to be separate property of either spouse, and all property not separate property is community property. Property acquired by either spouse before marriage, property acquired by either spouse after marriage by gift, will, or intestacy, and that property which is acquired by the exchange of such property, is separate property. Except for a few of these states, separate property includes the income and profits acquired during marriage from separate property.

The termination of the tenancy of community property and the transfer of interests in community property present difficulties. Community property cannot be partitioned, just as in tenancy by entirety, but divorce terminates the tenancy and partition then is possible. The extent to which community property and separate property are available to judgment creditors of either husband or wife, and the extent of the husband's control over community property, are complex and vary among the community property states. The death of either spouse causes the survivor to acquire at least half of the community property, the remaining half passing by the will or by the intestacy of the decedent, except as otherwise provided by statute in a few of these states.

Methods of Transferring Ownership

Ownership of land may be transferred in various ways, of which the following will be considered: by agreement; on death, by will or intestacy; by adverse possession; by prescription; by judicial process; and by eminent domain.

By Agreement. Ownership of land may be transferred pursuant to an agreement between the parties, and it occurs by the delivery of a deed by the grantor to the grantee and by the grantee's acceptance of the deed. A deed is a signed writing under seal transferring ownership of land. Today, in most states, a deed is effective without a seal.

Delivery of the deed by the grantor to the grantee and acceptance of the deed by the grantee are absolutely necessary to effect a conveyance of ownership. Death of the grantor prior to delivery renders the deed inoperative. Delivery of the deed by the grantor to a third person for delivery to the grantee may be an absolute delivery or a delivery in escrow, depending on the terms of the delivery. If delivery is to be made by the third person to the grantee unconditionally and immediately on the expiration of a specified period of time or on the occurrence of an event which is certain to happen, the delivery is absolute; the deed is irrevocable by the grantor and by his death. If delivery is to be made by the third person (called an "escrow holder") to the grantee on the occurrence of a condition (e.g., payment by the grantee), it is a delivery in escrow; on failure of the condition the grantor is entitled to the return of the deed; but, pending such failure, the deed is irrevocable by the granor or by his death, or by the death of the grantee. It should be noted that a purchaser, before finally closing the transaction with the seller, usually has his lawyer examine the abstract of title to ascertain the title of the seller. An abstract of title is a legal instrument describing, in chronological order, the history of ownership of particular land. Among the items found in an abstract are deeds, mortgages, and judgments. *An abstract of title should not be examined by an accountant for the purpose of giving an opinion regarding the same,* and an examination for this purpose should be made only by a lawyer. When a title search is made, the public records are searched carefully to determine who is the record owner of the land, all interests therein, and all encumbrances and restrictions thereon. Often the buyer of land obtains "title insurance," which is a contract of indemnity against loss or damage caused by defect or failure of title. The title insurance company is liable for errors in its title insurance policy.

The delivery and acceptance of a deed is effective to create a conveyance as between the parties but, by statute in the various states, such a *conveyance is void as to subsequent purchasers for value without notice of the conveyance unless the deed was recorded in the proper place*—usually the county clerk's office in the county where the land is located. While the statutes differ in the various states regarding the effect on creditors of a nonrecorded deed, nevertheless, in most states such a conveyance is void as to innocent judgment creditors or lien creditors; in some states it is void as to all innocent creditors. Under the "Torrens System" of registering titles in some states, a certificate of title issued pursuant to a court decree is conclusive concerning title and eliminates the necessity of the usual method of recording the deed. Liens and encumbrances are noted upon the certificate, and title is subject only to them. There is much dispute concerning the desirability of using the Torrens System.

Kinds of Deed. At Common Law, deeds of conveyance were either by "deed poll" or "deed indenture." *The deed poll is executed only by the grantor and is the type of deed commonly used today.* A deed indenture is a deed executed by both the grantor and the grantee. Three of the most common types of deed in common use today are the quitclaim deed, the bargain and sale deed, and the warranty deed. A *quitclaim deed purports to convey whatever title the grantor has* and contains no covenants by the grantor. Its purpose is to divest the grantor of any interest he might have and to clear title to a particular estate. A *bargain and sale deed is a deed for a valuable consideration,* although the consideration need not be stated in the deed. It conveys title but does not contain any covenants, or warranties. *A warranty deed is a deed which conveys title and contains covenants and warranties by the grantor;*

following are five usual covenants found in a warranty deed: that the grantor has title to the estate; that the grantor has the right to convey the estate; that the estate is free from encumbrances, except those named in the deed, if any; that the grantee shall have quiet enjoyment; that the grantor will warrant and defend the title to the estate. *The first three are personal covenants and do not run with the land, while the last two are covenants which run with the land and may be enforced by all subsequent grantees.*

Contents of Deeds. A deed consists of the following parts: the premises, habendum clause, terms and conditions, covenants, words indicating the execution of the deed and the date, the signature and seal (in the few states where required) of the grantor, and the signatures of the witnesses attesting to the grantor's signature. The premies include: the names of the parties, namely, the grantor and grantee;[11] an explanation for the conveyance, if any; the consideration for the conveyance and an acknowledgment of its receipt;[12] the words of conveyance or the granting clause; and, lastly, a description of the land conveyed. The habendum clause defines and limits the estate conveyed and usually begins with the words "To have and to hold." The terms and conditions include any reservations, called a "reddendum," to the grantor and any conditions to the conveyance (e.g., a condition on which the estate shall terminate). The covenants may be of various kinds—e.g., covenant of quiet enjoyment or covenant against encumbrances. The deed is followed by a certificate of acknowledgment signed by some proper public officer with authority to take acknowledgments, which is a statutory requirement in many of the states. The acknowledgment authenticates the deed and, in many states, is required in order to have the deed recorded.

On Death, by Will or by Intestacy. As distinguished from a transfer between living persons—i.e., *inter vivos*—ownership may be transferred on the death of the owner. Transfer may be effected either by will of the owner or, in the absence of any will, by operation of law. By his will the owner, called the "testator" if a man or "testatrix" if a woman, devises his ownership of land to a person called a "devisee," effective on the owner's death. The maker of a will may revoke it at any time prior to his death; a will is ambulatory and operative only at the time of his death. A person who dies without a will has died "intestate." Ownership if inheritable real property is transferred by intestacy in accordance with the statutes of descent and distribution in each state, and it passes to the intestate's heirs in the order as provided by statute. In contrast, personal property passes to the legal representative of the intestate for his distribution pursuant to law.

By Adverse Possession. Ownership or title to land may be acquired by actual, exclusive, and continuous possession of land under claim of right adverse or hostile to the true owner in an open and notorious manner for the

[11] Misspelling of the grantee's name or the absence of required federal revenue stamps on a deed conveying real property does not invalidate the deed.

[12] If the consideration was not paid, nevertheless, the deed is valid.

statutory period of time, which varies among the states. The acquisition of title to land by this method is called a transfer by "adverse possession." Title to incorporeal hereditaments (e.g., a right of way)[13] may be acquired in the same manner as adverse possession, except that the possession is not required to be exclusive; it is sufficient if the user of the land asserts the rights as his own. The acquisition of title to incorporeal hereditaments in this manner is called a transfer by "prescription."

By Judicial Process. Title to land may be transferred by reason of a judicial proceeding. Under the Bankruptcy Code, the trustee in bankruptcy acquires title to the debtor's property as of the date of the filing of the petition in bankruptcy. A sale of land pursuant to the levy of a writ of execution, issued at the instigation of the judgment creditor, and the issuance of a deed by the sheriff or other proper public official conveys the title to the purchaser. A court decree in a proper legal proceeding effectively transfers title to land.

By Eminent Domain. A state has the power to appropriate land from private persons for public use on payment of proper compensation therefor, called the "right of eminent domain," and the exercise of this power transfers title to such land to the state. The proceedings by which this right is exercised are called "condemnation proceedings."

PROBLEMS

1. A is a life tenant of land.
   (a) If A is unlawfully dispossessed by someone other than the remainderman, does the life tenant have the right to a possessory action for such dispossession? Why?
   (b) Does A have the right to crops or timber growing on the land?
   (c) May A assign his entire life estate? Why?
   (d) May A's creditors proceed against his life estate in satisfaction of their claims? Why?
   (e) Does A have the duty to pay for the following, do not explain:
      (1) Current taxes on the land?
      (2) Permanent improvements to the land?
      (3) Interest on encumbrances on the land?
      (4) Ordinary repairs to the land?
2. (a) A leases land to B, who is unlawfully dispossessed by C, who causes damage to the land. What rights do A and B each have against C?
   (b) A leases land to Y and fails to inform Y of a hidden danger on the premises known to X but unknown to Y, which causes injury to Y.
      (1) Does Y have any right against X?
      (2) Why?
   (c) The lessor covenanted to make repairs to the leased premises and failed to make necessary repairs. What are the rights of the lessee?
3. Write the numbers 1 to 10 in a column and write opposite each number the word

[13] See above, p. 768.

"True" if the statement is true and *"False"* if the statement is not true. Reasons are **not** to be given.

(1) The assignment of a lease of premises is not the same as subletting such premises.
(2) A lessor may assign his reversion.
(3) A lessee has the right to assign his lease without the consent of the lessor, unless the lease provides to the contrary.
(4) An assignee of a lessor or lessee acquires the rights and duties of his assignor and may enforce the covenants running with the land and conditions of the lease.
(5) Termination of the lessor's term terminates the lease.
(6) Neither the death of the lessor nor of the lessee terminates the lease, unless the lease provides to the contrary.
(7) Death of one of three joint tenants terminates the joint tenancy.
(8) On the death of one tenant in common his interest in land passes to the surviving tenants in common.
(9) Tenancy in common is terminable by agreement among the tenants.
(10) A joint tenancy is terminable by a joint tenant disposing of his interest during his lifetime.

4. (a) What is a fixture, and what tests are used to determine if there is a fixture?
   (b) Distinguish an easement from a license.
   (c) Enumerate three ways by which ownership of land may be transferred.
   (d) How do a quitclaim deed, a bargain and sale deed, and a warranty deed differ from one another?
5. (a) A executed a deed conveying ownership of his land to B and delivered the deed to B, who accepted it and placed it in his safe-deposit box. If A then executed another deed to the property in favor of C and delivered it to C, is it possible for C to divest B of his title to the land? Explain.
   (b) What is meant by "eminent domain"?

SOME PREVIOUS C.P.A. LAW EXAMINATION QUESTIONS AND AUTHOR'S MODEL ANSWERS

NOVEMBER, 1979

Number 1

Select the **best** answer for the following items.

10. Marcross and two business associates own real property as tenants in common that they have invested in as a speculation. The speculation proved to be highly successful, and the land is now worth substantially more than their investment. Which of the following is a correct legal incident of ownership of the property?

a. Upon the death of any of the other tenants, the deceased's interest passes to the survivor(s) unless there is a will.
b. Each of the co-tenants owns an undivided interest in the whole.
c. A co-tenant can **not** sell his interest in the property without the consent of the other tenants.
d. Upon the death of a co-tenant, his estate is entitled to the amount of the original investment, but **not** the appreciation.

41. Dunbar Dairy Farms, Inc., pursuant to an expansion of its operations in Tuberville, purchased from Moncrief a 140-acre farm strategically located in the general area in which Dunbar wishes to expand. Unknown to Dunbar, Cranston, an adjoining landowner, had fenced off approximately five acres of the land in question. Cranston installed a well, constructed a storage shed and garage on the fenced-off land, and continuously farmed and occupied the five acres for approximately 22 years prior to Dunbar's purchase. Cranston did this under the mistaken belief that the five acres of land belonged to him. Which of the following is a correct answer in regard to the five acres occupied by Cranston?

a. Under the circumstances Cranston has title to the five acres.
b. As long as Moncrief had properly recorded a deed which includes the five acres in dispute, Moncrief had good title to the five acres.
c. At best, the only right that Cranston could obtain is an easement.
d. If Dunbar is unaware of Cranston's presence and Cranston has failed to record, Dunbar can oust him as a trespasser.

Answer

1. 10.b(775) 41.a(778–79)

MAY, 1979

Number 5

Part a. Hammar Hardware Company, Inc., purchased all the assets and assumed all the liabilities of JoMar Hardware for $60,000. Among the assets and liabilities included in the sale was a lease of the building in which the business was located. The lessor-owner was Marathon Realty, Inc., and the remaining unexpired term of the lease was nine years. The lease did not contain a provision dealing with the assignment of the leasehold. Incidental to the purchase, Hammar expressly promised JoMar that it would pay the rental due Marathon over the life of the lease and would hold JoMar harmless from any future liability thereon.

When Marathon learned of the proposed transaction, it strenuously objected to the assignment of the lease and to the occupancy by Hammar. Later, after this dispute was resolved and prior to expiration of the lease, Hammar abandoned the building and ceased doing business in that area. Marathon has demanded payment by JoMar of the rent as it matures over the balance of the term of the lease.

Required:

Answer the following, setting forth reasons for any conclusions stated.

1. Was the consent of Marathon necessary in order to assign the lease?
2. Is JoMar liable on the lease?
3. If Marathon were to proceed against Hammar, would Hammar be liable under the lease?

Part b. The Merchants and Mechanics County Bank expanded its services and facilities as a result of the economic growth of the community it serves. In this connection, it provided safe deposit facilities for the first time. A large vault was constructed as a part of the renovation and expansion of the bank building. Merchants purchased a bank vault door from Foolproof Vault Doors, Inc., for $65,000 and installed it at the vault entrance. The state in which Merchants was located had a real property tax but did not have a personal property tax. When the tax assessor appriased the bank building after completion of the renovation and expansion, he included the bank vault door as a part of the real property. Merchants has filed an objection claiming the vault door was initially personal property and remains so after installation in the bank.

There are no specific statutes or regulations determinative of the issue. Therefore, the question will be decided according to common law principles of property law.

Required:

Answer the following, setting forth reasons for any conclusions stated.

1. What is the likely outcome as to the classification of the bank vault door?

2. The above situation involves a dispute between a tax authority and the owner of property. In what other circumstances might a dispute arise with respect to the classification of property as either real or personal property?

Answer

5.a.1. No. A lease of realty may be assigned without the landlord's consent, unless the lease expressly prohibits assignment. Here, the lease did not prohibit assignment and, therefore, JoMar could assign the lease without the consent of Marathon, landlord.

2. Yes. A lessee's assignment of the lease with its rights and duties and assumption by the assignee do not relieve the lessee of his contractual duties under the lease, which include payment of the rent to the landlord. Therefore, JoMar is still liable to Marathon on the lease.

3. Yes. Marathon is a third party creditor beneficiary of the assignment contract between JoMar and Hammar under which Hammar promised to perform JoMar's obligation to pay the rent to the creditor, Marathon. (pp. 771, 83, 75–76)

b.1. The vault door is real property. A chattel may be so annexed to land or structure on the land as to become a part of the land and, therefore, real property. The tests usually applied are: is the chattel so physically attached to the realty as to be a permanent part of the realty and its removal would materially damage the land or the structure; and is it the intention of the annexor that the chattel be a permanent part of the realty? Here, the door is definitely annexed to the bank building. The vault door is to further the purpose of a fixed safe deposit facility in the bank, and its removal materially adversely affects that purpose. Finally, the permanence of the door is intended by its intended use. Therefore, the tests have been met and the door is real property. (p. 766)

2.a. Between the mortgagor and the mortgagee of realty as to whether the annexed property is realty or chattel.

b. Between the mortgagee of a structure on land and a debtor's creditor who claims a security interest in a chattel annexed to the structure.

c. Between the seller and the buyer of realty as to whether a chattel affixed to the realty is removable by the seller.

d. Between the landlord and the lessee of realty as to who is entitled to a chattel annexed to the realty on the expiration of the lease.

e. Between different persons who would take property under a decedent's will depending on the nature of the annexed property as realty or chattel. (pp. 766)

NOVEMBER, 1978

Number 1

Select the **best** answer for the following item.

41. Winslow conveyed a 20-acre tract of land to his two children, George and Martha, "equally as tenants in common." What is the legal effect of this form of conveyance?
  a. George and Martha are joint owners with a right of survivorship.
  b. Each must first offer the other the right to purchase the property before he or she can sell to a third party.
  c. Neither may convey his or her interest in the property unless both join in the conveyance.
  d. Each owns an undivided interest in the whole, which he or she may dispose of by deed or by will.

Answer

1. 41.d(775)

MAY, 1978

Number 1

Select the **best** answer for the following item.

29. Donaldson, Inc., loaned Watson Enterprises $50,000 secured by a real estate mortgage which included the land, buildings, and "all other property which is added to the real property or which is considered as real property as a matter of law." Star Company also loaned Watson $25,000 and obtained a security interest in all of Watson's "inventory, accounts receivable, fixtures, and other tangible personal property." There is insufficient property to satisfy the two creditors. Consequently, Donaldson is attempting to include all property possible under the terms and scope of its real property mortgage. If Donaldson is successful in this regard, then Star will receive a lesser amount in satisfaction of its claim. What is the probable outcome of Donaldson's action?
  a. Donaldson will **not** prevail if the property in question is detachable trade fixtures.
  b. Donaldson will prevail if Star failed to file a financing statement.
  c. Donaldson will prevail if it was the first lender and duly filed its real property mortgage.
  d. The problem will be decided by taking all of Watson's property (real and personal) subject to the two secured creditors' claims and dividing it in proportion to the respective debts.

Answer

1. 29.a(766)

Part Ten: Wills and Decedents' Estates

Chapter 58

THE WILL

SECTION I. FORMAL REQUIREMENTS

Transfer of a decedent's property can occur by his will, or by his intestacy without a will. The law applicable to the making of a will is the law of the place where the testator was domiciled at the time of his death, except that the law of the place where land is situated governs. The "testator" (male) or "testatrix" (female) must have the capacity to make a will and he must express his testamentary intent thereby to make a will. The will must be in writing, except for a "nuncupative" will which is oral, and is valid and can transfer only personal property if: it was made during the testator's last illness, in his home or the house where he died, intending his words to be his will and published to the required number of witnesses who reduce his words to writing within a specified number of days thereafter. Nuncupative will statutes apply to military personnel in active service. A will entirely in the testator's handwriting is a "holographic" will, and usually does not require any witnesses. A will may include therein papers not attached to it by "incorporation by reference." In most states, the will must be signed by the testator; he need not "subscribe." His signature may be made in any manner as long as he intends it as his signature, and it must be witnessed by the required number of witnesses, usually two. In most states a beneficiary may be a witness, but if his testimony is necessary to prove the will he loses his interest under the will.

A will may be revoked by the testator himself or by operation of law. The testator's subsequent writing with the same formality as required to make a will indicating an intent to revoke his will accomplishes that result. A "codicil" changes or adds to the will and is a supplementary part thereto. The

testator's mutilation of his will with the intent thereby to revoke it accomplishes that result. When a material change in the circumstances of the testator occurs which would have caused him to revoke the will, such a change revokes the will by operation of law, e.g., divorce.

A "beneficiary" under a will is a person named in the will who is to receive property thereunder as a gift, and is a "devisee" of real property and a "legatee" of personal property. A "devise" is a gift of real property, and a "legacy" is of personal property. Inheritance by intestacy is governed by state statutes which vary from state to state. "Per capita" signifies by the heads, and means that all persons who stand in the same degree of relationship to the intestate share equally in the estate, while "per stirpes" signifies by stocks or by roots, and means that the survivors of their parent represent their parent and take his share by such representation for division among themselves—a right by representation.

The transfer of ownership of property may occur during the lifetime of the owner and on his death. The law reflects the desire of society to be able to effect a transfer of ownership at the time of a person's death in accordance with the wishes of the deceased and provides the method of a "will." Failure to execute a will causes the decedent's real property (in the sense of its being an inheritable freehold estate in land) to vest in his heirs,[1] and his personal property (in the sense of its being an interest in a thing other than a freehold estate in land)[2] to be transferred to his legal representative for distribution, according to the laws of descent and distribution as provided by statute in each particular state. A person who executes a will is called a "testator," if it is a man, and a "testatrix," if it is a woman; and a person with a will dies "testate," while a person without a will dies "intestate."

The Uniform Probate Code makes extensive changes in the law of wills and decedents' estates, but since the American Institute of Certified Public Accountants has not recognized it for purposes of coverage on the Uniform CPA Examination, as of the date of the publication of this book, it is not discussed in the Part.

Definition of a Will

A "will" is a person's expression in proper legal form of his desires and directions concerning the distribution of his property at the time of his death. It often is called a "testamentary disposition" of his property. The following elements in the formation of a will are to be considered: the law applicable; the capacity of the testator; the testamentary intent of the testator; the writing; the testator's signature; and attestation.

---

[1] For definition of "heirs" see above, p. 767, ftn. 6.

[2] For the concept of real and personal property, see above, pp. 765–66.

Law Applicable

The requirements for making a will are prescribed specifically by statute in each state and absolute compliance therewith is necessary. *The law applicable to the making of a will is the law of the place where the testator was domiciled at the time of his death, except that, in the case of an interest in land being transferred under a will, the law of the place where the land is situated governs.*

Capacity of Testator

Any person with mental capacity and who is above the statutory age, usually 21 years or 18 years, has legal capacity to make a will. A person has mental capacity to make a will when he has the *ability* to understand and comprehend the nature and extent of his property, the disposition he is making of his property, and to remember his relatives.

Testamentary Intent

The contents of a will consist of any written (except for nuncupative wills) manifestation of the testator's intent thereby to make a will and to dispose of his property. His expression is not required to be in any particular form and may be very informal. Although the writing may manifest such testamentary intent, nevertheless, after the testator's death it may be proved that the testator did not have such intent (e.g., because of fraud, undue influence, mistake) thereby disproving such writing as his will.

The Writing

A will must comply with statutory requirements in order to be effective as such. *Statutes require wills to be in writing, with the exception of the oral or "nuncupative" will* which is permitted only under certain circumstances. A nuncupative will is valid if: it was made during the last sickness of the testator; it was made in the testator's home or in the house where the testator died; the testator intended that his words constitute his will; the testator has published to the required number of witnesses, present at his request as witnesses, that his words were intended to be his will; and the witnesses have committed the will to writing within a specified number of days after the making thereof. Statutes in the various states make provision for soldiers' and sailors' nuncupative wills while soldiers are in actual service and sailors are at sea. *A nuncupative will can transfer only personal property.*

The writing may be made with ink or pencil, it may be typewritten or printed, and it may be a combination of these. *A will which is entirely in the testator's handwriting, including his signature, is called a "holographic" will.* The writing may be on one page of paper or on several pages if they clearly are a part of one instrument. In most states a will may include as a part thereof papers not attached to it but which are clearly described therein and which were in existence at the time the will was executed by the testator, even though such papers are not of the requisite formality of a will. *Such doctrine of inclusion is called "incorporation by reference."* The will must indicate an intention on the part of the testator to include such papers, which were not present at the time of the execution of the will, as a part of the will.

Testator's Signature

It is necessary that the testator's signature appear on the instrument to authenticate it as his will. His signature may be made by himself or, in most states, by another person at his request and direction and in his presence as his proxy. In most states the testator's signature is not required to be made at the end of the instrument, although usually it is placed there, but it may be placed anywhere on the instrument. An instrument on which the testator's signature must appear at the end must be "subscribed" by the testator. The signature may be made in ink or pencil, printed or stamped, and made by initials or any mark or device which is *intended by the testator to be his signature.*

Attestation

The signature of the testator, or his acknowledgment of a signature as his own, must be witnessed, called "attested," by the required number of witnesses, who are such pursuant to the testator's request. Most states require only two witnesses, although many require three. Witnesses must be competent to be such at the time of the execution of the will, and their subsequent incompetency does not cause the will to be invalid. They must be competent to testify concerning the facts surrounding the execution of the will and concerning the mental capacity and testamentary intent of the testator to execute the will. *In most states the interest of a person as a beneficiary under the will does not disqualify him from being a witness thereto; however, if his testimony is necessary in order to prove the will, although the witness may testify as such, he thereby loses his right to any interest under the will, except to the extent of his intestate share if there were no will.* A person who has an indirect interest under a will—e.g., a member of an association, church, or club which is a beneficiary under the will—is not an interested party; *only a person who is a direct beneficiary under the will is an interested party.*

After the testator has executed the instrument in their presence, the witnesses are required to sign their names as attesting witnesses anywhere upon a paper attached to the will and usually at the end of the will, although signing at the end is not required in most states. Statutes in most states do not require the witnesses to be present at the same time nor to sign in the presence of each other as witnesses. Usually an attestation clause follows immediately at the end of the will, but this is not required by statute in most of the states. An attestation clause describes the formalities which were observed at the time of the execution of the will, is an excellent method of proving the will, and is helpful to witnesses in recalling such execution. By statute in many states, a holographic will does not require any attesting witnesses. In most states, publication of the will by the testator—i.e., the testator's declaration to the witnesses that the instrument is his last will and testament—is not required. *In no state is it necessary that the witnesses know the contents of the will.*

SECTION II. REVOCATION

By Act of Testator

A will may be revoked by the act of the testator or by operation of law. *The will is ambulatory and speaks as of the time of death* and, until that event, the testator may revoke his will even though he has executed a contract not to do so. Revocation is accomplished by the expressed intent of the testator thereby to revoke the will and, in order to prove such revocation, statutes require that revocation be either: by a subsequent writing of the testator expressly or impliedly revoking a previously executed will; or by the testator's physical act to the instrument.

By Subsequent Writing. In most states, the testator's subsequent writing is required to be executed with the same formality as the will itself; however, in some states, a testator's alteration in his own hand of a holographic will revokes the portion altered. A will executed in the ordinary way is not revoked by a subsequent nuncupative will. The subsequent writing may be a new will or a "codicil." It may expressly or impliedly revoke a prior will. An express clause of revocation in a subsequent will or codicil may revoke a part of a prior will or codicil. A prior will may be revoked impliedly by a subsequent will which makes such a change in the terms of the prior will as to indicate the testator's intent to revoke the prior will. Inasmuch as a codicil is a part of a will, an expression of revocation of an entire will extends also to the codicil or codicils. *A codicil is an instrument executed by the testator subsequent to the execution of his will with the same formality as is required for the execution of a will, changing or adding to the will, and constituting a supplementary part of the will.* The loss of a will does not cause its revocation if it can be proved satisfactorily that the will had been executed properly. If the lost will contained an express clause of revocation of a prior will, such clause is effective to accomplish the revocation of the prior will.

By Act to the Instrument. Generally, *the testator's mutilation of a will with the intent thereby to revoke such will effectively revokes the same,* although the wording of the statutes varies among the states and the requirements for this method of revocation are different. The physical acts to the instrument may be done by the testator or by someone at his request and in his presence. Whether the revocation of the will by act to the instrument also revokes the codicil depends upon the testator's intent at the time the act occurred. In the absence of proof of intent to revoke the codicil also, the codicil is not revoked.

By Operation of Law

When a material change in the circumstances of a testator or a testatrix occurs which would have caused the testator or the testatrix to revoke the will, such change revokes the will by operation of law. Although in most states in the absence of statute a marriage subsequent to the will does not revoke the will, nevertheless, by statute in many states such marriage does effect a revocation unless the will was made in contemplation of such marriage or the will made provision for the widow or widower, respectively, thereby indicating an intent that such marriage was not to constitute a revocation of the will. However, in the absence of statute to the contrary, a will is revoked by a subsequent marriage *and* the subsequent birth of a child because the occurrence of both constitute a material change which would have caused the testator or testatrix to revoke the will.

In most states, a will by a *married* person is not revoked by the subsequent birth of a child from the marriage because the fact of marriage must have caused the testator or the testatrix to contemplate the possibility of having a child from the marriage and, the will having been made in the light of such contemplation, the subsequent birth is not such a change in circumstances implying an intention to revoke. However, the desire of society not to disinherit the after-born child when the will did not provide for it has caused almost all states by statute to accord to the child his intestate share as though there were no will, which is in effect a partial revocation of the will to such extent; but in almost all states the child does not acquire his intestate share if the child is provided for, or even merely mentioned, in the will because such provision or mention manifests a contemplation of the birth by the testator or testatrix precluding any implication of revocation by such birth.

In most states in the absence of statute, a divorce without a property settlement does not revoke a prior will of a former spouse or a provision in the will for a former spouse. However, in most states a divorce accompanied by a property settlement between the parties impliedly revokes that portion of the will providing for the other party.

SECTION III. BENEFICIARIES

By the Will

A "beneficiary" under a will is a person named in the will who is to receive property thereunder as a gift. The beneficiary of real property is called a "devisee," and the beneficiary of personal property is called a "legatee." A "legacy" is the name of the bequest of personal property, and "devise" describes the gift of real property. The interest of a beneficiary is a property interest which is available to his creditors. Legacies may be general, specific, or demonstrative. Today, devises may be general or specific. A "general legacy" is payable out of the general assets of the estate and does not require the delivery of any specific property. ("I give and bequeath to my sister, Anne Jones, the sum of $1,000, if she survives me.") A "specific legacy" is a gift of specific personal property. ("I give and bequeath to my brother, John Jones, if he survives me, the gold horse tie pin which I inherited from my father.") A "demonstrative legacy" is a gift of personal property, the testator having indicated a particular source of such gift but not having restricted the gift to such source in the event that the source is unavailable or inadequate. The demonstrative legacy is a charge on the source named and is payable in any event, unless the estate is inadequate after satisfying the specific legacies and devises.

By Intestacy

State statutes of descent and distribution prescribe the beneficiaries of the property of a decedent who died intestate, predicated upon their marital or blood relationship to the intestate. The word "descent" refers to real property descending and passing directly from the intestate to beneficiaries called "heirs," and the word "distribution" refers to the transfer of personal property from an intestate to the latter's legal representative and distributed by him to beneficiaries called "distributees," under the statutes of descent and distribution. Today the majority of state statutes of descent and distribution provide for the same persons as beneficiaries of real property and personal property of an intestate, and, accordingly, the word "heirs" refers, generally, to those persons to whom property, whether real or personal, passes by intestacy under these statutes.

Marital Relationship with Intestate. While statutes of descent and distribution differ among the various states, they do follow a general pattern. A spouse who survives the intestate generally receives a specified fractional share of the intestate's estate, and often the extent of the share is dependent upon whether or not there are surviving children or other specified heirs and their number. If children or other specified heirs survive, the surviving spouse shares in the estate with them and, generally, has a one-third or a one-half share. If no children or other specified heirs survive, the surviving spouse usually takes the entire estate. In community property states the statues vary, separate and community property often not passing in the same manner. By statute in most states a surviving spouse has a right, subject to limitation and variation among the states, to elect to disregard the provisions of the will of the decedent spouse and to take against the will, meaning an election to receive his or her intestate or fractional share as prescribed by statute.

Blood Relationship with Intestate. Blood relatives of the intestate may be lineal (by direct line) and be either descending (e.g., the intestate's children) or ascending (e.g., the intestate's parents), or the blood relatives of the intestate may be collateral, meaning they are of a common ancestor (e.g., first, brothers and sisters of the intestate and their descendants; second, uncles and aunts of the intestate and their descendants; and so on). The line of inheritance first descends for the purpose of intestate succession, and the children of the intestate have priority as beneficiaries, irrespective of the order of their birth and of their sex. If the intestate is survived by his only child, the latter takes the entire estate. If the intestate has more than one child, all the children share equally, and the issue (children) of the intestate's children who predeceased the testator take the share of their parent by representation (they representing their parent) and share equally among themselves. (A has three children, B, L, and W, each of which has three children: B having C, D, and E; L having M, N, and O; and W having X, Y, and Z. On A's death, there survive: B and all his children; L and all his children; and X, Y, and Z. A's estate is distributed: 1/3 to B; 1/3 to L: and 1/9 to each of X, Y, and Z.) If no children of the intestate survive the intestate, but their issue survive, the grandchildren of the intestate are in equal lineal degree of relationship with the intestate and in the majority of states they share *per capita*, while in a minority of states they share *per stirpes*. *Per capita*, signifying "by heads," means that all persons who stand in the same degree of relationship to the intestate share equally in the estate without consideration of any right of representation. *Per stirpes*, signifying "by stocks" or "by roots," is the antithesis of *per capita* and means that the survivors of their parent represent their parent and take his share by such representation for division among themselves; it is a right by representation. Thus, in the above illustration, if A's three children did not survive him but A was survived by B's three children, two of L's children, and one of W's children: if the grandchildren share *per capita*, each of the grandchildren would have an equal share in the estate; but if the grandchildren share *per stirpes*, B's three children take B's 1/3 share equally and each of them receives 1/9 of A's estate, L's two children take L's 1/3 share equally and each of them receives 1/6 of A's estate, and W's child takes W's 1/3 share of A's estate.

In the absence of a surviving spouse and of lineal descendants, the line of intestate succession ascends and, in most states, the parents of the intestate surviving the intestate share equally and a surviving parent takes the entire estate. If the intestate is survived only by brothers and sisters of the intestate, brothers and sisters are next in line, sharing equally; and when some of the brothers and sisters have predeceased the intestate but have left issue surviving, such issue share in like manner by representation as the surviving issue of children of the intestate share with surviving children of the intestate, as previously discussed. This process of priorities and sharing in intestate succession continues at great length and is prescribed by statute in each state.

Chapter 59

PROBATE AND ADMINISTRATION

Probate is the procedure of proving the authenticity of a will, which occurs in the state and county where the testator was domiciled at the time of his death. A probate in one state is effective in all states, except that the law of a state in which land is located will govern the validity of the will. The legal representative or "personal representative" of the decedent is appointed by the court. If he is named in the will, he is the "executor" (male) or "executrix" (female); if for an intestate, he is an "administrator" (male) or "administratrix" (female). If the executor is not available, the court appoints an "administrator (or administratrix) with the will annexed." Generally, the title to all of the decedent's personal property vests in the legal representative, and the title to all of the decedent's real property vests in the testator's devisees or the intestate's heirs, as of the time of the decedent's death.

"Administration" of the estate by the legal representative involves collecting the assets of the decedent's estate, paying the estate's debts and administration expenses, and distributing the remaining assets in accordance with the will or in intestacy under the court's supervision. The legal representative is responsible for reasonable care in administering the estate. He is a party personally to any contract made in his official capacity. In most states, he first resorts to personal property and then to real property to pay the estate's debts. The estate is closed after the legal representative has accounted to the court, which then issues a "decree of final settlement," distribution of the estate assets is made pursuant to the court decree, and the legal representative is discharged.

SECTION I. PROBATE

Nature

Probate means proof and is the term applied to the procedure of proving to a proper court that an instrument is the last will and testament of a decedent. Until the testator dies and the will subsequently is probated, the will lies dormant and does not have legal status or effect as such. Certain courts in each state have jurisdiction to handle the probate of wills, sometimes called "probate courts" and "surrogate courts." *A will is probated in the state and county in which the testator was domiciled at the time of his death.* If the testator has property located in other states, the will would be admitted to probate in such states; however, once a will is probated in one state, the probate is effective in all states, except in those states where land in which the testator has an interest is located, the law of the latter states governing the validity of the will. A petition for probate may be filed in the proper court by any interested person, although the executor usually makes the petition. After a petition has been filed for probate of a will, all interested parties notified, and the will admitted to probate, the will is certified by the court as the will of the testator; the legal representative, often called the "personal representative," then is appointed by the court.

The Legal Representative

The legal representative of the decedent is appointed by the court. An "executor" is the person named by the testator in his will and appointed by the court to represent the testator in the administration of his estate by carrying out his desires as provided in his will. If the testator's appointee is a woman, she is an "executrix." The legal representative of an intestate appointed by the court is called an "administrator," or an "administratrix" if a woman. If the person named in the will as an executor predeceases the testator or for some other reason is unavailable or cannot qualify as an executor, the legal representative of the testator is appointed by the court and is called an "administrator (or administratrix) with the will annexed." If an administrator or an executor has been unable to administer the estate completely, the person appointed by the court in his place is called an "administrator (or administratrix) *de bonis non*," who is an administrator of the property of the estate not administered previously. *Generally, the title to all of the decedent's personal property vests in the legal representative of the decedent's estate, and the title to all of the decedent's real property vests in the testator's devisees or the intestate's heirs, as of the time of the decedent's death.*

SECTION II. ADMINISTRATION

Function and Duties of the Legal Representative

Function. The function of the legal representative of a decedent is: to collect all the assets of the decedent's estate; to pay the debts of the estate and the administration expenses; and to distribute the remaining assets to the beneficiaries of the estate either pursuant to the direction of the testator as provided in his will, or pursuant to the statute of descent and distribution in the case of intestacy, under the court's supervision. This procedure is called "administration."

Duties. The legal representative has the duty to exercise that degree of care in administering the estate which would and should be exercised by a reasonable prudent person in his position in handling his own affairs. The legal representative's duties are confined to the conservation and distribution of the estate. He should maintain detailed accounts of his receipts and disbursements and, in the event that he is a trustee as well as a legal representative, he should keep separate trust accounts. He should use due care in selecting a proper depository for the funds of the estate and deposit the funds in the name of the estate; such funds should not be mixed with his own personal funds nor deposited in an account in his own name. He has the duty to collect assets of the estate and to sue for their collection if necessary; to discharge claims and, pursuant to court order as required in some states, to compromise claims against the estate; and to sell personal property of the estate pursuant to any express power of sale contained in the will or, in the absence of any such power, to sell either with or without court order depending upon the law of the state in which the estate is being administered. The legal representative has the duty to pay taxes and to pay all claims which must be presented within the time prescribed by law, regardless of whether or not they are mature or immature. A secured creditor is not required to prove his claim in order to recover against his security. Claims for the decedent's nonperformance of nonpersonal contracts made with the decedent may be asserted against the legal representative. (A's promissory note to B for $500 is overdue and unpaid. On A's death, B has a claim against A's estate for $500.) *In any contract made by the legal representative pursuant to authority, the legal representative personally is a party to such contract, which may be asserted against him personally.* In the latter case, the legal representative has a right of reimbursement against the estate for his outlay. The legal representative may not continue the business of the decedent unless the authority for temporary operation of such business in order to preserve the assets of the estate or to realize thereon is given expressly by the will, by the consent of interested parties in the estate, or by court order. He has no power to bind the estate by the issue or indorsement of negotiable instruments. *In most states he is to resort first to the personal property of the estate to pay its debts and, should that be insufficient, he then may resort to* *the real property either pursuant to testamentary power of sale contained in the will or pursuant to court order.* Devisees and heirs take the decedent's real property subject to this testamentary power of sale and the authority of the court to order its sale.

Final Settlement

On the expiration of the statutory period of time within which claims against the estate may be presented and after payment by the legal representative of such claims as have been presented, the legal representative has the duty to render to the court a final account of his administration of the estate. This is the last of several periodic accounts which may be required of the legal representative. Notice of the submission of the final account to the court is required to be given to all interested parties so that they may have an opportunity to object to it. After a court hearing, the final account is judicially allowed constituting a judicial approval and adjudication of such account, called a "decree of final settlement." A court order or decree of distribution then is rendered which specifies the persons to whom distribution is to be made and which orders such distribution. If the testator has created a trust in his will, called a "testamentary trust," the property of the trust is transferred at this point to the trustee, called a "testamentary trustee," to be held and administered by him in accordance with the terms of the testamentary trust. After distribution is made pursuant to the court decree, the legal representative is discharged and the estate is closed.

PROBLEMS

1. (a) The law of what place is applicable to the making of a will?
   (b) What is meant by the following in the law of wills:
      (1) A will.
      (2) A codicil.
      (3) "Incorporation by reference."
   (c) Name the essential elements of a will.
   (d) What is a nuncupative will, and when is it permitted?
   (e) What is a holographic will?
   (f) May a will be written in pencil? Answer "Yes" or "No."
2. (a) Must the testator's actual signature appear on his will?
   (b) Are a testator's initials sufficient as a signature to his will?
   (c) What is the purpose of witnesses to a will?
   (d) A and B are witnesses to T's will. Subsequently A and B became incompetent to be such witnesses.
      (1) Is the instrument invalid as a will because of such incompetency?
      (2) Why?
   (e) What is the effect of a beneficiary under a will also being a witness thereto?
   (f) Is it necessary that a witness to a will know the contents thereof? Answer "Yes" or "No."

3. (a) What is the effect of a testator's writing expressing an intent thereby to revoke his previously made will?
   (b) How may a testator revoke his will other than by a subsequent writing?
   (c) What is the effect of the following on a previously made will:
      (1) The testator's marriage.
      (2) The birth of the testator's child.
      (3) The testator's divorce from his wife.

SOME PREVIOUS C.P.A. LAW EXAMINATION QUESTIONS AND AUTHOR'S MODEL ANSWERS

NOVEMBER, 1979

Number 1

Select the **best** answer to the following item.

20. Woodrow died and left a will that named as co-executors the Fundamental Trust Company and Harlow, who is one of the residuary legatees. The will was silent on various points indicated below. Which of the following is correct?
   a. If Woodrow's will was **not** properly executed, it will **not** be admitted to probate and his property will be distributed according to the intestate succession laws even though this is contrary to Woodrow's wishes as stated in the will.
   b. Since Harlow is one of the residuary legatees, Harlow can **not** serve as executor since this would represent a conflict of interest and also would violate Harlow's fiduciary duty.
   c. All taxes paid will be allocated to the residuary estate and **not** apportioned.
   d. The executors have complete discretion insofar as investing the estate's assets during the term of their administration.

Answer

1. 20.a(785)

NOVEMBER, 1978

Number 1

Select the **best** answer to the following item.

34. The intestate succession distribution rules
   a. Do **not** apply to property held in joint tenancy.
   b. Do **not** apply to real property.
   c. Effectively prevent a decedent from totally disinheriting his wife and children.
   d. Apply to situations where the decedent failed to name an executor.

Answer

1. 34.a(774)

MAY, 1978

Number 1

Select the **best** answer to the following items.

34. Fifteen years ago Madison executed a valid will. He named his son, Walker, as the executor of his will and left two thirds of his estate to his wife and the balance equally

to his children. Madison is now dead and the approximate size of his estate is $1 million. Which of the following statements is correct?

a. The will is invalid because it was executed at a time which is beyond the general statute of limitations.
b. The estate is **not** recognized as a taxable entity for tax purposes.
c. All the property bequeathed to his wife will be excluded from the decedent's estate for federal estate tax purposes.
d. Walker must, in addition to being named in the will, be appointed or approved by the appropriate state court to serve as the executor.

Answer

1. 34.d(793)

Part Eleven: Trusts

Chapter 60

NATURE OF A TRUST

By trust is meant the legal relationship between one person who holds, and has a legal duty to deal with, property for the benefit of a beneficiary. There are 3 kinds of trust: (*1*) *Express trust,* whereby the "settlor," by his expressly manifested intent, cuases property to be held by a "trustee" for the benefit of a "beneficiary" called a "cestui que trust," the trustee being under a legal duty so to deal with the property. The settlor must manifestly intend to transfer the title *and* the beneficial interest for the benefit of someone. (*2*) "*Resulting trust,*" created by operation of law, whereby the person who holds title to the trust property holds it as a trustee for the transferor owner of the title who did not transfer the beneficial interest to the property to anyone. (*3*) "*Constructive trust,*" created by operation of law, whereby one person who holds title to property is subject to an equitable duty to transfer it to another person because he would be unjustly enriched if he were permitted to retain it. Emphasis is on the express trust here: the trust property can be real or personal property; the trustee has the legal title, and the beneficiary has the equitable title, to the trust property; the trustee is not subject to anyone's control, his death does not terminate the trust, and he cannot subject the beneficiary to liability; the trustee and the beneficiary are limited by the terms of the trust.

"A trust is one of several juridical devices whereby one person is enabled to deal with property for the benefit of another person."[1] Its distinguishing characteristics are: the separation of the legal title to property from the benefi-

[1] Restatement (Second) of Trusts, Introductory Note, p. 1.

cial equitable interest in the property; the flexibility of use of the trust device in a variety of transactions to which it is peculiarly suitable; the fiduciary relationship between the trustee and beneficiary; and a method of transferring property. The trust is a separate entity for both tax and non-tax purposes.

There are three kinds of trust—namely, "express," "resulting," and "constructive." *The ordinary kind of trust is the express trust,* and this part of the book is concerned mainly with it. First the three kinds of trust will be distinguished briefly from each other, and the express trust distinguished from a few other legal relationships; and then the creation, administration, modification, and termination of the express trust will be discussed.

Kinds of Trust

Express Trust. An express trust is a fiduciary relationship between persons in connection with property whereby one person called the "settlor" by his *manifestation of intention* causes property to be held by a person called the "trustee" for the benefit of a person called a "beneficiary" or "*cestui que trust,*" the trustee being under a duty so to deal with the property.[2] The fiduciary relationship of trust is between the trustee and the beneficiary. The property held in trust is called "trust property." An express trust may be private or charitable, the latter distinguished mainly by its charitable purpose. *Unless otherwise indicated in this portion of the book, the term "trust" refers solely to an express trust.*

Resulting Trust. *It is of the essence of an express trust that the settlor manifest an intent to transfer the beneficial interest as well as the title to trust property for the benefit of someone. If title alone is transferred and an intent to transfer the beneficial interest has not been expressed and cannot be implied, there is no express trust.* Accordingly, when the owner of property transfers title thereto without consideration and without intending to transfer the beneficial interest therein and the beneficial interest is not transferred to anyone else, there is no express trust and the person holding the title is a trustee of such title for the transferor by operation of law. Such trust is a resulting trust, resulting in the transferor being entitled to the return of the title to the property.

A resulting trust arises:

1. When an express trust fails, thereby causing the transferee to hold the trust property for the transferor under a resulting trust, in the absence of the transferor's manifestation of intent to the contrary; or
2. When some portion of the trust property remains after an express trust has been performed, thereby causing the trustee to hold the excess for the settlor under a resulting trust, in the absence of the settlor's manifestation of intent to the contrary; or
3. When property is purchased by one person and the seller delivers the property to a third person pursuant to the direction of the purchaser, it being

[2] See ibid., sec. 2.

presumed that, in the absence of the purchaser's manifestation of intent to the contrary, the purchaser does not intend a gift of the property to the transferee third person and, therefore, that the transferee holds the property for the purchaser under a resulting trust.

In all of these situations, inasmuch as there is no implication of an intent by the person causing the transfer of the property that the transferee of the title also is to have the beneficial interest, there is a resulting trust.

Constructive Trust. A constructive trust, like the resulting trust, is created by operation of law and arises regardless of the intention of the parties. *A constructive trust is imposed by law in order to prevent unjust enrichment to the party with the title to the trust property.* "A constructive trust arises where a person who holds title to property is subject to an equitable duty to convey it to another on the ground that he would be unjustly enriched if he were permitted to retain it."[3] (A fraudulently induced B to convey the title to B's land to A. A holds the title under a constructive trust for B, who is entitled to restitution of the land.)

Trust Distinguished

There are other legal relationships in which one person deals with property for the benefit of another which should be distinguished from a trust. Only bailment, agency, and sale of goods will be considered here. A bailment is concerned only with goods, is predicated on possession of such property, and the bailee does not have title to the property; in contrast, a trust may be concerned with real or personal property, and the trustee has title to the property. Agency is distinguishable from a trust, in that the agent usually does not have title to the property, he is subject to the control of his principal, his death terminates the agency, and he can subject his principal to liability to third persons. In contrast, a trustee has title to the property and is not subject to anyone's control, although the beneficiary can compel him to perform his trust duties, the trustee's death does not terminate the trust, and the trustee cannot subject the beneficiary to any liability. A sale of goods consists in the passing of title from the seller to the buyer for a price. A trust relationship consists of the transfer of legal title to any kind of property to a trustee to hold, use, and manage for the benefit of a beneficiary who has an equitable interest in the property. The subject of the sale can be only tangible, movable personal property; for a trust, it may be tangible or intangible personal or real property. In sale, the legal title is transferred; in trust, the title is split into legal title and a beneficial equitable title. In sale, the buyer can do with his property as he wishes; in trust, the trustee and beneficiary are limited by the terms of the trust.

---

[3] Austin W. Scott, *The Law of Trusts*, 3d ed. (Boston: Little, Brown & Co., 1967), Vol. V, p. 3413; also see Restatement of Restitution, 1937, sec. 160 and *Comment*.

Chapter 61

THE EXPRESS TRUST

Any person who can transfer title to property can, as a settlor, create an express trust. He must properly manifest his intent *thereby* to create a trust, not at a future time. His manifestation may be oral or in writing, except that a declaration of trust of an interest in land is within the Statute of Frauds and must be in writing. A testamentary trust is created by a will and arises on the testator's death. A trust may be created without any notice to the trustee or beneficiary and without their acceptance. Disclaimer by the trustee does not, but disclaimer by the beneficiary does, terminate the trust. No consideration is required, except that a promise *to create* a trust must have sufficient consideration. The trust must be for a legal purpose to be valid. The trust property must be specific, in existence, and transferable at the time the trust is created. Any person who has legal capacity to take, hold, and administer property as his own can be a trustee.

Only a person designated by the settlor as a beneficiary can be such, he must have legal capacity to take and hold particular property, and he must be identifiable at the time the trust is created or identifiable within the period of the rule against perpetuities. The settlor may be a beneficiary. A beneficiary's interest is personal property if the trust property is personal property, and real property if the trust property is real property, except for equitable conversion whereby: if the terms of the trust *require* sale of trust real property and distribution of the proceeds, the beneficiary's interest is personal property; and if the trust property *required* to be sold is personal property, the proceeds to be used to buy real property, the beneficiary's interest is real property.

The trustee is a fiduciary for the beneficiary, with the duty to administer the trust in a reasonable manner for the sole benefit of the beneficiary. He must

keep trust property separate from his own property. He has express and implied power in administering the trust, but this does not include any implied power to mortgage or pledge trust property nor to borrow on the credit of the trust estate. He has the duty to make proper allocations and charges to the principal and income accounts, and he is liable for loss from his failure to do so. Reference should be made to the text for a full discussion on this subject.[1] The trustee is liable to third persons on his contracts, as well as his torts, which have occurred while he was administering the trust.

A settlor may not modify or revoke a trust unless the terms of the trust so permit or the settlor has reserved such power. A settlor can revoke a trust created by his deposit of money in a bank account in his name as trustee for another person, in the absence of evidence to the contrary. A trust may terminate by its terms, as well as by court order and by consent of all the beneficiaries under certain circumstances.

SECTION I. CREATION OF AN EXPRESS TRUST

Methods

The Restatement of Trusts, section 17, describes various ways by which an express trust may be created:

> A trust may be created by
> (a) a declaration by the owner of property that he holds it as trustee for another person; or
> (b) a transfer *inter vivos* by the owner of property to another person as trustee for the transferor or for a third person; or
> (c) a transfer by will by the owner of property to another person as trustee for a third person; or
> (d) an appointment by one person having a power of appointment to another person as trustee for the donee of the power or for a third person;[2] or
> (e) a promise by one person to another person whose rights thereunder are to be held in trust for a third person.

Requirements

Capacity of Settlor. The settlor must have legal capacity to create a trust and *any person who can transfer title to property can create a trust,* which is essentially a transfer of property for the purpose of benefiting someone. If a person has legal capacity to make an *inter vivos* transfer, he has legal capacity to create a trust; if he has legal capacity to make a testamentary transfer, he has

[1] See below, pp. 805–8.

[2] E.g., A conveys land to B for B's life, the remainder to be determined by B. B creates a trust of the remainder for the benefit of D, naming C as trustee.

legal capacity to create a testamentary trust. The settlor may be the "remainderman," who is a person entitled to the principal.

Manifestation of Settlor's Intent to Create a Trust. The settlor must make a proper manifestation of his intent *thereby* to create a trust. His manifestation of an intent to create a trust other than at the time of the manifestation is ineffective to create a trust. Also, the settlor must manifest an intent to impose legally enforceable duties on the trustee.

Statute of Frauds. The settlor's manifestation of intent to create a trust may be written or oral, in the absence of statute to the contrary, and any words may be used which manifest such intent. The statutes of frauds in most states require that all declarations or creations of trusts of any *interest in land* shall be manifested and proved by some writing signed by the party who is by law enabled to declare such trust, or by his last will in writing, or else they are *void* and of no effect. The statute is satisfied if the signed memorandum specifies the trust property, the purpose of the trust, and the beneficiary. *Express trusts of personal property, and resulting and constructive trusts, are not within the purview of the Statute.* Except for nuncupative wills, statutes require a will to be in writing and, accordingly, a testamentary trust must be in writing.

Testamentary Trust. A testamentary trust is a trust created by a will which arises on the death of the testator. It is a testamentary disposition and, therefore, is governed by the law concerning Wills. A will is ambulatory and speaks as of the time of the testator's death. An *inter vivos* disposition which *does not transfer the beneficial interest to the property* and which is not to take effect until the death of the settlor is ineffective to create a trust and is a testamentary disposition which must comply with the law concerning Wills. A transfer *inter vivos* of the beneficial interest in trust, the enjoyment of which is postponed until the settlor's death, is effective to create a nontestamentary disposition. (A conveys property to B in trust for the benefit of C, who is to receive the trust property on A's death.)

No Notice or Acceptance Required. A trust may be created without any notice to the trustee or beneficiary and without their acceptance. *Disclaimer by the trustee does not terminate the trust;* its effect is to cause the title to the trust property to be transferred back to the settlor who then holds the property as a constructive trustee with the obligation to appoint another trustee and transfer the property to him. If one of several trustees disclaims, the title passes to those who did not disclaim. However, *disclaimer by the beneficiary terminates the trust;* and, if the settlor has declared himself as trustee, he holds the property free from the trust, while, if the settlor has transferred the title to another in trust, the trustee holds the title in a resulting trust for the settlor.

No Consideration Required. Consideration is not required as an ingredient in the creation of a trust and is not necessary in exchange for the settlor's declaration. However, a promise to create a trust is unenforceable unless it is supported by consideration, as required by the law of Contracts.

Legality. The *purpose* of the trust must be legal; and a purported trust, or a provision in an otherwise valid trust, for an illegal purpose is void. If only a *provision* in the trust is illegal, only that provision is void and the trust remains otherwise unaffected, unless the separation of the illegal provision would defeat the trust purpose in which event the purported trust is void.

Transfer of Property. *A trust involves the transfer of title and the beneficial interest in property,* so that the trustee has the title for the benefit of the beneficiary. A person may transfer the property to another as trustee, or he may declare himself as trustee and thereby transfer the property to himself as trustee (e.g., the settlor's deposit of money in a bank account in the settlor's name as trustee for another, in the absence of any evidence to indicate to the contrary, creates a revocable trust, revocable at the election of the depositor settlor). Failure to effect such a transfer precludes the creation of a trust.[3]

The Trust Property. The trust property must be specific, in existence, and capable of being transferred by the owner, *at the time the trust is created.* An interest in intangibles—e.g., a debt—and equitable as well as legal interests can be trust property. Under the Revised Uniform Principal and Income Act, section 1 (2), " 'inventory value' means the cost of property purchased by the trustee and the market value of other property at the time it became subject to the trust, but in the case of a testamentary trust the trustee may use any value finally determined for the purposes of an estate or inheritance tax."

The Trustee. *Any person who has legal capacity to take, hold, and administer property if it were his own has legal capacity to be a trustee of such property.* Infants, juristic persons (e.g., corporations), the beneficiary, or the settlor may be trustees. *The death of a trustee does not terminate the trust,* and the death of one of several trustees causes the title to vest in the surviving trustees. In the absence of statute to the contrary, the death intestate of a sole trustee causes the title to vest, *subject to the trust,* in his heirs if the trust property is real property and in his legal representative if it is personal property.

A trustee is removable pursuant to the terms of the trust or by a proper court. The appointment of a trustee is made in the same manner in the event that there is no trustee or one of several trustees has ceased to be a trustee. A trustee cannot resign a trust he had accepted previously, except either in accordance with the terms of the trust, with the consent of all the beneficiaries if they are capable of consenting, or by an order of a proper court.

Identifiable Beneficiary. Only those persons to receive beneficial interests as indicated by the settlor's manifested intention are beneficiaries. Persons who benefit incidentally from a trust are not beneficiaries. *Any person who has legal capacity to take and hold particular property can be a beneficiary of a*

---

[3] As an exception, a trust is created if the attempted transfer to another as trustee is ineffective *solely* because the trustee is not named in the instrument of conveyance (e.g., deed) or the named trustee is incapable of taking title to such property. The beneficiary may, by court order, compel the settlor to dispose of such property pursuant to such order. See Restatement (Second) of Trusts, 1959, sec. 32.

trust of such property. The beneficiary may be a natural person or a juristic person and *must be identifiable at the time that the trust is created, or identifiable within the period of the rule against perpetuities,*[4] i.e., in most states a period for the life of a person or persons in existence at the time the trust is created and 21 years after the death of such person or persons. A definite class of persons may be a beneficiary, provided that the members of the class are identifiable at the time of the creation of the trust or within the period of the rule against perpetuities. There may be more than one beneficiary, and the settlor himself may be a beneficiary. *A beneficiary's interest is personal property if the trust property is personal property, and it is real property if the trust property is real property, except for the principle of equitable conversion.* Under this principle:

> (1) If real property is held in trust and by the terms of the trust a duty is imposed upon the trustee to sell it and hold the proceeds in trust or distribute the proceeds, the interest of the beneficiary is personal property.
>
> (2) If personal property is held in trust and by the terms of the trust a duty is imposed upon the trustee to expend it or its proceeds for the purchase of real property, the interest of the beneficiary is real property unless it is so limited in duration that if it were a legal interest it would be personal property.[5]

SECTION II. ADMINISTRATION OF AN EXPRESS TRUST

Duties and Powers of Trustee

Duties. A trustee has the duty to act in accordance with the terms of the trust except for impossibility or illegality of performance. If the circumstances unknown to the settlor and not anticipated by him so change that compliance with the terms of the trust would defeat its purpose or substantially impair its implementation, a proper court may authorize or direct the trustee to act contrary to the terms of the trust. The trustee is a fiduciary with respect to the trust and the beneficiaries. *He owes a duty of loyalty to the beneficiary to administer the trust properly for the sole benefit of the beneficiary and to observe the fiduciary relationship between them in his dealings with the beneficiary for his personal gain.* The trustee has the duty, on request, to furnish to the beneficiary all information regarding the administration of the trust and to make all records available to the beneficiary for his examination.

The trustee has the duty to administer the trust in a reasonable manner. He is to exercise that care which would be exercised by a reasonable, prudent man in the care of *his own property* under the circumstances.[6] He may not delegate

---

[4] See Restatement (Second) of Trusts, 1959, sec. 112. Generally, the rule against perpetuities does not apply to charitable trusts.

[5] Ibid., sec. 131.

[6] *Cf.* the duty of care required of a trustee with that required of a corporate director, above, p. 707.

trust duties which he reasonably can do personally. He is required to control and preserve the trust property, collect on claims which he holds in trust, defend actions which subject the trust estate to loss when such defense appears to be reasonable, cause the trust property to produce returns when feasible, keep the trust property separate from his own property and make deposits of trust monies in a separate trust bank account, and keep accounts of the administration of the trust.

Powers. The powers of a trustee in administering the trust may be express or implied. A trustee has implied power to do only that which is reasonably necessary in order to execute the purpose of the trust and which is not prohibited by the terms of the trust. A trustee has implied power to incur reasonable expense in doing that which is reasonably necessary to administer the trust and not prohibited by the terms of the trust, and he has a right of reimbursement therefor. Although a trustee has implied power to sell trust property when reasonably required and not prohibited by the terms of the trust, *he does not have any implied authority to mortgage or pledge trust property nor to borrow on the credit of the trust estate.* In order to fulfill his duty to make the trust property productive, he has implied authority reasonably to lease the trust property, in the absence of any provisions to the contrary in the terms of the trust. He has implied power to exercise his reasonable discretion in compromising, arbitrating, or abandoning claims in connection with the trust estate and, in the absence of terms of the trust to the contrary, to vote and exercise those other powers inherent in shares of stock which are a part of the trust property. *If there is more than one trustee and the terms of the trust are not to the contrary, trust action is taken only by their unanimous consent; in charitable trusts, a majority of the trustees is sufficient.*

In carrying out his functions of preserving the trust property and of causing such property to produce returns, the trustee has the duty to exercise proper care in the investment of trust property not contrary to the terms of the trust. The trustee should make a reasonable distribution of the risk of loss by diversification of investment and dispose of improper investments in existence at the time of his appointment as trustee and of proper investments which subsequently become improper. Because of the trustee's duty to make the trust property productive, if certain of such property is unproductive it should be sold. Similarly, if some of the property is subject to depletion, i.e., wasting property—e.g., leaseholds, patents, copyrights—the trustee should sell the same or amortize the depreciation. It should be noted carefully that, in the absence of trust provision to the contrary, there is a conflict of view[7] on whether or not a trustee is permitted to amortize the depreciation or obsolescence of a building.

The trustee has the duty to make proper allocations and charges to the principal and income accounts, and his failure to do so resulting in loss

[7] See Austin W. Scott, *The Law of Trusts,* ed ed. (Boston: Little, Brown & Co., 1967), Vol. III, sec. 239.4.

subjects him to liability therefor. Under the Revised Uniform Principal and Income Act, section 3a,b, "income is the return in money or property derived from the use of principal," while "principal is the property which has been set aside by the owner or the person legally empowered so that it is held in trust eventually to be delivered to the remainderman while the return or use of the principal is in the meantime taken or received by or held for accumulation for an income beneficiary." The *trustee's* purchase of investments at a premium requires amortization of the premium out of the income from the investment, such amortization fund being *principal* and not income. However, the *settlor's* purchase of investments at a premium does not require amortization of the premium by the trustee, in the absence of trust provision to the contrary, and all income is available for distribution to the income beneficiary pursuant to the terms of the trust. Where *trust investments are acquired at a discount,* the benefit of such discount usually is considered as principal and is available to the principal beneficiary. However, the discount portion received on redemption of treasury bills is credited to income. When real property is held in trust, prepaid rent received from tenants is allocated to income, but insurance proceeds for the destruction of buildings (e.g., garage destroyed by fire) is allocated to principal. *Ordinary current administrative and operative expense is chargeable to income*—e.g., ordinary taxes, water rates, premiums on trustee's bond, insurance on the trust property, interest on a mortgage on trust property, and ordinary repairs to trust property. Other than ordinary current expense is chargeable to principal—e.g., the cost of purchasing or selling investments, the expense of litigation in protecting the trust property, the cost of setting up the trust, and the cost of permanent improvements.

While *income is allocated to the income account and made available to the income beneficiary and increase in principal is allocated to the principal account,* nevertheless, there often is difficulty in ascertaining whether receipts from shares of stock are principal or income. Although there are different rules in various states, under the Restatement of Trusts, section 236:

> Except as otherwise provided by the terms of the trust, if shares of stock of a corporation are held in trust to pay the income to a beneficiary for a designated period and thereafter to pay the principal to another beneficiary, the following rules are applicable:
>
> (a) Except as stated in Clauses (e) and (f), dividends payable in cash or in property other than in shares of the declaring corporation, including ordinary and extraordinary dividends, are income, if payable to shareholders of record on a designated date which is within the period; or, if no such date is designated, if declared at a date within the period.
>
> (b) Dividends payable in shares of the declaring corporation are principal.
>
> (c) If the trustee has the option of receiving a dividend either in cash or in shares of the declaring corporation, the dividend is income irrespective of the choice made by the trustee.
>
> (d) Rights to subscribe to the shares or other securities of the declaring corporation and the proceeds of any sale of such rights are principal, but rights to subscribe to the shares of other corporations are income.

(e) Upon the total or partial liquidation of the corporation during the period, amounts paid as cash dividends declared before such liquidation occurred or as arrears of preferred or guaranteed dividends are income; all other amounts paid upon corporate shares on distribution of the corporate assets to the shareholders are principal.

(f) A distribution by a corporation which is a return of capital and not a distribution of earnings is principal.

(g) The earnings of a corporation not distributed by the corporation during the period are not income.

Liability of Trustee

A trustee is liable to the beneficiary for his breach of trust and ". . . he is chargeable with (a) any loss or depreciation in value of the trust estate resulting from the breach of trust; or (b) any profit made by him through the breach of trust; or (c) any profit which would have accrued to the trust estate if there had been no breach of trust."[8] The beneficiary's consent to the trustee's breach of trust, either before or at the time of such breach, or his affirmance or release of such breach discharges the trustee from any liability to the beneficiary therefor. A trustee may incur personal liability to third persons while properly administering the trust, but this does not permit the claimants to proceed against the trust property in satisfaction of their claims. The trustee has a right of exoneration[9] against the trust property just as he has a right of reimbursement for his expenditures. *The trustee is liable to third persons on his contracts, as well as for his torts, which have occurred while he was administering the trust.*

SECTION III. MODIFICATION AND TERMINATION OF AN EXPRESS TRUST

A settlor may not modify or revoke a trust unless the terms of trust so permit or the settlor has reserved such power. The reason for this is that the beneficial interest in the trust property has been transferred to the beneficiary and he cannot be deprived of such interest without his consent. *In the absence of any evidence to indicate to the contrary, the power of the settlor to revoke is implied in a trust created by the settlor's deposit of money in a bank account in the settlor's name as trustee for another person.* If a trust is created by a writing and the settlor intended to reserve a power to modify or to revoke the trust but, by mistake, this power was omitted from inclusion in the writing, the settlor has the right to have the writing reformed so as to include this

---

[8] Restatement (Second) of Trusts, 1959, sec. 205.

[9] This is the trustee's right to have the trust property used to discharge his personal liability and thereby relieve him of the necessity of discharging the liability with his own property.

power. Also, the settlor has a right to rescind a trust or to have it reformed on the same grounds which permit any other transfer of property to be rescinded or reformed—e.g., fraud, undue influence, or mistake.

A trust may terminate in various ways. It may expire according to its terms.[10] If the circumstances unknown to the settlor and not anticipated by him so change that compliance with the terms of the trust would defeat its purpose or substantially impair its implementation, a court may order the termination of the trust. Impossibility of performance of the trust or supervening illegality are grounds for judicial termination of the trust. The consent of all the beneficiaries, if they are capable of consenting, may compel the termination of the trust, except when "the continuance of the trust is necessary to carry out a material purpose of the trust. . . ."[11] A spendthrift trust[12] is an illustration of a trust with a material purpose precluding termination by the consent of all the beneficiaries. However, if the settlor and all beneficiaries consent to the termination of the trust, then the trust is terminable even though there was a material purpose. The merger of the beneficial interest with the legal title to the trust property in one person terminates the trust.

PROBLEMS

1. (a) What is meant by the following:
   - (1) Settlor.
   - (2) *Cestui que trust.*
   - (3) Trust property.

   (b) Enumerate the requisites of an express trust of personal property.

   (c) A orally declared to B that, beginning from that moment, A held certain specified personal property of A in trust for B.
   - (1) Has a trust been created?
   - (2) Why?

2. (a) Who may create a trust?

   (b) A promised B to create a trust of certain specified personal property of A for B.
   - (1) Did A's promise create a trust? Why?
   - (2) Is A's promise enforceable? Why?

---

[10] *Cy pres* means as nearly as possible. *Cy pres* is an equitable doctrine of construction of instruments whereby the charitable intention of the settlor of a charitable trust is carried out as nearly as possible when circumstances prevent its being carried out exactly. It is applicable where the settlor's manifested intent indicates a particular, as well as a general, charitable purpose and the *particular* charitable purpose cannot, but the *general* charitable purpose can, be carried out. For example, if the settlor's manifested general intention was to improve medical facilities in a community and, in his will, he bequeathed property in trust for the establishment of a hospital in the community, and at the time of his death a hospital had been established in the community, a court could apply *cy pres* and direct that the trust property be applied in other ways to provide for the ill people in that community in furtherance of the settlor's general charitable purpose.

[11] Restatement (Second) of Trusts, (1959), sec. 337.

[12] A trust which, by statute or by valid trust provision, restrains the voluntary or involuntary transfer of the beneficial interest of the trust by the beneficiary or by his creditors is called a "spendthrift trust." Its purpose is to protect the beneficiary from his improvidence.

(c) X declared a trust of certain specified personal property of X for Y and named Z as trustee.
  (1) What is the effect of Z's refusal to act as trustee?
  (2) What is the effect of X's declaration if X was ignorant of the fact that Z was not alive at the time it was made?
(d) R delivers his property to S in trust for T. What is the effect of T's disclaimer of the trust?

3. (a) What is a testamentary trust?
   (b) May an *inter vivos* trust be created under the terms of which enjoyment of the trust by the beneficiary can be postponed until after the settlor's death? Why?
   (c) Can a trust of intangible personal property be created? Answer "Yes" or "No."
   (d) When must the beneficiary of a trust be identifiable?
   (e) What is the effect of the death of one of several trustees of a trust?
4. (a) Describe the relationship between the trustee and the beneficiary of a trust.
   (b) Describe the duties of a trustee.
   (c) May a trustee delegate trust duties? Explain.
   (d) How must the trustee allocate trust principal and income for trust expense and for investments of trust property acquired at a premium?

SOME PREVIOUS C.P.A. LAW EXAMINATION QUESTIONS AND AUTHOR'S MODEL ANSWERS

NOVEMBER, 1979

Number 1

Select the **best** answers for each of the following items.

44. James Gordon decided to create an inter vivos trust for the benefit of his grandchildren. He wished to bypass his own children, and to provide an independent income for his grandchildren. He did **not**, however, wish to completely part with the assets he would transfer to the trust. Therefore, he transferred the assets to the York Trust Company, in trust for the benefit of his grandchildren irrevocably for a period of 12 years. Which of the following is correct regarding the trust?
   a. The trust will fail for want of a proper purpose.
   b. The trust income will **not** be taxable to Gordon during its existence.
   c. Gordon retains beneficial title to the property transferred to the trust.
   d. If Gordon demands the return of the trust assets prior to the 12 years, York must return them to him since he created the trust and the assets will eventually be his again.

Items 46 and 47 are based on the following information:

Martin is the trustee of the Baker Trust which has assets in excess of $1 million. Martin has engaged the CPA firm of Hardy & Fox to prepare the annual accounting statement for the allocation of receipts and expenditures between income and principal. The trust indenture provides that "receipts and expenses are to be allocated to income or principal according to law."

46. Which of the following receipts should be allocated to income?
   a. Rights to subscribe to shares of the distributing corporation.
   b. Sale of rights to subscribe to shares of the distributing corporation.

c. A 2 percent stock dividend.
d. Rights to subscribe to shares of another corporation.

47. Which of the following receipts from real property should be allocated to principal?
a. An unexpected payment of nine months' arrears in rental payments.
b. A six-month prepayment of rent.
c. Insurance proceeds for the destruction of a garage on one of the properties.
d. Interest on a purchase money mortgage arising from the sale of a parcel of the trust's real property.

Answer

1. 44.b(805) 46.d(807) 47.c(807)

NOVEMBER, 1978

Number 1

Select the **best** answers for each of the following items.

37. Which of the following receipts should be allocated by a trustee exclusively to income?
a. A stock dividend.
b. An extraordinary year-end cash dividend.
c. A liquidating dividend whether in complete or partial liquidation.
d. A stock split.

38. The Unity Trust Company is the trustee of a trust which has large real estate investments. Which of the following receipts or charges should be allocated by the trustee to income?
a. Paving assessment for a new street.
b. Prepaid rent received from tenants.
c. A loss on the sale of one of the rental properties.
d. The proceeds from an eminent domain proceeding.

40. Which of the following receipts or disbursements by a trustee should be credited to or charged against income?
a. Amortization payment on real property subject to a mortgage.
b. Capital gain distributions received from a mutual fund.
c. Stock rights received from the distributing corporation.
d. The discount portion received on redemption of treasury bills.

Answer

1. 37.b(807) 38.b(807) 40.d(807)

MAY, 1978

Number 1

Select the **best** answers for each of the following items.

33. Kilgore created an irrevocable 15-year trust for the benefit of his minor children. At the end of the 15 years, the principal (corpus) reverts to Kilgore. Kilgore named the Reliable Trust Company as trustee and provided that Reliable would serve without the necessity of posting a bond. In understanding the trust and rules applicable to it, which of the following is correct?

a. The trust is **not** a separate legal entity for federal tax purposes.
b. The facts indicate that the trust is a separate legal entity for both tax and non-tax purposes.
c. Kilgore may revoke the trust after 11 years, since he created it, and the principal reverts to him at the expiration of the fifteen years.
d. If Kilgore dies ten years after creation of the trust, it is automatically revoked and the property is distributed to the beneficiaries of his trust upon their attaining age 21.

35. Hacker is considering the creation of either a lifetime (inter vivos) or testamentary (by his will) trust. In deciding what to do, which of the following statements is correct?
a. An inter vivos trust must meet the same legal requirements as one created by a will.
b. Property transferred to a testamentary trust upon the grantor's (creator's) death is **not** included in the decedent's gross estate for federal tax purposes.
c. Hacker can retain the power to revoke an inter vivos trust.
d. If the trust is an inter vivos trust, the trustee must file papers in the appropriate state office roughly similar to those required to be filed by a corporation.

Answer

1. 33.b(807) 35.c(808)

Part Twelve: Accountant's Legal Responsibility

Chapter 62

RESPONSIBILITY TO CLIENT AND THE PUBLIC

As an independent contractor, the public accountant has various responsibilities to his client and to third persons in connection with his work. He is to conduct a careful, independent examination of his client's *internal control system* and properly report in *understandable language* so that his certified financial statements *fairly present the financial condition of his client and are not materially false or misleading.* His ordinary examination of financial statements does not include special procedures to discover defalcations, but if such examination suggests suspicion of fraud then he has the responsibility to investigate and report. *With respect to his client:* he is not to practise law; he is to perform his work in a careful, competent and professional manner; he has no Common Law lien on the papers and other property of his client, but he owns and may retain working papers and copies of other papers; and unless state statute is to the contrary, his communications with his client are not privileged. *With respect to third persons,* although there is no privity of contract, yet if he has reason to believe that his accounting services to his client will be made available by his client to third persons, he has a varying duty of care toward them. *If he knows the specific identity of the third person* and that the latter intends to *rely* on his professional opinion, then he has the same duty of care toward the third person as he has to his client and is liable for his *ordinary negligence. If he does not know the specific identity of such third person,* then his liability is only for *actual fraud or constructive fraud.*

Any brief discussion of the status, duties, and liabilities of a public accountant must, of necessity, be limited to the high points and matters of dominant concern in this connection. First the status of a public accountant and then his duties and liabilities to his client and to third persons will be discussed. His responsibilities with respect to his involvement in the three areas of public law—Federal Securities Regulation, Antitrust, and Regulation of the Employer and Employee Relationship—will be discussed in Part Thirteen under those titles.

Status of the Public Accountant

An accountant has been well defined as a person "competent to design and control the systems of accounts required for records of multifarious transactions of business, trade, and finance."[1] If he serves more than one employer as an independent contractor, he is a public accountant. If he has been certified as a certified public accountant by a state regulatory body, usually an administrative board, he has such status.

The public accountant is a professional person and an independent contractor, except as he changes his status. An independent contractor is a person who contracts to render an agreed performance for another called an employer, does not act on his employer's behalf, has no authority to deal with third persons or to affect the employer's contractual relations with third persons, and whose manner of performance is not subject to any right of control by the employer. A public accountant renders professional services of a specialized nature involving the exercise of judgment not subject to his client's control, and he comes within the class of an independent contractor. However, if a public accountant should be hired and paid a salary as an employee, he is an agent of his employer principal. To the extent that a public accountant is retained for a fee to render an accounting service, he is an independent contractor; to the extent that he also has authority to contract in the name of his client, he is an agent of his client as a principal. The relationship between a public accountant and his client is of a personal character[2] and, therefore, the death or serious physical disability of the public accountant or the death of the client discharges the contract by operation of law because of impossibility of performance.[3]

Duties and Liabilities of the Public Accountant

The activities of a public accountant are the result of his relationship with his client and often affect third persons. *The primary responsibility of a public accountant is to ensure that, as a result of his careful, independent check on management's stewardship of a business, material relevant financial information is disclosed and disseminated without being misleading.* He is respon-

[1] I Am. Jur., *Accountants*, sec. 2 (1962).

[2] See above, pp. 79–80, 83.

[3] See above, pp. 123–25.

sible not only to his client, but also to third persons, who may rely with confidence on the financial statements which he has certified, that such financial statements fairly present the financial condition of his client and are not materially false or misleading.[4] In making his audit of a business, he must carefully examine its internal control system and properly report in understandable language the result of his audit and give his professional opinion. The American Institute of Certified Public Accountants has adopted the following as "generally accepted auditing standards":[5]

> ***General Standards***
>
> 1. The examination is to be performed by a person or persons having adequate technical training and proficiency as an auditor.
> 2. In all matters relating to the assignment, an independence in mental attitude is to be maintained by the auditor or auditors.
> 3. Due professional care is to be exercised in the performance of the examination and the preparation of the report.
>
> ***Standards of Field Work***
>
> 1. The work is to be adequately planned and assistants, if any, are to be properly supervised.
> 2. There is to be a proper study and evaluation of the existing internal control as a basis for reliance thereon and for the determination of the resultant extent of the tests to which auditing procedures are to be restricted.
> 3. Sufficient competent evidential matter is to be obtained through inspection, observation, inquiries and confirmations to afford a reasonable basis for an opinion regarding the financial statements under examination.
>
> ***Standards of Reporting***
>
> 1. The report shall state whether the financial statements are presented in accordance with generally accepted principles of accounting.
> 2. The report shall state whether such principles have been consistently observed in the current period in relation to the preceding period.
> 3. Informative disclosures in the financial statements are to be regarded as reasonably adequate unless otherwise stated in the report.
> 4. The report shall either contain an expression of opinion regarding the financial statements, taken as a whole, or an assertion to the effect that an opinion cannot be expressed. When an overall opinion cannot be expressed, the reasons therefor should be stated. In all cases, where an auditor's name is associated with financial statements, the report should contain a clear-cut indication of the character of the auditor's examination, if any, and the degree of responsibility he is taking.

An auditor is not an insurer against fraud or its discovery in the audit. Unless otherwise agreed, an engagement to perform an ordinary examination

[4] See *United States* v. *Simon* (known as the "Continental Vending" case), 425 F.2d 796 (2nd Cir. 1969), cert. denied 397 U.S. 1006 (1970).

[5] Reproduced with permission, *Code of Professional Ethics*, copyright March 1975, American Institute of Certified Public Accountants.

of financial statements does not include special procedural work to discover defalcations and other similar irregularities. His responsibility is to exercise reasonable care in performing his examination in a competent manner and properly reporting the same. However, if his negligence prevents his discovery of fraud resulting in loss which could have been prevented by his discovery, then he is subject to liability therefor. Suspicion suggested by circumstances or data during the course of the audit prompts responsibility to investigate further. On discovery, fraud must be reported by the auditor both to responsible business officers and in his report or financial statement. First the public accountant's duties and liabilities with respect to his client, and then with respect to third persons, will be discussed.

To His Client. ***Not to Practise Law.*** A public accountant is not licensed to practise law. However, he must be knowledgeable of the legal significance of the transactions and activities of his client so that he may properly reflect their nature and materiality in his audit, reports, and other accounting services rendered to his clients. It has been well stated that: "An accountant may apply legal knowledge and answer legal questions in connection with the practice of his ordinary work in the keeping of books and records and the preparation of tax returns and advising with respect to such matters, but where he undertakes to give legal advice and answer legal questions completely disconnected with such ordinary work in keeping and auditing books and preparing tax returns, he is guilty of practising law without a license."[6]

Generally. The public accountant's legal responsibility to clients is: to possess that ability and competence which a member of that profession and status professes to have and does have; to use the care, skill, and diligence of a reasonable man who is a public accountant; and to use his best prudence, discretion, and judgment as a public accountant. The professional man is an expert in the area of his profession and the layman retaining his services does not have (and cannot be expected to have) the knowledge to appraise properly the quality of the professional work being done. The client relies on the professional man's superior knowledge in such area and trusts in him. Accordingly, the law imposes a special duty upon a professional man. The public accountant's legal responsibility is to ascertain the facts pertinent to the performance required of him, to act reasonably in properly utilizing such facts in such performance, and to use reasonable care in communicating the performance to his client so that the client may understand and properly utilize such performance.

Communication to His Client. Numerous lawsuits against public accountants are based upon the premise that there has been a failure to communicate the information obtained in an audit to non-accountant laymen suitable, in *content* and *terminology,* to *their* needs as the users of such information. Generally, at the present time, it is not sufficient that the public accountant has complied with "generally accepted accounting principles," but he must in-

[6] I Am. Jur., *Accountants,* sec. 9 (1962).

form the layman user of what *he* needs to know in terms that *he* reasonably can understand. Only then is there a full, fair, and complete disclosure consistent with the public accountant's responsibility to his client. If he fails to do this and has made a misrepresentation, he is negligent and liable for damage proximately caused by his negligence. At the present time, it appears that whether or not there has been a fair disclosure will be determined by a layman's standard established by the jury, namely, has there been a disclosure of information adequately meaningful to the particular user?

Quality of Work. A public accountant has the legal duty toward his client to exercise reasonable care in accordance with the profession's standards, in good faith, without fraud or collusion, and to follow standard accounting practices. Except as otherwise provided by law, he exercises reasonable care when he employs that knowledge, skill, judgment, and discretion usually employed by public accountants in that particular locality under similar circumstances. Since he is in privity of contract with his client, the public accountant is liable to his client for damages for breach of contract and for loss proximately caused to his client by his ordinary negligence. However, he is not an insurer against damage to his client, and is not liable for small inaccuracies and errors of judgment. Inaccuracies of a serious character constitute a material breach of contract and preclude compensation for his services. A public accountant is to perform his work within the time expressly provided by the contract with his client, or in a reasonable time if the contract has not expressly so provided. Failure to perform within such time precludes any right to compensation for such services, unless delay is waived or excused by his client or his client's conduct caused such delay. For gross negligence, he may be liable for punitive damages.

Payment and Lien. The contract normally fixes the fee or compensation to be paid to the public accountant. In the absence of any express provision, e.g., an engagement letter, it is implied that his compensation will be for what his services are reasonably worth under the particular circumstances of that employment. He does not have a Common Law lien on his client's materials in his possession, but he may well acquire a statutory lien for services rendered on his client's materials (books, etc.) by their improvement.

Since a public accountant is an independent contractor employed to render accounting services, he owns and may retain *his own* copies of his client's books and records, copies of tax returns and working papers, in the absence of agreement to the contrary. Also, a public accountant may require his working papers and copies should his performance be questioned later, and such papers should be in his possession. He also owns the originals of letters written to him in connection with his work, copies of letters written by him, analyses, computations, and other such materials. Inasmuch as such materials contain data which are the subject of a confidential relationship between the public accountant and his client, their transfer or disclosure by the accountant without the client's permission would be improper as a violation of their confidential relationship and is not ethically or legally sanctioned. Of course, papers, records and other materials loaned by the client are the property of the client and are to be returned to him by the public accountant. It should be noted that if a public accountant becomes an employee and, therefore, an agent, the working and other papers belong to his employer principal.

Privileged Communications. Because of the confidential relationship existing between the public accountant and his client, communications between them in connection with the employment are confidential and *ethically* are not to be disclosed by the public accountant without his client's permission. However, unless such communications are recognized and privileged by statute, the public accountant can be compelled to testify in court concerning such communications. Such communications were not privileged at Common Law and, today, they are not privileged by statute in a majority of states nor by federal statute. A communication is privileged when, by statute, it is recognized as a confidential communication of such a nature as to be precluded from admission into evidence in court without the utterer's consent. The purpose of according a statutory privilege to communications between public accountant and his client is to encourage free discussion and exchange of information between the parties, even at the expense of making such communications unavailable in court under the rules of evidence. Today, most of the statutes which provide that communications between a public accountant and his client are privileged do not limit the privilege with respect to any particular proceedings; in some states the privilege is inapplicable in matters involving criminal law. When a statute causes communications between public accountant and his client to become privileged, the public accountant has a *legal* duty not to disclose such communications without his client's consent. The privilege is for the benefit of his client, and only the client can waive it. By statute, the client's permission to the accountant to testify is a wavier of the client's privilege and the accountant is relieved of his obligation not to testify. Although not a matter of specific statutory provision, it would seem that the client had waived his privilege if he sued the accountant on a privileged matter or if the client had published the otherwise privileged matter, especially if it were published to a third person who was suing the accountant in connection with such matter.

To Third Persons. While *a public accountant has duties towards his client because of their privity of contract,* since no such privity of contract exists between the public accountant and third persons there is no duty of care owing to them, with one exception. *When the public accountant has reason to believe that his accounting services which he has rendered to his client* (e.g., a certified balance sheet) *will be made available by his client to third persons, then a legal duty of care is imposed upon the public accountant.* The *extent* of his duty of care depends upon whether the public accountant knows the *specific identity* of the third person and that the latter *intends to rely* upon the public accountant's professional opinion.[7] If the specific identity of the third

[7] William L. Prosser, *Handbook of the Law of Torts*, 5th ed. (St. Paul, Minn.: West Publishing Co., 1971), pp. 718, 721–28.

person is known to the public accountant, then the latter has the same duty of care toward such identified third person as he has to his client, and he is liable for damage caused to such relying third person by his *ordinary negligence.* The third person is misnamed a "third party beneficiary." However, if the public accountant *does not know the specific identity* of the third person to whom his professional opinion is to be made available, then his liability to such third person is only for *actual fraud, or for gross negligence amounting to constructive fraud.* It should be noted that actual fraud exists when there is present an actual intent to mislead, legally called "scienter"; while constructive fraud exists when there is no such actual intent but there is reckless disregard for the truth. "A mere mistake in the balance sheet which is the result of negligence only is not ordinarily a basis for recovery by a third person, but a representation certified as true to the knowledge of the accountant when there is no knowledge, a reckless misstatement, or an opinion based on grounds so flimsy as to lead to the conclusion that there is no genuine belief in its truth, is a sufficient basis for liability."[8] In other words, a misrepresentation made recklessly, careless whether the matter misrepresented be true or false, is made without belief in its truth. A person's misrepresentation which expressly or impliedly asserts a particular basis for his knowledge or belief, such as his actual knowledge of the matter misrepresented or his personal investigation of it, when there is no such basis for his professed knowledge or belief, is made fraudulently. Quite apart from an accountant's liability for his negligence, he may be liable for the tort of deceit.[9]

The public accountant's responsibilities discussed here are continued with respect to his involvement in the preparation of certified financial statements in connection with federal securities regulation, discussed in Part Thirteen under that title.

PROBLEMS

1. Meglow Corporation manufactured ladies' dresses and blouses. Because its cash position was deteriorating, Meglow sought a loan from Busch Factors. Busch had previously extended $25,000 credit to Meglow but refused to lend any additional money without obtaining copies of Meglow's audited financial statements.

   Meglow contacted the C.P.A. firm of Watkins, Winslow & Watkins to perform the audit. In arranging for the examination, Meglow clearly indicated that its purpose was to satisfy Busch Factors as to the Corporation's sound financial condition and thus to obtain an additional loan of $50,000. Watkins, Winslow & Watkins accepted the engagement, performed the examination in a negligent manner and rendered an unqualified auditor's opinion. If an adequate examination had been performed, the financial statements would have been found to be misleading.

   Meglow submitted the audited financial statements to Busch Factors and obtained an additional loan of $35,000. Busch refused to lend more than that amount. After several other factors also refused, Meglow finally was able to persuade Max-

[8] I Am. Jur., *Accountants,* sec. 19 (1962).

[9] See above, p. 34, ftn. 28.

well Department Stores, one of its customers, to lend the additional $15,000. Maxwell relied upon the financial statements examined by Watkins, Winslow & Watkins.

Meglow is now in bankruptcy and Busch seeks to collect from Watkins, Winslow & Watkins the $60,000 it loaned Meglow. Maxwell seeks to recover from Watkins, Winslow & Watkins the $15,000 it loaned Meglow.

(1) Will Busch recover? Explain.

(2) Will Maxwell recover? Explain. (Former C.P.A. Examination question)

2. Barney & Co., CPAs, has been engaged to perform an examination of the financial statements of Waldo, Inc., for several years. The terms of the engagement have been set out in an annual engagement letter signed by both parties. The terms of each engagement included the following:

> This being an ordinary examination, it is not primarily or specifically designed, and cannot be relied upon, to disclose defalcations and other similar irregularities, although their discovery may result.

Three years ago Harold Zamp, head cashier of Waldo and an expert in computer operations, devised a previously unheard of method of embezzling funds from his employer. At first, Zamp's thefts were small but increased as time went on. During the current year, before Barney began working on the engagement, the thefts became so large that serious variances in certain accounts came to the attention of the controller. When questioned about the variances, Zamp confessed and explained his unique embezzlement scheme. Investigation revealed that Zamp had stolen $257,550. Zamp has no assets with which to repay the thefts.

Waldo submitted its claim for $257,550 to Multi-State Surety Company in accordance with the terms of the fidelity bond covering Zamp. Fulfilling its surety obligation, Multi-State paid the claim and now seeks to recover its losses from Barney.

In defense, Barney asserts, in the alternative, the following defenses:

1. Multi-State has no standing in court to sue because it was not a party to the contract (i.e., lacking in privity) between Barney and its client, Waldo.

2. Even if Multi-State had the standing to sue, its claim should be dismissed because Barney's engagements with Waldo did not specifically include the discovery of defalcations other than those which might arise in the process of an ordinary examination.

3. Even if Barney's contract had made it responsible for discoverable defalcations, it could not have discovered Zamp's defalcations with the exercise of reasonable care. Zamp's technique was so new, unique, and novel that no accounting firm could have discovered the defalcations in any event.

Required:

In separately numbered paragraphs, discuss the validity of each of Barney's defenses. (Former C.P.A. Examination question)

3. **Part a.** The partnership of Smith, Frank, & Clark, a CPA firm, has been the auditor of Greenleaf, Inc., for many years. During the annual examination of the financial statements for the year ended December 31, 1980, a dispute developed over whether certain disclosures should be made in the financial statements. The dispute resulted in Smith, Frank, & Clark's being dismissed and Greenleaf's engaging another firm. Greenleaf demanded that Smith, Frank, & Clark turn over all working

papers applicable to the Greenleaf audits to it or face a lawsuit. Smith, Frank, & Clark refused. Greenleaf has instituted a suit against Smith, Frank, & Clark to obtain the working papers.

Required:

1. Will Greenleaf succeed in its suit? Explain.

2. Discuss the rationale underlying the rule of law applicable to the ownership of working papers.

Part b. Parker Products, Inc., is suing Flagstone Specialties, Inc., your client, in the state court system, alleging a breach of contract. The contract provided for Flagstone to construct a piece of highly technical equipment at Flagstone's cost plus a fixed fee. Specifically, Parker alleges that Flagstone has calculated costs incorrectly, loading the contract billings with inappropriate costs. Parker seeks to recover the excess costs.

Charles Lake, your CPA firm's partner in charge of the Flagstone account, has been subpoenaed by Parker to testify. Neither Lake nor the firm wishes to become involved in the litigation. Furthermore, if Lake testifies, some of the facts he would reveal might be prejudicial to the client.

Required:

1. Must Lake testify? Explain.

2. If the cause of action had been such that the suit would have been brought in a federal court, must Lake testify? Explain. (Former C.P.A. Examination question)

SOME PREVIOUS C.P.A. LAW EXAMINATION QUESTIONS AND AUTHOR'S MODEL ANSWERS

NOVEMBER, 1979

Number 5

Part b. Farr & Madison, CPAs, audited Glamour, Inc. Their audit was deficient in several respects:

• Farr and Madison failed to verify properly certain receivables which later proved to be fictitious.

• With respect to other receivables, although they made a cursory check, they did not detect many accounts which were long overdue and obviously uncollectible.

• No physical inventory was taken of the securities claimed to be in Glamour's possession, which in fact had been sold. Both the securities and cash received from the sales were listed on the balance sheet as assets.

There is no indication that Farr & Madison actually believed that the financial statements were false. Subsequent creditors, not known to Farr & Madison, are now suing based upon the deficiencies in the audit described above. Farr and Madison moved to dismiss the lawsuit against it on the basis that the firm did not have actual knowledge of falsity and therefore did not commit fraud.

Required:

Answer the following, setting forth reasons for any conclusions stated.

May the creditors recover without demonstrating Farr & Madison had actual knowledge of falsity?

Part c. The Bigelow Corporation decided to liquidate. A board member suggested the possibility of electing a one calendar month liquidation pursuant to section 333 of the Internal Revenue Code. In order to determine whether this type of liquidation was desirable, Bigelow engaged Fanslow & Angelo, CPAs, to perform a tax analysis of the corporation's data and figures to ascertain the amount of dividend per share that would be taxable as dividend income to the shareholders if this method of liquidation were elected. Such a determination is largely dependent on the amount of earnings and profits present, both current and historical.

In making the computation, Fanslow and Angelo treated retained earnings as stated in the financial statements as earnings and profits for tax purposes. However, on two prior occasions transfers were made from retained earnings to stated capital upon the issuance of stock dividends. The result of failure to adjust earnings and profits to reflect these transfers was to understate the amount of taxable dividend income per share by some $20 per share.

Required:

Answer the following, setting forth reasons for any conclusions stated.
Do Fanslow & Angelo have any liability under the above-stated facts?

Answer

5.b. Yes. An accountant's liability to his client may be for actual fraud, or for gross negligence amounting to constructive fraud. Actual fraud exists when there is present an actual intent to mislead, called scienter. Constructive fraud exists when there is no such actual intent but there is reckless disregard for the truth. The three instances in which the CPA firm's audit was deficient are so much at variance with established auditing standards and procedures and are so insufficient for a professional accounting opinion as to justify a conclusion of reckless disregard for the truth amounting to constructive fraud, and also possibly amounting to actual fraud, as to cause subsequent creditors to rely on the audit to their damage. Therefore, the creditors should recover in their lawsuit. (p. 819)

c. Yes. The CPA firm is liable to Bigelow for damage it sustained, and also is liable to Bigelow's shareholders for any interest and penalties they experienced with the tax authorities, and also for any additional taxes they may have had to pay, because of the firm's negligence in providing such misleading, wrong advice. A tax accountant certainly knows or should know that the concept of retained earnings is different from the concept of earnings and profits for tax purposes, and that these two must be reconciled with each other. Stock dividends on previous occasions certainly affected retained earnings, but they do not affect earnings and profits if the stock dividends are nontaxable.

MAY, 1979

Number 2

Part a. Factory Discount Prices, Inc., is a chain store discount outlet which sells women's clothes. It has an excessively large inventory on hand and is in urgent need of additional cash. It is bordering on bankruptcy, especially if the inventory has to be liquidated by sale to other stores instead of the public. Furthermore, about 15 percent of the inventory is not resalable except at a drastic discount below cost. Faced with this financial crisis, Factory approached several of the manufacturers from whom it purchases. Dexter Apparel, Inc., one of the parties approached, indicated a willingness to loan Factory $300,000 under certain conditions. First, Factory was to submit audited financial statements for the express purpose of providing the correct financial condition of the company. The loan was to be predicated upon these financial statements and Factory's engagement letter with Dunn & Clark, its CPAs, expressly indicated this.

The second condition insisted upon by Dexter was that it obtain a secured position in all unsecured inventory, accounts, and other related personal property. In due course a security agreement was executed and a financing statement properly filed and recorded.

In preparing the financial statements, Factory valued the inventory at cost which was approximately $100,000 over the current fair market value. Also, Factory failed to disclose two secured creditors to whom substantial amounts are owed and who take priority over Dexter's security interests.

Dunn & Clark issued an unqualified opinion on the financial statements of Factory which they believed were fairly presented.

Six months later Factory filed a voluntary bankruptcy petition. Dexter received $125,000 as its share of the bankrupt's estate. It is suing Dunn & Clark for the loss of $175,000. Dunn & Clark deny liability based upon lack of privity and lack of negligence.

Required.

Answer the following, setting forth reasons for any conclusions stated.

Is Dexter entitled to recover its loss from Dunn & Clark?

Part c. Smith, CPA, is the auditor for Juniper Manufacturing Corporation, a privately owned company which has a June 30 fiscal year. Juniper arranged for a substantial bank loan which was dependent upon the bank receiving, by September 30, audited financial statements which showed a current ratio of at least 2 to 1. On September 25, just before the audit report was to be issued, Smith received an anonymous letter on Juniper's stationery indicating that a five-year lease by Juniper, as lessee, of a factory building which was accounted for in the financial statements as an operating lease was in fact a capital lease. The letter stated that there was a secret written agreement with the lessor modifying the lease and creating a capital lease.

Smith confronted the president of Juniper who admitted that a secret agreement existed but said it was necessary to treat the lease as an operating lease to meet the current ratio requirement of the pending loan and that nobody would ever discover the secret agreement with the lessor. The president said that if Smith did not issue his report by September 30, Juniper would sue Smith for substantial damages which would result from not getting the loan. Under this pressure and because the working papers contained a copy of the five-year lease agreement which supported the operating lease treatment, Smith issued his report with an unqualified opinion on September 29.

In spite of the fact that the loan was received, Juniper went bankrupt within two years. The bank is suing Smith to recover its losses on the loan and the lessor is suing Smith to recover uncollected rents.

Required:

Answer the following, setting forth reasons for any conclusions stated.

1. Is Smith liable to the bank?
2. Is Smith liable to the lessor?

Answer

2.a. Yes. There is no privity of contract between a public accountant and third persons and, therefore, there is no duty of care owing by him to third persons, with an exception. If the accountant knows that his accounting services rendered to his client will be made available by his client to a third person whose identity is known to the accountant and he knows that the third person intends to rely upon his professional opinion, he has a duty to exercise reasonable care to the third person and he will be liable for his ordinary negligence which proximately causes damage to the third person.

Here, the engagement letter proves that Dunn & Clark knew of Dexter's identity and that the audited financial statement was to be made available to Dexter as a condition for Dexter's making a loan to Factory. Dunn & Clark were negligent in two respects. First, they should have been careful to detect that the inventory was valued substantially higher on a cost basis than its fair market value. This is contrary to generally accepted accounting principles. Second, by reasonable examination they should have ascertained that there were two secured creditors of Factory and should have disclosed this information, particularly since they knew the purpose of their services for Factory. Accordingly, they are liable to Dexter for its loss (pp. 818–19, 815–16).

c.1. Yes. Since Smith knew of the fraud (scienter) and participated in its perpetration on the bank by his non-disclosure of the true character of the lease, he is liable to the bank for its damage caused by his misrepresentation by such non-disclosure. Smith's liability is on the basis of the tort of deceit, consisting of a misrepresentation of a material fact, made with knowledge of its falsity and with the intent to mislead another person, who relies thereon and suffers pecuniary damage. Smith is liable also for his negligence in not disclosing to the bank the true character of the lease, his liability to the bank being an exception to the privity rule as explained in the answer **2a** above.

2. No. The lessor was not deceived because he had not relied on that part of the financial statements concerning the lease since he knew its true character. Also, his participation in the fraud precludes any equitable recovery for loss for uncollected rents (pp. 818, 34 n.28).

NOVEMBER, 1978

Number 1

Select the **best** answers for each of the following items.

3. The Apex Surety Company wrote a general fidelity bond covering defalcations by the employees of Watson, Inc. Thereafter, Grand, an employee of Watson, embezzled $18,900 of company funds. When his activities were discovered, Apex paid Watson the full amount in accordance with the terms of the fidelity bond, and then sought recovery against Watson's auditors, Kane & Dobbs, CPAs. Which of the following would be Kane & Dobbs' best defense?

a. Apex is **not** in privity of contract.
b. The shortages were the result of clever forgeries and collusive fraud which would **not** be detected by an examination made in accordance with generally accepted auditing standards.
c. Kane & Dobbs was **not** guilty either of gross negligence or fraud.
d. Kane & Dobbs were **not** aware of the Apex-Watson surety relationship.

4. The CPA firm of Knox and Knox has been subpoenaed to testify and produce its correspondence and working papers in connection with a lawsuit brought against Johnson, one of its clients. Regarding the attempted resort to the privileged communication rule in seeking to avoid admission of such evidence in the lawsuit, which of the following is correct?

a. Federal law recognizes such a privilege if the accountant is a Certified Public Accountant.
b. The privilege is available regarding the working papers since the accountant is deemed to own them.
c. The privilege is as widely available as the attorney-client privilege.
d. In the absence of a specific statutory provision, the law does **not** recognize the existence of the privileged communication rule between an accountant and his client.

32. On July 25, 1978, Archer, the president of Post Corporation, with the approval of the board of directors, engaged Biggs, a CPA, to examine Post's July 31, 1978, financial statements and to issue a report in time for the annual stockholders' meeting to be held on September 5, 1978. Notwithstanding Biggs' reasonable efforts, the report was not ready until September 7 because of delays by Post's staff. Archer, acting on behalf of Post, refused to accept or to pay for the report since it no longer served its intended purpose. In the event Biggs brings a legal action against Post, what is the probable outcome?

a. The case would be dismissed because it is unethical for a CPA to sue for his fee.
b. Biggs will be entitled to recover only in quasi contract for the value of the services to the client.
c. Biggs will **not** recover since the completion by September 5th was a condition precedent to his recovery.
d. Biggs will recover because the delay by Post's staff prevented Biggs from performing on time and thereby eliminated the timely performance condition.

Answer

1. 3.b(815–16) 4.d(818) 32.d(817)

MAY, 1978

Number 3

Part a. A CPA firm was engaged to examine the financial statements of Martin Manufacturing Corporation for the year ending December 31, 1977. The facts revealed that Martin was in need of cash to continue its operations and agreed to sell its common stock investment in a subsidiary through a private placement. The buyers insisted that the proceeds be placed in escrow because of the possibility of a major contingent tax liability that might result from a pending government claim. The payment in escrow was completed in late November 1977. The president of Martin told the audit partner that the proceeds from the sale of the subsidiary's common stock, held in escrow, should be shown on the balance sheet as an unrestricted current account receivable. The president was of the opinion that the government's claim was groundless and that Martin needed an "uncluttered" balance sheet and a "clean" auditor's opinion to obtain additional working capital from lenders. The audit partner agreed with the president and issued an unqualified opinion on the Martin financial statements which did not refer to the contingent liability and did not properly describe the escrow arrangement.

The government's claim proved to be valid, and pursuant to the agreement with the buyers, the purchase price of the subsidiary was reduced by $450,000. This adverse development forced Martin into bankruptcy. The CPA firm is being sued for deceit (fraud) by several of Martin's unpaid creditors who extended credit in reliance upon the CPA firm's unqualified opinion on Martin's financial statements.

Required:

Answer the following, setting forth reasons for any conclusions stated.

Based on these facts, can Martin's unpaid creditors recover from the CPA firm?

Part b. A CPA firm has been named as a defendant in a class action by purchasers of the shares of stock of the Newly Corporation. The offering was a public offering of securities within the meaning of the Securities Act of 1933. The plaintiffs alleged that the firm was either negligent or fraudulent in connection with the preparation of the audited financial statements which accompanied the registration statement filed with the SEC. Specifically, they allege that the CPA firm either intentionally disregarded, or failed to exercise reasonable care to discover, material facts which occurred subsequent to January 31, 1978, the date of the auditor's report. The securities were sold to the public on March 16, 1978. The plaintiffs have subpoenaed copies of the CPA firm's working papers. The CPA firm is considering refusing to relinquish the papers, asserting that they contain privileged communication between the CPA firm and its client. The CPA firm will, of course, defend on the merits irrespective of the questions regarding the working papers.

Required:

Answer the following, setting forth reasons for any conclusions stated.

1. Can the CPA firm rightfully refuse to surrender its working papers?

Answer

3.a. Yes. Deceit is a tort consisting of a misrepresentation of a material fact made by a person with knowledge of its falsity and with intent to mislead another person by inducing the latter to act in a particular business transaction in reliance thereon, which causes the other person so to act in justifiable reliance thereon and thereby to suffer pecuniary damage. It does not require privity of contract between the misrepresenting party and the party to whom the misrepresentation was made.

Here, the CPA firm did knowingly misrepresent that the proceeds from the sale of Martin stock were unrestricted, which is not in accordance with the facts. The restricted character of the proceeds was a material fact in that it is of such importance that, if known to the creditors, it would likely have influenced their conduct in their subsequent extension of credit to Martin. The CPA firm reasonably could realize that persons could subsequently become creditors of Martin in reliance on the false financial statement and, therefore, the CPA firm would intend to mislead that class by the firm's misrepresentation, even though the firm did not know the identity of the persons in that class of which the creditors here are members. Here, the creditors subsequently innocently and justifiably relied on the CPA firm's misrepresentation and thereby suffered pecuniary damage through Martin's bankruptcy.

Under the law of Agency, a principal is liable to third persons for the misrepresentations of its agents while they are acting within the scope of their authority. Thus the CPA firm is liable for the misrepresentation made in its name by its audit partner. (pp. 34, 610)

b.1. No. Privileged communications between accountant and client were not recognized at Common Law and, today, they are not privileged by statute in a majority of the states nor by federal statute. The privilege is for the benefit of the client, and only the client can waive it. Here, even if the case is in a state granting this privilege, it cannot be exercised by the CPA firm without Newly's consent, which is not present. Therefore, the CPA firm must obey the subpoena and surrender its working papers. (818)

NOVEMBER, 1977

Number 3

Select the **best** answer for the following item.

42. If a CPA firm is engaged by a law firm to aid it in the administration of a decedent's estate, its duties will invariably **not** include

a. Preparation of the federal estate tax return.
b. Preparation of the estate's fiduciary income tax returns.
c. Presentation of the necessary schedules and summations to be used in rendering an accounting to interested parties.
d. Consideration of the validity of the surviving spouse's right to take against the will.

Answer

3. 42.d(816)

Part Thirteen:
Public Law

A. Federal Securities Regulation

Chapter 63

THE FEDERAL SECURITIES LAWS OF 1933 AND 1934

SECTION I. SECURITIES

Laws have been enacted by the various states and by the federal government regulating the sale and transfer of securities, including corporate securities. State laws commonly are called "blue-sky laws," and the best-known federal laws are the Securities Act of 1933 and the Securities Exchange Act of 1934. The *state* laws are concerned with *intra-state* transactions and the *federal* laws are concerned with *interstate* transactions. The purpose of these state and federal laws is to prevent fraud on investors and purchasers by requiring full public disclosure of all information relating to the securities being offered or sold and by regulation of dealers and brokers[1] engaged in the sale and marketing of securities. A registration statement containing certain specified information regarding the securities to be sold, together with a prospectus or circular containing information to be made available to purchasers and investors, is to be filed with the state commission or, in the case of the federal government, with the Securities and Exchange Commission. The Securities Exchange Act is concerned with the registration and regulation of national security exchanges and of brokers and dealers, and with other pertinent information. The necessity for federal regulation supplementing state regulation through federal jurisdiction over interstate commerce and the mails was emphasized by the financial collapse in the 1920s.

[1] Section 10(b) and Rule 10b–5 of the Securities Exchange Act of 1934 are concerned with requiring registered brokers to file audited financial statements in connection with their annual reports.

The federal securities laws generally apply to: (1) corporations whose securities are traded on a national securities exchange or in the over-the-counter market, and their officers, directors and principal stockholders (those in a control relationship with the issuer); (2) corporations and other issuers of securities by a primary (new) or secondary (by controlling shareholders) distribution to the public; (3) makers of tender offers for, and purchasers of, more than 5 percent of a company's shares; (4) persons in the business of buying and selling securities, and others.

The 1934 Act provides for the creation of the Securities and Exchange Commission which administers the regulations governing these securities laws. The purpose of the 1933 Act is "to provide full and fair disclosure of the character of securities sold in interstate and foreign commerce and through the mails, and to prevent frauds in the sale thereof." *Disclosure is made by the issuer through a registration statement and a prospectus.* Generally, an "issuer" is every person who issues or proposes to issue any security. A "security" is broadly defined as "any note, stock, treasury stock, bond, debenture, . . . evidence of indebtedness, certificate of interest or participation in any profit-sharing agreement, . . . transferable share, investment contract, voting trust certificate, . . . or in general any interest or instrument commonly known as a security. . . ." An "underwriter" means any person "who has purchased from an issuer with a view to, or offers or sells for an issuer in connection with, the distribution of any security, or participates in . . . any such undertaking. . . ." Issuer here also includes "any person directly or indirectly controlling or controlled by the issuer, or any person under direct or indirect common control with the issuer."

There are two types of exemption from the requirement of registration with the SEC and furnishing a prospectus to prospective buyers: certain kinds of *securities* are exempted; and certain *transactions* in securities are exempted. Among those *securities* exempted are: small issues[2] in which the aggregate amount of issue offered to the public does not exceed $1.5 million, by SEC regulation pursuant to sec. 3(b) of the 1933 Act; intrastate issues in which the security is a part of an issue offered and sold only to persons resident within a single state in which the issuer also is a resident and doing business there. Among those *transactions* in securities exempted are: transactions by any person other than an issuer, underwriter or dealer, meaning individual investors, except that officers, directors, or those in control of the issuer must register in order to sell their securities; transactions by an issuer not involving a "public offering," often called "private offerings" or "private placement," made to "sophisticated" investors; and brokers' transactions, where orders for particular securities are not solicited and the broker merely executed his customer's orders. Disclosure does not stop with the filed registration statement, but

[2] Regulation A is concerned, in part, with securities exempted from the requirement of registration with the SEC. The Regulation specifies the filing requirements for such small issues which are much less than for a full registration. For example, less documentation is required and the financial statements need not be audited.

annual reports must be filed by the issuer if 300 or more persons own a class of the issued securities.[3] Under the 1934 Act, *a security may not be traded on an exchange unless it is registered*, and it is unlawful so to do; use of interstate commerce or the mails is prohibited. Every issuer engaged in interstate commerce, or in a business affecting interstate commerce, or whose securities are traded by use of the mails or any means or instrumentality of interstate commerce shall register such security by filing with the SEC a registration statement if such issuer has total assets in excess of $1 million and 500 or more but less than 750 shareholders.

Securities are registered when the registration statement *becomes effective*, which is the twentieth day after filing. A registration statement must contain a full and accurate disclosure of all relevant information relating to the company's business, its directors and officers, its securities, its financial position and earnings, and details about the underwriting. It must be signed by the issuer, its principal executive officer or officers, its principal financial officer, its principal accounting officer, and a majority of its board of directors. Financial statements certified by independent public accountants are usually required as a part of the registration statement. *A registration statement must be amended if additional material pertinent facts requiring disclosure are discovered.* A prospectus is any notice, circular, advertisement, letter, or communication, written or by radio or television, which offers any security for sale. It has substantially the same information as in the registration statement but in a summary form, and must be filed with the registration statement.

The 1934 Act prohibits deceptive or fraudulent practices, and unfair practices by an "insider," who is a person directly or indirectly owning more than 10 percent of any class of equity security registered on a national securities exchange, or who is a director or an officer of the issuer of such security. He must file with the exchange, at the time of the registration of such security or within ten days after he becomes such a beneficial owner, his statement of his holdings of securities of the issuer. In order to prevent his unfair use of insider information by reason of his relationship to the issuer, any "short swing" profits he realizes from any purchase and sale or sale and purchase of any security of the issuer within any period of *less than six months*, unless such security was acquired in good faith in connection with a debt previously contracted, inures to and is recoverable by the issuer no later than two years after realization of such profits.

The 1933 Act provides for *civil penalties* for a false registration statement. If any part of the registration statement, *when such part became effective*, contained an *untrue statement of a material fact or omitted to state a material fact required to be stated therein or necessary to make the statements therein not misleading*, any innocent person acquiring such security may, sue: (1) every person who signed the registration statement; (2) every person who was a director of or partner in the issuer at the time of the filing of the part of

[3] Section 10(b) and Rule 10b(5) of the 1934 Act are concerned with fraud, which is an intentional tort consisting of an intentional misrepresentation of a material fact.

the registration statement with respect to which his liability is asserted; (3) every person who, with his consent, is named in the registration statement as being or about to become a director, person performing similar functions, or partner; (4) *every accountant,* engineer, or appraiser, . . . who has with his consent been named as having prepared or certified any part of the registration statement, or as having prepared or certified any report or valuation which is used in connection with the registration statement; (5) every underwriter with respect to such security. This liability cannot be disclaimed. However, *a public accountant may avoid liability if he can prove that he had made a reasonable investigation and had reasonable ground to believe and did believe that, at the time the registration statement became effective, the statements therein were true and that there was no omission to state a material fact.* A one-year statute of limitations is applicable within which time a complainant may, after he discovered or should have discovered such untrue statements or omissions, assert his claim in a United States District Court, which has jurisdiction over controversies of this nature. However, no such action may be brought more than three years after the security was bona fide offered to the public or from the date of sale. *Criminal penalties* may be imposed upon any person who: (1) under the 1933 Act, *wilfully,* in a registration statement filed under the Act, makes any untrue statement of a material fact or omits to state any material fact required to be stated therein or necessary to make the statements therein not misleading; (2) under the 1934 Act, *wilfully* makes a false or misleading statement with respect to any material fact in any application, report, or a document required to be filed under the Act.

This is a very brief overview of a very technical and complex area of the law demanding expertise of practitioners.

A careful reading of the following references should be very helpful—United States Code, Title 15: Chapter 2A "Securities and Trust Indentures," particularly sections 77a through 77aa; and Chapter 2B "Securities Exchanges," particularly sections 78p through 78ff. Also, examine the regulations of the SEC, particularly Regulation A concerning exemptions in the exercise of its discretion and administrative authority pursuant to the statute.

SECTION II. THE FOREIGN CORRUPT PRACTICES ACT OF 1977

Background

On December 19, 1977, the Securities Exchange Act of 1934 was amended by the Foreign Corrupt Practices Act an an anti-bribery law because of foreign payments made by American business concerns to influence foreign government officials in order to obtain or retain business. This practice is contrary to the free market system that the sale of products take place on the basis of price, quality, and service, and is destructive of this system. The resulting law covers "Accounting Standards," "Foreign Corrupt Practices by Issuers and Domestic Concerns," and "Disclosure."

Accounting Standards

Every issuer of securities registered under the Securities Exchange Act of 1934 or who is required to file reports under the Act is made subject to strict record-keeping and internal accounting control requirements. The user must: "(A) make and keep books, records, and accounts, which in reasonable detail, accurately and fairly reflect the transactions and dispositions of the assets of the issuer; and (B) devise and maintain a system of internal controls sufficient to provide reasonable assurances that:

1. transactions are executed in accordance with management's general or specific authorization;
2. transactions are recorded as necessary (I) to permit preparation of financial statements in conformity with generally accepted accounting principles or any other criteria applicable to such statements, and (II) to maintain accountability for assets;
3. access to assets is permitted only in accordance with management's general or specific authorization; and
4. the recorded accountability for assets is compared with the existing assets at reasonable intervals and appropriate action is taken with respect to any differences."

The reason for this requirement of accounting standards is to preclude corrupt payments through off-the-books slush funds without disclosure on the issuer's books.

Foreign Corrupt Practices by Issuers and by Domestic Concerns Other Than Issuers

Issuers. It is unlawful for any issuer, or for any officer, director, employee, or agent of such issuer or any stockholder thereof acting on behalf of such issuer, to make use of the mails or any means or instrumentality of interstate commerce corruptly in furtherance of an offer, payment, promise to pay, or authorization of the payment of any money, or offer, gift, promise to give, or authorization of the giving of anything of value to:

a. any foreign official, any foreign political party or official thereof, or any candidate for foreign political office for the purpose of influencing such person to act, fail to act, or to influence a foreign government or instrumentality in order to assist such issuer in obtaining or retaining business for, or with, or directing business to, any person;
b. any person, while knowing or having reason to know that all or a portion of such money or thing of value will be offered, given, or promised, directly or indirectly, to any foreign official, to any foreign political party or official thereof, or to any candidate for foreign political office, for the above described purpose.

A "foreign official" includes any foreign governmental officer or employee, but does not include any employee whose duties are essentially ministerial or clerical.

On conviction for violation: an issuer shall be fined not more than $1 million; an officer or director of an issuer, or a stockholder acting on behalf of such issuer, for willful violation, shall be fined up to $10,000 or/and imprisoned for not more than five years; and, on an issuer's violation, the latter penalty shall be imposed upon any employee or agent of such issuer who is a U.S. resident or citizen or otherwise subject to U.S. jurisdiction (other than an officer, director, or stockholder of such issuer) who wilfully carried out the act or practice constituting the violation. A fine so imposed upon such persons other than the issuer shall not be paid, directly or indirectly, by the issuer.

Domestic Concerns Other Than Issuers. The same prohibitions and penalties apply to domestic concerns who are not issuers as to issuers. An individual may be a domestic concern, but then the penalty for willful violation is a maximum of $10,000 or/and imprisonment up to five years. The Attorney General has the responsibility for enforcing the law with respect to domestic concerns, and may institute injunctive civil proceedings to enjoin such violations.

Disclosure. This part of the Foreign Corrupt Practices Act of 1977 may be cited as the Domestic and Foreign Investment Improved Disclosure Act of 1977. It supplements the Securities Exchange Act of 1934 regarding the requirement of disclosure in connection with filing periodic and other reports with the SEC, requiring more detail to be disclosed by the same beneficial owners. It provides that any person (domestic or foreign) who is, directly or indirectly, the beneficial owner of more than 5 percent of a registered security must send to the issuer of the security and must file with the SEC a statement containing a large amount of complex information, which basically consists of: the beneficial owner's identity, residence, and citizenship; the number and description of the shares in which such owner has an interest and the nature of the interest; the source and amount of the funds or other consideration used to purchase the shares and the purpose for such acquisition; and detailed information as to any contracts, arrangements, or understandings with any person with respect to any securities of the issuer. If any material changes in the statement occur, an amendment must be sent to the issuer and filed with the SEC. A group of persons, (e.g., partnership), constitutes a "person." The SEC has the responsibility for enforcement of this part of the law.

The 1977 Act places full responsibility on a firm's board of directors to ensure that there is compliance with the Act's requirements for proper record-keeping and a system of internal accounting controls, and to make provision for their continual review so as to detect illegal payments in violation of the Act.

On February 15, 1979, the SEC published the following implementing Regulation 13B–2: "Maintenance of Records and Preparation of Required Reports," effective March 23, 1979: "No person shall, directly or indirectly, falsify or cause to be falsified, any book, record or account subject to Section 13(b)(2)(A) of the Securities Exchange Act. No director or officer of an issuer shall, directly or indirectly:

1. make or cause to be made a materially false or misleading statement, or
2. omit to state, or cause another person to omit to state, any material fact necessary in order to make statements made, in light of the circumstances under which such statements were made, not misleading to an accountant in connection with (1) any audit or examination of the financial statements of the issuer required to be made pursuant to this subpart or (2) the preparation of filing of any document or report required to be filed with the Commission pursuant to this subpart or otherwise."

Under SEC Rule 3b–3, the term *officer* "means a president, vice president, treasurer, comptroller, and any other person who performs for an issuer, whether incorporated or unincorporated, functions corresponding to those performed by the foregoing officers."

PROBLEMS

1. Each of the lettered statements of facts below is followed by numbered sentences that state legal conclusions relating to those facts. You are to determine whether each legal conclusion is true or false according to **the general principles of accountant's legal responsibility and federal securities regulation.**

   E. Xavier, Francis, & Paul are a growing medium-sized partnership of CPAs located in the midwest. One of the firm's major clients is considering offering its stock to the public. This will be the firm's first client to go public.

   52. The firm should thoroughly familiarize itself with the Securities Act of 1933 and the Securities Exchange Act of 1934.
   53. If the client is unincorporated, the Securities Act of 1933 will **not** apply.
   54. If the client is going to be listed on an organized exchange, the Securities Exchange Act of 1934 will **not** apply.
   55. The Securities Act of 1933 imposes an additional potential liability on firms such as Xavier, Francis, & Paul.
   56. So long as the company engages in exclusively intrastate business, the federal securities law will **not** apply.

   F. The partnership of Maxwell, Plumb, & Fisk, CPAs, has been engaged by Vitrolic Partners, their largest client, to examine the financial statements in connection with the offering of 2,000 limited-partnership interests in Vitrolic to the public at $5,000 per subscription.

   57. Maxwell, Plumb, & Fisk may disclaim any liability under the federal securities acts by an unambiguous, bold-faced disclaimer of liability on their work.
   58. If the Securities Act of 1933 applies, Maxwell, Plumb, & Fisk have responsibility only for the financial statements as of the close of the fiscal year in question.
   59. The dollar amount in question is sufficiently small so as to provide an exemption from the Securities Act of 1933.
   60. The Securities Exchange Act of 1934 will apply to Vitrolic.

   (Former C.P.A. Examination question)

2. The Chriswell Corporation decided to raise additional long-term capital by issuing $3,000,000 of 8 percent subordinated debentures to the public. May, Clark & Co., CPAs, the company's auditors, were engaged to examine the June 30, 1980 financial statements which were included in the bond registration statement.

May, Clark & Co. completed its examination and submitted an unqualified auditor's report dated July 15, 1980. The registration statement was filed and became effective on September 1, 1980. Two weeks prior to the effective date one of the partners of May, Clark & Co. called on Chriswell Corporation and had lunch with the financial vice president and the controller. He questioned both officials on the company's operations since June 30 and inquired whether there had been any material changes in the company's financial position since that date. Both officers assured him that everything had proceeded normally and that the financial condition of the company had not changed materially.

Unfortunately, the officers' representation was not true. On July 30, a substantial debtor of the company failed to pay the $400,000 due on its account receivable and indicated to Chriswell that it would probably be forced into bankruptcy. This receivable was shown as a collateralized loan on the June 30 financial statements. It was secured by stock of the debtor corporation which had a value in excess of the loan at the time the financial statements were prepared but was virtually worthless at the effective date of the registration statement. This $400,000 account receivable was material to the financial condition of Chriswell Corporation, and the market price of the subordinated debentures decreased by nearly 50 percent after the foregoing facts were disclosed.

The debenture holders of Chriswell are seeking recovery of their loss against all parties connected with the debenture registration.

Required:

Is May, Clark & Co. liable to the Chriswell debenture holders? Explain.

(Former C.P.A. Examination question, dates changed)

3. Each of the following numbered statements states a legal conclusion relating to the lettered material. You are to determine whether each of the legal conclusions is true or false according to general principles of accountants' legal responsibility.

C. The Dandy Container Corporation engaged the accounting firm of Adams and Adams to examine financial statements to be used in connection with a public offering of securities. The audit was completed and an unqualified opinion was expressed on the financial statements which were submitted to the Securities and Exchange Commission along with the registration statement. Two hundred thousand shares of Dandy Container common stock were offered to the public at $11 a share. Eight months later the stock fell to $2 a share when it was disclosed that several large loans to two "paper" corporations owned by one of the directors were worthless. The loans were secured by the stock of the borrowing corporation which was owned by the director. These facts were not disclosed in the financial report. The director involved and the two corporations are insolvent.

11. The Securities Act of 1933 applies to the above described public offering of securities in interstate commerce.
12. The accounting firm has potential liability to any person who acquired the stock in reliance upon the registration statement.
13. An insider who had knowledge of all the facts regarding the loans to the two "paper" corporations could nevertheless recover from the accounting firm.
14. An investor who bought shares in Dandy Container would make a prima facie case if he alleges that the failure to explain the nature of the loans in question constituted a false statement or misleading omission in the financial statements.

15. The accountants could avoid liability if they could show they were neither negligent nor fraudulent.
16. Accountants' responsibility as to the fairness of the financial statements is determined as of the date of the auditor's report and not beyond.
17. The accountants could avoid or reduce the damages asserted against them if they could establish that the drop in price was due in whole or in part to other causes.
18. The Dandy investors would have to institute suit within one year after discovery of the alleged untrue statements or omissions.
19. It would appear that the accountants were negligent in respect to the handling of the secured loans in question—if they discovered the facts regarding the loans to the "paper" corporations and failed to disclose them in their financial statements.
20. The Securities and Exchange Commission would defend any action brought against the accountants in that the SEC examined and approved the registration statement. (Former C.P.A. Examination question)

SOME PREVIOUS C.P.A. LAW EXAMINATION QUESTIONS AND AUTHOR'S MODEL ANSWERS

NOVEMBER, 1979

Number 1

Select the **best** answers to the following items.

27. Taylor is the executive vice president for marketing of Reflex Corporation and a member of the board of directors. Based on information obtained during the course of his duties, Taylor concluded that Reflex's profits would fall by 50 percent for the quarter and 30 percent for the year. He quietly contacted his broker and disposed of 10,000 shares of his Reflex stock at a profit, some of which he had acquired within six months of the sale. In fact, Reflex's profits did **not** fall, but its stock price declined for unrelated reasons. Taylor had also advised a friend to sell her shares and repurchase the stock later. She followed Taylor's advice, sold for $21, and subsequently repurchased an equal number of shares at $11. A shareholder has commenced a shareholder derivative action against Taylor and the friend for violation of the Securities Exchange Act of 1934. Under these circumstances, which of the following is correct?
   a. Taylor is **not** an insider in relation to Reflex.
   b. Taylor must account to the corporation for his short-swing profit.
   c. Taylor and the friend must both account to the corporation for their short-swing profits.
   d. Neither Taylor nor the friend has incurred any liability under the 1934 Act.

28. Which of the following is exempt from registration under the Securities Act of 1933?
   a. First mortgage bonds.
   b. The usual annuity contract issued by an insurer.
   c. Convertible preferred stock.
   d. Limited partnership interests.

29. Under the Securities Act of 1933, an accountant may be held liable for any materially false or misleading financial statements, including an omission of a material fact therefrom, provided the purchaser

a. Proves reliance on the registration statement or prospectus.
b. Proves negligence or fraud on the part of the accountant.
c. Brings suit within four years after the security is offered to the public.
d. Proves a false statement or omission existed *and* the specific securities were the ones offered through the registration statement.

32. Whitworth has been charged by Bonanza Corporation with violating the Securities Exchange Act of 1934. Whitworth was formerly the president of Bonanza, but he was ousted as a result of a proxy battle. Bonanza seeks to recover from Whitworth any and all of his short-swing profits. Which of the following would be a valid defense to the charges?

a. Whitworth is a New York resident, Bonanza was incorporated in New York, and the transactions were all made through the New York Stock Exchange; therefore, interstate commerce was **not** involved.
b. Whitworth did **not** actually make use of any insider information in connection with the various stock transactions in question.
c. All the transactions alleged to be in violation of the 1934 Act were purchases made during February 1979 with the corresponding sales made in September 1979.
d. Whitworth's motivation in selling the stock was solely a result of the likelihood that he would be ousted as president of Bonanza.

Answer

1. 27.b(830) 28.b(829) 29.d(830–31) 32.c(830)

MAY, 1979

Number 1

Select the **best** answers for each of the following items.

48. Harvey Wilson is a senior vice president, 15 percent shareholder, and a member of the board of directors of Winslow, Inc. Wilson has decided to sell 10 percent of his stock in the company. Which of the following methods of disposition would subject him to SEC registration requirements?

a. A redemption of the stock by the corporation.
b. The sale by several brokerage houses of the stock in the ordinary course of business.
c. The sale of the stock to an insurance company which will hold the stock for long-term investment purposes.
d. The sale to a corporate officer who currently owns 5 percent of the stock of Winslow and who will hold the purchased stock for long-term investment.

49. The Securities Exchange Act of 1934 holds certain insiders liable for short-swing profits under section 16(b) of the Act. Which of the following classes of people would **not** be insiders in relation to the corporation in which they own securities?

a. An executive vice president.
b. A major debenture holder.
c. An 11 percent owner, 8 percent of which he owns in his or her own name and 3 percent in an irrevocable trust for his or her benefit for life.
d. A director who own less than 10 percent of the shares of stock of the corporation.

Answer

1. 48.b(829) 49.b(830)

NOVEMBER, 1978

Number 1

Select the **best** answers for each of the following items.

11. A CPA firm is being sued by a third party purchaser of securities sold in interstate commerce to the public. The third party is relying upon the Securities Act of 1933. The CPA firm had issued an unqualified opinion on incorrect financial statements. Which of the following represents the best defense available to the CPA firm?
   a. The securities sold had **not** been registered with the SEC.
   b. The CPA firm had returned the entire fee it charged for the engagement to the corporation.
   c. The third party was **not** in privity of contract with the CPA firm.
   d. The action had **not** been commenced within one year after the discovery of the material misrepresentation.

33. Young owns 200 shares of stock of Victory Manufacturing Company. Victory is listed on a national stock exchange and has in excess of one million shares outstanding. Young claims that Truegood, a Victory director, has purchased and sold shares in violation of the insider trading provisions of the Securities Exchange Act of 1934. Young has threatened legal action. Which of the following statements is correct.?
   a. Truegood will have a valid defense if he can show he did **not** have any insider information which influenced his purchases or sales.
   b. Young can sue Truegood personally, but his recovery will be limited to his proportionate share of Truegood's profits plus legal expenses.
   c. In order to prevail, Young must sue for and on behalf of the corporation and establish that the transactions in question occurred within less than six months of each other and at a profit to Truegood.
   d. Since Young's stock ownership is less than 1 percent his only recourse is to file a complaint with the SEC or obtain a sufficient number of other shareholders to join him so that the 1 percent requirement is met.

Answer

1. 11.d(831) 33.c(830)

Number 4

Part b. Gordon & Groton, CPAs, were the auditors of Bank & Company, a brokerage firm and member of a national stock exchange. Gordon & Groton examined and reported on the financial statements of Bank which were filed with the Securities and Exchange Commission.

Several of Bank's customers were swindled by a fraudulent scheme perpetrated by Bank's president who owned 90 percent of the voting stock of the company. The facts establish that Gordon & Groton were negligent but not reckless or grossly negligent in the conduct of the audit and neither participated in the fraudulent scheme nor knew of its existence.

The customers are suing Gordon & Groton under the anitfraud provisons of Section 10(b) and Rule 10b–5 of the Securities Exchange Act of 1934 for aiding and abetting the fraudulent scheme of the president. The customers' suit for fraud is predicated exclusively on the nonfeasance of the auditors in failing to conduct a proper audit, thereby failing to discover the fraudulent scheme.

Required:

Answer the following, setting forth reasons for any conclusions stated.
1. What is the probable outcome of the lawsuit?
2. What other theory of liability might the customers have asserted?

Answer

4.b.1. The customers' suit will be dismissed. The action is based on fraud under Section 10(b) and Rule 10b–5, which is an intentional tort consisting of an intentional misrepresentation of a material fact. Here, the CPA firm was negligent, which is nonintentional conduct. Also, the CPA firm did not participate in, nor know the existence of, the fraudulent scheme, so it did not act intentionally to mislead. Therefore, no violation of the Section and Rule occurred (pp. 830, 34).

2. Liability on the basis of the tort of negligence, which is concerned with failure to exercise proper care. However, such an action would not be successful because of the privity of contract rule. Since the CPA firm had contracted with Bank and not with the customers, its duty of care was owing only to Bank. However, if the CPA firm had reason to believe that its accounting services which it had rendered to Bank will be made available by Bank to third persons, namely the customers here, then the CPA firm has a legal duty of care to them and would be liable to them for ordinary negligence since it knew the identity of those persons as being customers of Bank.

Also, there may be liability under the 1934 Act's regulation of brokers requiring registered brokers to file audited financial statements in connection with their annual reports. Bank was a registered broker who filed its audited financial statement with the SEC. Since the audit was incorrect because of the CPA firm's negligence the financial statement was incorrect, causing damage to the customers for which the CPA firm may be liable (pp. 818–19, 828).

MAY, 1978

Number 3

Part b. A CPA firm has been named as a defendant in a class action by purchasers of the shares of stock of the Newly Corporation. The offering was a public offering of securities within the meaning of the Securities Act of 1933. The plaintiffs alleged that the firm was either negligent or fraudulent in connection with the preparation of the audited financial statements which accompanied the registration statement filed with the SEC. Specifically, they allege that the CPA firm either intentionally disregarded, or failed to exercise reasonable care to discover, material facts which occurred subsequent to January 31, 1978, the date of the auditor's report. The securities were sold to the public on March 16, 1978. The plaintiffs have subpoenaed copies of the CPA firm's working papers. The CPA firm is considering refusing to relinquish the papers, asserting that they contain privileged communication between the CPA firm and its client. The CPA firm will, of course, defend on the merits irrespective of the questions regarding the working papers.

Required:

Answer the following, setting forth reasons for any conclusions stated.

2. Discuss the liability of the CPA firm in respect to events which occur in the period between the date of the auditor's report and the effective date of the public offering of the securities.

Answer

3.b.2. Under the federal Securities Act of 1933, if any part of a registration statement contains an untrue statement of a material fact or omitted to state a material fact required to be stated therein or necessary to make the statements therein not misleading, any innocent person acquiring such security may sue an accountant who prepared any part of the registration statement. Here, the CPA firm's audited financial statement accompanied the registration statement as a part thereof. The statement must be reviewed by the auditor accountant up until the date the registration becomes effective in order to determine if subsequent facts will have a material effect on it. The statement must be amended if additional material pertinent facts requiring disclosure are discovered.

Under the Act, a CPA who has prepared a part of a registration statement has the burden of proof that he was not negligent nor fraudulent in his preparation. Here, the CPA firm will be liable unless it can prove that it had made a reasonable investigation and had reasonable ground to believe and did believe that, at the time the registration statement became effective, the statements therein were true and that there was no omission to state a material fact (pp. 830–31).

Part Thirteen:
Public Law

B. Federal Antitrust Laws

Chapter 64

FEDERAL ANTITRUST LAWS

In 1890 the Congress felt the necessity to exercise the federal constitutional power over interstate commerce to curb the increasing restraint of trade and monopolization which threatened to disrupt the country's system of fair competition, by enacting antitrust legislation. The four most important federal antitrust laws are the Sherman Act, Clayton Act, Federal Trade Commission Act, and the Robinson-Patman Act, which in large part is an amendment of the Clayton Act. The purposes of the Sherman and FTC Acts are stated in general terms, requiring judicial interpretation and amplification as cases came before the courts. In contrast, the Clayton and Robinson-Patman Acts are very specific in designating business practice and conduct of concern to the Congress. *All of them are to protect trade and commerce against unlawful restraints and monopolies.*

The Sherman Act

Sections 1 and 2 of the Sherman Act state the purpose of the Act:

Section 1. Every contract, combination in the form of trust or otherwise, or conspiracy, in restraint of trade or commerce among the several States, or with foreign nations, is hereby declared to be illegal. Every person who shall make any contract or engage in any combination or conspiracy hereby declared to be illegal shall be deemed guilty of a felony and, on conviction thereof, shall be punished by fine not exceeding one million dollars if a corporation, or, if any other person, one hundred thousand dollars, or by imprisonment not exceeding three years, or by both said punishments, in the discretion of the court.

Section 2. Every person who shall monopolize, or attempt to monopolize, or combine or conspire with any other person or persons, to monopolize any part of the trade or commerce among the several States, or with foreign nations, shall be deemed guilty of a felony, and, on conviction thereof, shall be punished by fine not exceeding one million dollars if a corporation, or, if any other person, one hundred thousand dollars, or by imprisonment not exceeding three years, or by both said punishments, in the discretion of the court.

Section 3 is similar to section 1, applicable to Territories and the District of Columbia.

Effective March 1976, the Miller-Tydings amendment to section 1, exempting vertical resale price fixing agreements valid under state fair trade laws from being an unfair method of competition, was repealed. The flat unqualified "in restraint of trade" phrase in section 1 has now, by federal judicial decision, become subject to the "rule of reason" and the phrase is interpreted to mean *unreasonable* restraint of trade. The federal district courts have jurisdiction to prevent and restrain violations of the federal antitrust acts. The Sherman Act also provides for forfeiture of property in transit when the Act is violated:

Section 6. Any property owned under any contract or by any combination, or pursuant to any conspiracy (and being the subject thereof) mentioned in section one of this act, and being in the course of transportation from one State to another, or to a foreign country, shall be forfeited to the United States, and may be seized and condemned by like proceedings as those provided by law for the forfeiture, seizure, and condemnation of property imported into the United States contrary to law.

The Sherman Act's prohibition has an impact on many kinds of business practices—e.g., price fixing agreements between competitors, agreements between competitors to divide markets or customers often described as "allocating markets," exclusive dealing contracts, tying arrangements, and many more. Many business practices resulting in unfair competition are violative of the Sherman, Clayton, and FTC Acts; the Robinson-Patman Act will be considered as an amending part of the Clayton Act. It should be observed carefully that, with certain *per se* exceptions, no business practice is unlawful; but when that business practice produces the *result* prohibited by the Act only then is it unlawful. For example, *under the Sherman Act* the business practice must produce an unreasonable "restraint of trade," or be violative of section 2 on "monopolies," in order to be unlawful. *Under the Clayton Act*, the specified conduct must be to "substantially lessen competition or tend to create a monopoly." *Under FTCA*, the business practice must be an "unfair method of competition, unfair or deceptive act or practice, in or affecting commerce." Some business practices are restraints which are unreasonable as a matter of law, or violative of the antitrust statutes *per se*, and only such business practice need be shown to prove a violation of the particular statutorily prohibited result.

The Clayton Act

The Clayton Act specifies various business practices which, on producing the prohibited statutory result, are unlawful. *It should be remembered that unlawfulness is produced by two factors, namely, the business practice, and its prohibited result.* Section 2 is concerned with price discrimination; section 3 with agreements not to use goods of a competitor; section 4 with suits by persons injured in their business or property by antitrust violation with triple damages, and actual damages to the United States for its injury; section 7 with corporate acquisition of stock or assets of another corporation; section 8 with interlocking bank directorates and officers; and section 16 with injunctive relief for private parties for threatened loss or damage by violation of the antitrust laws.

Federal Trade Commission Act

FCTA provides for the creation of the Federal Trade Commission with the authority to administer the federal antitrust laws. The prohibited business practices are stated in section 5 of the Act:

> **Section 5.** (a) (1) Unfair methods of competition in or affecting commerce, and unfair or deceptive acts or practices in or affecting commerce, are hereby declared unlawful.
>
> (6) The Commission is empowered and directed to prevent persons, partnerships, or corporations, except banks, common carriers subject to the Acts to regulate commerce, air carriers and foreign air carriers subject to the Federal Aviation Act of 1958, and persons, partnerships, or corporations insofar as they are subject to the Packers and Stockyards Act, 1921, as amended, except as provided in section 406(b) of said Act, from using unfair methods of competition in or affecting commerce and unfair or deceptive acts or practices in or affecting commerce.

Unlawful Restraints and Monopolies

Contracts, Combinations, and Conspiracies. Under the Sherman Act, every contract, combination, or conspiracy in restraint of trade or commerce among the several states or with foreign nations is hereby declared to be illegal, subject to the "rule of reason" test. Generally, whether or not a restraint is reasonable or unreasonable is determined by its effect on competition in a particular case. A person's motivation and intent do not affect the issue of lawfulness of a practice and is not a defense to unlawful conduct. Generally, a combination formed for the purpose and with the effect of raising, depressing, fixing, pegging, or stabilizing the price of a commodity in interstate or foreign commerce is illegal *per se.* The reasonableness of the restraint is immaterial for the purpose of determining its legality.

Price Fixing. Proof of a combination formed with the purpose of fixing prices and which caused the prices to be fixed is proof of a price fixing conspiracy violative of the Sherman Act. The combination is unlawful irrespective of reasonableness of purpose.

Restricting Distribution Systems. While a person may choose his own customers, he violates the Sherman Act if, in concert with his competitors, he *attempts* to control the channels of trade; the purpose is to support a particular price program of the members.

Monopolization. Under the Sherman Act, it is unlawful to monopolize, or attempt to monopolize, or combine or conspire with another person to monopolize any part of trade or commerce among the various states or with foreign nations. In order to prove monopoly it is necessary to prove the existence of monopoly power, namely, the power to control prices or to exclude competition.

Resale Price Fixing. This is the fixing of the price at which a purchaser is to resell the product he purchased. If two or more competitors agree to fix the price, there is "horizontal" price fixing. "Vertical" price fixing is controlled from the top downwards between seller and buyer and, with the repeal of the Miller-Tydings amendment to the Sherman Act, is an unlawful business practice.

Price Discrimination. Section 2(a) of the Clayton Act as amended by the Robinson-Patman Act is concerned primarily with price discrimination as a violation of the Clayton Act. It is concerned with contemporaneous transactions in interstate commerce between a seller and two or more purchasers from him who are competing with each other, the grade, quality, and quantity of the goods (not services) being the same but the seller's price terms to each purchaser being different. Such price discriminatory business practice is unlawful if it produces the statutorily prohibited result of illegal restraint or monopoly. Accordingly, section 2(a) provides that it is unlawful for (1) any person engaged in commerce, in the course of such commerce (2) either directly or indirectly, to discriminate in price between different purchasers of (3) commodites of like grade and quality, where such commodities (not services) are sold for use, consumption or resale within the United States, any Territory, the District of Columbia, or any place within the jurisdiction of the United States, and where (4) the effect of the discrimination *may be* (a) *substantially* to lessen competition, or (b) to *tend to create* a monopoly in any line of commerce, or (c) *to injure, destroy, or prevent competition* with any person who either grants or knowingly receives the benefit of such discrimination, or with customers of either of them. "Person" includes corporations and associations. Thus, it is unlawful and a crime to sell goods at unreasonably low prices for the purpose of destroying competition or eliminating a competitor. It should be carefully noted that it is sufficient to show that the price discrimination "*may*" cause the prohibited result; the unlawfulness of the price discrimination is not affected by whether or not the prohibited result occurs.

Price differentials are not unlawful where they reflect differences because of the grade or quality of the goods sold or in the cost of manufacture, sale, or delivery resulting from differing methods or quantities in which the goods are sold or delivered. Differences in price are not unlawful price discriminations, on the basis of actual cost differences, where sellers sell to their own subsidiaries or to buyers combining wholesale and retail functions. They are not unlawful if lower prices to a customer are shown to have been made in good faith to meet an equally low price of a competitor. The unlawful discrimination may be in the terms of sale other than the price. Discrimination in price occurs only if there are at least two contemporaneous purchases by different buyers. It is not unlawful for a person engaged in selling goods in commerce to select his own customers in bona fide transactions not in restraint of trade; the Act applies only when there is a discrimination in price. Quantity discounts in good faith to meet competition are not unlawful. Cooperative associations and non-profit institutions are exempted from the Clayton Act to the extent that they purchase supplies for their own use. Special laws govern price discrimination in particular industries (e.g., common carriers by water).

Exclusive Dealing. Section 3 of the Clayton Act is concerned with agreements not to use goods of a competitor, or of exclusive dealing:

> **Section 3.** It shall be unlawful for any person engaged in commerce, in the course of such commerce, to lease or make a sale or contract for sale of goods, wares, merchandise, machinery, supplies, or other commodities, whether patented or unpatented, for use, consumption, or resale within the United States or any Territory thereof or the District of Columbia or any insular possession or other place under the jurisdiction of the United States, or fix a price charged therefor, or discount from, or rebate upon, such price, on the condition, agreement, or understanding that the lessee or purchaser thereof shall not use or deal in the goods, wares, merchandise, machinery, supplies, or other commodities of a competitor or competitors of the lessor or seller, where the effect of such lease, sale, or contract for sale or such condition, agreement, or understanding may be to substantially lessen competition or tend to create a monopoly in any line of commerce.

This section makes "tying arrangements" unlawful if they produce the statutorily prohibited result. A tying arrangement occurs when a purchaser or a lessee is required as a condition of the sale or lease of a product, to purchase or lease some other product of the seller or lessor. The purchaser or lessee is required to take two or more products. Tying arrangements are unlawful because they have the effect of preventing the purchaser or lessee from buying or leasing products competitive with the tied product and thereby prevent sellers or lessors of products competitive with the tied product from selling or leasing them to the purchaser or lessee of the tying product arrangement. However, it is not unlawful to have an arrangement for "full-line forcing," whereby a seller or lessor requires a purchaser or lessee to buy or lease a *full line* of its products as a condition of receiving any one of its products.

Acquisition by One Corporation of Stock or Assets of Another Corporation. Section 7 of the Clayton Act, often referred to as the "Anti-merger Act," is designed to prevent corporate mergers or consolidations which *may* produce the statutorily prohibited result:

> No corporation shall acquire, directly or indirectly, the whole or any part of the stock or other share capital and no corporation subject to the jurisdiction of the Federal Trade Commission shall acquire the whole or any part of the assets of one or more corporations engaged in commerce, where in any line of commerce in any section of the country, the effect of such acquisition, of such stocks or assets, or of the use of such stock by the voting or granting of proxies or otherwise, may be substantially to lessen competition, or to tend to create a monopoly.

It is immaterial whether the acquisition is made from or through another corporation; the important point is the unlawful *acquisition* of the stock or assets. Section 7 applies to any acquisition or merger, whether horizontal, vertical, or conglomerate. Section 7 does not apply to corporations purchasing another's stock solely for investment, provided the stock is not used to bring about, or in attempting to bring about, the substantial lessening of competition. The section is applicable to the holding and subsequent use of the acquired stock, as well as to its original acquisition. While the original acquisition of stock may be lawful, nevertheless its holding and use may become unlawful in the future if there is a reasonable probability that such holding and use will substantially lessen competition or tend to create a monopoly. If an acquisition occurs with the *intent to restrain* interstate commerce or to bring about a substantial lessening of competition, the acquisition is violative of the section, even though commerce is not actually restrained. The effect of an acquisition must create a reasonable probability, and not a mere possibility, that competition will be substantially lessened or a monopoly created. The section is intended to arrest such a prohibited effect in its incipiency. The section also does not apply to acquisitions or mergers pursuant to governmental authority. Special federal laws govern acquisition in certain industries—e.g., air carriers and radio stations.

Interlocking Directorates. Section 8 of the Clayton Act deals with interlocking directorates, and provides that no one person at the same time may be a director in any two or more corporations, any one of which has capital, surplus, and undivided profits aggregating more than $1 million engaged in whole or in part in commerce, other than banks and certain other corporations, if such corporations are, or have been previously, by virtue of their business and location of operation, competitors, so that the elimination of competition by agreement between them would constitute a violation of any of the antitrust laws. The section makes special provision for interlocking bank directorates. The Federal Trade Commission is responsible for both bank and non-bank interlocking directorates. Special federal laws govern interlocking directorates in certain industries.

Unfair Methods of Competition and Unfair Practices

Section 5 of the Federal Trade Commission Act declares unlawful "unfair methods of competition in or affecting commerce, and unfair or deceptive acts or practices in or affecting commerce." As construed by the courts, this general statement is amplified to be applicable to a multitude of factual situations.

Misrepresentation. Various kinds of misrepresentation have been held to be violative of section 5: (1) the composition, quality, or character of a product; (2) misuse of names, phrases, or pictorial scenes regarding manufacturers and locations of supply of goods; (3) price or value of goods; (4) sales contracts or orders, particularly regarding ability to fill orders; (5) falsification of trade status, e.g., that the supplier is the manufacturer; (6) failure to make material disclosures, e.g., change in ingredients of a product; (7) passing off one product as that of another manufacturer.

Combinations or Conspiracies Between Competitors. Many combinations or conspiracies between competitors have been held violative of section 5 because they are to destroy some kind of competition. Some are: (1) eliminating competition among themselves; (2) allocating customers and sales territories; (3) appointing a common selling agency; (4) curtailing production or sales; (5) refusing to solicit each other's customers; (6) horizontal price fixing and maintaining prices—e.g., fixing or enhancing prices at which the competitors will sell, fixing uniform terms of sale; (7) group boycotts cutting off trade or supplies from certain persons or groups, or from other competitors; (8) by dealers or distributors to prevent manufacturers or wholesalers from selling to certain types of competitor e.g., chain stores, out-of-town dealers, nonmembers of an association; (9) by manufacturers to prevent rival manufacturers from securing necessary supplies or from selling their products; (10) activities to further such conspiracies—e.g., circulation of black or white lists, boycott. However, it is not unlawful for a single person to refuse to deal with others.

Unfair Practices Against Competitors. Many unfair practices against competitors have been held violative of section 5. Some are: (1) unfairly, by espionage, acquiring a competitor's trade secrets; (2) bribing competitors' purchasing agents; (3) inducing breaches of contracts between competitors and customers or suppliers; (4) circulation of false reports and statements misrepresenting and disparaging a competitor's products, methods, financial standing, etc.; (5) offering special benefits to retailers for cutting out competitive lines.

The Federal Trade Commission is administratively responsible not only for the antitrust area stated in section 5 of FTCA, but also, by court decision, for those prohibited unlawful business practices covered by the Sherman Act as unfair practices under the FTCA.

PROBLEMS

1. Each of the lettered statements of facts below is followed by numbered sentences that state legal conclusions relating to those facts. You are to determine whether each legal conclusion is true or false according to **the general principles of antitrust law.**

   A. The presidents of three competing manufacturing corporations engaged in interstate commerce decided to eliminate what they called "senseless price cutting" in the tri-state area in which they compete. Each agreed that prices should be determined on the basis of fairness to the public and to his company. To implement their verbal agreement, the three presidents have established a four-month rotating price-leadership arrangement. Each company has served four months of each year as the designated price leader. The price leader has set the minimum price for all competing products sold by the three companies. Each president has agreed that his company would abide strictly by the prices set by the price leader.

You are the CPA for one of these companies.

61. The government can bring criminal action against the presidents of the three companies.
62. The government can seek injunctive relief prohibiting the continuation of the agreement.
63. Private individuals who suffer damages as a result of the agreement can recover treble damages.
64. Any party suing the presidents of the three corporations would rely primarily on the Sherman Act.
65. If one of the corporations refused to abide by the agreement, the others could obtain damages for breach of contract.
66. If the corporations can show that "senseless price cutting" did exist in fact, they will **not** have violated antitrust law
67. If the corporations can show that the minimum prices established by the price leader were always fair to the public, the corporations will **not** have violated antitrust law.
68. If there is a violation of antitrust law, the government validly can seize any of the corporations' goods that are shipped in interstate commerce pursuant to the agreement.
69. The corporations will **not** have violated antitrust law if the value of goods shipped in interstate commerce is less than $50,000 each year.
70. There is **no** violation of antitrust law if the prices established under the agreement are uniformly beneath the prices charged prior to its implementation.

B. The following problems arose during the examination of the financial statements of Northup, Inc. Northup, a large manufacturer of industrial products, is attempting to acquire a controlling block of shares of Jackson, Inc., a competing manufacturer. Jackson's market share is about 40 percent in the section of the United States in which Northup and Jackson compete. Northup's share of this market is about 35 percent. Four other firms compete for the remaining 25 percent.

Northup is also considering the purchase of Keller Corporation, one of its major customers (Keller's average annual purchases from Northup have been about $12 million), to assure itself of an outlet for a substantial quantity of its products. Northup intends to have Keller continue as a subsidiary. Keller also purchases substantial dollar volumes (usually around $5 million per year) from Northup's competitors.

Some time ago, independent of its present acquisition activities, Northup stopped dealing with Lambert, one of its distributors. Lambert and Northup had entered into a distributorship agreement giving either party the right to terminate on at least 90 days prior written notice. Northup had given such notice. Lambert has nevertheless instituted a treble damage suit under the antitrust laws against Northup. Lambert alleges that it will lose a substantial capital investment made in connection with this distributorship.

Northup, Jackson, Keller, and Lambert are all in interstate commerce.

71. Northup would avoid an antitrust action by purchasing the assets rather than the stock of Jackson.
72. One of Northup's risks is the threat of injunction prior to the delivery of the Jackson shares.
73. Assuming that the acquisition of Jackson is completed without antitrust attack, the Department of Justice is thereafter precluded from instituting suit to divest the acquisition.
74. If the Jackson acquisition were attacked as anticompetitive, a possible defense would be available to Northup if Jackson were in bankruptcy and there were no other prospective purchaser of the Jackson shares.
75. If Northup abandoned the acquisition of Jackson, it would **not** be illegal per se for Northup and Jackson to agree to allocate customers and for each to refrain from soliciting customers of the other.
76. The acquisition of Jackson would violate the antimerger section of the Clayton Act if the merger merely tended to create, though it did not in fact yet create, a monopoly, absent any unique facts.
77. The acquisition of Keller would be illegal if Northup intended Keller to purchase only from Northup to the exclusion of Northup's competitors.
78. The acquisition of Keller is totally without legal justification; hence, the intent of Northup is totally irrelevant.
79. Northup's termination of the distributorship agreement with Lambert constitutes an illegal refusal to deal with or to boycott in violation of the antitrust law.

C. Cranston, Inc., a manufacturer of various electrical products, sells some of its goods to over 20 retailers in a five-state area. It has been selling to Allen, a retailer in this area, at lower prices than it charges other retailers in the area. This low price was made in good faith to meet equally low prices legally offered by competing manufacturers as evidenced by the competing manufacturers' sales invoices. Cranston has also been selling goods at reduced prices to Barry, another retailer within the area. The prices to Barry reflect savings to Cranston in the cost of manufacture and delivery accruing from Barry's purchases in large quantities. Two other retailers in the area, Coleman and Dixon, are being sold to at prices lower than Cranston sells outside the area.

Cranston and its retailers are engaged in interstate commerce. Each of Cranston's product lines contains only goods of like grade and quality. Cranston holds a substantial share (50 percent) of the market in the five-state area, but only has a small (4 percent) share of the national market. All of Cranston's retailers compete with one another. Each retailer buys substantial quantities (between $1 million to $2 million per year) of each of Cranston's products.

80. The sales to Allen violate the antitrust laws against price discrimination.
81. The sales to Barry violate the antitrust laws against price discrimination.
82. Cranston's competing manufacturers would have an antitrust action against Cranston.
83. Cranston could agree with Branston, a competing manufacturer, to sell to various retailers at certain specified prices so long as Cranston's prices were above its direct variable costs attributable to goods sold.
84. If Cranston's sales were attacked by its competitors as discriminatory, a valid defense would be to prove that the effect of such discrimination did not substantially lessen competition.

85. Cranston could legally adopt a merchandising plan to pay for or furnish services to all its customers in the five-state area on proportionally equally terms.
86. Cranston would violate antitrust law if it were to license certain of its unique products to retailers on condition that they purchase from Cranston all their major requirements of Cranston's other products.

D. Four corporations are the largest manufacturers in their industry. Their combined share of the market has constituted over 90 percent each year for many years. As members of a trade association, certain officers of these corporations meet periodically to discuss topics of mutual interest. Matters discussed include engineering design, production methods, product costs, product pricing, merchandising policy, and inventory levels. The representatives also usually see each other after the association meetings for cocktails where they discuss these and other business matters. These representatives have maintained prices in accordance with an informal oral agreement terminable at will by any company wishing to withdraw. However, they have never reduced their agreement to a written document or memorandum. The four corporations compete with each other in interstate commerce.

87. The members of the trade association validly may appoint the trade association as their representative to allocate manufacturing quotas.
88. An arrangement relating to price fixing would be illegal per se if the government merely proved the existence of the oral agreement.
89. The distributors of the four corporations legally could enter into price maintenance agreements among themselves to prescribe the minimum prices at which they would resell the products bearing the brand name, trademark, or trade name of any of the four corporations.
90. The retailers of the four corporations legally could enter into price maintenance agreements among themselves to prescribe the minimum prices at which they would resell the products bearing the brand name, trademark, or trade name of any of the four corporations. (Former C.P.A. Examination question)

SOME PREVIOUS C.P.A. LAW EXAMINATION QUESTIONS AND AUTHOR'S MODEL ANSWERS

NOVEMBER, 1979

Number 1

Select the **best** answers for each of the following items.

6. The Flick Corporation sold various interrelated products that it manufactured. One of the items was manufactured almost exclusively by Flick and sold throughout the United States. Flick realized the importance of this product to its purchasers and decided to capitalize on the situation by requiring all purchasers to take at least two other products in order to obtain the item over which it has almost complete market control. At Flick's spring sales meeting, its president informed the entire sales force that they were to henceforth sell only to those customers who agreed to take the additional products. As a result of this plan, gross sales of the additional items increased by more than $1 million. Which of the following **best** describes the legality of the above situation?

a. It is illegal only if the products are patented products.
b. It is an illegal tying arrangement.
c. It is legal as long as the price charged to retailers for the other products is competitive.
d. It is legal if the retailers do **not** complain about purchasing the other products.

21. Wanton Corporation, its president, and several other officers of the corporation are found guilty of conspiring with its major competitor to fix prices. Which of the following sanctions would **not** be applicable under federal antitrust laws?
a. Suspension of corporate right to engage in interstate commerce for **not** more than one year.
b. Treble damages.
c. Seizure of Wanton's property illegally shipped in interstate commerce.
d. Fines against Wanton and fines and imprisonment of its president and officers.

34. Which of the following activities engaged in by a corporation will **not** be deemed illegal under the antitrust law?
a. A price-fixing agreement with competitors aimed at lowering prices to a reasonable level.
b. The charging of a price aimed at maximizing its profits based upon economic analysis of supply and demand for its products.
c. Participating in a plan suggested by the trade association aimed at territorial allocations of markets to cut costs.
d. The payment of brokerage commissions to the purchasers of goods.

35. The Donner Corporation has obtained a patent on a revolutionary coin-operated washing machine. It is far superior to the existing machines currently in use. Which of the following actions taken by Donner will **not** result in a violation of federal antitrust law?
a. Maintaining the resale price for machines it sells to distributors.
b. Obtaining a near total monopolization of the market as a result of the patent.
c. Requiring the purchasers of the machines to buy from Donner all their other commonplace supplies connected with the use of the machine.
d. Joining in a boycott with other appliance manufacturers to eliminate a troublesome discount distributor.

36. Expansion Corporation is an aggressive, large-sized conglomerate. It is seeking to obtain control of several additional corporations including Resistance Corporation. Expansion does **not** currently buy from, sell to, or compete with Resistance. Which of the following statements applies to this proposed takeover?
a. Since Expansion does **not** buy from, sell to, or compete with Resistance, antitrust laws do **not** apply.
b. If Expansion can consummate the acquisition before there is an objection to it, the acquisition can **not** subsequently be set aside.
c. The acquisition is likely to be declared illegal if there will be reciprocal buying and there is a likelihood that other entrants into the market would be precluded.
d. The acquisition is legal on its face if there will be cost efficiency resulting from combined marketing and advertising.

37. The Justice Department is contemplating commencing an action against Lion Corporation for monopolizing the off-shore oil drilling business in violation of Section 2 of the Sherman Act. Which of the following would be Lion's **best** defense against such an action?

a. Since the drilling is off-shore, interstate commerce is not involved.
b. The monopoly was originally the result of a long since expired patent.
c. Lion had **no** specific wrongful intent to monopolize.
d. Lion's market share is such that it does **not** have the power to fix prices or to exclude competitors.

42. Nicks is a troublesome chain store furniture dealer. He constantly engaged in price cutting on widely advertised name products in order to lure customers to his store so that he could sell them other products. The "big three" manufacturers agreed that Nicks could no longer sell their products unless he ceased and desisted from such practices. Nicks refused and the three manufacturers promptly cut off his supply of their branded products. Which of the following is a correct statement?
a. Since a businessman has the freedom to choose with whom he will deal, the conduct in question is **not** illegal under the antitrust laws.
b. If the harm to the public was minor, and the products were readily available from other appliance dealers in a market marked by free and open competition, there would be **no** violation of the law.
c. The conduct described is a joint boycott, and as such is illegal per se.
d. Since the conduct described was unilateral, and Nicks did **not** agree to stop his price cutting, the manufacturers' conduct is legal.

Answer

1. 6.b(845) 21.a(842) 34.b(841) 35.b(136, ftn. 3)
36.c(845–46) 37.d(844) 42.c(847)

MAY, 1979

Number 1

Select the **best** answers for each of the following items.

41. Zebra Acquisitions, Inc., has been steadily acquiring the assets and stock of various corporations manufacturing brass. It also has been purchasing the stock of its customers and others who purchase substantial quantities of brass. It now has 8 percent of the brass manufacturing facilities in the United States and 22 percent in the tri-state area in which it is located. Which of the following claims is the United States Department of Justice likely to assert?
a. The relevant market in question is the entire United States.
b. It is illegal per se to purchase the stock of competitors.
c. It is illegal per se to purchase the stock of customers and other potential buyers.
d. The most recent acquisition substantially lessens competition in the tri-state area.

42. Drummond Company manufactures and sells distinctive clocks. Its best selling item is a reproduction of a rare antique grandfather clock. Adams purchased 100 of the clocks from Drummond at $79.50. Much to Adams' chagrin it discovered that Young, one of its competitors, had purchased the same clock at $74.50 per clock. Adams has complained and threatened legal action. In the event the issue is litigated,
a. Drummond will prevail if it can show it did **not** intend to harm Adams.
b. Adams has a presumption in its favor that it has been harmed by price discrimination.
c. Drummond will prevail if it can show that it sold the clocks at the lower price to all customers such as Young who had been doing business with it continuously for ten years or more.

d. Drummond will prevail if it can establish that there were several other clock companies with which Adams could deal if Adams were dissatisfied.

46. Research Development Corporation has made a major breakthrough in the development of a super TV antenna. It has patented the product and is seeking to maximize the profit potential. In this effort, Research can legally

a. Require its retailer to take stipulated quantities of its other products in addition to the antennas.
b. Require its retailers to sell only Research's products, including the antennas, and **not** sell similar competing products.
c. Sell the product to its retailers upon condition that they do **not** sell the antennas to the public for less than a stated price.
d. Sell the product at whatever price the traffic will bear even though it has a monopoly.

Answer

1. 41.d(845–46) 42.b(844) 46.d(842, 843)

NOVEMBER, 1978

Number 1

Select the **best** answer for the following item.

6. Wonder Electronix, Inc., entered into "reasonable" minimum price-resale-maintenance agreements with the distributors of its trademarked products. The distributors willingly accepted the minimum price and it was in fact a "reasonable" price for the products. What is the legal status of this arrangement?

a. It is subject to the rule of reason as contrasted with the per se illegality rule applicable to such price fixing among competitors.
b. It is subject to the per se illegality rule.
c. It will **not** be illegal if the product bears the label, trademark, or brand name of Wonder and it competes with like products of Wonder's competitors.
d. It is exempt from antitrust law if the product is patented.

Answer

1. 6.b(843)

MAY, 1978

Number 1

Select the **best** answer for the following item.

7. Over a six-year period, Yeats Corporation acquired 46 percent of the outstanding stock of Glick, Inc. More than 40 percent of the shares so acquired were purchased from Glick's past and present directors. Both Glick and Yeats have capital, surplus, and undivided profits aggregating more than $1 million. Yeats' current directors owned stock in both corporations and were on the board of directors of each. Yeats utilized its ownership control to elect the remaining members of the board of directors and its own slate of officers for Glick. Glick and Yeats are manufacturers of goods which are in competition with each other throughout the United States. Since Yeats acquired control of Glick, Yeats' percentage share of the nationwide market has remained relatively stable. However, Yeats and Glick each by agreement have ceased marketing in certain

geographical territories where it is more advantageous for the other to sell. Which of the following statements applies to the above situation?

a. There is nothing in the facts as revealed above which would constitute a violation of the federal antitrust laws.
b. The interlocking directorate is **not** illegal because less than 50 percent of the Glick stock is owned by Yeats.
c. The interlocking directorate is a clear violation of the federal antitrust laws.
d. There is **no** current violation of the federal antitrust law because there has been **no** marked improvement in the competitive position of Yeats or Glick.

Answer

1. 7.c(846)

Part Thirteen: Public Law

C. Regulation of the Employer and Employee Relationship

Chapter 65

STATE WORKMEN'S COMPENSATION LAWS

Four areas of the law concerned with regulation of the employer and employee relationship which will be considered very briefly here are State Workmen's Compensation Laws, the federal Fair Labor Standards Act, the federal Civil Rights Act on non-discriminatory employment, and a portion of the federal Social Security Act.

At Common Law, the master had a duty: to provide reasonably safe conditions for work; to provide reasonably safe tools and equipment; to exercise reasonable care in the selection of adequate, competent, fellow servants; and to exercise reasonable care in the operation of the business and in the formulation of reasonable operating rules. The master was liable to the servant for damage caused to him by negligence on the part of the master in the performance of his duties, except when such damage was caused: by the negligence of a fellow servant; by the servant's contributory negligence; or by known risks of the business voluntarily assumed by the servant. These three exceptions were often referred to, respectively, as the fellow-servant rule, the servant's contributory negligence rule, and the assumption-of-risk rule.

Today, under workmen's compensation statutes, society has imposed upon industry as an overhead operating expense the risk of personal injury to employees arising out of, and in the course of, employment. Employers are required to make adequate financial provision in order to assure payment for such damage. Usually the employer is required to take out insurance, either under a state insurance fund or with an insurance company; or the employer may self-insure by providing proof of financial ability to pay the compensation himself and depositing adequate securities with the state workmen's compensation commission. Essentially, the purpose of such statutes is to assure indemnity to employees in business for personal injuries arising out of, and in the course of, employment. Domestic servants and farm laborers usually are excluded from protection under such statutes. Generally, compensation is not allowed for self-inflicted injury or if the injured employee was intoxicated. The law in some states gives to business the election of coming within the terms of a workmen's compensation statute. In other states there are compulsory workmen's compensation laws in which industry must participate.

An employee cannot waive workmen's compensation coverage; it is obligatory for the employer. An employee's contributory negligence or his violation of his employer's rules do not preclude the employee from receiving benefits for his injury. An employee need only show that the accident, and consequent injury, arose out of and in the course of his employment. Also, workmen's compensation coverage does not preclude the injured employee from suing a third person who was responsible for causing the employee's injury, although he cannot sue his employer inasmuch as he has the workmen's compensation coverage.

Chapter 66

FEDERAL FAIR LABOR STANDARDS ACT

The federal Fair Labor Standards Act, also known as the Wage-Hour Law, was enacted to provide "for the establishment of fair labor standards in employments in and affecting interstate and foreign commerce, and for other purposes."

Definitions under the Act. *"Oppressive child labor"* means a condition of employment under which (1) any employee under the age of 16 years is employed by an employer (other than a parent under certain conditions) in any occupation, or (2) any employee between the ages of 16 and 18 years is employed by an employer in any occupation which the Secretary of Labor declares to be particularly hazardous for the employment of children between such ages or detrimental to their health or well-being. Oppressive child labor is not deemed to exist if the employer has an unexpired certificate from the Secretary of Labor certifying that the person named therein is above the oppressive child-labor age.

"Wage" paid to an employee includes the reasonable cost to the employer of furnishing such employee with board, lodging, or other facilities, if such board, lodging, or other facilities are customarily furnished by such employer to his employees. But such cost is not included in wages to the extent that it is excluded as a part of the wage by the terms of a bona fide collective-bargaining agreement applicable to that particular employee. The Secretary of Labor has the authority to determine the fair value of such board, lodging, or other facilities.

"Changing Clothes or Washing" Time, for the purpose of determining the hours for which an employee is employed, spent at the beginning or end of each workday, is excluded for such hours of employment only if it was ex-

cluded from measured working time during the week involved by the express terms of, or by custom or practice under, a bona fide collective-bargaining agreement applicable to the particular employee. "*Tipped Employee*" is an employee engaged in an occupation in which he customarily and regularly receives more than $20 a month in tips. "*Man-day*" means any day during which an employee performs any agricultural labor, for not less than an hour.

Minimum Wages. Effective 1978, this Act establishes the following minimum hourly wages for employees: "not less than $2.65 an hour during the year beginning January 1, 1978, not less than $2.90 an hour during the year beginning January 1, 1979, not less than $3.10 an hour during the year beginning January 1, 1980, and not less than $3.35 an hour after December 31, 1980, except as otherwise provided in this section." Special provisions are made for a committee to recommend minimum wage rates to be paid by employers in Puerto Rico or the Virgin Islands.

Under section 6(d)(1), which is the Equal Pay Act amendment to the Fair Labor Standards Act, wage discrimination based on sex is prohibited, except where such pay is made pursuant to a seniority system, a merit system, a system which measures earnings by quantity or quality of production, or a differential based on any other factor other than sex.

Maximum Hours. An employee is not to be employed by an employer for a workweek longer than 40 hours unless such employee receives compensation for his employment in excess of the 40 hours at a rate not less than one and one-half times the regular rate at which he is employed. However, exceptions are made if the employee is employed under a collective-bargaining agreement specifying and limiting the maximum number of hours for a specified period of time or under a guaranteed wage plan, for an employee at piece rates, and for other special situations.

Child Labor Provisions. Section 12 prohibits an employer from employing any "oppressive child labor" in commerce[1] or in the production of goods for commerce or in any enterprise engaged in commerce or in the production of goods for commerce. It also prohibits shipment of "oppressive child labor" goods and provides:

> (a) No producer, manufacturer, or dealer shall ship or deliver for shipment in commerce any goods produced in an establishment situated in the United States in or about which within 30 days prior to the removal of such goods therefrom any oppressive child labor has been employed: *Provided*, That any such shipment or delivery for shipment of such goods by a purchaser who acquired them in good faith in reliance on written assurance from a producer, manufacturer, or dealer that the goods were produced in compliance with the requirements of this section and who acquired such goods for value without notice of any such violation, shall not be deemed prohibited. . . .

Exemption from Wage-Hour Provisions. The provisions discussed above for wages (except for prohibition of wage based on sex) and maximum hours

[1] "Commerce" means trade or commerce among the several states or with foreign nations.

generally do not apply, with certain exceptions, to:an employee in a bona fide executive, administrative, or professional capacity, or as an outside salesman; an employee in a retail or service establishment with annual sales of less than $250,000; an employee in an amusement or recreational establishment not operating for more than seven months in a calendar year; an employee in the catching or production of fish. Also, the provisions with respect to child labor do not apply to an employee in agriculture outside of school hours if he is less than 12 years of age and is employed by his parent on a farm owned or operated by such parent, or in the parent's place on a farm under certain conditions.

Penalties. Criminal penalties may be imposed by a court for wilful violation of specified sections of the Act, and civil suit may be brought by an employee against his employer for unpaid minimum wages or overtime compensation as provided in the Act.

Chapter 67

NON-DISCRIMINATORY EMPLOYMENT

The Civil Rights Act as amended by the Equal Employment Opportunity Act, and the Age Discrimination In Employment Act are the two basic sources for federal legislative provision ensuring equal non-discriminatory opportunity for employment.

Equal Employment Opportunity Act. This Act prohibits employers—who are persons engaged in an industry affecting interstate commerce with 15 or more employees for each working day in each of 20 or more calendar weeks in the current or preceding calendar year—from unlawfully discriminating in employment, and states that it is "an unlawful employment practice for an employer (1) to fail or refuse to hire or to discharge any individual, or otherwise to discriminate against any individual with respect to his compensation, terms, conditions, or privileges of employment, because of such individual's race, color, religion, sex, or national origin; or (2) to limit, segregate, or classify his employees or applicants for employment in any way which would deprive or tend to deprive any individual of employment opportunities or otherwise adversely affect his status as an employee, because of such individual's race, color, religion, sex, or national origin." It is also an unlawful act to make such discrimination by employment agencies, labor organizations, apprenticeship programs, in advertising, and to cause or attempt to cause an employer to discriminate against an individual in violation of these provisions against such discrimination. However, it is *not* an unlawful employment practice:

> (1) for an employer to hire and employ employees, for an employment agency to classify or refer for employment an individual, for a labor organization to classify its membership or to classify or refer for employment any individual, or

> for an employer, labor organization, or joint labor-management committee controlling apprenticeship or other training or retraining programs to admit or employ any individual in any such program, on the basis of his religion, sex, or national origin in those certain instances where religion, sex, or national origin is a bona fide occupational qualification reasonably necessary to the normal operation of that particular business or enterprise, and
>
> (2) for a school, college, university, or other educational institution or institution of learning to hire and employ employees of a particular religion if such school, college, university, or other educational institution or institution of learning is, in whole or in substantial part, owned, supported, controlled, or managed by a particular religion or by a particular religious corporation, association, or society, or if the curriculum of such school, college, university, or other educational institution or institution of learning is directed toward the propagation of a particular religion.
>
> (3) for an employer to apply different standards of compensation, or different terms, conditions, or privileges of employment pursuant to a bona fide seniority or merit system, or a system which measures earnings by quantity or quality of production or to employees who work in different locations, provided that such differences are not the result of an intention to discriminate because of race, color, religion, sex, or national origin, nor shall it be an unlawful employment practice for an employer to give and to act upon the results of any professioanlly developed ability test provided that such test, its administration or action upon the results is not designed, intended or used to discriminate because of race, color, religion, sex or national origin. It shall not be an unlawful employment practice under this title for any employer to differentiate upon the basis of sex in determining the amount of the wages or compensation paid or to be paid to employees of such employer if such differentiation is authorized by the provisions of section 6(d) of the Fair Labor Standards Act of 1938, as amended (29 U.S.C. 206(d)).

It should be noted very carefully that *nothing* in the Act:

> shall be interpreted to require any employer, employment agency, labor organization, or joint labor-management committee subject to this title to grant preferential treatment to any individual or to any group because of the race, color, religion, sex, or national origin of such individual or group on account of an imbalance which may exist with respect to the total number or percentage of persons of any race, color, religion, sex, or national origin employed by any employer, refererred or classified for employment by any employment agency or labor organization, admitted to membership or classified by any labor organization, or admitted to, or employed in, any apprenticeship or other training program, in comparison with the total number or percentage of persons of such race, color, religion, sex, or national origin in any community, State, section, or other area, or in the available work force in any community, State, section, or other area.

Age Discrimination In Employment Act. This Act prohibits age discrimination in employment of an individual at least 40 years of age but less than 70 years of age by an employer, who is a person engaged in industry affecting interstate and foreign commerce who has 20 or more employees for each working day in each of 20 or more calendar weeks in the current or preceding calendar year.

Chapter 68

THE SOCIAL SECURITY ACT

The federal Social Security Act has as its purpose what is indicated in its title, the social security of people in society. This necessarily involves social insurance to cover the risks inherent in retirement, disability, death and its effect on surviving spouse or children, hospitalization, and unemployment. In order to provide some minimum measure of national security with respect to these areas of risk, insurance was needed and is provided by the federal government in the form of: old age, survivor's, and disability insurance; hospital insurance (Medicare); and unemployment insurance.

Old Age, Survivor's, and Disability Insurance. Equal contributions (taxes) are paid both by the employer and the employee under the Federal Insurance Contributions Act (FICA) for the compulsory federal insurance to provide for: loss of income benefits on retirement of the employee at age 65, or sooner at a reduced benefit at age 62; survivor benefits on his death; and financial assistance during physical disablement for some people under 65. Self-employed persons can voluntarily participate in such a program of insurance coverage, paid for by their contributions under the Self-Employment Contributions Act. The contributions are witheld by the employer from the wages of the employee as he is paid. The employee's "annual wage base" is the basis for determination of the contributions to be made by *both* the employer and employee with periodically increasing fixed percentages of a specified maximum portion of wages earned called the annual wage base. Inasmuch as the law provides for automatic benefit increases whenever the cost of living rises 3 percent or more between specified periods as shown by the consumer price index, the cost annually for such increased benefits causes an automatic adjustment in the annual wage base to pay for such increased costs. For 1981, the first $29,700 of wages (annual wage base) are taxable at a rate of 6.65 percent (5.35 percent for old age, survivor's, and disability insurance, 1.30 percent for hospital insurance). For 1982–84 the rate is 6.70 percent (5.40 and 1.30), for 1985 it is 7.05 percent (5.70 and 1.35), for 1986–89 it is 7.15 percent (5.70 and 1.45), and after 1989 it is 7.65 percent (6.20 and 1.45). If an employee works for two separate employers at the same time, he is entitled to a refund for the excess over the annual contribution that *he* has paid, because his wages are taxable up to a maximum percentage of a maximum amount; this is not true of either employer, who gets no refund. The employee's contribution is not a deductible item on his annual federal income tax return.

Hospital Insurance (Medicare). As described by the federal *Medicare Handbook* for 1976, "Medicare is a health income program for people 65 and older and some under 65 who are disabled. It is a federal government program run by the Social Security Administration. Medicare has two parts. One part is called *hospital* insurance. The other part is called *medical* insurance," which helps pay for medically necessary doctor's and other medical services not covered by the hospital insurance part of Medicare. "Most people who have Medicare's hospital insurance do not have to make monthly payments for this protection. They have hospital insurance because of credits for work under social security." If the person has Medicare hospital insurance he can acquire federal medical insurance by paying a relatively small monthly premium, payable quarterly, which will rise as the costs of medical care rise. The premium is never more than one-half the cost of the medical insurance protection.

Unemployment Insurance. Unemployment insurance is to provide for some financial assistance in the event of unemployment as provided by the Federal Unemployment Tax Act (FUTA). Compulsory contributions (taxes) are made quarterly by a non-exempt employer if he has at least one employee who meets the wage service requirement, namely, one employee (or more employees) in each of 20 weeks in a year, or a quarterly pay roll of at least $1,500. The federal government does not require a tax from an employee, but does not prohibit a state from imposing such a tax; as of 1976, three states impose a tax on the employee as well as on the employer. All funds are collected by the state unemployment insurance system and deposited in the Unemployment Trust Fund in the United States Treasury where each state system has a separate account. Disbursements are made from these individual accounts to the individual states who individually pay unemployment insurance benefits. The wage base and the percentage of contribution (tax) on such base are established by the federal government. Beginning 1978, the wage base is $6,000 and the federal tax on that base is 3.4 percent. There is a state unemployment insurance tax which is 2.7 percent in a majority of the states. An employer can receive an offset credit against the federal tax up to 2.75 percent of the state unemployment insurance tax. Also, if the employer has a good experience rating of a low unemployment pattern he can reduce his state tax and get an additional offset or credit. The federal government pays the costs of administering the unemployment insurance program federally and among the various states.

PROBLEMS

Select the **best** answers for each of the following items.

1. The Federal Social Security Act
   a. Applies to self-employed businessmen;
   b. Excludes professionals such as accountants, lawyers, and doctors;
   c. Provides for a deduction by the employee against his federal income tax.
   d. Applies to professionals at their option.
2. Markum was grossly negligent in the operation of a forklift. As a result he suffered permanent disability. His claim for workmen's compensation will be
   a. Denied.
   b. Limited to medical benefits;
   c. Reduced by the percentage share attributable to his own fault;
   d. Paid in full.
3. Which of the following classes of employees is **exempt** from both the minimum wage and maximum hours provisions of the Federal Fair Labor Standards Act?
   a. Members of a labor union.
   b. Administrative personnel.
   c. Hospital workers.
   d. **No** class of employees is exempt.
4. The Jax Corporation owned and operated a modern, highly efficient sawmill. Forrester was one of its saw operators. Jax Corporation was subject to periodic inspections of its operations by both governmental and insurance company inspectors regarding its safety standards. It was agreed by virtually everyone involved in examining Jax's safety standards and equipment that they were outstanding and far above the minimum level which most other mills in the state met. Forrester was an employee of long standing and a man of firm convictions. He believed that many of the rules and required safety equipment were nothing more than a "bloody nuisance." Forrester repeatedly disregarded them when he could do so without being caught. Unfortunately, one day Forrester was seriously injured while using a power saw. He lost his left hand. Had he followed proper procedures and used the required safety equipment the injury would **not** have occurred. What circumstance described above would preclude Forrester from recovering under workmen's compensation?
   a. Forrester's gross negligence.
   b. Agreement by all inspectors that safety standards were outstanding and far above minimum levels.
   c. Forrester's disregard of safety standards only when he could do it without being caught.
   d. None of the circumstances described above would preclude Forrester's recovery under workmen's compensation.
5. Which of the following payments is provided for under the Federal Fair Labor Standards Act?

a. Double-time pay for employees who work on Sunday if this is in excess of 40 hours worked during the week.
b. Payments of less than the minimum wage if the employees are represented by a bona fide union.
c. Piece-rate method in lieu of an hourly rate.
d. Penalty bonus to employees who work in excess of the maximum number of hours per day as set by the Act. (All former C.P.A. Examination questions)

SOME PREVIOUS C.P.A. LAW EXAMINATION QUESTIONS AND AUTHOR'S MODEL ANSWERS

NOVEMBER, 1979

Number 1

Select the **best** answer for the following item.
48. Yeats Manufacturing is engaged in the manufacture and sale of convertible furniture in interstate commerce. Yeats' manufacturing facilities are located in a jurisdiction which has a compulsory workmen's compensation Act. Hardwood, Yeats' president, decided that the company should, in light of its safety record, choose to ignore the requirement of providing workmen's compensation insurance. Instead, Hardwood indicated that a special account should be created to provide for such contingencies. Basset was severely injured as a result of his negligent operation of a lathe which accelerated and cut off his right arm. In assessing the potential liability of Yeats, which of the following is a correct answer?
a. Federal law applies since Yeats is engaged in interstate commerce.
b. Yeats has **no** liability, since Basset negligently operated the lathe.
c. Since Yeats did **not** provide workmen's compensation insurance, it can be sued by Basset and cannot resort to the usual common law defenses.
d. Yeats is a self-insurer, hence it has **no** liability beyond the amount of the money in the insurance fund.

Answer

1. 48.c(855–56)

MAY, 1979

Number 1

Select the **best** answer for the following item.
47. Wilton was grossly negligent in the operation of a drill press. As a result he suffered permanent disability. His claim for workmen's compensation will be
a. Reduced by the percentage share attributable to his own fault.
b. Limited to medical benefits;
c. Denied;
d. Paid in full.

Answer

1. 47.d(856)

MAY, 1978

Number 1

Select the **best** answers for each of the following items.

1. Wilcox works as a welder for Miracle Muffler, Inc. He was specially trained by Miracle in the procedures and safety precautions applicable to installing replacement mufflers on automobiles. One rule of which he was aware involved a prohibition against installing a muffler on any auto which had heavily congealed oil or grease or which had any leaks. Wilcox disregarded this rule, and as a result an auto caught fire causing extensive property damage and injury to Wilcox. Which of the following statements is correct?
   a. Miracle is **not** liable because its rule prohibited Wilcox from installing the muffler in question.
   b. Miracle is **not** liable to Wilcox under the workmen's compensation laws.
   c. Miracle is liable irrespective of its efforts to prevent such an occurrence and the fact that it exercised reasonable care.
   d. Wilcox does **not** have any personal liability for the loss because he was acting for and on behalf of his employer.

47. Barnaby is an employee of the Excelsior Manufacturing Company, a multi-state manufacturer of toys. The plant in which he works is unionized and Barnaby is a dues paying member. Which statement is correct insofar as the Federal Fair Labor Standards Act is concerned?
   a. Excelsior is permitted to pay less than the minimum wage to employees since they are represented by a bona fide union.
   b. The act allows a piece-rate method to be employed in lieu of the hourly rate method where appropriate.
   c. The act excludes from its coverage the employees of a labor union.
   d. The act sets the maximum number of hours that an employee can work in a given day or week.

Answer

1. 1.c(609, 856) 47.b(858)

NOVEMBER, 1977

Number 1

Select the **best** answers for each of the following items.

13. During the 1976 examination of the financial statements of Viscount Manufacturing Corporation, the CPAs noted that although Viscount had 860 full-time and part-time employees, it had completely overlooked its responsibilities under the Federal Insurance Contributions Act (FICA). Under these circumstances, which of the following is true?
   a. **No** liability under the act will attach if the employees voluntarily relinquish their rights under the act in exchange for a cash equivalent paid directly to them.
   b. If the union which represents the employees has a vested pension plan covering the employees which is equal to or exceeds the benefits available under the act, Viscount has **no** liability.
   c. Since employers and employees owe FICA taxes at the same rate and since the employer must withhold the employees' tax from their wages as paid, Viscount

must remit to the government a tax double the amount assessed directly against the employer.

d. The act does **not** apply to the part-time employees.

14. Fashion Industries, Inc., manufactures dresses which it sells throughout the United States and South America. Among its 5,000 employees in 1976 were 165 youngsters aged 14 and 15 who worked in a wide range of jobs and were paid at a rate less than the minimum wage. Which statement is correct in accordance with the general rules of the Fair Labor Standards Act?

a. Fashion was exempt from regulation because less than 5 percent of its employees were children.

b. Fashion did **not** violate the law since both male and female youngsters were paid at the same rate and only worked on Saturdays.

c. Fashion violated the law by employing children under 16 years of age.

d. Fashion was exempt from regulation if more than 10 percent of its sales were in direct competition with foreign goods.

Answer

1. 13.c(862) 14.c(857)

INDEX

D

E

F–G–H

This book is set VIP in 10 and 9 point Caledonia, leaded 2 points. Part numbers and titles are 12 point Optima Bold. Part divisions are 12 point Optima. Chapter numbers are 14 point Optima Bold, and chapter titles are 16 point Optima. The size of the type page is 30 × 46½ picas.